Java™ for Programmers
Second Edition
Deitel® Developer Series

The publisher offers excellent discounts on this book when ordered in quantity for bulk purchases or special sales, which may include electronic versions and/or custom covers and content particular to your business, training goals, marketing focus, and branding interests. For more information, please contact:

> U. S. Corporate and Government Sales
> (800) 382-3419
> corpsales@pearsontechgroup.com

For sales outside the U. S., please contact:

> International Sales
> international@pearsoned.com

Visit us on the Web: informit.com/ph

Library of Congress Cataloging-in-Publication Data

`On file`

> ISBN-13: 978-0-13282154-4
> ISBN-10: 0-13-282154-0

Text printed in the United States on recycled paper at RR Donnelley in Crawfordsville, Indiana.
First printing, March 2011

Java™ for Programmers
Second Edition
Deitel® Developer Series

Paul Deitel
Deitel & Associates, Inc.

Harvey Deitel
Deitel & Associates, Inc.

PRENTICE
HALL

Upper Saddle River, NJ • Boston • Indianapolis • San Francisco
New York • Toronto • Montreal • London • Munich • Paris • Madrid
Capetown • Sydney • Tokyo • Singapore • Mexico City

Trademarks

DEITEL, the double-thumbs-up bug and DIVE INTO are registered trademarks of Deitel and Associates, Inc.

Oracle and Java are registered trademarks of Oracle and/or its affiliates. Other names may be trademarks of their respective owners.

Microsoft, Internet Explorer and the Windows logo are either registered trademarks or trademarks of Microsoft Corporation in the United States and/or other countries.

UNIX is a registered trademark of The Open Group.

Apache is a trademark of The Apache Software Foundation.

CSS, XHTML and XML are registered trademarks of the World Wide Web Consortium.

Firefox is a registered trademark of the Mozilla Foundation.

Google is a trademark of Google, Inc.

Web 2.0 is a service mark of CMP Media.

Throughout this book, trademarks are used. Rather than put a trademark symbol in every occurrence of a trademarked name, we state that we are using the names in an editorial fashion only and to the benefit of the trademark owner, with no intention of infringement of the trademark.

In memory of Clifford "Spike" Stephens,
A dear friend who will be greatly missed.

Paul and Harvey Deitel

Contents

10 Object-Oriented Programming: Polymorphism 254

11 Exception Handling: A Deeper Look 292

12 ATM Case Study, Part 1: Object-Oriented Design with the UML   318

13 ATM Case Study Part 2: Implementing an Object-Oriented Design   359

14 GUI Components: Part 1 398

15 Graphics and Java 2D   468

16 Strings, Characters and Regular Expressions   502

17 Files, Streams and Object Serialization   539

18 Generic Collections   578

Preface

Live in fragments no longer, only connect.
—Edgar Morgan Foster

Welcome to Java and *Java for Programmers, Second Edition*! This book presents leading-edge computing technologies for software developers.

We focus on software engineering best practices. At the heart of the book is the Deitel signature "live-code approach"—concepts are presented in the context of complete working programs, rather than in code snippets. Each complete code example is accompanied by live sample executions. All the source code is available at

> `www.deitel.com/books/javafp2/`

As you read the book, if you have questions, send an e-mail to `deitel@deitel.com`; we'll respond promptly. For updates on this book, visit the website shown above, follow us on Facebook (`www.facebook.com/DeitelFan`) and Twitter (`@deitel`), and subscribe to the *Deitel® Buzz Online* newsletter (`www.deitel.com/newsletter/subscribe.html`).

Features

Here are the key features of *Java for Programmers, 2/e*:

Java Standard Edition (SE) 7

- *Easy to use as a Java SE 6 or Java SE 7 book.* We cover the new Java SE 7 features in modular sections. Here's some of the new functionality: `String`s in `switch` statements, the try-with-resources statement for managing `AutoClosable` objects, multi-`catch` for defining a single exception handler to replace multiple exception handlers that perform the same task and inferring the types of generic objects from the variable they're assigned to by using the `<>` notation. We also overview the new concurrency API features.

- *Java SE 7's `AutoClosable` versions of `Connection`, `Statement` and `ResultSet`.* With the source code for Chapter 25, Accessing Databases with JDBC, we provide a version of the chapter's first example that's implemented using Java SE 7's `AutoClosable` versions of `Connection`, `Statement` and `ResultSet`. `AutoClosable` objects reduce the likelihood of resource leaks when you use them with Java SE 7's try-with-resources statement, which automatically closes the `AutoClosable` objects allocated in the parentheses following the `try` keyword.

Object Technology

- *Object-oriented programming and design.* We review the basic concepts and terminology of object technology in Chapter 1. Readers develop their first customized classes and objects in Chapter 3.

- *Exception handling.* We integrate basic exception handling early in the book and cover it in detail in Chapter 11, Exception Handling: A Deeper Look.

- *Class `Arrays` and `ArrayList`.* Chapter 7 covers class `Arrays`—which contains methods for performing common array manipulations—and class `ArrayList`—which implements a dynamically resizable array-like data structure.

- *OO case studies.* The early classes and objects presentation features `Time`, `Employee` and `GradeBook` class case studies that weave their way through multiple sections and chapters, gradually introducing deeper OO concepts.

- *Case Study: Using the UML to Develop an Object-Oriented Design and Java Implementation of an ATM.* The UML™ (Unified Modeling Language™) is the industry-standard graphical language for modeling object-oriented systems. Chapters 12–13 include a case study on object-oriented design using the UML. We design and implement the software for a simple automated teller machine (ATM). We analyze a typical requirements document that specifies the system to be built. We determine the classes needed to implement that system, the attributes the classes need to have, the behaviors the classes need to exhibit and specify how the classes must interact with one another to meet the system requirements. From the design we produce a *complete* Java implementation. Readers often report having a "light-bulb moment"—the case study helps them "tie it all together" and really understand object orientation in Java.

- *Reordered generics presentation.* We begin with generic class `ArrayList` in Chapter 7. Because *you'll understand basic generics concepts early in the book*, our later data structures discussions provide a deeper treatment of generic collections—showing how to use the built-in collections of the Java API. We then show how to implement generic methods and classes.

Database and Web Development

- *JDBC 4.* Chapter 25, Accessing Databases with JDBC, covers JDBC 4 and uses the Java DB/Apache Derby and MySQL database management systems. The chapter features an OO case study on developing a database-driven address book that demonstrates prepared statements and JDBC 4's automatic driver discovery.

- *Java Server Faces (JSF) 2.0.* Chapters 26–27 have been updated with JavaServer Faces (JSF) 2.0 technology, which greatly simplifies building JSF web applications. Chapter 26 includes examples on building web application GUIs, validating forms and session tracking. Chapter 27 discusses data-driven and Ajax-enabled JSF applications. The chapter features a database-driven multitier web address book that allows users to add and search for contacts.

- *Web services.* Chapter 28, Web Services, demonstrates creating and consuming SOAP- *and* REST-based web services. Case studies include developing blackjack and airline reservation web services.

- *Java Web Start and the Java Network Launch Protocol (JNLP).* We introduce Java Web Start and JNLP, which enable applets *and* applications to be launched via a web browser. Users can install locally for later execution. Programs can also request the user's permission to access local system resources such as files—enabling you to develop more robust applets and applications that execute safely using Java's sandbox security model, which applies to downloaded code.

Multithreading

- *Multithreading.* We completely reworked Chapter 23, Multithreading [special thanks to the guidance of Brian Goetz and Joseph Bowbeer—two of the co-authors of *Java Concurrency in Practice,* Addison-Wesley, 2006].
- **SwingWorker** *class.* We use class SwingWorker to create *multithreaded user interfaces.*

GUI and Graphics

- *GUI and graphics presentation.* Chapters 14, 15 and 22, and Appendix H present Java GUI and Graphics programming.
- **GroupLayout** *layout manager.* We discuss the GroupLayout layout manager in the context of the GUI design tool in the NetBeans IDE.
- **JTable** *sorting and filtering capabilities.* Chapter 25 uses these capabilities to sort the data in a JTable and filter it by regular expressions.

Other Features

- *Android.* Because of the tremendous interest in Android-based smartphones and tablets, we've included a three-chapter introduction to Android app development online at www.deitel.com/books/javafp. These chapters are from our new Deitel Developer Series book *Android for Programmers: An App-Driven Approach.* After you learn Java, you'll find it straightforward to develop and run Android apps on the free Android emulator that you can download from developer.android.com.
- *Software engineering community concepts.* We discuss agile software development, refactoring, design patterns, LAMP, SaaS (Software as a Service), PaaS (Platform as a Service), cloud computing, open-source software and more.

Teaching Approach

Java for Programmers, 2/e, contains hundreds of complete working examples. We stress program clarity and concentrate on building well-engineered software.

Syntax Shading. For readability, we syntax shade the code, similar to the way most integrated-development environments and code editors syntax color the code. Our syntax-shading conventions are:

```
comments appear like this
keywords appear like this
constants and literal values appear like this
all other code appears in black
```

Code Highlighting. We place gray rectangles around each program's key code.

Using Fonts for Emphasis. We place the key terms and the index's page reference for each defining occurrence in **bold** text for easier reference. On-screen components are emphasized in the **bold Helvetica** font (e.g., the **File** menu) and Java program text in the Lucida font (e.g., int x = 5;).

Web Access. All of the source-code examples can be downloaded from:

```
www.deitel.com/books/javafp2
www.pearsonhighered.com/deitel
```

Objectives. The chapter opening quotations are followed by a list of chapter objectives.

Illustrations/Figures. Abundant tables, line drawings, UML diagrams, programs and program outputs are included.

Programming Tips. We include programming tips to help you focus on important aspects of program development. These tips and practices represent the best we've gleaned from a combined eight decades of programming and teaching experience.

Good Programming Practice

The Good Programming Practices *call attention to techniques that will help you produce programs that are clearer, more understandable and more maintainable.*

Common Programming Error

Pointing out these Common Programming Errors *reduces the likelihood that you'll make the same errors.*

Error-Prevention Tip

These tips contain suggestions for exposing and removing bugs from your programs; many of the tips describe aspects of Java that prevent bugs from getting into programs.

Performance Tip

These tips highlight opportunities for making your programs run faster or minimizing the amount of memory that they occupy.

Portability Tip

The Portability Tips *help you write code that will run on a variety of platforms.*

Software Engineering Observation

The Software Engineering Observations *highlight architectural and design issues that affect the construction of software systems, especially large-scale systems.*

Look-and-Feel Observation

These observations help you design attractive, user-friendly graphical user interfaces that conform to industry norms.

Thousands of Index Entries. We've included a comprehensive index, which is especially useful when you use the book as a reference.

Software Used in *Java for Programmers, 2/e*

All the software you'll need for this book is available free for download from the web. See the Before You Begin section that follows the Preface for links to each download.

We wrote most of the examples in *Java for Programmers, 2/e*, using the free Java Standard Edition Development Kit (JDK) 6. For the Java SE 7 modules, we used the OpenJDK's early access version of JDK 7 (`download.java.net/jdk7/`). In Chapters 26–28, we also used the Netbeans IDE, and in Chapter 25, we used MySQL and MySQL Connector/J. You can find additional resources and software downloads in our Java Resource Centers at:

`www.deitel.com/ResourceCenters.html`

Discounts on *Deitel Developer Series* Books

If you'd like to receive information on professional *Deitel Developer Series* titles, including *Android for Programmers: An App-Driven Approach*, please register your copy of *Java for Programmers, 2/e* at `informit.com/register`. You'll receive information on how to purchase *Android for Programmers* at a discount.

Java Fundamentals: Parts I, II and III, Second Edition LiveLessons Video Training Product

Our *Java Fundamentals: Parts I, II and III, Second Edition* LiveLessons video training product shows you what you need to know to start building robust, powerful software with Java. It includes 20+ hours of expert training synchronized with *Java for Programmers, 2/e*. Check out our growing list of LiveLessons video products:

- *Java Fundamentals I and II*
- *C# 2010 Fundamentals I, II, and III*
- *C# 2008 Fundamentals I and II*
- *C++ Fundamentals I and II*
- *iPhone App-Development Fundamentals I and II*
- *JavaScript Fundamentals I and II*
- *Visual Basic 2010 Fundamentals I and II*

Coming Soon
- *Java Fundamentals I, II and III, Second Edition*
- *C Fundamentals I and II*
- *Android App Development Fundamentals I and II*
- *iPhone and iPad App-Development Fundamentals I and II, Second Edition*

For additional information about Deitel LiveLessons video products, visit:

`www.deitel.com/livelessons`

Acknowledgments

We'd like to thank Abbey Deitel and Barbara Deitel for long hours devoted to this project. Barbara devoted long hours to Internet research to support our writing efforts. Abbey wrote the new engaging Chapter 1 and the new cover copy. We're fortunate to have worked on this project with the dedicated team of publishing professionals at Pearson. We appreciate the guidance, savvy and energy of Mark Taub, Editor-in-Chief of Computer Science. John Fuller managed the book's production. Sandra Schroeder did the cover design.

Reviewers

We wish to acknowledge the efforts of the reviewers who contributed to the recent editions of this content. They scrutinized the text and the programs and provided countless suggestions for improving the presentation: Lance Andersen (Oracle), Soundararajan Angusamy (Sun Microsystems), Joseph Bowbeer (Consultant), William E. Duncan (Louisiana State University), Diana Franklin (University of California, Santa Barbara), Edward F. Gehringer (North Carolina State University), Huiwei Guan (Northshore Community College), Ric Heishman (George Mason University), Dr. Heinz Kabutz (JavaSpecialists.eu), Patty Kraft (San Diego State University), Lawrence Premkumar (Sun Microsystems), Tim Margush (University of Akron), Sue McFarland Metzger (Villanova University), Shyamal Mitra (The University of Texas at Austin), Peter Pilgrim (Java Champion, Consultant), Manjeet Rege, Ph.D. (Rochester Institute of Technology), Manfred Riem (Java Champion, Consultant, Robert Half), Simon Ritter (Oracle), Susan Rodger (Duke University), Amr Sabry (Indiana University), José Antonio González Seco (Parliament of Andalusia), Sang Shin (Sun Microsystems), S. Sivakumar (Astra Infotech Private Limited), Raghavan "Rags" Srinivas (Intuit), Monica Sweat (Georgia Tech), Vinod Varma (Astra Infotech Private Limited) and Alexander Zuev (Sun Microsystems).

Well, there you have it! As you read the book, we'd appreciate your comments, criticisms, corrections and suggestions for improvement. Please address all correspondence to:

```
deitel@deitel.com
```

We'll respond promptly. We hope you enjoy working with *Java for Programmers, 2/e*. Good luck!

Paul and Harvey Deitel

About the Authors

Paul J. Deitel, CEO and Chief Technical Officer of Deitel & Associates, Inc., is a graduate of MIT, where he studied Information Technology. He holds the Sun (now Oracle) Certified Java Programmer and Certified Java Developer certifications, and is an Oracle Java Champion. Through Deitel & Associates, Inc., he has delivered Java, C#, Visual Basic, C++, C and Internet programming courses to industry clients, including Cisco, IBM, Sun Microsystems, Dell, Siemens, Lucent Technologies, Fidelity, NASA at the Kennedy Space Center, the National Severe Storm Laboratory, White Sands Missile Range, Rogue Wave Software, Boeing, SunGard Higher Education, Stratus, Cambridge Technology Partners, One Wave, Hyperion Software, Adra Systems, Entergy, CableData Systems, Nortel Networks, Puma, iRobot, Invensys and many more. He and his co-author, Dr. Harvey M. Deitel, are the world's best-selling programming-language textbook/professional book authors.

Dr. Harvey M. Deitel, Chairman and Chief Strategy Officer of Deitel & Associates, Inc., has 50 years of experience in the computer field. Dr. Deitel earned B.S. and M.S. degrees from MIT and a Ph.D. from Boston University. He has extensive industry and academic experience, including earning tenure and serving as the Chairman of the Computer Science Department at Boston College before founding Deitel & Associates, Inc., with his son, Paul J. Deitel. He and Paul are the co-authors of dozens of books and multi-media packages and they are writing many more. With translations published in Japanese, German, Russian, Chinese, Spanish, Korean, French, Polish, Italian, Portuguese, Greek, Urdu and Turkish, the Deitels' texts have earned international recognition. Dr. Deitel has delivered hundreds of professional seminars to major corporations, academic institutions, government organizations and the military.

About Deitel & Associates, Inc.

Deitel & Associates, Inc., founded by Paul Deitel and Harvey Deitel, is an internationally recognized authoring, corporate training and software development organization specializing in computer programming languages, object technology, Android and iPhone app development, and Internet and web software technology. The company offers instructor-led training courses delivered at client sites worldwide on major programming languages and platforms, such as Java™, C, C++, Visual C#®, Visual Basic®, Objective-C, and iPhone and iPad app development, Android app development, XML®, Python®, object technology, Internet and web programming, and a growing list of additional programming and software development courses. The company's clients include many of the world's largest companies, government agencies, branches of the military, and academic institutions.

Through its 35-year publishing partnership with Prentice Hall/Pearson, Deitel & Associates, Inc., publishes leading-edge programming professional books, college textbooks, and *LiveLessons* DVD- and web-based video courses. Deitel & Associates, Inc. and the authors can be reached at:

deitel@deitel.com

To learn more about Deitel's *Dive Into*® *Series* Corporate Training curriculum, visit:

www.deitel.com/training/

subscribe to the free *Deitel*® *Buzz Online* e-mail newsletter at:

www.deitel.com/newsletter/subscribe.html

and follow the authors on Facebook

www.facebook.com/DeitelFan

and Twitter

@deitel

To request a proposal for on-site, instructor-led training at your company or organization, e-mail

deitel@deitel.com

Individuals wishing to purchase Deitel books and *LiveLessons* DVD training courses can do so through www.deitel.com. Bulk orders by corporations, the government, the military and academic institutions should be placed directly with Pearson. For more information, visit www.pearsoned.com/professional/index.htm.

Before You Begin

This section contains information you should review before using this book and instructions to ensure that your computer is set up properly for use with this book. We'll post updates (if any) to the Before You Begin section on the book's website:

> www.deitel.com/books/javafp2/

Font and Naming Conventions

We use fonts to distinguish between on-screen components (such as menu names and menu items) and Java code or commands. Our convention is to emphasize on-screen components in a sans-serif bold Helvetica font (for example, **File** menu) and to emphasize Java code and commands in a sans-serif Lucida font (for example, System.out.println()).

Software Used in the Book

All the software you'll need for this book is available free for download from the web.

Java SE Software Development Kit (JDK) 6 and 7

We wrote most of the examples in *Java for Programmers, 2/e*, using the free Java Standard Edition Development Kit (JDK) 6, which is available from:

> www.oracle.com/technetwork/java/javase/downloads/index.html

For the Java SE 7 modules, we used the OpenJDK's early access version of JDK 7, which is available from:

> dlc.sun.com.edgesuite.net/jdk7/binaries-/index.html

Java DB, MySQL and MySQL Connector/J

In Chapter 25, we use the Java DB and MySQL Community Edition database management systems. Java DB is part of the JDK installation. At the time of this writing, the JDK's 64-bit installer was not properly installing Java DB. If you are using the 64-bit version of Java, you may need to install Java DB separately. You can download Java DB from:

> www.oracle.com/technetwork/java/javadb/downloads/index.html

At the time of this writing, the latest release of MySQL Community Edition was 5.5.8. To install MySQL Community Edition on Windows, Linux or Mac OS X, see the installation overview for your platform at:

- Windows: dev.mysql.com/doc/refman/5.5/en/windows-installation.html
- Linux: dev.mysql.com/doc/refman/5.5/en/linux-installation-rpm.html
- Mac OS X: dev.mysql.com/doc/refman/5.5/en/macosx-installation.html

Carefully follow the instructions for downloading and installing the software on your platform. The downloads are available from:

> `dev.mysql.com/downloads/mysql/`

You also need to install MySQL Connector/J (the J stands for Java), which allows programs to use JDBC to interact with MySQL. MySQL Connector/J can be downloaded from

> `dev.mysql.com/downloads/connector/j/`

At the time of this writing, the current generally available release of MySQL Connector/J is 5.1.14. The documentation for Connector/J is located at

> `dev.mysql.com/doc/refman/5.5/en/connector-j.html`

To install MySQL Connector/J, carefully follow the installation instructions at:

> `dev.mysql.com/doc/refman/5.5/en/connector-j-installing.html`

We *do not* recommend modifying your system's CLASSPATH environment variable, which is discussed in the installation instructions. Instead, we'll show you how use MySQL Connector/J by specifying it as a command-line option when you execute your applications.

Obtaining the Code Examples

The examples for *Java for Programmers, 2/e* are available for download at

> `www.deitel.com/books/javafp2/`

If you're not already registered at our website, go to `www.deitel.com` and click the **Register** link below our logo in the upper-left corner of the page. Fill in your information. There's no charge to register, and we do not share your information with anyone. We send you only account-management e-mails unless you register separately for our free *Deitel® Buzz Online* e-mail newsletter at `www.deitel.com/newsletter/subscribe.html`. After registering for the site, you'll receive a confirmation e-mail with your verification code. *Click the link in the confirmation e-mail to complete your registration.* Configure your e-mail client to allow e-mails from `deitel.com` to ensure that the confirmation email is not filtered as junk mail.

Next, go to `www.deitel.com` and sign in using the **Login** link below our logo in the upper-left corner of the page. Go to `www.deitel.com/books/javafp2/`. You'll find the link to download the examples under the heading **Download Code Examples and Other Premium Content for Registered Users**. Write down the location where you choose to save the ZIP file on your computer. We assume the examples are located at `C:\Examples` on your computer.

Setting the PATH Environment Variable

The PATH environment variable on your computer designates which directories the computer searches when looking for applications, such as the applications that enable you to compile and run your Java applications (called `javac` and `java`, respectively). *Carefully follow the installation instructions for Java on your platform to ensure that you set the PATH environment variable correctly.*

If you do not set the PATH variable correctly, when you use the JDK's tools, you'll receive a message like:

```
'java' is not recognized as an internal or external command,
operable program or batch file.
```

In this case, go back to the installation instructions for setting the PATH and recheck your steps. If you've downloaded a newer version of the JDK, you may need to change the name of the JDK's installation directory in the PATH variable.

Setting the CLASSPATH Environment Variable

If you attempt to run a Java program and receive a message like

```
Exception in thread "main" java.lang.NoClassDefFoundError: YourClass
```

then your system has a CLASSPATH environment variable that must be modified. To fix the preceding error, follow the steps in setting the PATH environment variable, to locate the CLASSPATH variable, then edit the variable's value to include the local directory—typically represented as a dot (.). On Windows add

```
.;
```

at the beginning of the CLASSPATH's value (with no spaces before or after these characters). On other platforms, replace the semicolon with the appropriate path separator characters—often a colon (:)

Java's Nimbus Look-and-Feel

Java comes bundled with an elegant, cross-platform look-and-feel known as Nimbus. For programs with graphical user interfaces, we've configured our systems to use Nimbus as the default look-and-feel.

To set Nimbus as the default for all Java applications, you must create a text file named swing.properties in the lib folder of both your JDK installation folder and your JRE installation folder. Place the following line of code in the file:

```
swing.defaultlaf=com.sun.java.swing.plaf.nimbus.NimbusLookAndFeel
```

For more information on locating these installation folders visit java.sun.com/javase/6/webnotes/install/index.html. [*Note:* In addition to the standalone JRE, there's a JRE nested in your JDK's installation folder. If you're using an IDE that depends on the JDK (e.g., NetBeans), you may also need to place the swing.properties file in the nested jre folder's lib folder.]

1

Introduction

> *Man is still the most extraordinary computer of all.*
> —John F. Kennedy

> *Good design is good business.*
> —Thomas J. Watson, Founder of IBM

> *How wonderful it is that nobody need wait a single moment before starting to improve the world.*
> —Anne Frank

Objectives

In this chapter you'll learn:

- Exciting recent developments in the computer field.
- Basic object-technology concepts.
- A typical Java program-development environment.
- To test-drive a Java application.
- Some key recent software technologies.

1.1 Introduction

Welcome to Java—the world's most widely used computer programming language. In this book, you'll learn *object-oriented programming*—today's key programming methodology. You'll create and work with many *software objects* in this text.

Java is the preferred language for meeting many organizations' enterprise programming needs. Java has also become the language of choice for implementing Internet-based applications and software for devices that communicate over a network.

In use today are more than a billion general-purpose computers and billions more Java-enabled cell phones, smartphones and handheld devices (such as tablet computers). According to a study by eMarketer, the number of mobile Internet users will reach approximately 134 million by 2013.[1] Other studies have projected smartphone sales to surpass personal computer sales in 2011[2] and tablet sales to account for over 20% of all personal computer sales by 2015.[3] By 2014, the smartphone applications market is expected to exceed $40 billion,[4] which is creating significant opportunities for programming mobile applications.

Java Editions: SE, EE and ME

Java for Programmers, Second Edition is based on **Java Standard Edition 6 (Java SE 6)** and **Java SE 7.** Java is used in such a broad spectrum of applications that it has two other editions. The **Java Enterprise Edition (Java EE)**, which we use later in the book, is geared toward developing large-scale, distributed networking applications and web-based applications.

The **Java Micro Edition (Java ME)** is geared toward developing applications for small, memory-constrained devices, such as BlackBerry smartphones. Google's Android operating system—used on numerous smartphones, tablets (small, lightweight mobile computers with touch screens), e-readers and other devices—uses a customized version of Java not based on Java ME.

1.2 Introduction to Object Technology

Building software quickly, correctly and economically remains an elusive goal at a time when demands for new and more powerful software are soaring. *Objects*, or more precisely—as we'll see in Chapter 3—the *classes* objects come from, are essentially *reusable* software components. There are date objects, time objects, audio objects, video objects,

---

1. www.circleid.com/posts/mobile_internet_users_to_reach_134_million_by_2013/.
2. www.pcworld.com/article/171380/more_smartphones_than_desktop_pcs_by_2011.html.
3. www.forrester.com/ER/Press/Release/0,1769,1340,00.html.
4. *Inc.*, December 2010/January 2011, pages 116–123.

automobile objects, people objects, etc. Almost any *noun* can be reasonably represented as a software object in terms of *attributes* (e.g., name, color and size) and *behaviors* (e.g., calculating, moving and communicating). Software developers are discovering that using a modular, object-oriented design and implementation approach can make software-development groups much more productive than was possible with earlier popular techniques like "structured programming"—object-oriented programs are often easier to understand, correct and modify.

The Automobile as an Object

To help you understand objects and their contents, let's begin with a simple analogy. Suppose you want to *drive a car and make it go faster by pressing its accelerator pedal.* What must happen before you can do this? Well, before you can drive a car, someone has to *design* it. A car typically begins as engineering drawings, similar to the *blueprints* that describe the design of a house. These drawings include the design for an accelerator pedal. The pedal *hides* from the driver the complex mechanisms that actually make the car go faster, just as the brake pedal hides the mechanisms that slow the car, and the steering wheel "hides" the mechanisms that turn the car. This enables people with little or no knowledge of how engines, braking and steering mechanisms work to drive a car easily.

Just as you cannot cook meals in the kitchen of a blueprint, you cannot drive a car's engineering drawings. Before you can drive a car, it must be *built* from the engineering drawings that describe it. A completed car has an *actual* accelerator pedal to make the car go faster, but even that's not enough—the car won't accelerate on its own (hopefully!), so the driver must *press* the pedal to accelerate the car.

Methods and Classes

Let's use our car example to introduce some key object-oriented programming concepts. Performing a task in a program requires a **method**. The method houses the program statements that actually perform its tasks. The method hides these statements from its user, just as the accelerator pedal of a car hides from the driver the mechanisms of making the car go faster. In Java, we create a program unit called a **class** to house the set of methods that perform the class's tasks. For example, a class that represents a bank account might contain one method to *deposit* money to an account, another to *withdraw* money from an account and a third to *inquire* what the account's current balance is. A class is similar in concept to a car's engineering drawings, which house the design of an accelerator pedal, steering wheel, and so on.

Instantiation

Just as someone has to *build a car* from its engineering drawings before you can actually drive a car, you must *build an object* of a class before a program can perform the tasks that the class's methods define. The process of doing this is called *instantiation*. An object is then referred to as an **instance** of its class.

Reuse

Just as a car's engineering drawings can be *reused* many times to build many cars, you can *reuse* a class many times to build many objects. Reuse of existing classes when building new classes and programs saves time and effort. Reuse also helps you build more reliable and effective systems, because existing classes and components often have gone through extensive *testing*, *debugging* and *performance* tuning. Just as the notion of *interchangeable parts* was crucial to the Industrial Revolution, reusable classes are crucial to the software revolution that has been spurred by object technology.

> **Software Engineering Observation 1.1**
>
> *Use a building-block approach to creating your programs. Avoid reinventing the wheel— use existing pieces wherever possible. This software reuse is a key benefit of object-oriented programming.*

Messages and Methods Calls

When you drive a car, pressing its gas pedal sends a *message* to the car to perform a task— that is, to go faster. Similarly, you *send messages to an object*. Each message is implemented as a **method call** that tells a method of the object to perform its task. For example, a program might call a particular bank account object's *deposit* method to increase the account's balance.

Attributes and Instance Variables

A car, besides having capabilities to accomplish tasks, also has *attributes*, such as its color, its number of doors, the amount of gas in its tank, its current speed and its record of total miles driven (i.e., its odometer reading). Like its capabilities, the car's attributes are represented as part of its design in its engineering diagrams (which, for example, include an odometer and a fuel gauge). As you drive an actual car, these attributes are carried along with the car. Every car maintains its *own* attributes. For example, each car knows how much gas is in its own gas tank, but *not* how much is in the tanks of *other* cars.

An object, similarly, has attributes that it carries along as it's used in a program. These attributes are specified as part of the object's class. For example, a bank account object has a *balance attribute* that represents the amount of money in the account. Each bank account object knows the balance in the account it represents, but *not* the balances of the *other* accounts in the bank. Attributes are specified by the class's **instance variables**.

Encapsulation

Classes **encapsulate** (i.e., wrap) attributes and methods into objects—an object's attributes and methods are intimately related. Objects may communicate with one another, but they're normally not allowed to know how other objects are implemented—implementation details are *hidden* within the objects themselves. This **information hiding**, as we'll see, is crucial to good software engineering.

Inheritance

A new class of objects can be created quickly and conveniently by **inheritance**—the new class absorbs the characteristics of an existing class, possibly customizing them and adding unique characteristics of its own. In our car analogy, an object of class "convertible" certainly *is an* object of the more *general* class "automobile," but more *specifically*, the roof can be raised or lowered.

Object-Oriented Analysis and Design (OOAD)

Soon you'll be writing programs in Java. How will you create the **code** (i.e., the program instructions) for your programs? Perhaps, like many programmers, you'll simply turn on your computer and start typing. This approach may work for small programs (like the ones we present in the early chapters of the book), but what if you were asked to create a software system to control thousands of automated teller machines for a major bank? Or suppose you were asked to work on a team of 1,000 software developers building the next U.S. air traffic control system? For projects so large and complex, you should not simply sit down and start writing programs.

To create the best solutions, you should follow a detailed **analysis** process for determining your project's **requirements** (i.e., defining *what* the system is supposed to do) and developing a **design** that satisfies them (i.e., deciding *how* the system should do it). Ideally, you'd go through this process and carefully review the design (and have your design reviewed by other software professionals) before writing any code. If this process involves analyzing and designing your system from an object-oriented point of view, it's called an **object-oriented analysis and design (OOAD) process**. Languages like Java are object oriented. Programming in such a language, called **object-oriented programming (OOP)**, allows you to implement an object-oriented design as a working system.

The UML (Unified Modeling Language)

Many different OOAD processes exist, but a single graphical language for communicating the results of *any* OOAD process has come into wide use. This language, known as the Unified Modeling Language (UML), is now the most widely used graphical scheme for modeling object-oriented systems. We present our first UML diagrams in Chapters 3 and 4, then use them in our deeper treatment of object-oriented programming through Chapter 11. In our ATM Software Engineering Case Study in Chapters 12–13 we present a simple subset of the UML's features as we guide you through an object-oriented design experience.

1.3 Open Source Software

The Linux operating system is perhaps the greatest success of the *open-source* movement. **Open-source software** is a software development style that departs from the *proprietary* development that dominated software's early years. With open-source development, individuals and companies contribute their efforts in developing, maintaining and evolving software in exchange for the right to use that software for their own purposes, typically at no charge. Open-source code is often scrutinized by a much larger audience than proprietary software, so errors often get removed faster. Open source also encourages more innovation. Sun open sourced its implementation of the Java Development Kit and many of its related Java technologies.

Some organizations in the open-source community are the Eclipse Foundation (the Eclipse Integrated Development Environment helps Java programmers conveniently develop software), the Mozilla Foundation (creators of the Firefox web browser), the Apache Software Foundation (creators of the Apache web server used to develop web-based applications) and SourceForge (which provides the tools for managing open source projects—it has over 260,000 of them under development). Rapid improvements to computing and communications, decreasing costs and open-source software have made it much easier and more economical to create a software-based business now than just a few decades ago. A great example is Facebook, which was launched from a college dorm room and built with open-source software.[5]

---

5. developers.facebook.com/opensource/.

The **Linux** kernel is the core of the operating system. It's developed by a loosely organized team of volunteers, and is popular in servers, personal computers and embedded systems. Unlike that of proprietary operating systems like Microsoft's Windows and Apple's Mac OS X, Linux source code (the program code) is available to the public for examination and modification and is free to download and install. As a result, users of the operating system benefit from a community of developers actively debugging and improving the kernel, an absence of licensing fees and restrictions, and the ability to completely customize the operating system to meet specific needs.

A variety of issues—such as Microsoft's market power, the small number of user-friendly Linux applications and the diversity of Linux distributions, such as Red Hat Linux, Ubuntu Linux and many others—have prevented widespread Linux use on desktop computers. But Linux has become extremely popular on servers and in embedded systems, such as Google's Android-based smartphones.

Android

Android—the fastest growing mobile and smartphone operating system—is based on the Linux kernel and Java. Experienced Java programmers can quickly dive into Android development. One benefit of developing Android apps is the openness of the platform. The operating system is open source and free.

The Android operating system was developed by Android, Inc., which was acquired by Google in 2005. In 2007, the Open Handset Alliance™—a consortium of 34 companies initially and 79 by 2010—was formed to continue developing Android. As of December 2010, more than 300,000 Android smartphones were being activated each day![6] Android smartphones are now outselling iPhones.[7] The Android operating system is used in numerous smartphones (such as the Motorola Droid, HTC EVO™ 4G, Samsung Vibrant™ and many more), e-reader devices (such as the Barnes and Noble Nook™), tablet computers (such as the Motorola Xoom, the Dell Streak, the Samsung Galaxy Tab and more), in-store touch-screen kiosks, cars, robots and multimedia players.

Android smartphones include the functionality of a mobile phone, Internet client (for web browsing and Internet communication), MP3 player, gaming console, digital camera and more, wrapped into handheld devices with full-color *multitouch screens*—these allow you to control the device with *gestures* involving one touch or multiple simultaneous touches. You can download apps directly onto your Android device through Android Market and other app marketplaces. As of early 2011, there were over 280,000 apps in Google's Android Market.

Android App-Development Chapters on the Companion Website

Because of the tremendous interest in Android-based devices and apps, we've included on the book's website a three-chapter introduction to Android app development from our new book, *Android for Programmers: An App-Driven Approach*. After you learn Java, you'll find it straightforward to begin developing and running Android apps. You can place your apps on the online Android Market (www.market.android.com).

---

6. www.pcmag.com/article2/0,2817,2374076,00.asp.
7. mashable.com/2010/08/02/android-outselling-iphone-2/.

1.4 Java and a Typical Java Development Environment

The microprocessor revolution's most important contribution to date is that it made possible the development of personal computers. Microprocessors are having a profound impact in intelligent consumer-electronic devices. Recognizing this, Sun Microsystems in 1991 funded an internal corporate research project led by James Gosling, which resulted in a C++-based object-oriented programming language Sun called Java.

A key goal of Java is to be able to write programs that will run on a great variety of computer systems and computer-control devices. This is sometimes called "write once, run anywhere."

The web exploded in popularity in 1993, and Sun saw the potential of using Java to add *dynamic content*, such as interactivity and animations, to web pages. Java garnered the attention of the business community because of the phenomenal interest in the web. Java is now used to develop large-scale enterprise applications, to enhance the functionality of web servers (the computers that provide the content we see in our web browsers), to provide applications for consumer devices (e.g., cell phones, smartphones, television set-top boxes and more) and for many other purposes. Sun Microsystems was acquired by Oracle in 2009. At the JavaOne 2010 conference, Oracle announced that 97% of enterprise desktops, three billion handsets, and 80 million television devices run Java. There are currently over 9 million Java developers, up from 4.5 million in 2005.[8] Java is now the most widely used software development language in the world.

Java Class Libraries

You can create each class and method you need to form your Java programs. However, most Java programmers take advantage of the rich collections of existing classes and methods in the **Java class libraries**, which are also known as the **Java APIs** (**Application Programming Interfaces**).

Performance Tip 1.1

Using Java API classes and methods instead of writing your own versions can improve program performance, because they're carefully written to perform efficiently. This also shortens program development time.

Portability Tip 1.1

Although it's easier to write portable programs (i.e., programs that can run on many different types of computers) in Java than in most other programming languages, differences between compilers, JVMs and computers can make portability difficult to achieve. Simply writing programs in Java does not *guarantee portability.*

We now explain the commonly used steps in creating and executing a Java application using a Java development environment (illustrated in Figs. 1.1–1.5). Java programs normally go through five phases—edit, compile, load, verify and execute. We discuss these phases in the context of the Java SE Development Kit (JDK). You can download the most up-to-date JDK and its documentation from www.oracle.com/technetwork/java/javase/downloads/index.html. *Read the Before You Begin section of this book to ensure that*

---

8.   jaxenter.com/how-many-java-developers-are-there-10462.html.

you set up your computer properly to compile and execute Java programs. You may also want to visit Oracle's New to Java Center at:

www.oracle.com/technetwork/topics/newtojava/overview/index.html

[*Note:* This website provides installation instructions for Windows, Linux and Mac OS X. If you aren't using one of these operating systems, refer to the documentation for your system's Java environment. If you encounter a problem with this link or any others referenced in this book, please check www.deitel.com/books/javafp2/ for errata and please notify us by e-mail at deitel@deitel.com.]

Phase 1: Creating a Program

Phase 1 consists of editing a file with an *editor program*, normally known simply as an *editor* (Fig. 1.1). You type a Java program (typically referred to as **source code**) using the editor, make any necessary corrections and save the program on a secondary storage device, such as your hard drive. A file name ending with the **.java extension** indicates that the file contains Java source code.

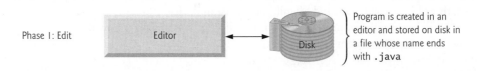

Fig. 1.1 | Typical Java development environment—editing phase.

Two editors widely used on Linux systems are vi and emacs. On Windows, Notepad will suffice. Many freeware and shareware editors are also available online, including Edit-Plus (www.editplus.com), TextPad (www.textpad.com) and jEdit (www.jedit.org).

For organizations that develop substantial information systems, **integrated development environments (IDEs)** are available from many major software suppliers. IDEs provide tools that support the software development process, including editors for writing and editing programs and debuggers for locating **logic errors**—errors that cause programs to execute incorrectly. Popular IDEs include Eclipse (www.eclipse.org) and NetBeans (www.netbeans.org).

Phase 2: Compiling a Java Program into Bytecodes

In Phase 2, you use the command **javac** (the **Java compiler**) to **compile** a program (Fig. 1.2). For example, to compile a program called Welcome.java, you'd type

```
javac Welcome.java
```

in the command window of your system (i.e., the **Command Prompt** in Windows, the *shell prompt* in Linux or the Terminal application in Mac OS X). If the program compiles, the compiler produces a **.class** file called Welcome.class that contains the compiled version of the program.

The Java compiler translates Java source code into **bytecodes** that represent the tasks to execute in the execution phase (Phase 5). Bytecodes are executed by the **Java Virtual Machine (JVM)**—a part of the JDK and the foundation of the Java platform. A **virtual**

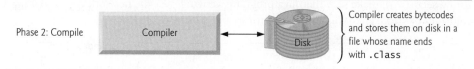

Fig. 1.2 | Typical Java development environment—compilation phase.

machine (VM) is a software application that simulates a computer but hides the underlying operating system and hardware from the programs that interact with it. If the same VM is implemented on many computer platforms, applications that it executes can be used on all those platforms. The JVM is one of the most widely used virtual machines. Microsoft's .NET uses a similar virtual-machine architecture.

Unlike machine language, which is dependent on specific computer hardware, byte-codes are platform independent—they do not depend on a particular hardware platform. So, Java's bytecodes are **portable**—without recompiling the source code, the same byte-codes can execute on any platform containing a JVM that understands the version of Java in which the bytecodes were compiled. The JVM is invoked by the **java** command. For example, to execute a Java application called Welcome, you'd type the command

```
java Welcome
```

in a command window to invoke the JVM, which would then initiate the steps necessary to execute the application. This begins Phase 3.

Phase 3: Loading a Program into Memory
In Phase 3, the JVM places the program in memory to execute it—this is known as **loading** (Fig. 1.3). The JVM's **class loader** takes the .class files containing the program's bytecodes and transfers them to primary memory. The class loader also loads any of the .class files provided by Java that your program uses. The .class files can be loaded from a disk on your system or over a network (e.g., your local college or company network, or the Internet).

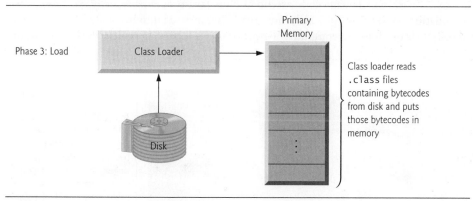

Fig. 1.3 | Typical Java development environment—loading phase.

Phase 4: Bytecode Verification
In Phase 4, as the classes are loaded, the **bytecode verifier** examines their bytecodes to ensure that they're valid and do not violate Java's security restrictions (Fig. 1.4). Java enforces

strong security to make sure that Java programs arriving over the network do not damage your files or your system (as computer viruses and worms might).

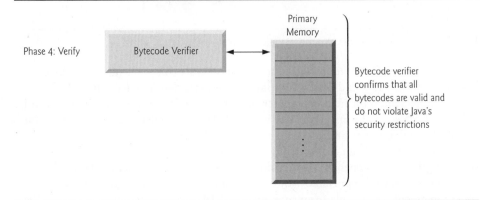

Fig. 1.4 | Typical Java development environment—verification phase.

Phase 5: Execution

In Phase 5, the JVM **executes** the program's bytecodes, thus performing the actions specified by the program (Fig. 1.5). In early Java versions, the JVM was simply an interpreter for Java bytecodes. This caused most Java programs to execute slowly, because the JVM would interpret and execute one bytecode at a time. Some modern computer architectures can execute several instructions in parallel. Today's JVMs typically execute bytecodes using a combination of interpretation and so-called **just-in-time (JIT) compilation**. In this process, the JVM analyzes the bytecodes as they're interpreted, searching for *hot spots*—parts of the bytecodes that execute frequently. For these parts, a **just-in-time (JIT) compiler**—known as the **Java HotSpot compiler**—translates the bytecodes into the underlying computer's machine language. When the JVM encounters these compiled parts again, the faster machine-language code executes. Thus Java programs actually go through *two* compilation phases—one in which source code is translated into bytecodes (for portability across JVMs on different computer platforms) and a second in which, during execution,

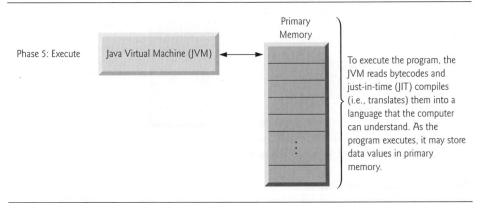

Fig. 1.5 | Typical Java development environment—execution phase.

the bytecodes are translated into machine language for the actual computer on which the program executes.

Problems That May Occur at Execution Time

Programs might not work on the first try. Each of the preceding phases can fail because of various errors that we'll discuss throughout this book. For example, an executing program might try to divide by zero (an illegal operation for whole-number arithmetic in Java). This would cause the Java program to display an error message. If this occurred, you'd have to return to the edit phase, make the necessary corrections and proceed through the remaining phases again to determine that the corrections fixed the problem(s). [*Note:* Most programs in Java input or output data. When we say that a program displays a message, we normally mean that it displays that message on your computer's screen. Messages and other data may be output to other devices, such as disks and hardcopy printers, or even to a network for transmission to other computers.]

Common Programming Error 1.1

*Errors such as division by zero occur as a program runs, so they're called **runtime errors** or **execution-time errors**. Fatal runtime errors cause programs to terminate immediately without having successfully performed their jobs. **Nonfatal runtime errors** allow programs to run to completion, often producing incorrect results.*

1.5 Test-Driving a Java Application

In this section, you'll run and interact with your first Java application. You'll begin by running an ATM application that simulates the transactions that take place when you use an ATM machine (e.g., withdrawing money, making deposits and checking your account balances). You'll learn how to build this application in the object-oriented case study included in Chapters 12–13. For the purpose of this section, we assume you're running Microsoft Windows.[9]

In the following steps, you'll run the application and perform various transactions. The elements and functionality you see here are typical of what you'll learn to program in this book. [*Note:* We use fonts to distinguish between features you see on a screen (e.g., the **Command Prompt**) and elements that are not directly related to a screen. Our convention is to emphasize screen features like titles and menus (e.g., the **File** menu) in a semibold sans-serif Helvetica font and to emphasize nonscreen elements, such as file names or input (e.g., `ProgramName.java`) in a sans-serif Lucida font. As you've already noticed, the defining occurrence of each key term in the text is set in **bold**. In the figures in this section, we highlight in gray the user input required by each step and point out significant parts of the application. To make these features more visible, we've changed the background color of the **Command Prompt** windows to white and the foreground color to black.] This is a simple text-only version. Later in the book, you'll learn the techniques to rework this using GUI (graphical user interface) techniques.

---

9. At `www.deitel.com/books/javafp2/`, we provide videos that help you get started with popular integrated development environments (IDEs) Eclipse and NetBeans.

1. *Checking your setup.* Read the Before You Begin section of the book to confirm that you've set up Java properly on your computer and that you've copied the book's examples to your hard drive.

2. *Locating the completed application.* Open a **Command Prompt** window. This can be done by selecting **Start > All Programs > Accessories > Command Prompt**. Change to the ATM application directory by typing cd C:\examples\ch01\ATM, then press *Enter* (Fig. 1.6). The command cd is used to change directories.

Using the **cd** command to
change directories   File location of the ATM application

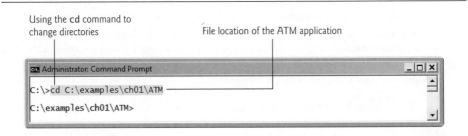

Fig. I.6 | Opening a **Command Prompt** and changing directories.

3. *Running the ATM application.* Type the command java ATMCaseStudy and press *Enter* (Fig. 1.7). Recall that the java command, followed by the name of the application's .class file (in this case, ATMCaseStudy), executes the application. Specifying the .class extension when using the java command results in an error. [*Note:* Java commands are case sensitive. It's important to type the name of this application with a capital A, T and M in "ATM," a capital C in "Case" and a capital S in "Study." Otherwise, the application will not execute.] If you receive the error message, "Exception in thread "main" java.lang.NoClass-DefFoundError: ATMCaseStudy," your system has a CLASSPATH problem. Please refer to the Before You Begin section of the book for instructions to help you fix this problem.

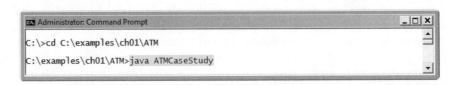

Fig. I.7 | Using the java command to execute the ATM application.

4. *Entering an account number.* When the application first executes, it displays a "Welcome!" greeting and prompts you for an account number. Type 12345 at the "Please enter your account number:" prompt (Fig. 1.8) and press *Enter*.

5. *Entering a PIN.* Once a valid account number is entered, the application displays the prompt "Enter your PIN:". Type "54321" as your valid PIN (Personal Identification Number) and press *Enter*. The ATM main menu containing a list of

options will be displayed (Fig. 1.9). We'll show how you can enter a PIN private-ly using a JPasswordField in Chapter 14.

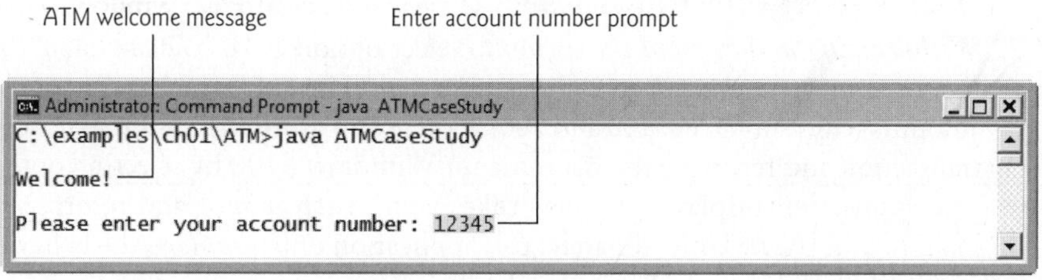

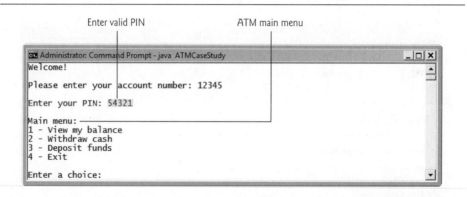

Fig. 1.8 | Prompting the user for an account number.

Fig. 1.9 | Entering a valid PIN number and displaying the ATM application's main menu.

6. *Viewing the account balance.* Select option 1, "View my balance", from the ATM menu (Fig. 1.10). The application then displays two numbers—the Available balance ($1000.00) and the Total balance ($1200.00). The avail-able balance is the maximum amount of money in your account which is available

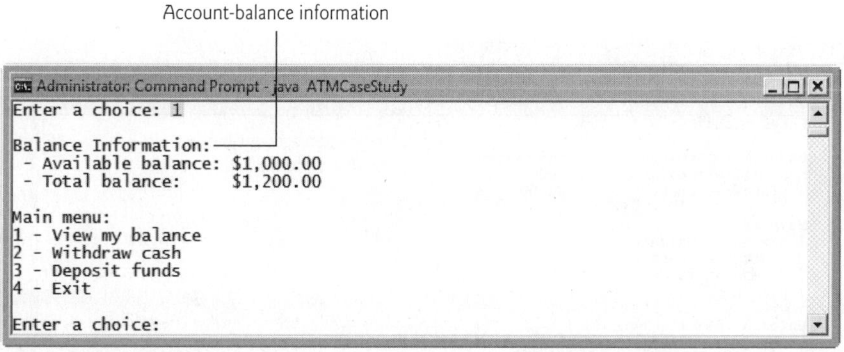

Fig. 1.10 | ATM application displaying user account-balance information.

for withdrawal at a given time. In some cases, certain funds, such as recent deposits, are not immediately available for the user to withdraw, so the available balance may be less than the total balance, as it is here. After the account-balance information is shown, the application's main menu is displayed again.

7. *Withdrawing money from the account.* Select option 2, "Withdraw cash", from the application menu. You're then presented (Fig. 1.11) with a list of dollar amounts (e.g., 20, 40, 60, 100 and 200). You're also given the option to cancel the transaction and return to the main menu. Withdraw $100 by selecting option 4. The application displays "Please take your cash now." and returns to the main menu. [*Note:* Unfortunately, this application only *simulates* the behavior of a real ATM and thus does not actually dispense money.]

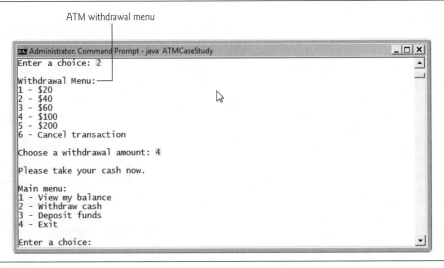

Fig. 1.11 | Withdrawing money from the account and returning to the main menu.

8. *Confirming that the account information has been updated.* From the main menu, select option 1 again to view your current account balance (Fig. 1.12). Both the available balance and the total balance have been updated to reflect your withdrawal transaction.

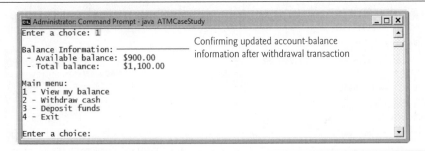

Fig. 1.12 | Checking the new balance.

9. *Ending the transaction.* To end your current ATM session, select option 4, "Exit", from the main menu (Fig. 1.13). The ATM will exit the system and display
   a goodbye message to the user. The application will then return to its original
   prompt, asking for the next user's account number.

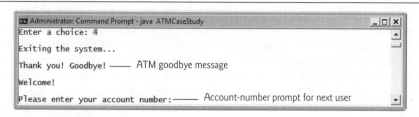

Fig. 1.13 | Ending an ATM transaction session.

10. *Exiting the ATM and closing the* **Command Prompt** *window.* Most applications
    provide an option to exit and return to the **Command Prompt** directory from
    which the application was run. A real ATM does not provide a user with the op-
    tion to turn off the ATM. Rather, when a user has completed all desired transac-
    tions and chosen the menu option to exit, the ATM resets itself and displays a
    prompt for the next user's account number. As Fig. 1.13 illustrates, the ATM ap-
    plication here behaves similarly. Choosing the menu option to exit ends only the
    current user's ATM session, not the entire ATM application. To actually exit the
    ATM application, click the close (**x**) button in the upper-right corner of the **Com-
    mand Prompt** window. Closing the window causes the running application to ter-
    minate.

1.6 Web 2.0: Going Social

The web literally exploded in the mid-to-late 1990s, but the "dot com" economic bust
brought hard times in the early 2000s. The resurgence that began in 2004 or so has been
named **Web 2.0**. Google is widely regarded as the signature company of Web 2.0. Some
other companies with "Web 2.0 characteristics" are YouTube (video sharing), FaceBook
(social networking), Twitter (microblogging), Groupon (social commerce), Foursquare
(mobile check-in), Salesforce (business software offered as online services), Craigslist (free
classified listings), Flickr (photo sharing), Second Life (a virtual world), Skype (Internet
telephony) and Wikipedia (a free online encyclopedia).

Google
In 1996, Stanford computer science Ph.D. candidates Larry Page and Sergey Brin began
collaborating on a new search engine. In 1997, they changed the name to Google—a play
on the mathematical term *googol*, a quantity represented by the number "one" followed by
100 "zeros" (or 10^{100})—a staggeringly large number. Google's ability to return extremely
accurate search results quickly helped it become the most widely used search engine and
one of the most popular websites in the world.

Google continues to be an innovator in search technologies. For example, Google
Goggles is a fascinating mobile app (available on Android and iPhone) that allows you to

perform a Google search using a photo rather than entering text. You simply take pictures of landmarks, books (covers or barcodes), logos, art or wine bottle labels, and Google Goggles scans the photos and returns search results. You can also take a picture of text (for example, a restaurant menu or a sign) and Google Goggles will translate it for you.

Web Services and Mashups

We include in this book a substantial treatment of web services (Chapter 28) and introduce the applications-development methodology of *mashups* in which you can rapidly develop powerful and intriguing applications by combining (often free) complementary web services and other forms of information feeds (Fig. 1.14). One of the first mashups was www.housingmaps.com, which quickly combines the real estate listings provided by www.craigslist.org with the mapping capabilities of *Google Maps* to offer maps that show the locations of apartments for rent in a given area.

Web services source	How it's used
Google Maps	Mapping services
Facebook	Social networking
Foursquare	Mobile check-in
LinkedIn	Social networking for business
YouTube	Video search
Twitter	Microblogging
Groupon	Social commerce
Netflix	Movie rentals
eBay	Internet auctions
Wikipedia	Collaborative encyclopedia
PayPal	Payments
Last.fm	Internet radio
Amazon eCommerce	Shopping for books and more
Salesforce.com	Customer Relationship Management (CRM)
Skype	Internet telephony
Microsoft Bing	Search
Flickr	Photo sharing
Zillow	Real estate pricing
Yahoo Search	Search
WeatherBug	Weather

Fig. 1.14 | Some popular web services (www.programmableweb.com/apis/directory/1?sort=mashups).

Ajax

Ajax is one of the premier Web 2.0 software technologies. Ajax helps Internet-based applications perform like desktop applications—a difficult task, given that such applications suffer transmission delays as data is shuttled back and forth between your computer and server computers on the Internet. Using Ajax, applications like Google Maps have achieved excellent performance and approach the look-and-feel of desktop applications. Although we don't discuss "raw" Ajax programming (which is quite complex) in this text, we do show in Chapter 27 how to build Ajax-enabled applications using JavaServer Faces (JSF) Ajax-enabled components.

Social Applications

Over the last several years, there's been a tremendous increase in the number of social applications on the web. Even though the computer industry is mature, these sites were still able to become phenomenally successful in a relatively short period of time. Figure 1.15 discusses a few of the social applications that are making an impact.

Company	Description
Facebook	Facebook was launched from a Harvard dorm room in 2004 by classmates Mark Zuckerberg, Chris Hughes, Dustin Moskovitz and Eduardo Saverin and is already worth an estimated $70 billion. By January 2011, Facebook was the most active site on the Internet with more than 600 million users—nearly 9% of the Earth's population—who spend 700 billion minutes on Facebook per month (`www.time.com/time/specials/packages/article/0,28804,2036683_2037183,00.html`). At its current growth rate (about 5% per month), Facebook will reach one billion users in 2012, out of the two billion Internet users! The activity on the site makes it extremely attractive for application developers. Each day, over 20 million applications are installed by Facebook users (`www.facebook.com/press/info.php?statistics`).
Twitter	Twitter was founded in 2006 by Jack Dorsey, Evan Williams and Isaac "Biz" Stone—all from the podcast company, Odeo. Twitter has revolutionized *microblogging*. Users post tweets—messages of up to 140 characters long. Approximately 95 million tweets are posted per day (`twitter.com/about`). You can follow the tweets of friends, celebrities, businesses, government representatives (including the U.S. President, who has 6.3 million followers), etc., or you can follow tweets by subject to track news, trends and more. At the time of this writing, Lady Gaga had the most followers (over 7.7 million). Twitter has become the point of origin for many breaking news stories worldwide.
Groupon	Groupon, a *social commerce* site, was launched by Andrew Mason in 2008. By January 2011, the company was valued around $15 billion, making it the fastest growing company ever! It's now available in hundreds of markets worldwide. Groupon offers one daily deal in each market for restaurants, retailers, services, attractions and more. Deals are activated only after a minimum number of people sign up to buy the product or service. If you sign up for a deal and it has yet to meet the minimum, you might be inclined to tell others about the deal by email, Facebook, Twitter, etc. If the deal does not meet the minimum sales, it's cancelled. One of the most successful national Groupon deals to date was a certificate for $50 worth of merchandise from a major apparel company for $25. Over 440,000 vouchers were sold in one day.

Fig. 1.15 | Social applications. (Part 1 of 2.)

Company	Description
Foursquare	Foursquare—launched in 2009 by Dennis Crowley and Naveen Selvadurai—is a mobile *check-in* application that allows you to notify your friends of your whereabouts. You can download the app to your smartphone and link it to your Facebook and Twitter accounts so your friends can follow you from multiple platforms. If you do not have a smartphone, you can check in by text message. Foursquare uses GPS to determine your exact location. Businesses use Foursquare to send offers to users in the area. Launched in March 2009, Foursquare already has over 5 million users worldwide.
Skype	Skype is a software product that allows you to make mostly free voice and video calls over the Internet using a technology called *VoIP (Voice over IP*; IP stands for Internet Protocol*)*. Skype was founded in 2003 by Niklas Zennström and Dane Janus Friis. Just two years later, the company was sold to eBay for $2.6 billion.
YouTube	YouTube is a video-sharing site that was founded in 2005. Within one year, the company was purchased by Google for $1.65 billion. YouTube now accounts for 10% of all Internet traffic (`www.webpronews.com/topnews/2010/04/16/ facebook-and-youtube-get-the-most-business-internet-traffic`). Within one week of the release of Apple's iPhone 3GS—the first iPhone model to offer video—mobile uploads to YouTube grew 400% (`www.hypebot.com/hypebot/ 2009/06/youtube-reports-1700-jump-in-mobile-video.html`).

Fig. 1.15 | Social applications. (Part 2 of 2.)

1.7 Software Technologies

Figure 1.16 lists a number of buzzwords that you'll hear in the software development community. We've created Resource Centers on most of these topics, with more on the way.

Technology	Description
Agile software development	**Agile software development** is a set of methodologies that try to get software implemented faster and using fewer resources than previous methodologies. Check out the Agile Alliance (`www.agilealliance.org`) and the Agile Manifesto (`www.agilemanifesto.org`).
Refactoring	**Refactoring** involves reworking programs to make them clearer and easier to maintain while preserving their correctness and functionality. It's widely employed with agile development methodologies. Many IDEs contain built-in *refactoring tools* to do major portions of the reworking automatically.
Design patterns	**Design patterns** are proven architectures for constructing flexible and maintainable object-oriented software. The field of design patterns tries to enumerate those recurring patterns, encouraging software designers to *reuse* them to develop better-quality software using less time, money and effort.

Fig. 1.16 | Software technologies. (Part 1 of 2.)

Technology	Description
LAMP	MySQL is an open-source database management system. PHP is the most popular open-source server-side "scripting" language for developing web applications. **LAMP** is an acronym for the open-source technologies that many developers use to build web applications—it stands for Linux, Apache, MySQL and PHP (or Perl or Python—two other scripting languages).
Software as a Service (SaaS)	Software has generally been viewed as a product; most software still is offered this way. To run an application, you buy it from a software vendor. You then install it on your computer and run it as needed. As new versions appear, you upgrade the software, often at considerable expense. This process can be cumbersome for organizations with tens of thousands of systems that must be maintained on a diverse array of computer equipment. With **Software as a Service (SaaS)**, the software runs on servers elsewhere on the Internet. When that server is updated, all clients worldwide see the new capabilities—no local installation is needed. You access the service through a browser. Browsers are quite portable, so you can run the same applications on a wide variety of computers from anywhere in the world. Salesforce.com, Google, and Microsoft's Office Live and Windows Live all offer SaaS.
Platform as a Service (PaaS)	**Platform as a Service (PaaS)** provides a computing platform for developing and running applications as a service over the web, rather than installing the tools on your computer. PaaS providers include Google App Engine, Amazon EC2, Bungee Labs and more.
Cloud computing	SaaS and PaaS are examples of **cloud computing** in which software, platforms and infrastructure (e.g., processing power and storage) are hosted on demand over the Internet. This provides users with flexibility, scalability and cost savings. For example, consider a company's data storage needs which can fluctuate significantly over the course of a year. Rather than investing in large-scale storage hardware—which can be costly to purchase, maintain and secure, and would most likely not be used to capacity at all times—the company could purchase cloud-based services (such as Amazon S3, Google Storage, Microsoft Windows Azure™, Nirvanix™ and others) dynamically as needed.
Software Development Kit (SDK)	**Software Development Kits (SDKs)** include the tools and documentation developers use to program applications. For example, you'll use the Java Development Kit (JDK) to build and run Java applications.

Fig. 1.16 | Software technologies. (Part 2 of 2.)

Figure 1.17 describes software product release categories.

Version	Description
Alpha	*Alpha* software is the earliest release of a software product that's still under active development. Alpha versions are often buggy, incomplete and unstable, and are released to a relatively small number of developers for testing new features, getting early feedback, etc.

Fig. 1.17 | Software product release terminology. (Part 1 of 2.)

Version	Description
Beta	*Beta* versions are released to a larger number of developers later in the development process after most major bugs have been fixed and new features are nearly complete. Beta software is more stable, but still subject to change.
Release candidates	*Release candidates* are generally *feature complete* and (supposedly) bug free, and ready for use by the community, which provides a diverse testing environment—the software is used on different systems, with varying constraints and for a variety of purposes. Any bugs that appear are corrected and eventually the final product is released to the general public. Software companies often distribute incremental updates over the Internet.
Continuous beta	Software that's developed using this approach generally does not have version numbers (for example, Google search or Gmail). The software, which is hosted in the cloud (not installed on your computer), is constantly evolving so that users always have the latest version.

Fig. 1.17 | Software product release terminology. (Part 2 of 2.)

1.8 Keeping Up to Date with Information Technologies

Figure 1.18 lists key technical and business publications that will help you stay up-to-date with the latest news and trends and technology. You can also find a growing list of Internet- and web-related Resource Centers at www.deitel.com/ResourceCenters.html.

Publication	URL
Bloomberg BusinessWeek	www.businessweek.com
CNET	news.cnet.com
Computer World	www.computerworld.com
Engadget	www.engadget.com
eWeek	www.eweek.com
Fast Company	www.fastcompany.com/
Fortune	money.cnn.com/magazines/fortune/
InfoWorld	www.infoworld.com
Mashable	mashable.com
PCWorld	www.pcworld.com
SD Times	www.sdtimes.com
Slashdot	slashdot.org/
Smarter Technology	www.smartertechnology.com
Technology Review	technologyreview.com
Techcrunch	techcrunch.com
Wired	www.wired.com

Fig. 1.18 | Technical and business publications.

1.9 Wrap-Up

In this chapter we discussed computer hardware, software, programming languages and operating systems. We overviewed a typical Java program development environment and you test-drove a Java application. We introduced the basics of object technology. We also discussed some key software development terminology.

In Chapter 2, you'll create your first Java applications. You'll see how programs display messages on the screen and obtain information from the user at the keyboard for processing. You'll use Java's primitive data types and arithmetic operators in calculations and use Java's equality and relational operators to write simple decision-making statements.

2

Introduction to Java Applications

Objectives

In this chapter you'll learn:

- To write simple Java applications.
- To use input and output statements.
- Java's primitive types.
- To use arithmetic operators.
- The precedence of arithmetic operators.
- To write decision-making statements.
- To use relational and equality operators.

What's in a name?
That which we call a rose
By any other name would
smell as sweet.
—William Shakespeare

When faced with a
decision,
I always ask, "What would
be the most fun?"
—Peggy Walker

The chief merit of language
is clearness.
—Galen

One person can make a
difference and every person
should try.
—John F. Kennedy

2.1 Introduction

This chapter introduces Java application programming. We begin with examples of programs that display messages on the screen. We then present a program that obtains two numbers from a user, calculates their sum and displays the result. The last example demonstrates how to make decisions. The application compares numbers, then displays messages that show the comparison results.

This chapter uses tools from the JDK to compile and run programs. We've also posted *Dive Into*® videos at www.deitel.com/books/javafp2/ to help you get started with the popular Eclipse and NetBeans integrated development environments.

2.2 Your First Program in Java: Printing a Line of Text

A Java **application** is a computer program that executes when you use the **java command** to launch the Java Virtual Machine (JVM). Later in this section we'll discuss how to compile and run a Java application. First we consider a simple application that displays a line of text. Figure 2.1 shows the program followed by a box that displays its output. The program includes line numbers. We've added these for instructional purposes—they're *not* part of a Java program. This example illustrates several important Java features. We'll see that line 9 does the real work—displaying the phrase Welcome to Java Programming! on the screen.

```
1   // Fig. 2.1: Welcome1.java
2   // Text-printing program.
3
4   public class Welcome1
5   {
6      // main method begins execution of Java application
7      public static void main( String[] args )
8      {
9         System.out.println( "Welcome to Java Programming!" );
10     } // end method main
11  } // end class Welcome1
```

```
Welcome to Java Programming!
```

Fig. 2.1 | Text-printing program.

Commenting Your Programs

By convention, we begin every program with a comment indicating the figure number and file name. The comment in line 1 begins with //, indicating that it is an **end-of-line com-**

ment—it terminates at the end of the line on which the // appears. An end-of-line comment need not begin a line; it also can begin in the middle of a line and continue until the end (as in lines 10 and 11). Line 2 is a comment that describes the purpose of the program.

Java also has **traditional comments**, which can be spread over several lines as in

```
/* This is a traditional comment. It
   can be split over multiple lines */
```

These begin and end with delimiters, /* and */. The compiler ignores all text between the delimiters. Java incorporated traditional comments and end-of-line comments from the C and C++ programming languages, respectively. In this book, we use only // comments.

Java provides comments of a third type, **Javadoc comments**. These are delimited by /** and */. The compiler ignores all text between the delimiters. Javadoc comments enable you to embed program documentation directly in your programs. Such comments are the preferred Java documenting format in industry. The **javadoc utility program** (part of the Java SE Development Kit) reads Javadoc comments and uses them to prepare your program's documentation in HTML format.

Using Blank Lines

Line 3 is a blank line. Blank lines, space characters and tabs make programs easier to read. Together, they're known as **white space** (or whitespace). The compiler ignores white space.

Declaring a Class

Line 4 begins a **class declaration** for class Welcome1. Every Java program consists of at least one class that you (the programmer) define. The **class keyword** introduces a class declaration and is immediately followed by the **class name** (Welcome1). **Keywords** are reserved for use by Java and are always spelled with all lowercase letters. The complete list of keywords is shown in Appendix C.

Class Names and Identifiers

By convention, class names begin with a capital letter and capitalize the first letter of each word they include (e.g., SampleClassName). A class name is an **identifier**—a series of characters consisting of letters, digits, underscores (_) and dollar signs ($) that does not begin with a digit and does not contain spaces. Some valid identifiers are Welcome1, $value, _value, m_inputField1 and button7. The name 7button is not a valid identifier because it begins with a digit, and the name input field is not a valid identifier because it contains a space. Normally, an identifier that does not begin with a capital letter is not a class name. Java is **case sensitive**—uppercase and lowercase letters are distinct—so value and Value are different (but both valid) identifiers.

In Chapters 4–7, every class we define begins with the **public** keyword. For now, we simply require this keyword. For our application, the file name is Welcome1.java. You'll learn more about public and non-public classes in Chapter 8.

Common Programming Error 2.1

A public class must be placed in a file that has the same name as the class (in terms of both spelling and capitalization) plus the .java extension; otherwise, a compilation error occurs. For example, public class Welcome must be placed in a file named Welcome.java.

A **left brace** (as in line 5), {, begins the **body** of every class declaration. A corresponding **right brace** (at line 11), }, must end each class declaration. Lines 6–10 are indented.

Good Programming Practice 2.1

Indent the entire body of each class declaration one "level" between the left brace and the right brace that delimit the body of the class. We recommend using three spaces to form a level of indent. This format emphasizes the class declaration's structure and makes it easier to read.

Good Programming Practice 2.2

Many IDEs insert indentation for you in all the right places. The Tab *key may also be used to indent code, but tab stops vary among text editors. Most IDEs allow you to configure tabs such that a specified number of spaces is inserted each time you press the* Tab *key.*

Declaring a Method

Line 6 is an end-of-line comment indicating the purpose of lines 7–10. Line 7 is the starting point of every Java application. The **parentheses** after the identifier `main` indicate that it's a **method**. Java class declarations normally contain one or more methods. For a Java application, one of the methods *must* be called `main` and must be defined as shown in line 7; otherwise, the Java Virtual Machine (JVM) will not execute the application. Methods perform tasks and can return information when they complete their tasks. Keyword **void** indicates that this method will *not* return any information. In line 7, the `String[] args` in parentheses is a required part of the method `main`'s declaration—we discuss this in Chapter 7.

The left brace in line 8 begins the **body of the method declaration**. A corresponding right brace ends it (line 10). Line 9 in the method body is indented between the braces.

Good Programming Practice 2.3

Indent the entire body of each method declaration one "level" between the braces that define the body of the method.

Performing Output with `System.out.println`

Line 9 instructs the computer to perform an action—namely, to print the **string** of characters contained between the double quotation marks (but not the quotation marks themselves). White-space characters in strings are *not* ignored by the compiler. Strings cannot span multiple lines of code, but as you'll see later, this does not restrict you from using long strings in your code.

The `System.out` object is known as the **standard output object**. It allows a Java applications to display information in the **command window** from which it executes. In recent versions of Microsoft Windows, the command window is the **Command Prompt**. In UNIX/Linux/Mac OS X, the command window is called a **terminal window** or a **shell**. Many programmers call it simply the **command line**.

Method `System.out.println` displays a line of text in the command window. The string in the parentheses in line 9 is the method's **argument**. When `System.out.println` completes its task, it positions the output cursor (the location where the next character will be displayed) at the beginning of the next line in the command window.

The entire line 9, including `System.out.println`, the argument `"Welcome to Java Programming!"` in the parentheses and the **semicolon** (`;`), is called a **statement**. A method typically contains one or more statements that perform its task. Most statements end with a semicolon. When the statement in line 9 executes, it displays Welcome to Java Programming! in the command window.

Using End-of-Line Comments on Right Braces for Readability

We include an end-of-line comment after a closing brace that ends a method declaration and after a closing brace that ends a class declaration. For example, line 10 indicates the closing brace of method main, and line 11 indicates the closing brace of class Welcome1. Each comment indicates the method or class that the right brace terminates.

Compiling and Executing Your First Java Application

We assume you're using the Java Development Kit's command-line tools, not an IDE. Our Java Resource Centers at www.deitel.com/ResourceCenters.html provide links to tutorials that help you get started with several popular Java development tools, including NetBeans™, Eclipse™ and others. We've also posted NetBeans and Eclipse videos at www.deitel.com/books/javafp2/ to help you get started using these popular IDEs.

To prepare to compile the program, open a command window and change to the directory where the program is stored. Many operating systems use the command cd to change directories. On Windows, for example,

```
cd c:\examples\ch02\fig02_01
```

changes to the fig02_01 directory. On UNIX/Linux/Max OS X, the command

```
cd ~/examples/ch02/fig02_01
```

changes to the fig02_01 directory.
   To compile the program, type

```
javac Welcome1.java
```

If the program contains no syntax errors, this command creates a new file called Welcome1.class (known as the **class file** for Welcome1) containing the platform-independent Java bytecodes that represent our application. When we use the java command to execute the application on a given platform, the JVM will translate these bytecodes into instructions that are understood by the underlying operating system and hardware.

Error-Prevention Tip 2.1

When attempting to compile a program, if you receive a message such as "bad command or filename," "javac: command not found" or "'javac' is not recognized as an internal or external command, operable program or batch file," then your Java software installation was not completed properly. If you're using the JDK, this indicates that the system's PATH environment variable was not set properly. Please carefully review the installation instructions in the Before You Begin section of this book. On some systems, after correcting the PATH, you may need to reboot your computer or open a new command window for these settings to take effect.

Error-Prevention Tip 2.2

Each syntax-error message contains the file name and line number where the error occurred. For example, Welcome1.java:6 indicates that an error occurred at line 6 in Welcome1.java. The rest of the message provides information about the syntax error.

Error-Prevention Tip 2.3

The compiler error message "`class Welcome1 is public, should be declared in a file`
`named Welcome1.java`" indicates that the file name does not match the name of the pub-
lic class in the file or that you typed the class name incorrectly when compiling the class.

Figure 2.2 shows the program of Fig. 2.1 executing in a Microsoft® Windows® 7
Command Prompt window. To execute the program, type java `Welcome1`. This command
launches the JVM, which loads the `.class` file for class `Welcome1`. The command omits
the `.class` file-name extension; otherwise, the JVM will not execute the program. The
JVM calls method `main`. Next, the statement at line 9 of `main` displays "`Welcome to Java`
`Programming!`" [*Note:* Many environments show command prompts with black back-
grounds and white text. We adjusted these settings in our environment to make our screen
captures more readable.]

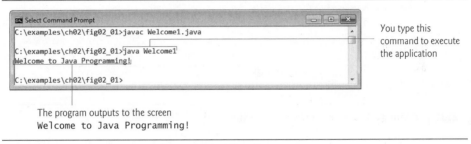

You type this
command to execute
the application

The program outputs to the screen
`Welcome to Java Programming!`

Fig. 2.2 | Executing `Welcome1` from the **Command Prompt**.

Error-Prevention Tip 2.4

When attempting to run a Java program, if you receive a message such as "`Exception in`
`thread "main" java.lang.NoClassDefFoundError: Welcome1`," your CLASSPATH envi-
ronment variable has not been set properly. Please carefully review the installation in-
structions in the Before You Begin section of this book. On some systems, you may need to
reboot your computer or open a new command window after configuring the CLASSPATH.

2.3 Modifying Your First Java Program

In this section, we modify the example in Fig. 2.1 to print text on one line by using multiple statements and to print text on several lines by using a single statement.

Displaying a Single Line of Text with Multiple Statements

`Welcome to Java Programming!` can be displayed several ways. Class `Welcome2`, shown in
Fig. 2.3, uses two statements (lines 9–10) to produce the output shown in Fig. 2.1. [*Note:*
From this point forward, we highlight the new and key features in each code listing, as
we've done for lines 9–10.]

The program is similar to Fig. 2.1, so we discuss only the changes here. Line 2 is an
end-of-line comment stating the purpose of the program. Line 4 begins the `Welcome2` class
declaration. Lines 9–10 of method `main` display one line of text. The first statement uses
`System.out`'s method `print` to display a string. Each `print` or `println` statement resumes
displaying characters from where the last `print` or `println` statement stopped displaying

characters. Unlike `println`, after displaying its argument, `print` does *not* position the output cursor at the beginning of the next line in the command window—the next character the program displays will appear *immediately after* the last character that `print` displays. Thus, line 10 positions the first character in its argument (the letter "J") immediately after the last character that line 9 displays (the *space character* before the string's closing double-quote character).

```
 1   // Fig. 2.3: Welcome2.java
 2   // Printing a line of text with multiple statements.
 3
 4   public class Welcome2
 5   {
 6      // main method begins execution of Java application
 7      public static void main( String[] args )
 8      {
 9         System.out.print( "Welcome to " );
10         System.out.println( "Java Programming!" );
11      } // end method main
12   } // end class Welcome2
```

```
Welcome to Java Programming!
```

Fig. 2.3 | Printing a line of text with multiple statements.

Displaying Multiple Lines of Text with a Single Statement

A single statement can display multiple lines by using **newline characters**, which indicate to `System.out`'s `print` and `println` methods when to position the output cursor at the beginning of the next line in the command window. Like blank lines, space characters and tab characters, newline characters are white-space characters. The program in Fig. 2.4 outputs four lines of text, using newline characters to determine when to begin each new line. Most of the program is identical to those in Fig. 2.1 and Fig. 2.3.

```
 1   // Fig. 2.4: Welcome3.java
 2   // Printing multiple lines of text with a single statement.
 3
 4   public class Welcome3
 5   {
 6      // main method begins execution of Java application
 7      public static void main( String[] args )
 8      {
 9         System.out.println( "Welcome\nto\nJava\nProgramming!" );
10      } // end method main
11   } // end class Welcome3
```

```
Welcome
to
Java
Programming!
```

Fig. 2.4 | Printing multiple lines of text with a single statement.

Line 2 is a comment stating the program's purpose. Line 4 begins the `Welcome3` class declaration. Line 9 displays four separate lines of text in the command window. Normally, the characters in a string are displayed *exactly* as they appear in the double quotes. Note, however, that the paired characters \ and n (repeated three times in the statement) do not appear on the screen. The **backslash** (\) is an **escape character**. which has special meaning to `System.out`'s `print` and `println` methods. When a backslash appears in a string, Java combines it with the next character to form an **escape sequence**. The escape sequence \n represents the newline character. When a newline character appears in a string being output with `System.out`, the newline character causes the screen's output cursor to move to the beginning of the next line in the command window.

Figure 2.5 lists several common escape sequences and describes how they affect the display of characters in the command window. For the complete list of escape sequences, visit `java.sun.com/docs/books/jls/third_edition/html/lexical.html#3.10.6`.

Escape sequence	Description
\n	Newline. Position the screen cursor at the beginning of the next line.
\t	Horizontal tab. Move the screen cursor to the next tab stop.
\r	Carriage return. Position the screen cursor at the beginning of the current line—do *not* advance to the next line. Any characters output after the carriage return overwrite the characters previously output on that line.
\\	Backslash. Used to print a backslash character.
\"	Double quote. Used to print a double-quote character. For example, `System.out.println( "\"in quotes\"" );` displays `"in quotes"`.

Fig. 2.5 | Some common escape sequences.

2.4 Displaying Text with `printf`

The **`System.out.printf`** method (f means "formatted") displays formatted data. Figure 2.6 uses this method to output the strings `"Welcome to"` and `"Java Programming!"`. Lines 9–10

```
System.out.printf( "%s\n%s\n",
    "Welcome to", "Java Programming!" );
```

call method `System.out.printf` to display the program's output. The method call specifies three arguments. When a method requires multiple arguments, they're placed in a **comma-separated list**.

Lines 9–10 represent only *one* statement. Java allows large statements to be split over many lines. We indent line 10 to indicate that it's a *continuation* of line 9.

 Common Programming Error 2.2
Splitting a statement in the middle of an identifier or a string is a syntax error.

```
 1   // Fig. 2.6: Welcome4.java
 2   // Displaying multiple lines with method System.out.printf.
 3
 4   public class Welcome4
 5   {
 6      // main method begins execution of Java application
 7      public static void main( String[] args )
 8      {
 9         System.out.printf( "%s\n%s\n",
10            "Welcome to", "Java Programming!" );
11      } // end method main
12   } // end class Welcome4
```

```
Welcome to
Java Programming!
```

Fig. 2.6 | Displaying multiple lines with method `System.out.printf`.

Method `printf`'s first argument is a **format string** that may consist of **fixed text** and **format specifiers**. Fixed text is output by `printf` just as it would be by `print` or `println`. Each format specifier is a placeholder for a value and specifies the type of data to output. Format specifiers also may include optional formatting information.

Format specifiers begin with a percent sign (%) followed by a character that represents the data type. For example, the format specifier **%s** is a placeholder for a string. The format string in line 9 specifies that `printf` should output two strings, each followed by a newline character. At the first format specifier's position, `printf` substitutes the value of the first argument after the format string. At each subsequent format specifier's position, `printf` substitutes the value of the next argument. So this example substitutes "Welcome to" for the first %s and "Java Programming!" for the second %s. The output shows that two lines of text are displayed.

We introduce various formatting features as they're needed in our examples. Appendix G presents the details of formatting output with `printf`.

2.5 Another Application: Adding Integers

Our next application reads (or inputs) two **integers** (whole numbers, such as –22, 7, 0 and 1024) typed by a user at the keyboard, computes their sum and displays it. This program must keep track of the numbers supplied by the user for the calculation later in the program. Programs remember numbers and other data in the computer's memory and access that data through program elements called **variables**. The program of Fig. 2.7 demonstrates these concepts. In the sample output, we use bold text to identify the user's input (i.e., **45** and **72**).

```
 1   // Fig. 2.7: Addition.java
 2   // Addition program that displays the sum of two numbers.
 3   import java.util.Scanner; // program uses class Scanner
 4
```

Fig. 2.7 | Addition program that displays the sum of two numbers. (Part 1 of 2.)

```
 5    public class Addition
 6    {
 7       // main method begins execution of Java application
 8       public static void main( String[] args )
 9       {
10          // create a Scanner to obtain input from the command window
11          Scanner input = new Scanner( System.in );
12
13          int number1; // first number to add
14          int number2; // second number to add
15          int sum; // sum of number1 and number2
16
17          System.out.print( "Enter first integer: " ); // prompt
18          number1 = input.nextInt(); // read first number from user
19
20          System.out.print( "Enter second integer: " ); // prompt
21          number2 = input.nextInt(); // read second number from user
22
23          sum = number1 + number2; // add numbers, then store total in sum
24
25          System.out.printf( "Sum is %d\n", sum ); // display sum
26       } // end method main
27    } // end class Addition
```

```
Enter first integer: 45
Enter second integer: 72
Sum is 117
```

Fig. 2.7 | Addition program that displays the sum of two numbers. (Part 2 of 2.)

Import Declarations
Lines 1–2

```
// Fig. 2.7: Addition.java
// Addition program that displays the sum of two numbers.
```

state the figure number, file name and purpose of the program.

A great strength of Java is its rich set of predefined classes that you can *reuse* rather than "reinventing the wheel." These classes are grouped into **packages**—named groups of related classes—and are collectively referred to as the **Java class library**, or the **Java Application Programming Interface (Java API)**. Line 3

```
import java.util.Scanner; // program uses class Scanner
```

is an **import declaration** that helps the compiler locate a class that's used in this program. It indicates that this example uses Java's predefined Scanner class (discussed shortly) from package **java.util**.

Common Programming Error 2.3

All import declarations must appear before the first class declaration in the file. Placing an import declaration inside or after a class declaration is a syntax error.

Error-Prevention Tip 2.5
Forgetting to include an import *declaration for a class used in your program typically re-sults in a compilation error containing a message such as "*cannot find symbol.*" When this occurs, check that you provided the proper* import *declarations and that the names in them are correct, including proper capitalization.*

Declaring Class Addition

Line 5 begins the declaration of class Addition. The file name for this public class must be Addition.java. Remember that the body of each class declaration starts with an opening left brace (line 6) and ends with a closing right brace (line 27).

The application begins execution with the main method (lines 8–26). The left brace (line 9) marks the beginning of method main's body, and the corresponding right brace (line 26) marks its end. Method main is indented one level in the body of class Addition, and the code in the body of main is indented another level for readability.

Declaring and Creating a Scanner to Obtain User Input from the Keyboard

All Java variables *must* be declared with a **name** and a **type** *before* they can be used. A variable's name can be any valid identifier. Like other statements, declaration statements end with a semicolon (;).

Line 11 is a **variable declaration statement** that specifies the name (input) and type (Scanner) of a variable that's used in this program. A **Scanner** enables a program to read data (e.g., numbers and strings) for use in a program. The data can come from many sources, such as the user at the keyboard or a file on disk. Before using a Scanner, you must create it and specify the source of the data.

Line 11 initalizes Scanner variable input in its declaration with the result of the expression to the right of the equals sign—new Scanner(System.in). This expression uses the **new** keyword to create a Scanner object that reads keystrokes from the keyboard. The **standard input object**, **System.in**, enables applications to read bytes of information typed by the user. The Scanner translates these bytes into types (like ints) that can be used in a program.

Declaring Variables to Store Integers

Lines 13–15 declare that variables number1, number2 and sum hold data of type **int**—they can hold integer values (whole numbers such as 72, -1127 and 0). These variables are not yet initialized. The range of values for an int is –2,147,483,648 to +2,147,483,647. [*Note:* Actual int values may not contain commas.]

Other types of data include **float** and **double**, for holding real numbers, and **char**, for holding character data. Real numbers contain decimal points, such as 3.4, 0.0 and -11.19. Variables of type char represent individual characters, such as an uppercase letter (e.g., A), a digit (e.g., 7), a special character (e.g., * or %) or an escape sequence (e.g., the newline character, \n). The types int, float, double and char are called **primitive types**.Primitive-type names are keywords and must appear in all lowercase letters. Appendix D summarizes the characteristics of the primitive types (boolean, byte, char, short, int, long, float and double).

Several variables of the same type may be declared in a single declaration with the variable names separated by commas (i.e., a comma-separated list of variable names). For example, lines 13–15 can also be written as:

```
int number1, // first number to add
    number2, // second number to add
    sum; // sum of number1 and number2
```

Prompting the User for Input

Line 17 uses System.out.print to display the message "Enter first integer: ". We use method print here rather than println so that the user's input appears on the same line as the prompt. Recall from Section 2.2 that identifiers starting with capital letters typically represent class names. Class System is part of package **java.lang**. Notice that class System is not imported with an import declaration at the beginning of the program.

Software Engineering Observation 2.1

By default, package java.lang *is imported in every Java program; thus, classes in* java.lang *are the only ones in the Java API that do not require an* import *declaration.*

Obtaining an **int** as Input from the User

Line 18 uses Scanner object input's nextInt method to obtain an integer from the user at the keyboard. At this point the program waits for the user to type the number and press the *Enter* key to submit the number to the program.

Our program assumes that the user enters a valid integer value. If not, a runtime logic error will occur and the program will terminate. Chapter 11, Exception Handling: A Deeper Look, discusses how to make your programs more robust by enabling them to handle such errors. This is also known as making your program *fault tolerant.*

In line 18, we place the result of the call to method nextInt (an int value) in variable number1 by using the **assignment operator**, =. The statement is read as "number1 gets the value of input.nextInt()." Everything to the *right* of the assignment operator, =, is always evaluated *before* the assignment is performed.

Prompting for and Inputting a Second **int**

Line 20 prompts the user to input the second integer. Line 21 reads the second integer and assigns it to variable number2.

Using Variables in a Calculation

Line 23 calculates the sum of the variables number1 and number2 then assigns the result to variable sum by using the assignment operator, =. When the program encounters the addition operation, it performs the calculation using the values stored in the variables number1 and number2. In the preceding statement, the addition operator is a *binary operator*—its *two* operands are the variables number1 and number2. Portions of statements that contain calculations are called **expressions**. In fact, an expression is any portion of a statement that has a *value* associated with it. For example, the value of the expression number1 + number2 is the *sum* of the numbers. Similarly, the value of the expression input.nextInt() is the integer typed by the user.

Displaying the Result of the Calculation

After the calculation has been performed, line 25 uses method System.out.printf to display the sum. The format specifier **%d** is a placeholder for an int value (in this case the value of sum)—the letter d stands for "decimal integer." The remaining characters in the format string are all fixed text. So, method `printf` displays `"Sum is "`, followed by the value of sum (in the position of the `%d` format specifier) and a newline.

Calculations can also be performed *inside* `printf` statements. We could have combined the statements at lines 23 and 25 into the statement

```
System.out.printf( "Sum is %d\n", ( number1 + number2 ) );
```

The parentheses around the expression `number1 + number2` are not required—they're included to emphasize that the value of the *entire* expression is output in the position of the `%d` format specifier.

Java API Documentation

For each new Java API class we use, we indicate the package in which it's located. This information helps you locate descriptions of each package and class in the Java API documentation. A web-based version of this documentation can be found at

```
download.oracle.com/javase/6/docs/api/
```

You can download it from

```
www.oracle.com/technetwork/java/javase/downloads/index.html
```

Appendix E shows how to use this documentation.

2.6 Arithmetic

The **arithmetic operators** are summarized in Fig. 2.8. The **asterisk** (*) indicates multiplication, and the percent sign (**%**) is the **remainder operator**, which we'll discuss shortly.

Java operation	Operator	Algebraic expression	Java expression
Addition	+	$f + 7$	`f + 7`
Subtraction	–	$p - c$	`p - c`
Multiplication	*	bm	`b * m`
Division	/	x / y or $\frac{x}{y}$ or $x \div y$	`x / y`
Remainder	%	$r \bmod s$	`r % s`

Fig. 2.8 | Arithmetic operators.

Integer division yields an integer quotient. For example, the expression 7 / 4 evaluates to 1, and the expression 17 / 5 evaluates to 3. Any fractional part in integer division is simply *discarded* (i.e., *truncated*)—no rounding occurs. Java provides the remainder operator, %, which yields the remainder after division. The expression x % y yields the remainder after x is divided by y. Thus, 7 % 4 yields 3, and 17 % 5 yields 2. This operator is most commonly used with integer operands but can also be used with other arithmetic types.

Rules of Operator Precedence

Java applies the operators in arithmetic expressions in a precise sequence determined by the **rules of operator precedence**, which are generally the same as those followed in algebra:

1. Multiplication, division and remainder operations are applied first. If an expression contains several such operations, they're applied from left to right. Multiplication, division and remainder operators have the same level of precedence.

2. Addition and subtraction operations are applied next. If an expression contains several such operations, the operators are applied from left to right. Addition and subtraction operators have the same level of precedence.

These rules enable Java to apply operators in the correct order.[1] When we say that operators are applied from left to right, we're referring to their **associativity**. Some operators associate from right to left. Figure 2.9 summarizes these rules of operator precedence. A complete precedence chart is included in Appendix A.

Operator(s)	Operation(s)	Order of evaluation (precedence)
* / %	Multiplication Division Remainder	Evaluated first. If there are several operators of this type, they're evaluated from left to right.
+ -	Addition Subtraction	Evaluated next. If there are several operators of this type, they're evaluated from left to right.
=	Assignment	Evaluated last.

Fig. 2.9 | Precedence of arithmetic operators.

2.7 Decision Making: Equality and Relational Operators

A **condition** is an expression that can be **true** or **false**. This section introduces Java's **if selection statement**, which allows a program to make a **decision** based on a condition's value. For example, the condition "grade is greater than or equal to 60" determines whether a student passed a test. If the condition in an `if` statement is true, the body of the `if` statement executes. If the condition is false, the body does not execute. We'll see an example shortly.

Conditions in `if` statements can be formed by using the **equality operators** (`==` and `!=`) and **relational operators** (`>`, `<`, `>=` and `<=`) summarized in Fig. 2.10. Both equality operators have the same level of precedence, which is *lower* than that of the relational operators. The equality operators associate from left to right. The relational operators all have the same level of precedence and also associate from left to right.

Figure 2.11 uses six `if` statements to compare two integers input by the user. If the condition in any of these `if` statements is true, the statement associated with that `if` statement executes; otherwise, the statement is skipped. We use a `Scanner` to input the integers from the user and store them in variables `number1` and `number2`. The program compares the numbers and displays the results of the comparisons that are true.

---

1. We use simple examples to explain the order of evaluation of expressions. Subtle issues occur in the more complex expressions you'll encounter later in the book. For more information on order of evaluation, see Chapter 15 of *The Java™ Language Specification* (`java.sun.com/docs/books/jls/`).

Standard algebraic equality or relational operator	Java equality or relational operator	Sample Java condition	Meaning of Java condition
Equality operators			
=	==	x == y	x is equal to y
≠	!=	x != y	x is not equal to y
Relational operators			
>	>	x > y	x is greater than y
<	<	x < y	x is less than y
≥	>=	x >= y	x is greater than or equal to y
≤	<=	x <= y	x is less than or equal to y

Fig. 2.10 | Equality and relational operators.

```
1   // Fig. 2.11: Comparison.java
2   // Compare integers using if statements, relational operators
3   // and equality operators.
4   import java.util.Scanner; // program uses class Scanner
5
6   public class Comparison
7   {
8      // main method begins execution of Java application
9      public static void main( String[] args )
10     {
11        // create Scanner to obtain input from command line
12        Scanner input = new Scanner( System.in );
13
14        int number1; // first number to compare
15        int number2; // second number to compare
16
17        System.out.print( "Enter first integer: " ); // prompt
18        number1 = input.nextInt(); // read first number from user
19
20        System.out.print( "Enter second integer: " ); // prompt
21        number2 = input.nextInt(); // read second number from user
22
23        if ( number1 == number2 )
24           System.out.printf( "%d == %d\n", number1, number2 );
25
26        if ( number1 != number2 )
27           System.out.printf( "%d != %d\n", number1, number2 );
28
29        if ( number1 < number2 )
30           System.out.printf( "%d < %d\n", number1, number2 );
31
```

Fig. 2.11 | Compare integers using if statements, relational operators and equality operators. (Part 1 of 2.)

```
32          if ( number1 > number2 )
33             System.out.printf( "%d > %d\n", number1, number2 );
34
35          if ( number1 <= number2 )
36             System.out.printf( "%d <= %d\n", number1, number2 );
37
38          if ( number1 >= number2 )
39             System.out.printf( "%d >= %d\n", number1, number2 );
40       } // end method main
41    } // end class Comparison
```

```
Enter first integer: 777
Enter second integer: 777
777 == 777
777 <= 777
777 >= 777
```

```
Enter first integer: 1000
Enter second integer: 2000
1000 != 2000
1000 < 2000
1000 <= 2000
```

```
Enter first integer: 2000
Enter second integer: 1000
2000 != 1000
2000 > 1000
2000 >= 1000
```

Fig. 2.11 | Compare integers using if statements, relational operators and equality operators. (Part 2 of 2.)

The declaration of class Comparison begins at line 6. The class's main method (lines 9–40) begins the execution of the program. Line 12 declares Scanner variable input and assigns it a Scanner that inputs data from the standard input (i.e., the keyboard).

Lines 14–15 declare the int variables used to store the values input from the user. Lines 17–18 prompt the user to enter the first integer and input the value, respectively. The input value is stored in variable number1.

Lines 20–21 prompt the user to enter the second integer and input the value, respectively. The input value is stored in variable number2.

Lines 23–24 compare the values of number1 and number2 to determine whether they're equal. An if statement always begins with keyword if, followed by a condition in parentheses. An if statement expects one statement in its body, but may contain multiple statements if they're enclosed in a set of braces ({}). The indentation of the body statement shown here is not required, but it improves the program's readability by emphasizing that the statement in line 24 *is part of* the if statement that begins at line 23. Line 24 executes only if the numbers stored in variables number1 and number2 are equal (i.e., the condition is true). The if statements in lines 26–27, 29–30, 32–33, 35–36 and 38–39 compare number1 and number2 using the operators !=, <, >, <= and >=, respectively. If the condition in one or more of the if statements is true, the corresponding body statement executes.

 Common Programming Error 2.4
Confusing the equality operator, ==, with the assignment operator, =, can cause a logic error or a syntax error. The equality operator should be read as "is equal to" and the assignment operator as "gets" or "gets the value of." To avoid confusion, some people read the equality operator as "double equals" or "equals equals."

There's no semicolon (;) at the end of the first line of each if statement. Such a semicolon would result in a logic error at execution time. For example,

```java
if ( number1 == number2 ); // logic error
    System.out.printf( "%d == %d\n", number1, number2 );
```

would actually be interpreted by Java as

```java
if ( number1 == number2 )
    ; // empty statement

System.out.printf( "%d == %d\n", number1, number2 );
```

where the semicolon on the line by itself—called the **empty statement**—is the statement to execute if the condition in the if statement is true. When the empty statement executes, no task is performed. The program then continues with the output statement, which always executes, regardless of whether the condition is true or false, because the output statement is not part of the if statement.

Figure 2.12 shows the operators discussed so far in decreasing order of precedence. All but the assignment operator, =, associate from left to right. The assignment operator, =, associates from right to left, so an expression like x = y = 0 is evaluated as if it had been written as x = (y = 0), which first assigns the value 0 to variable y, then assigns the result of that assignment, 0, to x.

Operators	Associativity	Type
* / %	left to right	multiplicative
+ −	left to right	additive
< <= > >=	left to right	relational
== !=	left to right	equality
=	right to left	assignment

Fig. 2.12 | Precedence and associativity of operators discussed.

2.8 Wrap-Up

In this chapter, you learned many important features of Java, including displaying data on the screen in a **Command Prompt**, inputting data from the keyboard, performing calculations and making decisions. The applications presented here introduced you to basic programming concepts. In Chapter 3, you'll learn how to implement your own classes and use objects of those classes in applications.

3

Introduction to Classes, Objects, Methods and Strings

*Nothing can have value
without being an object of
utility.*
—Karl Marx

*Your public servants serve
you right.*
—Adlai E. Stevenson

*You'll see something new.
Two things. And I call them
Thing One and Thing Two.*
—Dr. Theodor Seuss Geisel

Objectives

In this chapter you'll learn:

■ How to declare a class and use it to create an object.

■ How to implement a class's behaviors as methods.

■ How to implement a class's attributes as instance variables and properties.

■ How to call an object's methods to make them perform their tasks.

■ What instance variables of a class and local variables of a method are.

■ How to use a constructor to initialize an object's data.

■ The differences between primitive and reference types.

3.1 Introduction

We introduced the basic terminology and concepts of object-oriented programming in Section 1.2. In this chapter, we present a simple framework for organizing object-oriented applications in Java. First, we motivate the notion of classes with a real-world example. Then we present five applications to demonstrate creating and using your own classes.

3.2 Declaring a Class with a Method and Instantiating an Object of a Class

In Sections 2.5 and 2.7, you created an object of the *existing* class Scanner, then used that object to read data from the keyboard. In this section, you'll create a *new* class, then use it to create an object. We begin by delcaring classes GradeBook (Fig. 3.1) and GradeBook-Test (Fig. 3.2). Class GradeBook (declared in the file GradeBook.java) will be used to display a message on the screen (Fig. 3.2) welcoming the instructor to the grade book application. Class GradeBookTest (declared in the file GradeBookTest.java) is an application class in which the main method will create and use an object of class GradeBook. *Each class declaration that begins with keyword public must be stored in a file having the same name as the class and ending with the .java file-name extension.* Thus, classes GradeBook and GradeBookTest must be declared in *separate* files, because each class is declared public.

Class GradeBook
The GradeBook class declaration (Fig. 3.1) contains a displayMessage method (lines 7–10) that displays a message on the screen. We'll need to make an object of this class and call its method to execute line 9 and display the message.

```
1   // Fig. 3.1: GradeBook.java
2   // Class declaration with one method.
3
4   public class GradeBook
5   {
6      // display a welcome message to the GradeBook user
7      public void displayMessage()
8      {
9         System.out.println( "Welcome to the Grade Book!" );
10     } // end method displayMessage
11  } // end class GradeBook
```

Fig. 3.1 | Class declaration with one method.

The *class declaration* begins in line 4. The keyword `public` is an **access modifier**. For now, we'll simply declare every class `public`. Every class declaration contains keyword `class` followed immediately by the class's name. Every class's body is enclosed in a pair of left and right braces, as in lines 5 and 11 of class `GradeBook`.

In Chapter 2, each class we declared had one method named `main`. Class `GradeBook` also has one method—`displayMessage` (lines 7–10). Recall that `main` is a special method that's *always* called automatically by the Java Virtual Machine (JVM) when you execute an application. Most methods do not get called automatically. As you'll soon see, you must call method `displayMessage` explicitly to tell it to perform its task.

The method declaration begins with keyword `public` to indicate that the method is "available to the public"—it can be called from methods of other classes. Next is the method's **return type**, which specifies the type of data the method returns to its caller after performing its task. The return type `void` indicates that this method will perform a task but will *not* return (i.e., give back) any information to its **calling method**. You've used methods that return information—for example, in Chapter 2 you used `Scanner` method `nextInt` to input an integer typed by the user at the keyboard. When `nextInt` reads a value from the user, it returns that value for use in the program.

The name of the method, `displayMessage`, follows the return type. By convention, method names begin with a lowercase first letter and subsequent words in the name begin with a capital letter. The parentheses after the method name indicate that this is a method. Empty parentheses, as in line 7, indicate that this method does not require additional information to perform its task. Line 7 is commonly referred to as the **method header**. Every method's body is delimited by left and right braces, as in lines 8 and 10.

The body of a method contains one or more statements that perform the method's task. In this case, the method contains one statement (line 9) that displays the message `"Welcome to the Grade Book!"` followed by a newline (because of `println`) in the command window. After this statement executes, the method has completed its task.

Class *GradeBookTest*

Next, we'd like to use class `GradeBook` in an application. As you learned in Chapter 2, method `main` begins the execution of *every* application. A class that contains method `main` begins the execution of a Java application. Class `GradeBook` is *not* an application because it does *not* contain `main`. Therefore, if you try to execute `GradeBook` by typing `java Grade-Book` in the command window, an error will occur. This was not a problem in Chapter 2, because every class you declared had a `main` method. To fix this problem, we must either declare a separate class that contains a `main` method or place a `main` method in class `Grade-Book`. To help you prepare for the larger programs you'll encounter later in this book and in industry, we use a separate class (`GradeBookTest` in this example) containing method `main` to test each new class we create in this chapter. Some programmers refer to such a class as a *driver class*.

The `GradeBookTest` class declaration (Fig. 3.2) contains the `main` method that will control our application's execution. The `GradeBookTest` class declaration begins in line 4 and ends in line 15. The class, like many that begin an application's execution, contains *only* a `main` method.

Lines 7–14 declare method `main`. A key part of enabling the JVM to locate and call method `main` to begin the application's execution is the `static` keyword (line 7), which indicates that `main` is a `static` method. *A `static` method is special, because you can call it*

```
1   // Fig. 3.2: GradeBookTest.java
2   // Creating a GradeBook object and calling its displayMessage method.
3
4   public class GradeBookTest
5   {
6      // main method begins program execution
7      public static void main( String[] args )
8      {
9         // create a GradeBook object and assign it to myGradeBook
10        GradeBook myGradeBook = new GradeBook();
11
12        // call myGradeBook's displayMessage method
13        myGradeBook.displayMessage();
14     } // end main
15  } // end class GradeBookTest
```

```
Welcome to the Grade Book!
```

Fig. 3.2 | Creating a GradeBook object and calling its displayMessage method.

without first creating an object of the class in which the method is declared. We discuss static methods in detail in Chapter 6, Methods: A Deeper Look.

In this application, we'd like to call class GradeBook's displayMessage method to display the welcome message in the command window. Typically, you cannot call a method that belongs to another class until you create an object of that class, as shown in line 10. We begin by declaring variable myGradeBook. The variable's type is GradeBook—the class we declared in Fig. 3.1. Each new *class* you create becomes a new *type* that can be used to declare variables and create objects. You can declare new class types as needed; this is one reason why Java is known as an **extensible language**.

Variable myGradeBook is initialized (line 10) with the result of the **class instance creation expression** new GradeBook(). Keyword **new** creates a new object of the class specified to the right of the keyword (i.e., GradeBook). The parentheses to the right of GradeBook are required. As you'll learn in Section 3.6, those parentheses in combination with a class name represent a call to a **constructor**, which is similar to a method but is used only at the time an object is *created* to *initialize* the object's data. You'll see that data can be placed in the parentheses to specify *initial values* for the object's data. For now, we simply leave the parentheses empty.

Just as we can use object System.out to call its methods print, printf and println, we can use object myGradeBook to call its method displayMessage. Line 13 calls the method displayMessage (lines 7–10 of Fig. 3.1) using myGradeBook followed by a **dot separator** (.), the method name displayMessage and an empty set of parentheses. This call causes the displayMessage method to perform its task. This method call differs from those in Chapter 2 that displayed information in a command window—each of those method calls provided arguments that specified the data to display. At the beginning of line 13, "myGradeBook." indicates that main should use the myGradeBook object that was created in line 10. Line 7 of Fig. 3.1 indicates that method displayMessage has an *empty parameter list*—that is, displayMessage does *not* require additional information to perform its task. For this reason, the method call (line 13 of Fig. 3.2) specifies an empty set of parentheses after the method name to indicate that *no arguments* are being passed to method displayMessage. When method displayMessage completes its task, method main continues executing at line 14. This is the end of method main, so the program terminates.

Any class can contain a main method. The JVM invokes the main method *only* in the class used to execute the application. If an application has multiple classes that contain main, the one that's invoked is the one in the class named in the java command.

Compiling an Application with Multiple Classes

You must compile the classes in Fig. 3.1 and Fig. 3.2 before you can execute the application. First, change to the directory that contains the application's source-code files. Next, type the command

```
javac GradeBook.java GradeBookTest.java
```

to compile *both* classes at once. If the directory containing the application includes only this application's files, you can compile *all* the classes in the directory with the command

```
javac *.java
```

The asterisk (*) in *.java indicates that *all* files in the current directory that end with the file-name extension ".java" should be compiled.

UML Class Diagram for Class GradeBook

Figure 3.3 presents a **UML class diagram** for class GradeBook of Fig. 3.1. In the UML, each class is modeled in a class diagram as a rectangle with three compartments. The top compartment contains the name of the class centered horizontally in boldface type. The middle compartment contains the class's attributes, which correspond to instance variables (discussed in Section 3.4) in Java. In Fig. 3.3, the middle compartment is empty, because this GradeBook class does *not* have any attributes. The bottom compartment contains the class's **operations**, which correspond to methods in Java. The UML models operations by listing the operation name preceded by an access modifier (in this case +) and followed by a set of parentheses. Class GradeBook has one method, displayMessage, so the bottom compartment of Fig. 3.3 lists one operation with this name. Method displayMessage does *not* require additional information to perform its tasks, so the parentheses following the method name in the class diagram are *empty*, just as they were in the method's declaration in line 7 of Fig. 3.1. The plus sign (+) in front of the operation name indicates that displayMessage is a public operation in the UML (i.e., a public method in Java). We'll often use UML class diagrams to summarize a class's attributes and operations.

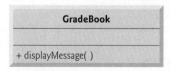

Fig. 3.3 | UML class diagram indicating that class GradeBook has a public displayMessage operation.

3.3 Declaring a Method with a Parameter

In our car analogy from Section 1.2, we discussed the fact that pressing a car's gas pedal sends a *message* to the car to *perform a task*—to go faster. But *how fast* should the car accelerate? As you know, the farther down you press the pedal, the faster the car accelerates. So the message to the car actually includes the *task to perform* and *additional information* that helps the car perform the task. This additional information is known as a **parameter**—the value of the parameter helps the car determine how fast to accelerate. Similarly, a method can require one or more parameters that represent additional information it needs to perform its task. Parameters are defined in a comma-separated **parameter list**, which is located inside the parentheses that follow the method name. Each parameter must specify a *type* and a variable name. The parameter list may contain any number of parameters, including none at all. Empty parentheses following the method name (as in Fig. 3.1, line 7) indicate that a method does *not* require any parameters.

Arguments to a Method
A method call supplies values—called *arguments*—for each of the method's parameters. For example, the method System.out.println requires an argument that specifies the data to output in a command window. Similarly, to make a deposit into a bank account, a deposit method specifies a parameter that represents the deposit amount. When the deposit method is called, an argument value representing the deposit amount is assigned to the method's parameter. The method then makes a deposit of that amount.

Class Declaration with a Method That Has One Parameter
We now declare class GradeBook (Fig. 3.4) with a displayMessage method that displays the course name as part of the welcome message. (See the sample execution in Fig. 3.5.) The new method requires a parameter that represents the course name to output.

```
1   // Fig. 3.4: GradeBook.java
2   // Class declaration with one method that has a parameter.
3
4   public class GradeBook
5   {
6      // display a welcome message to the GradeBook user
7      public void displayMessage( String courseName )
8      {
9         System.out.printf( "Welcome to the grade book for\n%s!\n",
10           courseName );
11     } // end method displayMessage
12  } // end class GradeBook
```

Fig. 3.4 | Class declaration with one method that has a parameter.

Before discussing the new features of class GradeBook, let's see how the new class is used from the main method of class GradeBookTest (Fig. 3.5). Line 12 creates a Scanner named input for reading the course name from the user. Line 15 creates the GradeBook object myGradeBook. Line 18 prompts the user to enter a course name. Line 19 reads the name from the user and assigns it to the nameOfCourse variable, using Scanner method **nextLine** to perform the input. The user types the course name and presses *Enter* to submit the course name to the program. Pressing *Enter* inserts a newline character at the end of the characters typed by the user. Method nextLine reads characters typed by the user until it encounters the newline character, then returns a String containing the characters up to, but *not* including, the newline. The newline character is *discarded*.

```
1   // Fig. 3.5: GradeBookTest.java
2   // Create GradeBook object and pass a String to
3   // its displayMessage method.
4   import java.util.Scanner; // program uses Scanner
5
6   public class GradeBookTest
7   {
8      // main method begins program execution
9      public static void main( String[] args )
10     {
11        // create Scanner to obtain input from command window
12        Scanner input = new Scanner( System.in );
13
14        // create a GradeBook object and assign it to myGradeBook
15        GradeBook myGradeBook = new GradeBook();
16
17        // prompt for and input course name
18        System.out.println( "Please enter the course name:" );
19        String nameOfCourse = input.nextLine(); // read a line of text
20        System.out.println(); // outputs a blank line
21
22        // call myGradeBook's displayMessage method
23        // and pass nameOfCourse as an argument
24        myGradeBook.displayMessage( nameOfCourse );
25     } // end main
26  } // end class GradeBookTest
```

```
Please enter the course name:
CS101 Introduction to Java Programming

Welcome to the grade book for
CS101 Introduction to Java Programming!
```

Fig. 3.5 | Create a GradeBook object and pass a String to its displayMessage method.

Class Scanner also provides a similar method—**next**—that reads individual words. When the user presses *Enter* after typing input, method next reads characters until it encounters a *white-space character* (such as a space, tab or newline), then returns a String containing the characters up to, but *not* including, the white-space character (which is discarded). All information after the first white-space character is not lost—it can be read by other statements that call the Scanner's methods later in the program. Line 20 outputs a blank line.

Line 24 calls myGradeBooks's displayMessage method. The variable nameOfCourse in parentheses is the *argument* that's passed to method displayMessage so that the method can perform its task. The value of variable nameOfCourse in main becomes the value of method displayMessage's *parameter* courseName in line 7 of Fig. 3.4. When you execute this application, notice that method displayMessage outputs the name you type as part of the welcome message (Fig. 3.5).

More on Arguments and Parameters
In Fig. 3.4, displayMessage's parameter list (line 7) declares one parameter indicating that the method requires a String to perform its task. When the method is called, the argument value in the call is assigned to the corresponding parameter (courseName) in the method header. Then, the method body uses the value of the courseName parameter. Lines 9–10 of Fig. 3.4 display parameter courseName's value, using the %s format specifier in printf's format string. The parameter variable's name (courseName in Fig. 3.4, line 7) can be the *same or different* from the argument variable's name (nameOfCourse in Fig. 3.5, line 24).

The number of arguments in a method call *must* match the number of parameters in the parameter list of the method's declaration. Also, the argument types in the method call must be "consistent with" the types of the corresponding parameters in the method's declaration—as you'll see in Chapter 6, an argument's type and its corresponding parameter's type are not always required to be *identical*. In our example, the method call passes one argument of type String (nameOfCourse is declared as a String in line 19 of Fig. 3.5) and the method declaration specifies one parameter of type String (courseName is declared as a String in line 7 of Fig. 3.4). So in this example the type of the argument in the method call exactly matches the type of the parameter in the method header.

*Updated UML Class Diagram for Class **GradeBook***
The UML class diagram of Fig. 3.6 models class GradeBook of Fig. 3.4. Like Fig. 3.1, this GradeBook class contains public operation displayMessage. However, this version of displayMessage has a parameter. The UML models a parameter a bit differently from Java by listing the parameter name, followed by a colon and the parameter type in the parentheses following the operation name. The UML has its own data types similar to those of Java (but, as you'll see, not all the UML data types have the same names as the corresponding Java types). The UML type String does correspond to the Java type String. GradeBook method displayMessage (Fig. 3.4) has a String parameter named courseName, so Fig. 3.6 lists courseName : String between the parentheses following displayMessage.

GradeBook
+ displayMessage(courseName : String)

Fig. 3.6 | UML class diagram indicating that class GradeBook has a displayMessage operation with a courseName parameter of UML type String.

*Notes on **import** Declarations*
Notice the import declaration in Fig. 3.5 (line 4). This indicates to the compiler that the program uses class Scanner. Why do we need to import class Scanner, but not classes System, String or GradeBook? Classes System and String are in package java.lang, which is implicitly imported into *every* Java program, so all programs can use that package's classes *without* explicitly importing them. Most other classes you'll use in Java programs must be imported explicitly.

There's a special relationship between classes that are compiled in the same directory on disk, like classes `GradeBook` and `GradeBookTest`. By default, such classes are considered to be in the same package—known as the **default package**. Classes in the same package are *implicitly imported* into the source-code files of other classes in the same package. Thus, an `import` declaration is *not* required when one class in a package uses another in the same package—such as when class `GradeBookTest` uses class `GradeBook`.

The `import` declaration in line 4 is *not* required if we always refer to class `Scanner` as `java.util.Scanner`, which includes the *full package name and class name*. This is known as the class's **fully qualified class name**. For example, line 12 could be written as

```
java.util.Scanner input = new java.util.Scanner( System.in );
```

Software Engineering Observation 3.1

The Java compiler does not require import *declarations in a Java source-code file if the fully qualified class name is specified every time a class name is used in the source code. Most Java programmers prefer to use* import *declarations.*

3.4 Instance Variables, *set* Methods and *get* Methods

In Chapter 2, we declared all of an application's variables in the application's `main` method. Variables declared in the body of a particular method are **local variables** and can be used only in that method. When that method terminates, the values of its local variables are lost. Recall from Section 1.2 that an object has *attributes* that are carried with it as it's used in a program. Such attributes exist before a method is called on an object, while the method is executing and after the method completes execution.

A class normally consists of one or more methods that manipulate the attributes that belong to a particular object of the class. Attributes are represented as variables in a class declaration. Such variables are called **fields** and are declared *inside* a class declaration but *outside* the bodies of the class's method declarations. When each object of a class maintains its own copy of an attribute, the field that represents the attribute is also known as an **instance variable**—each object (instance) of the class has a separate instance of the variable in memory. The example in this section demonstrates a `GradeBook` class that contains a `courseName` instance variable to represent a particular `GradeBook` object's course name.

GradeBook *Class with an Instance Variable, a* set *Method and a* get *Method*

In our next application (Figs. 3.7–3.8), class `GradeBook` (Fig. 3.7) maintains the course name as an instance variable so that it can be used or modified at any time during an application's execution. The class contains three methods—`setCourseName`, `getCourseName` and `displayMessage`. Method `setCourseName` stores a course name in a `GradeBook`. Method `getCourseName` obtains a `GradeBook`'s course name. Method `displayMessage`, which now specifies no parameters, still displays a welcome message that includes the course name; as you'll see, the method now obtains the course name by calling a method in the same class—`getCourseName`.

A typical instructor teaches more than one course, each with its own course name. Line 7 declares `courseName` as a variable of type `String`. Because the variable is declared *in* the body of the class but *outside* the bodies of the class's methods (lines 10–13, 16–19 and 22–28), line 7 is a declaration for an *instance variable*. Every instance (i.e., object) of

```
 1   // Fig. 3.7: GradeBook.java
 2   // GradeBook class that contains a courseName instance variable
 3   // and methods to set and get its value.
 4
 5   public class GradeBook
 6   {
 7      private String courseName; // course name for this GradeBook
 8
 9      // method to set the course name
10      public void setCourseName( String name )
11      {
12         courseName = name; // store the course name
13      } // end method setCourseName
14
15      // method to retrieve the course name
16      public String getCourseName()
17      {
18         return courseName;
19      } // end method getCourseName
20
21      // display a welcome message to the GradeBook user
22      public void displayMessage()
23      {
24         // calls getCourseName to get the name of
25         // the course this GradeBook represents
26         System.out.printf( "Welcome to the grade book for\n%s!\n",
27            getCourseName() );
28      } // end method displayMessage
29   } // end class GradeBook
```

Fig. 3.7 | GradeBook class that contains a courseName instance variable and methods to set and get its value.

class GradeBook contains one copy of each instance variable. For example, if there are two GradeBook objects, each object has its own copy of courseName. A benefit of making courseName an instance variable is that all the methods of the class (in this case, Grade-Book) can manipulate any instance variables that appear in the class (in this case, course-Name).

Access Modifiers public *and* private
Most instance-variable declarations are preceded with the keyword private (as in line 7). Like public, keyword **private** is an *access modifier. Variables or methods declared with access modifier private are accessible only to methods of the class in which they're declared.* Thus, variable courseName can be used only in methods setCourseName, getCourseName and displayMessage of (every object of) class GradeBook.

Declaring instance variables with access modifier private is known as **data hiding** or information hiding. When a program creates (instantiates) an object of class GradeBook, variable courseName is *encapsulated* (hidden) in the object and can be accessed only by methods of the object's class. This prevents courseName from being modified accidentally by a class in another part of the program. In class GradeBook, methods setCourseName and getCourseName manipulate the instance variable courseName.

Software Engineering Observation 3.2

Precede each field and method declaration with an access modifier. Generally, instance variables should be declared private *and methods* public. *(It's appropriate to declare certain methods* private, *if they'll be accessed only by other methods of the class.)*

Good Programming Practice 3.1

We prefer to list a class's fields first, so that, as you read the code, you see the names and types of the variables before they're used in the class's methods. You can list the class's fields anywhere in the class outside its method declarations, but scattering them can lead to hard-to-read code.

Methods *setCourseName* and *getCourseName*

Method setCourseName (lines 10–13) does not return any data when it completes its task, so its return type is void. The method receives one parameter—name—which represents the course name that will be passed to the method as an argument. Line 12 assigns name to instance variable courseName.

Method getCourseName (lines 16–19) returns a particular GradeBook object's courseName. The method has an empty parameter list, so it does not require additional information to perform its task. The method specifies that it returns a String—this is the method's return type. When a method that specifies a return type other than void is called and completes its task, the method returns a *result* to its calling method. For example, when you go to an automated teller machine (ATM) and request your account balance, you expect the ATM to give you back a value that represents your balance. Similarly, when a statement calls method getCourseName on a GradeBook object, the statement expects to receive the GradeBook's course name (in this case, a String, as specified in the method declaration's return type).

The **return** statement in line 18 passes the value of instance variable courseName back to the statement that calls method getCourseName. Consider, method displayMessage's line 27, which calls method getCourseName. When the value is returned, the statement in lines 26–27 uses that value to output the course name. Similarly, if you have a method square that returns the square of its argument, you'd expect the statement

```
int result = square( 2 );
```

to return 4 from method square and assign 4 to the variable result. If you have a method maximum that returns the largest of three integer arguments, you'd expect the statement

```
int biggest = maximum( 27, 114, 51 );
```

to return 114 from method maximum and assign 114 to variable biggest.

The statements in lines 12 and 18 each use courseName *even though it was not declared in any of the methods.* We can use courseName in GradeBook's methods because course-Name is an instance variable of the class.

Method *displayMessage*

Method displayMessage (lines 22–28) does *not* return any data when it completes its task, so its return type is void. The method does *not* receive parameters, so the parameter list is empty. Lines 26–27 output a welcome message that includes the value of instance variable courseName, which is returned by the call to method getCourseName in line 27.

Notice that one method of a class (displayMessage in this case) can call another method of the *same* class by using just the method name (getCourseName in this case).

GradeBookTest *Class That Demonstrates Class* GradeBook

Class GradeBookTest (Fig. 3.8) creates one object of class GradeBook and demonstrates its methods. Line 14 creates a GradeBook object and assigns it to local variable myGradeBook of type GradeBook. Lines 17–18 display the initial course name calling the object's getCourse-Name method. The first line of the output shows the name "null." *Unlike local variables, which are not automatically initialized, every field has a **default initial value**—a value provided by Java when you do not specify the field's initial value.* Thus, fields are *not* required to be explicitly initialized before they're used in a program—unless they must be initialized to values *other than* their default values. The default value for a field of type String (like courseName in this example) is null, which we say more about in Section 3.5.

```java
1   // Fig. 3.8: GradeBookTest.java
2   // Creating and manipulating a GradeBook object.
3   import java.util.Scanner; // program uses Scanner
4
5   public class GradeBookTest
6   {
7      // main method begins program execution
8      public static void main( String[] args )
9      {
10        // create Scanner to obtain input from command window
11        Scanner input = new Scanner( System.in );
12
13        // create a GradeBook object and assign it to myGradeBook
14        GradeBook myGradeBook = new GradeBook();
15
16        // display initial value of courseName
17        System.out.printf( "Initial course name is: %s\n\n",
18           myGradeBook.getCourseName() );
19
20        // prompt for and read course name
21        System.out.println( "Please enter the course name:" );
22        String theName = input.nextLine(); // read a line of text
23        myGradeBook.setCourseName( theName ); // set the course name
24        System.out.println(); // outputs a blank line
25
26        // display welcome message after specifying course name
27        myGradeBook.displayMessage();
28     } // end main
29  } // end class GradeBookTest
```

```
Initial course name is: null

Please enter the course name:
CS101 Introduction to Java Programming

Welcome to the grade book for
CS101 Introduction to Java Programming!
```

Fig. 3.8 | Creating and manipulating a GradeBook object.

Line 21 prompts the user to enter a course name. Local `String` variable `theName` (declared in line 22) is initialized with the course name entered by the user, which is returned by the call to the `nextLine` method of the `Scanner` object `input`. Line 23 calls object `myGradeBook`'s `setCourseName` method and supplies `theName` as the method's argument. When the method is called, the argument's value is assigned to parameter `name` (line 10, Fig. 3.7) of method `setCourseName` (lines 10–13, Fig. 3.7). Then the parameter's value is assigned to instance variable `courseName` (line 12, Fig. 3.7). Line 24 (Fig. 3.8) skips a line in the output, then line 27 calls object `myGradeBook`'s `displayMessage` method to display the welcome message containing the course name.

set *and* get *Methods*

A class's `private` fields can be manipulated *only* by the class's methods. So a **client of an object**—that is, any class that calls the object's methods—calls the class's `public` methods to manipulate the `private` fields of an object of the class. This is why the statements in method `main` (Fig. 3.8) call the `setCourseName`, `getCourseName` and `displayMessage` methods on a `GradeBook` object. Classes often provide `public` methods to allow clients to *set* (i.e., assign values to) or *get* (i.e., obtain the values of) `private` instance variables. The names of these methods need not begin with *set* or *get*, but this naming convention is recommended and is the convention for special Java software components called JavaBeans, which can simplify programming in many Java integrated development environments (IDEs). The method that *sets* instance variable `courseName` in this example is called `setCourseName`, and the method that *gets* its value is called `getCourseName`.

GradeBook *UML Class Diagram with an Instance Variable and* set *and* get *Methods*

Figure 3.9 contains an updated UML class diagram for the version of class `GradeBook` in Fig. 3.7. This diagram models class `GradeBook`'s instance variable `courseName` as an attribute in the middle compartment of the class. The UML represents instance variables as attributes by listing the attribute name, followed by a colon and the attribute type. The UML type of attribute `courseName` is `String`. Instance variable `courseName` is `private` in Java, so the class diagram lists a minus sign (–) access modifier in front of the corresponding attribute's name. Class `GradeBook` contains three `public` methods, so the class diagram lists three operations in the third compartment. Recall that the plus sign (+) before each operation name indicates that the operation is `public`. Operation `setCourseName` has a `String` parameter called `name`. The UML indicates the return type of an operation by placing a colon and the return type after the parentheses following the operation name. Meth-

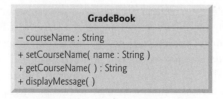

GradeBook
– courseName : String
+ setCourseName(name : String) + getCourseName( ) : String + displayMessage( )

Fig. 3.9 | UML class diagram indicating that class `GradeBook` has a private `courseName` attribute of UML type `String` and three public operations—`setCourseName` (with a `name` parameter of UML type `String`), `getCourseName` (which returns UML type `String`) and `displayMessage`.

od getCourseName of class GradeBook (Fig. 3.7) has a String return type in Java, so the class diagram shows a String return type in the UML. Operations setCourseName and displayMessage *do not* return values (i.e., they return void in Java), so the UML class diagram *does not* specify a return type after the parentheses of these operations.

3.5 Primitive Types vs. Reference Types

Java's types are divided into primitive types and **reference types**. The primitive types are boolean, byte, char, short, int, long, float and double. All nonprimitive types are reference types, so classes, which specify the types of objects, are reference types.

A primitive-type variable can store exactly one *value of its declared type* at a time. For example, an int variable can store one whole number (such as 7) at a time. When another value is assigned to that variable, its initial value is replaced. Primitive-type instance variables are *initialized by default*—variables of types byte, char, short, int, long, float and double are initialized to 0, and variables of type boolean are initialized to false. You can specify your own initial value for a primitive-type variable by assigning the variable a value in its declaration, as in

```
private int numberOfStudents = 10;
```

Recall that local variables are *not* initialized by default.

Error-Prevention Tip 3.1
An attempt to use an uninitialized local variable causes a compilation error.

Programs use variables of reference types (normally called **references**) to store the *locations* of objects in the computer's memory. Such a variable is said to **refer to an object** in the program. Objects that are referenced may each contain many instance variables. Line 14 of Fig. 3.8 creates an object of class GradeBook, and the variable myGradeBook contains a reference to that GradeBook object. *Reference-type instance variables are initialized by default to the value null*—a reserved word that represents a "reference to nothing." This is why the first call to getCourseName in line 18 of Fig. 3.8 returned null—the value of courseName had not been set, so the default initial value null was returned. The complete list of reserved words and keywords is listed in Appendix C.

When you use an object of another class, a reference to the object is required to **invoke** (i.e., call) its methods. In the application of Fig. 3.8, the statements in method main use the variable myGradeBook to send messages to the GradeBook object. These messages are calls to methods (like setCourseName and getCourseName) that enable the program to interact with the GradeBook object. For example, the statement in line 23 uses myGradeBook to send the setCourseName message to the GradeBook object. The message includes the argument that setCourseName requires to perform its task. The GradeBook object uses this information to set the courseName instance variable. Primitive-type variables do not refer to objects, so such variables cannot be used to invoke methods.

Software Engineering Observation 3.3
A variable's declared type (e.g., int, double or GradeBook) indicates whether the variable is of a primitive or a reference type. If a variable is not of one of the eight primitive types, then it's of a reference type.

3.6 Initializing Objects with Constructors

As mentioned in Section 3.4, when an object of class GradeBook (Fig. 3.7) is created, its instance variable courseName is initialized to null by default. What if you want to provide a course name when you create a GradeBook object? Each class you declare can provide a special method called a constructor that can be used to initialize an object of a class when the object is created. In fact, Java *requires* a constructor call for *every* object that's created. Keyword new requests memory from the system to store an object, then calls the corresponding class's constructor to initialize the object. The call is indicated by the parentheses after the class name. A constructor *must* have the *same name* as the class. For example, line 14 of Fig. 3.8 first uses new to create a GradeBook object. The empty parentheses after "new GradeBook" indicate a call to the class's constructor without arguments. By default, the compiler provides a **default constructor** with *no parameters* in any class that does *not* explicitly include a constructor. When a class has only the default constructor, its instance variables are initialized to their *default values*.

When you declare a class, you can provide your own constructor to specify custom initialization for objects of your class. For example, you might want to specify a course name for a GradeBook object when the object is created, as in

```
GradeBook myGradeBook =
    new GradeBook( "CS101 Introduction to Java Programming" );
```

In this case, the argument "CS101 Introduction to Java Programming" is passed to the GradeBook object's constructor and used to initialize the courseName. The preceding statement requires that the class provide a constructor with a String parameter. Figure 3.10 contains a modified GradeBook class with such a constructor.

```java
1   // Fig. 3.10: GradeBook.java
2   // GradeBook class with a constructor to initialize the course name.
3
4   public class GradeBook
5   {
6      private String courseName; // course name for this GradeBook
7
8      // constructor initializes courseName with String argument
9      public GradeBook( String name ) // constructor name is class name
10     {
11        courseName = name; // initializes courseName
12     } // end constructor
13
14     // method to set the course name
15     public void setCourseName( String name )
16     {
17        courseName = name; // store the course name
18     } // end method setCourseName
19
20     // method to retrieve the course name
21     public String getCourseName()
22     {
```

Fig. 3.10 | GradeBook class with a constructor to initialize the course name. (Part 1 of 2.)

```
23          return courseName;
24      } // end method getCourseName
25
26      // display a welcome message to the GradeBook user
27      public void displayMessage()
28      {
29          // this statement calls getCourseName to get the
30          // name of the course this GradeBook represents
31          System.out.printf( "Welcome to the grade book for\n%s!\n",
32              getCourseName() );
33      } // end method displayMessage
34  } // end class GradeBook
```

Fig. 3.10 | GradeBook class with a constructor to initialize the course name. (Part 2 of 2.)

Lines 9–12 declare GradeBook's constructor. Like a method, a constructor's parameter list specifies the data it requires to perform its task. When you create a new object (as we'll do in Fig. 3.11), this data is placed in the *parentheses that follow the class name*. Line 9 of Fig. 3.10 indicates that the constructor has a String parameter called name. The name passed to the constructor is assigned to instance variable courseName in line 11.

Figure 3.11 initializes GradeBook objects using the constructor. Lines 11–12 create and initialize the GradeBook object gradeBook1. The GradeBook constructor is called with the argument "CS101 Introduction to Java Programming" to initialize the course name. The class instance creation expression in lines 11–12 returns a reference to the new object, which is assigned to the variable gradeBook1. Lines 13–14 repeat this process, this time passing the argument "CS102 Data Structures in Java" to initialize the course name for gradeBook2. Lines 17–20 use each object's getCourseName method to obtain the course names and show that they were initialized when the objects were created. The output confirms that each GradeBook maintains its own copy of instance variable courseName.

Software Engineering Observation 3.4

Unless default initialization of your class's instance variables is acceptable, provide a constructor to ensure that they're properly initialized with meaningful values when each new object of your class is created.

```
1   // Fig. 3.11: GradeBookTest.java
2   // GradeBook constructor used to specify the course name at the
3   // time each GradeBook object is created.
4
5   public class GradeBookTest
6   {
7       // main method begins program execution
8       public static void main( String[] args )
9       {
10          // create GradeBook object
11          GradeBook gradeBook1 = new GradeBook(
12              "CS101 Introduction to Java Programming" );
```

Fig. 3.11 | GradeBook constructor used to specify the course name at the time each GradeBook object is created. (Part 1 of 2.)

```
13          GradeBook gradeBook2 = new GradeBook(
14             "CS102 Data Structures in Java" );
15
16          // display initial value of courseName for each GradeBook
17          System.out.printf( "gradeBook1 course name is: %s\n",
18             gradeBook1.getCourseName() );
19          System.out.printf( "gradeBook2 course name is: %s\n",
20             gradeBook2.getCourseName() );
21       } // end main
22    } // end class GradeBookTest
```

```
gradeBook1 course name is: CS101 Introduction to Java Programming
gradeBook2 course name is: CS102 Data Structures in Java
```

Fig. 3.11 | GradeBook constructor used to specify the course name at the time each GradeBook object is created. (Part 2 of 2.)

An important difference between constructors and methods is that constructors cannot return values, so they cannot specify a return type (not even void). Normally, constructors are declared public. If a class does not include a constructor, the class's instance variables are initialized to their default values. *If you declare any constructors for a class, the Java compiler will not create a default constructor for that class.* Thus, we can no longer create a GradeBook object with new GradeBook() as we did in the earlier examples.

Adding the Constructor to Class *GradeBook's* UML Class Diagram
The UML class diagram of Fig. 3.12 models class GradeBook of Fig. 3.10, which has a constructor that has a name parameter of type String. Like operations, the UML models constructors in the third compartment of a class in a class diagram. To distinguish a constructor from a class's operations, the UML requires that the word "constructor" be placed between **guillemets** (« and ») before the constructor's name. It's *customary* to list constructors *before* other operations in the third compartment.

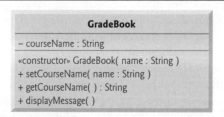

Fig. 3.12 | UML class diagram indicating that class GradeBook has a constructor that has a name parameter of UML type String.

Constructors with Multiple Parameters
Sometimes you'll want to initialize objects with multiple data items. For example, you could store the course name *and* the instructor's name in a GradeBook object. In this case, the GradeBook's constructor would be modified to receive two Strings, as in

```
public GradeBook( String courseName, String instructorName )
```

and you'd call the `GradeBook` constructor as follows:

```
GradeBook gradeBook = new GradeBook(
    "CS101 Introduction to Java Programming", "Sue Green" );
```

3.7 Floating-Point Numbers and Type `double`

We now depart temporarily from our `GradeBook` case study to declare an `Account` class that maintains the balance of a bank account. Most account balances are not whole numbers (such as 0, –22 and 1024). For this reason, class `Account` represents the account balance as a **floating-point number** (i.e., a number with a decimal point, such as 7.33, 0.0975 or 1000.12345). Java provides two primitive types for storing floating-point numbers in memory—`float` and `double`. They differ primarily in that `double` variables can store numbers with larger magnitude and finer detail (i.e., more digits to the right of the decimal point—also known as the number's **precision**) than `float` variables.

Floating-Point Number Precision and Memory Requirements
Variables of type **float** represent **single-precision floating-point numbers** and can represent up to *seven significant digits*. Variables of type **double** represent **double-precision floating-point numbers**. These require twice as much memory as `float` variables and provide *15 significant digits*—approximately double the precision of `float` variables. For the range of values required by most programs, variables of type `float` should suffice, but you can use `double` to "play it safe." In some applications, even `double` variables will be inadequate. Most programmers represent floating-point numbers with type `double`. In fact, Java treats all floating-point numbers you type in a program's source code (such as 7.33 and 0.0975) as `double` values by default. Such values in the source code are known as **floating-point literals**. See Appendix D, Primitive Types, for the ranges of values for `float`s and `double`s.

Although floating-point numbers are not always 100% precise, they have numerous applications. For example, when we speak of a "normal" body temperature of 98.6, we do not need to be precise to a large number of digits. When we read the temperature on a thermometer as 98.6, it may actually be 98.5999473210643. Calling this number simply 98.6 is fine for most applications involving body temperatures. Owing to the imprecise nature of floating-point numbers, type `double` is preferred over type `float`, because `double` variables can represent floating-point numbers more accurately. For this reason, we primarily use type `double` throughout the book. For precise floating-point numbers, Java provides class `BigDecimal` (package `java.math`).

Floating-point numbers also arise as a result of division. In conventional arithmetic, when we divide 10 by 3, the result is 3.3333333..., with the sequence of 3s repeating infinitely. The computer allocates only a fixed amount of space to hold such a value, so clearly the stored floating-point value can be only an approximation.

Account Class with an Instance Variable of Type `double`
Our next application (Figs. 3.13–3.14) contains a class named `Account` (Fig. 3.13) that maintains the balance of a bank account. A typical bank services many accounts, each with its own balance, so line 7 declares an instance variable named `balance` of type `double`. It's an instance variable because it's declared in the body of the class but outside the class's method declarations (lines 10–16, 19–22 and 25–28). Every instance (i.e., object) of class `Account` contains its own copy of `balance`.

```
 1   // Fig. 3.13: Account.java
 2   // Account class with a constructor to validate and
 3   // initialize instance variable balance of type double.
 4
 5   public class Account
 6   {
 7      private double balance; // instance variable that stores the balance
 8
 9      // constructor
10      public Account( double initialBalance )
11      {
12         // validate that initialBalance is greater than 0.0;
13         // if it is not, balance is initialized to the default value 0.0
14         if ( initialBalance > 0.0 )
15            balance = initialBalance;
16      } // end Account constructor
17
18      // credit (add) an amount to the account
19      public void credit( double amount )
20      {
21         balance = balance + amount; // add amount to balance
22      } // end method credit
23
24      // return the account balance
25      public double getBalance()
26      {
27         return balance; // gives the value of balance to the calling method
28      } // end method getBalance
29   } // end class Account
```

Fig. 3.13 | Account class with a constructor to validate and initialize instance variable balance of type double.

The class has a constructor and two methods. It's common for someone opening an account to deposit money immediately, so the constructor (lines 10–16) receives a parameter initialBalance of type double that represents the *starting balance*. Lines 14–15 ensure that initialBalance is greater than 0.0. If so, initialBalance's value is assigned to instance variable balance. Otherwise, balance remains at 0.0—its default initial value.

Method credit (lines 19–22) does *not* return any data when it completes its task, so its return type is void. The method receives one parameter named amount—a double value that will be added to the balance. Line 21 adds amount to the current value of balance, then assigns the result to balance (thus replacing the prior balance amount).

Method getBalance (lines 25–28) allows clients of the class (i.e., other classes that use this class) to obtain the value of a particular Account object's balance. The method specifies return type double and an empty parameter list. Once again, the statements in lines 15, 21 and 27 use instance variable balance even though it was *not* declared in any of the methods. We can use balance in these methods because it's an instance variable of the class.

AccountTest Class to Use Class Account
Class AccountTest (Fig. 3.14) creates two Account objects (lines 10–11) and initializes them with 50.00 and -7.53, respectively. Lines 14–17 output the balance in each Account

by calling the Account's getBalance method. When method getBalance is called for account1 from line 15, the value of account1's balance is returned from line 27 of Fig. 3.13 and displayed by the System.out.printf statement (Fig. 3.14, lines 14–15). Similarly, when method getBalance is called for account2 from line 17, the value of account2's balance is returned from line 27 of Fig. 3.13 and displayed by the System.out.printf statement (Fig. 3.14, lines 16–17). The balance of account2 is 0.00, because the constructor ensured that the account could *not* begin with a negative balance. The value is output by printf with the format specifier %.2f. The format specifier **%f** is used to output values of type float or double. The .2 between % and f represents the number of decimal places (2) that should be output to the right of the decimal point in the floating-point number—also known as the number's **precision**. Any floating-point value output with %.2f will be rounded to the hundredths position—for example, 123.457 would be rounded to 123.46, 27.333 would be rounded to 27.33 and 123.455 would be rounded to 123.46.

```
1   // Fig. 3.14: AccountTest.java
2   // Inputting and outputting floating-point numbers with Account objects.
3   import java.util.Scanner;
4
5   public class AccountTest
6   {
7      // main method begins execution of Java application
8      public static void main( String[] args )
9      {
10        Account account1 = new Account( 50.00 ); // create Account object
11        Account account2 = new Account( -7.53 ); // create Account object
12
13        // display initial balance of each object
14        System.out.printf( "account1 balance: $%.2f\n",
15           account1.getBalance() );
16        System.out.printf( "account2 balance: $%.2f\n\n",
17           account2.getBalance() );
18
19        // create Scanner to obtain input from command window
20        Scanner input = new Scanner( System.in );
21        double depositAmount; // deposit amount read from user
22
23        System.out.print( "Enter deposit amount for account1: " ); // prompt
24        depositAmount = input.nextDouble(); // obtain user input
25        System.out.printf( "\nadding %.2f to account1 balance\n\n",
26           depositAmount );
27        account1.credit( depositAmount ); // add to account1 balance
28
29        // display balances
30        System.out.printf( "account1 balance: $%.2f\n",
31           account1.getBalance() );
32        System.out.printf( "account2 balance: $%.2f\n\n",
33           account2.getBalance() );
34
35        System.out.print( "Enter deposit amount for account2: " ); // prompt
```

Fig. 3.14 | Inputting and outputting floating-point numbers with Account objects. (Part 1 of 2.)

```
36              depositAmount = input.nextDouble(); // obtain user input
37              System.out.printf( "\nadding %.2f to account2 balance\n\n",
38                 depositAmount );
39              account2.credit( depositAmount ); // add to account2 balance
40
41              // display balances
42              System.out.printf( "account1 balance: $%.2f\n",
43                 account1.getBalance() );
44              System.out.printf( "account2 balance: $%.2f\n",
45                 account2.getBalance() );
46          } // end main
47      } // end class AccountTest
```

```
account1 balance: $50.00
account2 balance: $0.00

Enter deposit amount for account1: 25.53

adding 25.53 to account1 balance

account1 balance: $75.53
account2 balance: $0.00

Enter deposit amount for account2: 123.45

adding 123.45 to account2 balance

account1 balance: $75.53
account2 balance: $123.45
```

Fig. 3.14 | Inputting and outputting floating-point numbers with Account objects. (Part 2 of 2.)

Line 21 declares local variable depositAmount to store each deposit amount entered by the user. Unlike the instance variable balance in class Account, local variable deposit-Amount in main is *not* initialized to 0.0 by default. However, this variable does not need to be initialized here, because its value will be determined by the user's input.

Line 23 prompts the user to enter a deposit amount for account1. Line 24 obtains the input from the user by calling Scanner object input's **nextDouble** method, which returns a double value entered by the user. Lines 25–26 display the deposit amount. Line 27 calls object account1's credit method and supplies depositAmount as the method's argument. When the method is called, the argument's value is assigned to parameter amount (line 19 of Fig. 3.13) of method credit (lines 19–22 of Fig. 3.13); then method credit adds that value to the balance (line 21 of Fig. 3.13). Lines 30–33 (Fig. 3.14) output the balances of both Accounts again to show that only account1's balance changed.

Line 35 prompts the user to enter a deposit amount for account2. Line 36 obtains the input from the user by calling Scanner object input's nextDouble method. Lines 37–38 display the deposit amount. Line 39 calls object account2's credit method and supplies depositAmount as the method's argument; then method credit adds that value to the balance. Finally, lines 42–45 output the balances of both Accounts again to show that only account2's balance changed.

*UML Class Diagram for Class **Account***

The UML class diagram in Fig. 3.15 models class Account of Fig. 3.13. The diagram models the private attribute balance with UML type Double to correspond to the class's instance variable balance of Java type double. The diagram models class Account's constructor with a parameter initialBalance of UML type Double in the third compartment of the class. The class's two public methods are modeled as operations in the third compartment as well. The diagram models operation credit with an amount parameter of UML type Double (because the corresponding method has an amount parameter of Java type double), and operation getBalance with a return type of Double (because the corresponding Java method returns a double value).

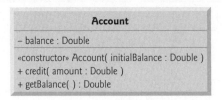

Fig. 3.15 | UML class diagram indicating that class Account has a private balance attribute of UML type Double, a constructor (with a parameter of UML type Double) and two public operations—credit (with an amount parameter of UML type Double) and getBalance (returns UML type Double).

3.8 Wrap-Up

In this chapter, you learned how to declare instance variables of a class to maintain data for each object of the class, and how to declare methods that operate on that data. You learned how to call a method to tell it to perform its task and how to pass information to methods as arguments. You learned the difference between a local variable of a method and an instance variable of a class and that only instance variables are initialized automatically. You also learned how to use a class's constructor to specify the initial values for an object's instance variables. Throughout the chapter, you saw how the UML can be used to create class diagrams that model the constructors, methods and attributes of classes. Finally, you learned about floating-point numbers—how to store them with variables of primitive type double, how to input them with a Scanner object and how to format them with printf and format specifier %f for display purposes. In the next chapter we begin our introduction to control statements, which specify the order in which a program's actions are performed. You'll use these in your methods to specify how they should perform their tasks.

4

Control Statements: Part 1

Let's all move one place on.
—Lewis Carroll

The wheel is come full circle.
—William Shakespeare

How many apples fell on Newton's head before he took the hint!
—Robert Frost

Objectives

In this chapter you'll learn:

- To use the `if` and `if...else` selection statements to choose among alternative actions.

- To use the `while` repetition statement to execute statements in a program repeatedly.

- To use counter-controlled repetition and sentinel-controlled repetition.

- To use the compound assignment, increment and decrement operators.

- The portability of primitive data types.

4.1 Introduction

In this chapter, we introduce Java's if, if...else and while statements, three of the building blocks that allow you to specify the logic required for methods to perform their tasks. We devote a portion of this chapter (and Chapters 5 and 7) to further developing the GradeBook class introduced in Chapter 3. In particular, we add a method to the GradeBook class that uses control statements to calculate the average of a set of student grades. Another example demonstrates additional ways to combine control statements to solve a similar problem. We introduce Java's compound assignment, increment and decrement operators. Finally, we discuss the portability of Java's primitive types.

4.2 Control Structures

Normally, statements in a program are executed one after the other in the order in which they're written. This process is called **sequential execution**. Various Java statements, which we'll soon discuss, enable you to specify that the next statement to execute is *not* necessarily the *next* one in sequence. This is called **transfer of control**.

During the 1960s, it became clear that the indiscriminate use of transfers of control was the root of much difficulty experienced by software development groups. The blame was pointed at the **goto statement** (used in most programming languages of the time), which allows you to specify a transfer of control to one of a wide range of destinations in a program. The term **structured programming** became almost synonymous with "goto elimination." [*Note:* Java does *not* have a goto statement; however, the word goto is *reserved* by Java and should *not* be used as an identifier in programs.]

Bohm and Jacopini's work demonstrated that all programs could be written in terms of only three control structures—the **sequence structure**, the **selection structure** and the **repetition structure**.[1] When we introduce Java's control structure implementations, we'll refer to them in the terminology of the *Java Language Specification* as "control statements."

Sequence Structure in Java
The sequence structure is built into Java. Unless directed otherwise, the computer executes Java statements one after the other in the order in which they're written—that is, in sequence. The **activity diagram** in Fig. 4.1 illustrates a typical sequence structure in which two calculations are performed in order. Java lets you have as many actions as you want in

---

1. Bohm, C., and G. Jacopini, "Flow Diagrams, Turing Machines, and Languages with Only Two Formation Rules," *Communications of the ACM*, Vol. 9, No. 5, May 1966, pp. 336–371.

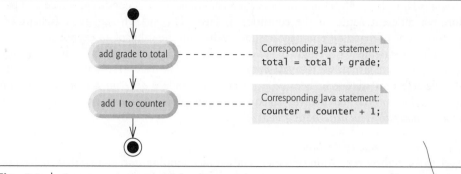

Fig. 4.1 | Sequence structure activity diagram.

a sequence structure. As we'll soon see, anywhere a single action may be placed, we may place several actions in sequence.

A UML activity diagram models the **workflow** (also called the **activity**) of a portion of a software system. Such workflows may include a portion of an algorithm, like the sequence structure in Fig. 4.1. Activity diagrams are composed of symbols, such as **action-state symbols** (rectangles with their left and right sides replaced with outward arcs), **diamonds** and **small circles**. These symbols are connected by **transition arrows**, which represent the flow of the activity—that is, the order in which the actions should occur.

Activity diagrams help you develop and represent algorithms. They also clearly show how control structures operate. We use the UML in this chapter and Chapter 5 to show control flow in control statements. In Chapters 12–13, we use the UML in a real-world automated-teller machine case study.

Consider the sequence structure activity diagram in Fig. 4.1. It contains two **action states** that represent actions to perform. Each action state contains an **action expression**—for example, "add grade to total" or "add 1 to counter"—that specifies a particular action to perform. Other actions might include calculations or input/output operations. The arrows in the activity diagram represent **transitions**, which indicate the *order* in which the actions represented by the action states occur. The program that implements the activities illustrated by the diagram in Fig. 4.1 first adds `grade` to `total`, then adds `1` to `counter`.

The **solid circle** at the top of the activity diagram represents the **initial state**—the *beginning* of the workflow *before* the program performs the modeled actions. The **solid circle surrounded by a hollow circle** that appears at the bottom of the diagram represents the **final state**—the *end* of the workflow *after* the program performs its actions.

Figure 4.1 also includes rectangles with the upper-right corners folded over. These are UML **notes** (like comments in Java)—explanatory remarks that describe the purpose of symbols in the diagram. Figure 4.1 uses UML notes to show the Java code associated with each action state. A **dotted line** connects each note with the element it describes. Activity diagrams normally do *not* show the Java code that implements the activity. We do this here to illustrate how the diagram relates to Java code. For more information on the UML, see our case study (Chapters 12–13) or visit `www.uml.org`.

Selection Statements in Java

Java has three types of **selection statements** (discussed in this chapter and Chapter 5). The `if` statement either performs (selects) an action, if a condition is true, or skips it, if the condition is false. The if...else statement performs an action if a condition is true and performs a different action if the condition is false. The switch statement (Chapter 5) performs one of many different actions, depending on the value of an expression.

The if statement is a **single-selection statement** because it selects or ignores a *single* action (or, as we'll soon see, a *single group of actions*). The if...else statement is called a **double-selection statement** because it selects between *two different actions* (or *groups of actions*). The switch statement is called a **multiple-selection statement** because it selects among *many different actions* (or *groups of actions*).

Repetition Statements in Java
Java provides three **repetition statements** (also called **looping statements**) that enable programs to perform statements repeatedly as long as a condition (called the **loop-continuation condition**) remains true. The repetition statements are the while, do...while and for statements. (Chapter 5 presents the do...while and for statements.) The while and for statements perform the action (or group of actions) in their bodies zero or more times—if the loop-continuation condition is initially false, the action (or group of actions) will not execute. The do...while statement performs the action (or group of actions) in its body *one or more* times. The words if, else, switch, while, do and for are Java keywords. A complete list of Java keywords appears in Appendix C.

Summary of Control Statements in Java
Java has only three kinds of control structures, which from this point forward we refer to as control statements: the sequence statement, selection statements (three types) and repetition statements (three types). Every program is formed by combining as many of these statements as is appropriate for the algorithm the program implements. We can model each control statement as an activity diagram. Like Fig. 4.1, each diagram contains an initial state and a final state that represent a control statement's entry point and exit point, respectively. **Single-entry/single-exit control statements** make it easy to build programs—we simply connect the exit point of one to the entry point of the next. We call this **control-statement stacking**. We'll learn that there's only one other way in which control statements may be connected—**control-statement nesting**—in which one control statement appears *inside* another. Thus, algorithms in Java programs are constructed from only three kinds of control statements, combined in only two ways. This is the essence of simplicity.

4.3 if Single-Selection Statement

Programs use selection statements to choose among alternative courses of action. For example, suppose that the passing grade on an exam is 60. The statement

```
if ( studentGrade >= 60 )
    System.out.println( "Passed" );
```

determines whether the condition studentGrade >= 60 is true. If so, "Passed" is printed, and the next statement in order is performed. If the condition is false, the body statement is ignored, and the next statement in order is performed.

Figure 4.2 illustrates the single-selection if statement. This figure contains the most important symbol in an activity diagram—the diamond, or **decision symbol**, which indicates that a decision is to be made. The workflow continues along a path determined by the symbol's associated **guard conditions**, which can be true or false. Each transition arrow emerging from a decision symbol has a guard condition (specified in square brackets next to the arrow). If a guard condition is true, the workflow enters the action state to which the transition arrow points. In Fig. 4.2, if the grade is greater than or equal to 60, the program prints "Passed," then transitions to the activity's final state. If the grade is less than 60, the program immediately transitions to the final state without displaying a message.

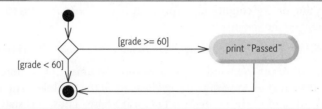

Fig. 4.2 | if single-selection statement UML activity diagram.

The if statement is a single-entry/single-exit control statement. We'll see that the activity diagrams for the remaining control statements also contain initial states, transition arrows, action states that indicate actions to perform, decision symbols (with associated guard conditions) that indicate decisions to be made, and final states.

4.4 if...else Double-Selection Statement

The if single-selection statement performs an indicated action only when the condition is true; otherwise, the action is skipped. The **if...else double-selection statement** allows you to specify an action to perform when the condition is true and a different action when the condition is false. For example, the statement

```
if ( grade >= 60 )
    System.out.println( "Passed" );
else
    System.out.println( "Failed" );
```

prints "Passed" if the student's grade is greater than or equal to 60, but prints "Failed" if it's less than 60. In either case, after printing occurs, the next statement in sequence is performed.

Figure 4.3 illustrates the flow of control in the if...else statement. Once again, the symbols in the UML activity diagram (besides the initial state, transition arrows and final state) represent action states and decisions.

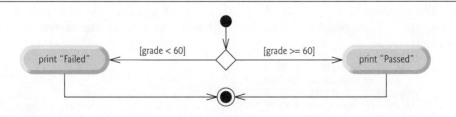

Fig. 4.3 | if...else double-selection statement UML activity diagram.

Conditional Operator (?:)

Java provides the **conditional operator** (**?:**) that can be used in place of an if...else statement. This is Java's only **ternary operator** (operator that takes three operands). Together, the operands and the ?: symbol form a **conditional expression.** The first operand (to the left of the ?) is a **boolean expression** (i.e., a condition that evaluates to a boolean value—**true** or **false**), the second operand (between the ? and :) is the value of the conditional expression if the boolean expression is true and the third operand (to the right of the :) is the value of the conditional expression if the boolean expression evaluates to false. For example, the statement

```
System.out.println( studentGrade >= 60 ? "Passed" : "Failed" );
```

prints the value of println's conditional-expression argument. The conditional expression in this statement evaluates to the string "Passed" if the boolean expression student-Grade >= 60 is true and to the string "Failed" if it's false. Thus, this statement with the conditional operator performs essentially the same function as the if...else statement shown earlier in this section. The precedence of the conditional operator is low, so the entire conditional expression is normally placed in parentheses. We'll see that conditional expressions can be used in some situations where if...else statements cannot.

Nested **if...else** *Statements*

A program can test multiple cases by placing if...else statements inside other if...else statements to create **nested if...else statements.** For example, the following nested if...else statements print A for exam grades greater than or equal to 90, B for grades 80 to 89, C for grades 70 to 79, D for grades 60 to 69 and F for all other grades:

```
if ( studentGrade >= 90 )
   System.out.println( "A" );
else
   if ( studentGrade >= 80 )
      System.out.println( "B" );
   else
      if ( studentGrade >= 70 )
         System.out.println( "C" );
      else
         if ( studentGrade >= 60 )
            System.out.println( "D" );
         else
            System.out.println( "F" );
```

If variable studentGrade is greater than or equal to 90, the first four conditions in the nested if...else statement will be true, but only the statement in the if part of the first if...else statement will execute. After that statement executes, the else part of the "outermost" if...else statement is skipped. Many programmers prefer to write the preceding nested if...else statement as

```
if ( studentGrade >= 90 )
   System.out.println( "A" );
else if ( studentGrade >= 80 )
   System.out.println( "B" );
else if ( studentGrade >= 70 )
   System.out.println( "C" );
```

```
   else if ( studentGrade >= 60 )
      System.out.println( "D" );
   else
      System.out.println( "F" );
```

The two forms are identical except for the spacing and indentation, which the compiler ignores. The latter form avoids deep indentation of the code to the right. Such indentation often leaves little room on a line of source code, forcing lines to be split.

Dangling-else Problem

The Java compiler always associates an else with the immediately preceding if unless told to do otherwise by the placement of braces ({ and }). This behavior can lead to what is referred to as the **dangling-else problem**. For example,

```
if ( x > 5 )
   if ( y > 5 )
      System.out.println( "x and y are > 5" );
else
   System.out.println( "x is <= 5" );
```

appears to indicate that if x is greater than 5, the nested if statement determines whether y is also greater than 5. If so, the string "x and y are > 5" is output. Otherwise, it appears that if x is not greater than 5, the else part of the if...else outputs the string "x is <= 5". Beware! This nested if...else statement does not execute as it appears. The compiler actually interprets the statement as

```
if ( x > 5 )
   if ( y > 5 )
      System.out.println( "x and y are > 5" );
   else
      System.out.println( "x is <= 5" );
```

in which the body of the first if is a nested if...else. The outer if statement tests whether x is greater than 5. If so, execution continues by testing whether y is also greater than 5. If the second condition is true, the proper string—"x and y are > 5"—is displayed. However, if the second condition is false, the string "x is <= 5" is displayed, even though we know that x is greater than 5. Equally bad, if the outer if statement's condition is false, the inner if...else is skipped and nothing is displayed.

To force the nested if...else statement to execute as it was intended, use:

```
if ( x > 5 )
{
   if ( y > 5 )
      System.out.println( "x and y are > 5" );
}
else
   System.out.println( "x is <= 5" );
```

The braces indicate that the second if is in the body of the first and that the else is associated with the *first* if.

Blocks

The if statement normally expects only one statement in its body. To include several statements in the body of an if (or the body of an else for an if...else statement), enclose the statements in braces. Statements contained in a pair of braces form a **block**. A block can be placed anywhere in a program that a single statement can be placed.

The following example includes a block in the else part of an if...else statement:

```
if ( grade >= 60 )
    System.out.println( "Passed" );
else
{
    System.out.println( "Failed" );
    System.out.println( "You must take this course again." );
}
```

In this case, if grade is less than 60, the program executes *both* statements in the body of the else and prints

```
Failed
You must take this course again.
```

Note the braces surrounding the two statements in the else clause. These braces are important. Without the braces, the statement

```
System.out.println( "You must take this course again." );
```

would be outside the body of the else part of the if...else statement and would execute *regardless* of whether the grade was less than 60.

Syntax errors (e.g., when one brace in a block is left out of the program) are caught by the compiler. A **logic error** (e.g., when both braces in a block are left out of the program) has its effect at execution time. A **fatal logic error** causes a program to fail and terminate prematurely. A **nonfatal logic error** allows a program to continue executing but causes it to produce incorrect results.

Just as a block can be placed anywhere a single statement can be placed, it's also possible to have an empty statement. Recall from Section 2.7 that the empty statement is represented by placing a semicolon (;) where a statement would normally be.

Common Programming Error 4.1

Placing a semicolon after the condition in an if or if...else statement leads to a logic error in single-selection if statements and a syntax error in double-selection if...else statements (when the if part contains an actual body statement).

4.5 while Repetition Statement

A **repetition** (or **looping**) **statement** allows you to specify that a program should repeat an action while some condition remains true. As an example of Java's **while repetition statement**, consider a program segment that finds the first power of 3 larger than 100. Suppose that the int variable product is initialized to 3. After the following while statement executes, product contains the result:

```
while ( product <= 100 )
    product = 3 * product;
```

When this while statement begins execution, the value of variable product is 3. Each iteration of the while statement multiplies product by 3, so product takes on the values 9,

27, 81 and 243 successively. When variable product becomes 243, the while-statement condition—product <= 100—becomes false. This terminates the repetition, so the final value of product is 243. At this point, program execution continues with the next statement after the while statement.

> ### Common Programming Error 4.2
> *Not providing in the body of a while statement an action that eventually causes the condition in the while to become false normally results in an infinite loop.*

The UML activity diagram in Fig. 4.4 illustrates the flow of control in the preceding while statement. Once again, the symbols in the diagram (besides the initial state, transition arrows, a final state and three notes) represent an action state and a decision. This diagram introduces the UML's **merge symbol**. The UML represents both the merge symbol and the decision symbol as diamonds. The merge symbol joins two flows of activity into one. In this diagram, the merge symbol joins the transitions from the initial state and from the action state, so they both flow into the decision that determines whether the loop should begin (or continue) executing. The decision and merge symbols can be distinguished by the number of "incoming" and "outgoing" transition arrows. A decision symbol has one transition arrow pointing to the diamond and two or more pointing out from it to indicate possible transitions from that point. In addition, each transition arrow pointing out of a decision symbol has a guard condition next to it. A merge symbol has two or more transition arrows pointing to the diamond and only one pointing from the diamond, to indicate multiple activity flows merging to continue the activity. *None* of the transition arrows associated with a merge symbol has a guard condition.

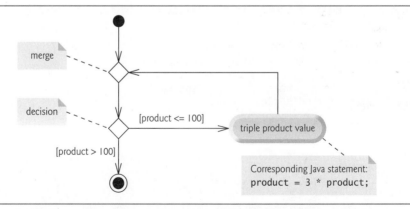

Fig. 4.4 | while repetition statement UML activity diagram.

Figure 4.4 clearly shows the repetition of the while statement discussed earlier in this section. The transition arrow emerging from the action state points back to the merge, from which program flow transitions back to the decision that's tested at the beginning of each iteration of the loop. The loop continues to execute until the guard condition product > 100 becomes true. Then the while statement exits (reaches its final state), and control passes to the next statement in sequence in the program.

4.6 Counter-Controlled Repetition

Consider the following problem statement:

> *A class of ten students took a quiz. The grades (integers in the range 0 to 100) for this quiz are available to you. Determine the class average on the quiz.*

The class average is equal to the sum of the grades divided by the number of students. The program for solving this problem must input each grade, keep track of the total of all grades input, perform the averaging calculation and print the result.

Implementing Counter-Controlled Repetition in Class GradeBook

Class GradeBook (Fig. 4.5) contains a constructor (lines 11–14) that assigns a value to the class's instance variable courseName (declared in line 8), and methods setCourseName (lines 17–20), getCourseName (lines 23–26) and displayMessage (lines 29–34). Lines 37–66 declare method determineClassAverage, which implements the class-averaging algorithm.

```java
1  // Fig. 4.5: GradeBook.java
2  // GradeBook class that solves class-average problem using
3  // counter-controlled repetition.
4  import java.util.Scanner; // program uses class Scanner
5
6  public class GradeBook
7  {
8     private String courseName; // name of course this GradeBook represents
9
10    // constructor initializes courseName
11    public GradeBook( String name )
12    {
13       courseName = name; // initializes courseName
14    } // end constructor
15
16    // method to set the course name
17    public void setCourseName( String name )
18    {
19       courseName = name; // store the course name
20    } // end method setCourseName
21
22    // method to retrieve the course name
23    public String getCourseName()
24    {
25       return courseName;
26    } // end method getCourseName
27
28    // display a welcome message to the GradeBook user
29    public void displayMessage()
30    {
31       // getCourseName gets the name of the course
32       System.out.printf( "Welcome to the grade book for\n%s!\n\n",
33          getCourseName() );
34    } // end method displayMessage
```

Fig. 4.5 | GradeBook class that solves class-average problem using counter-controlled repetition. (Part 1 of 2.)

```
35
36        // determine class average based on 10 grades entered by user
37        public void determineClassAverage()
38        {
39           // create Scanner to obtain input from command window
40           Scanner input = new Scanner( System.in );
41
42           int total; // sum of grades entered by user
43           int gradeCounter; // number of the grade to be entered next
44           int grade; // grade value entered by user
45           int average; // average of grades
46
47           // initialization phase
48           total = 0; // initialize total
49           gradeCounter = 1; // initialize loop counter
50
51           // processing phase uses counter-controlled repetition
52           while ( gradeCounter <= 10 ) // loop 10 times
53           {
54              System.out.print( "Enter grade: " ); // prompt
55              grade = input.nextInt(); // input next grade
56              total = total + grade; // add grade to total
57              gradeCounter = gradeCounter + 1; // increment counter by 1
58           } // end while
59
60           // termination phase
61           average = total / 10; // integer division yields integer result
62
63           // display total and average of grades
64           System.out.printf( "\nTotal of all 10 grades is %d\n", total );
65           System.out.printf( "Class average is %d\n", average );
66        } // end method determineClassAverage
67     } // end class GradeBook
```

Fig. 4.5 | GradeBook class that solves class-average problem using counter-controlled repetition. (Part 2 of 2.)

Line 40 declares and initializes Scanner variable input, which is used to read values entered by the user. Lines 42–45 declare local variables total, gradeCounter, grade and average to be of type int. Variable grade stores the user input.

The declarations (in lines 42–45) appear in the body of method determine-ClassAverage. Recall that variables declared in a method body are local variables and can be used only from the line of their declaration to the closing right brace of the method declaration. A local variable's declaration must appear before the variable is used in that method. A local variable cannot be accessed outside the method in which it's declared.

In this chapter, class GradeBook simply reads and processes a set of grades. The averaging calculation is performed in method determineClassAverage using local variables—we do not preserve any information about student grades in instance variables of the class.

The assignments (in lines 48–49) initialize total to 0 and gradeCounter to 1. These initializations occur *before* the variables are used in calculations. Variables grade and average (for the user input and calculated average, respectively) need not be initialized here—their values will be assigned as they're input or calculated later in the method.

Common Programming Error 4.3

Using the value of a local variable before it's initialized results in a compilation error. All local variables must be initialized before their values are used in expressions.

Line 52 indicates that the while statement should continue looping (also called **iterating**) as long as gradeCounter's value is less than or equal to 10. While this condition remains true, the while statement repeatedly executes the statements between the braces that delimit its body (lines 54–57).

Line 54 displays the prompt "Enter grade: ". Line 55 reads the grade entered by the user and assigns it to variable grade. Then line 56 adds the new grade entered by the user to the total and assigns the result to total, which replaces its previous value.

Line 57 adds 1 to gradeCounter to indicate that the program has processed a grade and is ready to input the next grade from the user. Incrementing gradeCounter eventually causes it to exceed 10. Then the loop terminates, because its condition (line 52) becomes false.

When the loop terminates, line 61 performs the averaging calculation and assigns its result to the variable average. Line 64 uses System.out's printf method to display the text "Total of all 10 grades is " followed by variable total's value. Line 65 then uses printf to display the text "Class average is " followed by variable average's value. After reaching line 66, method determineClassAverage returns control to the calling method (i.e., main in GradeBookTest of Fig. 4.6).

Class *GradeBookTest*

Class GradeBookTest (Fig. 4.6) creates an object of class GradeBook (Fig. 4.5) and demonstrates its capabilities. Lines 10–11 of Fig. 4.6 create a new GradeBook object and assign it to variable myGradeBook. The String in line 11 is passed to the GradeBook constructor (lines 11–14 of Fig. 4.5). Line 13 calls myGradeBook's displayMessage method to display a welcome message to the user. Line 14 then calls myGradeBook's determineClassAverage method to allow the user to enter 10 grades, for which the method then calculates and prints the average.

```
1   // Fig. 4.6: GradeBookTest.java
2   // Create GradeBook object and invoke its determineClassAverage method.
3
4   public class GradeBookTest
5   {
6      public static void main( String[] args )
7      {
8         // create GradeBook object myGradeBook and
9         // pass course name to constructor
10        GradeBook myGradeBook = new GradeBook(
11           "CS101 Introduction to Java Programming" );
12
13        myGradeBook.displayMessage(); // display welcome message
```

Fig. 4.6 | GradeBookTest class creates an object of class GradeBook (Fig. 4.5) and invokes its determineClassAverage method. (Part I of 2.)

```
14            myGradeBook.determineClassAverage(); // find average of 10 grades
15        } // end main
16    } // end class GradeBookTest
```

```
Welcome to the grade book for
CS101 Introduction to Java Programming!

Enter grade: 67
Enter grade: 78
Enter grade: 89
Enter grade: 67
Enter grade: 87
Enter grade: 98
Enter grade: 93
Enter grade: 85
Enter grade: 82
Enter grade: 100

Total of all 10 grades is 846
Class average is 84
```

Fig. 4.6 | GradeBookTest class creates an object of class GradeBook (Fig. 4.5) and invokes its determineClassAverage method. (Part 2 of 2.)

Notes on Integer Division and Truncation

The averaging calculation performed by method determineClassAverage in response to the method call at line 14 in Fig. 4.6 produces an integer result. The program's output indicates that the sum of the grade values in the sample execution is 846, which, when divided by 10, should yield the floating-point number 84.6. However, the result of the calculation total / 10 (line 61 of Fig. 4.5) is the integer 84, because total and 10 are both integers. Dividing two integers results in **integer division**—any fractional part of the calculation is lost (i.e., **truncated**). In the next section we'll see how to obtain a floating-point result from the averaging calculation.

Common Programming Error 4.4

Assuming that integer division rounds (rather than truncates) can lead to incorrect results. For example, 7 ÷ 4, which yields 1.75 in conventional arithmetic, truncates to 1 in integer arithmetic, rather than rounding to 2.

4.7 Sentinel-Controlled Repetition

Let's generalize Section 4.6's class-average problem. Consider the following problem:

> *Develop a class-averaging program that processes grades for an arbitrary number of students each time it's run.*

In the previous class-average example, the problem statement specified the number of students, so the number of grades (10) was known in advance. In this example, no indication is given of how many grades the user will enter during the program's execution. The program must process an arbitrary number of grades. How can it determine when to stop the input of grades? How will it know when to calculate and print the class average?

One way to solve this problem is to use a special value called a **sentinel value** (also called a **signal value**, a **dummy value** or a **flag value**) to indicate "end of data entry." The user enters grades until all legitimate grades have been entered. The user then types the sentinel value to indicate that no more grades will be entered. **Sentinel-controlled repetition** is often called **indefinite repetition** because the number of repetitions is *not* known before the loop begins executing.

Clearly, a sentinel value must be chosen that cannot be confused with an acceptable input value. Grades on a quiz are nonnegative integers, so –1 is an acceptable sentinel value for this problem. Thus, a run of the class-average program might process a stream of inputs such as 95, 96, 75, 74, 89 and –1. The program would then compute and print the class average for the grades 95, 96, 75, 74 and 89; since –1 is the sentinel value, it should *not* enter into the averaging calculation.

Implementing Sentinel-Controlled Repetition in Class GradeBook
Figure 4.7 shows the Java class GradeBook containing method determineClassAverage that implements the sentinel-controlled repetition algorithm. Although each grade is an integer, the averaging calculation is likely to produce a number with a decimal point—in other words, a real (i.e., floating-point) number. The type int cannot represent such a number, so this class uses type double to do so.

```java
1   // Fig. 4.7: GradeBook.java
2   // GradeBook class that solves the class-average problem using
3   // sentinel-controlled repetition.
4   import java.util.Scanner; // program uses class Scanner
5
6   public class GradeBook
7   {
8      private String courseName; // name of course this GradeBook represents
9
10     // constructor initializes courseName
11     public GradeBook( String name )
12     {
13        courseName = name; // initializes courseName
14     } // end constructor
15
16     // method to set the course name
17     public void setCourseName( String name )
18     {
19        courseName = name; // store the course name
20     } // end method setCourseName
21
22     // method to retrieve the course name
23     public String getCourseName()
24     {
25        return courseName;
26     } // end method getCourseName
27
```

Fig. 4.7 | GradeBook class that solves the class-average problem using sentinel-controlled repetition. (Part 1 of 3.)

```
28       // display a welcome message to the GradeBook user
29       public void displayMessage()
30       {
31          // getCourseName gets the name of the course
32          System.out.printf( "Welcome to the grade book for\n%s!\n\n",
33             getCourseName() );
34       } // end method displayMessage
35
36       // determine the average of an arbitrary number of grades
37       public void determineClassAverage()
38       {
39          // create Scanner to obtain input from command window
40          Scanner input = new Scanner( System.in );
41
42          int total; // sum of grades
43          int gradeCounter; // number of grades entered
44          int grade; // grade value
45          double average; // number with decimal point for average
46
47          // initialization phase
48          total = 0; // initialize total
49          gradeCounter = 0; // initialize loop counter
50
51          // processing phase
52          // prompt for input and read grade from user
53          System.out.print( "Enter grade or -1 to quit: " );
54          grade = input.nextInt();
55
56          // loop until sentinel value read from user
57          while ( grade != -1 )
58          {
59             total = total + grade; // add grade to total
60             gradeCounter = gradeCounter + 1; // increment counter
61
62             // prompt for input and read next grade from user
63             System.out.print( "Enter grade or -1 to quit: " );
64             grade = input.nextInt();
65          } // end while
66
67          // termination phase
68          // if user entered at least one grade...
69          if ( gradeCounter != 0 )
70          {
71             // calculate average of all grades entered
72             average = (double) total / gradeCounter;
73
74             // display total and average (with two digits of precision)
75             System.out.printf( "\nTotal of the %d grades entered is %d\n",
76                gradeCounter, total );
77             System.out.printf( "Class average is %.2f\n", average );
78          } // end if
```

Fig. 4.7 | GradeBook class that solves the class-average problem using sentinel-controlled repetition. (Part 2 of 3.)

```
79          else // no grades were entered, so output appropriate message
80             System.out.println( "No grades were entered" );
81       } // end method determineClassAverage
82    } // end class GradeBook
```

Fig. 4.7 | GradeBook class that solves the class-average problem using sentinel-controlled repetition. (Part 3 of 3.)

In this example, we see that control statements may be *stacked* on top of one another (in sequence). The `while` statement (lines 57–65) is followed in sequence by an `if...else` statement (lines 69–80). Much of the code in this program is identical to that in Fig. 4.5, so we concentrate on the new concepts.

Line 45 declares `double` variable `average`, which allows us to store the class average as a floating-point number. Line 49 initializes `gradeCounter` to 0, because no grades have been entered yet. Remember that this program uses sentinel-controlled repetition to input the grades. To keep an accurate record of the number of grades entered, the program increments `gradeCounter` only when the user enters a valid grade.

Program Logic for Sentinel-Controlled Repetition vs. Counter-Controlled Repetition
Compare the program logic for sentinel-controlled repetition in this application with that for counter-controlled repetition in Fig. 4.5. In counter-controlled repetition, each iteration of the `while` statement (e.g., lines 52–58 of Fig. 4.5) reads a value from the user, for the specified number of iterations. In sentinel-controlled repetition, the program reads the first value (lines 53–54 of Fig. 4.7) before reaching the `while`. This value determines whether the program's flow of control should enter the body of the `while`. If the condition of the `while` is false, the user entered the sentinel value, so the body of the `while` does not execute (i.e., no grades were entered). If, on the other hand, the condition is true, the body begins execution, and the loop adds the `grade` value to the `total` (line 59). Then lines 63–64 in the loop body input the next value from the user. Next, program control reaches the closing right brace of the loop body at line 65, so execution continues with the test of the `while`'s condition (line 57). The condition uses the most recent `grade` input by the user to determine whether the loop body should execute again. The value of variable `grade` is always input from the user immediately before the program tests the `while` condition. This allows the program to determine whether the value just input is the sentinel value *before* the program processes that value (i.e., adds it to the `total`). If the sentinel value is input, the loop terminates, and the program does not add –1 to the `total`.

Good Programming Practice 4.1
In a sentinel-controlled loop, prompts should remind the user of the sentinel.

After the loop terminates, the `if...else` statement at lines 69–80 executes. The condition at line 69 determines whether any grades were input. If none were input, the `else` part (lines 79–80) of the `if...else` statement executes and displays the message "No grades were entered" and the method returns control to the calling method.

Notice the `while` statement's block in Fig. 4.7 (lines 58–65). Without the braces, the loop would consider its body to be only the first statement, which adds the `grade` to the `total`. The last three statements in the block would fall outside the loop body, causing the computer to interpret the code incorrectly as follows:

```
while ( grade != -1 )
    total = total + grade; // add grade to total
gradeCounter = gradeCounter + 1; // increment counter

// prompt for input and read next grade from user
System.out.print( "Enter grade or -1 to quit: " );
grade = input.nextInt();
```

The preceding code would cause an infinite loop in the program if the user did not input the sentinel -1 at line 54 (before the `while` statement).

Common Programming Error 4.5

Omitting the braces that delimit a block can lead to logic errors, such as infinite loops. To prevent this problem, some programmers enclose the body of every control statement in braces, even if the body contains only a single statement.

Explicitly and Implicitly Converting Between Primitive Types

If at least one grade was entered, line 72 of Fig. 4.7 calculates the average of the grades. Recall from Fig. 4.5 that integer division yields an integer result. Even though variable average is declared as a `double` (line 45), the calculation

```
average = total / gradeCounter;
```

loses the fractional part of the quotient *before* the result of the division is assigned to average. This occurs because `total` and `gradeCounter` are *both* integers, and integer division yields an integer result. To perform a floating-point calculation with integer values, we must temporarily treat these values as floating-point numbers for use in the calculation. Java provides the **unary cast operator** to accomplish this task. Line 72 uses the **(double)** cast operator—a unary operator—to create a *temporary* floating-point copy of its operand `total` (which appears to the right of the operator). Using a cast operator in this manner is called **explicit conversion** or **type casting**. The value stored in `total` is still an integer.

The calculation now consists of a floating-point value (the temporary `double` version of `total`) divided by the integer `gradeCounter`. Java knows how to evaluate only arithmetic expressions in which the operands' types are *identical*. To ensure that the operands are of the same type, Java performs an operation called **promotion** (or **implicit conversion**) on selected operands. For example, in an expression containing values of the types `int` and `double`, the `int` values are promoted to `double` values for use in the expression. In this example, the value of `gradeCounter` is promoted to type `double`, then the floating-point division is performed and the result of the calculation is assigned to `average`. As long as the `(double)` cast operator is applied to *any* variable in the calculation, the calculation will yield a `double` result. Later in this chapter, we discuss all the primitive types. You'll learn more about the promotion rules in Section 6.6.

Common Programming Error 4.6

A cast operator can be used to convert between primitive numeric types, such as `int` and `double`, and between related reference types (as we discuss in Chapter 10, Object-Oriented Programming: Polymorphism). Casting to the wrong type may cause compilation errors or runtime errors.

A cast operator is formed by placing parentheses around any type's name. The operator is a **unary operator** (i.e., an operator that takes only one operand). Java also supports unary versions of the plus (+) and minus (–) operators, so you can write expressions like -7 or +5. Cast operators associate from right to left and have the same precedence as other unary operators, such as unary + and unary -. This precedence is one level higher than that of the **multiplicative operators** *, / and %. (See the operator precedence chart in Appendix A.) We indicate the cast operator with the notation (*type*) in our precedence charts, to indicate that any type name can be used to form a cast operator.

Line 77 displays the class average. In this example, we display the class average rounded to the nearest hundredth. The format specifier %.2f in printf's format control string indicates that variable average's value should be displayed with two digits of precision to the right of the decimal point—indicated by .2 in the format specifier. The three grades entered during the sample execution of class GradeBookTest (Fig. 4.8) total 257, which yields the average 85.666666.... Method printf uses the precision in the format specifier to round the value to the specified number of digits. In this program, the average is rounded to the hundredths position and is displayed as 85.67.

```java
1   // Fig. 4.8: GradeBookTest.java
2   // Create GradeBook object and invoke its determineClassAverage method.
3
4   public class GradeBookTest
5   {
6      public static void main( String[] args )
7      {
8         // create GradeBook object myGradeBook and
9         // pass course name to constructor
10        GradeBook myGradeBook = new GradeBook(
11           "CS101 Introduction to Java Programming" );
12
13        myGradeBook.displayMessage(); // display welcome message
14        myGradeBook.determineClassAverage(); // find average of grades
15     } // end main
16  } // end class GradeBookTest
```

```
Welcome to the grade book for
CS101 Introduction to Java Programming!

Enter grade or -1 to quit: 97
Enter grade or -1 to quit: 88
Enter grade or -1 to quit: 72
Enter grade or -1 to quit: -1

Total of the 3 grades entered is 257
Class average is 85.67
```

Fig. 4.8 | GradeBookTest class creates an object of class GradeBook (Fig. 4.7) and invokes its determineClassAverage method.

4.8 Nested Control Statements

We've seen that control statements can be stacked on top of one another (in sequence). In this case study, we examine the only other structured way control statements can be connected—namely, by **nesting** one control statement within another. Consider the following problem statement:

> *A college offers a course that prepares students for the state licensing exam for real estate brokers. Last year, ten of the students who completed this course took the exam. The college wants to know how well its students did on the exam. You've been asked to write a program to summarize the results. You've been given a list of these 10 students. Next to each name is written a 1 if the student passed the exam or a 2 if the student failed.*
>
> *Your program should analyze the results of the exam as follows:*
>
> *1. Input each test result (i.e., a 1 or a 2). Display the message "Enter result" on the screen each time the program requests another test result.*
>
> *2. Count the number of test results of each type.*
>
> *3. Display a summary of the test results, indicating the number of students who passed and the number who failed.*
>
> *4. If more than eight students passed the exam, print the message "Bonus to instructor!"*

After reading the problem statement carefully, we make the following observations:

1. The program must process test results for 10 students. A counter-controlled loop can be used, because the number of test results is known in advance.

2. Each test result has a numeric value—either a 1 or a 2. Each time it reads a test result, the program must determine whether it's a 1 or a 2. We test for a 1 in our algorithm. If the number is not a 1, we assume that it's a 2.

3. Two counters are used to keep track of the exam results—one to count the number of students who passed the exam and one to count the number who failed.

4. After the program has processed all the results, it must decide whether more than eight students passed the exam.

The Java class that solves this problem and two sample executions are shown in Fig. 4.9. Lines 13–16 of main declare the variables that method processExamResults of class Analysis uses to process the examination results. Several of these declarations use Java's ability to incorporate variable initialization into declarations (passes is assigned 0, failures 0 and studentCounter 1). Looping programs may require initialization at the beginning of each repetition—normally performed by assignment statements rather than in declarations.

Error-Prevention Tip 4.1

Initializing local variables when they're declared helps you avoid any compilation errors that might arise from attempts to use uninitialized variables. While Java does not require that local-variable initializations be incorporated into declarations, it does require that local variables be initialized before their values are used in an expression.

```
1   // Fig. 4.9: Analysis.java
2   // Analysis of examination results using nested control statements.
3   import java.util.Scanner; // class uses class Scanner
```

Fig. 4.9 | Analysis of examination results using nested control statements. (Part 1 of 3.)

```
4
5   public class Analysis
6   {
7      public static void main( String[] args )
8      {
9         // create Scanner to obtain input from command window
10        Scanner input = new Scanner( System.in );
11
12        // initializing variables in declarations
13        int passes = 0; // number of passes
14        int failures = 0; // number of failures
15        int studentCounter = 1; // student counter
16        int result; // one exam result (obtains value from user)
17
18        // process 10 students using counter-controlled loop
19        while ( studentCounter <= 10 )
20        {
21           // prompt user for input and obtain value from user
22           System.out.print( "Enter result (1 = pass, 2 = fail): " );
23           result = input.nextInt();
24
25           // if...else is nested in the while statement
26           if ( result == 1 )          // if result 1,
27              passes = passes + 1;      // increment passes;
28           else                         // else result is not 1, so
29              failures = failures + 1; // increment failures
30
31           // increment studentCounter so loop eventually terminates
32           studentCounter = studentCounter + 1;
33        } // end while
34
35        // termination phase; prepare and display results
36        System.out.printf( "Passed: %d\nFailed: %d\n", passes, failures );
37
38        // determine whether more than 8 students passed
39        if ( passes > 8 )
40           System.out.println( "Bonus to instructor!" );
41     } // end main
42  } // end class Analysis
```

```
Enter result (1 = pass, 2 = fail): 1
Enter result (1 = pass, 2 = fail): 2
Enter result (1 = pass, 2 = fail): 1
Enter result (1 = pass, 2 = fail): 1
Enter result (1 = pass, 2 = fail): 1
Enter result (1 = pass, 2 = fail): 1
Enter result (1 = pass, 2 = fail): 1
Enter result (1 = pass, 2 = fail): 1
Enter result (1 = pass, 2 = fail): 1
Enter result (1 = pass, 2 = fail): 1
Passed: 9
Failed: 1
Bonus to instructor!
```

Fig. 4.9 | Analysis of examination results using nested control statements. (Part 2 of 3.)

```
Enter result (1 = pass, 2 = fail): 1
Enter result (1 = pass, 2 = fail): 2
Enter result (1 = pass, 2 = fail): 1
Enter result (1 = pass, 2 = fail): 2
Enter result (1 = pass, 2 = fail): 1
Enter result (1 = pass, 2 = fail): 2
Enter result (1 = pass, 2 = fail): 2
Enter result (1 = pass, 2 = fail): 1
Enter result (1 = pass, 2 = fail): 1
Enter result (1 = pass, 2 = fail): 1
Passed: 6
Failed: 4
```

Fig. 4.9 | Analysis of examination results using nested control statements. (Part 3 of 3.)

The while statement (lines 19–33) loops 10 times. During each iteration, the loop inputs and processes one exam result. Notice that the if...else statement (lines 26–29) for processing each result is nested in the while statement. If the result is 1, the if...else statement increments passes; otherwise, it assumes the result is 2 and increments failures. Line 32 increments studentCounter before the loop condition is tested again at line 19. After 10 values have been input, the loop terminates and line 36 displays the number of passes and failures. The if statement at lines 39–40 determines whether more than eight students passed the exam and, if so, outputs the message "Bonus to instructor!".

Figure 4.9 shows the input and output from two sample excutions of the program. During the first, the condition at line 39 of method main is true—more than eight students passed the exam, so the program outputs a message to bonus the instructor.

This example contains only one class, with method main performing all the class's work. In this chapter and in Chapter 3, you've seen examples consisting of two classes—one containing methods that perform useful tasks and one containing method main, which creates an object of the other class and calls its methods. Occasionally, when it does not make sense to try to create a reusable class to demonstrate a concept, we'll place the program's statements entirely within the main method of a single class.

4.9 Compound Assignment Operators

The **compound assignment operators** abbreviate assignment expressions. Statements like

variable = variable operator expression;

where *operator* is one of the binary operators +, -, *, / or % (or others we discuss later in the text) can be written in the form

variable operator= expression;

For example, you can abbreviate the statement

c = c + 3;

with the **addition compound assignment operator**, +=, as

c += 3;

The += operator adds the value of the expression on its right to the value of the variable on its left and stores the result in the variable on the left of the operator. Thus, the assignment expression c += 3 adds 3 to c. Figure 4.10 shows the arithmetic compound assignment operators, sample expressions using the operators and explanations of what the operators do.

Assignment operator	Sample expression	Explanation	Assigns
Assume: int c = 3, d = 5, e = 4, f = 6, g = 12;			
+=	c += 7	c = c + 7	10 to c
-=	d -= 4	d = d - 4	1 to d
*=	e *= 5	e = e * 5	20 to e
/=	f /= 3	f = f / 3	2 to f
%=	g %= 9	g = g % 9	3 to g

Fig. 4.10 | Arithmetic compound assignment operators.

4.10 Increment and Decrement Operators

Java provides two unary operators (summarized in Fig. 4.11) for adding 1 to or subtracting 1 from the value of a numeric variable. These are the unary **increment operator**, **++**, and the unary **decrement operator**, **--**. A program can increment by 1 the value of a variable called c using the increment operator, ++, rather than the expression c = c + 1 or c += 1. An increment or decrement operator that's prefixed to (placed before) a variable is referred to as the **prefix increment** or **prefix decrement operator**, respectively. An increment or decrement operator that's postfixed to (placed after) a variable is referred to as the **postfix increment** or **postfix decrement operator**, respectively.

Operator	Operator name	Sample expression	Explanation
++	prefix increment	++a	Increment a by 1, then use the new value of a in the expression in which a resides.
++	postfix increment	a++	Use the current value of a in the expression in which a resides, then increment a by 1.
--	prefix decrement	--b	Decrement b by 1, then use the new value of b in the expression in which b resides.
--	postfix decrement	b--	Use the current value of b in the expression in which b resides, then decrement b by 1.

Fig. 4.11 | Increment and decrement operators.

Using the prefix increment (or decrement) operator to add 1 to (or subtract 1 from) a variable is known as **preincrementing** (or **predecrementing**). This causes the variable to be incremented (decremented) by 1; then the new value of the variable is used in the expression in which it appears. Using the postfix increment (or decrement) operator to add

1 to (or subtract 1 from) a variable is known as **postincrementing** (or **postdecrementing**). This causes the current value of the variable to be used in the expression in which it appears; then the variable's value is incremented (decremented) by 1.

Good Programming Practice 4.2

Unlike binary operators, the unary increment and decrement operators should be placed next to their operands, with no intervening spaces.

Figure 4.12 demonstrates the difference between the prefix increment and postfix increment versions of the ++ increment operator. The decrement operator (--) works similarly.

```java
1   // Fig. 4.12: Increment.java
2   // Prefix increment and postfix increment operators.
3
4   public class Increment
5   {
6      public static void main( String[] args )
7      {
8         int c;
9
10        // demonstrate postfix increment operator
11        c = 5; // assign 5 to c
12        System.out.println( c );    // prints 5
13        System.out.println( c++ ); // prints 5 then postincrements
14        System.out.println( c );    // prints 6
15
16        System.out.println(); // skip a line
17
18        // demonstrate prefix increment operator
19        c = 5; // assign 5 to c
20        System.out.println( c );    // prints 5
21        System.out.println( ++c ); // preincrements then prints 6
22        System.out.println( c );    // prints 6
23     } // end main
24  } // end class Increment
```

```
5
5
6

5
6
6
```

Fig. 4.12 | Preincrementing and postincrementing.

Line 11 initializes the variable c to 5, and line 12 outputs c's initial value. Line 13 outputs the value of the expression c++. This expression postincrements the variable c, so c's original value (5) is output, then c's value is incremented (to 6). Thus, line 13 outputs c's initial value (5) again. Line 14 outputs c's new value (6) to prove that the variable's value was indeed incremented in line 13.

Line 19 resets c's value to 5, and line 20 outputs c's value. Line 21 outputs the value of the expression ++c. This expression preincrements c, so its value is incremented; then the new value (6) is output. Line 22 outputs c's value again to show that the value of c is still 6 after line 21 executes.

The arithmetic compound assignment operators and the increment and decrement operators can be used to simplify program statements. For example, the three assignment statements in Fig. 4.9 (lines 27, 29 and 32)

```
passes = passes + 1;
failures = failures + 1;
studentCounter = studentCounter + 1;
```

can be written more concisely with compound assignment operators as

```
passes += 1;
failures += 1;
studentCounter += 1;
```

with prefix increment operators as

```
++passes;
++failures;
++studentCounter;
```

or with postfix increment operators as

```
passes++;
failures++;
studentCounter++;
```

When incrementing or decrementing a variable in a statement by itself, the prefix increment and postfix increment forms have the same effect, and the prefix decrement and postfix decrement forms have the same effect. It's only when a variable appears in the context of a larger expression that preincrementing and postincrementing the variable have different effects (and similarly for predecrementing and postdecrementing).

Common Programming Error 4.7

Attempting to use the increment or decrement operator on an expression other than one to which a value can be assigned is a syntax error. For example, writing ++(x + 1) is a syntax error, because (x + 1) is not a variable.

Figure 4.13 shows the precedence and associativity of the operators we've introduced. They're shown from top to bottom in decreasing order of precedence. The second column describes the associativity of the operators at each level of precedence.

Operators					Associativity	Type
++	--				right to left	unary postfix
++	--	+	-	(*type*)	right to left	unary prefix
*	/	%			left to right	multiplicative

Fig. 4.13 | Precedence and associativity of the operators discussed so far. (Part 1 of 2.)

Operators						Associativity	Type
+	–					left to right	additive
<	<=	>	>=			left to right	relational
==	!=					left to right	equality
?:						right to left	conditional
=	+=	-=	*=	/=	%=	right to left	assignment

Fig. 4.13 | Precedence and associativity of the operators discussed so far. (Part 2 of 2.)

4.11 Primitive Types

The table in Appendix D lists the eight primitive types in Java. Like its predecessor languages C and C++, Java requires all variables to have a type. For this reason, Java is referred to as a **strongly typed language**. In C and C++, programmers frequently have to write separate versions of programs to support different computer platforms, because the primitive types are not guaranteed to be identical from computer to computer. For example, an int value on one machine might be represented by 16 bits (2 bytes) of memory, on a second machine by 32 bits (4 bytes) of memory, and on another machine by 64 bits (8 bytes) of memory. In Java, int values are always 32 bits (4 bytes).

Portability Tip 4.1

The primitive types in Java are portable across all computer platforms that support Java.

Each type in Appendix D is listed with its size in bits and its value range. To ensure portability, Java uses internationally recognized standards for character formats (Unicode; for more information, visit www.unicode.org) and floating-point numbers (IEEE 754; for more information, visit grouper.ieee.org/groups/754/).

Recall from Section 3.4 that variables of primitive types declared outside of a method as fields of a class are automatically assigned default values unless explicitly initialized. Instance variables of types char, byte, short, int, long, float and double are all given the value 0 by default. Instance variables of type boolean are given the value false by default. Reference-type instance variables are initialized by default to the value null.

4.12 Wrap-Up

Only three types of control structures—sequence, selection and repetition—are needed to develop any problem-solving algorithm. Specifically, this chapter demonstrated the if single-selection statement, the if...else double-selection statement and the while repetition statement. These are some of the building blocks used to construct solutions to many problems. We used control-statement stacking to total and compute the average of a set of student grades with counter- and sentinel-controlled repetition, and we used control-statement nesting to analyze and make decisions based on a set of exam results. We introduced Java's compound assignment operators and its increment and decrement operators. Finally, we discussed Java's primitive types. In Chapter 5, we continue our discussion of control statements, introducing the for, do...while and switch statements.

5

Control Statements: Part 2

Objectives

In this chapter you'll learn:

- To use the **for** and **do...while** repetition statements to execute statements in a program repeatedly.

- To understand multiple selection using the **switch** selection statement.

- To use the **break** and **continue** program control statements to alter the flow of control.

- To use the logical operators to form complex conditional expressions in control statements.

The wheel is come full circle.
—William Shakespeare
—Robert Frost

All the evolution we know of proceeds from the vague to the definite.
—Charles Sanders Peirce

5.1 Introduction

This chapter introduces all but one of Java's remaining control statements. We demonstrate Java's for, do...while and `switch` statements. Through a series of short examples using while and for, we explore the essentials of counter-controlled repetition. We create a version of class GradeBook that uses a `switch` statement to count the number of A, B, C, D and F grade equivalents in a set of numeric grades entered by the user. We introduce the break and continue program-control statements. We discuss Java's logical operators, which enable you to use more complex conditional expressions in control statements. Finally, we summarize Java's control statements and the proven problem-solving techniques presented in this chapter and Chapter 4.

5.2 Essentials of Counter-Controlled Repetition

This section uses the while repetition statement introduced in Chapter 4 to formalize the elements required to perform counter-controlled repetition, which requires

1. a **control variable** (or loop counter)

2. the **initial value** of the control variable

3. the **increment** (or **decrement**) by which the control variable is modified each time through the loop (also known as **each iteration of the loop**)

4. the **loop-continuation condition** that determines if looping should continue.

To see these elements of counter-controlled repetition, consider the application of Fig. 5.1, which uses a loop to display the numbers from 1 through 10.

```
1  // Fig. 5.1: WhileCounter.java
2  // Counter-controlled repetition with the while repetition statement.
3
4  public class WhileCounter
5  {
6     public static void main( String[] args )
7     {
8        int counter = 1; // declare and initialize control variable
9
10       while ( counter <= 10 ) // loop-continuation condition
11       {
```

Fig. 5.1 | Counter-controlled repetition with the while repetition statement. (Part 1 of 2.)

```
12              System.out.printf( "%d  ", counter );
13              ++counter; // increment control variable by 1
14          } // end while
15
16          System.out.println(); // output a newline
17      } // end main
18  } // end class WhileCounter
```

```
1  2  3  4  5  6  7  8  9  10
```

Fig. 5.1 | Counter-controlled repetition with the `while` repetition statement. (Part 2 of 2.)

In Fig. 5.1, the elements of counter-controlled repetition are defined in lines 8, 10 and 13. Line 8 declares the control variable (`counter`) as an `int`, reserves space for it in memory and sets its initial value to 1. Variable `counter` also could have been declared and initialized with the following local-variable declaration and assignment statements:

```
int counter; // declare counter
counter = 1; // initialize counter to 1
```

Line 12 displays control variable `counter`'s value during each iteration of the loop. Line 13 increments the control variable by 1 for each iteration of the loop. The loop-continuation condition in the `while` (line 10) tests whether the value of the control variable is less than or equal to 10 (the final value for which the condition is `true`). The program performs the body of this `while` even when the control variable is 10. The loop terminates when the control variable exceeds 10 (i.e., `counter` becomes 11).

Common Programming Error 5.1

Because floating-point values may be approximate, controlling loops with floating-point variables may result in imprecise counter values and inaccurate termination tests.

Error-Prevention Tip 5.1

Use integers to control counting loops.

The program in Fig. 5.1 can be made more concise by initializing `counter` to 0 in line 8 and preincrementing `counter` in the `while` condition as follows:

```
while ( ++counter <= 10 ) // loop-continuation condition
    System.out.printf( "%d   ", counter );
```

This code saves a statement (and eliminates the need for braces around the loop's body), because the `while` condition performs the increment before testing the condition. (Recall from Section 4.10 that the precedence of `++` is higher than that of `<=`.) Coding in such a condensed fashion takes practice, might make code more difficult to read, debug, modify and maintain, and typically should be avoided.

Software Engineering Observation 5.1

"Keep it simple" is good advice for most of the code you'll write.

5.3 for Repetition Statement

Section 5.2 presented the essentials of counter-controlled repetition. The while statement can be used to implement any counter-controlled loop. Java also provides the **for repetition statement**, which specifies the counter-controlled-repetition details in a single line of code. Figure 5.2 reimplements the application of Fig. 5.1 using for.

```
1   // Fig. 5.2: ForCounter.java
2   // Counter-controlled repetition with the for repetition statement.
3
4   public class ForCounter
5   {
6      public static void main( String[] args )
7      {
8         // for statement header includes initialization,
9         // loop-continuation condition and increment
10        for ( int counter = 1; counter <= 10; counter++ )
11           System.out.printf( "%d  ", counter );
12
13        System.out.println(); // output a newline
14     } // end main
15  } // end class ForCounter
```

```
1  2  3  4  5  6  7  8  9  10
```

Fig. 5.2 | Counter-controlled repetition with the for repetition statement.

When the for statement (lines 10–11) begins executing, the control variable counter is declared and initialized to 1. Next, the program checks the loop-continuation condition, counter <= 10, which is between the two required semicolons. Because the initial value of counter is 1, the condition initially is true. Therefore, the body statement (line 11) displays control variable counter's value, namely 1. After executing the loop's body, the program increments counter in the expression counter++, which appears to the right of the second semicolon. Then the loop-continuation test is performed again to determine whether the program should continue with the next iteration of the loop. At this point, the control variable's value is 2, so the condition is still true (the final value is not exceeded)—thus, the program performs the body statement again (i.e., the next iteration of the loop). This process continues until the numbers 1 through 10 have been displayed and the counter's value becomes 11, causing the loop-continuation test to fail and repetition to terminate (after 10 repetitions of the loop body). Then the program performs the first statement after the for—in this case, line 13.

Figure 5.2 uses (in line 10) the loop-continuation condition counter <= 10. If you incorrectly specified counter < 10 as the condition, the loop would iterate only nine times. This is a common logic error called an **off-by-one error**.

A Closer Look at the for Statement's Header

Figure 5.3 takes a closer look at the for statement in Fig. 5.2. The for's first line (including the keyword for and everything in parentheses after for)—line 10 in Fig. 5.2—is sometimes called the **for statement header**. The for header "does it all"—it specifies each item needed for counter-controlled repetition with a control variable. If there's more than one statement in the body of the for, braces are required to define the body of the loop.

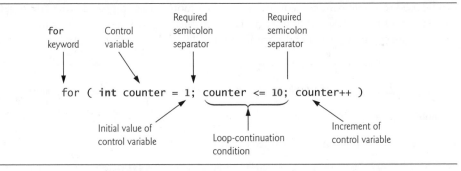

Fig. 5.3 | for statement header components.

*General Format of a **for** Statement*
The general format of the for statement is

> **for** (*initialization*; *loopContinuationCondition*; *increment*)
>   *statement*

where the *initialization* expression names the loop's control variable and optionally provides its initial value, *loopContinuationCondition* determines whether the loop should continue executing and *increment* modifies the control variable's value (possibly an increment or decrement), so that the loop-continuation condition eventually becomes false. The two semicolons in the for header are required. If the loop-continuation condition is initially false, the program does *not* execute the for statement's body. Instead, execution proceeds with the statement following the for.

*Representing a **for** Statement with an Equivalent **while** Statement*
In most cases, the for statement can be represented with an equivalent while statement as:

> *initialization*;
> **while** (*loopContinuationCondition*)
> {
>   *statement*
>   *increment*;
> }

Typically, for statements are used for counter-controlled repetition and while statements for sentinel-controlled repetition, but they can each be used for either repetition type.

*Scope of a **for** Statement's Control Variable*
If the *initialization* expression in the for header declares the control variable (i.e., the control variable's type is specified before the variable name, as in Fig. 5.2), the control variable can be used *only* in that for statement—it will not exist outside it. This restricted use is known as the variable's **scope**. The scope of a variable defines where it can be used in a program. For example, a local variable can be used *only* in the method that declares it and *only* from the point of declaration through the end of the method. Scope is discussed in detail in Chapter 6, Methods: A Deeper Look.

Common Programming Error 5.2

When a for *statement's control variable is declared in the initialization section of the* for's *header, using the control variable after the* for's *body is a compilation error.*

Expressions in a **for** *Statement's Header Are Optional*

All three expressions in a for header are optional. If the *loopContinuationCondition* is omitted, Java assumes that the loop-continuation condition is always true, thus creating an infinite loop. You might omit the *initialization* expression if the program initializes the control variable before the loop. You might omit the *increment* expression if the program calculates the increment with statements in the loop's body or if no increment is needed. The increment expression in a for acts as if it were a standalone statement at the end of the for's body. Therefore, the expressions

```
counter = counter + 1
counter += 1
++counter
counter++
```

are equivalent increment expressions in a for statement. Many programmers prefer counter++ because it's concise and because a for loop evaluates its increment expression *after* its body executes, so the postfix increment form seems more natural. In this case, the variable being incremented does not appear in a larger expression, so preincrementing and postincrementing actually have the same effect.

Placing Arithmetic Expressions in a **for** *Statement's Header*

The initialization, loop-continuation condition and increment portions of a for statement can contain arithmetic expressions. For example, assume that x = 2 and y = 10. If x and y are not modified in the body of the loop, the statement

```
for ( int j = x; j <= 4 * x * y; j += y / x )
```

is equivalent to the statement

```
for ( int j = 2; j <= 80; j += 5 )
```

The increment of a for statement may also be *negative*, in which case it's really a *decrement*, and the loop counts *downward*.

Using a **for** *Statement's Control Variable in the Statements's Body*

Programs frequently display the control-variable value or use it in calculations in the loop body, but this use is not required. The control variable is commonly used to control repetition without being mentioned in the body of the for.

Error-Prevention Tip 5.2

Although the value of the control variable can be changed in the body of a for *loop, avoid doing so, because this practice can lead to subtle errors.*

UML Activity Diagram for the **for** *Statement*

The for statement's UML activity diagram is similar to that of the while statement (Fig. 4.4). Figure 5.4 shows the activity diagram of the for statement in Fig. 5.2. The diagram makes it clear that initialization occurs *once before* the loop-continuation test is

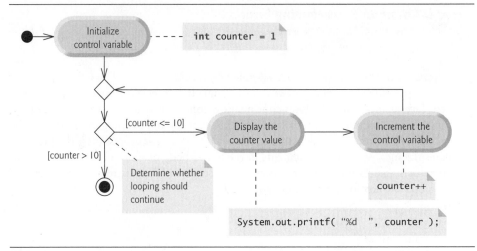

Fig. 5.4 | UML activity diagram for the `for` statement in Fig. 5.2.

evaluated the first time, and that incrementing occurs *each* time through the loop *after* the body statement executes.

5.4 Examples Using the for Statement

The following examples show techniques for varying the control variable in a `for` statement. In each case, we write the appropriate `for` header. Note the change in the relational operator for loops that decrement the control variable.

a) Vary the control variable from 1 to 100 in increments of 1.

```
for ( int i = 1; i <= 100; i++ )
```

b) Vary the control variable from 100 to 1 in decrements of 1.

```
for ( int i = 100; i >= 1; i-- )
```

c) Vary the control variable from 7 to 77 in increments of 7.

```
for ( int i = 7; i <= 77; i += 7 )
```

d) Vary the control variable from 20 to 2 in decrements of 2.

```
for ( int i = 20; i >= 2; i -= 2 )
```

e) Vary the control variable over the values 2, 5, 8, 11, 14, 17, 20.

```
for ( int i = 2; i <= 20; i += 3 )
```

f) Vary the control variable over the values 99, 88, 77, 66, 55, 44, 33, 22, 11, 0.

```
for ( int i = 99; i >= 0; i -= 11 )
```

Application: Summing the Even Integers from 2 to 20
We now consider two sample applications that demonstrate simple uses of `for`. The application in Fig. 5.5 uses a `for` statement to sum the even integers from 2 to 20 and store the result in an `int` variable called `total`.

```
1   // Fig. 5.5: Sum.java
2   // Summing integers with the for statement.
3
4   public class Sum
5   {
6      public static void main( String[] args )
7      {
8         int total = 0; // initialize total
9
10        // total even integers from 2 through 20
11        for ( int number = 2; number <= 20; number += 2 )
12           total += number;
13
14        System.out.printf( "Sum is %d\n", total ); // display results
15     } // end main
16  } // end class Sum
```

```
Sum is 110
```

Fig. 5.5 | Summing integers with the for statement.

The *initialization* and *increment* expressions can be comma-separated lists that enable you to use multiple initialization expressions or multiple increment expressions. For example, *although this is discouraged*, you could merge the body of the for statement in lines 11–12 of Fig. 5.5 into the increment portion of the for header by using a comma as follows:

```
for ( int number = 2; number <= 20; total += number, number += 2 )
   ; // empty statement
```

Application: Compound-Interest Calculations

Let's use the for statement to compute compound interest. Consider the following problem:

> A person invests $1000 in a savings account yielding 5% interest. Assuming that all the interest is left on deposit, calculate and print the amount of money in the account at the end of each year for 10 years. Use the following formula to determine the amounts:
>
> $a = p \, (1 + r)^n$
>
> where
>
>> p is the original amount invested (i.e., the principal)
>> r is the annual interest rate (e.g., use 0.05 for 5%)
>> n is the number of years
>> a is the amount on deposit at the end of the nth year.

The solution to this problem (Fig. 5.6) involves a loop that performs the indicated calculation for each of the 10 years the money remains on deposit. Lines 8–10 in method main declare double variables amount, principal and rate, and initialize principal to 1000.0 and rate to 0.05. Java treats floating-point constants like 1000.0 and 0.05 as type double. Similarly, Java treats whole-number constants like 7 and -22 as type int.

```java
1   // Fig. 5.6: Interest.java
2   // Compound-interest calculations with for.
3
4   public class Interest
5   {
6      public static void main( String[] args )
7      {
8         double amount; // amount on deposit at end of each year
9         double principal = 1000.0; // initial amount before interest
10        double rate = 0.05; // interest rate
11
12        // display headers
13        System.out.printf( "%s%20s\n", "Year", "Amount on deposit" );
14
15        // calculate amount on deposit for each of ten years
16        for ( int year = 1; year <= 10; year++ )
17        {
18           // calculate new amount for specified year
19           amount = principal * Math.pow( 1.0 + rate, year );
20
21           // display the year and the amount
22           System.out.printf( "%4d%,20.2f\n", year, amount );
23        } // end for
24     } // end main
25  } // end class Interest
```

```
Year    Amount on deposit
   1            1,050.00
   2            1,102.50
   3            1,157.63
   4            1,215.51
   5            1,276.28
   6            1,340.10
   7            1,407.10
   8            1,477.46
   9            1,551.33
  10            1,628.89
```

Fig. 5.6 | Compound-interest calculations with `for`.

Formatting Strings with Field Widths and Justification

Line 13 outputs the headers for two columns of output. The first column displays the year and the second column the amount on deposit at the end of that year. We use the format specifier %20s to output the String "Amount on Deposit". The integer 20 between the % and the conversion character s indicates that the value should be displayed with a **field width** of 20—that is, printf displays the value with at least 20 character positions. If the value to be output is less than 20 character positions wide (17 characters in this example), the value is **right justified** in the field by default. If the year value to be output were more than four character positions wide, the field width would be extended to the right to accommodate the entire value—this would push the amount field to the right, upsetting the neat columns of our tabular output. To output values **left justified**, simply precede the field width with the **minus sign (–) formatting flag** (e.g., %-20s).

Performing the Interest Calculations

The for statement (lines 16–23) executes its body
from 1 to 10 in increments of 1. This loop termin
year represents n in the problem statement.)

Classes provide methods that perform comm
methods must be called on a specific object. For exa
13 calls method printf on the System.out object. M
perform common tasks and do *not* require objects. T
example, Java does not include an exponentiation ope
class defined static method pow for raising a value
method by specifying the class name followed by a dot

ClassName.methodName(arguments)

In Chapter 6, you'll learn how to implement static me   ᴏwn classes.

We use static method **pow** of class **Math** to perform the compound-interest calculation in Fig. 5.6. Math.pow(x, y) calculates the value of x raised to the yth power. The
method receives two double arguments and returns a double value. Line 19 performs the
calculation $a = p(1 + r)^n$, where a is amount, p is principal, r is rate and n is year. Class
Math is defined in package java.lang, so you do *not* need to import class Math to use it.

The body of the for statement contains the calculation 1.0 + rate, which appears as
an argument to the Math.pow method. In fact, this calculation produces the same result
each time through the loop, so repeating it every iteration of the loop is wasteful.

Performance Tip 5.1

*In loops, avoid calculations for which the result never changes—such calculations should
typically be placed before the loop. Many of today's sophisticated optimizing compilers will
place such calculations outside loops in the compiled code.*

Formatting Floating-Point Numbers

After each calculation, line 22 outputs the year and the amount on deposit at the end of
that year. The year is output in a field width of four characters (as specified by %4d). The
amount is output as a floating-point number with the format specifier %,20.2f. The **comma (,) formatting flag** indicates that the floating-point value should be output with a
grouping separator. The actual separator used is specific to the user's locale (i.e., coun-
try). For example, in the United States, the number will be output using commas to separate every three digits and a decimal point to separate the fractional part of the number,
as in 1,234.45. The number 20 in the format specification indicates that the value should
be output right justified in a field width of 20 characters. The .2 specifies the formatted
number's precision—in this case, the number is rounded to the nearest hundredth and
output with two digits to the right of the decimal point.

A Warning about Displaying Rounded Values

We declared variables amount, principal and rate to be of type double in this example.
We're dealing with fractional parts of dollars and thus need a type that allows decimal
points in its values. Unfortunately, floating-point numbers can cause trouble. Here's a
simple explanation of what can go wrong when using double (or float) to represent dollar
amounts (assuming that dollar amounts are displayed with two digits to the right of the

double dollar amounts stored in the machine could be 14.234
nally be rounded to 14.23 for display purposes) and 18.673 (which
be rounded to 18.67 for display purposes). When these amounts are add-
duce the internal sum 32.907, which would normally be rounded to 32.91 for
urposes. Thus, your output could appear as

```
   14.23
 + 18.67
 -------
   32.91
```

but a person adding the individual numbers as displayed would expect the sum to be
32.90. You've been warned!

Error-Prevention Tip 5.3

*Do not use variables of type double (or float) to perform precise monetary calculations.
The imprecision of floating-point numbers can cause errors. Java provides class BigDec-
imal (package java.math) to perform precise monetary calculations. For more information, see download.oracle.com/javase/6/docs/api/java/math//BigDecimal.html.*

5.5 do...while Repetition Statement

The **do...while repetition statement** is similar to the while statement. In the while, the
program tests the loop-continuation condition at the beginning of the loop, before executing the loop's body; if the condition is false, the body *never* executes. The do...while statement tests the loop-continuation condition *after* executing the loop's body; therefore, *the
body always executes at least once*. When a do...while statement terminates, execution continues with the next statement in sequence. Figure 5.7 uses a do...while (lines 10–14) to
output the numbers 1–10.

```java
 1   // Fig. 5.7: DoWhileTest.java
 2   // do...while repetition statement.
 3
 4   public class DoWhileTest
 5   {
 6      public static void main( String[] args )
 7      {
 8         int counter = 1; // initialize counter
 9
10         do
11         {
12            System.out.printf( "%d  ", counter );
13            ++counter;
14         } while ( counter <= 10 ); // end do...while
15
16         System.out.println(); // outputs a newline
17      } // end main
18   } // end class DoWhileTest
```

Fig. 5.7 | do...while repetition statement. (Part 1 of 2.)

```
1   2   3   4   5   6   7   8   9   10
```

Fig. 5.7 | do...while repetition statement. (Part 2 of 2.)

Line 8 declares and initializes control variable counter. Upon entering the do...while statement, line 12 outputs counter's value and line 13 increments counter. Then the program evaluates the loop-continuation test at the *bottom* of the loop (line 14). If the condition is true, the loop continues from the first body statement (line 12). If the condition is false, the loop terminates and the program continues with the next statement after the loop.

Figure 5.8 contains the UML activity diagram for the do...while statement. This diagram makes it clear that the loop-continuation condition is not evaluated until *after* the loop performs the action state at least once. Compare this activity diagram with that of the while statement (Fig. 4.4).

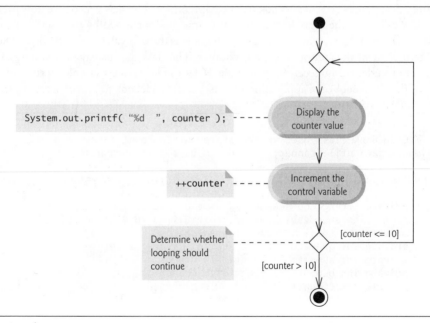

Fig. 5.8 | do...while repetition statement UML activity diagram.

It isn't necessary to use braces in the do...while repetition statement if there's only one statement in the body. However, many programmers include the braces, to avoid confusion between the while and do...while statements. For example,

while (*condition*)

is normally the first line of a while statement. A do...while statement with no braces around a single-statement body appears as:

do
    statement
while (*condition*);

which can be confusing. A reader may misinterpret the last line—while(*condition*);—
as a while statement containing an empty statement (the semicolon by itself). Thus, the
do...while statement with one body statement is usually written as follows:

```
do
{
    statement
} while ( condition );
```

5.6 switch Multiple-Selection Statement

Chapter 4 discussed the if single-selection statement and the if...else double-selection
statement. The **switch multiple-selection statement** performs different actions based on
the possible values of a **constant integral expression** of type byte, short, int or char.

GradeBook Class with switch Statement to Count A, B, C, D and F Grades

Figure 5.9 enhances class GradeBook from Chapters 3–4. The new version we now present
not only calculates the average of a set of numeric grades entered by the user, but uses a
switch statement to determine whether each grade is the equivalent of an A, B, C, D or F
and to increment the appropriate grade counter. The class also displays a summary of the
number of students who received each grade. Refer to Fig. 5.10 for sample inputs and outputs of the GradeBookTest application that uses class GradeBook to process a set of grades.

```
1    // Fig. 5.9: GradeBook.java
2    // GradeBook class uses switch statement to count letter grades.
3    import java.util.Scanner; // program uses class Scanner
4
5    public class GradeBook
6    {
7       private String courseName; // name of course this GradeBook represents
8       // int instance variables are initialized to 0 by default
9       private int total; // sum of grades
10      private int gradeCounter; // number of grades entered
11      private int aCount; // count of A grades
12      private int bCount; // count of B grades
13      private int cCount; // count of C grades
14      private int dCount; // count of D grades
15      private int fCount; // count of F grades
16
17      // constructor initializes courseName;
18      public GradeBook( String name )
19      {
20         courseName = name; // initializes courseName
21      } // end constructor
22
23      // method to set the course name
24      public void setCourseName( String name )
25      {
26         courseName = name; // store the course name
27      } // end method setCourseName
```

Fig. 5.9 | GradeBook class uses switch statement to count letter grades. (Part 1 of 3.)

```
28
29      // method to retrieve the course name
30      public String getCourseName()
31      {
32         return courseName;
33      } // end method getCourseName
34
35      // display a welcome message to the GradeE
36      public void displayMessage()
37      {
38         // getCourseName gets the name of the c
39         System.out.printf( "Welcome to the grad
40            getCourseName() );
41      } // end method displayMessage
42
43      // input arbitrary number of grades from user
44      public void inputGrades()
45      {
46         Scanner input = new Scanner( System.in );
47
48         int grade; // grade entered by user
49
50         System.out.printf( "%s\n%s\n    %s\n    %s\n",
51            "Enter the integer grades in the range 0-100.",
52            "Type the end-of-file indicator to terminate input:",
53            "On UNIX/Linux/Mac OS X type <Ctrl> d then press Enter",
54            "On Windows type <Ctrl> z then press Enter" );
55
56         // loop until user enters the end-of-file indicator
57         while ( input.hasNext() )
58         {
59            grade = input.nextInt(); // read grade
60            total += grade; // add grade to total
61            ++gradeCounter; // increment number of grades
62
63            // call method to increment appropriate counter
64            incrementLetterGradeCounter( grade );
65         } // end while
66      } // end method inputGrades
67
68      // add 1 to appropriate counter for specified grade
69      private void incrementLetterGradeCounter( int grade )
70      {
71         // determine which grade was entered
72         switch ( grade / 10 )
73         {
74            case 9:  // grade was between 90
75            case 10: // and 100, inclusive
76               ++aCount; // increment aCount
77               break; // necessary to exit switch
78
```

Fig. 5.9 | GradeBook class uses switch statement to count letter grades. (Part 2 of 3.)

```
        case 8: // grade was between 80 and 89
            ++bCount; // increment bCount
            break; // exit switch

        case 7: // grade was between 70 and 79
            ++cCount; // increment cCount
            break; // exit switch
86
87      case 6: // grade was between 60 and 69
88          ++dCount; // increment dCount
89          break; // exit switch
90
91      default: // grade was less than 60
92          ++fCount; // increment fCount
93          break; // optional; will exit switch anyway
94      } // end switch
95  } // end method incrementLetterGradeCounter
96
97  // display a report based on the grades entered by the user
98  public void displayGradeReport()
99  {
100     System.out.println( "\nGrade Report:" );
101
102     // if user entered at least one grade...
103     if ( gradeCounter != 0 )
104     {
105         // calculate average of all grades entered
106         double average = (double) total / gradeCounter;
107
108         // output summary of results
109         System.out.printf( "Total of the %d grades entered is %d\n",
110             gradeCounter, total );
111         System.out.printf( "Class average is %.2f\n", average );
112         System.out.printf( "%s\n%s%d\n%s%d\n%s%d\n%s%d\n%s%d\n",
113             "Number of students who received each grade:",
114             "A: ", aCount,   // display number of A grades
115             "B: ", bCount,   // display number of B grades
116             "C: ", cCount,   // display number of C grades
117             "D: ", dCount,   // display number of D grades
118             "F: ", fCount ); // display number of F grades
119     } // end if
120     else // no grades were entered, so output appropriate message
121         System.out.println( "No grades were entered" );
122     } // end method displayGradeReport
123 } // end class GradeBook
```

Fig. 5.9 | GradeBook class uses switch statement to count letter grades. (Part 3 of 3.)

Like earlier versions of the class, class GradeBook (Fig. 5.9) declares instance variable courseName (line 7) and contains methods setCourseName (lines 24–27), getCourseName (lines 30–33) and displayMessage (lines 36–41), which set the course name, store the course name and display a welcome message to the user, respectively. The class also contains a constructor (lines 18–21) that initializes the course name.

Class GradeBook also declares instance variables total (line 9) and gradeCounter (line 10), which keep track of the sum of the grades entered by the user and the number of grades entered, respectively. Lines 11–15 declare counter variables for each grade category. Class GradeBook maintains total, gradeCounter and the five letter-grade counters as instance variables so that they can be used or modified in any of the class's methods. The class's constructor (lines 18–21) sets only the course name, because the remaining seven instance variables are ints and are initialized to 0 by default.

Class GradeBook (Fig. 5.9) contains three additional methods—inputGrades, incrementLetterGradeCounter and displayGradeReport. Method inputGrades (lines 44–66) reads an arbitrary number of integer grades from the user using sentinel-controlled repetition and updates instance variables total and gradeCounter. This method calls method incrementLetterGradeCounter (lines 69–95) to update the appropriate letter-grade counter for each grade entered. Method displayGradeReport (lines 98–122) outputs a report containing the total of all grades entered, the average of the grades and the number of students who received each letter grade. Let's examine these methods in more detail.

Method inputGrades

Line 48 in method inputGrades declares variable grade, which will store the user's input. Lines 50–54 prompt the user to enter integer grades and to type the end-of-file indicator to terminate the input. The **end-of-file indicator** is a system-dependent keystroke combination which the user enters to indicate that there's no more data to input. In Chapter 17, Files, Streams and Object Serialization, we'll see how the end-of-file indicator is used when a program reads its input from a file.

On UNIX/Linux/Mac OS X systems, end-of-file is entered by typing the sequence

<*Ctrl*> *d*

on a line by itself. This notation means to simultaneously press both the *Ctrl* key and the *d* key. On Windows systems, end-of-file can be entered by typing

<*Ctrl*> *z*

[*Note:* On some systems, you must press *Enter* after typing the end-of-file key sequence. Also, Windows typically displays the characters ^Z on the screen when the end-of-file indicator is typed, as shown in the output of Fig. 5.10.]

Portability Tip 5.1
The keystroke combinations for entering end-of-file are system dependent.

The while statement (lines 57–65) obtains the user input. The condition at line 57 calls Scanner method **hasNext** to determine whether there's more data to input. This method returns the boolean value true if there's more data; otherwise, it returns false. The returned value is then used as the value of the condition in the while statement. Method hasNext returns false once the user types the end-of-file indicator.

Line 59 inputs a grade value from the user. Line 60 adds grade to total. Line 61 increments gradeCounter. The class's displayGradeReport method uses these variables to compute the average of the grades. Line 64 calls the class's incrementLetterGradeCounter method (declared in lines 69–95) to increment the appropriate letter-grade counter based on the numeric grade entered.

Method **incrementLetterGradeCounter**

Method incrementLetterGradeCounter contains a switch statement (lines 72–94) that determines which counter to increment. We assume that the user enters a valid grade in the range 0–100. A grade in the range 90–100 represents A, 80–89 represents B, 70–79 represents C, 60–69 represents D and 0–59 represents F. The switch statement consists of a block that contains a sequence of **case labels** and an optional **default case**. These are used in this example to determine which counter to increment based on the grade.

When the flow of control reaches the switch, the program evaluates the expression in the parentheses (grade / 10) following keyword switch. This is the switch's **controlling expression**. The program compares this expression's value (which must evaluate to an integral value of type byte, char, short or int) with each case label. The controlling expression in line 72 performs integer division, which *truncates the fractional part* of the result. Thus, when we divide a value from 0 to 100 by 10, the result is always a value from 0 to 10. We use several of these values in our case labels. For example, if the user enters the integer 85, the controlling expression evaluates to 8. The switch compares 8 with each case label. If a match occurs (case 8: at line 79), the program executes that case's statements. For the integer 8, line 80 increments bCount, because a grade in the 80s is a B. The **break statement** (line 81) causes program control to proceed with the first statement after the switch—in this program, we reach the end of method incrementLetterGrade-Counter's body, so the method terminates and control returns to line 65 in method inputGrades (the first line after the call to incrementLetterGradeCounter). Line 65 is the end of a while loop's body, so control flows to the while's condition (line 57) to determine whether the loop should continue executing.

The cases in our switch explicitly test for the values 10, 9, 8, 7 and 6. Note the cases at lines 74–75 that test for the values 9 and 10 (both of which represent the grade A). Listing cases consecutively in this manner with no statements between them enables the cases to perform the same set of statements—when the controlling expression evaluates to 9 or 10, the statements in lines 76–77 will execute. The switch statement does not provide a mechanism for testing ranges of values, so every value you need to test must be listed in a separate case label. Each case can have multiple statements. The switch statement differs from other control statements in that it does *not* require braces around multiple statements in a case.

Without break statements, each time a match occurs in the switch, the statements for that case and subsequent cases execute until a break statement or the end of the switch is encountered.

If no match occurs between the controlling expression's value and a case label, the default case (lines 91–93) executes. We use the default case in this example to process all controlling-expression values that are less than 6—that is, all failing grades. If no match occurs and the switch does not contain a default case, program control simply continues with the first statement after the switch.

GradeBookTest *Class That Demonstrates Class* *GradeBook*

Class GradeBookTest (Fig. 5.10) creates a GradeBook object (lines 10–11). Line 13 invokes the object's displayMessage method to output a welcome message to the user. Line 14 invokes the object's inputGrades method to read a set of grades from the user and keep track of the sum of all the grades entered and the number of grades. Recall that method input-Grades also calls method incrementLetterGradeCounter to keep track of the number of students who received each letter grade. Line 15 invokes method displayGradeReport of

```
 1   // Fig. 5.10: GradeBookTest.java
 2   // Create GradeBook object, input grades and display grade report.
 3
 4   public class GradeBookTest
 5   {
 6      public static void main( String[] args )
 7      {
 8         // create GradeBook object myGradeBook and
 9         // pass course name to constructor
10         GradeBook myGradeBook = new GradeBook(
11            "CS101 Introduction to Java Programming" );
12
13         myGradeBook.displayMessage(); // display welcome message
14         myGradeBook.inputGrades(); // read grades from user
15         myGradeBook.displayGradeReport(); // display report based on grades
16      } // end main
17   } // end class GradeBookTest
```

```
Welcome to the grade book for
CS101 Introduction to Java Programming!

Enter the integer grades in the range 0-100.
Type the end-of-file indicator to terminate input:
   On UNIX/Linux/Mac OS X type <Ctrl> d then press Enter
   On Windows type <Ctrl> z then press Enter
99
92
45
57
63
71
76
85
90
100
^Z

Grade Report:
Total of the 10 grades entered is 778
Class average is 77.80

Number of students who received each grade:
A: 4
B: 1
C: 2
D: 1
F: 2
```

Fig. 5.10 | Create GradeBook object, input grades and display grade report.

class GradeBook, which outputs a report based on the grades entered (as in the input/output window in Fig. 5.10). Line 103 of class GradeBook (Fig. 5.9) determines whether the user entered at least one grade—this helps us avoid dividing by zero. If so, line 106 calculates the average of the grades. Lines 109–118 then output the total of all the grades, the class average and the number of students who received each letter grade. If no grades were entered, line 121 outputs an appropriate message. The output in Fig. 5.10 shows a sample grade report based on 10 grades.

Class GradeBookTest (Fig. 5.10) does not directly call GradeBook method incrementLetterGradeCounter (lines 69–95 of Fig. 5.9). This method is used exclusively by method inputGrades of class GradeBook to update the appropriate letter-grade counter as each new grade is entered by the user. Method incrementLetterGradeCounter exists solely to support the operations of GradeBook's other methods, so it's declared private.

Software Engineering Observation 5.2

*Recall from Chapter 3 that methods declared with access modifier private can be called only by other methods of the class in which the private methods are declared. Such methods are commonly referred to as **utility methods** or **helper methods** because they're typically used to support the operation of the class's other methods.*

switch Statement UML Activity Diagram

Figure 5.11 shows the UML activity diagram for the general switch statement. Most switch statements use a break in each case to terminate the switch statement after processing the case. Figure 5.11 emphasizes this by including break statements in the activity diagram. The diagram makes it clear that the break statement at the end of a case causes control to exit the switch statement immediately.

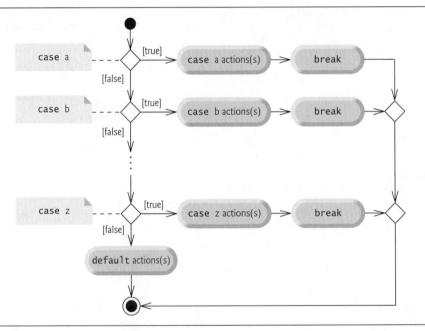

Fig. 5.11 | switch multiple-selection statement UML activity diagram with break statements.

The break statement is not required for the switch's last case (or the optional default case, when it appears last), because execution continues with the next statement after the switch.

Software Engineering Observation 5.3

Provide a default *case in* switch *statements. Including a* default *case focuses you on the need to process exceptional conditions.*

Good Programming Practice 5.1

Although each case *and the* default *case in a* switch *can occur in any order, place the default case last. When the* default *case is listed last, the* break *for that case is not required.*

Notes on the Expression in Each *case of a* switch

When using the switch statement, remember that each case must contain a constant integral expression—that is, any combination of integer constants that evaluates to a constant integer value (e.g., –7, 0 or 221). An integer constant is simply an integer value. In addition, you can use **character constants**—specific characters in single quotes, such as 'A', '7' or '$'—which represent the integer values of characters and enum constants (introduced in Section 6.9). (Appendix B shows the integer values of the characters in the ASCII character set, which is a subset of the Unicode character set used by Java.)

The expression in each case can also be a **constant variable**—a variable containing a value which does not change for the entire program. Such a variable is declared with keyword final (discussed in Chapter 6). Java has a feature called *enumerations*, which we also present in Chapter 6. Enumeration constants can also be used in case labels. In Chapter 10, Object-Oriented Programming: Polymorphism, we present a more elegant way to implement switch logic—we use a technique called *polymorphism* to create programs that are often clearer, easier to maintain and easier to extend than programs using switch logic.

Using *Strings in* switch *Statements (New in Java SE 7)*

As of Java SE 7, you can use Strings in a switch statement's controlling expression and in case labels. For example, you might want to use a city's name to obtain the corresponding ZIP code. Assuming that city and zipCode are String variables, the following switch statement performs this task for three cities:

```
switch( city )
{
   case "Maynard":
      zipCode = "01754";
      break;
   case "Marlborough":
      zipCode = "01752";
      break;
   case "Framingham":
      zipCode = "01701";
      break;
} // end switch
```

5.7 break and continue Statements

In addition to selection and repetition statements, Java provides statements break and **continue** to alter the flow of control. The preceding section showed how break can be used to terminate a switch statement's execution. This section discusses how to use break in repetition statements.

break *Statement*
The break statement, when executed in a while, for, do...while or switch, causes immediate exit from that statement. Execution continues with the first statement after the control statement. Common uses of the break statement are to escape early from a loop or to
skip the remainder of a switch (as in Fig. 5.9). Figure 5.12 demonstrates a break statement exiting a for.

When the if statement nested at lines 11–12 in the for statement (lines 9–15) detects
that count is 5, the break statement at line 12 executes. This terminates the for statement,
and the program proceeds to line 17 (immediately after the for statement), which displays
a message indicating the value of the control variable when the loop terminated. The loop
fully executes its body only four times instead of 10.

```
1   // Fig. 5.12: BreakTest.java
2   // break statement exiting a for statement.
3   public class BreakTest
4   {
5      public static void main( String[] args )
6      {
7         int count; // control variable also used after loop terminates
8
9         for ( count = 1; count <= 10; count++ ) // loop 10 times
10        {
11           if ( count == 5 ) // if count is 5,
12              break;            // terminate loop
13
14           System.out.printf( "%d ", count );
15        } // end for
16
17        System.out.printf( "\nBroke out of loop at count = %d\n", count );
18     } // end main
19  } // end class BreakTest
```

```
1 2 3 4
Broke out of loop at count = 5
```

Fig. 5.12 | break statement exiting a for statement.

continue *Statement*
The continue statement, when executed in a while, for or do...while, skips the remaining statements in the loop body and proceeds with the *next iteration* of the loop. In while
and do...while statements, the program evaluates the loop-continuation test immediately
after the continue statement executes. In a for statement, the increment expression executes, then the program evaluates the loop-continuation test.

```
1   // Fig. 5.13: ContinueTest.java
2   // continue statement terminating an iteration of a for statement.
3   public class ContinueTest
4   {
```

Fig. 5.13 | continue statement terminating an iteration of a for statement. (Part 1 of 2.)

```
 5      public static void main( String[] args )
 6      {
 7         for ( int count = 1; count <= 10; count++ ) // loop 10 times
 8         {
 9            if ( count == 5 ) // if count is 5,
10               continue; // skip remaining code in loop
11
12            System.out.printf( "%d ", count );
13         } // end for
14
15         System.out.println( "\nUsed continue to skip printing 5" );
16      } // end main
17   } // end class ContinueTest
```

```
1 2 3 4 6 7 8 9 10
Used continue to skip printing 5
```

Fig. 5.13 | continue statement terminating an iteration of a for statement. (Part 2 of 2.)

Figure 5.13 uses continue to skip the statement at line 12 when the nested if (line 9) determines that count's value is 5. When the continue statement executes, program control continues with the increment of the control variable in the for statement (line 7).

In Section 5.3, we stated that while could be used in most cases in place of for. This is *not* true when the increment expression in the while follows a continue statement. In this case, the increment does *not* execute before the program evaluates the repetition-continuation condition, so the while does not execute in the same manner as the for.

Software Engineering Observation 5.4

There's a tension between achieving quality software engineering and achieving the best-performing software. Sometimes one of these goals is achieved at the expense of the other. For all but the most performance-intensive situations, apply the following rule of thumb: First, make your code simple and correct; then make it fast and small, but only if necessary.

5.8 Logical Operators

The if, if...else, while, do...while and for statements each require a condition to determine how to continue a program's flow of control. So far, we've studied only simple conditions, such as count <= 10, number != sentinelValue and total > 1000. Simple conditions are expressed in terms of the relational operators >, <, >= and <= and the equality operators == and !=, and each expression tests only one condition. To test multiple conditions in the process of making a decision, we performed these tests in separate statements or in nested if or if...else statements. Sometimes control statements require more complex conditions to determine a program's flow of control.

Java's **logical operators** enable you to form more complex conditions by *combining* simple conditions. The logical operators are && (conditional AND), || (conditional OR), & (boolean logical AND), | (boolean logical inclusive OR), ∧ (boolean logical exclusive OR) and ! (logical NOT). [*Note:* The &, | and ∧ operators are also bitwise operators when they're applied to integral operands.]

Conditional AND (&&) Operator
Suppose we wish to ensure at some point in a program that two conditions are *both* true before we choose a certain path of execution. In this case, we can use the **&&** (**conditional AND**) operator, as follows:

```
if ( gender == FEMALE && age >= 65 )
   ++seniorFemales;
```

This if statement contains two simple conditions. The condition gender == FEMALE com-pares variable gender to the constant FEMALE to determine whether a person is female. The condition age >= 65 might be evaluated to determine whether a person is a senior citizen. The if statement considers the combined condition

```
gender == FEMALE && age >= 65
```

which is true if and only if *both* simple conditions are true. In this case, the if statement's body increments seniorFemales by 1. If either or both of the simple conditions are false, the program skips the increment. Some programmers find that the preceding combined condition is more readable when redundant parentheses are added, as in:

```
( gender == FEMALE ) && ( age >= 65 )
```

The table in Fig. 5.14 summarizes the && operator. The table shows all four possible combinations of false and true values for *expression1* and *expression2*. Such tables are called **truth tables**. Java evaluates to false or true all expressions that include relational operators, equality operators or logical operators.

expression1	expression2	expression1 && expression2
false	false	false
false	true	false
true	false	false
true	true	true

Fig. 5.14 | && (conditional AND) operator truth table.

Conditional OR (||) Operator
Now suppose we wish to ensure that *either or both* of two conditions are true before we choose a certain path of execution. In this case, we use the **||** (**conditional OR**) operator, as in the following program segment:

```
if ( ( semesterAverage >= 90 ) || ( finalExam >= 90 ) )
   System.out.println ( "Student grade is A" );
```

This statement also contains two simple conditions. The condition semesterAverage >= 90 evaluates to determine whether the student deserves an A in the course because of a sol-id performance throughout the semester. The condition finalExam >= 90 evaluates to de-termine whether the student deserves an A in the course because of an outstanding performance on the final exam. The if statement then considers the combined condition

```
( semesterAverage >= 90 ) || ( finalExam >= 90 )
```

and awards the student an A if *either or both* of the simple conditions are true. The only time the message "Student grade is A" is *not* printed is when *both* of the simple conditions are *false*. Figure 5.15 is a truth table for operator conditional OR (||). Operator && has a higher precedence than operator ||. Both operators associate from left to right.

expression1	expression2	expression1 || expression2
false	false	false
false	true	true
true	false	true
true	true	true

Fig. 5.15 | || (conditional OR) operator truth table.

Short-Circuit Evaluation of Complex Conditions

The parts of an expression containing && or || operators are evaluated *only* until it's known whether the condition is true or false. Thus, evaluation of the expression

```
( gender == FEMALE ) && ( age >= 65 )
```

stops immediately if gender is not equal to FEMALE (i.e., the entire expression is false) and continues if gender *is* equal to FEMALE (i.e., the entire expression could still be true if the condition age >= 65 is true). This feature of conditional AND and conditional OR expressions is called **short-circuit evaluation**.

Common Programming Error 5.3

In expressions using operator &&, a condition—we'll call this the dependent condition—may require another condition to be true for the evaluation of the dependent condition to be meaningful. In this case, the dependent condition should be placed after the other condition, or an error might occur. For example, in the expression (i != 0) && (10 / i == 2), the second condition must appear after the first condition, or a divide-by-zero error might occur.

Boolean Logical AND (&) and Boolean Logical Inclusive OR (|) Operators

The **boolean logical AND (&)** and **boolean logical inclusive OR (|)** operators are identical to the && and || operators, except that the & and | operators *always* evaluate *both* of their operands (i.e., they do *not* perform short-circuit evaluation). So, the expression

```
( gender == 1 ) & ( age >= 65 )
```

evaluates age >= 65 *regardless* of whether gender is equal to 1. This is useful if the right operand of the boolean logical AND or boolean logical inclusive OR operator has a required **side effect**—a modification of a variable's value. For example, the expression

```
( birthday == true ) | ( ++age >= 65 )
```

guarantees that the condition ++age >= 65 will be evaluated. Thus, the variable age is incremented, regardless of whether the overall expression is true or false.

Error-Prevention Tip 5.4

For clarity, avoid expressions with side effects in conditions. The side effects may seem clever, but they can make it harder to understand code and can lead to subtle logic errors.

Boolean Logical Exclusive OR (^)

A simple condition containing the **boolean logical exclusive OR** (^) operator is true *if and only if one of its operands is* true *and the other is* false. If both are true or both are false, the entire condition is false. Figure 5.16 is a truth table for the boolean logical exclusive OR operator (^). This operator is guaranteed to evaluate *both* of its operands.

expression1	expression2	expression1 ^ expression2
false	false	false
false	true	true
true	false	true
true	true	false

Fig. 5.16 | ^ (boolean logical exclusive OR) operator truth table.

Logical Negation (!) Operator

The **!** (**logical NOT**) operator "reverses" the meaning of a condition. Unlike the logical operators &&, ||, &, | and ^, which are *binary* operators that combine two conditions, the logical negation operator is a *unary* operator that has only a single condition as an operand. The operator is placed *before* a condition to choose a path of execution if the original condition (without the logical negation operator) is false, as in the program segment

```
if ( ! ( grade == sentinelValue ) )
    System.out.printf( "The next grade is %d\n", grade );
```

which executes the printf call only if grade is *not* equal to sentinelValue. The parentheses around the condition grade == sentinelValue are needed because the logical negation operator has a higher precedence than the equality operator. You can typically avoid using logical negation by expressing the condition differently with an appropriate relational or equality operator. For example, the previous statement may also be written as follows:

```
if ( grade != sentinelValue )
    System.out.printf( "The next grade is %d\n", grade );
```

This flexibility can help you express a condition in a more convenient manner. Figure 5.17 is a truth table for the logical negation operator.

expression	!expression
false	true
true	false

Fig. 5.17 | ! (logical negation, or logical NOT) operator truth table.

Logical Operators Example

Figure 5.18 uses logical operators to produce the truth tables discussed in this section. The output shows the boolean expression that was evaluated and its result. We used the **%b format specifier** to display the word "true" or the word "false" based on a boolean expression's value. Lines 9–13 produce the truth table for **&&**. Lines 16–20 produce the truth table for ||. Lines 23–27 produce the truth table for &. Lines 30–35 produce the truth table for |. Lines 38–43 produce the truth table for ∧. Lines 46–47 produce the truth table for !.

```
 1   // Fig. 5.18: LogicalOperators.java
 2   // Logical operators.
 3
 4   public class LogicalOperators
 5   {
 6      public static void main( String[] args )
 7      {
 8         // create truth table for && (conditional AND) operator
 9         System.out.printf( "%s\n%s: %b\n%s: %b\n%s: %b\n%s: %b\n\n",
10            "Conditional AND (&&)", "false && false", ( false && false ),
11            "false && true", ( false && true ),
12            "true && false", ( true && false ),
13            "true && true", ( true && true ) );
14
15         // create truth table for || (conditional OR) operator
16         System.out.printf( "%s\n%s: %b\n%s: %b\n%s: %b\n%s: %b\n\n",
17            "Conditional OR (||)", "false || false", ( false || false ),
18            "false || true", ( false || true ),
19            "true || false", ( true || false ),
20            "true || true", ( true || true ) );
21
22         // create truth table for & (boolean logical AND) operator
23         System.out.printf( "%s\n%s: %b\n%s: %b\n%s: %b\n%s: %b\n\n",
24            "Boolean logical AND (&)", "false & false", ( false & false ),
25            "false & true", ( false & true ),
26            "true & false", ( true & false ),
27            "true & true", ( true & true ) );
28
29         // create truth table for | (boolean logical inclusive OR) operator
30         System.out.printf( "%s\n%s: %b\n%s: %b\n%s: %b\n%s: %b\n\n",
31            "Boolean logical inclusive OR (|)",
32            "false | false", ( false | false ),
33            "false | true", ( false | true ),
34            "true | false", ( true | false ),
35            "true | true", ( true | true ) );
36
37         // create truth table for ∧ (boolean logical exclusive OR) operator
38         System.out.printf( "%s\n%s: %b\n%s: %b\n%s: %b\n%s: %b\n\n",
39            "Boolean logical exclusive OR (∧)",
40            "false ∧ false", ( false ∧ false ),
41            "false ∧ true", ( false ∧ true ),
42            "true ∧ false", ( true ∧ false ),
43            "true ∧ true", ( true ∧ true ) );
```

Fig. 5.18 | Logical operators. (Part 1 of 2.)

```
44
45          // create truth table for ! (logical negation) operator
46          System.out.printf( "%s\n%s: %b\n%s: %b\n", "Logical NOT (!)",
47             "!false", ( !false ), "!true", ( !true ) );
48       } // end main
49    } // end class LogicalOperators
```

```
Conditional AND (&&)
false && false: false
false && true: false
true && false: false
true && true: true

Conditional OR (||)
false || false: false
false || true: true
true || false: true
true || true: true

Boolean logical AND (&)
false & false: false
false & true: false
true & false: false
true & true: true

Boolean logical inclusive OR (|)
false | false: false
false | true: true
true | false: true
true | true: true

Boolean logical exclusive OR (^)
false ^ false: false
false ^ true: true
true ^ false: true
true ^ true: false

Logical NOT (!)
!false: true
!true: false
```

Fig. 5.18 | Logical operators. (Part 2 of 2.)

Figure 5.19 shows the precedence and associativity of the Java operators introduced so far. The operators are shown from top to bottom in decreasing order of precedence.

Operators						Associativity	Type
++ --						right to left	unary postfix
++ -- + - !					(type)	right to left	unary prefix
* / %						left to right	multiplicative
+ -						left to right	additive

Fig. 5.19 | Precedence/associativity of the operators discussed so far. (Part 1 of 2.)

Operators	Associativity	Type
< <= > >=	left to right	relational
== !=	left to right	equality
&	left to right	boolean logical AND
^	left to right	boolean logical exclusive OR
|	left to right	boolean logical inclusive OR
&&	left to right	conditional AND
||	left to right	conditional OR
?:	right to left	conditional
= += -= *= /= %=	right to left	assignment

Fig. 5.19 | Precedence/associativity of the operators discussed so far. (Part 2 of 2.)

5.9 Wrap-Up

In this chapter, we completed our introduction to Java's control statements, which enable you to control the flow of execution in methods. Chapter 4 discussed Java's if, if...else and while statements. The current chapter demonstrated the for, do...while and switch statements. We also introduced Java's logical operators, which enable you to use more complex conditional expressions in control statements. In Chapter 6, we examine methods in greater depth.

6

Methods:
A Deeper Look

Objectives

In this chapter you'll learn:

- How **static** methods and fields are associated with classes rather than objects.

- How the method call/return mechanism is supported by the method-call stack.

- How packages group related classes.

- How to use random-number generation to implement game-playing applications.

- How the visibility of declarations is limited to specific regions of programs.

- What method overloading is and how to create overloaded methods.

E pluribus unum.
(One composed of many.)
—Virgil

O! call back yesterday, bid time return.
—William Shakespeare

Call me Ishmael.
—Herman Melville

Answer me in one word.
—William Shakespeare

There is a point at which methods devour themselves.
—Frantz Fanon

6.1 Introduction

In this chapter, we study methods in more depth. You'll see that it's possible to call certain methods, called static methods, without the need for an object of the class to exist.

We'll take a brief diversion into simulation techniques with random-number generation and develop a version of the casino dice game called craps that uses most of the programming techniques you've used to this point in the book. You'll learn how to declare constants.

Many of the classes you'll use or create while developing applications will have more than one method of the same name. This technique, called overloading, is used to implement methods that perform similar tasks for arguments of different types or for different numbers of arguments.

6.2 Program Modules in Java

Your programs will combine methods and classes with predefined ones available in the **Java Application Programming Interface** (also referred to as the **Java API** or **Java class library**) and in various other class libraries. Related classes are typically grouped into packages so that they can be imported into programs and reused. You'll learn how to group your own classes into packages in Chapter 8. The Java API provides a rich collection of predefined classes that contain methods for performing common mathematical calculations, string manipulations, character manipulations, input/output operations, database operations, networking operations, file processing, error checking and many other useful tasks.

Software Engineering Observation 6.1

Familiarize yourself with the rich collection of classes and methods provided by the Java API (download.oracle.com/javase/6/docs/api/). Section 6.7 presents an overview of several common packages. Appendix E explains how to navigate the API documentation. Don't reinvent the wheel. When possible, reuse Java API classes and methods. This reduces program development time and avoids introducing programming errors.

6.3 static Methods, static Fields and Class Math

Although most methods execute in response to method calls on specific objects, this is not always the case. Sometimes a method performs a task that does not depend on the contents of any object. Such a method applies to the class in which it's declared as a whole and is known as a static method or a **class method**. It's common for classes to contain convenient static methods to perform common tasks. For example, recall that we used static method pow of class Math to raise a value to a power in Fig. 5.6. To declare a method as static, place the keyword static before the return type in the method's declaration. For any class imported into your program, you can call the class's static methods by specifying the name of the class in which the method is declared, followed by a dot (.) and the method name, as in

ClassName.methodName(arguments)

We use various Math class methods here to present the concept of static methods. Class Math provides a collection of methods that enable you to perform common mathematical calculations. For example, you can calculate the square root of 900.0 with the static method call

```
Math.sqrt( 900.0 )
```

The preceding expression evaluates to 30.0. Method sqrt takes an argument of type double and returns a result of type double. To output the value of the preceding method call in the command window, you might write the statement

```
System.out.println( Math.sqrt( 900.0 ) );
```

In this statement, the value that sqrt returns becomes the argument to method println. There was no need to create a Math object before calling method sqrt. Also *all* Math class methods are static—therefore, each is called by preceding its name with the class name Math and the dot (.) separator.

Software Engineering Observation 6.2

Class Math is part of the java.lang package, which is implicitly imported by the compiler, so it's not necessary to import class Math to use its methods.

Method arguments may be constants, variables or expressions. If c = 13.0, d = 3.0 and f = 4.0, then the statement

```
System.out.println( Math.sqrt( c + d * f ) );
```

calculates and prints the square root of 13.0 + 3.0 * 4.0 = 25.0—namely, 5.0. Figure 6.1 summarizes several Math class methods. In the figure, x and y are of type double.

Method	Description	Example
abs(x)	absolute value of x	abs(23.7) is 23.7 abs(0.0) is 0.0 abs(-23.7) is 23.7
ceil(x)	rounds x to the smallest integer not less than x	ceil(9.2) is 10.0 ceil(-9.8) is -9.0
cos(x)	trigonometric cosine of x (x in radians)	cos(0.0) is 1.0
exp(x)	exponential method e^x	exp(1.0) is 2.71828 exp(2.0) is 7.38906

Fig. 6.1 | Math class methods. (Part 1 of 2.)

Method	Description	Example
floor(x)	rounds x to the largest integer not greater than x	floor(9.2) is 9.0 floor(-9.8) is -10.0
log(x)	natural logarithm of x (base e)	log(Math.E) is 1.0 log(Math.E * Math.E) is 2.0
max(x, y)	larger value of x and y	max(2.3, 12.7) is 12.7 max(-2.3, -12.7) is -2.3
min(x, y)	smaller value of x and y	min(2.3, 12.7) is 2.3 min(-2.3, -12.7) is -12.7
pow(x, y)	x raised to the power y (i.e., x^y)	pow(2.0, 7.0) is 128.0 pow(9.0, 0.5) is 3.0
sin(x)	trigonometric sine of x (x in radians)	sin(0.0) is 0.0
sqrt(x)	square root of x	sqrt(900.0) is 30.0
tan(x)	trigonometric tangent of x (x in radians)	tan(0.0) is 0.0

Fig. 6.1 | Math class methods. (Part 2 of 2.)

Math Class Constants PI and E

Class Math declares two fields that represent commonly used mathematical constants—
Math.PI and Math.E. Math.PI (3.141592653589793) is the ratio of a circle's circumference to its diameter. Math.E (2.718281828459045) is the base value for natural logarithms (calculated with static Math method log). These fields are declared in class Math with the modifiers public, final and static. Making them public allows you to use these fields in your own classes. Any field declared with keyword **final** is constant—its value cannot change after the field is initialized. PI and E are declared final because their values never change. Making these fields static allows them to be accessed via the class name Math and a dot (.) separator, just like class Math's methods. Recall from Section 3.4 that when each object of a class maintains its own copy of an attribute, the field that represents the attribute is also known as an instance variable—each object (instance) of the class has a separate instance of the variable in memory. There are fields for which each object of a class does *not* have a separate instance of the field. That's the case with static fields, which are also known as **class variables**. When objects of a class containing static fields are created, all the objects of that class share one copy of the class's static fields. Together the class variables (i.e., static variables) and instance variables represent the fields of a class. You'll learn more about static fields in Section 8.11.

Why Is Method main Declared static?

When you execute the Java Virtual Machine (JVM) with the java command, the JVM attempts to invoke the main method of the class you specify—when no objects of the class have been created. Declaring main as static allows the JVM to invoke main without creating an instance of the class. When you execute your application, you specify its class name as an argument to the command java, as in

```
java ClassName argument1 argument2 ...
```

The JVM loads the class specified by *ClassName* and uses that class name to invoke method main. In the preceding command, *ClassName* is a **command-line argument** to the JVM that tells it which class to execute. Following the *ClassName*, you can also specify a list of Strings (separated by spaces) as command-line arguments that the JVM will pass to your application. Such arguments might be used to specify options (e.g., a file name) to run the application. As you'll learn in Chapter 7, Arrays and ArrayLists, your application can access those command-line arguments and use them to customize the application.

6.4 Declaring Methods with Multiple Parameters

We now consider how to write your own methods with multiple parameters. Figure 6.2 uses a method called maximum to determine and return the largest of *three* double values. In main, lines 14–18 prompt the user to enter three double values, then read them from the user. Line 21 calls method maximum (declared in lines 28–41) to determine the largest of the three values it receives as arguments. When method maximum returns the result to line 21, the program assigns maximum's return value to local variable result. Then line 24 outputs the maximum value. At the end of this section, we'll discuss the use of operator + in line 24.

```java
 1   // Fig. 6.2: MaximumFinder.java
 2   // Programmer-declared method maximum with three double parameters.
 3   import java.util.Scanner;
 4
 5   public class MaximumFinder
 6   {
 7      // obtain three floating-point values and locate the maximum value
 8      public static void main( String[] args )
 9      {
10         // create Scanner for input from command window
11         Scanner input = new Scanner( System.in );
12
13         // prompt for and input three floating-point values
14         System.out.print(
15            "Enter three floating-point values separated by spaces: " );
16         double number1 = input.nextDouble(); // read first double
17         double number2 = input.nextDouble(); // read second double
18         double number3 = input.nextDouble(); // read third double
19
20         // determine the maximum value
21         double result = maximum( number1, number2, number3 );
22
23         // display maximum value
24         System.out.println( "Maximum is: " + result );
25      } // end main
26
27      // returns the maximum of its three double parameters
28      public static double maximum( double x, double y, double z )
29      {
30         double maximumValue = x; // assume x is the largest to start
31
```

Fig. 6.2 | Programmer-declared method maximum with three double parameters. (Part 1 of 2.)

```
32          // determine whether y is greater than maximumValue
33          if ( y > maximumValue )
34             maximumValue = y;
35
36          // determine whether z is greater than maximumValue
37          if ( z > maximumValue )
38             maximumValue = z;
39
40          return maximumValue;
41       } // end method maximum
42    } // end class MaximumFinder
```

```
Enter three floating-point values separated by spaces: 9.35 2.74 5.1
Maximum is: 9.35
```

```
Enter three floating-point values separated by spaces: 5.8 12.45 8.32
Maximum is: 12.45
```

```
Enter three floating-point values separated by spaces: 6.46 4.12 10.54
Maximum is: 10.54
```

Fig. 6.2 | Programmer-declared method maximum with three double parameters. (Part 2 of 2.)

The *public* and *static* Keywords

Method maximum's declaration begins with keyword public to indicate that the method is "available to the public"—it can be called from methods of other classes. The keyword static enables the main method (another static method) to call maximum as shown in line 21 without qualifying the method name with the class name MaximumFinder—static methods in the same class can call each other directly. Any other class that uses maximum must fully qualify the method name with the class name.

Method *maximum*

Consider maximum's declaration (lines 28–41). Line 28 indicates that it returns a double value, that the method's name is maximum and that the method requires three double parameters (x, y and z) to accomplish its task. Multiple parameters are specified as a comma-separated list. When maximum is called from line 21, the parameters x, y and z are initialized with the values of arguments number1, number2 and number3, respectively. There must be one argument in the method call for each parameter in the method declaration. Also, each argument must be *consistent* with the type of the corresponding parameter. For example, a parameter of type double can receive values like 7.35, 22 or –0.03456, but not Strings like "hello" nor the boolean values true or false. Section 6.6 discusses the argument types that can be provided in a method call for each parameter of a primitive type.

To determine the maximum value, we begin with the assumption that parameter x contains the largest value, so line 30 declares local variable maximumValue and initializes it with the value of parameter x. Of course, it's possible that parameter y or z contains the actual largest value, so we must compare each of these values with maximumValue. The if statement at lines 33–34 determines whether y is greater than maximumValue. If so, line 34 assigns y to maximumValue. The if statement at lines 37–38 determines whether z is greater than maximumValue. If so, line 38 assigns z to maximumValue. At this point the largest of the three values resides in maximumValue, so line 40 returns that value to line 21. When program control returns to the point in the program where maximum was called, maximum's parameters x, y and z no longer exist in memory.

Software Engineering Observation 6.3

Methods can return at most one value, but the returned value could be a reference to an object that contains many values.

Software Engineering Observation 6.4

Variables should be declared as fields only if they're required for use in more than one method of the class or if the program should save their values between calls to the class's methods.

Implementing Method `maximum` by Reusing Method `Math.max`

The entire body of our maximum method could also be implemented with two calls to Math.max, as follows:

```
return Math.max( x, Math.max( y, z ) );
```

The first call to Math.max specifies arguments x and Math.max(y, z). *Before* any method can be called, its arguments must be evaluated to determine their values. If an argument is a method call, the method call must be performed to determine its return value. So, in the preceding statement, Math.max(y, z) is evaluated to determine the maximum of y and z. Then the result is passed as the second argument to the other call to Math.max, which returns the larger of its two arguments. This is a good example of software reuse—we find the largest of three values by reusing Math.max, which finds the larger of two values. Note how concise this code is compared to lines 30–38 of Fig. 6.2.

Assembling Strings with String Concatenation

Java allows you to assemble String objects into larger strings by using operators + or +=. This is known as **string concatenation**. When both operands of operator + are String objects, operator + creates a new String object in which the characters of the right operand are placed at the end of those in the left operand—e.g., the expression "hello " + "there" creates the String "hello there".

In line 24 of Fig. 6.2, the expression "Maximum is: " + result uses operator + with operands of types String and double. *Every primitive value and object in Java has a String representation.* When one of the + operator's operands is a String, the other is converted to a String, then the two are *concatenated*. In line 24, the double value is converted to its String representation and placed at the end of the String "Maximum is: ". If there are any *trailing zeros* in a double value, these will be *discarded* when the number is converted to a String—for example 9.3500 would be represented as 9.35.

Primitive values used in String concatenation are converted to Strings. A boolean concatenated with a String is converted to the String "true" or "false". All objects have a toString method that returns a String representation of the object. (We discuss toString in more detail in subsequent chapters.) When an object is concatenated with a

String, the object's toString method is implicitly called to obtain the String represen-tation of the object. ToString can be called explicitly.

You can break large String literals into several smaller Strings and place them on multiple lines of code for readability. In this case, the Strings can be reassembled using concatenation. We discuss the details of Strings in Chapter 16.

Common Programming Error 6.1

It's a syntax error to break a String literal across lines. If necessary, you can split a String into several smaller Strings and use concatenation to form the desired String.

Common Programming Error 6.2

Confusing the + operator used for string concatenation with the + operator used for addi-tion can lead to strange results. Java evaluates the operands of an operator from left to right. For example, if integer variable y has the value 5, the expression "y + 2 = " + y + 2 results in the string "y + 2 = 52", not "y + 2 = 7", because first the value of y (5) is con-catenated to the string "y + 2 = ", then the value 2 is concatenated to the new larger string "y + 2 = 5". The expression "y + 2 = " + (y + 2) produces the desired result "y + 2 = 7".

6.5 Notes on Declaring and Using Methods

There are three ways to call a method:

1. Using a method name by itself to call another method of the *same* class—such as maximum(number1, number2, number3) in line 21 of Fig. 6.2.

2. Using a variable that contains a reference to an object, followed by a dot (.) and the method name to call a non-static method of the referenced object—such as the method call in line 13 of Fig. 5.10, myGradeBook.displayMessage(), which calls a method of class GradeBook from the main method of GradeBookTest.

3. Using the class name and a dot (.) to call a static method of a class—such as Math.sqrt(900.0) in Section 6.3.

A static method can call *only* other static methods of the same class directly (i.e., using the method name by itself) and can manipulate *only* static variables in the same class directly. To access the class's non-static members, a static method must use a ref-erence to an object of the class. Recall that static methods relate to a class as a whole, whereas non-static methods are associated with a specific instance (object) of the class and may manipulate the instance variables of that object. Many objects of a class, each with its own copies of the instance variables, may exist at the same time. Suppose a static method were to invoke a non-static method directly. How would the method know which object's instance variables to manipulate? What would happen if no objects of the class existed at the time the non-static method was invoked? Thus, Java does not allow a static method to access non-static members of the same class directly.

There are three ways to return control to the statement that calls a method. If the method does not return a result, control returns when the program flow reaches the method-ending right brace or when the statement

```
return;
```

is executed. If the method returns a result, the statement

> **return** *expression*;

evaluates the *expression*, then returns the result to the caller.

Common Programming Error 6.3
Declaring a method outside the body of a class declaration or inside the body of another method is a syntax error.

Common Programming Error 6.4
Redeclaring a parameter as a local variable in the method's body is a compilation error.

Common Programming Error 6.5
Forgetting to return a value from a method that should return a value is a compilation error. If a return type other than void *is specified, the method* must *contain a* return *statement that returns a value consistent with the method's return type. Returning a value from a method whose return type has been declared* void *is a compilation error.*

6.6 Argument Promotion and Casting

Another important feature of method calls is **argument promotion**—converting an argument's value, if possible, to the type that the method expects to receive in its corresponding parameter. For example, a program can call Math method sqrt with an int argument even though a double argument is expected. The statement

```
System.out.println( Math.sqrt( 4 ) );
```

correctly evaluates Math.sqrt(4) and prints the value 2.0. The method declaration's parameter list causes Java to convert the int value 4 to the double value 4.0 before passing the value to method sqrt. Such conversions may lead to compilation errors if Java's **promotion rules** are not satisfied. These rules specify which conversions are allowed—that is, which ones can be performed without losing data. In the sqrt example above, an int is converted to a double without changing its value. However, converting a double to an int truncates the fractional part of the double value—thus, part of the value is lost. Converting large integer types to small integer types (e.g., long to int, or int to short) may also result in changed values.

The promotion rules apply to expressions containing values of two or more primitive types and to primitive-type values passed as arguments to methods. Each value is promoted to the "highest" type in the expression. Actually, the expression uses a temporary copy of each value—the types of the original values remain unchanged. Figure 6.3 lists the primitive types and the types to which each can be promoted. The valid promotions for a given type are always to a type higher in the table. For example, an int can be promoted to the higher types long, float and double.

Converting values to types lower in the table of Fig. 6.3 will result in different values if the lower type cannot represent the value of the higher type (e.g., the int value 2000000 cannot be represented as a short, and any floating-point number with digits after its decimal point cannot be represented in an integer type such as long, int or short). Therefore, in cases where information may be lost due to conversion, the Java compiler requires you to use a cast operator (introduced in Section 4.7) to explicitly force the conversion to occur—otherwise a compilation error occurs. This enables you to "take control" from the

Type	Valid promotions
double	None
float	double
long	float or double
int	long, float or double
char	int, long, float or double
short	int, long, float or double (but not char)
byte	short, int, long, float or double (but not char)
boolean	None (boolean values are not considered to be numbers in Java)

Fig. 6.3 | Promotions allowed for primitive types.

compiler. You essentially say, "I know this conversion might cause loss of information, but for my purposes here, that's fine." Suppose method `square` calculates the square of an integer and thus requires an `int` argument. To call `square` with a `double` argument named `doubleValue`, we would be required to write the method call as

```
square( (int) doubleValue )
```

This method call explicitly casts (converts) a *copy* of variable `doubleValue`'s value to an integer for use in method `square`. Thus, if `doubleValue`'s value is `4.5`, the method receives the value 4 and returns 16, not `20.25`.

Common Programming Error 6.6

Converting a primitive-type value to another primitive type may change the value if the new type is not a valid promotion. For example, converting a floating-point value to an integer value may introduce truncation errors (loss of the fractional part) into the result.

6.7 Java API Packages

As you've seen, Java contains many predefined classes that are grouped into categories of related classes called packages. Together, these are known as the Java Application Programming Interface (Java API), or the Java class library. A great strength of Java is the Java API's thousands of classes. Some key Java API packages are described in Fig. 6.4, which represents only a small portion of the reusable components in the Java API.

The set of packages available in Java SE is quite large. In addition to those summarized in Fig. 6.4, Java SE includes packages for complex graphics, advanced graphical user interfaces, printing, advanced networking, security, database processing, multimedia, accessibility (for people with disabilities), concurrent programming, cryptography, XML processing and many other capabilities. For an overview of the packages in Java SE, visit

```
download.oracle.com/javase/6/docs/api/overview-summary.html
```

Many other packages are also available for download at `java.sun.com`.

You can locate additional information about a predefined Java class's methods in the Java API documentation at `download.oracle.com/javase/6/docs/api/`. When you visit this site, click the **Index** link to see an alphabetical listing of all the classes and methods in the Java API. Locate the class name and click its link to see the online description of the class. Click the **METHOD** link to see a table of the class's methods. Each static method will be listed with the word "static" preceding its return type.

Package	Description
java.applet	The **Java Applet Package** contains a class and several interfaces required to create Java applets—programs that execute in web browsers. Applets are discussed in Chapter 20, Applets and Java Web Start; interfaces are discussed in Chapter 10, Object-Oriented Programming: Polymorphism.)
java.awt	The **Java Abstract Window Toolkit Package** contains the classes and interfaces required to create and manipulate GUIs in early versions of Java. In current versions, the Swing GUI components of the javax.swing packages are typically used instead. (Some elements of the java.awt package are discussed in Chapter 14, GUI Components: Part 1; Chapter 15, Graphics and Java 2D; and Chapter 22, GUI Components: Part 2.)
java.awt.event	The **Java Abstract Window Toolkit Event Package** contains classes and interfaces that enable event handling for GUI components in both the java.awt and javax.swing packages. (See Chapter 14, GUI Components: Part 1, and Chapter 22, GUI Components: Part 2.)
java.awt.geom	The **Java 2D Shapes Package** contains classes and interfaces for working with Java's advanced two-dimensional graphics capabilities. (See Chapter 15, Graphics and Java 2D.)
java.io	The **Java Input/Output Package** contains classes and interfaces that enable programs to input and output data. (See Chapter 17, Files, Streams and Object Serialization.)
java.lang	The **Java Language Package** contains classes and interfaces (discussed bookwide) that are required by many Java programs. This package is imported by the compiler into all programs.
java.net	The **Java Networking Package** contains classes and interfaces that enable programs to communicate via computer networks like the Internet. (See Chapter 24, Networking.)
java.sql	The **JDBC Package** contains classes and interfaces for working with databases. (See Chapter 25, Accessing Databases with JDBC.)
java.util	The **Java Utilities Package** contains utility classes and interfaces that enable such actions as date and time manipulations, random-number processing (class Random) and the storing and processing of large amounts of data. (See Chapter 18, Generic Collections.)
java.util. concurrent	The **Java Concurrency Package** contains utility classes and interfaces for implementing programs that can perform multiple tasks in parallel. (See Chapter 23, Multithreading.)
javax.media	The **Java Media Framework Package** contains classes and interfaces for working with Java's multimedia capabilities. (See Chapter 21, Multimedia: Applets and Applications.)

Fig. 6.4 | Java API packages (a subset). (Part 1 of 2.)

Package	Description
`javax.swing`	The **Java Swing GUI Components Package** contains classes and interfaces for Java's Swing GUI components that provide support for portable GUIs. (See Chapter 14, GUI Components: Part 1, and Chapter 22, GUI Components: Part 2.)
`javax.swing.event`	The **Java Swing Event Package** contains classes and interfaces that enable event handling (e.g., responding to button clicks) for GUI components in package `javax.swing`. (See Chapter 14, GUI Components: Part 1, and Chapter 22, GUI Components: Part 2.)
`javax.xml.ws`	The **JAX-WS Package** contains classes and interfaces for working with web services in Java. (See Chapter 28, Web Services.)

Fig. 6.4 | Java API packages (a subset). (Part 2 of 2.)

6.8 Case Study: Random-Number Generation

We now take a brief diversion into a popular type of programming application—simulation and game playing. In this and the next section, we develop a nicely structured game-playing program with multiple methods. The program uses most of the control statements presented thus far in the book and introduces several new programming concepts.

There's something in the air of a casino that invigorates people—from the high rollers at the plush mahogany-and-felt craps tables to the quarter poppers at the one-armed bandits. It's the **element of chance**, the possibility that luck will convert a pocketful of money into a mountain of wealth. The element of chance can be introduced in a program via an object of class **Random** (package `java.util`) or via the `static` method random of class Math. Objects of class Random can produce random boolean, byte, float, double, int, long and Gaussian values, whereas Math method random can produce only double values in the range $0.0 \leq x < 1.0$, where x is the value returned by method random. In the next several examples, we use objects of class Random to produce random values.

A new random-number generator object can be created as follows:

```
Random randomNumbers = new Random();
```

It can then be used to generate random boolean, byte, float, double, int, long and Gaussian values—we discuss only random int values here. For more information on the Random class, see `download.oracle.com/javase/6/docs/api/java/util/Random.html`.

Consider the following statement:

```
int randomValue = randomNumbers.nextInt();
```

Random method **nextInt** generates a random int value in the range −2,147,483,648 to +2,147,483,647, inclusive. If it truly produces values at random, then every value in the range should have an equal chance (or probability) of being chosen each time nextInt is called. The numbers are actually **pseudorandom numbers**—a sequence of values produced by a complex mathematical calculation. The calculation uses the current time of day (which, of course, changes constantly) to **seed** the random-number generator such that each execution of a program yields a different sequence of random values.

The range of values produced directly by method `nextInt` generally differs from the range of values required in a particular Java application. For example, a program that simulates coin tossing might require only 0 for "heads" and 1 for "tails." A program that simulates the rolling of a six-sided die might require random integers in the range 1–6. A program that randomly predicts the next type of spaceship (out of four possibilities) that will fly across the horizon in a video game might require random integers in the range 1–4. For cases like these, class `Random` provides another version of method `nextInt` that receives an `int` argument and returns a value from 0 up to, but not including, the argument's value. For example, for coin tossing, the following statement returns 0 or 1.

```
int randomValue = randomNumbers.nextInt( 2 );
```

Rolling a Six-Sided Die

To demonstrate random numbers, let's develop a program that simulates 20 rolls of a six-sided die and displays the value of each roll. We begin by using `nextInt` to produce random values in the range 0–5, as follows:

```
face = randomNumbers.nextInt( 6 );
```

The argument 6—called the **scaling factor**—represents the number of unique values that `nextInt` should produce (in this case six—0, 1, 2, 3, 4 and 5). This manipulation is called **scaling** the range of values produced by `Random` method `nextInt`.

A six-sided die has the numbers 1–6 on its faces, not 0–5. So we **shift** the range of numbers produced by adding a **shifting value**—in this case 1—to our previous result, as in

```
face = 1 + randomNumbers.nextInt( 6 );
```

The shifting value (1) specifies the *first* value in the desired range of random integers. The preceding statement assigns `face` a random integer in the range 1–6.

Figure 6.5 shows two sample outputs which confirm that the results of the preceding calculation are integers in the range 1–6, and that each run of the program can produce a different sequence of random numbers. Line 3 imports class `Random` from the `java.util` package. Line 9 creates the `Random` object `randomNumbers` to produce random values. Line 16 executes 20 times in a loop to roll the die. The `if` statement (lines 21–22) in the loop starts a new line of output after every five numbers.

```java
1   // Fig. 6.5: RandomIntegers.java
2   // Shifted and scaled random integers.
3   import java.util.Random; // program uses class Random
4
5   public class RandomIntegers
6   {
7      public static void main( String[] args )
8      {
9         Random randomNumbers = new Random(); // random number generator
10        int face; // stores each random integer generated
11
12        // loop 20 times
13        for ( int counter = 1; counter <= 20; counter++ )
14        {
```

Fig. 6.5 | Shifted and scaled random integers. (Part 1 of 2.)

```
15                    // pick random integer from 1 to 6
16                    face = 1 + randomNumbers.nextInt( 6 );
17
18                    System.out.printf( "%d  ", face ); // display generated value
19
20                    // if counter is divisible by 5, start a new line of output
21                    if ( counter % 5 == 0 )
22                       System.out.println();
23                 } // end for
24           } // end main
25     } // end class RandomIntegers
```

```
1  5  3  6  2
5  2  6  5  2
4  4  4  2  6
3  1  6  2  2
```

```
6  5  4  2  6
1  2  5  1  3
6  3  2  2  1
6  4  2  6  4
```

Fig. 6.5 | Shifted and scaled random integers. (Part 2 of 2.)

Rolling a Six-Sided Die 6,000,000 Times

To show that the numbers produced by nextInt occur with approximately equal likelihood, let's simulate 6,000,000 rolls of a die with the application in Fig. 6.6. Each integer from 1 to 6 should appear approximately 1,000,000 times.

```
1   // Fig. 6.6: RollDie.java
2   // Roll a six-sided die 6,000,000 times.
3   import java.util.Random;
4
5   public class RollDie
6   {
7      public static void main( String[] args )
8      {
9         Random randomNumbers = new Random(); // random number generator
10
11        int frequency1 = 0; // maintains count of 1s rolled
12        int frequency2 = 0; // count of 2s rolled
13        int frequency3 = 0; // count of 3s rolled
14        int frequency4 = 0; // count of 4s rolled
15        int frequency5 = 0; // count of 5s rolled
16        int frequency6 = 0; // count of 6s rolled
17
18        int face; // most recently rolled value
19
```

Fig. 6.6 | Roll a six-sided die 6,000,000 times. (Part 1 of 2.)

```
20          // tally counts for 6,000,000 rolls of a die
21          for ( int roll = 1; roll <= 6000000; roll++ )
22          {
23             face = 1 + randomNumbers.nextInt( 6 ); // number from 1 to 6
24
25             // determine roll value 1-6 and increment appropriate counter
26             switch ( face )
27             {
28                case 1:
29                   ++frequency1; // increment the 1s counter
30                   break;
31                case 2:
32                   ++frequency2; // increment the 2s counter
33                   break;
34                case 3:
35                   ++frequency3; // increment the 3s counter
36                   break;
37                case 4:
38                   ++frequency4; // increment the 4s counter
39                   break;
40                case 5:
41                   ++frequency5; // increment the 5s counter
42                   break;
43                case 6:
44                   ++frequency6; // increment the 6s counter
45                   break; // optional at end of switch
46             } // end switch
47          } // end for
48
49          System.out.println( "Face\tFrequency" ); // output headers
50          System.out.printf( "1\t%d\n2\t%d\n3\t%d\n4\t%d\n5\t%d\n6\t%d\n",
51             frequency1, frequency2, frequency3, frequency4,
52             frequency5, frequency6 );
53       } // end main
54    } // end class RollDie
```

Face	Frequency
1	999501
2	1000412
3	998262
4	1000820
5	1002245
6	998760

Face	Frequency
1	999647
2	999557
3	999571
4	1000376
5	1000701
6	1000148

Fig. 6.6 | Roll a six-sided die 6,000,000 times. (Part 2 of 2.)

As the sample outputs show, scaling and shifting the values produced by `nextInt` enables the program to simulate rolling a six-sided die. The application uses nested control statements (the `switch` is nested inside the `for`) to determine the number of times each side of the die appears. The `for` statement (lines 21–47) iterates 6,000,000 times. During each iteration, line 23 produces a random value from 1 to 6. That value is then used as the controlling expression (line 26) of the `switch` statement (lines 26–46). Based on the `face` value, the `switch` statement increments one of the six counter variables during each iteration of the loop. When we study arrays in Chapter 7, we'll show an elegant way to replace the entire `switch` statement in this program with a single statement! This `switch` statement has no `default` case, because we have a `case` for every possible die value that the expression in line 23 could produce. Run the program, and observe the results. As you'll see, every time you run this program, it produces different results.

6.8.1 Generalized Scaling and Shifting of Random Numbers

Previously, we simulated the rolling of a six-sided die with the statement

```
face = 1 + randomNumbers.nextInt( 6 );
```

This statement always assigns to variable `face` an integer in the range 1 ≤ `face` ≤6. The width of this range (i.e., the number of consecutive integers in the range) is 6, and the starting number in the range is 1. In the preceding statement, the width of the range is determined by the number 6 that's passed as an argument to `Random` method `nextInt`, and the starting number of the range is the number 1 that's added to `randomNumberGenerator.nextInt(6)`. We can generalize this result as

```
number = shiftingValue + randomNumbers.nextInt( scalingFactor );
```

where *shiftingValue* specifies the first number in the desired range of consecutive integers and *scalingFactor* specifies how many numbers are in the range.

It's also possible to choose integers at random from sets of values other than ranges of consecutive integers. For example, to obtain a random value from the sequence 2, 5, 8, 11 and 14, you could use the statement

```
number = 2 + 3 * randomNumbers.nextInt( 5 );
```

In this case, `randomNumberGenerator.nextInt(5)` produces values in the range 0–4. Each value produced is multiplied by 3 to produce a number in the sequence 0, 3, 6, 9 and 12. We add 2 to that value to shift the range of values and obtain a value from the sequence 2, 5, 8, 11 and 14. We can generalize this result as

```
number = shiftingValue +
    differenceBetweenValues * randomNumbers.nextInt( scalingFactor );
```

where *shiftingValue* specifies the first number in the desired range of values, *differenceBetweenValues* represents the constant difference between consecutive numbers in the sequence and *scalingFactor* specifies how many numbers are in the range.

6.8.2 Random-Number Repeatability for Testing and Debugging

Class `Random`'s methods actually generate pseudorandom numbers based on complex mathematical calculations—the sequence of numbers appears to be random. The calculation that produces the numbers uses the time of day as a **seed value** to change the sequence's starting point. Each new `Random` object seeds itself with a value based on the computer system's clock at the time the object is created, enabling each execution of a program to produce a different sequence of random numbers.

When debugging an application, it's often useful to repeat the exact same sequence of pseudorandom numbers during each execution of the program. This repeatability enables you to prove that your application is working for a specific sequence of random numbers before you test it with different sequences of random numbers. When repeatability is important, you can create a `Random` object as follows:

```
Random randomNumbers = new Random( seedValue );
```

The `seedValue` argument (of type `long`) seeds the random-number calculation. If the same `seedValue` is used every time, the `Random` object produces the same sequence of numbers. You can set a `Random` object's seed at any time during program execution by calling the object's set method, as in

```
randomNumbers.set( seedValue );
```

Error-Prevention Tip 6.1

While developing a program, create the `Random` object with a specific seed value to produce a repeatable sequence of numbers each time the program executes. If a logic error occurs, fix the error and test the program again with the same seed value—this allows you to reconstruct the same sequence of numbers that caused the error. Once the logic errors have been removed, create the `Random` object without using a seed value, causing the `Random` object to generate a new sequence of random numbers each time the program executes.

6.9 Case Study: A Game of Chance; Introducing Enumerations

A popular game of chance is a dice game known as craps, which is played in casinos and back alleys throughout the world. The rules of the game are straightforward:

> *You roll two dice. Each die has six faces, which contain one, two, three, four, five and six spots, respectively. After the dice have come to rest, the sum of the spots on the two upward faces is calculated. If the sum is 7 or 11 on the first throw, you win. If the sum is 2, 3 or 12 on the first throw (called "craps"), you lose (i.e., the "house" wins). If the sum is 4, 5, 6, 8, 9 or 10 on the first throw, that sum becomes your "point." To win, you must continue rolling the dice until you "make your point" (i.e., roll that same point value). You lose by rolling a 7 before making your point.*

Figure 6.7 simulates the game of craps, using methods to implement the game's logic. The `main` method (lines 21–65) calls the `rollDice` method (lines 68–81) as necessary to roll the dice and compute their sum. The sample outputs show winning and losing on the first roll, and winning and losing on a subsequent roll.

```
1   // Fig. 6.7: Craps.java
2   // Craps class simulates the dice game craps.
3   import java.util.Random;
```

Fig. 6.7 | Craps class simulates the dice game craps. (Part 1 of 3.)

```java
4
5   public class Craps
6   {
7      // create random number generator for use in method rollDice
8      private static final Random randomNumbers = new Random();
9
10     // enumeration with constants that represent the game status
11     private enum Status { CONTINUE, WON, LOST };
12
13     // constants that represent common rolls of the dice
14     private static final int SNAKE_EYES = 2;
15     private static final int TREY = 3;
16     private static final int SEVEN = 7;
17     private static final int YO_LEVEN = 11;
18     private static final int BOX_CARS = 12;
19
20     // plays one game of craps
21     public static void main( String[] args )
22     {
23        int myPoint = 0; // point if no win or loss on first roll
24        Status gameStatus; // can contain CONTINUE, WON or LOST
25
26        int sumOfDice = rollDice(); // first roll of the dice
27
28        // determine game status and point based on first roll
29        switch ( sumOfDice )
30        {
31           case SEVEN: // win with 7 on first roll
32           case YO_LEVEN: // win with 11 on first roll
33              gameStatus = Status.WON;
34              break;
35           case SNAKE_EYES: // lose with 2 on first roll
36           case TREY: // lose with 3 on first roll
37           case BOX_CARS: // lose with 12 on first roll
38              gameStatus = Status.LOST;
39              break;
40           default: // did not win or lose, so remember point
41              gameStatus = Status.CONTINUE; // game is not over
42              myPoint = sumOfDice; // remember the point
43              System.out.printf( "Point is %d\n", myPoint );
44              break; // optional at end of switch
45        } // end switch
46
47        // while game is not complete
48        while ( gameStatus == Status.CONTINUE ) // not WON or LOST
49        {
50           sumOfDice = rollDice(); // roll dice again
51
52           // determine game status
53           if ( sumOfDice == myPoint ) // win by making point
54              gameStatus = Status.WON;
```

Fig. 6.7 | Craps class simulates the dice game craps. (Part 2 of 3.)

```
55            else
56                if ( sumOfDice == SEVEN ) // lose by rolling 7 before point
57                    gameStatus = Status.LOST;
58          } // end while
59
60          // display won or lost message
61          if ( gameStatus == Status.WON )
62              System.out.println( "Player wins" );
63          else
64              System.out.println( "Player loses" );
65      } // end main
66
67      // roll dice, calculate sum and display results
68      public static int rollDice()
69      {
70          // pick random die values
71          int die1 = 1 + randomNumbers.nextInt( 6 ); // first die roll
72          int die2 = 1 + randomNumbers.nextInt( 6 ); // second die roll
73
74          int sum = die1 + die2; // sum of die values
75
76          // display results of this roll
77          System.out.printf( "Player rolled %d + %d = %d\n",
78              die1, die2, sum );
79
80          return sum; // return sum of dice
81      } // end method rollDice
82  } // end class Craps
```

```
Player rolled 5 + 6 = 11
Player wins
```

```
Player rolled 5 + 4 = 9
Point is 9
Player rolled 4 + 2 = 6
Player rolled 3 + 6 = 9
Player wins
```

```
Player rolled 1 + 2 = 3
Player loses
```

```
Player rolled 2 + 6 = 8
Point is 8
Player rolled 5 + 1 = 6
Player rolled 2 + 1 = 3
Player rolled 1 + 6 = 7
Player loses
```

Fig. 6.7 | Craps class simulates the dice game craps. (Part 3 of 3.)

Method `rollDice`

In the rules of the game, the player must roll two dice on the first roll and must do the same on all subsequent rolls. We declare method `rollDice` (Fig. 6.7, lines 68–81) to roll the dice and compute and print their sum. Method `rollDice` is declared once, but it's called from two places (lines 26 and 50) in `main`, which contains the logic for one complete game of craps. Method `rollDice` takes no arguments, so it has an empty parameter list. Each time it's called, `rollDice` returns the sum of the dice, so the return type `int` is indicated in the method header (line 68). Although lines 71 and 72 look the same (except for the die names), they do not necessarily produce the same result. Each of these statements produces a random value in the range 1–6. Variable `randomNumbers` (used in lines 71–72) is *not* declared in the method. Instead it's declared as a `private static final` variable of the class and initialized in line 8. This enables us to create one `Random` object that's reused in each call to `rollDice`. If there were a program that contained multiple instances of class `Craps`, they'd all share this one `Random` object.

Method `main`'s Local Variables

The game is reasonably involved. The player may win or lose on the first roll, or may win or lose on any subsequent roll. Method `main` (lines 21–65) uses local variable `myPoint` (line 23) to store the "point" if the player does not win or lose on the first roll, local variable `gameStatus` (line 24) to keep track of the overall game status and local variable `sumOfDice` (line 26) to hold the sum of the dice for the most recent roll. Variable `myPoint` is initialized to 0 to ensure that the application will compile. If you do not initialize `myPoint`, the compiler issues an error, because `myPoint` is not assigned a value in *every* case of the `switch` statement, and thus the program could try to use `myPoint` before it's assigned a value. By contrast, `gameStatus` *is* assigned a value in *every* case of the `switch` statement—thus, it's guaranteed to be initialized before it's used and does not need to be initialized.

enum *Type* `Status`

Local variable `gameStatus` (line 24) is declared to be of a new type called `Status` (declared at line 11). Type `Status` is a `private` member of class `Craps`, because `Status` will be used only in that class. `Status` is a type called an **enumeration**, which, in its simplest form, declares a set of constants represented by identifiers. An enumeration is a special kind of class that's introduced by the keyword **enum** and a type name (in this case, `Status`). As with classes, braces delimit an enum declaration's body. Inside the braces is a comma-separated list of **enumeration constants**, each representing a unique value. The identifiers in an enum must be unique. You'll learn more about enumerations in Chapter 8.

Good Programming Practice 6.1

By convention, we use only uppercase letters in the names of enumeration constants. This makes them stand out and reminds you that they're not variables.

Variables of type `Status` can be assigned only the three constants declared in the enumeration (line 11) or a compilation error will occur. When the game is won, the program sets local variable `gameStatus` to `Status.WON` (lines 33 and 54). When the game is lost, the program sets local variable `gameStatus` to `Status.LOST` (lines 38 and 57). Otherwise, the program sets local variable `gameStatus` to `Status.CONTINUE` (line 41) to indicate that the game is not over and the dice must be rolled again.

Good Programming Practice 6.2

Using enumeration constants (like Status.WON, Status.LOST *and* Status.CONTINUE*) rather than literal values (such as 0, 1 and 2) makes programs easier to read and maintain.*

Logic of the main Method

Line 26 in main calls rollDice, which picks two random values from 1 to 6, displays the values of the first die, the second die and their sum, and returns the sum. Method main next enters the switch statement (lines 29–45), which uses the sumOfDice value from line 26 to determine whether the game has been won or lost, or should continue with another roll. The values that result in a win or loss on the first roll are declared as public static final int constants in lines 14–18. The identifier names use casino parlance for these sums. These constants, like enum constants, are declared by convention with all capital letters, to make them stand out in the program. Lines 31–34 determine whether the player won on the first roll with SEVEN (7) or YO_LEVEN (11). Lines 35–39 determine whether the player lost on the first roll with SNAKE_EYES (2), TREY (3), or BOX_CARS (12). After the first roll, if the game is not over, the default case (lines 40–44) sets gameStatus to Status.CONTINUE, saves sumOfDice in myPoint and displays the point.

If we're still trying to "make our point" (i.e., the game is continuing from a prior roll), lines 48–58 execute. Line 50 rolls the dice again. If sumOfDice matches myPoint (line 53), line 54 sets gameStatus to Status.WON, then the loop terminates because the game is complete. If sumOfDice is SEVEN (line 56), line 57 sets gameStatus to Status.LOST, and the loop terminates because the game is complete. When the game completes, lines 61–64 display a message indicating whether the player won or lost, and the program terminates.

The program uses the various program-control mechanisms we've discussed. The Craps class uses two methods—main and rollDice (called twice from main)—and the switch, while, if...else and nested if control statements. Note also the use of multiple case labels in the switch statement to execute the same statements for sums of SEVEN and YO_LEVEN (lines 31–32) and for sums of SNAKE_EYES, TREY and BOX_CARS (lines 35–37).

Why Some Constants Are Not Defined as enum Constants

You might be wondering why we declared the sums of the dice as public final static int constants rather than as enum constants. The reason is that the program must compare the int variable sumOfDice (line 26) to these constants to determine the outcome of each roll. Suppose we declared enum Sum containing constants (e.g., Sum.SNAKE_EYES) representing the five sums used in the game, then used these constants in the switch statement (lines 29–45). Doing so would prevent us from using sumOfDice as the switch statement's controlling expression, because Java *does not allow an* int *to be compared to an enumeration constant.* To achieve the same functionality as the current program, we would have to use a variable currentSum of type Sum as the switch's controlling expression. Unfortunately, Java does not provide an easy way to convert an int value to a particular enum constant. This could be done with a separate switch statement. Clearly this would be cumbersome and not improve the program's readability (thus defeating the purpose of using an enum).

6.10 Scope of Declarations

You've seen declarations of various Java entities, such as classes, methods, variables and parameters. Declarations introduce names that can be used to refer to such Java entities. The

scope of a declaration is the portion of the program that can refer to the declared entity by its name. Such an entity is said to be "in scope" for that portion of the program. This section introduces several important scope issues.

The basic scope rules are as follows:

1. The scope of a parameter declaration is the body of the method in which the declaration appears.

2. The scope of a local-variable declaration is from the point at which the declaration appears to the end of that block.

3. The scope of a local-variable declaration that appears in the initialization section of a for statement's header is the body of the for statement and the other expressions in the header.

4. A method or field's scope is the entire body of the class. This enables non-static methods of a class to use the fields and other methods of the class.

Any block may contain variable declarations. If a local variable or parameter in a method has the same name as a field of the class, the field is "hidden" until the block terminates execution—this is called **shadowing**. In Chapter 8, we discuss how to access shadowed fields.

Error-Prevention Tip 6.2

Use different names for fields and local variables to help prevent subtle logic errors that occur when a method is called and a local variable of the method shadows a field in the class.

Figure 6.8 demonstrates scoping issues with fields and local variables. Line 7 declares and initializes the field x to 1. This field is shadowed (hidden) in any block (or method) that declares a local variable named x. Method main (lines 11–23) declares a local variable x (line 13) and initializes it to 5. This local variable's value is output to show that the field x (whose value is 1) is shadowed in main. The program declares two other methods—useLocalVariable (lines 26–35) and useField (lines 38–45)—that each take no arguments and return no results. Method main calls each method twice (lines 17–20). Method useLocalVariable declares local variable x (line 28). When useLocalVariable is first called (line 17), it creates local variable x and initializes it to 25 (line 28), outputs the value of x (lines 30–31), increments x (line 32) and outputs the value of x again (lines 33–34). When useLocalVariable is called a second time (line 19), it recreates local variable x and reinitializes it to 25, so the output of each useLocalVariable call is identical.

```
1   // Fig. 6.8: Scope.java
2   // Scope class demonstrates field and local variable scopes.
3
4   public class Scope
5   {
6      // field that is accessible to all methods of this class
7      private static int x = 1;
8
```

Fig. 6.8 | Scope class demonstrates field and local variable scopes. (Part 1 of 2.)

```
9       // method main creates and initializes local variable x
10      // and calls methods useLocalVariable and useField
11      public static void main( String[] args )
12      {
13          int x = 5; // method's local variable x shadows field x
14
15          System.out.printf( "local x in main is %d\n", x );
16
17          useLocalVariable(); // useLocalVariable has local x
18          useField(); // useField uses class Scope's field x
19          useLocalVariable(); // useLocalVariable reinitializes local x
20          useField(); // class Scope's field x retains its value
21
22          System.out.printf( "\nlocal x in main is %d\n", x );
23      } // end main
24
25      // create and initialize local variable x during each call
26      public static void useLocalVariable()
27      {
28          int x = 25; // initialized each time useLocalVariable is called
29
30          System.out.printf(
31              "\nlocal x on entering method useLocalVariable is %d\n", x );
32          ++x; // modifies this method's local variable x
33          System.out.printf(
34              "local x before exiting method useLocalVariable is %d\n", x );
35      } // end method useLocalVariable
36
37      // modify class Scope's field x during each call
38      public static void useField()
39      {
40          System.out.printf(
41              "\nfield x on entering method useField is %d\n", x );
42          x *= 10; // modifies class Scope's field x
43          System.out.printf(
44              "field x before exiting method useField is %d\n", x );
45      } // end method useField
46  } // end class Scope
```

```
local x in main is 5

local x on entering method useLocalVariable is 25
local x before exiting method useLocalVariable is 26

field x on entering method useField is 1
field x before exiting method useField is 10

local x on entering method useLocalVariable is 25
local x before exiting method useLocalVariable is 26

field x on entering method useField is 10
field x before exiting method useField is 100

local x in main is 5
```

Fig. 6.8 | Scope class demonstrates field and local variable scopes. (Part 2 of 2.)

Method useField does not declare any local variables. Therefore, when it refers to x, field x (line 7) of the class is used. When method useField is first called (line 18), it outputs the value (1) of field x (lines 40–41), multiplies the field x by 10 (line 42) and outputs the value (10) of field x again (lines 43–44) before returning. The next time method use-Field is called (line 20), the field has its modified value (10), so the method outputs 10, then 100. Finally, in method main, the program outputs the value of local variable x again (line 22) to show that none of the method calls modified main's local variable x, because the methods all referred to variables named x in other scopes.

6.11 Method Overloading

Methods of the same name can be declared in the same class, as long as they have different sets of parameters (determined by the number, types and order of the parameters)—this is called **method overloading**. When an overloaded method is called, the compiler selects the appropriate method by examining the number, types and order of the arguments in the call. Method overloading is commonly used to create several methods with the *same* name that perform the *same* or *similar* tasks, but on different types or different numbers of arguments. For example, Math methods abs, min and max (summarized in Section 6.3) are overloaded with four versions each:

1. One with two double parameters.
2. One with two float parameters.
3. One with two int parameters.
4. One with two long parameters.

Our next example demonstrates declaring and invoking overloaded methods. We demonstrate overloaded constructors in Chapter 8.

Declaring Overloaded Methods
Class MethodOverload (Fig. 6.9) includes two overloaded versions of method square—one that calculates the square of an int (and returns an int) and one that calculates the square of a double (and returns a double). Although these methods have the same name and similar parameter lists and bodies, think of them simply as *different* methods. It may help to think of the method names as "square of int" and "square of double," respectively.

```
1   // Fig. 6.9: MethodOverload.java
2   // Overloaded method declarations.
3
4   public class MethodOverload
5   {
6      // test overloaded square methods
7      public static void main( String[] args )
8      {
9         System.out.printf( "Square of integer 7 is %d\n", square( 7 ) );
10        System.out.printf( "Square of double 7.5 is %f\n", square( 7.5 ) );
11     } // end main
12
```

Fig. 6.9 | Overloaded method declarations. (Part 1 of 2.)

```
13        // square method with int argument
14        public static int square( int intValue )
15        {
16            System.out.printf( "\nCalled square with int argument: %d\n",
17                intValue );
18            return intValue * intValue;
19        } // end method square with int argument
20
21        // square method with double argument
22        public static double square( double doubleValue )
23        {
24            System.out.printf( "\nCalled square with double argument: %f\n",
25                doubleValue );
26            return doubleValue * doubleValue;
27        } // end method square with double argument
28    } // end class MethodOverload
```

```
Called square with int argument: 7
Square of integer 7 is 49

Called square with double argument: 7.500000
Square of double 7.5 is 56.250000
```

Fig. 6.9 | Overloaded method declarations. (Part 2 of 2.)

Line 9 invokes method square with the argument 7. Literal integer values are treated as type int, so the method call in line 9 invokes the version of square at lines 14–19 that specifies an int parameter. Similarly, line 10 invokes method square with the argument 7.5. Literal floating-point values are treated as type double, so the method call in line 10 invokes the version of square at lines 22–27 that specifies a double parameter. Each method first outputs a line of text to prove that the proper method was called in each case. The values in lines 10 and 24 are displayed with the format specifier %f. We did not specify a precision in either case. By default, floating-point values are displayed with six digits of precision if the precision is not specified in the format specifier.

Distinguishing Between Overloaded Methods

The compiler distinguishes overloaded methods by their **signature**—a combination of the method's name and the number, types and order of its parameters. If the compiler looked only at method names during compilation, the code in Fig. 6.9 would be ambiguous—the compiler would not know how to distinguish between the two square methods (lines 14–19 and 22–27). Internally, the compiler uses longer method names that include the original method name, the types of each parameter and the exact order of the parameters to determine whether the methods in a class are unique in that class.

For example, in Fig. 6.9, the compiler might use the logical name "square of int" for the square method that specifies an int parameter and "square of double" for the square method that specifies a double parameter (the actual names the compiler uses are messier). If method1's declaration begins as

```
void method1( int a, float b )
```

then the compiler might use the logical name "method1 of int and float." If the parameters are specified as

```
void method1( float a, int b )
```

then the compiler might use the logical name "method1 of float and int." The *order* of the parameter types is important—the compiler considers the preceding two method1 headers to be distinct.

Return Types of Overloaded Methods

In discussing the logical names of methods used by the compiler, we did not mention the return types of the methods. *Method calls cannot be distinguished by return type.* If you had overloaded methods that differed only by their return types and you called one of the methods in a standalone statement as in:

```
square( 2 );
```

the compiler would *not* be able to determine the version of the method to call, because the return value is ignored. When two methods have the same signature and different return types, the compiler issues an error message indicating that the method is already defined in the class. Overloaded methods *can* have different return types if the methods have different parameter lists. Also, overloaded methods need *not* have the same number of parameters.

Common Programming Error 6.7
Declaring overloaded methods with identical parameter lists is a compilation error regardless of whether the return types are different.

6.12 Wrap-Up

In this chapter, you learned more about method declarations. You also learned the difference between non-static and static methods and how to call static methods by preceding the method name with the name of the class in which it appears and the dot (.) separator. You learned how to use operators + and += to perform string concatenations. We also discussed Java's promotion rules for converting implicitly between primitive types and how to perform explicit conversions with cast operators. Next, you learned about some of the commonly used packages in the Java API.

You saw how to declare named constants using both enum types and public static final variables. You used class Random to generate random numbers for simulations. You learned about the scope of fields and local variables in a class. Finally, you learned that multiple methods in one class can be overloaded by providing methods with the same name and different signatures. Such methods can be used to perform the same or similar tasks using different types or different numbers of parameters.

In Chapter 7, we discuss how to maintain lists and tables of data in arrays. You'll see a more elegant implementation of the die-rolling application and two enhanced versions of our GradeBook case study that you studied in Chapters 3–5. You'll also learn how to access an application's command-line arguments that are passed to method main when an application begins execution.

7

Arrays and ArrayLists

Begin at the beginning, …
and go on till you come to
the end: then stop.
—Lewis Carroll

Now go, write it before
them in a table, and note it
in a book.
—Isaiah 30:8

To go beyond is as wrong as
to fall short.
—Confucius

Objectives

In this chapter you'll learn:

- To use arrays to store data in and retrieve data from lists and tables of values.

- To declare arrays, initialize arrays and refer to individual elements of arrays.

- To iterate through arrays with the enhanced **for** statement.

- To pass arrays to methods.

- To declare and manipulate multidimensional arrays.

- To use variable-length argument lists.

- To read command-line arguments into a program.

- To perform common array manipulations with the methods of class **Arrays**.

- To use class **ArrayList** to manipulate a dynamically resizable array-like data structure.

7.1 Introduction

Arrays are data structures consisting of related data items of the same type. Arrays make it convenient to process related groups of values. Arrays remain the same length once they're created, although an array variable may be reassigned such that it refers to a new array of a different length.

After discussing how arrays are declared, created and initialized, we present practical examples that demonstrate common array manipulations. We introduce Java's exception-handling mechanism and use it to allow a program to continue executing when the program attempts to access an array element that does not exist. We also present a case study that examines how arrays can help simulate the shuffling and dealing of playing cards in a card-game application. We introduce Java's enhanced for statement, which allows a program to access the data in an array more easily than does the counter-controlled for statement presented in Section 5.3. We enhance the GradeBook case study from Chapters 3–5. In particular, we use arrays to enable the class to maintain a set of grades *in memory* and analyze student grades from multiple exams. We show how to use variable-length argument lists to create methods that can be called with varying numbers of arguments, and we demonstrate how to process command-line arguments in method main. Next, we present some common array manipulations with static methods of class Arrays from the java.util package.

Although commonly used, arrays have limited capabilities. For instance, you must specify an array's size, and if at execution time you wish to modify that size, you must do so manually by creating a new array. At the end of this chapter, we introduce one of Java's prebuilt data structures from the Java API's collection classes. These offer greater capabilities than traditional arrays. They're reusable, reliable, powerful and efficient. We focus on the ArrayList collection. ArrayLists are similar to arrays but provide additional functionality, such as **dynamic resizing**—they automatically increase their size at execution time to accommodate additional elements.

7.2 Arrays

An array is a group of variables (called elements or components) containing values that all have the same type. Arrays are *objects*, so they're considered reference types. As you'll soon see, what we typically think of as an array is actually a reference to an array object in memory. The *elements* of an array can be either primitive types or reference types (including arrays, as we'll see in Section 7.9). To refer to a particular element in an array, we specify the name of the reference to the array and the *position number* of the element in the array. The position number of the element is called the element's **index** or **subscript**.

Figure 7.1 shows a logical representation of an integer array called c. This array contains 12 elements. A program refers to any one of these elements with an **array-access expression** that includes the name of the array followed by the index of the particular element in **square brackets ([ ])**. The first element in every array has **index zero** and is sometimes called the **zeroth element**. Thus, the elements of array c are c[0], c[1], c[2] and so on. The highest index in array c is 11, which is 1 less than 12—the number of elements in the array. Array names follow the same conventions as other variable names.

c[0]	−45
c[1]	6
c[2]	0
c[3]	72
c[4]	1543
c[5]	−89
c[6]	0
c[7]	62
c[8]	−3
c[9]	1
c[10]	6453
c[11]	78

Name of array (c) →

Index (or subscript) of the element in array c

Fig. 7.1 | A 12-element array.

An index must be a nonnegative integer. A program can use an expression as an index. For example, if we assume that variable a is 5 and variable b is 6, then the statement

```
c[ a + b ] += 2;
```

adds 2 to array element c[11]. An indexed array name is an array-access expression, which can be used on the left side of an assignment to place a new value into an array element.

Common Programming Error 7.1

An index must be an int value or a value of a type that can be promoted to int—namely, byte, short or char, but not long; otherwise, a compilation error occurs.

Let's examine array c in Fig. 7.1 more closely. The **name** of the array is c. Every array object knows its own length and stores it in a **length instance variable**. The expression c.length accesses array c's length field to determine the length of the array. Even though the length instance variable of an array is public, it cannot be changed because it's a final variable. This array's 12 elements are referred to as c[0], c[1], c[2], ..., c[11]. The value of c[0] is -45, the value of c[1] is 6, the value of c[2] is 0, the value of c[7] is 62 and the value of c[11] is 78. To calculate the sum of the values contained in the first three elements of array c and store the result in variable sum, we would write

```
sum = c[ 0 ] + c[ 1 ] + c[ 2 ];
```

To divide the value of c[6] by 2 and assign the result to the variable x, we would write

```
x = c[ 6 ] / 2;
```

7.3 Declaring and Creating Arrays

Array objects occupy space in memory. Like other objects, arrays are created with keyword new. To create an array object, you specify the type of the array elements and the number of elements as part of an **array-creation expression** that uses keyword new. Such an expression returns a reference that can be stored in an array variable. The following declaration and array-creation expression create an array object containing 12 int elements and store the array's reference in array variable c:

```
int[] c = new int[ 12 ];
```

This expression can be used to create the array shown in Fig. 7.1. When an array is created, each element of the array receives a default value—zero for the numeric primitive-type elements, false for boolean elements and null for references. As you'll soon see, you can provide nondefault initial element values when you create an array.

Creating the array in Fig. 7.1 can also be performed in two steps as follows:

```
int[] c; // declare the array variable
c = new int[ 12 ]; // create the array; assign to array variable
```

In the declaration, the square brackets following the type indicate that c is a variable that will refer to an array (i.e., the variable will store an array reference). In the assignment statement, the array variable c receives the reference to a new array of 12 int elements.

Common Programming Error 7.2

In an array declaration, specifying the number of elements in the square brackets of the declaration (e.g., int[12] c;) is a syntax error.

A program can create several arrays in a single declaration. The following declaration reserves 100 elements for b and 27 elements for x:

```
String[] b = new String[ 100 ], x = new String[ 27 ];
```

When the type of the array and the square brackets are combined at the beginning of the declaration, all the identifiers in the declaration are array variables. In this case, variables b and x refer to String arrays. For readability, we prefer to declare only one variable per declaration. The preceding declaration is equivalent to:

```
String[] b = new String[ 100 ]; // create array b
String[] x = new String[ 27 ]; // create array x
```

When only one variable is declared in each declaration, the square brackets can be placed either after the type or after the array variable name, as in:

```
String b[] = new String[ 100 ]; // create array b
String x[] = new String[ 27 ]; // create array x
```

Common Programming Error 7.3

Declaring multiple array variables in a single declaration can lead to subtle errors. Consider the declaration int[] a, b, c;. *If a, b and c should be declared as array variables, then this declaration is correct—placing square brackets directly following the type indicates that all the identifiers in the declaration are array variables. However, if only a is intended to be an array variable, and b and c are intended to be individual int variables, then this declaration is incorrect—the declaration* int a[], b, c; *would achieve the desired result.*

A program can declare arrays of any type. Every element of a primitive-type array contains a value of the array's declared element type. Similarly, in an array of a reference type, every element is a reference to an object of the array's declared element type. For example, every element of an int array is an int value, and every element of a String array is a reference to a String object.

7.4 Examples Using Arrays

This section presents several examples that demonstrate declaring arrays, creating arrays, initializing arrays and manipulating array elements.

Creating and Initializing an Array

The application of Fig. 7.2 uses keyword new to create an array of 10 int elements, which are initially zero (the default for int variables). Line 8 declares array—a reference capable of referring to an array of int elements. Line 10 creates the array object and assigns its reference to variable array. Line 12 outputs the column headings. The first column contains the index (0–9) of each array element, and the second column contains the default value (0) of each array element.

The for statement in lines 15–16 outputs the index number (represented by counter) and the value of each array element (represented by array[counter]). The loop-control variable counter is initially 0—index values start at 0, so using **zero-based counting** allows

```java
1   // Fig. 7.2: InitArray.java
2   // Initializing the elements of an array to default values of zero.
3
4   public class InitArray
5   {
6      public static void main( String[] args )
7      {
8         int[] array; // declare array named array
9
10        array = new int[ 10 ]; // create the array object
11
12        System.out.printf( "%s%8s\n", "Index", "Value" ); // column headings
13
14        // output each array element's value
15        for ( int counter = 0; counter < array.length; counter++ )
16           System.out.printf( "%5d%8d\n", counter, array[ counter ] );
17     } // end main
18  } // end class InitArray
```

Fig. 7.2 | Initializing the elements of an array to default values of zero. (Part 1 of 2.)

```
Index    Value
    0        0
    1        0
    2        0
    3        0
    4        0
    5        0
    6        0
    7        0
    8        0
    9        0
```

Fig. 7.2 | Initializing the elements of an array to default values of zero. (Part 2 of 2.)

the loop to access every element of the array. The for's loop-continuation condition uses the expression array.length (line 15) to determine the length of the array. In this example, the length of the array is 10, so the loop continues executing as long as the value of control variable counter is less than 10. The highest index value of a 10-element array is 9, so using the less-than operator in the loop-continuation condition guarantees that the loop does not attempt to access an element *beyond* the end of the array (i.e., during the final iteration of the loop, counter is 9). We'll soon see what Java does when it encounters such an *out-of-range index* at execution time.

Using an Array Initializer

You can create an array and initialize its elements with an **array initializer**—a comma-separated list of expressions (called an **initializer list**) enclosed in braces. In this case, the array length is determined by the number of elements in the initializer list. For example,

```java
int[] n = { 10, 20, 30, 40, 50 };
```

creates a five-element array with index values 0–4. Element n[0] is initialized to 10, n[1] is initialized to 20, and so on. When the compiler encounters an array declaration that includes an initializer list, it counts the number of initializers in the list to determine the size of the array, then sets up the appropriate new operation "behind the scenes."

The application in Fig. 7.3 initializes an integer array with 10 values (line 9) and displays the array in tabular format. The code for displaying the array elements (lines 14–15) is identical to that in Fig. 7.2 (lines 15–16).

```java
 1   // Fig. 7.3: InitArray.java
 2   // Initializing the elements of an array with an array initializer.
 3
 4   public class InitArray
 5   {
 6      public static void main( String[] args )
 7      {
 8         // initializer list specifies the value for each element
 9         int[] array = { 32, 27, 64, 18, 95, 14, 90, 70, 60, 37 };
10
11         System.out.printf( "%s%8s\n", "Index", "Value" ); // column headings
```

Fig. 7.3 | Initializing the elements of an array with an array initializer. (Part 1 of 2.)

```
12
13          // output each array element's value
14          for ( int counter = 0; counter < array.length; counter++ )
15              System.out.printf( "%5d%8d\n", counter, array[ counter ] );
16      } // end main
17  } // end class InitArray
```

```
Index   Value
   0      32
   1      27
   2      64
   3      18
   4      95
   5      14
   6      90
   7      70
   8      60
   9      37
```

Fig. 7.3 | Initializing the elements of an array with an array initializer. (Part 2 of 2.)

Calculating the Values to Store in an Array

The application in Fig. 7.4 creates a 10-element array and assigns to each element one of the even integers from 2 to 20 (2, 4, 6, ..., 20). Then the application displays the array in tabular format. The for statement at lines 12–13 calculates an array element's value by multiplying the current value of the control variable counter by 2, then adding 2.

Line 8 uses the modifier final to declare the constant variable ARRAY_LENGTH with the value 10. Constant variables must be initialized before they're used and cannot be modified thereafter. If you attempt to *modify* a final variable after it's initialized in its declaration, the compiler issues an error message like

    cannot assign a value to final variable *variableName*

If an attempt is made to access the value of a final variable before it's initialized, the compiler issues an error message like

    variable *variableName* might not have been initialized

Good Programming Practice 7.1

*Constant variables also are called **named constants**. They often make programs more readable than programs that use literal values (e.g., 10)—a named constant such as ARRAY_LENGTH clearly indicates its purpose, whereas a literal value could have different meanings based on its context.*

```
1   // Fig. 7.4: InitArray.java
2   // Calculating the values to be placed into the elements of an array.
3
4   public class InitArray
5   {
```

Fig. 7.4 | Calculating the values to be placed into the elements of an array. (Part 1 of 2.)

```
6        public static void main( String[] args )
7        {
8           final int ARRAY_LENGTH = 10; // declare constant
9           int[] array = new int[ ARRAY_LENGTH ]; // create array
10
11          // calculate value for each array element
12          for ( int counter = 0; counter < array.length; counter++ )
13             array[ counter ] = 2 + 2 * counter;
14
15          System.out.printf( "%s%8s\n", "Index", "Value" ); // column headings
16
17          // output each array element's value
18          for ( int counter = 0; counter < array.length; counter++ )
19             System.out.printf( "%5d%8d\n", counter, array[ counter ] );
20       } // end main
21    } // end class InitArray
```

```
Index   Value
    0       2
    1       4
    2       6
    3       8
    4      10
    5      12
    6      14
    7      16
    8      18
    9      20
```

Fig. 7.4 | Calculating the values to be placed into the elements of an array. (Part 2 of 2.)

Summing the Elements of an Array

Often, an array's elements represent a series of values to be used in a calculation. Figure 7.5 sums the values contained in a 10-element integer array. The program declares, creates and initializes the array at line 8. The for statement performs the calculations.

```
1    // Fig. 7.5: SumArray.java
2    // Computing the sum of the elements of an array.
3
4    public class SumArray
5    {
6       public static void main( String[] args )
7       {
8          int[] array = { 87, 68, 94, 100, 83, 78, 85, 91, 76, 87 };
9          int total = 0;
10
11         // add each element's value to total
12         for ( int counter = 0; counter < array.length; counter++ )
13            total += array[ counter ];
14
```

Fig. 7.5 | Computing the sum of the elements of an array. (Part 1 of 2.)

```
15            System.out.printf( "Total of array elements: %d\n", total );
16       } // end main
17    } // end class SumArray
```

```
Total of array elements: 849
```

Fig. 7.5 | Computing the sum of the elements of an array. (Part 2 of 2.)

Using Bar Charts to Display Array Data Graphically

Many programs present data to users in a graphical manner. For example, numeric values are often displayed as bars in a bar chart. In such a chart, longer bars represent proportionally larger numeric values. One simple way to display numeric data graphically is with a bar chart that shows each numeric value as a bar of asterisks (*).

Professors often like to examine the distribution of grades on an exam. A professor might graph the number of grades in each of several categories to visualize the grade distribution. Suppose the grades on an exam were 87, 68, 94, 100, 83, 78, 85, 91, 76 and 87. They include one grade of 100, two grades in the 90s, four grades in the 80s, two grades in the 70s, one grade in the 60s and no grades below 60. Our next application (Fig. 7.6) stores this grade distribution data in an array of 11 elements, each corresponding to a category of grades. For example, array[0] indicates the number of grades in the range 0–9, array[7] the number of grades in the range 70–79 and array[10] the number of 100 grades. The GradeBook classes later in the chapter (Figs. 7.14 and 7.18) contain code that calculates these grade frequencies based on a set of grades. For now, we manually create the array with the given grade frequencies.

```
1    // Fig. 7.6: BarChart.java
2    // Bar chart printing program.
3
4    public class BarChart
5    {
6       public static void main( String[] args )
7       {
8          int[] array = { 0, 0, 0, 0, 0, 0, 1, 2, 4, 2, 1 };
9
10         System.out.println( "Grade distribution:" );
11
12         // for each array element, output a bar of the chart
13         for ( int counter = 0; counter < array.length; counter++ )
14         {
15            // output bar label ( "00-09: ", ..., "90-99: ", "100: " )
16            if ( counter == 10 )
17               System.out.printf( "%5d: ", 100 );
18            else
19               System.out.printf( "%02d-%02d: ",
20                  counter * 10, counter * 10 + 9 );
21
```

Fig. 7.6 | Bar chart printing program. (Part 1 of 2.)

```
22              // print bar of asterisks
23              for ( int stars = 0; stars < array[ counter ]; stars++ )
24                 System.out.print( "*" );
25
26              System.out.println(); // start a new line of output
27           } // end outer for
28        } // end main
29     } // end class BarChart
```

```
Grade distribution:
00-09:
10-19:
20-29:
30-39:
40-49:
50-59:
60-69: *
70-79: **
80-89: ****
90-99: **
  100: *
```

Fig. 7.6 | Bar chart printing program. (Part 2 of 2.)

The application reads the numbers from the array and graphs the information as a bar chart. It displays each grade range followed by a bar of asterisks indicating the number of grades in that range. To label each bar, lines 16–20 output a grade range (e.g., "70-79: ") based on the current value of counter. When counter is 10, line 17 outputs 100 with a field width of 5, followed by a colon and a space, to align the label "100: " with the other bar labels. The nested for statement (lines 23–24) outputs the bars. Note the loop-continuation condition at line 23 (stars < array[counter]). Each time the program reaches the inner for, the loop counts from 0 up to array[counter], thus using a value in array to determine the number of asterisks to display. In this example, no students received a grade below 60, so array[0]–array[5] contain zeroes, and no asterisks are displayed next to the first six grade ranges. In line 19, the format specifier %02d indicates that an int value should be formatted as a field of two digits. The **0 flag** in the format specifier displays a leading 0 for values with fewer digits than the field width (2).

Using the Elements of an Array as Counters

Sometimes, programs use counter variables to summarize data, such as the results of a survey. In Fig. 6.6, we used separate counters in our die-rolling program to track the number of occurrences of each side of a six-sided die as the program rolled the die 6,000,000 times. An array version of this application is shown in Fig. 7.7.

```
1   // Fig. 7.7: RollDie.java
2   // Die-rolling program using arrays instead of switch.
3   import java.util.Random;
4
```

Fig. 7.7 | Die-rolling program using arrays instead of switch. (Part 1 of 2.)

```
5    public class RollDie
6    {
7       public static void main( String[] args )
8       {
9          Random randomNumbers = new Random(); // random number generator
10         int[] frequency = new int[ 7 ]; // array of frequency counters
11
12         // roll die 6,000,000 times; use die value as frequency index
13         for ( int roll = 1; roll <= 6000000; roll++ )
14            ++frequency[ 1 + randomNumbers.nextInt( 6 ) ];
15
16         System.out.printf( "%s%10s\n", "Face", "Frequency" );
17
18         // output each array element's value
19         for ( int face = 1; face < frequency.length; face++ )
20            System.out.printf( "%4d%10d\n", face, frequency[ face ] );
21      } // end main
22   } // end class RollDie
```

```
Face Frequency
   1    999690
   2    999512
   3   1000575
   4    999815
   5    999781
   6   1000627
```

Fig. 7.7 | Die-rolling program using arrays instead of `switch`. (Part 2 of 2.)

Figure 7.7 uses the array `frequency` (line 10) to count the occurrences of each side of the die. *The single statement in line 14 of this program replaces lines 23–46 of Fig. 6.6.* Line 14 uses the random value to determine which `frequency` element to increment during each iteration of the loop. The calculation in line 14 produces random numbers from 1 to 6, so the array `frequency` must be large enough to store six counters. However, we use a seven-element array in which we ignore `frequency[0]`—it's more logical to have the face value 1 increment `frequency[1]` than `frequency[0]`. Thus, each face value is used as an index for array `frequency`. In line 14, the calculation inside the square brackets evaluates first to determine which element of the array to increment, then the ++ operator adds one to that element. We also replaced lines 50–52 from Fig. 6.6 by looping through array `frequency` to output the results (lines 19–20).

Using Arrays to Analyze Survey Results

Our next example uses arrays to summarize data collected in a survey. Consider the following problem statement:

> *Twenty students were asked to rate on a scale of 1 to 5 the quality of the food in the student cafeteria, with 1 being "awful" and 5 being "excellent." Place the 20 responses in an integer array and determine the frequency of each rating.*

This is a typical array-processing application (Fig. 7.8). We wish to summarize the number of responses of each type (that is, 1–5). Array `responses` (lines 9–10) is a 20-element integer array containing the students' survey responses. The last value in the array is intentionally an incorrect response (14). When a Java program executes, array element indices are checked for validity—all indices must be greater than or equal to 0 and less than the array's length. Any attempt to access an element outside that range results in a runtime error that's known as an ArrayIndexOutOfBoundsException. At the end of this section, we'll discuss the invalid response value, demonstrate array **bounds checking** and introduce Java's exception-handling mechanism, which can be used to detect and handle an ArrayIndexOutOfBoundsException.

```java
 1  // Fig. 7.8: StudentPoll.java
 2  // Poll analysis program.
 3
 4  public class StudentPoll
 5  {
 6     public static void main( String[] args )
 7     {
 8        // student response array (more typically, input at runtime)
 9        int[] responses = { 1, 2, 5, 4, 3, 5, 2, 1, 3, 3, 1, 4, 3, 3, 3,
10           2, 3, 3, 2, 14 };
11        int[] frequency = new int[ 6 ]; // array of frequency counters
12
13        // for each answer, select responses element and use that value
14        // as frequency index to determine element to increment
15        for ( int answer = 0; answer < responses.length; answer++ )
16        {
17           try
18           {
19              ++frequency[ responses[ answer ] ];
20           } // end try
21           catch ( ArrayIndexOutOfBoundsException e )
22           {
23              System.out.println( e );
24              System.out.printf( "   responses[%d] = %d\n\n",
25                 answer, responses[ answer ] );
26           } // end catch
27        } // end for
28
29        System.out.printf( "%s%10s\n", "Rating", "Frequency" );
30
31        // output each array element's value
32        for ( int rating = 1; rating < frequency.length; rating++ )
33           System.out.printf( "%6d%10d\n", rating, frequency[ rating ] );
34     } // end main
35  } // end class StudentPoll
```

```
java.lang.ArrayIndexOutOfBoundsException: 14
   responses[19] = 14

Rating Frequency
     1        3
     2        4
     3        8
     4        2
     5        2
```

Fig. 7.8 | Poll analysis program.

The *frequency* Array

We use the *six-element* array frequency (line 11) to count the number of occurrences of each response. Each element is used as a counter for one of the possible types of survey responses—frequency[1] counts the number of students who rated the food as 1, frequency[2] counts the number of students who rated the food as 2, and so on.

Summarizing the Results

The for statement (lines 15–27) reads the responses from the array responses one at a time and increments one of the counters frequency[1] to frequency[5]; we ignore frequency[0] because the survey responses are limited to the range 1–5. The key statement in the loop appears in line 19. This statement increments the appropriate frequency counter as determined by the value of responses[answer].

Let's step through the first few iterations of the for statement:

- When the counter answer is 0, responses[answer] is the value of responses[0] (that is, 1—see line 9). In this case, frequency[responses[answer]] is interpreted as frequency[1], and the counter frequency[1] is incremented by one. To evaluate the expression, we begin with the value in the *innermost* set of brackets (answer, currently 0). The value of answer is plugged into the expression, and the next set of brackets (responses[answer]) is evaluated. That value is used as the index for the frequency array to determine which counter to increment (in this case, frequency[1]).

- The next time through the loop answer is 1, responses[answer] is the value of responses[1] (that is, 2—see line 9), so frequency[responses[answer]] is interpreted as frequency[2], causing frequency[2] to be incremented.

- When answer is 2, responses[answer] is the value of responses[2] (that is, 5—see line 9), so frequency[responses[answer]] is interpreted as frequency[5], causing frequency[5] to be incremented, and so on.

Regardless of the number of responses processed in the survey, only a six-element array (in which we ignore element zero) is required to summarize the results, because all the correct response values are between 1 and 5, and the index values for a six-element array are 0–5. In the program's output, the Frequency column summarizes only 19 of the 20 values in the responses array—the last element of the array responses contains an incorrect response that was not counted.

Exception Handling: Processing the Incorrect Response

An **exception** indicates a problem that occurs while a program executes. The name "exception" suggests that the problem occurs infrequently—if the "rule" is that a statement normally executes correctly, then the problem represents the "exception to the rule." **Exception handling** (introduced here and explained in detail in Chapter 11) enables you to create **fault-tolerant programs** that can resolve (or handle) exceptions. In many cases, this allows a program to continue executing as if no problems were encountered. For example, the StudentPoll application still displays results (Fig. 7.8), even though one of the responses was out of range. More severe problems might prevent a program from continuing normal execution, instead requiring the program to notify the user of the problem, then terminate. When the JVM or a method detects a problem, such as an invalid array index or an invalid method argument, it **throws** an exception—that is, an exception occurs.

The *try* Statement

To handle an exception, place any code that might throw an exception in a **try statement** (lines 17–26). The **try block** (lines 17–20) contains the code that might *throw* an exception, and the **catch block** (lines 21–26) contains the code that *handles* the exception if one occurs. You can have many catch blocks to handle different types of exceptions that might be thrown in the corresponding try block. When line 19 correctly increments an element of the frequency array, lines 21–26 are ignored. The braces that delimit the bodies of the try and catch blocks are required.

Executing the *catch* Block

When the program encounters the responses array value 14, it attempts to add 1 to frequency[14], which is *outside* the array's bounds—it has only six elements. Because array bounds checking is performed at execution time, the JVM generates an exception—specifically line 19 throws an **ArrayIndexOutOfBoundsException** to notify the program of this problem. At this point the try block terminates and the catch block begins executing—if you declared any variables in the try block, they're now out of scope and are not accessible in the catch block. The catch block declares a type (ArrayIndexOutOfBoundsException) and an exception parameter (e) and can handle exceptions of the specified type. In the catch block, you can use the parameter's identifier to interact with a caught exception object.

Error-Prevention Tip 7.1

When writing code to access an array element, ensure that the array index remains greater than or equal to 0 and less than the length of the array. This helps prevent ArrayIndex-OutOfBoundsException *in your program.*

toString Method of the Exception Parameter

When lines 21–26 *catch* the exception, the program displays a message indicating the problem that occurred. Line 23 implicitly calls the exception object's toString method to get the error message that is stored in the exception object and display it. Once the message is displayed in this example, the exception is considered handled and the program continues with the next statement after the catch block's closing brace. In this example, the end of the for statement is reached (line 27), so the program continues with the increment of the control variable in line 15.

7.5 Case Study: Card Shuffling and Dealing Simulation

So far we've focused on primitive-type arrays. Recall from Section 7.2 that the elements of an array can be either primitive types or reference types. This section uses random-number generation and an array of reference-type elements, namely objects representing playing cards, to develop a class that simulates card shuffling and dealing. This class can then be used to implement applications that play specific card games.

We first develop class Card (Fig. 7.9), which represents a playing card that has a face (e.g., "Ace", "Deuce", "Three", ..., "Jack", "Queen", "King") and a suit (e.g., "Hearts", "Diamonds", "Clubs", "Spades"). Next, we develop class DeckOfCards (Fig. 7.10), which creates a deck of 52 Cards. We then build a test application (Fig. 7.11) that demonstrates class DeckOfCards's card shuffling and dealing capabilities.

*Class **Card***

Class Card (Fig. 7.9) contains two String instance variables—face and suit—that are
used to store references to the face name and suit name for a specific Card. The constructor
for the class (lines 10–14) receives two Strings that it uses to initialize face and suit.
Method toString (lines 17–20) creates a String consisting of the face of the card, the
String " of " and the suit of the card. Card's toString method can be invoked explicitly
to obtain a string representation of a Card object (e.g., "Ace of Spades"). The toString
method of an object is called *implicitly* when the object is used where a String is expected
(e.g., when printf outputs the object as a String using the %s format specifier or when
the object is concatenated to a String using the + operator). For this behavior to occur,
toString must be declared with the header shown in Fig. 7.9.

```
1   // Fig. 7.9: Card.java
2   // Card class represents a playing card.
3
4   public class Card
5   {
6      private String face; // face of card ("Ace", "Deuce", ...)
7      private String suit; // suit of card ("Hearts", "Diamonds", ...)
8
9      // two-argument constructor initializes card's face and suit
10     public Card( String cardFace, String cardSuit )
11     {
12        face = cardFace; // initialize face of card
13        suit = cardSuit; // initialize suit of card
14     } // end two-argument Card constructor
15
16     // return String representation of Card
17     public String toString()
18     {
19        return face + " of " + suit;
20     } // end method toString
21  } // end class Card
```

Fig. 7.9 | Card class represents a playing card.

*Class **DeckOfCards***

Class DeckOfCards (Fig. 7.10) declares as an instance variable a Card array named deck
(line 7). An array of a reference type is declared like any other array. Class DeckOfCards
also declares an integer instance variable currentCard (line 8) representing the next Card
to be dealt from the deck array and a named constant NUMBER_OF_CARDS (line 9) indicating
the number of Cards in the deck (52).

```
1   // Fig. 7.10: DeckOfCards.java
2   // DeckOfCards class represents a deck of playing cards.
3   import java.util.Random;
4
```

Fig. 7.10 | DeckOfCards class represents a deck of playing cards. (Part 1 of 2.)

```
 5   public class DeckOfCards
 6   {
 7      private Card[] deck; // array of Card objects
 8      private int currentCard; // index of next Card to be dealt (0-51)
 9      private static final int NUMBER_OF_CARDS = 52; // constant # of Cards
10      // random number generator
11      private static final Random randomNumbers = new Random();
12
13      // constructor fills deck of Cards
14      public DeckOfCards()
15      {
16         String[] faces = { "Ace", "Deuce", "Three", "Four", "Five", "Six",
17            "Seven", "Eight", "Nine", "Ten", "Jack", "Queen", "King" };
18         String[] suits = { "Hearts", "Diamonds", "Clubs", "Spades" };
19
20         deck = new Card[ NUMBER_OF_CARDS ]; // create array of Card objects
21         currentCard = 0; // set currentCard so first Card dealt is deck[ 0 ]
22
23         // populate deck with Card objects
24         for ( int count = 0; count < deck.length; count++ )
25            deck[ count ] =
26               new Card( faces[ count % 13 ], suits[ count / 13 ] );
27      } // end DeckOfCards constructor
28
29      // shuffle deck of Cards with one-pass algorithm
30      public void shuffle()
31      {
32         // after shuffling, dealing should start at deck[ 0 ] again
33         currentCard = 0; // reinitialize currentCard
34
35         // for each Card, pick another random Card (0-51) and swap them
36         for ( int first = 0; first < deck.length; first++ )
37         {
38            // select a random number between 0 and 51
39            int second = randomNumbers.nextInt( NUMBER_OF_CARDS );
40
41            // swap current Card with randomly selected Card
42            Card temp = deck[ first ];
43            deck[ first ] = deck[ second ];
44            deck[ second ] = temp;
45         } // end for
46      } // end method shuffle
47
48      // deal one Card
49      public Card dealCard()
50      {
51         // determine whether Cards remain to be dealt
52         if ( currentCard < deck.length )
53            return deck[ currentCard++ ]; // return current Card in array
54         else
55            return null; // return null to indicate that all Cards were dealt
56      } // end method dealCard
57   } // end class DeckOfCards
```

Fig. 7.10 | DeckOfCards class represents a deck of playing cards. (Part 2 of 2.)

DeckOfCards *Constructor*

The class's constructor instantiates the deck array (line 20) with NUMBER_OF_CARDS (52) elements. The elements of deck are null by default, so the constructor uses a for statement (lines 24–26) to fill the deck with Cards. The loop initializes control variable count to 0 and loops while count is less than deck.length, causing count to take on each integer value from 0 to 51 (the indices of the deck array). Each Card is instantiated and initialized with two Strings—one from the faces array (which contains the Strings "Ace" through "King") and one from the suits array (which contains the Strings "Hearts", "Diamonds", "Clubs" and "Spades"). The calculation count % 13 always results in a value from 0 to 12 (the 13 indices of the faces array in lines 16–17), and the calculation count / 13 always results in a value from 0 to 3 (the four indices of the suits array in line 18). When the deck array is initialized, it contains the Cards with faces "Ace" through "King" in order for each suit ("Hearts" then "Diamonds" then "Clubs" then "Spades"). We use arrays of Strings to represent the faces and suits in this example.

DeckOfCards *Method* shuffle

Method shuffle (lines 30–46) shuffles the Cards in the deck. The method loops through all 52 Cards (array indices 0 to 51). For each Card, a number between 0 and 51 is picked randomly to select another Card. Next, the current Card object and the randomly selected Card object are swapped in the array. This exchange is performed by the three assignments in lines 42–44. The extra variable temp temporarily stores one of the two Card objects being swapped. The swap cannot be performed with only the two statements

```
deck[ first ] = deck[ second ];
deck[ second ] = deck[ first ];
```

If deck[first] is the "Ace" of "Spades" and deck[second] is the "Queen" of "Hearts", after the first assignment, both array elements contain the "Queen" of "Hearts" and the "Ace" of "Spades" is lost—hence, the extra variable temp is needed. After the for loop terminates, the Card objects are randomly ordered. A total of only 52 swaps are made in a single pass of the entire array, and the array of Card objects is shuffled!

[*Note:* It's recommended that you use a so-called unbiased shuffling algorithm for real card games. Such an algorithm ensures that all possible shuffled card sequences are equally likely to occur. A popular unbiased shuffling algorithm is the Fisher-Yates algorithm.]

DeckOfCards *Method* dealCard

Method dealCard (lines 49–56) deals one Card in the array. Recall that currentCard indicates the index of the next Card to be dealt (i.e., the Card at the top of the deck). Thus, line 52 compares currentCard to the length of the deck array. If the deck is not empty (i.e., currentCard is less than 52), line 53 returns the "top" Card and postincrements currentCard to prepare for the next call to dealCard—otherwise, null is returned. Recall from Chapter 3 that null represents a "reference to nothing."

Shuffling and Dealing Cards

Figure 7.11 demonstrates class DeckOfCards (Fig. 7.10). Line 9 creates a DeckOfCards object named myDeckOfCards. The DeckOfCards constructor creates the deck with the 52 Card objects in order by suit and face. Line 10 invokes myDeckOfCards's shuffle method to rearrange the Card objects. Lines 13–20 deal all 52 Cards and print them in four columns of 13 Cards each. Line 16 deals one Card object by invoking myDeckOfCards's deal-Card method, then displays the Card left justified in a field of 19 characters. When a Card is output as a String, the Card's toString method (lines 17–20 of Fig. 7.9) is implicitly invoked. Lines 18–19 start a new line after every four Cards.

```java
1   // Fig. 7.11: DeckOfCardsTest.java
2   // Card shuffling and dealing.
3
4   public class DeckOfCardsTest
5   {
6      // execute application
7      public static void main( String[] args )
8      {
9         DeckOfCards myDeckOfCards = new DeckOfCards();
10        myDeckOfCards.shuffle(); // place Cards in random order
11
12        // print all 52 Cards in the order in which they are dealt
13        for ( int i = 1; i <= 52; i++ )
14        {
15           // deal and display a Card
16           System.out.printf( "%-19s", myDeckOfCards.dealCard() );
17
18           if ( i % 4 == 0 ) // output a newline after every fourth card
19              System.out.println();
20        } // end for
21     } // end main
22  } // end class DeckOfCardsTest
```

Six of Spades	Eight of Spades	Six of Clubs	Nine of Hearts
Queen of Hearts	Seven of Clubs	Nine of Spades	King of Hearts
Three of Diamonds	Deuce of Clubs	Ace of Hearts	Ten of Spades
Four of Spades	Ace of Clubs	Seven of Diamonds	Four of Hearts
Three of Clubs	Deuce of Hearts	Five of Spades	Jack of Diamonds
King of Clubs	Ten of Hearts	Three of Hearts	Six of Diamonds
Queen of Clubs	Eight of Diamonds	Deuce of Diamonds	Ten of Diamonds
Three of Spades	King of Diamonds	Nine of Clubs	Six of Hearts
Ace of Spades	Four of Diamonds	Seven of Hearts	Eight of Clubs
Deuce of Spades	Eight of Hearts	Five of Hearts	Queen of Spades
Jack of Hearts	Seven of Spades	Four of Clubs	Nine of Diamonds
Ace of Diamonds	Queen of Diamonds	Five of Clubs	King of Spades
Five of Diamonds	Ten of Clubs	Jack of Spades	Jack of Clubs

Fig. 7.11 | Card shuffling and dealing.

7.6 Enhanced for Statement

The **enhanced for statement** iterates through the elements of an array *without* using a counter, thus avoiding the possibility of "stepping outside" the array. We show how to use the enhanced for statement with the Java API's prebuilt data structures (called collections) in Section 7.14. The syntax of an enhanced for statement is:

```
for ( parameter : arrayName )
   statement
```

where *parameter* has a type and an identifier (e.g., int number), and *arrayName* is the array through which to iterate. The type of the parameter must be consistent with the type of the elements in the array. As the next example illustrates, the identifier represents successive element values in the array on successive iterations of the loop.

Figure 7.12 uses the enhanced for statement (lines 12–13) to sum the integers in an array of student grades. The enhanced for's parameter is of type int, because array contains int values—the loop selects one int value from the array during each iteration. The enhanced for statement iterates through successive values in the array one by one. The statement's header can be read as "for each iteration, assign the next element of array to int variable number, then execute the following statement." Thus, for each iteration, identifier number represents an int value in array. Lines 12–13 are equivalent to the following counter-controlled repetition used in lines 12–13 of Fig. 7.5 to total the integers in array, except that counter cannot be accessed in the enhanced for statement:

```
for ( int counter = 0; counter < array.length; counter++ )
    total += array[ counter ];
```

```
 1   // Fig. 7.12: EnhancedForTest.java
 2   // Using the enhanced for statement to total integers in an array.
 3
 4   public class EnhancedForTest
 5   {
 6      public static void main( String[] args )
 7      {
 8         int[] array = { 87, 68, 94, 100, 83, 78, 85, 91, 76, 87 };
 9         int total = 0;
10
11         // add each element's value to total
12         for ( int number : array )
13            total += number;
14
15         System.out.printf( "Total of array elements: %d\n", total );
16      } // end main
17   } // end class EnhancedForTest
```

```
Total of array elements: 849
```

Fig. 7.12 | Using the enhanced for statement to total integers in an array.

The enhanced for statement simplifies the code for iterating through an array. Note, however, that *the enhanced for statement can be used only to obtain array elements—it cannot be used to modify elements.* If your program needs to modify elements, use the traditional counter-controlled for statement.

The enhanced for statement can be used in place of the counter-controlled for statement whenever code looping through an array does *not* require access to the counter indicating the index of the current array element. For example, totaling the integers in an array requires access only to the element values—the index of each element is irrelevant. However, if a program must use a counter for some reason other than simply to loop through an array (e.g., to print an index number next to each array element value, as in the examples earlier in this chapter), use the counter-controlled for statement.

7.7 Passing Arrays to Methods

This section demonstrates how to pass arrays and individual array elements as arguments to methods. To pass an array argument to a method, specify the name of the array without any brackets. For example, if array `hourlyTemperatures` is declared as

```
double[] hourlyTemperatures = new double[ 24 ];
```

then the method call

```
modifyArray( hourlyTemperatures );
```

passes the reference of array `hourlyTemperatures` to method `modifyArray`. Every array object "knows" its own length (via its `length` field). Thus, when we pass an array object's reference into a method, we need not pass the array length as an additional argument.

For a method to receive an array reference through a method call, the method's parameter list must specify an array parameter. For example, the method header for method `modifyArray` might be written as

```
void modifyArray( double[] b )
```

indicating that `modifyArray` receives the reference of a `double` array in parameter b. The method call passes array `hourlyTemperature`'s reference, so when the called method uses the array variable b, it *refers to* the same array object as `hourlyTemperatures` in the caller.

When an argument to a method is an entire array or an individual array element of a reference type, the called method receives a *copy* of the reference. However, when an argument to a method is an individual array element of a primitive type, the called method receives a copy of the element's *value*. Such primitive values are called **scalars** or **scalar quantities**. To pass an individual array element to a method, use the indexed name of the array element as an argument in the method call.

Figure 7.13 demonstrates the difference between passing an entire array and passing a primitive-type array element to a method. Notice that `main` invokes `static` methods `modifyArray` (line 19) and `modifyElement` (line 30) directly. Recall from Section 6.4 that a `static` method of a class can invoke other `static` methods of the same class directly.

```
1   // Fig. 7.13: PassArray.java
2   // Passing arrays and individual array elements to methods.
3
4   public class PassArray
5   {
6      // main creates array and calls modifyArray and modifyElement
7      public static void main( String[] args )
8      {
9         int[] array = { 1, 2, 3, 4, 5 };
10
11         System.out.println(
12            "Effects of passing reference to entire array:\n" +
13            "The values of the original array are:" );
14
```

Fig. 7.13 | Passing arrays and individual array elements to methods. (Part 1 of 2.)

```
15          // output original array elements
16          for ( int value : array )
17             System.out.printf( "   %d", value );
18
19          modifyArray( array ); // pass array reference
20          System.out.println( "\n\nThe values of the modified array are:" );
21
22          // output modified array elements
23          for ( int value : array )
24             System.out.printf( "   %d", value );
25
26          System.out.printf(
27             "\n\nEffects of passing array element value:\n" +
28             "array[3] before modifyElement: %d\n", array[ 3 ] );
29
30          modifyElement( array[ 3 ] ); // attempt to modify array[ 3 ]
31          System.out.printf(
32             "array[3] after modifyElement: %d\n", array[ 3 ] );
33       } // end main
34
35       // multiply each element of an array by 2
36       public static void modifyArray( int[] array2 )
37       {
38          for ( int counter = 0; counter < array2.length; counter++ )
39             array2[ counter ] *= 2;
40       } // end method modifyArray
41
42       // multiply argument by 2
43       public static void modifyElement( int element )
44       {
45          element *= 2;
46          System.out.printf(
47             "Value of element in modifyElement: %d\n", element );
48       } // end method modifyElement
49    } // end class PassArray
```

```
Effects of passing reference to entire array:
The values of the original array are:
   1   2   3   4   5

The values of the modified array are:
   2   4   6   8   10

Effects of passing array element value:
array[3] before modifyElement: 8
Value of element in modifyElement: 16
array[3] after modifyElement: 8
```

Fig. 7.13 | Passing arrays and individual array elements to methods. (Part 2 of 2.)

The enhanced for statement at lines 16–17 outputs the five int elements of array. Line 19 invokes method modifyArray, passing array as an argument. Method modify-Array (lines 36–40) receives a copy of array's reference and uses the reference to multiply each of array's elements by 2. To prove that array's elements were modified, lines 23–24 output the five elements of `array` again. As the output shows, method `modifyArray` doubled the value of each element. We could not use the enhanced `for` statement in lines 38–39 because we're modifying the array's elements.

Figure 7.13 next demonstrates that when a copy of an individual primitive-type array element is passed to a method, modifying the *copy* in the called method does *not* affect the original value of that element in the calling method's array. Lines 26–28 output the value of `array[3]` *before* invoking method `modifyElement`. Remember that the value of this element is now 8 after it was modified in the call to `modifyArray`. Line 30 calls method `modifyElement` and passes `array[3]` as an argument. Remember that `array[3]` is actually one `int` value (8) in `array`. Therefore, the program passes a copy of the value of `array[3]`. Method `modifyElement` (lines 43–48) multiplies the value received as an argument by 2, stores the result in its parameter `element`, then outputs the value of `element` (16). Since method parameters, like local variables, cease to exist when the method in which they're declared completes execution, the method parameter `element` is destroyed when method `modifyElement` terminates. When the program returns control to `main`, lines 31–32 output the *unmodified* value of `array[3]` (i.e., 8).

Notes on Passing Arguments to Methods
The preceding example demonstrated how arrays and primitive-type array elements are passed as arguments to methods. We now take a closer look at how arguments in general are passed to methods. Two ways to pass arguments in method calls in many programming languages are **pass-by-value** and **pass-by-reference** (also called **call-by-value** and **call-by-reference**). When an argument is passed by value, a copy of the argument's *value* is passed to the called method. The called method works exclusively with the copy. Changes to the called method's copy do *not* affect the original variable's value in the caller.

When an argument is passed by reference, the called method can access the argument's value in the caller directly and modify that data, if necessary. Pass-by-reference improves performance by eliminating the need to copy possibly large amounts of data.

Unlike some other languages, Java does *not* allow you to choose pass-by-value or pass-by-reference—*all arguments are passed by value*. A method call can pass two types of values to a method—copies of primitive values (e.g., values of type `int` and `double`) and copies of references to objects. Objects themselves cannot be passed to methods. When a method modifies a primitive-type parameter, changes to the parameter have no effect on the original argument value in the calling method. For example, when line 30 in `main` of Fig. 7.13 passes `array[3]` to method `modifyElement`, the statement in line 45 that doubles the value of parameter `element` has *no* effect on the value of `array[3]` in `main`. This is also true for reference-type parameters. If you modify a reference-type parameter so that it refers to another object, only the parameter refers to the new object—the reference stored in the caller's variable still refers to the original object.

Although an object's reference is passed by value, a method can still interact with the referenced object by calling its `public` methods using the copy of the object's reference. Since the reference stored in the parameter is a copy of the reference that was passed as an argument, the parameter in the called method and the argument in the calling method refer to the same object in memory. For example, in Fig. 7.13, both parameter `array2` in method `modifyArray` and variable `array` in `main` refer to the *same* array object in memory. Any changes made using the parameter `array2` are carried out on the object that `array` references in the calling method. In Fig. 7.13, the changes made in `modifyArray` using array2 affect the contents of the array object referenced by array in main. Thus, with a reference to an object, the called method *can* manipulate the caller's object directly.

Performance Tip 7.1

Passing arrays by reference makes sense for performance reasons. If arrays were passed by value, a copy of each element would be passed. For large, frequently passed arrays, this would waste time and consume considerable storage for the copies of the arrays.

7.8 Case Study: Class GradeBook Using an Array to Store Grades

Previous versions of class GradeBook process a set of grades entered by the user, but do not maintain the individual grade values in instance variables of the class. Thus, repeat calculations require the user to reenter the same grades. One way to solve this problem would be to store each grade entered in an individual instance of the class. For example, we could create instance variables grade1, grade2, ..., grade10 in class GradeBook to store 10 student grades. But this would make the code to total the grades and determine the class average cumbersome, and the class would not be able to process any more than 10 grades at a time. We solve this problem by storing grades in an array.

*Storing Student Grades in an Array in Class **GradeBook***

Class GradeBook (Fig. 7.14) uses an array of ints to store several students' grades on a single exam. This eliminates the need to repeatedly input the same set of grades. Array grades is declared as an instance variable (line 7), so each GradeBook object maintains its own set of grades. The constructor (lines 10–14) has two parameters—the name of the course and an array of grades. When an application (e.g., class GradeBookTest in Fig. 7.15) creates a GradeBook object, the application passes an existing int array to the constructor, which assigns the array's reference to instance variable grades (line 13). The grades array's size is determined by the length of the array that's passed to the constructor. Thus, a Grade-Book object can process a variable number of grades. The grade values in the passed array could have been input from a user or read from a file on disk (as discussed in Chapter 17). In our test application, we initialize an array with grade values (Fig. 7.15, line 10). Once the grades are stored in instance variable grades of class GradeBook, all the class's methods can access the elements of grades *as often as needed* to perform various calculations.

```
1   // Fig. 7.14: GradeBook.java
2   // GradeBook class using an array to store test grades.
3
4   public class GradeBook
5   {
6      private String courseName; // name of course this GradeBook represents
7      private int[] grades; // array of student grades
8
9      // two-argument constructor initializes courseName and grades array
10     public GradeBook( String name, int[] gradesArray )
11     {
```

Fig. 7.14 | GradeBook class using an array to store test grades. (Part 1 of 4.)

```
12          courseName = name; // initialize courseName
13          grades = gradesArray; // store grades
14      } // end two-argument GradeBook constructor
15
16      // method to set the course name
17      public void setCourseName( String name )
18      {
19          courseName = name; // store the course name
20      } // end method setCourseName
21
22      // method to retrieve the course name
23      public String getCourseName()
24      {
25          return courseName;
26      } // end method getCourseName
27
28      // display a welcome message to the GradeBook user
29      public void displayMessage()
30      {
31          // getCourseName gets the name of the course
32          System.out.printf( "Welcome to the grade book for\n%s!\n\n",
33              getCourseName() );
34      } // end method displayMessage
35
36      // perform various operations on the data
37      public void processGrades()
38      {
39          // output grades array
40          outputGrades();
41
42          // call method getAverage to calculate the average grade
43          System.out.printf( "\nClass average is %.2f\n", getAverage() );
44
45          // call methods getMinimum and getMaximum
46          System.out.printf( "Lowest grade is %d\nHighest grade is %d\n\n",
47              getMinimum(), getMaximum() );
48
49          // call outputBarChart to print grade distribution chart
50          outputBarChart();
51      } // end method processGrades
52
53      // find minimum grade
54      public int getMinimum()
55      {
56          int lowGrade = grades[ 0 ]; // assume grades[ 0 ] is smallest
57
58          // loop through grades array
59          for ( int grade : grades )
60          {
61              // if grade lower than lowGrade, assign it to lowGrade
62              if ( grade < lowGrade )
63                  lowGrade = grade; // new lowest grade
64          } // end for
```

Fig. 7.14 | GradeBook class using an array to store test grades. (Part 2 of 4.)

```
65
66         return lowGrade; // return lowest grade
67      } // end method getMinimum
68
69      // find maximum grade
70      public int getMaximum()
71      {
72         int highGrade = grades[ 0 ]; // assume grades[ 0 ] is largest
73
74         // loop through grades array
75         for ( int grade : grades )
76         {
77            // if grade greater than highGrade, assign it to highGrade
78            if ( grade > highGrade )
79               highGrade = grade; // new highest grade
80         } // end for
81
82         return highGrade; // return highest grade
83      } // end method getMaximum
84
85      // determine average grade for test
86      public double getAverage()
87      {
88         int total = 0; // initialize total
89
90         // sum grades for one student
91         for ( int grade : grades )
92            total += grade;
93
94         // return average of grades
95         return (double) total / grades.length;
96      } // end method getAverage
97
98      // output bar chart displaying grade distribution
99      public void outputBarChart()
100     {
101        System.out.println( "Grade distribution:" );
102
103        // stores frequency of grades in each range of 10 grades
104        int[] frequency = new int[ 11 ];
105
106        // for each grade, increment the appropriate frequency
107        for ( int grade : grades )
108           ++frequency[ grade / 10 ];
109
110        // for each grade frequency, print bar in chart
111        for ( int count = 0; count < frequency.length; count++ )
112        {
113           // output bar label ( "00-09: ", ..., "90-99: ", "100: " )
114           if ( count == 10 )
115              System.out.printf( "%5d: ", 100 );
```

Fig. 7.14 | GradeBook class using an array to store test grades. (Part 3 of 4.)

```
116            else
117               System.out.printf( "%02d-%02d: ",
118                  count * 10, count * 10 + 9  );
119
120            // print bar of asterisks
121            for ( int stars = 0; stars < frequency[ count ]; stars++ )
122               System.out.print( "*" );
123
124            System.out.println(); // start a new line of output
125         } // end outer for
126      } // end method outputBarChart
127
128      // output the contents of the grades array
129      public void outputGrades()
130      {
131         System.out.println( "The grades are:\n" );
132
133         // output each student's grade
134         for ( int student = 0; student < grades.length; student++ )
135            System.out.printf( "Student %2d: %3d\n",
136               student + 1, grades[ student ] );
137      } // end method outputGrades
138   } // end class GradeBook
```

Fig. 7.14 | GradeBook class using an array to store test grades. (Part 4 of 4.)

Method processGrades (lines 37–51) contains a series of method calls that output a report summarizing the grades. Line 40 calls method outputGrades to print the contents of the array grades. Lines 134–136 in method outputGrades use a for statement to output the students' grades. A counter-controlled for *must* be used in this case, because lines 135–136 use counter variable student's value to output each grade next to a particular student number (see output in Fig. 7.15). Although array indices start at 0, a professor would typically number students starting at 1. Thus, lines 135–136 output student + 1 as the student number to produce grade labels "Student 1: ", "Student 2: ", and so on.

Method processGrades next calls method getAverage (line 43) to obtain the average of the grades in the array. Method getAverage (lines 86–96) uses an enhanced for statement to total the values in array grades before calculating the average. The parameter in the enhanced for's header (e.g., int grade) indicates that for each iteration, the int variable grade takes on a value in the array grades. The averaging calculation in line 95 uses grades.length to determine the number of grades being averaged.

Lines 46–47 in method processGrades call methods getMinimum and getMaximum to determine the lowest and highest grades of any student on the exam, respectively. Each of these methods uses an enhanced for statement to loop through array grades. Lines 59–64 in method getMinimum loop through the array. Lines 62–63 compare each grade to lowGrade; if a grade is less than lowGrade, lowGrade is set to that grade. When line 66 executes, lowGrade contains the lowest grade in the array. Method getMaximum (lines 70–83) works similarly to method getMinimum.

Finally, line 50 in method processGrades calls method outputBarChart to print a distribution chart of the grade data using a technique similar to that in Fig. 7.6. In that example, we manually calculated the number of grades in each category (i.e., 0–9, 10–19,

..., 90–99 and 100) by simply looking at a set of grades. In this example, lines 107–108 use a technique similar to that in Figs. 7.7 and 7.8 to calculate the frequency of grades in each category. Line 104 declares and creates array frequency of 11 ints to store the frequency of grades in each grade category. For each grade in array grades, lines 107–108 increment the appropriate element of the frequency array. To determine which element to increment, line 108 divides the current grade by 10 using integer division. For example, if grade is 85, line 108 increments frequency[8] to update the count of grades in the range 80–89. Lines 111–125 next print the bar chart (see Fig. 7.15) based on the values in array frequency. Like lines 23–24 of Fig. 7.6, lines 121–122 of Fig. 7.14 use a value in array frequency to determine the number of asterisks to display in each bar.

Class **GradeBookTest** *That Demonstrates Class* **GradeBook**

The application of Fig. 7.15 creates an object of class GradeBook (Fig. 7.14) using the int array gradesArray (declared and initialized in line 10). Lines 12–13 pass a course name and gradesArray to the GradeBook constructor. Line 14 displays a welcome message, and line 15 invokes the GradeBook object's processGrades method. The output summarizes the 10 grades in myGradeBook.

Software Engineering Observation 7.1

A test harness (or test application) is responsible for creating an object of the class being tested and providing it with data. This data could come from any of several sources. Test data can be placed directly into an array with an array initializer, it can come from the user at the keyboard, it can come from a file (as you'll see in Chapter 17), or it can come from a network (as you'll see in Chapter 24). After passing this data to the class's constructor to instantiate the object, the test harness should call upon the object to test its methods and manipulate its data. Gathering data in the test harness like this allows the class to manipulate data from several sources.

```java
1   // Fig. 7.15: GradeBookTest.java
2   // GradeBookTest creates a GradeBook object using an array of grades,
3   // then invokes method processGrades to analyze them.
4   public class GradeBookTest
5   {
6      // main method begins program execution
7      public static void main( String[] args )
8      {
9         // array of student grades
10        int[] gradesArray = { 87, 68, 94, 100, 83, 78, 85, 91, 76, 87 };
11
12        GradeBook myGradeBook = new GradeBook(
13           "CS101 Introduction to Java Programming", gradesArray );
14        myGradeBook.displayMessage();
15        myGradeBook.processGrades();
16     } // end main
17  } // end class GradeBookTest
```

Fig. 7.15 | GradeBookTest creates a GradeBook object using an array of grades, then invokes method processGrades to analyze them. (Part 1 of 2.)

```
Welcome to the grade book for
CS101 Introduction to Java Programming!

The grades are:

Student  1:  87
Student  2:  68
Student  3:  94
Student  4: 100
Student  5:  83
Student  6:  78
Student  7:  85
Student  8:  91
Student  9:  76
Student 10:  87

Class average is 84.90
Lowest grade is 68
Highest grade is 100

Grade distribution:
00-09:
10-19:
20-29:
30-39:
40-49:
50-59:
60-69: *
70-79: **
80-89: ****
90-99: **
  100: *
```

Fig. 7.15 | GradeBookTest creates a GradeBook object using an array of grades, then invokes method processGrades to analyze them. (Part 2 of 2.)

7.9 Multidimensional Arrays

Multidimensional arrays with two dimensions are often used to represent *tables* of values consisting of information arranged in *rows* and *columns*. To identify a particular table element, we must specify two indices. *By convention*, the first identifies the element's row and the second its column. Arrays that require two indices to identify a particular element are called **two-dimensional arrays**. (Multidimensional arrays can have more than two dimensions.) Java does not support multidimensional arrays directly, but it does allow you to specify one-dimensional arrays whose elements are also one-dimensional arrays, thus achieving the same effect. Figure 7.16 illustrates a two-dimensional array named a that contains three rows and four columns (i.e., a three-by-four array). In general, an array with *m* rows and *n* columns is called an **m-by-n array**.

Every element in array a is identified in Fig. 7.16 by an *array-access expression* of the form a[*row*][*column*]; a is the name of the array, and *row* and *column* are the indices that uniquely identify each element in array a by row and column number. The names of the elements in *row* 0 all have a first index of 0, and the names of the elements in *column* 3 all have a second index of 3.

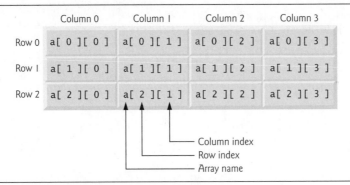

Fig. 7.16 | Two-dimensional array with three rows and four columns.

Arrays of One-Dimensional Arrays

Like one-dimensional arrays, multidimensional arrays can be initialized with array initializers in declarations. A two-dimensional array b with two rows and two columns could be declared and initialized with **nested array initializers** as follows:

```
int[][] b = { { 1, 2 }, { 3, 4 } };
```

The initial values are grouped by row in braces. So 1 and 2 initialize b[0][0] and b[0][1], respectively, and 3 and 4 initialize b[1][0] and b[1][1], respectively. The compiler counts the number of nested array initializers (represented by sets of braces within the outer braces) to determine the number of rows in array b. The compiler counts the initializer values in the nested array initializer for a row to determine the number of columns in that row. As we'll see momentarily, this means that *rows can have different lengths.*

Multidimensional arrays are maintained as arrays of one-dimensional arrays. Therefore array b in the preceding declaration is actually composed of two separate one-dimensional arrays—one containing the values in the first nested initializer list { 1, 2 } and one containing the values in the second nested initializer list { 3, 4 }. Thus, array b itself is an array of two elements, each a one-dimensional array of int values.

Two-Dimensional Arrays with Rows of Different Lengths

The manner in which multidimensional arrays are represented makes them quite flexible. In fact, the lengths of the rows in array b are *not* required to be the same. For example,

```
int[][] b = { { 1, 2 }, { 3, 4, 5 } };
```

creates integer array b with two elements (determined by the number of nested array initializers) that represent the rows of the two-dimensional array. Each element of b is a reference to a one-dimensional array of int variables. The int array for row 0 is a one-dimensional array with two elements (1 and 2), and the int array for row 1 is a one-dimensional array with three elements (3, 4 and 5).

Creating Two-Dimensional Arrays with Array-Creation Expressions

A multidimensional array with the same number of columns in every row can be created with an array-creation expression. For example, the following lines declare array b and assign it a reference to a three-by-four array:

```
int[][] b = new int[ 3 ][ 4 ];
```

In this case, we use the literal values 3 and 4 to specify the number of rows and number of columns, respectively, but this is not required. Programs can also use variables to specify array dimensions, because *new creates arrays at execution time—not at compile time.* As with one-dimensional arrays, the elements of a multidimensional array are initialized when the array object is created.

A multidimensional array in which each row has a different number of columns can be created as follows:

```
int[][] b = new int[ 2 ][ ];    // create 2 rows
b[ 0 ] = new int[ 5 ]; // create 5 columns for row 0
b[ 1 ] = new int[ 3 ]; // create 3 columns for row 1
```

The preceding statements create a two-dimensional array with two rows. Row 0 has five columns, and row 1 has three columns.

Two-Dimensional Array Example: Displaying Element Values

Figure 7.17 demonstrates initializing two-dimensional arrays with array initializers and using nested for loops to **traverse** the arrays (i.e., manipulate every element of each array). Class InitArray's main declares two arrays. The declaration of array1 (line 9) uses nested array initializers of the *same* length to initialize the first row to the values 1, 2 and 3, and the second row to the values 4, 5 and 6. The declaration of array2 (line 10) uses nested initializers of *different* lengths. In this case, the first row is initialized to two elements with the values 1 and 2, respectively. The second row is initialized to one element with the value 3. The third row is initialized to three elements with the values 4, 5 and 6, respectively.

```
1    // Fig. 7.17: InitArray.java
2    // Initializing two-dimensional arrays.
3
4    public class InitArray
5    {
6       // create and output two-dimensional arrays
7       public static void main( String[] args )
8       {
9          int[][] array1 = { { 1, 2, 3 }, { 4, 5, 6 } };
10         int[][] array2 = { { 1, 2 }, { 3 }, { 4, 5, 6 } };
11
12         System.out.println( "Values in array1 by row are" );
13         outputArray( array1 ); // displays array1 by row
14
15         System.out.println( "\nValues in array2 by row are" );
16         outputArray( array2 ); // displays array2 by row
17      } // end main
18
19      // output rows and columns of a two-dimensional array
20      public static void outputArray( int[][] array )
21      {
22         // loop through array's rows
23         for ( int row = 0; row < array.length; row++ )
24         {
```

Fig. 7.17 | Initializing two-dimensional arrays. (Part 1 of 2.)

```
25                    // loop through columns of current row
26                    for ( int column = 0; column < array[ row ].length; column++ )
27                       System.out.printf( "%d  ", array[ row ][ column ] );
28
29                    System.out.println(); // start new line of output
30                 } // end outer for
31        } // end method outputArray
32   } // end class InitArray
```

```
Values in array1 by row are
1  2  3
4  5  6

Values in array2 by row are
1  2
3
4  5  6
```

Fig. 7.17 | Initializing two-dimensional arrays. (Part 2 of 2.)

Lines 13 and 16 call method `outputArray` (lines 20–31) to output the elements of
`array1` and `array2`, respectively. Method `outputArray`'s parameter—`int[][] array`—
indicates that the method receives a two-dimensional array. The `for` statement (lines 23–
30) outputs the rows of a two-dimensional array. In the loop-continuation condition of
the outer `for` statement, the expression `array.length` determines the number of rows in
the array. In the inner `for` statement, the expression `array[row].length` determines the
number of columns in the current row of the array. The inner `for` statement's condition
enables the loop to determine the exact number of columns in each row.

Common Multidimensional-Array Manipulations Performed with for Statements
Many common array manipulations use `for` statements. As an example, the following `for`
statement sets all the elements in row 2 of array a in Fig. 7.16 to zero:

```
for ( int column = 0; column < a[ 2 ].length; column++)
    a[ 2 ][ column ] = 0;
```

We specified row 2; therefore, we know that the first index is always 2 (0 is the first row,
and 1 is the second row). This `for` loop varies only the second index (i.e., the column index). If row 2 of array a contains four elements, then the preceding `for` statement is equivalent to the assignment statements

```
a[ 2 ][ 0 ] = 0;
a[ 2 ][ 1 ] = 0;
a[ 2 ][ 2 ] = 0;
a[ 2 ][ 3 ] = 0;
```

The following nested `for` statement totals the values of all the elements in array a:

```
int total = 0;
for ( int row = 0; row < a.length; row++ )
{
    for ( int column = 0; column < a[ row ].length; column++ )
        total += a[ row ][ column ];
} // end outer for
```

These nested for statements total the array elements one row at a time. The outer for statement begins by setting the row index to 0 so that the first row's elements can be totaled by the inner for statement. The outer for then increments row to 1 so that the second row can be totaled. Then, the outer for increments row to 2 so that the third row can be totaled. The variable total can be displayed when the outer for statement terminates. In the next example, we show how to process a two-dimensional array in a similar manner using nested enhanced for statements.

7.10 Case Study: Class GradeBook Using a Two-Dimensional Array

In Section 7.8, we presented class GradeBook (Fig. 7.14), which used a one-dimensional array to store student grades on a single exam. In most semesters, students take several exams. Professors are likely to want to analyze grades across the entire semester, both for a single student and for the class as a whole.

Storing Student Grades in a Two-Dimensional Array in Class *GradeBook*
Figure 7.18 contains a GradeBook class that uses a two-dimensional array grades to store the grades of a number of students on multiple exams. Each row of the array represents a single student's grades for the entire course, and each column represents the grades of all the students who took a particular exam. Class GradeBookTest (Fig. 7.19) passes the array as an argument to the GradeBook constructor. In this example, we use a ten-by-three array for ten students' grades on three exams. Five methods perform array manipulations to process the grades. Each method is similar to its counterpart in the earlier one-dimensional array version of GradeBook (Fig. 7.14). Method getMinimum (lines 52–70) determines the lowest grade of any student for the semester. Method getMaximum (lines 73–91) determines the highest grade of any student for the semester. Method getAverage (lines 94–104) determines a particular student's semester average. Method outputBarChart (lines 107–137) outputs a grade bar chart for the entire semester's student grades. Method outputGrades (lines 140–164) outputs the array in a tabular format, along with each student's semester average.

```
1   // Fig. 7.18: GradeBook.java
2   // GradeBook class using a two-dimensional array to store grades.
3
4   public class GradeBook
5   {
6      private String courseName; // name of course this grade book represents
7      private int[][] grades; // two-dimensional array of student grades
8
9      // two-argument constructor initializes courseName and grades array
10     public GradeBook( String name, int[][] gradesArray )
11     {
12        courseName = name; // initialize courseName
13        grades = gradesArray; // store grades
14     } // end two-argument GradeBook constructor
15
```

Fig. 7.18 | GradeBook class using a two-dimensional array to store grades. (Part 1 of 4.)

```
16      // method to set the course name
17      public void setCourseName( String name )
18      {
19         courseName = name; // store the course name
20      } // end method setCourseName
21
22      // method to retrieve the course name
23      public String getCourseName()
24      {
25         return courseName;
26      } // end method getCourseName
27
28      // display a welcome message to the GradeBook user
29      public void displayMessage()
30      {
31         // getCourseName gets the name of the course
32         System.out.printf( "Welcome to the grade book for\n%s!\n\n",
33            getCourseName() );
34      } // end method displayMessage
35
36      // perform various operations on the data
37      public void processGrades()
38      {
39         // output grades array
40         outputGrades();
41
42         // call methods getMinimum and getMaximum
43         System.out.printf( "\n%s %d\n%s %d\n\n",
44            "Lowest grade in the grade book is", getMinimum(),
45            "Highest grade in the grade book is", getMaximum() );
46
47         // output grade distribution chart of all grades on all tests
48         outputBarChart();
49      } // end method processGrades
50
51      // find minimum grade
52      public int getMinimum()
53      {
54         // assume first element of grades array is smallest
55         int lowGrade = grades[ 0 ][ 0 ];
56
57         // loop through rows of grades array
58         for ( int[] studentGrades : grades )
59         {
60            // loop through columns of current row
61            for ( int grade : studentGrades )
62            {
63               // if grade less than lowGrade, assign it to lowGrade
64               if ( grade < lowGrade )
65                  lowGrade = grade;
66            } // end inner for
67         } // end outer for
68
```

Fig. 7.18 | GradeBook class using a two-dimensional array to store grades. (Part 2 of 4.)

```
69          return lowGrade; // return lowest grade
70      } // end method getMinimum
71
72      // find maximum grade
73      public int getMaximum()
74      {
75          // assume first element of grades array is largest
76          int highGrade = grades[ 0 ][ 0 ];
77
78          // loop through rows of grades array
79          for ( int[] studentGrades : grades )
80          {
81              // loop through columns of current row
82              for ( int grade : studentGrades )
83              {
84                  // if grade greater than highGrade, assign it to highGrade
85                  if ( grade > highGrade )
86                      highGrade = grade;
87              } // end inner for
88          } // end outer for
89
90          return highGrade; // return highest grade
91      } // end method getMaximum
92
93      // determine average grade for particular set of grades
94      public double getAverage( int[] setOfGrades )
95      {
96          int total = 0; // initialize total
97
98          // sum grades for one student
99          for ( int grade : setOfGrades )
100             total += grade;
101
102         // return average of grades
103         return (double) total / setOfGrades.length;
104     } // end method getAverage
105
106     // output bar chart displaying overall grade distribution
107     public void outputBarChart()
108     {
109         System.out.println( "Overall grade distribution:" );
110
111         // stores frequency of grades in each range of 10 grades
112         int[] frequency = new int[ 11 ];
113
114         // for each grade in GradeBook, increment the appropriate frequency
115         for ( int[] studentGrades : grades )
116         {
117             for ( int grade : studentGrades )
118                 ++frequency[ grade / 10 ];
119         } // end outer for
120
```

Fig. 7.18 | GradeBook class using a two-dimensional array to store grades. (Part 3 of 4.)

```
121          // for each grade frequency, print bar in chart
122          for ( int count = 0; count < frequency.length; count++ )
123          {
124             // output bar label ( "00-09: ", ..., "90-99: ", "100: " )
125             if ( count == 10 )
126                System.out.printf( "%5d: ", 100 );
127             else
128                System.out.printf( "%02d-%02d: ",
129                   count * 10, count * 10 + 9  );
130
131             // print bar of asterisks
132             for ( int stars = 0; stars < frequency[ count ]; stars++ )
133                System.out.print( "*" );
134
135             System.out.println(); // start a new line of output
136          } // end outer for
137       } // end method outputBarChart
138
139       // output the contents of the grades array
140       public void outputGrades()
141       {
142          System.out.println( "The grades are:\n" );
143          System.out.print( "              " ); // align column heads
144
145          // create a column heading for each of the tests
146          for ( int test = 0; test < grades[ 0 ].length; test++ )
147             System.out.printf( "Test %d  ", test + 1 );
148
149          System.out.println( "Average" ); // student average column heading
150
151          // create rows/columns of text representing array grades
152          for ( int student = 0; student < grades.length; student++ )
153          {
154             System.out.printf( "Student %2d", student + 1 );
155
156             for ( int test : grades[ student ] ) // output student's grades
157                System.out.printf( "%8d", test );
158
159             // call method getAverage to calculate student's average grade;
160             // pass row of grades as the argument to getAverage
161             double average = getAverage( grades[ student ] );
162             System.out.printf( "%9.2f\n", average );
163          } // end outer for
164       } // end method outputGrades
165    } // end class GradeBook
```

Fig. 7.18 | GradeBook class using a two-dimensional array to store grades. (Part 4 of 4.)

Methods *getMinimum* and *getMaximum*

Methods getMinimum, getMaximum, outputBarChart and outputGrades each loop through array grades by using nested for statements—for example, the nested enhanced for statement from the declaration of method getMinimum (lines 58–67). The outer enhanced for statement iterates through the two-dimensional array grades, assigning successive rows to parameter `studentGrades` on successive iterations. The square brackets following the parameter name indicate that `studentGrades` refers to a one-dimensional `int` array—namely, a row in array `grades` containing one student's grades. To find the lowest overall grade, the inner `for` statement compares the elements of the current one-dimensional array `studentGrades` to variable `lowGrade`. For example, on the first iteration of the outer `for`, row 0 of `grades` is assigned to parameter `studentGrades`. The inner enhanced `for` statement then loops through `studentGrades` and compares each grade value with `lowGrade`. If a grade is less than `lowGrade`, `lowGrade` is set to that grade. On the second iteration of the outer enhanced `for` statement, row 1 of `grades` is assigned to `studentGrades`, and the elements of this row are compared with variable `lowGrade`. This repeats until all rows of `grades` have been traversed. When execution of the nested statement is complete, `lowGrade` contains the lowest grade in the two-dimensional array. Method `getMaximum` works similarly to method `getMinimum`.

Method *outputBarChart*
Method `outputBarChart` in Fig. 7.18 is nearly identical to the one in Fig. 7.14. However, to output the overall grade distribution for a whole semester, the method here uses nested enhanced `for` statements (lines 115–119) to create the one-dimensional array `frequency` based on all the grades in the two-dimensional array. The rest of the code in each of the two `outputBarChart` methods that displays the chart is identical.

Method *outputGrades*
Method `outputGrades` (lines 140–164) uses nested `for` statements to output values of the array `grades` and each student's semester average. The output (Fig. 7.19) shows the result, which resembles the tabular format of a professor's physical grade book. Lines 146–147 print the column headings for each test. We use a counter-controlled `for` statement here so that we can identify each test with a number. Similarly, the `for` statement in lines 152–163 first outputs a row label using a counter variable to identify each student (line 154). Although array indices start at 0, lines 147 and 154 output `test + 1` and `student + 1`, respectively, to produce test and student numbers starting at 1 (see Fig. 7.19). The inner `for` statement (lines 156–157) uses the outer `for` statement's counter variable `student` to loop through a specific row of array `grades` and output each student's test grade. An enhanced `for` statement can be nested in a counter-controlled `for` statement, and vice versa. Finally, line 161 obtains each student's semester average by passing the current row of `grades` (i.e., `grades[student]`) to method `getAverage`.

Method *getAverage*
Method `getAverage` (lines 94–104) takes one argument—a one-dimensional array of test results for a particular student. When line 161 calls `getAverage`, the argument is `grades[student]`, which specifies that a particular row of the two-dimensional array `grades` should be passed to `getAverage`. For example, based on the array created in Fig. 7.19, the argument `grades[1]` represents the three values (a one-dimensional array of grades) stored in row 1 of the two-dimensional array `grades`. Recall that a two-dimensional array is one whose elements are one-dimensional arrays. Method `getAverage` calculates the sum of the array elements, divides the total by the number of test results and returns the floating-point result as a `double` value (line 103).

Class **GradeBookTest** *That Demonstrates Class* **GradeBook**

Figure 7.19 creates an object of class GradeBook (Fig. 7.18) using the two-dimensional array of ints named gradesArray (declared and initialized in lines 10–19). Lines 21–22 pass a course name and gradesArray to the GradeBook constructor. Lines 23–24 then invoke myGradeBook's displayMessage and processGrades methods to display a welcome message and obtain a report summarizing the students' grades for the semester, respectively.

```java
1  // Fig. 7.19: GradeBookTest.java
2  // GradeBookTest creates GradeBook object using a two-dimensional array
3  // of grades, then invokes method processGrades to analyze them.
4  public class GradeBookTest
5  {
6     // main method begins program execution
7     public static void main( String[] args )
8     {
9        // two-dimensional array of student grades
10       int[][] gradesArray = { { 87, 96, 70 },
11                               { 68, 87, 90 },
12                               { 94, 100, 90 },
13                               { 100, 81, 82 },
14                               { 83, 65, 85 },
15                               { 78, 87, 65 },
16                               { 85, 75, 83 },
17                               { 91, 94, 100 },
18                               { 76, 72, 84 },
19                               { 87, 93, 73 } };
20
21       GradeBook myGradeBook = new GradeBook(
22          "CS101 Introduction to Java Programming", gradesArray );
23       myGradeBook.displayMessage();
24       myGradeBook.processGrades();
25    } // end main
26 } // end class GradeBookTest
```

```
Welcome to the grade book for
CS101 Introduction to Java Programming!

The grades are:

            Test 1  Test 2  Test 3  Average
Student  1     87      96      70     84.33
Student  2     68      87      90     81.67
Student  3     94     100      90     94.67
Student  4    100      81      82     87.67
Student  5     83      65      85     77.67
Student  6     78      87      65     76.67
Student  7     85      75      83     81.00
Student  8     91      94     100     95.00
Student  9     76      72      84     77.33
Student 10     87      93      73     84.33
```

Fig. 7.19 | GradeBookTest creates GradeBook object using a two-dimensional array of grades, then invokes method processGrades to analyze them. (Part 1 of 2.)

```
Overall grade distribution:
00-09:
10-19:
20-29:
30-39:
40-49:
50-59:
60-69: ***
70-79: ******
80-89: ************
90-99: *******
  100: ***
```

Fig. 7.19 | GradeBookTest creates GradeBook object using a two-dimensional array of grades, then invokes method processGrades to analyze them. (Part 2 of 2.)

7.11 Variable-Length Argument Lists

With **variable-length argument lists**, you can create methods that receive an unspecified number of arguments. A type followed by an **ellipsis (...)** in a method's parameter list indicates that the method receives a variable number of arguments of that particular type. This use of the ellipsis can occur only once in a parameter list, and the ellipsis, together with its type, must be placed at the end of the parameter list. While you can use method overloading and array passing to accomplish much of what is accomplished with variable-length argument lists, using an ellipsis in a method's parameter list is more concise.

Figure 7.20 demonstrates method average (lines 7–16), which receives a variable-length sequence of doubles. Java treats the variable-length argument list as an array whose elements are all of the same type. Hence, the method body can manipulate the parameter numbers as an array of doubles. Lines 12–13 use the enhanced for loop to walk through the array and calculate the total of the doubles in the array. Line 15 accesses numbers.length to obtain the size of the numbers array for use in the averaging calculation. Lines 29, 31 and 33 in main call method average with two, three and four arguments, respectively. Method average has a variable-length argument list (line 7), so it can average as many double arguments as the caller passes. The output shows that each call to method average returns the correct value.

```
1   // Fig. 7.20: VarargsTest.java
2   // Using variable-length argument lists.
3
4   public class VarargsTest
5   {
6      // calculate average
7      public static double average( double... numbers )
8      {
9         double total = 0.0; // initialize total
10
```

Fig. 7.20 | Using variable-length argument lists. (Part 1 of 2.)

```
11          // calculate total using the enhanced for statement
12          for ( double d : numbers )
13             total += d;
14
15          return total / numbers.length;
16       } // end method average
17
18       public static void main( String[] args )
19       {
20          double d1 = 10.0;
21          double d2 = 20.0;
22          double d3 = 30.0;
23          double d4 = 40.0;
24
25          System.out.printf( "d1 = %.1f\nd2 = %.1f\nd3 = %.1f\nd4 = %.1f\n\n",
26             d1, d2, d3, d4 );
27
28          System.out.printf( "Average of d1 and d2 is %.1f\n",
29             average( d1, d2 ) );
30          System.out.printf( "Average of d1, d2 and d3 is %.1f\n",
31             average( d1, d2, d3 ) );
32          System.out.printf( "Average of d1, d2, d3 and d4 is %.1f\n",
33             average( d1, d2, d3, d4 ) );
34       } // end main
35   } // end class VarargsTest
```

```
d1 = 10.0
d2 = 20.0
d3 = 30.0
d4 = 40.0

Average of d1 and d2 is 15.0
Average of d1, d2 and d3 is 20.0
Average of d1, d2, d3 and d4 is 25.0
```

Fig. 7.20 | Using variable-length argument lists. (Part 2 of 2.)

Common Programming Error 7.4

Placing an ellipsis indicating a variable-length argument list in the middle of a parameter list is a syntax error. An ellipsis may be placed only at the end of the parameter list.

7.12 Using Command-Line Arguments

It's possible to pass arguments from the command line (these are known as **command-line arguments**) to an application by including a parameter of type String[] (i.e., an array of Strings) in the parameter list of main, exactly as we've done in every application in the book. By convention, this parameter is named args. When an application is executed using the java command, Java passes the command-line arguments that appear after the class name in the java command to the application's main method as Strings in the array args. The number of command-line arguments is obtained by accessing the array's length attribute. Common uses of command-line arguments include passing options and file names to applications.

Our next example uses command-line arguments to determine the size of an array, the value of its first element and the increment used to calculate the values of the array's remaining elements. The command

```
java InitArray 5 0 4
```

passes three arguments, 5, 0 and 4, to the application InitArray. Command-line arguments are separated by white space. When this command executes, InitArray's main method receives the three-element array args in which args[0] contains the String "5", args[1] contains the String "0" and args[2] contains the String "4". The program determines how to use these arguments—in Fig. 7.21 we convert them to int values and use them to initialize an array. When the program executes, if args.length is not 3, the program prints an error message and terminates (lines 9–12). Otherwise, lines 14–32 initialize and display the array based on the values of the command-line arguments.

```
 1   // Fig. 7.21: InitArray.java
 2   // Initializing an array using command-line arguments.
 3
 4   public class InitArray
 5   {
 6      public static void main( String[] args )
 7      {
 8         // check number of command-line arguments
 9         if ( args.length != 3 )
10            System.out.println(
11               "Error: Please re-enter the entire command, including\n" +
12               "an array size, initial value and increment." );
13         else
14         {
15            // get array size from first command-line argument
16            int arrayLength = Integer.parseInt( args[ 0 ] );
17            int[] array = new int[ arrayLength ]; // create array
18
19            // get initial value and increment from command-line arguments
20            int initialValue = Integer.parseInt( args[ 1 ] );
21            int increment = Integer.parseInt( args[ 2 ] );
22
23            // calculate value for each array element
24            for ( int counter = 0; counter < array.length; counter++ )
25               array[ counter ] = initialValue + increment * counter;
26
27            System.out.printf( "%s%8s\n", "Index", "Value" );
28
29            // display array index and value
30            for ( int counter = 0; counter < array.length; counter++ )
31               System.out.printf( "%5d%8d\n", counter, array[ counter ] );
32         } // end else
33      } // end main
34   } // end class InitArray
```

Fig. 7.21 | Initializing an array using command-line arguments. (Part 1 of 2.)

```
java InitArray
Error: Please re-enter the entire command, including
an array size, initial value and increment.
```

```
java InitArray 5 0 4
Index    Value
    0        0
    1        4
    2        8
    3       12
    4       16
```

```
java InitArray 8 1 2
Index    Value
    0        1
    1        3
    2        5
    3        7
    4        9
    5       11
    6       13
    7       15
```

Fig. 7.21 | Initializing an array using command-line arguments. (Part 2 of 2.)

Line 16 gets args[0]—a String that specifies the array size—and converts it to an int value that the program uses to create the array in line 17. The static method parseInt of class Integer converts its String argument to an int.

Lines 20–21 convert the args[1] and args[2] command-line arguments to int values and store them in initialValue and increment, respectively. Lines 24–25 calculate the value for each array element.

The output of the first execution shows that the application received an insufficient number of command-line arguments. The second execution uses command-line arguments 5, 0 and 4 to specify the size of the array (5), the value of the first element (0) and the increment of each value in the array (4), respectively. The corresponding output shows that these values create an array containing the integers 0, 4, 8, 12 and 16. The output from the third execution shows that the command-line arguments 8, 1 and 2 produce an array whose 8 elements are the nonnegative odd integers from 1 to 15.

7.13 Class Arrays

Class **Arrays** helps you avoid reinventing the wheel by providing static methods for common array manipulations. These methods include **sort** for sorting an array (i.e., arranging elements into increasing order), **binarySearch** for searching an array (i.e., determining whether an array contains a specific value and, if so, where the value is located), **equals** for comparing arrays and **fill** for placing values into an array. These methods are overloaded for primitive-type arrays and for arrays of objects. Our focus in this section is on using the built-in capabilities provided by the Java API.

Figure 7.22 uses Arrays methods sort, binarySearch, equals and fill, and shows how to copy arrays with class System's static **arraycopy method**. In main, line 11 sorts the elements of array doubleArray. The static method sort of class Arrays orders the array's elements in *ascending* order by default. We discuss how to sort in *descending* order later in the chapter. Overloaded versions of sort allow you to sort a specific range of elements. Lines 12–15 output the sorted array.

```java
1  // Fig. 7.22: ArrayManipulations.java
2  // Arrays class methods and System.arraycopy.
3  import java.util.Arrays;
4
5  public class ArrayManipulations
6  {
7     public static void main( String[] args )
8     {
9        // sort doubleArray into ascending order
10       double[] doubleArray = { 8.4, 9.3, 0.2, 7.9, 3.4 };
11       Arrays.sort( doubleArray );
12       System.out.printf( "\ndoubleArray: " );
13
14       for ( double value : doubleArray )
15          System.out.printf( "%.1f ", value );
16
17       // fill 10-element array with 7s
18       int[] filledIntArray = new int[ 10 ];
19       Arrays.fill( filledIntArray, 7 );
20       displayArray( filledIntArray, "filledIntArray" );
21
22       // copy array intArray into array intArrayCopy
23       int[] intArray = { 1, 2, 3, 4, 5, 6 };
24       int[] intArrayCopy = new int[ intArray.length ];
25       System.arraycopy( intArray, 0, intArrayCopy, 0, intArray.length );
26       displayArray( intArray, "intArray" );
27       displayArray( intArrayCopy, "intArrayCopy" );
28
29       // compare intArray and intArrayCopy for equality
30       boolean b = Arrays.equals( intArray, intArrayCopy );
31       System.out.printf( "\n\nintArray %s intArrayCopy\n",
32          ( b ? "==" : "!=" ) );
33
34       // compare intArray and filledIntArray for equality
35       b = Arrays.equals( intArray, filledIntArray );
36       System.out.printf( "intArray %s filledIntArray\n",
37          ( b ? "==" : "!=" ) );
38
39       // search intArray for the value 5
40       int location = Arrays.binarySearch( intArray, 5 );
41
42       if ( location >= 0 )
43          System.out.printf(
44             "Found 5 at element %d in intArray\n", location );
```

Fig. 7.22 | Arrays class methods. (Part 1 of 2.)

```
45              else
46                  System.out.println( "5 not found in intArray" );
47
48              // search intArray for the value 8763
49              location = Arrays.binarySearch( intArray, 8763 );
50
51              if ( location >= 0 )
52                  System.out.printf(
53                      "Found 8763 at element %d in intArray\n", location );
54              else
55                  System.out.println( "8763 not found in intArray" );
56          } // end main
57
58          // output values in each array
59          public static void displayArray( int[] array, String description )
60          {
61              System.out.printf( "\n%s: ", description );
62
63              for ( int value : array )
64                  System.out.printf( "%d ", value );
65          } // end method displayArray
66      } // end class ArrayManipulations
```

```
doubleArray: 0.2 3.4 7.9 8.4 9.3
filledIntArray: 7 7 7 7 7 7 7 7 7 7
intArray: 1 2 3 4 5 6
intArrayCopy: 1 2 3 4 5 6

intArray == intArrayCopy
intArray != filledIntArray
Found 5 at element 4 in intArray
8763 not found in intArray
```

Fig. 7.22 | Arrays class methods. (Part 2 of 2.)

Line 19 calls static method fill of class Arrays to populate all 10 elements of filledIntArray with 7s. Overloaded versions of fill allow you to populate a specific range of elements with the same value. Line 20 calls our class's displayArray method (declared at lines 59–65) to output the contents of filledIntArray.

Line 25 copies the elements of intArray into intArrayCopy. The first argument (intArray) passed to System method arraycopy is the array from which elements are to be copied. The second argument (0) is the index that specifies the starting point in the range of elements to copy from the array. This value can be any valid array index. The third argument (intArrayCopy) specifies the destination array that will store the copy. The fourth argument (0) specifies the index in the destination array where the first copied element should be stored. The last argument specifies the number of elements to copy from the array in the first argument. In this case, we copy all the elements in the array.

Lines 30 and 35 call static method equals of class Arrays to determine whether all the elements of two arrays are equivalent. If the arrays contain the same elements in the same order, the method returns true; otherwise, it returns false.

Lines 40 and 49 call static method binarySearch of class Arrays to perform a binary search on intArray, using the second argument (5 and 8763, respectively) as the key. If value is found, binarySearch returns the index of the element; otherwise, binarySearch returns a negative value. The negative value returned is based on the search key's insertion point—the index where the key would be inserted in the array if we were performing an insert operation. After binarySearch determines the insertion point, it changes its sign to negative and subtracts 1 to obtain the return value. For example, in Fig. 7.22, the insertion point for the value 8763 is the element with index 6 in the array. Method binarySearch changes the insertion point to -6, subtracts 1 from it and returns the value -7. Subtracting 1 from the insertion point guarantees that method binarySearch returns positive values (>= 0) if and only if the key is found. This return value is useful for inserting elements in a sorted array.

Common Programming Error 7.5

Passing an unsorted array to binarySearch is a logic error—the value returned is undefined.

7.14 Introduction to Collections and Class ArrayList

The Java API provides several predefined data structures, called **collections,** used to store groups of related objects. These classes provide efficient methods that organize, store and retrieve your data without requiring knowledge of how the data is being stored. This reduces application-development time.

You've used arrays to store sequences of objects. Arrays do not automatically change their size at execution time to accommodate additional elements. The collection class **ArrayList<T>** (from package java.util) provides a convenient solution to this problem—it can *dynamically* change its size to accommodate more elements. The T (by convention) is a *placeholder*—when declaring a new ArrayList, replace it with the type of elements that you want the ArrayList to hold. This is similar to specifying the type when declaring an array, except that *only nonprimitive types can be used with these collection classes*. For example,

```
ArrayList< String > list;
```

declares list as an ArrayList collection that can store only Strings. Classes with this kind of placeholder that can be used with any type are called **generic classes.** Additional generic collection classes and generics are discussed in Chapters 18 and 19, respectively. Figure 7.23 shows some common methods of class ArrayList<T>.

Method	Description
add	Adds an element to the end of the ArrayList.
clear	Removes all the elements from the ArrayList.
contains	Returns true if the ArrayList contains the specified element; otherwise, returns false.
get	Returns the element at the specified index.
indexOf	Returns the index of the first occurrence of the specified element in the ArrayList.

Fig. 7.23 | Some methods and properties of class ArrayList<T>. (Part 1 of 2.)

Method	Description
remove	Overloaded. Removes the first occurrence of the specified value or the element at the specified index.
size	Returns the number of elements stored in the ArrayList.
trimToSize	Trims the capacity of the ArrayList to current number of elements.

Fig. 7.23 | Some methods and properties of class ArrayList<T>. (Part 2 of 2.)

Figure 7.24 demonstrates some common ArrayList capabilities. Line 10 creates a new empty ArrayList of Strings with a default initial capacity of 10 elements. The capacity indicates how many items the ArrayList can hold without growing. ArrayList is implemented using an array behind the scenes. When the ArrayList grows, it must create a larger internal array and copy each element to the new array. This is a time-consuming operation. It would be inefficient for the ArrayList to grow each time an element is added. Instead, it grows only when an element is added *and* the number of elements is equal to the capacity—i.e., there's no space for the new element.

```
1    // Fig. 7.24: ArrayListCollection.java
2    // Generic ArrayList<T> collection demonstration.
3    import java.util.ArrayList;
4
5    public class ArrayListCollection
6    {
7       public static void main( String[] args )
8       {
9          // create a new ArrayList of Strings with an initial capacity of 10
10         ArrayList< String > items = new ArrayList< String >();
11
12         items.add( "red" ); // append an item to the list
13         items.add( 0, "yellow" ); // insert the value at index 0
14
15         // header
16         System.out.print(
17            "Display list contents with counter-controlled loop:" );
18
19         // display the colors in the list
20         for ( int i = 0; i < items.size(); i++ )
21            System.out.printf( " %s", items.get( i ) );
22
23         // display colors using foreach in the display method
24         display( items,
25            "\nDisplay list contents with enhanced for statement:" );
26
27         items.add( "green" ); // add "green" to the end of the list
28         items.add( "yellow" ); // add "yellow" to the end of the list
29         display( items, "List with two new elements:" );
30
```

Fig. 7.24 | Generic ArrayList<T> collection demonstration. (Part 1 of 2.)

```
31          items.remove( "yellow" ); // remove the first "yellow"
32          display( items, "Remove first instance of yellow:" );
33
34          items.remove( 1 ); // remove item at index 1
35          display( items, "Remove second list element (green):" );
36
37          // check if a value is in the List
38          System.out.printf( "\"red\" is %sin the list\n",
39             items.contains( "red" ) ? "": "not " );
40
41          // display number of elements in the List
42          System.out.printf( "Size: %s\n", items.size() );
43       } // end main
44
45       // display the ArrayList's elements on the console
46       public static void display( ArrayList< String > items, String header )
47       {
48          System.out.print( header ); // display header
49
50          // display each element in items
51          for ( String item : items )
52             System.out.printf( " %s", item );
53
54          System.out.println(); // display end of line
55       } // end method display
56    } // end class ArrayListCollection
```

```
Display list contents with counter-controlled loop: yellow red
Display list contents with enhanced for statement: yellow red
List with two new elements: yellow red green yellow
Remove first instance of yellow: red green yellow
Remove second list element (green): red yellow
"red" is in the list
Size: 2
```

Fig. 7.24 | Generic ArrayList<T> collection demonstration. (Part 2 of 2.)

The **add** method adds elements to the ArrayList (lines 12–13). The add method with *one* argument appends its argument to the end of the ArrayList. The add method with *two* arguments inserts a new element at the specified position. The first argument is an index. As with arrays, collection indices start at zero. The second argument is the value to insert at that index. The indices of all subsequent elements are incremented by one. Inserting an element is usually slower than adding an element to the end of the ArrayList

Lines 20–21 display the items in the ArrayList. The **size** method returns the number of elements currently in the ArrayList. ArrayLists method **get** (line 21) obtains the element at a specified index. Lines 24–25 display the elements again by invoking method display (defined at lines 46–55). Lines 27–28 add two more elements to the ArrayList, then line 29 displays the elements again to confirm that the two elements were added to the end of the collection.

The **remove** method is used to remove an element with a specific value (line 31). It removes only the first such element. If no such element is in the ArrayList, remove does nothing. An overloaded version of the method removes the element at the specified index (line 34). When an element is removed, the indices of all elements after the removed element decrease by one.

Line 39 uses the **contains** method to check if an item is in the ArrayList. The contains method returns true if the element is found in the ArrayList, and false otherwise. The method compares its argument to each element of the ArrayList in order, so using contains on a large ArrayList can be inefficient. Line 42 displays the ArrayList's size.

7.15 Wrap-Up

This chapter demonstrated how to declare an array, initialize an array and refer to individual elements of an array. We introduced the enhanced for statement to iterate through arrays. We used exception handling to test for ArrayIndexOutOfBoundsExceptions that occur when a program attempts to access an array element outside the bounds of an array (we'll take a deeper look at exception handling in Chapter 11). We also illustrated how to pass arrays to methods and how to declare and manipulate multidimensional arrays. Finally, the chapter showed how to write methods that use variable-length argument lists and how to read arguments passed to a program from the command line.

We introduced the ArrayList<T> generic collection, which provides all the functionality and performance of arrays, along with other useful capabilities such as dynamic resizing. We used the add methods to add new items to the end of an ArrayList and to insert items in an ArrayList. The remove method was used to remove the first occurrence of a specified item, and an overloaded version of remove was used to remove an item at a specified index. We used the size method to obtain number of items in the ArrayList.

We continue our coverage of data structures in Chapter 18, Generic Collections. Chapter 18 introduces the Java Collections Framework, which uses generics to allow you to specify the exact types of objects that a particular data structure will store. The Collections API provides class Arrays, which contains utility methods for array manipulation. Chapter 18 uses several static methods of class Arrays to perform such manipulations as sorting and searching the data in an array. You'll be able to use some of the Arrays methods discussed in Chapter 18 after reading the current chapter, but some of the Arrays methods require knowledge of concepts presented later in the book. Chapter 19 presents the topic of generics, which provide the means to create general models of methods and classes that can be declared once, but used with many different data types.

We've now introduced the basic concepts of classes, objects, control statements, methods, arrays and collections. In Chapter 8, we take a deeper look at classes and objects.

8

Classes and Objects: A Deeper Look

Instead of this absurd division into sexes, they ought to class people as static and dynamic.
—Evelyn Waugh

Is it a world to hide virtues in?
—William Shakespeare

But what, to serve our private ends, Forbids the cheating of our friends?
—Charles Churchill

This above all: to thine own self be true.
—William Shakespeare

Don't be "consistent," but be simply true.
—Oliver Wendell Holmes, Jr.

Objectives

In this chapter you'll learn:

- Encapsulation and data hiding.
- To use keyword **this**.
- To use **static** variables and methods.
- To import **static** members of a class.
- To use the **enum** type to create sets of constants with unique identifiers.
- To declare **enum** constants with parameters.
- To organize classes in packages to promote reuse.

8.1 Introduction

We now take a deeper look at building classes, controlling access to members of a class and creating constructors. We discuss composition—a capability that allows a class to have references to objects of other classes as members. We reexamine the use of *set* and *get* methods. Recall that Section 6.9 introduced the basic enum type to declare a set of constants. In this chapter, we discuss the relationship between enum types and classes, demonstrating that an enum, like a class, can be declared in its own file with constructors, methods and fields. The chapter also discusses static class members and final instance variables in detail. Finally, we explain how to organize classes in packages to help manage large applications and promote reuse, then show a special relationship between classes in the same package.

8.2 Time Class Case Study

Our first example consists of two classes—Time1 (Fig. 8.1) and Time1Test (Fig. 8.2). Class Time1 represents the time of day. Class Time1Test is an application class in which the main method creates one object of class Time1 and invokes its methods. These classes must be declared in *separate* files because they're both public classes. The output of this program appears in Fig. 8.2.

Time1 Class Declaration

Class Time1's private int instance variables hour, minute and second (Fig. 8.1, lines 6–8) represent the time in universal-time format (24-hour clock format in which hours are in the range 0–23). Class Time1 contains public methods setTime (lines 12–25), toUniversalString (lines 28–31) and toString (lines 34–39). These methods are also called the **public services** or the **public interface** that the class provides to its clients.

```
1   // Fig. 8.1: Time1.java
2   // Time1 class declaration maintains the time in 24-hour format.
3
4   public class Time1
5   {
```

Fig. 8.1 | Time1 class declaration maintains the time in 24-hour format. (Part 1 of 2.)

```
 6      private int hour; // 0 - 23
 7      private int minute; // 0 - 59
 8      private int second; // 0 - 59
 9
10      // set a new time value using universal time; throw an
11      // exception if the hour, minute or second is invalid
12      public void setTime( int h, int m, int s )
13      {
14         // validate hour, minute and second
15         if ( ( h >= 0 && h < 24 ) && ( m >= 0 && m < 60 ) &&
16            ( s >= 0 && s < 60 ) )
17         {
18            hour = h;
19            minute = m;
20            second = s;
21         } // end if
22         else
23            throw new IllegalArgumentException(
24               "hour, minute and/or second was out of range" );
25      } // end method setTime
26
27      // convert to String in universal-time format (HH:MM:SS)
28      public String toUniversalString()
29      {
30         return String.format( "%02d:%02d:%02d", hour, minute, second );
31      } // end method toUniversalString
32
33      // convert to String in standard-time format (H:MM:SS AM or PM)
34      public String toString()
35      {
36         return String.format( "%d:%02d:%02d %s",
37            ( ( hour == 0 || hour == 12 ) ? 12 : hour % 12 ),
38            minute, second, ( hour < 12 ? "AM" : "PM" ) );
39      } // end method toString
40   } // end class Time1
```

Fig. 8.1 | Time1 class declaration maintains the time in 24-hour format. (Part 2 of 2.)

Default Constructor

In this example, class Time1 does not declare a constructor, so the class has a default constructor that's supplied by the compiler. Each instance variable implicitly receives the default value 0 for an int. Instance variables also can be initialized when they're declared in the class body, using the same initialization syntax as with a local variable.

Method setTime and Throwing Exceptions

The public method setTime (lines 12–25) declares three int parameters and uses them to set the time. Lines 15–16 test each argument to determine whether the value is in range, and, if so, lines 18–20 assign the values to instance variables hour, minute and second. The hour value must be greater than or equal to 0 and less than 24, because universal-time format represents hours as integers from 0 to 23 (e.g., 1 PM is hour 13 and 11 PM is hour 23; midnight is hour 0 and noon is hour 12). Similarly, minute and second values must be greater than or equal to 0 and less than 60. For values outside these ranges, SetTime **throws an exception** of type **IllegalArgumentException** (lines 23–24), which notifies the client code that an invalid argument was passed to the method. As you learned in Chapter 7, you can use try...catch to catch exceptions and attempt to recover from them, which we'll do in Fig. 8.2. The **throw statement** (line 23) creates a new object of type IllegalArgumentException. The parentheses following the class name indicate a call to the IllegalArgumentException constructor. In this case, we call the constructor that allows us to specify a custom error message. After the exception object is created, the throw statement immediately terminates method set-Time and the exception is returned to the code that attempted to set the time.

Method *toUniversalString*

Method toUniversalString (lines 28–31) takes no arguments and returns a String in universal-time format, consisting of two digits each for the hour, minute and second. For example, if the time were 1:30:07 PM, the method would return 13:30:07. Line 22 uses static method **format** of class String to return a String containing the formatted hour, minute and second values, each with two digits and possibly a leading 0 (specified with the 0 flag). Method format is similar to method System.out.printf except that format *returns* a formatted String rather than displaying it in a command window. The formatted String is returned by method toUniversalString.

Method *toString*

Method toString (lines 34–39) takes no arguments and returns a String in standard-time format, consisting of the hour, minute and second values separated by colons and followed by AM or PM (e.g., 1:27:06 PM). Like method toUniversalString, method to-String uses static String method format to format the minute and second as two-digit values, with leading zeros if necessary. Line 29 uses a conditional operator (?:) to determine the value for hour in the String—if the hour is 0 or 12 (AM or PM), it appears as 12; otherwise, it appears as a value from 1 to 11. The conditional operator in line 30 determines whether AM or PM will be returned as part of the String.

Recall from Section 6.4 that all objects in Java have a toString method that returns a String representation of the object. We chose to return a String containing the time in standard-time format. Method toString is called implicitly whenever a Time1 object appears in the code where a String is needed, such as the value to output with a %s format specifier in a call to System.out.printf.

Using Class *Time1*

As you learned in Chapter 3, each class you declare represents a new *type* in Java. Therefore, after declaring class Time1, we can use it as a type in declarations such as

```
Time1 sunset; // sunset can hold a reference to a Time1 object
```

The Time1Test application class (Fig. 8.2) uses class Time1. Line 9 declares and creates a Time1 object and assigns it to local variable time. Operator new implicitly invokes class Time1's default constructor, since Time1 does not declare any constructors. Lines 12–16 output the time first in universal-time format (by invoking time's toUniversalString method in line 13), then in standard-time format (by explicitly invoking time's toString method in line 15) to confirm that the Time1 object was initialized properly. Next, line 19 invokes method setTime of the time object to change the time. Then lines 20–24 output the time again in both formats to confirm that it was set correctly.

```java
1   // Fig. 8.2: Time1Test.java
2   // Time1 object used in an application.
3
4   public class Time1Test
5   {
6      public static void main( String[] args )
7      {
8         // create and initialize a Time1 object
9         Time1 time = new Time1(); // invokes Time1 constructor
10
11        // output string representations of the time
12        System.out.print( "The initial universal time is: " );
13        System.out.println( time.toUniversalString() );
14        System.out.print( "The initial standard time is: " );
15        System.out.println( time.toString() );
16        System.out.println(); // output a blank line
17
18        // change time and output updated time
19        time.setTime( 13, 27, 6 );
20        System.out.print( "Universal time after setTime is: " );
21        System.out.println( time.toUniversalString() );
22        System.out.print( "Standard time after setTime is: " );
23        System.out.println( time.toString() );
24        System.out.println(); // output a blank line
25
26        // attempt to set time with invalid values
27        try
28        {
29           time.setTime( 99, 99, 99 ); // all values out of range
30        } // end try
31        catch ( IllegalArgumentException e )
32        {
33           System.out.printf( "Exception: %s\n\n", e.getMessage() );
34        } // end catch
35
36        // display time after attempt to set invalid values
37        System.out.println( "After attempting invalid settings:" );
38        System.out.print( "Universal time: " );
39        System.out.println( time.toUniversalString() );
40        System.out.print( "Standard time: " );
41        System.out.println( time.toString() );
42     } // end main
43  } // end class Time1Test
```

```
The initial universal time is: 00:00:00
The initial standard time is: 12:00:00 AM

Universal time after setTime is: 13:27:06
Standard time after setTime is: 1:27:06 PM

Exception: hour, minute and/or second was out of range

After attempting invalid settings:
Universal time: 13:27:06
Standard time: 1:27:06 PM
```

Fig. 8.2 | Time1 object used in an application.

Calling Time1 Method setTime with Invalid Values
To illustrate that method setTime validates its arguments, line 29 calls method setTime with invalid arguments of 99 for the hour, minute and second. This statement is placed in a try block (lines 27–30) in case setTime throws an IllegalArgumentException, which it will do since the arguments are all invalid. When this occurs, the exception is caught at lines 31–34, and line 33 displays the exception's error message by calling its getMessage method. Lines 37–41 output the time again in both formats to confirm that setTime did not change the time when invalid arguments were supplied.

Notes on the Time1 Class Declaration
Consider several issues of class design with respect to class Time1. The instance variables hour, minute and second are each declared private. The actual data representation used within the class is of no concern to the class's clients. For example, it would be perfectly reasonable for Time1 to represent the time internally as the number of seconds since midnight or the number of minutes and seconds since midnight. Clients could use the same public methods and get the same results without being aware of this.

Software Engineering Observation 8.1

Classes simplify programming, because the client can use only the public methods exposed by the class. Such methods are usually client oriented rather than implementation oriented. Clients are neither aware of, nor involved in, a class's implementation. Clients generally care about what the class does but not how the class does it.

Software Engineering Observation 8.2

Interfaces change less frequently than implementations. When an implementation changes, implementation-dependent code must change accordingly. Hiding the implementation reduces the possibility that other program parts will become dependent on class implementation details.

8.3 Controlling Access to Members

The access modifiers public and private control access to a class's variables and methods. In Chapter 9, we'll introduce the additional access modifier protected. As we stated in Section 8.2, the primary purpose of public methods is to present to the class's clients a view of the services the class provides (the class's public interface). Clients need not be concerned with how the class accomplishes its tasks. For this reason, the class's private variables and private methods (i.e., its implementation details) are *not* accessible to its clients.

Figure 8.3 demonstrates that private class members are not accessible outside the class. Lines 9–11 attempt to access directly the private instance variables hour, minute and second of the Time1 object time. When this program is compiled, the compiler generates error messages that these private members are not accessible. This program assumes that the Time1 class from Fig. 8.1 is used.

Common Programming Error 8.1

An attempt by a method that's not a member of a class to access a private member of that class is a compilation error.

```
 1   // Fig. 8.3: MemberAccessTest.java
 2   // Private members of class Time1 are not accessible.
 3   public class MemberAccessTest
 4   {
 5      public static void main( String[] args )
 6      {
 7         Time1 time = new Time1(); // create and initialize Time1 object
 8
 9         time.hour = 7; // error: hour has private access in Time1
10         time.minute = 15; // error: minute has private access in Time1
11         time.second = 30; // error: second has private access in Time1
12      } // end main
13   } // end class MemberAccessTest
```

```
MemberAccessTest.java:9: hour has private access in Time1
      time.hour = 7; // error: hour has private access in Time1
          ^
MemberAccessTest.java:10: minute has private access in Time1
      time.minute = 15; // error: minute has private access in Time1
          ^
MemberAccessTest.java:11: second has private access in Time1
      time.second = 30; // error: second has private access in Time1
          ^
3 errors
```

Fig. 8.3 | Private members of class Time1 are not accessible.

8.4 Referring to the Current Object's Members with the `this` Reference

Every object can access a reference to itself with keyword **this** (sometimes called the **this reference**). When a non-static method is called for a particular object, the method's body implicitly uses keyword this to refer to the object's instance variables and other methods. This enables the class's code to know which object should be manipulated. As you'll see in Fig. 8.4, you can also use keyword this explicitly in a non-static method's body. Section 8.5 shows another interesting use of keyword this. Section 8.11 explains why keyword this cannot be used in a static method.

```
 1   // Fig. 8.4: ThisTest.java
 2   // this used implicitly and explicitly to refer to members of an object.
 3
 4   public class ThisTest
 5   {
 6      public static void main( String[] args )
 7      {
 8         SimpleTime time = new SimpleTime( 15, 30, 19 );
 9         System.out.println( time.buildString() );
10      } // end main
11   } // end class ThisTest
```

Fig. 8.4 | this used implicitly and explicitly to refer to members of an object. (Part I of 2.)

```
12
13   // class SimpleTime demonstrates the "this" reference
14   class SimpleTime
15   {
16      private int hour; // 0-23
17      private int minute; // 0-59
18      private int second; // 0-59
19
20      // if the constructor uses parameter names identical to
21      // instance variable names the "this" reference is
22      // required to distinguish between the names
23      public SimpleTime( int hour, int minute, int second )
24      {
25         this.hour = hour; // set "this" object's hour
26         this.minute = minute; // set "this" object's minute
27         this.second = second; // set "this" object's second
28      } // end SimpleTime constructor
29
30      // use explicit and implicit "this" to call toUniversalString
31      public String buildString()
32      {
33         return String.format( "%24s: %s\n%24s: %s",
34            "this.toUniversalString()", this.toUniversalString(),
35            "toUniversalString()", toUniversalString() );
36      } // end method buildString
37
38      // convert to String in universal-time format (HH:MM:SS)
39      public String toUniversalString()
40      {
41         // "this" is not required here to access instance variables,
42         // because method does not have local variables with same
43         // names as instance variables
44         return String.format( "%02d:%02d:%02d",
45            this.hour, this.minute, this.second );
46      } // end method toUniversalString
47   } // end class SimpleTime
```

```
this.toUniversalString(): 15:30:19
    toUniversalString(): 15:30:19
```

Fig. 8.4 | this used implicitly and explicitly to refer to members of an object. (Part 2 of 2.)

We now demonstrate implicit and explicit use of the this reference (Fig. 8.4). This example is the first in which we declare *two* classes in one file—class ThisTest is declared in lines 4–11, and class SimpleTime in lines 14–47. We do this to demonstrate that when you compile a .java file containing more than one class, the compiler produces a separate class file with the .class extension for every compiled class. In this case, two separate files are produced—SimpleTime.class and ThisTest.class. When one source-code (.java) file contains multiple class declarations, the compiler places both class files for those classes in the same directory. Note also in Fig. 8.4 that only class ThisTest is declared public. A source-code file can contain only one public class—otherwise, a compilation error occurs.

Non-public classes can be used only by other classes in the same package. So, in this example, class SimpleTime can be used only by class ThisTest.

Class SimpleTime (lines 14–47) declares three private instance variables—hour, minute and second (lines 16–18). The constructor (lines 23–28) receives three int arguments to initialize a SimpleTime object. We used parameter names for the constructor (line 23) that are identical to the class's instance-variable names (lines 16–18). We don't recommend this practice, but we did it here to shadow (hide) the corresponding instance variables so that we could illustrate a case in which *explicit* use of the this reference is required. If a method contains a local variable with the *same* name as a field, that method will refer to the local variable rather than the field. In this case, the local variable shadows the field in the method's scope. However, the method can use the this reference to refer to the shadowed field explicitly, as shown on the left sides of the assignments in lines 25–27 for SimpleTime's shadowed instance variables.

Method buildString (lines 31–36) returns a String created by a statement that uses the this reference explicitly and implicitly. Line 34 uses it explicitly to call method toUniversalString. Line 35 uses it implicitly to call the same method. Both lines perform the same task. You typically will not use this explicitly to reference other methods within the current object. Also, line 45 in method toUniversalString explicitly uses the this reference to access each instance variable. This is *not* necessary here, because the method does *not* have any local variables that shadow the instance variables of the class.

Common Programming Error 8.2

It's often a logic error when a method contains a parameter or local variable that has the same name as a field of the class. In this case, use reference this if you wish to access the field of the class—otherwise, the method parameter or local variable will be referenced.

Error-Prevention Tip 8.1

Avoid method-parameter names or local-variable names that conflict with field names. This helps prevent subtle, hard-to-locate bugs.

Performance Tip 8.1

Java conserves storage by maintaining only one copy of each method per class—this method is invoked by every object of the class. Each object, on the other hand, has its own copy of the class's instance variables (i.e., non-static fields). Each method of the class implicitly uses this to determine the specific object of the class to manipulate.

Application class ThisTest (lines 4–11) demonstrates class SimpleTime. Line 8 creates an instance of class SimpleTime and invokes its constructor. Line 9 invokes the object's buildString method, then displays the results.

8.5 Time Class Case Study: Overloaded Constructors

As you know, you can declare your own constructor to specify how objects of a class should be initialized. Next, we demonstrate a class with several **overloaded constructors** that enable objects of that class to be initialized in different ways. To overload constructors, simply provide multiple constructor declarations with different signatures.

Class *Time2* with Overloaded Constructors

The default constructor for class Time1 (Fig. 8.1) initialized hour, minute and second to their default 0 values (which is midnight in universal time). The default constructor does not enable the class's clients to initialize the time with specific nonzero values. Class Time2 (Fig. 8.5) contains five overloaded constructors that provide convenient ways to initialize objects of the new class Time2. Each constructor initializes the object to begin in a consistent state. In this program, four of the constructors invoke a fifth, which in turn calls method setTime to ensure that the value supplied for hour is in the range 0 to 23, and the values for minute and second are each in the range 0 to 59. The compiler invokes the appropriate constructor by matching the number, types and order of the types of the arguments specified in the constructor call with the number, types and order of the types of the parameters specified in each constructor declaration. Class Time2 also provides *set* and *get* methods for each instance variable.

```
1   // Fig. 8.5: Time2.java
2   // Time2 class declaration with overloaded constructors.
3
4   public class Time2
5   {
6      private int hour; // 0 - 23
7      private int minute; // 0 - 59
8      private int second; // 0 - 59
9
10     // Time2 no-argument constructor:
11     // initializes each instance variable to zero
12     public Time2()
13     {
14        this( 0, 0, 0 ); // invoke Time2 constructor with three arguments
15     } // end Time2 no-argument constructor
16
17     // Time2 constructor: hour supplied, minute and second defaulted to 0
18     public Time2( int h )
19     {
20        this( h, 0, 0 ); // invoke Time2 constructor with three arguments
21     } // end Time2 one-argument constructor
22
23     // Time2 constructor: hour and minute supplied, second defaulted to 0
24     public Time2( int h, int m )
25     {
26        this( h, m, 0 ); // invoke Time2 constructor with three arguments
27     } // end Time2 two-argument constructor
28
29     // Time2 constructor: hour, minute and second supplied
30     public Time2( int h, int m, int s )
31     {
32        setTime( h, m, s ); // invoke setTime to validate time
33     } // end Time2 three-argument constructor
34
```

Fig. 8.5 | Time2 class with overloaded constructors. (Part 1 of 3.)

```
35        // Time2 constructor: another Time2 object supplied
36        public Time2( Time2 time )
37        {
38           // invoke Time2 three-argument constructor
39           this( time.getHour(), time.getMinute(), time.getSecond() );
40        } // end Time2 constructor with a Time2 object argument
41
42        // Set Methods
43        // set a new time value using universal time;
44        // validate the data
45        public void setTime( int h, int m, int s )
46        {
47           setHour( h ); // set the hour
48           setMinute( m ); // set the minute
49           setSecond( s ); // set the second
50        } // end method setTime
51
52        // validate and set hour
53        public void setHour( int h )
54        {
55           if ( h >= 0 && h < 24 )
56              hour = h;
57           else
58              throw new IllegalArgumentException( "hour must be 0-23" );
59        } // end method setHour
60
61        // validate and set minute
62        public void setMinute( int m )
63        {
64           if ( m >= 0 && m < 60 )
65              minute = m;
66           else
67              throw new IllegalArgumentException( "minute must be 0-59" );
68        } // end method setMinute
69
70        // validate and set second
71        public void setSecond( int s )
72        {
73           if ( s >= 0 && s < 60 )
74              second = ( ( s >= 0 && s < 60 ) ? s : 0 );
75           else
76              throw new IllegalArgumentException( "second must be 0-59" );
77        } // end method setSecond
78
79        // Get Methods
80        // get hour value
81        public int getHour()
82        {
83           return hour;
84        } // end method getHour
85
```

Fig. 8.5 | Time2 class with overloaded constructors. (Part 2 of 3.)

```
86      // get minute value
87      public int getMinute()
88      {
89         return minute;
90      } // end method getMinute
91
92      // get second value
93      public int getSecond()
94      {
95         return second;
96      } // end method getSecond
97
98      // convert to String in universal-time format (HH:MM:SS)
99      public String toUniversalString()
100     {
101        return String.format(
102           "%02d:%02d:%02d", getHour(), getMinute(), getSecond() );
103     } // end method toUniversalString
104
105     // convert to String in standard-time format (H:MM:SS AM or PM)
106     public String toString()
107     {
108        return String.format( "%d:%02d:%02d %s",
109           ( (getHour() == 0 || getHour() == 12) ? 12 : getHour() % 12 ),
110           getMinute(), getSecond(), ( getHour() < 12 ? "AM" : "PM" ) );
111     } // end method toString
112  } // end class Time2
```

Fig. 8.5 | Time2 class with overloaded constructors. (Part 3 of 3.)

Class *Time2's* Constructors

Lines 12–15 declare a so-called **no-argument constructor** that's invoked without arguments. Once you declare any constructors in a class, the compiler will *not* provide a default constructor. This no-argument constructor ensures that class Time2's clients can create Time2 objects with default values. Such a constructor simply initializes the object as specified in the constructor's body. In the body, we introduce a use of the this reference that's allowed only as the *first* statement in a constructor's body. Line 14 uses this in method-call syntax to invoke the Time2 constructor that takes three parameters (lines 30–33) with values of 0 for the hour, minute and second. Using the this reference as shown here is a popular way to reuse initialization code provided by another of the class's constructors rather than defining similar code in the no-argument constructor's body. We use this syntax in four of the five Time2 constructors to make the class easier to maintain and modify. If we need to change how objects of class Time2 are initialized, only the constructor that the class's other constructors call will need to be modified. In fact, even that constructor might not need modification in this example. That constructor simply calls the setTime method to perform the actual initialization, so it's possible that the changes the class might require would be localized to the *set* methods.

Common Programming Error 8.3

A constructor can call methods of the class. Instance variables might not yet be initialized, because the constructor is initializing the object. This can lead to logic errors.

Lines 18–21 declare a `Time2` constructor with a single `int` parameter representing the hour, which is passed with 0 for the `minute` and `second` to the constructor at lines 30–33. Lines 24–27 declare a `Time2` constructor that receives two `int` parameters representing the hour and `minute`, which are passed with 0 for the `second` to the constructor at lines 30–33. Like the no-argument constructor, each of these constructors invokes the constructor at lines 30–33 to minimize code duplication. Lines 30–33 declare the `Time2` constructor that receives three `int` parameters representing the hour, `minute` and `second`. This constructor calls `setTime` to initialize the instance variables.

Lines 36–40 declare a `Time2` constructor that receives a reference to another `Time2` object. In this case, the values from the `Time2` argument are passed to the three-argument constructor at lines 30–33 to initialize the hour, `minute` and `second`. Line 39 could have directly accessed the hour, `minute` and `second` values of the constructor's argument `time` with the expressions `time.hour`, `time.minute` and `time.second`—even though hour, `minute` and `second` are declared as `private` variables of class `Time2`. This is due to a special relationship between objects of the same class. We'll see in a moment why it's preferable to use the *get* methods.

Software Engineering Observation 8.3

When one object of a class has a reference to another object of the same class, the first object can access all the second object's data and methods (including those that are private).

Class Time2's setTime Method

Method `setTime` (lines 45–50) invokes the `setHour` (lines 53–59), `setMinute` (lines 62–68) and `setSecond` (lines 71–77) methods, which ensure that the value supplied for hour is in the range 0 to 23 and the values for `minute` and `second` are each in the range 0 to 59. If a value is out of range, each of these methods throws an `IllegalArgumentException` (lines 58, 67 and 76) indicating which value was out of range.

Notes Regarding Class Time2's set and get Methods and Constructors

`Time2`'s *set* and *get* methods are called throughout the class. In particular, method `setTime` calls methods `setHour`, `setMinute` and `setSecond` in lines 47–49, and methods `toUniversalString` and `toString` call methods `getHour`, `getMinute` and `getSecond` in line 93 and lines 100–101, respectively. In each case, these methods could have accessed the class's private data directly without calling the *set* and *get* methods. However, consider changing the representation of the time from three `int` values (requiring 12 bytes of memory) to a single `int` value representing the total number of seconds that have elapsed since midnight (requiring only 4 bytes of memory). If we made such a change, only the bodies of the methods that access the `private` data directly would need to change—in particular, the individual *set* and *get* methods for the hour, `minute` and `second`. There would be no need to modify the bodies of methods `setTime`, `toUniversalString` or `toString` because they do not access the data directly. Designing the class in this manner reduces the likelihood of programming errors when altering the class's implementation.

Similarly, each `Time2` constructor could include a copy of the appropriate statements from methods `setHour`, `setMinute` and `setSecond`. Doing so may be slightly more efficient, because the extra calls to the constructor and `setTime` are eliminated. However, *duplicating* statements in multiple methods or constructors makes changing the class's internal data representation more difficult. Having the `Time2` constructors call the constructor with three arguments (or even call setTime directly) requires that any changes to the implementation of setTime be made only once. Also, the compiler can optimize programs by removing calls to simple methods and replacing them with the expanded code of their declarations—a technique known as **inlining the code**, which improves program performance.

Software Engineering Observation 8.4

When implementing a method of a class, use the class's set *and* get *methods to access the class's* private *data. This simplifies code maintenance and reduces the likelihood of errors.*

Using Class Time2's Overloaded Constructors

Class Time2Test (Fig. 8.6) invokes the overloaded Time2 constructors (lines 8–12 and 40). Line 8 invokes the no-argument constructor (Fig. 8.5, lines 12–15). Lines 9–13 of the program demonstrate passing arguments to the other Time2 constructors. Line 9 invokes the single-argument constructor that receives an int at lines 18–21 of Fig. 8.5. Line 10 invokes the two-argument constructor at lines 24–27 of Fig. 8.5. Line 11 invokes the three-argument constructor at lines 30–33 of Fig. 8.5. Line 12 invokes the single-argument constructor that takes a Time2 at lines 36–40 of Fig. 8.5. Next, the application displays the String representations of each Time2 object to confirm that it was initialized properly. Line 40 attempts to intialize t6 by creating a new Time2 object and passing three invalid values to the constructor. When the constructor attempts to use the invalid hour value to initialize the object's hour, an IllegalArgumentException occurs. We catch this exception at line 42 and display its error message, which results in the last line of the output.

```
1   // Fig. 8.6: Time2Test.java
2   // Overloaded constructors used to initialize Time2 objects.
3
4   public class Time2Test
5   {
6      public static void main( String[] args )
7      {
8         Time2 t1 = new Time2(); // 00:00:00
9         Time2 t2 = new Time2( 2 ); // 02:00:00
10        Time2 t3 = new Time2( 21, 34 ); // 21:34:00
11        Time2 t4 = new Time2( 12, 25, 42 ); // 12:25:42
12        Time2 t5 = new Time2( t4 ); // 12:25:42
13
14        System.out.println( "Constructed with:" );
15        System.out.println( "t1: all arguments defaulted" );
16        System.out.printf( "   %s\n", t1.toUniversalString() );
17        System.out.printf( "   %s\n", t1.toString() );
18
19        System.out.println(
20           "t2: hour specified; minute and second defaulted" );
21        System.out.printf( "   %s\n", t2.toUniversalString() );
22        System.out.printf( "   %s\n", t2.toString() );
23
24        System.out.println(
25           "t3: hour and minute specified; second defaulted" );
26        System.out.printf( "   %s\n", t3.toUniversalString() );
```

Fig. 8.6 | Overloaded constructors used to initialize Time2 objects. (Part 1 of 2.)

```
27            System.out.printf( "   %s\n", t3.toString() );
28
29            System.out.println( "t4: hour, minute and second specified" );
30            System.out.printf( "   %s\n", t4.toUniversalString() );
31            System.out.printf( "   %s\n", t4.toString() );
32
33            System.out.println( "t5: Time2 object t4 specified" );
34            System.out.printf( "   %s\n", t5.toUniversalString() );
35            System.out.printf( "   %s\n", t5.toString() );
36
37            // attempt to initialize t6 with invalid values
38            try
39            {
40               Time2 t6 = new Time2( 27, 74, 99 ); // invalid values
41            } // end try
42            catch ( IllegalArgumentException e )
43            {
44               System.out.printf( "\nException while initializing t6: %s\n",
45                  e.getMessage() );
46            } // end catch
47        } // end main
48   } // end class Time2Test
```

```
Constructed with:
t1: all arguments defaulted
   00:00:00
   12:00:00 AM
t2: hour specified; minute and second defaulted
   02:00:00
   2:00:00 AM

t3: hour and minute specified; second defaulted
   21:34:00
   9:34:00 PM
t4: hour, minute and second specified
   12:25:42
   12:25:42 PM
t5: Time2 object t4 specified
   12:25:42
   12:25:42 PM

Exception while initializing t6: hour must be 0-23
```

Fig. 8.6 | Overloaded constructors used to initialize Time2 objects. (Part 2 of 2.)

8.6 Default and No-Argument Constructors

Every class must have at least one constructor. If you do not provide any in a class's declaration, the compiler creates a default constructor that takes no arguments when it's invoked. The default constructor initializes the instance variables to the initial values specified in their declarations or to their default values (zero for primitive numeric types, false for boolean values and null for references). In Section 9.4.1, you'll learn that the default constructor performs another task also.

If your class declares constructors, the compiler will *not* create a default constructor. In this case, you must declare a no-argument constructor if default initialization is required. Like a default constructor, a no-argument constructor is invoked with empty parentheses. The Time2 no-argument constructor (lines 12–15 of Fig. 8.5) explicitly initializes a Time2 object by passing to the three-argument constructor 0 for each parameter. Since 0 is the default value for int instance variables, the no-argument constructor in this example could actually be declared with an empty body. In this case, each instance variable would receive its default value when the no-argument constructor was called. If we omit the no-argument constructor, clients of this class would not be able to create a Time2 object with the expression new Time2().

Common Programming Error 8.4

A compilation error occurs if a program attempts to initialize an object of a class by passing the wrong number or types of arguments to the class's constructor.

Error-Prevention Tip 8.2

Ensure that you do not *include a return type in a constructor definition. Java allows other methods of the class besides its constructors to have the same name as the class and to specify return types. Such methods are* not *constructors and will not be called when an object of the class is instantiated.*

8.7 Notes on *Set* and *Get* Methods

As you know, a class's private fields can be manipulated only by its methods. A typical manipulation might be the adjustment of a customer's bank balance (e.g., a private instance variable of a class BankAccount) by a method computeInterest. Classes often provide public methods to allow clients of the class to *set* (i.e., assign values to) or *get* (i.e., obtain the values of) private instance variables.

As a naming example, a method that sets instance variable interestRate would typically be named setInterestRate and a method that gets the interestRate would typically be called getInterestRate. *Set* methods are also commonly called **mutator methods**, because they typically change an object's state—i.e., modify the values of instance variables. *Get* methods are also commonly called **accessor methods** or **query methods**.

Set *and* Get *Methods vs.* public *Data*

It would seem that providing *set* and *get* capabilities is essentially the same as making the instance variables public. This is one of the subtleties that makes Java so desirable for software engineering. A public instance variable can be read or written by any method that has a reference to an object containing that variable. If an instance variable is declared private, a public *get* method certainly allows other methods to access it, but the *get* method can *control* how the client can access it. For example, a *get* method might control the format of the data it returns and thus shield the client code from the actual data representation. A public *set* method can—and should—carefully scrutinize attempts to modify the variable's value and throw an exception if necessary. For example, an attempt to *set* the day of the month to 37 would be rejected, an attempt to *set* a person's weight to a negative value would be rejected, and so on. Although *set* and *get* methods provide access to private data, the access is restricted by the implementation of the methods. This helps promote good software engineering.

Validity Checking in Set *Methods*

The benefits of data integrity do not follow automatically simply because instance variables are declared `private`—you must provide validity checking. Java enables you to design better programs in a convenient manner. A class's *set* methods could return values indicating that attempts were made to assign invalid data to objects of the class. A client of the class could test the return value of a *set* method to determine whether the client's attempt to modify the object was successful and to take appropriate action. Typically, however, *set* methods have `void` return type and use exception handling to indicate attempts to assign invalid data. We discuss exception handling in detail in Chapter 11.

Software Engineering Observation 8.5

When appropriate, provide `public` methods to change and retrieve the values of `private` instance variables. This architecture helps hide the implementation of a class from its clients, which improves program modifiability.

Error-Prevention Tip 8.3

Using set *and* get *methods helps you create classes that are easier to debug and maintain. If only one method performs a particular task, such as setting the hour in a `Time2` object, it's easier to debug and maintain the class. If the hour is not being set properly, the code that actually modifies instance variable `hour` is localized to one method's body—`setHour`. Thus, your debugging efforts can be focused on method `setHour`.*

Predicate Methods

Another common use for accessor methods is to test whether a condition is true or false—such methods are often called **predicate methods**. An example would be class `ArrayList`'s `isEmpty` method, which returns `true` if the `ArrayList` is empty. A program might test `isEmpty` before attempting to read another item from an `ArrayList`.

8.8 Composition

A class can have references to objects of other classes as members. This is called **composition** and is sometimes referred to as a *has-a* **relationship**. For example, an `AlarmClock` object needs to know the current time *and* the time when it's supposed to sound its alarm, so it's reasonable to include *two* references to `Time` objects in an `AlarmClock` object.

Class **Date**

This composition example contains classes `Date` (Fig. 8.7), `Employee` (Fig. 8.8) and `EmployeeTest` (Fig. 8.9). Class `Date` (Fig. 8.7) declares instance variables month, day and year (lines 6–8) to represent a date. The constructor receives three `int` parameters. Line 17 invokes utility method `checkMonth` (lines 26–32) to validate the month—if the value is out-of-range the method throws an exception. Line 15 assumes that the value for year is correct and doesn't validate it. Line 19 invokes utility method `checkDay` (lines 35–48) to validate the day based on the current month and year. Line 38 determines whether the day is correct based on the number of days in the particular month. If the day is not correct, lines 42–43 determine whether the month is February, the day is 29 and the year is a leap year. If the day is still invalid, the method throws an exception. Lines 21–22 in the constructor output the `this` reference as a `String`. Since `this` is a reference to the current `Date` object, the object's toString method (lines 51–54) is called *implicitly* to obtain the object's String representation.

```
1   // Fig. 8.7: Date.java
2   // Date class declaration.
3
4   public class Date
5   {
6      private int month; // 1-12
7      private int day; // 1-31 based on month
8      private int year; // any year
9
10     private static final int[] daysPerMonth = // days in each month
11        { 0, 31, 28, 31, 30, 31, 30, 31, 31, 30, 31, 30, 31 };
12
13     // constructor: call checkMonth to confirm proper value for month;
14     // call checkDay to confirm proper value for day
15     public Date( int theMonth, int theDay, int theYear )
16     {
17        month = checkMonth( theMonth ); // validate month
18        year = theYear; // could validate year
19        day = checkDay( theDay ); // validate day
20
21        System.out.printf(
22           "Date object constructor for date %s\n", this );
23     } // end Date constructor
24
25     // utility method to confirm proper month value
26     private int checkMonth( int testMonth )
27     {
28        if ( testMonth > 0 && testMonth <= 12 ) // validate month
29           return testMonth;
30        else // month is invalid
31           throw new IllegalArgumentException( "month must be 1-12" );
32     } // end method checkMonth
33
34     // utility method to confirm proper day value based on month and year
35     private int checkDay( int testDay )
36     {
37        // check if day in range for month
38        if ( testDay > 0 && testDay <= daysPerMonth[ month ] )
39           return testDay;
40
41        // check for leap year
42        if ( month == 2 && testDay == 29 && ( year % 400 == 0 ||
43           ( year % 4 == 0 && year % 100 != 0 ) ) )
44           return testDay;
45
46        throw new IllegalArgumentException(
47           "day out-of-range for the specified month and year" );
48     } // end method checkDay
49
```

Fig. 8.7 | Date class declaration. (Part 1 of 2.)

```
50        // return a String of the form month/day/year
51        public String toString()
52        {
53           return String.format( "%d/%d/%d", month, day, year );
54        } // end method toString
55     } // end class Date
```

Fig. 8.7 | Date class declaration. (Part 2 of 2.)

Class Employee

Class Employee (Fig. 8.8) has instance variables firstName, lastName, birthDate and hireDate. Members firstName and lastName (lines 6–7) are references to String objects. Members birthDate and hireDate (lines 8–9) are references to Date objects. This demonstrates that a class can have as instance variables references to objects of other classes. The Employee constructor (lines 12–19) takes four parameters—first, last, dateOf-Birth and dateOfHire. The objects referenced by the parameters are assigned to the Employee object's instance variables. When class Employee's toString method is called, it returns a String containing the employee's name and the String representations of the two Date objects. Each of these Strings is obtained with an *implicit* call to the Date class's toString method.

```
1   // Fig. 8.8: Employee.java
2   // Employee class with references to other objects.
3
4   public class Employee
5   {
6      private String firstName;
7      private String lastName;
8      private Date birthDate;
9      private Date hireDate;
10
11     // constructor to initialize name, birth date and hire date
12     public Employee( String first, String last, Date dateOfBirth,
13        Date dateOfHire )
14     {
15        firstName = first;
16        lastName = last;
17        birthDate = dateOfBirth;
18        hireDate = dateOfHire;
19     } // end Employee constructor
20
21     // convert Employee to String format
22     public String toString()
23     {
24        return String.format( "%s, %s  Hired: %s  Birthday: %s",
25           lastName, firstName, hireDate, birthDate );
26     } // end method toString
27  } // end class Employee
```

Fig. 8.8 | Employee class with references to other objects.

Class EmployeeTest
Class EmployeeTest (Fig. 8.9) creates two Date objects (lines 8–9) to represent an Employee's birthday and hire date, respectively. Line 10 creates an Employee and initializes its instance variables by passing to the constructor two Strings (representing the Employee's first and last names) and two Date objects (representing the birthday and hire date). Line 12 implicitly invokes the Employee's toString method to display the values of its instance variables and demonstrate that the object was initialized properly.

```
1   // Fig. 8.9: EmployeeTest.java
2   // Composition demonstration.
3
4   public class EmployeeTest
5   {
6      public static void main( String[] args )
7      {
8         Date birth = new Date( 7, 24, 1949 );
9         Date hire = new Date( 3, 12, 1988 );
10        Employee employee = new Employee( "Bob", "Blue", birth, hire );
11
12        System.out.println( employee );
13     } // end main
14  } // end class EmployeeTest
```

```
Date object constructor for date 7/24/1949
Date object constructor for date 3/12/1988
Blue, Bob  Hired: 3/12/1988  Birthday: 7/24/1949
```

Fig. 8.9 | Composition demonstration.

8.9 Enumerations

In Fig. 6.7, we introduced the basic enum type, which defines a set of constants represented as unique identifiers. In that program the enum constants represented the game's status. In this section we discuss the relationship between enum types and classes. Like classes, all enum types are reference types. An enum type is declared with an **enum declaration**, which is a comma-separated list of enum constants—the declaration may optionally include other components of traditional classes, such as constructors, fields and methods. Each enum declaration declares an enum class with the following restrictions:

1. enum constants are implicitly final, because they declare constants that shouldn't be modified.

2. enum constants are implicitly static.

3. Any attempt to create an object of an enum type with operator new results in a compilation error.

The enum constants can be used anywhere constants can be used, such as in the case labels of switch statements and to control enhanced for statements.

Figure 8.10 illustrates how to declare instance variables, a constructor and methods in an enum type. The enum declaration (lines 5–37) contains two parts—the enum constants and the other members of the enum type. The first part (lines 8–13) declares six enum constants. Each is optionally followed by arguments which are passed to the **enum constructor** (lines 20–24). Like the constructors you've seen in classes, an enum constructor can specify any number of parameters and can be overloaded. In this example, the enum constructor requires two String parameters. To properly initialize each enum constant, we follow it with parentheses containing two String arguments, which are passed to the enum's constructor. The second part (lines 16–36) declares the other members of the enum type—two instance variables (lines 16–17), a constructor (lines 20–24) and two methods (lines 27–30 and 33–36).

```java
1   // Fig. 8.10: Book.java
2   // Declaring an enum type with constructor and explicit instance fields
3   // and accessors for these fields
4
5   public enum Book
6   {
7      // declare constants of enum type
8      JHTP( "Java How to Program", "2012" ),
9      CHTP( "C How to Program", "2007" ),
10     IW3HTP( "Internet & World Wide Web How to Program", "2008" ),
11     CPPHTP( "C++ How to Program", "2012" ),
12     VBHTP( "Visual Basic 2010 How to Program", "2011" ),
13     CSHARPHTP( "Visual C# 2010 How to Program", "2011" );
14
15     // instance fields
16     private final String title; // book title
17     private final String copyrightYear; // copyright year
18
19     // enum constructor
20     Book( String bookTitle, String year )
21     {
22        title = bookTitle;
23        copyrightYear = year;
24     } // end enum Book constructor
25
26     // accessor for field title
27     public String getTitle()
28     {
29        return title;
30     } // end method getTitle
31
32     // accessor for field copyrightYear
33     public String getCopyrightYear()
34     {
35        return copyrightYear;
36     } // end method getCopyrightYear
37  } // end enum Book
```

Fig. 8.10 | Declaring an enum type with constructor and explicit instance fields and accessors for these fields.

Lines 16–17 declare the instance variables title and copyrightYear. Each enum constant in Book is actually an object of type Book that has its own copy of instance variables title and copyrightYear. The constructor (lines 20–24) takes two String parameters, one that specifies the book's title and one that specifies its copyright year. Lines 22–23 assign these parameters to the instance variables. Lines 27–36 declare two methods, which return the book title and copyright year, respectively.

Figure 8.11 tests the enum type Book and illustrates how to iterate through a range of enum constants. For every enum, the compiler generates the static method **values** (called in line 12) that returns an array of the enum's constants in the order they were declared. Lines 12–14 use the enhanced for statement to display all the constants declared in the enum Book. Line 14 invokes the enum Book's getTitle and getCopyrightYear methods to get the title and copyright year associated with the constant. When an enum constant is converted to a String (e.g., book in line 13), the constant's identifier is used as the String representation (e.g., JHTP for the first enum constant).

```java
1   // Fig. 8.11: EnumTest.java
2   // Testing enum type Book.
3   import java.util.EnumSet;
4
5   public class EnumTest
6   {
7      public static void main( String[] args )
8      {
9         System.out.println( "All books:\n" );
10
11        // print all books in enum Book
12        for ( Book book : Book.values() )
13           System.out.printf( "%-10s%-45s%s\n", book,
14              book.getTitle(), book.getCopyrightYear() );
15
16        System.out.println( "\nDisplay a range of enum constants:\n" );
17
18        // print first four books
19        for ( Book book : EnumSet.range( Book.JHTP, Book.CPPHTP ) )
20           System.out.printf( "%-10s%-45s%s\n", book,
21              book.getTitle(), book.getCopyrightYear() );
22     } // end main
23  } // end class EnumTest
```

```
All books:

JHTP       Java How to Program                           2012
CHTP       C How to Program                              2007
IW3HTP     Internet & World Wide Web How to Program      2008
CPPHTP     C++ How to Program                            2012
VBHTP      Visual Basic 2010 How to Program              2011
CSHARPHTP  Visual C# 2010 How to Program                 2011

Display a range of enum constants:

JHTP       Java How to Program                           2012
CHTP       C How to Program                              2007
IW3HTP     Internet & World Wide Web How to Program      2008
CPPHTP     C++ How to Program                            2012
```

Fig. 8.11 | Testing an enum type.

Lines 19–21 use the `static` method **range** of class **EnumSet** (declared in package `java.util`) to display a range of the enum Book's constants. Method range takes two parameters—the first and the last `enum` constants in the range—and returns an `EnumSet` that contains all the constants between these two constants, inclusive. For example, the expression `EnumSet.range( Book.JHTP, Book.CPPHTP )` returns an `EnumSet` containing `Book.JHTP`, `Book.CHTP`, `Book.IW3HTP` and `Book.CPPHTP`. The enhanced for statement can be used with an `EnumSet` just as it can with an array, so lines 12–14 use it to display the title and copyright year of every book in the `EnumSet`. Class `EnumSet` provides several other `static` methods for creating sets of enum constants from the same enum type.

Common Programming Error 8.5

In an enum *declaration, it's a syntax error to declare* enum *constants after the* enum *type's constructors, fields and methods.*

8.10 Garbage Collection and Method `finalize`

Every class in Java has the methods of class `Object` (package `java.lang`), one of which is the `finalize` method. This method is rarely used because it can cause performance problems and there's some uncertainty as to whether it will get called. Nevertheless, because `finalize` is part of every class, we discuss it here to help you understand its intended purpose. The complete details of the `finalize` method are beyond the scope of this book, and most programmers should not use it—you'll soon see why. You'll learn more about class `Object` in Chapter 9.

Every object uses system resources, such as memory. We need a disciplined way to give resources back to the system when they're no longer needed; otherwise, "resource leaks" might occur that would prevent them from being reused by your program or possibly by other programs. The JVM performs automatic **garbage collection** to reclaim the memory occupied by objects that are no longer used. When there are no more references to an object, the object is eligible to be collected. This typically occurs when the JVM executes its **garbage collector**. So, memory leaks that are common in other languages like C and C++ (because memory is not automatically reclaimed in those languages) are less likely in Java, but some can still happen in subtle ways. Other types of resource leaks can occur. For example, an application may open a file on disk to modify its contents. If it does not close the file, the application must terminate before any other application can use it.

The **finalize method** is called by the garbage collector to perform **termination housekeeping** on an object just before the garbage collector reclaims the object's memory. Method `finalize` does not take parameters and has return type `void`. A problem with method `finalize` is that the garbage collector is not guaranteed to execute at a specified time. In fact, the garbage collector may never execute before a program terminates. Thus, it's unclear whether, or when, method `finalize` will be called. For this reason, most programmers should avoid method `finalize`.

Software Engineering Observation 8.6

A class that uses system resources, such as files on disk, should provide a method that programmers can call to release resources when they're no longer needed in a program. Many Java API classes provide close *or* dispose *methods for this purpose. We discuss new Java SE 7 features related to this in Section 11.13.*

8.11 static **Class Members**

Every object has its own copy of all the instance variables of the class. In certain cases, only one copy of a particular variable should be *shared* by all objects of a class. A **static field**—called a **class variable**—is used in such cases. A static variable represents **classwide information**—all objects of the class share the *same* piece of data. The declaration of a static variable begins with the keyword static.

Let's motivate static data with an example. Suppose that we have a video game with Martians and other space creatures. Each Martian tends to be brave and willing to attack other space creatures when the Martian is aware that at least four other Martians are present. If fewer than five Martians are present, each of them becomes cowardly. Thus, each Martian needs to know the martianCount. We could endow class Martian with martianCount as an instance variable. If we do this, then every Martian will have *a separate copy* of the instance variable, and every time we create a new Martian, we'll have to update the instance variable martianCount in every Martian object. This wastes space with the redundant copies, wastes time in updating the separate copies and is error prone. Instead, we declare martianCount to be static, making martianCount classwide data. Every Martian can see the martianCount as if it were an instance variable of class Martian, but only one copy of the static martianCount is maintained. This saves space. We save time by having the Martian constructor increment the static martianCount—there's only one copy, so we do not have to increment separate copies for each Martian object.

Software Engineering Observation 8.7

Use a static variable when all objects of a class must use the same copy of the variable.

Static variables have class scope. We can access a class's public static members through a reference to any object of the class, or by qualifying the member name with the class name and a dot (.), as in Math.random(). A class's private static class members can be accessed by client code only through methods of the class. Actually, *static class members exist even when no objects of the class exist*—they're available as soon as the class is loaded into memory at execution time. To access a public static member when no objects of the class exist (and even when they do), prefix the class name and a dot (.) to the static member, as in Math.PI. To access a private static member when no objects of the class exist, provide a public static method and call it by qualifying its name with the class name and a dot.

Software Engineering Observation 8.8

Static class variables and methods exist, and can be used, even if no objects of that class have been instantiated.

A static method cannot access non-static class members, because a static method can be called even when no objects of the class have been instantiated. For the same reason, the this reference cannot be used in a static method. The this reference must refer to a specific object of the class, and when a static method is called, there might not be any objects of its class in memory.

Common Programming Error 8.6

Referring to this *in a* static *method is a compilation error.*

Common Programming Error 8.7

A compilation error occurs if a static method calls an instance (non-static) method in the same class by using only the method name. Similarly, a compilation error occurs if a static method attempts to access an instance variable in the same class by using only the variable name.

Tracking the Number of Employee Objects That Have Been Created

Our next program declares two classes—Employee (Fig. 8.12) and EmployeeTest (Fig. 8.13). Class Employee declares private static variable count (Fig. 8.12, line 9) and public static method getCount (lines 36–39). The static variable count is initialized to zero in line 9. If a static variable is not initialized, the compiler assigns it a default value—in this case 0, the default value for type int. Variable count maintains a count of the number of objects of class Employee that have been created so far.

```
1   // Fig. 8.12: Employee.java
2   // Static variable used to maintain a count of the number of
3   // Employee objects in memory.
4
5   public class Employee
6   {
7      private String firstName;
8      private String lastName;
9      private static int count = 0; // number of Employees created
10
11     // initialize Employee, add 1 to static count and
12     // output String indicating that constructor was called
13     public Employee( String first, String last )
14     {
15        firstName = first;
16        lastName = last;
17
18        ++count;  // increment static count of employees
19        System.out.printf( "Employee constructor: %s %s; count = %d\n",
20           firstName, lastName, count );
21     } // end Employee constructor
22
23     // get first name
24     public String getFirstName()
25     {
26        return firstName;
27     } // end method getFirstName
28
29     // get last name
30     public String getLastName()
31     {
32        return lastName;
33     } // end method getLastName
34
```

Fig. 8.12 | static variable used to maintain a count of the number of Employee objects in memory. (Part 1 of 2.)

```
35      // static method to get static count value
36      public static int getCount()
37      {
38         return count;
39      } // end method getCount
40   } // end class Employee
```

Fig. 8.12 | static variable used to maintain a count of the number of Employee objects in memory. (Part 2 of 2.)

When Employee objects exist, variable count can be used in any method of an Employee object—this example increments count in the constructor (line 18). The public static method getCount (lines 36–39) returns the number of Employee objects that have been created so far. When no objects of class Employee exist, client code can access variable count by calling method getCount via the class name, as in Employee.getCount(). When objects exist, method getCount can also be called via any reference to an Employee object.

Good Programming Practice 8.1

Invoke every static method by using the class name and a dot (.) to emphasize that the method being called is a static method.

EmployeeTest method main (Fig. 8.13) instantiates two Employee objects (lines 13–14). When each Employee object's constructor is invoked, lines 15–16 of Fig. 8.12 assign the Employee's first name and last name to instance variables firstName and lastName. These two statements do *not* make copies of the original String arguments. Actually, String objects in Java are **immutable**—they cannot be modified after they're created. Therefore, it's safe to have many references to one String object. This is not normally the case for objects of most other classes in Java. If String objects are immutable, you might wonder why we're able to use operators + and += to concatenate String objects. String-concatenation operations actually result in a *new* Strings object containing the concatenated values. The original String objects are not modified.

```
1    // Fig. 8.13: EmployeeTest.java
2    // static member demonstration.
3
4    public class EmployeeTest
5    {
6       public static void main( String[] args )
7       {
8          // show that count is 0 before creating Employees
9          System.out.printf( "Employees before instantiation: %d\n",
10            Employee.getCount() );
11
12          // create two Employees; count should be 2
13          Employee e1 = new Employee( "Susan", "Baker" );
14          Employee e2 = new Employee( "Bob", "Blue" );
15
```

Fig. 8.13 | static member demonstration. (Part 1 of 2.)

```
16          // show that count is 2 after creating two Employees
17          System.out.println( "\nEmployees after instantiation: " );
18          System.out.printf( "via e1.getCount(): %d\n", e1.getCount() );
19          System.out.printf( "via e2.getCount(): %d\n", e2.getCount() );
20          System.out.printf( "via Employee.getCount(): %d\n",
21             Employee.getCount() );
22
23          // get names of Employees
24          System.out.printf( "\nEmployee 1: %s %s\nEmployee 2: %s %s\n",
25             e1.getFirstName(), e1.getLastName(),
26             e2.getFirstName(), e2.getLastName() );
27
28          // in this example, there is only one reference to each Employee,
29          // so the following two statements indicate that these objects
30          // are eligible for garbage collection
31          e1 = null;
32          e2 = null;
33       } // end main
34    } // end class EmployeeTest
```

```
Employees before instantiation: 0
Employee constructor: Susan Baker; count = 1
Employee constructor: Bob Blue; count = 2

Employees after instantiation:
via e1.getCount(): 2
via e2.getCount(): 2
via Employee.getCount(): 2

Employee 1: Susan Baker
Employee 2: Bob Blue
```

Fig. 8.13 | static member demonstration. (Part 2 of 2.)

When main has finished using the two Employee objects, the references e1 and e2 are set to null at lines 31–32. At this point, references e1 and e2 no longer refer to the objects that were instantiated in lines 13–14. The objects become "eligible for garbage collection" because there are no more references to them in the program.

Eventually, the garbage collector might reclaim the memory for these objects (or the operating system will reclaim the memory when the program terminates). The JVM does not guarantee when, or even whether, the garbage collector will execute. When it does, it's possible that no objects or only a subset of the eligible objects will be collected.

8.12 static Import

In Section 6.3, you learned about the static fields and methods of class Math. We invoked class Math's static fields and methods by preceding each with the class name Math and a dot (.). A **static import** declaration enables you to import the static members of a class or interface so you can access them via their unqualified names in your class—the class name and a dot (.) are not required to use an imported static member.

A static import declaration has two forms—one that imports a particular static member (which is known as **single static import**) and one that imports *all* static members of a class (known as **static import on demand**). The following syntax imports a particular static member:

> **import static** *packageName*. *ClassName*. *staticMemberName*;

where *packageName* is the package of the class (e.g., java.lang), *ClassName* is the name of the class (e.g., Math) and *staticMemberName* is the name of the static field or method (e.g., PI or abs). The following syntax imports all static members of a class:

> **import static** *packageName*. *ClassName*. *;

The asterisk (*) indicates that *all* static members of the specified class should be available for use in the file. static import declarations import only static class members. Regular import statements should be used to specify the classes used in a program.

Figure 8.14 demonstrates a static import. Line 3 is a static import declaration, which imports all static fields and methods of class Math from package java.lang. Lines 9–12 access the Math class's static fields E (line 11) and PI (line 12) and the static methods sqrt (line 9) and ceil (line 10) without preceding the field names or method names with class name Math and a dot.

Common Programming Error 8.8

A compilation error occurs if a program attempts to import two or more classes' static methods that have the same signature or static fields that have the same name.

```
 1   // Fig. 8.14: StaticImportTest.java
 2   // Static import of Math class methods.
 3   import static java.lang.Math.*;
 4
 5   public class StaticImportTest
 6   {
 7      public static void main( String[] args )
 8      {
 9         System.out.printf( "sqrt( 900.0 ) = %.1f\n", sqrt( 900.0 ) );
10         System.out.printf( "ceil( -9.8 ) = %.1f\n", ceil( -9.8 ) );
11         System.out.printf( "E = %f\n", E );
12         System.out.printf( "PI = %f\n", PI );
13      } // end main
14   } // end class StaticImportTest
```

```
sqrt( 900.0 ) = 30.0
ceil( -9.8 ) = -9.0
log( E ) = 1.0
cos( 0.0 ) = 1.0
```

Fig. 8.14 | Static import of Math class methods.

8.13 final Instance Variables

The **principle of least privilege** is fundamental to good software engineering. In the context of an application, it states that code should be granted only the amount of privilege and access that it needs to accomplish its designated task, but no more. This makes your programs more robust by preventing code from accidentally (or maliciously) modifying variable values and calling methods that should not be accessible.

Let's see how this principle applies to instance variables. Some of them need to be modifiable and some do not. You can use the keyword `final` to specify that a variable is not modifiable (i.e., it's a constant) and that any attempt to modify it is an error. For example,

```
private final int INCREMENT;
```

declares a `final` (constant) instance variable INCREMENT of type `int`. Such variables can be initialized when they're declared. If they are not, they *must* be initialized in every constructor of the class. Initializing constants in constructors enables each object of the class to have a different value for the constant. If a `final` variable is not initialized in its declaration or in every constructor, a compilation error occurs.

Software Engineering Observation 8.9

Declaring an instance variable as `final` helps enforce the principle of least privilege. If an instance variable should not be modified, declare it to be `final` to prevent modification.

Common Programming Error 8.9

Attempting to modify a `final` instance variable after it's initialized is a compilation error.

Error-Prevention Tip 8.4

Attempts to modify a `final` instance variable are caught at compilation time rather than causing execution-time errors. It's always preferable to get bugs out at compilation time, if possible, rather than allow them to slip through to execution time (where experience has found that repair is often many times more expensive).

Software Engineering Observation 8.10

A `final` field should also be declared `static` if it's initialized in its declaration to a value that's the same for all objects of the class. After this initialization, its value can never change. Therefore, we don't need a separate copy of the field for every object of the class. Making the field `static` enables all objects of the class to share the `final` field.

8.14 Time Class Case Study: Creating Packages

We've seen in almost every example in the text that classes from preexisting libraries, such as the Java API, can be imported into a Java program. Each class in the Java API belongs to a package that contains a group of related classes. These packages are defined once, but can be imported into many programs. As applications become more complex, packages help you manage the complexity of application components. Packages also facilitate software reuse by enabling programs to *import* classes from other packages (as we've done in most examples), rather than *copying* the classes into each program that uses them. Another benefit of packages is that they provide a convention for unique class names, which helps prevent class-name conflicts (discussed later in this section). This section introduces how to create your own packages.

Steps for Declaring a Reusable Class

Before a class can be imported into multiple applications, it must be placed in a package to make it reusable. Figure 8.15 shows how to specify the package in which a class should be placed. Figure 8.16 shows how to import our packaged class so that it can be used in an application. The steps for creating a reusable class are:

1. Declare a public class. If the class is not public, it can be used only by other classes in the same package.

2. Choose a unique package name and add a **package declaration** to the source-code file for the reusable class declaration. In each Java source-code file there can be only one package declaration, and it must precede all other declarations and statements. Comments are not statements, so comments can be placed before a package statement in a file. [*Note:* If no package statement is provided, the class is placed in the so-called default package and is accessible only to other classes in the default package that are located in the same directory. All prior programs in this book having two or more classes have used this default package.]

3. Compile the class so that it's placed in the appropriate package directory.

4. Import the reusable class into a program and use the class.

We'll now discuss each of these steps in detail.

*Steps 1 and 2: Creating a **public** Class and Adding the **package** Statement*

For *Step 1*, we modify the public class Time1 declared in Fig. 8.1. The new version is shown in Fig. 8.15. No modifications have been made to the implementation of the class, so we'll not discuss its implementation details again here.

```
1    // Fig. 8.15: Time1.java
2    // Time1 class declaration maintains the time in 24-hour format.
3    package com.deitel.javafp.ch08;
4
5    public class Time1
6    {
7       private int hour; // 0 - 23
8       private int minute; // 0 - 59
9       private int second; // 0 - 59
10
11      // set a new time value using universal time; throw an
12      // exception if the hour, minute or second is invalid
13      public void setTime( int h, int m, int s )
14      {
15         // validate hour, minute and second
16         if ( ( h >= 0 && h < 24 ) && ( m >= 0 && m < 60 ) &&
17            ( s >= 0 && s < 60 ) )
18         {
19            hour = h;
20            minute = m;
21            second = s;
22         } // end if
```

Fig. 8.15 | Packaging class Time1 for reuse. (Part 1 of 2.)

```
23            else
24                throw new IllegalArgumentException(
25                    "hour, minute and/or second was out of range" );
26        } // end method setTime
27
28        // convert to String in universal-time format (HH:MM:SS)
29        public String toUniversalString()
30        {
31            return String.format( "%02d:%02d:%02d", hour, minute, second );
32        } // end method toUniversalString
33
34        // convert to String in standard-time format (H:MM:SS AM or PM)
35        public String toString()
36        {
37            return String.format( "%d:%02d:%02d %s",
38                ( ( hour == 0 || hour == 12 ) ? 12 : hour % 12 ),
39                minute, second, ( hour < 12 ? "AM" : "PM" ) );
40        } // end method toString
41    } // end class Time1
```

Fig. 8.15 | Packaging class Time1 for reuse. (Part 2 of 2.)

For *Step 2*, we add a package declaration (line 3) that declares a package named com.deitel.javafp.ch08. Placing a package declaration at the beginning of a Java source file indicates that the class declared in the file is part of the specified package. Only package declarations, import declarations and comments can appear outside the braces of a class declaration. A Java source-code file must have the following order:

1. a package declaration (if any),

2. import declarations (if any), then

3. class declarations.

Only one of the class declarations in a particular file can be public. Other classes in the file are placed in the package and can be used only by the other classes in the package. Non-public classes are in a package to support the reusable classes in the package.

To provide unique package names, start each one with your Internet domain name in reverse order. For example, our domain name is deitel.com, so our package names begin with com.deitel. For the domain name *yourcollege*.edu, the package name should begin with edu.*yourcollege*. After the domain name is reversed, you can choose any other names you want for your package. If you're part of a company with many divisions or a university with many schools, you may want to use the name of your division or school as the next name in the package. We chose to use javafp as the next name in our package name to indicate that this class is from *Java for Programmer*. The last name in our package name specifies that this package is for Chapter 8 (ch08).

Step 3: Compiling the Packaged Class
Step 3 is to compile the class so that it's stored in the appropriate package. When a Java file containing a package declaration is compiled, the resulting class file is placed in the directory specified by the declaration. The package declaration in Fig. 8.15 indicates that class Time1 should be placed in the directory

```
com
    deitel
        javafp
            ch08
```

The names in the package declaration specify the exact location of the package's classes.

When compiling a class in a package, the javac command-line option **-d** causes the javac compiler to create appropriate directories based on the class's package declaration. The option also specifies where the directories should be stored. For example, in a command window, we used the compilation command

```
javac -d . Time1.java
```

to specify that the first directory in our package name should be placed in the current directory. The period (.) after -d in the preceding command represents the current directory on the Windows, UNIX, Linux and Mac OS X operating systems (and several others as well). After execution of the compilation command, the current directory contains a directory called com, com contains a directory called deitel, deitel contains a directory called javafp and javafp contains a directory called ch08. In the ch08 directory, you can find the file Time1.class. [*Note:* If you do not use the -d option, then you must copy or move the class file to the appropriate package directory after compiling it.]

The package name is part of the **fully qualified class name**, so the name of class Time1 is actually com.deitel.javafp.ch08.Time1. You can use this fully qualified name in your programs, or you can import the class and use its **simple name** (the class name by itself—Time1) in the program. If another package also contains a Time1 class, the fully qualified class names can be used to distinguish between the classes in the program and prevent a **name conflict** (also called a **name collision**).

Step 4: Importing the Reusable Class

Once it's compiled and stored in its package, the class can be imported into programs (*Step 4*). In the Time1PackageTest application of Fig. 8.16, line 3 specifies that class Time1 should be imported for use in class Time1PackageTest. This class is in the default package because its .java file does not contain a package declaration. Since the two classes are in different packages, the import at line 3 is required so that class Time1PackageTest can use class Time1.

```
1   // Fig. 8.16: Time1PackageTest.java
2   // Time1 object used in an application.
3   import com.deitel.javafp.ch08.Time1; // import class Time1
4
5   public class Time1PackageTest
6   {
7      public static void main( String[] args )
8      {
9         // create and initialize a Time1 object
10        Time1 time = new Time1(); // invokes Time1 constructor
11
12        // output string representations of the time
13        System.out.print( "The initial universal time is: " );
14        System.out.println( time.toUniversalString() );
```

Fig. 8.16 | Time1 object used in an application. (Part 1 of 2.)

```
15            System.out.print( "The initial standard time is: " );
16            System.out.println( time.toString() );
17            System.out.println(); // output a blank line
18
19            // change time and output updated time
20            time.setTime( 13, 27, 6 );
21            System.out.print( "Universal time after setTime is: " );
22            System.out.println( time.toUniversalString() );
23            System.out.print( "Standard time after setTime is: " );
24            System.out.println( time.toString() );
25            System.out.println(); // output a blank line
26
27            // attempt to set time with invalid values
28            try
29            {
30               time.setTime( 99, 99, 99 ); // all values out of range
31            } // end try
32            catch ( IllegalArgumentException e )
33            {
34               System.out.printf( "Exception: %s\n\n", e.getMessage() );
35            } // end catch
36
37            // display time after attempt to set invalid values
38            System.out.println( "After attempting invalid settings:" );
39            System.out.print( "Universal time: " );
40            System.out.println( time.toUniversalString() );
41            System.out.print( "Standard time: " );
42            System.out.println( time.toString() );
43         } // end main
44   } // end class Time1PackageTest
```

```
The initial universal time is: 00:00:00
The initial standard time is: 12:00:00 AM

Universal time after setTime is: 13:27:06
Standard time after setTime is: 1:27:06 PM

Exception: hour, minute and/or second was out of range

After attempting invalid settings:
Universal time: 13:27:06
Standard time: 1:27:06 PM
```

Fig. 8.16 | Time1 object used in an application. (Part 2 of 2.)

Line 3 is known as a **single-type-import declaration**—that is, the import declaration specifies one class to import. When your program uses multiple classes from the same package, you can import those classes with a single import declaration. For example, the import declaration

```
import java.util.*; // import classes from package java.util
```

uses an asterisk (*) at its end to inform the compiler that all public classes from the java.util package are available for use in the program. This is known as a **type-import-on-**

demand declaration. Only the classes from package java.util that are used in the program are loaded by the JVM. The preceding import allows you to use the simple name of any class from the java.util package in the program. Throughout this book, we use single-type-import declarations for clarity.

Common Programming Error 8.10

Using the import declaration import java.*; causes a compilation error. You must specify the exact name of the package from which you want to import classes.

Specifying the Classpath During Compilation

When compiling Time1PackageTest, javac must locate the .class file for Time1 to ensure that class Time1PackageTest uses class Time1 correctly. The compiler uses a special object called a **class loader** to locate the classes it needs. The class loader begins by searching the standard Java classes that are bundled with the JDK. Then it searches for **optional packages**. Java provides an **extension mechanism** that enables new (optional) packages to be added to Java for development and execution purposes. If the class is not found in the standard Java classes or in the extension classes, the class loader searches the **classpath**, which contains a list of locations in which classes are stored. The classpath consists of a list of directories or **archive files**, each separated by a **directory separator**—a semicolon (;) on Windows or a colon (:) on UNIX/Linux/Mac OS X. Archive files are individual files that contain directories of other files, typically in a compressed format. For example, the standard classes used by your programs are contained in the archive file rt.jar, which is installed with the JDK. Archive files normally end with the .jar or .zip file-name extensions. The directories and archive files specified in the classpath contain the classes you wish to make available to the Java compiler and the JVM.

By default, the classpath consists only of the current directory. However, the classpath can be modified by

1. providing the **-classpath** option to the javac compiler or

2. setting the **CLASSPATH environment variable** (a special variable that you define and the operating system maintains so that applications can search for classes in the specified locations).

For more information on the classpath, visit download.oracle.com/javase/6/docs/technotes/tools/index.html#general. The section entitled "General Information" contains information on setting the classpath for UNIX/Linux and Windows.

Common Programming Error 8.11

Specifying an explicit classpath eliminates the current directory from the classpath. This prevents classes in the current directory (including packages in the current directory) from loading properly. If classes must be loaded from the current directory, include a dot (.) in the classpath to specify the current directory.

Software Engineering Observation 8.11

In general, it's a better practice to use the -classpath option of the compiler, rather than the CLASSPATH environment variable, to specify the classpath for a program. This enables each application to have its own classpath.

> **Error-Prevention Tip 8.5**
>
> *Specifying the classpath with the CLASSPATH environment variable can cause subtle and difficult-to-locate errors in programs that use different versions of the same package.*

Figures 8.15–8.16 didn't specify an explicit classpath. Thus, to locate the classes in the `com.deitel.javafp.ch08` package from this example, the class loader looks in the current directory for the first name in the package—`com`—then navigates the directory structure. Directory `com` contains the subdirectory `deitel`, `deitel` contains the subdirectory `javafp`, and `javafp` contains subdirectory `ch08`. In the `ch08` directory is the file `Time1.class`, which is loaded by the class loader to ensure that the class is used properly in our program.

Specifying the Classpath When Executing an Application

When you execute an application, the JVM must be able to locate the `.class` files of the classes used in that application. Like the compiler, the `java` command uses a class loader that searches the standard classes and extension classes first, then searches the classpath (the current directory by default). The classpath can be specified explicitly by using either of the techniques discussed for the compiler. As with the compiler, it's better to specify an individual program's classpath via command-line JVM options. You can specify the classpath in the `java` command via the **-classpath** or **-cp** command-line options, followed by a list of directories or archive files separated by semicolons (;) on Microsoft Windows or by colons (:) on UNIX/Linux/Mac OS X. Again, if classes must be loaded from the current directory, be sure to include a dot (.) in the classpath to specify the current directory.

8.15 Package Access

If no access modifier (`public`, `protected` or `private`—we discuss `protected` in Chapter 9) is specified for a method or variable when it's declared in a class, the method or variable is considered to have **package access**. In a program that consists of one class declaration, this has no specific effect. However, if a program uses multiple classes from the same package (i.e., a group of related classes), these classes can access each other's package-access members directly through references to objects of the appropriate classes, or in the case of `static` members through the class name. Package access is rarely used.

The application in Fig. 8.17 demonstrates package access. The application contains two classes in one source-code file—the `PackageDataTest` application class (lines 5–21) and the `PackageData` class (lines 24–41). When you compile this program, the compiler produces two separate .class files—`PackageDataTest.class` and `PackageData.class`. The compiler places the two `.class` files in the same directory, so the classes are considered to be part of the same package. Consequently, class `PackageDataTest` is allowed to modify the package-access data of `PackageData` objects. You can also place class `Package-Data` (lines 24–41) in a separate source-code file. As long as both classes are compiled in the same directory on disk, the package-access relationship will still work.

In the `PackageData` class declaration, lines 26–27 declare the instance variables `number` and `string` with no access modifiers—therefore, these are package-access instance variables. The `PackageDataTest` application's `main` method creates an instance of the `PackageData` class (line 9) to demonstrate the ability to modify the `PackageData` instance variables directly (as shown in lines 15–16). The results of the modification can be seen in the output window.

```
 1   // Fig. 8.17: PackageDataTest.java
 2   // Package-access members of a class are accessible by other classes
 3   // in the same package.
 4
 5   public class PackageDataTest
 6   {
 7      public static void main( String[] args )
 8      {
 9         PackageData packageData = new PackageData();
10
11         // output String representation of packageData
12         System.out.printf( "After instantiation:\n%s\n", packageData );
13
14         // change package access data in packageData object
15         packageData.number = 77;
16         packageData.string = "Goodbye";
17
18         // output String representation of packageData
19         System.out.printf( "\nAfter changing values:\n%s\n", packageData );
20      } // end main
21   } // end class PackageDataTest
22
23   // class with package access instance variables
24   class PackageData
25   {
26      int number; // package-access instance variable
27      String string; // package-access instance variable
28
29      // constructor
30      public PackageData()
31      {
32         number = 0;
33         string = "Hello";
34      } // end PackageData constructor
35
36      // return PackageData object String representation
37      public String toString()
38      {
39         return String.format( "number: %d; string: %s", number, string );
40      } // end method toString
41   } // end class PackageData
```

```
After instantiation:
number: 0; string: Hello

After changing values:
number: 77; string: Goodbye
```

Fig. 8.17 | Package-access members of a class are accessible by other classes in the same package.

8.16 Wrap-Up

In this chapter, we presented additional class concepts. The Time class case study presented a complete class declaration consisting of private data, overloaded public constructors for initialization flexibility, *set* and *get* methods for manipulating the class's data, and methods that returned String representations of a Time object in two different formats. You also learned that every class can declare a toString method that returns a String representation of an object of the class and that method toString can be called implicitly whenever an object of a class appears in the code where a String is expected.

You learned that the this reference is used implicitly in a class's non-static methods to access the class's instance variables and other non-static methods. You also saw explicit uses of the this reference to access the class's members (including shadowed fields) and how to use keyword this in a constructor to call another constructor of the class.

We discussed the differences between default constructors provided by the compiler and no-argument constructors provided by the programmer. You learned that a class can have references to objects of other classes as members—a concept known as composition. You saw the enum class type and learned how it can be used to create a set of constants for use in a program. You learned about Java's garbage-collection capability and how it (unpredictably) reclaims the memory of objects that are no longer used. The chapter explained the motivation for static fields in a class and demonstrated how to declare and use static fields and methods in your own classes. You also learned how to declare and initialize final variables.

You learned how to package your own classes for reuse and how to import those classes into an application. Finally, you learned that fields declared without an access modifier are given package access by default. You saw the relationship between classes in the same package that allows each class in a package to access the package-access members of other classes in the package.

In the next chapter, you'll learn about an important aspect of object-oriented programming in Java—inheritance. You'll see that all classes in Java are related directly or indirectly to the class called Object. You'll also begin to understand how the relationships between classes enable you to build more powerful applications.

9

Object-Oriented Programming: Inheritance

Objectives

In this chapter you'll learn:

- How inheritance promotes software reusability.

- The notions of superclasses and subclasses and the relationship between them.

- To use keyword **extends** to create a class that inherits attributes and behaviors from another class.

- To use access modifier **protected** to give subclass methods access to superclass members.

- To access superclass members with **super**.

- How constructors are used in inheritance hierarchies.

- The methods of class **Object**, the direct or indirect superclass of all classes.

9.1 Introduction

This chapter continues our discussion of object-oriented programming (OOP) by introducing one of its primary capabilities—**inheritance**, which is a form of software reuse in which a new class is created by absorbing an existing class's members and embellishing them with new or modified capabilities. With inheritance, you can save time during program development by basing new classes on existing proven and debugged high-quality software. This also increases the likelihood that a system will be implemented and maintained effectively.

When creating a class, rather than declaring completely new members, you can designate that the new class should inherit the members of an existing class. The existing class is called the **superclass**, and the new class is the **subclass.** (The C++ programming language refers to the superclass as the **base class** and the subclass as the **derived class.**) Each subclass can become a superclass for future subclasses.

A subclass can add its own fields and methods. Therefore, a subclass is *more specific* than its superclass and represents a more specialized group of objects. The subclass exhibits the behaviors of its superclass and can modify those behaviors so that they operate appropriately for the subclass. This is why inheritance is sometimes referred to as **specialization**.

The **direct superclass** is the superclass from which the subclass explicitly inherits. An **indirect superclass** is any class above the direct superclass in the **class hierarchy**, which defines the inheritance relationships between classes. In Java, the class hierarchy begins with class Object (in package java.lang), which *every* class in Java directly or indirectly **extends** (or "inherits from"). Section 9.7 lists the methods of class Object that are inherited by all other Java classes. Java supports only **single inheritance**, in which each class is derived from exactly *one* direct superclass. Unlike C++, Java does *not* support multiple inheritance (which occurs when a class is derived from more than one direct superclass). Chapter 10, Object-Oriented Programming: Polymorphism, explains how to use Java interfaces to realize many of the benefits of multiple inheritance while avoiding the associated problems.

We distinguish between the *is-a* **relationship** and the *has-a* **relationship**. *Is-a* represents inheritance. In an *is-a* relationship, *an object of a subclass can also be treated as an object of its superclass*—e.g., a car *is a* vehicle. By contrast, *has-a* represents composition (see Chapter 8). In a *has-a* relationship, *an object contains as members references to other objects*—e.g., a car *has a* steering wheel (and a car object has a reference to a steering-wheel object).

New classes can inherit from classes in **class libraries**. Organizations develop their own class libraries and can take advantage of others available worldwide. Some day, most new software likely will be constructed from **standardized reusable components**, just as automobiles and most computer hardware are constructed today. This will facilitate the development of more powerful, abundant and economical software.

9.2 Superclasses and Subclasses

Often, an object of one class *is an* object of another class as well. Figure 9.1 lists several simple examples of superclasses and subclasses—superclasses tend to be "more general" and subclasses "more specific." For example, a CarLoan *is a* Loan as are HomeImprovementLoans and MortgageLoans. Thus, in Java, class CarLoan can be said to inherit from class Loan. In this context, class Loan is a superclass and class CarLoan is a subclass. A CarLoan *is a* specific type of Loan, but it's incorrect to claim that every Loan *is a* CarLoan—the Loan could be any type of loan.

Superclass	Subclasses
Student	GraduateStudent, UndergraduateStudent
Shape	Circle, Triangle, Rectangle, Sphere, Cube
Loan	CarLoan, HomeImprovementLoan, MortgageLoan
Employee	Faculty, Staff
BankAccount	CheckingAccount, SavingsAccount

Fig. 9.1 | Inheritance examples.

Because every subclass object *is an* object of its superclass, and one superclass can have many subclasses, the set of objects represented by a superclass is often larger than the set of objects represented by any of its subclasses. For example, the superclass Vehicle represents all vehicles, including cars, trucks, boats, bicycles and so on. By contrast, subclass Car represents a smaller, more specific subset of vehicles.

University Community Member Hierarchy
Inheritance relationships form treelike hierarchical structures. A superclass exists in a hierarchical relationship with its subclasses. Let's develop a sample class hierarchy (Fig. 9.2), also called an **inheritance hierarchy**. A university community has thousands of members, including employees, students and alumni. Employees are either faculty or staff members. Faculty members are either administrators (e.g., deans and department chairpersons) or teachers. The hierarchy could contain many other classes. For example, students can be graduate or undergraduate students. Undergraduate students can be freshmen, sophomores, juniors or seniors.

Each arrow in the hierarchy represents an *is-a* relationship. As we follow the arrows upward in this class hierarchy, we can state, for instance, that "an Employee *is a* CommunityMember" and "a Teacher *is a* Faculty member." CommunityMember is the direct superclass of Employee, Student and Alumnus and is an indirect superclass of all the other classes in the diagram. Starting from the bottom, you can follow the arrows and apply the

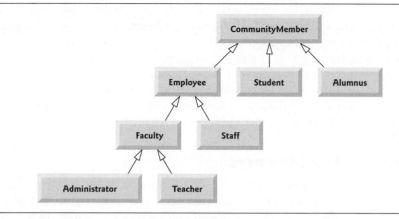

Fig. 9.2 | Inheritance hierarchy for university CommunityMembers.

is-a relationship up to the topmost superclass. For example, an Administrator *is a* Faculty member, *is an* Employee, *is a* CommunityMember and, of course, *is an* Object.

Shape Hierarchy

Now consider the Shape inheritance hierarchy in Fig. 9.3. This hierarchy begins with superclass Shape, which is extended by subclasses TwoDimensionalShape and ThreeDimensionalShape—Shapes are either TwoDimensionalShapes or ThreeDimensionalShapes. The third level of this hierarchy contains specific types of TwoDimensionalShapes and ThreeDimensionalShapes. As in Fig. 9.2, we can follow the arrows from the bottom of the diagram to the topmost superclass in this class hierarchy to identify several *is-a* relationships. For instance, a Triangle *is a* TwoDimensionalShape and *is a* Shape, while a Sphere *is a* ThreeDimensionalShape and *is a* Shape. This hierarchy could contain many other classes. For example, ellipses and trapezoids are TwoDimensionalShapes.

Not every class relationship is an inheritance relationship. In Chapter 8, we discussed the *has-a* relationship, in which classes have members that are references to objects of other classes. Such relationships create classes by composition of existing classes. For example, given the classes Employee, BirthDate and TelephoneNumber, it's improper to say that an Employee *is a* BirthDate or that an Employee *is a* TelephoneNumber. However, an Employee *has a* BirthDate, and an Employee *has a* TelephoneNumber.

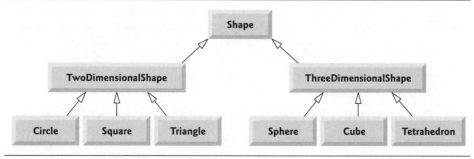

Fig. 9.3 | Inheritance hierarchy for Shapes.

It's possible to treat superclass objects and subclass objects similarly—their commonalities are expressed in the superclass's members. Objects of all classes that extend a common superclass can be treated as objects of that superclass—such objects have an *is-a* relationship with the superclass. Later in this chapter and in Chapter 10, we consider many examples that take advantage of the *is-a* relationship.

A subclass can customize methods that it inherits from its superclass. To do this, the subclass **overrides** (redefines) the superclass method with an appropriate implementation, as we'll see often in the chapter's code examples.

9.3 protected Members

Chapter 8 discussed access modifiers public and private. A class's public members are accessible wherever the program has a reference to an object of that class or one of its subclasses. A class's private members are accessible only within the class itself. In this section, we introduce access modifier **protected**. Using protected access offers an intermediate level of access between public and private. A superclass's protected members can be accessed by members of that superclass, by members of its subclasses and by members of other classes in the same package—protected members also have package access.

All public and protected superclass members retain their original access modifier when they become members of the subclass—public members of the superclass become public members of the subclass, and protected members of the superclass become protected members of the subclass. A superclass's private members are not accessible outside the class itself. Rather, they're *hidden* in its subclasses and can be accessed only through the public or protected methods inherited from the superclass.

Subclass methods can refer to public and protected members inherited from the superclass simply by using the member names. When a subclass method overrides an inherited superclass method, the *superclass* method can be accessed from the *subclass* by preceding the superclass method name with keyword **super** and a dot (.) separator. We discuss accessing overridden members of the superclass in Section 9.4.

Software Engineering Observation 9.1

Methods of a subclass cannot directly access private members of their superclass. A subclass can change the state of private superclass instance variables only through non-private methods provided in the superclass and inherited by the subclass.

Software Engineering Observation 9.2

Declaring private instance variables helps you test, debug and correctly modify systems. If a subclass could access its superclass's private instance variables, classes that inherit from that subclass could access the instance variables as well. This would propagate access to what should be private instance variables, and the benefits of information hiding would be lost.

9.4 Relationship between Superclasses and Subclasses

We now use an inheritance hierarchy containing types of employees in a company's payroll application to discuss the relationship between a superclass and its subclass. In this company, commission employees (who will be represented as objects of a superclass) are paid a percentage of their sales, while base-salaried commission employees (who will be represented as objects of a subclass) receive a base salary *plus* a percentage of their sales.

We divide our discussion of the relationship between these classes into five examples. The first declares class CommissionEmployee, which directly inherits from class Object and declares as private instance variables a first name, last name, social security number, commission rate and gross (i.e., total) sales amount.

The second example declares class BasePlusCommissionEmployee, which also directly inherits from class Object and declares as private instance variables a first name, last name, social security number, commission rate, gross sales amount *and* base salary. We create this class by *writing every line of code* the class requires—we'll soon see that it's much more efficient to create it by inheriting from class CommissionEmployee.

The third example declares a new BasePlusCommissionEmployee class that *extends* class CommissionEmployee (i.e., a BasePlusCommissionEmployee *is a* CommissionEmployee who also has a base salary). This *software reuse lets us write less code* when developing the new subclass. In this example, class BasePlusCommissionEmployee attempts to access class CommissionEmployee's private members—this results in compilation errors, because the subclass cannot access the superclass's private instance variables.

The fourth example shows that if CommissionEmployee's instance variables are declared as protected, the BasePlusCommissionEmployee subclass can access that data directly. Both BasePlusCommissionEmployee classes contain identical functionality, but we show how the inherited version is easier to create and manage.

After we discuss the convenience of using protected instance variables, we create the fifth example, which sets the CommissionEmployee instance variables back to private to enforce good software engineering. Then we show how the BasePlusCommissionEmployee subclass can use CommissionEmployee's public methods to manipulate (in a controlled manner) the private instance variables inherited from CommissionEmployee.

9.4.1 Creating and Using a CommissionEmployee Class

We first declare class CommissionEmployee (Fig. 9.4). Line 4 begins the class declaration and indicates that CommissionEmployee **extends** (i.e., inherits from) class **Object** (from package java.lang). This causes class CommissionEmployee to inherit the class Object's methods—class Object does not have any fields. If you don't explicitly specify which class a new class extends, the class extends Object implicitly. For this reason, you typically will not include "extends Object" in your code—we do so in this example only for demonstration purposes.

Overview of Class CommissionEmployee's Methods and Instance Variables
Class CommissionEmployee's public services include a constructor (lines 13–22) and methods earnings (lines 93–96) and toString (lines 99–107). Lines 25–90 declare public *get* and *set* methods for the class's instance variables (declared in lines 6–10) first-Name, lastName, socialSecurityNumber, grossSales and commissionRate. The class declares its instance variables as private, so objects of other classes cannot directly access these variables. Declaring instance variables as private and providing *get* and *set* methods to manipulate and validate them helps enforce good software engineering. Methods set-GrossSales and setCommissionRate, for example, validate their arguments before assigning the values to instance variables grossSales and commissionRate. In a real-world, business-critical application, we'd also perform validation in the class's other *set* methods.

```java
1   // Fig. 9.4: CommissionEmployee.java
2   // CommissionEmployee class represents an employee paid a
3   // percentage of gross sales.
4   public class CommissionEmployee extends Object
5   {
6      private String firstName;
7      private String lastName;
8      private String socialSecurityNumber;
9      private double grossSales; // gross weekly sales
10     private double commissionRate; // commission percentage
11
12     // five-argument constructor
13     public CommissionEmployee( String first, String last, String ssn,
14        double sales, double rate )
15     {
16        // implicit call to Object constructor occurs here
17        firstName = first;
18        lastName = last;
19        socialSecurityNumber = ssn;
20        setGrossSales( sales ); // validate and store gross sales
21        setCommissionRate( rate ); // validate and store commission rate
22     } // end five-argument CommissionEmployee constructor
23
24     // set first name
25     public void setFirstName( String first )
26     {
27        firstName = first; // should validate
28     } // end method setFirstName
29
30     // return first name
31     public String getFirstName()
32     {
33        return firstName;
34     } // end method getFirstName
35
36     // set last name
37     public void setLastName( String last )
38     {
39        lastName = last; // should validate
40     } // end method setLastName
41
42     // return last name
43     public String getLastName()
44     {
45        return lastName;
46     } // end method getLastName
47
48     // set social security number
49     public void setSocialSecurityNumber( String ssn )
50     {
51        socialSecurityNumber = ssn; // should validate
52     } // end method setSocialSecurityNumber
```

Fig. 9.4 | CommissionEmployee class represents an employee paid a percentage of gross sales. (Part 1 of 3.)

```
53
54      // return social security number
55      public String getSocialSecurityNumber()
56      {
57          return socialSecurityNumber;
58      } // end method getSocialSecurityNumber
59
60      // set gross sales amount
61      public void setGrossSales( double sales )
62      {
63          if ( sales >= 0.0 )
64              grossSales = sales;
65          else
66              throw new IllegalArgumentException(
67                  "Gross sales must be >= 0.0" );
68      } // end method setGrossSales
69
70      // return gross sales amount
71      public double getGrossSales()
72      {
73          return grossSales;
74      } // end method getGrossSales
75
76      // set commission rate
77      public void setCommissionRate( double rate )
78      {
79          if ( rate > 0.0 && rate < 1.0 )
80              commissionRate = rate;
81          else
82              throw new IllegalArgumentException(
83                  "Commission rate must be > 0.0 and < 1.0" );
84      } // end method setCommissionRate
85
86      // return commission rate
87      public double getCommissionRate()
88      {
89          return commissionRate;
90      } // end method getCommissionRate
91
92      // calculate earnings
93      public double earnings()
94      {
95          return commissionRate * grossSales;
96      } // end method earnings
97
98      // return String representation of CommissionEmployee object
99      @Override // indicates that this method overrides a superclass method
100     public String toString()
101     {
102         return String.format( "%s: %s %s\n%s: %s\n%s: %.2f\n%s: %.2f",
103             "commission employee", firstName, lastName,
```

Fig. 9.4 | CommissionEmployee class represents an employee paid a percentage of gross sales. (Part 2 of 3.)

```
104              "social security number", socialSecurityNumber,
105          "gross sales", grossSales,
106          "commission rate", commissionRate );
107     } // end method toString
108 } // end class CommissionEmployee
```

Fig. 9.4 | CommissionEmployee class represents an employee paid a percentage of gross sales. (Part 3 of 3.)

Class *CommissionEmployee's Constructor*

Constructors are *not* inherited, so class CommissionEmployee does not inherit class Object's constructor. However, a superclass's constructors are still available to subclasses. In fact, *the first task of any subclass constructor is to call its direct superclass's constructor*, either explicitly or implicitly (if no constructor call is specified), to ensure that the instance variables inherited from the superclass are initialized properly. In this example, class CommissionEmployee's constructor calls class Object's constructor implicitly. The syntax for calling a superclass constructor explicitly is discussed in Section 9.4.3. If the code does not include an explicit call to the superclass constructor, Java *implicitly* calls the superclass's default or no-argument constructor. The comment in line 16 of Fig. 9.4 indicates where the implicit call to the superclass Object's default constructor is made (you do not write the code for this call). Object's default (empty) constructor does nothing. Even if a class does not have constructors, the default constructor that the compiler implicitly declares for the class will call the superclass's default or no-argument constructor.

After the implicit call to Object's constructor, lines 17–21 of CommissionEmployee's constructor assign values to the class's instance variables. We do not validate the values of arguments first, last and ssn before assigning them to the corresponding instance variables. We could validate the first and last names—perhaps to ensure that they're of a reasonable length. Similarly, a social security number could be validated using regular expressions (Section 16.7) to ensure that it contains nine digits, with or without dashes (e.g., 123-45-6789 or 123456789).

Class *CommissionEmployee's earnings Method*

Method earnings (lines 93–96) calculates a CommissionEmployee's earnings. Line 95 multiplies the commissionRate by the grossSales and returns the result.

Class *CommissionEmployee's toString Method and the @Override Annotation*

Method toString (lines 99–107) is special—it's one of the methods that *every* class inherits directly or indirectly from class Object (summarized in Section 9.7). Method toString returns a String representing an object. It's called implicitly whenever an object must be converted to a String representation, such as when an object is output by printf or output by String method format via the %s format specifier. Class Object's toString method returns a String that includes the name of the object's class. It's primarily a placeholder that can be overridden by a subclass to specify an appropriate String representation of the data in a subclass object. Method toString of class CommissionEmployee overrides (redefines) class Object's toString method. When invoked, CommissionEmployee's toString method uses String method format to return a String containing information about the CommissionEmployee. To override a superclass method, a subclass must declare a method with the same signature (method name, number of parameters, parameter types and order of parameter types) as the superclass method—Object's toString method takes no parameters, so CommissionEmployee declares toString with no parameters.

Line 99 uses the **@Override annotation** to indicate that method toString should override a superclass method. Annotations have several purposes. For example, when you attempt to override a superclass method, common errors include naming the subclass method incorrectly, or using the wrong number or types of parameters in the parameter list. Each of these problems creates an *unintentional overload* of the superclass method. If you then attempt to call the method on a subclass object, the superclass's version is invoked and the subclass version is ignored—potentially leading to subtle logic errors. When the compiler encounters a method declared with @Override, it compares the method's signature with the superclass's method signatures. If there isn't an exact match, the compiler issues an error message, such as "method does not override or implement a method from a supertype." This indicates that you've accidentally overloaded a superclass method. You can then fix your method's signature so that it matches one in the superclass.

As you'll see when we discuss web applications and web services in Chapters 26–28, annotations can also add complex support code to your classes to simplify the development process and can be used by servers to configure certain aspects of web applications.

Common Programming Error 9.1

Using an incorrect method signature when attempting to override a superclass method causes an unintentional method overload that can lead to subtle logic errors.

Error-Prevention Tip 9.1

Declare overridden methods with the @Override annotation to ensure at compilation time that you defined their signatures correctly. It's always better to find errors at compile time rather than at runtime.

Common Programming Error 9.2

It's a syntax error to override a method with a more restricted access modifier—a public method of the superclass cannot become a protected or private method in the subclass; a protected method of the superclass cannot become a private method in the subclass. Doing so would break the is-a relationship in which it's required that all subclass objects be able to respond to method calls that are made to public methods declared in the superclass. If a public method, for example, could be overridden as a protected or private method, the subclass objects would not be able to respond to the same method calls as superclass objects. Once a method is declared public in a superclass, the method remains public for all that class's direct and indirect subclasses.

Class CommissionEmployeeTest

Figure 9.5 tests class CommissionEmployee. Lines 9–10 instantiate a CommissionEmployee object and invoke CommissionEmployee's constructor (lines 13–22 of Fig. 9.4) to initialize it with "Sue" as the first name, "Jones" as the last name, "222-22-2222" as the social security number, 10000 as the gross sales amount and .06 as the commission rate. Lines 15–24 use CommissionEmployee's *get* methods to retrieve the object's instance-variable values for output. Lines 26–27 invoke the object's methods setGrossSales and setCommissionRate to change the values of instance variables grossSales and commissionRate. Lines

29–30 output the String representation of the updated CommissionEmployee. When an object is output using the %s format specifier, the object's toString method is invoked implicitly to obtain the object's String representation. [*Note:* In this chapter, we do not use the earnings methods of our classes—they're used extensively in Chapter 10.]

```java
1   // Fig. 9.5: CommissionEmployeeTest.java
2   // CommissionEmployee class test program.
3
4   public class CommissionEmployeeTest
5   {
6      public static void main( String[] args )
7      {
8         // instantiate CommissionEmployee object
9         CommissionEmployee employee = new CommissionEmployee(
10           "Sue", "Jones", "222-22-2222", 10000, .06 );
11
12        // get commission employee data
13        System.out.println(
14           "Employee information obtained by get methods: \n" );
15        System.out.printf( "%s %s\n", "First name is",
16           employee.getFirstName() );
17        System.out.printf( "%s %s\n", "Last name is",
18           employee.getLastName() );
19        System.out.printf( "%s %s\n", "Social security number is",
20           employee.getSocialSecurityNumber() );
21        System.out.printf( "%s %.2f\n", "Gross sales is",
22           employee.getGrossSales() );
23        System.out.printf( "%s %.2f\n", "Commission rate is",
24           employee.getCommissionRate() );
25
26        employee.setGrossSales( 500 ); // set gross sales
27        employee.setCommissionRate( .1 ); // set commission rate
28
29        System.out.printf( "\n%s:\n\n%s\n",
30           "Updated employee information obtained by toString", employee );
31     } // end main
32  } // end class CommissionEmployeeTest
```

```
Employee information obtained by get methods:

First name is Sue
Last name is Jones
Social security number is 222-22-2222
Gross sales is 10000.00
Commission rate is 0.06

Updated employee information obtained by toString:

commission employee: Sue Jones
social security number: 222-22-2222
gross sales: 500.00
commission rate: 0.10
```

Fig. 9.5 | CommissionEmployee class test program.

9.4.2 Creating and Using a BasePlusCommissionEmployee Class

We now discuss the second part of our introduction to inheritance by declaring and testing (a completely new and independent) class BasePlusCommissionEmployee (Fig. 9.6), which contains a first name, last name, social security number, gross sales amount, commission rate *and* base salary. Class BasePlusCommissionEmployee's public services include a BasePlusCommissionEmployee constructor (lines 15–25) and methods earnings (lines 112–115) and toString (lines 118–127). Lines 28–109 declare public *get* and *set* methods for the class's private instance variables (declared in lines 7–12) firstName, lastName, socialSecurityNumber, grossSales, commissionRate *and* baseSalary. These variables and methods encapsulate all the necessary features of a base-salaried commission employee. Note the *similarity* between this class and class CommissionEmployee (Fig. 9.4)—in this example, we'll not yet exploit that similarity.

```
1   // Fig. 9.6: BasePlusCommissionEmployee.java
2   // BasePlusCommissionEmployee class represents an employee who receives
3   // a base salary in addition to commission.
4
5   public class BasePlusCommissionEmployee
6   {
7      private String firstName;
8      private String lastName;
9      private String socialSecurityNumber;
10     private double grossSales; // gross weekly sales
11     private double commissionRate; // commission percentage
12     private double baseSalary; // base salary per week
13
14     // six-argument constructor
15     public BasePlusCommissionEmployee( String first, String last,
16        String ssn, double sales, double rate, double salary )
17     {
18        // implicit call to Object constructor occurs here
19        firstName = first;
20        lastName = last;
21        socialSecurityNumber = ssn;
22        setGrossSales( sales ); // validate and store gross sales
23        setCommissionRate( rate ); // validate and store commission rate
24        setBaseSalary( salary ); // validate and store base salary
25     } // end six-argument BasePlusCommissionEmployee constructor
26
27     // set first name
28     public void setFirstName( String first )
29     {
30        firstName = first; // should validate
31     } // end method setFirstName
32
33     // return first name
34     public String getFirstName()
35     {
```

Fig. 9.6 | BasePlusCommissionEmployee class represents an employee who receives a base salary in addition to a commission. (Part 1 of 3.)

```
36              return firstName;
37          } // end method getFirstName
38
39          // set last name
40          public void setLastName( String last )
41          {
42              lastName = last; // should validate
43          } // end method setLastName
44
45          // return last name
46          public String getLastName()
47          {
48              return lastName;
49          } // end method getLastName
50
51          // set social security number
52          public void setSocialSecurityNumber( String ssn )
53          {
54              socialSecurityNumber = ssn; // should validate
55          } // end method setSocialSecurityNumber
56
57          // return social security number
58          public String getSocialSecurityNumber()
59          {
60              return socialSecurityNumber;
61          } // end method getSocialSecurityNumber
62
63          // set gross sales amount
64          public void setGrossSales( double sales )
65          {
66              if ( sales >= 0.0 )
67                  grossSales = sales;
68              else
69                  throw new IllegalArgumentException(
70                      "Gross sales must be >= 0.0" );
71          } // end method setGrossSales
72
73          // return gross sales amount
74          public double getGrossSales()
75          {
76              return grossSales;
77          } // end method getGrossSales
78
79          // set commission rate
80          public void setCommissionRate( double rate )
81          {
82              if ( rate > 0.0 && rate < 1.0 )
83                  commissionRate = rate;
84              else
85                  throw new IllegalArgumentException(
86                      "Commission rate must be > 0.0 and < 1.0" );
87          } // end method setCommissionRate
```

Fig. 9.6 | BasePlusCommissionEmployee class represents an employee who receives a base salary in addition to a commission. (Part 2 of 3.)

```
88
89      // return commission rate
90      public double getCommissionRate()
91      {
92         return commissionRate;
93      } // end method getCommissionRate
94
95      // set base salary
96      public void setBaseSalary( double salary )
97      {
98         if ( salary >= 0.0 )
99            baseSalary = salary;
100        else
101           throw new IllegalArgumentException(
102              "Base salary must be >= 0.0" );
103     } // end method setBaseSalary
104
105     // return base salary
106     public double getBaseSalary()
107     {
108        return baseSalary;
109     } // end method getBaseSalary
110
111     // calculate earnings
112     public double earnings()
113     {
114        return baseSalary + ( commissionRate * grossSales );
115     } // end method earnings
116
117     // return String representation of BasePlusCommissionEmployee
118     @Override // indicates that this method overrides a superclass method
119     public String toString()
120     {
121        return String.format(
122           "%s: %s %s\n%s: %s\n%s: %.2f\n%s: %.2f\n%s: %.2f",
123           "base-salaried commission employee", firstName, lastName,
124           "social security number", socialSecurityNumber,
125           "gross sales", grossSales, "commission rate", commissionRate,
126           "base salary", baseSalary );
127     } // end method toString
128 } // end class BasePlusCommissionEmployee
```

Fig. 9.6 | BasePlusCommissionEmployee class represents an employee who receives a base salary in addition to a commission. (Part 3 of 3.)

Class BasePlusCommissionEmployee does not specify "extends Object" in line 5, so the class implicitly extends Object. Also, like class CommissionEmployee's constructor (lines 13–22 of Fig. 9.4), class BasePlusCommissionEmployee's constructor invokes class Object's default constructor implicitly, as noted in the comment in line 18.

Class BasePlusCommissionEmployee's earnings method (lines 112–115) returns the result of adding the BasePlusCommissionEmployee's base salary to the product of the commission rate and the employee's gross sales.

Class BasePlusCommissionEmployee overrides Object method toString to return a String containing the BasePlusCommissionEmployee's information. Once again, we use format specifier %.2f to format the gross sales, commission rate and base salary with two digits of precision to the right of the decimal point (line 122).

Testing Class *BasePlusCommissionEmployee*

Figure 9.7 tests class BasePlusCommissionEmployee. Lines 9–11 create a BasePlusCommissionEmployee object and pass "Bob", "Lewis", "333-33-3333", 5000, .04 and 300 to the constructor as the first name, last name, social security number, gross sales, commission rate and base salary, respectively. Lines 16–27 use BasePlusCommissionEmployee's *get* methods to retrieve the values of the object's instance variables for output. Line 29 invokes the object's setBaseSalary method to change the base salary. Method setBaseSalary (Fig. 9.6, lines 88–91) ensures that instance variable baseSalary is not assigned a negative value. Lines 31–33 of Fig. 9.7 invoke method toString explicitly to get the object's String representation.

```java
1   // Fig. 9.7: BasePlusCommissionEmployeeTest.java
2   // BasePlusCommissionEmployee test program.
3
4   public class BasePlusCommissionEmployeeTest
5   {
6      public static void main( String[] args )
7      {
8         // instantiate BasePlusCommissionEmployee object
9         BasePlusCommissionEmployee employee =
10           new BasePlusCommissionEmployee(
11           "Bob", "Lewis", "333-33-3333", 5000, .04, 300 );
12
13        // get base-salaried commission employee data
14        System.out.println(
15           "Employee information obtained by get methods: \n" );
16        System.out.printf( "%s %s\n", "First name is",
17           employee.getFirstName() );
18        System.out.printf( "%s %s\n", "Last name is",
19           employee.getLastName() );
20        System.out.printf( "%s %s\n", "Social security number is",
21           employee.getSocialSecurityNumber() );
22        System.out.printf( "%s %.2f\n", "Gross sales is",
23           employee.getGrossSales() );
24        System.out.printf( "%s %.2f\n", "Commission rate is",
25           employee.getCommissionRate() );
26        System.out.printf( "%s %.2f\n", "Base salary is",
27           employee.getBaseSalary() );
28
29        employee.setBaseSalary( 1000 ); // set base salary
30
31        System.out.printf( "\n%s:\n\n%s\n",
32           "Updated employee information obtained by toString",
33           employee.toString() );
34     } // end main
35  } // end class BasePlusCommissionEmployeeTest
```

Fig. 9.7 | BasePlusCommissionEmployee test program. (Part 1 of 2.)

```
Employee information obtained by get methods:

First name is Bob
Last name is Lewis
Social security number is 333-33-3333
Gross sales is 5000.00
Commission rate is 0.04
Base salary is 300.00

Updated employee information obtained by toString:

base-salaried commission employee: Bob Lewis
social security number: 333-33-3333
gross sales: 5000.00
commission rate: 0.04
base salary: 1000.00
```

Fig. 9.7 | BasePlusCommissionEmployee test program. (Part 2 of 2.)

Notes on Class *BasePlusCommissionEmployee*

Much of class BasePlusCommissionEmployee's code (Fig. 9.6) is similar, or identical, to that of class CommissionEmployee (Fig. 9.4). For example, private instance variables firstName and lastName and methods setFirstName, getFirstName, setLastName and getLastName are identical to those of class CommissionEmployee. The classes also both contain private instance variables socialSecurityNumber, commissionRate and gross-Sales, and corresponding *get* and *set* methods. In addition, the BasePlusCommissionEmployee constructor is almost identical to that of class CommissionEmployee, except that BasePlusCommissionEmployee's constructor also sets the baseSalary. The other additions to class BasePlusCommissionEmployee are private instance variable baseSalary and methods setBaseSalary and getBaseSalary. Class BasePlusCommissionEmployee's toString method is nearly identical to that of class CommissionEmployee except that it also outputs instance variable baseSalary with two digits of precision to the right of the decimal point.

We literally *copied* code from class CommissionEmployee and *pasted* it into class Base-PlusCommissionEmployee, then modified class BasePlusCommissionEmployee to include a base salary and methods that manipulate the base salary. This *"copy-and-paste"* approach is often error prone and time consuming. Worse yet, it spreads copies of the same code throughout a system, creating a code-maintenance nightmare. Is there a way to "absorb" the instance variables and methods of one class in a way that makes them part of other classes *without duplicating code*? Next we answer this question, using a more elegant approach to building classes that emphasizes the benefits of inheritance.

Software Engineering Observation 9.3

With inheritance, the common instance variables and methods of all the classes in the hierarchy are declared in a superclass. When changes are made for these common features in the superclass—subclasses then inherit the changes. Without inheritance, changes would need to be made to all the source-code files that contain a copy of the code in question.

9.4.3 Creating a CommissionEmployee–BasePlusCommissionEmployee Inheritance Hierarchy

Now we redeclare class BasePlusCommissionEmployee (Fig. 9.8) to *extend* class CommissionEmployee (Fig. 9.4). A BasePlusCommissionEmployee object *is a* CommissionEmployee, because inheritance passes on class CommissionEmployee's capabilities. Class BasePlus-CommissionEmployee also has instance variable baseSalary (Fig. 9.8, line 6). Keyword extends (line 4) indicates inheritance. BasePlusCommissionEmployee *inherits* CommissionEmployee's instance variables and methods, but only the superclass's public and protected members are directly accessible in the subclass. The CommissionEmployee constructor is *not* inherited. So, the public BasePlusCommissionEmployee services include its constructor (lines 9–16), public methods inherited from CommissionEmployee, and methods setBaseSalary (lines 19–26), getBaseSalary (lines 29–32), earnings (lines 35–40) and toString (lines 43–53). Methods earnings and toString *override* the corresponding methods in class CommissionEmployee because their superclass versions do not properly calculate a BasePlusCommissionEmployee's earnings or return an appropriate String representation.

```java
1   // Fig. 9.8: BasePlusCommissionEmployee.java
2   // private superclass members cannot be accessed in a subclass.
3
4   public class BasePlusCommissionEmployee extends CommissionEmployee
5   {
6      private double baseSalary; // base salary per week
7
8      // six-argument constructor
9      public BasePlusCommissionEmployee( String first, String last,
10        String ssn, double sales, double rate, double salary )
11     {
12        // explicit call to superclass CommissionEmployee constructor
13        super( first, last, ssn, sales, rate );
14
15        setBaseSalary( salary ); // validate and store base salary
16     } // end six-argument BasePlusCommissionEmployee constructor
17
18     // set base salary
19     public void setBaseSalary( double salary )
20     {
21        if ( salary >= 0.0 )
22           baseSalary = salary;
23        else
24           throw new IllegalArgumentException(
25              "Base salary must be >= 0.0" );
26     } // end method setBaseSalary
27
28     // return base salary
29     public double getBaseSalary()
30     {
31        return baseSalary;
32     } // end method getBaseSalary
```

Fig. 9.8 | private superclass members cannot be accessed in a subclass. (Part 1 of 2.)

```
33
34      // calculate earnings
35      @Override // indicates that this method overrides a superclass method
36      public double earnings()
37      {
38         // not allowed: commissionRate and grossSales private in superclass
39         return baseSalary + ( commissionRate * grossSales );
40      } // end method earnings
41
42      // return String representation of BasePlusCommissionEmployee
43      @Override // indicates that this method overrides a superclass method
44      public String toString()
45      {
46         // not allowed: attempts to access private superclass members
47         return String.format(
48            "%s: %s %s\n%s: %s\n%s: %.2f\n%s: %.2f\n%s: %.2f",
49            "base-salaried commission employee", firstName, lastName,
50            "social security number", socialSecurityNumber,
51            "gross sales", grossSales, "commission rate", commissionRate,
52            "base salary", baseSalary );
53      } // end method toString
54   } // end class BasePlusCommissionEmployee
```

```
BasePlusCommissionEmployee.java:39: commissionRate has private access in
CommissionEmployee
      return baseSalary + ( commissionRate * grossSales );
                            ^
BasePlusCommissionEmployee.java:39: grossSales has private access in
CommissionEmployee
      return baseSalary + ( commissionRate * grossSales );
                                             ^
BasePlusCommissionEmployee.java:49: firstName has private access in
CommissionEmployee
         "base-salaried commission employee", firstName, lastName,
                                               ^
BasePlusCommissionEmployee.java:49: lastName has private access in
CommissionEmployee
         "base-salaried commission employee", firstName, lastName,
                                                          ^
BasePlusCommissionEmployee.java:50: socialSecurityNumber has private access
in CommissionEmployee
         "social security number", socialSecurityNumber,
                                   ^
BasePlusCommissionEmployee.java:51: grossSales has private access in
CommissionEmployee
         "gross sales", grossSales, "commission rate", commissionRate,
                        ^
BasePlusCommissionEmployee.java:51: commissionRate has private access in
CommissionEmployee
         "gross sales", grossSales, "commission rate", commissionRate,
                                                       ^
7 errors
```

Fig. 9.8 | private superclass members cannot be accessed in a subclass. (Part 2 of 2.)

A Subclass's Constructor Must Call Its Superclass's Constructor
Each subclass constructor must implicitly or explicitly call its superclass constructor to initialize the instance variables inherited from the superclass. Line 13 in BasePlusCommissionEmployee's six-argument constructor (lines 9–16) explicitly calls class CommissionEmployee's five-argument constructor (declared at lines 13–22 of Fig. 9.4) to initialize the superclass portion of a BasePlusCommissionEmployee object (i.e., variables firstName, lastName, socialSecurityNumber, grossSales and commissionRate). We do this by using the **superclass constructor call syntax**—keyword super, followed by a set of parentheses containing the superclass constructor arguments. The arguments first, last, ssn, sales and rate are used to initialize superclass members firstName, lastName, socialSecurityNumber, grossSales and commissionRate, respectively. If BasePlusCommissionEmployee's constructor did not invoke the superclass's constructor explicitly, Java would attempt to invoke the superclass's no-argument or default constructor. Class CommissionEmployee does not have such a constructor, so the compiler would issue an error. The explicit superclass constructor call in line 13 of Fig. 9.8 must be the *first* statement in the subclass constructor's body. When a superclass contains a no-argument constructor, you can use super() to call that constructor explicitly, but this is rarely done.

BasePlusCommissionEmployee Method Earnings
The compiler generates errors for line 39 because superclass CommissionEmployee's instance variables commissionRate and grossSales are private—subclass BasePlusCommissionEmployee's methods are not allowed to access superclass CommissionEmployee's private instance variables. The compiler issues additional errors at lines 49–51 of BasePlusCommissionEmployee's toString method for the same reason. The errors in BasePlusCommissionEmployee could have been prevented by using the *get* methods inherited from class CommissionEmployee. For example, line 39 could have used getCommissionRate and getGrossSales to access CommissionEmployee's private instance variables commissionRate and grossSales, respectively. Lines 49–51 also could have used appropriate *get* methods to retrieve the values of the superclass's instance variables.

9.4.4 CommissionEmployee–BasePlusCommissionEmployee Inheritance Hierarchy Using protected Instance Variables

To enable class BasePlusCommissionEmployee to directly access superclass instance variables firstName, lastName, socialSecurityNumber, grossSales and commissionRate, we can declare those members as protected in the superclass. As we discussed in Section 9.3, a superclass's protected members are accessible by all subclasses of that superclass. In the new CommissionEmployee class, we modified only lines 6–10 of Fig. 9.4 to declare the instance variables with the protected access modifier as follows:

```
protected String firstName;
protected String lastName;
protected String socialSecurityNumber;
protected double grossSales; // gross weekly sales
protected double commissionRate; // commission percentage
```

The rest of the class declaration (which is not shown here) is identical to that of Fig. 9.4.
We could have declared CommissionEmployee's instance variables public to enable subclass BasePlusCommissionEmployee to access them. However, declaring public

instance variables is poor software engineering because it allows unrestricted access to the these variables, greatly increasing the chance of errors. With `protected` instance variables, the subclass gets access to the instance variables, but classes that are not subclasses and classes that are not in the same package cannot access these variables directly—recall that protected class members are also visible to other classes in the same package.

Class *BasePlusCommissionEmployee*

Class `BasePlusCommissionEmployee` (Fig. 9.9) extends the new version of class `CommissionEmployee` with protected instance variables. `BasePlusCommissionEmployee` objects inherit `CommissionEmployee`'s protected instance variables `firstName`, `lastName`, `socialSecurityNumber`, `grossSales` and `commissionRate`—all these variables are now protected members of `BasePlusCommissionEmployee`. As a result, the compiler does not generate errors when compiling line 37 of method `earnings` and lines 46–48 of method `toString`. If another class extends this version of class `BasePlusCommissionEmployee`, the new subclass also can access the protected members.

```
 1   // Fig. 9.9: BasePlusCommissionEmployee.java
 2   // BasePlusCommissionEmployee inherits protected instance
 3   // variables from CommissionEmployee.
 4
 5   public class BasePlusCommissionEmployee extends CommissionEmployee
 6   {
 7      private double baseSalary; // base salary per week
 8
 9      // six-argument constructor
10      public BasePlusCommissionEmployee( String first, String last,
11         String ssn, double sales, double rate, double salary )
12      {
13         super( first, last, ssn, sales, rate );
14         setBaseSalary( salary ); // validate and store base salary
15      } // end six-argument BasePlusCommissionEmployee constructor
16
17      // set base salary
18      public void setBaseSalary( double salary )
19      {
20         if ( salary >= 0.0 )
21            baseSalary = salary;
22         else
23            throw new IllegalArgumentException(
24               "Base salary must be >= 0.0" );
25      } // end method setBaseSalary
26
27      // return base salary
28      public double getBaseSalary()
29      {
30         return baseSalary;
31      } // end method getBaseSalary
```

Fig. 9.9 | BasePlusCommissionEmployee inherits `protected` instance variables from CommissionEmployee. (Part 1 of 2.)

```
32
33     // calculate earnings
34     @Override // indicates that this method overrides a superclass method
35     public double earnings()
36     {
37        return baseSalary + ( commissionRate * grossSales );
38     } // end method earnings
39
40     // return String representation of BasePlusCommissionEmployee
41     @Override // indicates that this method overrides a superclass method
42     public String toString()
43     {
44        return String.format(
45           "%s: %s %s\n%s: %s\n%s: %.2f\n%s: %.2f\n%s: %.2f",
46           "base-salaried commission employee", firstName, lastName,
47           "social security number", socialSecurityNumber,
48           "gross sales", grossSales, "commission rate", commissionRate,
49           "base salary", baseSalary );
50     } // end method toString
51  } // end class BasePlusCommissionEmployee
```

Fig. 9.9 | BasePlusCommissionEmployee inherits protected instance variables from
CommissionEmployee. (Part 2 of 2.)

When you create a BasePlusCommissionEmployee object, it contains all instance variables declared in the class hierarchy to that point—i.e., those from classes Object, CommissionEmployee and BasePlusCommissionEmployee. Class BasePlusCommissionEmployee does not inherit class CommissionEmployee's constructor. However, class BasePlusCommissionEmployee's six-argument constructor (lines 10–15) calls class CommissionEmployee's five-argument constructor *explicitly* to initialize the instance variables that BasePlusCommissionEmployee inherited from class CommissionEmployee. Similarly, class CommissionEmployee's constructor *implicitly* calls class Object's constructor. BasePlusCommissionEmployee's constructor must do this *explicitly* because CommissionEmployee does *not* provide a no-argument constructor that could be invoked implicitly.

Testing Class *BasePlusCommissionEmployee*
The BasePlusCommissionEmployeeTest class for this example is identical to that of Fig. 9.7 and produces the same output, so we do not show it here. Although the version of class BasePlusCommissionEmployee in Fig. 9.6 does not use inheritance and the version in Fig. 9.9 does, *both classes provide the same functionality*. The source code in Fig. 9.9 (47 lines) is considerably shorter than that in Fig. 9.6 (116 lines), because most of BasePlusCommissionEmployee's functionality is now inherited from CommissionEmployee—there's now only one copy of the CommissionEmployee functionality. This makes the code easier to maintain, modify and debug, because the code related to a commission employee exists only in class CommissionEmployee.

Notes on Using *protected* Instance Variables
In this example, we declared superclass instance variables as protected so that subclasses could access them. Inheriting protected instance variables slightly increases performance, because we can directly access the variables in the subclass without incurring the overhead

of a *set* or *get* method call. In most cases, however, it's better to use `private` instance variables to encourage proper software engineering, and leave code optimization issues to the compiler. Your code will be easier to maintain, modify and debug.

Using `protected` instance variables creates several potential problems. First, the subclass object can set an inherited variable's value directly without using a *set* method. Therefore, a subclass object can assign an invalid value to the variable, possibly leaving the object in an inconsistent state. For example, if we were to declare `CommissionEmployee`'s instance variable `grossSales` as `protected`, a subclass object (e.g., `BasePlusCommissionEmployee`) could then assign a negative value to `grossSales`. Another problem with using `protected` instance variables is that subclass methods are more likely to be written so that they depend on the superclass's data implementation. In practice, subclasses should depend only on the superclass services (i.e., non-`private` methods) and not on the superclass data implementation. With `protected` instance variables in the superclass, we may need to modify all the subclasses of the superclass if the superclass implementation changes. For example, if for some reason we were to change the names of instance variables `firstName` and `lastName` to `first` and `last`, then we would have to do so for all occurrences in which a subclass directly references superclass instance variables `firstName` and `lastName`. In such a case, the software is said to be **fragile** or **brittle**, because a small change in the superclass can "break" subclass implementation. You should be able to change the superclass implementation while still providing the same services to the subclasses. Of course, if the superclass services change, we must reimplement our subclasses. A third problem is that a class's `protected` members are visible to all classes in the same package as the class containing the `protected` members—this is not always desirable.

Software Engineering Observation 9.4

Use the `protected` *access modifier when a superclass should provide a method only to its subclasses and other classes in the same package, but not to other clients.*

Software Engineering Observation 9.5

Declaring superclass instance variables `private` *(as opposed to* `protected`*) enables the superclass implementation of these instance variables to change without affecting subclass implementations.*

Error-Prevention Tip 9.2

When possible, do not include `protected` *instance variables in a superclass. Instead, include non-*`private` *methods that access* `private` *instance variables. This will help ensure that objects of the class maintain consistent states.*

9.4.5 CommissionEmployee–BasePlusCommissionEmployee Inheritance Hierarchy Using `private` Instance Variables

Let's reexamine our hierarchy once more, this time using good software engineering practices. Class `CommissionEmployee` (Fig. 9.10) declares instance variables `firstName`, `lastName`, `socialSecurityNumber`, `grossSales` and `commissionRate` as *private* (lines 6–10) and provides `public` methods `setFirstName`, `getFirstName`, `setLastName`, `getLastName`, `setSocialSecurityNumber`, `getSocialSecurityNumber`, `setGrossSales`, `getGrossSales`, `setCommissionRate`, `getCommissionRate`, `earnings` and `toString` for manipulating these values. Methods `earnings` (lines 93–96) and `toString` (lines 99–107) use the class's *get* methods to obtain the values of its instance variables. If we decide to change the instance-variable names, the earnings and toString declarations will not require modification—only the bodies of the *get* and *set* methods that directly manipulate the instance variables will need to change. These changes occur solely within the superclass—no changes to the subclass are needed. *Localizing the effects of changes* like this is a good software engineering practice.

```java
 1   // Fig. 9.10: CommissionEmployee.java
 2   // CommissionEmployee class uses methods to manipulate its
 3   // private instance variables.
 4   public class CommissionEmployee
 5   {
 6      private String firstName;
 7      private String lastName;
 8      private String socialSecurityNumber;
 9      private double grossSales; // gross weekly sales
10      private double commissionRate; // commission percentage
11
12      // five-argument constructor
13      public CommissionEmployee( String first, String last, String ssn,
14         double sales, double rate )
15      {
16         // implicit call to Object constructor occurs here
17         firstName = first;
18         lastName = last;
19         socialSecurityNumber = ssn;
20         setGrossSales( sales ); // validate and store gross sales
21         setCommissionRate( rate ); // validate and store commission rate
22      } // end five-argument CommissionEmployee constructor
23
24      // set first name
25      public void setFirstName( String first )
26      {
27         firstName = first; // should validate
28      } // end method setFirstName
29
30      // return first name
31      public String getFirstName()
32      {
33         return firstName;
34      } // end method getFirstName
35
36      // set last name
37      public void setLastName( String last )
38      {
39         la5stName = last; // should validate
40      } // end method setLastName
41
42      // return last name
43      public String getLastName()
44      {
```

Fig. 9.10 | CommissionEmployee class uses methods to manipulate its private instance variables. (Part 1 of 3.)

```
45          return lastName;
46       } // end method getLastName
47
48       // set social security number
49       public void setSocialSecurityNumber( String ssn )
50       {
51          socialSecurityNumber = ssn; // should validate
52       } // end method setSocialSecurityNumber
53
54       // return social security number
55       public String getSocialSecurityNumber()
56       {
57          return socialSecurityNumber;
58       } // end method getSocialSecurityNumber
59
60       // set gross sales amount
61       public void setGrossSales( double sales )
62       {
63          if ( sales >= 0.0 )
64             grossSales = sales;
65          else
66             throw new IllegalArgumentException(
67                "Gross sales must be >= 0.0" );
68       } // end method setGrossSales
69
70       // return gross sales amount
71       public double getGrossSales()
72       {
73          return grossSales;
74       } // end method getGrossSales
75
76       // set commission rate
77       public void setCommissionRate( double rate )
78       {
79          if ( rate > 0.0 && rate < 1.0 )
80             commissionRate = rate;
81          else
82             throw new IllegalArgumentException(
83                "Commission rate must be > 0.0 and < 1.0" );
84       } // end method setCommissionRate
85
86       // return commission rate
87       public double getCommissionRate()
88       {
89          return commissionRate;
90       } // end method getCommissionRate
91
92       // calculate earnings
93       public double earnings()
94       {
95          return getCommissionRate() * getGrossSales();
96       } // end method earnings
```

Fig. 9.10 | CommissionEmployee class uses methods to manipulate its private instance variables. (Part 2 of 3.)

```
97
98     // return String representation of CommissionEmployee object
99     @Override // indicates that this method overrides a superclass method
100    public String toString()
101    {
102       return String.format( "%s: %s %s\n%s: %s\n%s: %.2f\n%s: %.2f",
103          "commission employee", getFirstName(), getLastName(),
104          "social security number", getSocialSecurityNumber(),
105          "gross sales", getGrossSales(),
106          "commission rate", getCommissionRate() );
107    } // end method toString
108 } // end class CommissionEmployee
```

Fig. 9.10 | CommissionEmployee class uses methods to manipulate its private instance variables. (Part 3 of 3.)

Subclass BasePlusCommissionEmployee (Fig. 9.11) inherits CommissionEmployee's non-private methods and can access the private superclass members via those methods. Class BasePlusCommissionEmployee has several changes that distinguish it from Fig. 9.9. Methods earnings (lines 35–39) and toString (lines 42–47) each invoke method get-BaseSalary to obtain the base salary value, rather than accessing baseSalary directly. If we decide to rename instance variable baseSalary, only the bodies of method setBas-eSalary and getBaseSalary will need to change.

```
1   // Fig. 9.11: BasePlusCommissionEmployee.java
2   // BasePlusCommissionEmployee class inherits from CommissionEmployee
3   // and accesses the superclass's private data via inherited
4   // public methods.
5
6   public class BasePlusCommissionEmployee extends CommissionEmployee
7   {
8      private double baseSalary; // base salary per week
9
10     // six-argument constructor
11     public BasePlusCommissionEmployee( String first, String last,
12        String ssn, double sales, double rate, double salary )
13     {
14        super( first, last, ssn, sales, rate );
15        setBaseSalary( salary ); // validate and store base salary
16     } // end six-argument BasePlusCommissionEmployee constructor
17
18     // set base salary
19     public void setBaseSalary( double salary )
20     {
21        if ( salary >= 0.0 )
22           baseSalary = salary;
```

Fig. 9.11 | BasePlusCommissionEmployee class inherits from CommissionEmployee and accesses the superclass's private data via inherited public methods. (Part 1 of 2.)

```
23              else
24                  throw new IllegalArgumentException(
25                      "Base salary must be >= 0.0" );
26          } // end method setBaseSalary
27
28          // return base salary
29          public double getBaseSalary()
30          {
31              return baseSalary;
32          } // end method getBaseSalary
33
34          // calculate earnings
35          @Override // indicates that this method overrides a superclass method
36          public double earnings()
37          {
38              return getBaseSalary() + super.earnings();
39          } // end method earnings
40
41          // return String representation of BasePlusCommissionEmployee
42          @Override // indicates that this method overrides a superclass method
43          public String toString()
44          {
45              return String.format( "%s %s\n%s: %.2f", "base-salaried",
46                  super.toString(), "base salary", getBaseSalary() );
47          } // end method toString
48      } // end class BasePlusCommissionEmployee
```

Fig. 9.11 | BasePlusCommissionEmployee class inherits from CommissionEmployee and accesses the superclass's private data via inherited public methods. (Part 2 of 2.)

Class *BasePlusCommissionEmployee's earnings Method*

Method earnings (lines 35–39) overrides class CommissionEmployee's earnings method (Fig. 9.10, lines 93–96) to calculate a base-salaried commission employee's earnings. The new version obtains the portion of the earnings based on commission alone by calling CommissionEmployee's earnings method with super.earnings() (line 34), then adds the base salary to this value to calculate the total earnings. Note the syntax used to invoke an overridden superclass method from a subclass—place the keyword super and a dot (.) separator before the superclass method name. This method invocation is a good software engineering practice—if a method performs all or some of the actions needed by another method, call that method rather than duplicate its code. By having BasePlusCommissionEmployee's earnings method invoke CommissionEmployee's earnings method to calculate part of a BasePlusCommissionEmployee object's earnings, we *avoid duplicating the code* and *reduce code-maintenance problems*. If we did not use "super." then BasePlusCommissionEmployee's earnings method would *call itself* rather than the superclass version. This would result in *infinite recursion*, which would eventually cause the method-call stack to overflow—a fatal runtime error.

Class *BasePlusCommissionEmployee's toString Method*

Similarly, BasePlusCommissionEmployee's toString method (Fig. 9.11, lines 38–43) overrides class CommissionEmployee's toString method (Fig. 9.10, lines 91–99) to return a String representation that's appropriate for a base-salaried commission employee. The new version creates part of a BasePlusCommissionEmployee object's String representation (i.e., the String "commission employee" and the values of class CommissionEmployee's private instance variables) by calling CommissionEmployee's toString method with the expression super.toString() (Fig. 9.11, line 42). BasePlusCommissionEmployee's toString method then outputs the remainder of a BasePlusCommissionEmployee object's String representation (i.e., the value of class BasePlusCommissionEmployee's base salary).

Common Programming Error 9.3

When a superclass method is overridden in a subclass, the subclass version often calls the superclass version to do a portion of the work. Failure to prefix the superclass method name with the keyword super and a dot (.) separator when calling the superclass's method causes the subclass method to call itself, potentially creating an error called infinite recursion.

*Testing Class **BasePlusCommissionEmployee***
Class BasePlusCommissionEmployeeTest performs the same manipulations on a Base-PlusCommissionEmployee object as in Fig. 9.7 and produces the same output, so we do not show it here. Although each BasePlusCommissionEmployee class you've seen behaves identically, the version in Fig. 9.11 is the best engineered. By using inheritance and by calling methods that hide the data and ensure consistency, we've efficiently and effectively constructed a well-engineered class.

Summary of the Inheritance Examples in Sections 9.4.1–9.4.5
You've now seen a set of examples that were designed to teach good software engineering with inheritance. You used the keyword extends to create a subclass using inheritance, used protected superclass members to enable a subclass to access inherited superclass instance variables, and overrode superclass methods to provide versions that are more appropriate for subclass objects. In addition, you applied software engineering techniques from Chapter 8 and this chapter to create classes that are easy to maintain, modify and debug.

9.5 Constructors in Subclasses

As we explained in the preceding section, instantiating a subclass object begins a chain of constructor calls in which the subclass constructor, before performing its own tasks, invokes its direct superclass's constructor either explicitly via the super reference or implicitly calling the superclass's default constructor or no-argument constructor. Similarly, if the superclass is derived from another class—as is, of course, every class except Object—the superclass constructor invokes the constructor of the next class up the hierarchy, and so on. The last constructor called in the chain is *always* the constructor for class Object. The original subclass constructor's body finishes executing *last*. Each superclass's constructor manipulates the superclass instance variables that the subclass object inherits. For example, consider again the CommissionEmployee–BasePlusCommissionEmployee hierarchy from Fig. 9.10 and Fig. 9.11. When a program creates a BasePlusCommissionEmployee object, its constructor is called. That constructor calls CommissionEmployee's constructor, which in turn calls Object's constructor. Class Object's constructor has an empty body, so it immediately returns control to CommissionEmployee's constructor, which then initializes the CommissionEmployee private instance variables that are part of the Base-PlusCommissionEmployee object. When CommissionEmployee's constructor completes execution, it returns control to BasePlusCommissionEmployee's constructor, which initializes the BasePlusCommissionEmployee object's baseSalary.

Software Engineering Observation 9.6

Java ensures that even if a constructor does not assign a value to an instance variable, the variable is still initialized to its default value (e.g., 0 for primitive numeric types, false for booleans, null for references).

9.6 Software Engineering with Inheritance

When you extend a class, the new class inherits the superclass's members—though the private superclass members are *hidden* in the new class. You can *customize* the new class to meet your needs by *including additional members* and by *overriding* superclass members. Doing this does not require the subclass programmer to change (or even have access to) the superclass's source code. Java simply requires access to the superclass's .class file so it can compile and execute any program that uses or extends the superclass. This powerful capability is attractive to independent software vendors (ISVs), who can develop proprietary classes for sale or license and make them available to users in bytecode format. Users then can derive new classes from these library classes rapidly and without accessing the ISVs' proprietary source code.

Software Engineering Observation 9.7

Although inheriting from a class does not require access to the class's source code, developers often insist on seeing the source code to understand how the class is implemented. Developers in industry want to ensure that they're extending a solid class—for example, a class that performs well and is implemented robustly and securely.

It's sometimes difficult to appreciate the scope of the problems faced by designers who work on large-scale software projects. People experienced with such projects say that effective software reuse improves the software-development process. Object-oriented programming facilitates software reuse, often significantly shortening development time.

The availability of substantial and useful class libraries delivers the maximum benefits of software reuse through inheritance. The standard Java class libraries that are shipped with Java tend to be rather general purpose, encouraging broad software reuse. Many other class libraries exist.

Reading subclass declarations can be confusing, because inherited members are not declared explicitly in the subclasses but are nevertheless present in them. A similar problem exists in documenting subclass members.

Software Engineering Observation 9.8

At the design stage in an object-oriented system, you'll often find that certain classes are closely related. You should "factor out" common instance variables and methods and place them in a superclass. Then use inheritance to develop subclasses, specializing them with capabilities beyond those inherited from the superclass.

Software Engineering Observation 9.9

Declaring a subclass does not affect its superclass's source code. Inheritance preserves the integrity of the superclass.

Software Engineering Observation 9.10

Designers of object-oriented systems should avoid class proliferation. Such proliferation creates management problems and can hinder software reusability, because in a huge class library it becomes difficult to locate the most appropriate classes. The alternative is to create fewer classes that provide more substantial functionality, but such classes might prove cumbersome.

9.7 Class Object

As we discussed earlier in this chapter, all classes in Java inherit directly or indirectly from the Object class (package java.lang), so its 11 methods (some are overloaded) are inherited by all other classes. Figure 9.12 summarizes Object's methods. We discuss several Object methods throughout this book (as indicated in Fig. 9.12).

Method	Description
clone	This protected method, which takes no arguments and returns an Object reference, makes a copy of the object on which it's called. The default implementation performs a so-called **shallow copy**—instance-variable values in one object are copied into another object of the same type. For reference types, only the references are copied. A typical overridden clone method's implementation would perform a **deep copy** that creates a new object for each reference-type instance variable. Implementing clone correctly is difficult. For this reason, its use is discouraged. Many industry experts suggest that object serialization should be used instead. We discuss object serialization in Chapter 17, Files, Streams and Object Serialization.
equals	This method compares two objects for equality and returns true if they're equal and false otherwise. The method takes any Object as an argument. When objects of a particular class must be compared for equality, the class should override method equals to compare the *contents* of the two objects. For the requirements of implementing this method, refer to the method's documentation at download.oracle.com/javase/6/docs/api/java/lang/Object.html#equals(java.lang.Object). The default equals implementation uses operator == to determine whether two references *refer to the same object* in memory. Section 16.3.3 demonstrates class String's equals method and differentiates between comparing String objects with == and with equals.
finalize	This protected method (introduced in Section 8.10) is called by the garbage collector to perform termination housekeeping on an object just before the garbage collector reclaims the object's memory. Recall that it's unclear whether, or when, method finalize will be called. For this reason, most programmers should avoid method finalize.

Fig. 9.12 | Object methods. (Part 1 of 2.)

Method	Description
getClass	Every object in Java knows its own type at execution time. Method getClass (used in Sections 10.5 and 14.5) returns an object of class Class (package java.lang) that contains information about the object's type, such as its class name (returned by Class method getName).
hashCode	Hashcodes are int values that are useful for high-speed storage and retrieval of information stored in a data structure that's known as a hashtable (discussed in Section 18.11). This method is also called as part of class Object's default toString method implementation.
wait, notify, notifyAll	Methods notify, notifyAll and the three overloaded versions of wait are related to multithreading, which is discussed in Chapter 23.
toString	This method (introduced in Section 9.4.1) returns a String representation of an object. The default implementation of this method returns the package name and class name of the object's class followed by a hexadecimal representation of the value returned by the object's hashCode method.

Fig. 9.12 | Object methods. (Part 2 of 2.)

Recall from Chapter 7 that arrays are objects. As a result, like all other objects, arrays inherit the members of class Object. Every array has an overridden clone method that copies the array. However, if the array stores references to objects, the objects are not copied—a *shallow copy is* performed.

9.8 Wrap-Up

This chapter introduced inheritance—the ability to create classes by absorbing an existing class's members and embellishing them with new capabilities. You learned the notions of superclasses and subclasses and used keyword extends to create a subclass that inherits members from a superclass. We showed how to use the @Override annotation to prevent unintended overloading by indicating that a method overrides a superclass method. We introduced the access modifier protected; subclass methods can directly access protected superclass members. You learned how to use super to access overridden superclass members. You also saw how constructors are used in inheritance hierarchies. Finally, you learned about the methods of class Object, the direct or indirect superclass of all Java classes.

In Chapter 10, Object-Oriented Programming: Polymorphism, we build on our discussion of inheritance by introducing polymorphism—an object-oriented concept that enables us to write programs that conveniently handle, in a more general manner, objects of a wide variety of classes related by inheritance. After studying Chapter 10, you'll be familiar with classes, objects, encapsulation, inheritance and polymorphism—the key technologies of object-oriented programming.

10

Object-Oriented Programming: Polymorphism

Objectives

In this chapter you'll learn:

- The concept of polymorphism.

- To use overridden methods to effect polymorphism.

- To distinguish between abstract and concrete classes.

- To declare abstract methods to create abstract classes.

- How polymorphism makes systems extensible and maintainable.

- To determine an object's type at execution time.

- To declare and implement interfaces.

10.1 Introduction

We continue our study of object-oriented programming by explaining and demonstrating **polymorphism** with inheritance hierarchies. Polymorphism enables you to "program in the general" rather than "program in the specific." In particular, polymorphism enables you to write programs that process objects that share the same superclass (either directly or indirectly) as if they're all objects of the superclass; this can simplify programming.

Consider the following example of polymorphism. Suppose we create a program that simulates the movement of several types of animals for a biological study. Classes Fish, Frog and Bird represent the types of animals under investigation. Imagine that each class extends superclass Animal, which contains a method move and maintains an animal's current location as *x-y* coordinates. Each subclass implements method move. Our program maintains an Animal array containing references to objects of the various Animal subclasses. To simulate the animals' movements, the program sends each object the *same* message once per second—namely, move. Each specific type of Animal responds to a move message in its own way—a Fish might swim three feet, a Frog might jump five feet and a Bird might fly ten feet. Each object knows how to modify its *x-y* coordinates appropriately for its *specific* type of movement. Relying on each object to know how to "do the right thing" (i.e., do what is appropriate for that type of object) in response to the same method call is the key concept of polymorphism. The same message (in this case, move) sent to a variety of objects has "many forms" of results—hence the term polymorphism.

Implementing for Extensibility

With polymorphism, we can design and implement systems that are easily extensible—new classes can be added with little or no modification to the general portions of the program, as long as the new classes are part of the inheritance hierarchy that the program processes generically. The only parts of a program that must be altered are those that require direct knowledge of the new classes that we add to the hierarchy. For example, if we extend class `Animal` to create class `Tortoise` (which might respond to a move message by crawling one inch), we need to write only the `Tortoise` class and the part of the simulation that instantiates a `Tortoise` object. The portions of the simulation that tell each `Animal` to move generically can remain the same.

Chapter Overview

First, we discuss common examples of polymorphism. We then provide a simple example demonstrating polymorphic behavior. We use superclass references to manipulate *both* superclass objects and subclass objects polymorphically.

We then present a case study that revisits the employee hierarchy of Section 9.4.5. We develop a simple payroll application that polymorphically calculates the weekly pay of several different types of employees using each employee's `earnings` method. Though the earnings of each type of employee are calculated in a specific way, polymorphism allows us to process the employees "in the general." In the case study, we enlarge the hierarchy to include two new classes—`SalariedEmployee` (for people paid a fixed weekly salary) and `HourlyEmployee` (for people paid an hourly salary and "time-and-a-half" for overtime). We declare a common set of functionality for all the classes in the updated hierarchy in an "abstract" class, `Employee`, from which "concrete"classes `SalariedEmployee`, `HourlyEmployee` and `CommissionEmployee` inherit directly and "concrete" class `BasePlusCommissionEmployee` inherits indirectly. As you'll soon see, *when we invoke each employee's earnings method off a superclass Employee reference, the correct earnings subclass calculation is performed*, due to Java's polymorphic capabilities.

Programming in the Specific

Occasionally, when performing polymorphic processing, we need to program "in the specific." Our `Employee` case study demonstrates that a program can determine the type of an object at *execution time* and act on that object accordingly. In the case study, we've decided that `BasePlusCommissionEmployees` should receive 10% raises on their base salaries. So, we use these capabilities to determine whether a particular employee object *is a* `BasePlusCommissionEmployee`. If so, we increase that employee's base salary by 10%.

Interfaces

The chapter continues with an introduction to Java interfaces. An interface describes a set of methods that can be called on an object, but does *not* provide concrete implementations for all the methods. You can declare classes that **implement** (i.e., provide concrete implementations for the methods of) one or more interfaces. Each interface method must be declared in all the classes that explicitly implement the interface. Once a class implements an interface, all objects of that class have an *is-a* relationship with the interface type, and all objects of the class are guaranteed to provide the functionality described by the interface. This is true of all subclasses of that class as well.

Interfaces are particularly useful for assigning common functionality to possibly *unrelated* classes. This allows objects of unrelated classes to be processed polymorphically—objects of classes that implement the same interface can respond to all of the interface method calls. To demonstrate creating and using interfaces, we modify our payroll application to create a general accounts payable application that can calculate payments due for company employees and invoice amounts to be billed for purchased goods. As you'll see, interfaces enable polymorphic capabilities similar to those possible with inheritance.

10.2 Polymorphism Examples

We now consider several additional examples of polymorphism.

Quadrilaterals

If class `Rectangle` is derived from class `Quadrilateral`, then a `Rectangle` object is a more specific version of a `Quadrilateral`. Any operation (e.g., calculating the perimeter or the area) that can be performed on a `Quadrilateral` can also be performed on a `Rectangle`. These operations can also be performed on other `Quadrilaterals`, such as `Squares`, `Parallelograms` and `Trapezoids`. The polymorphism occurs when a program invokes a method through a superclass `Quadrilateral` variable—at execution time, the correct subclass version of the method is called, based on the type of the reference stored in the superclass variable. You'll see a simple code example that illustrates this process in Section 10.3.

Space Objects in a Video Game

Suppose we design a video game that manipulates objects of classes `Martian`, `Venusian`, `Plutonian`, `SpaceShip` and `LaserBeam`. Imagine that each class inherits from the superclass `SpaceObject`, which contains method `draw`. Each subclass implements this method. A screen manager maintains a collection (e.g., a `SpaceObject` array) of references to objects of the various classes. To refresh the screen, the screen manager periodically sends each object the same message—namely, `draw`. However, each object responds its own way, based on its class. For example, a `Martian` object might draw itself in red with green eyes and the appropriate number of antennae. A `SpaceShip` object might draw itself as a bright silver flying saucer. A `LaserBeam` object might draw itself as a bright red beam across the screen. Again, the *same* message (in this case, `draw`) sent to a variety of objects has "many forms" of results.

A screen manager might use polymorphism to facilitate adding new classes to a system with minimal modifications to the system's code. Suppose that we want to add `Mercurian` objects to our video game. To do so, we'd build a class `Mercurian` that extends `SpaceObject` and provides its own `draw` method implementation. When `Mercurian` objects appear in the `SpaceObject` collection, the screen manager code *invokes method draw, exactly as it does for every other object in the collection, regardless of its type.* So the new `Mercurian` objects simply "plug right in" without any modification of the screen manager code by the programmer. Thus, without modifying the system (other than to build new classes and modify the code that creates new objects), you can use polymorphism to conveniently include additional types that were not envisioned when the system was created.

Software Engineering Observation 10.1

Polymorphism enables you to deal in generalities and let the execution-time environment handle the specifics. You can command objects to behave in manners appropriate to those objects, without knowing their types (as long as the objects belong to the same inheritance hierarchy).

Software Engineering Observation 10.2

Polymorphism promotes extensibility: Software that invokes polymorphic behavior is independent of the object types to which messages are sent. New object types that can respond to existing method calls can be incorporated into a system without modifying the base system. Only client code that instantiates new objects must be modified to accommodate new types.

10.3 Demonstrating Polymorphic Behavior

Section 9.4 created a class hierarchy, in which class BasePlusCommissionEmployee inherited from CommissionEmployee. The examples in that section manipulated CommissionEmployee and BasePlusCommissionEmployee objects by using references to them to invoke their methods—we aimed superclass variables at superclass objects and subclass variables at subclass objects. These assignments are natural and straightforward—superclass variables are *intended* to refer to superclass objects, and subclass variables are *intended* to refer to subclass objects. However, as you'll soon see, other assignments are possible.

In the next example, we aim a *superclass* reference at *a subclass* object. We then show how invoking a method on a subclass object via a superclass reference invokes the *subclass* functionality—the type of the *referenced object*, not the type of the *variable*, determines which method is called. This example demonstrates that *an object of a subclass can be treated as an object of its superclass,* enabling various interesting manipulations. A program can create an array of superclass variables that refer to objects of many subclass types. This is allowed because each subclass object *is an* object of its superclass. For instance, we can assign the reference of a BasePlusCommissionEmployee object to a superclass CommissionEmployee variable, because a BasePlusCommissionEmployee *is a* CommissionEmployee—we can treat a BasePlusCommissionEmployee as a CommissionEmployee.

As you'll learn later in the chapter, you *cannot treat a superclass object as a subclass object,* because a superclass object is *not* an object of any of its subclasses. For example, we cannot assign the reference of a CommissionEmployee object to a subclass BasePlusCommissionEmployee variable, because a CommissionEmployee is *not* a BasePlusCommissionEmployee—a CommissionEmployee does *not* have a baseSalary instance variable and does *not* have methods setBaseSalary and getBaseSalary. The *is-a* relationship applies only *up the hierarchy* from a subclass to its direct (and indirect) superclasses, and *not* vice versa (i.e., not down the hierarchy from a superclass to its subclasses).

The Java compiler *does* allow the assignment of a superclass reference to a subclass variable if we explicitly cast the superclass reference to the subclass type—a technique we discuss in Section 10.5. Why would we ever want to perform such an assignment? A superclass reference can be used to invoke only the methods declared in the superclass—attempting to invoke subclass-only methods through a superclass reference results in compilation errors. If a program needs to perform a subclass-specific operation on a subclass object referenced by a superclass variable, the program must first cast the superclass reference to a subclass reference through a technique known as **downcasting**. This enables the program to invoke subclass methods that are not in the superclass. We show a downcasting example in Section 10.5.

The example in Fig. 10.1 demonstrates three ways to use superclass and subclass variables to store references to superclass and subclass objects. The first two are straightforward—as in Section 9.4, we assign a superclass reference to a superclass variable, and a subclass reference to a subclass variable. Then we demonstrate the relationship between subclasses and superclasses (i.e., the *is-a* relationship) by assigning a subclass reference to a superclass variable. This program uses classes CommissionEmployee and BasePlusCommissionEmployee from Fig. 9.10 and Fig. 9.11, respectively.

In Fig. 10.1, lines 10–11 create a CommissionEmployee object and assign its reference to a CommissionEmployee variable. Lines 14–16 create a BasePlusCommissionEmployee object and assign its reference to a BasePlusCommissionEmployee variable. These assign-

```
 1   // Fig. 10.1: PolymorphismTest.java
 2   // Assigning superclass and subclass references to superclass and
 3   // subclass variables.
 4
 5   public class PolymorphismTest
 6   {
 7      public static void main( String[] args )
 8      {
 9         // assign superclass reference to superclass variable
10         CommissionEmployee commissionEmployee = new CommissionEmployee(
11            "Sue", "Jones", "222-22-2222", 10000, .06 );
12
13         // assign subclass reference to subclass variable
14         BasePlusCommissionEmployee basePlusCommissionEmployee =
15            new BasePlusCommissionEmployee(
16            "Bob", "Lewis", "333-33-3333", 5000, .04, 300 );
17
18         // invoke toString on superclass object using superclass variable
19         System.out.printf( "%s %s:\n\n%s\n\n",
20            "Call CommissionEmployee's toString with superclass reference ",
21            "to superclass object", commissionEmployee.toString() );
22
23         // invoke toString on subclass object using subclass variable
24         System.out.printf( "%s %s:\n\n%s\n\n",
25            "Call BasePlusCommissionEmployee's toString with subclass",
26            "reference to subclass object",
27            basePlusCommissionEmployee.toString() );
28
29         // invoke toString on subclass object using superclass variable
30         CommissionEmployee commissionEmployee2 =
31            basePlusCommissionEmployee;
32         System.out.printf( "%s %s:\n\n%s\n",
33            "Call BasePlusCommissionEmployee's toString with superclass",
34            "reference to subclass object", commissionEmployee2.toString() );
35      } // end main
36   } // end class PolymorphismTest
```

```
Call CommissionEmployee's toString with superclass reference to superclass
object:

commission employee: Sue Jones
social security number: 222-22-2222
gross sales: 10000.00
commission rate: 0.06

Call BasePlusCommissionEmployee's toString with subclass reference to
subclass object:

base-salaried commission employee: Bob Lewis
social security number: 333-33-3333
gross sales: 5000.00
commission rate: 0.04
base salary: 300.00
```

Fig. 10.1 | Assigning superclass and subclass references to superclass and subclass variables. (Part 1 of 2.)

```
Call BasePlusCommissionEmployee's toString with superclass reference to
subclass object:

base-salaried commission employee: Bob Lewis
social security number: 333-33-3333
gross sales: 5000.00
commission rate: 0.04
base salary: 300.00
```

Fig. 10.1 | Assigning superclass and subclass references to superclass and subclass variables. (Part 2 of 2.)

ments are natural—for example, a CommissionEmployee variable's primary purpose is to hold a reference to a CommissionEmployee object. Lines 19–21 use commissionEmployee to invoke toString explicitly. Because commissionEmployee refers to a CommissionEmployee object, superclass CommissionEmployee's version of toString is called. Similarly, lines 24–27 use basePlusCommissionEmployee to invoke toString explicitly on the BasePlusCommissionEmployee object. This invokes subclass BasePlusCommissionEmployee's version of toString.

Lines 30–31 then assign the reference of subclass object basePlusCommissionEmployee to a superclass CommissionEmployee variable, which lines 32–34 use to invoke method toString. *When a superclass variable contains a reference to a subclass object, and that reference is used to call a method, the subclass version of the method is called.* Hence, commissionEmployee2.toString() in line 34 actually calls class BasePlusCommissionEmployee's toString method. The Java compiler allows this "crossover" because an object of a subclass *is an* object of its superclass (but not vice versa). When the compiler encounters a method call made through a variable, the compiler determines if the method can be called by checking the variable's class type. If that class contains the proper method declaration (or inherits one), the call is compiled. At execution time, the type of the object to which the variable refers determines the actual method to use. This process, called *dynamic binding*, is discussed in detail in Section 10.5.

10.4 Abstract Classes and Methods

When we think of a class, we assume that programs will create objects of that type. Sometimes it's useful to declare classes—called **abstract classes**—for which you *never* intend to create objects. Because they're used only as superclasses in inheritance hierarchies, we refer to them as **abstract superclasses**. These classes cannot be used to instantiate objects, because, as we'll soon see, abstract classes are *incomplete*. Subclasses must declare the "missing pieces" to become "concrete" classes, from which you can instantiate objects. Otherwise, these subclasses, too, will be abstract. We demonstrate abstract classes in Section 10.5.

Purpose of Abstract Classes
An abstract class's purpose is to provide an appropriate superclass from which other classes can inherit and thus share a common design. In the Shape hierarchy of Fig. 9.3, for example, subclasses inherit the notion of what it means to be a Shape—perhaps common attributes such as location, color and borderThickness, and behaviors such as draw, move, resize and changeColor. Classes that can be used to instantiate objects are called **concrete**

classes. Such classes provide implementations of *every* method they declare (some of the implementations can be inherited). For example, we could derive concrete classes Circle, Square and Triangle from abstract superclass TwoDimensionalShape. Similarly, we could derive concrete classes Sphere, Cube and Tetrahedron from abstract superclass ThreeDimensionalShape. Abstract superclasses are *too general* to create real objects—they specify only what is common among subclasses. We need to be more *specific* before we can create objects. For example, if you send the draw message to abstract class TwoDimensionalShape, the class knows that two-dimensional shapes should be drawable, but it does not know what specific shape to draw, so it cannot implement a real draw method. Concrete classes provide the specifics that make it reasonable to instantiate objects.

Not all hierarchies contain abstract classes. However, you'll often write client code that uses only abstract superclass types to reduce the client code's dependencies on a range of subclass types. For example, you can write a method with a parameter of an abstract superclass type. When called, such a method can receive an object of any concrete class that directly or indirectly extends the superclass specified as the parameter's type.

Abstract classes sometimes constitute several levels of a hierarchy. For example, the Shape hierarchy of Fig. 9.3 begins with abstract class Shape. On the next level of the hierarchy are *abstract* classes TwoDimensionalShape and ThreeDimensionalShape. The next level of the hierarchy declares *concrete* classes for TwoDimensionalShapes (Circle, Square and Triangle) and for ThreeDimensionalShapes (Sphere, Cube and Tetrahedron).

Declaring an Abstract Class and Abstract Methods

You make a class abstract by declaring it with keyword **abstract**. An abstract class normally contains one or more **abstract methods**. An abstract method is one with keyword abstract in its declaration, as in

```
public abstract void draw(); // abstract method
```

Abstract methods do *not* provide implementations. A class that contains *any* abstract methods must be explicitly declared abstract even if that class contains some concrete (nonabstract) methods. Each concrete subclass of an abstract superclass also must provide concrete implementations of each of the superclass's abstract methods. Constructors and static methods cannot be declared abstract. Constructors are not inherited, so an abstract constructor could never be implemented. Though non-private static methods are inherited, they cannot be overridden. Since abstract methods are meant to be overridden so that they can process objects based on their types, it would not make sense to declare a static method as abstract.

Software Engineering Observation 10.3

An abstract class declares common attributes and behaviors (both abstract and concrete) of the various classes in a class hierarchy. An abstract class typically contains one or more abstract methods that subclasses must override if they are to be concrete. The instance variables and concrete methods of an abstract class are subject to the normal rules of inheritance.

Common Programming Error 10.1

Attempting to instantiate an object of an abstract class is a compilation error.

Common Programming Error 10.2

Failure to implement a superclass's abstract methods in a subclass is a compilation error unless the subclass is also declared abstract.

Using Abstract Classes to Declare Variables

Although we cannot instantiate objects of abstract superclasses, you'll soon see that we *can* use abstract superclasses to declare variables that can hold references to objects of any concrete class derived from those abstract superclasses. Programs typically use such variables to manipulate subclass objects polymorphically. You also can use abstract superclass names to invoke static methods declared in those abstract superclasses.

Consider another application of polymorphism. A drawing program needs to display many shapes, including types of new shapes that you'll add to the system after writing the drawing program. The drawing program might need to display shapes, such as Circles, Triangles, Rectangles or others, that derive from abstract class Shape. The drawing program uses Shape variables to manage the objects that are displayed. To draw any object in this inheritance hierarchy, the drawing program uses a superclass Shape variable containing a reference to the subclass object to invoke the object's draw method. This method is declared abstract in superclass Shape, so each concrete subclass *must* implement method draw in a manner specific to that shape—each object in the Shape inheritance hierarchy *knows how to draw itself.* The drawing program does not have to worry about the type of each object or whether the program has ever encountered objects of that type.

Layered Software Systems

Polymorphism is particularly effective for implementing so-called layered software systems. In operating systems, for example, each type of physical device could operate quite differently from the others. Even so, commands to read or write data from and to devices may have a certain uniformity. For each device, the operating system uses a piece of software called a *device driver* to control all communication between the system and the device. The write message sent to a device-driver object needs to be interpreted specifically in the context of that driver and how it manipulates devices of a specific type. However, the write call itself really is no different from the write to any other device in the system—place some number of bytes from memory onto that device. An object-oriented operating system might use an abstract superclass to provide an "interface" appropriate for all device drivers. Then, through inheritance from that abstract superclass, subclasses are formed that all behave similarly. The device-driver methods are declared as abstract methods in the abstract superclass. The implementations of these abstract methods are provided in the concrete subclasses that correspond to the specific types of device drivers. New devices are always being developed, often long after the operating system has been released. When you buy a new device, it comes with a device driver provided by the device vendor. The device is immediately operational after you connect it to your computer and install the driver. This is another elegant example of how polymorphism makes systems *extensible.*

10.5 Case Study: Payroll System Using Polymorphism

This section reexamines the hierarchy that we explored throughout Section 9.4. Now we use an abstract method and polymorphism to perform payroll calculations based on an enhanced employee inheritance hierarchy that meets the following requirements:

A company pays its employees on a weekly basis. The employees are of four types: Salaried employees are paid a fixed weekly salary regardless of the number of hours worked, hourly employees are paid by the hour and receive overtime pay (i.e., 1.5 times their hourly salary rate) for all hours worked in excess of 40 hours, commission employees are paid a percentage of their sales and base-salaried commission employees receive a base salary plus a percentage of their sales. For the current pay period, the company has decided to reward salaried-commission employees by adding 10% to their base salaries. The company wants to write an application that performs its payroll calculations polymorphically.

We use abstract class Employee to represent the general concept of an employee. The classes that extend Employee are SalariedEmployee, CommissionEmployee and HourlyEmployee. Class BasePlusCommissionEmployee—which extends CommissionEmployee—represents the last employee type. The UML class diagram in Fig. 10.2 shows the inheritance hierarchy for our polymorphic employee-payroll application. Abstract class name Employee is italicized—a convention of the UML.

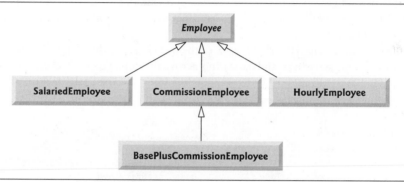

Fig. 10.2 | Employee hierarchy UML class diagram.

Abstract superclass Employee declares the "interface" to the hierarchy—that is, the set of methods that a program can invoke on all Employee objects. We use the term "interface" here in a general sense to refer to the various ways programs can communicate with objects of any Employee subclass. Be careful not to confuse the general notion of an "interface" with the formal notion of a Java interface, the subject of Section 10.7. Each employee, regardless of the way his or her earnings are calculated, has a first name, a last name and a social security number, so private instance variables firstName, lastName and socialSecurityNumber appear in abstract superclass Employee.

The following sections implement the Employee class hierarchy of Fig. 10.2. The first section implements abstract superclass Employee. The next four sections each implement one of the concrete classes. The last section implements a test program that builds objects of all these classes and processes those objects polymorphically.

10.5.1 Abstract Superclass Employee

Class Employee (Fig. 10.4) provides methods earnings and toString, in addition to the *get* and *set* methods that manipulate Employee's instance variables. An earnings method certainly applies generically to all employees. But each earnings calculation depends on the employee's class. So we declare earnings as abstract in superclass Employee because a default implementation does not make sense for that method—there isn't enough information to determine what amount `earnings` should return. Each subclass overrides `earnings` with an appropriate implementation. To calculate an employee's earnings, the program assigns to a superclass `Employee` variable a reference to the employee's object, then invokes the `earnings` method on that variable. We maintain an array of `Employee` variables, each holding a reference to an `Employee` object. (Of course, there cannot be `Employee` objects, because `Employee` is an abstract class. Because of inheritance, however, all objects of all subclasses of `Employee` may nevertheless be thought of as `Employee` objects.) The program will iterate through the array and call method `earnings` for each `Employee` object. Java processes these method calls polymorphically. Declaring `earnings` as an `abstract` method in `Employee` enables the calls to `earnings` through `Employee` variables to compile and forces every direct concrete subclass of `Employee` to override `earnings`.

Method `toString` in class `Employee` returns a `String` containing the first name, last name and social security number of the employee. As we'll see, each subclass of `Employee` overrides method `toString` to create a `String` representation of an object of that class that contains the employee's type (e.g., `"salaried employee:"`) followed by the rest of the employee's information.

The diagram in Fig. 10.3 shows each of the five classes in the hierarchy down the left side and methods `earnings` and `toString` across the top. For each class, the diagram

	earnings	toString
Employee	abstract	*firstName lastName* social security number: *SSN*
Salaried- Employee	weeklySalary	salaried employee: *firstName lastName* social security number: *SSN* weekly salary: *weeklySalary*

Hourly-
Employee
	if (hours <= 40)
	  wage * hours
	else if (hours > 40)
	{
	  40 * wage +
	  (hours - 40) *
	  wage * 1.5
	}
		hourly employee: *firstName lastName*
		social security number: *SSN*
		hourly wage: *wage*; hours worked: *hours*

Commission- Employee	commissionRate * grossSales	commission employee: *firstName lastName* social security number: *SSN* gross sales: *grossSales*; commission rate: *commissionRate*
BasePlus- Commission- Employee	(commissionRate * grossSales) + baseSalary	base salaried commission employee: *firstName lastName* social security number: *SSN* gross sales: *grossSales*; commission rate: *commissionRate*; base salary: *baseSalary*

Fig. 10.3 | Polymorphic interface for the `Employee` hierarchy classes.

shows the desired results of each method. We do not list superclass `Employee`'s *get* and *set* methods because they're not overridden in any of the subclasses—each of these methods is inherited and used "as is" by each subclass.

Let's consider class `Employee`'s declaration (Fig. 10.4). The class includes a constructor that takes the first name, last name and social security number as arguments (lines 11–16); *get* methods that return the first name, last name and social security number (lines 25–28, 37–40 and 49–52, respectively); *set* methods that set the first name, last name and social security number (lines 19–22, 31–34 and 43–46, respectively); method `toString` (lines 55–60), which returns the `String` representation of an `Employee`; and abstract method `earnings` (line 63), which will be implemented by each of the concrete subclasses. The `Employee` constructor does not validate its parameters in this example; normally, such validation should be provided.

Why did we decide to declare `earnings` as an `abstract` method? It simply does not make sense to provide an implementation of this method in class `Employee`. We cannot calculate the earnings for a *general* `Employee`—we first must know the *specific* type of `Employee` to determine the appropriate earnings calculation. By declaring this method abstract, we indicate that each concrete subclass *must* provide an appropriate `earnings` implementation and that a program will be able to use superclass `Employee` variables to invoke method `earnings` polymorphically for any type of `Employee`.

```
1   // Fig. 10.4: Employee.java
2   // Employee abstract superclass.
3
4   public abstract class Employee
5   {
6      private String firstName;
7      private String lastName;
8      private String socialSecurityNumber;
9
10     // three-argument constructor
11     public Employee( String first, String last, String ssn )
12     {
13        firstName = first;
14        lastName = last;
15        socialSecurityNumber = ssn;
16     } // end three-argument Employee constructor
17
18     // set first name
19     public void setFirstName( String first )
20     {
21        firstName = first; // should validate
22     } // end method setFirstName
23
24     // return first name
25     public String getFirstName()
26     {
27        return firstName;
28     } // end method getFirstName
29
```

Fig. 10.4 | `Employee` abstract superclass. (Part 1 of 2.)

```
30      // set last name
31      public void setLastName( String last )
32      {
33          lastName = last; // should validate
34      } // end method setLastName
35
36      // return last name
37      public String getLastName()
38      {
39          return lastName;
40      } // end method getLastName
41
42      // set social security number
43      public void setSocialSecurityNumber( String ssn )
44      {
45          socialSecurityNumber = ssn; // should validate
46      } // end method setSocialSecurityNumber
47
48      // return social security number
49      public String getSocialSecurityNumber()
50      {
51          return socialSecurityNumber;
52      } // end method getSocialSecurityNumber
53
54      // return String representation of Employee object
55      @Override
56      public String toString()
57      {
58          return String.format( "%s %s\nsocial security number: %s",
59              getFirstName(), getLastName(), getSocialSecurityNumber() );
60      } // end method toString
61
62      // abstract method overridden by concrete subclasses
63      public abstract double earnings(); // no implementation here
64  } // end abstract class Employee
```

Fig. 10.4 | Employee abstract superclass. (Part 2 of 2.)

10.5.2 Concrete Subclass SalariedEmployee

Class SalariedEmployee (Fig. 10.5) extends class Employee (line 4) and overrides abstract method earnings (lines 33–37), which makes SalariedEmployee a concrete class. The class includes a constructor (lines 9–14) that takes a first name, a last name, a social security number and a weekly salary as arguments; a *set* method to assign a new nonnegative value to instance variable weeklySalary (lines 17–24); a *get* method to return weeklySalary's value (lines 27–30); a method earnings (lines 33–37) to calculate a SalariedEmployee's earnings; and a method toString (lines 40–45), which returns a String including the employee's type, namely, "salaried employee: " followed by employee-specific information produced by superclass Employee's toString method and SalariedEmployee's getWeeklySalary method. Class SalariedEmployee's constructor passes the first name, last name and social security number to the Employee constructor (line 12) to initialize the private instance variables not inherited from the superclass. Method earnings overrides Employee's abstract method earnings to provide a concrete implementation that returns the SalariedEmployee's weekly salary. If we do not implement earnings, class SalariedEmployee must be declared abstract—otherwise, class SalariedEmployee will not compile. Of course, we want SalariedEmployee to be a concrete class in this example.

```java
1   // Fig. 10.5: SalariedEmployee.java
2   // SalariedEmployee concrete class extends abstract class Employee.
3
4   public class SalariedEmployee extends Employee
5   {
6      private double weeklySalary;
7
8      // four-argument constructor
9      public SalariedEmployee( String first, String last, String ssn,
10        double salary )
11     {
12        super( first, last, ssn ); // pass to Employee constructor
13        setWeeklySalary( salary ); // validate and store salary
14     } // end four-argument SalariedEmployee constructor
15
16     // set salary
17     public void setWeeklySalary( double salary )
18     {
19        if ( salary >= 0.0 )
20           baseSalary = salary;
21        else
22           throw new IllegalArgumentException(
23              "Weekly salary must be >= 0.0" );
24     } // end method setWeeklySalary
25
26     // return salary
27     public double getWeeklySalary()
28     {
29        return weeklySalary;
30     } // end method getWeeklySalary
31
32     // calculate earnings; override abstract method earnings in Employee
33     @Override
34     public double earnings()
35     {
36        return getWeeklySalary();
37     } // end method earnings
38
39     // return String representation of SalariedEmployee object
40     @Override
41     public String toString()
42     {
43        return String.format( "salaried employee: %s\n%s: $%,.2f",
44           super.toString(), "weekly salary", getWeeklySalary() );
45     } // end method toString
46  } // end class SalariedEmployee
```

Fig. 10.5 | SalariedEmployee concrete class extends abstract class Employee.

Method `toString` (lines 40–45) overrides `Employee` method `toString`. If class `SalariedEmployee` did not override `toString`, `SalariedEmployee` would have inherited the `Employee` version of `toString`. In that case, `SalariedEmployee`'s `toString` method would simply return the employee's full name and social security number, which does not adequately represent a `SalariedEmployee`. To produce a complete `String` representation of a `SalariedEmployee`, the subclass's `toString` method returns `"salaried employee: "` followed by the superclass `Employee`-specific information (i.e., first name, last name and social security number) obtained by invoking the superclass's `toString` method (line 44)—this is a nice example of code reuse. The `String` representation of a `SalariedEmployee` also contains the employee's weekly salary obtained by invoking the class's `getWeeklySalary` method.

10.5.3 Concrete Subclass HourlyEmployee

Class `HourlyEmployee` (Fig. 10.6) also extends `Employee` (line 4). The class includes a constructor (lines 10–16) that takes as arguments a first name, a last name, a social security number, an hourly wage and the number of hours worked. Lines 19–26 and 35–42 declare *set* methods that assign new values to instance variables `wage` and `hours`, respectively. Method `setWage` (lines 19–26) ensures that `wage` is nonnegative, and method `setHours` (lines 35–42) ensures that `hours` is between 0 and 168 (the total number of hours in a week) inclusive. Class `HourlyEmployee` also includes *get* methods (lines 29–32 and 45–48) to return the values of `wage` and `hours`, respectively; a method `earnings` (lines 51–58) to calculate an `HourlyEmployee`'s earnings; and a method `toString` (lines 61–67), which returns a `String` containing the employee's type (`"hourly employee: "`) and the employee-specific information. The `HourlyEmployee` constructor, like the `SalariedEmployee` constructor, passes the first name, last name and social security number to the superclass `Employee` constructor (line 13) to initialize the `private` instance variables. In addition, method `toString` calls superclass method `toString` (line 65) to obtain the `Employee`-specific information (i.e., first name, last name and social security number)—this is another nice example of code reuse.

```
1   // Fig. 10.6: HourlyEmployee.java
2   // HourlyEmployee class extends Employee.
3
4   public class HourlyEmployee extends Employee
5   {
6      private double wage; // wage per hour
7      private double hours; // hours worked for week
8
9      // five-argument constructor
10     public HourlyEmployee( String first, String last, String ssn,
11        double hourlyWage, double hoursWorked )
12     {
13        super( first, last, ssn );
14        setWage( hourlyWage ); // validate hourly wage
15        setHours( hoursWorked ); // validate hours worked
16     } // end five-argument HourlyEmployee constructor
17
```

Fig. 10.6 | `HourlyEmployee` class extends `Employee`. (Part 1 of 2.)

```
18       // set wage
19       public void setWage( double hourlyWage )
20       {
21          if ( hourlyWage >= 0.0 )
22             wage = hourlyWage;
23          else
24             throw new IllegalArgumentException(
25                "Hourly wage must be >= 0.0" );
26       } // end method setWage
27
28       // return wage
29       public double getWage()
30       {
31          return wage;
32       } // end method getWage
33
34       // set hours worked
35       public void setHours( double hoursWorked )
36       {
37          if ( ( hoursWorked >= 0.0 ) && ( hoursWorked <= 168.0 ) )
38             hours = hoursWorked;
39          else
40             throw new IllegalArgumentException(
41                "Hours worked must be >= 0.0 and <= 168.0" );
42       } // end method setHours
43
44       // return hours worked
45       public double getHours()
46       {
47          return hours;
48       } // end method getHours
49
50       // calculate earnings; override abstract method earnings in Employee
51       @Override
52       public double earnings()
53       {
54          if ( getHours() <= 40 ) // no overtime
55             return getWage() * getHours();
56          else
57             return 40 * getWage() + ( getHours() - 40 ) * getWage() * 1.5;
58       } // end method earnings
59
60       // return String representation of HourlyEmployee object
61       @Override
62       public String toString()
63       {
64          return String.format( "hourly employee: %s\n%s: $%,.2f; %s: %,.2f",
65             super.toString(), "hourly wage", getWage(),
66             "hours worked", getHours() );
67       } // end method toString
68    } // end class HourlyEmployee
```

Fig. 10.6 | HourlyEmployee class extends Employee. (Part 2 of 2.)

10.5.4 Concrete Subclass CommissionEmployee

Class CommissionEmployee (Fig. 10.7) extends class Employee (line 4). The class includes a constructor (lines 10–16) that takes a first name, a last name, a social security number, a sales amount and a commission rate; *set* methods (lines 19–26 and 35–42) to assign new values to instance variables commissionRate and grossSales, respectively; *get* methods (lines 29–32 and 45–48) that retrieve the values of these instance variables; method earnings (lines 51–55) to calculate a CommissionEmployee's earnings; and method toString (lines 58–65), which returns the employee's type, namely, "commission employee: " and employee-specific information. The constructor also passes the first name, last name and social security number to Employee's constructor (line 13) to initialize Employee's private instance variables. Method toString calls superclass method toString (line 62) to obtain the Employee-specific information (i.e., first name, last name and social security number).

```java
 1   // Fig. 10.7: CommissionEmployee.java
 2   // CommissionEmployee class extends Employee.
 3
 4   public class CommissionEmployee extends Employee
 5   {
 6      private double grossSales; // gross weekly sales
 7      private double commissionRate; // commission percentage
 8
 9      // five-argument constructor
10      public CommissionEmployee( String first, String last, String ssn,
11         double sales, double rate )
12      {
13         super( first, last, ssn );
14         setGrossSales( sales );
15         setCommissionRate( rate );
16      } // end five-argument CommissionEmployee constructor
17
18      // set commission rate
19      public void setCommissionRate( double rate )
20      {
21         if ( rate > 0.0 && rate < 1.0 )
22            commissionRate = rate;
23         else
24            throw new IllegalArgumentException(
25               "Commission rate must be > 0.0 and < 1.0" );
26      } // end method setCommissionRate
27
28      // return commission rate
29      public double getCommissionRate()
30      {
31         return commissionRate;
32      } // end method getCommissionRate
33
34      // set gross sales amount
35      public void setGrossSales( double sales )
36      {
```

Fig. 10.7 | CommissionEmployee class extends Employee. (Part 1 of 2.)

```
37          if ( sales >= 0.0 )
38             grossSales = sales;
39          else
40             throw new IllegalArgumentException(
41                "Gross sales must be >= 0.0" );
42       } // end method setGrossSales
43
44       // return gross sales amount
45       public double getGrossSales()
46       {
47          return grossSales;
48       } // end method getGrossSales
49
50       // calculate earnings; override abstract method earnings in Employee
51       @Override
52       public double earnings()
53       {
54          return getCommissionRate() * getGrossSales();
55       } // end method earnings
56
57       // return String representation of CommissionEmployee object
58       @Override
59       public String toString()
60       {
61          return String.format( "%s: %s\n%s: $%,.2f; %s: %.2f",
62             "commission employee", super.toString(),
63             "gross sales", getGrossSales(),
64             "commission rate", getCommissionRate() );
65       } // end method toString
66    } // end class CommissionEmployee
```

Fig. 10.7 | CommissionEmployee class extends Employee. (Part 2 of 2.)

10.5.5 Indirect Concrete Subclass BasePlusCommissionEmployee

Class BasePlusCommissionEmployee (Fig. 10.8) extends class CommissionEmployee (line 4) and therefore is an *indirect* subclass of class Employee. Class BasePlusCommissionEmployee has a constructor (lines 9–14) that takes as arguments a first name, a last name, a social security number, a sales amount, a commission rate and a base salary. It then passes all of these except the base salary to the CommissionEmployee constructor (line 12) to initialize the inherited members. BasePlusCommissionEmployee also contains a *set* method (lines 17–24) to assign a new value to instance variable baseSalary and a *get* method (lines 27–30) to return baseSalary's value. Method earnings (lines 33–37) calculates a BasePlusCommissionEmployee's earnings. Line 36 in method earnings calls superclass CommissionEmployee's earnings method to calculate the commission-based portion of the employee's earnings—this is another nice example of code reuse. BasePlusCommissionEmployee's toString method (lines 40–46) creates a String representation of a BasePlusCommissionEmployee that contains "base-salaried", followed by the String obtained by invoking superclass CommissionEmployee's toString method (another example of code reuse), then the base salary. The result is a String beginning with "base-salaried commission employee" followed by the rest of the BasePlusCommissionEmployee's information. Recall that CommissionEmployee's toString obtains the employee's first name, last name and social security number by invoking the toString method of its superclass (i.e., Employee)—yet another example of code reuse. BasePlusCommissionEmployee's toString initiates a chain of method calls that span all three levels of the Employee hierarchy.

```java
1   // Fig. 10.8: BasePlusCommissionEmployee.java
2   // BasePlusCommissionEmployee class extends CommissionEmployee.
3
4   public class BasePlusCommissionEmployee extends CommissionEmployee
5   {
6      private double baseSalary; // base salary per week
7
8      // six-argument constructor
9      public BasePlusCommissionEmployee( String first, String last,
10        String ssn, double sales, double rate, double salary )
11     {
12        super( first, last, ssn, sales, rate );
13        setBaseSalary( salary ); // validate and store base salary
14     } // end six-argument BasePlusCommissionEmployee constructor
15
16     // set base salary
17     public void setBaseSalary( double salary )
18     {
19        if ( salary >= 0.0 )
20           baseSalary = salary;
21        else
22           throw new IllegalArgumentException(
23              "Base salary must be >= 0.0" );
24     } // end method setBaseSalary
25
26     // return base salary
27     public double getBaseSalary()
28     {
29        return baseSalary;
30     } // end method getBaseSalary
31
32     // calculate earnings; override method earnings in CommissionEmployee
33     @Override
34     public double earnings()
35     {
36        return getBaseSalary() + super.earnings();
37     } // end method earnings
38
39     // return String representation of BasePlusCommissionEmployee object
40     @Override
41     public String toString()
42     {
43        return String.format( "%s %s; %s: $%,.2f",
44           "base-salaried", super.toString(),
45           "base salary", getBaseSalary() );
46     } // end method toString
47   } // end class BasePlusCommissionEmployee
```

Fig. 10.8 | BasePlusCommissionEmployee class extends CommissionEmployee.

10.5.6 Polymorphic Processing, Operator instanceof and Downcasting

To test our Employee hierarchy, the application in Fig. 10.9 creates an object of each of the four concrete classes SalariedEmployee, HourlyEmployee, CommissionEmployee and BasePlusCommissionEmployee. The program manipulates these objects nonpolymorphically, via variables of each object's own type, then polymorphically, using an array of Employee variables. While processing the objects polymorphically, the program increases the base salary of each BasePlusCommissionEmployee by 10%—this requires *determining the object's type at execution time*. Finally, the program polymorphically determines and outputs the type of each object in the Employee array. Lines 9–18 create objects of each of the four concrete Employee subclasses. Lines 22–30 output the String representation and earnings of each of these objects *nonpolymorphically*. Each object's toString method is called *implicitly* by printf when the object is output as a String with the %s format specifier.

```java
 1   // Fig. 10.9: PayrollSystemTest.java
 2   // Employee hierarchy test program.
 3
 4   public class PayrollSystemTest
 5   {
 6      public static void main( String[] args )
 7      {
 8         // create subclass objects
 9         SalariedEmployee salariedEmployee =
10            new SalariedEmployee( "John", "Smith", "111-11-1111", 800.00 );
11         HourlyEmployee hourlyEmployee =
12            new HourlyEmployee( "Karen", "Price", "222-22-2222", 16.75, 40 );
13         CommissionEmployee commissionEmployee =
14            new CommissionEmployee(
15            "Sue", "Jones", "333-33-3333", 10000, .06 );
16         BasePlusCommissionEmployee basePlusCommissionEmployee =
17            new BasePlusCommissionEmployee(
18            "Bob", "Lewis", "444-44-4444", 5000, .04, 300 );
19
20         System.out.println( "Employees processed individually:\n" );
21
22         System.out.printf( "%s\n%s: $%,.2f\n\n",
23            salariedEmployee, "earned", salariedEmployee.earnings() );
24         System.out.printf( "%s\n%s: $%,.2f\n\n",
25            hourlyEmployee, "earned", hourlyEmployee.earnings() );
26         System.out.printf( "%s\n%s: $%,.2f\n\n",
27            commissionEmployee, "earned", commissionEmployee.earnings() );
28         System.out.printf( "%s\n%s: $%,.2f\n\n",
29            basePlusCommissionEmployee,
30            "earned", basePlusCommissionEmployee.earnings() );
31
32         // create four-element Employee array
33         Employee[] employees = new Employee[ 4 ];
34
35         // initialize array with Employees
36         employees[ 0 ] = salariedEmployee;
37         employees[ 1 ] = hourlyEmployee;
```

Fig. 10.9 | Employee hierarchy test program. (Part 1 of 3.)

```
38          employees[ 2 ] = commissionEmployee;
39          employees[ 3 ] = basePlusCommissionEmployee;
40
41      System.out.println( "Employees processed polymorphically:\n" );
42
43      // generically process each element in array employees
44      for ( Employee currentEmployee : employees )
45      {
46          System.out.println( currentEmployee ); // invokes toString
47
48          // determine whether element is a BasePlusCommissionEmployee
49          if ( currentEmployee instanceof BasePlusCommissionEmployee )
50          {
51              // downcast Employee reference to
52              // BasePlusCommissionEmployee reference
53              BasePlusCommissionEmployee employee =
54                  ( BasePlusCommissionEmployee ) currentEmployee;
55
56              employee.setBaseSalary( 1.10 * employee.getBaseSalary() );
57
58              System.out.printf(
59                  "new base salary with 10%% increase is: $%,.2f\n",
60                  employee.getBaseSalary() );
61          } // end if
62
63          System.out.printf(
64              "earned $%,.2f\n\n", currentEmployee.earnings() );
65      } // end for
66
67      // get type name of each object in employees array
68      for ( int j = 0; j < employees.length; j++ )
69          System.out.printf( "Employee %d is a %s\n", j,
70              employees[ j ].getClass().getName() );
71   } // end main
72 } // end class PayrollSystemTest
```

```
Employees processed individually:

salaried employee: John Smith
social security number: 111-11-1111
weekly salary: $800.00
earned: $800.00

hourly employee: Karen Price
social security number: 222-22-2222
hourly wage: $16.75; hours worked: 40.00
earned: $670.00

commission employee: Sue Jones
social security number: 333-33-3333
gross sales: $10,000.00; commission rate: 0.06
earned: $600.00

base-salaried commission employee: Bob Lewis
social security number: 444-44-4444
```

Fig. 10.9 | Employee hierarchy test program. (Part 2 of 3.)

```
gross sales: $5,000.00; commission rate: 0.04; base salary: $300.00
earned: $500.00

Employees processed polymorphically:

salaried employee: John Smith
social security number: 111-11-1111
weekly salary: $800.00
earned $800.00

hourly employee: Karen Price
social security number: 222-22-2222
hourly wage: $16.75; hours worked: 40.00
earned $670.00

commission employee: Sue Jones
social security number: 333-33-3333
gross sales: $10,000.00; commission rate: 0.06
earned $600.00

base-salaried commission employee: Bob Lewis
social security number: 444-44-4444
gross sales: $5,000.00; commission rate: 0.04; base salary: $300.00
new base salary with 10% increase is: $330.00
earned $530.00

Employee 0 is a SalariedEmployee
Employee 1 is a HourlyEmployee
Employee 2 is a CommissionEmployee
Employee 3 is a BasePlusCommissionEmployee
```

Fig. 10.9 | Employee hierarchy test program. (Part 3 of 3.)

Creating the Array of Employees

Line 33 declares employees and assigns it an array of four Employee variables. Line 36 assigns the reference to a SalariedEmployee object to employees[0]. Line 37 assigns the reference to an HourlyEmployee object to employees[1]. Line 38 assigns the reference to a CommissionEmployee object to employees[2]. Line 39 assigns the reference to a BasePlusCommissionEmployee object to employee[3]. These assignments are allowed, because a SalariedEmployee *is an* Employee, an HourlyEmployee *is an* Employee, a CommissionEmployee *is an* Employee and a BasePlusCommissionEmployee *is an* Employee. Therefore, we can assign the references of SalariedEmployee, HourlyEmployee, CommissionEmployee and BasePlusCommissionEmployee objects to superclass Employee variables, *even though Employee is an abstract class.*

Polymorphically Processing Employees

Lines 44–65 iterate through array employees and invoke methods toString and earnings with Employee variable currentEmployee, which is assigned the reference to a different Employee in the array on each iteration. The output illustrates that the appropriate methods for each class are indeed invoked. All calls to method toString and earnings are resolved at execution time, based on the type of the object to which currentEmployee refers. This process is known as **dynamic binding** or **late binding**. For example, line 46 *implicitly* invokes method toString of the object to which currentEmployee refers. As a result of dynamic binding, Java decides which class's toString method to call *at execution time rather than at compile time*. Only the methods of class Employee can be called via an Employee variable (and Employee, of course, includes the methods of class Object). A superclass reference can be used to invoke only methods of the superclass—the subclass method implementations are invoked polymorphically.

*Performing Type-Specific Operations on **BasePlusCommissionEmployee**s*
We perform special processing on BasePlusCommissionEmployee objects—as we encounter these objects at execution time, we increase their base salary by 10%. When processing objects polymorphically, we typically do not need to worry about the "specifics," but to adjust the base salary, we *do* have to determine the specific type of Employee object at execution time. Line 49 uses the **instanceof** operator to determine whether a particular Employee object's type is BasePlusCommissionEmployee. The condition in line 49 is true if the object referenced by currentEmployee *is a* BasePlusCommissionEmployee. This would also be true for any object of a BasePlusCommissionEmployee subclass because of the *is-a* relationship a subclass has with its superclass. Lines 53–54 downcast currentEmployee from type Employee to type BasePlusCommissionEmployee—this cast is allowed only if the object has an *is-a* relationship with BasePlusCommissionEmployee. The condition at line 49 ensures that this is the case. This cast is required if we're to invoke subclass BasePlusCommissionEmployee methods getBaseSalary and setBaseSalary on the current Employee object—as you'll see momentarily, *attempting to invoke a subclass-only method directly on a superclass reference is a compilation error.*

Common Programming Error 10.3
Assigning a superclass variable to a subclass variable (without an explicit cast) is a compilation error.

Software Engineering Observation 10.4
If a subclass object's reference has been assigned to a variable of one of its direct or indirect superclasses at execution time, it's acceptable to downcast the reference stored in that superclass variable back to a subclass-type reference. Before performing such a cast, use the instanceof *operator to ensure that the object is indeed an object of an appropriate subclass.*

Common Programming Error 10.4
When downcasting a reference, a ClassCastException *occurs if the referenced object at execution time does not have an* is-a *relationship with the type specified in the cast operator.*

If the instanceof expression in line 49 is true, lines 53–60 perform the special processing required for the BasePlusCommissionEmployee object. Using BasePlusCommissionEmployee variable employee, line 56 invokes subclass-only methods getBaseSalary and setBaseSalary to retrieve and update the employee's base salary with the 10% raise.

*Calling **earnings** Polymorphically*
Lines 63–64 invoke method earnings on currentEmployee, which polymorphically calls the appropriate subclass object's earnings method. Obtaining the earnings of the SalariedEmployee, HourlyEmployee and CommissionEmployee polymorphically in lines 63–64 produces the same results as obtaining these employees' earnings individually in lines 22–27. The earnings amount obtained for the BasePlusCommissionEmployee in lines 63–64 is higher than that obtained in lines 28–30, due to the 10% increase in its base salary.

Using Reflection to Get Each Employee's Class Name

Lines 68–70 display each employee's type as a String, using basic features of Java's so-called reflection capabilities. Every object knows its own class and can access this information through the **getClass** method, which all classes inherit from class Object. Method getClass returns an object of type **Class** (from package java.lang), which contains information about the object's type, including its class name. Line 70 invokes getClass on the current object to get its runtime class. The result of the getClass call is used to invoke **getName** to get the object's class name.

Avoiding Compilation Errors with Downcasting

In the previous example, we avoided several compilation errors by downcasting an Employee variable to a BasePlusCommissionEmployee variable in lines 53–54. If you remove the cast operator (BasePlusCommissionEmployee) from line 54 and attempt to assign Employee variable currentEmployee directly to BasePlusCommissionEmployee variable employee, you'll receive an "incompatible types" compilation error. This error indicates that the attempt to assign the reference of superclass object currentEmployee to subclass variable employee is not allowed. The compiler prevents this assignment because a CommissionEmployee is not a BasePlusCommissionEmployee—*the* is-a *relationship applies only between the subclass and its superclasses, not vice versa.*

Similarly, if lines 56 and 60 used superclass variable currentEmployee to invoke subclass-only methods getBaseSalary and setBaseSalary, we'd receive "cannot find symbol" compilation errors at these lines. Attempting to invoke subclass-only methods via a superclass variable is not allowed—even though lines 56 and 60 execute only if instanceof in line 49 returns true to indicate that currentEmployee holds a reference to a BasePlusCommissionEmployee object. Using a superclass Employee variable, we can invoke only methods found in class Employee—earnings, toString and Employee's *get* and *set* methods.

Software Engineering Observation 10.5

Although the actual method that's called depends on the runtime type of the object to which a variable refers, a variable can be used to invoke only those methods that are members of that variable's type, which the compiler verifies.

10.5.7 Summary of the Allowed Assignments Between Superclass and Subclass Variables

Now that you've seen a complete application that processes diverse subclass objects polymorphically, we summarize what you can and cannot do with superclass and subclass objects and variables. Although a subclass object also *is a* superclass object, the two objects are nevertheless different. As discussed previously, subclass objects can be treated as objects of their superclass. But because the subclass can have additional subclass-only members, assigning a superclass reference to a subclass variable is not allowed without an explicit cast—such an assignment would leave the subclass members undefined for the superclass object.

We've discussed four ways to assign superclass and subclass references to variables of superclass and subclass types:

1. Assigning a superclass reference to a superclass variable is straightforward.

2. Assigning a subclass reference to a subclass variable is straightforward.

3. Assigning a subclass reference to a superclass variable is safe, because the subclass object *is an* object of its superclass. However, the superclass variable can be used to refer *only* to superclass members. If this code refers to subclass-only members through the superclass variable, the compiler reports errors.

4. Attempting to assign a superclass reference to a subclass variable is a compilation error. To avoid this error, the superclass reference must be cast to a subclass type explicitly. At *execution time*, if the object to which the reference refers is *not* a subclass object, an exception will occur. (For more on exception handling, see Chapter 11.) You should use the `instanceof` operator to ensure that such a cast is performed only if the object is a subclass object.

10.6 `final` Methods and Classes

We saw in Sections 6.3 and 6.9 that variables can be declared `final` to indicate that they cannot be modified after they're initialized—such variables represent constant values. It's also possible to declare methods, method parameters and classes with the `final` modifier.

Final Methods Cannot Be Overridden
A **final method** in a superclass *cannot* be overridden in a subclass—this guarantees that the `final` method implementation will be used by all direct and indirect subclasses in the hierarchy. Methods that are declared `private` are implicitly `final`, because it's not possible to override them in a subclass. Methods that are declared `static` are also implicitly `final`. A `final` method's declaration can never change, so all subclasses use the same method implementation, and calls to `final` methods are resolved at compile time—this is known as **static binding**.

Final Classes Cannot Be Superclasses
A **final class** that's declared `final` cannot be a superclass (i.e., a class cannot extend a `final` class). All methods in a `final` class are implicitly `final`. Class `String` is an example of a `final` class. If you were allowed to create a subclass of `String`, objects of that subclass could be used wherever `Strings` are expected. Since class `String` cannot be extended, programs that use `Strings` can rely on the functionality of `String` objects as specified in the Java API. Making the class `final` also prevents programmers from creating subclasses that might bypass security restrictions. For more insights on the use of keyword `final`, visit

```
download.oracle.com/javase/tutorial/java/IandI/final.html
```

and

```
www.ibm.com/developerworks/java/library/j-jtp1029.html
```

Common Programming Error 10.5

Attempting to declare a subclass of a `final` class is a compilation error.

Software Engineering Observation 10.6

In the Java API, the vast majority of classes are not *declared `final`. This enables inheritance and polymorphism. However, in some cases, it's important to declare classes `final`—typically for security reasons.*

10.7 Case Study: Creating and Using Interfaces

Our next example (Figs. 10.11–10.15) reexamines the payroll system of Section 10.5. Suppose that the company involved wishes to perform several accounting operations in a single accounts payable application—in addition to calculating the earnings that must be paid to each employee, the company must also calculate the payment due on each of several invoices (i.e., bills for goods purchased). Though applied to unrelated things (i.e., employees and invoices), both operations have to do with obtaining some kind of payment amount. For an employee, the payment refers to the employee's earnings. For an invoice, the payment refers to the total cost of the goods listed on the invoice. Can we calculate such *different* things as the payments due for employees and invoices in *a single* application polymorphically? Does Java offer a capability requiring that *unrelated* classes implement a set of *common* methods (e.g., a method that calculates a payment amount)? Java **interfaces** offer exactly this capability.

Standardizing Interactions

Interfaces define and standardize the ways in which things such as people and systems can interact with one another. For example, the controls on a radio serve as an interface between radio users and a radio's internal components. The controls allow users to perform only a limited set of operations (e.g., change the station, adjust the volume, choose between AM and FM), and different radios may implement the controls in different ways (e.g., using push buttons, dials, voice commands). The interface specifies *what* operations a radio must permit users to perform but does not specify *how* the operations are performed.

Software Objects Communicate Via Interfaces

Software objects also communicate via interfaces. A Java interface describes a set of methods that can be called on an object to tell it, for example, to perform some task or return some piece of information. The next example introduces an interface named `Payable` to describe the functionality of any object that must be capable of being paid and thus must offer a method to determine the proper payment amount due. An **interface declaration** begins with the keyword **interface** and contains only constants and `abstract` methods. Unlike classes, all interface members must be `public`, and *interfaces may not specify any implementation details*, such as concrete method declarations and instance variables. All methods declared in an interface are implicitly `public abstract` methods, and all fields are implicitly `public`, `static` and `final`. [*Note:* As of Java SE 5, it became a better programming practice to declare sets of constants as enumerations with keyword `enum`. See Section 6.9 for an introduction to `enum` and Section 8.9 for additional `enum` details.]

Good Programming Practice 10.1

According to Chapter 9 of the Java Language Specification, *it's proper style to declare an interface's methods without keywords* `public` *and* `abstract`, *because they're redundant in interface method declarations. Similarly, constants should be declared without keywords* `public`, `static` *and* `final`, *because they, too, are redundant.*

Using an Interface

To use an interface, a concrete class must specify that it `implements` the interface and must declare each method in the interface with the signature specified in the interface declaration. To specify that a class implements an interface add the `implements` keyword and the name of the interface to the end of your class declaration's first line. A class that does not implement *all* the methods of the interface is an *abstract* class and must be declared abstract. Implementing an interface is like signing a *contract* with the compiler that states, "I will declare all the methods specified by the interface or I will declare my class abstract."

Common Programming Error 10.6

Failing to implement any method of an interface in a concrete class that implements the interface results in a compilation error indicating that the class must be declared abstract.

Relating Disparate Types

An interface is often used when disparate (i.e., unrelated) classes need to share common methods and constants. This allows objects of unrelated classes to be processed polymorphically—objects of classes that implement the same interface can respond to the same method calls. You can create an interface that describes the desired functionality, then implement this interface in any classes that require that functionality. For example, in the accounts payable application developed in this section, we implement interface Payable in any class that must be able to calculate a payment amount (e.g., Employee, Invoice).

Interfaces vs. Abstract Classes

An interface is often used in place of an abstract class when there's no default implementation to inherit—that is, no fields and no default method implementations. Like public abstract classes, interfaces are typically public types. Like a public class, a public interface must be declared in a file with the same name as the interface and the .java file-name extension.

Tagging Interfaces

We'll see in Chapter 17, Files, Streams and Object Serialization, the notion of "tagging interfaces"—empty interfaces that have *no* methods or constant values. They're used to add *is-a* relationships to classes. For example, in Chapter 17 we'll discuss a mechanism called object serialization, which can convert objects to byte representations and can convert those byte representations back to objects. To enable this mechanism to work with your objects, you simply have to mark them as Serializable by adding implements Serializable to the end of your class declaration's first line. Then, all the objects of your class have the *is-a* relationship with Serializable.

10.7.1 Developing a Payable Hierarchy

To build an application that can determine payments for employees and invoices alike, we first create interface Payable, which contains method getPaymentAmount that returns a double amount that must be paid for an object of any class that implements the interface. Method getPaymentAmount is a general-purpose version of method earnings of the Employee hierarchy—method earnings calculates a payment amount specifically for an Employee, while getPaymentAmount can be applied to a broad range of unrelated objects. After declaring interface Payable, we introduce class Invoice, which implements interface Payable. We then modify class Employee such that it also implements interface Payable.

Finally, we update Employee subclass SalariedEmployee to "fit" into the Payable hierarchy by renaming SalariedEmployee method earnings as getPaymentAmount.

Good Programming Practice 10.2

When declaring a method in an interface, choose a method name that describes the method's purpose in a general *manner, because the method may be implemented by many unrelated classes.*

Classes Invoice and Employee both represent things for which the company must be able to calculate a payment amount. Both classes implement the Payable interface, so a program can invoke method getPaymentAmount on Invoice objects and Employee objects alike. As we'll soon see, this enables the polymorphic processing of Invoices and Employees required for the company's accounts payable application.

The UML class diagram in Fig. 10.10 shows the hierarchy used in our accounts payable application. The hierarchy begins with interface Payable. The UML distinguishes an interface from other classes by placing the word "interface" in guillemets (« and ») above the interface name. The UML expresses the relationship between a class and an interface through a relationship known as **realization**. A class is said to "realize," or implement, the methods of an interface. A class diagram models a realization as a dashed arrow with a hollow arrowhead pointing from the implementing class to the interface. The diagram in Fig. 10.10 indicates that classes Invoice and Employee each realize (i.e., implement) interface Payable. As in the class diagram of Fig. 10.2, class Employee appears in italics, indicating that it's an abstract class. Concrete class SalariedEmployee extends Employee and *inherits its superclass's realization relationship* with interface Payable.

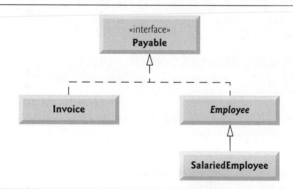

Fig. 10.10 | Payable interface hierarchy UML class diagram.

10.7.2 Interface Payable

The declaration of interface Payable begins in Fig. 10.11 at line 4. Interface Payable contains public abstract method getPaymentAmount (line 6). The method is not explicitly declared public or abstract. Interface methods are always public and abstract, so they do not need to be declared as such. Interface Payable has only one method—interfaces can have any number of methods. In addition, method getPaymentAmount has no parameters, but interface methods *can* have parameters. Interfaces may also contain fields that are implicitly final and static.

```
1   // Fig. 10.11: Payable.java
2   // Payable interface declaration.
3
4   public interface Payable
5   {
6      double getPaymentAmount(); // calculate payment; no implementation
7   } // end interface Payable
```

Fig. 10.11 | Payable interface declaration.

10.7.3 Class Invoice

We now create class Invoice (Fig. 10.12) to represent a simple invoice that contains billing information for only one kind of part. The class declares private instance variables partNumber, partDescription, quantity and pricePerItem (in lines 6–9) that indicate the part number, a description of the part, the quantity of the part ordered and the price per item. Class Invoice also contains a constructor (lines 12–19), *get* and *set* methods (lines 22–74) that manipulate the class's instance variables and a toString method (lines 77–83) that returns a String representation of an Invoice object. Methods setQuantity (lines 46–52) and setPricePerItem (lines 61–68) ensure that quantity and pricePerItem obtain only nonnegative values.

Line 4 indicates that class Invoice implements interface Payable. Like all classes, class Invoice also implicitly extends Object. Java does not allow subclasses to inherit from more than one superclass, but it allows a class to inherit from one superclass and implement as many interfaces as it needs. To implement more than one interface, use a comma-separated list of interface names after keyword implements in the class declaration, as in:

public class *ClassName* extends *SuperclassName* implements *FirstInterface*,
SecondInterface, ...

Software Engineering Observation 10.7

All objects of a class that implement multiple interfaces have the is-a *relationship with each implemented interface type.*

```
1   // Fig. 10.12: Invoice.java
2   // Invoice class that implements Payable.
3
4   public class Invoice implements Payable
5   {
6      private String partNumber;
7      private String partDescription;
8      private int quantity;
9      private double pricePerItem;
10
11     // four-argument constructor
12     public Invoice( String part, String description, int count,
13        double price )
14     {
15        partNumber = part;
```

Fig. 10.12 | Invoice class that implements Payable. (Part 1 of 3.)

```
16          partDescription = description;
17          setQuantity( count ); // validate and store quantity
18          setPricePerItem( price ); // validate and store price per item
19      } // end four-argument Invoice constructor
20
21      // set part number
22      public void setPartNumber( String part )
23      {
24          partNumber = part; // should validate
25      } // end method setPartNumber
26
27      // get part number
28      public String getPartNumber()
29      {
30          return partNumber;
31      } // end method getPartNumber
32
33      // set description
34      public void setPartDescription( String description )
35      {
36          partDescription = description; // should validate
37      } // end method setPartDescription
38
39      // get description
40      public String getPartDescription()
41      {
42          return partDescription;
43      } // end method getPartDescription
44
45      // set quantity
46      public void setQuantity( int count )
47      {
48          if ( count >= 0 )
49              quantity = count;
50          else
51              throw new IllegalArgumentException( "Quantity must be >= 0" );
52      } // end method setQuantity
53
54      // get quantity
55      public int getQuantity()
56      {
57          return quantity;
58      } // end method getQuantity
59
60      // set price per item
61      public void setPricePerItem( double price )
62      {
63          if ( price >= 0.0 )
64              pricePerItem = price;
65          else
66              throw new IllegalArgumentException(
67                  "Price per item must be >= 0" );
68      } // end method setPricePerItem
```

Fig. 10.12 | Invoice class that implements Payable. (Part 2 of 3.)

```
69
70      // get price per item
71      public double getPricePerItem()
72      {
73         return pricePerItem;
74      } // end method getPricePerItem
75
76      // return String representation of Invoice object
77      @Override
78      public String toString()
79      {
80         return String.format( "%s: \n%s: %s (%s) \n%s: %d \n%s: $%,.2f",
81            "invoice", "part number", getPartNumber(), getPartDescription(),
82            "quantity", getQuantity(), "price per item", getPricePerItem() );
83      } // end method toString
84
85      // method required to carry out contract with interface Payable
86      @Override
87      public double getPaymentAmount()
88      {
89         return getQuantity() * getPricePerItem(); // calculate total cost
90      } // end method getPaymentAmount
91   } // end class Invoice
```

Fig. 10.12 | Invoice class that implements Payable. (Part 3 of 3.)

Class Invoice implements the one method in interface Payable—method get-PaymentAmount is declared in lines 86–90. The method calculates the total payment required to pay the invoice. The method multiplies the values of quantity and pricePer-Item (obtained through the appropriate *get* methods) and returns the result (line 89). This method satisfies the implementation requirement for this method in interface Payable—we've fulfilled the interface contract with the compiler.

10.7.4 Modifying Class Employee to Implement Interface Payable

We now modify class Employee such that it implements interface Payable. Figure 10.13 contains the modified class, which is identical to that of Fig. 10.4 with two exceptions. First, line 4 of Fig. 10.13 indicates that class Employee now implements interface Payable. So we must rename earnings to getPaymentAmount throughout the Employee hierarchy. As with method earnings in the version of class Employee in Fig. 10.4, however, it does not make sense to implement method getPaymentAmount in class Employee because we cannot calculate the earnings payment owed to a general Employee—we must first know the specific type of Employee. In Fig. 10.4, we declared method earnings as abstract for this reason, so class Employee had to be declared abstract. This forced each Employee concrete subclass to override earnings with an implementation.

In Fig. 10.13, we handle this situation differently. Recall that when a class implements an interface, it makes a *contract* with the compiler stating either that the class will implement *each* of the methods in the interface or that the class will be declared abstract. If the latter option is chosen, we do not need to declare the interface methods as abstract in the abstract class—they're already implicitly declared as such in the interface. Any concrete subclass of the abstract class must implement the interface methods to fulfill the superclass's contract with the compiler. If the subclass does not do so, it too must be declared abstract. As indicated by the comments in lines 62–63, class Employee of Fig. 10.13 does *not* implement method getPaymentAmount, so the class is declared abstract. Each direct Employee subclass *inherits the superclass's contract* to implement method getPaymentAmount and thus must implement this method to become a concrete class for which objects can be instantiated. A class that extends one of Employee's concrete subclasses will inherit an implementation of getPaymentAmount and thus will also be a concrete class.

```java
1   // Fig. 10.13: Employee.java
2   // Employee abstract superclass that implements Payable.
3
4   public abstract class Employee implements Payable
5   {
6      private String firstName;
7      private String lastName;
8      private String socialSecurityNumber;
9
10     // three-argument constructor
11     public Employee( String first, String last, String ssn )
12     {
13        firstName = first;
14        lastName = last;
15        socialSecurityNumber = ssn;
16     } // end three-argument Employee constructor
17
18     // set first name
19     public void setFirstName( String first )
20     {
21        firstName = first; // should validate
22     } // end method setFirstName
23
24     // return first name
25     public String getFirstName()
26     {
27        return firstName;
28     } // end method getFirstName
29
30     // set last name
31     public void setLastName( String last )
32     {
33        lastName = last; // should validate
34     } // end method setLastName
35
36     // return last name
37     public String getLastName()
38     {
39        return lastName;
40     } // end method getLastName
41
```

Fig. 10.13 | Employee class that implements Payable. (Part I of 2.)

```
42       // set social security number
43       public void setSocialSecurityNumber( String ssn )
44       {
45          socialSecurityNumber = ssn; // should validate
46       } // end method setSocialSecurityNumber
47
48       // return social security number
49       public String getSocialSecurityNumber()
50       {
51          return socialSecurityNumber;
52       } // end method getSocialSecurityNumber
53
54       // return String representation of Employee object
55       @Override
56       public String toString()
57       {
58          return String.format( "%s %s\nsocial security number: %s",
59             getFirstName(), getLastName(), getSocialSecurityNumber() );
60       } // end method toString
61
62       // Note: We do not implement Payable method getPaymentAmount here so
63       // this class must be declared abstract to avoid a compilation error.
64    } // end abstract class Employee
```

Fig. 10.13 | Employee class that implements Payable. (Part 2 of 2.)

10.7.5 Modifying Class SalariedEmployee for Use in the Payable Hierarchy

Figure 10.14 contains a modified SalariedEmployee class that extends Employee and fulfills superclass Employee's contract to implement Payable method getPaymentAmount. This version of SalariedEmployee is identical to that of Fig. 10.5, but it replaces method earnings with method getPaymentAmount (lines 34–38). Recall that the Payable version of the method has a more *general* name to be applicable to possibly *disparate* classes. The remaining Employee subclasses (e.g., HourlyEmployee, CommissionEmployee and BasePlusCommissionEmployee) also must be modified to contain method getPaymentAmount in place of earnings to reflect the fact that Employee now implements Payable. We leave these modifications as an exercise.

```
1    // Fig. 10.14: SalariedEmployee.java
2    // SalariedEmployee class extends Employee, which implements Payable.
3
4    public class SalariedEmployee extends Employee
5    {
6       private double weeklySalary;
7
```

Fig. 10.14 | SalariedEmployee class that implements interface Payable method getPaymentAmount. (Part 1 of 2.)

```
 8      // four-argument constructor
 9      public SalariedEmployee( String first, String last, String ssn,
10         double salary )
11      {
12         super( first, last, ssn ); // pass to Employee constructor
13         setWeeklySalary( salary ); // validate and store salary
14      } // end four-argument SalariedEmployee constructor
15
16      // set salary
17      public void setWeeklySalary( double salary )
18      {
19         if ( salary >= 0.0 )
20            baseSalary = salary;
21         else
22            throw new IllegalArgumentException(
23               "Weekly salary must be >= 0.0" );
24      } // end method setWeeklySalary
25
26      // return salary
27      public double getWeeklySalary()
28      {
29         return weeklySalary;
30      } // end method getWeeklySalary
31
32      // calculate earnings; implement interface Payable method that was
33      // abstract in superclass Employee
34      @Override
35      public double getPaymentAmount()
36      {
37         return getWeeklySalary();
38      } // end method getPaymentAmount
39
40      // return String representation of SalariedEmployee object
41      @Override
42      public String toString()
43      {
44         return String.format( "salaried employee: %s\n%s: $%,.2f",
45            super.toString(), "weekly salary", getWeeklySalary() );
46      } // end method toString
47   } // end class SalariedEmployee
```

Fig. 10.14 | SalariedEmployee class that implements interface Payable method getPaymentAmount. (Part 2 of 2.)

When a class implements an interface, the same *is-a* relationship provided by inheritance applies. Class Employee implements Payable, so we can say that an Employee *is a* Payable. In fact, objects of any classes that extend Employee are also Payable objects. SalariedEmployee objects, for instance, are Payable objects. Objects of any subclasses of the class that implements the interface can also be thought of as objects of the interface type. Thus, just as we can assign the reference of a SalariedEmployee object to a superclass Employee variable, we can assign the reference of a SalariedEmployee object to an interface Payable variable. Invoice implements Payable, so an Invoice object also *is a* Payable object, and we can assign the reference of an Invoice object to a Payable variable.

Software Engineering Observation 10.8

When a method parameter is declared with a superclass or interface type, the method processes the object received as an argument polymorphically.

Software Engineering Observation 10.9

Using a superclass reference, we can polymorphically invoke any method declared in the superclass and its superclasses (e.g., class Object). Using an interface reference, we can polymorphically invoke any method declared in the interface, its superinterfaces (one interface can extend another) and in class Object—a variable of an interface type must refer to an object to call methods, and all objects have the methods of class Object.

10.7.6 Using Interface Payable to Process Invoices and Employees Polymorphically

PayableInterfaceTest (Fig. 10.15) illustrates that interface Payable can be used to process a set of Invoices and Employees polymorphically in a single application. Line 9 declares payableObjects and assigns it an array of four Payable variables. Lines 12–13 assign the references of Invoice objects to the first two elements of payableObjects. Lines 14–17 then assign the references of SalariedEmployee objects to the remaining two elements of payableObjects. These assignments are allowed because an Invoice *is a* Payable, a SalariedEmployee *is an* Employee and an Employee *is a* Payable. Lines 23–29 use the enhanced for statement to polymorphically process each Payable object in payableObjects, printing the object as a String, along with the payment amount due. Line 27 invokes method toString via a Payable interface reference, even though toString is not declared in interface Payable—*all references (including those of interface types) refer to objects that extend Object and therefore have a toString method.* (Method toString also can be invoked *implicitly* here.) Line 28 invokes Payable method getPaymentAmount to obtain the payment amount for each object in payableObjects, regardless of the actual type of the object. The output reveals that the method calls in lines 27–28 invoke the appropriate class's implementation of methods toString and getPaymentAmount. For instance, when currentPayable refers to an Invoice during the first iteration of the for loop, class Invoice's toString and getPaymentAmount execute.

```
1   // Fig. 10.15: PayableInterfaceTest.java
2   // Tests interface Payable.
3
4   public class PayableInterfaceTest
5   {
6      public static void main( String[] args )
7      {
8         // create four-element Payable array
9         Payable[] payableObjects = new Payable[ 4 ];
```

Fig. 10.15 | Payable interface test program processing Invoices and Employees polymorphically. (Part 1 of 2.)

```
10
11        // populate array with objects that implement Payable
12        payableObjects[ 0 ] = new Invoice( "01234", "seat", 2, 375.00 );
13        payableObjects[ 1 ] = new Invoice( "56789", "tire", 4, 79.95 );
14        payableObjects[ 2 ] =
15            new SalariedEmployee( "John", "Smith", "111-11-1111", 800.00 );
16        payableObjects[ 3 ] =
17            new SalariedEmployee( "Lisa", "Barnes", "888-88-8888", 1200.00 );
18
19        System.out.println(
20            "Invoices and Employees processed polymorphically:\n" );
21
22        // generically process each element in array payableObjects
23        for ( Payable currentPayable : payableObjects )
24        {
25            // output currentPayable and its appropriate payment amount
26            System.out.printf( "%s \n%s: $%,.2f\n\n",
27                currentPayable.toString(),
28                "payment due", currentPayable.getPaymentAmount() );
29        } // end for
30    } // end main
31 } // end class PayableInterfaceTest
```

```
Invoices and Employees processed polymorphically:

invoice:
part number: 01234 (seat)
quantity: 2
price per item: $375.00
payment due: $750.00

invoice:
part number: 56789 (tire)
quantity: 4
price per item: $79.95
payment due: $319.80

salaried employee: John Smith
social security number: 111-11-1111
weekly salary: $800.00
payment due: $800.00

salaried employee: Lisa Barnes
social security number: 888-88-8888
weekly salary: $1,200.00
payment due: $1,200.00
```

Fig. 10.15 | Payable interface test program processing Invoices and Employees polymorphically. (Part 2 of 2.)

10.7.7 Common Interfaces of the Java API

In this section, we overview several common interfaces found in the Java API. The power and flexibility of interfaces is used frequently throughout the Java API. These interfaces are implemented and used in the same manner as the interfaces you create (e.g., interface

`Payable` in Section 10.7.2). The Java API's interfaces enable you to use your own classes within the frameworks provided by Java, such as comparing objects of your own types and creating tasks that can execute concurrently with other tasks in the same program. Figure 10.16 overviews a few of the more popular interfaces of the Java API that we use in *Java for Programmers, 2/e.*

Interface	Description
Comparable	Java contains several comparison operators (e.g., <, <=, >, >=, ==, !=) that allow you to compare primitive values. However, these operators *cannot* be used to compare objects. Interface `Comparable` is used to allow objects of a class that `implements` the interface to be compared to one another. Interface `Comparable` is commonly used for ordering objects in a collection such as an array. We use `Comparable` in Chapter 18, Generic Collections, and Chapter 19, Generic Classes and Methods.
Serializable	An interface used to identify classes whose objects can be written to (i.e., serialized) or read from (i.e., deserialized) some type of storage (e.g., file on disk, database field) or transmitted across a network. We use `Serializable` in Chapter 17, Files, Streams and Object Serialization, and Chapter 24, Networking.
Runnable	Implemented by any class for which objects of that class should be able to execute in parallel using a technique called multithreading (discussed in Chapter 23, Multithreading). The interface contains one method, run, which describes the behavior of an object when executed.
GUI event-listener interfaces	You work with graphical user interfaces (GUIs) every day. In your web browser, you might type the address of a website to visit, or you might click a button to return to a previous site. The browser responds to your interaction and performs the desired task. Your interaction is known as an event, and the code that the browser uses to respond to an event is known as an event handler. In Chapter 14, GUI Components: Part 1, and Chapter 22, GUI Components: Part 2, you'll learn how to build GUIs and event handlers that respond to user interactions. Event handlers are declared in classes that implement an appropriate event-listener interface. Each event-listener interface specifies one or more methods that must be implemented to respond to user interactions.
SwingConstants	Contains a set of constants used in GUI programming to position GUI elements on the screen. We explore GUI programming in Chapters 14 and 22.

Fig. 10.16 | Common interfaces of the Java API.

10.8 Wrap-Up

This chapter introduced polymorphism—the ability to process objects that share the same superclass in a class hierarchy as if they're all objects of the superclass. The chapter discussed how polymorphism makes systems extensible and maintainable, then demonstrated how to use overridden methods to effect polymorphic behavior. We introduced abstract classes, which allow you to provide an appropriate superclass from which other classes can inherit. You learned that an abstract class can declare abstract methods that each subclass must implement to become a concrete class and that a program can use variables of an abstract class to invoke the subclasses' implementations of abstract methods polymorphically. You also learned how to determine an object's type at execution time. We discussed the concepts of `final` methods and classes. Finally, the chapter discussed declaring and implementing an interface as another way to achieve polymorphic behavior.

You should now be familiar with classes, objects, encapsulation, inheritance, interfaces and polymorphism—the most essential aspects of object-oriented programming.

In the next chapter, you'll learn about exceptions, useful for handling errors during a program's execution. Exception handling provides for more robust programs.

11

Exception Handling: A Deeper Look

Objectives

In this chapter you'll learn:

- What exceptions are and how they're handled.

- When to use exception handling.

- To use **try** blocks to delimit code in which exceptions might occur.

- To **throw** exceptions to indicate a problem.

- To use **catch** blocks to specify exception handlers.

- To use the **finally** block to release resources.

- The exception class hierarchy.

- To create user-defined exceptions.

It is common sense to take a method and try it. If it fails, admit it frankly and try another. But above all, try something.
—Franklin Delano Roosevelt

O! throw away the worser part of it, And live the purer with the other half.
—William Shakespeare

If they're running and they don't look where they're going I have to come out from somewhere and catch them.
—Jerome David Salinger

11.1 Introduction

As you know from Chapter 7, an `exception` is an indication of a problem that occurs during a program's execution. Exception handling enables you to create applications that can resolve (or handle) exceptions. In many cases, handling an exception allows a program to continue executing as if no problem had been encountered. The features presented in this chapter help you write robust and fault-tolerant programs that can deal with problems and continue executing or terminate gracefully. Java exception handling is based in part on the work of Andrew Koenig and Bjarne Stroustrup.[1]

First, we demonstrate basic exception-handling techniques by handling an exception that occurs when a method attempts to divide an integer by zero. Next, we introduce several classes at the top of Java's exception-handling class hierarchy. As you'll see, only classes that extend `Throwable` (package `java.lang`) directly or indirectly can be used with exception handling. We then show how to use chained exceptions. When you invoke a method that indicates an exception, you can throw another exception and chain the original one to the new one—this enables you to add application-specific information to the orginal exception. Next, we introduce preconditions and postconditions, which must be true when your methods are called and when they return, respectively. We then present assertions, which you can use at development time to help debug your code. Finally, we introduce two new Java SE 7 exception-handling features—catching multiple exceptions with one catch handler and the new `try`-with-resources statement that automatically releases a resource after it's used in the `try` block.

11.2 Example: Divide by Zero without Exception Handling

First we demonstrate what happens when errors arise in an application that does not use exception handling. Figure 11.1 prompts the user for two integers and passes them to method `quotient`, which calculates the integer quotient and returns an `int` result. In this

---

1. A. Koenig and B. Stroustrup, "Exception Handling for C++ (revised)," *Proceedings of the Usenix C++ Conference*, pp. 149–176, San Francisco, April 1990.

example, you'll see that exceptions are **thrown** (i.e., the exception occurs) when a method detects a problem and is unable to handle it.

```java
1   // Fig. 11.1: DivideByZeroNoExceptionHandling.java
2   // Integer division without exception handling.
3   import java.util.Scanner;
4
5   public class DivideByZeroNoExceptionHandling
6   {
7      // demonstrates throwing an exception when a divide-by-zero occurs
8      public static int quotient( int numerator, int denominator )
9      {
10        return numerator / denominator; // possible division by zero
11     } // end method quotient
12
13     public static void main( String[] args )
14     {
15        Scanner scanner = new Scanner( System.in ); // scanner for input
16
17        System.out.print( "Please enter an integer numerator: " );
18        int numerator = scanner.nextInt();
19        System.out.print( "Please enter an integer denominator: " );
20        int denominator = scanner.nextInt();
21
22        int result = quotient( numerator, denominator );
23        System.out.printf(
24           "\nResult: %d / %d = %d\n", numerator, denominator, result );
25     } // end main
26  } // end class DivideByZeroNoExceptionHandling
```

```
Please enter an integer numerator: 100
Please enter an integer denominator: 7

Result: 100 / 7 = 14
```

```
Please enter an integer numerator: 100
Please enter an integer denominator: 0
Exception in thread "main" java.lang.ArithmeticException: / by zero
        at DivideByZeroNoExceptionHandling.quotient(
           DivideByZeroNoExceptionHandling.java:10)
        at DivideByZeroNoExceptionHandling.main(
           DivideByZeroNoExceptionHandling.java:22)
```

```
Please enter an integer numerator: 100
Please enter an integer denominator: hello
Exception in thread "main" java.util.InputMismatchException
        at java.util.Scanner.throwFor(Unknown Source)
        at java.util.Scanner.next(Unknown Source)
        at java.util.Scanner.nextInt(Unknown Source)
        at java.util.Scanner.nextInt(Unknown Source)
        at DivideByZeroNoExceptionHandling.main(
           DivideByZeroNoExceptionHandling.java:20)
```

Fig. 11.1 | Integer division without exception handling.

The first sample execution in Fig. 11.1 shows a successful division. In the second execution, the user enters the value 0 as the denominator. Several lines of information are displayed in response to this invalid input. This information is known as a **stack trace**, which includes the name of the exception (`java.lang.ArithmeticException`) in a descriptive message that indicates the problem that occurred and the method-call stack (i.e., the call chain) at the time it occurred. The stack trace includes the path of execution that led to the exception method by method. This helps you debug the program. The first line specifies that an `ArithmeticException` has occurred. The text after the name of the exception ("`/ by zero`") indicates that this exception occurred as a result of an attempt to divide by zero. Java does not allow division by zero in integer arithmetic. When this occurs, Java throws an **ArithmeticException**. `ArithmeticException`s can arise from a number of different problems in arithmetic, so the extra data ("`/ by zero`") provides more specific information. Java *does* allow division by zero with floating-point values. Such a calculation results in the value positive or negative infinity, which is represented in Java as a floating-point value (but displays as the string `Infinity` or `-Infinity`). If 0.0 is divided by 0.0, the result is NaN (not a number), which is also represented in Java as a floating-point value (but displays as `NaN`).

Starting from the last line of the stack trace, we see that the exception was detected in line 22 of method `main`. Each line of the stack trace contains the class name and method (`DivideByZeroNoExceptionHandling.main`) followed by the file name and line number (`DivideByZeroNoExceptionHandling.java:22`). Moving up the stack trace, we see that the exception occurs in line 10, in method `quotient`. The top row of the call chain indicates the **throw point**—the initial point at which the exception occurs. The throw point of this exception is in line 10 of method `quotient`.

In the third execution, the user enters the string `"hello"` as the denominator. Notice again that a stack trace is displayed. This informs us that an `InputMismatchException` has occurred (package `java.util`). Our prior examples that read numeric values from the user assumed that the user would input a proper integer value. However, users sometimes make mistakes and input noninteger values. An **InputMismatchException** occurs when `Scanner` method `nextInt` receives a `string` that does not represent a valid integer. Starting from the end of the stack trace, we see that the exception was detected in line 20 of method `main`. Moving up the stack trace, we see that the exception occurred in method `nextInt`. Notice that in place of the file name and line number, we're provided with the text `Unknown Source`. This means that the so-called debugging symbols that provide the file-name and line number information for that method's class were not available to the JVM—this is typically the case for the classes of the Java API. Many IDEs have access to the Java API source code and will display file names and line numbers in stack traces.

In the sample executions of Fig. 11.1 when exceptions occur and stack traces are displayed, the program also exits. This does not always occur in Java—sometimes a program may continue even though an exception has occurred and a stack trace has been printed. In such cases, the application may produce unexpected results. For example, a graphical user interface (GUI) application will often continue executing. The next section demonstrates how to handle these exceptions.

In Fig. 11.1 both types of exceptions were detected in method `main`. In the next example, we'll see how to handle these exceptions to enable the program to run to normal completion.

11.3 Example: Handling ArithmeticExceptions and InputMismatchExceptions

The application in Fig. 11.2, which is based on Fig. 11.1, uses exception handling to process any ArithmeticExceptions and InputMistmatchExceptions that arise. The application still prompts the user for two integers and passes them to method quotient, which calculates the quotient and returns an int result. This version of the application uses exception handling so that if the user makes a mistake, the program catches and handles (i.e., deals with) the exception—in this case, allowing the user to enter the input again.

```java
 1   // Fig. 11.2: DivideByZeroWithExceptionHandling.java
 2   // Handling ArithmeticExceptions and InputMismatchExceptions.
 3   import java.util.InputMismatchException;
 4   import java.util.Scanner;
 5
 6   public class DivideByZeroWithExceptionHandling
 7   {
 8      // demonstrates throwing an exception when a divide-by-zero occurs
 9      public static int quotient( int numerator, int denominator )
10         throws ArithmeticException
11      {
12         return numerator / denominator; // possible division by zero
13      } // end method quotient
14
15      public static void main( String[] args )
16      {
17         Scanner scanner = new Scanner( System.in ); // scanner for input
18         boolean continueLoop = true; // determines if more input is needed
19
20         do
21         {
22            try // read two numbers and calculate quotient
23            {
24               System.out.print( "Please enter an integer numerator: " );
25               int numerator = scanner.nextInt();
26               System.out.print( "Please enter an integer denominator: " );
27               int denominator = scanner.nextInt();
28
29               int result = quotient( numerator, denominator );
30               System.out.printf( "\nResult: %d / %d = %d\n", numerator,
31                  denominator, result );
32               continueLoop = false; // input successful; end looping
33            } // end try
34            catch ( InputMismatchException inputMismatchException )
35            {
36               System.err.printf( "\nException: %s\n",
37                  inputMismatchException );
38               scanner.nextLine(); // discard input so user can try again
39               System.out.println(
40                  "You must enter integers. Please try again.\n" );
41            } // end catch
```

Fig. 11.2 | Handling ArithmeticExceptions and InputMismatchExceptions. (Part 1 of 2.)

```
42                    catch ( ArithmeticException arithmeticException )
43                    {
44                        System.err.printf( "\nException: %s\n", arithmeticException );
45                        System.out.println(
46                            "Zero is an invalid denominator. Please try again.\n" );
47                    } // end catch
48                } while ( continueLoop ); // end do...while
49          } // end main
50   } // end class DivideByZeroWithExceptionHandling
```

```
Please enter an integer numerator: 100
Please enter an integer denominator: 7

Result: 100 / 7 = 14
```

```
Please enter an integer numerator: 100
Please enter an integer denominator: 0

Exception: java.lang.ArithmeticException: / by zero
Zero is an invalid denominator. Please try again.

Please enter an integer numerator: 100
Please enter an integer denominator: 7

Result: 100 / 7 = 14
```

```
Please enter an integer numerator: 100
Please enter an integer denominator: hello

Exception: java.util.InputMismatchException
You must enter integers. Please try again.

Please enter an integer numerator: 100
Please enter an integer denominator: 7

Result: 100 / 7 = 14
```

Fig. 11.2 | Handling ArithmeticExceptions and InputMismatchExceptions. (Part 2 of 2.)

The first sample execution in Fig. 11.2 is a successful one that does not encounter any problems. In the second execution the user enters a zero denominator, and an ArithmeticException exception occurs. In the third execution the user enters the string "hello" as the denominator, and an InputMismatchException occurs. For each exception, the user is informed of the mistake and asked to try again, then is prompted for two new integers. In each sample execution, the program runs successfully to completion.

Class InputMismatchException is imported in line 3. Class ArithmeticException does not need to be imported because it's in package java.lang. Line 18 creates the boolean variable continueLoop, which is true if the user has not yet entered valid input. Lines 20–48 repeatedly ask users for input until a valid input is received.

*Enclosing Code in a **try** Block*

Lines 22–33 contain a **try block**, which encloses the code that might throw an exception and the code that should not execute if an exception occurs (i.e., if an exception occurs, the remaining code in the try block will be skipped). A try block consists of the keyword try followed by a block of code enclosed in curly braces. [*Note:* The term "try block" sometimes refers only to the block of code that follows the try keyword (not including the try keyword itself). For simplicity, we use the term "try block" to refer to the block of code that follows the try keyword, as well as the try keyword.] The statements that read the integers from the keyboard (lines 25 and 27) each use method nextInt to read an int value. Method nextInt throws an InputMismatchException if the value read in is not an integer.

The division that can cause an ArithmeticException is not performed in the try block. Rather, the call to method quotient (line 29) invokes the code that attempts the division (line 12); the JVM throws an ArithmeticException object when the denominator is zero.

Software Engineering Observation 11.1

Exceptions may surface through explicitly mentioned code in a try block, through calls to other methods, through deeply nested method calls initiated by code in a try block or from the Java Virtual Machine as it executes Java bytecodes.

Catching Exceptions

The try block in this example is followed by two catch blocks—one that handles an InputMismatchException (lines 34–41) and one that handles an ArithmeticException (lines 42–47). A **catch block** (also called a **catch clause** or **exception handler**) catches (i.e., receives) and handles an exception. A catch block begins with the keyword catch and is followed by a parameter in parentheses (called the exception parameter, discussed shortly) and a block of code enclosed in curly braces. [*Note:* The term "catch clause" is sometimes used to refer to the keyword catch followed by a block of code, whereas the term "catch block" refers to only the block of code following the catch keyword, but not including it. For simplicity, we use the term "catch block" to refer to the block of code following the catch keyword, as well as the keyword itself.]

At least one catch block or a **finally block** (discussed in Section 11.6) must immediately follow the try block. Each catch block specifies in parentheses an **exception parameter** that identifies the exception type the handler can process. When an exception occurs in a try block, the catch block that executes is the *first* one whose type matches the type of the exception that occurred (i.e., the type in the catch block matches the thrown exception type exactly or is a superclass of it). The exception parameter's name enables the catch block to interact with a caught exception object—e.g., to implicitly invoke the caught exception's toString method (as in lines 37 and 44), which displays basic information about the exception. Notice that we use the **System.err (standard error stream) object** to output error messages. By default, System.err's print methods, like those of System.out, display data to the command prompt.

Line 38 of the first catch block calls Scanner method nextLine. Because an InputMismatchException occurred, the call to method nextInt never successfully read in the user's data—so we read that input with a call to method nextLine. We do not do anything with the input at this point, because we know that it's invalid. Each catch block displays an error message and asks the user to try again. After either catch block terminates, the user is prompted for input. We'll soon take a deeper look at how this flow of control works in exception handling.

Common Programming Error 11.1
It's a syntax error to place code between a try *block and its corresponding* catch *blocks.*

Common Programming Error 11.2
Each catch *block can have only a single parameter—specifying a comma-separated list of exception parameters is a syntax error.*

An **uncaught exception** is one for which there are no matching catch blocks. You saw uncaught exceptions in the second and third outputs of Fig. 11.1. Recall that when exceptions occurred in that example, the application terminated early (after displaying the exception's stack trace). This does not always occur as a result of uncaught exceptions. Java uses a "multithreaded" model of program execution—each **thread** is a parallel activity. One program can have many threads. If a program has only one thread, an uncaught exception will cause the program to terminate. If a program has multiple threads, an uncaught exception will terminate *only* the thread where the exception occurred. In such programs, however, certain threads may rely on others, and if one thread terminates due to an uncaught exception, there may be adverse effects to the rest of the program. Chapter 23, Multithreading, discusses these issues in depth.

Termination Model of Exception Handling
If an exception occurs in a try block (such as an InputMismatchException being thrown as a result of the code at line 25 of Fig. 11.2), the try block terminates immediately and program control transfers to the *first* of the following catch blocks in which the exception parameter's type matches the thrown exception's type. In Fig. 11.2, the first catch block catches InputMismatchExceptions (which occur if invalid input is entered) and the second catch block catches ArithmeticExceptions (which occur if an attempt is made to divide by zero). After the exception is handled, program control does *not* return to the throw point, because the try block has *expired* (and its local variables have been lost). Rather, control resumes after the last catch block. This is known as the **termination model of exception handling**. Some languages use the **resumption model of exception handling**, in which, after an exception is handled, control resumes just after the throw point.

Notice that we name our exception parameters (inputMismatchException and arithmeticException) based on their type. Java programmers often simply use the letter e as the name of their exception parameters.

Good Programming Practice 11.1
Using an exception-parameter name that reflects the parameter's type promotes clarity by reminding you of the type of exception being handled.

After executing a catch block, this program's flow of control proceeds to the first statement after the last catch block (line 48 in this case). The condition in the do...while statement is true (variable continueLoop contains its initial value of true), so control returns to the beginning of the loop and the user is once again prompted for input. This control statement will loop until valid input is entered. At that point, program control reaches line 32, which assigns `false` to variable `continueLoop`. The `try` block then terminates. If no exceptions are thrown in the `try` block, the `catch` blocks are skipped and control continues with the first statement after the `catch` blocks (we'll learn about another possibility when we discuss the `finally` block in Section 11.6). Now the condition for the do...while loop is `false`, and method `main` ends.

The `try` block and its corresponding `catch` and/or `finally` blocks form a **try statement**. Do not confuse the terms "try block" and "try statement"—the latter includes the try block as well as the following `catch` blocks and/or `finally` block.

As with any other block of code, when a `try` block terminates, local variables declared in the block go out of scope and are no longer accessible; thus, the local variables of a `try` block are not accessible in the corresponding `catch` blocks. When a `catch` block terminates, local variables declared within the `catch` block (including the exception parameter of that `catch` block) also go out of scope and are destroyed. Any remaining `catch` blocks in the `try` statement are ignored, and execution resumes at the first line of code after the try...catch sequence—this will be a `finally` block, if one is present.

Using the **throws Clause**

Now let's examine method `quotient` (Fig. 11.2, lines 9–13). The portion of the method declaration located at line 10 is known as a **throws clause**. It specifies the exceptions the method throws. This clause appears *after* the method's parameter list and *before* the method's body. It contains a comma-separated list of the exceptions that the method will throw if various problems occur. Such exceptions may be thrown by statements in the method's body or by methods called from the body. A method can throw exceptions of the classes listed in its `throws` clause or of their subclasses. We've added the `throws` clause to this application to indicate to the rest of the program that this method may throw an `ArithmeticException`. Clients of method `quotient` are thus informed that the method may throw an `ArithmeticException`. You'll learn more about the `throws` clause in Section 11.5.

Error-Prevention Tip II.I
Read the online API documentation for a method before using it in a program. The documentation specifies the exceptions thrown by the method (if any) and indicates reasons why such exceptions may occur. Next, read the online API documentation for the specified exception classes. The documentation for an exception class typically contains potential reasons that such exceptions occur. Finally, provide for handling those exceptions in your program.

When line 12 executes, if the `denominator` is zero, the JVM throws an `ArithmeticException` object. This object will be caught by the `catch` block at lines 42–47, which displays basic information about the exception by implicitly invoking the exception's `toString` method, then asks the user to try again.

If the `denominator` is not zero, method `quotient` performs the division and returns the result to the point of invocation of method `quotient` in the `try` block (line 29). Lines 30–31 display the result of the calculation and line 32 sets `continueLoop` to `false`. In this case, the `try` block completes successfully, so the program skips the `catch` blocks and fails the condition at line 48, and method `main` completes execution normally.

When `quotient` throws an `ArithmeticException`, `quotient` terminates and does not return a value, and `quotient`'s local variables go out of scope (and are destroyed). If `quotient` contained local variables that were references to objects and there were no other references to those objects, the objects would be marked for garbage collection. Also, when an exception occurs, the `try` block from which `quotient` was called terminates before lines 30–32 can execute. Here, too, if local variables were created in the `try` block prior to the exception's being thrown, these variables would go out of scope.

If an `InputMismatchException` is generated by lines 25 or 27, the `try` block terminates and execution continues with the `catch` block at lines 34–41. In this case, method `quotient` is not called. Then method `main` continues after the last `catch` block (line 48).

11.4 When to Use Exception Handling

Exception handling is designed to process **synchronous errors**, which occur when a statement executes. Common examples we'll see throughout the book are out-of-range array indices, arithmetic overflow (i.e., a value outside the representable range of values), division by zero, invalid method parameters, thread interruption (as we'll see in Chapter 23) and unsuccessful memory allocation (due to lack of memory). Exception handling is not designed to process problems associated with **asynchronous events** (e.g., disk I/O completions, network message arrivals, mouse clicks and keystrokes), which occur in parallel with, and independent of, the program's flow of control.

Software Engineering Observation 11.2
Incorporate your exception-handling strategy into your system from the inception of the design process. Including exception handling after a system has been implemented can be difficult.

Software Engineering Observation 11.3
Exception handling provides a single, uniform technique for processing problems. This helps programmers working on large projects understand each other's error-processing code.

11.5 Java Exception Hierarchy

All Java exception classes inherit directly or indirectly from class **Exception**, forming an inheritance hierarchy. You can extend this hierarchy with your own exception classes.

Figure 11.3 shows a small portion of the inheritance hierarchy for class **Throwable** (a subclass of `Object`), which is the superclass of class `Exception`. Only `Throwable` objects can be used with the exception-handling mechanism. Class `Throwable` has two subclasses: `Exception` and `Error`. Class `Exception` and its subclasses—for instance, `RuntimeException` (package `java.lang`) and `IOException` (package `java.io`)—represent exceptional situations that can occur in a Java program and that can be caught by the application. Class **Error** and its subclasses represent abnormal situations that happen in the JVM. Most *Errors happen infrequently and should not be caught by applications—it's usually not possible for applications to recover from Errors.*

The Java exception hierarchy contains hundreds of classes. Information about Java's exception classes can be found throughout the Java API. You can view `Throwable`'s documentation at `download.oracle.com/javase/6/docs/api/java/lang/Throwable.html`. From there, you can look at this class's subclasses to get more information about Java's `Exceptions` and `Errors`.

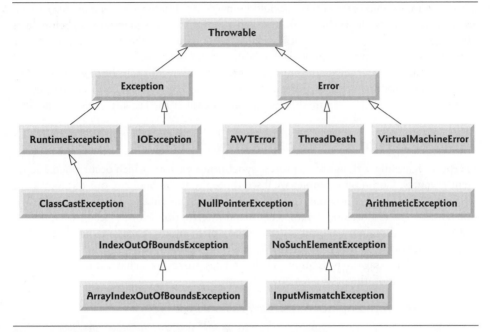

Fig. 11.3 | Portion of class `Throwable`'s inheritance hierarchy.

Checked vs. Unchecked Exceptions

Java distinguishes between **checked exceptions** and **unchecked exceptions**. This distinction is important, because the Java compiler enforces a **catch-or-declare requirement** for checked exceptions. An exception's type determines whether it's checked or unchecked. All exception types that are direct or indirect subclasses of class **RuntimeException** (package `java.lang`) are unchecked exceptions. These are typically caused by defects in your program's code. Examples of unchecked exceptions include `ArrayIndexOutOfBoundsExceptions` (discussed in Chapter 7) and `ArithmeticExceptions` (shown in Fig. 11.3). All classes that inherit from class `Exception` but not class `RuntimeException` are considered to be checked exceptions. Such exceptions are typically caused by conditions that are not under the control of the program—for example, in file processing, the program can't open a file because the file does not exist. Classes that inherit from class `Error` are considered to be unchecked.

The compiler *checks* each method call and method declaration to determine whether the method throws checked exceptions. If so, the compiler verifies that the checked exception is caught or is declared in a `throws` clause. We show how to catch and declare checked exceptions in the next several examples. Recall from Section 11.3 that the `throws` clause specifies the exceptions a method throws. Such exceptions are not caught in the method's body. To satisfy the *catch* part of the catch-or-declare requirement, the code that generates the exception must be wrapped in a `try` block and must provide a `catch` handler for the checked-exception type (or one of its superclass types). To satisfy the *declare* part of the catch-or-declare requirement, the method containing the code that generates the exception must provide a `throws` clause containing the checked-exception type after its parameter list and before its method body. If the catch-or-declare requirement is not satisfied, the compiler will issue an error message indicating that the exception must be caught or declared. This forces you to think about the problems that may occur when a method that throws checked exceptions is called.

Software Engineering Observation 11.4
You must deal with checked exceptions. This results in more robust code than would be created if you were able to simply ignore the exceptions.

Common Programming Error 11.3
A compilation error occurs if a method explicitly attempts to throw a checked exception (or calls another method that throws a checked exception) and that exception is not listed in that method's throws *clause.*

Common Programming Error 11.4
If a subclass method overrides a superclass method, it's an error for the subclass method to list more exceptions in its throws *clause than the overridden superclass method does. However, a subclass's* throws *clause can contain a subset of a superclass's* throws *list.*

Software Engineering Observation 11.5
If your method calls other methods that throw checked exceptions, those exceptions must be caught or declared in your method. If an exception can be handled meaningfully in a method, the method should catch the exception rather than declare it.

Unlike checked exceptions, the Java compiler does *not* check the code to determine whether an unchecked exception is caught or declared. Unchecked exceptions typically can be prevented by proper coding. For example, the unchecked ArithmeticException thrown by method quotient (lines 9–13) in Fig. 11.2 can be avoided if the method ensures that the denominator is not zero *before* attempting to perform the division. Unchecked exceptions are not required to be listed in a method's throws clause—even if they are, it's not required that such exceptions be caught by an application.

Software Engineering Observation 11.6
Although the compiler does not enforce the catch-or-declare requirement for unchecked exceptions, provide appropriate exception-handling code when it's known that such exceptions might occur. For example, a program should process the NumberFormatException *from* Integer *method* parseInt, *even though* NumberFormatException *(an indirect subclass of* RuntimeException*) is an unchecked exception type. This makes your programs more robust.*

Catching Subclass Exceptions
If a catch handler is written to catch superclass-type exception objects, it can also catch all objects of that class's subclasses. This enables catch to handle related errors with a concise notation and allows for polymorphic processing of related exceptions. You can certainly catch each subclass type individually if those exceptions require different processing.

Only the First Matching catch *Executes*
If there are *multiple* catch blocks that match a particular exception type, only the *first* matching catch block executes when an exception of that type occurs. It's a compilation error to catch the *exact same type* in two different catch blocks associated with a particular

try block. However, there may be several catch blocks that match an exception—i.e., several catch blocks whose types are the same as the exception type or a superclass of that type. For instance, we could follow a catch block for type ArithmeticException with a catch block for type Exception—both would match ArithmeticExceptions, but only the first matching catch block would execute.

Error-Prevention Tip 11.2

Catching subclass types individually is subject to error if you forget to test for one or more of the subclass types explicitly; catching the superclass guarantees that objects of all subclasses will be caught. Positioning a catch block for the superclass type after all other subclass catch blocks ensures that all subclass exceptions are eventually caught.

Common Programming Error 11.5

Placing a catch block for a superclass exception type before other catch blocks that catch subclass exception types would prevent those catch blocks from executing, so a compilation error occurs.

11.6 finally Block

Programs that obtain certain types of resources must return them to the system explicitly to avoid so-called **resource leaks.** In programming languages such as C and C++, the most common kind of resource leak is a memory leak. Java performs automatic garbage collection of memory no longer used by programs, thus avoiding most memory leaks. However, other types of resource leaks can occur. For example, files, database connections and network connections that are not closed properly after they're no longer needed might not be available for use in other programs.

Error-Prevention Tip 11.3

A subtle issue is that Java does not entirely eliminate memory leaks. Java will not garbage-collect an object until there are no remaining references to it. Thus, if you erroneously keep references to unwanted objects, memory leaks can occur. To help avoid this problem, set reference-type variables to null when they're no longer needed.

The finally block (which consists of the finally keyword, followed by code enclosed in curly braces), sometimes referred to as the **finally clause**, is optional. If it's present, it's placed after the last catch block. If there are no catch blocks, the finally block immediately follows the try block.

The finally block will execute whether or not an exception is thrown in the corresponding try block. The finally block also will execute if a try block exits by using a return, break or continue statement or simply by reaching its closing right brace. The finally block will *not* execute if the application exits early from a try block by calling method **System.exit**. This method, which we demonstrate in Chapter 17, immediately terminates an application.

Because a finally block almost always executes, it typically contains resource-release code. Suppose a resource is allocated in a try block. If no exception occurs, the catch blocks are skipped and control proceeds to the finally block, which frees the resource. Control then proceeds to the first statement after the finally block. If an exception occurs in the try block, the try block terminates. If the program catches the exception in one of the corresponding catch blocks, it processes the exception, then the finally block releases the resource and control proceeds to the first statement after the finally block. If the program doesn't catch the exception, the finally block *still* releases the resource and an attempt is made to catch the exception in a calling method.

Error-Prevention Tip 11.4

The finally block is an ideal place to release resources acquired in a try block (such as opened files), which helps eliminate resource leaks.

Performance Tip 11.1

Always release a resource explicitly and at the earliest possible moment at which it's no longer needed. This makes resources available for reuse as early as possible, thus improving resource utilization.

If an exception that occurs in a try block cannot be caught by one of that try block's catch handlers, the program skips the rest of the try block and control proceeds to the finally block. Then the program passes the exception to the next outer try block—normally in the calling method—where an associated catch block might catch it. This process can occur through many levels of try blocks. Also, the exception could go uncaught.

If a catch block throws an exception, the finally block still executes. Then the exception is passed to the next outer try block—again, normally in the calling method.

Figure 11.4 demonstrates that the finally block executes even if an exception is not thrown in the corresponding try block. The program contains static methods main (lines 6–18), throwException (lines 21–44) and doesNotThrowException (lines 47–64). Methods throwException and doesNotThrowException are declared static, so main can call them directly without instantiating a UsingExceptions object.

```java
1   // Fig. 11.4: UsingExceptions.java
2   // try...catch...finally exception handling mechanism.
3
4   public class UsingExceptions
5   {
6      public static void main( String[] args )
7      {
8         try
9         {
10           throwException(); // call method throwException
11        } // end try
12        catch ( Exception exception ) // exception thrown by throwException
13        {
14           System.err.println( "Exception handled in main" );
15        } // end catch
16
17        doesNotThrowException();
18     } // end main
19
20     // demonstrate try...catch...finally
21     public static void throwException() throws Exception
22     {
```

Fig. 11.4 | try...catch...finally exception-handling mechanism. (Part 1 of 2.)

```
23          try // throw an exception and immediately catch it
24          {
25             System.out.println( "Method throwException" );
26             throw new Exception(); // generate exception
27          } // end try
28          catch ( Exception exception ) // catch exception thrown in try
29          {
30             System.err.println(
31                "Exception handled in method throwException" );
32             throw exception; // rethrow for further processing
33
34             // code here would not be reached; would cause compilation errors
35
36          } // end catch
37          finally // executes regardless of what occurs in try...catch
38          {
39             System.err.println( "Finally executed in throwException" );
40          } // end finally
41
42          // code here would not be reached; would cause compilation errors
43
44       } // end method throwException
45
46       // demonstrate finally when no exception occurs
47       public static void doesNotThrowException()
48       {
49          try // try block does not throw an exception
50          {
51             System.out.println( "Method doesNotThrowException" );
52          } // end try
53          catch ( Exception exception ) // does not execute
54          {
55             System.err.println( exception );
56          } // end catch
57          finally // executes regardless of what occurs in try...catch
58          {
59             System.err.println(
60                "Finally executed in doesNotThrowException" );
61          } // end finally
62
63          System.out.println( "End of method doesNotThrowException" );
64       } // end method doesNotThrowException
65    } // end class UsingExceptions
```

```
Method throwException
Exception handled in method throwException
Finally executed in throwException
Exception handled in main
Method doesNotThrowException
Finally executed in doesNotThrowException
End of method doesNotThrowException
```

Fig. 11.4 | try...catch...finally exception-handling mechanism. (Part 2 of 2.)

System.out and System.err are **streams**—sequences of bytes. While System.out (known as the **standard output stream**) displays a program's output, System.err (known as the **standard error stream**) displays a program's errors. Output from these streams can be redirected (i.e., sent to somewhere other than the command prompt, such as to a file). Using two different streams enables you to easily separate error messages from other output. For instance, data output from System.err could be sent to a log file, while data output from System.out can be displayed on the screen. For simplicity, this chapter will not redirect output from System.err, but will display such messages to the command prompt. You'll learn more about streams in Chapter 17.

Throwing Exceptions Using the **throw** Statement

Method main (Fig. 11.4) begins executing, enters its try block and immediately calls method throwException (line 10). Method throwException throws an Exception. The statement at line 26 is known as a **throw statement**—it's executed to indicate that an exception has occurred. So far, you've only caught exceptions thrown by called methods. You can throw exceptions yourself by using the throw statement. Just as with exceptions thrown by the Java API's methods, this indicates to client applications that an error has occurred. A throw statement specifies an object to be thrown. The operand of a throw can be of any class derived from class Throwable.

Software Engineering Observation 11.7

When toString is invoked on any Throwable object, its resulting string includes the descriptive string that was supplied to the constructor, or simply the class name if no string was supplied.

Software Engineering Observation 11.8

An object can be thrown without containing information about the problem that occurred. In this case, simply knowing that an exception of a particular type occurred may provide sufficient information for the handler to process the problem correctly.

Software Engineering Observation 11.9

Exceptions can be thrown from constructors. When an error is detected in a constructor, an exception should be thrown to avoid creating an improperly formed object.

Rethrowing Exceptions

Line 32 of Fig. 11.4 **rethrows the exception**. Exceptions are rethrown when a catch block, upon receiving an exception, decides either that it cannot process that exception or that it can only partially process it. Rethrowing an exception defers the exception handling (or perhaps a portion of it) to another catch block associated with an outer try statement. An exception is rethrown by using the **throw keyword**, followed by a reference to the exception object that was just caught. Exceptions cannot be rethrown from a finally block, as the exception parameter (a local variable) from the catch block no longer exists.

When a rethrow occurs, the *next enclosing try block* detects the rethrown exception, and that try block's catch blocks attempt to handle it. In this case, the next enclosing try block is found at lines 8–11 in method main. Before the rethrown exception is handled, however, the finally block (lines 37–40) executes. Then method main detects the rethrown exception in the try block and handles it in the catch block (lines 12–15).

Next, main calls method doesNotThrowException (line 17). No exception is thrown in doesNotThrowException's try block (lines 49–52), so the program skips the catch block (lines 53–56), but the finally block (lines 57–61) nevertheless executes. Control proceeds to the statement after the finally block (line 63). Then control returns to main and the program terminates.

Common Programming Error 11.6

If an exception has not been caught when control enters a finally *block and the* finally *block throws an exception that's not caught in the* finally *block,* the first exception will be lost *and the exception from the* finally *block will be returned to the calling method.*

Error-Prevention Tip 11.5

Avoid placing code that can throw *an exception in a* finally *block. If such code is required, enclose the code in a* try...catch *within the* finally *block.*

Common Programming Error 11.7

Assuming that an exception thrown from a catch *block will be processed by that* catch *block or any other* catch *block associated with the same* try *statement can lead to logic errors.*

Good Programming Practice 11.2

Exception handling is intended to remove error-processing code from the main line of a program's code to improve program clarity. Do not place try...catch... finally *around every statement that may throw an exception. This makes programs difficult to read. Rather, place one* try *block around a significant portion of your code, follow that* try *block with* catch *blocks that handle each possible exception and follow the* catch *blocks with a single* finally *block (if one is required).*

11.7 Stack Unwinding and Obtaining Information from an Exception Object

When an exception is thrown but not caught in a particular scope, the method-call stack is "unwound," and an attempt is made to catch the exception in the next outer try block. This process is called **stack unwinding**. Unwinding the method-call stack means that the method in which the exception was not caught *terminates*, all local variables in that method go out of scope and control returns to the statement that originally invoked that method. If a try block encloses that statement, an attempt is made to catch the exception. If a try block does not enclose that statement or if the exception is not caught, stack unwinding occurs again. Figure 11.5 demonstrates stack unwinding, and the exception handler in main shows how to access the data in an exception object.

Stack Unwinding

In main, the try block (lines 8–11) calls method1 (declared at lines 35–38), which in turn calls method2 (declared at lines 41–44), which in turn calls method3 (declared at lines 47–50). Line 49 of method3 throws an Exception object—this is the *throw point*. Because the throw statement at line 49 is *not* enclosed in a try block, *stack unwinding* occurs—method3 terminates at line 49, then returns control to the statement in method2 that invoked method3 (i.e., line 43). Because *no* try block encloses line 43, *stack unwinding* occurs

```
 1   // Fig. 11.5: UsingExceptions.java
 2   // Stack unwinding and obtaining data from an exception object.
 3
 4   public class UsingExceptions
 5   {
 6      public static void main( String[] args )
 7      {
 8         try
 9         {
10            method1(); // call method1
11         } // end try
12         catch ( Exception exception ) // catch exception thrown in method1
13         {
14            System.err.printf( "%s\n\n", exception.getMessage() );
15            exception.printStackTrace(); // print exception stack trace
16
17            // obtain the stack-trace information
18            StackTraceElement[] traceElements = exception.getStackTrace();
19
20            System.out.println( "\nStack trace from getStackTrace:" );
21            System.out.println( "Class\t\tFile\t\t\tLine\tMethod" );
22
23            // loop through traceElements to get exception description
24            for ( StackTraceElement element : traceElements )
25            {
26               System.out.printf( "%s\t", element.getClassName() );
27               System.out.printf( "%s\t", element.getFileName() );
28               System.out.printf( "%s\t", element.getLineNumber() );
29               System.out.printf( "%s\n", element.getMethodName() );
30            } // end for
31         } // end catch
32      } // end main
33
34      // call method2; throw exceptions back to main
35      public static void method1() throws Exception
36      {
37         method2();
38      } // end method method1
39
40      // call method3; throw exceptions back to method1
41      public static void method2() throws Exception
42      {
43         method3();
44      } // end method method2
45
46      // throw Exception back to method2
47      public static void method3() throws Exception
48      {
49         throw new Exception( "Exception thrown in method3" );
50      } // end method method3
51   } // end class UsingExceptions
```

Fig. 11.5 | Stack unwinding and obtaining data from an exception object. (Part 1 of 2.)

```
Exception thrown in method3

java.lang.Exception: Exception thrown in method3
        at UsingExceptions.method3(UsingExceptions.java:49)
        at UsingExceptions.method2(UsingExceptions.java:43)
        at UsingExceptions.method1(UsingExceptions.java:37)
        at UsingExceptions.main(UsingExceptions.java:10)

Stack trace from getStackTrace:
Class           File                  Line     Method
UsingExceptions UsingExceptions.java    49     method3
UsingExceptions UsingExceptions.java    43     method2
UsingExceptions UsingExceptions.java    37     method1
UsingExceptions UsingExceptions.java    10     main
```

Fig. 11.5 | Stack unwinding and obtaining data from an exception object. (Part 2 of 2.)

again—method2 terminates at line 43 and returns control to the statement in method1 that invoked method2 (i.e., line 37). Because *no* try block encloses line 37, *stack unwinding* occurs one more time—method1 terminates at line 37 and returns control to the statement in main that invoked method1 (i.e., line 10). The try block at lines 8–11 encloses this statement. The exception has not been handled, so the try block terminates and the first matching catch block (lines 12–31) catches and processes the exception. If there were no matching catch blocks, and the exception is not declared in each method that throws it, a compilation error would occur. Remember that this is not always the case—for *unchecked* exceptions, the application will compile, but it will run with unexpected results.

Obtaining Data from an Exception Object
Recall that exceptions derive from class Throwable. Class Throwable offers a **printStackTrace** method that outputs to the standard error stream the stack trace (discussed in Section 11.2). Often, this is helpful in testing and debugging. Class Throwable also provides a **getStackTrace** method that retrieves the stack-trace information that might be printed by printStackTrace. Class Throwable's **getMessage** method returns the descriptive string stored in an exception.

Error-Prevention Tip 11.6
An exception that's not caught in an application causes Java's default exception handler to run. This displays the name of the exception, a descriptive message that indicates the problem that occurred and a complete execution stack trace. In an application with a single thread of execution, the application terminates. In an application with multiple threads, the thread that caused the exception terminates.

Error-Prevention Tip 11.7
Throwable method toString *(inherited by all* Throwable *subclasses) returns a* String *containing the name of the exception's class and a descriptive message.*

The catch handler in Fig. 11.5 (lines 12–31) demonstrates getMessage, printStackTrace and getStackTrace. If we wanted to output the stack-trace information to streams other than the standard error stream, we could use the information returned from getStackTrace and output it to another stream or use one of the overloaded versions of method printStackTrace. Sending data to other streams is discussed in Chapter 17.

Line 14 invokes the exception's getMessage method to get the exception description. Line 15 invokes the exception's printStackTrace method to output the stack trace that indicates where the exception occurred. Line 18 invokes the exception's getStackTrace method to obtain the stack-trace information as an array of **StackTraceElement** objects. Lines 24–30 get each StackTraceElement in the array and invoke its methods **getClassName**, **getFileName**, **getLineNumber** and **getMethodName** to get the class name, file name, line number and method name, respectively, for that StackTraceElement. Each StackTraceElement represents one method call on the method-call stack.

The program's output shows that the stack-trace information printed by printStackTrace follows the pattern: *className.methodName(fileName:lineNumber)*, where *className*, *methodName* and *fileName* indicate the names of the class, method and file in which the exception occurred, respectively, and the *lineNumber* indicates where in the file the exception occurred. You saw this in the output for Fig. 11.1. Method getStackTrace enables custom processing of the exception information. Compare the output of printStackTrace with the output created from the StackTraceElements to see that both contain the same stack-trace information.

Software Engineering Observation 11.10

Never provide a catch handler with an empty body—this effectively ignores the exception. At least use printStackTrace to output an error message to indicate that a problem exists.

11.8 Chained Exceptions

Sometimes a method responds to an exception by throwing a different exception type that's specific to the current application. If a catch block throws a new exception, the original exception's information and stack trace are *lost*. Earlier Java versions provided no mechanism to wrap the original exception information with the new exception's information to provide a complete stack trace showing where the original problem occurred. This made debugging such problems particularly difficult. **Chained exceptions** enable an exception object to maintain the complete stack-trace information from the original exception. Figure 11.6 demonstrates chained exceptions.

```
1   // Fig. 11.6: UsingChainedExceptions.java
2   // Chained exceptions.
3
4   public class UsingChainedExceptions
5   {
6      public static void main( String[] args )
7      {
8         try
9         {
10            method1(); // call method1
11         } // end try
12         catch ( Exception exception ) // exceptions thrown from method1
13         {
```

Fig. 11.6 | Chained exceptions. (Part 1 of 2.)

```
14              exception.printStackTrace();
15          } // end catch
16      } // end main
17
18      // call method2; throw exceptions back to main
19      public static void method1() throws Exception
20      {
21          try
22          {
23              method2(); // call method2
24          } // end try
25          catch ( Exception exception ) // exception thrown from method2
26          {
27              throw new Exception( "Exception thrown in method1", exception );
28          } // end catch
29      } // end method method1
30
31      // call method3; throw exceptions back to method1
32      public static void method2() throws Exception
33      {
34          try
35          {
36              method3(); // call method3
37          } // end try
38          catch ( Exception exception ) // exception thrown from method3
39          {
40              throw new Exception( "Exception thrown in method2", exception );
41          } // end catch
42      } // end method method2
43
44      // throw Exception back to method2
45      public static void method3() throws Exception
46      {
47          throw new Exception( "Exception thrown in method3" );
48      } // end method method3
49  } // end class UsingChainedExceptions
```

```
java.lang.Exception: Exception thrown in method1
        at UsingChainedExceptions.method1(UsingChainedExceptions.java:27)
        at UsingChainedExceptions.main(UsingChainedExceptions.java:10)
Caused by: java.lang.Exception: Exception thrown in method2
        at UsingChainedExceptions.method2(UsingChainedExceptions.java:40)
        at UsingChainedExceptions.method1(UsingChainedExceptions.java:23)
        ... 1 more
Caused by: java.lang.Exception: Exception thrown in method3
        at UsingChainedExceptions.method3(UsingChainedExceptions.java:47)
        at UsingChainedExceptions.method2(UsingChainedExceptions.java:36)
        ... 2 more
```

Fig. 11.6 | Chained exceptions. (Part 2 of 2.)

The program consists of four methods—main (lines 6–16), method1 (lines 19–29), method2 (lines 32–42) and method3 (lines 45–48). Line 10 in method main's try block calls method1. Line 23 in method1's try block calls method2. Line 36 in method2's try block calls method3. In method3, line 47 throws a new Exception. Because this statement is not in a try block, method3 terminates, and the exception is returned to the calling method (method2) at line 36. This statement *is* in a try block; therefore, the try block terminates and the exception is caught at lines 38–41. Line 40 in the catch block throws a new exception. In this case, the Exception constructor with *two* arguments is called. The second argument represents the exception that was the original cause of the problem. In this program, that exception occurred at line 47. Because an exception is thrown from the catch block, method2 terminates and returns the new exception to the calling method (method1) at line 23. Once again, this statement is in a try block, so the try block terminates and the exception is caught at lines 25–28. Line 27 in the catch block throws a new exception and uses the exception that was caught as the second argument to the Exception constructor. Because an exception is thrown from the catch block, method1 terminates and returns the new exception to the calling method (main) at line 10. The try block in main terminates, and the exception is caught at lines 12–15. Line 14 prints a stack trace.

Notice in the program output that the first three lines show the most recent exception that was thrown (i.e., the one from method1 at line 27). The next four lines indicate the exception that was thrown from method2 at line 40. Finally, the last four lines represent the exception that was thrown from method3 at line 47. Also notice that, as you read the output in reverse, it shows how many more chained exceptions remain.

11.9 Declaring New Exception Types

Most Java programmers use existing classes from the Java API, third-party vendors and freely available class libraries (usually downloadable from the Internet) to build Java applications. The methods of those classes typically are declared to throw appropriate exceptions when problems occur. You write code that processes these existing exceptions to make your programs more robust.

If you build classes that other programmers will use, you might find it useful to declare your own exception classes that are specific to the problems that can occur when another programmer uses your reusable classes.

Software Engineering Observation 11.11

If possible, indicate exceptions from your methods by using existing exception classes, rather than creating new ones. The Java API contains many exception classes that might be suitable for the type of problems your methods need to indicate.

A new exception class must extend an existing exception class to ensure that the class can be used with the exception-handling mechanism. Like any other class, an exception class can contain fields and methods. A typical new exception class contains only four constructors: one that takes no arguments and passes a default error message String to the superclass constructor; one that receives a customized error message as a String and passes it to the superclass constructor; one that receives a customized error message as a String and a Throwable (for chaining exceptions) and passes both to the superclass constructor; and one that receives a Throwable (for chaining exceptions) and passes it to the superclass constructor.

Good Programming Practice 11.3

Associating each type of serious execution-time malfunction with an appropriately named Exception class improves program clarity.

Software Engineering Observation 11.12

When defining your own exception type, study the existing exception classes in the Java API and try to extend a related exception class. For example, if you're creating a new class to represent when a method attempts a division by zero, you might extend class ArithmeticException *because division by zero occurs during arithmetic. If the existing classes are not appropriate superclasses for your new exception class, decide whether your new class should be a checked or an unchecked exception class. The new exception class should be a checked exception (i.e., extend* Exception *but not* RuntimeException*) if clients should be required to handle the exception. The client application should be able to reasonably recover from such an exception. The new exception class should extend* RuntimeException *if the client code should be able to ignore the exception (i.e., the exception is an unchecked one).*

In Chapter 19, Generic Classes and Methods, we provide an example of a custom exception class. We declare a generic class called Stack. Some operations typically performed on a Stack are not allowed if the Stack is empty, such as removing an item from the top of the stack. For this reason, some Stack methods throw exceptions of exception class EmptyStackException.

Good Programming Practice 11.4

By convention, all exception-class names should end with the word Exception.

11.10 Preconditions and Postconditions

Programmers spend significant time maintaining and debugging code. To facilitate these tasks and to improve the overall design, you can specify the expected states before and after a method's execution. These states are called preconditions and postconditions, respectively.

A **precondition** must be true when a method is *invoked*. Preconditions describe constraints on method parameters and any other expectations the method has about the current state of a program just before it begins executing. If the preconditions are not met, then the method's behavior is *undefined*—it may throw an exception, proceed with an illegal value or attempt to recover from the error. You should not expect consistent behavior if the preconditions are not satisfied.

A **postcondition** is true *after the method successfully returns*. Postconditions describe constraints on the return value and any other side effects the method may have. When defining a method, you should document all postconditions so that others know what to expect when they call your method, and you should make certain that your method honors all its postconditions if its preconditions are indeed met.

When their preconditions or postconditions are not met, methods typically throw exceptions. As an example, examine String method charAt, which has one int parameter—an index in the String. For a precondition, method charAt assumes that index is greater than or equal to zero and less than the length of the String. If the precondition is met, the postcondition states that the method will return the character at the position in the String specified by the parameter index. Otherwise, the method throws an IndexOutOfBoundsException. We trust that method charAt satisfies its postcondition, provided that we meet the precondition. We need not be concerned with the details of how the method actually retrieves the character at the index.

Typically, a method's preconditions and postconditions are described as part of its specification. When designing your own methods, you should state the preconditions and postconditions in a comment before the method declaration.

11.11 Assertions

When implementing and debugging a class, it's sometimes useful to state conditions that should be true at a particular point in a method. These conditions, called **assertions**, help ensure a program's validity by catching potential bugs and identifying possible logic errors during development. Preconditions and postconditions are two types of assertions. Preconditions are assertions about its state when a method is invoked, and postconditions are assertions about a program's state after a method finishes.

While assertions can be stated as comments to guide you during program development, Java includes two versions of the **assert** statement for validating assertions programatically. The assert statement evaluates a boolean expression and, if false, throws an **AssertionError** (a subclass of Error). The first form of the assert statement is

    assert *expression*;

which throws an AssertionError if *expression* is false. The second form is

    assert *expression1* : *expression2*;

which evaluates *expression1* and throws an AssertionError with *expression2* as the error message if *expression1* is false.

You can use assertions to implement preconditions and postconditions programmatically or to verify any other intermediate states that help you ensure that your code is working correctly. Figure 11.7 demonstrates the assert statement. Line 11 prompts the user to enter a number between 0 and 10, then line 12 reads the number. Line 15 determines whether the user entered a number within the valid range. If the number is out of range, the assert statement reports an error; otherwise, the program proceeds normally.

You use assertions primarily for debugging and identifying logic errors in an application. You must explicitly enable assertions when executing a program, because they reduce performance and are unnecessary for the program's user. To do so, use the java command's -ea command-line option, as in

    java -ea AssertTest

```
1   // Fig. 11.7: AssertTest.java
2   // Checking with assert that a value is within range
3   import java.util.Scanner;
4
5   public class AssertTest
6   {
7      public static void main( String[] args )
8      {
9         Scanner input = new Scanner( System.in );
10
11        System.out.print( "Enter a number between 0 and 10: " );
```

Fig. 11.7 | Checking with assert that a value is within range. (Part 1 of 2.)

```
12              int number = input.nextInt();
13
14              // assert that the value is >= 0 and <= 10
15              assert ( number >= 0 && number <= 10 ) : "bad number: " + number;
16
17              System.out.printf( "You entered %d\n", number );
18          } // end main
19      } // end class AssertTest
```

```
Enter a number between 0 and 10: 5
You entered 5
```

```
Enter a number between 0 and 10: 50
Exception in thread "main" java.lang.AssertionError: bad number: 50
        at AssertTest.main(AssertTest.java:15)
```

Fig. 11.7 | Checking with `assert` that a value is within range. (Part 2 of 2.)

Users should not encounter any `AssertionError`s through normal execution of a properly written program. Such errors should only indicate bugs in the implementation. As a result, you should never catch an `AssertionError`. Rather, you should allow the program to terminate when the error occurs, so you can see the error message, then locate and fix the source of the problem. Since application users can choose not to enable assertions at runtime, you should not use `assert` to indicate runtime problems in production code—use the exception mechanism for this purpose.

11.12 (New in Java SE 7) Multi-catch: Handling Multiple Exceptions in One catch

It's relatively common for a `try` block to be followed by several `catch` blocks to handle various types of exceptions. If the bodies of several `catch` blocks are identical, you can use the new Java SE 7 **multi-catch** feature to catch those exception types in a single `catch` handler and perform the same task. The syntax for a multi-catch is:

```
catch ( Type1 | Type2 | Type3 e )
```

Each exception type is separated from the next with a vertical bar (`|`). The preceding line of code indicates that one of the specified types (or any subclasses of those types) can be caught in the exception handler. Any number of `Throwable` types can be specified in a multi-catch.

11.13 (New in Java SE 7) try-with-Resources: Automatic Resource Deallocation

Typically resource-release code should be placed in a `finally` block to ensure that a resource is released, regardless of whether there were exceptions when the resource was used in the corresponding `try` block. An alternative notation—the **try-with-resources** statement (which is new in Java SE 7)—simplifies writing code in which you obtain one or more resources, use them in a `try` block and release them in a corresponding `finally` block. For example, a file-processing application (Chapter 17) could process a file with a try-with-resources statement to ensure that the file is closed properly when it's no longer needed. Each resource must be an object of a class that implements the **AutoCloseable** interface—such a class has a `close` method. The general form of a try-with-resources statement is

```
try ( ClassName theObject = new ClassName() )
{
    // use theObject here
}
catch ( Exception e )
{
    // catch exceptions that occur while using the resource
}
```

where *ClassName* is a class that implements the `AutoCloseable` interface. This code creates an object of type *ClassName* and uses it in the `try` block, then calls its `close` method to release any resources used by the object. The try-with-resources statement *implicitly* calls the theObject's `close` method *at the end of the try block*. You can allocate multiple resources in the parentheses following `try` by separating them with a semicolon (;).

11.14 Wrap-Up

In this chapter, you learned how to use exception handling to deal with errors. You learned that exception handling enables you to remove error-handling code from the "main line" of the program's execution. We showed how to use `try` blocks to enclose code that may throw an exception, and how to use `catch` blocks to deal with exceptions that may arise. You learned about the termination model of exception handling, which dictates that after an exception is handled, program control does not return to the throw point. We discussed checked vs. unchecked exceptions, and how to specify with the `throws` clause the exceptions that a method might throw. You learned how to use the `finally` block to release resources whether or not an exception occurs. You also learned how to throw and rethrow exceptions. We showed how to obtain information about an exception using methods `printStackTrace`, `getStackTrace` and `getMessage`. Next, we presented chained exceptions, which allow you to wrap original exception information with new exception information. Then, we showed how to create your own exception classes. We introduced preconditions and postconditions to help programmers using your methods understand conditions that must be true when the method is called and when it returns, respectively. When preconditions and postconditions are not met, methods typically throw exceptions. We discussed the `assert` statement and how it can be used to help you debug your programs. In particular, `assert` can be used to ensure that preconditions and postconditions are met. Finally, we introduced Java SE 7's new exception-handling features, including multi-`catch` for processing several types of exceptions in the same `catch` handler and the try-with-resources statement for automatically deallocating a resource after it's used in the `try` block. In the next chapter, we begin our two-chapter, optional case study on object-oriented design with the UML.

12

ATM Case Study, Part 1: Object-Oriented Design with the UML

Objectives

In this chapter you'll learn:

- A simple object-oriented design methodology.
- What a requirements document is.
- To identify classes and class attributes from a requirements document.
- To identify objects' states, activities and operations from a requirements document.
- To determine the collaborations among objects in a system.
- To work with the UML's use case, class, state, activity, communication and sequence diagrams to graphically model an object-oriented system.

Action speaks louder than words but not nearly as often.
—Mark Twain

Always design a thing by considering it in its next larger context.
—Eliel Saarinen

Oh, life is a glorious cycle of song.
—Dorothy Parker

The Wright brothers' design ... allowed them to survive long enough to learn how to fly.
—Michael Potts

12.1 Case Study Introduction

Now we begin our object-oriented design and implementation case study. In this chapter and Chapter 13, you'll design and implement an object-oriented automated teller machine (ATM) software system. The case study provides you with a concise, carefully paced, complete design and implementation experience. In Sections 12.2–12.7 and 13.2–13.3, you'll perform the steps of an object-oriented design (OOD) process using the UML while relating these steps to the object-oriented concepts discussed in Chapters 2–10. In this chapter, you'll work with six popular types of UML diagrams to graphically represent the design. In Chapter 13, you'll tune the design with inheritance, then fully implement the ATM in a 673-line Java application (Section 13.4).

This is not an exercise; rather, it's an end-to-end learning experience that concludes with a detailed walkthrough of the complete Java code that implements our design. It will begin to acquaint you with the kinds of substantial problems encountered in industry.

These chapters can be studied as a continuous unit after you've completed the introduction to object-oriented programming in Chapters 8–11. Or, you can pace the sections one at a time after Chapters 2–8 and 10. Each section of the case study begins with a note telling you the chapter after which it can be covered.

12.2 Examining the Requirements Document

We begin our design process by presenting a **requirements document** that specifies the purpose of the ATM system and *what* it must do. Throughout the case study, we refer often to this requirements document.

Requirements Document

A local bank intends to install a new automated teller machine (ATM) to allow users (i.e., bank customers) to perform basic financial transactions (Fig. 12.1). Each user can have only one account at the bank. ATM users should be able to view their account balance, withdraw cash (i.e., take money out of an account) and deposit funds (i.e., place money into an account). The user interface of the automated teller machine contains:

- a screen that displays messages to the user
- a keypad that receives numeric input from the user
- a cash dispenser that dispenses cash to the user and
- a deposit slot that receives deposit envelopes from the user.

The cash dispenser begins each day loaded with 500 $20 bills. [*Note:* Owing to the limited scope of this case study, certain elements of the ATM described here do not accurately mimic those of a real ATM. For example, a real ATM typically contains a device that reads a user's account number from an ATM card, whereas this ATM asks the user to type the account number on the keypad. A real ATM also usually prints a receipt at the end of a session, but all output from this ATM appears on the screen.]

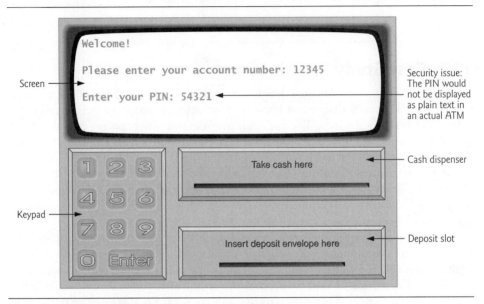

Fig. 12.1 | Automated teller machine user interface.

The bank wants you to develop software to perform the financial transactions initiated by bank customers through the ATM. The bank will integrate the software with the ATM's hardware at a later time. The software should encapsulate the functionality of the hardware devices (e.g., cash dispenser, deposit slot) within software components, but it need not concern itself with how these devices perform their duties. The ATM hardware has not been developed yet, so instead of writing your software to run on the ATM, you should develop a first version to run on a personal computer. This version should use the computer's monitor to simulate the ATM's screen, and the computer's keyboard to simulate the ATM's keypad.

An ATM session consists of authenticating a user (i.e., proving the user's identity) based on an account number and personal identification number (PIN), followed by creating and executing financial transactions. To authenticate a user and perform transactions, the ATM must interact with the bank's account information database (i.e., an organized collection of data stored on a computer; we study database access in Chapter 25). For each bank account, the database stores an account number, a PIN and a balance indicating the amount of money in the account. [*Note:* We assume that the bank plans to build only one ATM, so we need not worry about multiple ATMs accessing this database at the same time. Furthermore, we assume that the bank does not make any changes to the information in the database while a user is accessing the ATM. Also, any business system like an ATM faces complex and challenging security issues that are beyond the scope of this book. We make the simplifying assumption, however, that the bank trusts the ATM to access and manipulate the information in the database without significant security measures.]

Upon first approaching the ATM (assuming no one is currently using it), the user should experience the following sequence of events (shown in Fig. 12.1):

1. The screen displays Welcome! and prompts the user to enter an account number.

2. The user enters a five-digit account number using the keypad.

3. The screen prompts the user to enter the PIN (personal identification number) associated with the specified account number.

4. The user enters a five-digit PIN using the keypad.[1]

5. If the user enters a valid account number and the correct PIN for that account, the screen displays the main menu (Fig. 12.2). If the user enters an invalid account number or an incorrect PIN, the screen displays an appropriate message, then the ATM returns to *Step 1* to restart the authentication process.

Fig. 12.2 | ATM main menu.

After the ATM authenticates the user, the main menu (Fig. 12.2) should contain a numbered option for each of the three types of transactions: balance inquiry (option 1), withdrawal (option 2) and deposit (option 3). It also should contain an option to allow

---

1. In this simple, command-line, text-based ATM, as you type the PIN, it appears on the screen. This is an obvious security breach—you would not want someone looking over your shoulder at an ATM and seeing your PIN displayed on the screen. In Chapter 14, we introduce the JPasswordField GUI component, which displays asterisks as the user types—making it more appropriate for entering PIN numbers and passwords.

the user to exit the system (option 4). The user then chooses either to perform a transaction (by entering 1, 2 or 3) or to exit the system (by entering 4).

If the user enters 1 to make a balance inquiry, the screen displays the user's account balance. To do so, the ATM must retrieve the balance from the bank's database. The following steps describe what occurs when the user enters 2 to make a withdrawal:

1. The screen displays a menu (Fig. 12.3) containing standard withdrawal amounts: $20 (option 1), $40 (option 2), $60 (option 3), $100 (option 4) and $200 (option 5). The menu also contains an option to allow the user to cancel the transaction (option 6).

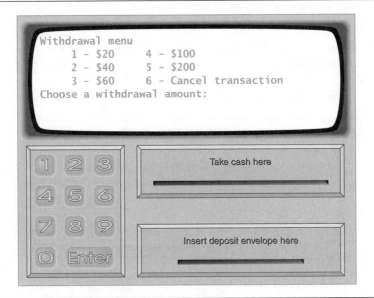

Fig. 12.3 | ATM withdrawal menu.

2. The user enters a menu selection using the keypad.

3. If the withdrawal amount chosen is greater than the user's account balance, the screen displays a message stating this and telling the user to choose a smaller amount. The ATM then returns to *Step 1*. If the withdrawal amount chosen is less than or equal to the user's account balance (i.e., an acceptable amount), the ATM proceeds to *Step 4*. If the user chooses to cancel the transaction (option 6), the ATM displays the main menu and waits for user input.

4. If the cash dispenser contains enough cash, the ATM proceeds to *Step 5*. Otherwise, the screen displays a message indicating the problem and telling the user to choose a smaller withdrawal amount. The ATM then returns to *Step 1*.

5. The ATM debits the withdrawal amount from the user's account in the bank's database (i.e., subtracts the withdrawal amount from the user's account balance).

6. The cash dispenser dispenses the desired amount of money to the user.

7. The screen displays a message reminding the user to take the money.

The following steps describe the actions that occur when the user enters 3 (when viewing the main menu of Fig. 12.2) to make a deposit:

1. The screen prompts the user to enter a deposit amount or type 0 (zero) to cancel.

2. The user enters a deposit amount or 0 using the keypad. [*Note:* The keypad does not contain a decimal point or a dollar sign, so the user cannot type a real dollar amount (e.g., $27.25). Instead, the user must enter a deposit amount as a number of cents (e.g., 2725). The ATM then divides this number by 100 to obtain a number representing a dollar amount (e.g., $2725 \div 100 = 27.25$).]

3. If the user specifies a deposit amount, the ATM proceeds to *Step 4*. If the user chooses to cancel the transaction (by entering 0), the ATM displays the main menu and waits for user input.

4. The screen displays a message telling the user to insert a deposit envelope.

5. If the deposit slot receives a deposit envelope within two minutes, the ATM credits the deposit amount to the user's account in the bank's database (i.e., adds the deposit amount to the user's account balance). [*Note:* This money is *not* immediately available for withdrawal. The bank first must physically verify the amount of cash in the deposit envelope, and any checks in the envelope must clear (i.e., money must be transferred from the check writer's account to the check recipient's account). When either of these events occurs, the bank appropriately updates the user's balance stored in its database. This occurs independently of the ATM system.] If the deposit slot does not receive a deposit envelope within this time period, the screen displays a message that the system has canceled the transaction due to inactivity. The ATM then displays the main menu and waits for user input.

After the system successfully executes a transaction, it should return to the main menu so that the user can perform additional transactions. If the user exits the system, the screen should display a thank you message, then display the welcome message for the next user.

Analyzing the ATM System

The preceding statement is a simplified example of a requirements document. Typically, such a document is the result of a detailed process of **requirements gathering**, which might include interviews with possible users of the system and specialists in fields related to the system. For example, a systems analyst who is hired to prepare a requirements document for banking software (e.g., the ATM system described here) might interview banking experts to gain a better understanding of what the software must do. The analyst would use the information gained to compile a list of **system requirements** to guide systems designers as they design the system.

The process of requirements gathering is a key task of the first stage of the software life cycle. The **software life cycle** specifies the stages through which software goes from the time it's first conceived to the time it's retired from use. These stages typically include: analysis, design, implementation, testing and debugging, deployment, maintenance and retirement. Several software life-cycle models exist, each with its own preferences and specifications for when and how often software engineers should perform each of these stages. **Waterfall models** perform each stage once in succession, whereas **iterative models** may *repeat* one or more stages several times throughout a product's life cycle.

The analysis stage focuses on defining the problem to be solved. When designing any system, one must *solve the problem right*, but of equal importance, one must *solve the right problem*. Systems analysts collect the requirements that indicate the specific problem to solve. Our requirements document describes the requirements of our ATM system in sufficient detail that you need not go through an extensive analysis stage—it's been done for you.

To capture what a proposed system should do, developers often employ a technique known as **use case modeling**. This process identifies the **use cases** of the system, each representing a different capability that the system provides to its clients. For example, ATMs typically have several use cases, such as "View Account Balance," "Withdraw Cash," "Deposit Funds," "Transfer Funds Between Accounts" and "Buy Postage Stamps." The simplified ATM system we build in this case study allows only the first three.

Each use case describes a typical scenario for which the user uses the system. You've already read descriptions of the ATM system's use cases in the requirements document; the lists of steps required to perform each transaction type (i.e., balance inquiry, withdrawal and deposit) actually described the three use cases of our ATM—"View Account Balance," "Withdraw Cash" and "Deposit Funds," respectively.

Use Case Diagrams

We now introduce the first of several UML diagrams in the case study. We create a **use case diagram** to model the interactions between a system's clients (in this case study, bank customers) and its use cases. The goal is to show the kinds of interactions users have with a system without providing the details—these are provided in other UML diagrams (which we present throughout this case study). Use case diagrams are often accompanied by informal text that gives more detail—like the text that appears in the requirements document. Use case diagrams are produced during the analysis stage of the software life cycle. In larger systems, use case diagrams are indispensable tools that help system designers remain focused on satisfying the users' needs.

Figure 12.4 shows the use case diagram for our ATM system. The stick figure represents an **actor**, which defines the roles that an external entity—such as a person or another system—plays when interacting with the system. For our automated teller machine, the actor is a User who can view an account balance, withdraw cash and deposit funds from the ATM. The User is not an actual person, but instead comprises the roles that a real person—when playing the part of a User—can play while interacting with the ATM. A

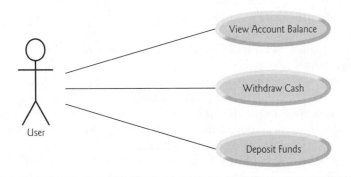

Fig. 12.4 | Use case diagram for the ATM system from the User's perspective.

use case diagram can include multiple actors. For example, the use case diagram for a real bank's ATM system might also include an actor named Administrator who refills the cash dispenser each day.

Our requirements document supplies the actors—"ATM users should be able to view their account balance, withdraw cash and deposit funds." Therefore, the actor in each of the three use cases is the user who interacts with the ATM. An external entity—a real person—plays the part of the user to perform financial transactions. Figure 12.4 shows one actor, whose name, User, appears below the actor in the diagram. The UML models each use case as an oval connected to an actor with a solid line.

Software engineers (more precisely, systems designers) must analyze the requirements document or a set of use cases and design the system before programmers implement it in a particular programming language. During the analysis stage, systems designers focus on understanding the requirements document to produce a high-level specification that describes *what* the system is supposed to do. The output of the design stage—a **design specification**—should specify clearly *how* the system should be constructed to satisfy these requirements. In the next several sections, we perform the steps of a simple object-oriented design (OOD) process on the ATM system to produce a design specification containing a collection of UML diagrams and supporting text.

The UML is designed for use with any OOD process. Many such processes exist, the best known of which is the Rational Unified Process™ (RUP) developed by Rational Software Corporation, now part of IBM. RUP is a rich process intended for designing "industrial strength" applications. For this case study, we present our own simplified design process.

Designing the ATM System

We now begin the design stage of our ATM system. A **system** is a set of components that interact to solve a problem. For example, to perform the ATM system's designated tasks, our ATM system has a user interface (Fig. 12.1), and contains software that executes financial transactions and interacts with a database of bank account information. **System structure** describes the system's objects and their interrelationships. **System behavior** describes how the system changes as its objects interact with one another.

Every system has both structure and behavior—designers must specify both. There are several types of system structures and behaviors. For example, the interactions among objects in the system differ from those between the user and the system, yet both constitute a portion of the system behavior.

The UML 2 standard specifies 13 diagram types for documenting the system models. Each models a distinct characteristic of a system's structure or behavior—six diagrams relate to system structure, the remaining seven to system behavior. We list here only the six diagram types used in our case study—one models system structure; the other five model system behavior. We provide an overview of the remaining seven UML diagram types in Appendix J, UML 2: Additional Diagram Types.

1. **Use case diagrams**, such as the one in Fig. 12.4, model the interactions between a system and its external entities (actors) in terms of use cases (system capabilities, such as "View Account Balance," "Withdraw Cash" and "Deposit Funds").

2. **Class diagrams**, which you'll study in Section 12.3, model the classes, or "building blocks," used in a system. Each noun or "thing" described in the requirements

document is a candidate to be a class in the system (e.g., `Account`, `Keypad`). Class diagrams help us specify the *structural relationships* between parts of the system. For example, the ATM system class diagram will specify that the ATM is physically *composed of* a screen, a keypad, a cash dispenser and a deposit slot.

3. **State machine diagrams**, which you'll study in Section 12.5, model the ways in which an object changes state. An object's **state** is indicated by the values of all its attributes at a given time. When an object changes state, it may behave differently in the system. For example, after validating a user's PIN, the ATM transitions from the "user not authenticated" state to the "user authenticated" state, at which point it allows the user to perform financial transactions (e.g., view account balance, withdraw cash, deposit funds).

4. **Activity diagrams**, which you'll also study in Section 12.5, model an object's **activity**—is workflow (sequence of events) during program execution. An activity diagram models the *actions* the object performs and specifies the *order* in which it performs them. For example, an activity diagram shows that the ATM must obtain the balance of the user's account (from the bank's account information database) *before* the screen can display the balance to the user.

5. **Communication diagrams** (called **collaboration diagrams** in earlier versions of the UML) model the interactions among objects in a system, with an emphasis on *what* interactions occur. You'll learn in Section 12.7 that these diagrams show which objects must interact to perform an ATM transaction. For example, the ATM must communicate with the bank's account information database to retrieve an account balance.

6. **Sequence diagrams** also model the interactions among the objects in a system, but unlike communication diagrams, they emphasize *when* interactions occur. You'll learn in Section 12.7 that these diagrams help show the order in which interactions occur in executing a financial transaction. For example, the screen prompts the user to enter a withdrawal amount before cash is dispensed.

In Section 12.3, we continue designing our ATM system by identifying the classes from the requirements document. We accomplish this by extracting key *nouns and noun phrases* from the requirements document. Using these classes, we develop our first draft of the class diagram that models the structure of our ATM system.

Web Resource

We've created an extensive UML Resource Center that contains many links to additional information, including introductions, tutorials, blogs, books, certification, conferences, developer tools, documentation, e-books, FAQs, forums, groups, UML in Java, podcasts, security, tools, downloads, training courses, videos and more. Browse our UML Resource Center at www.deitel.com/UML/.

Self-Review Exercises for Section 12.2

12.1   Suppose we enabled a user of our ATM system to transfer money between two bank accounts. Modify the use case diagram of Fig. 12.4 to reflect this change.

12.2   _____ model the interactions among objects in a system with an emphasis on *when* these interactions occur.

a) Class diagrams
b) Sequence diagrams
c) Communication diagrams
d) Activity diagrams

12.3 Which of the following choices lists stages of a typical software life cycle in sequential order?
a) design, analysis, implementation, testing
b) design, analysis, testing, implementation
c) analysis, design, testing, implementation
d) analysis, design, implementation, testing

12.3 Identifying the Classes in a Requirements Document

Now we begin designing the ATM system. In this section, we identify the classes that are needed to build the system by analyzing the *nouns* and *noun phrases* that appear in the requirements document. We introduce UML class diagrams to model these classes. This is an important first step in defining the system's structure.

Identifying the Classes in a System

We begin our OOD process by identifying the classes required to build the ATM system. We'll eventually describe these classes using UML class diagrams and implement these classes in Java. First, we review the requirements document of Section 12.2 and identify key nouns and noun phrases to help us identify classes that comprise the ATM system. We may decide that some of these are actually attributes of other classes in the system. We may also conclude that some of the nouns do not correspond to parts of the system and thus should not be modeled at all. Additional classes may become apparent to us as we proceed through the design process.

Figure 12.5 lists the nouns and noun phrases found in the requirements document. We list them from left to right in the order in which we first encounter them. We list only the singular form of each.

Nouns and noun phrases in the ATM requirements document			
bank	money / funds	account number	ATM
screen	PIN	user	keypad
bank database	customer	cash dispenser	balance inquiry
transaction	$20 bill / cash	withdrawal	account
deposit slot	deposit	balance	deposit envelope

Fig. 12.5 | Nouns and noun phrases in the ATM requirements document.

We create classes only for the nouns and noun phrases that have significance in the ATM system. We don't model "bank" as a class, because the bank is not a part of the ATM system—the bank simply wants us to build the ATM. "Customer" and "user" also represent outside entities—they're important because they *interact* with our ATM system, but we do not need to model them as classes in the ATM software. Recall that we modeled an ATM user (i.e., a bank customer) as the actor in the use case diagram of Fig. 12.4.

We do not model "$20 bill" or "deposit envelope" as classes. These are physical objects in the real world, but they're not part of what is being automated. We can adequately represent the presence of bills in the system using an attribute of the class that models the cash dispenser. (We assign attributes to the ATM system's classes in Section 12.4.) For example, the cash dispenser maintains a count of the number of bills it contains. The requirements document does not say anything about what the system should do with deposit envelopes after it receives them. We can assume that simply acknowledging the receipt of an envelope—an operation performed by the class that models the deposit slot—is sufficient to represent the presence of an envelope in the system. We assign operations to the ATM system's classes in Section 12.6.

In our simplified ATM system, representing various amounts of "money," including an account's "balance," as attributes of classes seems most appropriate. Likewise, the nouns "account number" and "PIN" represent significant pieces of information in the ATM system. They're important attributes of a bank account. They do not, however, exhibit behaviors. Thus, we can most appropriately model them as attributes of an account class.

Though the requirements document frequently describes a "transaction" in a general sense, we do not model the broad notion of a financial transaction at this time. Instead, we model the three types of transactions (i.e., "balance inquiry," "withdrawal" and "deposit") as individual classes. These classes possess specific attributes needed for executing the transactions they represent. For example, a withdrawal needs to know the amount of the withdrawal. A balance inquiry, however, does not require any additional data other than the account number. Furthermore, the three transaction classes exhibit unique behaviors. A withdrawal includes dispensing cash to the user, whereas a deposit involves receiving deposit envelopes from the user. In Section 13.3, we "factor out" common features of all transactions into a general "transaction" class using the object-oriented concept of inheritance.

We determine the classes for our system based on the remaining nouns and noun phrases from Fig. 12.5. Each of these refers to one or more of the following:

- ATM
- screen
- keypad
- cash dispenser
- deposit slot
- account
- bank database
- balance inquiry
- withdrawal
- deposit

The elements of this list are likely to be classes that we'll need to implement our system.

We can now model the classes in our system based on the list we've created. We capitalize class names in the design process—a UML convention—as we'll do when we write the actual Java code that implements our design. If the name of a class contains more than one word, we run the words together and capitalize each word (e.g., `MultipleWordName`). Using this convention, we create classes ATM, `Screen`, `Keypad`, `CashDispenser`, `Deposit-Slot`, `Account`, `BankDatabase`, `BalanceInquiry`, `Withdrawal` and `Deposit`. We construct our system using these classes as building blocks. Before we begin building the system, however, we must gain a better understanding of how the classes relate to one another.

Modeling Classes

The UML enables us to model, via **class diagrams**, the classes in the ATM system and their interrelationships. Figure 12.6 represents class ATM. Each class is modeled as a rectangle with three compartments. The top one contains the name of the class centered horizontally in boldface. The middle compartment contains the class's attributes. (We discuss attributes in Sections 12.4–12.5.) The bottom compartment contains the class's operations (discussed in Section 12.6). In Fig. 12.6, the middle and bottom compartments are empty because we've not yet determined this class's attributes and operations.

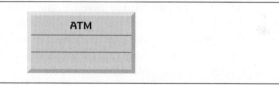

Fig. 12.6 | Representing a class in the UML using a class diagram.

Class diagrams also show the relationships between the classes of the system. Figure 12.7 shows how our classes ATM and `Withdrawal` relate to one another. For the moment, for simplicity, we choose to model only this subset of classes. We present a more complete class diagram later in this section. Notice that the rectangles representing classes in this diagram are not subdivided into compartments. The UML allows the suppression of class attributes and operations in this manner to create more readable diagrams, when appropriate. Such a diagram is said to be an **elided diagram**—one in which some information, such as the contents of the second and third compartments, is *not* modeled. We'll place information in these compartments in Sections 12.4–12.6.

Fig. 12.7 | Class diagram showing an association among classes.

In Fig. 12.7, the solid line that connects the two classes represents an **association**—a relationship between classes. The numbers near each end of the line are **multiplicity** values, which indicate how many objects of each class participate in the association. In this case, following the line from left to right reveals that, at any given moment, one ATM object participates in an association with either zero or one `Withdrawal` objects—zero if the current user is not currently performing a transaction or has requested a different type of transaction, and one if the user has requested a withdrawal. The UML can model many types of multiplicity. Figure 12.8 lists and explains the multiplicity types.

Symbol	Meaning
0	None
1	One
m	An integer value
0..1	Zero or one
m, n	m or n
$m..n$	At least m, but not more than n
*	Any nonnegative integer (zero or more)
0..*	Zero or more (identical to *)
1..*	One or more

Fig. 12.8 | Multiplicity types.

An association can be named. For example, the word `Executes` above the line connecting classes `ATM` and `Withdrawal` in Fig. 12.7 indicates the name of that association. This part of the diagram reads "one object of class `ATM` executes zero or one objects of class `Withdrawal`." Association names are *directional*, as indicated by the filled arrowhead—so it would be improper, for example, to read the preceding association from right to left as "zero or one objects of class `Withdrawal` execute one object of class `ATM`."

The word `currentTransaction` at the `Withdrawal` end of the association line in Fig. 12.7 is a **role name**, identifying the role the `Withdrawal` object plays in its relationship with the `ATM`. A role name adds meaning to an association between classes by identifying the role a class plays in the context of an association. A class can play several roles in the same system. For example, in a school personnel system, a person may play the role of "professor" when relating to students. The same person may take on the role of "colleague" when participating in an association with another professor, and "coach" when coaching student athletes. In Fig. 12.7, the role name `currentTransaction` indicates that the `Withdrawal` object participating in the `Executes` association with an object of class `ATM` represents the transaction currently being processed by the ATM. In other contexts, a `Withdrawal` object may take on other roles (e.g., the "previous transaction"). Notice that we do not specify a role name for the `ATM` end of the `Executes` association. Role names in class diagrams are often omitted when the meaning of an association is clear without them.

In addition to indicating simple relationships, associations can specify more complex relationships, such as objects of one class being *composed of* objects of other classes. Consider a real-world automated teller machine. What "pieces" does a manufacturer put together to build a working ATM? Our requirements document tells us that the ATM is composed of a screen, a keypad, a cash dispenser and a deposit slot.

In Fig. 12.9, the **solid diamonds** attached to the `ATM` class's association lines indicate that `ATM` has a **composition** relationship with classes `Screen`, `Keypad`, `CashDispenser` and `DepositSlot`. Composition implies a *whole/part relationship*. The class that has the composition symbol (the solid diamond) on its end of the association line is the *whole* (in this case, `ATM`), and the classes on the other end of the association lines are the *parts*—in this case, `Screen`, `Keypad`, `CashDispenser` and `DepositSlot`. The compositions in Fig. 12.9 indicate that an object of class `ATM` is formed from one object of class `Screen`, one object of class `CashDispenser`, one object of class `Keypad` and one object of class `DepositSlot`. The ATM *has a* screen, a keypad, a cash dispenser and a deposit slot. (As we saw in Chapter 9, the *is-a* relationship defines inheritance. We'll see in Section 13.3 that there's a nice opportunity to use inheritance in the ATM system design.)

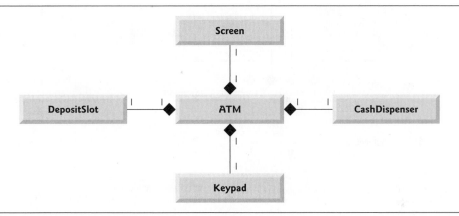

Fig. 12.9 | Class diagram showing composition relationships.

According to the UML specification (`www.omg.org/technology/documents/formal/uml.htm`), composition relationships have the following properties:

1. Only one class in the relationship can represent the *whole* (i.e., the diamond can be placed on only *one* end of the association line). For example, either the screen is part of the ATM or the ATM is part of the screen, but the screen and the ATM cannot both represent the whole in the relationship.

2. The *parts* in the composition relationship exist only as long as the whole does, and the whole is responsible for the creation and destruction of its parts. For example, the act of constructing an ATM includes manufacturing its parts. Also, if the ATM is destroyed, its screen, keypad, cash dispenser and deposit slot are also destroyed.

3. A *part* may belong to only one *whole* at a time, although it may be removed and attached to another whole, which then assumes responsibility for the part.

The solid diamonds in our class diagrams indicate composition relationships that fulfill these properties. If a *has-a* relationship does not satisfy one or more of these criteria, the UML specifies that **hollow diamonds** be attached to the ends of association lines to indicate **aggregation**—a weaker form of composition. For example, a personal computer and a computer monitor participate in an aggregation relationship—the computer *has a* monitor, but the two parts can exist independently, and the same monitor can be attached to multiple computers at once, thus violating composition's second and third properties.

Figure 12.10 shows a class diagram for the ATM system. This diagram models most of the classes that we've identified, as well as the associations between them that we can infer from the requirements document. Classes `BalanceInquiry` and `Deposit` participate in associations similar to those of class `Withdrawal`, so we've chosen to omit them from this diagram to keep it simple. In Section 13.3, we expand our class diagram to include all the classes in the ATM system.

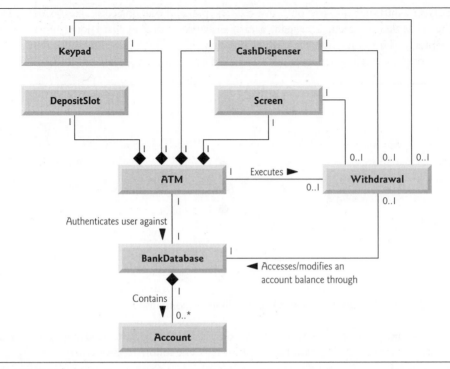

Fig. 12.10 | Class diagram for the ATM system model.

Figure 12.10 presents a graphical model of ATM system's structure. It includes classes BankDatabase and Account, and several associations that were not present in either Fig. 12.7 or Fig. 12.9. It shows that class ATM has a **one-to-one relationship** with class BankDatabase—one ATM object *authenticates users against* one BankDatabase object. In Fig. 12.10, we also model the fact that the bank's database contains information about many accounts—one BankDatabase object participates in a *composition* relationship with zero or more Account objects. The multiplicity value 0..* at the Account end of the association between class BankDatabase and class Account indicates that zero or more objects of class Account take part in the association. Class BankDatabase has a **one-to-many relationship** with class Account—the BankDatabase can contain many Accounts. Similarly, class Account has a **many-to-one relationship** with class BankDatabase—there can be many Accounts stored in the BankDatabase. Recall from Fig. 12.8 that the multiplicity value * is identical to 0..*. We include 0..* in our class diagrams for clarity.

Figure 12.10 also indicates that at any given time 0 or 1 Withdrawal objects can exist. If the user is performing a withdrawal, "one object of class Withdrawal accesses/modifies an account balance through one object of class BankDatabase." We could have created an association directly between class Withdrawal and class Account. The requirements document, however, states that the "ATM must interact with the bank's account information database" to perform transactions. A bank account contains sensitive information, and systems engineers must always consider the security of personal data when designing a system. Thus, only the BankDatabase can access and manipulate an account directly. All other parts of the system must interact with the database to retrieve or update account information (e.g., an account balance).

The class diagram in Fig. 12.10 also models associations between class `Withdrawal` and classes `Screen`, `CashDispenser` and `Keypad`. A withdrawal transaction includes prompting the user to choose a withdrawal amount, and receiving numeric input. These actions require the use of the screen and the keypad, respectively. Furthermore, dispensing cash to the user requires access to the cash dispenser.

Classes `BalanceInquiry` and `Deposit`, though not shown in Fig. 12.10, take part in several associations with the other classes of the ATM system. Like class `Withdrawal`, each of these classes associates with classes `ATM` and `BankDatabase`. An object of class `BalanceInquiry` also associates with an object of class `Screen` to display the balance of an account to the user. Class `Deposit` associates with classes `Screen`, `Keypad` and `DepositSlot`. Like withdrawals, deposit transactions require use of the screen and the keypad to display prompts and receive input, respectively. To receive deposit envelopes, an object of class `Deposit` accesses the deposit slot.

We've now identified the initial classes in our ATM system—we may discover others as we proceed with the design and implementation. In Section 12.4 we determine the attributes for each of these classes, and in Section 12.5 we use these attributes to examine how the system changes over time.

Self-Review Exercises for Section 12.3

12.4   Suppose we have a class `Car` that represents a car. Think of some of the different pieces that a manufacturer would put together to produce a whole car. Create a class diagram (similar to Fig. 12.9) that models some of the composition relationships of class `Car`.

12.5   Suppose we have a class `File` that represents an electronic document in a standalone, non-networked computer represented by class `Computer`. What sort of association exists between class `Computer` and class `File`?

    a) Class `Computer` has a one-to-one relationship with class `File`.
    b) Class `Computer` has a many-to-one relationship with class `File`.
    c) Class `Computer` has a one-to-many relationship with class `File`.
    d) Class `Computer` has a many-to-many relationship with class `File`.

12.6   State whether the following statement is *true* or *false*, and if *false*, explain why: A UML diagram in which a class's second and third compartments are not modeled is said to be an elided diagram.

12.7   Modify the class diagram of Fig. 12.10 to include class `Deposit` instead of class `Withdrawal`.

12.4 Identifying Class Attributes

Classes have attributes (data) and operations (behaviors). Class attributes are implemented as fields, and class operations are implemented as methods. In this section, we determine many of the attributes needed in the ATM system. In Section 12.5 we examine how these attributes represent an object's state. In Section 12.6 we determine class operations.

Identifying Attributes
Consider the attributes of some real-world objects: A person's attributes include height, weight and whether the person is left-handed, right-handed or ambidextrous. A radio's attributes include its station, volume and AM or FM settings. A car's attributes include its

speedometer and odometer readings, the amount of gas in its tank and what gear it's in. A personal computer's attributes include its manufacturer (e.g., Dell, Sun, Apple or IBM), type of screen (e.g., LCD or CRT), main memory size and hard disk size.

We can identify many attributes of the classes in our system by looking for descriptive words and phrases in the requirements document. For each such word and phrase we find that plays a significant role in the ATM system, we create an attribute and assign it to one or more of the classes identified in Section 12.3. We also create attributes to represent any additional data that a class may need, as such needs become clear throughout the design process.

Figure 12.11 lists the words or phrases from the requirements document that describe each class. We formed this list by reading the requirements document and identifying any words or phrases that refer to characteristics of the classes in the system. For example, the requirements document describes the steps taken to obtain a "withdrawal amount," so we list "amount" next to class Withdrawal.

Class	Descriptive words and phrases
ATM	user is authenticated
BalanceInquiry	account number
Withdrawal	account number
	amount
Deposit	account number
	amount
BankDatabase	*[no descriptive words or phrases]*
Account	account number
	PIN
	balance
Screen	*[no descriptive words or phrases]*
Keypad	*[no descriptive words or phrases]*
CashDispenser	begins each day loaded with 500 $20 bills
DepositSlot	*[no descriptive words or phrases]*

Fig. 12.11 | Descriptive words and phrases from the ATM requirements document.

Figure 12.11 leads us to create one attribute of class ATM. Class ATM maintains information about the state of the ATM. The phrase "user is authenticated" describes a state of the ATM (we introduce states in Section 12.5), so we include userAuthenticated as a **Boolean attribute** (i.e., an attribute that has a value of either true or false) in class ATM. The Boolean attribute type in the UML is equivalent to the boolean type in Java. This attribute indicates whether the ATM has successfully authenticated the current user—userAuthenticated must be true for the system to allow the user to perform transactions and access account information. This attribute helps ensure the security of the data in the system.

Classes BalanceInquiry, Withdrawal and Deposit share one attribute. Each transaction involves an "account number" that corresponds to the account of the user making the transaction. We assign an integer attribute `accountNumber` to each transaction class to identify the account to which an object of the class applies.

Descriptive words and phrases in the requirements document also suggest some differences in the attributes required by each transaction class. The requirements document indicates that to withdraw cash or deposit funds, users must input a specific "amount" of money to be withdrawn or deposited, respectively. Thus, we assign to classes `Withdrawal` and `Deposit` an attribute `amount` to store the value supplied by the user. The amounts of money related to a withdrawal and a deposit are defining characteristics of these transactions that the system requires for these transactions to take place. Class `BalanceInquiry`, however, needs no additional data to perform its task—it requires only an account number to indicate the account whose balance should be retrieved.

Class `Account` has several attributes. The requirements document states that each bank account has an "account number" and "PIN," which the system uses for identifying accounts and authenticating users. We assign to class `Account` two integer attributes: `accountNumber` and `pin`. The requirements document also specifies that an account maintains a "balance" of the amount of money in the account and that money the user deposits does not become available for a withdrawal until the bank verifies the amount of cash in the deposit envelope, and any checks in the envelope clear. An account must still record the amount of money that a user deposits, however. Therefore, we decide that an account should represent a balance using two attributes: `availableBalance` and `totalBalance`. Attribute `availableBalance` tracks the amount of money that a user can withdraw from the account. Attribute `totalBalance` refers to the total amount of money that the user has "on deposit" (i.e., the amount of money available, plus the amount waiting to be verified or cleared). For example, suppose an ATM user deposits $50.00 into an empty account. The `totalBalance` attribute would increase to $50.00 to record the deposit, but the `availableBalance` would remain at $0. [*Note:* We assume that the bank updates the `availableBalance` attribute of an `Account` some length of time after the ATM transaction occurs, in response to confirming that $50 worth of cash or checks was found in the deposit envelope. We assume that this update occurs through a transaction that a bank employee performs using some piece of bank software other than the ATM. Thus, we do not discuss this transaction in our case study.]

Class `CashDispenser` has one attribute. The requirements document states that the cash dispenser "begins each day loaded with 500 $20 bills." The cash dispenser must keep track of the number of bills it contains to determine whether enough cash is on hand to satisfy withdrawal requests. We assign to class `CashDispenser` an integer attribute `count`, which is initially set to 500.

For real problems in industry, there's no guarantee that requirements documents will be precise enough for the object-oriented systems designer to determine all the attributes or even all the classes. The need for additional classes, attributes and behaviors may become clear as the design process proceeds. As we progress through this case study, we will continue to add, modify and delete information about the classes in our system.

Modeling Attributes

The class diagram in Fig. 12.12 lists some of the attributes for the classes in our system—the descriptive words and phrases in Fig. 12.11 lead us to identify these attributes. For simplicity, Fig. 12.12 does not show the associations among classes—we showed these in Fig. 12.10. This is a common practice of systems designers when designs are being developed. Recall from Section 12.3 that in the UML, a class's attributes are placed in the middle compartment of the class's rectangle. We list each attribute's name and type separated by a colon (:), followed in some cases by an equal sign (=) and an initial value.

Consider the userAuthenticated attribute of class ATM:

> userAuthenticated : Boolean = false

This attribute declaration contains three pieces of information about the attribute. The **attribute name** is userAuthenticated. The **attribute type** is Boolean. In Java, an attribute can be represented by a primitive type, such as boolean, int or double, or a reference type like a class. We've chosen to model only primitive-type attributes in Fig. 12.12—we discuss the reasoning behind this decision shortly. The attribute types in Fig. 12.12 are in UML notation. We'll associate the types Boolean, Integer and Double in the UML diagram with the primitive types boolean, int and double in Java, respectively.

Fig. 12.12 | Classes with attributes.

We can also indicate an initial value for an attribute. The userAuthenticated attribute in class ATM has an initial value of false. This indicates that the system initially does not consider the user to be authenticated. If an attribute has no initial value specified, only its name and type (separated by a colon) are shown. For example, the accountNumber attribute of class BalanceInquiry is an integer. Here we show no initial value, because the value of this attribute is a number that we do not yet know. This number will be determined at execution time based on the account number entered by the current ATM user.

Figure 12.12 does not include attributes for classes Screen, Keypad and DepositSlot. These are important components of our system, for which our design process has not yet revealed any attributes. We may discover some, however, in the remaining phases of design or when we implement these classes in Java. This is perfectly normal.

Software Engineering Observation 12.1

At early stages in the design process, classes often lack attributes (and operations). Such classes should not be eliminated, however, because attributes (and operations) may become evident in the later phases of design and implementation.

Figure 12.12 also does not include attributes for class BankDatabase. Recall that attributes in Java can be represented by either primitive types or reference types. We've chosen to include only primitive-type attributes in the class diagram in Fig. 12.12 (and in similar class diagrams throughout the case study). A reference-type attribute is modeled more clearly as an association between the class holding the reference and the class of the object to which the reference points. For example, the class diagram in Fig. 12.10 indicates that class BankDatabase participates in a composition relationship with zero or more Account objects. From this composition, we can determine that when we implement the ATM system in Java, we'll be required to create an attribute of class BankDatabase to hold references to zero or more Account objects. Similarly, we can determine reference-type attributes of class ATM that correspond to its composition relationships with classes Screen, Keypad, CashDispenser and DepositSlot. These composition-based attributes would be redundant if modeled in Fig. 12.12, because the compositions modeled in Fig. 12.10 already convey the fact that the database contains information about zero or more accounts and that an ATM is composed of a screen, keypad, cash dispenser and deposit slot. Software developers typically model these whole/part relationships as compositions rather than as attributes required to implement the relationships.

The class diagram in Fig. 12.12 provides a solid basis for the structure of our model, but the diagram is not complete. In Section 12.5 we identify the states and activities of the objects in the model, and in Section 12.6 we identify the operations that the objects perform. As we present more of the UML and object-oriented design, we'll continue to strengthen the structure of our model.

Self-Review Exercises for Section 12.4

12.8 We typically identify the attributes of the classes in our system by analyzing the _____ in the requirements document.
    a) nouns and noun phrases
    b) descriptive words and phrases
    c) verbs and verb phrases
    d) All of the above.

12.9 Which of the following is *not* an attribute of an airplane?
    a) length
    b) wingspan
    c) fly
    d) number of seats

12.10   Describe the meaning of the following attribute declaration of class CashDispenser in the class diagram in Fig. 12.12:

```
count : Integer = 500
```

12.5 Identifying Objects' States and Activities

[*Note:* **This section can be taught after Chapter 5.**]
In Section 12.4, we identified many of the class attributes needed to implement the ATM system and added them to the class diagram in Fig. 12.12. We now show how these attributes represent an object's state. We identify some key states that our objects may occupy and discuss how objects *change state* in response to various events occurring in the system. We also discuss the workflow, or **activities**, that objects perform in the ATM system, and we present the activities of BalanceInquiry and Withdrawal transaction objects.

State Machine Diagrams
Each object in a system goes through a series of states. An object's state is indicated by the values of its attributes at a given time. **State machine diagrams** (commonly called **state diagrams**) model several states of an object and show under what circumstances the object changes state. Unlike the class diagrams presented in earlier case study sections, which focused primarily on the system's *structure*, state diagrams model some of the system's *behavior*.

Figure 12.13 is a simple state diagram that models some of the states of an object of class ATM. The UML represents each state in a state diagram as a **rounded rectangle** with the name of the state placed inside it. A **solid circle** with an attached stick (→) arrowhead designates the **initial state**. Recall that we modeled this state information as the Boolean attribute userAuthenticated in the class diagram of Fig. 12.12. This attribute is initialized to false, or the "User not authenticated" state, according to the state diagram.

Fig. 12.13 | State diagram for the ATM object.

The arrows with stick (→) arrowhead indicate **transitions** between states. An object can transition from one state to another in response to various *events* that occur in the system. The name or description of the event that causes a transition is written near the line that corresponds to the transition. For example, the ATM object changes from the "User not authenticated" to the "User authenticated" state after the database authenticates the user. Recall from the requirements document that the database authenticates a user by comparing the account number and PIN entered by the user with those of an account in the database. If the user has entered a valid account number and the correct PIN, the ATM object transitions to the "User authenticated" state and changes its userAuthenticated attribute to a value of true. When the user exits the system by choosing the "exit" option from the main menu, the ATM object returns to the "User not authenticated" state.

> ### Software Engineering Observation 12.2
> *Software designers do not generally create state diagrams showing every possible state and state transition for all attributes—there are simply too many of them. State diagrams typically show only key states and state transitions.*

Activity Diagrams

Like a state diagram, an activity diagram models aspects of system behavior. Unlike a state diagram, an activity diagram models an object's **workflow** (sequence of events) during program execution. An activity diagram models the **actions** the object will perform and in what *order*. The activity diagram in Fig. 12.14 models the actions involved in executing a balance-inquiry transaction. We assume that a `BalanceInquiry` object has already been initialized and assigned a valid account number (that of the current user), so the object knows which balance to retrieve. The diagram includes the actions that occur after the user selects a balance inquiry from the main menu and before the ATM returns the user to the main menu—a `BalanceInquiry` object does not perform or initiate these actions, so we do not model them here. The diagram begins with retrieving the balance of the account from the database. Next, the `BalanceInquiry` displays the balance on the screen. This action completes the execution of the transaction. Recall that we've chosen to represent an account balance as both the `availableBalance` and `totalBalance` attributes of class `Account`, so the actions modeled in Fig. 12.14 refer to the retrieval and display of *both* balance attributes.

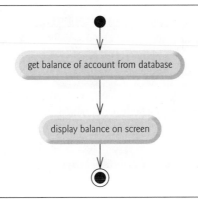

Fig. 12.14 | Activity diagram for a `BalanceInquiry` object.

The UML represents an action in an activity diagram as an action state modeled by a rectangle with its left and right sides replaced by arcs curving outward. Each action state contains an *action expression*—for example, "get balance of account from database"—that specifies an action to be performed. An arrow with a stick ($\rightarrow$) arrowhead connects two action states, indicating the order in which the actions represented by the action states occur. The solid circle (at the top of Fig. 12.14) represents the activity's *initial state*—the beginning of the workflow before the object performs the modeled actions. In this case, the transaction first executes the "get balance of account from database" action expression. The transaction then displays *both* balances on the screen. The solid circle enclosed in an open circle (at the bottom of Fig. 12.14) represents the *final state*—the end of the workflow after the object performs the modeled actions. We used UML activity diagrams to illustrate the flow of control for the control statements presented in Chapters 4–5.

Figure 12.15 shows an activity diagram for a withdrawal transaction. We assume that a Withdrawal object has been assigned a valid account number. We do not model the user

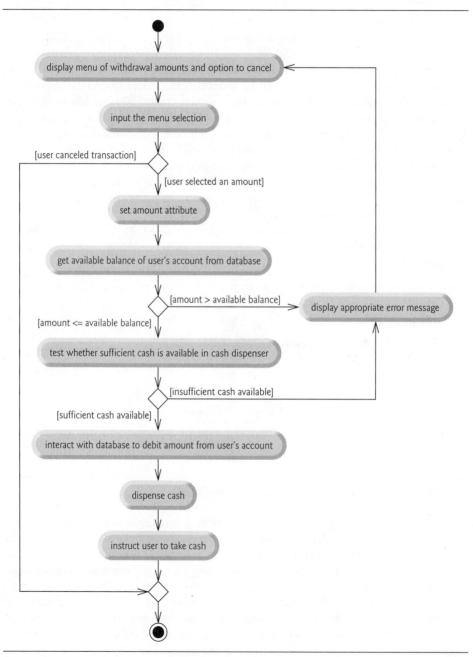

Fig. 12.15 | Activity diagram for a withdrawal transaction.

selecting a withdrawal from the main menu or the ATM returning the user to the main menu because these are not actions performed by a `Withdrawal` object. The transaction first displays a menu of standard withdrawal amounts (shown in Fig. 12.3) and an option to cancel the transaction. The transaction then receives a menu selection from the user. The activity flow now arrives at a decision (a fork indicated by the small diamond symbol). This point determines the next action based on the associated guard condition (in square brackets next to the transition), which states that the transition occurs if this guard condition is met. If the user cancels the transaction by choosing the "cancel" option from the menu, the activity flow immediately skips to the final state. Note the merge (indicated by the small diamond symbol) where the cancellation flow of activity joins the main flow of activity before reaching the activity's final state. If the user selects a withdrawal amount from the menu, `Withdrawal` sets `amount` (an attribute originally modeled in Fig. 12.12) to the value chosen by the user.

After setting the withdrawal amount, the transaction retrieves the available balance of the user's account (i.e., the `availableBalance` attribute of the user's `Account` object) from the database. The activity flow then arrives at another decision. If the requested withdrawal amount exceeds the user's available balance, the system displays an appropriate error message informing the user of the problem, then returns to the beginning of the activity diagram and prompts the user to input a new amount. If the requested withdrawal amount is less than or equal to the user's available balance, the transaction proceeds. The transaction next tests whether the cash dispenser has enough cash remaining to satisfy the withdrawal request. If it does not, the transaction displays an appropriate error message, then returns to the beginning of the activity diagram and prompts the user to choose a new amount. If sufficient cash is available, the transaction interacts with the database to debit the withdrawal amount from the user's account (i.e., subtract the amount from *both* the `availableBalance` and `totalBalance` attributes of the user's `Account` object). The transaction then dispenses the desired amount of cash and instructs the user to take it. Finally, the main flow of activity merges with the cancellation flow of activity before reaching the final state.

We've taken the first steps in modeling the ATM software system's behavior and have shown how an object's attributes participate in performing the object's activities. In Section 12.6, we investigate the behaviors for all classes to give a more accurate interpretation of the system behavior by filling in the third compartments of the classes in our class diagram.

Self-Review Exercises for Section 12.5

12.11   State whether the following statement is *true* or *false*, and if *false*, explain why: State diagrams model structural aspects of a system.

12.12   An activity diagram models the _____ that an object performs and the order in which it performs them.
   a)   actions
   b)   attributes
   c)   states
   d)   state transitions

12.13   Based on the requirements document, create an activity diagram for a deposit transaction.

12.6 Identifying Class Operations

[*Note:* **This section can be taught after Chapter 6.**]
In this section, we determine some of the class operations (or behaviors) needed to implement the ATM system. An operation is a service that objects of a class provide to clients (users) of the class. Consider the operations of some real-world objects. A radio's operations include setting its station and volume (typically invoked by a person's adjusting the radio's controls). A car's operations include accelerating (invoked by the driver's pressing the accelerator pedal), decelerating (invoked by the driver's pressing the brake pedal or releasing the gas pedal), turning and shifting gears. Software objects can offer operations as well—for example, a software graphics object might offer operations for drawing a circle, drawing a line, drawing a square and the like. A spreadsheet software object might offer operations like printing the spreadsheet, totaling the elements in a row or column and graphing information in the spreadsheet as a bar chart or pie chart.

We can derive many of the class operations by examining the key *verbs and verb phrases* in the requirements document. We then relate these verbs and verb phrases to classes in our system (Fig. 12.16). The verb phrases in Fig. 12.16 help us determine the operations of each class.

Class	Verbs and verb phrases
ATM	executes financial transactions
BalanceInquiry	*[none in the requirements document]*
Withdrawal	*[none in the requirements document]*
Deposit	*[none in the requirements document]*
BankDatabase	authenticates a user, retrieves an account balance, credits a deposit amount to an account, debits a withdrawal amount from an account
Account	retrieves an account balance, credits a deposit amount to an account, debits a withdrawal amount from an account
Screen	displays a message to the user
Keypad	receives numeric input from the user
CashDispenser	dispenses cash, indicates whether it contains enough cash to satisfy a withdrawal request
DepositSlot	receives a deposit envelope

Fig. 12.16 | Verbs and verb phrases for each class in the ATM system.

Modeling Operations
To identify operations, we examine the verb phrases listed for each class in Fig. 12.16. The "executes financial transactions" phrase associated with class ATM implies that class ATM instructs transactions to execute. Therefore, classes BalanceInquiry, Withdrawal and Deposit each need an operation to provide this service to the ATM. We place this operation (which we've named execute) in the third compartment of the three transaction classes in the updated class diagram of Fig. 12.17. During an ATM session, the ATM object will invoke these transaction operations as necessary.

Fig. 12.17 | Classes in the ATM system with attributes and operations.

The UML represents operations (that is, methods) by listing the operation name, followed by a comma-separated list of parameters in parentheses, a colon and the return type:

operationName(parameter1, parameter2, ..., parameterN) : return type

Each parameter in the comma-separated parameter list consists of a parameter name, followed by a colon and the parameter type:

parameterName : parameterType

For the moment, we do not list the parameters of our operations—we'll identify and model some of them shortly. For some of the operations, we do not yet know the return types, so we also omit them from the diagram. These omissions are perfectly normal at this point. As our design and implementation proceed, we'll add the remaining return types.

Authenticating a User

Figure 12.16 lists the phrase "authenticates a user" next to class BankDatabase—the database is the object that contains the account information necessary to determine whether the account number and PIN entered by a user match those of an account held at the bank. Therefore, class `BankDatabase` needs an operation that provides an authentication service to the ATM. We place the operation `authenticateUser` in the third compartment of class `BankDatabase` (Fig. 12.17). However, an object of class `Account`, not class `Bank-Database`, stores the account number and PIN that must be accessed to authenticate a user, so class `Account` must provide a service to validate a PIN obtained through user input against a PIN stored in an `Account` object. Therefore, we add a `validatePIN` operation to class `Account`. We specify a return type of `Boolean` for the `authenticateUser` and `validatePIN` operations. Each operation returns a value indicating either that the operation was successful in performing its task (i.e., a return value of `true`) or that it was not (i.e., a return value of `false`).

Other *BankDatabase* and *Account* Operations

Figure 12.16 lists several additional verb phrases for class `BankDatabase`: "retrieves an account balance," "credits a deposit amount to an account" and "debits a withdrawal amount from an account." Like "authenticates a user," these remaining phrases refer to services that the database must provide to the ATM, because the database holds all the account data used to authenticate a user and perform ATM transactions. However, objects of class `Account` actually perform the operations to which these phrases refer. Thus, we assign an operation to both class `BankDatabase` and class `Account` to correspond to each of these phrases. Recall from Section 12.3 that, because a bank account contains sensitive information, we do not allow the ATM to access accounts directly. The database acts as an intermediary between the ATM and the account data, thus preventing unauthorized access. As we'll see in Section 12.7, class `ATM` invokes the operations of class `BankDatabase`, each of which in turn invokes the operation with the same name in class `Account`.

Getting the Balances

The phrase "retrieves an account balance" suggests that classes `BankDatabase` and `Account` each need a `getBalance` operation. However, recall that we created *two* attributes in class `Account` to represent a balance—`availableBalance` and `totalBalance`. A balance inquiry requires access to *both* balance attributes so that it can display them to the user, but a withdrawal needs to check *only* the value of `availableBalance`. To allow objects in the system to obtain each balance attribute individually, we add operations `getAvailable-Balance` and `getTotalBalance` to the third compartment of classes `BankDatabase` and Account (Fig. 12.17). We specify a return type of `Double` for these operations because the balance attributes they retrieve are of type `Double`.

Crediting and Debiting an *Account*

The phrases "credits a deposit amount to an account" and "debits a withdrawal amount from an account" indicate that classes `BankDatabase` and `Account` must perform operations to update an account during a deposit and withdrawal, respectively. We therefore assign `credit` and `debit` operations to classes `BankDatabase` and `Account`. You may recall that crediting an account (as in a deposit) adds an amount only to the `totalBalance` attribute. Debiting an account (as in a withdrawal), on the other hand, subtracts the amount from *both* balance attributes. We hide these implementation details inside class `Account`. This is a good example of encapsulation and information hiding.

Deposit Confirmations Performed by Another Banking System

If this were a real ATM system, classes BankDatabase and Account would also provide a set of operations to allow another banking system to update a user's account balance after either confirming or rejecting all or part of a deposit. Operation confirmDepositAmount, for example, would add an amount to the availableBalance attribute, thus making deposited funds available for withdrawal. Operation rejectDepositAmount would subtract an amount from the totalBalance attribute to indicate that a specified amount, which had recently been deposited through the ATM and added to the totalBalance, was not found in the deposit envelope. The bank would invoke this operation after determining either that the user failed to include the correct amount of cash or that any checks did not clear (i.e., they "bounced"). While adding these operations would make our system more complete, we do *not* include them in our class diagrams or our implementation because they're beyond the scope of the case study.

Displaying Messages

Class Screen "displays a message to the user" at various times in an ATM session. All visual output occurs through the screen of the ATM. The requirements document describes many types of messages (e.g., a welcome message, an error message, a thank you message) that the screen displays to the user. The requirements document also indicates that the screen displays prompts and menus to the user. However, a prompt is really just a message describing what the user should input next, and a menu is essentially a type of prompt consisting of a series of messages (i.e., menu options) displayed consecutively. Therefore, rather than assign class Screen an individual operation to display each type of message, prompt and menu, we simply create one operation that can display any message specified by a parameter. We place this operation (displayMessage) in the third compartment of class Screen in our class diagram (Fig. 12.17). We do not worry about the parameter of this operation at this time—we model it later in this section.

Keyboard Input

From the phrase "receives numeric input from the user" listed by class Keypad in Fig. 12.16, we conclude that class Keypad should perform a getInput operation. Because the ATM's keypad, unlike a computer keyboard, contains only the numbers 0–9, we specify that this operation returns an integer value. Recall from the requirements document that in different situations the user may be required to enter a different type of number (e.g., an account number, a PIN, the number of a menu option, a deposit amount as a number of cents). Class Keypad simply obtains a numeric value for a client of the class— it does not determine whether the value meets any specific criteria. Any class that uses this operation must verify that the user entered an appropriate number in a given situation, then respond accordingly (i.e., display an error message via class Screen). [*Note:* When we implement the system, we simulate the ATM's keypad with a computer keyboard, and for simplicity we assume that the user does not enter nonnumeric input using keys on the computer keyboard that do not appear on the ATM's keypad.]

Dispensing Cash

Figure 12.16 lists "dispenses cash" for class CashDispenser. Therefore, we create operation dispenseCash and list it under class CashDispenser in Fig. 12.17. Class CashDispenser also "indicates whether it contains enough cash to satisfy a withdrawal request."

Thus, we include `isSufficientCashAvailable`, an operation that returns a value of UML type `Boolean`, in class `CashDispenser`.

Figure 12.16 also lists "receives a deposit envelope" for class `DepositSlot`. The deposit slot must indicate whether it received an envelope, so we place an operation `isEnvelopeReceived`, which returns a `Boolean` value, in the third compartment of class `DepositSlot`. [*Note:* A real hardware deposit slot would most likely send the ATM a signal to indicate that an envelope was received. We simulate this behavior, however, with an operation in class `DepositSlot` that class `ATM` can invoke to find out whether the deposit slot received an envelope.]

Class ATM

We do not list any operations for class `ATM` at this time. We're not yet aware of any services that class `ATM` provides to other classes in the system. When we implement the system with Java code, however, operations of this class, and additional operations of the other classes in the system, may emerge.

Identifying and Modeling Operation Parameters for Class BankDatabase

So far, we've not been concerned with the *parameters* of our operations—we've attempted to gain only a basic understanding of the operations of each class. Let's now take a closer look at some operation parameters. We identify an operation's parameters by examining what data the operation requires to perform its assigned task.

Consider `BankDatabase`'s `authenticateUser` operation. To authenticate a user, this operation must know the account number and PIN supplied by the user. So we specify that `authenticateUser` takes integer parameters `userAccountNumber` and `userPIN`, which the operation must compare to an `Account` object's account number and PIN in the database. We prefix these parameter names with "user" to avoid confusion between the operation's parameter names and class `Account`'s attribute names. We list these parameters in the class diagram in Fig. 12.18 that models only class `BankDatabase`. [*Note:* It's perfectly normal to model only one class. In this case, we're examining the parameters of this one class, so we omit the other classes. In class diagrams later in the case study, in which parameters are no longer the focus of our attention, we omit these parameters to save space. Remember, however, that the operations listed in these diagrams still have parameters.]

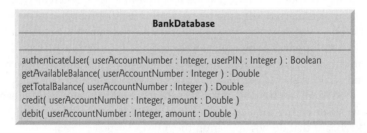

Fig. 12.18 | Class `BankDatabase` with operation parameters.

Recall that the UML models each parameter in an operation's comma-separated parameter list by listing the parameter name, followed by a colon and the parameter type (in UML notation). Figure 12.18 thus specifies that operation `authenticateUser` takes two parameters—`userAccountNumber` and `userPIN`, both of type `Integer`. When we implement the system in Java, we'll represent these parameters with `int` values.

Class `BankDatabase` operations `getAvailableBalance`, `getTotalBalance`, `credit` and `debit` also each require a `userAccountNumber` parameter to identify the account to which the database must apply the operations, so we include these parameters in the class diagram of Fig. 12.18. In addition, operations `credit` and `debit` each require a `Double` parameter `amount` to specify the amount of money to be credited or debited, respectively.

Identifying and Modeling Operation Parameters for Class ***Account***
Figure 12.19 models class `Account`'s operation parameters. Operation `validatePIN` requires only a `userPIN` parameter, which contains the user-specified PIN to be compared with the account's PIN. Like their `BankDatabase` counterparts, operations `credit` and `debit` in class `Account` each require a `Double` parameter `amount` that indicates the amount of money involved in the operation. Operations `getAvailableBalance` and `getTotal-Balance` in class `Account` require no additional data to perform their tasks. Class `Account`'s operations do *not* require an account-number parameter to distinguish between `Account`s, because these operations can be invoked only on a specific `Account` object.

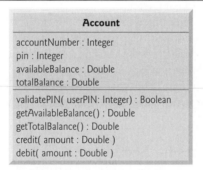

Fig. 12.19 | Class `Account` with operation parameters.

Identifying and Modeling Operation Parameters for Class ***Screen***
Figure 12.20 models class `Screen` with a parameter specified for operation `display-Message`. This operation requires only a `String` parameter `message` that indicates the text to be displayed. Recall that the parameter types listed in our class diagrams are in UML notation, so the `String` type listed in Fig. 12.20 refers to the UML type. When we implement the system in Java, we'll use the Java class `String` to represent this parameter.

Fig. 12.20 | Class `Screen` with operation parameters.

*Identifying and Modeling Operation Parameters for Class **CashDispenser***

Figure 12.21 specifies that operation dispenseCash of class CashDispenser takes a Double parameter amount to indicate the amount of cash (in dollars) to be dispensed. Operation isSufficientCashAvailable also takes a Double parameter amount to indicate the amount of cash in question.

CashDispenser
count : Integer = 500
dispenseCash(amount : Double) isSufficientCashAvailable(amount : Double) : Boolean

Fig. 12.21 | Class CashDispenser with operation parameters.

Identifying and Modeling Operation Parameters for Other Classes

We do not discuss parameters for operation execute of classes BalanceInquiry, Withdrawal and Deposit, operation getInput of class Keypad and operation isEnvelopeReceived of class DepositSlot. At this point in our design process, we cannot determine whether these operations require additional data, so we leave their parameter lists empty. Later, we may decide to add parameters.

In this section, we've determined many of the operations performed by the classes in the ATM system. We've identified the parameters and return types of some of the operations. As we continue our design process, the number of operations belonging to each class may vary—we might find that new operations are needed or that some current operations are unnecessary. We also might determine that some of our class operations need additional parameters and different return types, or that some parameters are unnecessary or require different types.

Self-Review Exercises for Section 12.6

12.14 Which of the following is *not* a behavior?
 a) reading data from a file
 b) printing output
 c) text output
 d) obtaining input from the user

12.15 If you were to add to the ATM system an operation that returns the amount attribute of class Withdrawal, how and where would you specify this operation in the class diagram of Fig. 12.17?

12.16 Describe the meaning of the following operation listing that might appear in a class diagram for an object-oriented design of a calculator:

```
add( x : Integer, y : Integer ) : Integer
```

12.7 Indicating Collaboration Among Objects

[*Note:* This section can be taught after Chapter 7.]

In this section, we concentrate on the collaborations (interactions) among objects. When two objects communicate with each other to accomplish a task, they're said to **collaborate**—objects do this by invoking one another's operations. A **collaboration** consists of an object of one class sending a **message** to an object of another class. Messages are sent in Java via method calls.

In Section 12.6, we determined many of the operations of the system's classes. Now, we concentrate on the messages that invoke these operations. To identify the collaborations in the system, we return to the requirements document in Section 12.2. Recall that this document specifies the range of activities that occur during an ATM session (e.g., authenticating a user, performing transactions). The steps used to describe how the system must perform each of these tasks are our first indication of the collaborations in our system. As we proceed through this section and Chapter 13, we may discover additional collaborations.

Identifying the Collaborations in a System

We identify the collaborations in the system by carefully reading the sections of the requirements document that specify what the ATM should do to authenticate a user and to perform each transaction type. For each action or step described, we decide which objects in our system must interact to achieve the desired result. We identify one object as the sending object and another as the receiving object. We then select one of the receiving object's operations (identified in Section 12.6) that must be invoked by the sending object to produce the proper behavior. For example, the ATM displays a welcome message when idle. We know that an object of class Screen displays a message to the user via its displayMessage operation. Thus, we decide that the system can display a welcome message by employing a collaboration between the ATM and the Screen in which the ATM sends a displayMessage message to the Screen by invoking the displayMessage operation of class Screen. [*Note:* To avoid repeating the phrase "an object of class...," we refer to an object by using its class name preceded by an article (e.g., "a," "an" or "the")—for example, "the ATM" refers to an object of class ATM.]

Figure 12.22 lists the collaborations that can be derived from the requirements document. For each sending object, we list the collaborations in the order in which they first occur during an ATM session (i.e., the order in which they're discussed in the requirements document). We list each collaboration involving a unique sender, message and recipient only once, even though the collaborations may occur at several different times throughout an ATM session. For example, the first row in Fig. 12.22 indicates that the ATM collaborates with the Screen whenever the ATM needs to display a message to the user.

Let's consider the collaborations in Fig. 12.22. Before allowing a user to perform any transactions, the ATM must prompt the user to enter an account number, then to enter a PIN. It accomplishes these tasks by sending a displayMessage message to the Screen. Both actions refer to the same collaboration between the ATM and the Screen, which is already listed in Fig. 12.22. The ATM obtains input in response to a prompt by sending a getInput message to the Keypad. Next, the ATM must determine whether the user-specified account number and PIN match those of an account in the database. It does so by sending an authenticateUser message to the BankDatabase. Recall that the BankDatabase cannot authenticate a user directly—only the user's Account (i.e., the Account that contains the account number specified by the user) can access the user's PIN on record to authenticate the user. Figure 12.22 therefore lists a collaboration in which the BankDatabase sends a validatePIN message to an Account.

After the user is authenticated, the ATM displays the main menu by sending a series of displayMessage messages to the Screen and obtains input containing a menu selection by sending a getInput message to the Keypad. We've already accounted for these collaborations, so we do not add anything to Fig. 12.22. After the user chooses a type of transaction to perform, the ATM executes the transaction by sending an execute message to an object of the appropriate transaction class (i.e., a BalanceInquiry, a Withdrawal or a Deposit). For example, if the user chooses to perform a balance inquiry, the ATM sends an execute message to a BalanceInquiry.

An object of class...	sends the message...	to an object of class...
ATM	displayMessage	Screen
	getInput	Keypad
	authenticateUser	BankDatabase
	execute	BalanceInquiry
	execute	Withdrawal
	execute	Deposit
BalanceInquiry	getAvailableBalance	BankDatabase
	getTotalBalance	BankDatabase
	displayMessage	Screen
Withdrawal	displayMessage	Screen
	getInput	Keypad
	getAvailableBalance	BankDatabase
	isSufficientCashAvailable	CashDispenser
	debit	BankDatabase
	dispenseCash	CashDispenser
Deposit	displayMessage	Screen
	getInput	Keypad
	isEnvelopeReceived	DepositSlot
	credit	BankDatabase
BankDatabase	validatePIN	Account
	getAvailableBalance	Account
	getTotalBalance	Account
	debit	Account
	credit	Account

Fig. 12.22 | Collaborations in the ATM system.

Further examination of the requirements document reveals the collaborations involved in executing each transaction type. A BalanceInquiry retrieves the amount of money available in the user's account by sending a getAvailableBalance message to the BankDatabase, which responds by sending a getAvailableBalance message to the user's Account. Similarly, the BalanceInquiry retrieves the amount of money on deposit by sending a getTotalBalance message to the BankDatabase, which sends the same message to the user's Account. To display both parts of the user's account balance at the same time, the BalanceInquiry sends a displayMessage message to the Screen.

A Withdrawal responds to an execute message by sending displayMessage messages to the Screen to display a menu of standard withdrawal amounts (i.e., $20, $40, $60,

$100, $200). The Withdrawal sends a getInput message to the Keypad to obtain the user's selection. Next, the Withdrawal determines whether the requested amount is less than or equal to the user's account balance. The Withdrawal can obtain the amount of money available by sending a getAvailableBalance message to the BankDatabase. The Withdrawal then tests whether the cash dispenser contains enough cash by sending an isSufficientCashAvailable message to the CashDispenser. A Withdrawal sends a debit message to the BankDatabase to decrease the user's account balance. The BankDatabase in turn sends the same message to the appropriate Account, which decreases both the totalBalance and the availableBalance. To dispense the requested amount of cash, the Withdrawal sends a dispenseCash message to the CashDispenser. Finally, the Withdrawal sends a displayMessage message to the Screen, instructing the user to take the cash.

A Deposit responds to an execute message first by sending a displayMessage message to the Screen to prompt the user for a deposit amount. The Deposit sends a getInput message to the Keypad to obtain the user's input. The Deposit then sends a displayMessage message to the Screen to tell the user to insert a deposit envelope. To determine whether the deposit slot received an incoming deposit envelope, the Deposit sends an isEnvelopeReceived message to the DepositSlot. The Deposit updates the user's account by sending a credit message to the BankDatabase, which subsequently sends a credit message to the user's Account. Recall that crediting funds to an Account increases the totalBalance but not the availableBalance.

Interaction Diagrams

Now that we've identified possible collaborations between our ATM system's objects, let's graphically model these interactions using the UML. The UML provides several types of **interaction diagrams** that model the behavior of a system by modeling how objects interact. The **communication diagram** emphasizes *which objects* participate in collaborations. Like the communication diagram, the **sequence diagram** shows collaborations among objects, but it emphasizes *when* messages are sent between objects *over time*.

Communication Diagrams

Figure 12.23 shows a communication diagram that models the ATM executing a BalanceInquiry. Objects are modeled in the UML as rectangles containing names in the form objectName : ClassName. In this example, which involves only one object of each type, we disregard the object name and list only a colon followed by the class name. [*Note:* Specifying each object's name in a communication diagram is recommended when modeling multiple objects of the same type.] Communicating objects are connected with solid lines, and messages are passed between objects along these lines in the direction shown by arrows. The name of the message, which appears next to the arrow, is the name of an operation (i.e., a method in Java) belonging to the receiving object—think of the name as a "service" that the receiving object provides to sending objects (its clients).

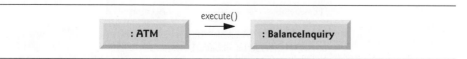

Fig. 12.23 | Communication diagram of the ATM executing a balance inquiry.

The solid filled arrow represents a message—or **synchronous call**—in the UML and a method call in Java. This arrow indicates that the flow of control is from the sending object (the ATM) to the receiving object (a BalanceInquiry). Since this is a synchronous call, the sending object can't send another message, or do anything at all, until the receiving object processes the message and returns control to the sending object. The sender just waits. In Fig. 12.23, the ATM calls BalanceInquiry method execute and can't send another message until execute has finished and returns control to the ATM. [*Note:* If this were an **asynchronous call**, represented by a stick ($\rightarrow$) arrowhead, the sending object would not have to wait for the receiving object to return control—it would continue sending additional messages immediately following the asynchronous call. Asynchronous calls are implemented in Java using a technique called multithreading, which is discussed in Chapter 23.]

Sequence of Messages in a Communication Diagram

Figure 12.24 shows a communication diagram that models the interactions among system objects when an object of class BalanceInquiry executes. We assume that the object's accountNumber attribute contains the account number of the current user. The collaborations in Fig. 12.24 begin after the ATM sends an execute message to a BalanceInquiry (i.e., the interaction modeled in Fig. 12.23). The number to the left of a message name indicates the order in which the message is passed. The **sequence of messages** in a communication diagram progresses in numerical order from least to greatest. In this diagram, the numbering starts with message 1 and ends with message 3. The BalanceInquiry first sends a getAvailableBalance message to the BankDatabase (message 1), then sends a getTotalBalance message to the BankDatabase (message 2). Within the parentheses following a message name, we can specify a comma-separated list of the names of the parameters sent with the message (i.e., arguments in a Java method call)—the BalanceInquiry passes attribute accountNumber with its messages to the BankDatabase to indicate which Account's balance information to retrieve. Recall from Fig. 12.18 that operations getAvailableBalance and getTotalBalance of class BankDatabase each require a parameter to identify an account. The BalanceInquiry next displays the availableBalance and

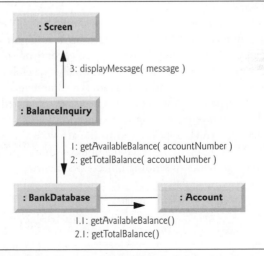

Fig. 12.24 | Communication diagram for executing a balance inquiry.

the totalBalance to the user by passing a displayMessage message to the Screen (message 3) that includes a parameter indicating the message to be displayed.

Figure 12.24 models two additional messages passing from the BankDatabase to an Account (message 1.1 and message 2.1). To provide the ATM with the *two* balances of the user's Account (as requested by messages 1 and 2), the BankDatabase must pass a getAvailableBalance and a getTotalBalance message to the user's Account. Such messages passed within the handling of another message are called **nested messages**. The UML recommends using a decimal numbering scheme to indicate nested messages. For example, message 1.1 is the first message nested in message 1—the BankDatabase passes a getAvailableBalance message during BankDatabase's processing of a message by the same name. [*Note:* If the BankDatabase needed to pass a second nested message while processing message 1, the second message would be numbered 1.2.] A message may be passed only when *all* the nested messages from the previous message have been passed. For example, the BalanceInquiry passes message 3 only after messages 2 and 2.1 have been passed, in that order.

The nested numbering scheme used in communication diagrams helps clarify precisely when and in what context each message is passed. For example, if we numbered the messages in Fig. 12.24 using a flat numbering scheme (i.e., 1, 2, 3, 4, 5), someone looking at the diagram might not be able to determine that BankDatabase passes the getAvailableBalance message (message 1.1) to an Account *during* the BankDatabase's processing of message 1, as opposed to *after* completing the processing of message 1. The nested decimal numbers make it clear that the second getAvailableBalance message (message 1.1) is passed to an Account within the handling of the first getAvailableBalance message (message 1) by the BankDatabase.

Sequence Diagrams

Communication diagrams emphasize the participants in collaborations, but model their timing a bit awkwardly. A sequence diagram helps model the timing of collaborations more clearly. Figure 12.25 shows a sequence diagram modeling the sequence of interactions that occur when a Withdrawal executes. The dotted line extending down from an object's rectangle is that object's **lifeline**, which represents the progression of time. Actions occur along an object's lifeline in chronological order from top to bottom—an action near the top happens before one near the bottom.

Message passing in sequence diagrams is similar to message passing in communication diagrams. A solid arrow with a filled arrowhead extending from the sending object to the receiving object represents a message between two objects. The arrowhead points to an activation on the receiving object's lifeline. An **activation**, shown as a thin vertical rectangle, indicates that an object is executing. When an object returns control, a return message, represented as a dashed line with a stick (⇢) arrowhead, extends from the activation of the object returning control to the activation of the object that initially sent the message. To eliminate clutter, we omit the return-message arrows—the UML allows this practice to make diagrams more readable. Like communication diagrams, sequence diagrams can indicate message parameters between the parentheses following a message name.

The sequence of messages in Fig. 12.25 begins when a Withdrawal prompts the user to choose a withdrawal amount by sending a displayMessage message to the Screen. The Withdrawal then sends a getInput message to the Keypad, which obtains input from the user. We've already modeled the control logic involved in a Withdrawal in the activity diagram of Fig. 12.15, so we do not show this logic in the sequence diagram of Fig. 12.25.

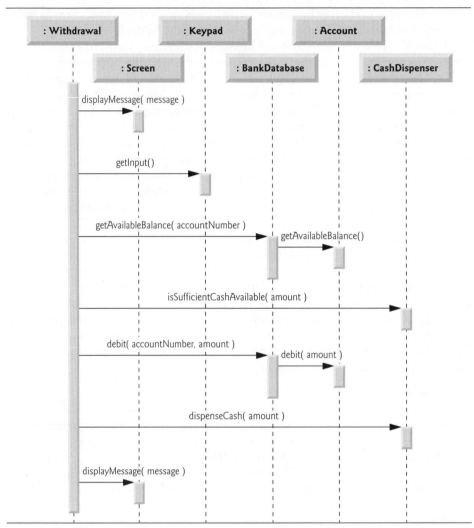

Fig. 12.25 | Sequence diagram that models a Withdrawal executing.

Instead, we model the best-case scenario in which the balance of the user's account is greater than or equal to the chosen withdrawal amount, and the cash dispenser contains a sufficient amount of cash to satisfy the request. You can model control logic in a sequence diagram with UML frames (which are not covered in this case study). For a quick overview of UML frames, visit www.agilemodeling.com/style/frame.htm.

After obtaining a withdrawal amount, the Withdrawal sends a getAvailableBalance message to the BankDatabase, which in turn sends a getAvailableBalance message to the user's Account. Assuming that the user's account has enough money available to permit the transaction, the Withdrawal next sends an isSufficientCashAvailable message to the CashDispenser. Assuming that there's enough cash available, the Withdrawal decreases the balance of the user's account (i.e., both the totalBalance and the availableBalance) by sending a debit message to the BankDatabase. The BankDatabase responds by sending a debit message to the user's Account. Finally, the Withdrawal sends a dispenseCash message to the CashDispenser and a displayMessage message to the Screen, telling the user to remove the cash from the machine.

We've identified the collaborations among objects in the ATM system and modeled some of them using UML interaction diagrams—both communication diagrams and sequence diagrams. In Section 13.2, we enhance the structure of our model to complete a preliminary object-oriented design, then we begin implementing the ATM system in Java.

Self-Review Exercises for Section 12.7

12.17 A(n) _____ consists of an object of one class sending a message to an object of another class.

   a) association   b) aggregation
   c) collaboration   d) composition

12.18 Which form of interaction diagram emphasizes *what* collaborations occur? Which form emphasizes *when* collaborations occur?

12.19 Create a sequence diagram that models the interactions among objects in the ATM system that occur when a Deposit executes successfully, and explain the sequence of messages modeled by the diagram.

12.8 Wrap-Up

In this chapter, you learned how to work from a detailed requirements document to develop an object-oriented design. You worked with six popular types of UML diagrams to graphically model an object-oriented automated teller machine software system. In Chapter 13, we tune the design using inheritance, then completely implement the design in a 673-line Java application.

Answers to Self-Review Exercises

12.1 Figure 12.26 contains a use case diagram for a modified version of our ATM system that also allows users to transfer money between accounts.

12.2 b.

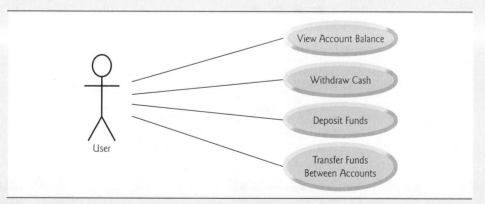

Fig. 12.26 | Use case diagram for a modified version of our ATM system that also allows users to transfer money between accounts.

12.3 d.

12.4 [*Note:* Answers may vary.] Figure 12.27 presents a class diagram that shows some of the composition relationships of a class Car.

12.5 c. [*Note:* In a computer network, this relationship could be many-to-many.]

12.6 True.

12.7 Figure 12.28 presents a class diagram for the ATM including class Deposit instead of class Withdrawal (as in Fig. 12.10). Deposit does not access CashDispenser, but does access DepositSlot.

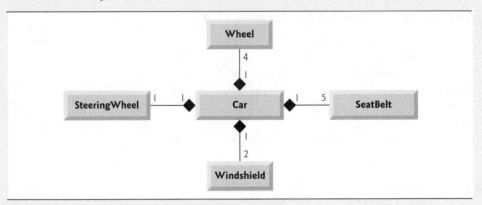

Fig. 12.27 | Class diagram showing composition relationships of a class Car.

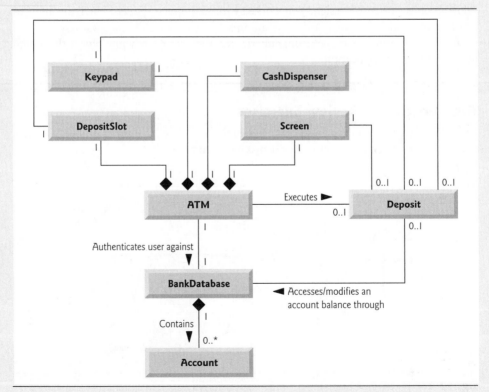

Fig. 12.28 | Class diagram for the ATM system model including class Deposit.

12.8 b.

12.9 c. Fly is an operation or behavior of an airplane, not an attribute.

12.10 This indicates that count is an Integer with an initial value of 500. This attribute keeps track of the number of bills available in the CashDispenser at any given time.

12.11 False. State diagrams model some of the behavior of a system.

12.12 a.

12.13 Figure 12.29 models the actions that occur after the user chooses the deposit option from the main menu and before the ATM returns the user to the main menu. Recall that part of receiving a deposit amount from the user involves converting an integer number of cents to a dollar amount. Also recall that crediting a deposit amount to an account increases only the totalBalance attribute of the user's Account object. The bank updates the availableBalance attribute of the user's Account object only after confirming the amount of cash in the deposit envelope and after the enclosed checks clear—this occurs independently of the ATM system.

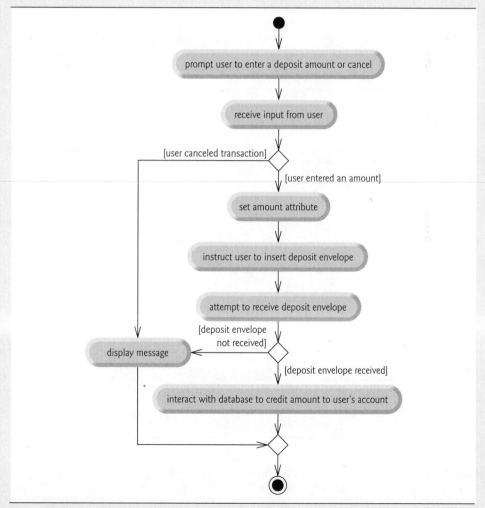

Fig. 12.29 | Activity diagram for a deposit transaction.

12.14 c.

12.15 To specify an operation that retrieves the amount attribute of class Withdrawal, the following operation listing would be placed in the operation (i.e., third) compartment of class Withdrawal:

```
getAmount( ) : Double
```

12.16 This operation listing indicates an operation named add that takes integers x and y as parameters and returns an integer value.

12.17 c.

12.18 Communication diagrams emphasize *what* collaborations occur. Sequence diagrams emphasize *when* collaborations occur.

12.19 Figure 12.30 presents a sequence diagram that models the interactions between objects in the ATM system that occur when a Deposit executes successfully. A Deposit first sends a displayMessage message to the Screen to ask the user to enter a deposit amount. Next the Deposit sends a getInput message to the Keypad to receive input from the user. The Deposit then instructs the user to enter a deposit envelope by sending a displayMessage message to the Screen. The Deposit next sends an isEnvelopeReceived message to the DepositSlot to confirm that the deposit envelope has been received by the ATM. Finally, the Deposit increases the totalBalance attribute (but not the availableBalance attribute) of the user's Account by sending a credit message to the BankDatabase. The BankDatabase responds by sending the same message to the user's Account.

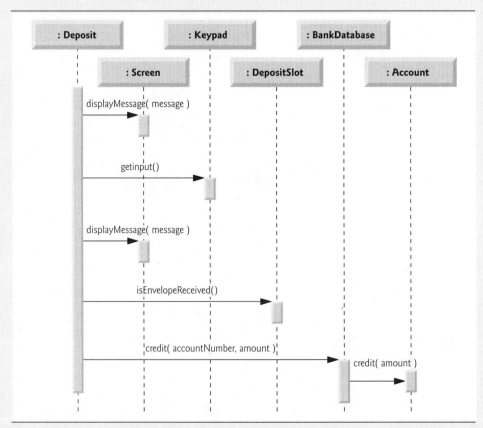

Fig. 12.30 | Sequence diagram that models a Deposit executing.

13

ATM Case Study Part 2: Implementing an Object-Oriented Design

You can't work in the abstract.
—I. M. Pei

To generalize means to think.
—Georg Wilhelm Friedrich Hegel

We are all gifted. That is our inheritance.
—Ethel Waters

Let me walk through the fields of paper touching with my wand dry stems and stunted butterflies...
—Denise Levertov

Objectives

In this chapter you'll learn:

- Incorporate inheritance into the design of the ATM.
- Incorporate polymorphism into the design of the ATM.
- Fully implement in Java the UML-based object-oriented design of the ATM software.
- Study a detailed code walkthrough of the ATM software system that explains the implementation issues.

13.1 Introduction

In Chapter 12, we developed an object-oriented design for our ATM system. We now implement our object-oriented design in Java. In Section 13.2, we show how to convert class diagrams to Java code. In Section 13.3, we tune the design with inheritance and polymorphism. Then we present a full Java code implementation of the ATM software in Section 13.4. The code is carefully commented and the discussions of the implementation are thorough and precise. Studying this application provides the opportunity for you to see a more substantial application of the kind you're likely to encounter in industry.

13.2 Starting to Program the Classes of the ATM System

Visibility

We now apply access modifiers to the members of our classes. We've introduced access modifiers public and private. Access modifiers determine the **visibility** or accessibility of an object's attributes and methods to other objects. Before we can begin implementing our design, we must consider which attributes and methods of our classes should be public and which should be private.

We've observed that attributes normally should be private and that methods invoked by clients of a given class should be public. Methods that are called as "utility methods" only by other methods of the same class normally should be private. The UML employs **visibility markers** for modeling the visibility of attributes and operations. Public visibility is indicated by placing a plus sign (+) before an operation or an attribute, whereas a minus sign (–) indicates private visibility. Figure 13.1 shows our updated class diagram with visibility markers included. [*Note:* We do not include any operation parameters in Fig. 13.1—this is perfectly normal. Adding visibility markers does not affect the parameters already modeled in the class diagrams of Figs. 12.17–12.21.]

Navigability

Before we begin implementing our design in Java, we introduce an additional UML notation. The class diagram in Fig. 13.2 further refines the relationships among classes in the ATM system by adding navigability arrows to the association lines. **Navigability arrows** (represented as arrows with stick (⤞) arrowheads in the class diagram) indicate in the

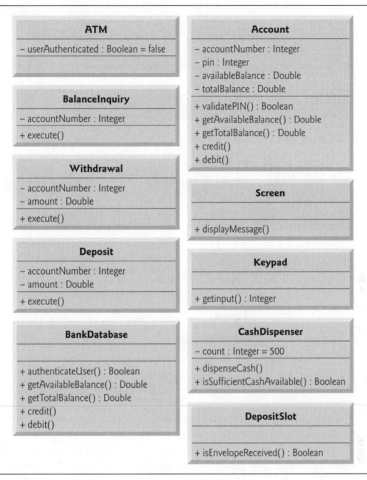

Fig. 13.1 | Class diagram with visibility markers.

direction which an association can be traversed. When implementing a system designed using the UML, you use navigability arrows to determine which objects need references to other objects. For example, the navigability arrow pointing from class ATM to class BankDatabase indicates that we can navigate from the former to the latter, thereby enabling the ATM to invoke the BankDatabase's operations. However, since Fig. 13.2 does *not* contain a navigability arrow pointing from class BankDatabase to class ATM, the BankDatabase cannot access the ATM's operations. Associations in a class diagram that have navigability arrows at both ends or have none at all indicate **bidirectional navigability**—navigation can proceed in either direction across the association.

Like the class diagram of Fig. 12.10, that of Fig. 13.2 omits classes BalanceInquiry and Deposit for simplicity. The navigability of the associations in which these classes participate closely parallels that of class Withdrawal. Recall from Section 12.3 that BalanceInquiry has an association with class Screen. We can navigate from class BalanceInquiry to class Screen along this association, but we cannot navigate from class Screen to class BalanceInquiry. Thus, if we were to model class BalanceInquiry in Fig. 13.2, we would place a navigability

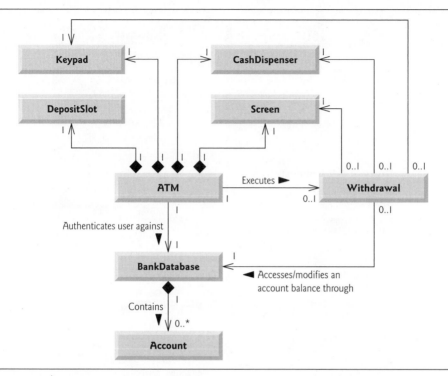

Fig. 13.2 | Class diagram with navigability arrows.

arrow at class Screen's end of this association. Also recall that class Deposit associates with classes Screen, Keypad and DepositSlot. We can navigate from class Deposit to each of these classes, but *not* vice versa. We therefore would place navigability arrows at the Screen, Keypad and DepositSlot ends of these associations. [*Note:* We model these additional classes and associations in our final class diagram in Section 13.3, after we've simplified the structure of our system by incorporating the object-oriented concept of inheritance.]

Implementing the ATM System from Its UML Design

We're now ready to begin implementing the ATM system. We first convert the classes in the diagrams of Fig. 13.1 and Fig. 13.2 into Java code. The code will represent the "skeleton" of the system. In Section 13.3, we modify the code to incorporate inheritance. In Section 13.4, we present the complete working Java code for our model.

As an example, we develop the code from our design of class Withdrawal in Fig. 13.1. We use this figure to determine the attributes and operations of the class. We use the UML model in Fig. 13.2 to determine the associations among classes. We follow the following four guidelines for each class:

1. Use the name located in the first compartment to declare the class as a public class with an empty no-argument constructor. We include this constructor simply as a placeholder to remind us that *most classes will indeed need custom constructors*. In Section 13.4, when we complete a working version of this class, we'll add arguments and code the body of the constructor as needed. For example, class

Withdrawal yields the code in Fig. 13.3. If we find that the class's instance variables require only default initialization, then we'll remove the empty no-argument constructor because it's unnecessary.

```java
1    // Class Withdrawal represents an ATM withdrawal transaction
2    public class Withdrawal
3    {
4       // no-argument constructor
5       public Withdrawal()
6       {
7       } // end no-argument Withdrawal constructor
8    } // end class Withdrawal
```

Fig. 13.3 | Java code for class Withdrawal based on Figs. 13.1–13.2.

2. Use the attributes located in the second compartment to declare the instance variables. For example, the private attributes accountNumber and amount of class Withdrawal yield the code in Fig. 13.4. [*Note:* The constructor of the complete working version of this class will assign values to these attributes.]

```java
1    // Class Withdrawal represents an ATM withdrawal transaction
2    public class Withdrawal
3    {
4       // attributes
5       private int accountNumber; // account to withdraw funds from
6       private double amount; // amount to withdraw
7
8       // no-argument constructor
9       public Withdrawal()
10      {
11      } // end no-argument Withdrawal constructor
12   } // end class Withdrawal
```

Fig. 13.4 | Java code for class Withdrawal based on Figs. 13.1–13.2.

3. Use the associations described in the class diagram to declare the references to other objects. For example, according to Fig. 13.2, Withdrawal can access one object of class Screen, one object of class Keypad, one object of class CashDispenser and one object of class BankDatabase. This yields the code in Fig. 13.5. [*Note:* The constructor of the complete working version of this class will initialize these instance variables with references to actual objects.]

4. Use the operations located in the third compartment of Fig. 13.1 to declare the shells of the methods. If we have not yet specified a return type for an operation, we declare the method with return type void. Refer to the class diagrams of Figs. 12.17–12.21 to declare any necessary parameters. For example, adding the public operation execute in class Withdrawal, which has an empty parameter list, yields the code in Fig. 13.6. [*Note:* We code the bodies of methods when we implement the complete system in Section 13.4.]

This concludes our discussion of the basics of generating classes from UML diagrams.

```
1   // Class Withdrawal represents an ATM withdrawal transaction
2   public class Withdrawal
3   {
4      // attributes
5      private int accountNumber; // account to withdraw funds from
6      private double amount; // amount to withdraw
7
8      // refere
9   nces to associated objects
10     private Screen screen; // ATM's screen
11     private Keypad keypad; // ATM's keypad
12     private CashDispenser cashDispenser; // ATM's cash dispenser
13     private BankDatabase bankDatabase; // account info database
14
15     // no-argument constructor
16     public Withdrawal()
17     {
18     } // end no-argument Withdrawal constructor
19  } // end class Withdrawal
```

Fig. 13.5 | Java code for class `Withdrawal` based on Figs. 13.1–13.2.

```
1   // Class Withdrawal represents an ATM withdrawal transaction
2   public class Withdrawal
3   {
4      // attributes
5      private int accountNumber; // account to withdraw funds from
6      private double amount; // amount to withdraw
7
8      // references to associated objects
9      private Screen screen; // ATM's screen
10     private Keypad keypad; // ATM's keypad
11     private CashDispenser cashDispenser; // ATM's cash dispenser
12     private BankDatabase bankDatabase; // account info database
13
14     // no-argument constructor
15     public Withdrawal()
16     {
17     } // end no-argument Withdrawal constructor
18
19     // operations
20     public void execute()
21     {
22     } // end method execute
23  } // end class Withdrawal
```

Fig. 13.6 | Java code for class `Withdrawal` based on Figs. 13.1–13.2.

Self-Review Exercises for Section 13.2

13.1   State whether the following statement is *true* or *false*, and if *false*, explain why: If an attribute of a class is marked with a minus sign (-) in a class diagram, the attribute is not directly accessible outside the class.

13.2   In Fig. 13.2, the association between the ATM and the Screen indicates that:
  a) we can navigate from the Screen to the ATM
  b) we can navigate from the ATM to the Screen
  c) Both (a) and (b); the association is bidirectional
  d) None of the above

13.3   Write Java code to begin implementing the design for class Keypad.

13.3 Incorporating Inheritance and Polymorphism into the ATM System

We now revisit our ATM system design to see how it might benefit from inheritance. To apply inheritance, we first look for *commonality among classes* in the system. We create an inheritance hierarchy to model similar (yet not identical) classes in a more elegant and efficient manner. We then modify our class diagram to incorporate the new inheritance relationships. Finally, we demonstrate how our updated design is translated into Java code.

In Section 12.3, we encountered the problem of representing a financial transaction in the system. Rather than create one class to represent all transaction types, we decided to create three individual transaction classes—BalanceInquiry, Withdrawal and Deposit—to represent the transactions that the ATM system can perform. Figure 13.7 shows the attributes and operations of classes BalanceInquiry, Withdrawal and Deposit. These classes have one attribute (accountNumber) and one operation (execute) in common. Each class requires attribute accountNumber to specify the account to which the transaction applies. Each class contains operation execute, which the ATM invokes to perform the transaction. Clearly, BalanceInquiry, Withdrawal and Deposit represent *types of* transactions. Figure 13.7 reveals commonality among the transaction classes, so using inheritance to factor out the common features seems appropriate for designing classes BalanceInquiry, Withdrawal and Deposit. We place the common functionality in a superclass, Transaction, that classes BalanceInquiry, Withdrawal and Deposit extend.

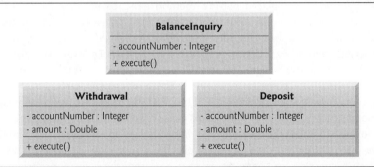

Fig. 13.7 | Attributes and operations of BalanceInquiry, Withdrawal and Deposit.

Generalization

The UML specifies a relationship called a **generalization** to model inheritance. Figure 13.8 is the class diagram that models the generalization of superclass Transaction and subclasses BalanceInquiry, Withdrawal and Deposit. The arrows with triangular hollow arrowheads indicate that classes BalanceInquiry, Withdrawal and Deposit extend class Transaction. Class Transaction is said to be a generalization of classes BalanceInquiry, Withdrawal and Deposit. Class BalanceInquiry, Withdrawal and Deposit are said to be **specializations** of class Transaction.

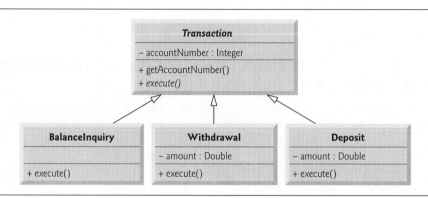

Fig. 13.8 | Class diagram modeling generalization of superclass Transaction and subclasses BalanceInquiry, Withdrawal and Deposit. Abstract class names (e.g., Transaction) and method names (e.g., execute in class Transaction) appear in italics.

Classes BalanceInquiry, Withdrawal and Deposit share integer attribute account-Number, so we *factor out* this *common attribute* and place it in superclass Transaction. We no longer list accountNumber in the second compartment of each subclass, because the three subclasses *inherit* this attribute from Transaction. Recall, however, that subclasses cannot directly access private attributes of a superclass. We therefore include public method getAccountNumber in class Transaction. Each subclass will inherit this method, enabling the subclass to access its accountNumber as needed to execute a transaction.

According to Fig. 13.7, classes BalanceInquiry, Withdrawal and Deposit also share operation execute, so we placed public method execute in superclass Transaction. However, it does *not* make sense to implement execute in class Transaction, because the functionality that this method provides *depends on the type of the actual transaction*. We therefore declare method execute as abstract in superclass Transaction. Any class that contains at least one abstract method must also be declared abstract. This forces any subclass of Transaction that must be a *concrete* class (i.e., BalanceInquiry, Withdrawal and Deposit) to implement method execute. The UML requires that we place abstract class names (and abstract methods) in italics, so Transaction and its method execute appear in italics in Fig. 13.8. Method execute is *not* italicized in subclasses BalanceInquiry, Withdrawal and Deposit. Each subclass overrides superclass Transaction's execute method with a concrete implementation that performs the steps appropriate for completing that type of transaction. Figure 13.8 includes operation execute in the third compartment of classes BalanceInquiry, Withdrawal and Deposit, because each class has a different concrete implementation of the overridden method.

Processing Transactions Polymorphically
Polymorphism provides the ATM with an elegant way to execute all transactions "in the general." For example, suppose a user chooses to perform a balance inquiry. The ATM sets a

Transaction reference to a new BalanceInquiry object. When the ATM uses its Transaction reference to invoke method execute, BalanceInquiry's version of execute is called.

This *polymorphic* approach also makes the system easily *extensible*. Should we wish to create a new transaction type (e.g., funds transfer or bill payment), we would just create an additional Transaction subclass that overrides the execute method with a version of the method appropriate for executing the new transaction type. We would need to make only minimal changes to the system code to allow users to choose the new transaction type from the main menu and for the ATM to instantiate and execute objects of the new subclass. The ATM could execute transactions of the new type using the current code, because it executes all transactions *polymorphically* using a general Transaction reference.

Recall that an abstract class like Transaction is one for which you never intend to instantiate objects. An abstract class simply declares common attributes and behaviors of its subclasses in an inheritance hierarchy. Class Transaction defines the concept of what it means to be a transaction that has an account number and executes. You may wonder why we bother to include abstract method execute in class Transaction if it lacks a concrete implementation. Conceptually, we include it because it corresponds to the defining behavior of *all* transactions—executing. Technically, we must include method execute in superclass Transaction so that the ATM (or any other class) can polymorphically invoke each subclass's *overridden* version of this method through a Transaction reference. Also, from a software engineering perspective, including an abstract method in a superclass forces the implementor of the subclasses to override that method with concrete implementations in the subclasses, or else the subclasses, too, will be abstract, preventing objects of those subclasses from being instantiated.

Additional Attribute of Classes Withdrawal *and* Deposit

Subclasses BalanceInquiry, Withdrawal and Deposit inherit attribute accountNumber from superclass Transaction, but classes Withdrawal and Deposit contain the additional attribute amount that distinguishes them from class BalanceInquiry. Classes Withdrawal and Deposit require this additional attribute to store the amount of money that the user wishes to withdraw or deposit. Class BalanceInquiry has no need for such an attribute and requires only an account number to execute. Even though two of the three Transaction subclasses share this attribute, we do *not* place it in superclass Transaction—we place only features *common* to all the subclasses in the superclass, otherwise subclasses could inherit attributes (and methods) that they do not need and should not have.

Class Diagram with Transaction *Hierarchy Incorporated*

Figure 13.9 presents an updated class diagram of our model that incorporates inheritance and introduces class Transaction. We model an association between class ATM and class Transaction to show that the ATM, at any given moment, either is executing a transaction or is not (i.e., zero or one objects of type Transaction exist in the system at a time). Because a Withdrawal is a type of Transaction, we no longer draw an association line directly between class ATM and class Withdrawal. Subclass Withdrawal inherits superclass Transaction's association with class ATM. Subclasses BalanceInquiry and Deposit inherit this association, too, so the previously omitted associations between ATM and classes BalanceInquiry and Deposit no longer exist either.

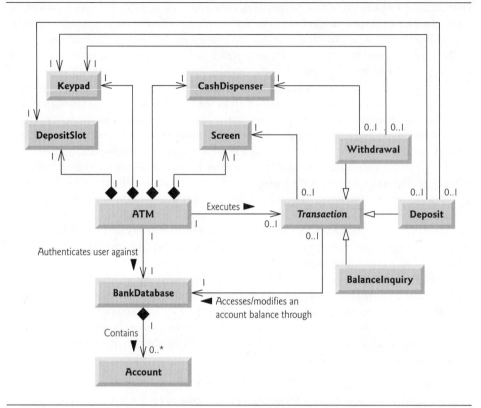

Fig. 13.9 | Class diagram of the ATM system (incorporating inheritance). The abstract class name Transaction appears in italics.

We also add an association between class Transaction and the BankDatabase (Fig. 13.9). All Transactions require a reference to the BankDatabase so they can access and modify account information. Because each Transaction subclass inherits this reference, we no longer model the association between class Withdrawal and the BankDatabase. Similarly, the previously omitted associations between the BankDatabase and classes BalanceInquiry and Deposit no longer exist.

We show an association between class Transaction and the Screen. All Transactions display output to the user via the Screen. Thus, we no longer include the association previously modeled between Withdrawal and the Screen, although Withdrawal still participates in associations with the CashDispenser and the Keypad. Our class diagram incorporating inheritance also models Deposit and BalanceInquiry. We show associations between Deposit and both the DepositSlot and the Keypad. Class BalanceInquiry takes part in no associations other than those inherited from class Transaction—a BalanceInquiry needs to interact only with the BankDatabase and with the Screen.

Figure 13.1 showed attributes and operations with visibility markers. Now in Fig. 13.10 we present a modified class diagram that incorporates inheritance. This abbreviated diagram does not show inheritance relationships, but instead shows the attributes and methods after we've employed inheritance in our system. To save space, as we did in

Fig. 12.12, we do not include those attributes shown by associations in Fig. 13.9—we do, however, include them in the Java implementation in Section 13.4. We also omit all operation parameters, as we did in Fig. 13.1—incorporating inheritance does not affect the parameters already modeled in Figs. 12.17–12.21.

Software Engineering Observation 13.1

A complete class diagram shows all the associations among classes and all the attributes and operations for each class. When the number of class attributes, methods and associations is substantial (as in Figs. 13.9 and 13.10), a good practice that promotes readability is to divide this information between two class diagrams—one focusing on associations and the other on attributes and methods.

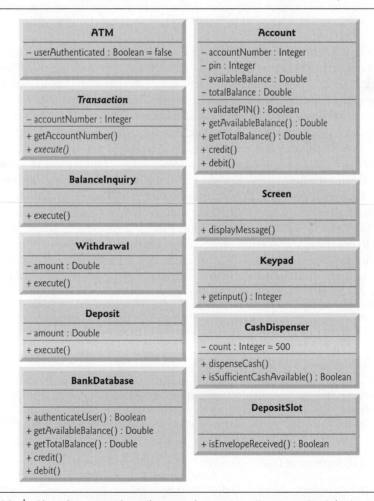

Fig. 13.10 | Class diagram with attributes and operations (incorporating inheritance). The abstract class name `Transaction` and the abstract method name `execute` in class `Transaction` appear in italics.

Implementing the ATM System Design (Incorporating Inheritance)
In Section 13.2, we began implementing the ATM system design in Java code. We now modify our implementation to incorporate inheritance, using class Withdrawal as an example.

1. If a class A is a generalization of class B, then class B extends class A in the class declaration. For example, abstract superclass Transaction is a generalization of class Withdrawal. Figure 13.11 shows the declaration of class Withdrawal.

```
1   // Class Withdrawal represents an ATM withdrawal transaction
2   public class Withdrawal extends Transaction
3   {
4   } // end class Withdrawal
```

Fig. 13.11 | Java code for shell of class Withdrawal.

2. If class A is an abstract class and class B is a subclass of class A, then class B must implement the *abstract* methods of class A if class B is to be a *concrete* class. For example, class Transaction contains abstract method execute, so class Withdrawal must implement this method if we want to instantiate a Withdrawal object. Figure 13.12 is the Java code for class Withdrawal from Fig. 13.9 and Fig. 13.10. Class Withdrawal inherits field accountNumber from superclass Transaction, so Withdrawal does not need to declare this field. Class Withdrawal also inherits references to the Screen and the BankDatabase from its superclass Transaction, so we do not include these references in our code. Figure 13.10 specifies attribute amount and operation execute for class Withdrawal. Line 6 of Fig. 13.12 declares a field for attribute amount. Lines 16–19 declare the shell of a method for operation execute. Recall that subclass Withdrawal must provide a concrete implementation of the abstract method execute in superclass Transaction. The keypad and cashDispenser references (lines 7–8) are fields derived from Withdrawal's associations in Fig. 13.9. The constructor in the complete working version of this class will initialize these references to actual objects.

```
1   // Withdrawal.java
2   // Generated using the class diagrams in Fig. 13.9 and Fig. 13.10
3   public class Withdrawal extends Transaction
4   {
5       // attributes
6       private double amount; // amount to withdraw
7       private Keypad keypad; // reference to keypad
8       private CashDispenser cashDispenser; // reference to cash dispenser
9
10      // no-argument constructor
11      public Withdrawal()
12      {
13      } // end no-argument Withdrawal constructor
14
```

Fig. 13.12 | Java code for class Withdrawal based on Figs. 13.9 and 13.10. (Part 1 of 2.)

```
15          // method overriding execute
16          @Override
17          public void execute()
18          {
19          } // end method execute
20      } // end class Withdrawal
```

Fig. 13.12 | Java code for class `Withdrawal` based on Figs. 13.9 and 13.10. (Part 2 of 2.)

 Software Engineering Observation 13.2

Several UML modeling tools can convert UML-based designs into Java code, speeding the implementation process considerably. For more information on these tools, visit our UML Resource Center at www.deitel.com/UML/.

Congratulations on completing the case study's design portion! We implement the ATM system in Java code in Section 13.4. We recommend that you carefully read the code and its description. The code is abundantly commented and precisely follows the design with which you're now familiar. The accompanying description is carefully written to guide your understanding of the implementation based on the UML design. Mastering this code is a wonderful culminating accomplishment after studying Sections 12.2–12.7 and 13.2–13.3.

Self-Review Exercises for Section 13.3

13.4 The UML uses an arrow with a _____ to indicate a generalization relationship.
a) solid filled arrowhead
b) triangular hollow arrowhead
c) diamond-shaped hollow arrowhead
d) stick arrowhead

13.5 State whether the following statement is *true* or *false*, and if *false*, explain why: The UML requires that we underline abstract class names and method names.

13.6 Write Java code to begin implementing the design for class `Transaction` specified in Figs. 13.9 and 13.10. Be sure to include `private` reference-type attributes based on class `Transaction`'s associations. Also be sure to include `public` *get* methods that provide access to any of these `private` attributes that the subclasses require to perform their tasks.

13.4 ATM Case Study Implementation

This section contains the complete working 673-line implementation of the ATM system. We consider the classes in the order in which we identified them in Section 12.3—ATM, Screen, Keypad, CashDispenser, DepositSlot, Account, BankDatabase, Transaction, BalanceInquiry, Withdrawal and Deposit.

We apply the guidelines discussed in Sections 13.2–13.3 to code these classes based on how we modeled them in the UML class diagrams of Figs. 13.9 and 13.10. To develop the bodies of class methods, we refer to the activity diagrams in Section 12.5 and the communication and sequence diagrams presented in Section 12.7. Our ATM design does *not* specify all the program logic and may not specify all the attributes and operations required to complete the ATM implementation. This is a *normal* part of the object-oriented design process. As we implement the system, we complete the program logic and add attributes and behaviors as necessary to construct the ATM system specified by the requirements document in Section 12.2.

We conclude the discussion by presenting a Java application (ATMCaseStudy) that starts the ATM and puts the other classes in the system in use. Recall that we're developing a first version of the ATM system that runs on a personal computer and uses the computer's keyboard and monitor to approximate the ATM's keypad and screen. We also simulate only the actions of the ATM's cash dispenser and deposit slot. We attempt to implement the system, however, so that real hardware versions of these devices could be integrated without significant changes in the code.

13.4.1 Class ATM

Class ATM (Fig. 13.13) represents the ATM as a whole. Lines 6–12 implement the class's attributes. We determine all but one of these attributes from the UML class diagrams of Figs. 13.9 and 13.10. We implement the UML Boolean attribute userAuthenticated in Fig. 13.10 as a boolean in Java (line 6). Line 7 declares an attribute not found in our UML design—an int attribute currentAccountNumber that keeps track of the account number of the current authenticated user. We'll soon see how the class uses this attribute. Lines 8–12 declare reference-type attributes corresponding to the ATM class's associations modeled in the class diagram of Fig. 13.9. These attributes allow the ATM to access its parts (i.e., its Screen, Keypad, CashDispenser and DepositSlot) and interact with the bank's account-information database (i.e., a BankDatabase object).

```java
1   // ATM.java
2   // Represents an automated teller machine
3
4   public class ATM
5   {
6      private boolean userAuthenticated; // whether user is authenticated
7      private int currentAccountNumber; // current user's account number
8      private Screen screen; // ATM's screen
9      private Keypad keypad; // ATM's keypad
10     private CashDispenser cashDispenser; // ATM's cash dispenser
11     private DepositSlot depositSlot; // ATM's deposit slot
12     private BankDatabase bankDatabase; // account information database
13
14     // constants corresponding to main menu options
15     private static final int BALANCE_INQUIRY = 1;
16     private static final int WITHDRAWAL = 2;
17     private static final int DEPOSIT = 3;
18     private static final int EXIT = 4;
19
20     // no-argument ATM constructor initializes instance variables
21     public ATM()
22     {
23        userAuthenticated = false; // user is not authenticated to start
24        currentAccountNumber = 0; // no current account number to start
25        screen = new Screen(); // create screen
```

Fig. 13.13 | Class ATM represents the ATM. (Part 1 of 4.)

```
26          keypad = new Keypad(); // create keypad
27          cashDispenser = new CashDispenser(); // create cash dispenser
28          depositSlot = new DepositSlot(); // create deposit slot
29          bankDatabase = new BankDatabase(); // create acct info database
30       } // end no-argument ATM constructor
31
32       // start ATM
33       public void run()
34       {
35          // welcome and authenticate user; perform transactions
36          while ( true )
37          {
38             // loop while user is not yet authenticated
39             while ( !userAuthenticated )
40             {
41                screen.displayMessageLine( "\nWelcome!" );
42                authenticateUser(); // authenticate user
43             } // end while
44
45             performTransactions(); // user is now authenticated
46             userAuthenticated = false; // reset before next ATM session
47             currentAccountNumber = 0; // reset before next ATM session
48             screen.displayMessageLine( "\nThank you! Goodbye!" );
49          } // end while
50       } // end method run
51
52       // attempts to authenticate user against database
53       private void authenticateUser()
54       {
55          screen.displayMessage( "\nPlease enter your account number: " );
56          int accountNumber = keypad.getInput(); // input account number
57          screen.displayMessage( "\nEnter your PIN: " ); // prompt for PIN
58          int pin = keypad.getInput(); // input PIN
59
60          // set userAuthenticated to boolean value returned by database
61          userAuthenticated =
62             bankDatabase.authenticateUser( accountNumber, pin );
63
64          // check whether authentication succeeded
65          if ( userAuthenticated )
66          {
67             currentAccountNumber = accountNumber; // save user's account #
68          } // end if
69          else
70             screen.displayMessageLine(
71                "Invalid account number or PIN. Please try again." );
72       } // end method authenticateUser
73
74       // display the main menu and perform transactions
75       private void performTransactions()
76       {
77          // local variable to store transaction currently being processed
78          Transaction currentTransaction = null;
```

Fig. 13.13 | Class ATM represents the ATM. (Part 2 of 4.)

```
79
80          boolean userExited = false; // user has not chosen to exit
81
82          // loop while user has not chosen option to exit system
83          while ( !userExited )
84          {
85             // show main menu and get user selection
86             int mainMenuSelection = displayMainMenu();
87
88             // decide how to proceed based on user's menu selection
89             switch ( mainMenuSelection )
90             {
91                // user chose to perform one of three transaction types
92                case BALANCE_INQUIRY:
93                case WITHDRAWAL:
94                case DEPOSIT:
95
96                   // initialize as new object of chosen type
97                   currentTransaction =
98                      createTransaction( mainMenuSelection );
99
100                  currentTransaction.execute(); // execute transaction
101                  break;
102               case EXIT: // user chose to terminate session
103                  screen.displayMessageLine( "\nExiting the system..." );
104                  userExited = true; // this ATM session should end
105                  break;
106               default: // user did not enter an integer from 1-4
107                  screen.displayMessageLine(
108                     "\nYou did not enter a valid selection. Try again." );
109                  break;
110            } // end switch
111         } // end while
112      } // end method performTransactions
113
114      // display the main menu and return an input selection
115      private int displayMainMenu()
116      {
117         screen.displayMessageLine( "\nMain menu:" );
118         screen.displayMessageLine( "1 - View my balance" );
119         screen.displayMessageLine( "2 - Withdraw cash" );
120         screen.displayMessageLine( "3 - Deposit funds" );
121         screen.displayMessageLine( "4 - Exit\n" );
122         screen.displayMessage( "Enter a choice: " );
123         return keypad.getInput(); // return user's selection
124      } // end method displayMainMenu
125
126      // return object of specified Transaction subclass
127      private Transaction createTransaction( int type )
128      {
129         Transaction temp = null; // temporary Transaction variable
130
```

Fig. 13.13 | Class ATM represents the ATM. (Part 3 of 4.)

```
131        // determine which type of Transaction to create
132        switch ( type )
133        {
134           case BALANCE_INQUIRY: // create new BalanceInquiry transaction
135              temp = new BalanceInquiry(
136                 currentAccountNumber, screen, bankDatabase );
137              break;
138           case WITHDRAWAL: // create new Withdrawal transaction
139              temp = new Withdrawal( currentAccountNumber, screen,
140                 bankDatabase, keypad, cashDispenser );
141              break;
142           case DEPOSIT: // create new Deposit transaction
143              temp = new Deposit( currentAccountNumber, screen,
144                 bankDatabase, keypad, depositSlot );
145              break;
146        } // end switch
147
148        return temp; // return the newly created object
149     } // end method createTransaction
150  } // end class ATM
```

Fig. 13.13 | Class ATM represents the ATM. (Part 4 of 4.)

Lines 15–18 declare integer constants that correspond to the four options in the ATM's main menu (i.e., balance inquiry, withdrawal, deposit and exit). Lines 21–30 declare the constructor, which initializes the class's attributes. When an ATM object is first created, no user is authenticated, so line 23 initializes userAuthenticated to false. Likewise, line 24 initializes currentAccountNumber to 0 because there's no current user yet. Lines 25–28 instantiate new objects to represent the ATM's parts. Recall that class ATM has composition relationships with classes Screen, Keypad, CashDispenser and DepositSlot, so class ATM is responsible for their creation. Line 29 creates a new BankDatabase. [*Note:* If this were a real ATM system, the ATM class would receive a reference to an existing database object created by the bank. However, in this implementation we're only simulating the bank's database, so class ATM creates the BankDatabase object with which it interacts.]

ATM *Method* run

The class diagram of Fig. 13.10 does not list any operations for class ATM. We now implement one operation (i.e., public method) in class ATM that allows an external client of the class (i.e., class ATMCaseStudy) to tell the ATM to run. ATM method run (lines 33–50) uses an infinite loop (lines 36–49) to repeatedly welcome a user, attempt to authenticate the user and, if authentication succeeds, allow the user to perform transactions. After an authenticated user performs the desired transactions and chooses to exit, the ATM resets itself, displays a goodbye message to the user and restarts the process. We use an infinite loop here to simulate the fact that an ATM appears to run continuously until the bank turns it off (an action beyond the user's control). An ATM user has the option to exit the system but not the ability to turn off the ATM completely.

Authenticating a User

In method run's infinite loop, lines 39–43 cause the ATM to repeatedly welcome and attempt to authenticate the user as long as the user has not been authenticated (i.e., !user-

Authenticated is true). Line 41 invokes method displayMessageLine of the ATM's screen to display a welcome message. Like Screen method displayMessage designed in the case study, method displayMessageLine (declared in lines 13–16 of Fig. 13.14) displays a message to the user, but this method also outputs a newline after the message. We've added this method during implementation to give class Screen's clients more control over the placement of displayed messages. Line 42 invokes class ATM's private utility method authenticateUser (declared in lines 53–72) to attempt to authenticate the user.

We refer to the requirements document to determine the steps necessary to authenticate the user before allowing transactions to occur. Line 55 of method authenticateUser invokes method displayMessage of the screen to prompt the user to enter an account number. Line 56 invokes method getInput of the keypad to obtain the user's input, then stores the integer value entered by the user in a local variable accountNumber. Method authenticateUser next prompts the user to enter a PIN (line 57), and stores the PIN input by the user in a local variable pin (line 58). Next, lines 61–62 attempt to authenticate the user by passing the accountNumber and pin entered by the user to the bankDatabase's authenticateUser method. Class ATM sets its userAuthenticated attribute to the boolean value returned by this method—userAuthenticated becomes true if authentication succeeds (i.e., accountNumber and pin match those of an existing Account in bankDatabase) and remains false otherwise. If userAuthenticated is true, line 67 saves the account number entered by the user (i.e., accountNumber) in the ATM attribute currentAccountNumber. The other ATM methods use this variable whenever an ATM session requires access to the user's account number. If userAuthenticated is false, lines 70–71 use the screen's displayMessageLine method to indicate that an invalid account number and/or PIN was entered and the user must try again. We set currentAccountNumber only after authenticating the user's account number and the associated PIN—if the database could not authenticate the user, currentAccountNumber remains 0.

After method run attempts to authenticate the user (line 42), if userAuthenticated is still false, the while loop in lines 39–43 executes again. If userAuthenticated is now true, the loop terminates and control continues with line 45, which calls class ATM's utility method performTransactions.

Performing Transactions

Method performTransactions (lines 75–112) carries out an ATM session for an authenticated user. Line 78 declares a local Transaction variable to which we'll assign a BalanceInquiry, Withdrawal or Deposit object representing the ATM transaction the user selected. We use a Transaction variable here to allow us to take advantage of polymorphism. Also, we name this variable after the *role name* included in the class diagram of Fig. 12.7—currentTransaction. Line 80 declares another local variable—a boolean called userExited that keeps track of whether the user has chosen to exit. This variable controls a while loop (lines 83–111) that allows the user to execute an unlimited number of transactions before choosing to exit. Within this loop, line 86 displays the main menu and obtains the user's menu selection by calling an ATM utility method displayMainMenu (declared in lines 115–124). This method displays the main menu by invoking methods of the ATM's screen and returns a menu selection obtained from the user through the ATM's keypad. Line 86 stores the user's selection returned by displayMainMenu in local variable mainMenuSelection.

After obtaining a main menu selection, method performTransactions uses a switch statement (lines 89–110) to respond to the selection appropriately. If mainMenuSelection is equal to any of the three integer constants representing transaction types (i.e., if the user chose to perform a transaction), lines 97–98 call utility method createTransaction (declared in lines 127–149) to return a newly instantiated object of the type that corresponds to the selected transaction. Variable currentTransaction is assigned the reference returned by createTransaction, then line 100 invokes method execute of this transaction to execute it. We'll discuss Transaction method execute and the three Transaction subclasses shortly. We assign the Transaction variable currentTransaction an object of one of the three Transaction subclasses so that we can execute transactions *polymorphically*. For example, if the user chooses to perform a balance inquiry, mainMenuSelection equals BALANCE_INQUIRY, leading createTransaction to return a BalanceInquiry object. Thus, currentTransaction refers to a BalanceInquiry, and invoking currentTransaction.execute() results in BalanceInquiry's version of execute being called.

Creating a Transaction
Method createTransaction (lines 127–149) uses a switch statement (lines 132–146) to instantiate a new Transaction subclass object of the type indicated by the parameter type. Recall that method performTransactions passes mainMenuSelection to this method only when mainMenuSelection contains a value corresponding to one of the three transaction types. Therefore type is BALANCE_INQUIRY, WITHDRAWAL or DEPOSIT. Each case in the switch statement instantiates a new object by calling the appropriate Transaction subclass constructor. Each constructor has a unique parameter list, based on the specific data required to initialize the subclass object. A BalanceInquiry requires only the account number of the current user and references to the ATM's screen and the bankDatabase. In addition to these parameters, a Withdrawal requires references to the ATM's keypad and cashDispenser, and a Deposit requires references to the ATM's keypad and depositSlot. We discuss the transaction classes in more detail in Sections 13.4.8–13.4.11.

Exiting the Main Menu and Processing Invalid Selections
After executing a transaction (line 100 in performTransactions), userExited remains false and lines 83–111 repeat, returning the user to the main menu. However, if a user does not perform a transaction and instead selects the main menu option to exit, line 104 sets userExited to true, causing the condition of the while loop (!userExited) to become false. This while is the final statement of method performTransactions, so control returns to the calling method run. If the user enters an invalid main menu selection (i.e., not an integer from 1–4), lines 107–108 display an appropriate error message, userExited remains false and the user returns to the main menu to try again.

Awaiting the Next ATM User
When performTransactions returns control to method run, the user has chosen to exit the system, so lines 46–47 reset the ATM's attributes userAuthenticated and currentAccountNumber to prepare for the next ATM user. Line 48 displays a goodbye message before the ATM starts over and welcomes the next user.

13.4.2 Class Screen

Class Screen (Fig. 13.14) represents the screen of the ATM and encapsulates all aspects of displaying output to the user. Class Screen approximates a real ATM's screen with a computer monitor and outputs text messages using standard console output methods

System.out.print, System.out.println and System.out.printf. In this case study, we designed class Screen to have one operation—displayMessage. For greater flexibility in displaying messages to the Screen, we now declare three Screen methods—displayMessage, displayMessageLine and displayDollarAmount.

```
1   // Screen.java
2   // Represents the screen of the ATM
3
4   public class Screen
5   {
6      // display a message without a carriage return
7      public void displayMessage( String message )
8      {
9         System.out.print( message );
10     } // end method displayMessage
11
12     // display a message with a carriage return
13     public void displayMessageLine( String message )
14     {
15        System.out.println( message );
16     } // end method displayMessageLine
17
18     // displays a dollar amount
19     public void displayDollarAmount( double amount )
20     {
21        System.out.printf( "$%,.2f", amount );
22     } // end method displayDollarAmount
23  } // end class Screen
```

Fig. 13.14 | Class Screen represents the screen of the ATM.

Method displayMessage (lines 7–10) takes a String argument and prints it to the console. The cursor stays on the same line, making this method appropriate for displaying prompts to the user. Method displayMessageLine (lines 13–16) does the same using System.out.println, which outputs a newline to move the cursor to the next line. Finally, method displayDollarAmount (lines 19–22) outputs a properly formatted dollar amount (e.g., $1,234.56). Line 21 uses System.out.printf to output a double value formatted with commas to increase readability and two decimal places.

13.4.3 Class Keypad

Class Keypad (Fig. 13.15) represents the keypad of the ATM and is responsible for receiving all user input. Recall that we're simulating this hardware, so we use the computer's keyboard to approximate the keypad. We use class Scanner to obtain console input from the user. A computer keyboard contains many keys not found on the ATM's keypad. However, we assume that the user presses only the keys on the computer keyboard that also appear on the keypad—the keys numbered 0–9 and the *Enter* key.

Line 3 of class Keypad imports class Scanner for use in class Keypad. Line 7 declares Scanner variable input as an instance variable. Line 12 in the constructor creates a new Scanner object that reads input from the standard input stream (System.in) and assigns the object's reference to variable input. Method getInput (lines 16–19) invokes Scanner

```
1   // Keypad.java
2   // Represents the keypad of the ATM
3   import java.util.Scanner; // program uses Scanner to obtain user input
4
5   public class Keypad
6   {
7      private Scanner input; // reads data from the command line
8
9      // no-argument constructor initializes the Scanner
10     public Keypad()
11     {
12        input = new Scanner( System.in );
13     } // end no-argument Keypad constructor
14
15     // return an integer value entered by user
16     public int getInput()
17     {
18        return input.nextInt(); // we assume that user enters an integer
19     } // end method getInput
20  } // end class Keypad
```

Fig. 13.15 | Class Keypad represents the ATM's keypad.

method nextInt (line 18) to return the next integer input by the user. [*Note:* Method nextInt can throw an InputMismatchException if the user enters non-integer input. Because the real ATM's keypad permits only integer input, we assume that no exception will occur and do not attempt to fix this problem. See Chapter 11, Exception Handling: A Deeper Look, for information on catching exceptions.] Recall that nextInt obtains all the input used by the ATM. Keypad's getInput method simply returns the integer input by the user. If a client of class Keypad requires input that satisfies some criteria (i.e., a number corresponding to a valid menu option), the client must perform the error checking.

13.4.4 Class CashDispenser

Class CashDispenser (Fig. 13.16) represents the cash dispenser of the ATM. Line 7 declares constant INITIAL_COUNT, which indicates the initial count of bills in the cash dispenser when the ATM starts (i.e., 500). Line 8 implements attribute count (modeled in Fig. 13.10), which keeps track of the number of bills remaining in the CashDispenser at any time. The constructor (lines 11–14) sets count to the initial count. CashDispenser has two public methods—dispenseCash (lines 17–21) and isSufficientCashAvailable (lines 24–32). The class trusts that a client (i.e., Withdrawal) calls dispenseCash only after establishing that sufficient cash is available by calling isSufficientCashAvailable. Thus, dispenseCash simply simulates dispensing the requested amount without checking whether sufficient cash is available.

```
1   // CashDispenser.java
2   // Represents the cash dispenser of the ATM
3
```

Fig. 13.16 | Class CashDispenser represents the ATM's cash dispenser. (Part 1 of 2.)

```
4   public class CashDispenser
5   {
6      // the default initial number of bills in the cash dispenser
7      private final static int INITIAL_COUNT = 500;
8      private int count; // number of $20 bills remaining
9
10     // no-argument CashDispenser constructor initializes count to default
11     public CashDispenser()
12     {
13        count = INITIAL_COUNT; // set count attribute to default
14     } // end CashDispenser constructor
15
16     // simulates dispensing of specified amount of cash
17     public void dispenseCash( int amount )
18     {
19        int billsRequired = amount / 20; // number of $20 bills required
20        count -= billsRequired; // update the count of bills
21     } // end method dispenseCash
22
23     // indicates whether cash dispenser can dispense desired amount
24     public boolean isSufficientCashAvailable( int amount )
25     {
26        int billsRequired = amount / 20; // number of $20 bills required
27
28        if ( count >= billsRequired  )
29           return true; // enough bills available
30        else
31           return false; // not enough bills available
32     } // end method isSufficientCashAvailable
33  } // end class CashDispenser
```

Fig. 13.16 | Class CashDispenser represents the ATM's cash dispenser. (Part 2 of 2.)

Method isSufficientCashAvailable (lines 24–32) has a parameter amount that specifies the amount of cash in question. Line 26 calculates the number of $20 bills required to dispense the specified amount. The ATM allows the user to choose only withdrawal amounts that are multiples of $20, so we divide amount by 20 to obtain the number of billsRequired. Lines 28–31 return true if the CashDispenser's count is greater than or equal to billsRequired (i.e., enough bills are available) and false otherwise (i.e., not enough bills). For example, if a user wishes to withdraw $80 (i.e., billsRequired is 4), but only three bills remain (i.e., count is 3), the method returns false.

Method dispenseCash (lines 17–21) simulates cash dispensing. If our system were hooked up to a real hardware cash dispenser, this method would interact with the device to physically dispense cash. Our version of the method simply decreases the count of bills remaining by the number required to dispense the specified amount (line 20). It's the responsibility of the client of the class (i.e., Withdrawal) to inform the user that cash has been dispensed—CashDispenser cannot interact directly with Screen.

13.4.5 Class DepositSlot

Class DepositSlot (Fig. 13.17) represents the ATM's deposit slot. Like class CashDispenser, class DepositSlot merely simulates the functionality of a real hardware deposit slot. DepositSlot has no attributes and only one method—isEnvelopeReceived (lines 8–11)—which indicates whether a deposit envelope was received.

```
1   // DepositSlot.java
2   // Represents the deposit slot of the ATM
3
4   public class DepositSlot
5   {
6      // indicates whether envelope was received (always returns true,
7      // because this is only a software simulation of a real deposit slot)
8      public boolean isEnvelopeReceived()
9      {
10        return true; // deposit envelope was received
11     } // end method isEnvelopeReceived
12  } // end class DepositSlot
```

Fig. 13.17 | Class DepositSlot represents the ATM's deposit slot.

Recall from the requirements document that the ATM allows the user up to two minutes to insert an envelope. The current version of method isEnvelopeReceived simply returns true immediately (line 10), because this is only a software simulation, and we assume that the user has inserted an envelope within the required time frame. If an actual hardware deposit slot were connected to our system, method isEnvelopeReceived might be implemented to wait for a maximum of two minutes to receive a signal from the hardware deposit slot indicating that the user has indeed inserted a deposit envelope. If isEnvelopeReceived were to receive such a signal within two minutes, the method would return true. If two minutes elapsed and the method still had not received a signal, then the method would return false.

13.4.6 Class Account

Class Account (Fig. 13.18) represents a bank account. Each Account has four attributes (modeled in Fig. 13.10)—accountNumber, pin, availableBalance and totalBalance. Lines 6–9 implement these attributes as private fields. Variable availableBalance represents the amount of funds available for withdrawal. Variable totalBalance represents the amount of funds available, plus the amount of deposited funds still pending confirmation or clearance.

```
1   // Account.java
2   // Represents a bank account
3
4   public class Account
5   {
6      private int accountNumber; // account number
7      private int pin; // PIN for authentication
8      private double availableBalance; // funds available for withdrawal
9      private double totalBalance; // funds available + pending deposits
```

Fig. 13.18 | Class Account represents a bank account. (Part 1 of 2.)

```
10
11        // Account constructor initializes attributes
12        public Account( int theAccountNumber, int thePIN,
13           double theAvailableBalance, double theTotalBalance )
14        {
15           accountNumber = theAccountNumber;
16           pin = thePIN;
17           availableBalance = theAvailableBalance;
18           totalBalance = theTotalBalance;
19        } // end Account constructor
20
21        // determines whether a user-specified PIN matches PIN in Account
22        public boolean validatePIN( int userPIN )
23        {
24           if ( userPIN == pin )
25              return true;
26           else
27              return false;
28        } // end method validatePIN
29
30        // returns available balance
31        public double getAvailableBalance()
32        {
33           return availableBalance;
34        } // end getAvailableBalance
35
36        // returns the total balance
37        public double getTotalBalance()
38        {
39           return totalBalance;
40        } // end method getTotalBalance
41
42        // credits an amount to the account
43        public void credit( double amount )
44        {
45           totalBalance += amount; // add to total balance
46        } // end method credit
47
48        // debits an amount from the account
49        public void debit( double amount )
50        {
51           availableBalance -= amount; // subtract from available balance
52           totalBalance -= amount; // subtract from total balance
53        } // end method debit
54
55        // returns account number
56        public int getAccountNumber()
57        {
58           return accountNumber;
59        } // end method getAccountNumber
60     } // end class Account
```

Fig. 13.18 | Class Account represents a bank account. (Part 2 of 2.)

The Account class has a constructor (lines 12–19) that takes an account number, the PIN established for the account, the account's initial available balance and the account's initial total balance as arguments. Lines 15–18 assign these values to the class's attributes (i.e., fields).

Method validatePIN (lines 22–28) determines whether a user-specified PIN (i.e., parameter userPIN) matches the PIN associated with the account (i.e., attribute pin). Recall that we modeled this method's parameter userPIN in Fig. 12.19. If the two PINs match, the method returns true (line 25); otherwise, it returns false (line 27).

Methods getAvailableBalance (lines 31–34) and getTotalBalance (lines 37–40) return the values of double attributes availableBalance and totalBalance, respectively.

Method credit (lines 43–46) adds an amount of money (i.e., parameter amount) to an Account as part of a deposit transaction. This method adds the amount only to attribute totalBalance (line 45). The money credited to an account during a deposit does *not* become available immediately, so we modify only the total balance. We assume that the bank updates the available balance appropriately at a later time. Our implementation of class Account includes only methods required for carrying out ATM transactions. Therefore, we omit the methods that some other bank system would invoke to add to attribute availableBalance (to confirm a deposit) or subtract from attribute totalBalance (to reject a deposit).

Method debit (lines 49–53) subtracts an amount of money (i.e., parameter amount) from an Account as part of a withdrawal transaction. This method subtracts the amount from *both* attribute availableBalance (line 51) and attribute totalBalance (line 52), because a withdrawal affects *both* measures of an account balance.

Method getAccountNumber (lines 56–59) provides access to an Account's accountNumber. We include this method in our implementation so that a client of the class (i.e., BankDatabase) can identify a particular Account. For example, BankDatabase contains many Account objects, and it can invoke this method on each of its Account objects to locate the one with a specific account number.

13.4.7 Class BankDatabase

Class BankDatabase (Fig. 13.19) models the bank's database with which the ATM interacts to access and modify a user's account information. We study database access in Chapter 25. For now we model the database as an array. An exercise in Chapter 25 asks you to reimplement this portion of the ATM using an actual database.

```
1   // BankDatabase.java
2   // Represents the bank account information database
3
4   public class BankDatabase
5   {
6      private Account[] accounts; // array of Accounts
7
8      // no-argument BankDatabase constructor initializes accounts
9      public BankDatabase()
10     {
```

Fig. 13.19 | Class BankDatabase represents the bank's account information database. (Part 1 of 3.)

```
11          accounts = new Account[ 2 ]; // just 2 accounts for testing
12          accounts[ 0 ] = new Account( 12345, 54321, 1000.0, 1200.0 );
13          accounts[ 1 ] = new Account( 98765, 56789, 200.0, 200.0 );
14       } // end no-argument BankDatabase constructor
15
16       // retrieve Account object containing specified account number
17       private Account getAccount( int accountNumber )
18       {
19          // loop through accounts searching for matching account number
20          for ( Account currentAccount : accounts )
21          {
22             // return current account if match found
23             if ( currentAccount.getAccountNumber() == accountNumber )
24                return currentAccount;
25          } // end for
26
27          return null; // if no matching account was found, return null
28       } // end method getAccount
29
30       // determine whether user-specified account number and PIN match
31       // those of an account in the database
32       public boolean authenticateUser( int userAccountNumber, int userPIN )
33       {
34          // attempt to retrieve the account with the account number
35          Account userAccount = getAccount( userAccountNumber );
36
37          // if account exists, return result of Account method validatePIN
38          if ( userAccount != null )
39             return userAccount.validatePIN( userPIN );
40          else
41             return false; // account number not found, so return false
42       } // end method authenticateUser
43
44       // return available balance of Account with specified account number
45       public double getAvailableBalance( int userAccountNumber )
46       {
47          return getAccount( userAccountNumber ).getAvailableBalance();
48       } // end method getAvailableBalance
49
50       // return total balance of Account with specified account number
51       public double getTotalBalance( int userAccountNumber )
52       {
53          return getAccount( userAccountNumber ).getTotalBalance();
54       } // end method getTotalBalance
55
56       // credit an amount to Account with specified account number
57       public void credit( int userAccountNumber, double amount )
58       {
59          getAccount( userAccountNumber ).credit( amount );
60       } // end method credit
61
```

Fig. 13.19 | Class BankDatabase represents the bank's account information database. (Part 2 of 3.)

```
62        // debit an amount from Account with specified account number
63        public void debit( int userAccountNumber, double amount )
64        {
65            getAccount( userAccountNumber ).debit( amount );
66        } // end method debit
67    } // end class BankDatabase
```

Fig. 13.19 | Class BankDatabase represents the bank's account information database. (Part 3 of 3.)

We determine one reference-type attribute for class BankDatabase based on its composition relationship with class Account. Recall from Fig. 13.9 that a BankDatabase is composed of zero or more objects of class Account. Line 6 implements attribute accounts—an array of Account objects—to implement this composition relationship. Class BankDatabase has a no-argument constructor (lines 9–14) that initializes accounts to contain a set of new Account objects. For the sake of testing the system, we declare accounts to hold just two array elements (line 11), which we instantiate as new Account objects with test data (lines 12–13). The Account constructor has four parameters—the account number, the PIN assigned to the account, the initial available balance and the initial total balance. Recall that class BankDatabase serves as an intermediary between class ATM and the actual Account objects that contain a user's account information. Thus, the methods of class BankDatabase do nothing more than invoke the corresponding methods of the Account object belonging to the current ATM user.

We include private utility method getAccount (lines 17–28) to allow the BankDatabase to obtain a reference to a particular Account within array accounts. To locate the user's Account, the BankDatabase compares the value returned by method getAccountNumber for each element of accounts to a specified account number until it finds a match. Lines 20–25 traverse the accounts array. If the account number of currentAccount equals the value of parameter accountNumber, the method immediately returns the currentAccount. If no account has the given account number, then line 27 returns null.

Method authenticateUser (lines 32–42) proves or disproves the identity of an ATM user. This method takes a user-specified account number and PIN as arguments and indicates whether they match the account number and PIN of an Account in the database. Line 35 calls method getAccount, which returns either an Account with userAccountNumber as its account number or null to indicate that userAccountNumber is invalid. If getAccount returns an Account object, line 39 returns the boolean value returned by that object's validatePIN method. BankDatabase's authenticateUser method does not perform the PIN comparison itself—rather, it forwards userPIN to the Account object's validatePIN method to do so. The value returned by Account method validatePIN indicates whether the user-specified PIN matches the PIN of the user's Account, so method authenticateUser simply returns this value to the class's client (i.e., ATM).

BankDatabase trusts the ATM to invoke method authenticateUser and receive a return value of true before allowing the user to perform transactions. BankDatabase also trusts that each Transaction object created by the ATM contains the valid account number of the current authenticated user and that this is the account number passed to the remaining BankDatabase methods as argument userAccountNumber. Methods getAvailableBalance (lines 45–48), getTotalBalance (lines 51–54), credit (lines 57–60) and debit (lines 63–66) therefore simply retrieve the user's Account object with utility method getAccount, then invoke the appropriate Account method on that object. We know that the calls to getAccount from these methods will never return null, because userAccount-Number must refer to an existing Account. Methods getAvailableBalance and getTotal-Balance return the values returned by the corresponding Account methods. Also, credit and debit simply redirect parameter amount to the Account methods they invoke.

13.4.8 Class Transaction

Class Transaction (Fig. 13.20) is an abstract superclass that represents the notion of an ATM transaction. It contains the common features of subclasses BalanceInquiry, With-drawal and Deposit. This class expands upon the "skeleton" code first developed in Section 13.3. Line 4 declares this class to be abstract. Lines 6–8 declare the class's private attributes. Recall from the class diagram of Fig. 13.10 that class Transaction contains an attribute accountNumber (line 6) that indicates the account involved in the Transaction. We derive attributes screen (line 7) and bankDatabase (line 8) from class Transaction's associations modeled in Fig. 13.9—all transactions require access to the ATM's screen and the bank's database.

```
1    // Transaction.java
2    // Abstract superclass Transaction represents an ATM transaction
3
4    public abstract class Transaction
5    {
6       private int accountNumber; // indicates account involved
7       private Screen screen; // ATM's screen
8       private BankDatabase bankDatabase; // account info database
9
10      // Transaction constructor invoked by subclasses using super()
11      public Transaction( int userAccountNumber, Screen atmScreen,
12         BankDatabase atmBankDatabase )
13      {
14         accountNumber = userAccountNumber;
15         screen = atmScreen;
16         bankDatabase = atmBankDatabase;
17      } // end Transaction constructor
18
19      // return account number
20      public int getAccountNumber()
21      {
22         return accountNumber;
23      } // end method getAccountNumber
24
25      // return reference to screen
26      public Screen getScreen()
27      {
28         return screen;
29      } // end method getScreen
30
```

Fig. 13.20 | Abstract superclass Transaction represents an ATM transaction. (Part 1 of 2.)

```
31      // return reference to bank database
32      public BankDatabase getBankDatabase()
33      {
34         return bankDatabase;
35      } // end method getBankDatabase
36
37      // perform the transaction (overridden by each subclass)
38      abstract public void execute();
39   } // end class Transaction
```

Fig. 13.20 | Abstract superclass Transaction represents an ATM transaction. (Part 2 of 2.)

Class Transaction has a constructor (lines 11–17) that takes as arguments the current user's account number and references to the ATM's screen and the bank's database. Because Transaction is an *abstract* class, this constructor will be called only by the constructors of the Transaction subclasses.

The class has three public *get* methods—getAccountNumber (lines 20–23), getScreen (lines 26–29) and getBankDatabase (lines 32–35). These are inherited by Transaction subclasses and used to gain access to class Transaction's private attributes.

Class Transaction also declares abstract method execute (line 38). It does not make sense to provide this method's implementation, because a generic transaction cannot be executed. So, we declare this method abstract and force each Transaction subclass to provide a concrete implementation that executes that particular type of transaction.

13.4.9 Class BalanceInquiry

Class BalanceInquiry (Fig. 13.21) extends Transaction and represents a balance-inquiry ATM transaction. BalanceInquiry does not have any attributes of its own, but it inherits Transaction attributes accountNumber, screen and bankDatabase, which are accessible through Transaction's public *get* methods. The BalanceInquiry constructor takes arguments corresponding to these attributes and simply forwards them to Transaction's constructor using super (line 10).

```
 1   // BalanceInquiry.java
 2   // Represents a balance inquiry ATM transaction
 3
 4   public class BalanceInquiry extends Transaction
 5   {
 6      // BalanceInquiry constructor
 7      public BalanceInquiry( int userAccountNumber, Screen atmScreen,
 8         BankDatabase atmBankDatabase )
 9      {
10         super( userAccountNumber, atmScreen, atmBankDatabase );
11      } // end BalanceInquiry constructor
12
13      // performs the transaction
14      @Override
15      public void execute()
16      {
```

Fig. 13.21 | Class BalanceInquiry represents a balance-inquiry ATM transaction. (Part 1 of 2.)

```
17          // get references to bank database and screen
18          BankDatabase bankDatabase = getBankDatabase();
19          Screen screen = getScreen();
20
21          // get the available balance for the account involved
22          double availableBalance =
23              bankDatabase.getAvailableBalance( getAccountNumber() );
24
25          // get the total balance for the account involved
26          double totalBalance =
27              bankDatabase.getTotalBalance( getAccountNumber() );
28
29          // display the balance information on the screen
30          screen.displayMessageLine( "\nBalance Information:" );
31          screen.displayMessage( " - Available balance: " );
32          screen.displayDollarAmount( availableBalance );
33          screen.displayMessage( "\n - Total balance:      " );
34          screen.displayDollarAmount( totalBalance );
35          screen.displayMessageLine( "" );
36      } // end method execute
37  } // end class BalanceInquiry
```

Fig. 13.21 | Class `BalanceInquiry` represents a balance-inquiry ATM transaction. (Part 2 of 2.)

Class `BalanceInquiry` overrides `Transaction`'s abstract method `execute` to provide a concrete implementation (lines 14–36) that performs the steps involved in a balance inquiry. Lines 18–19 get references to the bank database and the ATM's screen by invoking methods inherited from superclass `Transaction`. Lines 22–23 retrieve the available balance of the account involved by invoking method `getAvailableBalance` of bank-Database. Line 23 uses inherited method `getAccountNumber` to get the account number of the current user, which it then passes to `getAvailableBalance`. Lines 26–27 retrieve the total balance of the current user's account. Lines 30–35 display the balance information on the ATM's screen. Recall that `displayDollarAmount` takes a `double` argument and outputs it to the screen formatted as a dollar amount. For example, if a user's available-Balance is 1000.5, line 32 outputs $1,000.50. Line 35 inserts a blank line of output to separate the balance information from subsequent output (i.e., the main menu repeated by class `ATM` after executing the `BalanceInquiry`).

13.4.10 Class `Withdrawal`

Class `Withdrawal` (Fig. 13.22) extends `Transaction` and represents a withdrawal ATM transaction. This class expands upon the "skeleton" code for this class developed in Fig. 13.12. Recall from the class diagram of Fig. 13.10 that class `Withdrawal` has one attribute, amount, which line 6 implements as an `int` field. Figure 13.9 models associations between class `Withdrawal` and classes `Keypad` and `CashDispenser`, for which lines 7–8 implement reference-type attributes keypad and cashDispenser, respectively. Line 11 declares a constant corresponding to the cancel menu option. We'll soon discuss how the class uses this constant.

```java
1   // Withdrawal.java
2   // Represents a withdrawal ATM transaction
3
4   public class Withdrawal extends Transaction
5   {
6      private int amount; // amount to withdraw
7      private Keypad keypad; // reference to keypad
8      private CashDispenser cashDispenser; // reference to cash dispenser
9
10     // constant corresponding to menu option to cancel
11     private final static int CANCELED = 6;
12
13     // Withdrawal constructor
14     public Withdrawal( int userAccountNumber, Screen atmScreen,
15        BankDatabase atmBankDatabase, Keypad atmKeypad,
16        CashDispenser atmCashDispenser )
17     {
18        // initialize superclass variables
19        super( userAccountNumber, atmScreen, atmBankDatabase );
20
21        // initialize references to keypad and cash dispenser
22        keypad = atmKeypad;
23        cashDispenser = atmCashDispenser;
24     } // end Withdrawal constructor
25
26     // perform transaction
27     @Override
28     public void execute()
29     {
30        boolean cashDispensed = false; // cash was not dispensed yet
31        double availableBalance; // amount available for withdrawal
32
33        // get references to bank database and screen
34        BankDatabase bankDatabase = getBankDatabase();
35        Screen screen = getScreen();
36
37        // loop until cash is dispensed or the user cancels
38        do
39        {
40           // obtain a chosen withdrawal amount from the user
41           amount = displayMenuOfAmounts();
42
43           // check whether user chose a withdrawal amount or canceled
44           if ( amount != CANCELED )
45           {
46              // get available balance of account involved
47              availableBalance =
48                 bankDatabase.getAvailableBalance( getAccountNumber() );
49
50              // check whether the user has enough money in the account
51              if ( amount <= availableBalance )
52              {
```

Fig. 13.22 | Class `Withdrawal` represents a withdrawal ATM transaction. (Part 1 of 3.)

```
53              // check whether the cash dispenser has enough money
54              if ( cashDispenser.isSufficientCashAvailable( amount ) )
55              {
56                  // update the account involved to reflect the withdrawal
57                  bankDatabase.debit( getAccountNumber(), amount );
58
59                  cashDispenser.dispenseCash( amount ); // dispense cash
60                  cashDispensed = true; // cash was dispensed
61
62                  // instruct user to take cash
63                  screen.displayMessageLine( "\nYour cash has been" +
64                      " dispensed. Please take your cash now." );
65              } // end if
66              else // cash dispenser does not have enough cash
67                  screen.displayMessageLine(
68                      "\nInsufficient cash available in the ATM." +
69                      "\n\nPlease choose a smaller amount." );
70          } // end if
71          else // not enough money available in user's account
72          {
73              screen.displayMessageLine(
74                  "\nInsufficient funds in your account." +
75                  "\n\nPlease choose a smaller amount." );
76          } // end else
77      } // end if
78      else // user chose cancel menu option
79      {
80          screen.displayMessageLine( "\nCanceling transaction..." );
81          return; // return to main menu because user canceled
82      } // end else
83  } while ( !cashDispensed );
84
85  } // end method execute
86
87  // display a menu of withdrawal amounts and the option to cancel;
88  // return the chosen amount or 0 if the user chooses to cancel
89  private int displayMenuOfAmounts()
90  {
91      int userChoice = 0; // local variable to store return value
92
93      Screen screen = getScreen(); // get screen reference
94
95      // array of amounts to correspond to menu numbers
96      int[] amounts = { 0, 20, 40, 60, 100, 200 };
97
98      // loop while no valid choice has been made
99      while ( userChoice == 0 )
100     {
101         // display the withdrawal menu
102         screen.displayMessageLine( "\nWithdrawal Menu:" );
103         screen.displayMessageLine( "1 - $20" );
104         screen.displayMessageLine( "2 - $40" );
105         screen.displayMessageLine( "3 - $60" );
```

Fig. 13.22 | Class `Withdrawal` represents a withdrawal ATM transaction. (Part 2 of 3.)

```
106                screen.displayMessageLine( "4 - $100" );
107                screen.displayMessageLine( "5 - $200" );
108                screen.displayMessageLine( "6 - Cancel transaction" );
109                screen.displayMessage( "\nChoose a withdrawal amount: " );
110
111                int input = keypad.getInput(); // get user input through keypad
112
113                // determine how to proceed based on the input value
114                switch ( input )
115                {
116                   case 1: // if the user chose a withdrawal amount
117                   case 2: // (i.e., chose option 1, 2, 3, 4 or 5), return the
118                   case 3: // corresponding amount from amounts array
119                   case 4:
120                   case 5:
121                      userChoice = amounts[ input ]; // save user's choice
122                      break;
123                   case CANCELED: // the user chose to cancel
124                      userChoice = CANCELED; // save user's choice
125                      break;
126                   default: // the user did not enter a value from 1-6
127                      screen.displayMessageLine(
128                         "\nInvalid selection. Try again." );
129                } // end switch
130             } // end while
131
132             return userChoice; // return withdrawal amount or CANCELED
133          } // end method displayMenuOfAmounts
134       } // end class Withdrawal
```

Fig. 13.22 | Class Withdrawal represents a withdrawal ATM transaction. (Part 3 of 3.)

Class Withdrawal's constructor (lines 14–24) has five parameters. It uses super to pass parameters userAccountNumber, atmScreen and atmBankDatabase to superclass Transaction's constructor to set the attributes that Withdrawal inherits from Transaction. The constructor also takes references atmKeypad and atmCashDispenser as parameters and assigns them to reference-type attributes keypad and cashDispenser.

Class Withdrawal overrides Transaction method execute with a concrete implementation (lines 27–85) that performs the steps of a withdrawal. Line 30 declares and initializes a local boolean variable cashDispensed, which indicates whether cash has been dispensed (i.e., whether the transaction has completed successfully) and is initially false. Line 31 declares local double variable availableBalance, which will store the user's available balance during a withdrawal transaction. Lines 34–35 get references to the bank database and the ATM's screen by invoking methods inherited from superclass Transaction.

Lines 38–83 contain a do...while that executes its body until cash is dispensed (i.e., until cashDispensed becomes true) or until the user chooses to cancel (in which case, the loop terminates). We use this loop to continuously return the user to the start of the transaction if an error occurs (i.e., the requested withdrawal amount is greater than the user's available balance or greater than the amount of cash in the cash dispenser). Line 41 displays a menu of withdrawal amounts and obtains a user selection by calling private utility method displayMenuOfAmounts (declared in lines 89–133). This method displays the menu of amounts and returns either an `int` withdrawal amount or an `int` constant `CANCELED` to indicate that the user has chosen to cancel the transaction.

Method `displayMenuOfAmounts` (lines 89–133) first declares local variable `user-Choice` (initially 0) to store the value that the method will return (line 91). Line 93 gets a reference to the screen by calling method `getScreen` inherited from superclass `Transaction`. Line 96 declares an integer array of withdrawal amounts that correspond to the amounts displayed in the withdrawal menu. We ignore the first element in the array (index 0) because the menu has no option 0. The `while` statement at lines 99–130 repeats until `userChoice` takes on a value other than 0. We'll see shortly that this occurs when the user makes a valid selection from the menu. Lines 102–109 display the withdrawal menu on the screen and prompt the user to enter a choice. Line 111 obtains integer input through the keypad. The `switch` statement at lines 114–129 determines how to proceed based on the user's input. If the user selects a number between 1 and 5, line 121 sets `userChoice` to the value of the element in `amounts` at index `input`. For example, if the user enters 3 to withdraw $60, line 121 sets `userChoice` to the value of `amounts[ 3 ]` (i.e., 60). Line 122 terminates the `switch`. Variable `userChoice` no longer equals 0, so the `while` at lines 99–130 terminates and line 132 returns `userChoice`. If the user selects the cancel menu option, lines 124–125 execute, setting `userChoice` to `CANCELED` and causing the method to return this value. If the user does not enter a valid menu selection, lines 127–128 display an error message and the user is returned to the withdrawal menu.

Line 44 in method `execute` determines whether the user has selected a withdrawal amount or chosen to cancel. If the user cancels, lines 80–81 execute and display an appropriate message to the user before returning control to the calling method (i.e., ATM method `performTransactions`). If the user has chosen a withdrawal amount, lines 47–48 retrieve the available balance of the current user's `Account` and store it in variable `availableBalance`. Next, line 51 determines whether the selected amount is less than or equal to the user's available balance. If it's not, lines 73–75 display an appropriate error message. Control then continues to the end of the `do...while`, and the loop repeats because `cashDispensed` is still `false`. If the user's balance is high enough, the `if` statement at line 54 determines whether the cash dispenser has enough money to satisfy the withdrawal request by invoking the `cashDispenser`'s `isSufficientCashAvailable` method. If this method returns `false`, lines 67–69 display an appropriate error message and the `do...while` repeats. If sufficient cash is available, then the requirements for the withdrawal are satisfied, and line 57 debits `amount` from the user's account in the database. Lines 59–60 then instruct the cash dispenser to dispense the cash to the user and set `cashDispensed` to `true`. Finally, lines 63–64 display a message to the user that cash has been dispensed. Because `cashDispensed` is now `true`, control continues after the `do...while`. No additional statements appear below the loop, so the method returns.

13.4.11 Class `Deposit`

Class `Deposit` (Fig. 13.23) extends `Transaction` and represents a deposit transaction. Recall from Fig. 13.10 that class `Deposit` has one attribute `amount`, which line 6 implements as an `int` field. Lines 7–8 create reference attributes `keypad` and `depositSlot` that implement the associations between class `Deposit` and classes `Keypad` and `DepositSlot` modeled in Fig. 13.9. Line 9 declares a constant `CANCELED` that corresponds to the value a user enters to cancel. We'll soon discuss how the class uses this constant.

```java
1    // Deposit.java
2    // Represents a deposit ATM transaction
3
4    public class Deposit extends Transaction
5    {
6       private double amount; // amount to deposit
7       private Keypad keypad; // reference to keypad
8       private DepositSlot depositSlot; // reference to deposit slot
9       private final static int CANCELED = 0; // constant for cancel option
10
11      // Deposit constructor
12      public Deposit( int userAccountNumber, Screen atmScreen,
13         BankDatabase atmBankDatabase, Keypad atmKeypad,
14         DepositSlot atmDepositSlot )
15      {
16         // initialize superclass variables
17         super( userAccountNumber, atmScreen, atmBankDatabase );
18
19         // initialize references to keypad and deposit slot
20         keypad = atmKeypad;
21         depositSlot = atmDepositSlot;
22      } // end Deposit constructor
23
24      // perform transaction
25      @Override
26      public void execute()
27      {
28         BankDatabase bankDatabase = getBankDatabase(); // get reference
29         Screen screen = getScreen(); // get reference
30
31         amount = promptForDepositAmount(); // get deposit amount from user
32
33         // check whether user entered a deposit amount or canceled
34         if ( amount != CANCELED )
35         {
36            // request deposit envelope containing specified amount
37            screen.displayMessage(
38               "\nPlease insert a deposit envelope containing " );
39            screen.displayDollarAmount( amount );
40            screen.displayMessageLine( "." );
41
42            // receive deposit envelope
43            boolean envelopeReceived = depositSlot.isEnvelopeReceived();
44
45            // check whether deposit envelope was received
46            if ( envelopeReceived )
47            {
48               screen.displayMessageLine( "\nYour envelope has been " +
49                  "received.\nNOTE: The money just deposited will not " +
50                  "be available until we verify the amount of any " +
51                  "enclosed cash and your checks clear." );
52
```

Fig. 13.23 | Class Deposit represents a deposit ATM transaction. (Part 1 of 2.)

```
53                    // credit account to reflect the deposit
54                    bankDatabase.credit( getAccountNumber(), amount );
55                 } // end if
56                 else // deposit envelope not received
57                 {
58                    screen.displayMessageLine( "\nYou did not insert an " +
59                       "envelope, so the ATM has canceled your transaction." );
60                 } // end else
61              } // end if
62              else // user canceled instead of entering amount
63              {
64                 screen.displayMessageLine( "\nCanceling transaction..." );
65              } // end else
66           } // end method execute
67
68           // prompt user to enter a deposit amount in cents
69           private double promptForDepositAmount()
70           {
71              Screen screen = getScreen(); // get reference to screen
72
73              // display the prompt
74              screen.displayMessage( "\nPlease enter a deposit amount in " +
75                 "CENTS (or 0 to cancel): " );
76              int input = keypad.getInput(); // receive input of deposit amount
77
78              // check whether the user canceled or entered a valid amount
79              if ( input == CANCELED )
80                 return CANCELED;
81              else
82              {
83                 return ( double ) input / 100; // return dollar amount
84              } // end else
85           } // end method promptForDepositAmount
86        } // end class Deposit
```

Fig. 13.23 | Class Deposit represents a deposit ATM transaction. (Part 2 of 2.)

Like Withdrawal, class Deposit contains a constructor (lines 12–22) that passes three parameters to superclass Transaction's constructor. The constructor also has parameters atmKeypad and atmDepositSlot, which it assigns to corresponding attributes (lines 20–21).

Method execute (lines 25–66) overrides the abstract version in superclass Transaction with a concrete implementation that performs the steps required in a deposit transaction. Lines 28–29 get references to the database and the screen. Line 31 prompts the user to enter a deposit amount by invoking private utility method promptForDepositAmount (declared in lines 69–85) and sets attribute amount to the value returned. Method promptForDepositAmount asks the user to enter a deposit amount as an integer number of cents (because the ATM's keypad does not contain a decimal point; this is consistent with many real ATMs) and returns the double value representing the dollar amount to be deposited.

Line 71 in method promptForDepositAmount gets a reference to the ATM's screen. Lines 74–75 display a message asking the user to input a deposit amount as a number of cents or "0" to cancel the transaction. Line 76 receives the user's input from the keypad. Lines 79–84 determine whether the user has entered a real deposit amount or chosen to cancel. If the latter, line 80 returns the constant CANCELED. Otherwise, line 83 returns the deposit amount after converting from the number of cents to a dollar amount by casting input to a double, then dividing by 100. For example, if the user enters 125 as the number of cents, line 83 returns 125.0 divided by 100, or 1.25—125 cents is $1.25.

Lines 34–65 in method execute determine whether the user has chosen to cancel the transaction instead of entering a deposit amount. If the user cancels, line 64 displays an appropriate message, and the method returns. If the user enters a deposit amount, lines 37–40 instruct the user to insert a deposit envelope with the correct amount. Recall that Screen method displayDollarAmount outputs a double formatted as a dollar amount.

Line 43 sets a local boolean variable to the value returned by depositSlot's isEnvelopeReceived method, indicating whether a deposit envelope has been received. Recall that we coded method isEnvelopeReceived (lines 8–11 of Fig. 13.17) to always return true, because we're simulating the functionality of the deposit slot and assume that the user always inserts an envelope. However, we code method execute of class Deposit to test for the possibility that the user does not insert an envelope—good software engineering demands that programs account for *all* possible return values. Thus, class Deposit is prepared for future versions of isEnvelopeReceived that could return false. Lines 48–54 execute if the deposit slot receives an envelope. Lines 48–51 display an appropriate message to the user. Line 54 then credits the deposit amount to the user's account in the database. Lines 58–59 will execute if the deposit slot does not receive a deposit envelope. In this case, we display a message to the user stating that the ATM has canceled the transaction. The method then returns without modifying the user's account.

13.4.12 Class ATMCaseStudy

Class ATMCaseStudy (Fig. 13.24) is a simple class that allows us to start, or "turn on," the ATM and test the implementation of our ATM system model. Class ATMCaseStudy's main method (lines 7–11) does nothing more than instantiate a new ATM object named theATM (line 9) and invoke its run method (line 10) to start the ATM.

```
1   // ATMCaseStudy.java
2   // Driver program for the ATM case study
3
4   public class ATMCaseStudy
5   {
6      // main method creates and runs the ATM
7      public static void main( String[] args )
8      {
9         ATM theATM = new ATM();
10        theATM.run();
11     } // end main
12  } // end class ATMCaseStudy
```

Fig. 13.24 | ATMCaseStudy.java starts the ATM.

13.5 Wrap-Up

In this chapter, you used inheritance to tune the design of the ATM software system, and you fully implemented the ATM in Java. Congratulations on completing the entire ATM case study! We hope you found this experience to be valuable and that it reinforced many of the object-oriented programming concepts that you've learned. In the next chapter, we take a deeper look at graphical user interfaces (GUIs).

Answers to Self-Review Exercises

13.1 True. The minus sign (-) indicates private visibility.

13.2 b.

13.3 The design for class Keypad yields the code in Fig. 13.25. Recall that class Keypad has no attributes for the moment, but attributes may become apparent as we continue the implementation. Also, if we were designing a real ATM, method getInput would need to interact with the ATM's keypad hardware. We'll actually read input from the keyboard of a personal computer when we write the complete Java code in Section 13.4.

```
1   // Class Keypad represents an ATM's keypad
2   public class Keypad
3   {
4      // no attributes have been specified yet
5
6      // no-argument constructor
7      public Keypad()
8      {
9      } // end no-argument Keypad constructor
10
11     // operations
12     public int getInput()
13     {
14     } // end method getInput
15  } // end class Keypad
```

Fig. 13.25 | Java code for class Keypad based on Figs. 13.1–13.2.

13.4 b.

13.5 False. The UML requires that we italicize abstract class names and method names.

13.6 The design for class Transaction yields the code in Fig. 13.26. The bodies of the class constructor and methods are completed in Section 13.4. When fully implemented, methods getScreen and getBankDatabase will return superclass Transaction's private reference attributes screen and bankDatabase, respectively. These methods allow the Transaction subclasses to access the ATM's screen and interact with the bank's database.

```
1   // Abstract class Transaction represents an ATM transaction
2   public abstract class Transaction
3   {
4      // attributes
5      private int accountNumber; // indicates account involved
6      private Screen screen; // ATM's screen
7      private BankDatabase bankDatabase; // account info database
```

Fig. 13.26 | Java code for class Transaction based on Figs. 13.9 and 13.10. (Part 1 of 2.)

```
 8
 9        // no-argument constructor invoked by subclasses using super()
10        public Transaction()
11        {
12        } // end no-argument Transaction constructor
13
14        // return account number
15        public int getAccountNumber()
16        {
17        } // end method getAccountNumber
18
19        // return reference to screen
20        public Screen getScreen()
21        {
22        } // end method getScreen
23
24        // return reference to bank database
25        public BankDatabase getBankDatabase()
26        {
27        } // end method getBankDatabase
28
29        // abstract method overridden by subclasses
30        public abstract void execute();
31   } // end class Transaction
```

Fig. 13.26 | Java code for class Transaction based on Figs. 13.9 and 13.10. (Part 2 of 2.)

14

GUI Components: Part 1

Objectives

In this chapter you'll learn:

- How to use Java's elegant, cross-platform Nimbus look-and-feel.

- To build GUIs and handle events generated by user interactions with GUIs.

- To understand the packages containing GUI components, event-handling classes and interfaces.

- To create and manipulate buttons, labels, lists, text fields and panels.

- To handle mouse events and keyboard events.

- To use layout managers to arrange GUI components.

14.1 Introduction

A **graphical user interface (GUI)** presents a user-friendly mechanism for interacting with an application. A GUI (pronounced "GOO-ee") gives an application a distinctive "look and feel." GUIs are built from **GUI components**. These are sometimes called controls or widgets—short for window gadgets. A GUI component is an object with which the user interacts via the mouse, the keyboard or another form of input, such as voice recognition. In this chapter and Chapter 22, GUI Components: Part 2, you'll learn about many of Java's so-called **Swing GUI components** from the `javax.swing` package. We cover other GUI components as they're needed throughout the rest of the book.

Look-and-Feel Observation 14.1

Providing different applications with consistent, intuitive user-interface components gives users a sense of familiarity with a new application, so that they can learn it more quickly and use it more productively.

IDE Support for GUI Design
Many IDEs provide GUI design tools with which you can specify a component's exact size and location in a visual manner by using the mouse. The IDE generates the GUI code for you. Though this greatly simplifies creating GUIs, each IDE generates this code differently. For this reason, we wrote the GUI code by hand.

Sample GUI: The SwingSet3 Demo Application
As an example of a GUI, consider Fig. 14.1, which shows the SwingSet3 application that's available at `download.java.net/javadesktop/swingset3/SwingSet3.jnlp`. This application is a nice way for you to browse through the various GUI components provided by Java's Swing GUI APIs. Simply click a component name (e.g., `JFrame`, `JTabbedPane`, etc.)

in the **GUI Components** area at the left of the window to see a demonstration of the GUI component in the right side of the window. The source code for each demo is shown in the text area at the bottom of the window. We've labeled a few of the GUI components in the application. At the top of the window is a **title bar** that contains the window's title. Below that is a **menu bar** containing **menus** (**File** and **View**). In the top-right region of the window is a set of **buttons**—typically, users press buttons to perform tasks. In the **GUI Components** area of the window is a **combo box**; the user can click the down arrow at the right side of the box to select from a list of items. The menus, buttons and combo box are part of the application's GUI. They enable you to interact with the application.

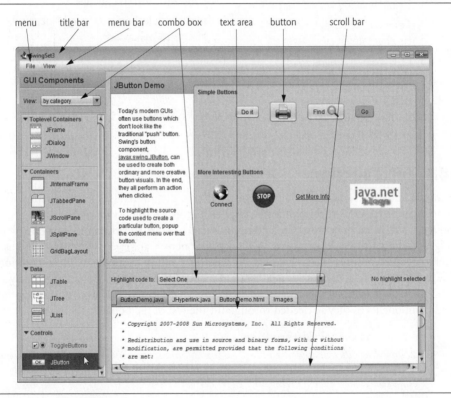

Fig. 14.1 | **SwingSet3** application demonstrates many of Java's Swing GUI components.

14.2 Java's New Nimbus Look-and-Feel

In Java SE 6 update 10, Java's elegant, cross-platform look-and-feel known as **Nimbus** was introduced. For GUI screen captures like Fig. 14.1, we've configured our systems to use Nimbus as the default look-and-feel. There are three ways that you can use Nimbus:

1. Set it as the default for all Java applications that run on your computer.
2. Set it as the look-and-feel at the time that you launch an application by passing a command-line argument to the java command.
3. Set it as the look-and-feel programatically in your application (see Section 22.6).

To set Nimbus as the default for all Java applications, you must create a text file named swing.properties in the lib folder of both your JDK installation folder and your JRE installation folder. Place the following line of code in the file:

```
swing.defaultlaf=com.sun.java.swing.plaf.nimbus.NimbusLookAndFeel
```

For more information on locating these installation folders visit

```
bit.ly/JavaInstallationInstructions
```

In addition to the standalone JRE, there is a JRE nested in your JDK's installation folder. If you're using an IDE that depends on the JDK, you may also need to place the swing.properties file in the nested jre folder's lib folder.

If you prefer to select Nimbus on an application-by-application basis, place the following command-line argument after the java command and before the application's name when you run the application:

```
-Dswing.defaultlaf=com.sun.java.swing.plaf.nimbus.NimbusLookAndFeel
```

14.3 Simple GUI-Based Input/Output with JOptionPane

The applications in Chapters 2–10 display text in the command window and obtain input from the command window. Most applications you use on a daily basis use windows or **dialog boxes** (also called **dialogs**) to interact with the user. For example, an e-mail program allows you to type and read messages in a window the program provides. Dialog boxes are windows in which programs display important messages to the user or obtain information from the user. Java's **JOptionPane** class (package javax.swing) provides prebuilt dialog boxes for both input and output. These are displayed by invoking static JOptionPane methods. Figure 14.2 presents a simple addition application that uses two **input dialogs** to obtain integers from the user and a **message dialog** to display the sum of the integers the user enters.

```java
1   // Fig. 14.2: Addition.java
2   // Addition program that uses JOptionPane for input and output.
3   import javax.swing.JOptionPane; // program uses JOptionPane
4
5   public class Addition
6   {
7      public static void main( String[] args )
8      {
9         // obtain user input from JOptionPane input dialogs
10        String firstNumber =
11           JOptionPane.showInputDialog( "Enter first integer" );
12        String secondNumber =
13           JOptionPane.showInputDialog( "Enter second integer" );
14
15        // convert String inputs to int values for use in a calculation
16        int number1 = Integer.parseInt( firstNumber );
17        int number2 = Integer.parseInt( secondNumber );
```

Fig. 14.2 | Addition program that uses JOptionPane for input and output. (Part 1 of 2.)

```
18
19      int sum = number1 + number2; // add numbers
20
21      // display result in a JOptionPane message dialog
22      JOptionPane.showMessageDialog( null, "The sum is " + sum,
23         "Sum of Two Integers", JOptionPane.PLAIN_MESSAGE );
24   } // end method main
25 } // end class Addition
```

(a) Input dialog displayed by lines 10–11

Prompt to the user

When the user clicks **OK**, showInputDialog returns to the program the 100 typed by the user as a String; the program must convert the String to an int

Input

Enter first integer

100

OK Cancel

Text field in which the user types a value

(b) Input dialog displayed by lines 12–13

Input

Enter second integer

23

OK Cancel

(c) Message dialog displayed by lines 22–23

Sum of Two Integers

The sum is 123

OK

When the user clicks **OK**, the message dialog is dismissed (removed from the screen).

Fig. 14.2 | Addition program that uses JOptionPane for input and output. (Part 2 of 2.)

Input Dialogs

Line 3 imports class JOptionPane. Lines 10–11 declare the local String variable first-Number and assign it the result of the call to JOptionPane static method **showInputDialog**. This method displays an input dialog (see the first screen capture in Fig. 14.2), using the method's String argument ("Enter first integer") as a prompt.

Look-and-Feel Observation 14.2

*The prompt in an input dialog typically uses **sentence-style capitalization**—a style that capitalizes only the first letter of the first word in the text unless the word is a proper noun (for example, Jones).*

The user types characters in the text field, then clicks **OK** or presses the *Enter* key to submit the String to the program. Clicking **OK** also **dismisses (hides) the dialog**. [*Note:* If you type in the text field and nothing appears, activate the text field by clicking it with the mouse.] Unlike Scanner, which can be used to input values of *several* types from the user at the keyboard, an input dialog can input only Strings. This is typical of most GUI components. The user can type any characters in the input dialog's text field. Our program assumes that the user enters a valid integer. If the user clicks **Cancel**, showInputDialog returns null. If the user either types a noninteger value or clicks the **Cancel** button in the input dialog, an exception will occur and the program will not operate correctly. Chapter 11 discussed how to handle such errors. Lines 12–13 display another input dialog that prompts the user to enter the second integer. Each JOptionPane dialog that you display is a so called **modal dialog**—while the dialog is on the screen, the user *cannot* interact with the rest of the application.

Look-and-Feel Observation 14.3

Do not overuse modal dialogs, as they can reduce the usability of your applications. Use a modal dialog only when it's necessary to prevent users from interacting with the rest of an application until they dismiss the dialog.

Converting *Strings* to *int* Values

To perform the calculation, we convert the Strings that the user entered to int values. Recall that the Integer class's static method parseInt converts its String argument to an int value. Lines 16–17 assign the converted values to local variables number1 and number2, and line 19 sums these values.

Message Dialogs

Lines 22–23 use JOptionPane static method **showMessageDialog** to display a message dialog (the last screen of Fig. 14.2) containing the sum. The first argument helps the Java application determine where to position the dialog box. A dialog is typically displayed from a GUI application with its own window. The first argument refers to that window (known as the parent window) and causes the dialog to appear centered over the parent (as we'll do in Section 14.9). If the first argument is null, the dialog box is displayed at the center of your screen. The second argument is the message to display—in this case, the result of concatenating the String "The sum is " and the value of sum. The third argument—"Sum of Two Integers"—is the String that should appear in the *title bar* at the top of the dialog. The fourth argument—**JOptionPane.PLAIN_MESSAGE**—is the type of message dialog to display. A PLAIN_MESSAGE dialog does not display an icon to the left of the message. Class JOptionPane provides several overloaded versions of methods showInputDialog and showMessageDialog, as well as methods that display other dialog types. For complete information on class JOptionPane, visit download.oracle.com/javase/6/docs/api/javax/swing/JOptionPane.html.

Look-and-Feel Observation 14.4

*The title bar of a window typically uses **book-title capitalization**—a style that capitalizes the first letter of each significant word in the text and does not end with any punctuation (for example, Capitalization in a Book Title).*

JOptionPane Message Dialog Constants

The constants that represent the message dialog types are shown in Fig. 14.3. All message dialog types except PLAIN_MESSAGE display an icon to the left of the message. These icons provide a visual indication of the message's importance to the user. A QUESTION_MESSAGE icon is the *default icon* for an input dialog box (see Fig. 14.2).

Message dialog type	Icon	Description
ERROR_MESSAGE		Indicates an error.
INFORMATION_MESSAGE		Indicates an informational message.
WARNING_MESSAGE		Warns of a potential problem.
QUESTION_MESSAGE		Poses a question. This dialog normally requires a response, such as clicking a **Yes** or a **No** button.
PLAIN_MESSAGE	no icon	A dialog that contains a message, but no icon.

Fig. 14.3 | JOptionPane static constants for message dialogs.

14.4 Overview of Swing Components

Though it's possible to perform input and output using the JOptionPane dialogs, most GUI applications require more elaborate user interfaces. The remainder of this chapter discusses many GUI components that enable application developers to create robust GUIs. Figure 14.4 lists several basic Swing GUI components that we discuss.

Component	Description
JLabel	Displays uneditable text and/or icons.
JTextField	Typically receives input from the user.
JButton	Triggers an event when clicked with the mouse.
JCheckBox	Specifies an option that can be selected or not selected.
JComboBox	A drop-down list of items from which the user can make a selection.
JList	A list of items from which the user can make a selection by clicking on any one of them. Multiple elements can be selected.
JPanel	An area in which components can be placed and organized.

Fig. 14.4 | Some basic GUI components.

Swing vs. AWT
There are actually two sets of Java GUI components. In Java's early days, GUIs were built with components from the **Abstract Window Toolkit (AWT)** in package **java.awt**. These look like the native GUI components of the platform on which a Java program executes. For example, a Button object displayed in a Java program running on Microsoft Windows looks like those in other *Windows* applications. On Apple Mac OS X, the Button looks like those in other *Mac* applications. Sometimes, even the manner in which a user can interact with an AWT component *differs between platforms*. The component's appearance and the way in which the user interacts with it are known as its **look-and-feel**.

Look-and-Feel Observation 14.5

Swing GUI components allow you to specify a uniform look-and-feel for your application across all *platforms or to use each platform's custom look-and-feel. An application can even change the look-and-feel during execution to enable users to choose their own preferred look-and-feel.*

Lightweight vs. Heavyweight GUI Components
Most Swing components are **lightweight components**—they're written, manipulated and displayed completely in Java. AWT components are **heavyweight components**, because they rely on the local platform's **windowing system** to determine their functionality and their look-and-feel. Several Swing components are heavyweight components.

Superclasses of Swing's Lightweight GUI Components
The UML class diagram of Fig. 14.5 shows an inheritance hierarchy of classes from which lightweight Swing components inherit their common attributes and behaviors.

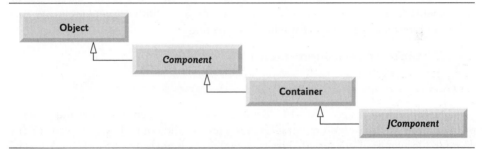

Fig. 14.5 | Common superclasses of the lightweight Swing components.

Class **Component** (package java.awt) is a superclass that declares the common features of GUI components in packages java.awt and javax.swing. Any object that *is a* **Container** (package java.awt) can be used to organize Components by attaching the Components to the Container. Containers can be placed in other Containers to organize a GUI.

Class **JComponent** (package javax.swing) is a subclass of Container. JComponent is the superclass of all lightweight Swing components and declares their common attributes and behaviors. Because JComponent is a subclass of Container, all lightweight Swing components are also Containers. Some common features supported by JComponent include:

1. A **pluggable look-and-feel** for customizing the appearance of components (e.g., for use on particular platforms). You'll see an example of this in Section 22.6.

2. Shortcut keys (called **mnemonics**) for direct access to GUI components through the keyboard. You'll see an example of this in Section 22.4.

3. Brief descriptions of a GUI component's purpose (called **tool tips**) that are displayed when the mouse cursor is positioned over the component for a short time. You'll see an example of this in the next section.

4. Support for accessibility, such as braille screen readers for the visually impaired.

5. Support for user-interface **localization**—that is, customizing the user interface to display in different languages and use local cultural conventions.

14.5 Displaying Text and Images in a Window

Our next example introduces a framework for building GUI applications. Several concepts in this framework will appear in many of our GUI applications. This is our first example in which the application appears in its own window. Most windows you'll create that can contain Swing GUI components are instances of class JFrame or a subclass of JFrame. JFrame is an indirect subclass of class java.awt.Window that provides the basic attributes and behaviors of a window—a title bar at the top, and buttons to minimize, maximize and close the window. Since an application's GUI is typically specific to the application, most of our examples will consist of two classes—a subclass of JFrame that helps us demonstrate new GUI concepts and an application class in which main creates and displays the application's primary window.

Labeling GUI Components

A typical GUI consists of many components. GUI designers often provide text stating the purpose of each. Such text is known as a **label** and is created with a **JLabel**—a subclass of JComponent. A JLabel displays read-only text, an image, or both text and an image. Applications rarely change a label's contents after creating it.

Look-and-Feel Observation 14.6

Text in a JLabel normally uses sentence-style capitalization.

The application of Figs. 14.6–14.7 demonstrates several JLabel features and presents the framework we use in most of our GUI examples. We did not highlight the code in this example, since most of it is new. [*Note:* There are many more features for each GUI component than we can cover in our examples. To learn the complete details of each GUI component, visit its page in the online documentation. For class JLabel, visit download.oracle.com/javase/6/docs/api/javax/swing/JLabel.html.]

```
1   // Fig. 14.6: LabelFrame.java
2   // Demonstrating the JLabel class.
3   import java.awt.FlowLayout; // specifies how components are arranged
4   import javax.swing.JFrame; // provides basic window features
5   import javax.swing.JLabel; // displays text and images
6   import javax.swing.SwingConstants; // common constants used with Swing
7   import javax.swing.Icon; // interface used to manipulate images
8   import javax.swing.ImageIcon; // loads images
9
10  public class LabelFrame extends JFrame
11  {
12     private JLabel label1; // JLabel with just text
13     private JLabel label2; // JLabel constructed with text and icon
14     private JLabel label3; // JLabel with added text and icon
15
16     // LabelFrame constructor adds JLabels to JFrame
17     public LabelFrame()
18     {
```

Fig. 14.6 | JLabels with text and icons. (Part 1 of 2.)

```
19          super( "Testing JLabel" );
20          setLayout( new FlowLayout() ); // set frame layout
21
22          // JLabel constructor with a string argument
23          label1 = new JLabel( "Label with text" );
24          label1.setToolTipText( "This is label1" );
25          add( label1 ); // add label1 to JFrame
26
27          // JLabel constructor with string, Icon and alignment arguments
28          Icon bug = new ImageIcon( getClass().getResource( "bug1.png" ) );
29          label2 = new JLabel( "Label with text and icon", bug,
30             SwingConstants.LEFT );
31          label2.setToolTipText( "This is label2" );
32          add( label2 ); // add label2 to JFrame
33
34          label3 = new JLabel(); // JLabel constructor no arguments
35          label3.setText( "Label with icon and text at bottom" );
36          label3.setIcon( bug ); // add icon to JLabel
37          label3.setHorizontalTextPosition( SwingConstants.CENTER );
38          label3.setVerticalTextPosition( SwingConstants.BOTTOM );
39          label3.setToolTipText( "This is label3" );
40          add( label3 ); // add label3 to JFrame
41       } // end LabelFrame constructor
42    } // end class LabelFrame
```

Fig. 14.6 | JLabels with text and icons. (Part 2 of 2.)

```
1    // Fig. 14.7: LabelTest.java
2    // Testing LabelFrame.
3    import javax.swing.JFrame;
4
5    public class LabelTest
6    {
7       public static void main( String[] args )
8       {
9          LabelFrame labelFrame = new LabelFrame(); // create LabelFrame
10         labelFrame.setDefaultCloseOperation( JFrame.EXIT_ON_CLOSE );
11         labelFrame.setSize( 260, 180 ); // set frame size
12         labelFrame.setVisible( true ); // display frame
13      } // end main
14   } // end class LabelTest
```

Fig. 14.7 | Test class for LabelFrame.

Class `LabelFrame` (Fig. 14.6) is a subclass of `JFrame`. We'll use an instance of class `LabelFrame` to display a window containing three `JLabel`s. Lines 3–8 import the classes used in class `LabelFrame`. The class extends `JFrame` to inherit the features of a window. Lines 12–14 declare the three `JLabel` instance variables that are instantiated in the `LabelFrame` constructor (lines 17–41). Typically, the `JFrame` subclass's constructor builds the GUI that's displayed in the window when the application executes. Line 19 invokes superclass `JFrame`'s constructor with the argument `"Testing JLabel"`. `JFrame`'s constructor uses this `String` as the text in the window's title bar.

Specifying the Layout

When building a GUI, you must attach each GUI component to a container, such as a window created with a `JFrame`. Also, you typically must decide *where* to position each GUI component—known as specifying the layout. Java provides several **layout managers** that can help you position components, as you'll learn at the end of this chapter and in Chapter 22.

Many IDEs provide GUI design tools in which you can specify components' exact sizes and locations in a visual manner by using the mouse; then the IDE will generate the GUI code for you. Such IDEs can greatly simplify GUI creation.

To ensure that our GUIs can be used with *any* IDE, we did *not* use an IDE to create the GUI code. We use Java's layout managers to size and position components. With the **FlowLayout** layout manager, components are placed on a container from left to right in the order in which they're added. When no more components can fit on the current line, they continue to display left to right on the next line. If the container is resized, a FlowLayout *reflows* the components, possibly with fewer or more rows based on the new container width. Every container has a default layout, which we're changing for `LabelFrame` to a `FlowLayout` (line 20). Method **setLayout** is inherited into class `LabelFrame` indirectly from class `Container`. The argument to the method must be an object of a class that implements the `LayoutManager` interface (e.g., `FlowLayout`). Line 20 creates a new `FlowLayout` object and passes its reference as the argument to `setLayout`.

Creating and Attaching `label1`

Now that we've specified the window's layout, we can begin creating and attaching GUI components to the window. Line 23 creates a `JLabel` object and passes `"Label with text"` to the constructor. The `JLabel` displays this text on the screen as part of the application's GUI. Line 24 uses method **setToolTipText** (inherited by `JLabel` from `JComponent`) to specify the tool tip that's displayed when the user positions the mouse cursor over the `JLabel` in the GUI. You can see a sample tool tip in the second screen capture of Fig. 14.7. When you execute this application, try positioning the mouse over each `JLabel` to see its tool tip. Line 25 attaches `label1` to the `LabelFrame` by passing `label1` to the **add** method, which is inherited indirectly from class `Container`.

Common Programming Error 14.1

If you do not explicitly add a GUI component to a container, the GUI component will not be displayed when the container appears on the screen.

Look-and-Feel Observation 14.7

Use tool tips to add descriptive text to your GUI components. This text helps the user determine the GUI component's purpose in the user interface.

The `Icon` Interface and Class `ImageIcon`

Icons are a popular way to enhance the look-and-feel of an application and are also commonly used to indicate functionality. For example, the same icon is used to play most of today's media on devices like DVD players and MP3 players. Several Swing components can display images. An icon is normally specified with an **Icon** argument to a constructor or to the component's **setIcon** method. An Icon is an object of any class that implements interface Icon (package javax.swing). Class **ImageIcon** supports several image formats, including Graphics Interchange Format (GIF), Portable Network Graphics (PNG) and Joint Photographic Experts Group (JPEG).

Line 28 declares an ImageIcon. The file bug1.png contains the image to load and store in the ImageIcon object. This image is included in the directory for this example. The ImageIcon object is assigned to Icon reference bug.

Loading an Image Resource

In line 28, the expression getClass().getResource("bug1.png") invokes method **getClass** (inherited indirectly from class Object) to retrieve a reference to the Class object that represents the LabelFrame class declaration. That reference is then used to invoke Class method **getResource**, which returns the location of the image as a URL. The ImageIcon constructor uses the URL to locate the image, then loads it into memory. As we discussed in Chapter 1, the JVM loads class declarations into memory, using a class loader. The class loader knows where each class it loads is located on disk. Method getResource uses the Class object's class loader to determine the location of a resource, such as an image file. In this example, the image file is stored in the same location as the LabelFrame.class file. The techniques described here enable an application to load image files from locations that are relative to the class file's location.

Creating and Attaching `label2`

Lines 29–30 use another JLabel constructor to create a JLabel that displays the text "Label with text and icon" and the Icon bug created in line 28. The last constructor argument indicates that the label's contents are left justified, or left aligned (i.e., the icon and text are at the left side of the label's area on the screen). Interface **SwingConstants** (package javax.swing) declares a set of common integer constants (such as SwingConstants.LEFT) that are used with many Swing components. By default, the text appears to the right of the image when a label contains both text and an image. The horizontal and vertical alignments of a JLabel can be set with methods **setHorizontalAlignment** and **setVerticalAlignment**, respectively. Line 31 specifies the tool-tip text for label2, and line 32 adds label2 to the JFrame.

Creating and Attaching `label3`

Class JLabel provides methods to change a label's appearance after it's been instantiated. Line 34 creates an empty JLabel with the no-argument constructor. Line 35 uses JLabel method **setText** to set the text displayed on the label. Method **getText** can be used to retrieve the current text displayed on a label. Line 36 uses JLabel method setIcon to specify the Icon to display on the label. Method **getIcon** can be used to retrieve the current Icon displayed on a label. Lines 37–38 use JLabel methods **setHorizontalTextPosition** and **setVerticalTextPosition** to specify the text position in the label. In this case, the text will be centered horizontally and will appear at the bottom of the label. Thus, the Icon will appear above the text. The horizontal-position constants in SwingConstants are LEFT, CENTER and RIGHT (Fig. 14.8). The vertical-position constants in SwingConstants are TOP, CENTER and BOTTOM (Fig. 14.8). Line 39 sets the tool-tip text for label3. Line 40 adds label3 to the JFrame.

Constant	Description	Constant	Description
Horizontal-position constants		*Vertical-position constants*	
LEFT	Place text on the left	TOP	Place text at the top
CENTER	Place text in the center	CENTER	Place text in the center
RIGHT	Place text on the right	BOTTOM	Place text at the bottom

Fig. 14.8 | Positioning constants (static members of interface SwingConstants).

Creating and Displaying a LabelFrame Window

Class LabelTest (Fig. 14.7) creates an object of class LabelFrame (line 9), then specifies the default close operation for the window. By default, closing a window simply hides the window. However, when the user closes the LabelFrame window, we would like the application to terminate. Line 10 invokes LabelFrame's **setDefaultCloseOperation** method (inherited from class JFrame) with constant **JFrame.EXIT_ON_CLOSE** as the argument to indicate that the program should terminate when the window is closed by the user. This line is important. Without it the application will not terminate when the user closes the window. Next, line 11 invokes LabelFrame's **setSize** method to specify the width and height of the window in pixels. Finally, line 12 invokes LabelFrame's **setVisible** method with the argument true to display the window on the screen. Try resizing the window to see how the FlowLayout changes the JLabel positions as the window width changes.

14.6 Text Fields and an Introduction to Event Handling with Nested Classes

Normally, a user interacts with an application's GUI to indicate the tasks that the application should perform. For example, when you write an e-mail in an e-mail application, clicking the **Send** button tells the application to send the e-mail to the specified e-mail addresses. GUIs are **event driven**. When the user interacts with a GUI component, the interaction—known as an **event**—drives the program to perform a task. Some common user interactions that cause an application to perform a task include clicking a button, typing in a text field, selecting an item from a menu, closing a window and moving the mouse. The code that performs a task in response to an event is called an **event handler**, and the overall process of responding to events is known as **event handling**.

Let's consider two other GUI components that can generate events—**JTextFields** and **JPasswordFields** (package javax.swing). Class JTextField extends class **JTextComponent** (package javax.swing.text), which provides many features common to Swing's text-based components. Class JPasswordField extends JTextField and adds methods that are specific to processing passwords. Each of these components is a single-line area in which the user can enter text via the keyboard. Applications can also display text in a JTextField (see the output of Fig. 14.10). A JPasswordField shows that characters are being typed as the user enters them, but hides the actual characters with an **echo character**, assuming that they represent a password that should remain known only to the user.

When the user types in a JTextField or a JPasswordField, then presses *Enter*, an event occurs. Our next example demonstrates how a program can perform a task in response to that event. The techniques shown here are applicable to all GUI components that generate events.

The application of Figs. 14.9–14.10 uses classes JTextField and JPasswordField to create and manipulate four text fields. When the user types in one of the text fields, then presses *Enter*, the application displays a message dialog box containing the text the user typed. You can type only in the text field that's "in **focus**." When you click a component, it *receives the focus*. This is important, because the text field with the focus is the one that generates an event when you press *Enter*. In this example, you press *Enter* in the JPasswordField, the password is revealed. We begin by discussing the setup of the GUI, then discuss the event-handling code.

Lines 3–9 import the classes and interfaces we use in this example. Class TextFieldFrame extends JFrame and declares three JTextField variables and a JPasswordField variable (lines 13–16). Each of the corresponding text fields is instantiated and attached to the TextFieldFrame in the constructor (lines 19–47).

```java
1   // Fig. 14.9: TextFieldFrame.java
2   // Demonstrating the JTextField class.
3   import java.awt.FlowLayout;
4   import java.awt.event.ActionListener;
5   import java.awt.event.ActionEvent;
6   import javax.swing.JFrame;
7   import javax.swing.JTextField;
8   import javax.swing.JPasswordField;
9   import javax.swing.JOptionPane;
10
11  public class TextFieldFrame extends JFrame
12  {
13     private JTextField textField1; // text field with set size
14     private JTextField textField2; // text field constructed with text
15     private JTextField textField3; // text field with text and size
16     private JPasswordField passwordField; // password field with text
17
18     // TextFieldFrame constructor adds JTextFields to JFrame
19     public TextFieldFrame()
20     {
21        super( "Testing JTextField and JPasswordField" );
22        setLayout( new FlowLayout() ); // set frame layout
23
24        // construct textfield with 10 columns
25        textField1 = new JTextField( 10 );
26        add( textField1 ); // add textField1 to JFrame
27
28        // construct textfield with default text
29        textField2 = new JTextField( "Enter text here" );
30        add( textField2 ); // add textField2 to JFrame
```

Fig. 14.9 | JTextFields and JPasswordFields. (Part 1 of 2.)

```
31
32          // construct textfield with default text and 21 columns
33          textField3 = new JTextField( "Uneditable text field", 21 );
34          textField3.setEditable( false ); // disable editing
35          add( textField3 ); // add textField3 to JFrame
36
37          // construct passwordfield with default text
38          passwordField = new JPasswordField( "Hidden text" );
39          add( passwordField ); // add passwordField to JFrame
40
41          // register event handlers
42          TextFieldHandler handler = new TextFieldHandler();
43          textField1.addActionListener( handler );
44          textField2.addActionListener( handler );
45          textField3.addActionListener( handler );
46          passwordField.addActionListener( handler );
47      } // end TextFieldFrame constructor
48
49      // private inner class for event handling
50      private class TextFieldHandler implements ActionListener
51      {
52          // process text field events
53          public void actionPerformed( ActionEvent event )
54          {
55              String string = ""; // declare string to display
56
57              // user pressed Enter in JTextField textField1
58              if ( event.getSource() == textField1 )
59                  string = String.format( "textField1: %s",
60                      event.getActionCommand() );
61
62              // user pressed Enter in JTextField textField2
63              else if ( event.getSource() == textField2 )
64                  string = String.format( "textField2: %s",
65                      event.getActionCommand() );
66
67              // user pressed Enter in JTextField textField3
68              else if ( event.getSource() == textField3 )
69                  string = String.format( "textField3: %s",
70                      event.getActionCommand() );
71
72              // user pressed Enter in JTextField passwordField
73              else if ( event.getSource() == passwordField )
74                  string = String.format( "passwordField: %s",
75                      event.getActionCommand() );
76
77              // display JTextField content
78              JOptionPane.showMessageDialog( null, string );
79          } // end method actionPerformed
80      } // end private inner class TextFieldHandler
81  } // end class TextFieldFrame
```

Fig. 14.9 | JTextFields and JPasswordFields. (Part 2 of 2.)

Creating the GUI
Line 22 sets the TextFieldFrame's layout to FlowLayout. Line 25 creates textField1 with 10 columns of text. A text column's width in *pixels* is determined by the average width of a character in the text field's current font. When text is displayed in a text field and the text is wider than the field itself, a portion of the text at the right side is not visible. If you're typing in a text field and the cursor reaches the right edge, the text at the left edge is pushed off the left side of the field and is no longer visible. Users can use the left and right arrow keys to move through the complete text. Line 26 adds textField1 to the JFrame.

Line 29 creates textField2 with the initial text "Enter text here" to display in the text field. The width of the field is determined by the width of the default text specified in the constructor. Line 30 adds textField2 to the JFrame.

Line 33 creates textField3 and calls the JTextField constructor with two arguments—the default text "Uneditable text field" to display and the text field's width in columns (21). Line 34 uses method **setEditable** (inherited by JTextField from class JTextComponent) to make the text field *uneditable*—i.e., the user cannot modify the text in the field. Line 35 adds textField3 to the JFrame.

Line 38 creates passwordField with the text "Hidden text" to display in the text field. The width of the field is determined by the width of the default text. When you execute the application, notice that the text is displayed as a string of asterisks. Line 39 adds passwordField to the JFrame.

Steps Required to Set Up Event Handling for a GUI Component
This example should display a message dialog containing the text from a text field when the user presses *Enter* in that text field. Before an application can respond to an event for a particular GUI component, you must:

1. Create a class that represents the event handler and implements an appropriate interface—known as an **event-listener interface**.

2. Indicate that an object of the class from *Step 1* should be notified when the event occurs—known as **registering the event handler**.

Using a Nested Class to Implement an Event Handler
All the classes discussed so far were so-called **top-level classes**—that is, they were not declared inside another class. Java allows you to declare classes *inside* other classes—these are called **nested classes**. Nested classes can be static or non-static. Non-static nested classes are called **inner classes** and are frequently used to implement *event handlers*.

An inner-class object must be created by an object of the top-level class that contains the inner class. Each inner-class object *implicitly* has a reference to an object of its top-level class. The inner-class object is allowed to use this implicit reference to directly access all the variables and methods of the top-level class. A nested class that's static does not require an object of its top-level class and does not implicitly have a reference to an object of the top-level class. As you'll see in Chapter 15, Graphics and Java 2D, the Java 2D graphics API uses static nested classes extensively.

Inner Class **TextFieldHandler**
The event handling in this example is performed by an object of the private inner class TextFieldHandler (lines 50–80). This class is private because it will be used only to cre-

ate event handlers for the text fields in top-level class TextFieldFrame. As with other class members, *inner classes* can be declared public, protected or private. Since event handlers tend to be specific to the application in which they're defined, they're often implemented as private inner classes or as *anonymous inner classes* (Section 14.11).

GUI components can generate many events in response to user interactions. Each event is represented by a class and can be processed only by the appropriate type of event handler. Normally, a component's supported events are described in the Java API documentation for that component's class and its superclasses. When the user presses *Enter* in a JTextField or JPasswordField, an **ActionEvent** (package java.awt.event) occurs. Such an event is processed by an object that implements the interface **ActionListener** (package java.awt.event). The information discussed here is available in the Java API documentation for classes JTextField and ActionEvent. Since JPasswordField is a subclass of JTextField, JPasswordField supports the same events.

To prepare to handle the events in this example, inner class TextFieldHandler implements interface ActionListener and declares the only method in that interface—actionPerformed (lines 53–79). This method specifies the tasks to perform when an ActionEvent occurs. So, inner class TextFieldHandler satisfies *Step 1* listed earlier in this section. We'll discuss the details of method actionPerformed shortly.

Registering the Event Handler for Each Text Field
In the TextFieldFrame constructor, line 42 creates a TextFieldHandler object and assigns it to variable handler. This object's actionPerformed method will be called automatically when the user presses *Enter* in any of the GUI's text fields. However, before this can occur, the program must register this object as the event handler for each text field. Lines 43–46 are the event-registration statements that specify handler as the event handler for the three JTextFields and the JPasswordField. The application calls JTextField method **addActionListener** to register the event handler for each component. This method receives as its argument an ActionListener object, which can be an object of any class that implements ActionListener. The object handler *is an* ActionListener, because class TextFieldHandler implements ActionListener. After lines 43–46 execute, the object handler **listens for events**. Now, when the user presses *Enter* in any of these four text fields, method actionPerformed (line 53–79) in class TextFieldHandler is called to handle the event. If an event handler is not registered for a particular text field, the event that occurs when the user presses *Enter* in that text field is **consumed**—i.e., it's simply ignored by the application.

Software Engineering Observation 14.1
The event listener for an event must implement the appropriate event-listener interface.

Common Programming Error 14.2
Forgetting to register an event-handler object for a particular GUI component's event type causes events of that type to be ignored.

Details of Class TextFieldHandler's actionPerformed Method
In this example, we're using one event-handling object's actionPerformed method (lines 53–79) to handle the events generated by four text fields. Since we'd like to output the

name of each text field's instance variable for demonstration purposes, we must determine which text field generated the event each time `actionPerformed` is called. The **event source** is the GUI component with which the user interacted. When the user presses *Enter* while one of the text fields or the password field *has the focus*, the system creates a unique `ActionEvent` object that contains information about the event that just occurred, such as the event source and the text in the text field. The system passes this `ActionEvent` object to the event listener's `actionPerformed` method. Line 55 declares the `String` that will be displayed. The variable is initialized with the **empty string**—a `String` containing no characters. The compiler requires the variable to be initialized in case none of the branches of the nested `if` in lines 58–75 executes.

`ActionEvent` method `getSource` (called in lines 58, 63, 68 and 73) returns a reference to the event source. The condition in line 58 asks, "Is the event source `textField1`?" This condition compares references with the `==` operator to determine if they refer to the same object. If they *both* refer to `textField1`, the user pressed *Enter* in `textField1`. Then, lines 59–60 create a `String` containing the message that line 78 displays in a message dialog. Line 60 uses `ActionEvent` method **getActionCommand** to obtain the text the user typed in the text field that generated the event.

In this example, we display the text of the password in the `JPasswordField` when the user presses *Enter* in that field. Sometimes it's necessary to programatically process the characters in a password. Class `JPasswordField` method **getPassword** returns the password's characters as an array of type `char`.

Class *TextFieldTest*

Class `TextFieldTest` (Fig. 14.10) contains the `main` method that executes this application and displays an object of class `TextFieldFrame`. When you execute the application, even the uneditable `JTextField` (`textField3`) can generate an `ActionEvent`. To test this, click the text field to give it the focus, then press *Enter*. Also, the actual text of the password is displayed when you press *Enter* in the `JPasswordField`. Of course, you would normally not display the password!

This application used a single object of class `TextFieldHandler` as the event listener for four text fields. Starting in Section 14.10, you'll see that it's possible to declare several event-listener objects of the same type and register each object for a separate GUI component's event. This technique enables us to eliminate the `if...else` logic used in this example's event handler by providing separate event handlers for each component's events.

```
1   // Fig. 14.10: TextFieldTest.java
2   // Testing TextFieldFrame.
3   import javax.swing.JFrame;
4
5   public class TextFieldTest
6   {
7      public static void main( String[] args )
8      {
9         TextFieldFrame textFieldFrame = new TextFieldFrame();
10        textFieldFrame.setDefaultCloseOperation( JFrame.EXIT_ON_CLOSE );
11        textFieldFrame.setSize( 350, 100 ); // set frame size
```

Fig. 14.10 | Test class for `TextFieldFrame`. (Part 1 of 2.)

```
12          textFieldFrame.setVisible( true ); // display frame
13      } // end main
14  } // end class TextFieldTest
```

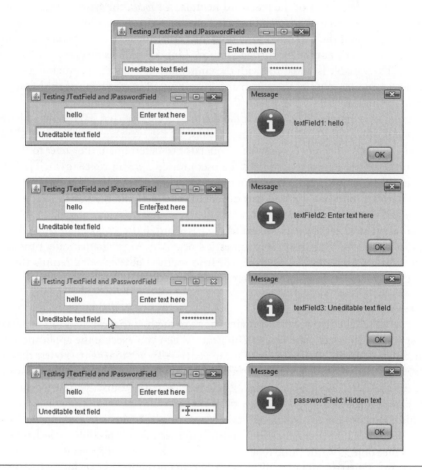

Fig. 14.10 | Test class for `TextFieldFrame`. (Part 2 of 2.)

14.7 Common GUI Event Types and Listener Interfaces

In Section 14.6, you learned that information about the event that occurs when the user presses *Enter* in a text field is stored in an `ActionEvent` object. Many different types of events can occur when the user interacts with a GUI. The event information is stored in an object of a class that extends `AWTEvent` (from package java.awt). Figure 14.11 illustrates a hierarchy containing many event classes from the package **java.awt.event**. Some of these are discussed in this chapter and Chapter 22. These event types are used with both AWT and Swing components. Additional event types that are specific to Swing GUI components are declared in package **javax.swing.event**.

Let's summarize the three parts to the event-handling mechanism that you saw in Section 14.6—the *event source*, the *event object* and the *event listener*. The event source is

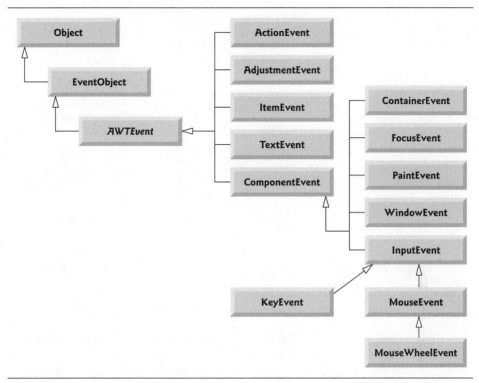

Fig. 14.11 | Some event classes of package `java.awt.event`.

the GUI component with which the user interacts. The event object encapsulates information about the event that occurred, such as a reference to the event source and any event-specific information that may be required by the event listener for it to handle the event. The event listener is an object that's notified by the event source when an event occurs; in effect, it "listens" for an event, and one of its methods executes in response to the event. A method of the event listener receives an event object when the event listener is notified of the event. The event listener then uses the event object to respond to the event. This event-handling model is known as the **delegation event model**—an event's processing is delegated to an object (the event listener) in the application.

For each event-object type, there's typically a corresponding event-listener interface. An event listener for a GUI event is an object of a class that implements one or more of the event-listener interfaces from packages `java.awt.event` and `javax.swing.event`. Many of the event-listener types are common to both Swing and AWT components. Such types are declared in package `java.awt.event`, and some of them are shown in Fig. 14.12. Additional event-listener types that are specific to Swing components are declared in package `javax.swing.event`.

Each event-listener interface specifies one or more event-handling methods that *must* be declared in the class that implements the interface. Recall from Section 10.7 that any class which implements an interface must declare *all* the abstract methods of that interface; otherwise, the class is an abstract class and cannot be used to create objects.

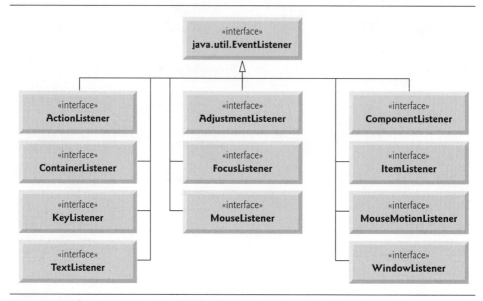

Fig. 14.12 | Some common event-listener interfaces of package `java.awt.event`.

When an event occurs, the GUI component with which the user interacted notifies its *registered listeners* by calling each listener's appropriate *event-handling method*. For example, when the user presses the *Enter* key in a JTextField, the registered listener's actionPerformed method is called. How did the event handler get registered? How does the GUI component know to call actionPerformed rather than another event-handling method? We answer these questions and diagram the interaction in the next section.

14.8 How Event Handling Works

Let's illustrate how the event-handling mechanism works, using textField1 from the example of Fig. 14.9. We have two remaining open questions from Section 14.7:

1. How did the *event handler* get *registered*?

2. How does the GUI component know to call actionPerformed rather than some other event-handling method?

The first question is answered by the event registration performed in lines 43–46 of Fig. 14.9. Figure 14.13 diagrams JTextField variable textField1, TextFieldHandler variable handler and the objects to which they refer.

Registering Events

Every JComponent has an instance variable called listenerList that refers to an object of class **EventListenerList** (package javax.swing.event). Each object of a JComponent subclass maintains references to its registered listeners in the listenerList. For simplicity, we've diagrammed listenerList as an array below the JTextField object in Fig. 14.13.

When line 43 of Fig. 14.9

```
textField1.addActionListener( handler );
```

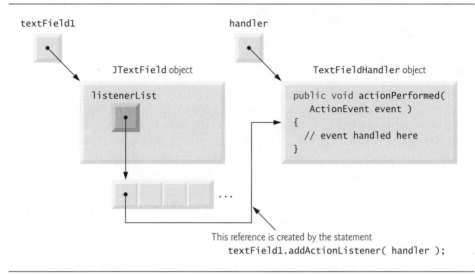

Fig. 14.13 | Event registration for JTextField textField1.

executes, a new entry containing a reference to the TextFieldHandler object is placed in textField1's listenerList. Although not shown in the diagram, this new entry also includes the listener's type (in this case, ActionListener). Using this mechanism, each lightweight Swing GUI component maintains its own list of *listeners* that were *registered* to *handle* the component's *events*.

Event-Handler Invocation

The event-listener type is important in answering the second question: How does the GUI component know to call actionPerformed rather than another method? Every GUI component supports several *event types*, including **mouse events**, **key events** and others. When an event occurs, the event is **dispatched** only to the *event listeners* of the appropriate type. Dispatching is simply the process by which the GUI component calls an event-handling method on each of its listeners that are registered for the event type that occurred.

Each *event type* has one or more corresponding *event-listener interfaces*. For example, ActionEvents are handled by ActionListeners, **MouseEvents** by **MouseListeners** and **MouseMotionListeners**, and **KeyEvents** by **KeyListeners**. When an event occurs, the GUI component receives (from the JVM) a unique *event ID* specifying the event type. The GUI component uses the event ID to decide the listener type to which the event should be dispatched and to decide which method to call on each listener object. For an ActionEvent, the event is dispatched to *every* registered ActionListener's actionPerformed method (the only method in interface ActionListener). For a MouseEvent, the event is dispatched to *every* registered MouseListener or MouseMotionListener, depending on the mouse event that occurs. The MouseEvent's event ID determines which of the several mouse event-handling methods are called. All these decisions are handled for you by the GUI components. All you need to do is register an event handler for the particular event type that your application requires, and the GUI component will ensure that the event handler's appropriate method gets called when the event occurs. We discuss other event types and event-listener interfaces as they're needed with each new component we introduce.

14.9 JButton

A **button** is a component the user clicks to trigger a specific action. A Java application can use several types of buttons, including **command buttons**, **checkboxes**, **toggle buttons** and **radio buttons**. Figure 14.14 shows the inheritance hierarchy of the Swing buttons we cover in this chapter. As you can see, all the button types are subclasses of **AbstractButton** (package javax.swing), which declares the common features of Swing buttons. In this section, we concentrate on buttons that are typically used to initiate a command.

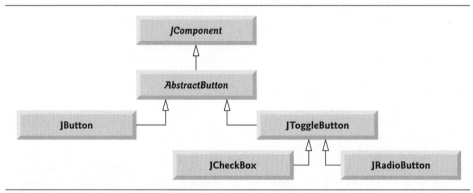

Fig. 14.14 | Swing button hierarchy.

A command button (see Fig. 14.16's output) generates an ActionEvent when the user clicks it. Command buttons are created with class **JButton**. The text on the face of a JButton is called a **button label**. A GUI can have many JButtons, but each button label should be unique in the portion of the GUI that's currently displayed.

Look-and-Feel Observation 14.8
The text on buttons typically uses book-title capitalization.

Look-and-Feel Observation 14.9
Having more than one JButton with the same label makes the JButtons ambiguous to the user. Provide a unique label for each button.

The application of Figs. 14.15 and 14.16 creates two JButtons and demonstrates that JButtons support the display of Icons. Event handling for the buttons is performed by a single instance of *inner class* ButtonHandler (lines 39–47).

Lines 14–15 declare JButton variables plainJButton and fancyJButton. The corresponding objects are instantiated in the constructor. Line 23 creates plainJButton with the button label "Plain Button". Line 24 adds the JButton to the JFrame.

A JButton can display an Icon. To provide the user with an extra level of visual interaction with the GUI, a JButton can also have a **rollover Icon**—an Icon that's displayed

```
 1   // Fig. 14.15: ButtonFrame.java
 2   // Creating JButtons.
 3   import java.awt.FlowLayout;
 4   import java.awt.event.ActionListener;
 5   import java.awt.event.ActionEvent;
 6   import javax.swing.JFrame;
 7   import javax.swing.JButton;
 8   import javax.swing.Icon;
 9   import javax.swing.ImageIcon;
10   import javax.swing.JOptionPane;
11
12   public class ButtonFrame extends JFrame
13   {
14      private JButton plainJButton; // button with just text
15      private JButton fancyJButton; // button with icons
16
17      // ButtonFrame adds JButtons to JFrame
18      public ButtonFrame()
19      {
20         super( "Testing Buttons" );
21         setLayout( new FlowLayout() ); // set frame layout
22
23         plainJButton = new JButton( "Plain Button" ); // button with text
24         add( plainJButton ); // add plainJButton to JFrame
25
26         Icon bug1 = new ImageIcon( getClass().getResource( "bug1.gif" ) );
27         Icon bug2 = new ImageIcon( getClass().getResource( "bug2.gif" ) );
28         fancyJButton = new JButton( "Fancy Button", bug1 ); // set image
29         fancyJButton.setRolloverIcon( bug2 ); // set rollover image
30         add( fancyJButton ); // add fancyJButton to JFrame
31
32         // create new ButtonHandler for button event handling
33         ButtonHandler handler = new ButtonHandler();
34         fancyJButton.addActionListener( handler );
35         plainJButton.addActionListener( handler );
36      } // end ButtonFrame constructor
37
38      // inner class for button event handling
39      private class ButtonHandler implements ActionListener
40      {
41         // handle button event
42         public void actionPerformed( ActionEvent event )
43         {
44            JOptionPane.showMessageDialog( ButtonFrame.this, String.format(
45               "You pressed: %s", event.getActionCommand() ) );
46         } // end method actionPerformed
47      } // end private inner class ButtonHandler
48   } // end class ButtonFrame
```

Fig. 14.15 | Command buttons and action events.

when the user positions the mouse over the JButton. The icon on the JButton changes as the mouse moves in and out of the JButton's area on the screen. Lines 26–27 (Fig. 14.15) create two ImageIcon objects that represent the default Icon and rollover Icon for the

```
 1   // Fig. 14.16: ButtonTest.java
 2   // Testing ButtonFrame.
 3   import javax.swing.JFrame;
 4
 5   public class ButtonTest
 6   {
 7      public static void main( String[] args )
 8      {
 9         ButtonFrame buttonFrame = new ButtonFrame(); // create ButtonFrame
10         buttonFrame.setDefaultCloseOperation( JFrame.EXIT_ON_CLOSE );
11         buttonFrame.setSize( 275, 110 ); // set frame size
12         buttonFrame.setVisible( true ); // display frame
13      } // end main
14   } // end class ButtonTest
```

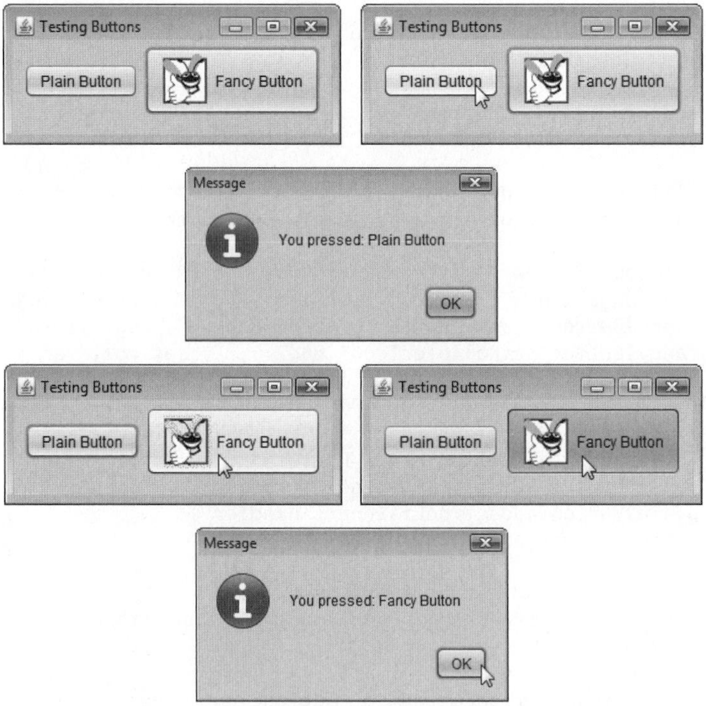

Fig. 14.16 | Test class for ButtonFrame.

JButton created at line 28. Both statements assume that the image files are stored in the same directory as the application. Images are commonly placed in the same directory as the application or a subdirectory like images). These image files have been provided for you with the example.

Line 28 creates fancyButton with the text "Fancy Button" and the icon bug1. By default, the text is displayed to the right of the icon. Line 29 uses **setRolloverIcon** (inherited from class AbstractButton) to specify the image displayed on the JButton when the user positions the mouse over it. Line 30 adds the JButton to the JFrame.

Look-and-Feel Observation 14.10
Because class AbstractButton supports displaying text and images on a button, all subclasses of AbstractButton also support displaying text and images.

Look-and-Feel Observation 14.11
Using rollover icons for JButtons provides users with visual feedback indicating that when they click the mouse while the cursor is positioned over the JButton, an action will occur.

JButtons, like JTextFields, generate ActionEvents that can be processed by any ActionListener object. Lines 33–35 create an object of private *inner class* ButtonHandler and use addActionListener to *register* it as the *event handler* for each JButton. Class ButtonHandler (lines 39–47) declares actionPerformed to display a message dialog box containing the label for the button the user pressed. For a JButton event, ActionEvent method getActionCommand returns the label on the JButton.

*Accessing the **this** Reference in an Object of a Top-Level Class From an Inner Class*
When you execute this application and click one of its buttons, notice that the message dialog that appears is centered over the application's window. This occurs because the call to JOptionPane method showMessageDialog (lines 44–45 of Fig. 14.15) uses ButtonFrame.this rather than null as the first argument. When this argument is not null, it represents the so-called *parent GUI component* of the message dialog (in this case the application window is the parent component) and enables the dialog to be centered over that component when the dialog is displayed. ButtonFrame.this represents the this reference of the object of top-level class ButtonFrame.

Software Engineering Observation 14.2
When used in an inner class, keyword this refers to the current inner-class object being manipulated. An inner-class method can use its outer-class object's this by preceding this with the outer-class name and a dot, as in ButtonFrame.this.

14.10 Buttons That Maintain State

The Swing GUI components contain three types of **state buttons**—**JToggleButton**, **JCheckBox** and **JRadioButton**—that have on/off or true/false values. Classes JCheckBox and JRadioButton are subclasses of JToggleButton (Fig. 14.14). A JRadioButton is different from a JCheckBox in that normally several JRadioButtons are grouped together and are mutually exclusive—only one in the group can be selected at any time, just like the buttons on a car radio. We first discuss class JCheckBox.

14.10.1 JCheckBox

The application of Figs. 14.17–14.18 uses two JCheckBoxes to select the desired font style of the text displayed in a JTextField. When selected, one applies a bold style and the other an italic style. If *both* are selected, the style is bold and italic. When the application initially executes, neither JCheckBox is checked (i.e., they're both false), so the font is plain. Class CheckBoxTest (Fig. 14.18) contains the main method that executes this application.

```java
1   // Fig. 14.17: CheckBoxFrame.java
2   // Creating JCheckBox buttons.
3   import java.awt.FlowLayout;
4   import java.awt.Font;
5   import java.awt.event.ItemListener;
6   import java.awt.event.ItemEvent;
7   import javax.swing.JFrame;
8   import javax.swing.JTextField;
9   import javax.swing.JCheckBox;
10
11  public class CheckBoxFrame extends JFrame
12  {
13     private JTextField textField; // displays text in changing fonts
14     private JCheckBox boldJCheckBox; // to select/deselect bold
15     private JCheckBox italicJCheckBox; // to select/deselect italic
16
17     // CheckBoxFrame constructor adds JCheckBoxes to JFrame
18     public CheckBoxFrame()
19     {
20        super( "JCheckBox Test" );
21        setLayout( new FlowLayout() ); // set frame layout
22
23        // set up JTextField and set its font
24        textField = new JTextField( "Watch the font style change", 20 );
25        textField.setFont( new Font( "Serif", Font.PLAIN, 14 ) );
26        add( textField ); // add textField to JFrame
27
28        boldJCheckBox = new JCheckBox( "Bold" ); // create bold checkbox
29        italicJCheckBox = new JCheckBox( "Italic" ); // create italic
30        add( boldJCheckBox ); // add bold checkbox to JFrame
31        add( italicJCheckBox ); // add italic checkbox to JFrame
32
33        // register listeners for JCheckBoxes
34        CheckBoxHandler handler = new CheckBoxHandler();
35        boldJCheckBox.addItemListener( handler );
36        italicJCheckBox.addItemListener( handler );
37     } // end CheckBoxFrame constructor
38
39     // private inner class for ItemListener event handling
40     private class CheckBoxHandler implements ItemListener
41     {
42        // respond to checkbox events
43        public void itemStateChanged( ItemEvent event )
44        {
45           Font font = null; // stores the new Font
46
47           // determine which CheckBoxes are checked and create Font
48           if ( boldJCheckBox.isSelected() && italicJCheckBox.isSelected() )
49              font = new Font( "Serif", Font.BOLD + Font.ITALIC, 14 );
50           else if ( boldJCheckBox.isSelected() )
51              font = new Font( "Serif", Font.BOLD, 14 );
52           else if ( italicJCheckBox.isSelected() )
53              font = new Font( "Serif", Font.ITALIC, 14 );
```

Fig. 14.17 | JCheckBox buttons and item events. (Part 1 of 2.)

```
54                  else
55                     font = new Font( "Serif", Font.PLAIN, 14 );
56
57                  textField.setFont( font ); // set textField's font
58            } // end method itemStateChanged
59         } // end private inner class CheckBoxHandler
60   } // end class CheckBoxFrame
```

Fig. 14.17 | JCheckBox buttons and item events. (Part 2 of 2.)

```
 1   // Fig. 14.18: CheckBoxTest.java
 2   // Testing CheckBoxFrame.
 3   import javax.swing.JFrame;
 4
 5   public class CheckBoxTest
 6   {
 7      public static void main( String[] args )
 8      {
 9         CheckBoxFrame checkBoxFrame = new CheckBoxFrame();
10         checkBoxFrame.setDefaultCloseOperation( JFrame.EXIT_ON_CLOSE );
11         checkBoxFrame.setSize( 275, 100 ); // set frame size
12         checkBoxFrame.setVisible( true ); // display frame
13      } // end main
14   } // end class CheckBoxTest
```

Fig. 14.18 | Test class for CheckBoxFrame.

After the JTextField is created and initialized (Fig. 14.17, line 24), line 25 uses method **setFont** (inherited by JTextField indirectly from class Component) to set the font of the JTextField to a new object of class **Font** (package java.awt). The new Font is initialized with "Serif" (a generic font name that represents a font such as Times and is supported on all Java platforms), Font.PLAIN style and 14-point size. Next, lines 28–29 create two JCheckBox objects. The String passed to the JCheckBox constructor is the **checkbox label** that appears to the right of the JCheckBox by default.

When the user clicks a JCheckBox, an **ItemEvent** occurs. This event can be handled by an **ItemListener** object, which *must* implement method **itemStateChanged**. In this example, the event handling is performed by an instance of private *inner class* CheckBox-Handler (lines 40–59). Lines 34–36 create an instance of class CheckBoxHandler and register it with method **addItemListener** as the listener for both the JCheckBox objects.

CheckBoxHandler method itemStateChanged (lines 43–58) is called when the user clicks the boldJCheckBox or the italicJCheckBox. In this example, we don't need to know which of the two JCheckBoxes was clicked, just whether or not each one is checked. Line 48 uses JCheckBox method **isSelected** to determine if both JCheckBoxes are selected. If so, line 49 creates a bold italic font by adding the Font constants Font.BOLD and Font.ITALIC for the font-style argument of the Font constructor. Line 50 determines whether the boldJCheckBox is selected, and if so line 51 creates a bold font. Line 52 determines whether the italicJCheckBox is selected, and if so line 53 creates an italic font. If none of the preceding conditions are true, line 55 creates a plain font using the Font constant Font.PLAIN. Finally, line 57 sets textField's new font, which changes the font in the JTextField on the screen.

Relationship Between an Inner Class and Its Top-Level Class

Class CheckBoxHandler used variables boldJCheckBox (Fig. 14.17, lines 48 and 50), italicJCheckBox (lines 48 and 52) and textField (line 57) even though they are *not* declared in the inner class. Recall that an inner class has a special relationship with its top-level class—it's allowed to access *all* the variables and methods of the top-level class. CheckBoxHandler method itemStateChanged (line 43–58) uses this relationship to determine which JCheckBoxes are checked and to set the font on the JTextField. Notice that none of the code in inner class CheckBoxHandler requires an explicit reference to the top-level class object.

14.10.2 JRadioButton

Radio buttons (declared with class JRadioButton) are similar to checkboxes in that they have two states—selected and not selected (also called deselected). However, radio buttons normally appear as a **group** in which only one button can be selected at a time (see the output of Fig. 14.20). Selecting a different radio button forces all others to be deselected. Radio buttons are used to represent **mutually exclusive options** (i.e., multiple options in the group *cannot* be selected at the same time). The logical relationship between radio buttons is maintained by a **ButtonGroup** object (package javax.swing), which itself is not a GUI component. A ButtonGroup object organizes a group of buttons and is not itself displayed in a user interface. Rather, the individual JRadioButton objects from the group are displayed in the GUI.

Common Programming Error 14.3

Adding a ButtonGroup object (or an object of any other class that does not derive from Component) to a container results in a compilation error.

The application of Figs. 14.19–14.20 is similar to that of Figs. 14.17–14.18. The user can alter the font style of a JTextField's text. The application uses radio buttons that permit only a single font style in the group to be selected at a time. Class RadioButtonTest (Fig. 14.20) contains the main method that executes this application.

```
1   // Fig. 14.19: RadioButtonFrame.java
2   // Creating radio buttons using ButtonGroup and JRadioButton.
3   import java.awt.FlowLayout;
4   import java.awt.Font;
```

Fig. 14.19 | JRadioButtons and ButtonGroups. (Part 1 of 3.)

```
 5   import java.awt.event.ItemListener;
 6   import java.awt.event.ItemEvent;
 7   import javax.swing.JFrame;
 8   import javax.swing.JTextField;
 9   import javax.swing.JRadioButton;
10   import javax.swing.ButtonGroup;
11
12   public class RadioButtonFrame extends JFrame
13   {
14      private JTextField textField; // used to display font changes
15      private Font plainFont; // font for plain text
16      private Font boldFont; // font for bold text
17      private Font italicFont; // font for italic text
18      private Font boldItalicFont; // font for bold and italic text
19      private JRadioButton plainJRadioButton; // selects plain text
20      private JRadioButton boldJRadioButton; // selects bold text
21      private JRadioButton italicJRadioButton; // selects italic text
22      private JRadioButton boldItalicJRadioButton; // bold and italic
23      private ButtonGroup radioGroup; // buttongroup to hold radio buttons
24
25      // RadioButtonFrame constructor adds JRadioButtons to JFrame
26      public RadioButtonFrame()
27      {
28         super( "RadioButton Test" );
29         setLayout( new FlowLayout() ); // set frame layout
30
31         textField = new JTextField( "Watch the font style change", 25 );
32         add( textField ); // add textField to JFrame
33
34         // create radio buttons
35         plainJRadioButton = new JRadioButton( "Plain", true );
36         boldJRadioButton = new JRadioButton( "Bold", false );
37         italicJRadioButton = new JRadioButton( "Italic", false );
38         boldItalicJRadioButton = new JRadioButton( "Bold/Italic", false );
39         add( plainJRadioButton ); // add plain button to JFrame
40         add( boldJRadioButton ); // add bold button to JFrame
41         add( italicJRadioButton ); // add italic button to JFrame
42         add( boldItalicJRadioButton ); // add bold and italic button
43
44         // create logical relationship between JRadioButtons
45         radioGroup = new ButtonGroup(); // create ButtonGroup
46         radioGroup.add( plainJRadioButton ); // add plain to group
47         radioGroup.add( boldJRadioButton ); // add bold to group
48         radioGroup.add( italicJRadioButton ); // add italic to group
49         radioGroup.add( boldItalicJRadioButton ); // add bold and italic
50
51         // create font objects
52         plainFont = new Font( "Serif", Font.PLAIN, 14 );
53         boldFont = new Font( "Serif", Font.BOLD, 14 );
54         italicFont = new Font( "Serif", Font.ITALIC, 14 );
55         boldItalicFont = new Font( "Serif", Font.BOLD + Font.ITALIC, 14 );
56         textField.setFont( plainFont ); // set initial font to plain
57
```

Fig. 14.19 | JRadioButtons and ButtonGroups. (Part 2 of 3.)

```
58          // register events for JRadioButtons
59          plainJRadioButton.addItemListener(
60             new RadioButtonHandler( plainFont ) );
61          boldJRadioButton.addItemListener(
62             new RadioButtonHandler( boldFont ) );
63          italicJRadioButton.addItemListener(
64             new RadioButtonHandler( italicFont ) );
65          boldItalicJRadioButton.addItemListener(
66             new RadioButtonHandler( boldItalicFont ) );
67       } // end RadioButtonFrame constructor
68
69       // private inner class to handle radio button events
70       private class RadioButtonHandler implements ItemListener
71       {
72          private Font font; // font associated with this listener
73
74          public RadioButtonHandler( Font f )
75          {
76             font = f; // set the font of this listener
77          } // end constructor RadioButtonHandler
78
79          // handle radio button events
80          public void itemStateChanged( ItemEvent event )
81          {
82             textField.setFont( font ); // set font of textField
83          } // end method itemStateChanged
84       } // end private inner class RadioButtonHandler
85    } // end class RadioButtonFrame
```

Fig. 14.19 | JRadioButtons and ButtonGroups. (Part 3 of 3.)

```
 1   // Fig. 14.20: RadioButtonTest.java
 2   // Testing RadioButtonFrame.
 3   import javax.swing.JFrame;
 4
 5   public class RadioButtonTest
 6   {
 7      public static void main( String[] args )
 8      {
 9         RadioButtonFrame radioButtonFrame = new RadioButtonFrame();
10         radioButtonFrame.setDefaultCloseOperation( JFrame.EXIT_ON_CLOSE );
11         radioButtonFrame.setSize( 300, 100 ); // set frame size
12         radioButtonFrame.setVisible( true ); // display frame
13      } // end main
14   } // end class RadioButtonTest
```

Fig. 14.20 | Test class for RadioButtonFrame. (Part 1 of 2.)

Fig. 14.20 | Test class for `RadioButtonFrame`. (Part 2 of 2.)

Lines 35–42 in the constructor (Fig. 14.19) create four `JRadioButton` objects and add them to the `JFrame`. Each `JRadioButton` is created with a constructor call like that in line 35. This constructor specifies the label that appears to the right of the `JRadioButton` by default and the initial state of the `JRadioButton`. A `true` second argument indicates that the `JRadioButton` should appear selected when it's displayed.

Line 45 instantiates `ButtonGroup` object `radioGroup`. This object is the "glue" that forms the logical relationship between the four `JRadioButton` objects and allows only one of the four to be selected at a time. It's possible that no `JRadioButtons` in a `ButtonGroup` are selected, but this can occur *only* if no preselected `JRadioButtons` are added to the `ButtonGroup` and the user has not selected a `JRadioButton` yet. Lines 46–49 use `ButtonGroup` method **add** to associate each of the `JRadioButtons` with `radioGroup`. If more than one selected `JRadioButton` object is added to the group, the selected one that was added first will be selected when the GUI is displayed.

`JRadioButtons`, like `JCheckBoxes`, generate `ItemEvents` when they're clicked. Lines 59–66 create four instances of inner class `RadioButtonHandler` (declared at lines 70–84). In this example, each event-listener object is registered to handle the `ItemEvent` generated when the user clicks a particular `JRadioButton`. Notice that each `RadioButtonHandler` object is initialized with a particular `Font` object (created in lines 52–55).

Class `RadioButtonHandler` (line 70–84) implements interface `ItemListener` so it can handle `ItemEvents` generated by the `JRadioButtons`. The constructor stores the `Font` object it receives as an argument in the event-listener object's instance variable `font` (declared at line 72). When the user clicks a `JRadioButton`, `radioGroup` turns off the previously selected `JRadioButton`, and method `itemStateChanged` (line 80–83) sets the font in the `JTextField` to the `Font` stored in the `JRadioButton`'s corresponding event-listener object. Notice that line 82 of inner class `RadioButtonHandler` uses the top-level class's `textField` instance variable to set the font.

14.11 JComboBox; Using an Anonymous Inner Class for Event Handling

A combo box (sometimes called a **drop-down list**) enables the user to select one item from a list (Fig. 14.22). Combo boxes are implemented with class **JComboBox**, which extends class `JComponent`. `JComboBoxes` generate `ItemEvents` just as `JCheckBoxes` and `JRadioButtons` do. This example also demonstrates a special form of inner class that's used frequently in event handling. The application (Figs. 14.21–14.22) uses a `JComboBox` to provide a list of four image-file names from which the user can select one image to display. When the user selects a name, the application displays the corresponding image as an `Icon` on a `JLabel`. Class `ComboBoxTest` (Fig. 14.22) contains the `main` method that executes this application. The screen captures for this application show the JComboBox list after the selection was made to illustrate which image-file name was selected.

Lines 19–23 (Fig. 14.21) declare and initialize array icons with four new ImageIcon objects. String array names (lines 17–18) contains the names of the four image files that are stored in the same directory as the application.

```java
1   // Fig. 14.21: ComboBoxFrame.java
2   // JComboBox that displays a list of image names.
3   import java.awt.FlowLayout;
4   import java.awt.event.ItemListener;
5   import java.awt.event.ItemEvent;
6   import javax.swing.JFrame;
7   import javax.swing.JLabel;
8   import javax.swing.JComboBox;
9   import javax.swing.Icon;
10  import javax.swing.ImageIcon;
11
12  public class ComboBoxFrame extends JFrame
13  {
14     private JComboBox imagesJComboBox; // combobox to hold names of icons
15     private JLabel label; // label to display selected icon
16
17     private static final String[] names =
18        { "bug1.gif", "bug2.gif", "travelbug.gif", "buganim.gif" };
19     private Icon[] icons = {
20        new ImageIcon( getClass().getResource( names[ 0 ] ) ),
21        new ImageIcon( getClass().getResource( names[ 1 ] ) ),
22        new ImageIcon( getClass().getResource( names[ 2 ] ) ),
23        new ImageIcon( getClass().getResource( names[ 3 ] ) ) };
24
25     // ComboBoxFrame constructor adds JComboBox to JFrame
26     public ComboBoxFrame()
27     {
28        super( "Testing JComboBox" );
29        setLayout( new FlowLayout() ); // set frame layout
30
31        imagesJComboBox = new JComboBox( names ); // set up JComboBox
32        imagesJComboBox.setMaximumRowCount( 3 ); // display three rows
33
34        imagesJComboBox.addItemListener(
35           new ItemListener() // anonymous inner class
36           {
37              // handle JComboBox event
38              public void itemStateChanged( ItemEvent event )
39              {
40                 // determine whether item selected
41                 if ( event.getStateChange() == ItemEvent.SELECTED )
42                    label.setIcon( icons[
43                       imagesJComboBox.getSelectedIndex() ] );
44              } // end method itemStateChanged
45           } // end anonymous inner class
46        ); // end call to addItemListener
```

Fig. 14.21 | JComboBox that displays a list of image names. (Part 1 of 2.)

```
47
48            add( imagesJComboBox ); // add combobox to JFrame
49            label = new JLabel( icons[ 0 ] ); // display first icon
50            add( label ); // add label to JFrame
51        } // end ComboBoxFrame constructor
52    } // end class ComboBoxFrame
```

Fig. 14.21 | JComboBox that displays a list of image names. (Part 2 of 2.)

```
 1    // Fig. 14.22: ComboBoxTest.java
 2    // Testing ComboBoxFrame.
 3    import javax.swing.JFrame;
 4
 5    public class ComboBoxTest
 6    {
 7        public static void main( String[] args )
 8        {
 9            ComboBoxFrame comboBoxFrame = new ComboBoxFrame();
10            comboBoxFrame.setDefaultCloseOperation( JFrame.EXIT_ON_CLOSE );
11            comboBoxFrame.setSize( 350, 150 ); // set frame size
12            comboBoxFrame.setVisible( true ); // display frame
13        } // end main
14    } // end class ComboBoxTest
```

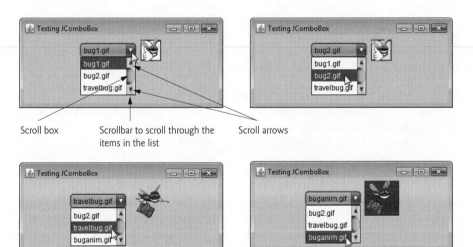

Scroll box   Scrollbar to scroll through the   Scroll arrows
                  items in the list

Fig. 14.22 | Testing ComboBoxFrame.

At line 31, the constructor initializes a JComboBox object with the Strings in array names as the elements in the list. Each item in the list has an **index**. The first item is added at index 0, the next at index 1 and so forth. The first item added to a JComboBox appears as the currently selected item when the JComboBox is displayed. Other items are selected by clicking the JComboBox, then selecting an item from the list that appears.

Line 32 uses JComboBox method **setMaximumRowCount** to set the maximum number of elements that are displayed when the user clicks the JComboBox. If there are additional items, the JComboBox provides a **scrollbar** (see the first screen) that allows the user to scroll through all the elements in the list. The user can click the **scroll arrows** at the top and bottom of the scrollbar to move up and down through the list one element at a time, or else drag the **scroll box** in the middle of the scrollbar up and down. To drag the scroll box, position the mouse cursor on it, hold the mouse button down and move the mouse. In this example, the drop-down list is too short to drag the scroll box, so you can click the up and down arrows or use your mouse's wheel to scroll through the four items in the list.

Look-and-Feel Observation 14.12

Set the maximum row count for a JComboBox to a number of rows that prevents the list from expanding outside the bounds of the window in which it's used.

Line 48 attaches the JComboBox to the ComboBoxFrame's FlowLayout (set in line 29). Line 49 creates the JLabel that displays ImageIcons and initializes it with the first Image-Icon in array icons. Line 50 attaches the JLabel to the ComboBoxFrame's FlowLayout.

Using an Anonymous Inner Class for Event Handling

Lines 34–46 are one statement that declares the event listener's class, creates an object of that class and registers it as the listener for imagesJComboBox's ItemEvents. This event-listener object is an instance of an **anonymous inner class**—an inner class that's declared without a name and typically appears inside a method declaration. *As with other inner classes, an anonymous inner class can access its top-level class's members.* However, an anonymous inner class has limited access to the local variables of the method in which it's declared. Since an anonymous inner class has no name, one object of the class must be created at the point where the class is declared (starting at line 35).

Software Engineering Observation 14.3

An anonymous inner class declared in a method can access the instance variables and methods of the top-level class object that declared it, as well as the method's final local variables, but cannot access the method's non-final local variables.

Lines 34–46 are a call to imagesJComboBox's addItemListener method. The argument to this method must be an object that *is an* ItemListener (i.e., any object of a class that implements ItemListener). Lines 35–45 are a class-instance creation expression that declares an anonymous inner class and creates one object of that class. A reference to that object is then passed as the argument to addItemListener. The syntax ItemListener() after new begins the declaration of an anonymous inner class that implements interface ItemListener. This is similar to beginning a class declaration with

```
public class MyHandler implements ItemListener
```

The opening left brace at 36 and the closing right brace at line 45 delimit the body of the anonymous inner class. Lines 38–44 declare the ItemListener's itemStateChanged method. When the user makes a selection from imagesJComboBox, this method sets label's Icon. The Icon is selected from array icons by determining the index of the selected item in the JComboBox with method **getSelectedIndex** in line 43. For each item selected from a JComboBox, another item is first deselected—so two ItemEvents occur when an item is selected. We wish to display only the icon for the item the user just selected. For this reason, line 41 determines whether ItemEvent method **getStateChange** returns ItemEvent.SELECTED. If so, lines 42–43 set label's icon.

> ### Software Engineering Observation 14.4
> *Like any other class, when an anonymous inner class implements an interface, the class must implement every method in the interface.*

The syntax shown in lines 35–45 for creating an event handler with an anonymous inner class is similar to the code that would be generated by a Java integrated development environment (IDE). Typically, an IDE enables you to design a GUI visually, then it generates code that implements the GUI. You simply insert statements in the event-handling methods that declare how to handle each event.

14.12 JList

A list displays a series of items from which the user may *select one or more items* (see the output of Fig. 14.24). Lists are created with class JList, which directly extends class JComponent. Class JList supports **single-selection lists** (which allow only one item to be selected at a time) and **multiple-selection lists** (which allow any number of items to be selected). In this section, we discuss single-selection lists.

The application of Figs. 14.23–14.24 creates a JList containing 13 color names. When a color name is clicked in the JList, a **ListSelectionEvent** occurs and the application changes the background color of the application window to the selected color. Class ListTest (Fig. 14.24) contains the main method that executes this application.

```java
1   // Fig. 14.23: ListFrame.java
2   // JList that displays a list of colors.
3   import java.awt.FlowLayout;
4   import java.awt.Color;
5   import javax.swing.JFrame;
6   import javax.swing.JList;
7   import javax.swing.JScrollPane;
8   import javax.swing.event.ListSelectionListener;
9   import javax.swing.event.ListSelectionEvent;
10  import javax.swing.ListSelectionModel;
11
12  public class ListFrame extends JFrame
13  {
14     private JList colorJList; // list to display colors
15     private static final String[] colorNames = { "Black", "Blue", "Cyan",
16        "Dark Gray", "Gray", "Green", "Light Gray", "Magenta",
17        "Orange", "Pink", "Red", "White", "Yellow" };
18     private static final Color[] colors = { Color.BLACK, Color.BLUE,
19        Color.CYAN, Color.DARK_GRAY, Color.GRAY, Color.GREEN,
20        Color.LIGHT_GRAY, Color.MAGENTA, Color.ORANGE, Color.PINK,
21        Color.RED, Color.WHITE, Color.YELLOW };
22
```

Fig. 14.23 | JList that displays a list of colors. (Part 1 of 2.)

```
23      // ListFrame constructor add JScrollPane containing JList to JFrame
24      public ListFrame()
25      {
26         super( "List Test" );
27         setLayout( new FlowLayout() ); // set frame layout
28
29         colorJList = new JList( colorNames ); // create with colorNames
30         colorJList.setVisibleRowCount( 5 ); // display five rows at once
31
32         // do not allow multiple selections
33         colorJList.setSelectionMode( ListSelectionModel.SINGLE_SELECTION );
34
35         // add a JScrollPane containing JList to frame
36         add( new JScrollPane( colorJList ) );
37
38         colorJList.addListSelectionListener(
39            new ListSelectionListener() // anonymous inner class
40            {
41               // handle list selection events
42               public void valueChanged( ListSelectionEvent event )
43               {
44                  getContentPane().setBackground(
45                     colors[ colorJList.getSelectedIndex() ] );
46               } // end method valueChanged
47            } // end anonymous inner class
48         ); // end call to addListSelectionListener
49      } // end ListFrame constructor
50   } // end class ListFrame
```

Fig. 14.23 | JList that displays a list of colors. (Part 2 of 2.)

```
1    // Fig. 14.24: ListTest.java
2    // Selecting colors from a JList.
3    import javax.swing.JFrame;
4
5    public class ListTest
6    {
7       public static void main( String[] args )
8       {
9          ListFrame listFrame = new ListFrame(); // create ListFrame
10         listFrame.setDefaultCloseOperation( JFrame.EXIT_ON_CLOSE );
11         listFrame.setSize( 350, 150 ); // set frame size
12         listFrame.setVisible( true ); // display frame
13      } // end main
14   } // end class ListTest
```

Fig. 14.24 | Test class for ListFrame.

Line 29 (Fig. 14.23) creates JList object colorJList. The argument to the JList constructor is the array of Objects (in this case Strings) to display in the list. Line 30 uses JList method **setVisibleRowCount** to determine the number of items visible in the list.

Line 33 uses JList method **setSelectionMode** to specify the list's **selection mode**. Class **ListSelectionModel** (of package javax.swing) declares three constants that specify a JList's selection mode—**SINGLE_SELECTION** (which allows only one item to be selected at a time), **SINGLE_INTERVAL_SELECTION** (for a multiple-selection list that allows selection of several contiguous items) and **MULTIPLE_INTERVAL_SELECTION** (for a multiple-selection list that does not restrict the items that can be selected).

Unlike a JComboBox, a JList *does not provide a scrollbar* if there are more items in the list than the number of visible rows. In this case, a **JScrollPane** object is used to provide the scrolling capability. Line 36 adds a new instance of class JScrollPane to the JFrame. The JScrollPane constructor receives as its argument the JComponent that needs scrolling functionality (in this case, colorJList). Notice in the screen captures that a scrollbar created by the JScrollPane appears at the right side of the JList. By default, the scrollbar appears only when the number of items in the JList exceeds the number of visible items.

Lines 38–48 use JList method **addListSelectionListener** to register an object that implements **ListSelectionListener** (package javax.swing.event) as the listener for the JList's selection events. Once again, we use an instance of an anonymous inner class (lines 39–47) as the listener. In this example, when the user makes a selection from colorJList, method **valueChanged** (line 42–46) should change the background color of the List-Frame to the selected color. This is accomplished in lines 44–45. Note the use of JFrame method **getContentPane** in line 44. Each JFrame actually consists of *three layers*—the *background*, the *content pane* and the *glass pane*. The content pane appears in front of the background and is where the GUI components in the JFrame are displayed. The glass pane is used to display tool tips and other items that should appear in front of the GUI components on the screen. The content pane completely hides the background of the JFrame; thus, to change the background color behind the GUI components, you must change the content pane's background color. Method getContentPane returns a reference to the JFrame's content pane (an object of class Container). In line 44, we then use that reference to call method **setBackground**, which sets the content pane's background color to an element in the colors array. The color is selected from the array by using the selected item's index. JList method **getSelectedIndex** returns the selected item's index. As with arrays and JComboBoxes, JList indexing is zero based.

14.13 Multiple-Selection Lists

A **multiple-selection list** enables the user to select many items from a JList (see the output of Fig. 14.26). A SINGLE_INTERVAL_SELECTION list allows selecting a contiguous range of items. To do so, click the first item, then press and hold the *Shift* key while clicking the last item in the range. A MULTIPLE_INTERVAL_SELECTION list (the default) allows continuous range selection as described for a SINGLE_INTERVAL_SELECTION list. Such a list also allows miscellaneous items to be selected by pressing and holding the *Ctrl* key while clicking each item to select. To deselect an item, press and hold the *Ctrl* key while clicking the item a second time.

The application of Figs. 14.25–14.26 uses multiple-selection lists to copy items from one JList to another. One list is a MULTIPLE_INTERVAL_SELECTION list and the other is a

SINGLE_INTERVAL_SELECTION list. When you execute the application, try using the selection techniques described previously to select items in both lists.

```java
1   // Fig. 14.25: MultipleSelectionFrame.java
2   // Copying items from one List to another.
3   import java.awt.FlowLayout;
4   import java.awt.event.ActionListener;
5   import java.awt.event.ActionEvent;
6   import javax.swing.JFrame;
7   import javax.swing.JList;
8   import javax.swing.JButton;
9   import javax.swing.JScrollPane;
10  import javax.swing.ListSelectionModel;
11
12  public class MultipleSelectionFrame extends JFrame
13  {
14     private JList colorJList; // list to hold color names
15     private JList copyJList; // list to copy color names into
16     private JButton copyJButton; // button to copy selected names
17     private static final String[] colorNames = { "Black", "Blue", "Cyan",
18        "Dark Gray", "Gray", "Green", "Light Gray", "Magenta", "Orange",
19        "Pink", "Red", "White", "Yellow" };
20
21     // MultipleSelectionFrame constructor
22     public MultipleSelectionFrame()
23     {
24        super( "Multiple Selection Lists" );
25        setLayout( new FlowLayout() ); // set frame layout
26
27        colorJList = new JList( colorNames ); // holds names of all colors
28        colorJList.setVisibleRowCount( 5 ); // show five rows
29        colorJList.setSelectionMode(
30           ListSelectionModel.MULTIPLE_INTERVAL_SELECTION );
31        add( new JScrollPane( colorJList ) ); // add list with scrollpane
32
33        copyJButton = new JButton( "Copy >>>" ); // create copy button
34        copyJButton.addActionListener(
35
36           new ActionListener() // anonymous inner class
37           {
38              // handle button event
39              public void actionPerformed( ActionEvent event )
40              {
41                 // place selected values in copyJList
42                 copyJList.setListData( colorJList.getSelectedValues() );
43              } // end method actionPerformed
44           } // end anonymous inner class
45        ); // end call to addActionListener
46
47        add( copyJButton ); // add copy button to JFrame
48
49        copyJList = new JList(); // create list to hold copied color names
```

Fig. 14.25 | JList that allows multiple selections. (Part 1 of 2.)

```
50          copyJList.setVisibleRowCount( 5 ); // show 5 rows
51          copyJList.setFixedCellWidth( 100 ); // set width
52          copyJList.setFixedCellHeight( 15 ); // set height
53          copyJList.setSelectionMode(
54             ListSelectionModel.SINGLE_INTERVAL_SELECTION );
55          add( new JScrollPane( copyJList ) ); // add list with scrollpane
56       } // end MultipleSelectionFrame constructor
57    } // end class MultipleSelectionFrame
```

Fig. 14.25 | JList that allows multiple selections. (Part 2 of 2.)

```
1    // Fig. 14.26: MultipleSelectionTest.java
2    // Testing MultipleSelectionFrame.
3    import javax.swing.JFrame;
4
5    public class MultipleSelectionTest
6    {
7       public static void main( String[] args )
8       {
9          MultipleSelectionFrame multipleSelectionFrame =
10             new MultipleSelectionFrame();
11          multipleSelectionFrame.setDefaultCloseOperation(
12             JFrame.EXIT_ON_CLOSE );
13          multipleSelectionFrame.setSize( 350, 150 ); // set frame size
14          multipleSelectionFrame.setVisible( true ); // display frame
15       } // end main
16    } // end class MultipleSelectionTest
```

Fig. 14.26 | Test class for MultipleSelectionFrame.

Line 27 of Fig. 14.25 creates JList colorJList and initializes it with the Strings in the array colorNames. Line 28 sets the number of visible rows in colorJList to 5. Lines 29–30 specify that colorJList is a MULTIPLE_INTERVAL_SELECTION list. Line 31 adds a new JScrollPane containing colorJList to the JFrame. Lines 49–55 perform similar tasks for copyJList, which is declared as a SINGLE_INTERVAL_SELECTION list. If a JList does not contain items, it will not diplay in a FlowLayout. For this reason, lines 51–52 use JList methods **setFixedCellWidth** and **setFixedCellHeight** to set copyJList's width to 100 pixels and the height of each item in the JList to 15 pixels, respectively.

Normally, an event generated by another GUI component (known as an **external event**) specifies when the multiple selections in a JList should be processed. In this example, the user clicks the JButton called copyJButton to trigger the event that copies the selected items in colorJList to copyJList.

Lines 34–45 declare, create and register an ActionListener for the copyJButton. When the user clicks copyJButton, method actionPerformed (lines 39–43) uses JList method **setListData** to set the items displayed in copyJList. Line 42 calls colorJList's method **getSelectedValues**, which returns an array of Objects representing the selected items in colorJList. In this example, the returned array is passed as the argument to copyJList's setListData method.

You might be wondering why copyJList can be used in line 42 even though the application does not create the object to which it refers until line 49. Remember that method actionPerformed (lines 39–43) does not execute until the user presses the copy-JButton, which cannot occur until after the constructor completes execution and the application displays the GUI. At that point in the application's execution, copyJList is already initialized with a new JList object.

14.14 Mouse Event Handling

This section presents the **MouseListener** and **MouseMotionListener** event-listener inter-faces for handling **mouse events**. Mouse events can be processed for any GUI component that derives from java.awt.Component. The methods of interfaces MouseListener and MouseMotionListener are summarized in Figure 14.27. Package javax.swing.event contains interface **MouseInputListener**, which extends interfaces MouseListener and MouseMotionListener to create a single interface containing all the MouseListener and MouseMotionListener methods. The MouseListener and MouseMotionListener meth-ods are called when the mouse interacts with a Component if appropriate event-listener ob-jects are registered for that Component.

Each of the mouse event-handling methods receives as an argument a **MouseEvent** object that contains information about the mouse event that occurred, including the *x*- and *y*-coordinates of its location. These coordinates are measured from the upper-left corner of the GUI component on which the event occurred. The *x*-coordinates start at 0 and increase from left to right. The *y*-coordinates start at 0 and increase from top to bottom. The methods and constants of class **InputEvent** (MouseEvent's superclass) enable you to determine which mouse button the user clicked.

MouseListener and MouseMotionListener interface methods
Methods of interface MouseListener
public void mousePressed(MouseEvent event)
Called when a mouse button is *pressed* while the mouse cursor is on a component.
public void mouseClicked(MouseEvent event)
Called when a mouse button is *pressed and released* while the mouse cursor remains sta-tionary on a component. This event is always preceded by a call to mousePressed.
public void mouseReleased(MouseEvent event)
Called when a mouse button is *released after being pressed*. This event is always preceded by a call to mousePressed and one or more calls to mouseDragged.

Fig. 14.27 | MouseListener and MouseMotionListener interface methods. (Part 1 of 2.)

MouseListener and MouseMotionListener interface methods

`public void mouseEntered( MouseEvent event )`

Called when the mouse cursor *enters* the bounds of a component.

`public void mouseExited( MouseEvent event )`

Called when the mouse cursor *leaves* the bounds of a component.

Methods of interface MouseMotionListener

`public void mouseDragged( MouseEvent event )`

Called when the mouse button is *pressed* while the mouse cursor is on a component and the mouse is *moved* while the mouse button *remains pressed*. This event is always preceded by a call to `mousePressed`. All drag events are sent to the component on which the user began to drag the mouse.

`public void mouseMoved( MouseEvent event )`

Called when the mouse is *moved* (with no mouse buttons pressed) when the mouse cursor is on a component. All move events are sent to the component over which the mouse is currently positioned.

Fig. 14.27 | MouseListener and MouseMotionListener interface methods. (Part 2 of 2.)

Software Engineering Observation 14.5

Calls to mouseDragged are sent to the MouseMotionListener for the Component on which the drag started. Similarly, the mouseReleased call at the end of a drag operation is sent to the MouseListener for the Component on which the drag operation started.

Java also provides interface **MouseWheelListener** to enable applications to respond to the *rotation of a mouse wheel*. This interface declares method **mouseWheelMoved**, which receives a **MouseWheelEvent** as its argument. Class MouseWheelEvent (a subclass of MouseEvent) contains methods that enable the event handler to obtain information about the amount of wheel rotation.

Tracking Mouse Events on a JPanel

The MouseTracker application (Figs. 14.28–14.29) demonstrates the MouseListener and MouseMotionListener interface methods. The event-handler class (lines 36–90) implements both interfaces. You *must* declare all seven methods from these two interfaces when your class implements them both. Each mouse event in this example displays a String in the JLabel called statusBar that is attached to the bottom of the window.

```
1   // Fig. 14.28: MouseTrackerFrame.java
2   // Demonstrating mouse events.
3   import java.awt.Color;
4   import java.awt.BorderLayout;
5   import java.awt.event.MouseListener;
6   import java.awt.event.MouseMotionListener;
7   import java.awt.event.MouseEvent;
```

Fig. 14.28 | Mouse event handling. (Part 1 of 3.)

```
 8   import javax.swing.JFrame;
 9   import javax.swing.JLabel;
10   import javax.swing.JPanel;
11
12   public class MouseTrackerFrame extends JFrame
13   {
14      private JPanel mousePanel; // panel in which mouse events will occur
15      private JLabel statusBar; // label that displays event information
16
17      // MouseTrackerFrame constructor sets up GUI and
18      // registers mouse event handlers
19      public MouseTrackerFrame()
20      {
21         super( "Demonstrating Mouse Events" );
22
23         mousePanel = new JPanel(); // create panel
24         mousePanel.setBackground( Color.WHITE ); // set background color
25         add( mousePanel, BorderLayout.CENTER ); // add panel to JFrame
26
27         statusBar = new JLabel( "Mouse outside JPanel" );
28         add( statusBar, BorderLayout.SOUTH ); // add label to JFrame
29
30         // create and register listener for mouse and mouse motion events
31         MouseHandler handler = new MouseHandler();
32         mousePanel.addMouseListener( handler );
33         mousePanel.addMouseMotionListener( handler );
34      } // end MouseTrackerFrame constructor
35
36      private class MouseHandler implements MouseListener,
37         MouseMotionListener
38      {
39         // MouseListener event handlers
40         // handle event when mouse released immediately after press
41         public void mouseClicked( MouseEvent event )
42         {
43            statusBar.setText( String.format( "Clicked at [%d, %d]",
44               event.getX(), event.getY() ) );
45         } // end method mouseClicked
46
47         // handle event when mouse pressed
48         public void mousePressed( MouseEvent event )
49         {
50            statusBar.setText( String.format( "Pressed at [%d, %d]",
51               event.getX(), event.getY() ) );
52         } // end method mousePressed
53
54         // handle event when mouse released
55         public void mouseReleased( MouseEvent event )
56         {
57            statusBar.setText( String.format( "Released at [%d, %d]",
58               event.getX(), event.getY() ) );
59         } // end method mouseReleased
60
```

Fig. 14.28 | Mouse event handling. (Part 2 of 3.)

```
61            // handle event when mouse enters area
62            public void mouseEntered( MouseEvent event )
63            {
64               statusBar.setText( String.format( "Mouse entered at [%d, %d]",
65                  event.getX(), event.getY() ) );
66               mousePanel.setBackground( Color.GREEN );
67            } // end method mouseEntered
68
69            // handle event when mouse exits area
70            public void mouseExited( MouseEvent event )
71            {
72               statusBar.setText( "Mouse outside JPanel" );
73               mousePanel.setBackground( Color.WHITE );
74            } // end method mouseExited
75
76            // MouseMotionListener event handlers
77            // handle event when user drags mouse with button pressed
78            public void mouseDragged( MouseEvent event )
79            {
80               statusBar.setText( String.format( "Dragged at [%d, %d]",
81                  event.getX(), event.getY() ) );
82            } // end method mouseDragged
83
84            // handle event when user moves mouse
85            public void mouseMoved( MouseEvent event )
86            {
87               statusBar.setText( String.format( "Moved at [%d, %d]",
88                  event.getX(), event.getY() ) );
89            } // end method mouseMoved
90         } // end inner class MouseHandler
91      } // end class MouseTrackerFrame
```

Fig. 14.28 | Mouse event handling. (Part 3 of 3.)

Line 23 in Fig. 14.28 creates JPanel mousePanel. This JPanel's mouse events will be tracked by the application. Line 24 sets mousePanel's background color to white. When the user moves the mouse into the mousePanel, the application will change mousePanel's background color to green. When the user moves the mouse out of the mousePanel, the application will change the background color back to white. Line 25 attaches mousePanel to the JFrame. As you learned in Section 14.5, you typically must specify the layout of the GUI components in a JFrame. In that section, we introduced the layout manager Flow-Layout. Here we use the default layout of a JFrame's content pane—**BorderLayout**. This layout manager arranges components into five regions: **NORTH**, **SOUTH**, **EAST**, **WEST** and **CENTER**. NORTH corresponds to the top of the container. This example uses the CENTER and SOUTH regions. Line 25 uses a two-argument version of method add to place mousePanel in the CENTER region. The BorderLayout automatically sizes the component in the CENTER to use all the space in the JFrame that is not occupied by components in the other regions. Section 14.18.2 discusses BorderLayout in more detail.

Lines 27–28 in the constructor declare JLabel statusBar and attach it to the JFrame's SOUTH region. This JLabel occupies the width of the JFrame. The region's height is determined by the JLabel.

```
 1   // Fig. 14.29: MouseTrackerFrame.java
 2   // Testing MouseTrackerFrame.
 3   import javax.swing.JFrame;
 4
 5   public class MouseTracker
 6   {
 7      public static void main( String[] args )
 8      {
 9         MouseTrackerFrame mouseTrackerFrame = new MouseTrackerFrame();
10         mouseTrackerFrame.setDefaultCloseOperation( JFrame.EXIT_ON_CLOSE );
11         mouseTrackerFrame.setSize( 300, 100 ); // set frame size
12         mouseTrackerFrame.setVisible( true ); // display frame
13      } // end main
14   } // end class MouseTracker
```

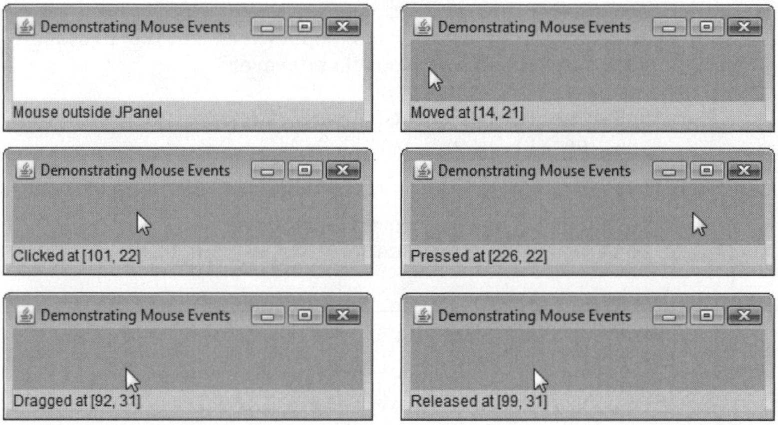

Fig. 14.29 | Test class for `MouseTrackerFrame`.

Line 31 creates an instance of inner class `MouseHandler` (lines 36–90) called `handler` that responds to mouse events. Lines 32–33 register `handler` as the listener for mouse-Panel's mouse events. Methods **addMouseListener** and **addMouseMotionListener** are inherited indirectly from class `Component` and can be used to register `MouseListeners` and `MouseMotionListeners`, respectively. A `MouseHandler` object *is a* `MouseListener` and *is a* `MouseMotionListener` because the class implements *both* interfaces. We chose to implement both interfaces here to demonstrate a class that implements more than one interface, but we could have implemented interface `MouseInputListener` instead.]

When the mouse enters and exits `mousePanel`'s area, methods `mouseEntered` (lines 62–67) and `mouseExited` (lines 70–74) are called, respectively. Method `mouseEntered` displays a message in the `statusBar` indicating that the mouse entered the `JPanel` and changes the background color to green. Method `mouseExited` displays a message in the `statusBar` indicating that the mouse is outside the `JPanel` (see the first sample output window) and changes the background color to white.

The other five events display a string in the `statusBar` that includes the event and the coordinates at which it occurred. `MouseEvent` methods **getX** and **getY** return the *x*- and *y*-coordinates, respectively, of the mouse at the time the event occurred.

14.15 Adapter Classes

Many event-listener interfaces, such as MouseListener and MouseMotionListener, contain multiple methods. It's not always desirable to declare every method in an event-listener interface. For instance, an application may need only the mouseClicked handler from MouseListener or the mouseDragged handler from MouseMotionListener. Interface WindowListener specifies seven window event-handling methods. For many of the listener interfaces that have multiple methods, packages java.awt.event and javax.swing.event provide event-listener adapter classes. An **adapter class** implements an interface and provides a default implementation (with an empty method body) of each method in the interface. Figure 14.30 shows several java.awt.event adapter classes and the interfaces they implement. You can extend an adapter class to inherit the default implementation of every method and subsequently override only the method(s) you need for event handling.

> **Software Engineering Observation 14.6**
>
> *When a class implements an interface, the class has an is-a relationship with that interface. All direct and indirect subclasses of that class inherit this interface. Thus, an object of a class that extends an event-adapter class is an object of the corresponding event-listener type (e.g., an object of a subclass of MouseAdapter is a MouseListener).*

Event-adapter class in `java.awt.event`	Implements interface
ComponentAdapter	ComponentListener
ContainerAdapter	ContainerListener
FocusAdapter	FocusListener
KeyAdapter	KeyListener
MouseAdapter	MouseListener
MouseMotionAdapter	MouseMotionListener
WindowAdapter	WindowListener

Fig. 14.30 | Event-adapter classes and the interfaces they implement in package java.awt.event.

Extending *MouseAdapter*

The application of Figs. 14.31–14.32 demonstrates how to determine the number of mouse clicks (i.e., the click count) and how to distinguish between the different mouse buttons. The event listener in this application is an object of inner class MouseClickHandler (lines 25–45) that extends MouseAdapter, so we can declare just the mouseClicked method we need in this example.

```
1  // Fig. 14.31: MouseDetailsFrame.java
2  // Demonstrating mouse clicks and distinguishing between mouse buttons.
3  import java.awt.BorderLayout;
4  import java.awt.event.MouseAdapter;
```

Fig. 14.31 | Left, center and right mouse-button clicks. (Part 1 of 2.)

```java
5   import java.awt.event.MouseEvent;
6   import javax.swing.JFrame;
7   import javax.swing.JLabel;
8
9   public class MouseDetailsFrame extends JFrame
10  {
11     private String details; // String that is displayed in the statusBar
12     private JLabel statusBar; // JLabel that appears at bottom of window
13
14     // constructor sets title bar String and register mouse listener
15     public MouseDetailsFrame()
16     {
17        super( "Mouse clicks and buttons" );
18
19        statusBar = new JLabel( "Click the mouse" );
20        add( statusBar, BorderLayout.SOUTH );
21        addMouseListener( new MouseClickHandler() ); // add handler
22     } // end MouseDetailsFrame constructor
23
24     // inner class to handle mouse events
25     private class MouseClickHandler extends MouseAdapter
26     {
27        // handle mouse-click event and determine which button was pressed
28        public void mouseClicked( MouseEvent event )
29        {
30           int xPos = event.getX(); // get x-position of mouse
31           int yPos = event.getY(); // get y-position of mouse
32
33           details = String.format( "Clicked %d time(s)",
34              event.getClickCount() );
35
36           if ( event.isMetaDown() ) // right mouse button
37              details += " with right mouse button";
38           else if ( event.isAltDown() ) // middle mouse button
39              details += " with center mouse button";
40           else // left mouse button
41              details += " with left mouse button";
42
43           statusBar.setText( details ); // display message in statusBar
44        } // end method mouseClicked
45     } // end private inner class MouseClickHandler
46  } // end class MouseDetailsFrame
```

Fig. 14.31 | Left, center and right mouse-button clicks. (Part 2 of 2.)

```java
1   // Fig. 14.32: MouseDetails.java
2   // Testing MouseDetailsFrame.
3   import javax.swing.JFrame;
4
5   public class MouseDetails
6   {
```

Fig. 14.32 | Test class for MouseDetailsFrame. (Part 1 of 2.)

```
 7     public static void main( String[] args )
 8     {
 9        MouseDetailsFrame mouseDetailsFrame = new MouseDetailsFrame();
10        mouseDetailsFrame.setDefaultCloseOperation( JFrame.EXIT_ON_CLOSE );
11        mouseDetailsFrame.setSize( 400, 150 ); // set frame size
12        mouseDetailsFrame.setVisible( true ); // display frame
13     } // end main
14  } // end class MouseDetails
```

Fig. 14.32 | Test class for `MouseDetailsFrame`. (Part 2 of 2.)

Common Programming Error 14.4

If you extend an adapter class and misspell the name of the method you're overriding, your method simply becomes another method in the class. This is a logic error that is difficult to detect, since the program will call the empty version of the method inherited from the adapter class.

A user of a Java application may be on a system with a one-, two- or three-button mouse. Java provides a mechanism to distinguish among mouse buttons. Class `MouseEvent` inherits several methods from class `InputEvent` that can distinguish among mouse buttons on a multibutton mouse or can mimic a multibutton mouse with a combined keystroke and mouse-button click. Figure 14.33 shows the `InputEvent` methods used to distinguish among mouse-button clicks. Java assumes that every mouse contains a left mouse button. Thus, it's simple to test for a left-mouse-button click. However, users with a one- or two-button mouse must use a combination of keystrokes and mouse-button clicks at the same time to simulate the missing buttons on the mouse. In the case of a one- or two-button mouse, a Java application assumes that the center mouse button is clicked if the user holds down the *Alt* key and clicks the left mouse button on a two-button mouse or the only mouse button on a one-button mouse. In the case of a one-button mouse, a Java application assumes that the right mouse button is clicked if the user holds down the *Meta* key (sometimes called the *Command* key or the "Apple" key on a Mac) and clicks the mouse button.

InputEvent method	Description
isMetaDown()	Returns true when the user clicks the *right mouse button* on a mouse with two or three buttons. To simulate a right-mouse-button click on a one-button mouse, the user can hold down the *Meta* key on the keyboard and click the mouse button.
isAltDown()	Returns true when the user clicks the *middle mouse button* on a mouse with three buttons. To simulate a middle-mouse-button click on a one- or two-button mouse, the user can press the *Alt* key and click the only or left mouse button, respectively.

Fig. 14.33 | InputEvent methods that help determine whether the right or center mouse button was clicked.

Line 21 of Fig. 14.31 registers a MouseListener for the MouseDetailsFrame. The event listener is an object of class MouseClickHandler, which extends MouseAdapter. This enables us to declare only method mouseClicked (lines 28–44). This method first captures the coordinates where the event occurred and stores them in local variables xPos and yPos (lines 30–31). Lines 33–34 create a String called details containing the number of consecutive mouse clicks, which is returned by MouseEvent method **getClickCount** at line 34. Lines 36–41 use methods **isMetaDown** and **isAltDown** to determine which mouse button the user clicked and append an appropriate String to details in each case. The resulting String is displayed in the statusBar. Class MouseDetails (Fig. 14.32) contains the main method that executes the application. Try clicking with each of your mouse's buttons repeatedly to see the click count increment.

14.16 JPanel Subclass for Drawing with the Mouse

Section 14.14 showed how to track mouse events in a JPanel. In this section, we use a JPanel as a **dedicated drawing area** in which the user can draw by dragging the mouse. In addition, this section demonstrates an event listener that extends an adapter class.

*Method **paintComponent***
Lightweight Swing components that extend class JComponent (such as JPanel) contain method **paintComponent**, which is called when a lightweight Swing component is displayed. By overriding this method, you can specify how to draw shapes using Java's graphics capabilities. When customizing a JPanel for use as a dedicated drawing area, the subclass should override method paintComponent and call the superclass version of paint-Component as the first statement in the body of the overridden method to ensure that the component displays correctly. The reason is that subclasses of JComponent support **transparency**. To display a component correctly, the program must determine whether the component is transparent. The code that determines this is in superclass JComponent's paintComponent implementation. When a component is transparent, paintComponent will not clear its background when the program displays the component. When a component is **opaque**, paintComponent clears the component's background before the component is displayed. The transparency of a Swing lightweight component can be set with method **setOpaque** (a false argument indicates that the component is transparent).

Error-Prevention Tip 14.1

In a JComponent subclass's paintComponent method, the first statement should always call the superclass's paintComponent method to ensure that an object of the subclass displays correctly.

Common Programming Error 14.5

If an overridden paintComponent method does not call the superclass's version, the subclass component may not display properly. If an overridden paintComponent method calls the superclass's version after other drawing is performed, the drawing will be erased.

Defining the Custom Drawing Area

The Painter application of Figs. 14.34–14.35 demonstrates a customized subclass of JPanel that is used to create a dedicated drawing area. The application uses the mouse-Dragged event handler to create a simple drawing application. The user can draw pictures by dragging the mouse on the JPanel. This example does not use method mouseMoved, so our *event-listener class* (the *anonymous inner class* at lines 22–34) extends Mouse-MotionAdapter. Since this class already declares both mouseMoved and mouseDragged, we can simply override mouseDragged to provide the event handling this application requires.

```java
1   // Fig. 14.34: PaintPanel.java
2   // Using class MouseMotionAdapter.
3   import java.awt.Point;
4   import java.awt.Graphics;
5   import java.awt.event.MouseEvent;
6   import java.awt.event.MouseMotionAdapter;
7   import javax.swing.JPanel;
8
9   public class PaintPanel extends JPanel
10  {
11     private int pointCount = 0; // count number of points
12
13     // array of 10000 java.awt.Point references
14     private Point[] points = new Point[ 10000 ];
15
16     // set up GUI and register mouse event handler
17     public PaintPanel()
18     {
19        // handle frame mouse motion event
20        addMouseMotionListener(
21
22           new MouseMotionAdapter() // anonymous inner class
23           {
24              // store drag coordinates and repaint
25              public void mouseDragged( MouseEvent event )
26              {
27                 if ( pointCount < points.length )
28                 {
```

Fig. 14.34 | Adapter class used to implement event handlers. (Part 1 of 2.)

```
29                              points[ pointCount ] = event.getPoint(); // find point
30                              ++pointCount; // increment number of points in array
31                              repaint(); // repaint JFrame
32                           } // end if
33                        } // end method mouseDragged
34                     } // end anonymous inner class
35                  ); // end call to addMouseMotionListener
36            } // end PaintPanel constructor
37
38            // draw ovals in a 4-by-4 bounding box at specified locations on window
39            public void paintComponent( Graphics g )
40            {
41               super.paintComponent( g ); // clears drawing area
42
43               // draw all points in array
44               for ( int i = 0; i < pointCount; i++ )
45                  g.fillOval( points[ i ].x, points[ i ].y, 4, 4 );
46            } // end method paintComponent
47      } // end class PaintPanel
```

Fig. 14.34 | Adapter class used to implement event handlers. (Part 2 of 2.)

Class PaintPanel (Fig. 14.34) extends JPanel to create the dedicated drawing area. Lines 3–7 import the classes used in class PaintPanel. Class **Point** (package java.awt) represents an *x-y* coordinate. We use objects of this class to store the coordinates of each mouse drag event. Class **Graphics** is used to draw.

In this example, we use an array of 10,000 Points (line 14) to store the location at which each mouse drag event occurs. As you'll see, method paintComponent uses these Points to draw. Instance variable pointCount (line 11) maintains the total number of Points captured from mouse drag events so far.

Lines 20–35 register a MouseMotionListener to listen for the PaintPanel's mouse motion events. Lines 22–34 create an object of an anonymous inner class that extends the adapter class MouseMotionAdapter. Recall that MouseMotionAdapter implements Mouse-MotionListener, so the *anonymous inner class* object is a MouseMotionListener. The anonymous inner class inherits default mouseMoved and mouseDragged implementations, so it already implements all the interface's methods. However, the default methods do nothing when they're called. So, we override method mouseDragged at lines 25–33 to capture the coordinates of a mouse drag event and store them as a Point object. Line 27 ensures that we store the event's coordinates *only* if there are still empty elements in the array. If so, line 29 invokes the MouseEvent's **getPoint** method to obtain the Point where the event occurred and stores it in the array at index pointCount. Line 30 increments the pointCount, and line 31 calls method **repaint** (inherited indirectly from class Component) to indicate that the PaintPanel should be refreshed on the screen as soon as possible with a call to the PaintPanel's paintComponent method.

Method paintComponent (lines 39–46), which receives a Graphics parameter, is called automatically any time the PaintPanel needs to be displayed on the screen—such as when the GUI is first displayed—or refreshed on the screen—such as when method repaint is called or when the GUI component has been hidden by another window on the screen and subsequently becomes visible again.

Look-and-Feel Observation 14.13

Calling repaint *for a Swing GUI component indicates that the component should be refreshed on the screen as soon as possible. The component's background is cleared only if the component is opaque.* JComponent *method* setOpaque *can be passed a* boolean *argument indicating whether the component is opaque (*true*) or transparent (*false*).*

Line 41 invokes the superclass version of paintComponent to clear the PaintPanel's background (JPanels are opaque by default). Lines 44–45 draw an oval at the location specified by each Point in the array (up to the pointCount). Graphics method **fillOval** draws a solid oval. The method's four parameters represent a rectangular area (called the bounding box) in which the oval is displayed. The first two parameters are the upper-left *x*-coordinate and the upper-left *y*-coordinate of the rectangular area. The last two coordinates represent the rectangular area's width and height. Method fillOval draws the oval so it touches the middle of each side of the rectangular area. In line 45, the first two arguments are specified by using class Point's two public instance variables—x and y. The loop terminates when pointCount points have been displayed. You'll learn more Graphics features in Chapter 15.

Look-and-Feel Observation 14.14

Drawing on any GUI component is performed with coordinates that are measured from the upper-left corner (0, 0) of that GUI component, not *the upper-left corner of the screen.*

Using the Custom JPanel in an Application

Class Painter (Fig. 14.35) contains the main method that executes this application. Line 14 creates a PaintPanel object on which the user can drag the mouse to draw. Line 15 attaches the PaintPanel to the JFrame.

```
 1  // Fig. 14.35: Painter.java
 2  // Testing PaintPanel.
 3  import java.awt.BorderLayout;
 4  import javax.swing.JFrame;
 5  import javax.swing.JLabel;
 6
 7  public class Painter
 8  {
 9     public static void main( String[] args )
10     {
11        // create JFrame
12        JFrame application = new JFrame( "A simple paint program" );
13
14        PaintPanel paintPanel = new PaintPanel(); // create paint panel
15        application.add( paintPanel, BorderLayout.CENTER ); // in center
16
17        // create a label and place it in SOUTH of BorderLayout
18        application.add( new JLabel( "Drag the mouse to draw" ),
19           BorderLayout.SOUTH );
20
21        application.setDefaultCloseOperation( JFrame.EXIT_ON_CLOSE );
```

Fig. 14.35 | Test class for PaintPanel. (Part 1 of 2.)

```
22            application.setSize( 400, 200 ); // set frame size
23            application.setVisible( true ); // display frame
24        } // end main
25    } // end class Painter
```

Fig. 14.35 | Test class for `PaintPanel`. (Part 2 of 2.)

14.17 Key Event Handling

This section presents the `KeyListener` interface for handling **key events**. Key events are generated when keys on the keyboard are pressed and released. A class that implements `KeyListener` must provide declarations for methods **keyPressed**, **keyReleased** and **key-Typed**, each of which receives a `KeyEvent` as its argument. Class `KeyEvent` is a subclass of `InputEvent`. Method `keyPressed` is called in response to pressing any key. Method `key-Typed` is called in response to pressing any key that is not an **action key**. (The action keys are any arrow key, *Home, End, Page Up, Page Down*, any function key, etc.) Method `key-Released` is called when the key is released after any `keyPressed` or `keyTyped` event.

The application of Figs. 14.36–14.37 demonstrates the `KeyListener` methods. Class `KeyDemoFrame` implements the `KeyListener` interface, so all three methods are declared in the application. The constructor (Fig. 14.36, lines 17–28) registers the application to handle its own key events by using method **addKeyListener** at line 27. Method addKey-Listener is declared in class `Component`, so every subclass of `Component` can notify Key-Listener objects of key events for that `Component`.

```
1   // Fig. 14.36: KeyDemoFrame.java
2   // Demonstrating keystroke events.
3   import java.awt.Color;
4   import java.awt.event.KeyListener;
5   import java.awt.event.KeyEvent;
6   import javax.swing.JFrame;
7   import javax.swing.JTextArea;
8
9   public class KeyDemoFrame extends JFrame implements KeyListener
10  {
11      private String line1 = ""; // first line of textarea
12      private String line2 = ""; // second line of textarea
13      private String line3 = ""; // third line of textarea
14      private JTextArea textArea; // textarea to display output
15
```

Fig. 14.36 | Key event handling. (Part 1 of 2.)

```
16         // KeyDemoFrame constructor
17         public KeyDemoFrame()
18         {
19            super( "Demonstrating Keystroke Events" );
20
21            textArea = new JTextArea( 10, 15 ); // set up JTextArea
22            textArea.setText( "Press any key on the keyboard..." );
23            textArea.setEnabled( false ); // disable textarea
24            textArea.setDisabledTextColor( Color.BLACK ); // set text color
25            add( textArea ); // add textarea to JFrame
26
27            addKeyListener( this ); // allow frame to process key events
28         } // end KeyDemoFrame constructor
29
30         // handle press of any key
31         public void keyPressed( KeyEvent event )
32         {
33            line1 = String.format( "Key pressed: %s",
34               KeyEvent.getKeyText( event.getKeyCode() ) ); // show pressed key
35            setLines2and3( event ); // set output lines two and three
36         } // end method keyPressed
37
38         // handle release of any key
39         public void keyReleased( KeyEvent event )
40         {
41            line1 = String.format( "Key released: %s",
42               KeyEvent.getKeyText( event.getKeyCode() ) ); // show released key
43            setLines2and3( event ); // set output lines two and three
44         } // end method keyReleased
45
46         // handle press of an action key
47         public void keyTyped( KeyEvent event )
48         {
49            line1 = String.format( "Key typed: %s", event.getKeyChar() );
50            setLines2and3( event ); // set output lines two and three
51         } // end method keyTyped
52
53         // set second and third lines of output
54         private void setLines2and3( KeyEvent event )
55         {
56            line2 = String.format( "This key is %san action key",
57               ( event.isActionKey() ? "" : "not " ) );
58
59            String temp = KeyEvent.getKeyModifiersText( event.getModifiers() );
60
61            line3 = String.format( "Modifier keys pressed: %s",
62               ( temp.equals( "" ) ? "none" : temp ) ); // output modifiers
63
64            textArea.setText( String.format( "%s\n%s\n%s\n",
65               line1, line2, line3 ) ); // output three lines of text
66         } // end method setLines2and3
67      } // end class KeyDemoFrame
```

Fig. 14.36 | Key event handling. (Part 2 of 2.)

```
1   // Fig. 14.37: KeyDemo.java
2   // Testing KeyDemoFrame.
3   import javax.swing.JFrame;
4
5   public class KeyDemo
6   {
7      public static void main( String[] args )
8      {
9         KeyDemoFrame keyDemoFrame = new KeyDemoFrame();
10        keyDemoFrame.setDefaultCloseOperation( JFrame.EXIT_ON_CLOSE );
11        keyDemoFrame.setSize( 350, 100 ); // set frame size
12        keyDemoFrame.setVisible( true ); // display frame
13     } // end main
14  } // end class KeyDemo
```

Fig. 14.37 | Test class for KeyDemoFrame.

At line 25, the constructor adds the JTextArea textArea (where the application's output is displayed) to the JFrame. A JTextArea is a *multiline area* in which you can display text. (We discuss JTextAreas in more detail in Section 14.20.) Notice in the screen captures that textArea occupies the *entire window*. This is due to the JFrame's default BorderLayout (discussed in Section 14.18.2 and demonstrated in Fig. 14.41). When a single Component is added to a BorderLayout, the Component occupies the entire Container. Line 23 disables the JTextArea so the user cannot type in it. This causes the text in the JTextArea to become gray. Line 24 uses method **setDisabledTextColor** to change the text color in the JTextArea to black for readability.

Methods keyPressed (lines 31–36) and keyReleased (lines 39–44) use KeyEvent method **getKeyCode** to get the **virtual key code** of the pressed key. Class KeyEvent contains virtual key-code constants that represent every key on the keyboard. These constants can be compared with getKeyCode's return value to test for individual keys on the keyboard. The value returned by getKeyCode is passed to static KeyEvent method **getKeyText**, which returns a string containing the name of the key that was pressed. For a complete list of virtual key constants, see the on-line documentation for class KeyEvent (package java.awt.event). Method keyTyped (lines 47–51) uses KeyEvent method **getKeyChar** (which returns a char) to get the Unicode value of the character typed.

All three event-handling methods finish by calling method setLines2and3 (lines 54–66) and passing it the KeyEvent object. This method uses KeyEvent method **isActionKey** (line 57) to determine whether the key in the event was an action key. Also, InputEvent method **getModifiers** is called (line 59) to determine whether any modifier keys (such as *Shift*, *Alt* and *Ctrl*) were pressed when the key event occurred. The result of this method is passed to static KeyEvent method **getKeyModifiersText**, which produces a string containing the names of the pressed modifier keys.

[*Note:* If you need to test for a specific key on the keyboard, class KeyEvent provides a **key constant** for each one. These constants can be used from the key event handlers to determine whether a particular key was pressed. Also, to determine whether the *Alt*, *Ctrl*, *Meta* and *Shift* keys are pressed individually, InputEvent methods **isAltDown**, **isControlDown**, **isMetaDown** and **isShiftDown** each return a boolean indicating whether the particular key was pressed during the key event.]

14.18 Introduction to Layout Managers

Layout managers arrange GUI components in a container for presentation purposes. You can use the layout managers for basic layout capabilities instead of determining every GUI component's exact position and size. This functionality enables you to concentrate on the basic look-and-feel and lets the layout managers process most of the layout details. All layout managers implement the interface **LayoutManager** (in package java.awt). Class Container's setLayout method takes an object that implements the LayoutManager interface as an argument. There are basically three ways for you to arrange components in a GUI:

1. *Absolute positioning:* This provides the greatest level of control over a GUI's appearance. By setting a Container's layout to null, you can specify the absolute position of each GUI component with respect to the upper-left corner of the Container by using Component methods setSize and setLocation or setBounds. If you do this, you also must specify each GUI component's size. Programming a GUI with absolute positioning can be tedious, unless you have an integrated development environment (IDE) that can generate the code for you.

2. *Layout managers:* Using layout managers to position elements can be simpler and faster than creating a GUI with absolute positioning, but you lose some control over the size and the precise positioning of GUI components.

3. *Visual programming in an IDE:* IDEs provide tools that make it easy to create GUIs. Each IDE typically provides a **GUI design tool** that allows you to drag and drop GUI components from a tool box onto a design area. You can then position, size and align GUI components as you like. The IDE generates the Java code that creates the GUI. In addition, you can typically add event-handling code for a particular component by double-clicking the component. Some design tools also allow you to use the layout managers described in this chapter and in Chapter 22.

Look-and-Feel Observation 14.15

Most Java IDEs provide GUI design tools for visually designing a GUI; the tools then write Java code that creates the GUI. Such tools often provide greater control over the size, position and alignment of GUI components than do the built-in layout managers.

Look-and-Feel Observation 14.16

It's possible to set a Container's layout to null*, which indicates that no layout manager should be used. In a* Container *without a layout manager, you must position and size the components in the given container and take care that, on resize events, all components are repositioned as necessary. A component's resize events can be processed by a* Component-Listener.

Figure 14.38 summarizes the layout managers presented in this chapter. Others are discussed in Chapter 22, and the powerful GroupLayout layout manager is discussed in Appendix H.

Layout manager	Description
FlowLayout	Default for javax.swing.JPanel. Places components sequentially (left to right) in the order they were added. It's also possible to specify the order of the components by using the Container method add, which takes a Component and an integer index position as arguments.
BorderLayout	Default for JFrames (and other windows). Arranges the components into five areas: NORTH, SOUTH, EAST, WEST and CENTER.
GridLayout	Arranges the components into rows and columns.

Fig. 14.38 | Layout managers.

14.18.1 FlowLayout

FlowLayout is the *simplest* layout manager. GUI components are placed on a container from left to right in the order in which they're added to the container. When the edge of the container is reached, components continue to display on the next line. Class FlowLayout allows GUI components to be *left aligned*, *centered* (the default) and *right aligned*.

The application of Figs. 14.39–14.40 creates three JButton objects and adds them to the application, using a FlowLayout layout manager. The components are center aligned by default. When the user clicks **Left**, the alignment for the layout manager is changed to a left-aligned FlowLayout. When the user clicks **Right**, the alignment for the layout manager is changed to a right-aligned FlowLayout. When the user clicks **Center**, the alignment for the layout manager is changed to a center-aligned FlowLayout. Each button has its own event handler that's declared with an anonymous inner class that implements ActionListener. The sample output windows show each of the FlowLayout alignments. Also, the last sample output window shows the centered alignment after the window has been resized to a smaller width. Notice that the button **Right** flows onto a new line.

As seen previously, a container's layout is set with method setLayout of class Container. Line 25 sets the layout manager to the FlowLayout declared at line 23. Normally, the layout is set before any GUI components are added to a container.

Look-and-Feel Observation 14.17

Each individual container can have only one layout manager, but multiple containers in the same application can each use different layout managers.

```
1   // Fig. 14.39: FlowLayoutFrame.java
2   // Demonstrating FlowLayout alignments.
3   import java.awt.FlowLayout;
4   import java.awt.Container;
5   import java.awt.event.ActionListener;
6   import java.awt.event.ActionEvent;
7   import javax.swing.JFrame;
8   import javax.swing.JButton;
9
10  public class FlowLayoutFrame extends JFrame
11  {
12     private JButton leftJButton; // button to set alignment left
13     private JButton centerJButton; // button to set alignment center
14     private JButton rightJButton; // button to set alignment right
15     private FlowLayout layout; // layout object
16     private Container container; // container to set layout
17
18     // set up GUI and register button listeners
19     public FlowLayoutFrame()
20     {
21        super( "FlowLayout Demo" );
22
23        layout = new FlowLayout(); // create FlowLayout
24        container = getContentPane(); // get container to layout
25        setLayout( layout ); // set frame layout
26
27        // set up leftJButton and register listener
28        leftJButton = new JButton( "Left" ); // create Left button
29        add( leftJButton ); // add Left button to frame
30        leftJButton.addActionListener(
31
32           new ActionListener() // anonymous inner class
33           {
34              // process leftJButton event
35              public void actionPerformed( ActionEvent event )
36              {
37                 layout.setAlignment( FlowLayout.LEFT );
38
39                 // realign attached components
40                 layout.layoutContainer( container );
41              } // end method actionPerformed
42           } // end anonymous inner class
43        ); // end call to addActionListener
44
45        // set up centerJButton and register listener
46        centerJButton = new JButton( "Center" ); // create Center button
47        add( centerJButton ); // add Center button to frame
```

Fig. 14.39 | FlowLayout allows components to flow over multiple lines. (Part 1 of 2.)

```
48          centerJButton.addActionListener(
49
50             new ActionListener() // anonymous inner class
51             {
52                // process centerJButton event
53                public void actionPerformed( ActionEvent event )
54                {
55                   layout.setAlignment( FlowLayout.CENTER );
56
57                   // realign attached components
58                   layout.layoutContainer( container );
59                } // end method actionPerformed
60             } // end anonymous inner class
61          ); // end call to addActionListener
62
63          // set up rightJButton and register listener
64          rightJButton = new JButton( "Right" ); // create Right button
65          add( rightJButton ); // add Right button to frame
66          rightJButton.addActionListener(
67
68             new ActionListener() // anonymous inner class
69             {
70                // process rightJButton event
71                public void actionPerformed( ActionEvent event )
72                {
73                   layout.setAlignment( FlowLayout.RIGHT );
74
75                   // realign attached components
76                   layout.layoutContainer( container );
77                } // end method actionPerformed
78             } // end anonymous inner class
79          ); // end call to addActionListener
80       } // end FlowLayoutFrame constructor
81    } // end class FlowLayoutFrame
```

Fig. 14.39 | FlowLayout allows components to flow over multiple lines. (Part 2 of 2.)

```
1    // Fig. 14.40: FlowLayoutDemo.java
2    // Testing FlowLayoutFrame.
3    import javax.swing.JFrame;
4
5    public class FlowLayoutDemo
6    {
7       public static void main( String[] args )
8       {
9          FlowLayoutFrame flowLayoutFrame = new FlowLayoutFrame();
10         flowLayoutFrame.setDefaultCloseOperation( JFrame.EXIT_ON_CLOSE );
11         flowLayoutFrame.setSize( 300, 75 ); // set frame size
12         flowLayoutFrame.setVisible( true ); // display frame
13      } // end main
14   } // end class FlowLayoutDemo
```

Fig. 14.40 | Test class for FlowLayoutFrame. (Part 1 of 2.)

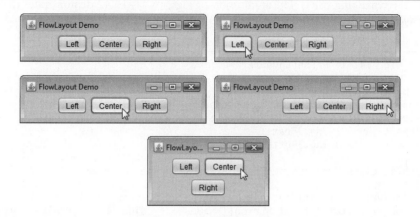

Fig. 14.40 | Test class for `FlowLayoutFrame`. (Part 2 of 2.)

Each button's event handler is specified with a separate anonymous inner-class object (Fig. 14.39, lines 30–43, 48–61 and 66–79, respectively), and method `actionPerformed` in each case executes two statements. For example, line 37 in the event handler for `leftJButton` uses `FlowLayout` method **`setAlignment`** to change the alignment for the `FlowLayout` to a left-aligned (**`FlowLayout.LEFT`**) `FlowLayout`. Line 40 uses `LayoutManager` interface method **`layoutContainer`** (which is inherited by all layout managers) to specify that the `JFrame` should be rearranged based on the adjusted layout. According to which button was clicked, the `actionPerformed` method for each button sets the `FlowLayout`'s alignment to `FlowLayout.LEFT` (line 37), **`FlowLayout.CENTER`** (line 55) or **`FlowLayout.RIGHT`** (line 73).

14.18.2 BorderLayout

The `BorderLayout` layout manager (the default layout manager for a `JFrame`) arranges components into five regions: NORTH, SOUTH, EAST, WEST and CENTER. NORTH corresponds to the top of the container. Class `BorderLayout` extends `Object` and implements interface **`LayoutManager2`** (a subinterface of `LayoutManager` that adds several methods for enhanced layout processing).

A `BorderLayout` limits a `Container` to containing at most five components—one in each region. The component placed in each region can be a container to which other components are attached. The components placed in the NORTH and SOUTH regions extend horizontally to the sides of the container and are as tall as the components placed in those regions. The EAST and WEST regions expand vertically between the NORTH and SOUTH regions and are as wide as the components placed in those regions. The component placed in the CENTER region expands to fill all remaining space in the layout (which is the reason the `JTextArea` in Fig. 14.37 occupies the entire window). If all five regions are occupied, the entire container's space is covered by GUI components. If the NORTH or SOUTH region is not occupied, the GUI components in the EAST, CENTER and WEST regions expand vertically to fill the remaining space. If the EAST or WEST region is not occupied, the GUI component in the CENTER region expands horizontally to fill the remaining space. If the CENTER region is not occupied, the area is left empty—the other GUI components do *not* expand to fill the remaining space. The application of Figs. 14.41–14.42 demonstrates the BorderLayout layout manager by using five JButtons.

```java
 1   // Fig. 14.41: BorderLayoutFrame.java
 2   // Demonstrating BorderLayout.
 3   import java.awt.BorderLayout;
 4   import java.awt.event.ActionListener;
 5   import java.awt.event.ActionEvent;
 6   import javax.swing.JFrame;
 7   import javax.swing.JButton;
 8
 9   public class BorderLayoutFrame extends JFrame implements ActionListener
10   {
11      private JButton[] buttons; // array of buttons to hide portions
12      private static final String[] names = { "Hide North", "Hide South",
13         "Hide East", "Hide West", "Hide Center" };
14      private BorderLayout layout; // borderlayout object
15
16      // set up GUI and event handling
17      public BorderLayoutFrame()
18      {
19         super( "BorderLayout Demo" );
20
21         layout = new BorderLayout( 5, 5 ); // 5 pixel gaps
22         setLayout( layout ); // set frame layout
23         buttons = new JButton[ names.length ]; // set size of array
24
25         // create JButtons and register listeners for them
26         for ( int count = 0; count < names.length; count++ )
27         {
28            buttons[ count ] = new JButton( names[ count ] );
29            buttons[ count ].addActionListener( this );
30         } // end for
31
32         add( buttons[ 0 ], BorderLayout.NORTH ); // add button to north
33         add( buttons[ 1 ], BorderLayout.SOUTH ); // add button to south
34         add( buttons[ 2 ], BorderLayout.EAST ); // add button to east
35         add( buttons[ 3 ], BorderLayout.WEST ); // add button to west
36         add( buttons[ 4 ], BorderLayout.CENTER ); // add button to center
37      } // end BorderLayoutFrame constructor
38
39      // handle button events
40      public void actionPerformed( ActionEvent event )
41      {
42         // check event source and lay out content pane correspondingly
43         for ( JButton button : buttons )
44         {
45            if ( event.getSource() == button )
46               button.setVisible( false ); // hide button clicked
47            else
48               button.setVisible( true ); // show other buttons
49         } // end for
```

Fig. 14.41 | BorderLayout containing five buttons. (Part 1 of 2.)

```
50
51          layout.layoutContainer( getContentPane() ); // lay out content pane
52      } // end method actionPerformed
53  } // end class BorderLayoutFrame
```

Fig. 14.41 | BorderLayout containing five buttons. (Part 2 of 2.)

```
1   // Fig. 14.42: BorderLayoutDemo.java
2   // Testing BorderLayoutFrame.
3   import javax.swing.JFrame;
4
5   public class BorderLayoutDemo
6   {
7      public static void main( String[] args )
8      {
9         BorderLayoutFrame borderLayoutFrame = new BorderLayoutFrame();
10        borderLayoutFrame.setDefaultCloseOperation( JFrame.EXIT_ON_CLOSE );
11        borderLayoutFrame.setSize( 300, 200 ); // set frame size
12        borderLayoutFrame.setVisible( true ); // display frame
13     } // end main
14  } // end class BorderLayoutDemo
```

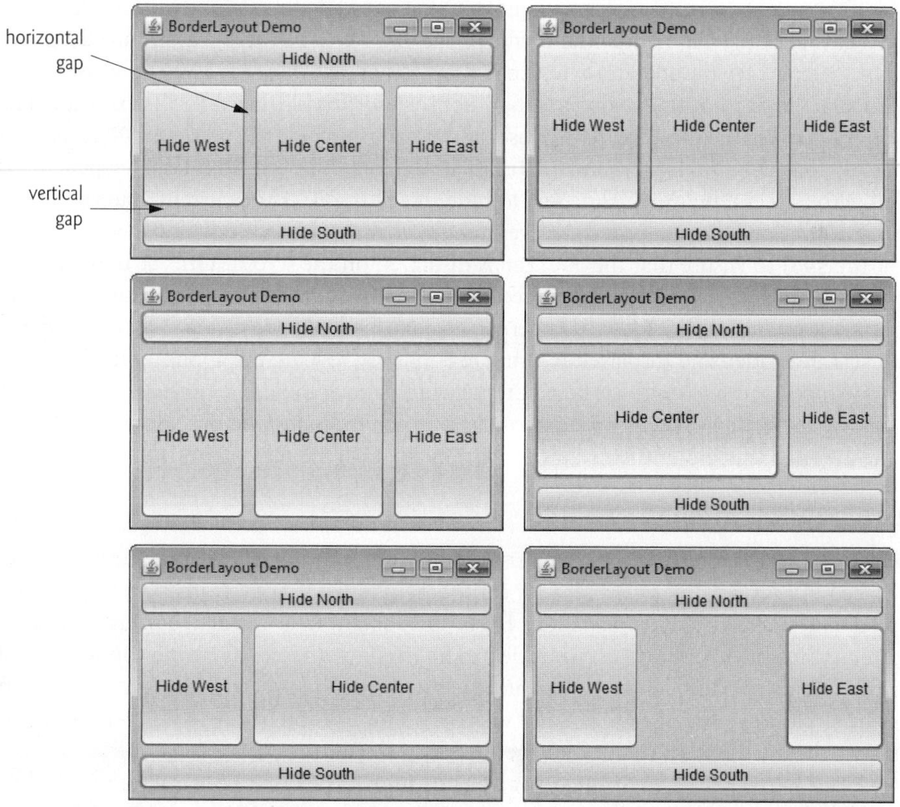

Fig. 14.42 | Test class for BorderLayoutFrame.

Line 21 of Fig. 14.41 creates a BorderLayout. The constructor arguments specify the number of pixels between components that are arranged horizontally (**horizontal gap space**) and between components that are arranged vertically (**vertical gap space**), respectively. The default is one pixel of gap space horizontally and vertically. Line 22 uses method setLayout to set the content pane's layout to layout.

We add Components to a BorderLayout with another version of Container method add that takes two arguments—the Component to add and the region in which the Component should appear. For example, line 32 specifies that buttons[0] should appear in the NORTH region. The components can be added in any order, but only one component should be added to each region.

Look-and-Feel Observation 14.18

If no region is specified when adding a Component to a BorderLayout, the layout manager assumes that the Component should be added to region BorderLayout.CENTER.

Common Programming Error 14.6

When more than one component is added to a region in a BorderLayout, only the last component added to that region will be displayed. There's no error that indicates this problem.

Class BorderLayoutFrame implements ActionListener directly in this example, so the BorderLayoutFrame will handle the events of the JButtons. For this reason, line 29 passes the this reference to the addActionListener method of each JButton. When the user clicks a particular JButton in the layout, method actionPerformed (lines 40–52) executes. The enhanced for statement at lines 43–49 uses an if...else to hide the particular JButton that generated the event. Method **setVisible** (inherited into JButton from class Component) is called with a false argument (line 46) to hide the JButton. If the current JButton in the array is not the one that generated the event, method setVisible is called with a true argument (line 48) to ensure that the JButton is displayed on the screen. Line 51 uses Layout-Manager method layoutContainer to recalculate the layout of the content pane. Notice in the screen captures of Fig. 14.42 that certain regions in the BorderLayout change shape as JButtons are hidden and displayed in other regions. Try resizing the application window to see how the various regions resize based on the window's width and height. *For more complex layouts, group components in JPanels, each with a separate layout manager.* Place the JPanels on the JFrame using either the default BorderLayout or some other layout.

14.18.3 GridLayout

The **GridLayout** layout manager divides the container into *a grid* so that components can be placed in *rows* and *columns*. Class GridLayout inherits directly from class Object and implements interface LayoutManager. Every Component in a GridLayout has the *same* width and height. Components are added to a GridLayout starting at the top-left cell of the grid and proceeding left to right until the row is full. Then the process continues left to right on the next row of the grid, and so on. The application of Figs. 14.43–14.44 demonstrates the GridLayout layout manager by using six JButtons.

Lines 24–25 create two GridLayout objects. The GridLayout constructor used at line 24 specifies a GridLayout with 2 rows, 3 columns, 5 pixels of horizontal-gap space between Components in the grid and 5 pixels of vertical-gap space between Components in the grid.

```
 1   // Fig. 14.43: GridLayoutFrame.java
 2   // Demonstrating GridLayout.
 3   import java.awt.GridLayout;
 4   import java.awt.Container;
 5   import java.awt.event.ActionListener;
 6   import java.awt.event.ActionEvent;
 7   import javax.swing.JFrame;
 8   import javax.swing.JButton;
 9
10   public class GridLayoutFrame extends JFrame implements ActionListener
11   {
12      private JButton[] buttons; // array of buttons
13      private static final String[] names =
14         { "one", "two", "three", "four", "five", "six" };
15      private boolean toggle = true; // toggle between two layouts
16      private Container container; // frame container
17      private GridLayout gridLayout1; // first gridlayout
18      private GridLayout gridLayout2; // second gridlayout
19
20      // no-argument constructor
21      public GridLayoutFrame()
22      {
23         super( "GridLayout Demo" );
24         gridLayout1 = new GridLayout( 2, 3, 5, 5 ); // 2 by 3; gaps of 5
25         gridLayout2 = new GridLayout( 3, 2 ); // 3 by 2; no gaps
26         container = getContentPane(); // get content pane
27         setLayout( gridLayout1 ); // set JFrame layout
28         buttons = new JButton[ names.length ]; // create array of JButtons
29
30         for ( int count = 0; count < names.length; count++ )
31         {
32            buttons[ count ] = new JButton( names[ count ] );
33            buttons[ count ].addActionListener( this ); // register listener
34            add( buttons[ count ] ); // add button to JFrame
35         } // end for
36      } // end GridLayoutFrame constructor
37
38      // handle button events by toggling between layouts
39      public void actionPerformed( ActionEvent event )
40      {
41         if ( toggle )
42            container.setLayout( gridLayout2 ); // set layout to second
43         else
44            container.setLayout( gridLayout1 ); // set layout to first
45
46         toggle = !toggle; // set toggle to opposite value
47         container.validate(); // re-lay out container
48      } // end method actionPerformed
49   } // end class GridLayoutFrame
```

Fig. 14.43 | GridLayout containing six buttons.

The GridLayout constructor used at line 25 specifies a GridLayout with 3 rows and 2 columns that uses the default gap space (1 pixel).

```
 I   // Fig. 14.44: GridLayoutDemo.java
 2   // Testing GridLayoutFrame.
 3   import javax.swing.JFrame;
 4
 5   public class GridLayoutDemo
 6   {
 7      public static void main( String[] args )
 8      {
 9         GridLayoutFrame gridLayoutFrame = new GridLayoutFrame();
10         gridLayoutFrame.setDefaultCloseOperation( JFrame.EXIT_ON_CLOSE );
11         gridLayoutFrame.setSize( 300, 200 ); // set frame size
12         gridLayoutFrame.setVisible( true ); // display frame
13      } // end main
14   } // end class GridLayoutDemo
```

Fig. 14.44 | Test class for `GridLayoutFrame`.

The `JButton` objects in this example initially are arranged using `gridLayout1` (set for the content pane at line 27 with method `setLayout`). The first component is added to the first column of the first row. The next component is added to the second column of the first row, and so on. When a `JButton` is pressed, method `actionPerformed` (lines 39–48) is called. Every call to `actionPerformed` toggles the layout between `gridLayout2` and `gridLayout1`, using `boolean` variable `toggle` to determine the next layout to set.

Line 47 shows another way to reformat a container for which the layout has changed. `Container` method **`validate`** recomputes the container's layout based on the current layout manager for the `Container` and the current set of displayed GUI components.

14.19 Using Panels to Manage More Complex Layouts

Complex GUIs (like Fig. 14.1) require that each component be placed in an exact location. They often consist of multiple panels, with each panel's components arranged in a specific layout. Class `JPanel` extends `JComponent` and `JComponent` extends class `Container`, so every `JPanel` is a `Container`. Thus, every `JPanel` may have components, including other panels, attached to it with `Container` method `add`. The application of Figs. 14.45–14.46 demonstrates how a `JPanel` can be used to create a more complex layout in which several `JButtons` are placed in the `SOUTH` region of a `BorderLayout`.

After `JPanel` `buttonJPanel` is declared (line 11) and created (line 19), line 20 sets `buttonJPanel`'s layout to a `GridLayout` of one row and five columns (there are five `JButtons` in array `buttons`). Lines 23–27 add the `JButtons` in the array to the `JPanel`. Line 26 adds the buttons directly to the `JPanel`—class `JPanel` does not have a content pane, unlike a `JFrame`. Line 29 uses the `JFrame`'s default `BorderLayout` to add `buttonJPanel` to the `SOUTH` region. The `SOUTH` region is as tall as the buttons on `buttonJPanel`. A `JPanel` is sized to the components it contains. As more components are added, the JPanel grows (according to the restrictions of its layout manager) to accommodate the components. Resize the window to see how the layout manager affects the size of the JButtons.

```java
 1  // Fig. 14.45: PanelFrame.java
 2  // Using a JPanel to help lay out components.
 3  import java.awt.GridLayout;
 4  import java.awt.BorderLayout;
 5  import javax.swing.JFrame;
 6  import javax.swing.JPanel;
 7  import javax.swing.JButton;
 8
 9  public class PanelFrame extends JFrame
10  {
11     private JPanel buttonJPanel; // panel to hold buttons
12     private JButton[] buttons; // array of buttons
13
14     // no-argument constructor
15     public PanelFrame()
16     {
17        super( "Panel Demo" );
18        buttons = new JButton[ 5 ]; // create buttons array
19        buttonJPanel = new JPanel(); // set up panel
20        buttonJPanel.setLayout( new GridLayout( 1, buttons.length ) );
21
22        // create and add buttons
23        for ( int count = 0; count < buttons.length; count++ )
24        {
25           buttons[ count ] = new JButton( "Button " + ( count + 1 ) );
26           buttonJPanel.add( buttons[ count ] ); // add button to panel
27        } // end for
28
29        add( buttonJPanel, BorderLayout.SOUTH ); // add panel to JFrame
30     } // end PanelFrame constructor
31  } // end class PanelFrame
```

Fig. 14.45 | JPanel with five JButtons in a GridLayout attached to the SOUTH region of a BorderLayout.

```java
 1  // Fig. 14.46: PanelDemo.java
 2  // Testing PanelFrame.
 3  import javax.swing.JFrame;
 4
 5  public class PanelDemo extends JFrame
 6  {
 7     public static void main( String[] args )
 8     {
 9        PanelFrame panelFrame = new PanelFrame();
10        panelFrame.setDefaultCloseOperation( JFrame.EXIT_ON_CLOSE );
11        panelFrame.setSize( 450, 200 ); // set frame size
```

Fig. 14.46 | Test class for PanelFrame. (Part 1 of 2.)

```
12          panelFrame.setVisible( true ); // display frame
13       } // end main
14    } // end class PanelDemo
```

Fig. 14.46 | Test class for PanelFrame. (Part 2 of 2.)

14.20 JTextArea

A **JTextArea** provides an area for *manipulating multiple lines of text*. Like class JTextField, JTextArea is a subclass of JTextComponent, which declares common methods for JText-Fields, JTextAreas and several other text-based GUI components.

The application in Figs. 14.47–14.48 demonstrates JTextAreas. One JTextArea displays text that the user can select. The other is uneditable and is used to display the text the user selected in the first JTextArea. Unlike JTextFields, JTextAreas do not have action events—when you press *Enter* while typing in a JTextArea, the cursor simply moves to the next line. As with multiple-selection JLists (Section 14.13), an external event from another GUI component indicates when to process the text in a JTextArea. For example, when typing an e-mail message, you normally click a **Send** button to send the text of the message to the recipient. Similarly, when editing a document in a word processor, you normally save the file by selecting a **Save** or **Save As...** menu item. In this program, the button **Copy >>>** generates the external event that copies the selected text in the left JTextArea and displays it in the right JTextArea.

```
1   // Fig. 14.47: TextAreaFrame.java
2   // Copying selected text from one textarea to another.
3   import java.awt.event.ActionListener;
4   import java.awt.event.ActionEvent;
5   import javax.swing.Box;
6   import javax.swing.JFrame;
7   import javax.swing.JTextArea;
8   import javax.swing.JButton;
9   import javax.swing.JScrollPane;
10
11  public class TextAreaFrame extends JFrame
12  {
13     private JTextArea textArea1; // displays demo string
14     private JTextArea textArea2; // highlighted text is copied here
15     private JButton copyJButton; // initiates copying of text
16
```

Fig. 14.47 | Copying selected text from one JTextArea to another. (Part 1 of 2.)

```
17      // no-argument constructor
18      public TextAreaFrame()
19      {
20         super( "TextArea Demo" );
21         Box box = Box.createHorizontalBox(); // create box
22         String demo = "This is a demo string to\n" +
23            "illustrate copying text\nfrom one textarea to \n" +
24            "another textarea using an\nexternal event\n";
25
26         textArea1 = new JTextArea( demo, 10, 15 ); // create textArea1
27         box.add( new JScrollPane( textArea1 ) ); // add scrollpane
28
29         copyJButton = new JButton( "Copy >>>" ); // create copy button
30         box.add( copyJButton ); // add copy button to box
31         copyJButton.addActionListener(
32
33            new ActionListener() // anonymous inner class
34            {
35               // set text in textArea2 to selected text from textArea1
36               public void actionPerformed( ActionEvent event )
37               {
38                  textArea2.setText( textArea1.getSelectedText() );
39               } // end method actionPerformed
40            } // end anonymous inner class
41         ); // end call to addActionListener
42
43         textArea2 = new JTextArea( 10, 15 ); // create second textarea
44         textArea2.setEditable( false ); // disable editing
45         box.add( new JScrollPane( textArea2 ) ); // add scrollpane
46
47         add( box ); // add box to frame
48      } // end TextAreaFrame constructor
49   } // end class TextAreaFrame
```

Fig. 14.47 | Copying selected text from one JTextArea to another. (Part 2 of 2.)

```
1   // Fig. 14.48: TextAreaDemo.java
2   // Copying selected text from one textarea to another.
3   import javax.swing.JFrame;
4
5   public class TextAreaDemo
6   {
7      public static void main( String[] args )
8      {
9         TextAreaFrame textAreaFrame = new TextAreaFrame();
10        textAreaFrame.setDefaultCloseOperation( JFrame.EXIT_ON_CLOSE );
11        textAreaFrame.setSize( 425, 200 ); // set frame size
12        textAreaFrame.setVisible( true ); // display frame
13     } // end main
14  } // end class TextAreaDemo
```

Fig. 14.48 | Test class for TextAreaFrame. (Part 1 of 2.)

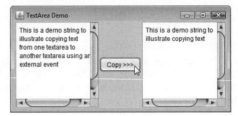

Fig. 14.48 | Test class for `TextAreaFrame`. (Part 2 of 2.)

In the constructor (lines 18–48), line 21 creates a **Box** container (package `javax.swing`) to organize the GUI components. `Box` is a subclass of `Container` that uses a **BoxLayout** layout manager (discussed in detail in Section 22.9) to arrange the GUI components either horizontally or vertically. `Box`'s `static` method **createHorizontalBox** creates a `Box` that arranges components from left to right in the order that they're attached.

Lines 26 and 43 create `JTextArea`s `textArea1` and `textArea2`. Line 26 uses `JTextArea`'s three-argument constructor, which takes a `String` representing the initial text and two `int`s specifying that the `JTextArea` has 10 rows and 15 columns. Line 43 uses `JTextArea`'s two-argument constructor, specifying that the `JTextArea` has 10 rows and 15 columns. Line 26 specifies that `demo` should be displayed as the default `JTextArea` content. A `JTextArea` does not provide scrollbars if it cannot display its complete contents. So, line 27 creates a `JScrollPane` object, initializes it with `textArea1` and attaches it to container `box`. By default, horizontal and vertical scrollbars appear as necessary in a `JScrollPane`.

Lines 29–41 create `JButton` object `copyJButton` with the label `"Copy >>>"`, add `copyJButton` to container `box` and register the event handler for `copyJButton`'s `ActionEvent`. This button provides the external event that determines when the program should copy the selected text in `textArea1` to `textArea2`. When the user clicks `copyJButton`, line 38 in `actionPerformed` indicates that method **getSelectedText** (inherited into `JTextArea` from `JTextComponent`) should return the selected text from `textArea1`. The user selects text by dragging the mouse over the desired text to highlight it. Method `setText` changes the text in `textArea2` to the string returned by `getSelectedText`.

Lines 43–45 create `textArea2`, set its editable property to `false` and add it to container `box`. Line 47 adds `box` to the `JFrame`. Recall from Section 14.18 that the default layout of a `JFrame` is a `BorderLayout` and that the `add` method by default attaches its argument to the `CENTER` of the `BorderLayout`.

When text reaches the right edge of a `JTextArea` the text can wrap to the next line. This is referred to as **line wrapping**. By default, `JTextArea` does *not* wrap lines.

 Look-and-Feel Observation 14.19

*To provide line wrapping functionality for a `JTextArea`, invoke `JTextArea` method **setLineWrap** with a `true` argument.*

JScrollPane Scrollbar Policies

This example uses a `JScrollPane` to provide scrolling for a `JTextArea`. By default, `JScrollPane` displays scrollbars only if they're required. You can set the horizontal and vertical **scrollbar policies** of a `JScrollPane` when it's constructed. If a program has a reference to a JScrollPane, the program can use JScrollPane methods **setHorizontal-ScrollBarPolicy** and **setVerticalScrollBarPolicy** to change the scrollbar policies at any time. Class JScrollPane declares the constants

```
JScrollPane.VERTICAL_SCROLLBAR_ALWAYS
JScrollPane.HORIZONTAL_SCROLLBAR_ALWAYS
```

to indicate that *a scrollbar should always appear*, constants

```
JScrollPane.VERTICAL_SCROLLBAR_AS_NEEDED
JScrollPane.HORIZONTAL_SCROLLBAR_AS_NEEDED
```

to indicate that *a scrollbar should appear only if necessary* (the defaults) and constants

```
JScrollPane.VERTICAL_SCROLLBAR_NEVER
JScrollPane.HORIZONTAL_SCROLLBAR_NEVER
```

to indicate that *a scrollbar should never appear*. If the horizontal scrollbar policy is set to JScrollPane.HORIZONTAL_SCROLLBAR_NEVER, a JTextArea attached to the JScrollPane will automatically wrap lines.

14.21 Wrap-Up

In this chapter, you learned many GUI components and how to implement event handling. You also learned about nested classes, inner classes and anonymous inner classes. You saw the special relationship between an inner-class object and an object of its top-level class. You learned how to use JOptionPane dialogs to obtain text input from the user and how to display messages to the user. You also learned how to create applications that execute in their own windows. We discussed class JFrame and components that enable a user to interact with an application. We also showed you how to display text and images to the user. You learned how to customize JPanels to create custom drawing areas, which you'll use extensively in the next chapter. You saw how to organize components on a window using layout managers and how to creating more complex GUIs by using JPanels to organize components. Finally, you learned about the JTextArea component in which a user can enter text and an application can display text. In Chapter 22, you'll learn about more advanced GUI components, such as sliders, menus and more complex layout managers. In the next chapter, you'll learn how to add graphics to your GUI application. Graphics allow you to draw shapes and text with colors and styles.

15

Graphics and Java 2D

Objectives

In this chapter you'll learn:

- To understand graphics contexts and graphics objects.

- To manipulate colors and fonts.

- To use methods of class `Graphics` to draw various shapes.

- To use methods of class `Graphics2D` from the Java 2D API to draw various shapes.

- To specify `Paint` and `Stroke` characteristics of shapes displayed with `Graphics2D`.

15.1 Introduction

In this chapter, we overview several of Java's capabilities for drawing two-dimensional shapes, controlling colors and controlling fonts. Part of Java's initial appeal was its support for graphics that enabled programmers to visually enhance their applications. Java now contains many more sophisticated drawing capabilities as part of the Java 2D API. This chapter begins by introducing many of Java's original drawing capabilities. Next we present several of the more powerful Java 2D capabilities, such as controlling the style of lines used to draw shapes and the way shapes are filled with colors and patterns. The classes that were part of Java's original graphics capabilities are now considered to be part of the Java 2D API.

Figure 15.1 shows a portion of the Java class hierarchy that includes several of the basic graphics classes and Java 2D API classes and interfaces covered in this chapter. Class **Color** contains methods and constants for manipulating colors. Class JComponent contains method paintComponent, which is used to draw graphics on a component. Class **Font** contains methods and constants for manipulating fonts. Class **FontMetrics** contains methods for obtaining font information. Class **Graphics** contains methods for drawing strings, lines, rectangles and other shapes. Class **Graphics2D**, which extends class Graphics, is used for drawing with the Java 2D API. Class **Polygon** contains methods for creating polygons. The bottom half of the figure lists several classes and interfaces from the Java 2D API. Class **BasicStroke** helps specify the drawing characteristics of lines. Classes **GradientPaint** and **TexturePaint** help specify the characteristics for filling shapes with colors or patterns. Classes GeneralPath, Line2D, Arc2D, Ellipse2D, Rectangle2D and RoundRectangle2D represent several Java 2D shapes.

To begin drawing in Java, we must first understand Java's **coordinate system** (Fig. 15.2), which is a scheme for identifying every point on the screen. By default, the upper-left corner of a GUI component (e.g., a window) has the coordinates (0, 0). A coordinate pair is composed of an *x*-coordinate (the **horizontal coordinate**) and a *y*-coordinate (the **vertical coordinate**). The *x*-coordinate is the horizontal distance moving *right* from the left of the screen. The *y*-coordinate is the vertical distance moving *down* from the top of the screen. The *x*-axis describes every horizontal coordinate, and the *y*-axis every vertical coordinate. The coordinates are used to indicate where graphics should be displayed on a screen. Coordinate units are measured in **pixels** (which stands for "picture element"). A pixel is a display monitor's smallest unit of resolution.

Portability Tip 15.1

Different display monitors have different resolutions (i.e., the density of the pixels varies). This can cause graphics to appear in different sizes on different monitors or on the same monitor with different settings.

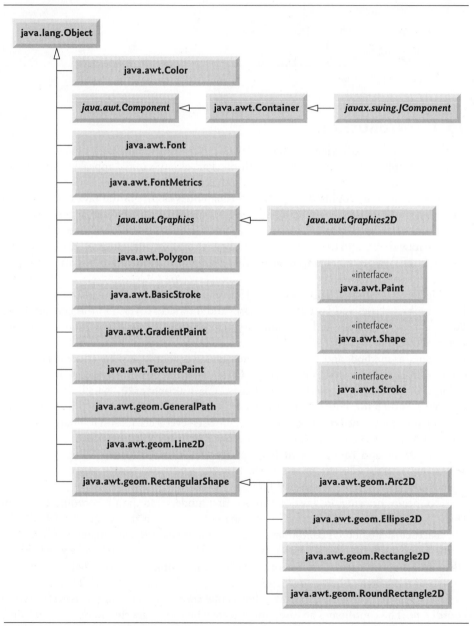

Fig. 15.1 | Classes and interfaces used in this chapter from Java's original graphics capabilities and from the Java 2D API.

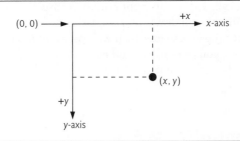

Fig. 15.2 | Java coordinate system. Units are measured in pixels.

15.2 Graphics Contexts and Graphics Objects

A **graphics context** enables drawing on the screen. A Graphics object manages a graphics context and draws pixels on the screen that represent text and other graphical objects (e.g., lines, ellipses, rectangles and other polygons). Graphics objects contain methods for drawing, font manipulation, color manipulation and the like.

Class Graphics is an abstract class (i.e., Graphics objects cannot be instantiated). This contributes to Java's portability. Because drawing is performed differently on every platform that supports Java, there cannot be only one implementation of the drawing capabilities across all systems. For example, the graphics capabilities that enable a PC running Microsoft Windows to draw a rectangle are different from those that enable a Linux workstation to draw a rectangle—and they're both different from the graphics capabilities that enable a Macintosh to draw a rectangle. When Java is implemented on each platform, a subclass of Graphics is created that implements the drawing capabilities. This implementation is hidden by class Graphics, which supplies the interface that enables us to use graphics in a platform-independent manner.

Recall from Chapter 14 that class Component is the superclass for many of the classes in package java.awt. Class JComponent (package javax.swing), which inherits indirectly from class Component, contains a paintComponent method that can be used to draw graphics. Method paintComponent takes a Graphics object as an argument. This object is passed to the paintComponent method by the system when a lightweight Swing component needs to be repainted. The header for the paintComponent method is

```
public void paintComponent( Graphics g )
```

Parameter g receives a reference to an instance of the system-specific subclass that Graphics extends. The preceding method header should look familiar to you—it's the same one we used in some of the applications in Chapter 14. Actually, class JComponent is a superclass of JPanel. Many capabilities of class JPanel are inherited from class JComponent.

You seldom call method paintComponent directly, because drawing graphics is an event-driven process. As we mentioned in Chapter 11, Java uses a multithreaded model of program execution. Each thread is a parallel activity. Each program can have many threads. When you create a GUI-based application, one of those threads is known as the **event-dispatch thread (EDT)**—it's used to process all GUI events. All drawing and manipulation of GUI components should be performed in that thread. When a GUI application executes, the application container calls method paintComponent (in the event-dispatch thread) for each lightweight component as the GUI is displayed. For paintComponent to be called again, an event must occur (such as covering and uncovering the component with another window).

If you need paintComponent to execute (i.e., if you want to update the graphics drawn on a Swing component), you can call method **repaint**, which is inherited by all JComponents indirectly from class Component (package java.awt). The header for repaint is

```
public void repaint()
```

15.3 Color Control

Class Color declares methods and constants for manipulating colors in a Java program. The predeclared color constants are summarized in Fig. 15.3, and several color methods and constructors are summarized in Fig. 15.4. Two of the methods in Fig. 15.4 are Graphics methods that are specific to colors.

Color constant	RGB value
public final static Color RED	255, 0, 0
public final static Color GREEN	0, 255, 0
public final static Color BLUE	0, 0, 255
public final static Color ORANGE	255, 200, 0
public final static Color PINK	255, 175, 175
public final static Color CYAN	0, 255, 255
public final static Color MAGENTA	255, 0, 255
public final static Color YELLOW	255, 255, 0
public final static Color BLACK	0, 0, 0
public final static Color WHITE	255, 255, 255
public final static Color GRAY	128, 128, 128
public final static Color LIGHT_GRAY	192, 192, 192
public final static Color DARK_GRAY	64, 64, 64

Fig. 15.3 | Color constants and their RGB values.

Method	Description
Color constructors and methods	
public Color(int r, int g, int b)	Creates a color based on red, green and blue components expressed as integers from 0 to 255.
public Color(float r, float g, float b)	Creates a color based on red, green and blue components expressed as floating-point values from 0.0 to 1.0.

Fig. 15.4 | Color methods and color-related Graphics methods. (Part 1 of 2.)

Method	Description
`public int getRed()`	
	Returns a value between 0 and 255 representing the red content.
`public int getGreen()`	
	Returns a value between 0 and 255 representing the green content.
`public int getBlue()`	
	Returns a value between 0 and 255 representing the blue content.
Graphics methods for manipulating `Color`s	
`public Color getColor()`	
	Returns `Color` object representing current color for the graphics context.
`public void setColor( Color c )`	
	Sets the current color for drawing with the graphics context.

Fig. 15.4 | `Color` methods and color-related `Graphics` methods. (Part 2 of 2.)

Every color is created from a red, a green and a blue component. Together these components are called **RGB values**. All three RGB components can be integers from 0 to 255, or all three can be floating-point values from 0.0 to 1.0. The first RGB component specifies the amount of red, the second the amount of green and the third the amount of blue. The larger the RGB value, the greater the amount of that particular color. Java enables you to choose from $256 \times 256 \times 256$ (approximately 16.7 million) colors. Not all computers are capable of displaying all these colors. The computer will display the closest color it can.

Two of class `Color`'s constructors are shown in Fig. 15.4—one that takes three `int` arguments and one that takes three `float` arguments, with each argument specifying the amount of red, green and blue. The `int` values must be in the range 0–255 and the `float` values in the range 0.0–1.0. The new `Color` object will have the specified amounts of red, green and blue. `Color` methods **getRed**, **getGreen** and **getBlue** return integer values from 0 to 255 representing the amounts of red, green and blue, respectively. `Graphics` method **getColor** returns a `Color` object representing the current drawing color. `Graphics` method **setColor** sets the current drawing color.

Drawing in Different Colors

Figures 15.5–15.6 demonstrate several methods from Fig. 15.4 by drawing filled rectangles and `String`s in several different colors. When the application begins execution, class `ColorJPanel`'s `paintComponent` method (lines 10–37 of Fig. 15.5) is called to paint the window. Line 17 uses `Graphics` method `setColor` to set the drawing color. Method `setColor` receives a `Color` object. The expression `new Color( 255, 0, 0 )` creates a new `Color` object that represents red (red value 255, and 0 for the green and blue values). Line 18 uses `Graphics` method **fillRect** to draw a filled rectangle in the current color. Method `fillRect` draws a rectangle based on its four arguments. The first two integer values represent the upper-left x-coordinate and upper-left y-coordinate, where the `Graphics` object begins drawing the rectangle. The third and fourth arguments are nonnegative integers that represent the width and the height of the rectangle in pixels, respectively. A rectangle drawn using method `fillRect` is filled by the current color of the `Graphics` object.

```
1   // Fig. 15.5: ColorJPanel.java
2   // Demonstrating Colors.
3   import java.awt.Graphics;
4   import java.awt.Color;
5   import javax.swing.JPanel;
6
7   public class ColorJPanel extends JPanel
8   {
9      // draw rectangles and Strings in different colors
10     public void paintComponent( Graphics g )
11     {
12        super.paintComponent( g ); // call superclass's paintComponent
13
14        this.setBackground( Color.WHITE );
15
16        // set new drawing color using integers
17        g.setColor( new Color( 255, 0, 0 ) );
18        g.fillRect( 15, 25, 100, 20 );
19        g.drawString( "Current RGB: " + g.getColor(), 130, 40 );
20
21        // set new drawing color using floats
22        g.setColor( new Color( 0.50f, 0.75f, 0.0f ) );
23        g.fillRect( 15, 50, 100, 20 );
24        g.drawString( "Current RGB: " + g.getColor(), 130, 65 );
25
26        // set new drawing color using static Color objects
27        g.setColor( Color.BLUE );
28        g.fillRect( 15, 75, 100, 20 );
29        g.drawString( "Current RGB: " + g.getColor(), 130, 90 );
30
31        // display individual RGB values
32        Color color = Color.MAGENTA;
33        g.setColor( color );
34        g.fillRect( 15, 100, 100, 20 );
35        g.drawString( "RGB values: " + color.getRed() + ", " +
36           color.getGreen() + ", " + color.getBlue(), 130, 115 );
37     } // end method paintComponent
38  } // end class ColorJPanel
```

Fig. 15.5 | Color changed for drawing.

```
1   // Fig. 15.6: ShowColors.java
2   // Demonstrating Colors.
3   import javax.swing.JFrame;
4
5   public class ShowColors
6   {
7      // execute application
8      public static void main( String[] args )
9      {
10        // create frame for ColorJPanel
11        JFrame frame = new JFrame( "Using colors" );
```

Fig. 15.6 | Creating JFrame to display colors on JPanel. (Part 1 of 2.)

```
12          frame.setDefaultCloseOperation( JFrame.EXIT_ON_CLOSE );
13
14          ColorJPanel colorJPanel = new ColorJPanel(); // create ColorJPanel
15          frame.add( colorJPanel ); // add colorJPanel to frame
16          frame.setSize( 400, 180 ); // set frame size
17          frame.setVisible( true ); // display frame
18       } // end main
19    } // end class ShowColors
```

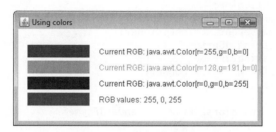

Fig. 15.6 | Creating JFrame to display colors on JPanel. (Part 2 of 2.)

Line 19 (Fig. 15.5) uses Graphics method **drawString** to draw a String in the current color. The expression g.getColor() retrieves the current color from the Graphics object. We then concatenate the Color with string "Current RGB: ", resulting in an implicit call to class Color's toString method. The String representation of a Color contains the class name and package (java.awt.Color) and the red, green and blue values.

Look-and-Feel Observation 15.1

People perceive colors differently. Choose your colors carefully to ensure that your application is readable, both for people who can perceive color and for those who are color blind. Try to avoid using many different colors in close proximity.

Lines 22–24 and 27–29 perform the same tasks again. Line 22 uses the Color constructor with three float arguments to create a dark green color (0.50f for red, 0.75f for green and 0.0f for blue). Note the syntax of the values. The letter f appended to a floating-point literal indicates that the literal should be treated as type float. Recall that by default, floating-point literals are treated as type double.

Line 27 sets the current drawing color to one of the predeclared Color constants (Color.BLUE). The Color constants are static, so they're created when class Color is loaded into memory at execution time.

The statement in lines 35–36 makes calls to Color methods getRed, getGreen and getBlue on the predeclared Color.MAGENTA constant. Method main of class ShowColors (lines 8–18 of Fig. 15.6) creates the JFrame that will contain a ColorJPanel object where the colors will be displayed.

Software Engineering Observation 15.1

To change the color, you must create a new Color object (or use one of the predeclared Color constants). Like String objects, Color objects are immutable (not modifiable).

Package javax.swing provides the **JColorChooser** GUI component that enables application users to select colors. Figures 15.7–15.8 demonstrates a JColorChooser dialog. When you click the **Change Color** button, a JColorChooser dialog appears. When you select a color and press the dialog's **OK** button, the background color of the application window changes.

```java
1   // Fig. 15.7: ShowColors2JFrame.java
2   // Choosing colors with JColorChooser.
3   import java.awt.BorderLayout;
4   import java.awt.Color;
5   import java.awt.event.ActionEvent;
6   import java.awt.event.ActionListener;
7   import javax.swing.JButton;
8   import javax.swing.JFrame;
9   import javax.swing.JColorChooser;
10  import javax.swing.JPanel;
11
12  public class ShowColors2JFrame extends JFrame
13  {
14     private JButton changeColorJButton;
15     private Color color = Color.LIGHT_GRAY;
16     private JPanel colorJPanel;
17
18     // set up GUI
19     public ShowColors2JFrame()
20     {
21        super( "Using JColorChooser" );
22
23        // create JPanel for display color
24        colorJPanel = new JPanel();
25        colorJPanel.setBackground( color );
26
27        // set up changeColorJButton and register its event handler
28        changeColorJButton = new JButton( "Change Color" );
29        changeColorJButton.addActionListener(
30
31           new ActionListener() // anonymous inner class
32           {
33              // display JColorChooser when user clicks button
34              public void actionPerformed( ActionEvent event )
35              {
36                 color = JColorChooser.showDialog(
37                    ShowColors2JFrame.this, "Choose a color", color );
38
39                 // set default color, if no color is returned
40                 if ( color == null )
41                    color = Color.LIGHT_GRAY;
42
43                 // change content pane's background color
44                 colorJPanel.setBackground( color );
45              } // end method actionPerformed
46           } // end anonymous inner class
47        ); // end call to addActionListener
```

Fig. 15.7 | JColorChooser dialog. (Part 1 of 2.)

```
48
49          add( colorJPanel, BorderLayout.CENTER ); // add colorJPanel
50          add( changeColorJButton, BorderLayout.SOUTH ); // add button
51
52          setSize( 400, 130 ); // set frame size
53          setVisible( true ); // display frame
54       } // end ShowColor2JFrame constructor
55    } // end class ShowColors2JFrame
```

Fig. 15.7 | JColorChooser dialog. (Part 2 of 2.)

```
1   // Fig. 15.8: ShowColors2.java
2   // Choosing colors with JColorChooser.
3   import javax.swing.JFrame;
4
5   public class ShowColors2
6   {
7      // execute application
8      public static void main( String[] args )
9      {
10         ShowColors2JFrame application = new ShowColors2JFrame();
11         application.setDefaultCloseOperation( JFrame.EXIT_ON_CLOSE );
12      } // end main
13   } // end class ShowColors2
```

(a) Initial application window

(b) JColorChooser window

Select a color from one of the color swatches

(c) Application window after changing JPanel's background color

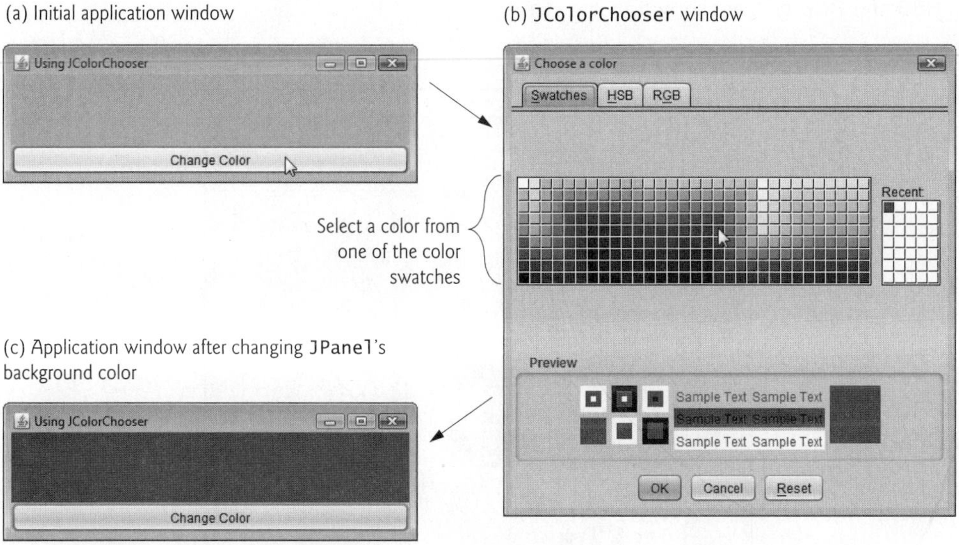

Fig. 15.8 | Choosing colors with JColorChooser.

Class JColorChooser provides static method **showDialog**, which creates a JColor-Chooser object, attaches it to a dialog box and displays the dialog. Lines 36–37 of Fig. 15.7 invoke this method to display the color chooser dialog. Method showDialog returns the selected `Color` object, or `null` if the user presses **Cancel** or closes the dialog without pressing **OK**. The method takes three arguments—a reference to its parent `Component`, a `String` to display in the title bar of the dialog and the initial selected `Color` for the dialog. The parent component is a reference to the window from which the dialog is displayed (in this case the `JFrame`, with the reference name `frame`). The dialog will be centered on the parent. If the parent is `null`, the dialog is centered on the screen. While the color chooser dialog is on the screen, the user cannot interact with the parent component until the dialog is dismissed. This type of dialog is called a modal dialog.

After the user selects a color, lines 40–41 determine whether `color` is `null`, and, if so, set `color` to `Color.LIGHT_GRAY`. Line 44 invokes method `setBackground` to change the background color of the `JPanel`. Method `setBackground` is one of the many `Component` methods that can be used on most GUI components. The user can continue to use the **Change Color** button to change the background color of the application. Figure 15.8 contains method `main`, which executes the program.

JColorChooser's Tabs

Figure 15.8(b) shows the default `JColorChooser` dialog that allows the user to select a color from a variety of **color swatches**. There are three tabs across the top of the dialog—**Swatches**, **HSB** and **RGB**. These represent three different ways to select a color. The **HSB** tab allows you to select a color based on **hue**, **saturation** and **brightness**—values that are used to define the amount of light in a color. We do not discuss HSB values. For more information on them, visit `en.wikipedia.org/wiki/HSL_and_HSV`. The **RGB** tab allows you to select a color by using sliders to select the red, green and blue components. The **HSB** and **RGB** tabs are shown in Fig. 15.9.

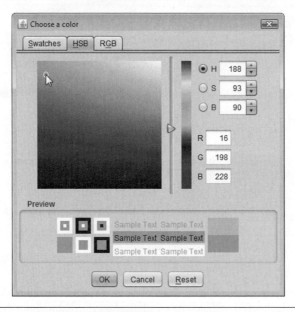

Fig. 15.9 | HSB and RGB tabs of the `JColorChooser` dialog.l

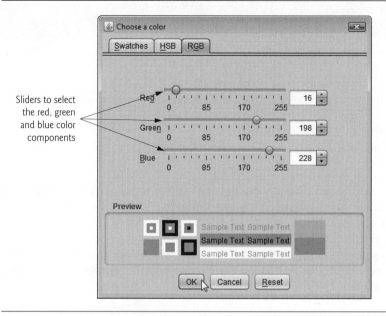

Fig. 15.9 | HSB and RGB tabs of the JColorChooser dialog.l

15.4 Manipulating Fonts

This section introduces methods and constants for manipulating fonts. Most font methods and font constants are part of class Font. Some methods of class Font and class Graphics are summarized in Fig. 15.10.

Method or constant	Description
Font constants, constructors and methods	
public final static int PLAIN	A constant representing a plain font style.
public final static int BOLD	A constant representing a bold font style.
public final static int ITALIC	A constant representing an italic font style.
public Font(String name, **int** style, **int** size)	Creates a Font object with the specified font name, style and size.
public int getStyle()	Returns an int indicating the current font style.
public int getSize()	Returns an int indicating the current font size.
public String getName()	Returns the current font name as a string.
public String getFamily()	Returns the font's family name as a string.
public boolean isPlain()	Returns true if the font is plain, else false.
public boolean isBold()	Returns true if the font is bold, else false.
public boolean isItalic()	Returns true if the font is italic, else false.

Fig. 15.10 | Font-related methods and constants. (Part 1 of 2.)

Method or constant	Description
Graphics methods for manipulating Fonts	
public Font getFont()	Returns a Font object reference representing the current font.
public void setFont(Font f)	Sets the current font to the font, style and size specified by the Font object reference f.

Fig. 15.10 | Font-related methods and constants. (Part 2 of 2.)

Class Font's constructor takes three arguments—the **font name**, **font style** and **font size**. The font name is any font currently supported by the system on which the program is running, such as standard Java fonts Monospaced, SansSerif and Serif. The font style is **Font.PLAIN**, **Font.ITALIC** or **Font.BOLD** (each is a static field of class Font). Font styles can be used in combination (e.g., Font.ITALIC + Font.BOLD). The font size is measured in points. A **point** is 1/72 of an inch. Graphics method **setFont** sets the current drawing font—the font in which text will be displayed—to its Font argument.

Portability Tip 15.2

The number of fonts varies across systems. Java provides five font names—Serif, Monospaced, SansSerif, Dialog and DialogInput—that can be used on all Java platforms. The Java runtime environment (JRE) on each platform maps these logical font names to actual fonts installed on the platform. The actual fonts used may vary by platform.

The application of Figs. 15.11–15.12 displays text in four different fonts, with each font in a different size. Figure 15.11 uses the Font constructor to initialize Font objects (in lines 16, 20, 24 and 29) that are each passed to Graphics method setFont to change the drawing font. Each call to the Font constructor passes a font name (Serif, Monospaced or SansSerif) as a string, a font style (Font.PLAIN, Font.ITALIC or Font.BOLD) and a font size. Once Graphics method setFont is invoked, all text displayed following the call will appear in the new font until the font is changed. Each font's information is displayed in lines 17, 21, 25 and 30–31 using method drawString. The coordinates passed to drawString corresponds to the lower-left corner of the baseline of the font. Line 28 changes the drawing color to red, so the next string displayed appears in red. Lines 30–31 display information about the final Font object. Method **getFont** of class Graphics returns a Font object representing the current font. Method **getName** returns the current font name as a string. Method **getSize** returns the font size in points.

Software Engineering Observation 15.2

To change the font, you must create a new Font object. Font objects are immutable—class Font has no set methods to change the characteristics of the current font.

Figure 15.12 contains the main method, which creates a JFrame to display a FontJPanel. We add a FontJPanel object to this JFrame (line 15), which displays the graphics created in Fig. 15.11.

```
 1   // Fig. 15.11: FontJPanel.java
 2   // Display strings in different fonts and colors.
 3   import java.awt.Font;
 4   import java.awt.Color;
 5   import java.awt.Graphics;
 6   import javax.swing.JPanel;
 7
 8   public class FontJPanel extends JPanel
 9   {
10      // display Strings in different fonts and colors
11      public void paintComponent( Graphics g )
12      {
13         super.paintComponent( g ); // call superclass's paintComponent
14
15         // set font to Serif (Times), bold, 12pt and draw a string
16         g.setFont( new Font( "Serif", Font.BOLD, 12 ) );
17         g.drawString( "Serif 12 point bold.", 20, 30 );
18
19         // set font to Monospaced (Courier), italic, 24pt and draw a string
20         g.setFont( new Font( "Monospaced", Font.ITALIC, 24 ) );
21         g.drawString( "Monospaced 24 point italic.", 20, 50 );
22
23         // set font to SansSerif (Helvetica), plain, 14pt and draw a string
24         g.setFont( new Font( "SansSerif", Font.PLAIN, 14 ) );
25         g.drawString( "SansSerif 14 point plain.", 20, 70 );
26
27         // set font to Serif (Times), bold/italic, 18pt and draw a string
28         g.setColor( Color.RED );
29         g.setFont( new Font( "Serif", Font.BOLD + Font.ITALIC, 18 ) );
30         g.drawString( g.getFont().getName() + " " + g.getFont().getSize() +
31            " point bold italic.", 20, 90 );
32      } // end method paintComponent
33   } // end class FontJPanel
```

Fig. 15.11 | Graphics method `setFont` changes the drawing font.

```
 1   // Fig. 15.12: Fonts.java
 2   // Using fonts.
 3   import javax.swing.JFrame;
 4
 5   public class Fonts
 6   {
 7      // execute application
 8      public static void main( String[] args )
 9      {
10         // create frame for FontJPanel
11         JFrame frame = new JFrame( "Using fonts" );
12         frame.setDefaultCloseOperation( JFrame.EXIT_ON_CLOSE );
13
14         FontJPanel fontJPanel = new FontJPanel(); // create FontJPanel
15         frame.add( fontJPanel ); // add fontJPanel to frame
```

Fig. 15.12 | Creating a `JFrame` to display fonts. (Part 1 of 2.)

```
16            frame.setSize( 420, 150 ); // set frame size
17            frame.setVisible( true ); // display frame
18       } // end main
19    } // end class Fonts
```

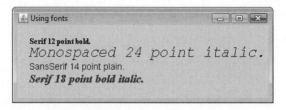

Fig. 15.12 | Creating a JFrame to display fonts. (Part 2 of 2.)

Font Metrics

Sometimes it's necessary to get information about the current drawing font, such as its name, style and size. Several Font methods used to get font information are summarized in Fig. 15.10. Method **getStyle** returns an integer value representing the current style. The integer value returned is either Font.PLAIN, Font.ITALIC, Font.BOLD or the combination of Font.ITALIC and Font.BOLD. Method **getFamily** returns the name of the font family to which the current font belongs. The name of the font family is platform specific. Font methods are also available to test the style of the current font, and these too are summarized in Fig. 15.10. Methods **isPlain**, **isBold** and **isItalic** return true if the current font style is plain, bold or italic, respectively.

Figure 15.13 illustrates some of the common **font metrics**, which provide precise information about a font, such as **height**, **descent** (the amount a character dips below the baseline), **ascent** (the amount a character rises above the baseline) and **leading** (the difference between the descent of one line of text and the ascent of the line of text below it—that is, the interline spacing).

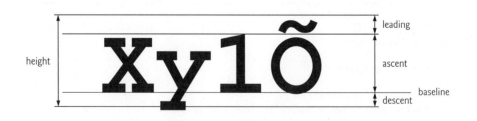

Fig. 15.13 | Font metrics.

Class **FontMetrics** declares several methods for obtaining font metrics. These methods and Graphics method **getFontMetrics** are summarized in Fig. 15.14. The application of Figs. 15.15–15.16 uses the methods of Fig. 15.14 to obtain font metric information for two fonts.

Method	Description
FontMetrics methods	
public int getAscent()	Returns the ascent of a font in points.
public int getDescent()	Returns the descent of a font in points.
public int getLeading()	Returns the leading of a font in points.
public int getHeight()	Returns the height of a font in points.
Graphics methods for getting a Font's FontMetrics	
public FontMetrics getFontMetrics()	
	Returns the FontMetrics object for the current drawing Font.
public FontMetrics getFontMetrics(Font f)	
	Returns the FontMetrics object for the specified Font argument.

Fig. 15.14 | FontMetrics and Graphics methods for obtaining font metrics.

```java
1   // Fig. 15.15: MetricsJPanel.java
2   // FontMetrics and Graphics methods useful for obtaining font metrics.
3   import java.awt.Font;
4   import java.awt.FontMetrics;
5   import java.awt.Graphics;
6   import javax.swing.JPanel;
7
8   public class MetricsJPanel extends JPanel
9   {
10     // display font metrics
11     public void paintComponent( Graphics g )
12     {
13       super.paintComponent( g ); // call superclass's paintComponent
14
15       g.setFont( new Font( "SansSerif", Font.BOLD, 12 ) );
16       FontMetrics metrics = g.getFontMetrics();
17       g.drawString( "Current font: " + g.getFont(), 10, 30 );
18       g.drawString( "Ascent: " + metrics.getAscent(), 10, 45 );
19       g.drawString( "Descent: " + metrics.getDescent(), 10, 60 );
20       g.drawString( "Height: " + metrics.getHeight(), 10, 75 );
21       g.drawString( "Leading: " + metrics.getLeading(), 10, 90 );
22
23       Font font = new Font( "Serif", Font.ITALIC, 14 );
24       metrics = g.getFontMetrics( font );
25       g.setFont( font );
26       g.drawString( "Current font: " + font, 10, 120 );
27       g.drawString( "Ascent: " + metrics.getAscent(), 10, 135 );
28       g.drawString( "Descent: " + metrics.getDescent(), 10, 150 );
29       g.drawString( "Height: " + metrics.getHeight(), 10, 165 );
30       g.drawString( "Leading: " + metrics.getLeading(), 10, 180 );
31     } // end method paintComponent
32   } // end class MetricsJPanel
```

Fig. 15.15 | Font metrics.

```
 1   // Fig. 15.16: Metrics.java
 2   // Displaying font metrics.
 3   import javax.swing.JFrame;
 4
 5   public class Metrics
 6   {
 7      // execute application
 8      public static void main( String[] args )
 9      {
10         // create frame for MetricsJPanel
11         JFrame frame = new JFrame( "Demonstrating FontMetrics" );
12         frame.setDefaultCloseOperation( JFrame.EXIT_ON_CLOSE );
13
14         MetricsJPanel metricsJPanel = new MetricsJPanel();
15         frame.add( metricsJPanel ); // add metricsJPanel to frame
16         frame.setSize( 510, 240 ); // set frame size
17         frame.setVisible( true ); // display frame
18      } // end main
19   } // end class Metrics
```

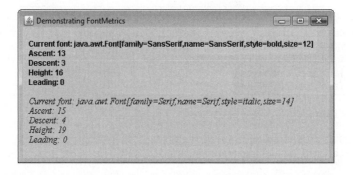

Fig. 15.16 | Creating JFrame to display font metric information.

Line 15 of Fig. 15.15 creates and sets the current drawing font to a SansSerif, bold, 12-point font. Line 16 uses Graphics method getFontMetrics to obtain the FontMetrics object for the current font. Line 17 outputs the String representation of the Font returned by g.getFont(). Lines 18–21 use FontMetric methods to obtain the ascent, descent, height and leading for the font.

Line 23 creates a new Serif, italic, 14-point font. Line 24 uses a second version of Graphics method getFontMetrics, which accepts a Font argument and returns a corresponding FontMetrics object. Lines 27–30 obtain the ascent, descent, height and leading for the font. The font metrics are slightly different for the two fonts.

15.5 Drawing Lines, Rectangles and Ovals

This section presents Graphics methods for drawing lines, rectangles and ovals. The methods and their parameters are summarized in Fig. 15.17. For each drawing method that requires a width and height parameter, the width and height must be nonnegative values. Otherwise, the shape will not display.

Method	Description
public void drawLine(int x1, int y1, int x2, int y2)	
	Draws a line between the point (x1, y1) and the point (x2, y2).
public void drawRect(int x, int y, int width, int height)	
	Draws a rectangle of the specified width and height. The rectangle's top-left corner is located at (x, y). Only the outline of the rectangle is drawn using the Graphics object's color—the body of the rectangle is not filled with this color.
public void fillRect(int x, int y, int width, int height)	
	Draws a filled rectangle in the current color with the specified width and height. The rectangle's top-left corner is located at (x, y).
public void clearRect(int x, int y, int width, int height)	
	Draws a filled rectangle with the specified width and height in the current background color. The rectangle's top-left corner is located at (x, y). This method is useful if you want to remove a portion of an image.
public void drawRoundRect(int x, int y, int width, int height, int arcWidth, int arcHeight)	
	Draws a rectangle with rounded corners in the current color with the specified width and height. The arcWidth and arcHeight determine the rounding of the corners (see Fig. 15.20). Only the outline of the shape is drawn.
public void fillRoundRect(int x, int y, int width, int height, int arcWidth, int arcHeight)	
	Draws a filled rectangle in the current color with rounded corners with the specified width and height. The arcWidth and arcHeight determine the rounding of the corners (see Fig. 15.20).
public void draw3DRect(int x, int y, int width, int height, boolean b)	
	Draws a three-dimensional rectangle in the current color with the specified width and height. The rectangle's top-left corner is located at (x, y). The rectangle appears raised when b is true and lowered when b is false. Only the outline of the shape is drawn.
public void fill3DRect(int x, int y, int width, int height, boolean b)	
	Draws a filled three-dimensional rectangle in the current color with the specified width and height. The rectangle's top-left corner is located at (x, y). The rectangle appears raised when b is true and lowered when b is false.
public void drawOval(int x, int y, int width, int height)	
	Draws an oval in the current color with the specified width and height. The bounding rectangle's top-left corner is located at (x, y). The oval touches all four sides of the bounding rectangle at the center of each side (see Fig. 15.21). Only the outline of the shape is drawn.
public void fillOval(int x, int y, int width, int height)	
	Draws a filled oval in the current color with the specified width and height. The bounding rectangle's top-left corner is located at (x, y). The oval touches the center of all four sides of the bounding rectangle (see Fig. 15.21).

Fig. 15.17 | Graphics methods that draw lines, rectangles and ovals.

The application of Figs. 15.18–15.19 demonstrates drawing a variety of lines, rectangles, three-dimensional rectangles, rounded rectangles and ovals. In Fig. 15.18, line 17 draws a red line, line 20 draws an empty blue rectangle and line 21 draws a filled blue rectangle. Methods **fillRoundRect** (line 24) and **drawRoundRect** (line 25) draw rectangles with rounded corners. Their first two arguments specify the coordinates of the upper-left corner of the **bounding rectangle**—the area in which the rounded rectangle will be drawn. The upper-left corner coordinates are *not* the edge of the rounded rectangle, but the coordinates where the edge would be if the rectangle had square corners. The third and fourth arguments specify the width and height of the rectangle. The last two arguments determine the horizontal and vertical diameters of the arc (i.e., the arc width and arc height) used to represent the corners.

Figure 15.20 labels the arc width, arc height, width and height of a rounded rectangle. Using the same value for the arc width and arc height produces a quarter-circle at each

```java
1   // Fig. 15.18: LinesRectsOvalsJPanel.java
2   // Drawing lines, rectangles and ovals.
3   import java.awt.Color;
4   import java.awt.Graphics;
5   import javax.swing.JPanel;
6
7   public class LinesRectsOvalsJPanel extends JPanel
8   {
9      // display various lines, rectangles and ovals
10     public void paintComponent( Graphics g )
11     {
12        super.paintComponent( g ); // call superclass's paint method
13
14        this.setBackground( Color.WHITE );
15
16        g.setColor( Color.RED );
17        g.drawLine( 5, 30, 380, 30 );
18
19        g.setColor( Color.BLUE );
20        g.drawRect( 5, 40, 90, 55 );
21        g.fillRect( 100, 40, 90, 55 );
22
23        g.setColor( Color.CYAN );
24        g.fillRoundRect( 195, 40, 90, 55, 50, 50 );
25        g.drawRoundRect( 290, 40, 90, 55, 20, 20 );
26
27        g.setColor( Color.GREEN );
28        g.draw3DRect( 5, 100, 90, 55, true );
29        g.fill3DRect( 100, 100, 90, 55, false );
30
31        g.setColor( Color.MAGENTA );
32        g.drawOval( 195, 100, 90, 55 );
33        g.fillOval( 290, 100, 90, 55 );
34     } // end method paintComponent
35  } // end class LinesRectsOvalsJPanel
```

Fig. 15.18 | Drawing lines, rectangles and ovals.

```
 1   // Fig. 15.19: LinesRectsOvals.java
 2   // Drawing lines, rectangles and ovals.
 3   import java.awt.Color;
 4   import javax.swing.JFrame;
 5
 6   public class LinesRectsOvals
 7   {
 8      // execute application
 9      public static void main( String[] args )
10      {
11         // create frame for LinesRectsOvalsJPanel
12         JFrame frame =
13            new JFrame( "Drawing lines, rectangles and ovals" );
14         frame.setDefaultCloseOperation( JFrame.EXIT_ON_CLOSE );
15
16         LinesRectsOvalsJPanel linesRectsOvalsJPanel =
17            new LinesRectsOvalsJPanel();
18         linesRectsOvalsJPanel.setBackground( Color.WHITE );
19         frame.add( linesRectsOvalsJPanel ); // add panel to frame
20         frame.setSize( 400, 210 ); // set frame size
21         frame.setVisible( true ); // display frame
22      } // end main
23   } // end class LinesRectsOvals
```

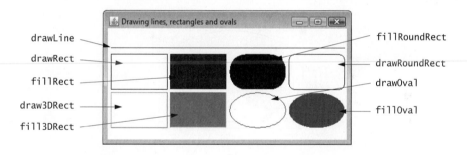

Fig. 15.19 | Creating JFrame to display lines, rectangles and ovals.

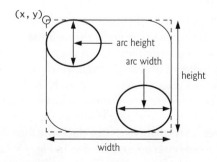

Fig. 15.20 | Arc width and arc height for rounded rectangles.

corner. When the arc width, arc height, width and height have the same values, the result is a circle. If the values for width and height are the same and the values of arcWidth and arcHeight are 0, the result is a square.

Methods **draw3DRect** (line 28) and **fill3DRect** (line 29) take the same arguments. The first two specify the top-left corner of the rectangle. The next two arguments specify the width and height of the rectangle, respectively. The last argument determines whether the rectangle is **raised** (true) or **lowered** (false). The three-dimensional effect of draw3DRect appears as two edges of the rectangle in the original color and two edges in a slightly darker color. The three-dimensional effect of fill3DRect appears as two edges of the rectangle in the original drawing color and the fill and other two edges in a slightly darker color. Raised rectangles have the original drawing color edges at the top and left of the rectangle. Lowered rectangles have the original drawing color edges at the bottom and right of the rectangle. The three-dimensional effect is difficult to see in some colors.

Methods **drawOval** and **fillOval** (Fig. 15.18, lines 32–33) take the same four arguments. The first two specify the top-left coordinate of the bounding rectangle that contains the oval. The last two specify the width and height of the bounding rectangle, respectively. Figure 15.21 shows an oval bounded by a rectangle. The oval touches the center of all four sides of the bounding rectangle. (The bounding rectangle is not displayed on the screen.)

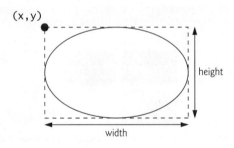

Fig. 15.21 | Oval bounded by a rectangle.

15.6 Drawing Arcs

An **arc** is drawn as a portion of an oval. Arc angles are measured in degrees. Arcs **sweep** (i.e., move along a curve) from a **starting angle** through the number of degrees specified by their **arc angle**. The starting angle indicates in degrees where the arc begins. The arc angle specifies the total number of degrees through which the arc sweeps. Figure 15.22 illustrates two arcs. The left set of axes shows an arc sweeping from zero degrees to approximately 110 degrees. Arcs that sweep in a counterclockwise direction are measured in **positive degrees**. The set of axes on the right shows an arc sweeping from zero degrees to approximately –110 degrees. Arcs that sweep in a clockwise direction are measured in **negative degrees**. Note the dashed boxes around the arcs in Fig. 15.22. When drawing an arc, we specify a bounding rectangle for an oval. The arc will sweep along part of the oval. Graphics methods **drawArc** and **fillArc** for drawing arcs are summarized in Fig. 15.23.

Fig. 15.22 | Positive and negative arc angles.

Method	Description
public void drawArc(**int** x, **int** y, **int** width, **int** height, **int** startAngle, **int** arcAngle)	
	Draws an arc relative to the bounding rectangle's top-left x- and y-coordinates with the specified width and height. The arc segment is drawn starting at startAngle and sweeps arcAngle degrees.
public void fillArc(**int** x, **int** y, **int** width, **int** height, **int** startAngle, **int** arcAngle)	
	Draws a filled arc (i.e., a sector) relative to the bounding rectangle's top-left x- and y-coordinates with the specified width and height. The arc segment is drawn starting at startAngle and sweeps arcAngle degrees.

Fig. 15.23 | Graphics methods for drawing arcs.

Figures 15.24–15.25 demonstrate the arc methods of Fig. 15.23. The application draws six arcs (three unfilled and three filled). To illustrate the bounding rectangle that helps determine where the arc appears, the first three arcs are displayed inside a red rectangle that has the same x, y, width and height arguments as the arcs.

```
 1   // Fig. 15.24: ArcsJPanel.java
 2   // Drawing arcs.
 3   import java.awt.Color;
 4   import java.awt.Graphics;
 5   import javax.swing.JPanel;
 6
 7   public class ArcsJPanel extends JPanel
 8   {
 9      // draw rectangles and arcs
10      public void paintComponent( Graphics g )
11      {
12         super.paintComponent( g ); // call superclass's paintComponent
13
```

Fig. 15.24 | Arcs displayed with drawArc and fillArc. (Part 1 of 2.)

```
14          // start at 0 and sweep 360 degrees
15          g.setColor( Color.RED );
16          g.drawRect( 15, 35, 80, 80 );
17          g.setColor( Color.BLACK );
18          g.drawArc( 15, 35, 80, 80, 0, 360 );
19
20          // start at 0 and sweep 110 degrees
21          g.setColor( Color.RED );
22          g.drawRect( 100, 35, 80, 80 );
23          g.setColor( Color.BLACK );
24          g.drawArc( 100, 35, 80, 80, 0, 110 );
25
26          // start at 0 and sweep -270 degrees
27          g.setColor( Color.RED );
28          g.drawRect( 185, 35, 80, 80 );
29          g.setColor( Color.BLACK );
30          g.drawArc( 185, 35, 80, 80, 0, -270 );
31
32          // start at 0 and sweep 360 degrees
33          g.fillArc( 15, 120, 80, 40, 0, 360 );
34
35          // start at 270 and sweep -90 degrees
36          g.fillArc( 100, 120, 80, 40, 270, -90 );
37
38          // start at 0 and sweep -270 degrees
39          g.fillArc( 185, 120, 80, 40, 0, -270 );
40       } // end method paintComponent
41    } // end class ArcsJPanel
```

Fig. 15.24 | Arcs displayed with drawArc and fillArc. (Part 2 of 2.)

```
1    // Fig. 15.25: DrawArcs.java
2    // Drawing arcs.
3    import javax.swing.JFrame;
4
5    public class DrawArcs
6    {
7       // execute application
8       public static void main( String[] args )
9       {
10          // create frame for ArcsJPanel
11          JFrame frame = new JFrame( "Drawing Arcs" );
12          frame.setDefaultCloseOperation( JFrame.EXIT_ON_CLOSE );
13
14          ArcsJPanel arcsJPanel = new ArcsJPanel(); // create ArcsJPanel
15          frame.add( arcsJPanel ); // add arcsJPanel to frame
16          frame.setSize( 300, 210 ); // set frame size
17          frame.setVisible( true ); // display frame
18       } // end main
19    } // end class DrawArcs
```

Fig. 15.25 | Creating JFrame to display arcs. (Part 1 of 2.)

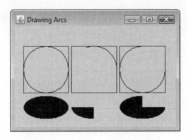

Fig. 15.25 | Creating JFrame to display arcs. (Part 2 of 2.)

15.7 Drawing Polygons and Polylines

Polygons are closed multisided shapes composed of straight-line segments. **Polylines** are sequences of connected points. Figure 15.26 discusses methods for drawing polygons and polylines. Some methods require a **Polygon** object (package java.awt). Class Polygon's constructors are also described in Fig. 15.26. The application of Figs. 15.27–15.28 draws polygons and polylines.

Method	Description
Graphics methods for drawing polygons	
public void drawPolygon(**int**[] xPoints, **int**[] yPoints, **int** points)	
	Draws a polygon. The *x*-coordinate of each point is specified in the xPoints array and the *y*-coordinate of each point in the yPoints array. The last argument specifies the number of points. This method draws a closed polygon. If the last point is different from the first, the polygon is closed by a line that connects the last point to the first.
public void drawPolyline(**int**[] xPoints, **int**[] yPoints, **int** points)	
	Draws a sequence of connected lines. The *x*-coordinate of each point is specified in the xPoints array and the *y*-coordinate of each point in the yPoints array. The last argument specifies the number of points. If the last point is different from the first, the polyline is not closed.
public void drawPolygon(Polygon p)	
	Draws the specified polygon.
public void fillPolygon(**int**[] xPoints, **int**[] yPoints, **int** points)	
	Draws a filled polygon. The *x*-coordinate of each point is specified in the xPoints array and the *y*-coordinate of each point in the yPoints array. The last argument specifies the number of points. This method draws a closed polygon. If the last point is different from the first, the polygon is closed by a line that connects the last point to the first.
public void fillPolygon(Polygon p)	
	Draws the specified filled polygon. The polygon is closed.

Fig. 15.26 | Graphics methods for polygons and class Polygon methods. (Part 1 of 2.)

Method	Description
Polygon constructors and methods	
`public Polygon()`	
	Constructs a new polygon object. The polygon does not contain any points.
`public Polygon( int[] xValues, int[] yValues, int numberOfPoints )`	
	Constructs a new polygon object. The polygon has `numberOfPoints` sides, with each point consisting of an *x*-coordinate from xValues and a *y*-coordinate from yValues.
`public void addPoint( int x, int y )`	
	Adds pairs of *x*- and *y*-coordinates to the `Polygon`.

Fig. 15.26 | `Graphics` methods for polygons and class `Polygon` methods. (Part 2 of 2.)

```
1   // Fig. 15.27: PolygonsJPanel.java
2   // Drawing polygons.
3   import java.awt.Graphics;
4   import java.awt.Polygon;
5   import javax.swing.JPanel;
6
7   public class PolygonsJPanel extends JPanel
8   {
9      // draw polygons and polylines
10     public void paintComponent( Graphics g )
11     {
12        super.paintComponent( g ); // call superclass's paintComponent
13
14        // draw polygon with Polygon object
15        int[] xValues = { 20, 40, 50, 30, 20, 15 };
16        int[] yValues = { 50, 50, 60, 80, 80, 60 };
17        Polygon polygon1 = new Polygon( xValues, yValues, 6 );
18        g.drawPolygon( polygon1 );
19
20        // draw polylines with two arrays
21        int[] xValues2 = { 70, 90, 100, 80, 70, 65, 60 };
22        int[] yValues2 = { 100, 100, 110, 110, 130, 110, 90 };
23        g.drawPolyline( xValues2, yValues2, 7 );
24
25        // fill polygon with two arrays
26        int[] xValues3 = { 120, 140, 150, 190 };
27        int[] yValues3 = { 40, 70, 80, 60 };
28        g.fillPolygon( xValues3, yValues3, 4 );
29
30        // draw filled polygon with Polygon object
31        Polygon polygon2 = new Polygon();
32        polygon2.addPoint( 165, 135 );
33        polygon2.addPoint( 175, 150 );
34        polygon2.addPoint( 270, 200 );
```

Fig. 15.27 | Polygons displayed with `drawPolygon` and `fillPolygon`. (Part 1 of 2.)

```
35          polygon2.addPoint( 200, 220 );
36          polygon2.addPoint( 130, 180 );
37          g.fillPolygon( polygon2 );
38       } // end method paintComponent
39    } // end class PolygonsJPanel
```

Fig. 15.27 | Polygons displayed with **drawPolygon** and **fillPolygon**. (Part 2 of 2.)

```
 1    // Fig. 15.28: DrawPolygons.java
 2    // Drawing polygons.
 3    import javax.swing.JFrame;
 4
 5    public class DrawPolygons
 6    {
 7       // execute application
 8       public static void main( String[] args )
 9       {
10          // create frame for PolygonsJPanel
11          JFrame frame = new JFrame( "Drawing Polygons" );
12          frame.setDefaultCloseOperation( JFrame.EXIT_ON_CLOSE );
13
14          PolygonsJPanel polygonsJPanel = new PolygonsJPanel();
15          frame.add( polygonsJPanel ); // add polygonsJPanel to frame
16          frame.setSize( 280, 270 ); // set frame size
17          frame.setVisible( true ); // display frame
18       } // end main
19    } // end class DrawPolygons
```

Fig. 15.28 | Creating JFrame to display polygons.

Lines 15–16 of Fig. 15.27 create two int arrays and use them to specify the points for Polygon polygon1. The Polygon constructor call in line 17 receives array xValues, which contains the *x*-coordinate of each point; array yValues, which contains the *y*-coordinate of each point; and 6 (the number of points in the polygon). Line 18 displays polygon1 by passing it as an argument to Graphics method **drawPolygon**.

Lines 21–22 create two int arrays and use them to specify the points for a series of connected lines. Array xValues2 contains the *x*-coordinate of each point and array yValues2 the *y*-coordinate of each point. Line 23 uses Graphics method **drawPolyline** to display the series of connected lines specified with the arguments xValues2, yValues2 and 7 (the number of points).

Lines 26–27 create two int arrays and use them to specify the points of a polygon. Array xValues3 contains the *x*-coordinate of each point and array yValues3 the *y*-coordinate of each point. Line 28 displays a polygon by passing to Graphics method **fill-Polygon** the two arrays (xValues3 and yValues3) and the number of points to draw (4).

> **Common Programming Error 15.1**
>
> *An ArrayIndexOutOfBoundsException is thrown if the number of points specified in the third argument to method drawPolygon or method fillPolygon is greater than the number of elements in the arrays of coordinates that specify the polygon to display.*

Line 31 creates Polygon polygon2 with no points. Lines 32–36 use Polygon method **addPoint** to add pairs of *x*- and *y*-coordinates to the Polygon. Line 37 displays Polygon polygon2 by passing it to Graphics method fillPolygon.

15.8 Java 2D API

The **Java 2D API** provides advanced two-dimensional graphics capabilities for programmers who require detailed and complex graphical manipulations. The API includes features for processing line art, text and images in packages java.awt, java.awt.image, java.awt.color, java.awt.font, java.awt.geom, java.awt.print and java.awt.image.renderable. The capabilities of the API are far too broad to cover in this textbook. For an overview, see the Java 2D demo (discussed in Chapter 20, Applets and Java Web Start) or visit download.oracle.com/javase/6/docs/technotes/guides/2d/. In this section, we overview several Java 2D capabilities.

Drawing with the Java 2D API is accomplished with a **Graphics2D** reference (package java.awt). Graphics2D is an abstract subclass of class Graphics, so it has all the graphics capabilities demonstrated earlier in this chapter. In fact, the actual object used to draw in every paintComponent method is an instance of a subclass of Graphics2D that is passed to method paintComponent and accessed via the superclass Graphics. To access Graphics2D capabilities, we must cast the Graphics reference (g) passed to paintComponent into a Graphics2D reference with a statement such as

```
Graphics2D g2d = ( Graphics2D ) g;
```

The next two examples use this technique.

Lines, Rectangles, Round Rectangles, Arcs and Ellipses
This example demonstrates several Java 2D shapes from package java.awt.geom, including **Line2D.Double**, **Rectangle2D.Double**, **RoundRectangle2D.Double**, **Arc2D.Double** and **Ellipse2D.Double**. Note the syntax of each class name. Each class represents a shape with dimensions specified as double values. There's a separate version of each represented with float values (e.g., **Ellipse2D.Float**). In each case, Double is a public static nested class of the class specified to the left of the dot (e.g., Ellipse2D). To use the static nested class, we simply qualify its name with the outer class name.

In Figs. 15.29–15.30, we draw Java 2D shapes and modify their drawing characteristics, such as changing line thickness, filling shapes with patterns and drawing dashed lines. These are just a few of the many capabilities provided by Java 2D.

Line 25 of Fig. 15.29 casts the Graphics reference received by paintComponent to a Graphics2D reference and assigns it to g2d to allow access to the Java 2D features.

```java
1   // Fig. 15.29: ShapesJPanel.java
2   // Demonstrating some Java 2D shapes.
3   import java.awt.Color;
4   import java.awt.Graphics;
5   import java.awt.BasicStroke;
6   import java.awt.GradientPaint;
7   import java.awt.TexturePaint;
8   import java.awt.Rectangle;
9   import java.awt.Graphics2D;
10  import java.awt.geom.Ellipse2D;
11  import java.awt.geom.Rectangle2D;
12  import java.awt.geom.RoundRectangle2D;
13  import java.awt.geom.Arc2D;
14  import java.awt.geom.Line2D;
15  import java.awt.image.BufferedImage;
16  import javax.swing.JPanel;
17
18  public class ShapesJPanel extends JPanel
19  {
20     // draw shapes with Java 2D API
21     public void paintComponent( Graphics g )
22     {
23        super.paintComponent( g ); // call superclass's paintComponent
24
25        Graphics2D g2d = ( Graphics2D ) g; // cast g to Graphics2D
26
27        // draw 2D ellipse filled with a blue-yellow gradient
28        g2d.setPaint( new GradientPaint( 5, 30, Color.BLUE, 35, 100,
29           Color.YELLOW, true ) );
30        g2d.fill( new Ellipse2D.Double( 5, 30, 65, 100 ) );
31
32        // draw 2D rectangle in red
33        g2d.setPaint( Color.RED );
34        g2d.setStroke( new BasicStroke( 10.0f ) );
35        g2d.draw( new Rectangle2D.Double( 80, 30, 65, 100 ) );
36
37        // draw 2D rounded rectangle with a buffered background
38        BufferedImage buffImage = new BufferedImage( 10, 10,
39           BufferedImage.TYPE_INT_RGB );
40
41        // obtain Graphics2D from buffImage and draw on it
42        Graphics2D gg = buffImage.createGraphics();
43        gg.setColor( Color.YELLOW ); // draw in yellow
44        gg.fillRect( 0, 0, 10, 10 ); // draw a filled rectangle
45        gg.setColor( Color.BLACK );  // draw in black
46        gg.drawRect( 1, 1, 6, 6 ); // draw a rectangle
47        gg.setColor( Color.BLUE ); // draw in blue
48        gg.fillRect( 1, 1, 3, 3 ); // draw a filled rectangle
49        gg.setColor( Color.RED ); // draw in red
```

Fig. 15.29 | Java 2D shapes. (Part 1 of 2.)

```
50        gg.fillRect( 4, 4, 3, 3 ); // draw a filled rectangle
51
52        // paint buffImage onto the JFrame
53        g2d.setPaint( new TexturePaint( buffImage,
54           new Rectangle( 10, 10 ) ) );
55        g2d.fill(
56           new RoundRectangle2D.Double( 155, 30, 75, 100, 50, 50 ) );
57
58        // draw 2D pie-shaped arc in white
59        g2d.setPaint( Color.WHITE );
60        g2d.setStroke( new BasicStroke( 6.0f ) );
61        g2d.draw(
62           new Arc2D.Double( 240, 30, 75, 100, 0, 270, Arc2D.PIE ) );
63
64        // draw 2D lines in green and yellow
65        g2d.setPaint( Color.GREEN );
66        g2d.draw( new Line2D.Double( 395, 30, 320, 150 ) );
67
68        // draw 2D line using stroke
69        float[] dashes = { 10 }; // specify dash pattern
70        g2d.setPaint( Color.YELLOW );
71        g2d.setStroke( new BasicStroke( 4, BasicStroke.CAP_ROUND,
72           BasicStroke.JOIN_ROUND, 10, dashes, 0 ) );
73        g2d.draw( new Line2D.Double( 320, 30, 395, 150 ) );
74     } // end method paintComponent
75  } // end class ShapesJPanel
```

Fig. 15.29 | Java 2D shapes. (Part 2 of 2.)

```
1   // Fig. 15.30: Shapes.java
2   // Demonstrating some Java 2D shapes.
3   import javax.swing.JFrame;
4
5   public class Shapes
6   {
7      // execute application
8      public static void main( String[] args )
9      {
10        // create frame for ShapesJPanel
11        JFrame frame = new JFrame( "Drawing 2D shapes" );
12        frame.setDefaultCloseOperation( JFrame.EXIT_ON_CLOSE );
13
14        // create ShapesJPanel
15        ShapesJPanel shapesJPanel = new ShapesJPanel();
16
17        frame.add( shapesJPanel ); // add shapesJPanel to frame
18        frame.setSize( 425, 200 ); // set frame size
19        frame.setVisible( true ); // display frame
20     } // end main
21  } // end class Shapes
```

Fig. 15.30 | Creating JFrame to display shapes. (Part 1 of 2.)

Fig. 15.30 | Creating JFrame to display shapes. (Part 2 of 2.)

Ovals, Gradient Fills and **Paint** *Objects*
The first shape we draw is an oval filled with gradually changing colors. Lines 28–29 invoke Graphics2D method **setPaint** to set the **Paint** object that determines the color for the shape to display. A Paint object implements interface java.awt.Paint. It can be something as simple as one of the predeclared Color objects introduced in Section 15.3 (class Color implements Paint), or it can be an instance of the Java 2D API's Gradient-Paint, **SystemColor**, TexturePaint, LinearGradientPaint or RadialGradientPaint classes. In this case, we use a GradientPaint object.

Class GradientPaint helps draw a shape in gradually changing colors—called a **gradient**. The GradientPaint constructor used here requires seven arguments. The first two specify the starting coordinate for the gradient. The third specifies the starting Color for the gradient. The fourth and fifth specify the ending coordinate for the gradient. The sixth specifies the ending Color for the gradient. The last argument specifies whether the gradient is **cyclic** (true) or **acyclic** (false). The two sets of coordinates determine the direction of the gradient. Because the second coordinate (35, 100) is down and to the right of the first coordinate (5, 30), the gradient goes down and to the right at an angle. Because this gradient is cyclic (true), the color starts with blue, gradually becomes yellow, then gradually returns to blue. If the gradient is acyclic, the color transitions from the first color specified (e.g., blue) to the second color (e.g., yellow).

Line 30 uses Graphics2D method **fill** to draw a filled **Shape** object—an object that implements interface Shape (package java.awt). In this case, we display an Ellipse2D.Double object. The Ellipse2D.Double constructor receives four arguments specifying the bounding rectangle for the ellipse to display.

Rectangles, **Stroke**s
Next we draw a red rectangle with a thick border. Line 33 invokes setPaint to set the Paint object to Color.RED. Line 34 uses Graphics2D method **setStroke** to set the characteristics of the rectangle's border (or the lines for any other shape). Method setStroke requires as its argument an object that implements interface **Stroke** (package java.awt). In this case, we use an instance of class BasicStroke. Class BasicStroke provides several constructors to specify the width of the line, how the line ends (called the **end caps**), how lines join together (called **line joins**) and the dash attributes of the line (if it's a dashed line). The constructor here specifies that the line should be 10 pixels wide.

Line 35 uses Graphics2D method **draw** to draw a Shape object—in this case, a Rectangle2D.Double. The Rectangle2D.Double constructor receives arguments specifying the rectangle's upper-left *x*-coordinate, upper-left *y*-coordinate, width and height.

Rounded Rectangles, **BufferedImages** *and* **TexturePaint** *Objects*

Next we draw a rounded rectangle filled with a pattern created in a **BufferedImage** (package java.awt.image) object. Lines 38–39 create the BufferedImage object. Class BufferedImage can be used to produce images in color and grayscale. This particular BufferedImage is 10 pixels wide and 10 pixels tall (as specified by the first two arguments of the constructor). The third argument **BufferedImage.TYPE_INT_RGB** indicates that the image is stored in color using the RGB color scheme.

To create the rounded rectangle's fill pattern, we must first draw into the BufferedImage. Line 42 creates a Graphics2D object (by calling BufferedImage method **createGraphics**) that can be used to draw into the BufferedImage. Lines 43–50 use methods setColor, fillRect and drawRect to create the pattern.

Lines 53–54 set the Paint object to a new TexturePaint (package java.awt) object. A TexturePaint object uses the image stored in its associated BufferedImage (the first constructor argument) as the fill texture for a filled-in shape. The second argument specifies the Rectangle area from the BufferedImage that will be replicated through the texture. In this case, the Rectangle is the same size as the BufferedImage. However, a smaller portion of the BufferedImage can be used.

Lines 55–56 use Graphics2D method fill to draw a filled Shape object—in this case, a RoundRectangle2D.Double. The constructor for class RoundRectangle2D.Double receives six arguments specifying the rectangle dimensions and the arc width and arc height used to determine the rounding of the corners.

Arcs

Next we draw a pie-shaped arc with a thick white line. Line 59 sets the Paint object to Color.WHITE. Line 60 sets the Stroke object to a new BasicStroke for a line 6 pixels wide. Lines 61–62 use Graphics2D method draw to draw a Shape object—in this case, an Arc2D.Double. The Arc2D.Double constructor's first four arguments specify the upper-left *x*-coordinate, upper-left *y*-coordinate, width and height of the bounding rectangle for the arc. The fifth argument specifies the start angle. The sixth argument specifies the arc angle. The last argument specifies how the arc is closed. Constant **Arc2D.PIE** indicates that the arc is closed by drawing two lines—one line from the arc's starting point to the center of the bounding rectangle and one line from the center of the bounding rectangle to the ending point. Class Arc2D provides two other static constants for specifying how the arc is closed. Constant **Arc2D.CHORD** draws a line from the starting point to the ending point. Constant **Arc2D.OPEN** specifies that the arc should *not* be closed.

Lines

Finally, we draw two lines using **Line2D** objects—one solid and one dashed. Line 65 sets the Paint object to Color.GREEN. Line 66 uses Graphics2D method draw to draw a Shape object—in this case, an instance of class Line2D.Double. The Line2D.Double constructor's arguments specify the starting coordinates and ending coordinates of the line.

Line 69 declares a one-element float array containing the value 10. This array describes the dashes in the dashed line. In this case, each dash will be 10 pixels long. To create dashes of different lengths in a pattern, simply provide the length of each dash as an element in the array. Line 70 sets the Paint object to Color.YELLOW. Lines 71–72 set the Stroke object to a new BasicStroke. The line will be 4 pixels wide and will have rounded ends (**BasicStroke.CAP_ROUND**). If lines join together (as in a rectangle at the corners), their joining will be rounded (**BasicStroke.JOIN_ROUND**). The dashes argument specifies the dash lengths for the line. The last argument indicates the starting index in the dashes array for the first dash in the pattern. Line 73 then draws a line with the current Stroke.

Creating Your Own Shapes with General Paths

Next we present a **general path**—a shape constructed from straight lines and complex curves. A general path is represented with an object of class **GeneralPath** (package java.awt.geom). The application of Figs. 15.31 and 15.32 demonstrates drawing a general path in the shape of a five-pointed star.

```java
1   // Fig. 15.31: Shapes2JPanel.java
2   // Demonstrating a general path.
3   import java.awt.Color;
4   import java.awt.Graphics;
5   import java.awt.Graphics2D;
6   import java.awt.geom.GeneralPath;
7   import java.util.Random;
8   import javax.swing.JPanel;
9
10  public class Shapes2JPanel extends JPanel
11  {
12     // draw general paths
13     public void paintComponent( Graphics g )
14     {
15        super.paintComponent( g ); // call superclass's paintComponent
16        Random random = new Random(); // get random number generator
17
18        int[] xPoints = { 55, 67, 109, 73, 83, 55, 27, 37, 1, 43 };
19        int[] yPoints = { 0, 36, 36, 54, 96, 72, 96, 54, 36, 36 };
20
21        Graphics2D g2d = ( Graphics2D ) g;
22        GeneralPath star = new GeneralPath(); // create GeneralPath object
23
24        // set the initial coordinate of the General Path
25        star.moveTo( xPoints[ 0 ], yPoints[ 0 ] );
26
27        // create the star--this does not draw the star
28        for ( int count = 1; count < xPoints.length; count++ )
29           star.lineTo( xPoints[ count ], yPoints[ count ] );
30
31        star.closePath(); // close the shape
32
33        g2d.translate( 150, 150 ); // translate the origin to (150, 150)
34
35        // rotate around origin and draw stars in random colors
36        for ( int count = 1; count <= 20; count++ )
37        {
38           g2d.rotate( Math.PI / 10.0 ); // rotate coordinate system
39
```

Fig. 15.31 | Java 2D general paths. (Part 1 of 2.)

```
40          // set random drawing color
41          g2d.setColor( new Color( random.nextInt( 256 ),
42             random.nextInt( 256 ), random.nextInt( 256 ) ) );
43
44          g2d.fill( star ); // draw filled star
45       } // end for
46    } // end method paintComponent
47 } // end class Shapes2JPanel
```

Fig. 15.31 | Java 2D general paths. (Part 2 of 2.)

```
 1 // Fig. 15.32: Shapes2.java
 2 // Demonstrating a general path.
 3 import java.awt.Color;
 4 import javax.swing.JFrame;
 5
 6 public class Shapes2
 7 {
 8    // execute application
 9    public static void main( String[] args )
10    {
11       // create frame for Shapes2JPanel
12       JFrame frame = new JFrame( "Drawing 2D Shapes" );
13       frame.setDefaultCloseOperation( JFrame.EXIT_ON_CLOSE );
14
15       Shapes2JPanel shapes2JPanel = new Shapes2JPanel();
16       frame.add( shapes2JPanel ); // add shapes2JPanel to frame
17       frame.setBackground( Color.WHITE ); // set frame background color
18       frame.setSize( 315, 330 ); // set frame size
19       frame.setVisible( true ); // display frame
20    } // end main
21 } // end class Shapes2
```

Fig. 15.32 | Creating JFrame to display stars.

Lines 18–19 declare two int arrays representing the *x*- and *y*-coordinates of the points in the star. Line 22 creates GeneralPath object star. Line 25 uses GeneralPath method **moveTo** to specify the first point in the star. The for statement in lines 28–29 uses GeneralPath method **lineTo** to draw a line to the next point in the star. Each new call to lineTo draws a line from the previous point to the current point. Line 31 uses General-Path method **closePath** to draw a line from the last point to the point specified in the last call to moveTo. This completes the general path.

Line 33 uses Graphics2D method **translate** to move the drawing origin to location (150, 150). All drawing operations now use location (150, 150) as (0, 0).

The for statement in lines 36–45 draws the star 20 times by rotating it around the new origin point. Line 38 uses Graphics2D method **rotate** to rotate the next displayed shape. The argument specifies the rotation angle in radians (with $360° = 2\pi$ radians). Line 44 uses Graphics2D method fill to draw a filled version of the star.

15.9 Wrap-Up

In this chapter, you learned how to use Java's graphics capabilities to produce colorful drawings. You learned how to specify the location of an object using Java's coordinate system, and how to draw on a window using the paintComponent method. You were introduced to class Color, and you learned how to use this class to specify different colors using their RGB components. You used the JColorChooser dialog to allow users to select colors in a program. You then learned how to work with fonts when drawing text on a window. You learned how to create a Font object from a font name, style and size, as well as how to access the metrics of a font. From there, you learned how to draw various shapes on a window, such as rectangles (regular, rounded and 3D), ovals and polygons, as well as lines and arcs. You then used the Java 2D API to create more complex shapes and to fill them with gradients or patterns. The chapter concluded with a discussion of general paths, used to construct shapes from straight lines and complex curves. In the next chapter, we discuss class String and its methods. We introduce regular expressions for pattern matching in strings and demonstrate how to validate user input with regular expressions.

16

Strings, Characters and Regular Expressions

Objectives

In this chapter you'll learn:

- To create and manipulate immutable character-string objects of class String.

- To create and manipulate mutable character-string objects of class StringBuilder.

- To create and manipulate objects of class Character.

- To break a String object into tokens using String method split.

- To use regular expressions to validate String data entered into an application.

*The chief defect of
Henry King
Was chewing little
bits of string.*
—Hilaire Belloc

*Vigorous writing is concise.
A sentence should contain
no unnecessary words, a
paragraph no unnecessary
sentences.*
—William Strunk, Jr.

*I have made this letter
longer than usual, because I
lack the time to make it
short.*
—Blaise Pascal

16.1 Introduction

This chapter introduces Java's string- and character-processing capabilities. The techniques discussed here are appropriate for validating program input, displaying information to users and other text-based manipulations. They're also appropriate for developing text editors, word processors, page-layout software, computerized typesetting systems and other kinds of text-processing software. We've presented several string-processing capabilities in earlier chapters. This chapter discusses in detail the capabilities of classes String, StringBuilder and Character from the java.lang package. These classes provide the foundation for string and character manipulation in Java.

The chapter also discusses regular expressions that provide applications with the capability to validate input. The functionality is located in the String class along with classes Matcher and Pattern located in the java.util.regex package.

16.2 Fundamentals of Characters and Strings

Characters are the fundamental building blocks of Java source programs. Every program is composed of a sequence of characters that—when grouped together meaningfully—are interpreted by the Java compiler as a series of instructions used to accomplish a task. A program may contain **character literals**. A character literal is an integer value represented as a character in single quotes. For example, 'z' represents the integer value of z, and '\n' represents the integer value of newline. The value of a character literal is the integer value of the character in the **Unicode character set**. Appendix B presents the integer equivalents of the characters in the ASCII character set, which is a subset of Unicode.

Recall from Section 2.2 that a string is a sequence of characters treated as a single unit. A string may include letters, digits and various **special characters**, such as +, -, *, / and $. A string is an object of class String. **String literals** (stored in memory as String objects) are written as a sequence of characters in double quotation marks, as in:

"John Q. Doe"	(a name)
"9999 Main Street"	(a street address)
"Waltham, Massachusetts"	(a city and state)
"(201) 555-1212"	(a telephone number)

A string may be assigned to a `String` reference. The declaration

```
String color = "blue";
```

initializes `String` variable `color` to refer to a `String` object that contains the string "blue".

Performance Tip 16.1

To conserve memory, Java treats all string literals with the same contents as a single String object that has many references to it.

16.3 Class String

Class `String` is used to represent strings in Java. The next several subsections cover many of class `String`'s capabilities.

16.3.1 String Constructors

Class `String` provides constructors for initializing `String` objects in a variety of ways. Four of the constructors are demonstrated in the `main` method of Fig. 16.1.

```
 1   // Fig. 16.1: StringConstructors.java
 2   // String class constructors.
 3
 4   public class StringConstructors
 5   {
 6      public static void main( String[] args )
 7      {
 8         char[] charArray = { 'b', 'i', 'r', 't', 'h', ' ', 'd', 'a', 'y' };
 9         String s = new String( "hello" );
10
11         // use String constructors
12         String s1 = new String();
13         String s2 = new String( s );
14         String s3 = new String( charArray );
15         String s4 = new String( charArray, 6, 3 );
16
17         System.out.printf(
18            "s1 = %s\ns2 = %s\ns3 = %s\ns4 = %s\n",
19            s1, s2, s3, s4 ); // display strings
20      } // end main
21   } // end class StringConstructors
```

```
s1 =
s2 = hello
s3 = birth day
s4 = day
```

Fig. 16.1 | String class constructors.

Line 12 instantiates a new String using class String's no-argument constructor and assigns its reference to s1. The new String object contains no characters (i.e., the **empty string**, which can also be represented as "") and has a length of 0. Line 13 instantiates a new String object using class String's constructor that takes a String object as an argument and assigns its reference to s2. The new String object contains the same sequence of characters as the String object s that's passed as an argument to the constructor.

> **Software Engineering Observation 16.1**
>
> *It's not necessary to copy an existing String object. String objects are **immutable**—their character contents cannot be changed after they're created, because class String does not provide methods that allow the contents of a String object to be modified.*

Line 14 instantiates a new String object and assigns its reference to s3 using class String's constructor that takes a char array as an argument. The new String object contains a copy of the characters in the array.

Line 15 instantiates a new String object and assigns its reference to s4 using class String's constructor that takes a char array and two integers as arguments. The second argument specifies the starting position (the offset) from which characters in the array are accessed. Remember that the first character is at position 0. The third argument specifies the number of characters (the count) to access in the array. The new String object is formed from the accessed characters. If the offset or the count specified as an argument results in accessing an element outside the bounds of the character array, a StringIndexOutOfBoundsException is thrown.

> **Common Programming Error 16.1**
>
> *Accessing a character outside the bounds of a String (i.e., an index less than 0 or an index greater than or equal to the String's length) results in a StringIndexOutOfBoundsException.*

16.3.2 String Methods length, charAt and getChars

String methods **length**, **charAt** and **getChars** return the length of a String, obtain the character at a specific location in a String and retrieve a set of characters from a String as a char array, respectively. Figure 16.2 demonstrates each of these methods.

```
1   // Fig. 16.2: StringMiscellaneous.java
2   // This application demonstrates the length, charAt and getChars
3   // methods of the String class.
4
5   public class StringMiscellaneous
6   {
7      public static void main( String[] args )
8      {
9         String s1 = "hello there";
10        char[] charArray = new char[ 5 ];
11
12        System.out.printf( "s1: %s", s1 );
13
```

Fig. 16.2 | String methods length, charAt and getChars. (Part 1 of 2.)

```
14            // test length method
15            System.out.printf( "\nLength of s1: %d", s1.length() );
16
17            // loop through characters in s1 with charAt and display reversed
18            System.out.print( "\nThe string reversed is: " );
19
20            for ( int count = s1.length() - 1; count >= 0; count-- )
21                System.out.printf( "%c ", s1.charAt( count ) );
22
23            // copy characters from string into charArray
24            s1.getChars( 0, 5, charArray, 0 );
25            System.out.print( "\nThe character array is: " );
26
27            for ( char character : charArray )
28                System.out.print( character );
29
30            System.out.println();
31        } // end main
32    } // end class StringMiscellaneous
```

```
s1: hello there
Length of s1: 11
The string reversed is: e r e h t   o l l e h
The character array is: hello
```

Fig. 16.2 | String methods `length`, `charAt` and `getChars`. (Part 2 of 2.)

Line 15 uses `String` method `length` to determine the number of characters in `String` s1. Like arrays, strings know their own length. However, unlike arrays, you access a `String`'s length via class `String`'s `length` method.

Lines 20–21 print the characters of the `String` s1 in reverse order (and separated by spaces). `String` method `charAt` (line 21) returns the character at a specific position in the `String`. Method `charAt` receives an integer argument that's used as the index and returns the character at that position. Like arrays, the first element of a `String` is at position 0.

Line 24 uses `String` method `getChars` to copy the characters of a `String` into a character array. The first argument is the starting index from which characters are to be copied. The second argument is the index that's one past the last character to be copied from the `String`. The third argument is the character array into which the characters are to be copied. The last argument is the starting index where the copied characters are placed in the target character array. Next, lines 27–28 print the char array contents one character at a time.

16.3.3 Comparing Strings

Chapter 19 discusses sorting and searching arrays. Frequently, the information being sorted or searched consists of `Strings` that must be compared to place them into order or to determine whether a string appears in an array (or other collection). Class `String` provides methods for comparing strings, as demonstrated in the next two examples.

To understand what it means for one string to be greater than or less than another, consider the process of alphabetizing a series of last names. No doubt, you'd place "Jones" before "Smith" because the first letter of "Jones" comes before the first letter of "Smith" in the alphabet. But the alphabet is more than just a list of 26 letters—it's an ordered set of characters. Each letter occurs in a specific position within the set. Z is more than just a letter of the alphabet—it's specifically the twenty-sixth letter of the alphabet.

How does the computer know that one letter "comes before" another? All characters are represented in the computer as numeric codes (see Appendix B). When the computer compares Strings, it actually compares the numeric codes of the characters in the Strings.

Figure 16.3 demonstrates String methods equals, equalsIgnoreCase, compareTo and **regionMatches** and using the equality operator == to compare String objects.

```
1   // Fig. 16.3: StringCompare.java
2   // String methods equals, equalsIgnoreCase, compareTo and regionMatches.
3
4   public class StringCompare
5   {
6      public static void main( String[] args )
7      {
8         String s1 = new String( "hello" ); // s1 is a copy of "hello"
9         String s2 = "goodbye";
10        String s3 = "Happy Birthday";
11        String s4 = "happy birthday";
12
13        System.out.printf(
14           "s1 = %s\ns2 = %s\ns3 = %s\ns4 = %s\n\n", s1, s2, s3, s4 );
15
16        // test for equality
17        if ( s1.equals( "hello" ) )   // true
18           System.out.println( "s1 equals \"hello\"" );
19        else
20           System.out.println( "s1 does not equal \"hello\"" );
21
22        // test for equality with ==
23        if ( s1 == "hello" )   // false; they are not the same object
24           System.out.println( "s1 is the same object as \"hello\"" );
25        else
26           System.out.println( "s1 is not the same object as \"hello\"" );
27
28        // test for equality (ignore case)
29        if ( s3.equalsIgnoreCase( s4 ) )   // true
30           System.out.printf( "%s equals %s with case ignored\n", s3, s4 );
31        else
32           System.out.println( "s3 does not equal s4" );
33
34        // test compareTo
35        System.out.printf(
36           "\ns1.compareTo( s2 ) is %d", s1.compareTo( s2 ) );
37        System.out.printf(
38           "\ns2.compareTo( s1 ) is %d", s2.compareTo( s1 ) );
39        System.out.printf(
40           "\ns1.compareTo( s1 ) is %d", s1.compareTo( s1 ) );
```

Fig. 16.3 | String methods equals, equalsIgnoreCase, compareTo and regionMatches. (Part 1 of 2.)

```
41          System.out.printf(
42             "\ns3.compareTo( s4 ) is %d", s3.compareTo( s4 ) );
43          System.out.printf(
44             "\ns4.compareTo( s3 ) is %d\n\n", s4.compareTo( s3 ) );
45
46          // test regionMatches (case sensitive)
47          if ( s3.regionMatches( 0, s4, 0, 5 ) )
48             System.out.println( "First 5 characters of s3 and s4 match" );
49          else
50             System.out.println(
51                "First 5 characters of s3 and s4 do not match" );
52
53          // test regionMatches (ignore case)
54          if ( s3.regionMatches( true, 0, s4, 0, 5 ) )
55             System.out.println(
56                "First 5 characters of s3 and s4 match with case ignored" );
57          else
58             System.out.println(
59                "First 5 characters of s3 and s4 do not match" );
60       } // end main
61    } // end class StringCompare
```

```
s1 = hello
s2 = goodbye
s3 = Happy Birthday
s4 = happy birthday

s1 equals "hello"
s1 is not the same object as "hello"
Happy Birthday equals happy birthday with case ignored

s1.compareTo( s2 ) is 1
s2.compareTo( s1 ) is -1
s1.compareTo( s1 ) is 0
s3.compareTo( s4 ) is -32
s4.compareTo( s3 ) is 32

First 5 characters of s3 and s4 do not match
First 5 characters of s3 and s4 match with case ignored
```

Fig. 16.3 | String methods equals, equalsIgnoreCase, compareTo and regionMatches. (Part 2 of 2.)

String *Method* equals

The condition at line 17 uses method equals to compare String s1 and the String literal "hello" for equality. Method equals (a method of class Object overridden in String) tests any two objects for equality—the strings contained in the two objects are identical. The method returns true if the contents of the objects are equal, and false otherwise. The preceding condition is true because String s1 was initialized with the string literal "hello". Method equals uses a **lexicographical comparison**—it compares the integer Unicode values that represent each character in each String. Thus, if the String "hello" is compared with the string "HELLO", the result is false, because the integer representation of a lowercase letter is different from that of the corresponding uppercase letter.

Comparing Strings with the == Operator

The condition at line 23 uses the equality operator == to compare String s1 for equality with the String literal "hello". When primitive-type values are compared with ==, the result is true if *both values are identical*. When references are compared with ==, the result is true if *both references refer to the same object in memory*. To compare the actual contents (or state information) of objects for equality, a method must be invoked. In the case of Strings, that method is equals. The preceding condition evaluates to false at line 23 because the reference s1 was initialized with the statement

```
s1 = new String( "hello" );
```

which creates a new String object with a copy of string literal "hello" and assigns the new object to variable s1. If s1 had been initialized with the statement

```
s1 = "hello";
```

which directly assigns the string literal "hello" to variable s1, the condition would be true. Remember that Java treats all string literal objects with the same contents as one String object to which there can be many references. Thus, lines 8, 17 and 23 all refer to the same String object "hello" in memory.

Common Programming Error 16.2

Comparing references with == can lead to logic errors, because == compares the references to determine whether they refer to the same object, not whether two objects have the same contents. *When two identical (but separate) objects are compared with ==, the result will be* false. *When comparing objects to determine whether they have the same contents, use method* equals.

String Method equalsIgnoreCase

If you're sorting Strings, you may compare them for equality with method equalsIgnoreCase, which ignores whether the letters in each String are uppercase or lowercase when performing the comparison. Thus, "hello" and "HELLO" compare as equal. Line 29 uses String method equalsIgnoreCase to compare String s3—Happy Birthday—for equality with String s4—happy birthday. The result of this comparison is true because the comparison ignores case sensitivity.

String Method compareTo

Lines 35–44 use method compareTo to compare Strings. Method compareTo is declared in the Comparable interface and implemented in the String class. Line 36 compares String s1 to String s2. Method compareTo returns 0 if the Strings are equal, a negative number if the String that invokes compareTo is less than the String that's passed as an argument and a positive number if the String that invokes compareTo is greater than the String that's passed as an argument. Method compareTo uses a lexicographical comparison—it compares the numeric values of corresponding characters in each String.

String Method regionMatches

The condition at line 47 uses String method regionMatches to compare portions of two Strings for equality. The first argument is the starting index in the String that invokes the method. The second argument is a comparison String. The third argument is the starting index in the comparison String. The last argument is the number of characters to compare between the two Strings. The method returns true only if the specified number of characters are lexicographically equal.

Finally, the condition at line 54 uses a five-argument version of String method regionMatches to compare portions of two Strings for equality. When the first argument is true, the method ignores the case of the characters being compared. The remaining arguments are identical to those described for the four-argument regionMatches method.

String Methods startsWith and endsWith

The next example (Fig. 16.4) demonstrates String methods **startsWith** and **endsWith**. Method main creates array strings containing "started", "starting", "ended" and "ending". The remainder of method main consists of three for statements that test the elements of the array to determine whether they start with or end with a particular set of characters.

```java
// Fig. 16.4: StringStartEnd.java
// String methods startsWith and endsWith.

public class StringStartEnd
{
   public static void main( String[] args )
   {
      String[] strings = { "started", "starting", "ended", "ending" };

      // test method startsWith
      for ( String string : strings )
      {
         if ( string.startsWith( "st" ) )
            System.out.printf( "\"%s\" starts with \"st\"\n", string );
      } // end for

      System.out.println();

      // test method startsWith starting from position 2 of string
      for ( String string : strings )
      {
         if ( string.startsWith( "art", 2 ) )
            System.out.printf(
               "\"%s\" starts with \"art\" at position 2\n", string );
      } // end for

      System.out.println();

      // test method endsWith
      for ( String string : strings )
      {
         if ( string.endsWith( "ed" ) )
            System.out.printf( "\"%s\" ends with \"ed\"\n", string );
      } // end for
   } // end main
} // end class StringStartEnd
```

Fig. 16.4 | String methods startsWith and endsWith. (Part 1 of 2.)

```
"started" starts with "st"
"starting" starts with "st"

"started" starts with "art" at position 2
"starting" starts with "art" at position 2

"started" ends with "ed"
"ended" ends with "ed"
```

Fig. 16.4 | String methods startsWith and endsWith. (Part 2 of 2.)

Lines 11–15 use the version of method startsWith that takes a String argument. The condition in the if statement (line 13) determines whether each String in the array starts with the characters "st". If so, the method returns true and the application prints that String. Otherwise, the method returns false and nothing happens.

Lines 20–25 use the startsWith method that takes a String and an integer as arguments. The integer specifies the index at which the comparison should begin in the String. The condition in the if statement (line 22) determines whether each String in the array has the characters "art" beginning with the third character in each String. If so, the method returns true and the application prints the String.

The third for statement (lines 30–34) uses method endsWith, which takes a String argument. The condition at line 32 determines whether each String in the array ends with the characters "ed". If so, the method returns true and the application prints the String.

16.3.4 Locating Characters and Substrings in Strings

Often it's useful to search a string for a character or set of characters. For example, if you're creating your own word processor, you might want to provide a capability for searching through documents. Figure 16.5 demonstrates the many versions of String methods **indexOf** and **lastIndexOf** that search for a specified character or substring in a String.

```
1   // Fig. 16.5: StringIndexMethods.java
2   // String searching methods indexOf and lastIndexOf.
3
4   public class StringIndexMethods
5   {
6      public static void main( String[] args )
7      {
8         String letters = "abcdefghijklmabcdefghijklm";
9
10        // test indexOf to locate a character in a string
11        System.out.printf(
12           "'c' is located at index %d\n", letters.indexOf( 'c' ) );
13        System.out.printf(
14           "'a' is located at index %d\n", letters.indexOf( 'a', 1 ) );
15        System.out.printf(
16           "'$' is located at index %d\n\n", letters.indexOf( '$' ) );
17
```

Fig. 16.5 | String-searching methods indexOf and lastIndexOf. (Part 1 of 2.)

```
18          // test lastIndexOf to find a character in a string
19          System.out.printf( "Last 'c' is located at index %d\n",
20             letters.lastIndexOf( 'c' ) );
21          System.out.printf( "Last 'a' is located at index %d\n",
22             letters.lastIndexOf( 'a', 25 ) );
23          System.out.printf( "Last '$' is located at index %d\n\n",
24             letters.lastIndexOf( '$' ) );
25
26          // test indexOf to locate a substring in a string
27          System.out.printf( "\"def\" is located at index %d\n",
28             letters.indexOf( "def" ) );
29          System.out.printf( "\"def\" is located at index %d\n",
30             letters.indexOf( "def", 7 ) );
31          System.out.printf( "\"hello\" is located at index %d\n\n",
32             letters.indexOf( "hello" ) );
33
34          // test lastIndexOf to find a substring in a string
35          System.out.printf( "Last \"def\" is located at index %d\n",
36             letters.lastIndexOf( "def" ) );
37          System.out.printf( "Last \"def\" is located at index %d\n",
38             letters.lastIndexOf( "def", 25 ) );
39          System.out.printf( "Last \"hello\" is located at index %d\n",
40             letters.lastIndexOf( "hello" ) );
41       } // end main
42    } // end class StringIndexMethods
```

```
'c' is located at index 2
'a' is located at index 13
'$' is located at index -1

Last 'c' is located at index 15
Last 'a' is located at index 13
Last '$' is located at index -1

"def" is located at index 3
"def" is located at index 16
"hello" is located at index -1

Last "def" is located at index 16
Last "def" is located at index 16
Last "hello" is located at index -1
```

Fig. 16.5 | String-searching methods `indexOf` and `lastIndexOf`. (Part 2 of 2.)

All the searches in this example are performed on the String `letters` (initialized with `"abcdefghijklmabcdefghijklm"`). Lines 11–16 use method `indexOf` to locate the first occurrence of a character in a String. If the method finds the character, it returns the character's index in the String—otherwise, it returns –1. There are two versions of `indexOf` that search for characters in a String. The expression in line 12 uses the version of method `indexOf` that takes an integer representation of the character to find. The expression at line 14 uses another version of method `indexOf`, which takes two integer arguments—the character and the starting index at which the search of the String should begin.

Lines 19–24 use method `lastIndexOf` to locate the last occurrence of a character in a String. The method searches from the end of the String toward the beginning. If it finds the character, it returns the character's index in the String—otherwise, it returns −1. There are two versions of lastIndexOf that search for characters in a String. The expression at line 20 uses the version that takes the integer representation of the character. The expression at line 22 uses the version that takes two integer arguments—the integer representation of the character and the index from which to begin searching backward.

Lines 27–40 demonstrate versions of methods indexOf and lastIndexOf that each take a String as the first argument. These versions perform identically to those described earlier except that they search for sequences of characters (or substrings) that are specified by their String arguments. If the substring is found, these methods return the index in the String of the first character in the substring.

16.3.5 Extracting Substrings from Strings

Class String provides two substring methods to enable a new String object to be created by copying part of an existing String object. Each method returns a new String object. Both methods are demonstrated in Fig. 16.6.

```
1  // Fig. 16.6: SubString.java
2  // String class substring methods.
3
4  public class SubString
5  {
6     public static void main( String[] args )
7     {
8        String letters = "abcdefghijklmabcdefghijklm";
9
10       // test substring methods
11       System.out.printf( "Substring from index 20 to end is \"%s\"\n",
12          letters.substring( 20 ) );
13       System.out.printf( "%s \"%s\"\n",
14          "Substring from index 3 up to, but not including 6 is",
15          letters.substring( 3, 6 ) );
16    } // end main
17 } // end class SubString
```

```
Substring from index 20 to end is "hijklm"
Substring from index 3 up to, but not including 6 is "def"
```

Fig. 16.6 | String class substring methods.

The expression letters.substring(20) at line 12 uses the substring method that takes one integer argument. The argument specifies the starting index in the original String letters from which characters are to be copied. The substring returned contains a copy of the characters from the starting index to the end of the String. Specifying an index outside the bounds of the String causes a **StringIndexOutOfBoundsException**.

Line 15 uses the substring method that takes two integer arguments—the starting index from which to copy characters in the original String and the index one beyond the last character to copy (i.e., copy up to, but not including, that index in the String). The substring returned contains a copy of the specified characters from the original String. An index outside the bounds of the String causes a StringIndexOutOfBoundsException.

16.3.6 Concatenating Strings

String method **concat** (Fig. 16.7) concatenates two String objects and returns a new String object containing the characters from both original Strings. The expression s1.concat(s2) at line 13 forms a String by appending the characters in s2 to the characters in s1. The original Strings to which s1 and s2 refer are not modified.

```
 1    // Fig. 16.7: StringConcatenation.java
 2    // String method concat.
 3
 4    public class StringConcatenation
 5    {
 6       public static void main( String[] args )
 7       {
 8          String s1 = "Happy ";
 9          String s2 = "Birthday";
10
11          System.out.printf( "s1 = %s\ns2 = %s\n\n",s1, s2 );
12          System.out.printf(
13             "Result of s1.concat( s2 ) = %s\n", s1.concat( s2 ) );
14          System.out.printf( "s1 after concatenation = %s\n", s1 );
15       } // end main
16    } // end class StringConcatenation
```

```
s1 = Happy
s2 = Birthday

Result of s1.concat( s2 ) = Happy Birthday
s1 after concatenation = Happy
```

Fig. 16.7 | String method concat.

16.3.7 Miscellaneous String Methods

Class String provides several methods that return modified copies of Strings or that return character arrays. These methods are demonstrated in the application in Fig. 16.8.

Line 16 uses String method replace to return a new String object in which every occurrence in s1 of character '1' (lowercase el) is replaced with character 'L'. Method replace leaves the original String unchanged. If there are no occurrences of the first argument in the String, method replace returns the original String. An overloaded version of method replace enables you to replace substrings rather than individual characters.

```
 1    // Fig. 16.8: StringMiscellaneous2.java
 2    // String methods replace, toLowerCase, toUpperCase, trim and toCharArray.
 3
 4    public class StringMiscellaneous2
 5    {
 6       public static void main( String[] args )
 7       {
```

Fig. 16.8 | String methods replace, toLowerCase, toUpperCase, trim and toCharArray. (Part 1 of 2.)

```
 8              String s1 = "hello";
 9              String s2 = "GOODBYE";
10              String s3 = "   spaces   ";
11
12              System.out.printf( "s1 = %s\ns2 = %s\ns3 = %s\n\n", s1, s2, s3 );
13
14              // test method replace
15              System.out.printf(
16                 "Replace 'l' with 'L' in s1: %s\n\n", s1.replace( 'l', 'L' ) );
17
18              // test toLowerCase and toUpperCase
19              System.out.printf( "s1.toUpperCase() = %s\n", s1.toUpperCase() );
20              System.out.printf( "s2.toLowerCase() = %s\n\n", s2.toLowerCase() );
21
22              // test trim method
23              System.out.printf( "s3 after trim = \"%s\"\n\n", s3.trim() );
24
25              // test toCharArray method
26              char[] charArray = s1.toCharArray();
27              System.out.print( "s1 as a character array = " );
28
29              for ( char character : charArray )
30                 System.out.print( character );
31
32              System.out.println();
33           } // end main
34        } // end class StringMiscellaneous2
```

```
s1 = hello
s2 = GOODBYE
s3 =    spaces

Replace 'l' with 'L' in s1: heLLo

s1.toUpperCase() = HELLO
s2.toLowerCase() = goodbye

s3 after trim = "spaces"

s1 as a character array = hello
```

Fig. 16.8 | String methods replace, toLowerCase, toUpperCase, trim and toCharArray. (Part 2 of 2.)

Line 19 uses String method **toUpperCase** to generate a new String with uppercase letters where corresponding lowercase letters exist in s1. The method returns a new String object containing the converted String and leaves the original String unchanged. If there are no characters to convert, method toUpperCase returns the original String.

Line 20 uses String method **toLowerCase** to return a new String object with lowercase letters where corresponding uppercase letters exist in s2. The original String remains unchanged. If there are no characters in the original String to convert, toLowerCase returns the original String.

Line 23 uses String method **trim** to generate a new String object that removes all white-space characters that appear at the beginning and/or end of the String on which trim operates. The method returns a new String object containing the String without leading or trailing white space. The original String remains unchanged. If there are no whitespace characters at the beginning and/or end, trim returns the original String.

Line 26 uses String method **toCharArray** to create a new character array containing a copy of the characters in s1. Lines 29–30 output each char in the array.

16.3.8 String Method valueOf

As we've seen, every object in Java has a toString method that enables a program to obtain the object's string representation. Unfortunately, this technique cannot be used with primitive types because they do not have methods. Class String provides static methods that take an argument of any type and convert it to a String object. Figure 16.9 demonstrates the String class **valueOf** methods.

The expression String.valueOf(charArray) at line 18 uses the character array char-Array to create a new String object. The expression String.valueOf(charArray, 3, 3) at line 20 uses a portion of the character array charArray to create a new String object. The second argument specifies the starting index from which the characters are used. The third argument specifies the number of characters to be used.

```
 1    // Fig. 16.9: StringValueOf.java
 2    // String valueOf methods.
 3
 4    public class StringValueOf
 5    {
 6       public static void main( String[] args )
 7       {
 8          char[] charArray = { 'a', 'b', 'c', 'd', 'e', 'f' };
 9          boolean booleanValue = true;
10          char characterValue = 'Z';
11          int integerValue = 7;
12          long longValue = 10000000000L; // L suffix indicates long
13          float floatValue = 2.5f; // f indicates that 2.5 is a float
14          double doubleValue = 33.333; // no suffix, double is default
15          Object objectRef = "hello"; // assign string to an Object reference
16
17          System.out.printf(
18             "char array = %s\n", String.valueOf( charArray ) );
19          System.out.printf( "part of char array = %s\n",
20             String.valueOf( charArray, 3, 3 ) );
21          System.out.printf(
22             "boolean = %s\n", String.valueOf( booleanValue ) );
23          System.out.printf(
24             "char = %s\n", String.valueOf( characterValue ) );
25          System.out.printf( "int = %s\n", String.valueOf( integerValue ) );
26          System.out.printf( "long = %s\n", String.valueOf( longValue ) );
27          System.out.printf( "float = %s\n", String.valueOf( floatValue ) );
28          System.out.printf(
29             "double = %s\n", String.valueOf( doubleValue ) );
```

Fig. 16.9 | String valueOf methods. (Part 1 of 2.)

```
30            System.out.printf( "Object = %s", String.valueOf( objectRef ) );
31      } // end main
32 } // end class StringValueOf
```

```
char array = abcdef
part of char array = def
boolean = true
char = Z
int = 7
long = 10000000000
float = 2.5
double = 33.333
Object = hello
```

Fig. 16.9 | String valueOf methods. (Part 2 of 2.)

There are seven other versions of method valueOf, which take arguments of type boolean, char, int, long, float, double and Object, respectively. These are demonstrated in lines 21–30. The version of valueOf that takes an Object as an argument can do so because all Objects can be converted to Strings with method toString.

[*Note:* Lines 12–13 use literal values 10000000000L and 2.5f as the initial values of long variable longValue and float variable floatValue, respectively. By default, Java treats integer literals as type int and floating-point literals as type double. Appending the letter L to the literal 10000000000 and appending letter f to the literal 2.5 indicates to the compiler that 10000000000 should be treated as a long and 2.5 as a float. An uppercase L or lowercase l can be used to denote a variable of type long and an uppercase F or lowercase f can be used to denote a variable of type float.]

16.4 Class StringBuilder

We now discuss the features of class **StringBuilder** for creating and manipulating *dynamic* string information—that is, *modifiable* strings. Every StringBuilder is capable of storing a number of characters specified by its capacity. If a StringBuilder's capacity is exceeded, the capacity expands to accommodate the additional characters.

Performance Tip 16.2
Java can perform certain optimizations involving String objects (such as referring to one String object from multiple variables) because it knows these objects will not change. Strings (not StringBuilders) should be used if the data will not change.

Performance Tip 16.3
In programs that frequently perform string concatenation, or other string modifications, it's often more efficient to implement the modifications with class StringBuilder.

Software Engineering Observation 16.2
*StringBuilders are not thread safe. If multiple threads require access to the same dynamic string information, use class **StringBuffer** in your code. Classes StringBuilder and StringBuffer provide identical capabilities, but class StringBuffer is thread safe. For more details on threading, see Chapter 23.*

16.4.1 StringBuilder Constructors

Class StringBuilder provides four constructors. We demonstrate three of these in Fig. 16.10. Line 8 uses the no-argument StringBuilder constructor to create a String-Builder with no characters in it and an initial capacity of 16 characters (the default for a StringBuilder). Line 9 uses the StringBuilder constructor that takes an integer argument to create a StringBuilder with no characters in it and the initial capacity specified by the integer argument (i.e., 10). Line 10 uses the StringBuilder constructor that takes a String argument to create a StringBuilder containing the characters in the String argument. The initial capacity is the number of characters in the String argument plus 16.

Lines 12–14 implicitly use the method toString of class StringBuilder to output the StringBuilders with the printf method. In Section 16.4.4, we discuss how Java uses StringBuilder objects to implement the + and += operators for string concatenation.

```
1  // Fig. 16.10: StringBuilderConstructors.java
2  // StringBuilder constructors.
3
4  public class StringBuilderConstructors
5  {
6     public static void main( String[] args )
7     {
8        StringBuilder buffer1 = new StringBuilder();
9        StringBuilder buffer2 = new StringBuilder( 10 );
10       StringBuilder buffer3 = new StringBuilder( "hello" );
11
12       System.out.printf( "buffer1 = \"%s\"\n", buffer1 );
13       System.out.printf( "buffer2 = \"%s\"\n", buffer2 );
14       System.out.printf( "buffer3 = \"%s\"\n", buffer3 );
15    } // end main
16 } // end class StringBuilderConstructors
```

```
buffer1 = ""
buffer2 = ""
buffer3 = "hello"
```

Fig. 16.10 | StringBuilder constructors.

16.4.2 StringBuilder Methods length, capacity, setLength and ensureCapacity

Class StringBuilder provides methods **length** and **capacity** to return the number of characters currently in a StringBuilder and the number of characters that can be stored in a StringBuilder without allocating more memory, respectively. Method **ensure-Capacity** guarantees that a StringBuilder has at least the specified capacity. Method setLength increases or decreases the length of a StringBuilder. Figure 16.11 demonstrates these methods.

The application contains one StringBuilder called buffer. Line 8 uses the String-Builder constructor that takes a String argument to initialize the StringBuilder with "Hello, how are you?". Lines 10–11 print the contents, length and capacity of the StringBuilder. Note in the output window that the capacity of the StringBuilder is

```
 1   // Fig. 16.11: StringBuilderCapLen.java
 2   // StringBuilder length, setLength, capacity and ensureCapacity methods.
 3
 4   public class StringBuilderCapLen
 5   {
 6      public static void main( String[] args )
 7      {
 8         StringBuilder buffer = new StringBuilder( "Hello, how are you?" );
 9
10         System.out.printf( "buffer = %s\nlength = %d\ncapacity = %d\n\n",
11            buffer.toString(), buffer.length(), buffer.capacity() );
12
13         buffer.ensureCapacity( 75 );
14         System.out.printf( "New capacity = %d\n\n", buffer.capacity() );
15
16         buffer.setLength( 10 );
17         System.out.printf( "New length = %d\nbuffer = %s\n",
18            buffer.length(), buffer.toString() );
19      } // end main
20   } // end class StringBuilderCapLen
```

```
buffer = Hello, how are you?
length = 19
capacity = 35

New capacity = 75

New length = 10
buffer = Hello, how
```

Fig. 16.11 | StringBuilder length, setLength, capacity and ensureCapacity methods.

initially 35. Recall that the StringBuilder constructor that takes a String argument initializes the capacity to the length of the string passed as an argument plus 16.

Line 13 uses method ensureCapacity to expand the capacity of the StringBuilder to a minimum of 75 characters. Actually, if the original capacity is less than the argument, the method ensures a capacity that's the greater of the number specified as an argument and twice the original capacity plus 2. The StringBuilder's current capacity remains unchanged if it's more than the specified capacity.

Performance Tip 16.4

Dynamically increasing the capacity of a StringBuilder can take a relatively long time. Executing a large number of these operations can degrade the performance of an application. If a StringBuilder is going to increase greatly in size, possibly multiple times, setting its capacity high at the beginning will increase performance.

Line 16 uses method setLength to set the length of the StringBuilder to 10. If the specified length is less than the current number of characters in the StringBuilder, the buffer is truncated to the specified length (i.e., the characters in the StringBuilder after the specified length are discarded). If the specified length is greater than the number of characters currently in the StringBuilder, null characters (characters with the numeric representation 0) are appended until the total number of characters in the StringBuilder is equal to the specified length.

16.4.3 StringBuilder Methods charAt, setCharAt, getChars and reverse

Class StringBuilder provides methods **charAt**, **setCharAt**, **getChars** and **reverse** to manipulate the characters in a StringBuilder (Fig. 16.12). Method charAt (line 12) takes an integer argument and returns the character in the StringBuilder at that index. Method getChars (line 15) copies characters from a StringBuilder into the character array passed as an argument. This method takes four arguments—the starting index from which characters should be copied in the StringBuilder, the index one past the last character to be copied from the StringBuilder, the character array into which the characters are to be copied and the starting location in the character array where the first character should be placed. Method setCharAt (lines 21 and 22) takes an integer and a character argument and sets the character at the specified position in the StringBuilder to the character argument. Method reverse (line 25) reverses the contents of the StringBuilder.

Common Programming Error 16.3

Attempting to access a character that's outside the bounds of a StringBuilder (i.e., with an index less than 0 or greater than or equal to the StringBuilder's length) results in a StringIndexOutOfBoundsException.

```
1   // Fig. 16.12: StringBuilderChars.java
2   // StringBuilder methods charAt, setCharAt, getChars and reverse.
3
4   public class StringBuilderChars
5   {
6      public static void main( String[] args )
7      {
8         StringBuilder buffer = new StringBuilder( "hello there" );
9
10        System.out.printf( "buffer = %s\n", buffer.toString() );
11        System.out.printf( "Character at 0: %s\nCharacter at 4: %s\n\n",
12           buffer.charAt( 0 ), buffer.charAt( 4 ) );
13
14        char[] charArray = new char[ buffer.length() ];
15        buffer.getChars( 0, buffer.length(), charArray, 0 );
16        System.out.print( "The characters are: " );
17
18        for ( char character : charArray )
19           System.out.print( character );
20
21        buffer.setCharAt( 0, 'H' );
22        buffer.setCharAt( 6, 'T' );
23        System.out.printf( "\n\nbuffer = %s", buffer.toString() );
24
25        buffer.reverse();
```

Fig. 16.12 | StringBuilder methods charAt, setCharAt, getChars and reverse. (Part 1 of 2.)

```
26            System.out.printf( "\n\nbuffer = %s\n", buffer.toString() );
27        } // end main
28    } // end class StringBuilderChars
```

```
buffer = hello there
Character at 0: h
Character at 4: o

The characters are: hello there

buffer = Hello There

buffer = erehT olleH
```

Fig. 16.12 | StringBuilder methods charAt, setCharAt, getChars and reverse. (Part 2 of 2.)

16.4.4 StringBuilder append Methods

Class StringBuilder provides overloaded **append** methods (Fig. 16.13) to allow values of various types to be appended to the end of a StringBuilder. Versions are provided for each of the primitive types, and for character arrays, Strings, Objects, and more. (Remember that method toString produces a string representation of any Object.) Each method takes its argument, converts it to a string and appends it to the StringBuilder.

```
1    // Fig. 16.13: StringBuilderAppend.java
2    // StringBuilder append methods.
3
4    public class StringBuilderAppend
5    {
6        public static void main( String[] args )
7        {
8            Object objectRef = "hello";
9            String string = "goodbye";
10           char[] charArray = { 'a', 'b', 'c', 'd', 'e', 'f' };
11           boolean booleanValue = true;
12           char characterValue = 'Z';
13           int integerValue = 7;
14           long longValue = 10000000000L;
15           float floatValue = 2.5f;
16           double doubleValue = 33.333;
17
18           StringBuilder lastBuffer = new StringBuilder( "last buffer" );
19           StringBuilder buffer = new StringBuilder();
20
21           buffer.append( objectRef );
22           buffer.append( "\n" );
23           buffer.append( string );
24           buffer.append( "\n" );
25           buffer.append( charArray );
26           buffer.append( "\n" );
```

Fig. 16.13 | StringBuilder append methods. (Part 1 of 2.)

```
27          buffer.append( charArray, 0, 3 );
28          buffer.append( "\n" );
29          buffer.append( booleanValue );
30          buffer.append( "\n" );
31          buffer.append( characterValue );
32          buffer.append( "\n" );
33          buffer.append( integerValue );
34          buffer.append( "\n" );
35          buffer.append( longValue );
36          buffer.append( "\n" );
37          buffer.append( floatValue );
38          buffer.append( "\n" );
39          buffer.append( doubleValue );
40          buffer.append( "\n" );
41          buffer.append( lastBuffer );
42
43          System.out.printf( "buffer contains %s\n", buffer.toString() );
44      } // end main
45  } // end StringBuilderAppend
```

```
buffer contains hello
goodbye
abcdef
abc
true
Z
7
10000000000
2.5
33.333
last buffer
```

Fig. 16.13 | StringBuilder append methods. (Part 2 of 2.)

Actually, a compiler can use StringBuilder (or StringBuffer) and the append methods to implement the + and += String concatenation operators. For example, assuming the declarations

```
String string1 = "hello";
String string2 = "BC";
int value = 22;
```

the statement

```
String s = string1 + string2 + value;
```

concatenates "hello", "BC" and 22. The concatenation can be performed as follows:

```
String s = new StringBuilder().append( "hello" ).append( "BC" ).
    append( 22 ).toString();
```

First, the preceding statement creates an empty StringBuilder, then appends to it the strings "hello" and "BC" and the integer 22. Next, StringBuilder's toString method converts the StringBuilder to a String object to be assigned to String s. The statement

```
s += "!";
```

can be performed as follows (this may differ by compiler):

```
s = new StringBuilder().append( s ).append( "!" ).toString();
```

This creates an empty StringBuilder, then appends to it the current contents of s followed by "!". Next, StringBuilder's method toString (which must be called explicitly here) returns the StringBuilder's contents as a String, and the result is assigned to s.

16.4.5 StringBuilder Insertion and Deletion Methods

StringBuilder provides overloaded **insert** methods to insert values of various types at any position in a StringBuilder. Versions are provided for the primitive types and for character arrays, Strings, Objects and CharSequences. Each method takes its second argument and inserts it at the index specified by the first argument. If the first argument is less than 0 or greater than the StringBuilder's length, a StringIndexOutOfBoundsException occurs. Class StringBuilder also provides methods **delete** and **deleteCharAt** to delete characters at any position in a StringBuilder. Method delete takes two arguments—the starting index and the index one past the end of the characters to delete. All characters beginning at the starting index up to but not including the ending index are deleted. Method deleteCharAt takes one argument—the index of the character to delete. Invalid indices cause both methods to throw a StringIndexOutOfBoundsException. Figure 16.14 demonstrates methods insert, delete and deleteCharAt.

```
1   // Fig. 16.14: StringBuilderInsertDelete.java
2   // StringBuilder methods insert, delete and deleteCharAt.
3
4   public class StringBuilderInsertDelete
5   {
6      public static void main( String[] args )
7      {
8         Object objectRef = "hello";
9         String string = "goodbye";
10        char[] charArray = { 'a', 'b', 'c', 'd', 'e', 'f' };
11        boolean booleanValue = true;
12        char characterValue = 'K';
13        int integerValue = 7;
14        long longValue = 10000000;
15        float floatValue = 2.5f; // f suffix indicates that 2.5 is a float
16        double doubleValue = 33.333;
17
18        StringBuilder buffer = new StringBuilder();
19
20        buffer.insert( 0, objectRef );
21        buffer.insert( 0, "  " ); // each of these contains two spaces
22        buffer.insert( 0, string );
23        buffer.insert( 0, "  " );
24        buffer.insert( 0, charArray );
25        buffer.insert( 0, "  " );
26        buffer.insert( 0, charArray, 3, 3 );
27        buffer.insert( 0, "  " );
28        buffer.insert( 0, booleanValue );
```

Fig. 16.14 | StringBuilder methods insert, delete and deleteCharAt. (Part 1 of 2.)

```
29          buffer.insert( 0, "   " );
30          buffer.insert( 0, characterValue );
31          buffer.insert( 0, "   " );
32          buffer.insert( 0, integerValue );
33          buffer.insert( 0, "   " );
34          buffer.insert( 0, longValue );
35          buffer.insert( 0, "   " );
36          buffer.insert( 0, floatValue );
37          buffer.insert( 0, "   " );
38          buffer.insert( 0, doubleValue );
39
40          System.out.printf(
41             "buffer after inserts:\n%s\n\n", buffer.toString() );
42
43          buffer.deleteCharAt( 10 ); // delete 5 in 2.5
44          buffer.delete( 2, 6 ); // delete .333 in 33.333
45
46          System.out.printf(
47             "buffer after deletes:\n%s\n", buffer.toString() );
48       } // end main
49    } // end class StringBuilderInsertDelete
```

```
buffer after inserts:
33.333  2.5  10000000  7  K  true  def  abcdef  goodbye  hello

buffer after deletes:
33  2.  10000000  7  K  true  def  abcdef  goodbye  hello
```

Fig. 16.14 | StringBuilder methods insert, delete and deleteCharAt. (Part 2 of 2.)

16.5 Class Character

Java provides eight type-wrapper classes—Boolean, Character, Double, Float, Byte, Short, Integer and Long—that enable primitive-type values to be treated as objects. In this section, we present class Character—the type-wrapper class for primitive type char.

Most Character methods are static methods designed for convenience in processing individual char values. These methods take at least a character argument and perform either a test or a manipulation of the character. Class Character also contains a constructor that receives a char argument to initialize a Character object. Most of the methods of class Character are presented in the next three examples. For more information on class Character (and all the type-wrapper classes), see the java.lang package in the Java API documentation.

Figure 16.15 demonstrates static methods that test characters to determine whether they're a specific character type and the static methods that perform case conversions on characters. You can enter any character and apply the methods to the character.

Line 15 uses Character method **isDefined** to determine whether character c is defined in the Unicode character set. If so, the method returns true; otherwise, it returns false. Line 16 uses Character method **isDigit** to determine whether character c is a defined Unicode digit. If so, the method returns true, and otherwise, false.

Line 18 uses Character method **isJavaIdentifierStart** to determine whether c is a character that can be the first character of an identifier in Java—that is, a letter, an underscore (_) or a dollar sign ($). If so, the method returns true, and otherwise, false. Line 20 uses Character method **isJavaIdentifierPart** to determine whether character c is a character that can be used in an identifier in Java—that is, a digit, a letter, an underscore (_) or a dollar sign ($). If so, the method returns true, and otherwise, false.

```java
1   // Fig. 16.15: StaticCharMethods.java
2   // Character static methods for testing characters and converting case.
3   import java.util.Scanner;
4
5   public class StaticCharMethods
6   {
7      public static void main( String[] args )
8      {
9         Scanner scanner = new Scanner( System.in ); // create scanner
10        System.out.println( "Enter a character and press Enter" );
11        String input = scanner.next();
12        char c = input.charAt( 0 ); // get input character
13
14        // display character info
15        System.out.printf( "is defined: %b\n", Character.isDefined( c ) );
16        System.out.printf( "is digit: %b\n", Character.isDigit( c ) );
17        System.out.printf( "is first character in a Java identifier: %b\n",
18           Character.isJavaIdentifierStart( c ) );
19        System.out.printf( "is part of a Java identifier: %b\n",
20           Character.isJavaIdentifierPart( c ) );
21        System.out.printf( "is letter: %b\n", Character.isLetter( c ) );
22        System.out.printf(
23           "is letter or digit: %b\n", Character.isLetterOrDigit( c ) );
24        System.out.printf(
25           "is lower case: %b\n", Character.isLowerCase( c ) );
26        System.out.printf(
27           "is upper case: %b\n", Character.isUpperCase( c ) );
28        System.out.printf(
29           "to upper case: %s\n", Character.toUpperCase( c ) );
30        System.out.printf(
31           "to lower case: %s\n", Character.toLowerCase( c ) );
32     } // end main
33  } // end class StaticCharMethods
```

```
Enter a character and press Enter
A
is defined: true
is digit: false
is first character in a Java identifier: true
is part of a Java identifier: true
is letter: true
is letter or digit: true
is lower case: false
is upper case: true
to upper case: A
to lower case: a
```

Fig. 16.15 | Character static methods for testing characters and converting case. (Part 1 of 2.)

```
Enter a character and press Enter
8
is defined: true
is digit: true
is first character in a Java identifier: false
is part of a Java identifier: true
is letter: false
is letter or digit: true
is lower case: false
is upper case: false
to upper case: 8
to lower case: 8
```

```
Enter a character and press Enter
$
is defined: true
is digit: false
is first character in a Java identifier: true
is part of a Java identifier: true
is letter: false
is letter or digit: false
is lower case: false
is upper case: false
to upper case: $
to lower case: $
```

Fig. 16.15 | Character static methods for testing characters and converting case. (Part 2 of 2.)

Line 21 uses Character method **isLetter** to determine whether character c is a letter. If so, the method returns true, and otherwise, false. Line 23 uses Character method **isLetterOrDigit** to determine whether character c is a letter or a digit. If so, the method returns true, and otherwise, false.

Line 25 uses Character method **isLowerCase** to determine whether character c is a lowercase letter. If so, the method returns true, and otherwise, false. Line 27 uses Character method **isUpperCase** to determine whether character c is an uppercase letter. If so, the method returns true, and otherwise, false.

Line 29 uses Character method **toUpperCase** to convert the character c to its uppercase equivalent. The method returns the converted character if the character has an uppercase equivalent, and otherwise, the method returns its original argument. Line 31 uses Character method **toLowerCase** to convert the character c to its lowercase equivalent. The method returns the converted character if the character has a lowercase equivalent, and otherwise, the method returns its original argument.

Figure 16.16 demonstrates static Character methods **digit** and **forDigit**, which convert characters to digits and digits to characters, respectively, in different number systems. Common number systems include decimal (base 10), octal (base 8), hexadecimal (base 16) and binary (base 2). The base of a number is also known as its **radix**. For more information on conversions between number systems, see Appendix H.

Line 28 uses method forDigit to convert the integer digit into a character in the number system specified by the integer radix (the base of the number). For example, the decimal integer 13 in base 16 (the radix) has the character value 'd'. Lowercase and upper-case letters represent the same value in number systems. Line 35 uses method digit to con-

```
1   // Fig. 16.16: StaticCharMethods2.java
2   // Character class static conversion methods.
3   import java.util.Scanner;
4
5   public class StaticCharMethods2
6   {
7      // executes application
8      public static void main( String[] args )
9      {
10        Scanner scanner = new Scanner( System.in );
11
12        // get radix
13        System.out.println( "Please enter a radix:" );
14        int radix = scanner.nextInt();
15
16        // get user choice
17        System.out.printf( "Please choose one:\n1 -- %s\n2 -- %s\n",
18           "Convert digit to character", "Convert character to digit" );
19        int choice = scanner.nextInt();
20
21        // process request
22        switch ( choice )
23        {
24           case 1: // convert digit to character
25              System.out.println( "Enter a digit:" );
26              int digit = scanner.nextInt();
27              System.out.printf( "Convert digit to character: %s\n",
28                 Character.forDigit( digit, radix ) );
29              break;
30
31           case 2: // convert character to digit
32              System.out.println( "Enter a character:" );
33              char character = scanner.next().charAt( 0 );
34              System.out.printf( "Convert character to digit: %s\n",
35                 Character.digit( character, radix ) );
36              break;
37        } // end switch
38     } // end main
39  } // end class StaticCharMethods2
```

```
Please enter a radix:
16
Please choose one:
1 -- Convert digit to character
2 -- Convert character to digit
2
Enter a character:
A
Convert character to digit: 10
```

Fig. 16.16 | Character class static conversion methods. (Part 1 of 2.)

```
Please enter a radix:
16
Please choose one:
1 -- Convert digit to character
2 -- Convert character to digit
1
Enter a digit:
13
Convert digit to character: d
```

Fig. 16.16 | Character class static conversion methods. (Part 2 of 2.)

vert variable character into an integer in the number system specified by the integer radix (the base of the number). For example, the character 'A' is the base 16 (the radix) representation of the base 10 value 10. The radix must be between 2 and 36, inclusive.

Figure 16.17 demonstrates the constructor and several non-static methods of class Character—**charValue**, toString and equals. Lines 7–8 instantiate two Character objects by assigning the character constants 'A' and 'a', respectively, to the Character variables. Java automatically converts these char literals into Character objects—a process known as *autoboxing* that we discuss in more detail in Section 18.4. Line 11 uses Character method charValue to return the char value stored in Character object c1. Line 11 returns a string representation of Character object c2 using method toString. The condition in line 13 uses method equals to determine whether the object c1 has the same contents as the object c2 (i.e., the characters inside each object are equal).

```
 1    // Fig. 16.17: OtherCharMethods.java
 2    // Character class non-static methods.
 3    public class OtherCharMethods
 4    {
 5       public static void main( String[] args )
 6       {
 7          Character c1 = 'A';
 8          Character c2 = 'a';
 9
10          System.out.printf(
11             "c1 = %s\nc2 = %s\n\n", c1.charValue(), c2.toString() );
12
13          if ( c1.equals( c2 ) )
14             System.out.println( "c1 and c2 are equal\n" );
15          else
16             System.out.println( "c1 and c2 are not equal\n" );
17       } // end main
18    } // end class OtherCharMethods
```

```
c1 = A
c2 = a

c1 and c2 are not equal
```

Fig. 16.17 | Character class non-static methods.

16.6 Tokenizing Strings

When you read a sentence, your mind breaks it into **tokens**—individual words and punctuation marks that convey meaning to you. Compilers also perform tokenization. They break up statements into individual pieces like keywords, identifiers, operators and other programming-language elements. We now study class String's **split** method, which breaks a String into its component tokens. Tokens are separated from one another by **delimiters**, typically white-space characters such as space, tab, newline and carriage return. Other characters can also be used as delimiters to separate tokens. The application in Fig. 16.18 demonstrates String's split method.

```
1   // Fig. 16.18: TokenTest.java
2   // StringTokenizer object used to tokenize strings.
3   import java.util.Scanner;
4   import java.util.StringTokenizer;
5
6   public class TokenTest
7   {
8      // execute application
9      public static void main( String[] args )
10     {
11        // get sentence
12        Scanner scanner = new Scanner( System.in );
13        System.out.println( "Enter a sentence and press Enter" );
14        String sentence = scanner.nextLine();
15
16        // process user sentence
17        String[] tokens = sentence.split( " " );
18        System.out.printf( "Number of elements: %d\nThe tokens are:\n",
19           tokens.length );
20
21        for ( String token : tokens )
22           System.out.println( token );
23     } // end main
24  } // end class TokenTest
```

```
Enter a sentence and press Enter
This is a sentence with seven tokens
Number of elements: 7
The tokens are:
This
is
a
sentence
with
seven
tokens
```

Fig. 16.18 | StringTokenizer object used to tokenize strings.

When the user presses the *Enter* key, the input sentence is stored in variable sentence. Line 17 invokes String method split with the String argument " ", which returns an array of `Strings`. The space character in the argument `String` is the delimiter that method `split` uses to locate the tokens in the `String`. As you'll learn in the next section, the argument to method split can be a regular expression for more complex tokenizing. Line 19 displays the length of the array `tokens`—i.e., the number of tokens in `sentence`. Lines 21–22 output each token on a separate line.

16.7 Regular Expressions, Class Pattern and Class Matcher

A **regular expression** is a `String` that describes a search pattern for matching characters in other `Strings`. Such expressions are useful for validating input and ensuring that data is in a particular format. For example, a ZIP code must consist of five digits, and a last name must contain only letters, spaces, apostrophes and hyphens. One application of regular expressions is to facilitate the construction of a compiler. Often, a large and complex regular expression is used to validate the syntax of a program. If the program code does not match the regular expression, the compiler knows that there's a syntax error in the code.

Class `String` provides several methods for performing regular-expression operations, the simplest of which is the matching operation. `String` method **matches** receives a `String` that specifies the regular expression and matches the contents of the `String` object on which it's called to the regular expression. The method returns a `boolean` indicating whether the match succeeded.

A regular expression consists of literal characters and special symbols. Figure 16.19 specifies some **predefined character classes** that can be used with regular expressions. A character class is an escape sequence that represents a group of characters. A digit is any numeric character. A **word character** is any letter (uppercase or lowercase), any digit or the underscore character. A white-space character is a space, a tab, a carriage return, a newline or a form feed. Each character class matches a single character in the `String` we're attempting to match with the regular expression.

Character	Matches	Character	Matches
\d	any digit	\D	any nondigit
\w	any word character	\W	any nonword character
\s	any white-space character	\S	any nonwhite-space character

Fig. 16.19 | Predefined character classes.

Regular expressions are not limited to these predefined character classes. The expressions employ various operators and other forms of notation to match complex patterns. We examine several of these techniques in the application in Figs. 16.20 and 16.21, which validates user input via regular expressions. [*Note:* This application is not designed to match all possible valid user input.]

Figure 16.20 validates user input. Line 9 validates the first name. To match a set of characters that does not have a predefined character class, use square brackets, []. For example, the pattern "[aeiou]" matches a single character that's a vowel. Character ranges are repre-

```
1    // Fig. 16.20: ValidateInput.java
2    // Validate user information using regular expressions.
3
4    public class ValidateInput
5    {
6       // validate first name
7       public static boolean validateFirstName( String firstName )
8       {
9          return firstName.matches( "[A-Z][a-zA-Z]*" );
10      } // end method validateFirstName
11
12      // validate last name
13      public static boolean validateLastName( String lastName )
14      {
15         return lastName.matches( "[a-zA-z]+([ '-][a-zA-Z]+)*" );
16      } // end method validateLastName
17
18      // validate address
19      public static boolean validateAddress( String address )
20      {
21         return address.matches(
22            "\\d+\\s+([a-zA-Z]+|[a-zA-Z]+\\s[a-zA-Z]+)" );
23      } // end method validateAddress
24
25      // validate city
26      public static boolean validateCity( String city )
27      {
28         return city.matches( "([a-zA-Z]+|[a-zA-Z]+\\s[a-zA-Z]+)" );
29      } // end method validateCity
30
31      // validate state
32      public static boolean validateState( String state )
33      {
34         return state.matches( "([a-zA-Z]+|[a-zA-Z]+\\s[a-zA-Z]+)" ) ;
35      } // end method validateState
36
37      // validate zip
38      public static boolean validateZip( String zip )
39      {
40         return zip.matches( "\\d{5}" );
41      } // end method validateZip
42
43      // validate phone
44      public static boolean validatePhone( String phone )
45      {
46         return phone.matches( "[1-9]\\d{2}-[1-9]\\d{2}-\\d{4}" );
47      } // end method validatePhone
48   } // end class ValidateInput
```

Fig. 16.20 | Validating user information using regular expressions.

sented by placing a dash (-) between two characters. In the example, "[A-Z]" matches a single uppercase letter. If the first character in the brackets is "^", the expression accepts any character other than those indicated. However, "[^Z]" is not the same as "[A-Y]", which matches uppercase letters A–Y—"[^Z]" matches any character other than capital Z, including lowercase letters and nonletters such as the newline character. Ranges in character classes are determined by the letters' integer values. In this example, "[A-Za-z]" matches all uppercase and lowercase letters. The range "[A-z]" matches all letters and also matches those characters (such as [and \) with an integer value between uppercase Z and lowercase a (for more information on integer values of characters see Appendix B). Like predefined character classes, character classes delimited by square brackets match a single character in the search object.

```java
1   // Fig. 16.21: Validate.java
2   // Validate user information using regular expressions.
3   import java.util.Scanner;
4
5   public class Validate
6   {
7      public static void main( String[] args )
8      {
9         // get user input
10        Scanner scanner = new Scanner( System.in );
11        System.out.println( "Please enter first name:" );
12        String firstName = scanner.nextLine();
13        System.out.println( "Please enter last name:" );
14        String lastName = scanner.nextLine();
15        System.out.println( "Please enter address:" );
16        String address = scanner.nextLine();
17        System.out.println( "Please enter city:" );
18        String city = scanner.nextLine();
19        System.out.println( "Please enter state:" );
20        String state = scanner.nextLine();
21        System.out.println( "Please enter zip:" );
22        String zip = scanner.nextLine();
23        System.out.println( "Please enter phone:" );
24        String phone = scanner.nextLine();
25
26        // validate user input and display error message
27        System.out.println( "\nValidate Result:" );
28
29        if ( !ValidateInput.validateFirstName( firstName ) )
30           System.out.println( "Invalid first name" );
31        else if ( !ValidateInput.validateLastName( lastName ) )
32           System.out.println( "Invalid last name" );
33        else if ( !ValidateInput.validateAddress( address ) )
34           System.out.println( "Invalid address" );
35        else if ( !ValidateInput.validateCity( city ) )
36           System.out.println( "Invalid city" );
37        else if ( !ValidateInput.validateState( state ) )
38           System.out.println( "Invalid state" );
39        else if ( !ValidateInput.validateZip( zip ) )
40           System.out.println( "Invalid zip code" );
41        else if ( !ValidateInput.validatePhone( phone ) )
42           System.out.println( "Invalid phone number" );
```

Fig. 16.21 | Inputs and validates data from user using the ValidateInput class. (Part 1 of 2.)

```
43              else
44                  System.out.println( "Valid input.   Thank you." );
45      } // end main
46  } // end class Validate
```

```
Please enter first name:
Jane
Please enter last name:
Doe
Please enter address:
123 Some Street
Please enter city:
Some City
Please enter state:
SS
Please enter zip:
123
Please enter phone:
123-456-7890

Validate Result:
Invalid zip code
```

```
Please enter first name:
Jane
Please enter last name:
Doe
Please enter address:
123 Some Street
Please enter city:
Some City
Please enter state:
SS
Please enter zip:
12345
Please enter phone:
123-456-7890

Validate Result:
Valid input.   Thank you.
```

Fig. 16.21 | Inputs and validates data from user using the ValidateInput class. (Part 2 of 2.)

In line 9, the asterisk after the second character class indicates that any number of letters can be matched. In general, when the regular-expression operator "*" appears in a regular expression, the application attempts to match zero or more occurrences of the subexpression immediately preceding the "*". Operator "+" attempts to match one or more occurrences of the subexpression immediately preceding "+". So both "A*" and "A+" will match "AAA" or "A", but only "A*" will match an empty string.

If method validateFirstName returns true (line 29 of Fig. 16.21), the application attempts to validate the last name (line 31) by calling validateLastName (lines 13–16 of Fig. 16.20). The regular expression to validate the last name matches any number of letters split by spaces, apostrophes or hyphens.

Line 33 of Fig. 16.21 calls method `validateAddress` (lines 19–23 of Fig. 16.20) to validate the address. The first character class matches any digit one or more times (\\d+). Two \ characters are used, because \ normally starts an escape sequence in a string. So \\d in a `String` represents the regular expression pattern \d. Then we match one or more white-space characters (\\s+). The character "|" matches the expression to its left or to its right. For example, `"Hi (John|Jane)"` matches both `"Hi John"` and `"Hi Jane"`. The parentheses are used to group parts of the regular expression. In this example, the left side of | matches a single word, and the right side matches two words separated by any amount of white space. So the address must contain a number followed by one or two words. Therefore, `"10 Broadway"` and `"10 Main Street"` are both valid addresses in this example. The city (lines 26–29 of Fig. 16.20) and state (lines 32–35 of Fig. 16.20) methods also match any word of at least one character or, alternatively, any two words of at least one character if the words are separated by a single space, so both `Waltham` and `West Newton` would match.

Quantifiers

The asterisk (*) and plus (+) are formally called **quantifiers**. Figure 16.22 lists all the quantifiers. We've already discussed how the asterisk (*) and plus (+) quantifiers work. All quantifiers affect only the subexpression immediately preceding the quantifier. Quantifier question mark (?) matches zero or one occurrences of the expression that it quantifies. A set of braces containing one number ({*n*}) matches exactly *n* occurrences of the expression it quantifies. We demonstrate this quantifier to validate the zip code in Fig. 16.20 at line 40. Including a comma after the number enclosed in braces matches at least *n* occurrences of the quantified expression. The set of braces containing two numbers ({*n*, *m*}), matches between *n* and *m* occurrences of the expression that it qualifies. Quantifiers may be applied to patterns enclosed in parentheses to create more complex regular expressions.

Quantifier	Matches
*	Matches zero or more occurrences of the pattern.
+	Matches one or more occurrences of the pattern.
?	Matches zero or one occurrences of the pattern.
{*n*}	Matches exactly *n* occurrences.
{*n*,}	Matches at least *n* occurrences.
{*n*,*m*}	Matches between *n* and *m* (inclusive) occurrences.

Fig. 16.22 | Quantifiers used in regular expressions.

All of the quantifiers are **greedy**. This means that they'll match as many occurrences as they can as long as the match is still successful. However, if any of these quantifiers is followed by a question mark (?), the quantifier becomes **reluctant** (sometimes called **lazy**). It then will match as few occurrences as possible as long as the match is still successful.

The zip code (line 40 in Fig. 16.20) matches a digit five times. This regular expression uses the digit character class and a quantifier with the digit 5 between braces. The phone number (line 46 in Fig. 16.20) matches three digits (the first one cannot be zero) followed by a dash followed by three more digits (again the first one cannot be zero) followed by four more digits.

String method matches checks whether an entire String conforms to a regular expression. For example, we want to accept "Smith" as a last name, but not "9@Smith#". If only a substring matches the regular expression, method matches returns false.

Replacing Substrings and Splitting Strings
Sometimes it's useful to replace parts of a string or to split a string into pieces. For this purpose, class String provides methods **replaceAll**, **replaceFirst** and **split**. These methods are demonstrated in Fig. 16.23.

```
1   // Fig. 16.23: RegexSubstitution.java
2   // String methods replaceFirst, replaceAll and split.
3   import java.util.Arrays;
4
5   public class RegexSubstitution
6   {
7      public static void main( String[] args )
8      {
9         String firstString = "This sentence ends in 5 stars *****";
10        String secondString = "1, 2, 3, 4, 5, 6, 7, 8";
11
12        System.out.printf( "Original String 1: %s\n", firstString );
13
14        // replace '*' with '^'
15        firstString = firstString.replaceAll( "\\*", "^" );
16
17        System.out.printf( "^ substituted for *: %s\n", firstString );
18
19        // replace 'stars' with 'carets'
20        firstString = firstString.replaceAll( "stars", "carets" );
21
22        System.out.printf(
23           "\"carets\" substituted for \"stars\": %s\n", firstString );
24
25        // replace words with 'word'
26        System.out.printf( "Every word replaced by \"word\": %s\n\n",
27           firstString.replaceAll( "\\w+", "word" ) );
28
29        System.out.printf( "Original String 2: %s\n", secondString );
30
31        // replace first three digits with 'digit'
32        for ( int i = 0; i < 3; i++ )
33           secondString = secondString.replaceFirst( "\\d", "digit" );
34
35        System.out.printf(
36           "First 3 digits replaced by \"digit\" : %s\n", secondString );
37
38        System.out.print( "String split at commas: " );
39        String[] results = secondString.split( ",\\s*" ); // split on commas
40        System.out.println( Arrays.toString( results ) );
41     } // end main
42  } // end class RegexSubstitution
```

Fig. 16.23 | String methods replaceFirst, replaceAll and split. (Part 1 of 2.)

```
Original String 1: This sentence ends in 5 stars *****
∧ substituted for *: This sentence ends in 5 stars ∧∧∧∧∧
"carets" substituted for "stars": This sentence ends in 5 carets ∧∧∧∧∧
Every word replaced by "word": word word word word word word ∧∧∧∧∧

Original String 2: 1, 2, 3, 4, 5, 6, 7, 8
First 3 digits replaced by "digit" : digit, digit, digit, 4, 5, 6, 7, 8
String split at commas: ["digit", "digit", "digit", "4", "5", "6", "7", "8"]
```

Fig. 16.23 | String methods `replaceFirst`, `replaceAll` and `split`. (Part 2 of 2.)

Method `replaceAll` replaces text in a `String` with new text (the second argument) wherever the original `String` matches a regular expression (the first argument). Line 15 replaces every instance of "*" in `firstString` with "∧". The regular expression ("*") precedes character * with two backslashes. Normally, * is a quantifier indicating that a regular expression should match any number of occurrences of a preceding pattern. However, in line 15, we want to find all occurrences of the literal character *—to do this, we must escape character * with character \. Escaping a special regular-expression character with \ instructs the matching engine to find the actual character. Since the expression is stored in a Java `String` and \ is a special character in Java `Strings`, we must include an additional \. So the Java `String` "*" represents the regular-expression pattern * which matches a single * character in the search string. In line 20, every match for the regular expression "stars" in `firstString` is replaced with "carets". Line 27 uses `replaceAll` to replace all words in the string with "word".

Method `replaceFirst` (line 33) replaces the first occurrence of a pattern match. Java `Strings` are immutable; therefore, method `replaceFirst` returns a new `String` in which the appropriate characters have been replaced. This line takes the original `String` and replaces it with the `String` returned by `replaceFirst`. By iterating three times we replace the first three instances of a digit (\d) in `secondString` with the text "digit".

Method `split` divides a `String` into several substrings. The original is broken in any location that matches a specified regular expression. Method `split` returns an array of `Strings` containing the substrings between matches for the regular expression. In line 39, we use method `split` to tokenize a `String` of comma-separated integers. The argument is the regular expression that locates the delimiter. In this case, we use the regular expression ",\\s*" to separate the substrings wherever a comma occurs. By matching any white-space characters, we eliminate extra spaces from the resulting substrings. The commas and white-space characters are not returned as part of the substrings. Again, the Java `String` ",\\s*" represents the regular expression ,\s*. Line 40 uses `Arrays` method `toString` to display the contents of array `results` in square brackets and separated by commas.

Classes *Pattern* and *Matcher*

In addition to the regular-expression capabilities of class `String`, Java provides other classes in package `java.util.regex` that help developers manipulate regular expressions. Class **Pattern** represents a regular expression. Class **Matcher** contains both a regular-expression pattern and a `CharSequence` in which to search for the pattern.

CharSequence (package `java.lang`) is an interface that allows read access to a sequence of characters. The interface requires that the methods `charAt`, `length`, `subSe-`

quence and toString be declared. Both String and StringBuilder implement interface CharSequence, so an instance of either of these classes can be used with class Matcher.

Common Programming Error 16.4

A regular expression can be tested against an object of any class that implements interface CharSequence, but the regular expression must be a String. Attempting to create a regular expression as a StringBuilder is an error.

If a regular expression will be used only once, static Pattern method **matches** can be used. This method takes a String that specifies the regular expression and a CharSequence on which to perform the match. This method returns a boolean indicating whether the search object (the second argument) matches the regular expression.

If a regular expression will be used more than once (in a loop, for example), it's more efficient to use static Pattern method **compile** to create a specific Pattern object for that regular expression. This method receives a String representing the pattern and returns a new Pattern object, which can then be used to call method **matcher**. This method receives a CharSequence to search and returns a Matcher object.

Matcher provides method **matches**, which performs the same task as Pattern method matches, but receives no arguments—the search pattern and search object are encapsulated in the Matcher object. Class Matcher provides other methods, including **find**, **lookingAt**, **replaceFirst** and **replaceAll**.

Figure 16.24 presents a simple example that employs regular expressions. This program matches birthdays against a regular expression. The expression matches only birthdays that do not occur in April and that belong to people whose names begin with "J".

Lines 11–12 create a Pattern by invoking static Pattern method compile. The dot character "." in the regular expression (line 12) matches any single character except a newline character.

```
1   // Fig. 16.24: RegexMatches.java
2   // Classes Pattern and Matcher.
3   import java.util.regex.Matcher;
4   import java.util.regex.Pattern;
5
6   public class RegexMatches
7   {
8      public static void main( String[] args )
9      {
10        // create regular expression
11        Pattern expression =
12           Pattern.compile( "J.*\\d[0-35-9]-\\d\\d-\\d\\d" );
13
14        String string1 = "Jane's Birthday is 05-12-75\n" +
15           "Dave's Birthday is 11-04-68\n" +
16           "John's Birthday is 04-28-73\n" +
17           "Joe's Birthday is 12-17-77";
18
19        // match regular expression to string and print matches
20        Matcher matcher = expression.matcher( string1 );
```

Fig. 16.24 | Classes Pattern and Matcher. (Part 1 of 2.)

```
21
22          while ( matcher.find() )
23             System.out.println( matcher.group() );
24      } // end main
25   } // end class RegexMatches
```

```
Jane's Birthday is 05-12-75
Joe's Birthday is 12-17-77
```

Fig. 16.24 | Classes Pattern and Matcher. (Part 2 of 2.)

Line 20 creates the Matcher object for the compiled regular expression and the matching sequence (string1). Lines 22–23 use a while loop to iterate through the String. Line 22 uses Matcher method find to attempt to match a piece of the search object to the search pattern. Each call to this method starts at the point where the last call ended, so multiple matches can be found. Matcher method lookingAt performs the same way, except that it always starts from the beginning of the search object and will always find the first match if there is one.

Common Programming Error 16.5

Method matches (from class String, Pattern or Matcher) will return true only if the entire search object matches the regular expression. Methods find and lookingAt (from class Matcher) will return true if a portion of the search object matches the regular expression.

Line 23 uses Matcher method **group**, which returns the String from the search object that matches the search pattern. The String that's returned is the one that was last matched by a call to find or lookingAt. The output in Fig. 16.24 shows the two matches that were found in string1.

For more information on regular expressions, visit our Regular Expressions Resource Center at www.deitel.com/regularexpressions/.

16.8 Wrap-Up

In this chapter, you learned about more String methods for selecting portions of Strings and manipulating Strings. You learned about the Character class and some of the methods it declares to handle chars. The chapter also discussed the capabilities of the String-Builder class for creating Strings. The end of the chapter discussed regular expressions, which provide a powerful capability to search and match portions of Strings that fit a particular pattern. In the next chapter, you'll learn about file processing, including how persistent data is stored and and retrieved.

17

Files, Streams and Object Serialization

Objectives

In this chapter you'll learn:

- To create, read, write and update files.

- To retrieve information about files and directories.

- The Java input/output stream class hierarchy.

- The differences between text files and binary files.

- To use classes `Scanner` and `Formatter` to process text files.

- To use classes `FileInputStream` and `FileOutputStream` to read from and write to files.

- To use classes `ObjectInputStream` and `ObjectOutputStream` to read objects from and write objects to files.

- To use a `JFileChooser` dialog.

17.1 Introduction

Data stored in variables and arrays is temporary—it's lost when a local variable goes out of scope or when the program terminates. For long-term retention of data, even after the programs that create the data terminate, computers use **files**. You use files every day for tasks such as writing a document or creating a spreadsheet. Computers store files on **secondary storage devices** such as hard disks, optical disks, flash drives and magnetic tapes. Data maintained in files is **persistent data**—it exists beyond the duration of program execution. In this chapter, we explain how Java programs create, update and process files.

We begin with a discussion of Java's architecture for handling files programmatically. Next we explain that data can be stored in text files and binary files—and we cover the differences between them. We demonstrate retrieving information about files and directories using class `File`, then devote several sections to the different mechanisms for writing data to and reading data from files. We show how to create and manipulate sequential-access text files. Working with text files allows you to quickly and easily start manipulating files. As you'll learn, however, it's difficult to read data from text files back into object form. Fortunately, many object-oriented languages (including Java) provide ways to write objects to and read objects from files (known as object serialization and deserialization). To demonstrate this, we recreate some of our sequential-access programs that used text files, this time by storing objects in binary files.

17.2 Files and Streams

Java views each file as a sequential **stream of bytes** (Fig. 17.1). Every operating system provides a mechanism to determine the end of a file, such as an **end-of-file marker** or a count of the total bytes in the file that's recorded in a system-maintained administrative data structure. A Java program processing a stream of bytes simply receives an indication from the operating system when it reaches the end of the stream—the program does *not* need

Fig. 17.1 | Java's view of a file of *n* bytes.

to know how the underlying platform represents files or streams. In some cases, the end-of-file indication occurs as an exception. In other cases, the indication is a return value from a method invoked on a stream-processing object.

Byte-Based and Character-Based Streams

File streams can be used to input and output data as bytes or characters. **Byte-based streams** input and output data in its binary format. **Character-based streams** input and output data as a sequence of characters. If the value 5 were being stored using a byte-based stream, it would be stored in the binary format of the numeric value 5, or 101. If the value 5 were being stored using a character-based stream, it would be stored in the binary format of the character 5, or 00000000 00110101 (this is the binary representation for the numeric value 53, which indicates the Unicode® character 5). The difference between the two forms is that the numeric value can be used as an integer in calculations, whereas the character 5 is simply a character that can be used in a string of text, as in "Sarah Miller is 15 years old". Files that are created using byte-based streams are referred to as **binary files**, while files created using character-based streams are referred to as **text files**. Text files can be read by text editors, while binary files are read by programs that understand the file's specific content and its ordering.

Standard Input, Standard Output and Standard Error Streams

A Java program **opens** a file by creating an object and associating a stream of bytes or characters with it. The object's constructor interacts with the operating system to open the file. Java can also associate streams with different devices. When a Java program begins executing, in fact, it creates three stream objects that are associated with devices—System.in, System.out and System.err. System.in (the standard input stream object) normally enables a program to input bytes from the keyboard; object System.out (the standard output stream object) normally enables a program to output character data to the screen; and object System.err (the standard error stream object) normally enables a program to output character-based error messages to the screen. Each stream can be redirected. For System.in, this capability enables the program to read bytes from a different source. For System.out and System.err, it enables the output to be sent to a different location, such as a file on disk. Class System provides methods **setIn**, **setOut** and **setErr** to **redirect** the standard input, output and error streams, respectively.

The `java.io` Package

Java programs perform file processing by using classes from package **java.io**. This package includes definitions for stream classes, such as **FileInputStream** (for byte-based input from a file), **FileOutputStream** (for byte-based output to a file), **FileReader** (for character-based input from a file) and **FileWriter** (for character-based output to a file), which inherit from classes InputStream, OutputStream, Reader and Writer, respectively. Thus, the methods of the these stream classes can also be applied to file streams.

Java contains classes that enable you to perform input and output of objects or variables of primitive data types. The data will still be stored as bytes or characters behind the scenes, allowing you to read or write data in the form of ints, Strings, or other types without having to worry about the details of converting such values to byte format. To perform such input and output, objects of classes **ObjectInputStream** and **ObjectOutput-Stream** can be used together with the byte-based file stream classes FileInputStream and

`FileOutputStream` (these classes will be discussed in more detail shortly). The complete hierarchy of types in package `java.io` can be viewed in the online documentation at

```
download.oracle.com/javase/6/docs/api/java/io/package-tree.html
```

As you can see in the hierarchy, Java offers many classes for performing input/output operations. We use several of these classes in this chapter to implement file-processing programs that create and manipulate sequential-access files. In Chapter 24, we use stream classes extensively to implement networking applications.

In addition to the `java.io` classes, character-based input and output can be performed with classes `Scanner` and **`Formatter`**. Class `Scanner` is used extensively to input data from the keyboard—it can also read data from a file. Class `Formatter` enables formatted data to be output to any text-based stream in a manner similar to method `System.out.printf`. Appendix G presents the details of formatted output with `printf`. All these features can be used to format text files as well.

17.3 Class `File`

This section presents class **`File`**, which is useful for retrieving information about files or directories from disk. Objects of class `File` do not open files or provide any file-processing capabilities. However, `File` objects are used frequently with objects of other `java.io` classes to specify files or directories to manipulate.

Creating `File` Objects

Class `File` provides four constructors. The one with a `String` argument specifies the name of a file or directory to associate with the `File` object. The name can contain **path information** as well as a file or directory name. A file or directory's path specifies its location on disk. The path includes some or all of the directories leading to the file or directory. An **absolute path** contains all the directories, starting with the **root directory**, that lead to a specific file or directory. Every file or directory on a particular disk drive has the same root directory in its path. A **relative path** normally starts from the directory in which the application began executing and is therefore "relative" to the current directory. The constructor with two `String` arguments specifies an absolute or relative path as the first argument and the file or directory to associate with the `File` object as the second argument. The constructor with `File` and `String` arguments uses an existing `File` object that specifies the parent directory of the file or directory specified by the `String` argument. The fourth constructor uses a `URI` object to locate the file. A **Uniform Resource Identifier (URI)** is a more general form of the **Uniform Resource Locators (URLs)** that are used to locate websites. For example, `http://www.deitel.com/` is the URL for the Deitel & Associates website. URIs for locating files vary across operating systems. On Windows platforms, the URI

```
file://C:/data.txt
```

identifies the file `data.txt` stored in the root directory of the C: drive. On UNIX/Linux platforms, the URI

```
file:/home/student/data.txt
```

identifies the file `data.txt` stored in the home directory of the user `student`.

Figure 17.2 lists some common `File` methods. The complete list can be viewed at `download.oracle.com/javase/6/docs/api/java/io/File.html`.

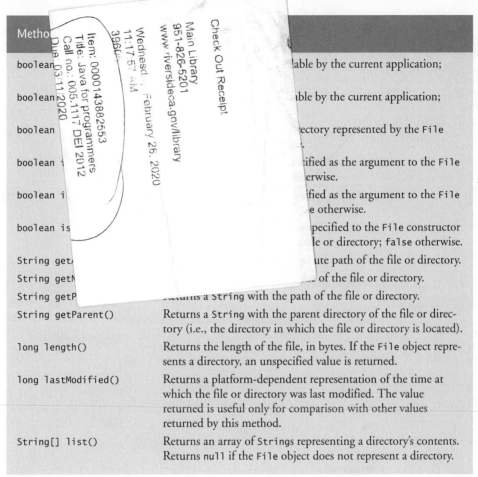

Method	Description
boolean ...	...able by the current application;
boolean ...	...ble by the current application;
boolean ...	...ectory represented by the `File` ...
boolean i...	...ified as the argument to the `File` ...erwise.
boolean i...	...ified as the argument to the `File` ...e otherwise.
boolean is...	...pecified to the `File` constructor ...le or directory; `false` otherwise.
String get...	...ute path of the file or directory.
String getN...	... of the file or directory.
String getP...	...eturns a `String` with the path of the file or directory.
String getParent()	Returns a `String` with the parent directory of the file or directory (i.e., the directory in which the file or directory is located).
long length()	Returns the length of the file, in bytes. If the `File` object represents a directory, an unspecified value is returned.
long lastModified()	Returns a platform-dependent representation of the time at which the file or directory was last modified. The value returned is useful only for comparison with other values returned by this method.
String[] list()	Returns an array of `Strings` representing a directory's contents. Returns `null` if the `File` object does not represent a directory.

Fig. 17.2 | `File` methods.

Demonstrating Class `File`

Figure 17.3 prompts the user to enter the name of a file or directory, then uses class `File` to output information about the file or directory.

```java
 1   // Fig. 17.3: FileDemonstration.java
 2   // File class used to obtain file and directory information.
 3   import java.io.File;
 4   import java.util.Scanner;
 5
 6   public class FileDemonstration
 7   {
 8      public static void main( String[] args )
 9      {
10         Scanner input = new Scanner( System.in );
11
```

Fig. 17.3 | `File` class used to obtain file and directory information. (Part 1 of 3.)

```
12              System.out.print( "Enter file or directory name: " );
13              analyzePath( input.nextLine() );
14      } // end main
15
16      // display information about file user specifies
17      public static void analyzePath( String path )
18      {
19          // create File object based on user input
20          File name = new File( path );
21
22          if ( name.exists() ) // if name exists, output information about it
23          {
24              // display file (or directory) information
25              System.out.printf(
26                  "%s%s\n%s\n%s\n%s\n%s%s\n%s%s\n%s%s\n%s%s\n%s%s",
27                  name.getName(), " exists",
28                  ( name.isFile() ? "is a file" : "is not a file" ),
29                  ( name.isDirectory() ? "is a directory" :
30                      "is not a directory" ),
31                  ( name.isAbsolute() ? "is absolute path" :
32                      "is not absolute path" ), "Last modified: ",
33                  name.lastModified(), "Length: ", name.length(),
34                  "Path: ", name.getPath(), "Absolute path: ",
35                  name.getAbsolutePath(), "Parent: ", name.getParent() );
36
37              if ( name.isDirectory() ) // output directory listing
38              {
39                  String[] directory = name.list();
40                  System.out.println( "\n\nDirectory contents:\n" );
41
42                  for ( String directoryName : directory )
43                      System.out.println( directoryName );
44              } // end if
45          } // end outer if
46          else // not file or directory, output error message
47          {
48              System.out.printf( "%s %s", path, "does not exist." );
49          } // end else
50      } // end method analyzePath
51  } // end class FileDemonstration
```

```
Enter file or directory name: E:\Program Files\Java\jdk1.6.0_11\demo\jfc
jfc exists
is not a file
is a directory
is absolute path
Last modified: 1228404395024
Length: 4096
Path: E:\Program Files\Java\jdk1.6.0_11\demo\jfc
Absolute path: E:\Program Files\Java\jdk1.6.0_11\demo\jfc
Parent: E:\Program Files\Java\jdk1.6.0_11\demo
```

Fig. 17.3 | File class used to obtain file and directory information. (Part 2 of 3.)

```
Directory contents:

CodePointIM
FileChooserDemo
Font2DTest
Java2D
Laffy
Metalworks
Notepad
SampleTree
Stylepad
SwingApplet
SwingSet2
SwingSet3
```

```
Enter file or directory name: C:\Program Files\Java\jdk1.6.0_11\demo\jfc
\Java2D\README.txt
README.txt exists
is a file
is not a directory
is absolute path
Last modified: 1228404384270
Length: 7518
Path: E:\Program Files\Java\jdk1.6.0_11\demo\jfc\Java2D\README.txt
Absolute path: E:\Program Files\Java\jdk1.6.0_11\demo\jfc\Java2D\README.txt
Parent: E:\Program Files\Java\jdk1.6.0_11\demo\jfc\Java2D
```

Fig. 17.3 | File class used to obtain file and directory information. (Part 3 of 3.)

The program begins by prompting the user for a file or directory (line 12). Line 13 inputs the file name or directory name and passes it to method analyzePath (lines 17–50). The method creates a new File object (line 20) and assigns its reference to name. Line 22 invokes File method exists to determine whether the name input by the user exists (either as a file or as a directory) on the disk. If the name does not exist, control proceeds to lines 46–49 and displays a message to the screen containing the name the user typed, followed by "does not exist." Otherwise, the if statement (lines 22–45) executes. The program outputs the name of the file or directory (line 27), followed by the results of testing the File object with isFile (line 28), isDirectory (line 29) and isAbsolute (line 31). Next, the program displays the values returned by lastModified (line 33), length (line 33), getPath (line 34), getAbsolutePath (line 35) and getParent (line 35). If the File object represents a directory (line 37), the program obtains a list of the directory's contents as an array of Strings by using File method list (line 39) and displays the list on the screen.

The first output of this program demonstrates a File object associated with the jfc directory from the JDK. The second output demonstrates a File object associated with the README.txt file from the Java 2D example that comes with the JDK. In both cases, we specified an absolute path on our computer.

A **separator character** is used to separate directories and files in the path. On a Windows computer, the separator character is a backslash (\). On a UNIX system, it's a forward slash (/). Java processes both characters identically in a path name. For example, if we were to use the path

```
c:\Program Files\Java\jdk1.6.0_11\demo/jfc
```

which employs each separator character, Java would still process the path properly. When building Strings that represent path information, use File.separator to obtain the local computer's proper separator character rather than explicitly using / or \. This constant returns a String consisting of one character—the proper separator for the system.

Common Programming Error 17.1

Using \ as a directory separator rather than \\ in a string literal is a logic error. A single \ indicates that the \ followed by the next character represents an escape sequence. Use \\ to insert a \ in a string literal.

17.4 Sequential-Access Text Files

Next, we create and manipulate sequential-access files in which records are stored in order by the record-key field. We begin with text files, enabling the reader to quickly create and edit human-readable files. We discuss creating, writing data to, reading data from and updating sequential-access text files. We also include a credit-inquiry program that retrieves specific data from a file.

17.4.1 Creating a Sequential-Access Text File

Java imposes no structure on a file—notions such as records do not exist as part of the Java language. Therefore, you must structure files to meet the requirements of your applications. In the following example, we see how to impose a keyed record structure on a file.

The program in Figs. 17.4, 17.5 and 17.8 creates a simple sequential-access file that might be used in an accounts receivable system to keep track of the amounts owed to a company by its credit clients. For each client, the program obtains from the user an account number and the client's name and balance (i.e., the amount the client owes the company for goods and services received). Each client's data constitutes a "record" for that client. This application uses the account number as the record key—the file will be created and maintained in account-number order. The program assumes that the user enters the records in account-number order. In a comprehensive accounts receivable system (based on sequential-access files), a sorting capability would be provided so that the user could enter the records in any order. The records would then be sorted and written to the file.

Class *AccountRecord*

Class AccountRecord (Fig. 17.4) encapsulates the client record information used by the examples in this chapter. AccountRecord is declared in package com.deitel.ch17 (line 3), so that it can be imported into several of this chapter's examples for reuse. (Section 8.14 provides information on compiling and using your own packages.) Class AccountRecord contains private instance variables account, firstName, lastName and balance (lines 7–10) and *set* and *get* methods for accessing these fields. Though the *set* methods do not validate the data in this example, they should do so in an "industrial-strength" system.

```java
 1   // Fig. 17.4: AccountRecord.java
 2   // AccountRecord class maintains information for one account.
 3   package com.deitel.ch17; // packaged for reuse
 4
 5   public class AccountRecord
 6   {
 7      private int account;
 8      private String firstName;
 9      private String lastName;
10      private double balance;
11
12      // no-argument constructor calls other constructor with default values
13      public AccountRecord()
14      {
15         this( 0, "", "", 0.0 ); // call four-argument constructor
16      } // end no-argument AccountRecord constructor
17
18      // initialize a record
19      public AccountRecord( int acct, String first, String last, double bal )
20      {
21         setAccount( acct );
22         setFirstName( first );
23         setLastName( last );
24         setBalance( bal );
25      } // end four-argument AccountRecord constructor
26
27      // set account number
28      public void setAccount( int acct )
29      {
30         account = acct;
31      } // end method setAccount
32
33      // get account number
34      public int getAccount()
35      {
36         return account;
37      } // end method getAccount
38
39      // set first name
40      public void setFirstName( String first )
41      {
42         firstName = first;
43      } // end method setFirstName
44
45      // get first name
46      public String getFirstName()
47      {
48         return firstName;
49      } // end method getFirstName
50
51      // set last name
52      public void setLastName( String last )
53      {
```

Fig. 17.4 | AccountRecord class maintains information for one account. (Part 1 of 2.)

```
54            lastName = last;
55       } // end method setLastName
56
57       // get last name
58       public String getLastName()
59       {
60          return lastName;
61       } // end method getLastName
62
63       // set balance
64       public void setBalance( double bal )
65       {
66          balance = bal;
67       } // end method setBalance
68
69       // get balance
70       public double getBalance()
71       {
72          return balance;
73       } // end method getBalance
74    } // end class AccountRecord
```

Fig. 17.4 | AccountRecord class maintains information for one account. (Part 2 of 2.)

To compile class AccountRecord, open a command window, change directories to this chapter's fig17_05 directory (which contains AccountRecord.java), then type:

```
javac -d .. AccountRecord.java
```

This places AccountRecord.class in its package directory structure and places the package in the ch17 folder that contains all the examples for this chapter. When you compile class AccountRecord (or any other classes that will be reused in this chapter), you should place them in a common directory. When you compile or execute classes that use class AccountRecord (e.g., CreateTextFile in Fig. 17.5), you must specify the command-line argument -classpath to both javac and java, as in

```
javac -classpath .;c:\examples\ch17 CreateTextFile.java
java -classpath .;c:\examples\ch17 CreateTextFile
```

The current directory (specified with .) is included in the classpath to ensure that the compiler can locate other classes in the same directory as the class being compiled. The path separator used in the preceding commands must be appropriate for your platform—a semicolon (;) on Windows and a colon (:) on UNIX/Linux/Mac OS X. The preceding commands assume that the package containing AccountRecord is located at in the directory C:\examples\ch17 on a Windows computer.

Class CreateTextFile

Now let's examine class CreateTextFile (Fig. 17.5). Line 14 declares Formatter variable output. As discussed in Section 17.2, a Formatter object outputs formatted Strings, using the same formatting capabilities as method System.out.printf. A Formatter object can output to various locations, such as the screen or a file, as is done here. The Formatter object is instantiated in line 21 in method openFile (lines 17–34). The constructor used in line 21 takes one argument—a String containing the name of the file, including its path. If a path is not specified, as is the case here, the JVM assumes that the file is in the directory from which the program was executed. For text files, we use the .txt file extension. If the file does not exist, it will be created. If an existing file is opened, its contents are **truncated**—all the data in the file is discarded. At this point the file is open for writing, and the resulting Formatter object can be used to write data to the file.

```java
1   // Fig. 17.5: CreateTextFile.java
2   // Writing data to a sequential text file with class Formatter.
3   import java.io.FileNotFoundException;
4   import java.lang.SecurityException;
5   import java.util.Formatter;
6   import java.util.FormatterClosedException;
7   import java.util.NoSuchElementException;
8   import java.util.Scanner;
9
10  import com.deitel.ch17.AccountRecord;
11
12  public class CreateTextFile
13  {
14     private Formatter output; // object used to output text to file
15
16     // enable user to open file
17     public void openFile()
18     {
19        try
20        {
21           output = new Formatter( "clients.txt" ); // open the file
22        } // end try
23        catch ( SecurityException securityException )
24        {
25           System.err.println(
26              "You do not have write access to this file." );
27           System.exit( 1 ); // terminate the program
28        } // end catch
29        catch ( FileNotFoundException fileNotFoundException )
30        {
31           System.err.println( "Error opening or creating file." );
32           System.exit( 1 ); // terminate the program
33        } // end catch
34     } // end method openFile
35
36     // add records to file
37     public void addRecords()
38     {
39        // object to be written to file
40        AccountRecord record = new AccountRecord();
41
42        Scanner input = new Scanner( System.in );
43
```

Fig. 17.5 | Writing data to a sequential text file with class Formatter. (Part 1 of 3.)

```
44          System.out.printf( "%s\n%s\n%s\n%s\n\n",
45             "To terminate input, type the end-of-file indicator ",
46             "when you are prompted to enter input.",
47             "On UNIX/Linux/Mac OS X type <ctrl> d then press Enter",
48             "On Windows type <ctrl> z then press Enter" );
49
50          System.out.printf( "%s\n%s",
51             "Enter account number (> 0), first name, last name and balance.",
52             "? " );
53
54          while ( input.hasNext() ) // loop until end-of-file indicator
55          {
56             try // output values to file
57             {
58                // retrieve data to be output
59                record.setAccount( input.nextInt() ); // read account number
60                record.setFirstName( input.next() ); // read first name
61                record.setLastName( input.next() ); // read last name
62                record.setBalance( input.nextDouble() ); // read balance
63
64                if ( record.getAccount() > 0 )
65                {
66                   // write new record
67                   output.format( "%d %s %s %.2f\n", record.getAccount(),
68                      record.getFirstName(), record.getLastName(),
69                      record.getBalance() );
70                } // end if
71                else
72                {
73                   System.out.println(
74                      "Account number must be greater than 0." );
75                } // end else
76             } // end try
77             catch ( FormatterClosedException formatterClosedException )
78             {
79                System.err.println( "Error writing to file." );
80                return;
81             } // end catch
82             catch ( NoSuchElementException elementException )
83             {
84                System.err.println( "Invalid input. Please try again." );
85                input.nextLine(); // discard input so user can try again
86             } // end catch
87
88             System.out.printf( "%s %s\n%s", "Enter account number (>0),",
89                "first name, last name and balance.", "? " );
90          } // end while
91       } // end method addRecords
92
93       // close file
94       public void closeFile()
95       {
```

Fig. 17.5 | Writing data to a sequential text file with class Formatter. (Part 2 of 3.)

```
96              if ( output != null )
97                 output.close();
98           } // end method closeFile
99     } // end class CreateTextFile
```

Fig. 17.5 | Writing data to a sequential text file with class `Formatter`. (Part 3 of 3.)

Lines 23–28 handle the **SecurityException**, which occurs if the user does not have permission to write data to the file. Lines 29–33 handle the **FileNotFoundException**, which occurs if the file does not exist and a new file cannot be created. This exception may also occur if there's an error opening the file. In both exception handlers we call `static` method **System.exit** and pass the value 1. This method terminates the application. An argument of 0 to method `exit` indicates successful program termination. A nonzero value, such as 1 in this example, normally indicates that an error has occurred. This value is passed to the command window that executed the program. The argument is useful if the program is executed from a **batch file** on Windows systems or a **shell script** on UNIX/Linux/Mac OS X systems. Batch files and shell scripts offer a convenient way of executing several programs in sequence. When the first program ends, the next program begins execution. It's possible to use the argument to method `exit` in a batch file or shell script to determine whether other programs should execute. For more information on batch files or shell scripts, see your operating system's documentation.

Method `addRecords` (lines 37–91) prompts the user to enter the various fields for each record or to enter the end-of-file key sequence when data entry is complete. Figure 17.6 lists the key combinations for entering end-of-file for various computer systems.

Operating system	Key combination
UNIX/Linux/Mac OS X	*<Enter> <Ctrl> d*
Windows	*<Ctrl> z*

Fig. 17.6 | End-of-file key combinations.

Line 40 creates an `AccountRecord` object, which will be used to store the values of the current record entered by the user. Line 42 creates a `Scanner` object to read input from the user at the keyboard. Lines 44–48 and 50–52 prompt the user for input.

Line 54 uses `Scanner` method `hasNext` to determine whether the end-of-file key combination has been entered. The loop executes until `hasNext` encounters end-of-file.

Lines 59–62 read data from the user, storing the record information in the `AccountRecord` object. Each statement throws a **NoSuchElementException** (handled in lines 82–86) if the data is in the wrong format (e.g., a `String` when an `int` is expected) or if there's no more data to input. If the account number is greater than 0 (line 64), the record's information is written to `clients.txt` (lines 67–69) using method **format**, which can perform identical formatting to the `System.out.printf` method used extensively in earlier chapters. Method `format` outputs a formatted `String` to the output destination of the `Formatter` object—the file `clients.txt`. The format string `"%d %s %s %.2f\n"` indicates that the current record will be stored as an integer (the account number) followed by a String (the first name), another String (the last name) and a floating-point value (the balance). Each piece of information is separated from the next by a space, and the double value (the balance) is output with two digits to the right of the decimal point (as indicated by the .2 in %.2f). The data in the text file can be viewed with a text editor or retrieved later by a program designed to read the file (Section 17.4.2).

When lines 67–69 execute, if the Formatter object is closed, a **FormatterClosedException** will be thrown. This exception is handled in lines 77–81. [*Note:* You can also output data to a text file using class **java.io.PrintWriter**, which provides format and printf methods for outputting formatted data.]

Lines 94–98 declare method closeFile, which closes the Formatter and the underlying output file. Line 97 closes the object by simply calling method **close**. If method close is not called explicitly, the operating system normally will close the file when program execution terminates—this is an example of operating-system "housekeeping." However, you should always explicitly close a file when it's no longer needed.

Platform-Specific Line-Separator Characters

Lines 67–69 output a line of text followed by a newline (\n). If you use a text editor to open the clients.txt file produced, each record might not display on a separate line. For example, in Notepad (Microsoft Windows), users will see one continuous line of text. This occurs because different platforms use different line-separator characters. On UNIX/Linux/Mac OS X, the line separator is a newline (\n). On Windows, it's a combination of a carriage return and a line feed—represented as \r\n. You can use the **%n** format specifier in a format control string to output a platform-specific line separator, thus ensuring that the text file can be opened and viewed correctly in a text editor for the platform on which the file was created. The method System.out.println outputs a platform-specific line separator after its argument. Also, regardless of the line separator used in a text file, a Java program can still recognize the lines of text and read them.

Class *CreateTextFileTest*

Figure 17.7 runs the program. Line 8 creates a CreateTextFile object, which is then used to open, add records to and close the file (lines 10–12). The sample data for this application is shown in Fig. 17.8. In the sample execution for this program, the user enters information for five accounts, then enters end-of-file to signal that data entry is complete. The sample execution does not show how the data records actually appear in the file. In the next section, to verify that the file has been created successfully, we present a program that reads the file and prints its contents. Because this is a text file, you can also verify the information simply by opening the file in a text editor.

```
1   // Fig. 17.7: CreateTextFileTest.java
2   // Testing the CreateTextFile class.
3
4   public class CreateTextFileTest
5   {
6      public static void main( String[] args )
7      {
8         CreateTextFile application = new CreateTextFile();
```

Fig. 17.7 | Testing the CreateTextFile class. (Part 1 of 2.)

```
 9
10          application.openFile();
11          application.addRecords();
12          application.closeFile();
13      } // end main
14  } // end class CreateTextFileTest
```

```
To terminate input, type the end-of-file indicator
when you are prompted to enter input.
On UNIX/Linux/Mac OS X type <ctrl> d then press Enter
On Windows type <ctrl> z then press Enter

Enter account number (> 0), first name, last name and balance.
? 100 Bob Jones 24.98
Enter account number (> 0), first name, last name and balance.
? 200 Steve Doe -345.67
Enter account number (> 0), first name, last name and balance.
? 300 Pam White 0.00
Enter account number (> 0), first name, last name and balance.
? 400 Sam Stone -42.16
Enter account number (> 0), first name, last name and balance.
? 500 Sue Rich 224.62
Enter account number (> 0), first name, last name and balance.
? ^Z
```

Fig. 17.7 | Testing the `CreateTextFile` class. (Part 2 of 2.)

Sample data			
100	Bob	Jones	24.98
200	Steve	Doe	-345.67
300	Pam	White	0.00
400	Sam	Stone	-42.16
500	Sue	Rich	224.62

Fig. 17.8 | Sample data for the program in Figs. 17.5–17.7.

17.4.2 Reading Data from a Sequential-Access Text File

Data is stored in files so that it may be retrieved for processing when needed. Section 17.4.1 demonstrated how to create a file for sequential access. This section shows how to read data sequentially from a text file. We demonstrate how class Scanner can be used to input data from a file rather than the keyboard.

The application in Figs. 17.9 and 17.10 reads records from the file "clients.txt" created by the application of Section 17.4.1 and displays the record contents. Line 13 of Fig. 17.9 declares a Scanner that will be used to retrieve input from the file.

Method openFile (lines 16–27) opens the file for reading by instantiating a Scanner object in line 20. We pass a File object to the constructor, which specifies that the Scanner object will read from the file "clients.txt" located in the directory from which the application executes. If the file cannot be found, a FileNotFoundException occurs. The exception is handled in lines 22–26.

```
1   // Fig. 17.9: ReadTextFile.java
2   // This program reads a text file and displays each record.
3   import java.io.File;
4   import java.io.FileNotFoundException;
5   import java.lang.IllegalStateException;
6   import java.util.NoSuchElementException;
7   import java.util.Scanner;
8
9   import com.deitel.ch17.AccountRecord;
10
11  public class ReadTextFile
12  {
13     private Scanner input;
14
15     // enable user to open file
16     public void openFile()
17     {
18        try
19        {
20           input = new Scanner( new File( "clients.txt" ) );
21        } // end try
22        catch ( FileNotFoundException fileNotFoundException )
23        {
24           System.err.println( "Error opening file." );
25           System.exit( 1 );
26        } // end catch
27     } // end method openFile
28
29     // read record from file
30     public void readRecords()
31     {
32        // object to be written to screen
33        AccountRecord record = new AccountRecord();
34
35        System.out.printf( "%-10s%-12s%-12s%10s\n", "Account",
36           "First Name", "Last Name", "Balance" );
37
38        try // read records from file using Scanner object
39        {
40           while ( input.hasNext() )
41           {
42              record.setAccount( input.nextInt() ); // read account number
43              record.setFirstName( input.next() ); // read first name
44              record.setLastName( input.next() ); // read last name
45              record.setBalance( input.nextDouble() ); // read balance
46
47              // display record contents
48              System.out.printf( "%-10d%-12s%-12s%10.2f\n",
49                 record.getAccount(), record.getFirstName(),
50                 record.getLastName(), record.getBalance() );
51           } // end while
52        } // end try
```

Fig. 17.9 | Sequential file reading using a Scanner. (Part 1 of 2.)

```
53              catch ( NoSuchElementException elementException )
54              {
55                 System.err.println( "File improperly formed." );
56                 input.close();
57                 System.exit( 1 );
58              } // end catch
59              catch ( IllegalStateException stateException )
60              {
61                 System.err.println( "Error reading from file." );
62                 System.exit( 1 );
63              } // end catch
64           } // end method readRecords
65
66           // close file and terminate application
67           public void closeFile()
68           {
69              if ( input != null )
70                 input.close(); // close file
71           } // end method closeFile
72        } // end class ReadTextFile
```

Fig. 17.9 | Sequential file reading using a Scanner. (Part 2 of 2.)

```
1     // Fig. 17.10: ReadTextFileTest.java
2     // Testing the ReadTextFile class.
3
4     public class ReadTextFileTest
5     {
6        public static void main( String[] args )
7        {
8           ReadTextFile application = new ReadTextFile();
9
10          application.openFile();
11          application.readRecords();
12          application.closeFile();
13       } // end main
14    } // end class ReadTextFileTest
```

```
Account   First Name  Last Name    Balance
100       Bob         Jones          24.98
200       Steve       Doe          -345.67
300       Pam         White           0.00
400       Sam         Stone         -42.16
500       Sue         Rich          224.62
```

Fig. 17.10 | Testing the ReadTextFile class.

Method readRecords (lines 30–64) reads and displays records from the file. Line 33 creates AccountRecord object record to store the current record's information. Lines 35–36 display headers for the columns in the application's output. Lines 40–51 read data from the file until the end-of-file marker is reached (in which case, method hasNext will return false at line 40). Lines 42–45 use Scanner methods nextInt, next and nextDouble to input an int (the account number), two Strings (the first and last names) and a double value (the balance). Each record is one line of data in the file. The values are stored in object record. If the information in the file is not properly formed (e.g., there's a last name where there should be a balance), a NoSuchElementException occurs when the record is input. This exception is handled in lines 53–58. If the Scanner was closed before the data was input, an **IllegalStateException** occurs (handled in lines 59–63). If no exceptions occur, the record's information is displayed on the screen (lines 48–50). Note in the format string in line 48 that the account number, first name and last name are left justified, while the balance is right justified and output with two digits of precision. Each iteration of the loop inputs one line of text from the text file, which represents one record.

Lines 67–71 define method closeFile, which closes the Scanner. Method main is defined in Fig. 17.10 in lines 6–13. Line 8 creates a ReadTextFile object, which is then used to open, add records to and close the file (lines 10–12).

17.4.3 Case Study: A Credit-Inquiry Program

To retrieve data sequentially from a file, programs start from the beginning of the file and read all the data consecutively until the desired information is found. It might be necessary to process the file sequentially several times (from the beginning of the file) during the execution of a program. Class Scanner does *not* allow repositioning to the beginning of the file. If it's necessary to read the file again, the program must close the file and reopen it.

The program in Figs. 17.11–17.13 allows a credit manager to obtain lists of customers with zero balances (i.e., customers who do not owe any money), customers with credit balances (i.e., customers to whom the company owes money) and customers with debit balances (i.e., customers who owe the company money for goods and services received). A credit balance is a negative amount, a debit balance a positive amount.

MenuOption Enumeration

We begin by creating an enum type (Fig. 17.11) to define the different menu options the user will have. The options and their values are listed in lines 7–10. Method getValue (lines 19–22) retrieves the value of a specific enum constant.

```
1   // Fig. 17.11: MenuOption.java
2   // Enumeration for the credit-inquiry program's options.
3
4   public enum MenuOption
5   {
6      // declare contents of enum type
7      ZERO_BALANCE( 1 ),
8      CREDIT_BALANCE( 2 ),
9      DEBIT_BALANCE( 3 ),
10     END( 4 );
11
12     private final int value; // current menu option
13
14     // constructor
15     MenuOption( int valueOption )
16     {
```

Fig. 17.11 | Enumeration for the credit-inquiry program's menu options. (Part 1 of 2.)

```
17            value = valueOption;
18        } // end MenuOptions enum constructor
19
20        // return the value of a constant
21        public int getValue()
22        {
23            return value;
24        } // end method getValue
25    } // end enum MenuOption
```

Fig. 17.11 | Enumeration for the credit-inquiry program's menu options. (Part 2 of 2.)

CreditInquiry Class

Figure 17.12 contains the functionality for the credit-inquiry program, and Fig. 17.13 contains the main method that executes the program. The program displays a text menu and allows the credit manager to enter one of three options to obtain credit information. Option 1 (ZERO_BALANCE) displays accounts with zero balances. Option 2 (CREDIT_BAL-ANCE) displays accounts with credit balances. Option 3 (DEBIT_BALANCE) displays accounts with debit balances. Option 4 (END) terminates program execution.

```
 1    // Fig. 17.12: CreditInquiry.java
 2    // This program reads a file sequentially and displays the
 3    // contents based on the type of account the user requests
 4    // (credit balance, debit balance or zero balance).
 5    import java.io.File;
 6    import java.io.FileNotFoundException;
 7    import java.lang.IllegalStateException;
 8    import java.util.NoSuchElementException;
 9    import java.util.Scanner;
10
11    import com.deitel.ch17.AccountRecord;
12
13    public class CreditInquiry
14    {
15        private MenuOption accountType;
16        private Scanner input;
17        private final static MenuOption[] choices = { MenuOption.ZERO_BALANCE,
18            MenuOption.CREDIT_BALANCE, MenuOption.DEBIT_BALANCE,
19            MenuOption.END };
20
21        // read records from file and display only records of appropriate type
22        private void readRecords()
23        {
24            // object to store data that will be written to file
25            AccountRecord record = new AccountRecord();
26
27            try // read records
28            {
29                // open file to read from beginning
30                input = new Scanner( new File( "clients.txt" ) );
```

Fig. 17.12 | Credit-inquiry program. (Part 1 of 4.)

```
31
32              while ( input.hasNext() ) // input the values from the file
33              {
34                 record.setAccount( input.nextInt() ); // read account number
35                 record.setFirstName( input.next() ); // read first name
36                 record.setLastName( input.next() ); // read last name
37                 record.setBalance( input.nextDouble() ); // read balance
38
39                 // if proper acount type, display record
40                 if ( shouldDisplay( record.getBalance() ) )
41                    System.out.printf( "%-10d%-12s%-12s%10.2f\n",
42                       record.getAccount(), record.getFirstName(),
43                       record.getLastName(), record.getBalance() );
44              } // end while
45           } // end try
46           catch ( NoSuchElementException elementException )
47           {
48              System.err.println( "File improperly formed." );
49              input.close();
50              System.exit( 1 );
51           } // end catch
52           catch ( IllegalStateException stateException )
53           {
54              System.err.println( "Error reading from file." );
55              System.exit( 1 );
56           } // end catch
57           catch ( FileNotFoundException fileNotFoundException )
58           {
59              System.err.println( "File cannot be found." );
60              System.exit( 1 );
61           } // end catch
62           finally
63           {
64              if ( input != null )
65                 input.close(); // close the Scanner and the file
66           } // end finally
67        } // end method readRecords
68
69        // use record type to determine if record should be displayed
70        private boolean shouldDisplay( double balance )
71        {
72           if ( ( accountType == MenuOption.CREDIT_BALANCE )
73              && ( balance < 0 ) )
74              return true;
75
76           else if ( ( accountType == MenuOption.DEBIT_BALANCE )
77              && ( balance > 0 ) )
78              return true;
79
80           else if ( ( accountType == MenuOption.ZERO_BALANCE )
81              && ( balance == 0 ) )
82              return true;
83
```

Fig. 17.12 | Credit-inquiry program. (Part 2 of 4.)

```
 84          return false;
 85       } // end method shouldDisplay
 86
 87       // obtain request from user
 88       private MenuOption getRequest()
 89       {
 90          Scanner textIn = new Scanner( System.in );
 91          int request = 1;
 92
 93          // display request options
 94          System.out.printf( "\n%s\n%s\n%s\n%s\n%s\n",
 95             "Enter request", " 1 - List accounts with zero balances",
 96             " 2 - List accounts with credit balances",
 97             " 3 - List accounts with debit balances", " 4 - End of run" );
 98
 99          try // attempt to input menu choice
100          {
101             do // input user request
102             {
103                System.out.print( "\n? " );
104                request = textIn.nextInt();
105             } while ( ( request < 1 ) || ( request > 4 ) );
106          } // end try
107          catch ( NoSuchElementException elementException )
108          {
109             System.err.println( "Invalid input." );
110             System.exit( 1 );
111          } // end catch
112
113          return choices[ request - 1 ]; // return enum value for option
114       } // end method getRequest
115
116       public void processRequests()
117       {
118          // get user's request (e.g., zero, credit or debit balance)
119          accountType = getRequest();
120
121          while ( accountType != MenuOption.END )
122          {
123             switch ( accountType )
124             {
125                case ZERO_BALANCE:
126                   System.out.println( "\nAccounts with zero balances:\n" );
127                   break;
128                case CREDIT_BALANCE:
129                   System.out.println( "\nAccounts with credit balances:\n" );
130                   break;
131                case DEBIT_BALANCE:
132                   System.out.println( "\nAccounts with debit balances:\n" );
133                   break;
134             } // end switch
135
136             readRecords();
```

Fig. 17.12 | Credit-inquiry program. (Part 3 of 4.)

```
137              accountType = getRequest();
138         } // end while
139      } // end method processRequests
140  } // end class CreditInquiry
```

Fig. 17.12 | Credit-inquiry program. (Part 4 of 4.)

```
1   // Fig. 17.13: CreditInquiryTest.java
2   // This program tests class CreditInquiry.
3
4   public class CreditInquiryTest
5   {
6      public static void main( String[] args )
7      {
8         CreditInquiry application = new CreditInquiry();
9         application.processRequests();
10      } // end main
11   } // end class CreditInquiryTest
```

Fig. 17.13 | Testing the CreditInquiry class.

```
Enter request
 1 - List accounts with zero balances
 2 - List accounts with credit balances
 3 - List accounts with debit balances
 4 - End of run

? 1

Accounts with zero balances:
300      Pam         White           0.00

Enter request
 1 - List accounts with zero balances
 2 - List accounts with credit balances
 3 - List accounts with debit balances
 4 - End of run

? 2

Accounts with credit balances:
200      Steve       Doe          -345.67
400      Sam         Stone         -42.16

Enter request
 1 - List accounts with zero balances
 2 - List accounts with credit balances
 3 - List accounts with debit balances
 4 - End of run

? 3
```

Fig. 17.14 | Sample output of the credit-inquiry program in Fig. 17.13. (Part 1 of 2.)

```
Accounts with debit balances:
100        Bob         Jones           24.98
500        Sue         Rich           224.62

? 4
```

Fig. 17.14 | Sample output of the credit-inquiry program in Fig. 17.13. (Part 2 of 2.)

The record information is collected by reading through the file and determining if each record satisfies the criteria for the selected account type. Method processRequests (lines 116–139 of Fig. 17.12) calls method getRequest to display the menu options (line 119), translates the number typed by the user into a MenuOption and stores the result in MenuOption variable accountType. Lines 121–138 loop until the user specifies that the program should terminate. Lines 123–134 display a header for the current set of records to be output to the screen. Line 136 calls method readRecords (lines 22–67), which loops through the file and reads every record.

Line 30 of method readRecords opens the file for reading with a Scanner. The file will be opened for reading with a new Scanner object each time this method is called, so that we can again read from the beginning of the file. Lines 34–37 read a record. Line 40 calls method shouldDisplay (lines 70–85) to determine whether the current record satisfies the account type requested. If shouldDisplay returns true, the program displays the account information. When the end-of-file marker is reached, the loop terminates and line 65 calls the Scanner's close method to close the Scanner and the file. Notice that this occurs in a finally block, which will execute whether or not the file was successfully read. Once all the records have been read, control returns to method processRequests and getRequest is again called (line 137) to retrieve the user's next menu option. Figure 17.13 contains method main, and calls method processRequests in line 9.

17.4.4 Updating Sequential-Access Files

The data in many sequential files cannot be modified without the risk of destroying other data in the file. For example, if the name "White" needs to be changed to "Worthington," the old name cannot simply be overwritten, because the new name requires more space. The record for White was written to the file as

```
300 Pam White 0.00
```

If the record is rewritten beginning at the same location in the file using the new name, the record will be

```
300 Pam Worthington 0.00
```

The new record is larger (has more characters) than the original record. The characters beyond the second "o" in "Worthington" will overwrite the beginning of the next sequential record in the file. The problem here is that fields in a text file—and hence records—can vary in size. For example, 7, 14, –117, 2074 and 27383 are all ints stored in the same number of bytes (4) internally, but they're different-sized fields when displayed on the screen or written to a file as text. Therefore, records in a sequential-access file are not usually updated in place. Instead, the entire file is usually rewritten. To make the preceding name change, the records before 300 Pam White 0.00 would be copied to a new file, the new record (which can be of a different size than the one it replaces) would be written and the records after 300 Pam White 0.00 would be copied to the new file. Rewriting the entire file is uneconomical to update just one record, but reasonable if a substantial number of records need to be updated.

17.5 Object Serialization

In Section 17.4, we demonstrated how to write the individual fields of an AccountRecord object into a file as text, and how to read those fields from a file and place their values into an AccountRecord object in memory. In the examples, AccountRecord was used to aggregate the information for one record. When the instance variables for an AccountRecord were output to a disk file, certain information was lost, such as the type of each value. For instance, if the value "3" is read from a file, there's no way to tell whether it came from an int, a String or a double. We have only data, not type information, on a disk. If the program that's going to read this data "knows" what object type the data corresponds to, then the data is simply read into objects of that type. For example, in Section 17.4.2, we know that we're inputting an int (the account number), followed by two Strings (the first and last name) and a double (the balance). We also know that these values are separated by spaces, with only one record on each line. Sometimes we'll not know exactly how the data is stored in a file. In such cases, we want to read or write an entire object from a file. Java provides such a mechanism, called **object serialization**. A so-called **serialized object** is an object represented as a sequence of bytes that includes the object's data as well as information about the object's type and the types of data stored in the object. After a serialized object has been written into a file, it can be read from the file and **deserialized**—that is, the type information and bytes that represent the object and its data can be used to recreate the object in memory.

Software Engineering Observation 17.1

The serialization mechanism makes exact copies of objects. This makes it a simple way to clone objects without having to override Object method clone.

Classes *ObjectInputStream and ObjectOutputStream*

Classes ObjectInputStream and ObjectOutputStream, which respectively implement the **ObjectInput** and **ObjectOutput** interfaces, enable entire objects to be read from or written to a stream (possibly a file). To use serialization with files, we initialize ObjectInputStream and ObjectOutputStream objects with stream objects that read from and write to files—objects of classes FileInputStream and FileOutputStream, respectively. Initializing stream objects with other stream objects in this manner is sometimes called **wrapping**—the new stream object being created wraps the stream object specified as a constructor argument. To wrap a FileInputStream in an ObjectInputStream, for instance, we pass the FileInputStream object to the ObjectInputStream's constructor.

Interfaces *ObjectOutput and ObjectInput*

The ObjectOutput interface contains method **writeObject**, which takes an Object as an argument and writes its information to an OutputStream. A class that implements interface ObjectOutput (such as ObjectOutputStream) declares this method and ensures that the object being output implements interface Serializable (discussed shortly). Correspondingly, the ObjectInput interface contains method **readObject**, which reads and returns a reference to an Object from an InputStream. After an object has been read, its reference can be cast to the object's actual type. As you'll see in Chapter 24, applications that communicate via a network, such as the Internet, can also transmit entire objects across the network.

17.5.1 Creating a Sequential-Access File Using Object Serialization

This section and Section 17.5.2 create and manipulate sequential-access files using object serialization. The object serialization we show here is performed with byte-based streams, so the sequential files created and manipulated will be binary files. Recall that binary files typically cannot be viewed in standard text editors. For this reason, we write a separate application that knows how to read and display serialized objects. We begin by creating and writing serialized objects to a sequential-access file. The example is similar to the one in Section 17.4, so we focus only on the new features.

Defining Class AccountRecordSerializable
Let's begin by modifying our AccountRecord class so that objects of this class can be serialized. Class AccountRecordSerializable (Fig. 17.15) implements interface **Serializable** (line 7), which allows objects of AccountRecordSerializable to be serialized and deserialized with ObjectOutputStreams and ObjectInputStreams, respectively. Interface Serializable is a **tagging interface**. Such an interface does not contain methods. A class that implements Serializable is tagged as being a Serializable object. This is important, because an ObjectOutputStream will *not* output an object unless it *is a* Serializable object, which is the case for any object of a class that implements Serializable.

```
1   // Fig. 17.15: AccountRecordSerializable.java
2   // AccountRecordSerializable class for serializable objects.
3   package com.deitel.ch17; // packaged for reuse
4
5   import java.io.Serializable;
6
7   public class AccountRecordSerializable implements Serializable
8   {
9      private int account;
10     private String firstName;
11     private String lastName;
12     private double balance;
13
14     // no-argument constructor calls other constructor with default values
15     public AccountRecordSerializable()
16     {
17        this( 0, "", "", 0.0 );
18     } // end no-argument AccountRecordSerializable constructor
19
```

Fig. 17.15 | AccountRecordSerializable class for serializable objects. (Part 1 of 3.)

```
20      // four-argument constructor initializes a record
21      public AccountRecordSerializable(
22         int acct, String first, String last, double bal )
23      {
24         setAccount( acct );
25         setFirstName( first );
26         setLastName( last );
27         setBalance( bal );
28      } // end four-argument AccountRecordSerializable constructor
29
30      // set account number
31      public void setAccount( int acct )
32      {
33         account = acct;
34      } // end method setAccount
35
36      // get account number
37      public int getAccount()
38      {
39         return account;
40      } // end method getAccount
41
42      // set first name
43      public void setFirstName( String first )
44      {
45         firstName = first;
46      } // end method setFirstName
47
48      // get first name
49      public String getFirstName()
50      {
51         return firstName;
52      } // end method getFirstName
53
54      // set last name
55      public void setLastName( String last )
56      {
57         lastName = last;
58      } // end method setLastName
59
60      // get last name
61      public String getLastName()
62      {
63         return lastName;
64      } // end method getLastName
65
66      // set balance
67      public void setBalance( double bal )
68      {
69         balance = bal;
70      } // end method setBalance
71
```

Fig. 17.15 | AccountRecordSerializable class for serializable objects. (Part 2 of 3.)

```
72      // get balance
73      public double getBalance()
74      {
75         return balance;
76      } // end method getBalance
77   } // end class AccountRecordSerializable
```

Fig. 17.15 | AccountRecordSerializable class for serializable objects. (Part 3 of 3.)

In a Serializable class, every instance variable must be Serializable. Non-Serializable instance variables must be declared **transient** to indicate that they should be ignored during the serialization process. *By default, all primitive-type variables are serializable.* For reference-type variables, you must check the class's documentation (and possibly its superclasses) to ensure that the type is Serializable. For example, Strings are Serializable. By default, arrays are serializable; however, in a reference-type array, the referenced objects might not be. Class AccountRecordSerializable contains private data members account, firstName, lastName and balance—all of which are Serializable. This class also provides public *get* and *set* methods for accessing the private fields.

Writing Serialized Objects to a Sequential-Access File

Now let's discuss the code that creates the sequential-access file (Figs. 17.16–17.17). We concentrate only on new concepts here. As stated in Section 17.2, a program can open a file by creating an object of stream class FileInputStream or FileOutputStream. In this example, the file is to be opened for output, so the program creates a FileOutputStream (line 21 of Fig. 17.16). The String argument that's passed to the FileOutputStream's constructor represents the name and path of the file to be opened. Existing files that are opened for output in this manner are truncated. We chose the .ser file extension for binary files that contain serialized objects, but this is not required.

Common Programming Error 17.2

It's a logic error to open an existing file for output when, in fact, you wish to preserve the file. Class FileOutputStream provides an overloaded constructor that enables you to open a file and append data to the end of the file. This will preserve the file's contents.

```
1   // Fig. 17.16: CreateSequentialFile.java
2   // Writing objects sequentially to a file with class ObjectOutputStream.
3   import java.io.FileOutputStream;
4   import java.io.IOException;
5   import java.io.ObjectOutputStream;
6   import java.util.NoSuchElementException;
7   import java.util.Scanner;
8
9   import com.deitel.ch17.AccountRecordSerializable;
10
11  public class CreateSequentialFile
12  {
13     private ObjectOutputStream output; // outputs data to file
```

Fig. 17.16 | Sequential file created using ObjectOutputStream. (Part 1 of 3.)

```
14
15      // allow user to specify file name
16      public void openFile()
17      {
18         try // open file
19         {
20            output = new ObjectOutputStream(
21               new FileOutputStream( "clients.ser" ) );
22         } // end try
23         catch ( IOException ioException )
24         {
25            System.err.println( "Error opening file." );
26         } // end catch
27      } // end method openFile
28
29      // add records to file
30      public void addRecords()
31      {
32         AccountRecordSerializable record; // object to be written to file
33         int accountNumber = 0; // account number for record object
34         String firstName; // first name for record object
35         String lastName; // last name for record object
36         double balance; // balance for record object
37
38         Scanner input = new Scanner( System.in );
39
40         System.out.printf( "%s\n%s\n%s\n%s\n\n",
41            "To terminate input, type the end-of-file indicator ",
42            "when you are prompted to enter input.",
43            "On UNIX/Linux/Mac OS X type <ctrl> d then press Enter",
44            "On Windows type <ctrl> z then press Enter" );
45
46         System.out.printf( "%s\n%s",
47            "Enter account number (> 0), first name, last name and balance.",
48            "? " );
49
50         while ( input.hasNext() ) // loop until end-of-file indicator
51         {
52            try // output values to file
53            {
54               accountNumber = input.nextInt(); // read account number
55               firstName = input.next(); // read first name
56               lastName = input.next(); // read last name
57               balance = input.nextDouble(); // read balance
58
59               if ( accountNumber > 0 )
60               {
61                  // create new record
62                  record = new AccountRecordSerializable( accountNumber,
63                     firstName, lastName, balance );
64                  output.writeObject( record ); // output record
65               } // end if
```

Fig. 17.16 | Sequential file created using `ObjectOutputStream`. (Part 2 of 3.)

```
66              else
67              {
68                 System.out.println(
69                    "Account number must be greater than 0." );
70              } // end else
71           } // end try
72           catch ( IOException ioException )
73           {
74              System.err.println( "Error writing to file." );
75              return;
76           } // end catch
77           catch ( NoSuchElementException elementException )
78           {
79              System.err.println( "Invalid input. Please try again." );
80              input.nextLine(); // discard input so user can try again
81           } // end catch
82
83           System.out.printf( "%s %s\n%s", "Enter account number (>0),",
84              "first name, last name and balance.", "? " );
85        } // end while
86     } // end method addRecords
87
88     // close file and terminate application
89     public void closeFile()
90     {
91        try // close file
92        {
93           if ( output != null )
94              output.close();
95        } // end try
96        catch ( IOException ioException )
97        {
98           System.err.println( "Error closing file." );
99           System.exit( 1 );
100        } // end catch
101     } // end method closeFile
102 } // end class CreateSequentialFile
```

Fig. 17.16 | Sequential file created using ObjectOutputStream. (Part 3 of 3.)

```
1  // Fig. 17.17: CreateSequentialFileTest.java
2  // Testing class CreateSequentialFile.
3
4  public class CreateSequentialFileTest
5  {
6     public static void main( String[] args )
7     {
8        CreateSequentialFile application = new CreateSequentialFile();
9
10        application.openFile();
11        application.addRecords();
```

Fig. 17.17 | Testing class CreateSequentialFile. (Part 1 of 2.)

```
12          application.closeFile();
13      } // end main
14  } // end class CreateSequentialFileTest
```

```
To terminate input, type the end-of-file indicator
when you are prompted to enter input.
On UNIX/Linux/Mac OS X type <ctrl> d then press Enter
On Windows type <ctrl> z then press Enter

Enter account number (> 0), first name, last name and balance.
? 100 Bob Jones 24.98
Enter account number (> 0), first name, last name and balance.
? 200 Steve Doe -345.67
Enter account number (> 0), first name, last name and balance.
? 300 Pam White 0.00
Enter account number (> 0), first name, last name and balance.
? 400 Sam Stone -42.16
Enter account number (> 0), first name, last name and balance.
? 500 Sue Rich 224.62
Enter account number (> 0), first name, last name and balance.
? ^Z
```

Fig. 17.17 | Testing class CreateSequentialFile. (Part 2 of 2.)

Class FileOutputStream provides methods for writing byte arrays and individual bytes to a file, but we wish to write objects to a file. For this reason, we wrap a FileOutputStream in an ObjectOutputStream by passing the new FileOutputStream object to the ObjectOutputStream's constructor (lines 20–21). The ObjectOutputStream object uses the FileOutputStream object to write objects into the file. Lines 20–21 may throw an **IOException** if a problem occurs while opening the file (e.g., when a file is opened for writing on a drive with insufficient space or when a read-only file is opened for writing). If so, the program displays an error message (lines 23–26). If no exception occurs, the file is open, and variable output can be used to write objects to it.

This program assumes that data is input correctly and in the proper record-number order. Method addRecords (lines 30–86) performs the write operation. Lines 62–63 create an AccountRecordSerializable object from the data entered by the user. Line 64 calls ObjectOutputStream method writeObject to write the record object to the output file. Only one statement is required to write the entire object.

Method closeFile (lines 89–101) calls ObjectOutputStream method **close** on output to close both the ObjectOutputStream and its underlying FileOutputStream (line 94). The call to method close is contained in a try block. Method close throws an IOException if the file cannot be closed properly. In this case, it's important to notify the user that the information in the file might be corrupted. When using wrapped streams, closing the outermost stream also closes the underlying file.

In the sample execution for the program in Fig. 17.17, we entered information for five accounts—the same information shown in Fig. 17.8. The program does not show how the data records actually appear in the file. Remember that now we're using binary files, which are not humanly readable. To verify that the file has been created successfully, the next section presents a program to read the file's contents.

17.5.2 Reading and Deserializing Data from a Sequential-Access File

The preceding section showed how to create a file for sequential access using object serialization. In this section, we discuss how to read serialized data sequentially from a file.

The program in Figs. 17.18–17.19 reads records from a file created by the program in Section 17.5.1 and displays the contents. The program opens the file for input by creating a FileInputStream object (line 21). The name of the file to open is specified as an argument to the FileInputStream constructor. In Fig. 17.16, we wrote objects to the file, using an ObjectOutputStream object. Data must be read from the file in the same format in which it was written. Therefore, we use an ObjectInputStream wrapped around a FileInputStream in this program (lines 20–21). If no exceptions occur when opening the file, variable input can be used to read objects from the file.

```java
1   // Fig. 17.18: ReadSequentialFile.java
2   // Reading a file of objects sequentially with ObjectInputStream
3   // and displaying each record.
4   import java.io.EOFException;
5   import java.io.FileInputStream;
6   import java.io.IOException;
7   import java.io.ObjectInputStream;
8
9   import com.deitel.ch17.AccountRecordSerializable;
10
11  public class ReadSequentialFile
12  {
13     private ObjectInputStream input;
14
15     // enable user to select file to open
16     public void openFile()
17     {
18        try // open file
19        {
20           input = new ObjectInputStream(
21              new FileInputStream( "clients.ser" ) );
22        } // end try
23        catch ( IOException ioException )
24        {
25           System.err.println( "Error opening file." );
26        } // end catch
27     } // end method openFile
28
29     // read record from file
30     public void readRecords()
31     {
32        AccountRecordSerializable record;
33        System.out.printf( "%-10s%-12s%-12s%10s\n", "Account",
34           "First Name", "Last Name", "Balance" );
35
36        try // input the values from the file
37        {
```

Fig. 17.18 | Reading a file of objects sequentially with ObjectInputStream and displaying each record. (Part 1 of 2.)

```
38              while ( true )
39              {
40                 record = ( AccountRecordSerializable ) input.readObject();
41
42                 // display record contents
43                 System.out.printf( "%-10d%-12s%-12s%10.2f\n",
44                    record.getAccount(), record.getFirstName(),
45                    record.getLastName(), record.getBalance() );
46              } // end while
47           } // end try
48           catch ( EOFException endOfFileException )
49           {
50              return; // end of file was reached
51           } // end catch
52           catch ( ClassNotFoundException classNotFoundException )
53           {
54              System.err.println( "Unable to create object." );
55           } // end catch
56           catch ( IOException ioException )
57           {
58              System.err.println( "Error during read from file." );
59           } // end catch
60        } // end method readRecords
61
62        // close file and terminate application
63        public void closeFile()
64        {
65           try // close file and exit
66           {
67              if ( input != null )
68                 input.close();
69           } // end try
70           catch ( IOException ioException )
71           {
72              System.err.println( "Error closing file." );
73              System.exit( 1 );
74           } // end catch
75        } // end method closeFile
76  } // end class ReadSequentialFile
```

Fig. 17.18 | Reading a file of objects sequentially with `ObjectInputStream` and displaying each record. (Part 2 of 2.)

The program reads records from the file in method readRecords (lines 30–60). Line 40 calls ObjectInputStream method readObject to read an Object from the file. To use AccountRecordSerializable-specific methods, we downcast the returned Object to type AccountRecordSerializable. Method readObject throws an **EOFException** (processed at lines 48–51) if an attempt is made to read beyond the end of the file. Method readObject throws a ClassNotFoundException if the class for the object being read cannot be located. This may occur if the file is accessed on a computer that does not have the class. Figure 17.19 contains method main (lines 6–13), which opens the file, calls method readRecords and closes the file.

```
 1    // Fig. 17.19: ReadSequentialFileTest.java
 2    // Testing class ReadSequentialFile.
 3
 4    public class ReadSequentialFileTest
 5    {
 6       public static void main( String[] args )
 7       {
 8          ReadSequentialFile application = new ReadSequentialFile();
 9
10          application.openFile();
11          application.readRecords();
12          application.closeFile();
13       } // end main
14    } // end class ReadSequentialFileTest
```

Account	First Name	Last Name	Balance
100	Bob	Jones	24.98
200	Steve	Doe	-345.67
300	Pam	White	0.00
400	Sam	Stone	-42.16
500	Sue	Rich	224.62

Fig. 17.19 | Testing class ReadSequentialFile.

17.6 Additional java.io Classes

This section overviews additional interfaces and classes (from package java.io) for byte-based input and output streams and character-based input and output streams.

17.6.1 Interfaces and Classes for Byte-Based Input and Output

InputStream and OutputStream are abstract classes that declare methods for performing byte-based input and output, respectively. We used various concrete subclasses FileInputStream InputStream and OutputStream to manipulate files in this chapter.

Pipe Streams

Pipes are synchronized communication channels between threads. We discuss threads in Chapter 23. Java provides **PipedOutputStream** (a subclass of OutputStream) and **PipedInputStream** (a subclass of InputStream) to establish pipes between two threads in a program. One thread sends data to another by writing to a PipedOutputStream. The target thread reads information from the pipe via a PipedInputStream.

Filter Streams

A **FilterInputStream** filters an InputStream, and a FilterOutputStream filters an OutputStream. **Filtering** means simply that the filter stream provides additional functionality, such as aggregating data bytes into meaningful primitive-type units. FilterInputStream and FilterOutputStream are typically extended, so some of their filtering capabilities are provided by their subclasses.

A **PrintStream** (a subclass of FilterOutputStream) performs text output to the specified stream. Actually, we've been using PrintStream output throughout the text to this point—System.out and System.err are PrintStream objects.

Data Streams

Reading data as raw bytes is fast, but crude. Usually, programs read data as aggregates of bytes that form ints, floats, doubles and so on. Java programs can use several classes to input and output data in aggregate form.

Interface DataInput describes methods for reading primitive types from an input stream. Classes **DataInputStream** and RandomAccessFile each implement this interface to read sets of bytes and view them as primitive-type values. Interface DataInput includes methods such as readBoolean, readByte, readChar, readDouble, readFloat, readFully (for byte arrays), readInt, readLong, readShort, readUnsignedByte, readUnsigned-Short, readUTF (for reading Unicode characters encoded by Java.

Interface DataOutput describes a set of methods for writing primitive types to an output stream. Classes **DataOutputStream** (a subclass of FilterOutputStream) and RandomAccessFile each implement this interface to write primitive-type values as bytes. Interface DataOutput includes overloaded versions of method write (for a byte or for a byte array) and methods writeBoolean, writeByte, writeBytes, writeChar, writeChars (for Unicode Strings), writeDouble, writeFloat, writeInt, writeLong, writeShort and writeUTF (to output text modified for Unicode).

Buffered Streams

Buffering is an I/O-performance-enhancement technique. With a **BufferedOutputStream** (a subclass of class FilterOutputStream), each output statement does *not* necessarily result in an actual physical transfer of data to the output device (which is a slow operation compared to processor and main memory speeds). Rather, each output operation is directed to a region in memory called a **buffer** that's large enough to hold the data of many output operations. Then, actual transfer to the output device is performed in one large **physical output operation** each time the buffer fills. The output operations directed to the output buffer in memory are often called **logical output operations**. With a BufferedOutputStream, a partially filled buffer can be forced out to the device at any time by invoking the stream object's **flush** method.

Using buffering can greatly increase the performance of an application. Typical I/O operations are extremely slow compared with the speed of accessing data in computer memory. Buffering reduces the number of I/O operations by first combining smaller outputs together in memory. The number of actual physical I/O operations is small compared with the number of I/O requests issued by the program. Thus, the program that's using buffering is more efficient.

Performance Tip 17.1

Buffered I/O can yield significant performance improvements over unbuffered I/O.

With a **BufferedInputStream** (a subclass of class FilterInputStream), many "logical" chunks of data from a file are read as one large **physical input operation** into a memory buffer. As a program requests each new chunk of data, it's taken from the buffer. (This procedure is sometimes referred to as a **logical input operation**.) When the buffer is empty, the next actual physical input operation from the input device is performed to read in the next group of "logical" chunks of data. Thus, the number of actual physical input operations is small compared with the number of read requests issued by the program.

Memory-Based *byte* Array Steams

Java stream I/O includes capabilities for inputting from byte arrays in memory and outputting to byte arrays in memory. A ByteArrayInputStream (a subclass of InputStream) reads from a byte array in memory. A ByteArrayOutputStream (a subclass of Output-Stream) outputs to a byte array in memory. One use of byte-array I/O is *data validation*. A program can input an entire line at a time from the input stream into a byte array. Then a validation routine can scrutinize the contents of the byte array and correct the data if necessary. Finally, the program can proceed to input from the byte array, "knowing" that the input data is in the proper format. Outputting to a byte array is a nice way to take advantage of the powerful output-formatting capabilities of Java streams. For example, data can be stored in a byte array, using the same formatting that will be displayed at a later time, and the byte array can then be output to a file to preserve the formatting.

Sequencing Input from Multiple Streams

A SequenceInputStream (a subclass of InputStream) logically concatenates several Input-Streams—the program sees the group as one continuous InputStream. When the program reaches the end of one input stream, that stream closes, and the next stream in the sequence opens.

17.6.2 Interfaces and Classes for Character-Based Input and Output

In addition to the byte-based streams, Java provides the **Reader** and **Writer** abstract classes, which are Unicode two-byte, character-based streams. Most of the byte-based streams have corresponding character-based concrete Reader or Writer classes.

Character-Based Buffering *Readers and Writers*

Classes **BufferedReader** (a subclass of abstract class Reader) and **BufferedWriter** (a subclass of abstract class Writer) enable buffering for character-based streams. Remember that character-based streams use Unicode characters—such streams can process data in any language that the Unicode character set represents.

Memory-Based *char* Array *Readers and Writers*

Classes **CharArrayReader** and **CharArrayWriter** read and write, respectively, a stream of characters to a char array. A **LineNumberReader** (a subclass of BufferedReader) is a buffered character stream that keeps track of the number of lines read—newlines, returns and carriage-return–line-feed combinations increment the line count. Keeping track of line numbers can be useful if the program needs to inform the reader of an error on a specific line.

Character-Based File, Pipe and String *Readers and Writers*

An InputStream can be converted to a Reader via class **InputStreamReader**. Similarly, an OuputStream can be converted to a Writer via class **OutputStreamWriter**. Class File-Reader (a subclass of InputStreamReader) and class FileWriter (a subclass of Output-StreamWriter) read characters from and write characters to a file, respectively. Class **PipedReader** and class **PipedWriter** implement piped-character streams for transfering data between threads. Class **StringReader** and **StringWriter** read characters from and write characters to Strings, respectively. A PrintWriter writes characters to a stream.

17.7 Opening Files with JFileChooser

Class **JFileChooser** displays a dialog (known as the JFileChooser dialog) that enables the user to easily select files or directories. To demonstrate this dialog, we enhance the example in Section 17.3, as shown in Figs. 17.20–17.21. The example now contains a graphical user interface, but still displays the same data as before. The constructor calls method an- alyzePath in line 34. This method then calls method getFile in line 68 to retrieve the File object.

```java
1   // Fig. 17.20: FileDemonstration.java
2   // Demonstrating JFileChooser.
3   import java.awt.BorderLayout;
4   import java.awt.event.ActionEvent;
5   import java.awt.event.ActionListener;
6   import java.io.File;
7   import javax.swing.JFileChooser;
8   import javax.swing.JFrame;
9   import javax.swing.JOptionPane;
10  import javax.swing.JScrollPane;
11  import javax.swing.JTextArea;
12  import javax.swing.JTextField;
13
14  public class FileDemonstration extends JFrame
15  {
16     private JTextArea outputArea; // used for output
17     private JScrollPane scrollPane; // used to provide scrolling to output
18
19     // set up GUI
20     public FileDemonstration()
21     {
22        super( "Testing class File" );
23
24        outputArea = new JTextArea();
25
26        // add outputArea to scrollPane
27        scrollPane = new JScrollPane( outputArea );
28
29        add( scrollPane, BorderLayout.CENTER ); // add scrollPane to GUI
30
31        setSize( 400, 400 ); // set GUI size
32        setVisible( true ); // display GUI
33
34        analyzePath(); // create and analyze File object
35     } // end FileDemonstration constructor
36
37     // allow user to specify file or directory name
38     private File getFileOrDirectory()
39     {
40        // display file dialog, so user can choose file or directory to open
41        JFileChooser fileChooser = new JFileChooser();
42        fileChooser.setFileSelectionMode(
43           JFileChooser.FILES_AND_DIRECTORIES );
```

Fig. 17.20 | Demonstrating JFileChooser. (Part 1 of 3.)

```
44
45          int result = fileChooser.showOpenDialog( this );
46
47          // if user clicked Cancel button on dialog, return
48          if ( result == JFileChooser.CANCEL_OPTION )
49             System.exit( 1 );
50
51          File fileName = fileChooser.getSelectedFile(); // get File
52
53          // display error if invalid
54          if ( ( fileName == null ) || ( fileName.getName().equals( "" ) ) )
55          {
56             JOptionPane.showMessageDialog( this, "Invalid Name",
57                "Invalid Name", JOptionPane.ERROR_MESSAGE );
58             System.exit( 1 );
59          } // end if
60
61          return fileName;
62       } // end method getFile
63
64       // display information about file or directory user specifies
65       public void analyzePath()
66       {
67          // create File object based on user input
68          File name = getFileOrDirectory();
69
70          if ( name.exists() ) // if name exists, output information about it
71          {
72             // display file (or directory) information
73             outputArea.setText( String.format(
74                "%s%s\n%s\n%s\n%s%s\n%s%s\n%s%s\n%s%s\n%s%s",
75                name.getName(), " exists",
76                ( name.isFile() ? "is a file" : "is not a file" ),
77                ( name.isDirectory() ? "is a directory" :
78                   "is not a directory" ),
79                ( name.isAbsolute() ? "is absolute path" :
80                   "is not absolute path" ), "Last modified: ",
81                name.lastModified(), "Length: ", name.length(),
82                "Path: ", name.getPath(), "Absolute path: ",
83                name.getAbsolutePath(), "Parent: ", name.getParent() ) );
84
85             if ( name.isDirectory() ) // output directory listing
86             {
87                String[] directory = name.list();
88                outputArea.append( "\n\nDirectory contents:\n" );
89
90                for ( String directoryName : directory )
91                   outputArea.append( directoryName + "\n" );
92             } // end else
93          } // end outer if
94          else // not file or directory, output error message
95          {
```

Fig. 17.20 | Demonstrating JFileChooser. (Part 2 of 3.)

```
96              JOptionPane.showMessageDialog( this, name +
97                 " does not exist.", "ERROR", JOptionPane.ERROR_MESSAGE );
98          } // end else
99      } // end method analyzePath
100 } // end class FileDemonstration
```

Fig. 17.20 | Demonstrating JFileChooser. (Part 3 of 3.)

```
1   // Fig. 17.21: FileDemonstrationTest.java
2   // Testing class FileDemonstration.
3   import javax.swing.JFrame;
4
5   public class FileDemonstrationTest
6   {
7      public static void main( String[] args )
8      {
9         FileDemonstration application = new FileDemonstration();
10        application.setDefaultCloseOperation( JFrame.EXIT_ON_CLOSE );
11     } // end main
12  } // end class FileDemonstrationTest
```

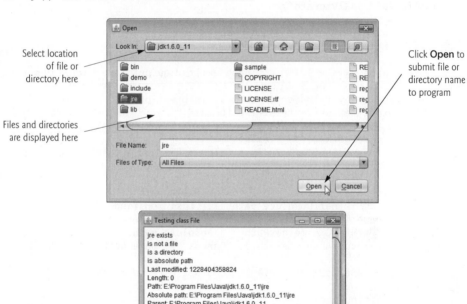

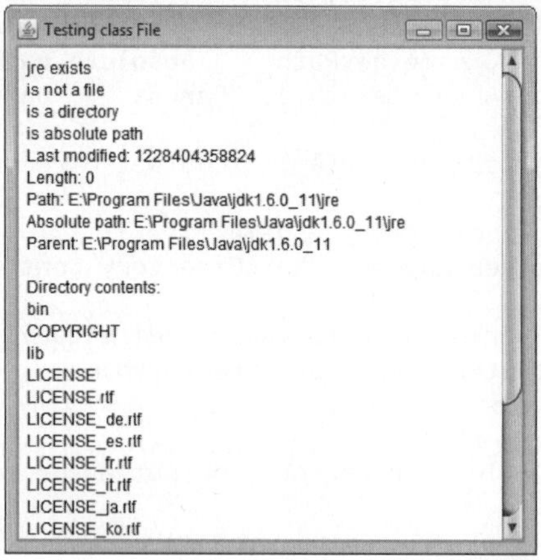

Fig. 17.21 | Testing class FileDemonstration.

Method getFile is defined in lines 38–62 of Fig. 17.20. Line 41 creates a JFile-Chooser and assigns its reference to fileChooser. Lines 42–43 call method **setFileSelectionMode** to specify what the user can select from the fileChooser. For this program, we use JFileChooser static constant **FILES_AND_DIRECTORIES** to indicate that files and directories can be selected. Other static constants include **FILES_ONLY** (the default) and **DIRECTORIES_ONLY**.

Line 45 calls method **showOpenDialog** to display the JFileChooser dialog titled **Open**. Argument this specifies the JFileChooser dialog's parent window, which determines the position of the dialog on the screen. If null is passed, the dialog is displayed in the center of the screen—otherwise, the dialog is centered over the application window (specified by the argument this). A JFileChooser dialog is a *modal dialog* that does not allow the user to interact with any other window in the program until the user closes the JFileChooser by clicking the **Open** or **Cancel** button. The user selects the drive, directory or file name, then clicks **Open**. Method showOpenDialog returns an integer specifying which button (**Open** or **Cancel**) the user clicked to close the dialog. Line 48 tests whether the user clicked **Cancel** by comparing the result with static constant **CANCEL_OPTION**. If they're equal, the program terminates. Line 51 retrieves the file the user selected by calling JFileChooser method **getSelectedFile**. The program then displays information about the selected file or directory.

17.8 Wrap-Up

In this chapter, you learned how to manipulate persistent data. We compared character-based and byte-based streams, and introduced several file-processing classes from the java.io package. You used class File to retrieve information about a file or directory. You used sequential-access file processing to manipulate records that are stored in order by the record-key field. You learned the differences between text-file processing and object serialization, and used serialization to store and retrieve entire objects. The chapter concluded with a small example of using a JFileChooser dialog to allow users to easily select files from a GUI. The next two chapters continue our discussion of dynamic data structures that can grow or shrink at execution time.

18

Generic Collections

Objectives

In this chapter you'll learn:

- What collections are.

- To use class **Arrays** for array manipulations.

- The type-wrapper classes that enable programs to process primitive data values as objects.

- To use the prebuilt generic data structures of the collections framework.

- To use iterators to "walk through" a collection.

- To use persistent hash tables manipulated with objects of class **Properties**.

- To use synchronization and modifiability wrappers.

I think this is the most extraordinary collection of talent, of human knowledge, that has ever been gathered together at the White House—with the possible exception of when Thomas Jefferson dined alone.
—John F. Kennedy

Journey over all the universe in a map.
—Miguel de Cervantes

Not by age but by capacity is wisdom acquired.
—Titus Maccius Plautus

18.1 Introduction

In Section 7.14, we introduced the generic ArrayList collection—a dynamically resizable array-like data structure that stores references to objects of a type that you specify when you create the ArrayList. In this chapter, we continue our discussion of the Java **collections framework**, which contains many other prebuilt generic data structures and various methods for manipulating them.

Because you specify the type to store in a collection at compile time, generic collections provide compile-time type safety that allows the compiler to catch attempts to use invalid types. For example, you cannot store Employees in a collection of Strings. Some examples of collections are the cards you hold in a card game, your favorite songs stored in your computer, the members of a sports team and the real-estate records in your local registry of deeds (which map book numbers and page numbers to property owners).

We discuss the collections-framework interfaces that declare the capabilities of each collection type, the implementation classes, the methods that process collection objects, and the so-called **iterators** that "walk through" collections. This chapter provides an introduction to the collections framework. For complete details, visit download.oracle.com/javase/6/docs/technotes/guides/collections/index.html.

18.2 Collections Overview

A **collection** is a data structure—actually, an object—that can hold references to other objects. Usually, collections contain references to objects that are all of the same type. The collections-framework interfaces declare the operations to be performed generically on various types of collections. Figure 18.1 lists some of the interfaces of the collections framework. Several implementations of these interfaces are provided within the framework. You may also provide implementations specific to your own requirements.

Interface	Description
Collection	The root interface in the collections hierarchy from which interfaces Set, Queue and List are derived.
Set	A collection that does not contain duplicates.
List	An ordered collection that can contain duplicate elements.
Map	A collection that associates keys to values and cannot contain duplicate keys.
Queue	Typically a first-in, first-out collection that models a waiting line; other orders can be specified.

Fig. 18.1 | Some collections-framework interfaces.

The classes and interfaces of the collections framework are members of package java.util. In the next section, we begin our discussion by examining the collections-framework capabilities for array manipulation. In earlier versions of Java, the classes in the collections framework stored and manipulated Object references, enabling you to store *any* object in a collection. One inconvenient aspect of this approach occurs when retrieving Object references from a collection. A program normally needs to process specific types of objects. As a result, the Object references obtained from a collection typically need to be *cast* to an appropriate type to allow the program to process the objects correctly.

In Java SE 5, the collections framework was enhanced with the *generics* capabilities we introduced in Chapter 7 when discussing generic ArrayLists. This means that you can specify the *exact type* that will be stored in a collection. You also receive the benefits of compile-time type checking—the compiler ensures that you're using appropriate types with your collection and, if not, issues compile-time error messages. Also, once you specify the type stored in a collection, any reference you retrieve from the collection will have the specified type. This eliminates the need for explicit type casts that can throw ClassCastExceptions if the referenced object is *not* of the appropriate type. In addition, the generic collections are *backward compatible* with Java code that was written before generics were introduced.

18.3 Type-Wrapper Classes for Primitive Types

Each primitive type (listed in Appendix D) has a corresponding **type-wrapper class** (in package java.lang). These classes are called **Boolean**, **Byte**, **Character**, **Double**, **Float**, **Integer**, **Long** and **Short**. These enable you to manipulate primitive-type values as objects. The data structures that we reuse or develop in Chapters 18–22 manipulate and share *objects*—they cannot manipulate variables of primitive types. However, they can manipulate objects of the type-wrapper classes, because every class ultimately derives from Object.

Each of the numeric type-wrapper classes—Byte, Short, Integer, Long, Float and Double—extends class Number. Also, the type-wrapper classes are final classes, so you cannot extend them.

Primitive types do not have methods, so the methods related to a primitive type are located in the corresponding type-wrapper class (e.g., method parseInt, which converts a String to an int value, is located in class Integer). If you need to manipulate a primitive value in your program, first refer to the documentation for the type-wrapper classes—the method you need might already be declared.

18.4 **Autoboxing and Auto-Unboxing**

Prior to Java SE 5, if you wanted to insert a primitive value into a data structure, you had to create a new object of the corresponding type-wrapper class, then insert it in the collection. Similarly, if you wanted to retrieve an object of a type-wrapper class from a collection and manipulate its primitive value, you had to invoke a method on the object to obtain its corresponding primitive-type value. For example, suppose you wanted to add an `int` to an array that stores only references to `Integer` objects. Prior to Java SE 5, you'd be required to "wrap" an `int` value in an `Integer` object before adding the integer to the array and to "unwrap" the `int` value to retrieve it from the array, as in

```
Integer[] integerArray = new Integer[ 5 ]; // create integerArray

// assign Integer 10 to integerArray[ 0 ]
integerArray[ 0 ] = new Integer( 10 );

// get int value of Integer
int value = integerArray[ 0 ].intValue();
```

Notice that the `int` primitive value 10 is used to initialize an `Integer` object. This achieves the desired result but requires extra code and is cumbersome. We then need to invoke method `intValue` of class `Integer` to obtain the `int` value in the `Integer` object.

Java SE 5 introduced two new conversions—the *boxing conversion* and the *unboxing conversion*—to simplify converting between primitive-type values and type-wrapper objects with no additional coding on the part of the programmer. A **boxing conversion** converts a value of a primitive type to an object of the corresponding type-wrapper class. An **unboxing conversion** converts an object of a type-wrapper class to a value of the corresponding primitive type. These conversions can be performed automatically (called **autoboxing** and **auto-unboxing**). For example, the previous statements can be rewritten as

```
Integer[] integerArray = new Integer[ 5 ]; // create integerArray
integerArray[ 0 ] = 10; // assign Integer 10 to integerArray[ 0 ]
int value = integerArray[ 0 ]; // get int value of Integer
```

In this case, *autoboxing* occurs when assigning an `int` value (10) to `integerArray[0]`, because `integerArray` stores references to `Integer` objects, not `int` values. *Auto-unboxing* occurs when assigning `integerArray[0]` to `int` variable `value`, because variable `value` stores an `int` value, not a reference to an `Integer` object. Boxing conversions also occur in conditions, which can evaluate to primitive `boolean` values or `Boolean` objects. Many of the examples in Chapters 18–22 use these conversions to store primitive values in and retrieve them from data structures.

18.5 **Interface `Collection` and Class `Collections`**

Interface **`Collection`** is the root interface in the collection hierarchy from which interfaces `Set`, `Queue` and `List` are derived. Interface **`Set`** defines a collection that does not contain duplicates. Interface **`Queue`** defines a collection that represents a waiting line—typically, insertions are made at the back of a queue and deletions from the front, though other orders can be specified. We discuss `Queue` and `Set` in Sections 18.9–18.10. Interface `Collection` contains **bulk operations** (i.e., operations performed on an entire collection) for operations such as adding, clearing and comparing objects (or elements) in a collection. A `Collection` can also be converted to an array. In addition, interface `Collection` provides a method that returns an **Iterator** object, which allows a program to walk through the collection and remove elements from it during the iteration. We discuss class Iterator in Section 18.6.1. Other methods of interface Collection enable a program to determine a collection's size and whether a collection is empty.

Software Engineering Observation 18.1

Collection is used commonly as a parameter type in methods to allow polymorphic processing of all objects that implement interface Collection.

Software Engineering Observation 18.2

Most collection implementations provide a constructor that takes a Collection argument, thereby allowing a new collection to be constructed containing the elements of the specified collection.

Class **Collections** provides static methods that search, sort and perform other operations on collections. Section 18.7 discusses more about the methods that are available in class Collections. We also cover this class's **wrapper methods** that enable you to treat a collection as a *synchronized collection* (Section 18.13) or an *unmodifiable collection* (Section 18.14). Unmodifiable collections are useful when clients of a class need to view a collection's elements, but they should not be allowed to modify the collection by adding and removing elements. Synchronized collections are for use with multithreading (discussed in Chapter 23), which enables programs to perform operations in parallel. When two or more threads of a program *share* a collection, problems might occur. As an analogy, consider a traffic intersection. If all cars were allowed to access the intersection at the same time, collisions might occur. For this reason, traffic lights are provided to control access to the intersection. Similarly, we can *synchronize* access to a collection to ensure that only *one* thread manipulates the collection at a time. The synchronization wrapper methods of class Collections return synchronized versions of collections that can be shared among threads in a program.

18.6 Lists

A List (sometimes called a **sequence**) is an ordered Collection that can contain duplicate elements. Like array indices, List indices are zero based (i.e., the first element's index is zero). In addition to the methods inherited from Collection, List provides methods for manipulating elements via their indices, manipulating a specified range of elements, searching for elements and obtaining a **ListIterator** to access the elements.

Interface List is implemented by several classes, including **ArrayList, LinkedList** and **Vector**. *Autoboxing* occurs when you add primitive-type values to objects of these classes, because they store only *references* to objects. Class ArrayList and Vector are resizable-array implementations of List. Inserting an element between existing elements of an ArrayList or Vector is an *inefficient* operation—all elements after the new one must be moved out of the way, which could be an expensive operation in a collection with a large number of elements. A LinkedList enables efficient insertion (or removal) of elements in the middle of a collection. We discuss the architecture of linked lists in Chapter 22.

ArrayList and Vector have nearly identical behaviors. Vectors are synchronized by default, whereas ArrayLists are not. Also, class Vector is from Java 1.0, before the collections framework was added to Java. As such, Vector has some methods that are not part of interface List and are not implemented in class ArrayList but perform identical tasks. For example, Vector methods addElement and add both append an element to a Vector, but only method add is specified in interface List and implemented by ArrayList. *Unsynchronized collections provide better performance than synchronized ones.* For this reason, ArrayList is typically preferred over Vector in programs that do not share a collection among threads. Separately, the Java collections API provides *synchronization wrappers* (Section 18.13) that can be used to add synchronization to the unsynchronized collections, and several powerful synchronized collections are available in the Java concurrency APIs.

Performance Tip 18.1

ArrayLists behave like Vectors without synchronization and therefore execute faster than Vectors, because ArrayLists do not have the overhead of thread synchronization.

Software Engineering Observation 18.3

LinkedLists can be used to create stacks, queues and deques (double-ended queues, pronounced "decks"). The collections framework provides implementations of some of these data structures.

The following three subsections demonstrate the List and Collection capabilities. Section 18.6.1 removes elements from an ArrayList with an Iterator. Section 18.6.2 uses ListIterator and several List- and LinkedList-specific methods.

18.6.1 ArrayList and Iterator

Figure 18.2 uses an ArrayList (introduced in Section 7.14) to demonstrate several capabilities of interface Collection. The program places two Color arrays in ArrayLists and uses an Iterator to remove elements in the second ArrayList collection from the first.

```
 1   // Fig. 18.2: CollectionTest.java
 2   // Collection interface demonstrated via an ArrayList object.
 3   import java.util.List;
 4   import java.util.ArrayList;
 5   import java.util.Collection;
 6   import java.util.Iterator;
 7
 8   public class CollectionTest
 9   {
10      public static void main( String[] args )
11      {
12         // add elements in colors array to list
13         String[] colors = { "MAGENTA", "RED", "WHITE", "BLUE", "CYAN" };
14         List< String > list = new ArrayList< String >();
15
16         for ( String color : colors )
17            list.add( color ); // adds color to end of list
18
19         // add elements in removeColors array to removeList
20         String[] removeColors = { "RED", "WHITE", "BLUE" };
```

Fig. 18.2 | Collection interface demonstrated via an ArrayList object. (Part 1 of 2.)

```
21              List< String > removeList = new ArrayList< String >();
22
23              for ( String color : removeColors )
24                 removeList.add( color );
25
26              // output list contents
27              System.out.println( "ArrayList: " );
28
29              for ( int count = 0; count < list.size(); count++ )
30                 System.out.printf( "%s ", list.get( count ) );
31
32              // remove from list the colors contained in removeList
33              removeColors( list, removeList );
34
35              // output list contents
36              System.out.println( "\n\nArrayList after calling removeColors: " );
37
38              for ( String color : list )
39                 System.out.printf( "%s ", color );
40           } // end main
41
42           // remove colors specified in collection2 from collection1
43           private static void removeColors( Collection< String > collection1,
44              Collection< String > collection2 )
45           {
46              // get iterator
47              Iterator< String > iterator = collection1.iterator();
48
49              // loop while collection has items
50              while ( iterator.hasNext() )
51              {
52                 if ( collection2.contains( iterator.next() ) )
53                    iterator.remove(); // remove current Color
54              } // end while
55           } // end method removeColors
56  } // end class CollectionTest
```

```
ArrayList:
MAGENTA RED WHITE BLUE CYAN

ArrayList after calling removeColors:
MAGENTA CYAN
```

Fig. 18.2 | `Collection` interface demonstrated via an `ArrayList` object. (Part 2 of 2.)

Lines 13 and 20 declare and initialize `String` arrays `colors` and `removeColors`. Lines 14 and 21 create `ArrayList<String>` objects and assign their references to `List<String>` variables `list` and `removeList`, respectively. Recall that `ArrayList` is a *generic* class, so we can specify a type argument (`String` in this case) to indicate the type of the elements in each list. We refer to the `ArrayList`s in this example via `List` variables. This makes our code more flexible and easier to modify. If we later decide that `LinkedList`s would be more appropriate, we'll need to modify only lines 14 and 21 where we created the `ArrayList` objects.

Lines 16–17 populate list with Strings stored in array colors, and lines 23–24 populate removeList with Strings stored in array removeColors using **List method add**. Lines 29–30 output each element of list. Line 29 calls **List method size** to get the number of elements in the ArrayList. Line 30 uses **List method get** to retrieve individual element values. Lines 29–30 also could have used the enhanced for statement (which we'll demonstrate with collections in other examples).

Line 33 calls method removeColors (lines 43–55), passing list and removeList as arguments. Method removeColors deletes the Strings in removeList from the Strings in list. Lines 38–39 print list's elements after removeColors completes its task.

Method removeColors declares two Collection<String> parameters (lines 43–44) that allow any two Collections containing strings to be passed as arguments to this method. The method accesses the elements of the first Collection (collection1) via an Iterator. Line 47 calls **Collection method iterator** to get an Iterator for the Collection. Interfaces Collection and Iterator are generic types. The loop-continuation condition (line 50) calls **Iterator method hasNext** to determine whether the Collection contains more elements. Method hasNext returns true if another element exists and false otherwise.

The if condition in line 52 calls **Iterator method next** to obtain a reference to the next element, then uses method **contains** of the second Collection (collection2) to determine whether collection2 contains the element returned by next. If so, line 53 calls **Iterator method remove** to remove the element from the Collection collection1.

Common Programming Error 18.1

If a collection is modified by one of its methods after an iterator is created for that collection, the iterator immediately becomes invalid—operations performed with the iterator after this point throw ConcurrentModificationExceptions. For this reason, iterators are said to be "fail fast."

New in Java SE 7: Type Inference with the <> Notation

Lines 14 and 21 specify the type stored in the ArrayList (that is, String) on the left and right sides of the initialization statements. Java SE 7 supports type inferencing with the <> notation in statements that declare and create generic type variables and objects. For example, line 14 can be written as:

```
List< String > list = new ArrayList<>();
```

In this case, Java uses the type in angle brackets on the left of the declaration (that is, String) as the type stored int the ArrayList created on the right side of the declaration.

18.6.2 LinkedList

Figure 18.3 demonstrates various operations on LinkedLists. The program creates two LinkedLists of Strings. The elements of one List are added to the other. Then all the Strings are converted to uppercase, and a range of elements is deleted.

```
1   // Fig. 18.3: ListTest.java
2   // Lists, LinkedLists and ListIterators.
3   import java.util.List;
```

Fig. 18.3 | Lists, LinkedLists and ListIterators. (Part 1 of 3.)

```
4    import java.util.LinkedList;
5    import java.util.ListIterator;
6
7    public class ListTest
8    {
9       public static void main( String[] args )
10      {
11         // add colors elements to list1
12         String[] colors =
13            { "black", "yellow", "green", "blue", "violet", "silver" };
14         List< String > list1 = new LinkedList< String >();
15
16         for ( String color : colors )
17            list1.add( color );
18
19         // add colors2 elements to list2
20         String[] colors2 =
21            { "gold", "white", "brown", "blue", "gray", "silver" };
22         List< String > list2 = new LinkedList< String >();
23
24         for ( String color : colors2 )
25            list2.add( color );
26
27         list1.addAll( list2 ); // concatenate lists
28         list2 = null; // release resources
29         printList( list1 ); // print list1 elements
30
31         convertToUppercaseStrings( list1 ); // convert to uppercase string
32         printList( list1 ); // print list1 elements
33
34         System.out.print( "\nDeleting elements 4 to 6..." );
35         removeItems( list1, 4, 7 ); // remove items 4-6 from list
36         printList( list1 ); // print list1 elements
37         printReversedList( list1 ); // print list in reverse order
38      } // end main
39
40      // output List contents
41      private static void printList( List< String > list )
42      {
43         System.out.println( "\nlist: " );
44
45         for ( String color : list )
46            System.out.printf( "%s ", color );
47
48         System.out.println();
49      } // end method printList
50
51      // locate String objects and convert to uppercase
52      private static void convertToUppercaseStrings( List< String > list )
53      {
54         ListIterator< String > iterator = list.listIterator();
55
```

Fig. 18.3 | Lists, LinkedLists and ListIterators. (Part 2 of 3.)

```
56          while ( iterator.hasNext() )
57          {
58             String color = iterator.next(); // get item
59             iterator.set( color.toUpperCase() ); // convert to upper case
60          } // end while
61       } // end method convertToUppercaseStrings
62
63       // obtain sublist and use clear method to delete sublist items
64       private static void removeItems( List< String > list,
65          int start, int end )
66       {
67          list.subList( start, end ).clear(); // remove items
68       } // end method removeItems
69
70       // print reversed list
71       private static void printReversedList( List< String > list )
72       {
73          ListIterator< String > iterator = list.listIterator( list.size() );
74
75          System.out.println( "\nReversed List:" );
76
77          // print list in reverse order
78          while ( iterator.hasPrevious() )
79             System.out.printf( "%s ", iterator.previous() );
80       } // end method printReversedList
81    } // end class ListTest
```

```
list:
black yellow green blue violet silver gold white brown blue gray silver

list:
BLACK YELLOW GREEN BLUE VIOLET SILVER GOLD WHITE BROWN BLUE GRAY SILVER

Deleting elements 4 to 6...
list:
BLACK YELLOW GREEN BLUE WHITE BROWN BLUE GRAY SILVER

Reversed List:
SILVER GRAY BLUE BROWN WHITE BLUE GREEN YELLOW BLACK
```

Fig. 18.3 | Lists, LinkedLists and ListIterators. (Part 3 of 3.)

Lines 14 and 22 create LinkedLists list1 and list2 of type String. LinkedList is a generic class that has one type parameter for which we specify the type argument String in this example. Lines 16–17 and 24–25 call List method add to append elements from arrays colors and colors2 to the end of list1 and list2, respectively.

Line 27 calls **List method addAll** to append all elements of list2 to the end of list1. Line 28 sets list2 to null, so the LinkedList to which list2 referred can be garbage collected. Line 29 calls method printList (lines 41–49) to output list1's contents. Line 31 calls method convertToUppercaseStrings (lines 52–61) to convert each String element to uppercase, then line 32 calls printList again to display the modified Strings. Line 35 calls method removeItems (lines 64–68) to remove the elements starting at index 4 up to, but not including, index 7 of the list. Line 37 calls method printReversedList (lines 71–80) to print the list in reverse order.

Method convertToUppercaseStrings

Method convertToUppercaseStrings (lines 52–61) changes lowercase String elements in its List argument to uppercase Strings. Line 54 calls **List method listIterator** to get the List's **bidirectional iterator** (i.e., one that can traverse a List backward or forward). ListIterator is also a generic class. In this example, the ListIterator references String objects, because method listIterator is called on a List of Strings. Line 56 calls method hasNext to determine whether the List contains another element. Line 58 gets the next String in the List. Line 59 calls **String method toUpperCase** to get an uppercase version of the String and calls **ListIterator method set** to replace the current String to which iterator refers with the String returned by method toUpperCase. Like method toUpper-Case, **String method toLowerCase** returns a lowercase version of the String.

Method removeItems

Method removeItems (lines 64–68) removes a range of items from the list. Line 67 calls **List method subList** to obtain a portion of the List (called a **sublist**). This is a so-called **range-view method**, which enables the program to view a portion of the list. The sublist is simply a view into the List on which subList is called. Method subList takes as arguments the beginning and ending index for the sublist. The ending index is not part of the range of the sublist. In this example, line 35 passes 4 for the beginning index and 7 for the ending index to subList. The sublist returned is the set of elements with indices 4 through 6. Next, the program calls **List method clear** on the sublist to remove the elements of the sublist from the List. Any changes made to a sublist are also made to the original List.

Method printReversedList

Method printReversedList (lines 71–80) prints the list backward. Line 73 calls List method listIterator with the starting position as an argument (in our case, the last element in the list) to get a bidirectional iterator for the list. **List method size** returns the number of items in the List. The while condition (line 78) calls **ListIterator's hasPrevious method** to determine whether there are more elements while traversing the list backward. Line 79 calls **ListIterator's previous method** to get the previous element from the list and outputs it to the standard output stream.

Views into Collections and Arrays Method asList

An important feature of the collections framework is the ability to manipulate the elements of one collection type (such as a set) through a different collection type (such as a list), regardless of the collection's internal implementation. The set of public methods through which collections are manipulated is called a **view**.

Class Arrays provides static method **asList** to view an array (sometimes called the **backing array**) as a **List** collection. A List view allows you to manipulate the array as if it were a list. This is useful for adding the elements in an array to a collection and for sorting array elements. The next example demonstrates how to create a LinkedList with a List view of an array, because we cannot pass the array to a LinkedList constructor. Sorting array elements with a List view is demonstrated in Fig. 18.7. Any modifications made through the List view change the array, and any modifications made to the array change the List view. The only operation permitted on the view returned by asList is *set*, which changes the value of the view and the backing array. Any other attempts to change the view (such as adding or removing elements) result in an **UnsupportedOperationException**.

Viewing Arrays as Lists and Converting Lists to Arrays
Figure 18.4 uses Arrays method asList to view an array as a List and uses **List method toArray** to get an array from a LinkedList collection. The program calls method asList to create a List view of an array, which is used to initialize a LinkedList object, then adds a series of strings to the LinkedList and calls method toArray to obtain an array containing references to the Strings.

```java
1   // Fig. 18.4: UsingToArray.java
2   // Viewing arrays as Lists and converting Lists to arrays.
3   import java.util.LinkedList;
4   import java.util.Arrays;
5
6   public class UsingToArray
7   {
8      // creates a LinkedList, adds elements and converts to array
9      public static void main( String[] args )
10     {
11        String[] colors = { "black", "blue", "yellow" };
12
13        LinkedList< String > links =
14           new LinkedList< String >( Arrays.asList( colors ) );
15
16        links.addLast( "red" ); // add as last item
17        links.add( "pink" ); // add to the end
18        links.add( 3, "green" ); // add at 3rd index
19        links.addFirst( "cyan" ); // add as first item
20
21        // get LinkedList elements as an array
22        colors = links.toArray( new String[ links.size() ] );
23
24        System.out.println( "colors: " );
25
26        for ( String color : colors )
27           System.out.println( color );
28     } // end main
29  } // end class UsingToArray
```

```
colors:
cyan
black
blue
yellow
green
red
pink
```

Fig. 18.4 | Viewing arrays as Lists and converting Lists to arrays.

Lines 13–14 construct a LinkedList of Strings containing the elements of array colors. Line 14 uses Arrays method asList to return a List view of the array, then uses that to initialize the LinkedList with its constructor that receives a Collection as an argument (a List *is a* Collection). Line 16 calls **LinkedList method addLast** to add "red" to the end of links. Lines 17–18 call **LinkedList method add** to add "pink" as the last element and "green" as the element at index 3 (i.e., the fourth element). Method addLast (line 16) functions identically to method add (line 17). Line 19 calls **LinkedList method addFirst** to add "cyan" as the new first item in the LinkedList. The add operations are permitted because they operate on the LinkedList object, not the view returned by asList. [*Note:* When "cyan" is added as the first element, "green" becomes the fifth element in the LinkedList.]

Line 22 calls the List interface's toArray method to get a String array from links. The array is a copy of the list's elements—modifying the array's contents does *not* modify the list. The array passed to method toArray is of the same type that you'd like method toArray to return. If the number of elements in that array is greater than or equal to the number of elements in the LinkedList, toArray copies the list's elements into its array argument and returns that array. If the LinkedList has more elements than the number of elements in the array passed to toArray, toArray allocates a new array of the same type it receives as an argument, copies the list's elements into the new array and returns the new array.

Common Programming Error 18.2

Passing an array that contains data to toArray *can cause logic errors. If the number of elements in the array is smaller than the number of elements in the list on which* toArray *is called, a new array is allocated to store the list's elements—without preserving the array argument's elements. If the number of elements in the array is greater than the number of elements in the list, the elements of the array (starting at index zero) are overwritten with the list's elements. Array elements that are not overwritten retain their values.*

18.7 Collections Methods

Class Collections provides several high-performance algorithms for manipulating collection elements. The algorithms (Fig. 18.5) are implemented as static methods. The methods sort, binarySearch, reverse, shuffle, fill and copy operate on Lists. Methods min, max, addAll, frequency and disjoint operate on Collections.

Method	Description
sort	Sorts the elements of a List.
binarySearch	Locates an object in a List.
reverse	Reverses the elements of a List.
shuffle	Randomly orders a List's elements.
fill	Sets every List element to refer to a specified object.
copy	Copies references from one List into another.
min	Returns the smallest element in a Collection.
max	Returns the largest element in a Collection.
addAll	Appends all elements in an array to a Collection.
frequency	Calculates how many collection elements are equal to the specified element.
disjoint	Determines whether two collections have no elements in common.

Fig. 18.5 | Collections methods.

> ### Software Engineering Observation 18.4
> *The collections framework methods are polymorphic. That is, each can operate on objects that implement specific interfaces, regardless of the underlying implementations.*

18.7.1 Method sort

Method **sort** sorts the elements of a List, which must implement the **Comparable** interface. The order is determined by the natural order of the elements' type as implemented by a compareTo method. Method compareTo is declared in interface Comparable and is sometimes called the **natural comparison method**. The sort call may specify as a second argument a **Comparator** object that determines an alternative ordering of the elements.

Sorting in Ascending Order
Figure 18.6 uses Collections method sort to order the elements of a List in ascending order (line 17). Recall that List is a generic type and accepts one type argument that specifies the list element type—line 14 creates list as a List of Strings. Lines 15 and 20 each use an implicit call to the list's toString method to output the list contents in the format shown in the output.

```
1   // Fig. 18.6: Sort1.java
2   // Collections method sort.
3   import java.util.List;
4   import java.util.Arrays;
5   import java.util.Collections;
6
7   public class Sort1
8   {
9      public static void main( String[] args )
10     {
11        String[] suits = { "Hearts", "Diamonds", "Clubs", "Spades" };
12
13        // Create and display a list containing the suits array elements
14        List< String > list = Arrays.asList( suits ); // create List
15        System.out.printf( "Unsorted array elements: %s\n", list );
16
17        Collections.sort( list ); // sort ArrayList
18
19        // output list
20        System.out.printf( "Sorted array elements: %s\n", list );
21     } // end main
22  } // end class Sort1
```

```
Unsorted array elements: [Hearts, Diamonds, Clubs, Spades]
Sorted array elements: [Clubs, Diamonds, Hearts, Spades]
```

Fig. 18.6 | Collections method sort.

Sorting in Descending Order
Figure 18.7 sorts the same list of strings used in Fig. 18.6 in descending order. The example introduces the Comparator interface, which is used for sorting a Collection's elements in a different order. Line 18 calls Collections's method sort to order the List in de-

scending order. The static **Collections** method **reverseOrder** returns a Comparator object that orders the collection's elements in reverse order.

```
 1   // Fig. 18.7: Sort2.java
 2   // Using a Comparator object with method sort.
 3   import java.util.List;
 4   import java.util.Arrays;
 5   import java.util.Collections;
 6
 7   public class Sort2
 8   {
 9      public static void main( String[] args )
10      {
11         String[] suits = { "Hearts", "Diamonds", "Clubs", "Spades" };
12
13         // Create and display a list containing the suits array elements
14         List< String > list = Arrays.asList( suits ); // create List
15         System.out.printf( "Unsorted array elements: %s\n", list );
16
17         // sort in descending order using a comparator
18         Collections.sort( list, Collections.reverseOrder() );
19
20         // output List elements
21         System.out.printf( "Sorted list elements: %s\n", list );
22      } // end main
23   } // end class Sort2
```

```
Unsorted array elements: [Hearts, Diamonds, Clubs, Spades]
Sorted list elements: [Spades, Hearts, Diamonds, Clubs]
```

Fig. 18.7 | Collections method sort with a Comparator object.

Sorting with a *Comparator*
Figure 18.8 creates a custom Comparator class, named TimeComparator, that implements interface Comparator to compare two Time2 objects. Class Time2, declared in Fig. 8.5, represents times with hours, minutes and seconds.

```
 1   // Fig. 18.8: TimeComparator.java
 2   // Custom Comparator class that compares two Time2 objects.
 3   import java.util.Comparator;
 4
 5   public class TimeComparator implements Comparator< Time2 >
 6   {
 7      public int compare( Time2 time1, Time2 time2 )
 8      {
 9         int hourCompare = time1.getHour() - time2.getHour(); // compare hour
10
11         // test the hour first
12         if ( hourCompare != 0 )
13            return hourCompare;
14
```

Fig. 18.8 | Custom Comparator class that compares two Time2 objects. (Part 1 of 2.)

```
15        int minuteCompare =
16            time1.getMinute() - time2.getMinute(); // compare minute
17
18        // then test the minute
19        if ( minuteCompare != 0 )
20            return minuteCompare;
21
22        int secondCompare =
23            time1.getSecond() - time2.getSecond(); // compare second
24
25        return secondCompare; // return result of comparing seconds
26    } // end method compare
27 } // end class TimeComparator
```

Fig. 18.8 | Custom `Comparator` class that compares two `Time2` objects. (Part 2 of 2.)

Class `TimeComparator` implements interface `Comparator`, a generic type that takes one type argument (in this case `Time2`). A class that implements `Comparator` must declare a `compare` method that receives two arguments and returns a negative integer if the first argument is less than the second, 0 if the arguments are equal or a positive integer if the first argument is greater than the second. Method `compare` (lines 7–26) performs comparisons between `Time2` objects. Line 9 compares the two hours of the `Time2` objects. If the hours are different (line 12), then we return this value. If this value is positive, then the first hour is greater than the second and the first time is greater than the second. If this value is negative, then the first hour is less than the second and the first time is less than the second. If this value is zero, the hours are the same and we must test the minutes (and maybe the seconds) to determine which time is greater.

Figure 18.9 sorts a list using the custom `Comparator` class `TimeComparator`. Line 11 creates an `ArrayList` of `Time2` objects. Recall that both `ArrayList` and `List` are generic types and accept a type argument that specifies the element type of the collection. Lines 13–17 create five `Time2` objects and add them to this list. Line 23 calls method `sort`, passing it an object of our `TimeComparator` class (Fig. 18.8).

```
1  // Fig. 18.9: Sort3.java
2  // Collections method sort with a custom Comparator object.
3  import java.util.List;
4  import java.util.ArrayList;
5  import java.util.Collections;
6
7  public class Sort3
8  {
9     public static void main( String[] args )
10    {
11       List< Time2 > list = new ArrayList< Time2 >(); // create List
12
13       list.add( new Time2(  6, 24, 34 ) );
14       list.add( new Time2( 18, 14, 58 ) );
15       list.add( new Time2(  6, 05, 34 ) );
16       list.add( new Time2( 12, 14, 58 ) );
```

Fig. 18.9 | Collections method `sort` with a custom `Comparator` object. (Part 1 of 2.)

```
17          list.add( new Time2( 6, 24, 22 ) );
18
19          // output List elements
20          System.out.printf( "Unsorted array elements:\n%s\n", list );
21
22          // sort in order using a comparator
23          Collections.sort( list, new TimeComparator() );
24
25          // output List elements
26          System.out.printf( "Sorted list elements:\n%s\n", list );
27       } // end main
28    } // end class Sort3
```

```
Unsorted array elements:
[6:24:34 AM, 6:14:58 PM, 6:05:34 AM, 12:14:58 PM, 6:24:22 AM]
Sorted list elements:
[6:05:34 AM, 6:24:22 AM, 6:24:34 AM, 12:14:58 PM, 6:14:58 PM]
```

Fig. 18.9 | Collections method sort with a custom Comparator object. (Part 2 of 2.)

18.7.2 Method shuffle

Method **shuffle** randomly orders a List's elements. Chapter 7 presented a card shuffling and dealing simulation that shuffled a deck of cards with a loop. Figure 18.10 uses method shuffle to shuffle a deck of Card objects that might be used in a card-game simulator.

Class Card (lines 8–41) represents a card in a deck of cards. Each Card has a face and a suit. Lines 10–12 declare two enum types—Face and Suit—which represent the face and the suit of the card, respectively. Method toString (lines 37–40) returns a String containing the face and suit of the Card separated by the string " of ". When an enum constant is converted to a string, the constant's identifier is used as the string representation. Normally we would use all uppercase letters for enum constants. In this example, we chose to use capital letters for only the first letter of each enum constant because we want the card to be displayed with initial capital letters for the face and the suit (e.g., "Ace of Spades").

```
1    // Fig. 18.10: DeckOfCards.java
2    // Card shuffling and dealing with Collections method shuffle.
3    import java.util.List;
4    import java.util.Arrays;
5    import java.util.Collections;
6
7    // class to represent a Card in a deck of cards
8    class Card
9    {
10       public static enum Face { Ace, Deuce, Three, Four, Five, Six,
11          Seven, Eight, Nine, Ten, Jack, Queen, King };
12       public static enum Suit { Clubs, Diamonds, Hearts, Spades };
13
14       private final Face face; // face of card
15       private final Suit suit; // suit of card
```

Fig. 18.10 | Card shuffling and dealing with Collections method shuffle. (Part 1 of 3.)

```
16
17          // two-argument constructor
18          public Card( Face cardFace, Suit cardSuit )
19          {
20              face = cardFace; // initialize face of card
21              suit = cardSuit; // initialize suit of card
22          } // end two-argument Card constructor
23
24          // return face of the card
25          public Face getFace()
26          {
27              return face;
28          } // end method getFace
29
30          // return suit of Card
31          public Suit getSuit()
32          {
33              return suit;
34          } // end method getSuit
35
36          // return String representation of Card
37          public String toString()
38          {
39              return String.format( "%s of %s", face, suit );
40          } // end method toString
41      } // end class Card
42
43   // class DeckOfCards declaration
44   public class DeckOfCards
45   {
46       private List< Card > list; // declare List that will store Cards
47
48       // set up deck of Cards and shuffle
49       public DeckOfCards()
50       {
51           Card[] deck = new Card[ 52 ];
52           int count = 0; // number of cards
53
54           // populate deck with Card objects
55           for ( Card.Suit suit : Card.Suit.values() )
56           {
57               for ( Card.Face face : Card.Face.values() )
58               {
59                   deck[ count ] = new Card( face, suit );
60                   ++count;
61               } // end for
62           } // end for
63
64           list = Arrays.asList( deck ); // get List
65           Collections.shuffle( list );   // shuffle deck
66       } // end DeckOfCards constructor
67
```

Fig. 18.10 | Card shuffling and dealing with Collections method shuffle. (Part 2 of 3.)

```
68        // output deck
69        public void printCards()
70        {
71           // display 52 cards in two columns
72           for ( int i = 0; i < list.size(); i++ )
73              System.out.printf( "%-19s%s", list.get( i ),
74                 ( ( i + 1 ) % 4 == 0 ) ? "\n" : "" );
75        } // end method printCards
76
77        public static void main( String[] args )
78        {
79           DeckOfCards cards = new DeckOfCards();
80           cards.printCards();
81        } // end main
82     } // end class DeckOfCards
```

Deuce of Clubs	Six of Spades	Nine of Diamonds	Ten of Hearts
Three of Diamonds	Five of Clubs	Deuce of Diamonds	Seven of Clubs
Three of Spades	Six of Diamonds	King of Clubs	Jack of Hearts
Ten of Spades	King of Diamonds	Eight of Spades	Six of Hearts
Nine of Clubs	Ten of Diamonds	Eight of Diamonds	Eight of Hearts
Ten of Clubs	Five of Hearts	Ace of Clubs	Deuce of Hearts
Queen of Diamonds	Ace of Diamonds	Four of Clubs	Nine of Hearts
Ace of Spades	Deuce of Spades	Ace of Hearts	Jack of Diamonds
Seven of Diamonds	Three of Hearts	Four of Spades	Four of Diamonds
Seven of Spades	King of Hearts	Seven of Hearts	Five of Diamonds
Eight of Clubs	Three of Clubs	Queen of Clubs	Queen of Spades
Six of Clubs	Nine of Spades	Four of Hearts	Jack of Clubs
Five of Spades	King of Spades	Jack of Spades	Queen of Hearts

Fig. 18.10 | Card shuffling and dealing with `Collections` method `shuffle`. (Part 3 of 3.)

Lines 55–62 populate the deck array with cards that have unique face and suit combinations. Both `Face` and `Suit` are `public static` enum types of class `Card`. To use these enum types outside of class `Card`, you must qualify each enum's type name with the name of the class in which it resides (i.e., `Card`) and a dot (.) separator. Hence, lines 55 and 57 use `Card.Suit` and `Card.Face` to declare the control variables of the for statements. Recall that method `values` of an enum type returns an array that contains all the constants of the enum type. Lines 55–62 use enhanced for statements to construct 52 new `Card`s.

The shuffling occurs in line 65, which calls `static` method `shuffle` of class `Collections` to shuffle the elements of the array. Method `shuffle` requires a `List` argument, so we must obtain a `List` view of the array before we can shuffle it. Line 64 invokes `static` method `asList` of class `Arrays` to get a `List` view of the deck array.

Method `printCards` (lines 69–75) displays the deck of cards in four columns. In each iteration of the loop, lines 73–74 output a card left justified in a 19-character field followed by either a newline or an empty string based on the number of cards output so far. If the number of cards is divisible by 4, a newline is output; otherwise, the empty string is output.

18.7.3 Methods reverse, fill, copy, max and min

Class `Collections` provides methods for reversing, filling and copying `List`s. **Collections method reverse** reverses the order of the elements in a `List`, and **method fill** overwrites elements in a List with a specified value. The fill operation is useful for re-initializing a List. **Method copy** takes two arguments—a destination List and a source List. Each source List element is copied to the destination List. The destination List must be at least as long as the source List; otherwise, an IndexOutOfBoundsException occurs. If the destination List is longer, the elements not overwritten are unchanged.

Each method we've seen so far operates on Lists. Methods **min** and **max** each operate on any Collection. Method min returns the smallest element in a Collection, and method max returns the largest element in a Collection. Both of these methods can be called with a Comparator object as a second argument to perform custom comparisons of objects, such as the TimeComparator in Fig. 18.9. Figure 18.11 demonstrates methods reverse, fill, copy, max and min.

```java
1   // Fig. 18.11: Algorithms1.java
2   // Collections methods reverse, fill, copy, max and min.
3   import java.util.List;
4   import java.util.Arrays;
5   import java.util.Collections;
6
7   public class Algorithms1
8   {
9      public static void main( String[] args )
10     {
11        // create and display a List< Character >
12        Character[] letters = { 'P', 'C', 'M' };
13        List< Character > list = Arrays.asList( letters ); // get List
14        System.out.println( "list contains: " );
15        output( list );
16
17        // reverse and display the List< Character >
18        Collections.reverse( list ); // reverse order the elements
19        System.out.println( "\nAfter calling reverse, list contains: " );
20        output( list );
21
22        // create copyList from an array of 3 Characters
23        Character[] lettersCopy = new Character[ 3 ];
24        List< Character > copyList = Arrays.asList( lettersCopy );
25
26        // copy the contents of list into copyList
27        Collections.copy( copyList, list );
28        System.out.println( "\nAfter copying, copyList contains: " );
29        output( copyList );
30
31        // fill list with Rs
32        Collections.fill( list, 'R' );
33        System.out.println( "\nAfter calling fill, list contains: " );
34        output( list );
35     } // end main
36
37     // output List information
38     private static void output( List< Character > listRef )
39     {
```

Fig. 18.11 | Collections methods reverse, fill, copy, max and min. (Part 1 of 2.)

```
40              System.out.print( "The list is: " );
41
42              for ( Character element : listRef )
43                  System.out.printf( "%s ", element );
44
45              System.out.printf( "\nMax: %s", Collections.max( listRef ) );
46              System.out.printf( "  Min: %s\n", Collections.min( listRef ) );
47          } // end method output
48      } // end class Algorithms1
```

```
list contains:
The list is: P C M
Max: P  Min: C

After calling reverse, list contains:
The list is: M C P
Max: P  Min: C

After copying, copyList contains:
The list is: M C P
Max: P  Min: C

After calling fill, list contains:
The list is: R R R
Max: R  Min: R
```

Fig. 18.11 | Collections methods reverse, fill, copy, max and min. (Part 2 of 2.)

Line 13 creates List<Character> variable list and initializes it with a List view of the Character array letters. Lines 14–15 output the current contents of the List. Line 18 calls Collections method reverse to reverse the order of list. Method reverse takes one List argument. Since list is a List view of array letters, the array's elements are now in reverse order. The reversed contents are output in lines 19–20. Line 27 uses Collections method copy to copy list's elements into copyList. Changes to copyList do not change letters, because copyList is a separate List that is not a List view of the array letters. Method copy requires two List arguments—the destination List and the source List. Line 32 calls Collections method fill to place the character 'R' in each list element. Because list is a List view of the array letters, this operation changes each element in letters to 'R'. Method fill requires a List for the first argument and an Object for the second argument—in this case, the Object is the boxed version of the character 'R'. Lines 45–46 call Collections methods max and min to find the largest and the smallest element of a Collection, respectively. Recall that interface List extends interface Collection, so a List *is a* Collection.

18.7.4 Method binarySearch

In Section 19.2.2, we studied the high-speed binary search algorithm. This algorithm is built into the Java collections framework as a static **Collections method binarySearch**, which locates an object in a List (e.g., a LinkedList or an ArrayList). If the object is found, its index is returned. If the object is not found, binarySearch returns a negative value. Method `binarySearch` determines this negative value by first calculating the insertion point and making its sign negative. Then, `binarySearch` subtracts 1 from the insertion point to obtain the return value, which guarantees that method `binarySearch` returns positive numbers (>= 0) if and only if the object is found. If multiple elements in the list match the search key, there's no guarantee which one will be located first. Figure 18.12 uses method `binarySearch` to search for a series of strings in an `ArrayList`.

```java
1   // Fig. 18.12: BinarySearchTest.java
2   // Collections method binarySearch.
3   import java.util.List;
4   import java.util.Arrays;
5   import java.util.Collections;
6   import java.util.ArrayList;
7
8   public class BinarySearchTest
9   {
10     public static void main( String[] args )
11     {
12        // create an ArrayList< String > from the contents of colors array
13        String[] colors = { "red", "white", "blue", "black", "yellow",
14           "purple", "tan", "pink" };
15        List< String > list =
16           new ArrayList< String >( Arrays.asList( colors ) );
17
18        Collections.sort( list ); // sort the ArrayList
19        System.out.printf( "Sorted ArrayList: %s\n", list );
20
21        // search list for various values
22        printSearchResults( list, colors[ 3 ] ); // first item
23        printSearchResults( list, colors[ 0 ] ); // middle item
24        printSearchResults( list, colors[ 7 ] ); // last item
25        printSearchResults( list, "aqua" ); // below lowest
26        printSearchResults( list, "gray" ); // does not exist
27        printSearchResults( list, "teal" ); // does not exist
28     } // end main
29
30     // perform search and display result
31     private static void printSearchResults(
32        List< String > list, String key )
33     {
34        int result = 0;
35
36        System.out.printf( "\nSearching for: %s\n", key );
37        result = Collections.binarySearch( list, key );
38
39        if ( result >= 0 )
40           System.out.printf( "Found at index %d\n", result );
41        else
42           System.out.printf( "Not Found (%d)\n", result );
43     } // end method printSearchResults
44  } // end class BinarySearchTest
```

Fig. 18.12 | Collections method `binarySearch`. (Part 1 of 2.)

```
Sorted ArrayList: [black, blue, pink, purple, red, tan, white, yellow]

Searching for: black
Found at index 0

Searching for: red
Found at index 4

Searching for: pink
Found at index 2

Searching for: aqua
Not Found (-1)

Searching for: gray
Not Found (-3)

Searching for: teal
Not Found (-7)
```

Fig. 18.12 | Collections method binarySearch. (Part 2 of 2.)

Lines 15–16 initialize list with an ArrayList containing a copy of the elements in array colors. Collections method binarySearch expects its List argument's elements to be sorted in ascending order, so line 18 uses Collections method sort to sort the list. If the List argument's elements are not sorted, the result of using binarySearch is undefined. Line 19 outputs the sorted list. Lines 22–27 call method printSearchResults (lines 31–43) to perform searches and output the results. Line 37 calls Collections method binarySearch to search list for the specified key. Method binarySearch takes a List as the first argument and an Object as the second argument. Lines 39–42 output the results of the search. An overloaded version of binarySearch takes a Comparator object as its third argument, which specifies how binarySearch should compare the search key to the List's elements.

18.7.5 Methods addAll, frequency and disjoint

Class Collections also provides the methods addAll, frequency and disjoint. **Collections method addAll** takes two arguments—a Collection into which to insert the new element(s) and an array that provides elements to be inserted. **Collections method frequency** takes two arguments—a Collection to be searched and an Object to be searched for in the collection. Method frequency returns the number of times that the second argument appears in the collection. **Collections method disjoint** takes two Collections and returns true if they have no elements in common. Figure 18.13 demonstrates the use of methods addAll, frequency and disjoint.

```
1   // Fig. 18.13: Algorithms2.java
2   // Collections methods addAll, frequency and disjoint.
3   import java.util.ArrayList;
4   import java.util.List;
5   import java.util.Arrays;
6   import java.util.Collections;
```

Fig. 18.13 | Collections methods addAll, frequency and disjoint. (Part 1 of 2.)

```
7
8   public class Algorithms2
9   {
10     public static void main( String[] args )
11     {
12        // initialize list1 and list2
13        String[] colors = { "red", "white", "yellow", "blue" };
14        List< String > list1 = Arrays.asList( colors );
15        ArrayList< String > list2 = new ArrayList< String >();
16
17        list2.add( "black" ); // add "black" to the end of list2
18        list2.add( "red" ); // add "red" to the end of list2
19        list2.add( "green" ); // add "green" to the end of list2
20
21        System.out.print( "Before addAll, list2 contains: " );
22
23        // display elements in list2
24        for ( String s : list2 )
25           System.out.printf( "%s ", s );
26
27        Collections.addAll( list2, colors ); // add colors Strings to list2
28
29        System.out.print( "\nAfter addAll, list2 contains: " );
30
31        // display elements in list2
32        for ( String s : list2 )
33           System.out.printf( "%s ", s );
34
35        // get frequency of "red"
36        int frequency = Collections.frequency( list2, "red" );
37        System.out.printf(
38           "\nFrequency of red in list2: %d\n", frequency );
39
40        // check whether list1 and list2 have elements in common
41        boolean disjoint = Collections.disjoint( list1, list2 );
42
43        System.out.printf( "list1 and list2 %s elements in common\n",
44           ( disjoint ? "do not have" : "have" ) );
45     } // end main
46  } // end class Algorithms2
```

```
Before addAll, list2 contains: black red green
After addAll, list2 contains: black red green red white yellow blue
Frequency of red in list2: 2
list1 and list2 have elements in common
```

Fig. 18.13 | Collections methods addAll, frequency and disjoint. (Part 2 of 2.)

Line 14 initializes list1 with elements in array colors, and lines 17–19 add Strings "black", "red" and "green" to list2. Line 27 invokes method addAll to add elements in array colors to list2. Line 36 gets the frequency of String "red" in list2 using method frequency. Line 41 invokes method disjoint to test whether Collections list1 and list2 have elements in common, which they do in this example.

18.8 Stack Class of Package `java.util`

In a world of software reuse, rather than building data structures as we need them, we can often take advantage of existing data structures. In this section, we investigate class **Stack** in the Java utilities package (`java.util`).

The Stack class extends the Vector class to implement a stack data structure. Because class Stack extends class Vector, the entire `public` interface of class Vector is available to clients of class Stack. Figure 18.14 demonstrates several of the Stack class's methods. For the details of class Stack, visit `download.oracle.com/javase/6/docs/api/java/util/Stack.html`.

Error-Prevention Tip 18.1

Because Stack extends Vector, all public Vector methods can be called on Stack objects, even if the methods do not represent conventional stack operations. For example, Vector method add can be used to insert an element anywhere in a stack—an operation that could "corrupt" the stack. When manipulating a Stack, only methods push and pop should be used to add elements to and remove elements from the Stack, respectively.

```
1   // Fig. 18.14: StackTest.java
2   // Stack class of package java.util.
3   import java.util.Stack;
4   import java.util.EmptyStackException;
5
6   public class StackTest
7   {
8      public static void main( String[] args )
9      {
10        Stack< Number > stack = new Stack< Number >(); // create a Stack
11
12        // use push method
13        stack.push( 12L ); // push long value 12L
14        System.out.println( "Pushed 12L" );
15        printStack( stack );
16        stack.push( 34567 ); // push int value 34567
17        System.out.println( "Pushed 34567" );
18        printStack( stack );
19        stack.push( 1.0F ); // push float value 1.0F
20        System.out.println( "Pushed 1.0F" );
21        printStack( stack );
22        stack.push( 1234.5678 ); // push double value 1234.5678
23        System.out.println( "Pushed 1234.5678 " );
24        printStack( stack );
25
26        // remove items from stack
27        try
28        {
29           Number removedObject = null;
30
```

Fig. 18.14 | Stack class of package `java.util`. (Part 1 of 2.)

```
31                // pop elements from stack
32                while ( true )
33                {
34                    removedObject = stack.pop(); // use pop method
35                    System.out.printf( "Popped %s\n", removedObject );
36                    printStack( stack );
37                } // end while
38            } // end try
39            catch ( EmptyStackException emptyStackException )
40            {
41                emptyStackException.printStackTrace();
42            } // end catch
43        } // end main
44
45        // display Stack contents
46        private static void printStack( Stack< Number > stack )
47        {
48            if ( stack.isEmpty() )
49                System.out.println( "stack is empty\n" ); // the stack is empty
50            else // stack is not empty
51                System.out.printf( "stack contains: %s (top)\n", stack );
52        } // end method printStack
53    } // end class StackTest
```

```
Pushed 12L
stack contains: [12] (top)
Pushed 34567
stack contains: [12, 34567] (top)
Pushed 1.0F
stack contains: [12, 34567, 1.0] (top)
Pushed 1234.5678
stack contains: [12, 34567, 1.0, 1234.5678] (top)
Popped 1234.5678
stack contains: [12, 34567, 1.0] (top)
Popped 1.0
stack contains: [12, 34567] (top)
Popped 34567
stack contains: [12] (top)
Popped 12
stack is empty

java.util.EmptyStackException
        at java.util.Stack.peek(Unknown Source)
        at java.util.Stack.pop(Unknown Source)
        at StackTest.main(StackTest.java:34)
```

Fig. 18.14 | Stack class of package java.util. (Part 2 of 2.)

Line 10 creates an empty Stack of Numbers. Class Number (in package java.lang) is the superclass of the type-wrapper classes for the primitive numeric types (e.g., Integer, Double). By creating a Stack of Numbers, objects of any class that extends Number can be pushed onto the Stack. Lines 13, 16, 19 and 22 each call Stack method **push** to add a Number object to the top of the stack. Note the literals 12L (line 13) and 1.0F (line 19). Any integer literal that has the **suffix L** is a long value. An integer literal without a suffix is an int value. Similarly, any floating-point literal that has the **suffix F** is a float value. A floating-point literal without a suffix is a double value. You can learn more about numeric literals in the *Java Language Specification* at java.sun.com/docs/books/jls/third_edition/html/expressions.html#15.8.1.

An infinite loop (lines 32–37) calls **Stack method pop** to remove the top element of the stack. The method returns a Number reference to the removed element. If there are no elements in the Stack, method pop throws an **EmptyStackException**, which terminates the loop. Class Stack also declares **method peek**. This method returns the top element of the stack without popping the element off the stack.

Method printStack (lines 46–52) displays the stack's contents. The current top of the stack (the last value pushed onto the stack) is the first value printed. Line 48 calls **Stack method isEmpty** (inherited by Stack from class Vector) to determine whether the stack is empty. If it's empty, the method returns true; otherwise, false.

18.9 Class PriorityQueue and Interface Queue

Recall that a queue is a collection that represents a waiting line—typically, insertions are made at the back of a queue and deletions are made from the front. In Section 22.6, we'll discuss and implement a queue data structure. In this section, we investigate Java's **Queue** interface and **PriorityQueue** class from package java.util. Interface Queue extends interface Collection and provides additional operations for inserting, removing and inspecting elements in a queue. PriorityQueue, which implements the Queue interface, orders elements by their natural ordering as specified by Comparable elements' compareTo method or by a Comparator object that is supplied to the constructor.

Class PriorityQueue provides functionality that enables insertions in sorted order into the underlying data structure and deletions from the front of the underlying data structure. When adding elements to a PriorityQueue, the elements are inserted in priority order such that the highest-priority element (i.e., the largest value) will be the first element removed from the PriorityQueue.

The common PriorityQueue operations are **offer** to insert an element at the appropriate location based on priority order, **poll** to remove the highest-priority element of the priority queue (i.e., the head of the queue), **peek** to get a reference to the highest-priority element of the priority queue (without removing that element), **clear** to remove all elements in the priority queue and **size** to get the number of elements in the priority queue. Figure 18.15 demonstrates the PriorityQueue class.

```
1   // Fig. 18.15: PriorityQueueTest.java
2   // PriorityQueue test program.
3   import java.util.PriorityQueue;
4
5   public class PriorityQueueTest
6   {
7      public static void main( String[] args )
8      {
9         // queue of capacity 11
10        PriorityQueue< Double > queue = new PriorityQueue< Double >();
```

Fig. 18.15 | PriorityQueue test program. (Part 1 of 2.)

```
11
12          // insert elements to queue
13          queue.offer( 3.2 );
14          queue.offer( 9.8 );
15          queue.offer( 5.4 );
16
17          System.out.print( "Polling from queue: " );
18
19          // display elements in queue
20          while ( queue.size() > 0 )
21          {
22             System.out.printf( "%.1f ", queue.peek() ); // view top element
23             queue.poll(); // remove top element
24          } // end while
25       } // end main
26    } // end class PriorityQueueTest
```

```
Polling from queue: 3.2 5.4 9.8
```

Fig. 18.15 | PriorityQueue test program. (Part 2 of 2.)

Line 10 creates a PriorityQueue that stores Doubles with an initial capacity of 11 elements and orders the elements according to the object's natural ordering (the defaults for a PriorityQueue). PriorityQueue is a generic class. Line 10 instantiates a PriorityQueue with a type argument Double. Class PriorityQueue provides five additional constructors. One of these takes an int and a Comparator object to create a PriorityQueue with the initial capacity specified by the int and the ordering by the Comparator. Lines 13–15 use method offer to add elements to the priority queue. Method offer throws a NullPointerException if the program attempts to add a null object to the queue. The loop in lines 20–24 uses method size to determine whether the priority queue is empty (line 20). While there are more elements, line 22 uses PriorityQueue method peek to retrieve the highest-priority element in the queue for output (without actually removing it from the queue). Line 23 removes the highest-priority element in the queue with method poll, which returns the removed element.

18.10 Sets

A **Set** is an unordered Collection of unique elements (i.e., no duplicate elements). The collections framework contains several Set implementations, including **HashSet** and **TreeSet**. HashSet stores its elements in a hash table, and TreeSet stores its elements in a tree. Hash tables are presented in Section 18.11.

Figure 18.16 uses a HashSet to remove duplicate strings from a List. Recall that both List and Collection are generic types, so line 16 creates a List that contains String objects, and line 20 passes a Collection of Strings to method printNonDuplicates.

Method printNonDuplicates (lines 24–35) takes a Collection argument. Line 27 constructs a HashSet<String> from the Collection<String> argument. By definition, Sets do not contain duplicates, so when the HashSet is constructed, it removes any duplicates in the Collection. Lines 31–32 output elements in the Set.

```
 1   // Fig. 18.16: SetTest.java
 2   // HashSet used to remove duplicate values from array of strings.
 3   import java.util.List;
 4   import java.util.Arrays;
 5   import java.util.HashSet;
 6   import java.util.Set;
 7   import java.util.Collection;
 8
 9   public class SetTest
10   {
11      public static void main( String[] args )
12      {
13         // create and display a List< String >
14         String[] colors = { "red", "white", "blue", "green", "gray",
15            "orange", "tan", "white", "cyan", "peach", "gray", "orange" };
16         List< String > list = Arrays.asList( colors );
17         System.out.printf( "List: %s\n", list );
18
19         // eliminate duplicates then print the unique values
20         printNonDuplicates( list );
21      } // end main
22
23      // create a Set from a Collection to eliminate duplicates
24      private static void printNonDuplicates( Collection< String > values )
25      {
26         // create a HashSet
27         Set< String > set = new HashSet< String >( values );
28
29         System.out.print( "\nNonduplicates are: " );
30
31         for ( String value : set )
32            System.out.printf( "%s ", value );
33
34         System.out.println();
35      } // end method printNonDuplicates
36   } // end class SetTest
```

```
List: [red, white, blue, green, gray, orange, tan, white, cyan, peach, gray,
orange]

Nonduplicates are: orange green white peach gray cyan red blue tan
```

Fig. 18.16 | HashSet used to remove duplicate values from an array of strings.

Sorted Sets

The collections framework also includes the **SortedSet interface** (which extends Set) for sets that maintain their elements in sorted order—either the elements' natural order (e.g., numbers are in ascending order) or an order specified by a Comparator. Class TreeSet implements SortedSet. The program in Fig. 18.17 places strings into a TreeSet. The strings are sorted as they're added to the TreeSet. This example also demonstrates range-view methods, which enable a program to view a portion of a collection.

Lines 14–15 of create a TreeSet<String> that contains the elements of array colors, then assigns the new TreeSet<String> to SortedSet<String> variable tree. Line 18

```
 1    // Fig. 18.17: SortedSetTest.java
 2    // Using SortedSets and TreeSets.
 3    import java.util.Arrays;
 4    import java.util.SortedSet;
 5    import java.util.TreeSet;
 6
 7    public class SortedSetTest
 8    {
 9       public static void main( String[] args )
10       {
11          // create TreeSet from array colors
12          String[] colors = { "yellow", "green", "black", "tan", "grey",
13             "white", "orange", "red", "green" };
14          SortedSet< String > tree =
15             new TreeSet< String >( Arrays.asList( colors ) );
16
17          System.out.print( "sorted set: " );
18          printSet( tree ); // output contents of tree
19
20          // get headSet based on "orange"
21          System.out.print( "headSet (\"orange\"):  " );
22          printSet( tree.headSet( "orange" ) );
23
24          // get tailSet based upon "orange"
25          System.out.print( "tailSet (\"orange\"):  " );
26          printSet( tree.tailSet( "orange" ) );
27
28          // get first and last elements
29          System.out.printf( "first: %s\n", tree.first() );
30          System.out.printf( "last : %s\n", tree.last() );
31       } // end main
32
33       // output SortedSet using enhanced for statement
34       private static void printSet( SortedSet< String > set )
35       {
36          for ( String s : set )
37             System.out.printf( "%s ", s );
38
39          System.out.println();
40       } // end method printSet
41    } // end class SortedSetTest
```

```
sorted set: black green grey orange red tan white yellow
headSet ("orange"):  black green grey
tailSet ("orange"):  orange red tan white yellow
first: black
last : yellow
```

Fig. 18.17 | Using SortedSets and TreeSets.

outputs the initial set of strings using method printSet (lines 34–40), which we discuss
momentarily. Line 22 calls **TreeSet method headSet** to get a subset of the TreeSet in
which every element is less than "orange". The view returned from headSet is then output

with printSet. If any changes are made to the subset, they'll also be made to the original TreeSet, because the subset returned by headSet is a view of the TreeSet.

Line 26 calls **TreeSet method tailSet** to get a subset in which each element is greater than or equal to "orange", then outputs the result. Any changes made through the tailSet view are made to the original TreeSet. Lines 29–30 call **SortedSet methods first** and **last** to get the smallest and largest elements of the set, respectively.

Method printSet (lines 34–40) accepts a SortedSet as an argument and prints it. Lines 36–37 print each element of the SortedSet using the enhanced for statement.

18.11 Maps

Maps associate keys to values. The keys in a Map must be unique, but the associated values need not be. If a Map contains both unique keys and unique values, it's said to implement a **one-to-one mapping**. If only the keys are unique, the Map is said to implement a **many-to-one mapping**—many keys can map to one value.

Maps differ from Sets in that Maps contain keys and values, whereas Sets contain only values. Three of the several classes that implement interface Map are **Hashtable**, **HashMap** and **TreeMap**. Hashtables and HashMaps store elements in hash tables, and TreeMaps store elements in trees. This section discusses hash tables and provides an example that uses a HashMap to store key/value pairs. **Interface SortedMap** extends Map and maintains its keys in sorted order—either the elements' natural order or an order specified by a Comparator. Class TreeMap implements SortedMap.

Map Implementation with Hash Tables

When a program creates objects of new or existing types, it may need to store and retrieve them efficiently. Storing and retrieving information with arrays is efficient if some aspect of your data directly matches a numerical key value and if the keys are unique and tightly packed. If you have 100 employees with nine-digit social security numbers and you want to store and retrieve employee data by using the social security number as a key, the task will require an array with over 700 million elements, because nine-digit Social Security numbers must begin with 001–733 as per the Social Security Administration's website

```
www.socialsecurity.gov/employer/stateweb.htm
```

This is impractical for virtually all applications that use social security numbers as keys. A program having an array that large could achieve high performance for both storing and retrieving employee records by simply using the social security number as the array index.

Numerous applications have this problem—namely, that either the keys are of the wrong type (e.g., not positive integers that correspond to array subscripts) or they're of the right type, but sparsely spread over a huge range. What is needed is a high-speed scheme for converting keys such as social security numbers, inventory part numbers and the like into unique array indices. Then, when an application needs to store something, the scheme could convert the application's key rapidly into an index, and the record could be stored at that slot in the array. Retrieval is accomplished the same way: Once the application has a key for which it wants to retrieve a data record, the application simply applies the conversion to the key—this produces the array index where the data is stored and retrieved.

The scheme we describe here is the basis of a technique called **hashing**. Why the name? When we convert a key into an array index, we literally scramble the bits, forming a kind of "mishmashed," or hashed, number. The number actually has no real significance beyond its usefulness in storing and retrieving a particular data record.

A glitch in the scheme is called a **collision**—this occurs when two different keys "hash into" the same cell (or element) in the array. We cannot store two values in the same space, so we need to find an alternative home for all values beyond the first that hash to a particular array index. There are many schemes for doing this. One is to "hash again" (i.e., to apply another hashing transformation to the key to provide a next candidate cell in the array). The hashing process is designed to distribute the values throughout the table, so the assumption is that an available cell will be found with just a few hashes.

Another scheme uses one hash to locate the first candidate cell. If that cell is occupied, successive cells are searched in order until an available cell is found. Retrieval works the same way: The key is hashed once to determine the initial location and check whether it contains the desired data. If it does, the search is finished. If it does not, successive cells are searched linearly until the desired data is found.

The most popular solution to hash-table collisions is to have each cell of the table be a hash "bucket," typically a linked list of all the key/value pairs that hash to that cell. This is the solution that Java's Hashtable and HashMap classes (from package java.util) implement. Both Hashtable and HashMap implement the Map interface. The primary differences between them are that HashMap is unsynchronized (multiple threads should not modify a HashMap concurrently) and allows null keys and null values.

A hash table's **load factor** affects the performance of hashing schemes. The load factor is the ratio of the number of occupied cells in the hash table to the total number of cells in the hash table. The closer this ratio gets to 1.0, the greater the chance of collisions.

Performance Tip 18.2

The load factor in a hash table is a classic example of a memory-space/execution-time trade-off: By increasing the load factor, we get better memory utilization, but the program runs slower, due to increased hashing collisions. By decreasing the load factor, we get better program speed, because of reduced hashing collisions, but we get poorer memory utilization, because a larger portion of the hash table remains empty.

Hash tables are complex to program. Classes Hashtable and HashMap enable you to use hashing without having to implement hash-table mechanisms. This concept is profoundly important in our study of object-oriented programming. As discussed in earlier chapters, classes encapsulate and hide complexity (i.e., implementation details) and offer user-friendly interfaces. Properly crafting classes to exhibit such behavior is one of the most valued skills in the field of object-oriented programming. Figure 18.18 uses a HashMap to count the number of occurrences of each word in a string.

```
1   // Fig. 18.18: WordTypeCount.java
2   // Program counts the number of occurrences of each word in a String.
3   import java.util.Map;
4   import java.util.HashMap;
5   import java.util.Set;
6   import java.util.TreeSet;
```

Fig. 18.18 | Program counts the number of occurrences of each word in a String. (Part 1 of 3.)

```
 7   import java.util.Scanner;
 8
 9   public class WordTypeCount
10   {
11      public static void main( String[] args )
12      {
13         // create HashMap to store String keys and Integer values
14         Map< String, Integer > myMap = new HashMap< String, Integer >();
15
16         createMap( myMap ); // create map based on user input
17         displayMap( myMap ); // display map content
18      } // end main
19
20      // create map from user input
21      private static void createMap( Map< String, Integer > map )
22      {
23         Scanner scanner = new Scanner( System.in ); // create scanner
24         System.out.println( "Enter a string:" ); // prompt for user input
25         String input = scanner.nextLine();
26
27         // tokenize the input
28         String[] tokens = input.split( " " );
29
30         // processing input text
31         for ( String token : tokens )
32         {
33            String word = token.toLowerCase(); // get lowercase word
34
35            // if the map contains the word
36            if ( map.containsKey( word ) ) // is word in map
37            {
38               int count = map.get( word ); // get current count
39               map.put( word, count + 1 ); // increment count
40            } // end if
41            else
42               map.put( word, 1 ); // add new word with a count of 1 to map
43         } // end for
44      } // end method createMap
45
46      // display map content
47      private static void displayMap( Map< String, Integer > map )
48      {
49         Set< String > keys = map.keySet(); // get keys
50
51         // sort keys
52         TreeSet< String > sortedKeys = new TreeSet< String >( keys );
53
54         System.out.println( "\nMap contains:\nKey\t\tValue" );
55
56         // generate output for each key in map
57         for ( String key : sortedKeys )
58            System.out.printf( "%-10s%10s\n", key, map.get( key ) );
59
```

Fig. 18.18 | Program counts the number of occurrences of each word in a String. (Part 2 of 3.)

```
60          System.out.printf(
61              "\nsize: %d\nisEmpty: %b\n", map.size(), map.isEmpty() );
62     } // end method displayMap
63 } // end class WordTypeCount
```

```
Enter a string:
this is a sample sentence with several words this is another sample
sentence with several different words

Map contains:
Key             Value
a               1
another         1
different       1
is              2
sample          2
sentence        2
several         2
this            2
with            2
words           2

size: 10
isEmpty: false
```

Fig. 18.18 | Program counts the number of occurrences of each word in a `String`. (Part 3 of 3.)

Line 14 creates an empty `HashMap` with a default initial capacity (16 elements) and a default load factor (0.75)—these defaults are built into the implementation of `HashMap`. When the number of occupied slots in the `HashMap` becomes greater than the capacity times the load factor, the capacity is doubled automatically. `HashMap` is a generic class that takes two type arguments—the type of key (i.e., `String`) and the type of value (i.e., `Integer`). Recall that the type arguments passed to a generic class must be reference types, hence the second type argument is `Integer`, not `int`.

Line 16 calls method `createMap` (lines 21–44), which uses a map to store the number of occurrences of each word in the sentence. Line 25 obtains the user input, and line 28 tokenizes it. The loop in lines 31–43 converts the next token to lowercase letters (line 33), then calls **Map method containsKey** (line 36) to determine whether the word is in the map (and thus has occurred previously in the string). If the Map does not contain a mapping for the word, line 42 uses **Map method put** to create a new entry in the map, with the word as the key and an `Integer` object containing 1 as the value. Autoboxing occurs when the program passes integer 1 to method put, because the map stores the number of occurrences of the word as an `Integer`. If the word does exist in the map, line 38 uses **Map method get** to obtain the key's associated value (the count) in the map. Line 39 increments that value and uses put to replace the key's associated value in the map. Method put returns the key's prior associated value, or `null` if the key was not in the map.

Method `displayMap` (lines 47–62) displays all the entries in the map. It uses **HashMap method keySet** (line 49) to get a set of the keys. The keys have type `String` in the map, so method keySet returns a generic type Set with type parameter specified to be `String`. Line 52 creates a `TreeSet` of the keys, in which the keys are sorted. The loop in lines 57–58 accesses each key and its value in the map. Line 58 displays each key and its value using format specifier %-10s to left justify each key and format specifier %10s to right justify each value. The keys are displayed in ascending order. Line 61 calls **Map method size** to get the number of key/value pairs in the Map. Line 61 also calls **Map method isEmpty**, which returns a boolean indicating whether the Map is empty.

18.12 Properties Class

A **Properties** object is a persistent Hashtable that normally stores key/value pairs of strings—assuming that you use methods **setProperty** and **getProperty** to manipulate the table rather than inherited Hashtable methods put and get. By "persistent," we mean that the Properties object can be written to an output stream (possibly a file) and read back in through an input stream. A common use of Properties objects in prior versions of Java was to maintain application-configuration data or user preferences for applications. [*Note:* The **Preferences API** (package **java.util.prefs**) is meant to replace this particular use of class Properties but is beyond the scope of this book. To learn more, visit bit.ly/ JavaPreferences.]

Class Properties extends class Hashtable<Object, Object>. Figure 18.19 demonstrates several methods of class Properties.

```
1   // Fig. 18.19: PropertiesTest.java
2   // Demonstrates class Properties of the java.util package.
3   import java.io.FileOutputStream;
4   import java.io.FileInputStream;
5   import java.io.IOException;
6   import java.util.Properties;
7   import java.util.Set;
8
9   public class PropertiesTest
10  {
11     public static void main( String[] args )
12     {
13        Properties table = new Properties(); // create Properties table
14
15        // set properties
16        table.setProperty( "color", "blue" );
17        table.setProperty( "width", "200" );
18
19        System.out.println( "After setting properties" );
20        listProperties( table ); // display property values
21
22        // replace property value
23        table.setProperty( "color", "red" );
24
25        System.out.println( "After replacing properties" );
26        listProperties( table ); // display property values
27
28        saveProperties( table ); // save properties
29
```

Fig. 18.19 | Properties class of package java.util. (Part 1 of 3.)

```
30          table.clear(); // empty table
31
32          System.out.println( "After clearing properties" );
33          listProperties( table ); // display property values
34
35          loadProperties( table ); // load properties
36
37          // get value of property color
38          Object value = table.getProperty( "color" );
39
40          // check if value is in table
41          if ( value != null )
42             System.out.printf( "Property color's value is %s\n", value );
43          else
44             System.out.println( "Property color is not in table" );
45       } // end main
46
47       // save properties to a file
48       private static void saveProperties( Properties props )
49       {
50          // save contents of table
51          try
52          {
53             FileOutputStream output = new FileOutputStream( "props.dat" );
54             props.store( output, "Sample Properties" ); // save properties
55             output.close();
56             System.out.println( "After saving properties" );
57             listProperties( props ); // display property values
58          } // end try
59          catch ( IOException ioException )
60          {
61             ioException.printStackTrace();
62          } // end catch
63       } // end method saveProperties
64
65       // load properties from a file
66       private static void loadProperties( Properties props )
67       {
68          // load contents of table
69          try
70          {
71             FileInputStream input = new FileInputStream( "props.dat" );
72             props.load( input ); // load properties
73             input.close();
74             System.out.println( "After loading properties" );
75             listProperties( props ); // display property values
76          } // end try
77          catch ( IOException ioException )
78          {
79             ioException.printStackTrace();
80          } // end catch
81       } // end method loadProperties
82
```

Fig. 18.19 | Properties class of package `java.util`. (Part 2 of 3.)

```
83        // output property values
84        private static void listProperties( Properties props )
85        {
86           Set< Object > keys = props.keySet(); // get property names
87
88           // output name/value pairs
89           for ( Object key : keys )
90              System.out.printf(
91                 "%s\t%s\n", key, props.getProperty( ( String ) key ) );
92
93           System.out.println();
94        } // end method listProperties
95     } // end class PropertiesTest
```

```
After setting properties
color    blue
width    200

After replacing properties
color    red
width    200

After saving properties
color    red
width    200

After clearing properties

After loading properties
color    red
width    200

Property color's value is red
```

Fig. 18.19 | Properties class of package java.util. (Part 3 of 3.)

Line 13 uses the no-argument constructor to create an empty Properties table with no default properties. Class Properties also provides an overloaded constructor that receives a reference to a Properties object containing default property values. Lines 16 and 17 each call Properties method setProperty to store a value for the specified key. If the key does not exist in the table, setProperty returns null; otherwise, it returns the previous value for that key.

Line 38 calls Properties method getProperty to locate the value associated with the specified key. If the key is not found in this Properties object, getProperty returns null. An overloaded version of this method receives a second argument that specifies the default value to return if getProperty cannot locate the key.

Line 54 calls **Properties method store** to save the Properties object's contents to the OutputStream specified as the first argument (in this case, a FileOutputStream). The second argument, a String, is a description written into the file. **Properties method list**, which takes a PrintStream argument, is useful for displaying the list of properties.

Line 72 calls **Properties method load** to restore the contents of the Properties object from the InputStream specified as the first argument (in this case, a FileInput-Stream). Line 86 calls Properties method keySet to obtain a Set of the property names.

Because class `Properties` stores its contents as `Object`s, a `Set` of `Object` references is returned. Line 91 obtains the value of a property by passing a key to method `getProperty`.

18.13 Synchronized Collections

In Chapter 23, we discuss multithreading. Except for `Vector` and `Hashtable`, the collections in the collections framework are unsynchronized by default, so they can operate efficiently when multithreading is not required. Because they're unsynchronized, however, concurrent access to a `Collection` by multiple threads could cause indeterminate results or fatal errors. To prevent potential threading problems, **synchronization wrappers** are used for collections that might be accessed by multiple threads. A **wrapper** object receives method calls, adds thread synchronization (to prevent concurrent access to the collection) and delegates the calls to the wrapped collection object. The `Collections` API provides a set of `static` methods for wrapping collections as synchronized versions. Method headers for the synchronization wrappers are listed in Fig. 18.20. Details about these methods are available at `download.oracle.com/javase/6/docs/api/java/util/Collections.html`. All these methods take a generic type and return a synchronized view of the generic type. For example, the following code creates a synchronized `List` (`list2`) that stores `String` objects:

```
List< String > list1 = new ArrayList< String >();
List< String > list2 = Collections.synchronizedList( list1 );
```

public static method headers

```
< T > Collection< T > synchronizedCollection( Collection< T > c )
< T > List< T > synchronizedList( List< T > aList )
< T > Set< T > synchronizedSet( Set< T > s )
< T > SortedSet< T > synchronizedSortedSet( SortedSet< T > s )
< K, V > Map< K, V > synchronizedMap( Map< K, V > m )
< K, V > SortedMap< K, V > synchronizedSortedMap( SortedMap< K, V > m )
```

Fig. 18.20 | Synchronization wrapper methods.

18.14 Unmodifiable Collections

The `Collections` class provides a set of `static` methods that create **unmodifiable wrappers** for collections. Unmodifiable wrappers throw `UnsupportedOperationException`s if attempts are made to modify the collection. Headers for these methods are listed in Fig. 18.21. Details about these methods are available at `download.oracle.com/javase/6/docs/api/java/util/Collections.html`. All these methods take a generic type and return an unmodifiable view of the generic type. For example, the following code creates an unmodifiable `List` (`list2`) that stores `String` objects:

```
List< String > list1 = new ArrayList< String >();
List< String > list2 = Collections.unmodifiableList( list1 );
```

public static method headers
< T > Collection< T > unmodifiableCollection(Collection< T > c)
< T > List< T > unmodifiableList(List< T > aList)
< T > Set< T > unmodifiableSet(Set< T > s)
< T > SortedSet< T > unmodifiableSortedSet(SortedSet< T > s)
< K, V > Map< K, V > unmodifiableMap(Map< K, V > m)
< K, V > SortedMap< K, V > unmodifiableSortedMap(SortedMap< K, V > m)

Fig. 18.21 | Unmodifiable wrapper methods.

Software Engineering Observation 18.5

You can use an unmodifiable wrapper to create a collection that offers read-only access to others, while allowing read/write access to yourself. You do this simply by giving others a reference to the unmodifiable wrapper while retaining for yourself a reference to the original collection.

18.15 Abstract Implementations

The collections framework provides various abstract implementations of Collection interfaces from which you can quickly "flesh out" complete customized implementations. These abstract implementations include a thin Collection implementation called an **AbstractCollection**, a List implementation that allows random access to its elements called an **AbstractList**, a Map implementation called an **AbstractMap**, a List implementation that allows sequential access to its elements called an **AbstractSequentialList**, a Set implementation called an **AbstractSet** and a Queue implementation called **AbstractQueue**. You can learn more about these classes at download.oracle.com/javase/6/docs/api/java/util/package-summary.html.

To write a custom implementation, you can extend the abstract implementation that best meets your needs, and implement each of the class's abstract methods. Then, if your collection is to be modifiable, override any concrete methods that prevent modification.

18.16 Wrap-Up

This chapter introduced the Java collections framework. You learned the collection hierarchy and how to use the collections-framework interfaces to program with collections polymorphically. You used classes ArrayList and LinkedList, which both implement the List interface. We presented Java's built-in interfaces and classes for manipulating stacks and queues. You used several predefined methods for manipulating collections. Next, you learned how to use the Set interface and class HashSet to manipulate an unordered collection of unique values. We continued our presentation of sets with the SortedSet interface and class TreeSet for manipulating a sorted collection of unique values. You then learned about Java's interfaces and classes for manipulating key/value pairs—Map, SortedMap, Hashtable, HashMap and TreeMap. We discussed the specialized Properties class for manipulating key/value pairs of Strings that can be stored to a file and retrieved from a file.

Finally, we discussed the Collections class's static methods for obtaining unmodifiable and synchronized views of collections. Chapter 19 demonstrates how to use Java's generics capabilities to implement your own generic methods and classes.

19

Generic Classes and Methods

Every man of genius sees the world at a different angle from his fellows.
—Havelock Ellis

…our special individuality, as distinguished from our generic humanity.
—Oliver Wendell Holmes, Sr.

Born under one law, to another bound.
—Lord Brooke

Objectives

In this chapter you'll learn:

- To create generic methods that perform identical tasks on arguments of different types.

- To create a generic Stack class that can be used to store objects of any class or interface type.

- To understand how to overload generic methods with nongeneric methods or with other generic methods.

- To understand raw types and how they help achieve backward compatibility.

- To use wildcards when precise type information about a parameter is not required in the method body.

Outline

19.1 Introduction

You've used existing generic methods and classes in Chapters 7 and 18. In this chapter, you'll learn how to write your own. You'll also learn the relationships between generics and other Java features, such as overloading and inheritance.

It would be nice if we could write a single `sort` method to sort the elements in an `Integer` array, a `String` array or an array of any type that supports ordering (i.e., its elements can be compared). It would also be nice if we could write a single `Stack` class that could be used as a `Stack` of integers, a `Stack` of floating-point numbers, a `Stack` of `String`s or a `Stack` of any other type. It would be even nicer if we could detect type mismatches at *compile time*—known as **compile-time type safety**. For example, if a `Stack` stores only integers, attempting to push a `String` onto that `Stack` should issue a *compile-time* error.

This chapter discusses **generics**, which provide the means to create the general models mentioned above. **Generic methods** enable you to specify, with a single method declaration, a set of related methods. **Generic classes** (and interfaces) enable you to specify, with a single class (or interface) declaration, a set of related types, respectively. Generics also provide compile-time type safety that allows you to catch invalid types at compile time.

We might write a generic method for sorting an array of objects, then invoke the generic method with `Integer` arrays, `Double` arrays, `String` arrays and so on, to sort the array elements. The compiler could perform type checking to ensure that the array passed to the sorting method contains the same type elements. We might write a single generic `Stack` class that manipulates a stack of objects, then instantiate `Stack` objects for a stack of `Integer`s, a stack of `Double`s, a stack of `String`s and so on. The compiler could perform type checking to ensure that the `Stack` stores elements of the same type.

Software Engineering Observation 19.1

Generic methods and classes are among Java's most powerful capabilities for software reuse with compile-time type safety.

19.2 Motivation for Generic Methods

Overloaded methods are often used to perform *similar* operations on *different* types of data. To motivate generic methods, let's begin with an example (Fig. 19.1) containing overloaded `printArray` methods (lines 21–28, 31–38 and 41–48) that print the `String` representations of the elements of an `Integer` array, a `Double` array and a `Character` array, respectively. We could have used arrays of primitive types `int`, `double` and `char`. We're using arrays of the type-wrapper classes to set up our generic method example, because *only reference types can be used with generic methods and classes.*

```java
1   // Fig. 19.1: OverloadedMethods.java
2   // Printing array elements using overloaded methods.
3   public class OverloadedMethods
4   {
5      public static void main( String[] args )
6      {
7         // create arrays of Integer, Double and Character
8         Integer[] integerArray = { 1, 2, 3, 4, 5, 6 };
9         Double[] doubleArray = { 1.1, 2.2, 3.3, 4.4, 5.5, 6.6, 7.7 };
10        Character[] characterArray = { 'H', 'E', 'L', 'L', 'O' };
11
12        System.out.println( "Array integerArray contains:" );
13        printArray( integerArray ); // pass an Integer array
14        System.out.println( "\nArray doubleArray contains:" );
15        printArray( doubleArray ); // pass a Double array
16        System.out.println( "\nArray characterArray contains:" );
17        printArray( characterArray ); // pass a Character array
18     } // end main
19
20     // method printArray to print Integer array
21     public static void printArray( Integer[] inputArray )
22     {
23        // display array elements
24        for ( Integer element : inputArray )
25           System.out.printf( "%s ", element );
26
27        System.out.println();
28     } // end method printArray
29
30     // method printArray to print Double array
31     public static void printArray( Double[] inputArray )
32     {
33        // display array elements
34        for ( Double element : inputArray )
35           System.out.printf( "%s ", element );
36
37        System.out.println();
38     } // end method printArray
39
40     // method printArray to print Character array
41     public static void printArray( Character[] inputArray )
42     {
43        // display array elements
44        for ( Character element : inputArray )
45           System.out.printf( "%s ", element );
46
47        System.out.println();
48     } // end method printArray
49  } // end class OverloadedMethods
```

Fig. 19.1 | Printing array elements using overloaded methods. (Part 1 of 2.)

```
Array integerArray contains:
1 2 3 4 5 6

Array doubleArray contains:
1.1 2.2 3.3 4.4 5.5 6.6 7.7

Array characterArray contains:
H E L L O
```

Fig. 19.1 | Printing array elements using overloaded methods. (Part 2 of 2.)

The program begins by declaring and initializing three arrays—six-element `Integer` array `integerArray` (line 8), seven-element `Double` array `doubleArray` (line 9) and five-element `Character` array `characterArray` (line 10). Then lines 12–17 display the contents of each array.

When the compiler encounters a method call, it attempts to locate a method declaration with the same name and parameters that match the argument types in the call. In this example, each `printArray` call matches one of the `printArray` method declarations. For example, line 13 calls `printArray` with `integerArray` as its argument. The compiler determines the argument's type (i.e., `Integer[]`) and attempts to locate a `printArray` method that specifies an `Integer[]` parameter (lines 21–28), then sets up a call to that method. Similarly, when the compiler encounters the call at line 15, it determines the argument's type (i.e., `Double[]`), then attempts to locate a `printArray` method that specifies a `Double[]` parameter (lines 31–38), then sets up a call to that method. Finally, when the compiler encounters the call at line 17, it determines the argument's type (i.e., `Character[]`), then attempts to locate a `printArray` method that specifies a `Character[]` parameter (lines 41–48), then sets up a call to that method.

Study each `printArray` method. The array element type appears in each method's header (lines 21, 31 and 41) and `for`-statement header (lines 24, 34 and 44). If we were to replace the element types in each method with a generic name—`T` by convention—then all three methods would look like the one in Fig. 19.2. It appears that if we can replace the array element type in each of the three methods with a *single generic type*, then we should be able to declare *one* `printArray` method that can display the `String` representations of the elements of *any* array that contains objects. The method in Fig. 19.2 is similar to the generic `printArray` method declaration we discuss in Section 19.3.

```
1  public static void printArray( T[] inputArray )
2  {
3     // display array elements
4     for ( T element : inputArray )
5        System.out.printf( "%s ", element );
6
7     System.out.println();
8  } // end method printArray
```

Fig. 19.2 | `printArray` method in which actual type names are replaced by convention with the generic name T.

19.3 Generic Methods: Implementation and Compile-Time Translation

If the operations performed by several overloaded methods are *identical* for each argument type, the overloaded methods can be more compactly and conveniently coded using a generic method. You can write a single generic method declaration that can be called with arguments of different types. Based on the types of the arguments passed to the generic method, the compiler handles each method call appropriately.

Figure 19.3 reimplements the application of Fig. 19.1 using a generic printArray method (lines 22–29). The printArray method calls in lines 14, 16 and 18 are identical to those of Fig. 19.1 (lines 14, 16 and 18) and the outputs of the two applications are identical. This dramatically demonstrates the expressive power of generics.

```java
 1   // Fig. 19.3: GenericMethodTest.java
 2   // Printing array elements using generic method printArray.
 3
 4   public class GenericMethodTest
 5   {
 6      public static void main( String[] args )
 7      {
 8         // create arrays of Integer, Double and Character
 9         Integer[] intArray = { 1, 2, 3, 4, 5 };
10         Double[] doubleArray = { 1.1, 2.2, 3.3, 4.4, 5.5, 6.6, 7.7 };
11         Character[] charArray = { 'H', 'E', 'L', 'L', 'O' };
12
13         System.out.println( "Array integerArray contains:" );
14         printArray( integerArray ); // pass an Integer array
15         System.out.println( "\nArray doubleArray contains:" );
16         printArray( doubleArray ); // pass a Double array
17         System.out.println( "\nArray characterArray contains:" );
18         printArray( characterArray ); // pass a Character array
19      } // end main
20
21      // generic method printArray
22      public static < T > void printArray( T[] inputArray )
23      {
24         // display array elements
25         for ( T element : inputArray )
26            System.out.printf( "%s ", element );
27
28         System.out.println();
29      } // end method printArray
30   } // end class GenericMethodTest
```

```
Array integerArray contains:
1 2 3 4 5 6

Array doubleArray contains:
1.1 2.2 3.3 4.4 5.5 6.6 7.7

Array characterArray contains:
H E L L O
```

Fig. 19.3 | Printing array elements using generic method printArray.

Line 22 begins method `printArray`'s declaration. All generic method declarations have a **type-parameter section** delimited by **angle brackets** (< and >) that precedes the method's return type (< T > in this example). Each type-parameter section contains one or more **type parameters** (also called **formal type parameters**), separated by commas. A type parameter, also known as a **type variable**, is an identifier that specifies a generic type name. The type parameters can be used to declare the return type, parameter types and local variable types in a generic method declaration, and they act as placeholders for the types of the arguments passed to the generic method, which are known as **actual type arguments**. A generic method's body is declared like that of any other method. *Type parameters can represent only reference types*—not primitive types (like `int`, `double` and `char`). Note, too, that the type-parameter names throughout the method declaration must match those declared in the type-parameter section. For example, line 25 declares `element` as type `T`, which matches the type parameter (`T`) declared in line 22. Also, a type parameter can be declared only once in the type-parameter section but can appear more than once in the method's parameter list. For example, the type-parameter name `T` appears twice in the following method's parameter list:

```
public static < T > void printTwoArrays( T[] array1, T[] array2 )
```

Type-parameter names need not be unique among different generic methods.

> **Common Programming Error 19.1**
> *When declaring a generic method, failing to place a type-parameter section before the return type of a method is a syntax error—the compiler will not understand the type-parameter names when they're encountered in the method.*

Method `printArray`'s type-parameter section declares type parameter `T` as the *placeholder* for the array element type that `printArray` will output. `T` appears in the parameter list as the array element type (line 22). The for-statement header (line 25) also uses `T` as the element type. These are the same two locations where the overloaded `printArray` methods of Fig. 19.1 specified `Integer`, `Double` or `Character` as the array element type. The remainder of `printArray` is identical to the versions presented in Fig. 19.1.

> **Good Programming Practice 19.1**
> *It's recommended that type parameters be specified as individual capital letters. Typically, a type parameter that represents an array element's type (or other collection) is named T.*

As in Fig. 19.1, the program begins by declaring and initializing six-element `Integer` array `integerArray` (line 9), seven-element `Double` array `doubleArray` (line 10) and five-element `Character` array `characterArray` (line 11). Then the program outputs each array by calling `printArray` (lines 14, 16 and 18)—once with argument `integerArray`, once with argument `doubleArray` and once with argument `characterArray`.

When the compiler encounters line 14, it first determines argument `integerArray`'s type (i.e., `Integer[]`) and attempts to locate a method named `printArray` that specifies a single `Integer[]` parameter. There's no such method in this example. Next, the compiler determines whether there's a generic method named `printArray` that specifies a single array parameter and uses a type parameter to represent the array element type. The compiler determines that `printArray` (lines 22–29) is a match and sets up a call to the method. The same process is repeated for the calls to method `printArray` at lines 16 and 18.

Common Programming Error 19.2

If the compiler cannot match a method call to a nongeneric or a generic method declaration, a compilation error occurs.

Common Programming Error 19.3

If the compiler doesn't find a method declaration that matches a method call exactly, but does find two or more methods that can satisfy the method call, a compilation error occurs.

In addition to setting up the method calls, the compiler also determines whether the operations in the method body can be applied to elements of the type stored in the array argument. The only operation performed on the array elements in this example is to output their `String` representation. Line 26 performs an *implicit toString call* on every element. *To work with generics, every element of the array must be an object of a class or interface type.* Since all objects have a `toString` method, the compiler is satisfied that line 26 performs a *valid* operation for any object in `printArray`'s array argument. The `toString` methods of classes `Integer`, `Double` and `Character` return the `String` representation of the underlying `int`, `double` or `char` value, respectively.

Erasure at Compilation Time

When the compiler translates generic method `printArray` into Java bytecodes, it removes the type-parameter section and *replaces the type parameters with actual types*. This process is known as **erasure**. By default all generic types are replaced with type `Object`. So the compiled version of method `printArray` appears as shown in Fig. 19.4—there's only *one* copy of this code, which is used for all `printArray` calls in the example. This is quite different from other, similar mechanisms, such as C++'s templates, in which a *separate copy of the source code* is generated and compiled for *every* type passed as an argument to the method. As you'll see in Section 19.4, the translation and compilation of generics is a bit more involved than what we've discussed in this section.

By declaring `printArray` as a generic method in Fig. 19.3, we eliminated the need for the overloaded methods of Fig. 19.1, saving 19 lines of code and creating a reusable method that can output the `String` representations of the elements in any array that contains objects. However, this particular example could have simply declared the `printArray` method as shown in Fig. 19.4, using an `Object` array as the parameter. This would have yielded the same results, because any `Object` can be output as a `String`. In a generic method, the benefits become apparent when the method also uses a type parameter as the method's return type, as we demonstrate in the next section.

```
1   public static void printArray( Object[] inputArray )
2   {
3       // display array elements
4       for ( Object element : inputArray )
5           System.out.printf( "%s ", element );
6
7       System.out.println();
8   } // end method printArray
```

Fig. 19.4 | Generic method `printArray` after erasure is performed by the compiler.

19.4 Additional Compile-Time Translation Issues: Methods That Use a Type Parameter as the Return Type

Let's consider a generic method example in which type parameters are used in the return type and in the parameter list (Fig. 19.5). The application uses a generic method maximum to determine and return the largest of its three arguments of the same type. Unfortunately, *the relational operator > cannot be used with reference types*. However, it's possible to compare two objects of the same class if that class implements the generic **interface Comparable\<T>** (package java.lang). All the type-wrapper classes for primitive types implement this interface. Like generic classes, **generic interfaces** enable you to specify, with a single interface declaration, a set of related types. Comparable\<T> objects have a **compareTo method**. For example, if we have two Integer objects, integer1 and integer2, they can be compared with the expression:

```
integer1.compareTo( integer2 )
```

It's your responsibility when you declare a class that implements Comparable\<T> to declare method compareTo such that it compares the contents of two objects of that class and returns the comparison results. As specified in interface Comparable\<T>'s documentation, compareTo *must* return 0 if the objects are equal, a negative integer if object1 is less than object2 or a positive integer if object1 is greater than object2. For example, class Integer's compareTo method compares the int values stored in two Integer objects. A benefit of implementing interface Comparable\<T> is that Comparable\<T> objects can be used with the sorting and searching methods of class Collections (package java.util). We discussed those methods in Chapter 18. In this example, we'll use method compareTo in method maximum to help determine the largest value.

```
1   // Fig. 19.5: MaximumTest.java
2   // Generic method maximum returns the largest of three objects.
3
4   public class MaximumTest
5   {
6      public static void main( String[] args )
7      {
8         System.out.printf( "Maximum of %d, %d and %d is %d\n\n", 3, 4, 5,
9            maximum( 3, 4, 5 ) );
10        System.out.printf( "Maximum of %.1f, %.1f and %.1f is %.1f\n\n",
11           6.6, 8.8, 7.7, maximum( 6.6, 8.8, 7.7 ) );
12        System.out.printf( "Maximum of %s, %s and %s is %s\n", "pear",
13           "apple", "orange", maximum( "pear", "apple", "orange" ) );
14     } // end main
15
16     // determines the largest of three Comparable objects
17     public static < T extends Comparable< T > > T maximum( T x, T y, T z )
18     {
19        T max = x; // assume x is initially the largest
20
21        if ( y.compareTo( max ) > 0 )
22           max = y; // y is the largest so far
```

Fig. 19.5 | Generic method maximum with an upper bound on its type parameter. (Part 1 of 2.)

```
23
24        if ( z.compareTo( max ) > 0 )
25           max = z; // z is the largest
26
27        return max; // returns the largest object
28    } // end method maximum
29  } // end class MaximumTest
```

```
Maximum of 3, 4 and 5 is 5

Maximum of 6.6, 8.8 and 7.7 is 8.8

Maximum of pear, apple and orange is pear
```

Fig. 19.5 | Generic method `maximum` with an upper bound on its type parameter. (Part 2 of 2.)

Generic Method `maximum`

Generic method `maximum` (lines 17–28) uses type parameter T as the return type of the method (line 17), as the type of method parameters x, y and z (line 17), and as the type of local variable max (line 19). The type-parameter section specifies that T extends Comparable<T>—only objects of classes that implement interface Comparable<T> can be used with this method. In this case, Comparable is known as the **upper bound** of the type parameter. By default, Object is the upper bound. Type-parameter declarations that bound the parameter always use keyword extends regardless of whether the type parameter extends a class or implements an interface. This type parameter is more restrictive than the one specified for printArray in Fig. 19.3, which was able to output arrays containing any type of object. The restriction of using Comparable<T> objects is important, because not all objects can be compared. However, Comparable<T> objects are guaranteed to have a compareTo method.

Method maximum uses the same algorithm that we used in Section 6.4 to determine the largest of its three arguments. The method assumes that its first argument (x) is the largest and assigns it to local variable max (line 19). Next, the if statement at lines 21–22 determines whether y is greater than max. The condition invokes y's compareTo method with the expression y.compareTo(max), which returns a negative integer, 0 or a positive integer, to determine y's relationship to max. If the return value of the compareTo is greater than 0, then y is greater and is assigned to variable max. Similarly, the if statement at lines 24–25 determines whether z is greater than max. If so, line 25 assigns z to max. Then line 27 returns max to the caller.

Calling Method `maximum`

In main (lines 6–14), line 9 calls maximum with the integers 3, 4 and 5. When the compiler encounters this call, it first looks for a maximum method that takes three arguments of type int. There's no such method, so the compiler looks for a generic method that can be used and finds generic method maximum. However, recall that the arguments to a generic method must be of a *reference type*. So the compiler autoboxes the three int values as Integer objects and specifies that the three Integer objects will be passed to maximum. Class Integer (package java.lang) implements the Comparable<Integer> interface such that method compareTo compares the int values in two Integer objects. Therefore, Integers are valid arguments to method maximum. When the Integer representing the maximum is returned, we attempt to output it with the %d format specifier, which outputs an int primitive-type value. So maximum's return value is output as an int value.

A similar process occurs for the three double arguments passed to maximum in line 11. Each double is autoboxed as a Double object and passed to maximum. Again, this is allowed because class Double (package java.lang) implements the Comparable<Double> interface. The Double returned by maximum is output with the format specifier %.1f, which outputs a double primitive-type value. So maximum's return value is auto-unboxed and output as a double. The call to maximum in line 13 receives three Strings, which are also Comparable<String> objects. We intentionally placed the largest value in a different position in each method call (lines 9, 11 and 13) to show that the generic method always finds the maximum value, regardless of its position in the argument list.

Upper Bound of a Type Parameter

When the compiler translates method maximum into bytecodes, it uses erasure (introduced in Section 19.3) to replace the type parameters with actual types. In Fig. 19.3, all generic types were replaced with type Object. Actually, all type parameters are replaced with the so-called *upper bound* of the type parameter, which is specified in the type-parameter section. To indicate the upper bound, follow the type parameter's name with the keyword extends and the class or interface name that represents the upper bound, or a comma-separated list of the types that represent the upper bound. The list may contain zero or one class and zero or more interfaces. For example, in method maximum's type-parameter section (Fig. 19.5), we specified the upper bound of the type parameter T as type Comparable<T> as follows:

```
T extends Comparable< T >
```

Thus, only Comparable<T> objects can be passed as arguments to maximum—anything that is not a Comparable<T> will result in compilation errors. Unless specified otherwise, Object is the default upper bound. Figure 19.6 simulates the erasure of method maximum's types by showing the method's source code after the type-parameter section is removed and type parameter T is replaced with the upper bound, Comparable, throughout the method declaration. The erasure of Comparable<T> is simply Comparable.

```
1   public static Comparable maximum(Comparable x, Comparable y, Comparable z)
2   {
3      Comparable max = x; // assume x is initially the largest
4
5      if ( y.compareTo( max ) > 0 )
6         max = y; // y is the largest so far
7
8      if ( z.compareTo( max ) > 0 )
9         max = z; // z is the largest
10
11     return max; // returns the largest object
12  } // end method maximum
```

Fig. 19.6 | Generic method maximum after erasure is performed by the compiler.

After erasure, method maximum specifies that it returns type Comparable. However, the calling method does not expect to receive a Comparable. It expects to receive an object of the same type that was passed to maximum as an argument—Integer, Double or String in this example. When the compiler replaces the type-parameter information with the upper-bound type in the method declaration, it also inserts *explicit cast operations* in front of each method call to ensure that the returned value is of the type expected by the caller. Thus, the call to maximum in line 9 (Fig. 19.5) is preceded by an Integer cast, as in

```
(Integer) maximum( 3, 4, 5 )
```

the call to maximum in line 11 is preceded by a Double cast, as in

```
(Double) maximum( 6.6, 8.8, 7.7 )
```

and the call to maximum in line 13 is preceded by a String cast, as in

```
(String) maximum( "pear", "apple", "orange" )
```

In each case, the type of the cast for the return value is *inferred* from the types of the method arguments in the particular method call, because, according to the method declaration, the return type and the argument types match.

Possible *ClassCastExceptions*
In this example, you cannot use a method that accepts Objects, because class Object provides only an equality comparison. Also, without generics, you'd be responsible for implementing the cast operation. Using generics ensures that the inserted cast will never throw a ClassCastException, assuming that generics are used throughout your code (i.e., you do not mix old code with new generics code).

19.5 Overloading Generic Methods

A generic method may be overloaded. A class can provide two or more generic methods that specify the same method name but different method parameters. For example, generic method printArray of Fig. 19.3 could be overloaded with another printArray generic method with the additional parameters lowSubscript and highSubscript to specify the portion of the array to output.

A generic method can also be overloaded by nongeneric methods. When the compiler encounters a method call, it searches for the method declaration that most precisely matches the method name and the argument types specified in the call. For example, generic method printArray of Fig. 19.3 could be overloaded with a version that's specific to Strings, which outputs the Strings in neat, tabular format.

When the compiler encounters a method call, it performs a matching process to determine which method to invoke. The compiler tries to find and use a precise match in which the method name and argument types of the method call match those of a specific method declaration. If there's no such method, the compiler attempts to find a method with compatible types or a matching generic method.

19.6 Generic Classes

The concept of a data structure, such as a stack, can be understood *independently* of the element type it manipulates. Generic classes provide a means for describing the concept of a stack (or any other class) in a type-independent manner. We can then instantiate type-specific objects of the generic class. This capability provides a wonderful opportunity for software reusability.

Once you have a generic class, you can use a simple, concise notation to indicate the type(s) that should be used in place of the class's type parameter(s). At compilation time, the compiler ensures the *type safety* of your code and uses the *erasure* techniques described in Sections 19.3–19.4 to enable your client code to interact with the generic class.

One generic Stack class, for example, could be the basis for creating many logical Stack classes (e.g., "Stack of Double," "Stack of Integer," "Stack of Character," "Stack of Employee"). These classes are known as **parameterized classes** or **parameterized types** because they accept one or more type parameters. Recall that type parameters represent only *reference types*, which means the Stack generic class cannot be instantiated with primitive types. However, we can instantiate a Stack that stores objects of Java's type-wrapper classes and allow Java to use *autoboxing* to convert the primitive values into objects. Recall that autoboxing occurs when a value of a primitive type (e.g., int) is pushed onto a Stack that contains wrapper-class objects (e.g., Integer). *Auto-unboxing* occurs when an object of the wrapper class is popped off the Stack and assigned to a primitive-type variable.

Implementing a Generic Stack Class

Figure 19.7 presents a generic Stack class declaration. A generic class declaration looks like a nongeneric one, but the class name is followed by *a type-parameter section* (line 5). In this case, type parameter T represents the element type the Stack will manipulate. As with generic methods, the type-parameter section of a generic class can have one or more type parameters separated by commas. Type parameter T is used throughout the Stack class declaration to represent the element type. This example implements a Stack as an ArrayList.

```java
1   // Fig. 19.7: Stack.java
2   // Stack generic class declaration.
3   import java.util.ArrayList;
4
5   public class Stack< T >
6   {
7      private ArrayList< T > elements; // ArrayList stores stack elements
8
9      // no-argument constructor creates a stack of the default size
10     public Stack()
11     {
12        this( 10 ); // default stack size
13     } // end no-argument Stack constructor
14
15     // constructor creates a stack of the specified number of elements
16     public Stack( int capacity )
17     {
18        int initCapacity = capacity > 0 ? capacity : 10; // validate
19        elements = new ArrayList< T >( initCapacity ); // create ArrayList
20     } // end one-argument Stack constructor
21
22     // push element onto stack
23     public void push( T pushValue )
24     {
```

Fig. 19.7 | Stack generic class declaration. (Part 1 of 2.)

```
25            elements.add( pushValue ); // place pushValue on Stack
26    } // end method push
27
28    // return the top element if not empty; else throw EmptyStackException
29    public T pop()
30    {
31       if ( elements.isEmpty() ) // if stack is empty
32          throw new EmptyStackException( "Stack is empty, cannot pop" );
33
34       // remove and return top element of Stack
35       return elements.remove( elements.size() - 1 );
36    } // end method pop
37 } // end class Stack< T >
```

Fig. 19.7 | Stack generic class declaration. (Part 2 of 2.)

Class `Stack` declares variable `elements` as an `ArrayList<T>` (line 7). This `ArrayList` will store the `Stack`'s elements. As you know, an `ArrayList` can grow dynamically, so objects of our `Stack` class can also grow dynamically. The `Stack` class's no-argument constructor (lines 10–13) invokes the one-argument constructor (lines 16–20) to create a `Stack` in which the underlying `ArrayList` has a capacity of 10 elements. The one-argument constructor can also be called directly to create a `Stack` with a specified initial capacity. Line 18 validates the constructor's argument. Line 19 creates the `ArrayList` of the specified capacity (or 10 if the capacity was invalid).

Method `push` (lines 23–26) uses `ArrayList` method `add` to append the pushed item to the end of the `ArrayList` `elements`. The last element in the `ArrayList` represents the *top* of the stack.

Method `pop` (lines 29–36) first determines whether an attempt is being made to pop an element from an empty `Stack`. If so, line 32 throws an `EmptyStackException` (declared in Fig. 19.8). Otherwise, line 35 returns the top element of the `Stack` by removing the last element in the underlying `ArrayList`.

Class `EmptyStackException` (Fig. 19.8) provides a no-argument constructor and a one-argument constructor. The no-argument constructor sets the default error message, and the one-argument constructor sets a custom error message.

```
1  // Fig. 19.8: EmptyStackException.java
2  // EmptyStackException class declaration.
3  public class EmptyStackException extends RuntimeException
4  {
5     // no-argument constructor
6     public EmptyStackException()
7     {
8        this( "Stack is empty" );
9     } // end no-argument EmptyStackException constructor
10
11    // one-argument constructor
12    public EmptyStackException( String message )
13    {
```

Fig. 19.8 | EmptyStackException class declaration. (Part 1 of 2.)

```
14          super( message );
15       } // end one-argument EmptyStackException constructor
16    } // end class EmptyStackException
```

Fig. 19.8 | EmptyStackException class declaration. (Part 2 of 2.)

As with generic methods, when a generic class is compiled, the compiler performs *erasure* on the class's type parameters and replaces them with their upper bounds. For class Stack (Fig. 19.7), no upper bound is specified, so the default upper bound, Object, is used. The scope of a generic class's type parameter is the entire class. However, type parameters *cannot* be used in a class's static variable declarations.

Testing the Generic *Stack* Class of Fig. 19.7

Now, let's consider the application (Fig. 19.9) that uses the Stack generic class (Fig. 19.7). Lines 12–13 create and initialize variables of type Stack<Double> (pronounced "Stack of Double") and Stack<Integer> (pronounced "Stack of Integer"). The types Double and Integer are known as the Stack's **type arguments**. The compiler uses them to replace the type parameters so that it can perform type checking and insert cast operations as necessary. We'll discuss the cast operations in more detail shortly. Lines 12–13 instantiate doubleStack with a capacity of 5 and integerStack with a capacity of 10 (the default). Lines 16–17 and 20–21 call methods testPushDouble (lines 25–36), testPopDouble (lines 39–59), testPushInteger (lines 62–73) and testPopInteger (lines 76–96), respectively, to demonstrate the two Stacks in this example.

```
1    // Fig. 19.9: StackTest.java
2    // Stack generic class test program.
3
4    public class StackTest
5    {
6       public static void main( String[] args )
7       {
8          double[] doubleElements = { 1.1, 2.2, 3.3, 4.4, 5.5 };
9          int[] integerElements = { 1, 2, 3, 4, 5, 6, 7, 8, 9, 10 };
10
11         // Create a Stack< Double > and a Stack< Integer >
12         Stack< Double > doubleStack = new Stack< Double >( 5 );
13         Stack< Integer > integerStack = new Stack< Integer >();
14
15         // push elements of doubleElements onto doubleStack
16         testPushDouble( doubleStack, doubleElements );
17         testPopDouble( doubleStack ); // pop from doubleStack
18
19         // push elements of integerElements onto integerStack
20         testPushInteger( integerStack, integerElements );
21         testPopInteger( integerStack ); // pop from integerStack
22      } // end main
23
```

Fig. 19.9 | Stack generic class test program. (Part 1 of 3.)

```
24       // test push method with double stack
25       private static void testPushDouble(
26          Stack< Double > stack, double[] values )
27       {
28          System.out.println( "\nPushing elements onto doubleStack" );
29
30          // push elements to Stack
31          for ( double value : values )
32          {
33             System.out.printf( "%.1f ", value );
34             stack.push( value ); // push onto doubleStack
35          } // end for
36       } // end method testPushDouble
37
38       // test pop method with double stack
39       private static void testPopDouble( Stack< Double > stack )
40       {
41          // pop elements from stack
42          try
43          {
44             System.out.println( "\nPopping elements from doubleStack" );
45             double popValue; // store element removed from stack
46
47             // remove all elements from Stack
48             while ( true )
49             {
50                popValue = stack.pop(); // pop from doubleStack
51                System.out.printf( "%.1f ", popValue );
52             } // end while
53          } // end try
54          catch( EmptyStackException emptyStackException )
55          {
56             System.err.println();
57             emptyStackException.printStackTrace();
58          } // end catch EmptyStackException
59       } // end method testPopDouble
60
61       // test push method with integer stack
62       private static void testPushInteger(
63          Stack< Integer > stack, int[] values )
64       {
65          System.out.println( "\nPushing elements onto integerStack" );
66
67          // push elements to Stack
68          for ( int value : values )
69          {
70             System.out.printf( "%d ", value );
71             stack.push( value ); // push onto integerStack
72          } // end for
73       } // end method testPushInteger
74
```

Fig. 19.9 | Stack generic class test program. (Part 2 of 3.)

```
75    // test pop method with integer stack
76    private static void testPopInteger( Stack< Integer > stack )
77    {
78       // pop elements from stack
79       try
80       {
81          System.out.println( "\nPopping elements from integerStack" );
82          int popValue; // store element removed from stack
83
84          // remove all elements from Stack
85          while ( true )
86          {
87             popValue = stack.pop(); // pop from intStack
88             System.out.printf( "%d ", popValue );
89          } // end while
90       } // end try
91       catch( EmptyStackException emptyStackException )
92       {
93          System.err.println();
94          emptyStackException.printStackTrace();
95       } // end catch EmptyStackException
96    } // end method testPopInteger
97 } // end class StackTest
```

```
Pushing elements onto doubleStack
1.1 2.2 3.3 4.4 5.5
Popping elements from doubleStack
5.5 4.4 3.3 2.2 1.1
EmptyStackException: Stack is empty, cannot pop
        at Stack.pop(Stack.java:32)
        at StackTest.testPopDouble(StackTest.java:50)
        at StackTest.main(StackTest.java:17)

Pushing elements onto integerStack
1 2 3 4 5 6 7 8 9 10
Popping elements from integerStack
10 9 8 7 6 5 4 3 2 1
EmptyStackException: Stack is empty, cannot pop
        at Stack.pop(Stack.java:32)
        at StackTest.testPopInteger(StackTest.java:87)
        at StackTest.main(StackTest.java:21)
```

Fig. 19.9 | Stack generic class test program. (Part 3 of 3.)

Methods testPushDouble *and* testPopDouble

Method testPushDouble (lines 25–36) invokes method push (line 34) to place the double values 1.1, 2.2, 3.3, 4.4 and 5.5 from array doubleElements onto doubleStack. *Autoboxing* occurs in line 34 when the program tries to push a primitive double value onto the doubleStack, which stores only references to Double objects.

Method testPopDouble (lines 39–59) invokes Stack method pop (line 50) in an infinite while loop (lines 48–52) to remove all the values from the stack. Note in the output that the values indeed pop off in last-in, first-out order (the defining characteristic of stacks). When the loop attempts to pop a sixth value, the doubleStack is empty, so the pop throws an `EmptyStackException`, which causes the program to proceed to the `catch` block (lines 54–58) to handle the exception. The stack trace indicates the exception that occurred and shows that `Stack` method `pop` generated the exception at line 32 of the file `Stack.java` (Fig. 19.7). The trace also shows that method `pop` was called by `StackTest` method `testPopDouble` at line 50 of `StackTest.java` and that method `testPopDouble` was called from method `main` at line 17 of `StackTest.java`. This information enables you to determine the methods that were on the method-call stack at the time that the exception occurred. Because the program catches the exception, the exception is considered to have been handled and the program can continue executing.

Auto-unboxing occurs in line 50 when the program assigns the `Double` object popped from the stack to a `double` primitive variable. Recall from Section 19.4 that the compiler inserts casts to ensure that the proper types are returned from generic methods. After erasure, `Stack` method `pop` returns type `Object`, but the client code in `testPopDouble` expects to receive a `double` when method `pop` returns. So the compiler inserts a `Double` cast, as in

```
popValue = ( Double ) stack.pop();
```

The value assigned to `popValue` will be *unboxed* from the `Double` object returned by `pop`.

Methods *testPushInteger* and *testPopInteger*
Method `testPushInteger` (lines 62–73) invokes `Stack` method `push` to place values onto `integerStack` until it's full. Method `testPopInteger` (lines 76–96) invokes `Stack` method `pop` to remove values from `integerStack`. Once again, the values are popped in last-in, first-out order. During *erasure*, the compiler recognizes that the client code in method `testPopInteger` expects to receive an `int` when method `pop` returns. So the compiler inserts an `Integer` cast, as in

```
popValue = ( Integer ) stack.pop();
```

The value assigned to `popValue` will be unboxed from the `Integer` object returned by `pop`.

Creating Generic Methods to Test Class *Stack<T>*
The code in methods `testPushDouble` and `testPushInteger` is *almost identical* for pushing values onto a `Stack<Double>` or a `Stack<Integer>`, respectively, and the code in methods `testPopDouble` and `testPopInteger` is almost identical for popping values from a `Stack<Double>` or a `Stack<Integer>`, respectively. This presents another opportunity to use generic methods. Figure 19.10 declares generic method `testPush` (lines 24–35) to perform the same tasks as `testPushDouble` and `testPushInteger` in Fig. 19.9—that is, push values onto a `Stack<T>`. Similarly, generic method `testPop` (lines 38–58) performs the same tasks as `testPopDouble` and `testPopInteger` in Fig. 19.9—that is, pop values off a `Stack<T>`. The output of Fig. 19.10 precisely matches that of Fig. 19.9.

```
1   // Fig. 19.10: StackTest2.java
2   // Passing generic Stack objects to generic methods.
3   public class StackTest2
4   {
5      public static void main( String[] args )
6      {
```

Fig. 19.10 | Passing generic `Stack` objects to generic methods. (Part 1 of 3.)

```
 7          Double[] doubleElements = { 1.1, 2.2, 3.3, 4.4, 5.5 };
 8          Integer[] integerElements = { 1, 2, 3, 4, 5, 6, 7, 8, 9, 10 };
 9
10          // Create a Stack< Double > and a Stack< Integer >
11          Stack< Double > doubleStack = new Stack< Double >( 5 );
12          Stack< Integer > integerStack = new Stack< Integer >();
13
14          // push elements of doubleElements onto doubleStack
15          testPush( "doubleStack", doubleStack, doubleElements );
16          testPop( "doubleStack", doubleStack ); // pop from doubleStack
17
18          // push elements of integerElements onto integerStack
19          testPush( "integerStack", integerStack, integerElements );
20          testPop( "integerStack", integerStack ); // pop from integerStack
21       } // end main
22
23       // generic method testPush pushes elements onto a Stack
24       public static < T > void testPush( String name , Stack< T > stack,
25          T[] elements )
26       {
27          System.out.printf( "\nPushing elements onto %s\n", name );
28
29          // push elements onto Stack
30          for ( T element : elements )
31          {
32             System.out.printf( "%s ", element );
33             stack.push( element ); // push element onto stack
34          } // end for
35       } // end method testPush
36
37       // generic method testPop pops elements from a Stack
38       public static < T > void testPop( String name, Stack< T > stack )
39       {
40          // pop elements from stack
41          try
42          {
43             System.out.printf( "\nPopping elements from %s\n", name );
44             T popValue; // store element removed from stack
45
46             // remove all elements from Stack
47             while ( true )
48             {
49                popValue = stack.pop();
50                System.out.printf( "%s ", popValue );
51             } // end while
52          } // end try
53          catch( EmptyStackException emptyStackException )
54          {
55             System.out.println();
56             emptyStackException.printStackTrace();
57          } // end catch EmptyStackException
58       } // end method testPop
59    } // end class StackTest2
```

Fig. 19.10 | Passing generic Stack objects to generic methods. (Part 2 of 3.)

```
Pushing elements onto doubleStack
1.1 2.2 3.3 4.4 5.5
Popping elements from doubleStack
5.5 4.4 3.3 2.2 1.1
EmptyStackException: Stack is empty, cannot pop
        at Stack.pop(Stack.java:32)
        at StackTest2.testPop(StackTest2.java:50)
        at StackTest2.main(StackTest2.java:17)

Pushing elements onto integerStack
1 2 3 4 5 6 7 8 9 10
Popping elements from integerStack
10 9 8 7 6 5 4 3 2 1
EmptyStackException: Stack is empty, cannot pop
        at Stack.pop(Stack.java:32)
        at StackTest2.testPop(StackTest2.java:50)
        at StackTest2.main(StackTest2.java:21)
```

Fig. 19.10 | Passing generic `Stack` objects to generic methods. (Part 3 of 3.)

Lines 11–12 create the `Stack<Double>` and `Stack<Integer>` objects, respectively. Lines 15–16 and 19–20 invoke generic methods `testPush` and `testPop` to test the `Stack` objects. Because type parameters can represent only reference types, to be able to pass arrays `doubleElements` and `integerElements` to generic method `testPush`, the arrays declared in lines 7–8 must be declared with the wrapper types `Double` and `Integer`. When these arrays are initialized with primitive values, the compiler *autoboxes* each primitive value.

Generic method `testPush` (lines 24–35) uses type parameter T (specified at line 24) to represent the data type stored in the `Stack<T>`. The generic method takes three arguments—a `String` that represents the name of the `Stack<T>` object for output purposes, a reference to an object of type `Stack<T>` and an array of type T—the type of elements that will be pushed onto `Stack<T>`. The compiler enforces *consistency* between the type of the `Stack` and the elements that will be pushed onto the `Stack` when `push` is invoked, which is the real value of the generic method call. Generic method `testPop` (lines 38–58) takes two arguments—a `String` that represents the name of the `Stack<T>` object for output purposes and a reference to an object of type `Stack<T>`.

19.7 Raw Types

The test programs for generic class `Stack` in Section 19.6 instantiate `Stack`s with type arguments `Double` and `Integer`. It's also possible to instantiate generic class `Stack` without specifying a type argument, as follows:

```
Stack objectStack = new Stack( 5 ); // no type-argument specified
```

In this case, the `objectStack` is said to have a **raw type**, which means that the compiler implicitly uses type `Object` throughout the generic class for each type argument. Thus the preceding statement creates a `Stack` that can store objects of any type. This is important for *backward compatibility* with prior versions of Java. For example, the data structures of the Java Collections Framework (see Chapter 18) all stored references to `Object`s, but are now implemented as generic types.

A raw-type Stack variable can be assigned a Stack that specifies a type argument, such as a Stack<Double> object, as follows:

```
Stack rawTypeStack2 = new Stack< Double >( 5 );
```

because type Double is a subclass of Object. This assignment is allowed because the elements in a Stack<Double> (i.e., Double objects) are certainly objects—class Double is an indirect subclass of Object.

Similarly, a Stack variable that specifies a type argument in its declaration can be assigned a raw-type Stack object, as in:

```
Stack< Integer > integerStack = new Stack( 10 );
```

Although this assignment is permitted, it's *unsafe*, because a Stack of raw type might store types other than Integer. In this case, the compiler issues a warning message which indicates the unsafe assignment.

Using Raw Types with Generic Class Stack

The test program of Fig. 19.11 uses the notion of raw type. Line 11 instantiates generic class Stack with raw type, which indicates that rawTypeStack1 can hold objects of any type. Line 14 assigns a Stack<Double> to variable rawTypeStack2, which is declared as a Stack of raw type. Line 17 assigns a Stack of raw type to Stack<Integer> variable, which is legal but causes the compiler to issue a warning message (Fig. 19.12) indicating a *potentially unsafe assignment*—again, this occurs because a Stack of raw type might store types other than Integer. Also, the calls to generic methods testPush and testPop in lines 19–22 result in compiler warning messages (Fig. 19.12). These occur because rawTypeStack1 and rawTypeStack2 are declared as Stacks of raw type, but methods testPush and testPop each expect a second argument that is a Stack with a specific type argument. The warnings indicate that the compiler cannot guarantee the types manipulated by the stacks to be the correct types, since we did not supply a variable declared with a type argument. Methods testPush (lines 28–39) and testPop (lines 42–62) are the same as in Fig. 19.10.

Figure 19.12 shows the warning messages generated by the compiler when the file RawTypeTest.java (Fig. 19.11) is compiled with the -Xlint:unchecked option, which provides more information about potentially unsafe operations in code that uses generics. The first warning is generated for line 17, which assigned a raw-type Stack to a Stack<Integer> variable—the compiler cannot ensure that all objects in the Stack will be Integer objects. The next warning occurs at line 19. The compiler determines method testPush's type argument from the Double array passed as the third argument, because the second method argument is a raw-type Stack variable. In this case, Double is the type argument, so the compiler expects a Stack<Double> as the second argument. The warning occurs because the compiler cannot ensure that a raw-type Stack contains only Doubles. The warning at line 21 occurs for the same reason, even though the actual Stack that rawTypeStack2 references is a Stack<Double>. The compiler cannot guarantee that the variable will always refer to the same Stack object, so it must use the variable's declared type to perform all type checking. Lines 20 and 22 each generate warnings because method testPop expects as an argument a Stack for which a type argument has been specified. However, in each call to testPop, we pass a raw-type Stack variable. Thus, the compiler indicates a warning because it cannot check the types used in the body of the method. In general, you should avoid using raw types.

```
 1   // Fig. 19.11: RawTypeTest.java
 2   // Raw type test program.
 3   public class RawTypeTest
 4   {
 5      public static void main( String[] args )
 6      {
 7         Double[] doubleElements = { 1.1, 2.2, 3.3, 4.4, 5.5 };
 8         Integer[] integerElements = {  1, 2, 3, 4, 5, 6, 7, 8, 9, 10 };
 9
10         // Stack of raw types assigned to Stack of raw types variable
11         Stack rawTypeStack1 = new Stack( 5 );
12
13         // Stack< Double > assigned to Stack of raw types variable
14         Stack rawTypeStack2 = new Stack< Double >( 5 );
15
16         // Stack of raw types assigned to Stack< Integer > variable
17         Stack< Integer > integerStack = new Stack( 10 );
18
19         testPush( "rawTypeStack1", rawTypeStack1, doubleElements );
20         testPop( "rawTypeStack1", rawTypeStack1 );
21         testPush( "rawTypeStack2", rawTypeStack2, doubleElements );
22         testPop( "rawTypeStack2", rawTypeStack2 );
23         testPush( "integerStack", integerStack, integerElements );
24         testPop( "integerStack", integerStack );
25      } // end main
26
27      // generic method pushes elements onto stack
28      public static < T > void testPush( String name, Stack< T > stack,
29         T[] elements )
30      {
31         System.out.printf( "\nPushing elements onto %s\n", name );
32
33         // push elements onto Stack
34         for ( T element : elements )
35         {
36            System.out.printf( "%s ", element );
37            stack.push( element ); // push element onto stack
38         } // end for
39      } // end method testPush
40
41      // generic method testPop pops elements from stack
42      public static < T > void testPop( String name, Stack< T > stack )
43      {
44         // pop elements from stack
45         try
46         {
47            System.out.printf( "\nPopping elements from %s\n", name );
48            T popValue; // store element removed from stack
49
50            // remove elements from Stack
51            while ( true )
52            {
53               popValue = stack.pop(); // pop from stack
```

Fig. 19.11 | Raw-type test program. (Part 1 of 2.)

```
54                    System.out.printf( "%s ", popValue );
55                } // end while
56            } // end try
57            catch( EmptyStackException emptyStackException )
58            {
59                System.out.println();
60                emptyStackException.printStackTrace();
61            } // end catch EmptyStackException
62        } // end method testPop
63    } // end class RawTypeTest
```

```
Pushing elements onto rawTypeStack1
1.1 2.2 3.3 4.4 5.5
Popping elements from rawTypeStack1
5.5 4.4 3.3 2.2 1.1
EmptyStackException: Stack is empty, cannot pop
        at Stack.pop(Stack.java:32)
        at RawTypeTest.testPop(RawTypeTest.java:53)
        at RawTypeTest.main(RawTypeTest.java:20)

Pushing elements onto rawTypeStack2
1.1 2.2 3.3 4.4 5.5
Popping elements from rawTypeStack2
5.5 4.4 3.3 2.2 1.1
EmptyStackException: Stack is empty, cannot pop
        at Stack.pop(Stack.java:32)
        at RawTypeTest.testPop(RawTypeTest.java:53)
        at RawTypeTest.main(RawTypeTest.java:22)

Pushing elements onto integerStack
1 2 3 4 5 6 7 8 9 10
Popping elements from integerStack
10 9 8 7 6 5 4 3 2 1
EmptyStackException: Stack is empty, cannot pop
        at Stack.pop(Stack.java:32)
        at RawTypeTest.testPop(RawTypeTest.java:53)
        at RawTypeTest.main(RawTypeTest.java:24)
```

Fig. 19.11 | Raw-type test program. (Part 2 of 2.)

```
RawTypeTest.java:17: warning: [unchecked] unchecked conversion
found   : Stack
required: Stack<java.lang.Integer>
      Stack< Integer > integerStack = new Stack( 10 );
                                          ^

RawTypeTest.java:19: warning: [unchecked] unchecked conversion
found   : Stack
required: Stack<java.lang.Double>
      testPush( "rawTypeStack1", rawTypeStack1, doubleElements );
                                      ^
```

Fig. 19.12 | Warning messages from the compiler. (Part 1 of 2.)

```
RawTypeTest.java:19: warning: [unchecked] unchecked method invocation:
<T>testPush(java.lang.String,Stack<T>,T[]) in RawTypeTest is applied to
(java.lang.String,Stack,java.lang.Double[])
      testPush( "rawTypeStack1", rawTypeStack1, doubleElements );
           ^
RawTypeTest.java:20: warning: [unchecked] unchecked conversion
found    : Stack
required: Stack<T>
      testPop( "rawTypeStack1", rawTypeStack1 );
                              ^
RawTypeTest.java:20: warning: [unchecked] unchecked method invocation:
<T>testPop(java.lang.String,Stack<T>) in RawTypeTest is applied to
(java.lang.String,Stack)
      testPop( "rawTypeStack1", rawTypeStack1 );
          ^
RawTypeTest.java:21: warning: [unchecked] unchecked conversion
found    : Stack
required: Stack<java.lang.Double>
      testPush( "rawTypeStack2", rawTypeStack2, doubleElements );
                              ^
RawTypeTest.java:21: warning: [unchecked] unchecked method invocation:
<T>testPush(java.lang.String,Stack<T>,T[]) in RawTypeTest is applied to
(java.lang.String,Stack,java.lang.Double[])
      testPush( "rawTypeStack2", rawTypeStack2, doubleElements );
           ^
RawTypeTest.java:22: warning: [unchecked] unchecked conversion
found    : Stack
required: Stack<T>
      testPop( "rawTypeStack2", rawTypeStack2 );
                              ^
RawTypeTest.java:22: warning: [unchecked] unchecked method invocation:
<T>testPop(java.lang.String,Stack<T>) in RawTypeTest is applied to
(java.lang.String,Stack)
      testPop( "rawTypeStack2", rawTypeStack2 );
          ^
9 warnings
```

Fig. 19.12 | Warning messages from the compiler. (Part 2 of 2.)

19.8 Wildcards in Methods That Accept Type Parameters

In this section, we introduce a powerful generics concept known as **wildcards**. For this purpose, we'll also introduce a new data structure from package java.util. In Chapter 18, we discussed the Java Collections Framework, which provides many generic data structures and algorithms that manipulate the elements of those data structures. Perhaps the simplest of these data structures is class ArrayList—a dynamically resizable, arraylike data structure. As part of this discussion, you'll learn how to create an ArrayList, add elements to it and traverse those elements using an enhanced for statement.

Let's consider an example that motivates wildcards. Suppose that you'd like to implement a generic method sum that totals the numbers in a collection, such as an ArrayList. You'd begin by inserting the numbers in the collection. Because generic classes can be used only with class or interface types, the numbers would be *autoboxed* as objects of the type-wrapper classes. For example, any int value would be *autoboxed* as an Integer object, and any double value would be *autoboxed* as a Double object. We'd like to be able to total all the numbers in the ArrayList regardless of their type. For this reason, we'll declare the Array-List with the type argument Number, which is the superclass of both Integer and Double. In addition, method sum will receive a parameter of type ArrayList<Number> and total its elements. Figure 19.13 demonstrates totaling the elements of an ArrayList of Numbers.

```java
1  // Fig. 19.13: TotalNumbers.java
2  // Totaling the numbers in an ArrayList<Number>.
3  import java.util.ArrayList;
4
5  public class TotalNumbers
6  {
7     public static void main( String[] args )
8     {
9        // create, initialize and output ArrayList of Numbers containing
10       // both Integers and Doubles, then display total of the elements
11       Number[] numbers = { 1, 2.4, 3, 4.1 }; // Integers and Doubles
12       ArrayList< Number > numberList = new ArrayList< Number >();
13
14       for ( Number element : numbers )
15          numberList.add( element ); // place each number in numberList
16
17       System.out.printf( "numberList contains: %s\n", numberList );
18       System.out.printf( "Total of the elements in numberList: %.1f\n",
19          sum( numberList ) );
20    } // end main
21
22    // calculate total of ArrayList elements
23    public static double sum( ArrayList< Number > list )
24    {
25       double total = 0; // initialize total
26
27       // calculate sum
28       for ( Number element : list )
29          total += element.doubleValue();
30
31       return total;
32    } // end method sum
33 } // end class TotalNumbers
```

```
numberList contains: [1, 2.4, 3, 4.1]
Total of the elements in numberList: 10.5
```

Fig. 19.13 | Totaling the numbers in an ArrayList<Number>.

Line 11 declares and initializes an array of Numbers. Because the initializers are primitive values, Java *autoboxes* each primitive value as an object of its corresponding wrapper type. The int values 1 and 3 are *autoboxed* as Integer objects, and the double values 2.4 and 4.1 are *autoboxed* as Double objects. Line 12 declares and creates an ArrayList object that stores Numbers and assigns it to variable numberList. We do not have to specify the size of the ArrayList because it will grow automatically as we insert objects.

Lines 14–15 traverse array numbers and place each element in numberList. Line 17 outputs the contents of the ArrayList as a String. This statement implicitly invokes the ArrayList's toString method, which returns a String of the form "[*elements*]" in which *elements* is a comma-separated list of the elements' String representations. Lines 18–19 display the sum of the elements that is returned by the call to method sum.

Method sum (lines 23–32) receives an ArrayList of Numbers and calculates the total of the Numbers in the collection. The method uses double values to perform the calculations and returns the result as a double. Lines 28–29 use the enhanced for statement, which is designed to work with both arrays and the collections of the Collections Framework, to total the elements of the ArrayList. The for statement assigns each Number in the ArrayList to variable element, then uses **Number method doubleValue** to obtain the Number's underlying primitive value as a double value. The result is added to total. When the loop terminates, the method returns the total.

Implementing Method **sum** *With a Wildcard Type Argument in Its Parameter*

Recall that the purpose of method sum in Fig. 19.13 was to total any type of Numbers stored in an ArrayList. We created an ArrayList of Numbers that contained both Integer and Double objects. The output of Fig. 19.13 demonstrates that method sum worked properly. Given that method sum can total the elements of an ArrayList of Numbers, you might expect that the method would also work for ArrayLists that contain elements of only one numeric type, such as ArrayList<Integer>. So we modified class TotalNumbers to create an ArrayList of Integers and pass it to method sum. When we compile the program, the compiler issues the following error message:

```
sum(java.util.ArrayList<java.lang.Number>) in TotalNumbersErrors
cannot be applied to (java.util.ArrayList<java.lang.Integer>)
```

Although Number is the superclass of Integer, the compiler does not consider the parameterized type ArrayList<Number> to be a superclass of ArrayList<Integer>. If it were, then every operation we could perform on ArrayList<Number> would also work on an ArrayList<Integer>. Consider the fact that you can add a Double object to an ArrayList<Number> because a Double *is a* Number, but you cannot add a Double object to an ArrayList<Integer> because a Double *is not an* Integer. Thus, the subtype relationship does not hold.

How do we create a more flexible version of the sum method that can total the elements of any ArrayList containing elements of any subclass of Number? This is where **wildcard type arguments** are important. Wildcards enable you to specify method parameters, return values, variables or fields, and so on, that act as supertypes or subtypes of parameterized types. In Fig. 19.14, method sum's parameter is declared in line 50 with the type:

```
ArrayList< ? extends Number >
```

A wildcard type argument is denoted by a question mark (**?**), which by itself represents an "unknown type." In this case, the wildcard extends class Number, which means that the wildcard has an upper bound of Number. Thus, the unknown-type argument must be either Number or a subclass of Number. With the parameter type shown here, method sum can receive an ArrayList argument that contains any type of Number, such as ArrayList<Integer> (line 20), ArrayList<Double> (line 33) or ArrayList<Number> (line 46).

```java
1    // Fig. 19.14: WildcardTest.java
2    // Wildcard test program.
3    import java.util.ArrayList;
4
5    public class WildcardTest
6    {
7       public static void main( String[] args )
8       {
9          // create, initialize and output ArrayList of Integers, then
10         // display total of the elements
11         Integer[] integers = { 1, 2, 3, 4, 5 };
12         ArrayList< Integer > integerList = new ArrayList< Integer >();
13
14         // insert elements in integerList
15         for ( Integer element : integers )
16            integerList.add( element );
17
18         System.out.printf( "integerList contains: %s\n", integerList );
19         System.out.printf( "Total of the elements in integerList: %.0f\n\n",
20            sum( integerList ) );
21
22         // create, initialize and output ArrayList of Doubles, then
23         // display total of the elements
24         Double[] doubles = { 1.1, 3.3, 5.5 };
25         ArrayList< Double > doubleList = new ArrayList< Double >();
26
27         // insert elements in doubleList
28         for ( Double element : doubles )
29            doubleList.add( element );
30
31         System.out.printf( "doubleList contains: %s\n", doubleList );
32         System.out.printf( "Total of the elements in doubleList: %.1f\n\n",
33            sum( doubleList ) );
34
35         // create, initialize and output ArrayList of Numbers containing
36         // both Integers and Doubles, then display total of the elements
37         Number[] numbers = { 1, 2.4, 3, 4.1 }; // Integers and Doubles
38         ArrayList< Number > numberList = new ArrayList< Number >();
39
40         // insert elements in numberList
41         for ( Number element : numbers )
42            numberList.add( element );
43
44         System.out.printf( "numberList contains: %s\n", numberList );
45         System.out.printf( "Total of the elements in numberList: %.1f\n",
46            sum( numberList ) );
47      } // end main
48
49      // total the elements; using a wildcard in the ArrayList parameter
50      public static double sum( ArrayList< ? extends Number > list )
51      {
52         double total = 0; // initialize total
53
```

Fig. 19.14 | Generic wildcard test program. (Part 1 of 2.)

```
54            // calculate sum
55            for ( Number element : list )
56               total += element.doubleValue();
57
58            return total;
59         } // end method sum
60    } // end class WildcardTest
```

```
integerList contains: [1, 2, 3, 4, 5]
Total of the elements in integerList: 15

doubleList contains: [1.1, 3.3, 5.5]
Total of the elements in doubleList: 9.9

numberList contains: [1, 2.4, 3, 4.1]
Total of the elements in numberList: 10.5
```

Fig. 19.14 | Generic wildcard test program. (Part 2 of 2.)

Lines 11–20 create and initialize an `ArrayList<Integer>`, output its elements and total them by calling method sum (line 20). Lines 24–33 perform the same operations for an `ArrayList<Double>`. Lines 37–46 perform the same operations for an `Array-List<Number>` that contains `Integers` and `Doubles`.

In method sum (lines 50–59), although the `ArrayList` argument's element types are not directly known by the method, they're known to be at least of type `Number`, because the wildcard was specified with the upper bound `Number`. For this reason line 56 is allowed, because all `Number` objects have a `doubleValue` method.

Although wildcards provide flexibility when passing parameterized types to a method, they also have some disadvantages. Because the wildcard (?) in the method's header (line 50) does not specify a type-parameter name, you cannot use it as a type name throughout the method's body (i.e., you cannot replace `Number` with ? in line 55). You could, however, declare method sum as follows:

public static `<T` **extends** `Number> ` **double** `sum( ArrayList< T > list )`

which allows the method to receive an `ArrayList` that contains elements of any `Number` subclass. You could then use the type parameter `T` throughout the method body.

If the wildcard is specified without an upper bound, then only the methods of type `Object` can be invoked on values of the wildcard type. Also, methods that use wildcards in their parameter's type arguments cannot be used to add elements to a collection referenced by the parameter.

Common Programming Error 19.4

Using a wildcard in a method's type-parameter section or using a wildcard as an explicit type of a variable in the method body is a syntax error.

19.9 Generics and Inheritance: Notes

Generics can be used with inheritance in several ways:

- A generic class can be derived from a nongeneric class. For example, the `Object` class is a direct or indirect superclass of every generic class.

- A generic class can be derived from another generic class. For example, generic class Stack (in package java.util) is a subclass of generic class Vector (in package java.util). We discussed these classes in Chapter 18.

- A nongeneric class can be derived from a generic class. For example, nongeneric class Properties (in package java.util) is a subclass of generic class Hashtable (in package java.util). We also discussed these classes in Chapter 18.

- Finally, a generic method in a subclass can override a generic method in a superclass if both methods have the same signatures.

19.10 Wrap-Up

This chapter introduced generics. You learned how to declare generic methods and classes. We discussed how backward compatibility is achieved via raw types. You also learned how to use wildcards in a generic method or a generic class. For more information on generics, please visit our Java Resource Center at www.deitel.com/Java/ and click the topic **Java Generics** under the heading **Resource Center Contents**. Next, we introduce Java applets—Java programs that typically execute in a browser. We overview the JDK's sample applets, then show you how to write and execute your own applets. We then introduce the Java Web Start capabilities for launching an applet and installing a desktop shortcut to relaunch the applet in the future without having to revisit the applet's website.

20

Applets and Java Web Start

Objectives

In this chapter you'll learn:

- What applets are and how they're used in web pages.

- To observe some of Java's exciting capabilities through the JDK's demonstration applets.

- To write simple applets.

- To write a simple HyperText Markup Language (HTML) document to load an applet into an applet container and execute the applet.

- Applet life-cycle methods.

- About the sandbox security model for running downloaded code safely.

- What Java Web Start is and how to use it to download, install and run applets outside of the web browser.

20.1 Introduction

[*Note:* This chapter is intentionally small and simple for readers who wish to study applets after reading only the book's first few chapters. We present more complex applets in Chapter 21, Multimedia: Applets and Applications, and Chapter 24, Networking. Also, the examples in this chapter require some knowledge of HTML to create a web page that loads an applet. With each example we supply sample HTML documents that you can modify for your own purposes.

This chapter introduces **applets**—Java programs that are typically embedded in **HTML (HyperText Markup Language) documents**—also called web pages. When a Java-enabled web browser loads a web page containing an applet, the applet downloads into the browser and executes.

Applet Containers

The application in which an applet executes is known as the **applet container**. It's the applet container's responsibility to load the applet's class(es), create an instance of the applet and manage its life cycle (which we discuss in more detail in Section 20.4). The Java Development Kit (JDK) includes one called the **appletviewer** for testing applets as you develop them and before you embed them in web pages. We demonstrate applets using both the **appletviewer** and web browsers, which execute Java applets via the **Java Plug-In**. Some browsers don't come with the plug-in by default. You can visit java.com to determine whether your browser is ready to execute Java applets. If not, you can click the **Free Java Download** button to install Java for your browser. Several popular browsers are supported. We tested our applets in Mozilla's Firefox 3.6, Microsoft's Internet Explorer 8, Google's Chrome, Opera 11 and Apple's Safari 5.

Java Web Start and the Java Network Launch Protocol (JNLP)

This chapter concludes with an introduction to Java Web Start and the Java Network Launch Protocol (JNLP). Together, these enable you to package your applets and applications so that they can be installed onto the user's desktop. As you'll learn in Chapter 21, Java Web Start also enables you to give the user control over whether an applet or application downloaded from the web can have limited access to resources on the local file system. For example, if you create a downloadable text-editor program in Java, users would probably want to store their documents on their own computers.

20.2 Sample Applets Provided with the JDK

Before we discuss our own applets, let's consider several demonstration applets provided with the JDK. Each sample applet comes with its source code.

The demonstration programs provided with the JDK are located in a directory called demo. For Windows, the default location of the JDK 6.0's demo directory is

```
C:\Program Files\Java\jdk1.6.0_##\demo
```

where _## represents the JDK update number. On UNIX/Linux, the default location is the directory in which you install the JDK followed by jdk1.6.0_##/demo—for example,

```
/usr/local/jdk1.6.0_##/demo
```

Other platforms use a similar directory (or folder) structure. You may need to update the locations specified here to reflect your chosen installation directory and disk drive, or a different version of the JDK. The demonstration programs are also available on JDK 7.

If you're using a Java development tool that does not come with the Java demos, you can download the current JDK from www.oracle.com/technetwork/java/javase/down-loads/index.html. Mac OS X users should visit developer.apple.com/java for information about Java SE on the Mac, or use virtualization software to run the Windows or Linux versions of Java in a virtual machine. Apple recently joined the OpenJDK project (openjdk.java.net). Eventually a Mac OS X version of the JDK for Java SE 7 will be available from this project's website.

Overview of the Demonstration Applets

Open a command window and use the cd command to change directories to the JDK's demo directory. The demo directory contains several subdirectories. You can list them by issuing the dir command on Windows or the ls command on UNIX/Linux/Max OS X. We discuss sample programs in the applets and jfc subdirectories. The applets directory contains demonstration applets. The jfc (Java Foundation Classes) directory contains applets and applications that demonstrate Java's powerful graphics and GUI capabilities.

Change to the applets directory and list its contents to see the directory names for the demonstration applets. Figure 20.1 provides a brief description of each. If your browser supports Java, you can test an applet by opening the HTML document for it in the applet's directory. We'll demonstrate three of these applets by using the appletviewer command in a command window.

Example	Description
Animator	Performs one of four separate animations.
ArcTest	Demonstrates drawing arcs. You can interact with the applet to change attributes of the arc that's displayed.
BarChart	Draws a simple bar chart.
Blink	Displays blinking text in different colors.
CardTest	Demonstrates several GUI components and layouts.

Fig. 20.1 | The examples from the applets directory. (Part 1 of 2.)

Example	Description
Clock	Draws a clock with rotating hands, the current date and the current time. The clock updates once per second.
DitherTest	Demonstrates drawing with a graphics technique known as *dithering* that allows gradual transformation from one color to another.
DrawTest	Allows the user to draw lines and points in different colors by dragging the mouse.
Fractal	Draws a fractal. Fractals typically require complex calculations to determine how they're displayed. We discuss fractals in Section 18.8.
GraphicsTest	Draws shapes to illustrate graphics capabilities.
GraphLayout	Draws a graph consisting of many nodes (represented as rectangles) connected by lines. Drag a node to see the other nodes in the graph adjust on the screen and demonstrate complex graphical interactions.
JumpingBox	Moves a rectangle randomly around the screen. Try to catch it by clicking it with the mouse!
MoleculeViewer	Presents a three-dimensional view of several chemical molecules. Drag the mouse to view the molecule from different angles.
NervousText	Draws text that jumps around the applet.
SimpleGraph	Draws a complex curve.
SortDemo	Compares three sorting techniques. Sorting (described in Chapter 19) arranges information in order—like alphabetizing words. When you execute this example with the appletviewer, three windows appear. When you execute it in a browser, the three demos appear side by side. Click in each demo to start the sort. The sorts all operate at different speeds.
SpreadSheet	Demonstrates a simple spreadsheet of rows and columns.
TicTacToe	Allows the user to play Tic-Tac-Toe against the computer.
WireFrame	Draws a three-dimensional shape as a wire frame. Drag the mouse to view the shape from different angles.

Fig. 20.1 | The examples from the applets directory. (Part 2 of 2.)

TicTacToe *Applet*

This TicTacToe demonstration applet allows you to play Tic-Tac-Toe against the computer. Change directories to subdirectory TicTacToe, where you'll find the file example1.html that loads the applet. In the command window, type the command

```
appletviewer example1.html
```

and press *Enter*. This executes the appletviewer applet container, which loads the HTML document example1.html specified as its command-line argument. The appletviewer determines from the document which applet to load and executes it. Figure 20.2 shows several screen captures of playing Tic-Tac-Toe with this applet. You can open the HTML document in your browser to execute the applet in the browser.

You are player **X**. To interact with the applet, point the mouse at the square where you want to place an **X** and click the mouse button. The applet plays a sound and places an **X**

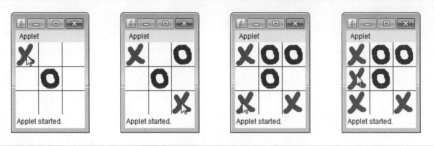

Fig. 20.2 | `TicTacToe` applet sample execution.

in the square if it's open. If the square is occupied, this is an invalid move, and the applet plays a different sound, indicating that you cannot make the specified move. After you make a valid move, the applet responds by making its own move.

To play again, click the `appletviewer`'s **Applet** menu and select the **Reload** menu item (Fig. 20.3), or click the applet again when the game is over. To terminate the `applet-viewer`, click the `appletviewer`'s **Applet** menu and select the **Quit** menu item.

Reload the applet to execute it again

Select **Quit** to terminate the `appletviewer`

Fig. 20.3 | **Applet** menu in the `appletviewer`.

DrawTest *Applet*

The `DrawTest` applet allows you to draw lines and points in different colors. In the command window, change directories to directory `applets`, then to subdirectory `DrawTest`. You can move up the directory tree incrementally toward `demo` by issuing the command "cd .." in the command window. The `DrawTest` directory contains the `example1.html` document that's used to execute the applet. In the command window, type the command

```
appletviewer example1.html
```

and press *Enter*. The `appletviewer` loads `example1.html`, determines from the document which applet to load and executes it. Figure 20.4 shows a screen capture after some lines and points have been drawn.

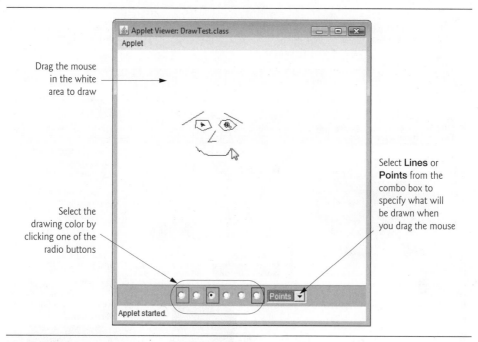

Fig. 20.4 | DrawTest applet sample execution.

By default the applet allows you to draw black lines by dragging the mouse across the applet. When you drag the mouse, the line's start point always remains in the same place and its endpoint follows the mouse pointer around the applet. The line is not permanent until you release the mouse button.

Select a color by clicking one of the radio buttons at the bottom of the applet. You can select from red, green, blue, pink, orange and black. Change the shape to draw from **Lines** to **Points** by selecting **Points** from the combo box. To start a new drawing, select **Reload** from the appletviewer's **Applet** menu.

Java2D *Applet*

The Java2D applet demonstrates many features of the Java 2D API, which we introduced in Chapter 15. This demo can also be found at java.sun.com/products/java-media/2D/samples/index.html. Change directories to the jfc directory in the JDK's demo directory, then change to the Java2D directory. In the command window, type the command

```
appletviewer Java2Demo.html
```

and press *Enter*. The appletviewer loads Java2Demo.html, determines from the document which applet to load and executes it. Figure 20.5 shows a screen capture of one of this applet's many demonstrations of Java's two-dimensional graphics capabilities.

At the top of the applet are tabs that look like file folders in a filing cabinet. This demo provides 12 tabs, each demonstrating Java 2D API features. To change to a different part of the demo, simply click a different tab. Also, try changing the options in the upper-right corner of the applet. Some of these affect the speed with which the applet draws the graphics. For example, click the checkbox to the left of the word **Anti-Aliasing** to turn off

Click a tab to select a
two-dimensional graphics demo

Try changing the options to see
their effect on the demonstration

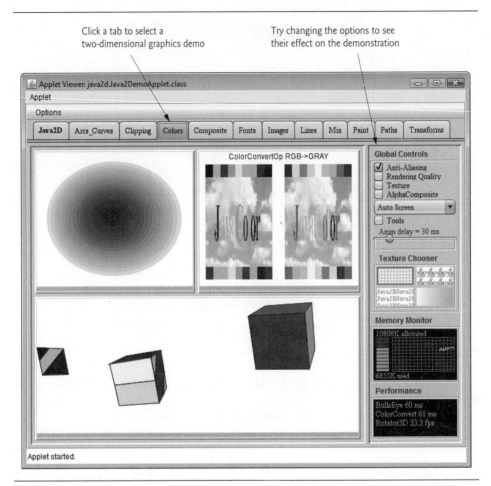

Fig. 20.5 | Java2D applet sample execution.

antialiasing (a graphics technique for producing smoother on-screen graphics in which the edges are blurred). Shapes that are not antialiased are less complex to draw. Accordingly, when the antialiasing feature is turned off, the animation speed increases for the animated shapes at the bottom of the demo (Fig. 20.5).

20.3 Simple Java Applet: Drawing a String

Every Java applet is a graphical user interface on which you can place GUI components using the techniques introduced in Chapter 14 or draw using the techniques demonstrated in Chapter 15. In this chapter, we'll demonstrate drawing on an applet. Examples in Chapters 21 and 24 demonstrate building an applet's graphical user interface.

Now let's build an applet of our own. We begin with a simple applet (Fig. 20.6) that draws "Welcome to Java Programming!" on the applet. We show this applet executing in two applet containers—the appletviewer and the Mozilla Firefox web browser. At the end of this section, you'll learn how to execute the applet in a web browser.

```
 1   // Fig. 20.6: WelcomeApplet.java
 2   // Applet that draws a String.
 3   import java.awt.Graphics;    // program uses class Graphics
 4   import javax.swing.JApplet; // program uses class JApplet
 5
 6   public class WelcomeApplet extends JApplet
 7   {
 8      // draw text on applet's background
 9      public void paint( Graphics g )
10      {
11         // call superclass version of method paint
12         super.paint( g );
13
14         // draw a String at x-coordinate 25 and y-coordinate 25
15         g.drawString( "Welcome to Java Programming!", 25, 25 );
16      } // end method paint
17   } // end class WelcomeApplet
```

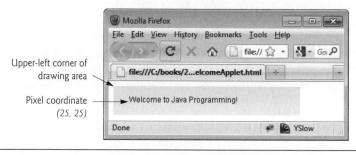

WelcomeApplet executing in the appletviewer

x-axis

y-axis

Upper-left corner of drawing
area is location (0, 0).
Drawing area extends from
below the **Applet** menu to
above the status bar. x-
coordinates increase from left
to right. y-coordinates
increase from top to bottom.

Applet menu

Status bar mimics what would
be displayed in the browser's
status bar as the applet loads
and begins executing

Pixel coordinate (25, 25) at which
the string is displayed

WelcomeApplet executing in Mozilla Firefox

Upper-left corner of
drawing area

Pixel coordinate
(25, 25)

Fig. 20.6 | Applet that draws a String.

Creating the Applet Class

Line 3 imports class Graphics to enable the applet to draw graphics, such as lines, rectangles, ovals and strings of characters. Class **JApplet** (imported at line 4) from package java.swing is used to create applets. As with applications, every Java applet contains at least one public class declaration. An applet container can create only objects of classes that are public and extend JApplet (or its superclass Applet). For this reason, class WelcomeApplet (lines 6–17) extends JApplet.

An applet container expects every Java applet to have methods named **init**, **start**, **paint**, **stop** and **destroy**, each of which is declared in class JApplet. Each new applet class you create inherits default implementations of these methods from class JApplet. These methods can be overridden (redefined) to perform tasks that are specific to your applet. Section 20.4 discusses each method in more detail.

When an applet container loads class WelcomeApplet, the container creates a WelcomeApplet object, then calls its methods init, start and paint in sequence. If you do not declare these methods in your applet, the applet container calls the inherited versions. The superclass methods init and start have empty bodies, so they do not perform any tasks. The superclass method paint does not draw anything on the applet.

You might wonder why it's necessary to inherit methods init, start and paint if their default implementations do not perform tasks. Some applets do not use all three of these methods. However, the applet container does not know that. Thus, it expects every applet to have these methods, so that it can provide a consistent start-up sequence. This is similar to applications' always starting execution with main. Inheriting the "default" versions of these methods guarantees that the applet container can execute each applet uniformly. Also, inheriting default implementations of these methods allows you to concentrate on defining only the methods required for a particular applet.

Overriding Method **paint** *for Drawing*
To enable our applet to draw, class WelcomeApplet overrides method paint (lines 9–16) by placing statements in the body of paint that draw a message on the screen. Method paint receives a parameter of type Graphics (called g by convention), which is used to draw graphics on the applet. You do not call method paint explicitly in an applet. Rather, the applet container calls paint to tell the applet when to draw, and the applet container is responsible for passing a Graphics object as an argument.

Line 12 calls the superclass version of method paint that was inherited from JApplet. This should be the first statement in every applet's paint method. Omitting it can cause subtle drawing errors in applets that combine drawing and GUI components.

Line 15 uses Graphics method drawString to draw Welcome to Java Programming! on the applet. The method receives as arguments the String to draw and the *x-y* coordinates at which the bottom-left corner of the String should appear in the drawing area. When line 15 executes, it draws the String on the applet at the coordinates 25 and 25.

20.3.1 Executing WelcomeApplet in the appletviewer
After creating class WelcomeApplet and saving it in the file WelcomeApplet.java, open a command window, change to the directory in which you saved the applet class declaration and compile class WelcomeApplet.

Recall that applets are embedded in web pages for execution in an applet container (appletviewer or a browser). Before you can execute the applet, you must create an HTML document that specifies which applet to execute in the applet container. Typically, an HTML document ends with an **.html** or **.htm** file-name extension. Figure 20.7 shows a simple HTML document—WelcomeApplet.html—that loads the applet defined in Fig. 20.6 into an applet container.

Most HTML elements are delimited by pairs of **tags**—e.g., lines 1 and 6 delimit the HTML document's beginning and end, respectively. Each tag is enclosed in angle brackets

```
1    <html>
2       <body>
3          <applet code = "WelcomeApplet.class" width = "300" height = "45">
4          </applet>
5       </body>
6    </html>
```

Fig. 20.7 | `WelcomeApplet.html` loads `WelcomeApplet` (Fig. 20.6) into an applet container.

(< and >). Lines 2–5 specify the **body element** element of the document—this represents the elements that will be displayed in the web page. Lines 3–4 specify an **applet element** that tells the applet container to load a specific applet and defines the size of its display area (its width and height in pixels) in the applet container.

The applet and its corresponding HTML document are normally stored in the same directory on disk. Typically, a browser loads an HTML document from a computer (other than your own) connected to the Internet. However, HTML documents also can reside on your computer (as in Section 20.2). When an applet container encounters an `applet` element in an HTML document, it loads the applet's `.class` file (or files) from the same location that contains the HTML document.

The `applet` element has several **attributes**. The first attribute in line 3, code = `"WelcomeApplet.class"`, indicates that the file `WelcomeApplet.class` contains the compiled applet class. The second and third attributes in line 3 indicate the **width** (300) and the **height** (45) of the applet in pixels. The `</applet>` tag (line 4) terminates the `applet` element that began at line 2. The `</html>` tag (line 6) terminates the HTML document.

Common Programming Error 20.1

Forgetting the ending `</applet>` tag prevents the applet from executing in some applet containers. The `appletviewer` terminates without indicating an error. Some web browsers simply ignore the incomplete `applet` element.

Error-Prevention Tip 20.1

If you receive a `MissingResourceException` error message when loading an applet into the `appletviewer` or a browser, check the `<applet>` tag in the HTML document carefully for syntax errors, such as commas (,) between the attributes.

The `appletviewer` understands only the `<applet>` and `</applet>` HTML tags and ignores all other tags in the document. The `appletviewer` is an ideal place to test an applet and ensure that it executes properly. Once the applet's execution is verified, you can add its HTML tags to a web page that others can view in their web browsers.

To execute `WelcomeApplet` in the `appletviewer`, open a command window, change to the directory containing your applet and HTML document, then type

```
appletviewer WelcomeApplet.html
```

Error-Prevention Tip 20.2

Test your applets in the `appletviewer` before executing them in a web browser. Browsers often save a copy of an applet in memory until all the browser's windows are closed. If you change an applet, recompile it, then reload it in your browser, the browser may still execute the original version of the applet.

Error-Prevention Tip 20.3

Test your applets in every web browser in which they'll execute to ensure that they operate correctly.

20.3.2 Executing an Applet in a Web Browser

The sample program executions in Fig. 20.6 demonstrate `WelcomeApplet` executing in the `appletviewer` and in the Mozilla Firefox web browser. To execute an applet in Firefox, perform the following steps:

1. Select **Open File...** from the **File** menu.

2. In the dialog box that appears, locate the directory containing the HTML document for the applet you wish to execute.

3. Select the HTML document.

4. Click the **Open** button.

The steps for executing applets in other web browsers are similar. In most browsers, you can simply type *<Ctrl> O* to open a dialog that enables you to select an HTML document from your local computer.

Error-Prevention Tip 20.4

*If your applet executes in the `appletviewer` but not in your web browser, Java may not be installed and configured for your browser. In this case, visit the website `java.com` and click the **Free Java Download** button to install Java for your browser.*

20.4 Applet Life-Cycle Methods

Now that you've created an applet, let's consider the five applet methods that are called by the applet container from the time the applet is loaded into the browser to the time it's terminated by the browser. These methods correspond to various aspects of an applet's life cycle. Figure 20.8 lists these methods, which are inherited into your applet classes from class `JApplet`. The table specifies when each method gets called and explains its purpose. Other than method `paint`, these methods have empty bodies by default. If you'd like to declare any of them in your applets and have the applet container call them, you must use the method headers shown in Fig. 20.8.

Method	Description
`public void init()`	
	Called *once* by the applet container when an applet is loaded for execution. This method initializes an applet. Typical actions performed here are initializing fields, creating GUI components, loading sounds to play, loading images to display (see Chapter 21) and creating threads (see Chapter 23).

Fig. 20.8 | `JApplet` life-cycle methods that are called by an applet container during an applet's execution. (Part 1 of 2.)

Method	Description

public void start()

Called by the applet container after method `init` completes execution. In addition, if the user browses to another website and later returns to the applet's HTML page, method `start` is called again. The method performs any tasks that must be completed when the applet is loaded for the first time and that must be performed every time the applet's HTML page is revisited. Actions performed here might include starting an animation or starting other threads of execution.

public void paint(Graphics g)

Called by the applet container after methods `init` and `start`. Method `paint` is also called when the applet needs to be repainted. For example, if the user covers the applet with another open window on the screen and later uncovers it, the `paint` method is called. Typical actions performed here involve drawing with the `Graphics` object g that's passed to the `paint` method by the applet container.

public void stop()

This method is called by the applet container when the user leaves the applet's web page by browsing to another web page. Since it's possible that the user might return to the web page containing the applet, method `stop` performs tasks that might be required to suspend the applet's execution, so that the applet does not use computer processing time when it's not displayed on the screen. Typical actions performed here would stop the execution of animations and threads.

public void destroy()

This method is called by the applet container when the applet is being removed from memory. This occurs when the user exits the browsing session by closing all the browser windows and may also occur at the browser's discretion when the user has browsed to other web pages. The method performs any tasks that are required to clean up resources allocated to the applet.

Fig. 20.8 | `JApplet` life-cycle methods that are called by an applet container during an applet's execution. (Part 2 of 2.)

Common Programming Error 20.2

Declaring methods `init`, `start`, `paint`, `stop` *or* `destroy` *with method headers that differ from those shown in Fig. 20.8 results in methods that will not be called by the applet container. The code specified in your versions of the methods will not execute. The* `@Override` *annotation can be applied to each method to prevent this problem.*

20.5 Initialization with Method `init`

Our next applet (Fig. 20.9) computes the sum of two values entered into input dialogs by the user and displays the result by drawing a `String` inside a rectangle on the applet. The sum is stored in an instance variable of the `AdditionApplet` class, so it can be used in both the `init` method and the `paint` method. The HTML document that you can use to load this applet into an applet container (i.e., the `appletviewer` or a web browser) is shown in Fig. 20.10.

```
 1    // Fig. 20.9: AdditionApplet.java
 2    // Applet that adds two double values entered via input dialogs.
 3    import java.awt.Graphics; // program uses class Graphics
 4    import javax.swing.JApplet; // program uses class JApplet
 5    import javax.swing.JOptionPane; // program uses class JOptionPane
 6
 7    public class AdditionApplet extends JApplet
 8    {
 9       private double sum; // sum of values entered by user
10
11       // initialize applet by obtaining values from user
12       public void init()
13       {
14          // obtain first number from user
15          String firstNumber = JOptionPane.showInputDialog(
16             "Enter first floating-point value" );
17
18          // obtain second number from user
19          String secondNumber = JOptionPane.showInputDialog(
20             "Enter second floating-point value" );
21
22          // convert numbers from type String to type double
23          double number1 = Double.parseDouble( firstNumber );
24          double number2 = Double.parseDouble( secondNumber );
25
26          sum = number1 + number2; // add numbers
27       } // end method init
28
29       // draw results in a rectangle on applet's background
30       public void paint( Graphics g )
31       {
32          super.paint( g ); // call superclass version of method paint
33
34          // draw rectangle starting from (15, 10) that is 270
35          // pixels wide and 20 pixels tall
36          g.drawRect( 15, 10, 270, 20 );
37
38          // draw results as a String at (25, 25)
39          g.drawString( "The sum is " + sum, 25, 25 );
40       } // end method paint
41    } // end class AdditionApplet
```

Fig. 20.9 | Applet that adds two `double` values entered via input dialogs. (Part 1 of 2.)

Fig. 20.9 | Applet that adds two `double` values entered via input dialogs. (Part 2 of 2.)

```
I   <html>
2   <body>
3   <applet code = "AdditionApplet.class" width = "300" height = "50">
4   </applet>
5   </body>
6   </html>
```

Fig. 20.10 | `AdditionApplet.html` loads class `AdditionApplet` of Fig. 20.9 into an applet container.

The applet requests that the user enter two floating-point numbers. In Fig. 20.9, line 9 declares instance variable `sum` of type `double`. The applet contains two methods—`init` (lines 12–27) and `paint` (lines 30–40). When an applet container loads this applet, the container creates an instance of class `AdditionApplet` and calls its `init` method—this occurs only *once* during an applet's execution. Method `init` normally initializes the applet's fields (if they need to be initialized to values other than their defaults) and performs other tasks that should occur only once when the applet begins execution. The first line of `init` always appears as shown in line 12, which indicates that `init` is a `public` method that receives no arguments and returns no information when it completes.

Lines 15–24 declare variables to store the values entered by the user, obtain the user input and convert the `Strings` entered by the user to `double` values. Line 26 adds the values stored in variables `number1` and `number2`, and assigns the result to instance variable `sum`. At this point, the applet's `init` method returns program control to the applet container, which then calls the applet's `start` method. We did not declare `start` in this applet, so the one inherited from class `JApplet` is called here.

Next, the applet container calls the applet's `paint` method, which draws a rectangle (line 36) where the addition result will appear. Line 39 calls the `Graphics` object's `drawString` method to display the results. The statement concatenates the value of instance variable `sum` to the `String "The sum is "` and displays the concatenated `String`.

Software Engineering Observation 20.1

The only statements that should be placed in an applet's `init` method are those that should execute only once when the applet is initialized.

20.6 Sandbox Security Model

For security reasons, it's generally considered dangerous to allow applets or any other program that you execute from a web browser to access your local computer. So, you must decide whether *you trust the source*. For example, if you choose to download a new version of the Firefox web browser from Mozilla's `firefox.com` website, you must decide whether you trust Mozilla. After all, their installer program is going to modify your system and place the files to execute Firefox on your computer. Once it's installed, Firefox will be able to access files and other local resources. Most of what you do with your web browsers—such as shopping, browsing the web and downloading software—requires you to trust the sites you visit and to trust the organizations that maintain those sites. If you're not careful, a malicious downloaded program could gain control of your computer, access personal information stored there, corrupt your data and possibly even be used to attack other computers on the Internet—as so often happens with computer viruses today.

Preventing Malicious Applets

Applets are typically downloaded from the Internet. What would happen if you downloaded a malicious applet? Consider the fact that a browser downloads and executes a Java applet automatically—the user *is not asked for approval.* In fact, an applet typically downloads *without the user's knowledge*—it's just another element of the web page the user happens to be visiting.

The designers of Java considered this issue thoroughly, since Java was intended for use in networked environments. To combat malicious code, the Java platform uses a so-called **sandbox security model** that provides a mechanism for executing downloaded code safely. Such code executes in the "sandbox" and is not allowed to "play outside the sandbox." *By default, downloaded code cannot access local system resources, and an applet can interact only with the server from which the applet was downloaded.*

Digitally Signed Applets

Unfortunately, executing in a sandbox makes it difficult for applets to perform useful tasks. It's possible, however, for an organization that wishes to create applets with access to the local system to obtain a security certificate (also called a digital certificate) from one of several certificate authorities (see `en.wikipedia.org/wiki/Certificate_Authority` for a list of authorities and more information about certificate authorities). The organization can then use tools provided with the JDK to *digitally sign* an applet that requires access to local system resources. When a user downloads a digitally signed applet, a dialog prompts the user asking whether he or she trusts the applet's source. In that dialog, the user can view the organization's security certificate and see which certificate authority issued it. If the user indicates that he/she trusts the source, only then will the applet be able to access to the local computer's resources.

In the next section, we introduce Java Web Start and the Java Network Launch Protocol (JNLP). These technologies enable applets or applications to interact with the user to request access to specific local system resources. With the user's permission, this enables Java programmers to *extend the sandbox*, but it does *not* give their programs access to all of the user's local resources—so the sandbox principles are still in effect. For example, it would be useful for a downloadable text editor program to store the user's files in a folder on the user's computer. The text editor can prompt the user to ask for permission to do this. If the user grants permission for a specific directory on disk, the program can then access *only* that local directory and its subdirectories.

For more information on digitally signed applets, visit `java.sun.com/developer/onlineTraining/Programming/JDCBook/signed.html`. For information on the Java security model, visit `download.oracle.com/javase/6/docs/technotes/guides/security/`.

20.7 Java Web Start and the Java Network Launch Protocol (JNLP)

Java Web Start is a framework for running downloaded applets and applications outside the browser. Typically, such programs are stored on a web server for access via the Internet, but they can also be stored on an organization's network for internal distribution, or even on CDs, DVDs or other media. As you'll learn in Chapter 21, Java Web Start enables you to ask the user if a downloaded program can have access to the resources of the user's computer.

Java Web Start Features
Some key Java Web Start features include:

- *Desktop integration:* Users can launch robust applets and applications by clicking a hyperlink in a web page, and can quickly and easily install the programs on their computers. *Java Web Start can be configured to ask the user if a desktop icon should be created so the user can launch the program directly from the desktop.* Downloaded programs can also have an "offline mode" for execution when the computer is not connected to the Internet.

- *Automatic updating:* When you execute a program via Java Web Start, the program is downloaded and cached (stored) on the user's computer. The next time the user executes that program, Java Web Start launches it from the cache. If the program has been updated since it was last launched, Java Web Start can automatically download the updates, so a user always has the most up-to-date version. This makes installing and updating software simple and seamless to the user.

- *Draggable applets:* With a small change to the `applet` element that invokes an applet from an HTML document, you can allow users to execute an applet in its own window by holding the *Alt* key and dragging the applet out of the web browser. The applet continues to execute even after the web browser closes.

Java Network Launch Protocol (JNLP)
A **Java Network Launch Protocol** (**JNLP**) document provides the information that Java Web Start needs in order to download and run a program. Also, you must package your program in one or more *Java archive (JAR) files* that contain the program's code and resources (e.g., images, media files, text files).

By default, programs launched via Java Web Start execute using the sandbox security model. If the user gives permission, such programs *can* access the local file system, the clipboard and other services via the JNLP APIs of package `javax.jnlp`. We discuss some of these features in Chapter 21. *Digitally signed programs can gain greater access to the local system if the user trusts the source.*

20.7.1 Packaging the DrawTest Applet for Use with Java Web Start

Let's package the JDK's `DrawTest` demonstration applet (discussed in Section 20.2) so that you can execute it via Java Web Start. To do so, you must first wrap the applet's `.class` files and the resources it uses (if any) into a Java archive (JAR) file. In a command window, change to the `DrawTest` directory, as you did in Section 20.2. Once in that folder, execute the following command:

```
jar cvf DrawTest.jar *.class
```

which creates in the current directory a JAR file named `DrawTest.jar` containing the applet's `.class` files—`DrawControls.class`, `DrawPanel.class` and `DrawTest.class`. If the program had other resources, you'd simply add the file names or the folder names in which those resources are stored to the end of the preceding command. The letters `cvf` are command-line options to the **jar command**. The **c option** indicates that the command should create a new JAR file. The **v option** indicates that the command should produce verbose output so you can see the list of files and directories being included in the JAR file. The **f option** indicates that the next argument in the command line (`DrawTest.jar`) is the new JAR file's name. Figure 20.11 shows the preceding command's verbose output, which shows the files that were placed into the JAR.

```
added manifest
adding: DrawControls.class(in = 2611) (out= 1488)(deflated 43%)
adding: DrawPanel.class(in = 2703) (out= 1406)(deflated 47%)
adding: DrawTest.class(in = 1170) (out= 706)(deflated 39%)
```

Fig. 20.11 | Output of the `jar` command.

20.7.2 JNLP Document for the DrawTest Applet

Next, you must create a JNLP document that describes the contents of the JAR file and specifies which file in the JAR is the so-called **main-class** that begins the program's execution. For an applet, the `main-class` is the one that extends `JApplet` (i.e., `DrawTest` in this example). For an application, the `main-class` is the one that contains the `main` method. A basic JNLP document for the `DrawTest` applet is shown in Fig. 20.12. We describe this document's elements momentarily.

```
 1    <?xml version="1.0" encoding="UTF-8"?>
 2    <jnlp
 3       codebase=PathToJNLPFile
 4       href="DrawTest.jnlp">
 5
 6       <information>
 7          <title>DrawTest Applet</title>
 8          <vendor>Oracle Corporation</vendor>
 9          <shortcut>
10             <desktop/>
11          </shortcut>
12          <offline-allowed/>
13       </information>
14
15       <resources>
16          <java version="1.6+"/>
17          <jar href="DrawTest.jar" main="true"/>
18       </resources>
```

Fig. 20.12 | `DrawTest.jnlp` document for launching the `DrawTest` applet. (Part 1 of 2.)

```
19
20      <applet-desc
21         name="DrawTest"
22         main-class="DrawTest"
23         width="400"
24         height="400">
25      </applet-desc>
26   </jnlp>
```

Fig. 20.12 | DrawTest.jnlp document for launching the DrawTest applet. (Part 2 of 2.)

Overview of XML

JNLP documents are written in **Extensible Markup Language (XML)**—a widely supported standard for describing data. XML is commonly used to exchange data between applications over the Internet, and many applications now use XML to specify configuration information as well—as is the case with JNLP documents for Java Web Start. XML permits you to create markup for virtually any type of information. This enables you to create entirely new markup languages for describing any type of data, such as mathematical formulas, software-configuration instructions, chemical molecular structures, music, news, recipes and financial reports. XML describes data in a way that both humans and computers can understand. JNLP is a so-called XML vocabulary that describes the information Java Web Start needs to launch a program.

XML documents contain **elements** that specify the document's structure, such as title (line 7), and text that represents content (i.e., data), such as DrawTest Applet (line 7). XML documents delimit elements with **start tags** and **end tags**. A start tag consists of the element name in **angle brackets** (e.g., <title> and <vendor> in lines 7 and 8). Start tags may also contain attributes of the form *name=value*—for example, the jnlp start tag contains the attribute href="DrawTest.jnlp". An end tag consists of the element name preceded by a **forward slash** (/) in angle brackets (e.g., </title> and </vendor> in lines 7 and 8). An element's start and end tags enclose text that represents a piece of data (e.g., the vendor of the program—Oracle Corporation—in line 8, which is enclosed by the <vendor> start tag and </vendor> end tag) or other elements (e.g., the title, vendor, shortcut and offline-allowed elements in the information element of lines 6–13). Every XML document must have exactly one **root element** that contains all the other elements. In Fig. 20.12, the **jnlp element** (lines 2–26) is the root element.

JNLP Document: jnlp Element

The jnlp element's start tag (lines 2–4) has two attributes—codebase and href. The codebase attribute's value is a URL that specifies the path where the JNLP document and the JAR file are stored—this is specified in Fig. 20.12 as *PathToJNLPFile*, since this value depends on the location from which the applet is loaded. The href attribute specifies the JNLP file that launches the program. We saved the JNLP file and the JAR file in the Draw-Test demonstration applet's directory within the JDK's directory structure. We used the following local file system URL as the codebase:

```
file:.
```

which indicates that the code is in the current directory (.). Typically, the codebase references a directory on a web server with an http:// URL. If you'd like to serve your applet or application from a web server so users can access it online, you'll need to configure your web server correctly, as described at java.sun.com/javase/6/docs/technotes/guides/javaws/developersguide/setup.html.

JNLP Document: `information` Element

The **information** element (lines 6–13) provides details about the program. The **title** element specifies a title for the program. The **vendor element** specifies who created the program. The values of these elements appear in Java Web Start's security warnings and errors that are presented to the user. The title's value also appears in the title bar of the window in which the program executes.

The **desktop element** that's nested in the **shortcut** element (lines 9–11) tells Java Web Start to ask whether the user wishes to install a desktop shortcut. If the user accepts, an icon will appear on the desktop. The user can then launch the program in its own window by double-clicking the desktop icon. Note the syntax of the <desktop/> element—a so-called empty XML element. When nothing appears between an element's start and end tags, the element can be written using one tag that ends with />.

The **offline-allowed element** (line 12) indicates that once the program is installed on the user's computer, it can be launched via Java Web Start—even when the computer is not connected to the Internet. This is particularly useful for any program that can be used with files stored on the user's computer.

JNLP Document: `resources` Element

The **resources element** (lines 15–18) contains two nested elements. The **java element** lists the minimum version of Java required to execute the program (line 16) and the **jar element** (line 17) specifies the location of the JAR file that contains the program and whether that JAR file contains the class that launches the program. There can be multiple jar elements, as you'll see in the next chapter.

JNLP Document: `applet-desc` Element

The **applet-desc element** (lines 20–25) is similar to the applet element in HTML. The name attribute specifies the applet's name. The main-class attribute specifies the main applet class (the one that extends JApplet). The width and height attributes specify the width and height in pixels, respectively, of the window in which the applet will execute. Chapter 21 discusses a similar element for applications—application-desc.

Launching the Applet with Java Web Start

You're now ready to launch the applet via Java Web Start. There are several ways to do this. You can use the **javaws command** in a command window from the folder that contains the JNLP document, as in

```
javaws DrawTest.jnlp
```

You can also use your operating system's file manager to locate the JNLP on your computer and double click its file name. Normally, the JNLP file is referenced from a web page via a hyperlink. The DrawTestWebPage.html document in Fig. 20.13 (which was saved in the same directory as the JNLP file) contains an anchor (a) element (line 4), which links to the DrawTest.jnlp file. Clicking this hyperlink in the web page downloads the JNLP file (in this case, it's loaded from the local file system) and executes the corresponding applet.

```
1    <html>
2       <head><title>DrawTest Launcher Page</title></head>
3       <body>
4          <a href="DrawTest.jnlp">Launch DrawTest via Java Web Start</a>
5       </body>
6    </html>
```

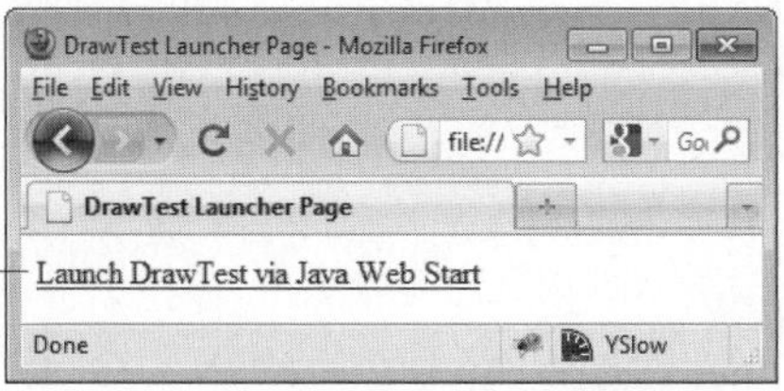

hyperlink to
DrawTest.jnlp

Fig. 20.13 | HTML document that launches the DrawTest applet when the user clicks the link.

When you run the applet via Java Web Start the first time, you'll be presented with the dialog in Fig. 20.14. This dialog enables the user to decide if a desktop icon will be installed. If the user clicks **OK**, a new icon labeled with the title specified in the JNLP document appears on the user's desktop. The applet is also cached for future use. After the user clicks **OK** or **Skip** in this dialog, the program executes (Fig. 20.15).

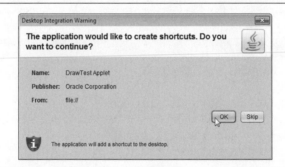

Fig. 20.14 | Dialog asking whether the user wishes to install a desktop shortcut.

Viewing the Installed Java Web Start Programs
You can view the installed Java Web Start programs in the **Java Cache Viewer** by typing the following command in a command window:

```
    javaws -viewer
```

This displays the window in Fig. 20.16. The **Java Cache Viewer** enables you to manage the Java Web Start programs on your system. You can run a selected program, create a desktop shortcut for a program (if there isn't one already), delete installed programs, and more.

For more information on Java Web Start, visit download.oracle.com/javase/6/docs/technotes/guides/javaws/. This site provides an overview of Java Web Start and includes links to the Developer's Guide, an FAQ, the JNLP Specification and the API documentation for the javax.jnlp package.

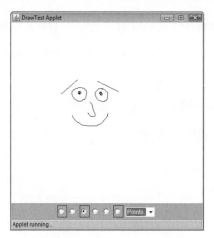

Fig. 20.15 | `DrawTest` applet running with Java Web Start.

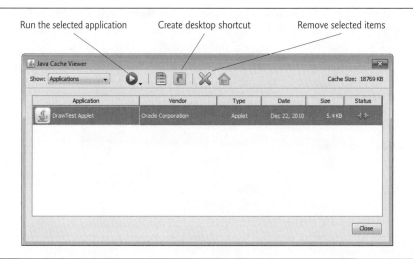

Fig. 20.16 | Viewing installed Java Web Start programs in the **Java Cache Viewer**.

20.8 Wrap-Up

In this chapter, you learned the fundamentals of Java applets and Java Web Start. You leaned HTML concepts for embedding an applet in a web page and executing it in an applet container such as the `appletviewer` or a web browser. You learned the five methods that are called automatically by the applet container during an applet's life cycle. We discussed Java's sandbox security model for executing downloaded code. Then we introduced Java Web Start and the Java Network Launch Protocol (JNLP). You packaged a program into a JAR file so that it could be executed via Java Web Start. We also discussed the basic elements of a JNLP document. Next, you'll see additional applets as we present basic multimedia capabilities. You'll also learn more features of Java Web Start and JNLP.

Multimedia: Applets and Applications

The wheel that squeaks the loudest ... gets the grease.
—John Billings (Henry Wheeler Shaw)

We'll use a signal I have tried and found far-reaching and easy to yell. Waa-hoo!
—Zane Grey

There is a natural hootchy-kootchy motion to a goldfish.
—Walt Disney

Between the motion and the act falls the shadow.
—Thomas Stearns Eliot

Objectives

In this chapter you'll learn:

- How to get, display and scale images.

- How to create animations from sequences of images.

- How to create image maps that can sense when the cursor is over them.

- How to get, play, loop and stop sounds using an AudioClip.

- How to play video using interface Player.

21.1 Introduction

Multimedia—using sound, images, graphics, animation and video—makes applications "come alive." Although most multimedia in Java applications is two-dimensional, you can use the **Java 3D API** to create 3D graphics applications (`www.oracle.com/technetwork/java/javase/tech/index-jsp-138252.html`).

Most new computers sold today are "multimedia ready," with DVD drives and audio and video capabilities. Economical desktop computers, laptops and smartphones are so powerful that they can store and play DVD-quality (and often, HD-quality) sound and video.

Among users who want graphics, many now want three-dimensional, high-resolution, color graphics. True three-dimensional imaging is already available. We expect high-resolution, "theater-in-the-round," three-dimensional television to eventually become common. Sporting and entertainment events will seem to take place on your living room floor! Medical students worldwide will see operations being performed thousands of miles away, as if they were occurring in the same room. People will learn how to drive with incredibly realistic driving simulators in their homes before they get behind the wheel. The possibilities are endless and exciting.

Multimedia demands extraordinary computing power. Today's ultrapowerful processors make effective multimedia economical. Users are eager to own faster processors, larger memories and wider communications channels that support demanding multimedia applications. Ironically, these enhanced capabilities may not cost more—fierce competition keeps driving prices down.

The Java APIs provide multimedia facilities that enable you to start developing powerful multimedia applications immediately. This chapter presents several examples, including:

1. the basics of manipulating images

2. creating smooth animations

3. playing audio files with the `AudioClip` interface

4. creating image maps that can sense when the cursor is over them, even without a mouse click

5. playing video files using the `Player` interface

We introduce additional JNLP features that, with the user's permission, enable an applet or application to access files on the user's local computer. [*Note:* Java's multimedia capabilities go far beyond those presented in this chapter. They include the **Java Media Framework (JMF) API** (for adding audio and video media to an application), **Java Sound API** (for playing, recording and modifying audio), Java 3D API (for creating and modifying 3D graphics), **Java Advanced Imaging API** (for image-processing capabilities, such as cropping and scaling), **Java Speech API** (for inputting speech from the user and converting it to text, or outputting text to the user as speech), Java 2D API (for creating and modifying 2D graphics, covered in Chapter 15) and **Java Image I/O API** (for reading images from and outputting images to files). Section 21.8 provides web links for these APIs.]

21.2 Loading, Displaying and Scaling Images

We begin our discussion with images. We'll use several different images in this chapter. You can create your own images with software such as Adobe® Photoshop®, Corel® Paint Shop Pro®, Microsoft® Paint and G.I.M.P. (gimp.org).

The applet of Fig. 21.1 uses Java Web Start and the JNLP **FileOpenService** (package javax.jnlp) to allow the user to select an image, then displays that image and allows the user to scale it. After the user selects an image, the applet gets the bytes from the file, then passes them to the ImageIcon (package javax.swing) constructor to create the image that will be displayed. Class ImageIcon's constructors can receive arguments of several different formats, including a byte array containing the bytes of an image, an **Image** (package java.awt) already loaded in memory, or a String or a URL representing the image's location. Java supports various image formats, including **Graphics Interchange Format (GIF)**, **Joint Photographic Experts Group (JPEG)** and **Portable Network Graphics (PNG)**. File names for these types typically end with **.gif**, **.jpg** (or **.jpeg**) and **.png**, respectively.

```
 1   // Fig. 21.1: LoadImageAndScale.java
 2   // Loading, displaying and scaling an image in an applet
 3   import java.awt.BorderLayout;
 4   import java.awt.Graphics;
 5   import java.awt.event.ActionEvent;
 6   import java.awt.event.ActionListener;
 7   import javax.jnlp.FileContents;
 8   import javax.jnlp.FileOpenService;
 9   import javax.jnlp.ServiceManager;
10   import javax.swing.ImageIcon;
11   import javax.swing.JApplet;
12   import javax.swing.JButton;
13   import javax.swing.JFrame;
14   import javax.swing.JLabel;
15   import javax.swing.JOptionPane;
16   import javax.swing.JPanel;
17   import javax.swing.JTextField;
18
19   public class LoadImageAndScale extends JApplet
20   {
21      private ImageIcon image; // references image to display
22      private JPanel scaleJPanel; // JPanel containing the scale-selector
```

Fig. 21.1 | Loading, displaying and scaling an image in an applet. (Part 1 of 4.)

```
23      private JLabel percentJLabel; // label for JTextField
24      private JTextField scaleInputJTextField; // obtains user's input
25      private JButton scaleChangeJButton; // initiates scaling of image
26      private double scaleValue = 1.0;  //scale percentage for image
27
28      // load image when applet is loaded
29      public void init()
30      {
31         scaleJPanel = new JPanel();
32         percentJLabel = new JLabel( "scale percent:" );
33         scaleInputJTextField = new JTextField( "100" );
34         scaleChangeJButton = new JButton( "Set Scale" );
35
36         // add components and place scaleJPanel in applet's NORTH region
37         scaleJPanel.add( percentJLabel );
38         scaleJPanel.add( scaleInputJTextField );
39         scaleJPanel.add( scaleChangeJButton );
40         add( scaleJPanel, BorderLayout.NORTH );
41
42         // register event handler for scaleChangeJButton
43         scaleChangeJButton.addActionListener(
44            new ActionListener()
45            {
46               // when the JButton is pressed, set scaleValue and repaint
47               public void actionPerformed( ActionEvent e )
48               {
49                  scaleValue = Double.parseDouble(
50                     scaleInputJTextField.getText() ) / 100.0;
51                  repaint(); // causes image to be redisplayed at new scale
52               } // end method actionPerformed
53            } // end anonymous inner class
54         ); // end call to addActionListener
55
56         // use JNLP services to open an image file that the user selects
57         try
58         {
59            // get a reference to the FileOpenService
60            FileOpenService fileOpenService =
61               (FileOpenService) ServiceManager.lookup(
62                  "javax.jnlp.FileOpenService" );
63
64            // get file's contents from the FileOpenService
65            FileContents contents =
66               fileOpenService.openFileDialog( null, null );
67
68            // byte array to store image's data
69            byte[] imageData = new byte[ (int) contents.getLength() ];
70            contents.getInputStream().read( imageData ); // read image bytes
71            image = new ImageIcon( imageData ); // create the image
72
73            // if image successfully loaded, create and add DrawJPanel
74            add( new DrawJPanel(), BorderLayout.CENTER );
75         } // end try
```

Fig. 21.1 | Loading, displaying and scaling an image in an applet. (Part 2 of 4.)

```
76          catch( Exception e )
77          {
78             e.printStackTrace();
79          } // end catch
80       } // end method init
81
82       // DrawJPanel used to display loaded image
83       private class DrawJPanel extends JPanel
84       {
85          // display image
86          public void paintComponent( Graphics g )
87          {
88             super.paintComponent( g );
89
90             // the following values are used to center the image
91             double spareWidth =
92                getWidth() - scaleValue * image.getIconWidth();
93             double spareHeight =
94                getHeight() - scaleValue * image.getIconHeight();
95
96             // draw image with scaled width and height
97             g.drawImage( image.getImage(),
98                (int) ( spareWidth ) / 2, (int) ( spareHeight ) / 2,
99                (int) ( image.getIconWidth() * scaleValue ),
100               (int) ( image.getIconHeight() * scaleValue ), this );
101         } // end method paint
102      } // end class DrawJPanel
103   } // end class LoadImageAndScale
```

(a) Java Web Start security dialog that appears because this applet is requesting access to a file on the local computer

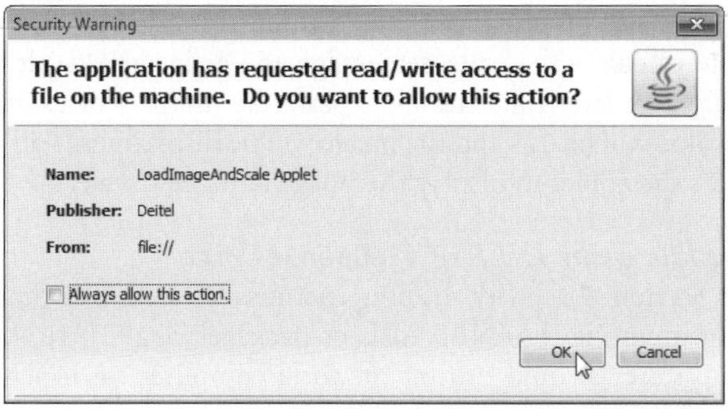

(b) **Open** dialog that appears if the user clicks **OK** in the security dialog

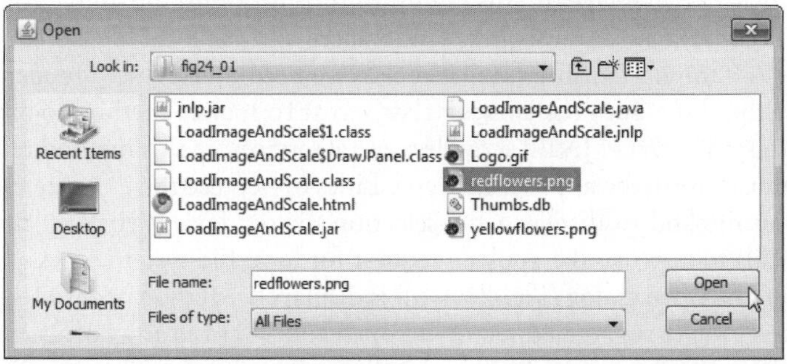

Fig. 21.1 | Loading, displaying and scaling an image in an applet. (Part 3 of 4.)

(c) Scaling the image

Fig. 21.1 | Loading, displaying and scaling an image in an applet. (Part 4 of 4.)

Configuring the GUI and the `JButton`'s Event Handler

The applet's `init` method (lines 29–80) configures the GUI and an event handler. It also uses JNLP services to enable the user to select an image to display from the local computer. Line 31 creates the `JPanel` that will contain the `JLabel`, `JTextField` and `JButton` created in lines 32–34. Lines 37–39 add these components to the `JPanel`'s default `FlowLayout`. Line 40 places this `JPanel` in the `NORTH` region of the `JApplet`'s default `BorderLayout`.

Lines 43–54 create the event handler for the `scaleChangeJButton`. When the user clicks this `JButton`, lines 49–50 obtain the user's input from the `scaleInputJTextField`, divide it by `100.0` to calculate the scale percentage and assign the result to `scaleValue`. This value will be used in later calculations to scale the image. For example, if the user enters 50, the scale value will be `0.5` and the image will be displayed at half its original size. Line 51 then repaints the applet to display the image at its new scale.

Opening the Image File Using JNLP's `FileOpenService`

As we mentioned in Section 20.7, with the user's permission, Java Web Start programs can access the local file system via the JNLP APIs of package `javax.jnlp`. In this example, we'd like the user to select an image from the local computer to display in the applet. (We've provided two images in this example's directory with the source code.) You can use JNLP's `FileOpenService` to request limited access to the local file system.

Lines 7–9 import the interfaces and class we need to use the `FileOpenService`. Lines 60–62 use the JNLP **ServiceManager** class's `static` `lookup` method to obtain a reference to the `FileOpenService`. JNLP provides several services, so this method returns an `Object` that you must cast to the appropriate type. Lines 65–66 use the `FileOpenService`'s **open-FileDialog** method to display a file-selection dialog. Java Web Start prompts the user (Fig. 21.1(a)) to approve the applet's request for local file-system access. If the user gives permission, the **Open** dialog (Fig. 21.1(b)) is displayed. Method `openFileDialog`'s parameters are a `String` to suggest a directory to open and a `String` array of acceptable file extensions (such as `"png"` and `"jpg"`). For simplicity, we passed `null` for each, which displays an open dialog showing the user's default directory and allows any file type to be selected.

When the user selects an image file and clicks the **Open** button in the dialog, method openFileDialog returns a FileContents object, which for security reasons does not give the program access to the file's exact location on disk. Instead, the program can get an InputStream and read the file's bytes. Line 69 creates a byte array in which the image's data will be stored. FileContents method **getLength** returns the number of bytes (as a long) in the file. Line 70 obtains the InputStream, then invokes its **read** method to fill the imageData byte array. Line 71 creates an ImageIcon using the byte array as the source of the image's data. Finally, line 74 adds a new DrawJPanel to the CENTER of the applet's BorderLayout. When the applet is displayed, its components' paintComponent methods are called, which causes the DrawJPanel to display the image. You can learn more about the JNLP APIs at download.oracle.com/javase/6/docs/jre/api/javaws/jnlp/.

Displaying the Image with Class **DrawJPanel**'s **paintComponent** Method

To separate the GUI from the area in which the image is displayed, we use a subclass of JPanel named DrawJPanel (lines 83–102). Its paintComponent method (lines 86–101) displays the image. We'd like to center the image in the DrawJPanel, so lines 91–94 calculate the difference between the width of the DrawJPanel and that of the scaled image, then the height of the DrawJPanel and that of the scaled image. DrawJPanel's **getWidth** and **getHeight** methods (inherited indirectly from class Component) return the DrawJPanel's width and height, respectively. The ImageIcon's **getIconWidth** and **getIconHeight** methods return the image's width and height, respectively. The scaleValue is set to 1.0 by default (line 26), and is changed when the user clicks the **Set Scale** JButton.

Lines 97–100 use Graphics's method **drawImage** to display a scaled ImageIcon. The first argument invokes the ImageIcon's **getImage** method to obtain the Image to draw. The second and third arguments represent the image's *upper-left* corner coordinates with respect to the DrawJPanel's upper-left corner. The fourth and fifth arguments specify the Image's scaled width and height, respectively. Line 99 scales the image's width by invoking the ImageIcon's getIconWidth method and multiplying its return value by scaleValue. Similarly, line 100 scales the image's height. The last argument is an **ImageObserver**—an interface implemented by class Component. Since class DrawJPanel indirectly extends Component, a DrawJPanel *is an* ImageObserver. This argument is important when displaying large images that require a long time to load (or download from the Internet). It's possible that a program will attempt to display the image before it has completely loaded (or downloaded). As the Image loads, the ImageObserver receives notifications and updates the image on the screen as necessary. In this example, the images are being loaded from the user's computer, so it's likely that entire image will be displayed immediately.

Compiling the Applet

Compiling and running this applet requires the jnlp.jar file that contains the JNLP APIs. This file can be found in your JDK installation directory under the directories

```
sample
   jnlp
      servlet
```

To compile the applet, use the following command:

```
javac -classpath PathToJnlpJarFile LoadImageAndScale.java
```

where *PathToJnlpJarFile* includes both the path and the file name jnlp.jar. For example, on our Windows Vista computer, the *PathToJnlpJarFile* is

```
"C:\Program Files\Java\jdk1.6.0_11\sample\jnlp\servlet\jnlp.jar"
```

Packaging the Applet for Use with Java Web Start
To package the applet for use with Java Web Start, you must create a JAR file that contains the applet's code and the jnlp.jar file. To do so, use the command

```
jar cvf LoadImageAndScale.jar *.class PathToJnlpJarFile
```

where *PathToJnlpJarFile* includes both the path and the file name jnlp.jar. This will place all the .class files for the applet and a copy of the jnlp.jar file in the new JAR file LoadImageAndScale.jar.

JNLP Document for **LoadImageAndScale** Applet
The JNLP document in Fig. 21.2 is similar to the one introduced in Fig. 20.12. The only new feature in this document is that the resources element (lines 10–14) contains a second jar element (line 13) that references the jnlp.jar file, which is embedded in the file LoadImageAndScale.jar.

```
 1   <?xml version="1.0" encoding="UTF-8"?>
 2   <jnlp codebase="file:." href="LoadImageAndScale.jnlp">
 3
 4      <information>
 5         <title>LoadImageAndScale Applet</title>
 6         <vendor>Deitel</vendor>
 7         <offline-allowed/>
 8      </information>
 9
10      <resources>
11         <java version="1.6+"/>
12         <jar href="LoadImageAndScale.jar" main="true"/>
13         <jar href="jnlp.jar"/>
14      </resources>
15
16      <applet-desc
17         name="LoadImageAndScale"
18         main-class="LoadImageAndScale"
19         width="400"
20         height="300">
21      </applet-desc>
22   </jnlp>
```

Fig. 21.2 | JNLP document for the LoadImageAndScale applet.

Making the Applet Draggable Outside the Browser Window
The HTML document in Fig. 21.3 loads the applet into a web browser. In this example, we use an applet element to specify the applet's class and provide two param elements between the applet element's tags. The first (line 4) specifies that this applet should be **draggable**. That is, the user can hold the *Alt* key and use the mouse to drag the applet outside the browser window. The applet will then continue executing, even if the browser is

closed. Clicking the close box on the applet when it's executing outside the browser causes the applet to move back into the browser window if it's still open, or to terminate otherwise. The second param element shows an alternate way to specify the JNLP file that launches an applet. We discuss applet parameters in more detail in Section 24.2.

```html
<html>
23    <body>
24    <applet code="LoadImageAndScale.class" width="400" height="300">
25        <param name="draggable" value="true">
26        <param name="jnlp_href" value="LoadImageAndScale.jnlp">
27    </applet>
28    </body>
29    </html>
```

Fig. 21.3 | HTML document to load the LoadImageAndScale applet and make it draggable outside the browser window.

21.3 Animating a Series of Images

Next, we animate a series of images stored in an array of ImageIcons. In this example, we use the JNLP FileOpenService to enable the user to choose a group of images that will be animated by displaying one image at a time at 50-millisecond intervals. The animation presented in Figs. 21.4–21.5 is implemented using a subclass of JPanel called LogoAnimatorJPanel (Fig. 21.4) that can be attached to an application window or a JApplet. Class LogoAnimator (Fig. 21.5) declares a main method (lines 8–20 of Fig. 21.5) to execute the animation as an application. Method main declares an instance of class JFrame and attaches a LogoAnimatorJPanel object to the JFrame to display the animation.

```java
1    // Fig. 21.4: LogoAnimatorJPanel.java
2    // Animating a series of images.
3    import java.awt.Dimension;
4    import java.awt.event.ActionEvent;
5    import java.awt.event.ActionListener;
6    import java.awt.Graphics;
7    import javax.jnlp.FileContents;
8    import javax.jnlp.FileOpenService;
9    import javax.jnlp.ServiceManager;
10   import javax.swing.ImageIcon;
11   import javax.swing.JPanel;
12   import javax.swing.Timer;
13
14   public class LogoAnimatorJPanel extends JPanel
15   {
16       protected ImageIcon images[]; // array of images
17       private int currentImage = 0; // current image index
18       private final int ANIMATION_DELAY = 50; // millisecond delay
19       private int width; // image width
20       private int height; // image height
21
```

Fig. 21.4 | Animating a series of images. (Part 1 of 3.)

```
22       private Timer animationTimer; // Timer drives animation
23
24       // constructor initializes LogoAnimatorJPanel by loading images
25       public LogoAnimatorJPanel()
26       {
27          try
28          {
29             // get reference to FileOpenService
30             FileOpenService fileOpenService =
31                (FileOpenService) ServiceManager.lookup(
32                   "javax.jnlp.FileOpenService" );
33
34             // display dialog that allows user to select multiple files
35             FileContents[] contents =
36                fileOpenService.openMultiFileDialog( null, null );
37
38             // create array to store ImageIcon references
39             images = new ImageIcon[ contents.length ];
40
41             // load the selected images
42             for ( int count = 0; count < images.length; count++ )
43             {
44                // create byte array to store an image's data
45                byte[] imageData =
46                   new byte[ (int) contents[ count ].getLength() ];
47
48                // get image's data and create image
49                contents[ count ].getInputStream().read( imageData );
50                images[ count ] = new ImageIcon( imageData );
51             } // end for
52
53             // this example assumes all images have the same width and height
54             width = images[ 0 ].getIconWidth();   // get icon width
55             height = images[ 0 ].getIconHeight(); // get icon height
56          } // end try
57          catch( Exception e )
58          {
59             e.printStackTrace();
60          } // end catch
61       } // end LogoAnimatorJPanel constructor
62
63       // display current image
64       public void paintComponent( Graphics g )
65       {
66          super.paintComponent( g ); // call superclass paintComponent
67
68          images[ currentImage ].paintIcon( this, g, 0, 0 );
69
70          // set next image to be drawn only if Timer is running
71          if ( animationTimer.isRunning() )
72             currentImage = ( currentImage + 1 ) % images.length;
73       } // end method paintComponent
```

Fig. 21.4 | Animating a series of images. (Part 2 of 3.)

```
74
75        // start animation, or restart if window is redisplayed
76        public void startAnimation()
77        {
78           if ( animationTimer == null )
79           {
80              currentImage = 0; // display first image
81
82              // create timer
83              animationTimer =
84                 new Timer( ANIMATION_DELAY, new TimerHandler() );
85
86              animationTimer.start(); // start Timer
87           } // end if
88           else // animationTimer already exists, restart animation
89           {
90              if ( ! animationTimer.isRunning() )
91                 animationTimer.restart();
92           } // end else
93        } // end method startAnimation
94
95        // stop animation Timer
96        public void stopAnimation()
97        {
98           animationTimer.stop();
99        } // end method stopAnimation
100
101       // return minimum size of animation
102       public Dimension getMinimumSize()
103       {
104          return getPreferredSize();
105       } // end method getMinimumSize
106
107       // return preferred size of animation
108       public Dimension getPreferredSize()
109       {
110          return new Dimension( width, height );
111       } // end method getPreferredSize
112
113       // inner class to handle action events from Timer
114       private class TimerHandler implements ActionListener
115       {
116          // respond to Timer's event
117          public void actionPerformed( ActionEvent actionEvent )
118          {
119             repaint(); // repaint animator
120          } // end method actionPerformed
121       } // end class TimerHandler
122    } // end class LogoAnimatorJPanel
```

Fig. 21.4 | Animating a series of images. (Part 3 of 3.)

```
 1  // Fig. 21.5: LogoAnimator.java
 2  // Displaying animated images on a JFrame.
 3  import javax.swing.JFrame;
 4
 5  public class LogoAnimator
 6  {
 7     // execute animation in a JFrame
 8     public static void main( String args[] )
 9     {
10        LogoAnimatorJPanel animation = new LogoAnimatorJPanel();
11
12        JFrame window = new JFrame( "Animator test" ); // set up window
13        window.setDefaultCloseOperation( JFrame.EXIT_ON_CLOSE );
14        window.add( animation ); // add panel to frame
15
16        window.pack();   // make window just large enough for its GUI
17        window.setVisible( true );   // display window
18
19        animation.startAnimation(); // begin animation
20     } // end main
21  } // end class LogoAnimator
```

Fig. 21.5 | Displaying animated images on a JFrame.

Class *LogoAnimatorPanel*

Class LogoAnimatorJPanel (Fig. 21.4) maintains an array of ImageIcons (declared at line 16) that are loaded in the constructor (lines 25–61). The constructor begins by using the JNLP FileOpenService's **openMultiFileDialog** method to display a file-selection dialog that allows the user to select multiple files at once. We named our sample images such that they all have the same base name ("deitel") followed by a two-digit number from 00–29. This ensures that our images are in the proper order for the animation. As in this chapter's first example, first the user is prompted to give permission, then the **Open** dialog appears if permission is granted. FileOpenService method openMultiFileDialog takes the same arguments as method openFileDialog but returns an array of FileContents objects representing the set of files selected by the user. When you run this application, navigate to a folder containing the images you wish to use and select the images. If you wish, you can use the 30 images we provide in this example's subdirectory named images.

Line 39 creates the array of ImageIcons, then lines 42–51 populate the array by creating a byte array (lines 45–46) for the current image's data, reading the bytes of the image into the array (line 49) and creating an ImageIcon object from the byte array. Lines 54–55 determine the width and height of the animation from the size of the first image in array images—we assume that all the images have the same width and height.

Method startAnimation

After the LogoAnimatorJPanel constructor loads the images, method main of Fig. 21.5 sets up the window in which the animation will appear (lines 12–17), and line 19 calls the LogoAnimatorJPanel's startAnimation method (declared at lines 76–93 of Fig. 21.4). This method starts the program's animation for the first time or restarts the animation that the program stopped previously. The animation is driven by an instance of class **Timer** (from package javax.swing).

When the program is first run, method startAnimation is called to begin the animation. Although we provide the functionality for this method to restart the animation if it has been stopped, the example does not call the method for this purpose. We've added the functionality, however, should the reader choose to add GUI components that enable the user to start and stop the animation.

A Timer generates ActionEvents at a fixed interval in milliseconds (normally specified as an argument to the Timer's constructor) and notifies all its ActionListeners each time an ActionEvent occurs. Line 78 determines whether the Timer reference animationTimer is null. If it is, method startAnimation is being called for the first time, and a Timer needs to be created so that the animation can begin. Line 80 sets currentImage to 0, which indicates that the animation should begin with the first element of array images. Lines 83–84 assign a new Timer object to animationTimer. The Timer constructor receives two arguments—the delay in milliseconds (ANIMATION_DELAY is 50, as specified in line 18) and the ActionListener that will respond to the Timer's ActionEvents. For the second argument, an object of class TimerHandler is created. This class, which implements Action-Listener, is declared in lines 114–121. Line 86 calls the Timer object's **start** method to start the Timer. Once started, animationTimer will generate an ActionEvent every 50 milliseconds and call the Timer's event handler actionPerformed (lines 117–120). Line 119 calls LogoAnimatorJPanel's repaint method to schedule a call to LogoAnimatorJPanel's paintComponent method (lines 64–73). Remember that any subclass of JComponent that draws should do so in its paintComponent method. Recall that the first statement in any paintComponent method should be a call to the superclass's paintComponent method, to ensure that Swing components are displayed correctly.

If the animation started earlier, then our Timer was created and the condition in line 78 evaluates to false. The program continues with lines 90–91, which restarts the animation that the program stopped previously. The if condition at line 90 uses Timer method **isRunning** to determine whether the Timer is running (i.e., generating events). If it's not running, line 91 calls Timer method **restart** to indicate that the Timer should start generating events again. Once this occurs, method actionPerformed (the Timer's event handler) is again called at regular intervals.

Method paintComponent

Line 68 calls the ImageIcon's **paintIcon** method to display the image stored at element currentImage in the array. The arguments represent the Component on which to draw (this), the Graphics object that performs the drawing (g) and the coordinates of the image's upper-left corner. Lines 71–72 determine whether the animationTimer is running and, if so, prepare for the next image to be displayed by incrementing currentImage by 1. The remainder calculation ensures that the value of currentImage is set to 0 (to repeat the animation sequence) when it's incremented past the last element index in the array. The if statement ensures that the same image will be displayed if paintComponent is called while the Timer is stopped. This can be useful if a GUI is provided that enables the user to start and stop the animation. For example, if the animation is stopped and the user covers it with another window, then uncovers it, method paintComponent will be called. In this case, we do not want the animation to show the next image (because the animation has been stopped). We simply want the window to display the same image until the animation is restarted.

Method *stopAnimation*

Method stopAnimation (lines 96–99) stops the animation by calling Timer method **stop** to indicate that the Timer should stop generating events. This prevents actionPerformed from calling repaint to initiate the painting of the next image in the array. Just as with restarting the animation, this example defines but does not use method stopAnimation. We've provided this method for demonstration purposes, or to allow the user to modify this example to stop and restart the animation.

> **Software Engineering Observation 21.1**
>
> *When creating an animation for use in an applet, provide a mechanism for disabling the animation when the user browses a new web page different from the one on which the animation applet resides.*

Methods *getPreferredSize* and *getMinimumSize*

By extending class JPanel, we're creating a new GUI component. So, we must ensure that it works like other components for layout purposes. Layout managers often use a component's **getPreferredSize** method (inherited from class java.awt.Component) to determine the component's preferred width and height. If a new component has a preferred width and height, it should override method getPreferredSize (lines 108–111) to return that width and height as an object of class **Dimension** (package java.awt). The Dimension class represents the width and height of a GUI component. In this example, the images we provide are 160 pixels wide and 80 pixels tall, so method getPreferredSize would return a Dimension object containing the numbers 160 and 80 (if you use these images).

> **Look-and-Feel Observation 21.1**
>
> *The default size of a JPanel object is 10 pixels wide and 10 pixels tall.*

> **Look-and-Feel Observation 21.2**
>
> *When subclassing JPanel (or any other JComponent), override method getPreferredSize if the new component is to have a specific preferred width and height.*

Lines 102–105 override method **getMinimumSize**. This method determines the minimum width and height of the component. As with method getPreferredSize, new components should override method getMinimumSize (also inherited from class Component). Method getMinimumSize simply calls getPreferredSize (a common programming practice) to indicate that the minimum size and preferred size are the same. Some layout managers ignore the dimensions specified by these methods. For example, a BorderLayout's NORTH and SOUTH regions use only the component's preferred height.

Look-and-Feel Observation 21.3
If a new GUI component has a minimum width and height (i.e., smaller dimensions would render the component ineffective on the display), override method getMinimumSize to return the minimum width and height as an instance of class Dimension.

Look-and-Feel Observation 21.4
For many GUI components, method getMinimumSize is implemented to return the result of a call to the component's getPreferredSize method.

Compiling the Application
Compiling and running this application requires the jnlp.jar file that contains the JNLP APIs. To compile the application use the following command:

```
javac -classpath PathToJnlpJarFile *.java
```

where *PathToJnlpJarFile* includes both the path and the file name jnlp.jar.

Packaging the Application for Use with Java Web Start
To package the application for use with Java Web Start, you must create a JAR file that contains the applet's code and the jnlp.jar file. To do so, use the command

```
jar cvf LogoAnimator.jar *.class PathToJnlpJarFile
```

where *PathToJnlpJarFile* includes both the path and the file name jnlp.jar.

*JNLP Document for **LoadImageAndScale** Applet*
The JNLP document in Fig. 21.6 is similar to the one in Fig. 21.2. The only new feature in this document is the application-desc element (lines 16–19), which specifies the name of the application and its main class. To run this application, use the command

```
javaws LogoAnimator.jnlp
```

Recall that you can also run Java Web Start applications via a link in a web page, as we showed in Fig. 20.13.

```
1   <?xml version="1.0" encoding="UTF-8"?>
2   <jnlp codebase="file:." href="LogoAnimator.jnlp">
3
4      <information>
5         <title>LogoAnimator</title>
6         <vendor>Deitel</vendor>
7         <offline-allowed/>
8      </information>
9
10     <resources>
11        <java version="1.6+"/>
12        <jar href="LogoAnimator.jar" main="true"/>
13        <jar href="jnlp.jar"/>
14     </resources>
15
```

Fig. 21.6 | JNLP document for the LoadImageAndScale applet. (Part 1 of 2.)

```
16    <application-desc
17       name="LogoAnimator"
18       main-class="LogoAnimator">
19    </application-desc>
20  </jnlp>
```

Fig. 21.6 | JNLP document for the LoadImageAndScale applet. (Part 2 of 2.)

21.4 Image Maps

Image maps are commonly used to create interactive web pages. An image map is an image with **hot areas** that the user can click to accomplish a task, such as loading a different web page into a browser. When the user positions the mouse pointer over a hot area, normally a descriptive message appears in the status area of the browser or in a tool tip.

Figure 21.7 loads an image containing several of the programming-tip icons used in this book. The program allows the user to position the mouse pointer over an icon to display a descriptive message associated with it. Event handler mouseMoved (lines 39–43) takes the mouse coordinates and passes them to method translateLocation (lines 58–69). Method translateLocation tests the coordinates to determine the icon over which the mouse was positioned when the mouseMoved event occurred—the method then returns a message indicating what the icon represents. This message is displayed in the applet container's status bar using method **showStatus** of class Applet.

```
1   // Fig. 21.7: ImageMap.java
2   // Image map.
3   import java.awt.event.MouseAdapter;
4   import java.awt.event.MouseEvent;
5   import java.awt.event.MouseMotionAdapter;
6   import java.awt.Graphics;
7   import javax.swing.ImageIcon;
8   import javax.swing.JApplet;
9
10  public class ImageMap extends JApplet
11  {
12     private ImageIcon mapImage;
13
14     private static final String captions[] = { "Common Programming Error",
15        "Good Programming Practice", "Look-and-Feel Observation",
16        "Performance Tip", "Portability Tip",
17        "Software Engineering Observation", "Error-Prevention Tip" };
18
19     // sets up mouse listeners
20     public void init()
21     {
22        addMouseListener(
23
24           new MouseAdapter() // anonymous inner class
25           {
```

Fig. 21.7 | Image map. (Part 1 of 3.)

```
26              // indicate when mouse pointer exits applet area
27              public void mouseExited( MouseEvent event )
28              {
29                  showStatus( "Pointer outside applet" );
30              } // end method mouseExited
31          } // end anonymous inner class
32      ); // end call to addMouseListener
33
34      addMouseMotionListener(
35
36          new MouseMotionAdapter() // anonymous inner class
37          {
38              // determine icon over which mouse appears
39              public void mouseMoved( MouseEvent event )
40              {
41                  showStatus( translateLocation(
42                      event.getX(), event.getY() ) );
43              } // end method mouseMoved
44          } // end anonymous inner class
45      ); // end call to addMouseMotionListener
46
47      mapImage = new ImageIcon( "icons.png" ); // get image
48  } // end method init
49
50  // display mapImage
51  public void paint( Graphics g )
52  {
53      super.paint( g );
54      mapImage.paintIcon( this, g, 0, 0 );
55  } // end method paint
56
57  // return tip caption based on mouse coordinates
58  public String translateLocation( int x, int y )
59  {
60      // if coordinates outside image, return immediately
61      if ( x >= mapImage.getIconWidth() || y >= mapImage.getIconHeight() )
62          return "";
63
64      // determine icon number (0 - 6)
65      double iconWidth = ( double ) mapImage.getIconWidth() / 7.0;
66      int iconNumber = ( int )( ( double ) x / iconWidth );
67
68      return captions[ iconNumber ]; // return appropriate icon caption
69  } // end method translateLocation
70 } // end class ImageMap
```

Fig. 21.7 | Image map. (Part 2 of 3.)

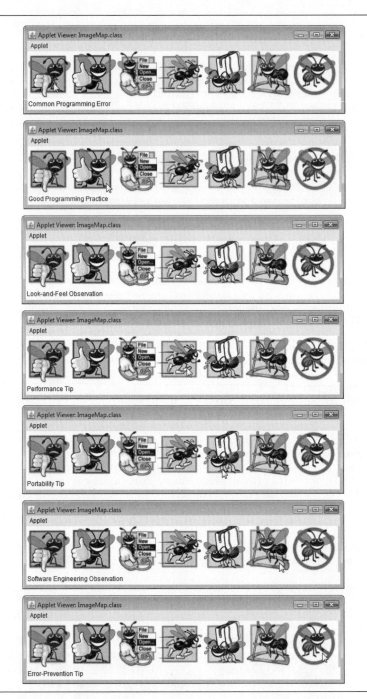

Fig. 21.7 | Image map. (Part 3 of 3.)

Clicking in the applet of Fig. 21.7 will not cause any action. In Chapter 24, we discuss the techniques for loading another web page into a browser via URLs and the AppletContext interface. Using those techniques, this applet could associate each icon with a URL that the browser would display when the user clicks the icon.

21.5 Loading and Playing Audio Clips

Java programs can manipulate and play **audio clips**. Users can capture their own audio clips, and many clips are available in software products and over the Internet. Your system needs to be equipped with audio hardware (speakers and a sound card) to be able to play the audio clips.

Java provides several mechanisms for playing sounds in an applet. The two simplest are the Applet's **play** method and the **play** method of the **AudioClip** interface. Additional audio capabilities are available in the Java Media Framework and Java Sound APIs. If you'd like to play a sound once in a program, the Applet method play loads the sound and plays it once, then the sound can be garbage collected. The Applet method play has two versions:

```
public void play( URL location, String soundFileName );
public void play( URL soundURL );
```

The first version loads the audio clip stored in file soundFileName from location and plays the sound. The first argument is normally a call to the applet's getDocumentBase or **getCodeBase** method. Method getDocumentBase returns the location of the HTML file that loaded the applet. (If the applet is in a package, the method returns the location of the package or the JAR file containing the package.) Method getCodeBase indicates the location of the applet's .class file. The second version of method play takes a URL that contains the location and the file name of the audio clip. The statement

```
play( getDocumentBase(), "hi.au" );
```

loads the audio clip in file hi.au and plays it once.

The **sound engine** that plays the audio clips supports several audio file formats, including **Sun Audio file format** (.au extension), **Windows Wave file format** (.wav extension), **Macintosh AIFF file format** (.aif or .aiff extensions) and **Musical Instrument Digital Interface (MIDI) file format** (.mid or .rmi extensions). The Java Media Framework (JMF) and Java Sound APIs support additional formats.

The program of Fig. 21.8 demonstrates loading and playing an AudioClip (package java.applet). This technique is more flexible than Applet method play. An applet can use an AudioClip to store audio for repeated use throughout a program's execution. Applet method **getAudioClip** has two forms that take the same arguments as method play described previously. Method getAudioClip returns a reference to an AudioClip. An AudioClip has three methods—play, loop and stop. As mentioned earlier, method play plays the audio clip once. Method **loop** continuously loops through the audio clip in the background. Method **stop** terminates an audio clip that is currently playing. In the program, each of these methods is associated with a button on the applet.

```
1   // Fig. 21.8: LoadAudioAndPlay.java
2   // Loading and playing an AudioClip.
3   import java.applet.AudioClip;
4   import java.awt.event.ItemListener;
```

Fig. 21.8 | Loading and playing an AudioClip. (Part I of 3.)

```
 5    import java.awt.event.ItemEvent;
 6    import java.awt.event.ActionListener;
 7    import java.awt.event.ActionEvent;
 8    import java.awt.FlowLayout;
 9    import javax.swing.JApplet;
10    import javax.swing.JButton;
11    import javax.swing.JComboBox;
12
13    public class LoadAudioAndPlay extends JApplet
14    {
15       private AudioClip sound1, sound2, currentSound;
16       private JButton playJButton, loopJButton, stopJButton;
17       private JComboBox soundJComboBox;
18
19       // load the audio when the applet begins executing
20       public void init()
21       {
22          setLayout( new FlowLayout() );
23
24          String choices[] = { "Welcome", "Hi" };
25          soundJComboBox = new JComboBox( choices ); // create JComboBox
26
27          soundJComboBox.addItemListener(
28
29             new ItemListener() // anonymous inner class
30             {
31                // stop sound and change sound to user's selection
32                public void itemStateChanged( ItemEvent e )
33                {
34                   currentSound.stop();
35                   currentSound = soundJComboBox.getSelectedIndex() == 0 ?
36                      sound1 : sound2;
37                } // end method itemStateChanged
38             } // end anonymous inner class
39          ); // end addItemListener method call
40
41          add( soundJComboBox ); // add JComboBox to applet
42
43          // set up button event handler and buttons
44          ButtonHandler handler = new ButtonHandler();
45
46          // create Play JButton
47          playJButton = new JButton( "Play" );
48          playJButton.addActionListener( handler );
49          add( playJButton );
50
51          // create Loop JButton
52          loopJButton = new JButton( "Loop" );
53          loopJButton.addActionListener( handler );
54          add( loopJButton );
55
56          // create Stop JButton
57          stopJButton = new JButton( "Stop" );
```

Fig. 21.8 | Loading and playing an AudioClip. (Part 2 of 3.)

```
58          stopJButton.addActionListener( handler );
59          add( stopJButton );
60
61          // load sounds and set currentSound
62          sound1 = getAudioClip( getDocumentBase(), "welcome.wav" );
63          sound2 = getAudioClip( getDocumentBase(), "hi.au" );
64          currentSound = sound1;
65       } // end method init
66
67       // stop the sound when the user switches web pages
68       public void stop()
69       {
70          currentSound.stop(); // stop AudioClip
71       } // end method stop
72
73       // private inner class to handle button events
74       private class ButtonHandler implements ActionListener
75       {
76          // process play, loop and stop button events
77          public void actionPerformed( ActionEvent actionEvent )
78          {
79             if ( actionEvent.getSource() == playJButton )
80                currentSound.play(); // play AudioClip once
81             else if ( actionEvent.getSource() == loopJButton )
82                currentSound.loop(); // play AudioClip continuously
83             else if ( actionEvent.getSource() == stopJButton )
84                currentSound.stop(); // stop AudioClip
85          } // end method actionPerformed
86       } // end class ButtonHandler
87 } // end class LoadAudioAndPlay
```

Fig. 21.8 | Loading and playing an `AudioClip`. (Part 3 of 3.)

Lines 62–63 in the applet's `init` method use `getAudioClip` to load two audio files—a Windows Wave file (`welcome.wav`) and a Sun Audio file (`hi.au`). The user can select which audio clip to play from the `JComboBox` `soundJComboBox`. The applet's `stop` method is overridden at lines 68–71. When the user switches web pages, the applet container calls the applet's `stop` method. This enables the applet to stop playing the audio clip. Otherwise, it continues to play in the background—even if the applet is not displayed in the browser. This is not necessarily a problem, but it can be annoying to the user if the audio clip is looping. The `stop` method is provided here as a convenience to the user.

Look-and-Feel Observation 21.5
When playing audio clips in an applet or application, provide a mechanism for the user to disable the audio.

21.6 Playing Video and Other Media with Java Media Framework

A simple video can concisely and effectively convey a great deal of information. Using the Java Media Framework (JMF) API, you can create Java applications that play, edit, stream and capture many popular media types. This section briefly introduces some popular media formats and demonstrates playing video using the JMF API.

JMF 2.1.1e supports media file types such as **Microsoft Audio/Video Interleave** (**.avi**), **Macromedia Flash movies** (**.swf**), **Future Splash** (**.spl**), **MPEG Layer 3 Audio** (**.mp3**), Musical Instrument Digital Interface (MIDI; .mid or .rmi extensions), **MPEG-1 videos** (**.mpeg**, **.mpg**), **QuickTime** (**.mov**), Sun Audio file format (.au extension), and Macintosh AIFF file format (.aif or .aiff extensions). You've already seen some of these file types.

Currently, JMF is available as an extension separate from the JDK. The most recent JMF implementation (2.1.1e) can be downloaded from:

www.oracle.com/technetwork/java/javase/download-142937.html

[*Note:* Keep track of where you install the Java Media Framework on your computer. To compile and run this application, you must include in the class path the jmf.jar file that is installed with the Java Media Framework. Recall that you can specify the class path with both the javac and java commands via the -classpath command-line option.]

The JMF website provides versions of the JMF that take advantage of the performance features of certain platforms. For example, the JMF Windows Performance Pack provides extensive media and device support for Java programs running on Microsoft Windows platforms. The JMF's website (www.oracle.com/technetwork/java/javase/tech/index-jsp-140239.html) provides information and resources for JMF programmers.

Creating a Simple Media Player
JMF offers several mechanisms for playing media. The simplest is using objects that implement interface **Player** declared in package **javax.media**. Package javax.media and its subpackages contain the classes that compose the Java Media Framework. To play a media clip, you must first create a URL object that refers to it. Then pass the URL as an argument to static method **createRealizedPlayer** of class Manager to obtain a Player for the media clip. Class **Manager** declares utility methods for accessing system resources to play and to manipulate media. Figure 21.9 declares a JPanel that demonstrates some of these methods.

```
1   // Fig. 21.9: MediaPanel.java
2   // JPanel that plays a media file from a URL.
3   import java.awt.BorderLayout;
4   import java.awt.Component;
5   import java.io.IOException;
6   import java.net.URL;
7   import javax.media.CannotRealizeException;
8   import javax.media.Manager;
9   import javax.media.NoPlayerException;
```

Fig. 21.9 | JPanel that plays a media file from a URL. (Part 1 of 2.)

```
10   import javax.media.Player;
11   import javax.swing.JPanel;
12
13   public class MediaPanel extends JPanel
14   {
15      public MediaPanel( URL mediaURL )
16      {
17         setLayout( new BorderLayout() ); // use a BorderLayout
18
19         // Use lightweight components for Swing compatibility
20         Manager.setHint( Manager.LIGHTWEIGHT_RENDERER, true );
21
22         try
23         {
24            // create a player to play the media specified in the URL
25            Player mediaPlayer = Manager.createRealizedPlayer( mediaURL );
26
27            // get the components for the video and the playback controls
28            Component video = mediaPlayer.getVisualComponent();
29            Component controls = mediaPlayer.getControlPanelComponent();
30
31            if ( video != null )
32               add( video, BorderLayout.CENTER ); // add video component
33
34            if ( controls != null )
35               add( controls, BorderLayout.SOUTH ); // add controls
36
37            mediaPlayer.start(); // start playing the media clip
38         } // end try
39         catch ( NoPlayerException noPlayerException )
40         {
41            System.err.println( "No media player found" );
42         } // end catch
43         catch ( CannotRealizeException cannotRealizeException )
44         {
45            System.err.println( "Could not realize media player" );
46         } // end catch
47         catch ( IOException iOException )
48         {
49            System.err.println( "Error reading from the source" );
50         } // end catch
51      } // end MediaPanel constructor
52   } // end class MediaPanel
```

Fig. 21.9 | JPanel that plays a media file from a URL. (Part 2 of 2.)

The constructor (lines 15–51) sets up the JPanel to play the media file specified by the constructor's URL parameter. MediaPanel uses a BorderLayout (line 17). Line 20 invokes static method **setHint** to set the flag **Manager.LIGHTWEIGHT_RENDERER** to true. This instructs the Manager to use a lightweight renderer that is compatible with lightweight Swing components, as opposed to the default heavyweight renderer. Inside the try block (lines 22–38), line 25 invokes static method createRealizedPlayer of class Manager to create and realize a Player that plays the media file. When a Player realizes, it identifies the system resources it needs to play the media. Depending on the file, realizing can be a resource-consuming and time-consuming process. Method createRealizedPlayer throws three checked exceptions, **NoPlayerException**, **CannotRealizeException** and IOException. A NoPlayerException indicates that the system could not find a player that can play the file format. A CannotRealizeException indicates that the system could not properly identify the resources a media file needs. An IOException indicates that there was an error while reading the file. These exceptions are handled in the catch block in lines 39–50.

Line 28 invokes method **getVisualComponent** of Player to get a Component that displays the visual (generally video) aspect of the media file. Line 29 invokes method **getControlPanelComponent** of Player to get a Component that provides playback and media controls. These components are assigned to local variables video and controls, respectively. The if statements in lines 31–32 and lines 34–35 add the video and the controls if they exist. The video Component is added to the CENTER region (line 32), so it fills any available space on the JPanel. The controls Component, which is added to the SOUTH region, typically provides the following controls:

1. A *positioning slider* to jump to certain points in the media clip

2. A *pause button*

3. A *volume button* that provides volume control by right clicking and a mute function by left clicking

4. A *media properties button* that provides detailed media information by left clicking and frame-rate control by right clicking

Line 37 calls Player method **start** to begin playing the media file. Lines 39–50 handle the various exceptions that createRealizedPlayer throws.

The application in Fig. 21.10 displays a JFileChooser dialog for the user to choose a media file. It then creates a MediaPanel that plays the selected file and creates a JFrame to display the MediaPanel.

```
1   // Fig. 21.10: MediaTest.java
2   // Test application that creates a MediaPanel from a user-selected file.
3   import java.io.File;
4   import java.net.MalformedURLException;
5   import java.net.URL;
6   import javax.swing.JFileChooser;
7   import javax.swing.JFrame;
8
9   public class MediaTest
10  {
11     // launch the application
12     public static void main( String args[] )
13     {
14        // create a file chooser
15        JFileChooser fileChooser = new JFileChooser();
16
17        // show open file dialog
18        int result = fileChooser.showOpenDialog( null );
```

Fig. 21.10 | Test application that creates a MediaPanel from a user-selected file. (Part 1 of 2.)

```
19
20          if ( result == JFileChooser.APPROVE_OPTION ) // user chose a file
21          {
22             URL mediaURL = null;
23
24             try
25             {
26                // get the file as URL
27                mediaURL = fileChooser.getSelectedFile().toURI().toURL();
28             } // end try
29             catch ( MalformedURLException malformedURLException )
30             {
31                System.err.println( "Could not create URL for the file" );
32             } // end catch
33
34             if ( mediaURL != null ) // only display if there is a valid URL
35             {
36                JFrame mediaTest = new JFrame( "Media Tester" );
37                mediaTest.setDefaultCloseOperation( JFrame.EXIT_ON_CLOSE );
38
39                MediaPanel mediaPanel = new MediaPanel( mediaURL );
40                mediaTest.add( mediaPanel );
41
42                mediaTest.setSize( 300, 300 );
43                mediaTest.setVisible( true );
44             } // end inner if
45          } // end outer if
46       } // end main
47    } // end class MediaTest
```

Fig. 21.10 | Test application that creates a MediaPanel from a user-selected file. (Part 2 of 2.)

Method main (lines 12–46) assigns a new JFileChooser to local variable fileChooser (line 15), shows an open-file dialog (line 18) and assigns the return value to result. Line 20 checks result to determine whether the user chose a file. To create a

Player to play the selected media file, you must convert the File object returned by JFileChooser to a URL object. Method **toURI** of class File returns a URI that points to the File on the system. We then invoke method **toURL** of class URI to get the file's URL. The try statement (lines 24–32) creates a URL for the selected file and assigns it to mediaURL. The if statement in lines 34–44 checks that mediaURL is not null and creates the GUI components to play the media.

21.7 Wrap-Up

In this chapter, you learned how to build multimedia-rich applications with sound, images, graphics and video. We introduced Java's multimedia capabilities, including the Java Media Framework API and Java Sound API. You used class ImageIcon to display and manipulate images stored in files, and you learned about the different image formats supported by Java. You used the JNLP FileOpenService to enable the user of a Java Web Start application to select files from the local file system, then used streams to load the contents of those files for use in your programs. You created an animation by displaying a series of images in a specific order. You used image maps to make an application more interactive. You learned how to load audio clips and how to play them either once or in a continuous loop. The chapter concluded with a demonstration of loading and playing video. In the next chapter, you'll continue your study of GUI concepts, building on the techniques you learned in Chapter 14.

21.8 Web Resources

www.nasa.gov/multimedia/index.html
The *NASA Multimedia Gallery* contains a wide variety of images, audio clips and video clips that you can download and use to test your Java multimedia programs.

commons.wikimedia.org/wiki/Main_Page
The *Wikimedia Commons* site provides access to millions of media files.

www.anbg.gov.au/gardens/index.html
The *Australian National Botanic Gardens* website provides links to the sounds of many animals. Try, for example, the *Common Birds* link under the "Animals in the Gardens" section.

www.thefreesite.com
This site has links to free sounds and clip art.

www.soundcentral.com
SoundCentral provides audio clips in WAV, AU, AIFF and MIDI formats.

www.animationfactory.com
The *Animation Factory* provides thousands of free GIF animations for personal use.

www.clipart.com
This site is a subscription-based service for images and sounds.

java.sun.com/developer/techDocs/hi/repository/
The *Java look-and-feel Graphics Repository* provides images designed for use in a Swing GUI, including toolbar button images.

www.freebyte.com/graphicprograms/
This guide contains links to several free graphics software programs. The software can be used to modify images and draw graphics.

graphicssoft.about.com/od/pixelbasedfreewin/
This site provides links to free graphics programs designed for use on Windows machines.

Java Multimedia API References

www.oracle.com/technetwork/java/javase/tech/media-141984.html
The online home of the Java Media APIs.

www.oracle.com/technetwork/java/index-139508.html
The *Java Sound API* home page. Java Sound provides capabilities for playing and recording audio.

java3d.dev.java.net/
The *Java 3D API* home page. This API can be used to produce three-dimensional images typical of today's video games.

java.sun.com/products/java-media/speech/
The *Java Speech API* enables programs to perform speech synthesis and speech recognition.

freetts.sourceforge.net/docs/index.php
FreeTTS is an implementation of the Java Speech API.

22

GUI Components:
Part 2

Objectives

In this chapter you'll learn:

- To create and manipulate sliders, menus, pop-up menus and windows.

- To programatically change the look-and-feel of a GUI, using Swing's pluggable look-and-feel.

- To create a multiple-document interface with `JDesktopPane` and `JInternalFrame`.

- To use additional layout managers.

An actor entering through the door, you've got nothing. But if he enters through the window, you've got a situation.
—Billy Wilder

...the force of events wakes slumberous talents.
—Edward Hoagland

You and I would see more interesting photography if they would stop worrying, and instead, apply horse-sense to the problem of recording the look and feel of their own era.
—Jessie Tarbox Beals

22.1 Introduction

In this chapter, we continue our study of GUIs. We discuss additional components and layout managers and lay the groundwork for building more complex GUIs.

We begin our discussion with sliders that enable you to select from a range of integer values. Next, we discuss some additional details of windows. You'll learn to use menus that enable the user to effectively perform tasks in the program. The look-and-feel of a Swing GUI can be uniform across all platforms on which a Java program executes, or the GUI can be customized by using Swing's **pluggable look-and-feel** (**PLAF**). We provide an example that illustrates how to change between Swing's default metal look-and-feel (which looks and behaves the same across platforms), the Nimbus look-and-feel (introduced in Chapter 14), a look-and-feel that simulates **Motif** (a popular UNIX look-and-feel) and one that simulates Microsoft's Windows look-and-feel.

Many of today's applications use a multiple-document interface (MDI)—a main window (often called the *parent window*) containing other windows (often called *child windows*) to manage several open documents in parallel. For example, many e-mail programs allow you to have several e-mail windows open at the same time so that you can compose or read multiple e-mail messages. We demonstrate Swing's classes for creating multiple-document interfaces. The chapter finishes with a series of examples discussing additional layout managers for organizing graphical user interfaces.

Swing is a large and complex topic. There are many more GUI components and capabilities than can be presented here. Several more Swing GUI components are introduced in the remaining chapters of this book as they're needed.

22.2 JSlider

JSliders enable a user to select from a range of integer values. Class JSlider inherits from JComponent. Figure 22.1 shows a horizontal JSlider with **tick marks** and the **thumb** that allows a user to select a value. JSliders can be customized to display *major tick marks*, *minor tick marks* and labels for the tick marks. They also support **snap-to ticks**, which cause the *thumb*, when positioned between two tick marks, to snap to the closest one.

Thumb ———   ———— Tick mark

Fig. 22.1 | JSlider component with horizontal orientation.

Most Swing GUI components support user interactions through the mouse and the keyboard. For example, if a JSlider has the focus (i.e., it's the currently selected GUI component in the user interface), the left arrow key and right arrow key cause the thumb of the JSlider to decrease or increase by 1, respectively. The down arrow key and up arrow key also cause the thumb to decrease or increase by 1 tick, respectively. The *PgDn* (page down) *key* and *PgUp* (page up) *key* cause the thumb to decrease or increase by **block increments** of one-tenth of the range of values, respectively. The *Home key* moves the thumb to the minimum value of the JSlider, and the *End key* moves the thumb to the maximum value of the JSlider.

JSliders have either a horizontal or a vertical orientation. For a horizontal JSlider, the minimum value is at the left end and the maximum is at the right end. For a vertical JSlider, the minimum value is at the bottom and the maximum is at the top. The minimum and maximum value positions on a JSlider can be reversed by invoking JSlider method **setInverted** with boolean argument true. The relative position of the thumb indicates the current value of the JSlider.

The program in Figs. 22.2–22.4 allows the user to size a circle drawn on a subclass of JPanel called OvalPanel (Fig. 22.2). The user specifies the circle's diameter with a horizontal JSlider. Class OvalPanel knows how to draw a circle on itself, using its own instance variable diameter to determine the diameter of the circle—the diameter is used as the width and height of the bounding box in which the circle is displayed. The diameter value is set when the user interacts with the JSlider. The event handler calls method setDiameter in class OvalPanel to set the diameter and calls repaint to draw the new circle. The repaint call results in a call to OvalPanel's paintComponent method.

```java
1   // Fig. 22.2: OvalPanel.java
2   // A customized JPanel class.
3   import java.awt.Graphics;
4   import java.awt.Dimension;
5   import javax.swing.JPanel;
6
7   public class OvalPanel extends JPanel
8   {
9      private int diameter = 10; // default diameter of 10
10
11     // draw an oval of the specified diameter
12     public void paintComponent( Graphics g )
13     {
14        super.paintComponent( g );
15
16        g.fillOval( 10, 10, diameter, diameter ); // draw circle
17     } // end method paintComponent
18
19     // validate and set diameter, then repaint
20     public void setDiameter( int newDiameter )
21     {
22        // if diameter invalid, default to 10
23        diameter = ( newDiameter >= 0 ? newDiameter : 10 );
```

Fig. 22.2 | JPanel subclass for drawing circles of a specified diameter. (Part 1 of 2.)

```
24            repaint(); // repaint panel
25         } // end method setDiameter
26
27         // used by layout manager to determine preferred size
28         public Dimension getPreferredSize()
29         {
30            return new Dimension( 200, 200 );
31         } // end method getPreferredSize
32
33         // used by layout manager to determine minimum size
34         public Dimension getMinimumSize()
35         {
36            return getPreferredSize();
37         } // end method getMinimumSize
38      } // end class OvalPanel
```

Fig. 22.2 | JPanel subclass for drawing circles of a specified diameter. (Part 2 of 2.)

```
 1      // Fig. 22.3: SliderFrame.java
 2      // Using JSliders to size an oval.
 3      import java.awt.BorderLayout;
 4      import java.awt.Color;
 5      import javax.swing.JFrame;
 6      import javax.swing.JSlider;
 7      import javax.swing.SwingConstants;
 8      import javax.swing.event.ChangeListener;
 9      import javax.swing.event.ChangeEvent;
10
11      public class SliderFrame extends JFrame
12      {
13         private JSlider diameterJSlider; // slider to select diameter
14         private OvalPanel myPanel; // panel to draw circle
15
16         // no-argument constructor
17         public SliderFrame()
18         {
19            super( "Slider Demo" );
20
21            myPanel = new OvalPanel(); // create panel to draw circle
22            myPanel.setBackground( Color.YELLOW ); // set background to yellow
23
24            // set up JSlider to control diameter value
25            diameterJSlider =
26               new JSlider( SwingConstants.HORIZONTAL, 0, 200, 10 );
27            diameterJSlider.setMajorTickSpacing( 10 ); // create tick every 10
28            diameterJSlider.setPaintTicks( true ); // paint ticks on slider
29
30            // register JSlider event listener
31            diameterJSlider.addChangeListener(
32
33               new ChangeListener() // anonymous inner class
34               {
```

Fig. 22.3 | JSlider value used to determine the diameter of a circle. (Part 1 of 2.)

```
35              // handle change in slider value
36              public void stateChanged( ChangeEvent e )
37              {
38                  myPanel.setDiameter( diameterJSlider.getValue() );
39              } // end method stateChanged
40          } // end anonymous inner class
41      ); // end call to addChangeListener
42
43      add( diameterJSlider, BorderLayout.SOUTH ); // add slider to frame
44      add( myPanel, BorderLayout.CENTER ); // add panel to frame
45   } // end SliderFrame constructor
46 } // end class SliderFrame
```

Fig. 22.3 | JSlider value used to determine the diameter of a circle. (Part 2 of 2.)

```
1  // Fig. 22.4: SliderDemo.java
2  // Testing SliderFrame.
3  import javax.swing.JFrame;
4
5  public class SliderDemo
6  {
7     public static void main( String[] args )
8     {
9        SliderFrame sliderFrame = new SliderFrame();
10       sliderFrame.setDefaultCloseOperation( JFrame.EXIT_ON_CLOSE );
11       sliderFrame.setSize( 220, 270 ); // set frame size
12       sliderFrame.setVisible( true ); // display frame
13    } // end main
14 } // end class SliderDemo
```

Fig. 22.4 | Test class for SliderFrame.

Class OvalPanel (Fig. 22.2) contains a paintComponent method (lines 12–17) that draws a filled oval (a circle in this example), a setDiameter method (lines 20–25) that changes the circle's diameter and repaints the OvalPanel, a getPreferredSize method (lines 28–31) that returns the preferred width and height of an OvalPanel and a getMinimumSize method (lines 34–37) that returns an OvalPanel's minimum width and height. Section 21.3 introduced getPreferredSize and getMinimumSize, which are used by some layout managers to determine the size of a component.

Class SliderFrame (Fig. 22.3) creates the JSlider that controls the diameter of the circle. Class SliderFrame's constructor (lines 17–45) creates OvalPanel object myPanel (line 21) and sets its background color (line 22). Lines 25–26 create JSlider object diameterSlider to control the diameter of the circle drawn on the OvalPanel. The JSlider constructor takes four arguments. The first argument specifies the orientation of diameterSlider, which is HORIZONTAL (a constant in interface SwingConstants). The second and third arguments indicate the minimum and maximum integer values in the range of values for this JSlider. The last argument indicates that the initial value of the JSlider (i.e., where the thumb is displayed) should be 10.

Lines 27–28 customize the appearance of the JSlider. Method **setMajorTickSpacing** indicates that each major tick mark represents 10 values in the range of values supported by the JSlider. Method **setPaintTicks** with a true argument indicates that the tick marks should be displayed (they aren't displayed by default). For other methods that are used to customize a JSlider's appearance, see the JSlider on-line documentation (download.oracle.com/javase/6/docs/api/javax/swing/JSlider.html).

JSliders generate **ChangeEvents** (package javax.swing.event) in response to user interactions. An object of a class that implements interface **ChangeListener** (package javax.swing.event) and declares method **stateChanged** can respond to ChangeEvents. Lines 31–41 register a ChangeListener to handle diameterSlider's events. When method stateChanged (lines 36–39) is called in response to a user interaction, line 38 calls myPanel's setDiameter method and passes the current value of the JSlider as an argument. JSlider method **getValue** returns the current thumb position.

22.3 Windows: Additional Notes

A JFrame is a **window** with a **title bar** and a **border**. Class JFrame is a subclass of Frame (package java.awt), which is a subclass of Window (package java.awt). As such, JFrame is one of the *heavyweight* Swing GUI components. When you display a window from a Java program, the window is provided by the local platform's windowing toolkit, and therefore the window will look like every other window displayed on that platform. When a Java application executes on a Macintosh and displays a window, the window's title bar and borders will look like those of other Macintosh applications. When a Java application executes on a Microsoft Windows system and displays a window, the window's title bar and borders will look like those of other Microsoft Windows applications. And when a Java application executes on a UNIX platform and displays a window, the window's title bar and borders will look like other UNIX applications on that platform.

By default, when the user closes a JFrame window, it's hidden (i.e., removed from the screen), but you can control this with JFrame method **setDefaultCloseOperation**. Interface **WindowConstants** (package javax.swing), which class JFrame implements, declares three constants—DISPOSE_ON_CLOSE, DO_NOTHING_ON_CLOSE and HIDE_ON_CLOSE (the default)—for use with this method. Some platforms allow only a limited number of windows to be displayed on the screen. Thus, a window is a valuable resource that should be given back to the system when it's no longer needed. Class Window (an indirect superclass of JFrame) declares method **dispose** for this purpose. When a Window is no longer needed in an application, you should explicitly dispose of it. This can be done by calling the Window's dispose method or by calling method setDefaultCloseOperation with the argument WindowConstants.DISPOSE_ON_CLOSE. Terminating an application also returns window resources to the system. Using DO_NOTHING_ON_CLOSE indicates that the program will determine what to do when the user attempts to close the window. For example, the program might want to ask whether to save a file's changes before closing a window.

Performance Tip 22.1

A window is an expensive system resource. Return it to the system by calling its dispose *method when the window is no longer needed.*

By default, a window is not displayed on the screen until the program invokes the window's setVisible method (inherited from class java.awt.Component) with a true argument. A window's size should be set with a call to method setSize (inherited from class java.awt.Component). The position of a window when it appears on the screen is specified with method **setLocation** (inherited from class java.awt.Component).

Common Programming Error 22.1

Forgetting to call method setVisible *on a window is a runtime logic error—the window is not displayed.*

Common Programming Error 22.2

Forgetting to call the setSize *method on a window is a runtime logic error—only the title bar appears.*

When the user manipulates the window, this action generates **window events**. Event listeners are registered for window events with Window method **addWindowListener**. Interface **WindowListener** provides seven window-event-handling methods—**windowActivated** (called when the user makes a window the active window), **windowClosed** (called after the window is closed), **windowClosing** (called when the user initiates closing of the window), **windowDeactivated** (called when the user makes another window the active window), **windowDeiconified** (called when the user restores a window from being minimized), **windowIconified** (called when the user minimizes a window) and **windowOpened** (called when a program first displays a window on the screen).

22.4 Using Menus with Frames

Menus are an integral part of GUIs. They allow the user to perform actions without unnecessarily cluttering a GUI with extra components. In Swing GUIs, menus can be attached only to objects of the classes that provide method **setJMenuBar**. Two such classes are JFrame and JApplet. The classes used to declare menus are JMenuBar, JMenu, JMenuItem, JCheckBoxMenuItem and class JRadioButtonMenuItem.

Look-and-Feel Observation 22.1

Menus simplify GUIs because components can be hidden within them. These components will be visible only when the user looks for them by selecting the menu.

Overview of Several Menu-Related Components

Class **JMenuBar** (a subclass of JComponent) contains the methods necessary to manage a **menu bar**, which is a container for menus. Class **JMenu** (a subclass of javax.swing.JMenuItem) contains the methods necessary for managing menus. Menus contain menu items and are added to menu bars or to other menus as submenus. When a menu is clicked, it expands to show its list of menu items.

Class **JMenuItem** (a subclass of javax.swing.AbstractButton) contains the methods necessary to manage **menu items**. A menu item is a GUI component inside a menu that, when selected, causes an action event. A menu item can be used to initiate an action, or it can be a **submenu** that provides more menu items from which the user can select. Submenus are useful for grouping related menu items in a menu.

Class **JCheckBoxMenuItem** (a subclass of javax.swing.JMenuItem) contains the methods necessary to manage menu items that can be toggled on or off. When a JCheckBoxMenuItem is selected, a check appears to the left of the menu item. When the JCheckBoxMenuItem is selected again, the check is removed.

Class **JRadioButtonMenuItem** (a subclass of javax.swing.JMenuItem) contains the methods necessary to manage menu items that can be toggled on or off like JCheckBoxMenuItems. When multiple JRadioButtonMenuItems are maintained as part of a ButtonGroup, only one item in the group can be selected at a given time. When a JRadioButtonMenuItem is selected, a filled circle appears to the left of the menu item. When another JRadioButtonMenuItem is selected, the filled circle of the previously selected menu item is removed.

Using Menus in an Application

Figures 22.5–22.6 demonstrate various menu items and how to specify special characters called **mnemonics** that can provide quick access to a menu or menu item from the keyboard. Mnemonics can be used with all subclasses of javax.swing.AbstractButton. Class MenuFrame (Fig. 22.5) creates the GUI and handles the menu-item events. Most of the code in this application appears in the class's constructor (lines 34–151).

```java
1   // Fig. 22.5: MenuFrame.java
2   // Demonstrating menus.
3   import java.awt.Color;
4   import java.awt.Font;
5   import java.awt.BorderLayout;
6   import java.awt.event.ActionListener;
7   import java.awt.event.ActionEvent;
8   import java.awt.event.ItemListener;
9   import java.awt.event.ItemEvent;
10  import javax.swing.JFrame;
11  import javax.swing.JRadioButtonMenuItem;
12  import javax.swing.JCheckBoxMenuItem;
13  import javax.swing.JOptionPane;
14  import javax.swing.JLabel;
15  import javax.swing.SwingConstants;
16  import javax.swing.ButtonGroup;
17  import javax.swing.JMenu;
18  import javax.swing.JMenuItem;
19  import javax.swing.JMenuBar;
20
21  public class MenuFrame extends JFrame
22  {
```

Fig. 22.5 | JMenus and mnemonics. (Part 1 of 5.)

```java
23        private final Color[] colorValues =
24            { Color.BLACK, Color.BLUE, Color.RED, Color.GREEN };
25        private JRadioButtonMenuItem[] colorItems; // color menu items
26        private JRadioButtonMenuItem[] fonts; // font menu items
27        private JCheckBoxMenuItem[] styleItems; // font style menu items
28        private JLabel displayJLabel; // displays sample text
29        private ButtonGroup fontButtonGroup; // manages font menu items
30        private ButtonGroup colorButtonGroup; // manages color menu items
31        private int style; // used to create style for font
32
33        // no-argument constructor set up GUI
34        public MenuFrame()
35        {
36            super( "Using JMenus" );
37
38            JMenu fileMenu = new JMenu( "File" ); // create file menu
39            fileMenu.setMnemonic( 'F' ); // set mnemonic to F
40
41            // create About... menu item
42            JMenuItem aboutItem = new JMenuItem( "About..." );
43            aboutItem.setMnemonic( 'A' ); // set mnemonic to A
44            fileMenu.add( aboutItem ); // add about item to file menu
45            aboutItem.addActionListener(
46
47                new ActionListener() // anonymous inner class
48                {
49                    // display message dialog when user selects About...
50                    public void actionPerformed( ActionEvent event )
51                    {
52                        JOptionPane.showMessageDialog( MenuFrame.this,
53                            "This is an example\nof using menus",
54                            "About", JOptionPane.PLAIN_MESSAGE );
55                    } // end method actionPerformed
56                } // end anonymous inner class
57            ); // end call to addActionListener
58
59            JMenuItem exitItem = new JMenuItem( "Exit" ); // create exit item
60            exitItem.setMnemonic( 'x' ); // set mnemonic to x
61            fileMenu.add( exitItem ); // add exit item to file menu
62            exitItem.addActionListener(
63
64                new ActionListener() // anonymous inner class
65                {
66                    // terminate application when user clicks exitItem
67                    public void actionPerformed( ActionEvent event )
68                    {
69                        System.exit( 0 ); // exit application
70                    } // end method actionPerformed
71                } // end anonymous inner class
72            ); // end call to addActionListener
73
74            JMenuBar bar = new JMenuBar(); // create menu bar
75            setJMenuBar( bar ); // add menu bar to application
```

Fig. 22.5 | JMenus and mnemonics. (Part 2 of 5.)

```
76          bar.add( fileMenu ); // add file menu to menu bar
77
78          JMenu formatMenu = new JMenu( "Format" ); // create format menu
79          formatMenu.setMnemonic( 'r' ); // set mnemonic to r
80
81          // array listing string colors
82          String[] colors = { "Black", "Blue", "Red", "Green" };
83
84          JMenu colorMenu = new JMenu( "Color" ); // create color menu
85          colorMenu.setMnemonic( 'C' ); // set mnemonic to C
86
87          // create radio button menu items for colors
88          colorItems = new JRadioButtonMenuItem[ colors.length ];
89          colorButtonGroup = new ButtonGroup(); // manages colors
90          ItemHandler itemHandler = new ItemHandler(); // handler for colors
91
92          // create color radio button menu items
93          for ( int count = 0; count < colors.length; count++ )
94          {
95             colorItems[ count ] =
96                new JRadioButtonMenuItem( colors[ count ] ); // create item
97             colorMenu.add( colorItems[ count ] ); // add item to color menu
98             colorButtonGroup.add( colorItems[ count ] ); // add to group
99             colorItems[ count ].addActionListener( itemHandler );
100         } // end for
101
102         colorItems[ 0 ].setSelected( true ); // select first Color item
103
104         formatMenu.add( colorMenu ); // add color menu to format menu
105         formatMenu.addSeparator(); // add separator in menu
106
107         // array listing font names
108         String[] fontNames = { "Serif", "Monospaced", "SansSerif" };
109         JMenu fontMenu = new JMenu( "Font" ); // create font menu
110         fontMenu.setMnemonic( 'n' ); // set mnemonic to n
111
112         // create radio button menu items for font names
113         fonts = new JRadioButtonMenuItem[ fontNames.length ];
114         fontButtonGroup = new ButtonGroup(); // manages font names
115
116         // create Font radio button menu items
117         for ( int count = 0; count < fonts.length; count++ )
118         {
119            fonts[ count ] = new JRadioButtonMenuItem( fontNames[ count ] );
120            fontMenu.add( fonts[ count ] ); // add font to font menu
121            fontButtonGroup.add( fonts[ count ] ); // add to button group
122            fonts[ count ].addActionListener( itemHandler ); // add handler
123         } // end for
124
125         fonts[ 0 ].setSelected( true ); // select first Font menu item
126         fontMenu.addSeparator(); // add separator bar to font menu
127
128         String[] styleNames = { "Bold", "Italic" }; // names of styles
```

Fig. 22.5 | JMenus and mnemonics. (Part 3 of 5.)

```
129            styleItems = new JCheckBoxMenuItem[ styleNames.length ];
130            StyleHandler styleHandler = new StyleHandler(); // style handler
131
132            // create style checkbox menu items
133            for ( int count = 0; count < styleNames.length; count++ )
134            {
135               styleItems[ count ] =
136                  new JCheckBoxMenuItem( styleNames[ count ] ); // for style
137               fontMenu.add( styleItems[ count ] ); // add to font menu
138               styleItems[ count ].addItemListener( styleHandler ); // handler
139            } // end for
140
141            formatMenu.add( fontMenu ); // add Font menu to Format menu
142            bar.add( formatMenu ); // add Format menu to menu bar
143
144            // set up label to display text
145            displayJLabel = new JLabel( "Sample Text", SwingConstants.CENTER );
146            displayJLabel.setForeground( colorValues[ 0 ] );
147            displayJLabel.setFont( new Font( "Serif", Font.PLAIN, 72 ) );
148
149            getContentPane().setBackground( Color.CYAN ); // set background
150            add( displayJLabel, BorderLayout.CENTER ); // add displayJLabel
151         } // end MenuFrame constructor
152
153         // inner class to handle action events from menu items
154         private class ItemHandler implements ActionListener
155         {
156            // process color and font selections
157            public void actionPerformed( ActionEvent event )
158            {
159               // process color selection
160               for ( int count = 0; count < colorItems.length; count++ )
161               {
162                  if ( colorItems[ count ].isSelected() )
163                  {
164                     displayJLabel.setForeground( colorValues[ count ] );
165                     break;
166                  } // end if
167               } // end for
168
169               // process font selection
170               for ( int count = 0; count < fonts.length; count++ )
171               {
172                  if ( event.getSource() == fonts[ count ] )
173                  {
174                     displayJLabel.setFont(
175                        new Font( fonts[ count ].getText(), style, 72 ) );
176                  } // end if
177               } // end for
178
179               repaint(); // redraw application
180            } // end method actionPerformed
181         } // end class ItemHandler
```

Fig. 22.5 | JMenus and mnemonics. (Part 4 of 5.)

```
182
183      // inner class to handle item events from checkbox menu items
184      private class StyleHandler implements ItemListener
185      {
186         // process font style selections
187         public void itemStateChanged( ItemEvent e )
188         {
189            String name = displayJLabel.getFont().getName(); // current Font
190            Font font; // new font based on user selections
191
192            // determine which items are checked and create Font
193            if ( styleItems[ 0 ].isSelected() &&
194                 styleItems[ 1 ].isSelected() )
195               font = new Font( name, Font.BOLD + Font.ITALIC, 72 );
196            else if ( styleItems[ 0 ].isSelected() )
197               font = new Font( name, Font.BOLD, 72 );
198            else if ( styleItems[ 1 ].isSelected() )
199               font = new Font( name, Font.ITALIC, 72 );
200            else
201               font = new Font( name, Font.PLAIN, 72 );
202
203            displayJLabel.setFont( font );
204            repaint(); // redraw application
205         } // end method itemStateChanged
206      } // end class StyleHandler
207   } // end class MenuFrame
```

Fig. 22.5 | JMenus and mnemonics. (Part 5 of 5.)

```
1    // Fig. 22.6: MenuTest.java
2    // Testing MenuFrame.
3    import javax.swing.JFrame;
4
5    public class MenuTest
6    {
7       public static void main( String[] args )
8       {
9          MenuFrame menuFrame = new MenuFrame(); // create MenuFrame
10         menuFrame.setDefaultCloseOperation( JFrame.EXIT_ON_CLOSE );
11         menuFrame.setSize( 500, 200 ); // set frame size
12         menuFrame.setVisible( true ); // display frame
13      } // end main
14   } // end class MenuTest
```

Fig. 22.6 | Test class for MenuFrame. (Part 1 of 2.)

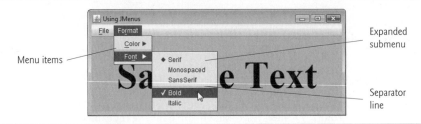

Fig. 22.6 | Test class for `MenuFrame`. (Part 2 of 2.)

Setting Up the File Menu
Lines 38–76 set up the **File** menu and attach it to the menu bar. The **File** menu contains an **About...** menu item that displays a message dialog when the menu item is selected and an **Exit** menu item that can be selected to terminate the application.

Line 38 creates a `JMenu` and passes to the constructor the string `"File"` as the name of the menu. Line 39 uses `JMenu` method **setMnemonic** (inherited from class `Abstract-Button`) to indicate that F is the mnemonic for this menu. Pressing the *Alt* key and the letter *F* opens the menu, just as clicking the menu name with the mouse would. In the GUI, the mnemonic character in the menu's name is displayed with an underline. (See the screen captures in Fig. 22.6.)

Look-and-Feel Observation 22.2
Mnemonics provide quick access to menu commands and button commands through the keyboard.

Look-and-Feel Observation 22.3
*Different mnemonics should be used for each button or menu item. Normally, the first letter in the label on the menu item or button is used as the mnemonic. If several buttons or menu items start with the same letter, choose the next most prominent letter in the name (e.g., x is commonly chosen for an **Exit** button or menu item). Mnemonics are case insensitive.*

Lines 42–43 create `JMenuItem aboutItem` with the text "`About...`" and set its mnemonic to the letter A. This menu item is added to `fileMenu` at line 44 with `JMenu` method **add**. To access the **About...** menu item through the keyboard, press the *Alt* key and letter *F* to open the **File** menu, then press *A* to select the **About...** menu item. Lines 47–56 create an `ActionListener` to process `aboutItem`'s action event. Lines 52–54 display a message dialog box. In most prior uses of `showMessageDialog`, the first argument was `null`. The purpose of the first argument is to specify the **parent window** that helps determine where the dialog box will be displayed. If the parent window is specified as `null`, the dialog box appears in the center of the screen. Otherwise, it appears centered over the specified parent window. In this example, the program specifies the parent window with `Menu-Frame.this`—the `this` reference of the `MenuFrame` object. When using the `this` reference in an inner class, specifying `this` by itself refers to the inner-class object. To reference the outer-class object's `this` reference, qualify `this` with the outer-class name and a dot (.).

Dialog boxes are typically modal. A modal dialog box does not allow any other window in the application to be accessed until the dialog box is dismissed. The dialogs displayed with class JOptionPane are modal dialogs. Class **JDialog** can be used to create your own modal or nonmodal dialogs.

Lines 59–72 create menu item exitItem, set its mnemonic to x, add it to fileMenu and register an ActionListener that terminates the program when the user selects exit-Item.

Lines 74–76 create the JMenuBar, attach it to the window with JFrame method set-JMenuBar and use JMenuBar method **add** to attach the fileMenu to the JMenuBar.

Common Programming Error 22.3

Forgetting to set the menu bar with JFrame method setJMenuBar prevents the menu bar from displaying in the JFrame.

Look-and-Feel Observation 22.4

Menus appear left to right in the order they're added to a JMenuBar.

Setting Up the Format Menu

Lines 78–79 create menu formatMenu and set its mnemonic to r. (F is not used because that is the **File** menu's mnemonic.)

Lines 84–85 create menu colorMenu (this will be a submenu in the **Format** menu) and set its mnemonic to C. Line 88 creates JRadioButtonMenuItem array colorItems, which refers to the menu items in colorMenu. Line 89 creates ButtonGroup colorButtonGroup, which will ensure that only one of the menu items in the **Color** submenu is selected at a time. Line 90 creates an instance of inner class ItemHandler (declared at lines 154–181) that responds to selections from the **Color** and **Font** submenus (discussed shortly). The for statement at lines 93–100 creates each JRadioButtonMenuItem in array colorItems, adds each menu item to colorMenu and to colorButtonGroup and registers the ActionListener for each menu item.

Line 102 invokes AbstractButton method **setSelected** to select the first element in array colorItems. Line 104 adds colorMenu as a submenu of formatMenu. Line 105 invokes JMenu method **addSeparator** to add a horizontal **separator** line to the menu.

Look-and-Feel Observation 22.5

A submenu is created by adding a menu as a menu item in another menu. When the mouse is positioned over a submenu (or the submenu's mnemonic is pressed), the submenu expands to show its menu items.

Look-and-Feel Observation 22.6

Separators can be added to a menu to group menu items logically.

Look-and-Feel Observation 22.7

Any lightweight GUI component (i.e., a component that is a subclass of JComponent) can be added to a JMenu or to a JMenuBar.

Lines 108–126 create the **Font** submenu and several JRadioButtonMenuItems and select the first element of JRadioButtonMenuItem array fonts. Line 129 creates a JCheckBoxMenu-

Item array to represent the menu items for specifying bold and italic styles for the fonts. Line 130 creates an instance of inner class StyleHandler (declared at lines 184–206) to respond to the JCheckBoxMenuItem events. The for statement at lines 133–139 creates each JCheck-BoxMenuItem, adds it to fontMenu and registers its ItemListener. Line 141 adds fontMenu as a submenu of formatMenu. Line 142 adds the formatMenu to bar (the menu bar).

Creating the Rest of the GUI and Defining the Event Handlers

Lines 145–147 create a JLabel for which the **Format** menu items control the font, font color and font style. The initial foreground color is set to the first element of array color-Values (Color.BLACK) by invoking JComponent method **setForeground**. The initial font is set to Serif with PLAIN style and 72-point size. Line 149 sets the background color of the window's content pane to cyan, and line 150 attaches the JLabel to the CENTER of the content pane's BorderLayout.

ItemHandler method actionPerformed (lines 157–180) uses two for statements to determine which font or color menu item generated the event and sets the font or color of the JLabel displayLabel, respectively. The if condition at line 162 uses Abstract-Button method **isSelected** to determine the selected JRadioButtonMenuItem. The if condition at line 172 invokes the event object's getSource method to get a reference to the JRadioButtonMenuItem that generated the event. Line 175 invokes AbstractButton method getText to obtain the name of the font from the menu item.

StyleHandler method itemStateChanged (lines 187–205) is called if the user selects a JCheckBoxMenuItem in the fontMenu. Lines 193–201 determine which JCheckBoxMenu-Items are selected and use their combined state to determine the new font style.

22.5 JPopupMenu

Many of today's computer applications provide so-called **context-sensitive pop-up menus**. In Swing, such menus are created with class **JPopupMenu** (a subclass of JCompo-nent). These menus provide options that are specific to the component for which the **pop-up trigger event** was generated. On most systems, the pop-up trigger event occurs when the user presses and releases the right mouse button.

Look-and-Feel Observation 22.8

The pop-up trigger event is platform specific. On most platforms that use a mouse with multiple buttons, the pop-up trigger event occurs when the user clicks the right mouse button on a component that supports a pop-up menu.

The application in Figs. 22.7–22.8 creates a JPopupMenu that allows the user to select one of three colors and change the background color of the window. When the user clicks the right mouse button on the PopupFrame window's background, a JPopupMenu containing colors appears. If the user clicks a JRadioButtonMenuItem for a color, ItemHandler method actionPerformed changes the background color of the window's content pane.

Line 25 of the PopupFrame constructor (Fig. 22.7, lines 21–69) creates an instance of class ItemHandler (declared in lines 72–87) that will process the item events from the menu items in the pop-up menu. Line 29 creates the JPopupMenu. The for statement (lines 33–39) creates a JRadioButtonMenuItem object (line 35), adds it to popupMenu (line 36), adds it to ButtonGroup colorGroup (line 37) to maintain one selected JRadioButton-

MenuItem at a time and registers its ActionListener (line 38). Line 41 sets the initial background to white by invoking method setBackground.

```java
1   // Fig. 22.7: PopupFrame.java
2   // Demonstrating JPopupMenus.
3   import java.awt.Color;
4   import java.awt.event.MouseAdapter;
5   import java.awt.event.MouseEvent;
6   import java.awt.event.ActionListener;
7   import java.awt.event.ActionEvent;
8   import javax.swing.JFrame;
9   import javax.swing.JRadioButtonMenuItem;
10  import javax.swing.JPopupMenu;
11  import javax.swing.ButtonGroup;
12
13  public class PopupFrame extends JFrame
14  {
15     private JRadioButtonMenuItem[] items; // holds items for colors
16     private final Color[] colorValues =
17        { Color.BLUE, Color.YELLOW, Color.RED }; // colors to be used
18     private JPopupMenu popupMenu; // allows user to select color
19
20     // no-argument constructor sets up GUI
21     public PopupFrame()
22     {
23        super( "Using JPopupMenus" );
24
25        ItemHandler handler = new ItemHandler(); // handler for menu items
26        String[] colors = { "Blue", "Yellow", "Red" }; // array of colors
27
28        ButtonGroup colorGroup = new ButtonGroup(); // manages color items
29        popupMenu = new JPopupMenu(); // create pop-up menu
30        items = new JRadioButtonMenuItem[ colors.length ]; // color items
31
32        // construct menu item, add to pop-up menu, enable event handling
33        for ( int count = 0; count < items.length; count++ )
34        {
35           items[ count ] = new JRadioButtonMenuItem( colors[ count ] );
36           popupMenu.add( items[ count ] ); // add item to pop-up menu
37           colorGroup.add( items[ count ] ); // add item to button group
38           items[ count ].addActionListener( handler ); // add handler
39        } // end for
40
41        setBackground( Color.WHITE ); // set background to white
42
43        // declare a MouseListener for the window to display pop-up menu
44        addMouseListener(
45
46           new MouseAdapter() // anonymous inner class
47           {
48              // handle mouse press event
49              public void mousePressed( MouseEvent event )
50              {
```

Fig. 22.7 | JPopupMenu for selecting colors. (Part 1 of 2.)

```
51              checkForTriggerEvent( event ); // check for trigger
52           } // end method mousePressed
53
54           // handle mouse release event
55           public void mouseReleased( MouseEvent event )
56           {
57              checkForTriggerEvent( event ); // check for trigger
58           } // end method mouseReleased
59
60           // determine whether event should trigger pop-up menu
61           private void checkForTriggerEvent( MouseEvent event )
62           {
63              if ( event.isPopupTrigger() )
64                 popupMenu.show(
65                    event.getComponent(), event.getX(), event.getY() );
66           } // end method checkForTriggerEvent
67        } // end anonymous inner class
68     ); // end call to addMouseListener
69   } // end PopupFrame constructor
70
71   // private inner class to handle menu item events
72   private class ItemHandler implements ActionListener
73   {
74      // process menu item selections
75      public void actionPerformed( ActionEvent event )
76      {
77         // determine which menu item was selected
78         for ( int i = 0; i < items.length; i++ )
79         {
80            if ( event.getSource() == items[ i ] )
81            {
82               getContentPane().setBackground( colorValues[ i ] );
83               return;
84            } // end if
85         } // end for
86      } // end method actionPerformed
87   } // end private inner class ItemHandler
88 } // end class PopupFrame
```

Fig. 22.7 | JPopupMenu for selecting colors. (Part 2 of 2.)

```
1  // Fig. 22.8: PopupTest.java
2  // Testing PopupFrame.
3  import javax.swing.JFrame;
4
5  public class PopupTest
6  {
7     public static void main( String[] args )
8     {
9        PopupFrame popupFrame = new PopupFrame(); // create PopupFrame
10       popupFrame.setDefaultCloseOperation( JFrame.EXIT_ON_CLOSE );
```

Fig. 22.8 | Test class for PopupFrame. (Part 1 of 2.)

```
11              popupFrame.setSize( 300, 200 ); // set frame size
12              popupFrame.setVisible( true ); // display frame
13       } // end main
14   } // end class PopupTest
```

Fig. 22.8 | Test class for PopupFrame. (Part 2 of 2.)

Lines 44–68 register a MouseListener to handle the mouse events of the application window. Methods mousePressed (lines 49–52) and mouseReleased (lines 55–58) check for the pop-up trigger event. Each method calls private utility method checkForTrigger-Event (lines 61–66) to determine whether the pop-up trigger event occurred. If it did, MouseEvent method **isPopupTrigger** returns true, and JPopupMenu method **show** displays the JPopupMenu. The first argument to method show specifies the **origin component**, whose position helps determine where the JPopupMenu will appear on the screen. The last two arguments are the *x-y* coordinates (measured from the origin component's upper-left corner) at which the JPopupMenu is to appear.

Look-and-Feel Observation 22.9

Displaying a JPopupMenu for the pop-up trigger event of multiple GUI components requires registering mouse-event handlers for each of those GUI components.

When the user selects a menu item from the pop-up menu, class ItemHandler's method actionPerformed (lines 75–86) determines which JRadioButtonMenuItem the user selected and sets the background color of the window's content pane.

22.6 Pluggable Look-and-Feel

A program that uses Java's AWT GUI components (package java.awt) takes on the look-and-feel of the platform on which the program executes. A Java application running on a Mac OS X looks like other Mac OS X applications. One running on Microsoft Windows looks like other Windows applications. One running on a Linux platform looks like other applications on that Linux platform. This is sometimes desirable, because it allows users of the application on each platform to use GUI components with which they're already familiar. However, it also introduces interesting portability issues.

Portability Tip 22.1

GUI components look different on different platforms and may require different amounts of space to display. This could change their layout and alignments.

Portability Tip 22.2

GUI components on different platforms have different default functionality (e.g., some platforms allow a button with the focus to be "pressed" with the space bar, and some don't).

Swing's lightweight GUI components eliminate many of these issues by providing uniform functionality across platforms and by defining a uniform cross-platform look-and-feel. Recent versions of Java SE 6 and Java SE 7 include the *Nimbus* look-and-feel that we discussed in Section 14.2. Earlier versions of Java used the **metal look-and-feel**, which is still the default. Swing also provides the flexibility to customize the look-and-feel to appear as a Microsoft Windows-style look-and-feel (only on Window systems), a Motif-style (UNIX) look-and-feel (across all platforms) or a Macintosh look-and-feel (only on Mac systems).

Figures 22.9–22.10 demonstrate a way to change the look-and-feel of a Swing GUI. It creates several GUI components, so you can see the change in their look-and-feel at the same time. The output windows show the Metal, Nimbus, CDE/Motif, Windows and Windows Classic look-and-feels that are available on Windows systems. The installed look-and-feels will vary by platform.

```java
1   // Fig. 22.9: LookAndFeelFrame.java
2   // Changing the look-and-feel.
3   import java.awt.GridLayout;
4   import java.awt.BorderLayout;
5   import java.awt.event.ItemListener;
6   import java.awt.event.ItemEvent;
7   import javax.swing.JFrame;
8   import javax.swing.UIManager;
9   import javax.swing.JRadioButton;
10  import javax.swing.ButtonGroup;
11  import javax.swing.JButton;
12  import javax.swing.JLabel;
13  import javax.swing.JComboBox;
14  import javax.swing.JPanel;
15  import javax.swing.SwingConstants;
16  import javax.swing.SwingUtilities;
17
18  public class LookAndFeelFrame extends JFrame
19  {
20     private UIManager.LookAndFeelInfo[] looks; // look and feels
21     private String[] lookNames; // names of look and feels
22     private JRadioButton[] radio; // radio buttons to select look-and-feel
23     private ButtonGroup group; // group for radio buttons
24     private JButton button; // displays look of button
25     private JLabel label; // displays look of label
26     private JComboBox comboBox; // displays look of combo box
27
28     // set up GUI
29     public LookAndFeelFrame()
30     {
```

Fig. 22.9 | Look-and-feel of a Swing-based GUI. (Part 1 of 3.)

```
31          super( "Look and Feel Demo" );
32
33          // get installed look-and-feel information
34          looks = UIManager.getInstalledLookAndFeels();
35          lookNames = new String[ looks.length ];
36
37          // get names of installed look-and-feels
38          for ( int i = 0; i < looks.length; i++ )
39             lookNames[ i ] = looks[ i ].getName();
40
41          JPanel northPanel = new JPanel(); // create north panel
42          northPanel.setLayout( new GridLayout( 3, 1, 0, 5 ) );
43
44          label = new JLabel( "This is a " + lookNames[0] + " look-and-feel",
45             SwingConstants.CENTER ); // create label
46          northPanel.add( label ); // add label to panel
47
48          button = new JButton( "JButton" ); // create button
49          northPanel.add( button ); // add button to panel
50
51          comboBox = new JComboBox( lookNames ); // create combobox
52          northPanel.add( comboBox ); // add combobox to panel
53
54          // create array for radio buttons
55          radio = new JRadioButton[ looks.length ];
56
57          JPanel southPanel = new JPanel(); // create south panel
58
59          // use a GridLayout with 3 buttons in each row
60          int rows = (int) Math.ceil( radio.length / 3.0 );
61          southPanel.setLayout( new GridLayout( rows, 3 ) );
62
63          group = new ButtonGroup(); // button group for looks-and-feels
64          ItemHandler handler = new ItemHandler(); // look-and-feel handler
65
66          for ( int count = 0; count < radio.length; count++ )
67          {
68             radio[ count ] = new JRadioButton( lookNames[ count ] );
69             radio[ count ].addItemListener( handler ); // add handler
70             group.add( radio[ count ] ); // add radio button to group
71             southPanel.add( radio[ count ] ); // add radio button to panel
72          } // end for
73
74          add( northPanel, BorderLayout.NORTH ); // add north panel
75          add( southPanel, BorderLayout.SOUTH ); // add south panel
76
77          radio[ 0 ].setSelected( true ); // set default selection
78       } // end LookAndFeelFrame constructor
79
80       // use UIManager to change look-and-feel of GUI
81       private void changeTheLookAndFeel( int value )
82       {
```

Fig. 22.9 | Look-and-feel of a Swing-based GUI. (Part 2 of 3.)

```
83            try // change look-and-feel
84            {
85               // set look-and-feel for this application
86               UIManager.setLookAndFeel( looks[ value ].getClassName() );
87
88               // update components in this application
89               SwingUtilities.updateComponentTreeUI( this );
90            } // end try
91            catch ( Exception exception )
92            {
93               exception.printStackTrace();
94            } // end catch
95         } // end method changeTheLookAndFeel
96
97         // private inner class to handle radio button events
98         private class ItemHandler implements ItemListener
99         {
100           // process user's look-and-feel selection
101           public void itemStateChanged( ItemEvent event )
102           {
103              for ( int count = 0; count < radio.length; count++ )
104              {
105                 if ( radio[ count ].isSelected() )
106                 {
107                    label.setText( String.format(
108                       "This is a %s look-and-feel", lookNames[ count ] ) );
109                    comboBox.setSelectedIndex( count ); // set combobox index
110                    changeTheLookAndFeel( count ); // change look-and-feel
111                 } // end if
112              } // end for
113           } // end method itemStateChanged
114        } // end private inner class ItemHandler
115  } // end class LookAndFeelFrame
```

Fig. 22.9 | Look-and-feel of a Swing-based GUI. (Part 3 of 3.)

```
1   // Fig. 22.10: LookAndFeelDemo.java
2   // Changing the look-and-feel.
3   import javax.swing.JFrame;
4
5   public class LookAndFeelDemo
6   {
7      public static void main( String[] args )
8      {
9         LookAndFeelFrame lookAndFeelFrame = new LookAndFeelFrame();
10        lookAndFeelFrame.setDefaultCloseOperation( JFrame.EXIT_ON_CLOSE );
11        lookAndFeelFrame.setSize( 400, 220 ); // set frame size
12        lookAndFeelFrame.setVisible( true ); // display frame
13     } // end main
14  } // end class LookAndFeelDemo
```

Fig. 22.10 | Test class for LookAndFeelFrame. (Part 1 of 2.)

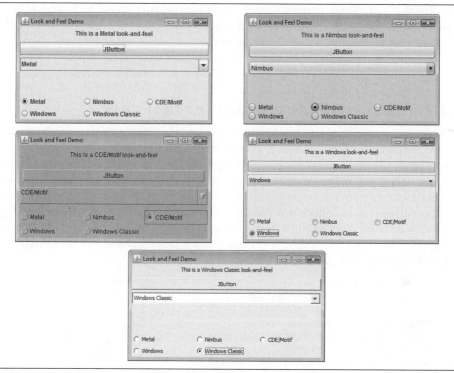

Fig. 22.10 | Test class for `LookAndFeelFrame`. (Part 2 of 2.)

We've covered the GUI components and event-handling concepts in this example previously, so we focus here on the mechanism for changing the look-and-feel. Class **UIManager** (package `javax.swing`) contains nested class **LookAndFeelInfo** (a public static class) that maintains information about a look-and-feel. Line 20 declares an array of type `UIManager.LookAndFeelInfo` (note the syntax used to identify the `static` inner class `LookAndFeelInfo`). Line 34 uses `UIManager` static method **getInstalledLookAnd-Feels** to get the array of `UIManager.LookAndFeelInfo` objects that describe each look-and-feel available on your system.

Performance Tip 22.2
Each look-and-feel is represented by a Java class. `UIManager` method `getInstalled-LookAndFeels` does not load each class. Rather, it provides the names of the available look-and-feel classes so that a choice can be made (presumably once at program start-up). This reduces the overhead of having to load all the look-and-feel classes even if the program will not use some of them.

Our utility method `changeTheLookAndFeel` (lines 81–95) is called by the event handler for the `JRadioButtons` at the bottom of the user interface. The event handler (declared in `private` inner class `ItemHandler` at lines 98–114) passes an integer representing the element in array `looks` that should be used to change the look-and-feel. Line 86 invokes static method **setLookAndFeel** of `UIManager` to change the look-and-feel. Method **get-ClassName** of class `UIManager.LookAndFeelInfo` determines the name of the look-and-feel class that corresponds to the UIManager.LookAndFeelInfo object. If the look-and-feel class is not already loaded, it will be loaded as part of the call to setLookAndFeel. Line 89 invokes static method **updateComponentTreeUI** of class **SwingUtilities** (package javax.swing) to change the look-and-feel of every GUI component attached to its argument (this instance of our application class LookAndFeelFrame) to the new look-and-feel.

22.7 JDesktopPane and JInternalFrame

Many of today's applications use a **multiple-document interface** (MDI)—a main window (called the **parent window**) containing other windows (called **child windows**), to manage several open documents that are being processed in parallel. For example, many e-mail programs allow you to have several windows open at the same time, so you can compose or read multiple e-mail messages simultaneously. Similarly, many word processors allow the user to open multiple documents in separate windows within a main window, making it possible to switch between them without having to close one to open another. The application in Figs. 22.11–22.12 demonstrates Swing's **JDesktopPane** and **JInternalFrame** classes for implementing multiple-document interfaces.

```
 1   // Fig. 22.11: DesktopFrame.java
 2   // Demonstrating JDesktopPane.
 3   import java.awt.BorderLayout;
 4   import java.awt.Dimension;
 5   import java.awt.Graphics;
 6   import java.awt.event.ActionListener;
 7   import java.awt.event.ActionEvent;
 8   import java.util.Random;
 9   import javax.swing.JFrame;
10   import javax.swing.JDesktopPane;
11   import javax.swing.JMenuBar;
12   import javax.swing.JMenu;
13   import javax.swing.JMenuItem;
14   import javax.swing.JInternalFrame;
15   import javax.swing.JPanel;
16   import javax.swing.ImageIcon;
17
18   public class DesktopFrame extends JFrame
19   {
20      private JDesktopPane theDesktop;
21
22      // set up GUI
23      public DesktopFrame()
24      {
25         super( "Using a JDesktopPane" );
26
27         JMenuBar bar = new JMenuBar(); // create menu bar
28         JMenu addMenu = new JMenu( "Add" ); // create Add menu
29         JMenuItem newFrame = new JMenuItem( "Internal Frame" );
30
31         addMenu.add( newFrame ); // add new frame item to Add menu
32         bar.add( addMenu ); // add Add menu to menu bar
```

Fig. 22.11 | Multiple-document interface. (Part I of 3.)

```
33            setJMenuBar( bar ); // set menu bar for this application
34
35            theDesktop = new JDesktopPane(); // create desktop pane
36            add( theDesktop ); // add desktop pane to frame
37
38            // set up listener for newFrame menu item
39            newFrame.addActionListener(
40
41               new ActionListener() // anonymous inner class
42               {
43                  // display new internal window
44                  public void actionPerformed( ActionEvent event )
45                  {
46                     // create internal frame
47                     JInternalFrame frame = new JInternalFrame(
48                        "Internal Frame", true, true, true, true );
49
50                     MyJPanel panel = new MyJPanel(); // create new panel
51                     frame.add( panel, BorderLayout.CENTER ); // add panel
52                     frame.pack(); // set internal frame to size of contents
53
54                     theDesktop.add( frame ); // attach internal frame
55                     frame.setVisible( true ); // show internal frame
56                  } // end method actionPerformed
57               } // end anonymous inner class
58            ); // end call to addActionListener
59         } // end DesktopFrame constructor
60   } // end class DesktopFrame
61
62   // class to display an ImageIcon on a panel
63   class MyJPanel extends JPanel
64   {
65      private static Random generator = new Random();
66      private ImageIcon picture; // image to be displayed
67      private final static String[] images = { "yellowflowers.png",
68         "purpleflowers.png", "redflowers.png", "redflowers2.png",
69         "lavenderflowers.png" };
70
71      // load image
72      public MyJPanel()
73      {
74         int randomNumber = generator.nextInt( images.length );
75         picture = new ImageIcon( images[ randomNumber ] ); // set icon
76      } // end MyJPanel constructor
77
78      // display imageIcon on panel
79      public void paintComponent( Graphics g )
80      {
81         super.paintComponent( g );
82         picture.paintIcon( this, g, 0, 0 ); // display icon
83      } // end method paintComponent
84
```

Fig. 22.11 | Multiple-document interface. (Part 2 of 3.)

```
85    // return image dimensions
86    public Dimension getPreferredSize()
87    {
88        return new Dimension( picture.getIconWidth(),
89            picture.getIconHeight() );
90    } // end method getPreferredSize
91 } // end class MyJPanel
```

Fig. 22.11 | Multiple-document interface. (Part 3 of 3.)

Lines 27–33 create a JMenuBar, a JMenu and a JMenuItem, add the JMenuItem to the JMenu, add the JMenu to the JMenuBar and set the JMenuBar for the application window. When the user selects the JMenuItem newFrame, the application creates and displays a new JInternalFrame object containing an image.

Line 35 assigns JDesktopPane (package javax.swing) variable theDesktop a new JDesktopPane object that will be used to manage the JInternalFrame child windows. Line 36 adds the JDesktopPane to the JFrame. By default, the JDesktopPane is added to the center of the content pane's BorderLayout, so the JDesktopPane expands to fill the entire application window.

Lines 39–58 register an ActionListener to handle the event when the user selects the newFrame menu item. When the event occurs, method actionPerformed (lines 44–56) creates a JInternalFrame object in lines 47–48. The JInternalFrame constructor used here takes five arguments—a String for the title bar of the internal window, a boolean indicating whether the internal frame can be resized by the user, a boolean indicating whether the internal frame can be closed by the user, a boolean indicating whether the internal frame can be maximized by the user and a boolean indicating whether the internal frame can be minimized by the user. For each of the boolean arguments, a true value indicates that the operation should be allowed (as is the case here).

As with JFrames and JApplets, a JInternalFrame has a content pane to which GUI components can be attached. Line 50 (Fig. 22.11) creates an instance of our class MyJPanel (declared at lines 63–91) that is added to the JInternalFrame at line 51.

```
1    // Fig. 22.12: DesktopTest.java
2    // Demonstrating JDesktopPane.
3    import javax.swing.JFrame;
4
5    public class DesktopTest
6    {
7        public static void main( String[] args )
8        {
9            DesktopFrame desktopFrame = new DesktopFrame();
10           desktopFrame.setDefaultCloseOperation( JFrame.EXIT_ON_CLOSE );
11           desktopFrame.setSize( 600, 480 ); // set frame size
12           desktopFrame.setVisible( true ); // display frame
13       } // end main
14   } // end class DesktopTest
```

Fig. 22.12 | Test class for DeskTopFrame. (Part 1 of 2.)

Internal frames   Minimize   Maximize   Close

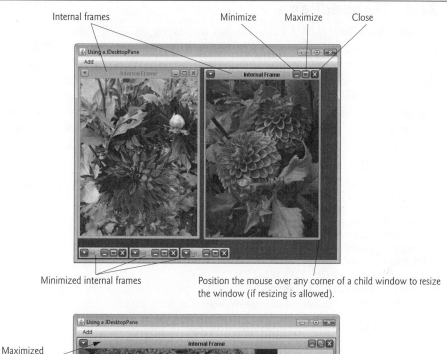

Minimized internal frames   Position the mouse over any corner of a child window to resize the window (if resizing is allowed).

Maximized internal frame

Fig. 22.12 | Test class for `DeskTopFrame`. (Part 2 of 2.)

Line 52 uses `JInternalFrame` method **pack** to set the size of the child window. Method pack uses the preferred sizes of the components to determine the window's size. Class `MyJPanel` declares method `getPreferredSize` (lines 86–90) to specify the panel's preferred size for use by the pack method. Line 54 adds the `JInternalFrame` to the `JDesktopPane`, and line 55 displays the `JInternalFrame`.

Classes `JInternalFrame` and `JDesktopPane` provide many methods for managing child windows. See the `JInternalFrame` and `JDesktopPane` online API documentation for complete lists of these methods:

```
download.oracle.com/javase/6/docs/api/javax/swing/JInternalFrame.html
download.oracle.com/javase/6/docs/api/javax/swing/JDesktopPane.html
```

22.8 JTabbedPane

A **JTabbedPane** arranges GUI components into layers, of which only one is visible at a time. Users access each layer via a tab—similar to folders in a file cabinet. When the user clicks a tab, the appropriate layer is displayed. The tabs appear at the top by default but also can be positioned at the left, right or bottom of the JTabbedPane. Any component can be placed on a tab. If the component is a container, such as a panel, it can use any layout manager to lay out several components on the tab. Class JTabbedPane is a subclass of JComponent. The application in Figs. 22.13–22.14 creates one tabbed pane with three tabs. Each tab displays one of the JPanels—panel1, panel2 or panel3.

```java
1   // Fig. 22.13: JTabbedPaneFrame.java
2   // Demonstrating JTabbedPane.
3   import java.awt.BorderLayout;
4   import java.awt.Color;
5   import javax.swing.JFrame;
6   import javax.swing.JTabbedPane;
7   import javax.swing.JLabel;
8   import javax.swing.JPanel;
9   import javax.swing.JButton;
10  import javax.swing.SwingConstants;
11
12  public class JTabbedPaneFrame extends JFrame
13  {
14     // set up GUI
15     public JTabbedPaneFrame()
16     {
17        super( "JTabbedPane Demo " );
18
19        JTabbedPane tabbedPane = new JTabbedPane(); // create JTabbedPane
20
21        // set up panel1 and add it to JTabbedPane
22        JLabel label1 = new JLabel( "panel one", SwingConstants.CENTER );
23        JPanel panel1 = new JPanel(); // create first panel
24        panel1.add( label1 ); // add label to panel
25        tabbedPane.addTab( "Tab One", null, panel1, "First Panel" );
26
27        // set up panel2 and add it to JTabbedPane
28        JLabel label2 = new JLabel( "panel two", SwingConstants.CENTER );
29        JPanel panel2 = new JPanel(); // create second panel
30        panel2.setBackground( Color.YELLOW ); // set background to yellow
31        panel2.add( label2 ); // add label to panel
32        tabbedPane.addTab( "Tab Two", null, panel2, "Second Panel" );
33
34        // set up panel3 and add it to JTabbedPane
35        JLabel label3 = new JLabel( "panel three" );
36        JPanel panel3 = new JPanel(); // create third panel
37        panel3.setLayout( new BorderLayout() ); // use borderlayout
38        panel3.add( new JButton( "North" ), BorderLayout.NORTH );
39        panel3.add( new JButton( "West" ), BorderLayout.WEST );
40        panel3.add( new JButton( "East" ), BorderLayout.EAST );
```

Fig. 22.13 | JTabbedPane used to organize GUI components. (Part 1 of 2.)

```
41            panel3.add( new JButton( "South" ), BorderLayout.SOUTH );
42            panel3.add( label3, BorderLayout.CENTER );
43            tabbedPane.addTab( "Tab Three", null, panel3, "Third Panel" );
44
45            add( tabbedPane ); // add JTabbedPane to frame
46         } // end JTabbedPaneFrame constructor
47    } // end class JTabbedPaneFrame
```

Fig. 22.13 | JTabbedPane used to organize GUI components. (Part 2 of 2.)

```
 1    // Fig. 22.14: JTabbedPaneDemo.java
 2    // Demonstrating JTabbedPane.
 3    import javax.swing.JFrame;
 4
 5    public class JTabbedPaneDemo
 6    {
 7       public static void main( String[] args )
 8       {
 9          JTabbedPaneFrame tabbedPaneFrame = new JTabbedPaneFrame();
10          tabbedPaneFrame.setDefaultCloseOperation( JFrame.EXIT_ON_CLOSE );
11          tabbedPaneFrame.setSize( 250, 200 ); // set frame size
12          tabbedPaneFrame.setVisible( true ); // display frame
13       } // end main
14    } // end class JTabbedPaneDemo
```

Fig. 22.14 | Test class for JTabbedPaneFrame.

The constructor (lines 15–46) builds the GUI. Line 19 creates an empty JTabbedPane with default settings—that is, tabs across the top. If the tabs do not fit on one line, they'll wrap to form additional lines of tabs. Next the constructor creates the JPanels panel1, panel2 and panel3 and their GUI components. As we set up each panel, we add it to tabbedPane, using JTabbedPane method **addTab** with four arguments. The first argument is a String that specifies the title of the tab. The second argument is an Icon reference that specifies an icon to display on the tab. If the Icon is a null reference, no image is displayed. The third argument is a Component reference that represents the GUI component to display when the user clicks the tab. The last argument is a String that specifies the tool tip for the tab. For example, line 25 adds JPanel panel1 to tabbedPane with title "Tab One" and the tool tip "First Panel". JPanels panel2 and panel3 are added to tabbedPane at lines 32 and 43. To view a tab, click it with the mouse or use the arrow keys to cycle through the tabs.

22.9 Layout Managers: BoxLayout and GridBagLayout

In Chapter 14, we introduced three layout managers—FlowLayout, BorderLayout and GridLayout. This section presents two additional layout managers (summarized in Fig. 22.15). We discuss them in the examples that follow. We also discuss the extremely flexible GroupLayout in Appendix H.

Layout manager	Description
BoxLayout	A layout manager that allows GUI components to be arranged left-to-right or top-to-bottom in a container. Class Box declares a container with BoxLayout as its default layout manager and provides static methods to create a Box with a horizontal or vertical BoxLayout.
GridBagLayout	A layout manager similar to GridLayout, but the components can vary in size and can be added in any order.

Fig. 22.15 | Additional layout managers.

BoxLayout Layout Manager

The BoxLayout layout manager (in package javax.swing) arranges GUI components horizontally along a container's *x*-axis or vertically along its *y*-axis. The application in Figs. 22.16–22.17 demonstrates BoxLayout and the container class Box that uses BoxLayout as its default layout manager.

```
1   // Fig. 22.16: BoxLayoutFrame.java
2   // Demonstrating BoxLayout.
3   import java.awt.Dimension;
4   import javax.swing.JFrame;
5   import javax.swing.Box;
6   import javax.swing.JButton;
7   import javax.swing.BoxLayout;
8   import javax.swing.JPanel;
9   import javax.swing.JTabbedPane;
10
11  public class BoxLayoutFrame extends JFrame
12  {
13     // set up GUI
14     public BoxLayoutFrame()
15     {
16        super( "Demonstrating BoxLayout" );
17
18        // create Box containers with BoxLayout
19        Box horizontal1 = Box.createHorizontalBox();
20        Box vertical1 = Box.createVerticalBox();
21        Box horizontal2 = Box.createHorizontalBox();
22        Box vertical2 = Box.createVerticalBox();
23
24        final int SIZE = 3; // number of buttons on each Box
25
```

Fig. 22.16 | BoxLayout layout manager. (Part 1 of 2.)

```
26              // add buttons to Box horizontal1
27              for ( int count = 0; count < SIZE; count++ )
28                 horizontal1.add( new JButton( "Button " + count ) );
29
30              // create strut and add buttons to Box vertical1
31              for ( int count = 0; count < SIZE; count++ )
32              {
33                 vertical1.add( Box.createVerticalStrut( 25 ) );
34                 vertical1.add( new JButton( "Button " + count ) );
35              } // end for
36
37              // create horizontal glue and add buttons to Box horizontal2
38              for ( int count = 0; count < SIZE; count++ )
39              {
40                 horizontal2.add( Box.createHorizontalGlue() );
41                 horizontal2.add( new JButton( "Button " + count ) );
42              } // end for
43
44              // create rigid area and add buttons to Box vertical2
45              for ( int count = 0; count < SIZE; count++ )
46              {
47                 vertical2.add( Box.createRigidArea( new Dimension( 12, 8 ) ) );
48                 vertical2.add( new JButton( "Button " + count ) );
49              } // end for
50
51              // create vertical glue and add buttons to panel
52              JPanel panel = new JPanel();
53              panel.setLayout( new BoxLayout( panel, BoxLayout.Y_AXIS ) );
54
55              for ( int count = 0; count < SIZE; count++ )
56              {
57                 panel.add( Box.createGlue() );
58                 panel.add( new JButton( "Button " + count ) );
59              } // end for
60
61              // create a JTabbedPane
62              JTabbedPane tabs = new JTabbedPane(
63                 JTabbedPane.TOP, JTabbedPane.SCROLL_TAB_LAYOUT );
64
65              // place each container on tabbed pane
66              tabs.addTab( "Horizontal Box", horizontal1 );
67              tabs.addTab( "Vertical Box with Struts", vertical1 );
68              tabs.addTab( "Horizontal Box with Glue", horizontal2 );
69              tabs.addTab( "Vertical Box with Rigid Areas", vertical2 );
70              tabs.addTab( "Vertical Box with Glue", panel );
71
72              add( tabs ); // place tabbed pane on frame
73           } // end BoxLayoutFrame constructor
74        } // end class BoxLayoutFrame
```

Fig. 22.16 | BoxLayout layout manager. (Part 2 of 2.)

Lines 19–22 create Box containers. References horizontal1 and horizontal2 are initialized with static Box method createHorizontalBox, which returns a Box container

```
 1   // Fig. 22.17: BoxLayoutDemo.java
 2   // Demonstrating BoxLayout.
 3   import javax.swing.JFrame;
 4
 5   public class BoxLayoutDemo
 6   {
 7      public static void main( String[] args )
 8      {
 9         BoxLayoutFrame boxLayoutFrame = new BoxLayoutFrame();
10         boxLayoutFrame.setDefaultCloseOperation( JFrame.EXIT_ON_CLOSE );
11         boxLayoutFrame.setSize( 400, 220 ); // set frame size
12         boxLayoutFrame.setVisible( true ); // display frame
13      } // end main
14   } // end class BoxLayoutDemo
```

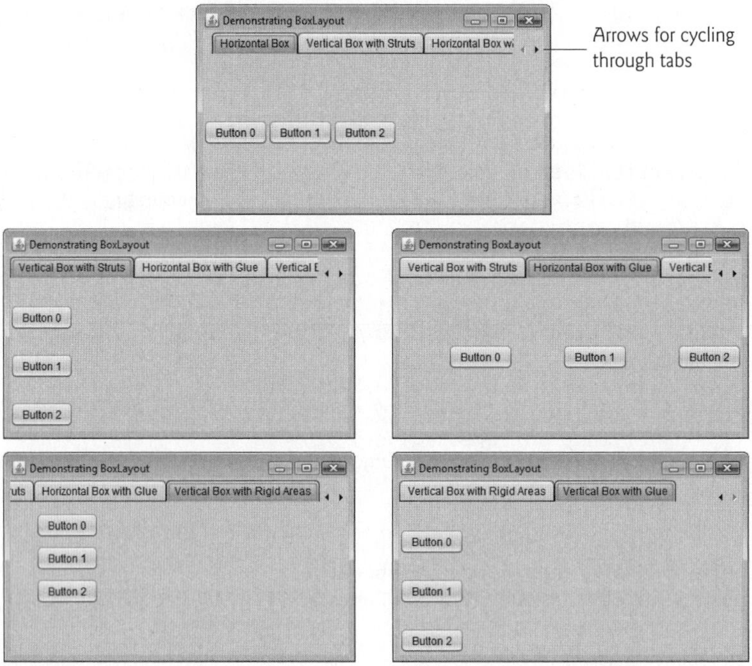

Arrows for cycling through tabs

Fig. 22.17 | Test class for `BoxLayoutFrame`.

with a horizontal `BoxLayout` in which GUI components are arranged left-to-right. Variables `vertical1` and `vertical2` are initialized with `static` `Box` method **createVerticalBox**, which returns references to `Box` containers with a vertical `BoxLayout` in which GUI components are arranged top-to-bottom.

The loop at lines 27–28 adds three `JButton`s to `horizontal1`. The `for` statement at lines 31–35 adds three `JButton`s to `vertical1`. Before adding each button, line 33 adds a **vertical strut** to the container with `static` `Box` method **createVerticalStrut**. A vertical strut is an invisible GUI component that has a fixed pixel height and is used to guarantee a fixed amount of space between GUI components. The `int` argument to method `create-VerticalStrut` determines the height of the strut in pixels. When the container is resized, the distance between GUI components separated by struts does not change. Class Box also declares method **createHorizontalStrut** for horizontal BoxLayouts.

The for statement at lines 38–42 adds three JButtons to horizontal2. Before adding each button, line 40 adds **horizontal glue** to the container with static Box method **createHorizontalGlue**. Horizontal glue is an invisible GUI component that can be used between fixed-size GUI components to occupy additional space. Normally, extra space appears to the right of the last horizontal GUI component or below the last vertical one in a BoxLayout. Glue allows the extra space to be placed between GUI components. When the container is resized, components separated by glue components remain the same size, but the glue stretches or contracts to occupy the space between them. Class Box also declares method **createVerticalGlue** for vertical BoxLayouts.

The for statement at lines 45–49 adds three JButtons to vertical2. Before each button is added, line 47 adds a **rigid area** to the container with static Box method **createRigidArea**. A rigid area is an invisible GUI component that always has a fixed pixel width and height. The argument to method createRigidArea is a Dimension object that specifies the area's width and height.

Lines 52–53 create a JPanel object and set its layout to a BoxLayout in the conventional manner, using Container method setLayout. The BoxLayout constructor receives a reference to the container for which it controls the layout and a constant indicating whether the layout is horizontal (**BoxLayout.X_AXIS**) or vertical (**BoxLayout.Y_AXIS**).

The for statement at lines 55–59 adds three JButtons to panel. Before adding each button, line 57 adds a glue component to the container with static Box method **createGlue**. This component expands or contracts based on the size of the Box.

Lines 62–63 create a JTabbedPane to display the five containers in this program. The argument **JTabbedPane.TOP** sent to the constructor indicates that the tabs should appear at the top of the JTabbedPane. The argument **JTabbedPane.SCROLL_TAB_LAYOUT** specifies that the tabs should wrap to a new line if there are too many to fit on one line.

The Box containers and the JPanel are attached to the JTabbedPane at lines 66–70. Try executing the application. When the window appears, resize the window to see how the glue components, strut components and rigid area affect the layout on each tab.

GridBagLayout Layout Manager

One of the most powerful predefined layout managers is **GridBagLayout** (in package java.awt). This layout is similar to GridLayout in that it arranges components in a grid, but it's more flexible. The components can vary in size (i.e., they can occupy multiple rows and columns) and can be added in any order.

The first step in using GridBagLayout is determining the appearance of the GUI. For this step you need only a piece of paper. Draw the GUI, then draw a grid over it, dividing the components into rows and columns. The initial row and column numbers should be 0, so that the GridBagLayout layout manager can use the row and column numbers to properly place the components in the grid. Figure 22.18 demonstrates drawing the lines for the rows and columns over a GUI.

A **GridBagConstraints** object describes how a component is placed in a GridBagLayout. Several GridBagConstraints fields are summarized in Fig. 22.19.

GridBagConstraints field **anchor** specifies the relative position of the component in an area that it does not fill. The variable anchor is assigned one of the following GridBag-

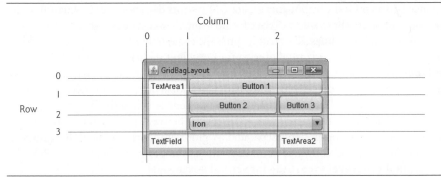

Fig. 22.18 | Designing a GUI that will use `GridBagLayout`.

Field	Description
anchor	Specifies the relative position (NORTH, NORTHEAST, EAST, SOUTHEAST, SOUTH, SOUTHWEST, WEST, NORTHWEST, CENTER) of the component in an area that it does not fill.
fill	Resizes the component in the specified direction (NONE, HORIZONTAL, VERTICAL, BOTH) when the display area is larger than the component.
gridx	The column in which the component will be placed.
gridy	The row in which the component will be placed.
gridwidth	The number of columns the component occupies.
gridheight	The number of rows the component occupies.
weightx	The amount of extra space to allocate horizontally. The grid slot can become wider when extra space is available.
weighty	The amount of extra space to allocate vertically. The grid slot can become taller when extra space is available.

Fig. 22.19 | `GridBagConstraints` fields.

Constraints constants: **NORTH, NORTHEAST, EAST, SOUTHEAST, SOUTH, SOUTHWEST, WEST, NORTHWEST** or **CENTER**. The default value is CENTER.

GridBagConstraints field `fill` defines how the component grows if the area in which it can be displayed is larger than the component. The variable `fill` is assigned one of the following GridBagConstraints constants: **NONE, VERTICAL, HORIZONTAL** or **BOTH**. The default value is NONE, which indicates that the component will not grow in either direction. VERTICAL indicates that it will grow vertically. HORIZONTAL indicates that it will grow horizontally. BOTH indicates that it will grow in both directions.

Variables **gridx** and **gridy** specify where the upper-left corner of the component is placed in the grid. Variable `gridx` corresponds to the column, and variable `gridy` corresponds to the row. In Fig. 22.18, the JComboBox (displaying "Iron") has a `gridx` value of 1 and a `gridy` value of 2.

Variable **gridwidth** specifies the number of columns a component occupies. The JComboBox occupies two columns. Variable **gridheight** specifies the number of rows a component occupies. The JTextArea on the left side of Fig. 22.18 occupies three rows.

Variable **weightx** specifies how to distribute extra horizontal space to grid slots in a GridBagLayout when the container is resized. A zero value indicates that the grid slot does not grow horizontally on its own. However, if the component spans a column containing a component with nonzero weightx value, the component with zero weightx value will grow horizontally in the same proportion as the other component(s) in that column. This is because each component must be maintained in the same row and column in which it was originally placed.

Variable **weighty** specifies how to distribute extra vertical space to grid slots in a Grid-BagLayout when the container is resized. A zero value indicates that the grid slot does not grow vertically on its own. However, if the component spans a row containing a component with nonzero weighty value, the component with zero weighty value grows vertically in the same proportion as the other component(s) in the same row.

In Fig. 22.18, the effects of weighty and weightx cannot easily be seen until the container is resized and additional space becomes available. Components with larger weight values occupy more of the additional space than those with smaller weight values.

Components should be given nonzero positive weight values—otherwise they'll "huddle" together in the middle of the container. Figure 22.20 shows the GUI of Fig. 22.18 with all weights set to zero.

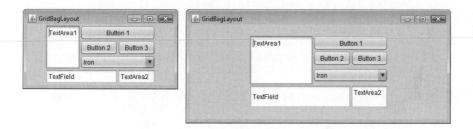

Fig. 22.20 | GridBagLayout with the weights set to zero.

The application in Figs. 22.21–22.22 uses the GridBagLayout layout manager to arrange the components of the GUI in Fig. 22.18. The application does nothing except demonstrate how to use GridBagLayout.

```
1   // Fig. 22.21: GridBagFrame.java
2   // Demonstrating GridBagLayout.
3   import java.awt.GridBagLayout;
4   import java.awt.GridBagConstraints;
5   import java.awt.Component;
6   import javax.swing.JFrame;
7   import javax.swing.JTextArea;
8   import javax.swing.JTextField;
```

Fig. 22.21 | GridBagLayout layout manager. (Part 1 of 3.)

```
 9   import javax.swing.JButton;
10   import javax.swing.JComboBox;
11
12   public class GridBagFrame extends JFrame
13   {
14      private GridBagLayout layout; // layout of this frame
15      private GridBagConstraints constraints; // constraints of this layout
16
17      // set up GUI
18      public GridBagFrame()
19      {
20         super( "GridBagLayout" );
21         layout = new GridBagLayout();
22         setLayout( layout ); // set frame layout
23         constraints = new GridBagConstraints(); // instantiate constraints
24
25         // create GUI components
26         JTextArea textArea1 = new JTextArea( "TextArea1", 5, 10 );
27         JTextArea textArea2 = new JTextArea( "TextArea2", 2, 2 );
28
29         String[] names = { "Iron", "Steel", "Brass" };
30         JComboBox comboBox = new JComboBox( names );
31
32         JTextField textField = new JTextField( "TextField" );
33         JButton button1 = new JButton( "Button 1" );
34         JButton button2 = new JButton( "Button 2" );
35         JButton button3 = new JButton( "Button 3" );
36
37         // weightx and weighty for textArea1 are both 0: the default
38         // anchor for all components is CENTER: the default
39         constraints.fill = GridBagConstraints.BOTH;
40         addComponent( textArea1, 0, 0, 1, 3 );
41
42         // weightx and weighty for button1 are both 0: the default
43         constraints.fill = GridBagConstraints.HORIZONTAL;
44         addComponent( button1, 0, 1, 2, 1 );
45
46         // weightx and weighty for comboBox are both 0: the default
47         // fill is HORIZONTAL
48         addComponent( comboBox, 2, 1, 2, 1 );
49
50         // button2
51         constraints.weightx = 1000;  // can grow wider
52         constraints.weighty = 1;      // can grow taller
53         constraints.fill = GridBagConstraints.BOTH;
54         addComponent( button2, 1, 1, 1, 1 );
55
56         // fill is BOTH for button3
57         constraints.weightx = 0;
58         constraints.weighty = 0;
59         addComponent( button3, 1, 2, 1, 1 );
60
```

Fig. 22.21 | GridBagLayout layout manager. (Part 2 of 3.)

```
61          // weightx and weighty for textField are both 0, fill is BOTH
62          addComponent( textField, 3, 0, 2, 1 );
63
64          // weightx and weighty for textArea2 are both 0, fill is BOTH
65          addComponent( textArea2, 3, 2, 1, 1 );
66       } // end GridBagFrame constructor
67
68       // method to set constraints on
69       private void addComponent( Component component,
70          int row, int column, int width, int height )
71       {
72          constraints.gridx = column; // set gridx
73          constraints.gridy = row; // set gridy
74          constraints.gridwidth = width; // set gridwidth
75          constraints.gridheight = height; // set gridheight
76          layout.setConstraints( component, constraints ); // set constraints
77          add( component ); // add component
78       } // end method addComponent
79    } // end class GridBagFrame
```

Fig. 22.21 | GridBagLayout layout manager. (Part 3 of 3.)

```
1    // Fig. 22.22: GridBagDemo.java
2    // Demonstrating GridBagLayout.
3    import javax.swing.JFrame;
4
5    public class GridBagDemo
6    {
7       public static void main( String[] args )
8       {
9          GridBagFrame gridBagFrame = new GridBagFrame();
10         gridBagFrame.setDefaultCloseOperation( JFrame.EXIT_ON_CLOSE );
11         gridBagFrame.setSize( 300, 150 ); // set frame size
12         gridBagFrame.setVisible( true ); // display frame
13      } // end main
14   } // end class GridBagDemo
```

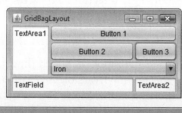

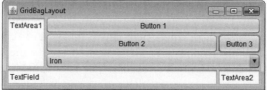

Fig. 22.22 | Test class for GridBagFrame. (Part 1 of 2.)

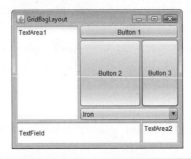

Fig. 22.22 | Test class for `GridBagFrame`. (Part 2 of 2.)

The GUI contains three `JButton`s, two `JTextArea`s, a `JComboBox` and a `JTextField`. The layout manager is `GridBagLayout`. Lines 21–22 create the `GridBagLayout` object and set the layout manager for the `JFrame` to layout. Line 23 creates the `GridBagConstraints` object used to determine the location and size of each component in the grid. Lines 26–35 create each GUI component that will be added to the content pane.

Lines 39–40 configure `JTextArea textArea1` and add it to the content pane. The values for `weightx` and `weighty` values are not specified in `constraints`, so each has the value zero by default. Thus, the `JTextArea` will not resize itself even if space is available. However, it spans multiple rows, so the vertical size is subject to the `weighty` values of `JButton`s `button2` and `button3`. When either button is resized vertically based on its `weighty` value, the `JTextArea` is also resized.

Line 39 sets variable `fill` in `constraints` to `GridBagConstraints.BOTH`, causing the `JTextArea` to always fill its entire allocated area in the grid. An anchor value is not specified in `constraints`, so the default `CENTER` is used. We do not use variable `anchor` in this application, so all the components will use the default. Line 40 calls our utility method `addComponent` (declared at lines 69–78). The `JTextArea` object, the row, the column, the number of columns to span and the number of rows to span are passed as arguments.

`JButton button1` is the next component added (lines 43–44). By default, the `weightx` and `weighty` values are still zero. The `fill` variable is set to `HORIZONTAL`—the component will always fill its area in the horizontal direction. The vertical direction is not filled. The `weighty` value is zero, so the button will become taller only if another component in the same row has a nonzero `weighty` value. `JButton button1` is located at row 0, column 1. One row and two columns are occupied.

`JComboBox comboBox` is the next component added (line 48). By default, the `weightx` and `weighty` values are zero, and the `fill` variable is set to `HORIZONTAL`. The `JComboBox` button will grow only in the horizontal direction. The `weightx`, `weighty` and `fill` variables retain the values set in `constraints` until they're changed. The `JComboBox` button is placed at row 2, column 1. One row and two columns are occupied.

`JButton button2` is the next component added (lines 51–54). It's given a `weightx` value of 1000 and a `weighty` value of 1. The area occupied by the button is capable of growing in the vertical and horizontal directions. The `fill` variable is set to `BOTH`, which specifies that the button will always fill the entire area. When the window is resized, `button2` will grow. The button is placed at row 1, column 1. One row and one column are occupied.

JButton button3 is added next (lines 57–59). Both the weightx value and weighty value are set to zero, and the value of fill is BOTH. JButton button3 will grow if the window is resized—it's affected by the weight values of button2. The weightx value for button2 is much larger than that for button3. When resizing occurs, button2 will occupy a larger percentage of the new space. The button is placed at row 1, column 2. One row and one column are occupied.

Both the JTextField textField (line 62) and JTextArea textArea2 (line 65) have a weightx value of 0 and a weighty value of 0. The value of fill is BOTH. The JTextField is placed at row 3, column 0, and the JTextArea at row 3, column 2. The JTextField occupies one row and two columns, the JTextArea one row and one column.

Method addComponent's parameters are a Component reference component and integers row, column, width and height. Lines 72–73 set the GridBagConstraints variables gridx and gridy. The gridx variable is assigned the column in which the Component will be placed, and the gridy value is assigned the row in which the Component will be placed. Lines 74–75 set the GridBagConstraints variables gridwidth and gridheight. The gridwidth variable specifies the number of columns the Component will span in the grid, and the gridheight variable specifies the number of rows the Component will span in the grid. Line 76 sets the GridBagConstraints for a component in the GridBagLayout. Method **setConstraints** of class GridBagLayout takes a Component argument and a GridBagConstraints argument. Line 77 adds the component to the JFrame.

When you execute this application, try resizing the window to see how the constraints for each GUI component affect its position and size in the window.

GridBagConstraints *Constants* RELATIVE *and* REMAINDER

Instead of gridx and gridy, a variation of GridBagLayout uses GridBagConstraints constants **RELATIVE** and **REMAINDER**. RELATIVE specifies that the next-to-last component in a particular row should be placed to the right of the previous component in the row. REMAINDER specifies that a component is the last component in a row. Any component that is not the second-to-last or last component on a row must specify values for GridbagConstraints variables gridwidth and gridheight. The application in Figs. 22.23–22.24 arranges components in GridBagLayout, using these constants.

```
 1    // Fig. 22.23: GridBagFrame2.java
 2    // Demonstrating GridBagLayout constants.
 3    import java.awt.GridBagLayout;
 4    import java.awt.GridBagConstraints;
 5    import java.awt.Component;
 6    import javax.swing.JFrame;
 7    import javax.swing.JComboBox;
 8    import javax.swing.JTextField;
 9    import javax.swing.JList;
10    import javax.swing.JButton;
11
12    public class GridBagFrame2 extends JFrame
13    {
14       private GridBagLayout layout; // layout of this frame
15       private GridBagConstraints constraints; // constraints of this layout
```

Fig. 22.23 | GridBagConstraints constants RELATIVE and REMAINDER. (Part 1 of 3.)

```
16
17      // set up GUI
18      public GridBagFrame2()
19      {
20         super( "GridBagLayout" );
21         layout = new GridBagLayout();
22         setLayout( layout ); // set frame layout
23         constraints = new GridBagConstraints(); // instantiate constraints
24
25         // create GUI components
26         String[] metals = { "Copper", "Aluminum", "Silver" };
27         JComboBox comboBox = new JComboBox( metals );
28
29         JTextField textField = new JTextField( "TextField" );
30
31         String[] fonts = { "Serif", "Monospaced" };
32         JList list = new JList( fonts );
33
34         String[] names = { "zero", "one", "two", "three", "four" };
35         JButton[] buttons = new JButton[ names.length ];
36
37         for ( int count = 0; count < buttons.length; count++ )
38            buttons[ count ] = new JButton( names[ count ] );
39
40         // define GUI component constraints for textField
41         constraints.weightx = 1;
42         constraints.weighty = 1;
43         constraints.fill = GridBagConstraints.BOTH;
44         constraints.gridwidth = GridBagConstraints.REMAINDER;
45         addComponent( textField );
46
47         // buttons[0] -- weightx and weighty are 1: fill is BOTH
48         constraints.gridwidth = 1;
49         addComponent( buttons[ 0 ] );
50
51         // buttons[1] -- weightx and weighty are 1: fill is BOTH
52         constraints.gridwidth = GridBagConstraints.RELATIVE;
53         addComponent( buttons[ 1 ] );
54
55         // buttons[2] -- weightx and weighty are 1: fill is BOTH
56         constraints.gridwidth = GridBagConstraints.REMAINDER;
57         addComponent( buttons[ 2 ] );
58
59         // comboBox -- weightx is 1: fill is BOTH
60         constraints.weighty = 0;
61         constraints.gridwidth = GridBagConstraints.REMAINDER;
62         addComponent( comboBox );
63
64         // buttons[3] -- weightx is 1: fill is BOTH
65         constraints.weighty = 1;
66         constraints.gridwidth = GridBagConstraints.REMAINDER;
67         addComponent( buttons[ 3 ] );
68
```

Fig. 22.23 | GridBagConstraints constants RELATIVE and REMAINDER. (Part 2 of 3.)

```
69          // buttons[4] -- weightx and weighty are 1: fill is BOTH
70          constraints.gridwidth = GridBagConstraints.RELATIVE;
71          addComponent( buttons[ 4 ] );
72
73          // list -- weightx and weighty are 1: fill is BOTH
74          constraints.gridwidth = GridBagConstraints.REMAINDER;
75          addComponent( list );
76       } // end GridBagFrame2 constructor
77
78       // add a component to the container
79       private void addComponent( Component component )
80       {
81          layout.setConstraints( component, constraints );
82          add( component ); // add component
83       } // end method addComponent
84    } // end class GridBagFrame2
```

Fig. 22.23 | GridBagConstraints constants RELATIVE and REMAINDER. (Part 3 of 3.)

```
 1    // Fig. 22.24: GridBagDemo2.java
 2    // Demonstrating GridBagLayout constants.
 3    import javax.swing.JFrame;
 4
 5    public class GridBagDemo2
 6    {
 7       public static void main( String[] args )
 8       {
 9          GridBagFrame2 gridBagFrame = new GridBagFrame2();
10          gridBagFrame.setDefaultCloseOperation( JFrame.EXIT_ON_CLOSE );
11          gridBagFrame.setSize( 300, 200 ); // set frame size
12          gridBagFrame.setVisible( true ); // display frame
13       } // end main
14    } // end class GridBagDemo2
```

 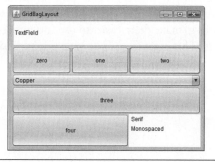

Fig. 22.24 | Test class for GridBagDemo2.

Lines 21–22 create a GridBagLayout and use it to set the JFrame's layout manager. The components that are placed in GridBagLayout are created in lines 27–38—they are a JComboBox, a JTextField, a JList and five JButtons.

The JTextField is added first (lines 41–45). The weightx and weighty values are set to 1. The fill variable is set to BOTH. Line 44 specifies that the JTextField is the last component on the line. The JTextField is added to the content pane with a call to our utility method addComponent (declared at lines 79–83). Method addComponent takes a Component argument and uses GridBagLayout method setConstraints to set the constraints for the Component. Method add attaches the component to the content pane.

JButton buttons[0] (lines 48–49) has weightx and weighty values of 1. The fill variable is BOTH. Because buttons[0] is not one of the last two components on the row, it's given a gridwidth of 1 and so will occupy one column. The JButton is added to the content pane with a call to utility method addComponent.

JButton buttons[1] (lines 52–53) has weightx and weighty values of 1. The fill variable is BOTH. Line 52 specifies that the JButton is to be placed relative to the previous component. The Button is added to the JFrame with a call to addComponent.

JButton buttons[2] (lines 56–57) has weightx and weighty values of 1. The fill variable is BOTH. This JButton is the last component on the line, so REMAINDER is used. The JButton is added to the content pane with a call to addComponent.

The JComboBox (lines 60–62) has a weightx of 1 and a weighty of 0. The JComboBox will not grow vertically. The JComboBox is the only component on the line, so REMAINDER is used. The JComboBox is added to the content pane with a call to addComponent.

JButton buttons[3] (lines 65–67) has weightx and weighty values of 1. The fill variable is BOTH. This JButton is the only component on the line, so REMAINDER is used. The JButton is added to the content pane with a call to addComponent.

JButton buttons[4] (lines 70–71) has weightx and weighty values of 1. The fill variable is BOTH. This JButton is the next-to-last component on the line, so RELATIVE is used. The JButton is added to the content pane with a call to addComponent.

The JList (lines 74–75) has weightx and weighty values of 1. The fill variable is BOTH. The JList is added to the content pane with a call to addComponent.

22.10 Wrap-Up

This chapter completes our introduction to GUIs. In this chapter, we discussed additional GUI topics, such as menus, sliders, pop-up menus, multiple-document interfaces, tabbed panes and Java's pluggable look-and-feel. All these components can be added to existing applications to make them easier to use and understand. We also presented additional layout managers for organizing and sizing GUI components. In the next chapter, you'll learn about multithreading, which allows you to specify that an application should perform multiple tasks at once.

Multithreading

Objectives

In this chapter you'll learn:

- What threads are and why they're useful.

- How threads enable you to manage concurrent activities.

- The life cycle of a thread.

- To create and execute `Runnable`s.

- Thread synchronization.

- What producer/consumer relationships are and how they're implemented with multithreading.

- To enable multiple threads to update Swing GUI components in a thread-safe manner.

23.1 Introduction

It would be nice if we could focus our attention on performing only one action at a time and performing it well, but that's usually difficult to do. The human body performs a great variety of operations *in parallel*—or, as we'll say throughout this chapter, **concurrently**. Respiration, blood circulation, digestion, thinking and walking, for example, can occur concurrently, as can all the senses—sight, touch, smell, taste and hearing.

Computers, too, can perform operations concurrently. It's common for personal computers to compile a program, send a file to a printer and receive electronic mail messages over a network concurrently. Only computers that have multiple processors can truly execute multiple instructions concurrently. Operating systems on single-processor computers create the illusion of concurrent execution by rapidly switching between activities, but on such computers only a single instruction can execute at once. Today's multicore computers have multiple processors that enable computers to perform tasks truly concurrently. Multicore smartphones are starting to appear.

Historically, concurrency has been implemented with operating system primitives available only to experienced systems programmers. The Ada programming language—developed by the United States Department of Defense—made concurrency primitives widely available to defense contractors building military command-and-control systems. However, Ada has not been widely used in academia and industry.

Java Concurrency

Java makes concurrency available to you through the language and APIs. Java programs can have multiple **threads of execution**, where each thread has its own method-call stack and program counter, allowing it to execute concurrently with other threads while sharing with them application-wide resources such as memory. This capability is called **multithreading**.

Performance Tip 23.1

A problem with single-threaded applications that can lead to poor responsiveness is that lengthy activities must complete before others can begin. In a multithreaded application, threads can be distributed across multiple processors (if available) so that multiple tasks execute truly concurrently and the application can operate more efficiently. Multithreading can also increase performance on single-processor systems that simulate concurrency—when one thread cannot proceed (because, for example, it's waiting for the result of an I/O operation), another can use the processor.

Concurrent Programming Uses

We'll discuss many applications of **concurrent programming**. For example, when downloading a large file (e.g., an image, an audio clip or a video clip) over the Internet, the user may not want to wait until the entire clip downloads before starting the playback. To solve this problem, multiple threads can be used—one to download the clip, and another to play it. These activities proceed concurrently. To avoid choppy playback, the threads are **synchronized** (that is, their actions are coordinated) so that the player thread doesn't begin until there's a sufficient amount of the clip in memory to keep the player thread busy. The Java Virtual Machine (JVM) creates threads to run programs and threads to perform housekeeping tasks such as garbage collection.

Concurrent Programming Is Difficult

Writing multithreaded programs can be tricky. Although the human mind can perform functions concurrently, people find it difficult to jump between parallel trains of thought. To see why multithreaded programs can be difficult to write and understand, try the following experiment: Open three books to page 1, and try reading the books concurrently. Read a few words from the first book, then a few from the second, then a few from the third, then loop back and read the next few words from the first book, and so on. After this experiment, you'll appreciate many of the challenges of multithreading—switching between the books, reading briefly, remembering your place in each book, moving the book you're reading closer so that you can see it and pushing the books you're not reading aside—and, amid all this chaos, trying to comprehend the content of the books!

Use the Prebuilt Classes of the Concurrency APIs Whenever Possible

Programming concurrent applications is difficult and error prone. If you must use synchronization in a program, you should follow some simple guidelines. *Use existing classes from the Concurrency APIs (such as the `ArrayBlockingQueue` class we discuss in Section 23.6) that manage synchronization for you.* These classes are written by experts, have been thoroughly tested and debugged, operate efficiently and help you avoid common traps and pitfalls.

If you need even more complex capabilities, use interfaces `Lock` and `Condition` that we introduce in Section 23.9. These interfaces should be used only by advanced programmers who are familiar with concurrent programming's common traps and pitfalls. We explain these topics in this chapter for several reasons:

- They provide a solid basis for understanding how concurrent applications synchronize access to shared memory.
- The concepts are important to understand, even if an application does not use these tools explicitly.

- By showing you the complexity involved in using these low-level features, we hope to impress upon you the importance of *using prebuilt concurrency capabilities whenever possible.*

Section 23.10 provides an overview of Java's pre-built concurrent collections.

23.2 Thread States: Life Cycle of a Thread

At any time, a thread is said to be in one of several **thread states**—illustrated in the UML state diagram in Fig. 23.1. Several of the terms in the diagram are defined in later sections. We include this discussion to help you understand what's going on "under the hood" in a Java multithreaded environment. Java hides most of this detail from you, greatly simplifying the task of developing multithreaded applications.

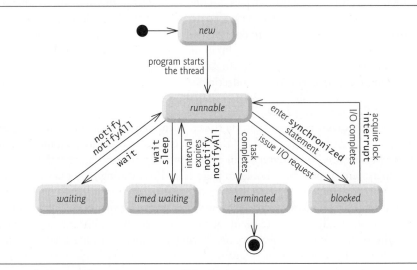

Fig. 23.1 | Thread life-cycle UML state diagram.

New *and* Runnable *States*
A new thread begins its life cycle in the *new* state. It remains in this state until the program starts the thread, which places it in the *runnable* state. A thread in the *runnable* state is considered to be executing its task.

Waiting *State*
Sometimes a *runnable* thread transitions to the *waiting* state while it waits for another thread to perform a task. A *waiting* thread transitions back to the *runnable* state only when another thread notifies it to continue executing.

Timed Waiting *State*
A *runnable* thread can enter the *timed waiting* state for a specified interval of time. It transitions back to the *runnable* state when that time interval expires or when the event it's waiting for occurs. *Timed waiting* and *waiting* threads cannot use a processor, even if one

is available. A *runnable* thread can transition to the *timed waiting* state if it provides an optional wait interval when it's waiting for another thread to perform a task. Such a thread returns to the *runnable* state when it's notified by another thread or when the timed interval expires—whichever comes first. Another way to place a thread in the *timed waiting* state is to put a *runnable* thread to sleep. A **sleeping thread** remains in the *timed waiting* state for a designated period of time (called a **sleep interval**), after which it returns to the *runnable* state. Threads sleep when they momentarily do not have work to perform. For example, a word processor may contain a thread that periodically backs up (i.e., writes a copy of) the current document to disk for recovery purposes. If the thread did not sleep between successive backups, it would require a loop in which it continually tested whether it should write a copy of the document to disk. This loop would consume processor time without performing productive work, thus reducing system performance. In this case, it's more efficient for the thread to specify a sleep interval (equal to the period between successive backups) and enter the *timed waiting* state. This thread is returned to the *runnable* state when its sleep interval expires, at which point it writes a copy of the document to disk and reenters the *timed waiting* state.

Blocked *State*

A *runnable* thread transitions to the ***blocked*** state when it attempts to perform a task that cannot be completed immediately and it must temporarily wait until that task completes. For example, when a thread issues an input/output request, the operating system blocks the thread from executing until that I/O request completes—at that point, the *blocked* thread transitions to the *runnable* state, so it can resume execution. A *blocked* thread cannot use a processor, even if one is available.

Terminated *State*

A *runnable* thread enters the ***terminated*** state (sometimes called the ***dead*** state) when it successfully completes its task or otherwise terminates (perhaps due to an error). In the UML state diagram of Fig. 23.1, the *terminated* state is followed by the UML final state (the bull's-eye symbol) to indicate the end of the state transitions.

Operating-System View of the Runnable *State*

At the operating system level, Java's *runnable* state typically encompasses *two separate* states (Fig. 23.2). The operating system hides these states from the Java Virtual Machine (JVM), which sees only the *runnable* state. When a thread first transitions to the *runnable* state from the *new* state, it's in the **ready** state. A *ready* thread enters the **running** state (i.e., begins executing) when the operating system assigns it to a processor—also known as **dispatching the thread**. In most operating systems, each thread is given a small amount of processor time—called a **quantum** or **timeslice**—with which to perform its task. When its quantum expires, the thread returns to the *ready* state, and the operating system assigns another thread to the processor. Transitions between the *ready* and *running* states are handled solely by the operating system. The JVM does not "see" the transitions—it simply views the thread as being *runnable* and leaves it up to the operating system to transition the thread between *ready* and *running*. The process that an operating system uses to determine which thread to dispatch is called **thread scheduling** and is dependent on thread priorities.

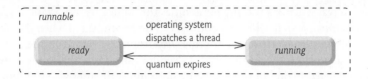

Fig. 23.2 | Operating system's internal view of Java's *runnable* state.

Thread Priorities and Thread Scheduling

Every Java thread has a **thread priority** that helps determine the order in which threads are scheduled. Each new thread inherits the priority of the thread that created it. Informally, higher-priority threads are more important to a program and should be allocated processor time before lower-priority threads. *Nevertheless, thread priorities cannot guarantee the order in which threads execute.*

It's recommended that you do not explicitly create and use Thread *objects to implement concurrency, but rather use the* Executor *interface (which is described in Section 23.3).* The Thread class does contain some useful static methods, which you *will* use later in the chapter.

Most operating systems support timeslicing, which enables threads of equal priority to share a processor. Without timeslicing, each thread in a set of equal-priority threads runs to completion (unless it leaves the *runnable* state and enters the *waiting* or *timed waiting* state, or gets interrupted by a higher-priority thread) before other threads of equal priority get a chance to execute. With timeslicing, even if a thread has *not* finished executing when its quantum expires, the processor is taken away from the thread and given to the next thread of equal priority, if one is available.

An *operating system's* **thread scheduler** determines which thread runs next. One simple thread-scheduler implementation keeps the highest-priority thread *running* at all times and, if there's more than one highest-priority thread, ensures that all such threads execute for a quantum each in **round-robin** fashion. This process continues until all threads run to completion.

When a higher-priority thread enters the *ready* state, the operating system generally preempts the currently *running* thread (an operation known as **preemptive scheduling**). Depending on the operating system, higher-priority threads could postpone—possibly indefinitely—the execution of lower-priority threads. Such **indefinite postponement** is sometimes referred to more colorfully as **starvation**. Operating systems employ a technique called *aging* to prevent starvation—as a thread waits in the *ready* state, the operating system gradually increases the thread's priority, thus ensuring that the thread will eventually run.

Java provides higher-level concurrency utilities to hide much of this complexity and make multithreaded programming less error prone. Thread priorities are used behind the scenes to interact with the operating system, but most programmers who use Java multithreading will not be concerned with setting and adjusting thread priorities.

Portability Tip 23.1

Thread scheduling is platform dependent—the behavior of a multithreaded program could vary across different Java implementations.

23.3 Creating and Executing Threads with Executor Framework

This section demonstrates how to perform concurrent tasks in an application by using Executors and Runnable objectss.

*Creating Concurrent Tasks with the **Runnable** Interface*
You implement the **Runnable** interface (of package java.lang) to specify a task that can execute concurrently with other tasks. The Runnable interface declares the single method **run**, which contains the code that defines the task that a Runnable object should perform.

*Executing **Runnable** Objects with an **Executor***
To allow a Runnable to perform its task, you must execute it. An **Executor** object executes Runnables. An Executor does this by creating and managing a group of threads called a **thread pool**. When an Executor begins executing a Runnable, the Executor calls the Runnable object's run method, which executes in the new thread.

The Executor interface declares a single method named **execute** which accepts a Runnable as an argument. The Executor assigns every Runnable passed to its execute method to one of the available threads in the thread pool. If there are no available threads, the Executor creates a new thread or waits for a thread to become available and assigns that thread the Runnable that was passed to method execute.

Using an Executor has many advantages over creating threads yourself. Executors can *reuse existing threads* to eliminate the overhead of creating a new thread for each task and can improve performance by *optimizing the number of threads* to ensure that the processor stays busy, without creating so many threads that the application runs out of resources.

Software Engineering Observation 23.1
Though it's possible to create threads explicitly, it's recommended that you use the Executor interface to manage the execution of Runnable objects.

*Using Class **Executors** to Obtain an **ExecutorService***
The **ExecutorService** interface (of package java.util.concurrent) *extends* Executor and declares various methods for managing the life cycle of an Executor. An object that implements the ExecutorService interface can be created using static methods declared in class **Executors** (of package java.util.concurrent). We use interface ExecutorService and a method of class Executors in our example, which executes three tasks.

*Implementing the **Runnable** Interface*
Class PrintTask (Fig. 23.3) implements Runnable (line 5), *so that multiple PrintTasks can execute concurrently*. Variable sleepTime (line 7) stores a random integer value from 0 to 5 seconds created in the PrintTask constructor (line 17). Each thread running a PrintTask sleeps for the amount of time specified by sleepTime, then outputs its task's name and a message indicating that it's done sleeping.

A PrintTask executes when a thread calls the PrintTask's run method. Lines 25–26 display a message indicating the name of the currently executing task and that the task is going to sleep for sleepTime milliseconds. Line 27 invokes static method **sleep** of class Thread to place the thread in the *timed waiting* state for the specified amount of time. At this point, the thread loses the processor, and the system allows another thread to execute.

```
1   // Fig. 23.3: PrintTask.java
2   // PrintTask class sleeps for a random time from 0 to 5 seconds
3   import java.util.Random;
4
5   public class PrintTask implements Runnable
6   {
7      private final int sleepTime; // random sleep time for thread
8      private final String taskName; // name of task
9      private final static Random generator = new Random();
10
11     // constructor
12     public PrintTask( String name )
13     {
14        taskName = name; // set task name
15
16        // pick random sleep time between 0 and 5 seconds
17        sleepTime = generator.nextInt( 5000 ); // milliseconds
18     } // end PrintTask constructor
19
20     // method run contains the code that a thread will execute
21     public void run()
22     {
23        try // put thread to sleep for sleepTime amount of time
24        {
25           System.out.printf( "%s going to sleep for %d milliseconds.\n",
26              taskName, sleepTime );
27           Thread.sleep( sleepTime ); // put thread to sleep
28        } // end try
29        catch ( InterruptedException exception )
30        {
31           System.out.printf( "%s %s\n", taskName,
32              "terminated prematurely due to interruption" );
33        } // end catch
34
35        // print task name
36        System.out.printf( "%s done sleeping\n", taskName );
37     } // end method run
38  } // end class PrintTask
```

Fig. 23.3 | PrintTask class sleeps for a random time from 0 to 5 seconds.

When the thread awakens, it reenters the *runnable* state. When the PrintTask is assigned to a processor again, line 36 outputs a message indicating that the task is done sleeping, then method run terminates. The catch at lines 29–33 is required because method sleep might throw a *checked* exception of type **InterruptedException** if a sleeping thread's **interrupt** method is called.

Using the ExecutorService to Manage Threads that Execute PrintTasks

Figure 23.4 uses an ExecutorService object to manage threads that execute PrintTasks (as defined in Fig. 23.3). Lines 11–13 create and name three PrintTasks to execute. Line 18 uses Executors method **newCachedThreadPool** to obtain an ExecutorService that's capable of creating new threads as they're needed by the application. These threads are used by ExecutorService (threadExecutor) to execute the Runnables.

```
 1   // Fig. 23.4: TaskExecutor.java
 2   // Using an ExecutorService to execute Runnables.
 3   import java.util.concurrent.Executors;
 4   import java.util.concurrent.ExecutorService;
 5
 6   public class TaskExecutor
 7   {
 8      public static void main( String[] args )
 9      {
10         // create and name each runnable
11         PrintTask task1 = new PrintTask( "task1" );
12         PrintTask task2 = new PrintTask( "task2" );
13         PrintTask task3 = new PrintTask( "task3" );
14
15         System.out.println( "Starting Executor" );
16
17         // create ExecutorService to manage threads
18         ExecutorService threadExecutor = Executors.newCachedThreadPool();
19
20         // start threads and place in runnable state
21         threadExecutor.execute( task1 ); // start task1
22         threadExecutor.execute( task2 ); // start task2
23         threadExecutor.execute( task3 ); // start task3
24
25         // shut down worker threads when their tasks complete
26         threadExecutor.shutdown();
27
28         System.out.println( "Tasks started, main ends.\n" );
29      } // end main
30   } // end class TaskExecutor
```

```
Starting Executor
Tasks started, main ends

task1 going to sleep for 4806 milliseconds
task2 going to sleep for 2513 milliseconds
task3 going to sleep for 1132 milliseconds
task3 done sleeping
task2 done sleeping
task1 done sleeping
```

```
Starting Executor
task1 going to sleep for 3161 milliseconds.
task3 going to sleep for 532 milliseconds.
task2 going to sleep for 3440 milliseconds.
Tasks started, main ends.

task3 done sleeping
task1 done sleeping
task2 done sleeping
```

Fig. 23.4 | Using an ExecutorService to execute Runnables.

Lines 21–23 each invoke the ExecutorService's execute method, which executes the Runnable passed to it as an argument (in this case a PrintTask) some time in the future. The specified task may execute in one of the threads in the ExecutorService's thread pool, in a new thread created to execute it, or in the thread that called the execute method—the ExecutorService manages these details. Method execute returns immediately from each invocation—the program does *not* wait for each PrintTask to finish. Line 26 calls ExecutorService method **shutdown**, which notifies the ExecutorService to *stop accepting new tasks, but continues executing tasks that have already been submitted.* Once all of the previously submitted Runnables have completed, the threadExecutor terminates. Line 28 outputs a message indicating that the tasks were started and the main thread is finishing its execution.

The code in main executes in the **main thread**, a thread created by the JVM. The code in the run method of PrintTask (lines 21–37 of Fig. 23.3) executes whenever the Executor starts each PrintTask—again, this is sometime after they're passed to the ExecutorService's execute method (Fig. 23.4, lines 21–23). When main terminates, the program itself continues running because there are still tasks that must finish executing. The program will not terminate until these tasks complete.

The sample outputs show each task's name and sleep time as the thread goes to sleep. The thread with the shortest sleep time *normally* awakens first, indicates that it's done sleeping and terminates. In Section 23.8, we discuss multithreading issues that could prevent the thread with the shortest sleep time from awakening first. In the first output, the main thread terminates *before* any of the PrintTasks output their names and sleep times. This shows that the main thread runs to completion before any of the PrintTasks gets a chance to run. In the second output, all of the PrintTasks output their names and sleep times *before* the main thread terminates. This shows that the PrintTasks started executing before the main thread terminated. Also, notice in the second example output, task3 goes to sleep before task2 last, even though we passed task2 to the ExecutorService's execute method before task3. This illustrates the fact that *we cannot predict the order in which the tasks will start executing, even if we know the order in which they were created and started.*

23.4 Thread Synchronization

When multiple threads share an object and it's modified by one or more of them, indeterminate results may occur (as we'll see in the examples) unless access to the shared object is managed properly. If one thread is in the process of updating a shared object and another thread also tries to update it, it's unclear which thread's update takes effect. When this happens, the program's behavior cannot be trusted—sometimes the program will produce the correct results, and sometimes it won't. In either case, there'll be no indication that the shared object was manipulated incorrectly.

The problem can be solved by giving only one thread at a time *exclusive access* to code that manipulates the shared object. During that time, other threads desiring to manipulate the object are kept waiting. When the thread with exclusive access to the object finishes manipulating it, one of the threads that was waiting is allowed to proceed. This process, called **thread synchronization**, coordinates access to shared data by multiple concurrent threads. By synchronizing threads in this manner, you can ensure that each thread accessing a shared object excludes all other threads from doing so simultaneously—this is called **mutual exclusion**.

Monitors

A common way to perform synchronization is to use Java's built-in **monitors**. Every object has a monitor and a **monitor lock** (or **intrinsic lock**). The monitor ensures that its object's monitor lock is held by a maximum of only one thread at any time. Monitors and monitor locks can thus be used to enforce mutual exclusion. If an operation requires the executing thread to hold a lock while the operation is performed, a thread must acquire the lock before proceeding with the operation. Other threads attempting to perform an operation that requires the same lock will be *blocked* until the first thread releases the lock, at which point the *blocked* threads may attempt to acquire the lock and proceed with the operation.

To specify that a thread must hold a monitor lock to execute a block of code, the code should be placed in a **synchronized statement**. Such code is said to be **guarded** by the monitor lock; a thread must **acquire the lock** to execute the guarded statements. The monitor allows only one thread at a time to execute statements within synchronized statements that lock on the same object, as only one thread at a time can hold the monitor lock. The synchronized statements are declared using the **synchronized** keyword:

```
synchronized ( object )
{
    statements
} // end synchronized statement
```

where *object* is the object whose monitor lock will be acquired; *object* is normally this if it's the object in which the synchronized statement appears. If several synchronized statements are trying to execute on an object at the same time, only one of them may be active on the object—all the other threads attempting to enter a synchronized statement on the same object are placed in the *blocked* state.

When a synchronized statement finishes executing, the object's monitor lock is released and one of the *blocked* threads attempting to enter a synchronized statement can be allowed to acquire the lock to proceed. Java also allows **synchronized methods**. Before executing, a non-static synchronized method must acquire the lock on the object that's used to call the method. Similary, a static synchronized method must acquire the lock on the class that's used to call the method.

23.4.1 Unsynchronized Data Sharing

First, we illustrate the dangers of sharing an object across threads without proper synchronization. In this example, two Runnables maintain references to a single integer array. Each Runnable writes three values to the array, then terminates. This may seem harmless, but we'll see that it can result in errors if the array is manipulated without synchronization.

Class SimpleArray

A SimpleArray object (Fig. 23.5) will be *shared* across multiple threads. SimpleArray will enable those threads to place int values into array (declared at line 8). Line 9 initializes variable writeIndex, which will be used to determine the array element that should be written to next. The constructor (lines 13–16) creates an integer array of the desired size.

Method add (lines 19–40) allows new values to be inserted at the end of the array. Line 21 stores the current writeIndex value. Line 26 puts the thread that invokes add to sleep for a random interval from 0 to 499 milliseconds. This is done to make the problems associated with *unsynchronized access to shared data* more obvious. After the thread is done

```
 1    // Fig. 23.5: SimpleArray.java
 2    // Class that manages an integer array to be shared by multiple threads.
 3    import java.util.Arrays;
 4    import java.util.Random;
 5
 6    public class SimpleArray // CAUTION: NOT THREAD SAFE!
 7    {
 8       private final int[] array; // the shared integer array
 9       private int writeIndex = 0; // index of next element to be written
10       private final static Random generator = new Random();
11
12       // construct a SimpleArray of a given size
13       public SimpleArray( int size )
14       {
15          array = new int[ size ];
16       } // end constructor
17
18       // add a value to the shared array
19       public void add( int value )
20       {
21          int position = writeIndex; // store the write index
22
23          try
24          {
25             // put thread to sleep for 0-499 milliseconds
26             Thread.sleep( generator.nextInt( 500 ) );
27          } // end try
28          catch ( InterruptedException ex )
29          {
30             ex.printStackTrace();
31          } // end catch
32
33          // put value in the appropriate element
34          array[ position ] = value;
35          System.out.printf( "%s wrote %2d to element %d.\n",
36             Thread.currentThread().getName(), value, position );
37
38          ++writeIndex; // increment index of element to be written next
39          System.out.printf( "Next write index: %d\n", writeIndex );
40       } // end method add
41
42       // used for outputting the contents of the shared integer array
43       public String toString()
44       {
45          return "\nContents of SimpleArray:\n" + Arrays.toString( array );
46       } // end method toString
47    } // end class SimpleArray
```

Fig. 23.5 | Class that manages an integer array to be shared by multiple threads.

sleeping, line 34 inserts the value passed to add into the array at the element specified by position. Lines 35–36 output a message indicating the executing thread's name, the value that was inserted in the array and where it was inserted. The expression Thread.current-Thread.getName() (line 36) first obtains a reference to the currently executing Thread, then uses that Thread's getName method to obtain its name. Line 38 increments writeIndex so that the next call to add will insert a value in the array's next element. Lines 43–46 override method toString to create a String representation of the array's contents.

Class *ArrayWriter*

Class ArrayWriter (Fig. 23.6) implements the interface Runnable to define a task for inserting values in a SimpleArray object. The constructor (lines 10–14) takes two arguments—an integer value, which is the first value this task will insert in the SimpleArray object, and a reference to the SimpleArray object. Line 20 invokes method add on the SimpleArray object. The task completes after three consecutive integers beginning with startValue are added to the SimpleArray object.

```
1   // Fig. 23.6: ArrayWriter.java
2   // Adds integers to an array shared with other Runnables
3   import java.lang.Runnable;
4
5   public class ArrayWriter implements Runnable
6   {
7      private final SimpleArray sharedSimpleArray;
8      private final int startValue;
9
10     public ArrayWriter( int value, SimpleArray array )
11     {
12        startValue = value;
13        sharedSimpleArray = array;
14     } // end constructor
15
16     public void run()
17     {
18        for ( int i = startValue; i < startValue + 3; i++ )
19        {
20           sharedSimpleArray.add( i ); // add an element to the shared array
21        } // end for
22     } // end method run
23  } // end class ArrayWriter
```

Fig. 23.6 | Adds integers to an array shared with other Runnables.

Class *SharedArrayTest*

Class SharedArrayTest (Fig. 23.7) executes two ArrayWriter tasks that add values to a single SimpleArray object. Line 12 constructs a six-element SimpleArray object. Lines 15–16 create two new ArrayWriter tasks, one that places the values 1–3 in the SimpleArray object, and one that places the values 11–13. Lines 19–21 create an ExecutorService and execute the two ArrayWriters. Line 23 invokes the ExecutorService's shutDown method to *prevent additional tasks from starting* and to enable the application to terminate when the currently executing tasks complete execution.

Recall that ExecutorService method shutdown returns immediately. Thus any code that appears *after* the call to ExecutorService method shutdown in line 23 *will continue executing as long as the main thread is still assigned to a processor.* We'd like to output the SimpleArray object to show you the results *after* the threads complete their tasks. So, we need the program to wait for the threads to complete before main outputs the SimpleArray object's contents. Interface ExecutorService provides the **awaitTermination** method for this purpose. This method returns control to its caller either when all tasks executing in the ExecutorService complete or when the specified timeout elapses. If all tasks are completed before awaitTermination times out, this method returns true; otherwise it returns false. The two arguments to awaitTermination represent a timeout value and a unit of measure specified with a constant from class TimeUnit (in this case, TimeUnit.MINUTES).

```java
1   // Fig 23.7: SharedArrayTest.java
2   // Executes two Runnables to add elements to a shared SimpleArray.
3   import java.util.concurrent.Executors;
4   import java.util.concurrent.ExecutorService;
5   import java.util.concurrent.TimeUnit;
6
7   public class SharedArrayTest
8   {
9      public static void main( String[] arg )
10     {
11        // construct the shared object
12        SimpleArray sharedSimpleArray = new SimpleArray( 6 );
13
14        // create two tasks to write to the shared SimpleArray
15        ArrayWriter writer1 = new ArrayWriter( 1, sharedSimpleArray );
16        ArrayWriter writer2 = new ArrayWriter( 11, sharedSimpleArray );
17
18        // execute the tasks with an ExecutorService
19        ExecutorService executor = Executors.newCachedThreadPool();
20        executor.execute( writer1 );
21        executor.execute( writer2 );
22
23        executor.shutdown();
24
25        try
26        {
27           // wait 1 minute for both writers to finish executing
28           boolean tasksEnded = executor.awaitTermination(
29              1, TimeUnit.MINUTES );
30
31           if ( tasksEnded )
32              System.out.println( sharedSimpleArray ); // print contents
33           else
34              System.out.println(
35                 "Timed out while waiting for tasks to finish." );
36        } // end try
37        catch ( InterruptedException ex )
38        {
39           System.out.println(
40              "Interrupted while waiting for tasks to finish." );
41        } // end catch
42     } // end main
43  } // end class SharedArrayTest
```

Fig. 23.7 | Executes two Runnables to insert values in a shared array. (Part 1 of 2.)

```
pool-1-thread-1 wrote  1 to element 0.
Next write index: 1
pool-1-thread-1 wrote  2 to element 1.
Next write index: 2
pool-1-thread-1 wrote  3 to element 2.
Next write index: 3
pool-1-thread-2 wrote 11 to element 0.
Next write index: 4
pool-1-thread-2 wrote 12 to element 4.
Next write index: 5
pool-1-thread-2 wrote 13 to element 5.
Next write index: 6

Contents of SimpleArray:
[11, 2, 3, 0, 12, 13]
```

First `pool-1-thread-1` wrote the value 1 to element 0. Later `pool-1-thread-2` wrote the value 11 to element 0, thus *overwriting* the previously stored value.

Fig. 23.7 | Executes two `Runnables` to insert values in a shared array. (Part 2 of 2.)

In this example, if *both* tasks complete before `awaitTermination` times out, line 32 displays the `SimpleArray` object's contents. Otherwise, lines 34–35 print a message indicating that the tasks did not finish executing before `awaitTermination` timed out.

The output in Fig. 23.7 demonstrates the problems (highlighted in the output) that can be *caused by failure to synchronize access to shared data*. The value 1 was written to element 0, then *overwritten* later by the value 11. Also, when `writeIndex` was incremented to 3, *nothing was written to that element*, as indicated by the 0 in that element of the printed array.

Recall that we added calls to `Thread` method `sleep` between operations on the shared data to emphasize the *unpredictability of thread scheduling* and increase the likelihood of producing erroneous output. Even if these operations were allowed to proceed at their normal pace, you could still see errors in the program's output. However, modern processors can handle the simple operations of the `SimpleArray` method `add` so quickly that you might not see the errors caused by the two threads executing this method concurrently, even if you tested the program dozens of times. *One of the challenges of multithreaded programming is spotting the errors—they may occur so infrequently that a broken program does not produce incorrect results during testing, creating the illusion that the program is correct.*

23.4.2 Synchronized Data Sharing—Making Operations Atomic

The output errors of Fig. 23.7 can be attributed to the fact that the shared object, `Simple-Array`, is not **thread safe**—`SimpleArray` is susceptible to errors if it's *accessed concurrently by multiple threads*. The problem lies in method `add`, which stores the value of `writeIndex`, places a new value in that element, then increments `writeIndex`. Such a method would present no problem in a single-threaded program. However, if one thread obtains the value of `writeIndex`, there's no guarantee that another thread cannot come along and increment `writeIndex` *before* the first thread has had a chance to place a value in the array. If this happens, the first thread will be writing to the array based on a **stale value** of `writeIndex`—a value that's no longer valid. Another possibility is that one thread might obtain the value of `writeIndex` *after* another thread adds an element to the array but *before* `writeIndex` is incremented. In this case, too, the first thread would write to the array based on an invalid value for `writeIndex`.

SimpleArray is *not thread safe because it allows any number of threads to read and modify shared data concurrently*, which can cause errors. To make SimpleArray thread safe, we must ensure that no two threads can access it at the same time. We also must ensure that while one thread is in the process of storing writeIndex, adding a value to the array, and incrementing writeIndex, no other thread may read or change the value of writeIndex or modify the contents of the array at any point during these three operations. In other words, we want these three operations—storing writeIndex, writing to the array, incrementing writeIndex—to be an **atomic operation**, which cannot be divided into smaller suboperations. We can simulate atomicity by ensuring that only one thread carries out the three operations at a time. Any other threads that need to perform the operation must *wait* until the first thread has finished the add operation in its entirety.

Atomicity can be achieved using the synchronized keyword. By placing our three suboperations in a synchronized statement or synchronized method, we allow only one thread at a time to acquire the lock and perform the operations. When that thread has completed all of the operations in the synchronized block and releases the lock, another thread may acquire the lock and begin executing the operations. This ensures that a thread executing the operations will see the actual values of the shared data and that *these values will not change unexpectedly in the middle of the operations as a result of another thread's modifying them.*

Software Engineering Observation 23.2

Place all accesses to mutable data that may be shared by multiple threads inside synchronized statements or synchronized methods that synchronize on the same lock. When performing multiple operations on shared data, hold the lock for the entirety of the operation to ensure that the operation is effectively atomic.

Class *SimpleArray* with Synchronization

Figure 23.8 displays class SimpleArray with the proper synchronization. Notice that it's identical to the SimpleArray class of Fig. 23.5, except that add is now a synchronized method (line 20). So, only one thread at a time can execute this method. We reuse classes ArrayWriter (Fig. 23.6) and SharedArrayTest (Fig. 23.7) from the previous example.

```
1   // Fig. 23.8: SimpleArray.java
2   // Class that manages an integer array to be shared by multiple
3   // threads with synchronization.
4   import java.util.Arrays;
5   import java.util.Random;
6
7   public class SimpleArray
8   {
9      private final int[] array; // the shared integer array
10     private int writeIndex = 0; // index of next element to be written
11     private final static Random generator = new Random();
12
```

Fig. 23.8 | Class that manages an integer array to be shared by multiple threads with synchronization. (Part 1 of 2.)

```
13        // construct a SimpleArray of a given size
14        public SimpleArray( int size )
15        {
16           array = new int[ size ];
17        } // end constructor
18
19        // add a value to the shared array
20        public synchronized void add( int value )
21        {
22           int position = writeIndex; // store the write index
23
24           try
25           {
26              // put thread to sleep for 0-499 milliseconds
27              Thread.sleep( generator.nextInt( 500 ) );
28           } // end try
29           catch ( InterruptedException ex )
30           {
31              ex.printStackTrace();
32           } // end catch
33
34           // put value in the appropriate element
35           array[ position ] = value;
36           System.out.printf( "%s wrote %2d to element %d.\n",
37              Thread.currentThread().getName(), value, position );
38
39           ++writeIndex; // increment index of element to be written next
40           System.out.printf( "Next write index: %d\n", writeIndex );
41        } // end method add
42
43        // used for outputting the contents of the shared integer array
44        public String toString()
45        {
46           return "\nContents of SimpleArray:\n" + Arrays.toString( array );
47        } // end method toString
48     } // end class SimpleArray
```

```
pool-1-thread-1 wrote  1 to element 0.
Next write index: 1
pool-1-thread-2 wrote 11 to element 1.
Next write index: 2
pool-1-thread-2 wrote 12 to element 2.
Next write index: 3
pool-1-thread-2 wrote 13 to element 3.
Next write index: 4
pool-1-thread-1 wrote  2 to element 4.
Next write index: 5
pool-1-thread-1 wrote  3 to element 5.
Next write index: 6

Contents of SimpleArray:
1 11 12 13 2 3
```

Fig. 23.8 | Class that manages an integer array to be shared by multiple threads with synchronization. (Part 2 of 2.)

Line 20 declares method as `synchronized`, making all of the operations in this method behave as a single, atomic operation. Line 22 performs the first suboperation—storing the value of `writeIndex`. Line 35 defines the second suboperation, writing an element to the element at the index `position`. Line 39 increments `writeIndex`. When the method finishes executing at line 41, the executing thread implicitly releases the `Simple-Array` lock, making it possible for another thread to begin executing the `add` method.

In the `synchronized` `add` method, we print messages to the console indicating the progress of threads as they execute this method, in addition to performing the actual operations required to insert a value in the array. We do this so that the messages will be printed in the correct order, allowing us to see whether the method is properly synchronized by comparing these outputs with those of the previous, unsynchronized example. We continue to output messages from `synchronized` blocks in later examples for demonstration purposes only; typically, however, I/O *should not* be performed in `synchronized` blocks, because it's important to minimize the amount of time that an object is "locked." Also, line 27 in this example calls `Thread` method `sleep` to emphasize the *unpredictability of thread scheduling. You should never call `sleep` while holding a lock in a real application.*

Performance Tip 23.2

Keep the duration of `synchronized` statements as short as possible while maintaining the needed synchronization. This minimizes the wait time for blocked threads. Avoid performing I/O, lengthy calculations and operations that do not require synchronization while holding a lock.

Another note on thread safety: We've said that it's necessary to synchronize access to all data that may be shared across multiple threads. Actually, this synchronization is necessary only for **mutable data**, or data that may *change* in its lifetime. If the shared data will not change in a multithreaded program, then it's not possible for a thread to see old or incorrect values as a result of another thread's manipulating that data.

When you share immutable data across threads, declare the corresponding data fields `final` to indicate that the values of the variables will *not* change after they're initialized. This prevents accidental modification of the shared data later in a program, which could compromise thread safety. *Labeling object references as `final` indicates that the reference will not change, but it does not guarantee that the object itself is immutable—this depends entirely on the object's properties.* However, it's still good practice to mark references that will not change as `final`, as doing so forces the object's constructor to be atomic—the object will be fully constructed with all its fields initialized before the program accesses it.

Good Programming Practice 23.1

Always declare data fields that you do not expect to change as `final`. Primitive variables that are declared as `final` can safely be shared across threads. An object reference that's declared as `final` ensures that the object it refers to will be fully constructed and initialized before it's used by the program, and prevents the reference from pointing to another object.

23.5 Producer/Consumer Relationship without Synchronization

In a **producer/consumer relationship**, the **producer** portion of an application generates data and *stores it in a shared object*, and the **consumer** portion of the application *reads data* *from the shared object.* The producer/consumer relationship separates the task of identifying work to be done from the tasks involved in actually carrying out the work. One example of a common producer/consumer relationship is **print spooling**. Although a printer might not be available when you want to print from an application (i.e., the producer), you can still "complete" the print task, as the data is temporarily placed on disk until the printer becomes available. Similarly, when the printer (i.e., a consumer) is available, it doesn't have to wait until a current user wants to print. The spooled print jobs can be printed as soon as the printer becomes available. Another example of the producer/consumer relationship is an application that copies data onto DVDs by placing data in a fixed-size buffer, which is emptied as the DVD drive "burns" the data onto the DVD.

In a multithreaded producer/consumer relationship, a **producer thread** generates data and places it in a shared object called a **buffer**. A **consumer thread** reads data from the buffer. This relationship requires *synchronization* to ensure that values are produced and consumed properly. All operations on mutable data that's shared by multiple threads (e.g., the data in the buffer) must be guarded with a lock to prevent corruption, as discussed in Section 23.4. Operations on the buffer data shared by a producer and consumer thread are also **state dependent**—the operations should proceed only if the buffer is in the correct state. If the buffer is in a *not-full state*, the producer may produce; if the buffer is in a *not-empty state*, the consumer may consume. All operations that access the buffer must use synchronization to ensure that data is written to the buffer or read from the buffer only if the buffer is in the proper state. If the producer attempting to put the next data into the buffer determines that it's full, the producer thread must *wait* until there's space to write a new value. If a consumer thread finds the buffer empty or finds that the previous data has already been read, the consumer must also *wait* for new data to become available.

Consider how logic errors can arise if we do not synchronize access among multiple threads manipulating shared data. Our next example (Fig. 23.9–Fig. 23.13) implements a producer/consumer relationship without the proper synchronization. A producer thread writes the numbers 1 through 10 into a shared buffer—a single memory location shared between two threads (a single int variable called buffer in line 6 of Fig. 23.12 in this example). The consumer thread reads this data from the shared buffer and displays the data. The program's output shows the values that the producer writes (produces) into the shared buffer and the values that the consumer reads (consumes) from the shared buffer.

Each value the producer thread writes to the shared buffer must be consumed *exactly once* by the consumer thread. However, the threads in this example are not synchronized. Therefore, *data can be lost or garbled if the producer places new data into the shared buffer before the consumer reads the previous data.* Also, data can be incorrectly *duplicated* if the consumer consumes data again before the producer produces the next value. To show these possibilities, the consumer thread in the following example keeps a total of all the values it reads. The producer thread produces values from 1 through 10. If the consumer reads each value produced once and only once, the total will be 55. However, if you execute this program several times, you'll see that the total is not always 55 (as shown in the outputs in Fig. 23.13). To emphasize the point, the producer and consumer threads in the example each sleep for random intervals of up to three seconds between performing their tasks. Thus, we do not know when the producer thread will attempt to write a new value, or when the consumer thread will attempt to read a value.

Implementing the Producer/Consumer Relationship

The program consists of interface `Buffer` (Fig. 23.9) and classes `Producer` (Fig. 23.10), `Consumer` (Fig. 23.11), `UnsynchronizedBuffer` (Fig. 23.12) and `SharedBufferTest` (Fig. 23.13). Interface `Buffer` (Fig. 23.9) declares methods `set` (line 6) and `get` (line 9) that a `Buffer` (such as `UnsynchronizedBuffer`) must implement to enable the `Producer` thread to place a value in the `Buffer` and the `Consumer` thread to retrieve a value from the `Buffer`, respectively. In subsequent examples, methods `set` and `get` will call methods that throw `InterruptedException`s. We declare each method with a `throws` clause here so that we don't have to modify this interface for the later examples.

```
 1   // Fig. 23.9: Buffer.java
 2   // Buffer interface specifies methods called by Producer and Consumer.
 3   public interface Buffer
 4   {
 5      // place int value into Buffer
 6      public void set( int value ) throws InterruptedException;
 7
 8      // return int value from Buffer
 9      public int get() throws InterruptedException;
10   } // end interface Buffer
```

Fig. 23.9 | Buffer interface specifies methods called by `Producer` and `Consumer`.

Class `Producer` (Fig. 23.10) implements the `Runnable` interface, allowing it to be executed as a task in a separate thread. The constructor (lines 11–14) initializes the `Buffer` reference `sharedLocation` with an object created in `main` (line 14 of Fig. 23.13) and passed to the constructor. As we'll see, this is an `UnsynchronizedBuffer` object that implements interface `Buffer` *without synchronizing access to the shared object*. The `Producer` thread in this program executes the tasks specified in the method `run` (lines 17–39). Each iteration of the loop (lines 21–35) invokes `Thread` method `sleep` (line 25) to place the `Producer` thread into the *timed waiting* state for a random time interval between 0 and 3 seconds. When the thread awakens, line 26 passes the value of control variable `count` to the `Buffer` object's `set` method to set the shared buffer's value. Lines 27–28 keep a total of all the values produced so far and output that value. When the loop completes, lines 37–38 display a message indicating that the `Producer` has finished producing data and is terminating. Next, method `run` terminates, which indicates that the `Producer` completed its task. Any method called from a `Runnable`'s run method (e.g., `Buffer` method `set`) executes as part of that task's thread of execution. This fact becomes important in Sections 23.6–23.8 when we add synchronization to the producer/consumer relationship.

```
 1   // Fig. 23.10: Producer.java
 2   // Producer with a run method that inserts the values 1 to 10 in buffer.
 3   import java.util.Random;
 4
 5   public class Producer implements Runnable
 6   {
```

Fig. 23.10 | Producer with a run method that inserts the values 1 to 10 in buffer. (Part 1 of 2.)

```
 7        private final static Random generator = new Random();
 8        private final Buffer sharedLocation; // reference to shared object
 9
10        // constructor
11        public Producer( Buffer shared )
12        {
13            sharedLocation = shared;
14        } // end Producer constructor
15
16        // store values from 1 to 10 in sharedLocation
17        public void run()
18        {
19            int sum = 0;
20
21            for ( int count = 1; count <= 10; count++ )
22            {
23                try // sleep 0 to 3 seconds, then place value in Buffer
24                {
25                    Thread.sleep( generator.nextInt( 3000 ) ); // random sleep
26                    sharedLocation.set( count ); // set value in buffer
27                    sum += count; // increment sum of values
28                    System.out.printf( "\t%2d\n", sum );
29                } // end try
30                // if lines 25 or 26 get interrupted, print stack trace
31                catch ( InterruptedException exception )
32                {
33                    exception.printStackTrace();
34                } // end catch
35            } // end for
36
37            System.out.println(
38                "Producer done producing\nTerminating Producer" );
39        } // end method run
40    } // end class Producer
```

Fig. 23.10 | Producer with a run method that inserts the values 1 to 10 in buffer. (Part 2 of 2.)

Class Consumer (Fig. 23.11) also implements interface Runnable, allowing the Consumer to execute concurrently with the Producer. Lines 11–14 initialize Buffer reference sharedLocation with an object that implements the Buffer interface (created in main, Fig. 23.13) and passed to the constructor as the parameter shared. As we'll see, this is the same UnsynchronizedBuffer object that's used to initialize the Producer object—thus, the two threads share the same object. The Consumer thread in this program performs the tasks specified in method run (lines 17–39). Lines 21–35 iterate 10 times. Each iteration invokes Thread method sleep (line 26) to put the Consumer thread into the *timed waiting* state for up to 3 seconds. Next, line 27 uses the Buffer's get method to retrieve the value in the shared buffer, then adds the value to variable sum. Line 28 displays the total of all the values consumed so far. When the loop completes, lines 37–38 display a line indicating the sum of the consumed values. Then method run terminates, which indicates that the Consumer completed its task. Once both threads enter the *terminated* state, the program ends.

```
 1   // Fig. 23.11: Consumer.java
 2   // Consumer with a run method that loops, reading 10 values from buffer.
 3   import java.util.Random;
 4
 5   public class Consumer implements Runnable
 6   {
 7      private final static Random generator = new Random();
 8      private final Buffer sharedLocation; // reference to shared object
 9
10      // constructor
11      public Consumer( Buffer shared )
12      {
13         sharedLocation = shared;
14      } // end Consumer constructor
15
16      // read sharedLocation's value 10 times and sum the values
17      public void run()
18      {
19         int sum = 0;
20
21         for ( int count = 1; count <= 10; count++ )
22         {
23            // sleep 0 to 3 seconds, read value from buffer and add to sum
24            try
25            {
26               Thread.sleep( generator.nextInt( 3000 ) );
27               sum += sharedLocation.get();
28               System.out.printf( "\t\t\t%2d\n", sum );
29            } // end try
30            // if lines 26 or 27 get interrupted, print stack trace
31            catch ( InterruptedException exception )
32            {
33               exception.printStackTrace();
34            } // end catch
35         } // end for
36
37         System.out.printf( "\n%s %d\n%s\n",
38            "Consumer read values totaling", sum, "Terminating Consumer" );
39      } // end method run
40   } // end class Consumer
```

Fig. 23.11 | Consumer with a run method that loops, reading 10 values from buffer.

[*Note:* We call method sleep in method run of the Producer and Consumer classes to emphasize the fact that, *in multithreaded applications, it's unpredictable when each thread will perform its task and for how long it will perform the task when it has a processor.* Normally, these thread scheduling issues are beyond the control of the Java developer. In this program, our thread's tasks are quite simple—the Producer writes the values 1 to 10 to the buffer, and the Consumer reads 10 values from the buffer and adds each value to variable sum. Without the sleep method call, and if the Producer executes first, given today's phenomenally fast processors, the Producer would likely complete its task before the Consumer got a chance to execute. If the Consumer executed first, it would likely consume garbage data ten times, then terminate before the Producer could produce the first real value.]

Class `UnsynchronizedBuffer` (Fig. 23.12) implements interface `Buffer` (line 4). An object of this class is shared between the `Producer` and the `Consumer`. Line 6 declares instance variable `buffer` and initializes it with the value -1. This value is used to demonstrate the case in which the `Consumer` attempts to consume a value *before* the `Producer` ever places a value in `buffer`. Methods `set` (lines 9–13) and `get` (lines 16–20) do *not* synchronize access to the field `buffer`. Method `set` simply assigns its argument to `buffer` (line 12), and method `get` simply returns the value of `buffer` (line 19).

```
1    // Fig. 23.12: UnsynchronizedBuffer.java
2    // UnsynchronizedBuffer maintains the shared integer that is accessed by
3    // a producer thread and a consumer thread via methods set and get.
4    public class UnsynchronizedBuffer implements Buffer
5    {
6       private int buffer = -1; // shared by producer and consumer threads
7
8       // place value into buffer
9       public void set( int value ) throws InterruptedException
10      {
11         System.out.printf( "Producer writes\t%2d", value );
12         buffer = value;
13      } // end method set
14
15      // return value from buffer
16      public int get() throws InterruptedException
17      {
18         System.out.printf( "Consumer reads\t%2d", buffer );
19         return buffer;
20      } // end method get
21   } // end class UnsynchronizedBuffer
```

Fig. 23.12 | `UnsynchronizedBuffer` maintains the shared integer that is accessed by a producer thread and a consumer thread via methods `set` and `get`.

In class `SharedBufferTest` (Fig. 23.13), line 11 creates an `ExecutorService` to execute the `Producer` and `Consumer` `Runnable`s. Line 14 creates an `UnsynchronizedBuffer` object and assigns it to `Buffer` variable `sharedLocation`. This object stores the data that the `Producer` and `Consumer` threads will share. Lines 23–24 create and execute the `Producer` and `Consumer`. The `Producer` and `Consumer` constructors are each passed the same `Buffer` object (`sharedLocation`), so each object is initialized with a reference to the same `Buffer`. These lines also implicitly launch the threads and call each `Runnable`'s run method. Finally, line 26 calls method `shutdown` so that the application can terminate when the threads executing the `Producer` and `Consumer` complete their tasks. When `main` terminates (line 27), the main thread of execution enters the *terminated* state.

```
1    // Fig. 23.13: SharedBufferTest.java
2    // Application with two threads manipulating an unsynchronized buffer.
3    import java.util.concurrent.ExecutorService;
4    import java.util.concurrent.Executors;
```

Fig. 23.13 | Application with two threads manipulating an unsynchronized buffer. (Part 1 of 3.)

```
5
6    public class SharedBufferTest
7    {
8       public static void main( String[] args )
9       {
10          // create new thread pool with two threads
11          ExecutorService application = Executors.newCachedThreadPool();
12
13          // create UnsynchronizedBuffer to store ints
14          Buffer sharedLocation = new UnsynchronizedBuffer();
15
16          System.out.println(
17             "Action\t\tValue\tSum of Produced\tSum of Consumed" );
18          System.out.println(
19             "------\t\t-----\t---------------\t---------------\n" );
20
21          // execute the Producer and Consumer, giving each of them access
22          // to sharedLocation
23          application.execute( new Producer( sharedLocation ) );
24          application.execute( new Consumer( sharedLocation ) );
25
26          application.shutdown(); // terminate application when tasks complete
27       } // end main
28   } // end class SharedBufferTest
```

Action	Value	Sum of Produced	Sum of Consumed	
Producer writes	1	1		
Producer writes	2	3		—— 1 is lost
Producer writes	3	6		—— 2 is lost
Consumer reads	3		3	
Producer writes	4	10		
Consumer reads	4		7	
Producer writes	5	15		
Producer writes	6	21		—— 5 is lost
Producer writes	7	28		—— 6 is lost
Consumer reads	7		14	
Consumer reads	7		21	—— 7 read again
Producer writes	8	36		
Consumer reads	8		29	
Consumer reads	8		37	—— 8 read again
Producer writes	9	45		
Producer writes	10	55		—— 9 is lost
Producer done producing				
Terminating Producer				
Consumer reads	10		47	
Consumer reads	10		57	—— 10 read again
Consumer reads	10		67	—— 10 read again
Consumer reads	10		77	—— 10 read again
Consumer read values totaling 77				
Terminating Consumer				

Fig. 23.13 | Application with two threads manipulating an unsynchronized buffer. (Part 2 of 3.)

```
Action          Value   Sum of Produced Sum of Consumed
------          -----   --------------- ---------------

Consumer reads  -1                            -1 ——— reads -I bad data
Producer writes  1       1
Consumer reads   1                             0
Consumer reads   1                             1 ——— I read again
Consumer reads   1                             2 ——— I read again
Consumer reads   1                             3 ——— I read again
Consumer reads   1                             4 ——— I read again
Producer writes  2       3
Consumer reads   2                             6
Producer writes  3       6
Consumer reads   3                             9
Producer writes  4      10
Consumer reads   4                            13
Producer writes  5      15
Producer writes  6      21                        ——— 5 is lost
Consumer reads   6                            19

Consumer read values totaling 19
Terminating Consumer
Producer writes  7      28                        ——— 7 never read
Producer writes  8      36                        ——— 8 never read
Producer writes  9      45                        ——— 9 never read
Producer writes 10      55                        ——— I0 never read

Producer done producing
Terminating Producer
```

Fig. 23.13 | Application with two threads manipulating an unsynchronized buffer. (Part 3 of 3.)

Recall from the overview of this example that we would like the Producer to execute first and every value produced by the Producer to be consumed exactly once by the Consumer. However, when we study the first output of Fig. 23.13, we see that the Producer writes the values 1, 2 and 3 before the Consumer reads its first value (3). Therefore, the values 1 and 2 are lost. Later, the values 5, 6 and 9 are lost, while 7 and 8 are read twice and 10 is read four times. So the first output produces an incorrect total of 77, instead of the correct total of 55. In the second output, the Consumer reads the value -1 before the Producer ever writes a value. The Consumer reads the value 1 five times before the Producer writes the value 2. Meanwhile, the values 5, 7, 8, 9 and 10 are all lost—the last four because the Consumer terminates before the Producer. An incorrect consumer total of 19 is displayed. (Lines in the output where the Producer or Consumer has acted out of order are highlighted.)

Error-Prevention Tip 23.1

Access to a shared object by concurrent threads must be controlled carefully or a program may produce incorrect results.

To solve the problems of lost and duplicated data, Section 23.6 presents an example in which we use an ArrayBlockingQueue (from package java.util.concurrent) to synchronize access to the shared object, guaranteeing that each and every value will be processed once and only once.

23.6 Producer/Consumer Relationship: ArrayBlockingQueue

One way to synchronize producer and consumer threads is to use classes from Java's concurrency package that *encapsulate the synchronization for you*. Java includes the class **ArrayBlockingQueue** (from package java.util.concurrent)—a fully implemented, *thread-safe buffer class* that implements interface **BlockingQueue**. This interface extends the Queue interface discussed in Chapter 18 and declares methods **put** and **take**, the blocking equivalents of Queue methods offer and poll, respectively. Method put places an element at the end of the BlockingQueue, waiting if the queue is full. Method take removes an element from the head of the BlockingQueue, waiting if the queue is empty. These methods make class ArrayBlockingQueue a good choice for implementing a shared buffer. Because method put blocks until there's room in the buffer to write data, and method take blocks until there's new data to read, the producer must produce a value first, the consumer correctly consumes only after the producer writes a value and the producer correctly produces the next value (after the first) only after the consumer reads the previous (or first) value. ArrayBlockingQueue stores the shared data in an array. The array's size is specified as an argument to the ArrayBlockingQueue constructor. Once created, an ArrayBlockingQueue is fixed in size and will not expand to accommodate extra elements.

Figures 23.14–23.15 demonstrate a Producer and a Consumer accessing an Array-BlockingQueue. Class BlockingBuffer (Fig. 23.14) uses an ArrayBlockingQueue object that stores an Integer (line 7). Line 11 creates the ArrayBlockingQueue and passes 1 to the constructor so that the object holds a single value, as we did with the Unsynchronized-Buffer of Fig. 23.12. Lines 7 and 11 use generics, which we discussed in Chapters 18–19. We discuss multiple-element buffers in Section 23.8. Because our BlockingBuffer class uses the thread-safe ArrayBlockingQueue class to manage access to the shared buffer, BlockingBuffer is itself *thread safe*, even though we have not implemented the synchronization ourselves.

```
1   // Fig. 23.14: BlockingBuffer.java
2   // Creating a synchronized buffer using an ArrayBlockingQueue.
3   import java.util.concurrent.ArrayBlockingQueue;
4
5   public class BlockingBuffer implements Buffer
6   {
7      private final ArrayBlockingQueue<Integer> buffer; // shared buffer
8
9      public BlockingBuffer()
10     {
11        buffer = new ArrayBlockingQueue<Integer>( 1 );
12     } // end BlockingBuffer constructor
13
14     // place value into buffer
15     public void set( int value ) throws InterruptedException
16     {
17        buffer.put( value ); // place value in buffer
```

Fig. 23.14 | Creating a synchronized buffer using an ArrayBlockingQueue. (Part 1 of 2.)

```
18              System.out.printf( "%s%2d\t%s%d\n", "Producer writes ", value,
19                 "Buffer cells occupied: ", buffer.size() );
20          } // end method set
21
22          // return value from buffer
23          public int get() throws InterruptedException
24          {
25              int readValue = buffer.take(); // remove value from buffer
26              System.out.printf( "%s %2d\t%s%d\n", "Consumer reads ",
27                 readValue, "Buffer cells occupied: ", buffer.size() );
28
29              return readValue;
30          } // end method get
31      } // end class BlockingBuffer
```

Fig. 23.14 | Creating a synchronized buffer using an `ArrayBlockingQueue`. (Part 2 of 2.)

`BlockingBuffer` implements interface `Buffer` (Fig. 23.9) and uses classes `Producer` (Fig. 23.10 modified to remove line 28) and `Consumer` (Fig. 23.11 modified to remove line 28) from the example in Section 23.5. This approach demonstrates that *the threads accessing the shared object are unaware that their buffer accesses are now synchronized.* The synchronization is handled entirely in the `set` and `get` methods of `BlockingBuffer` by calling the synchronized `ArrayBlockingQueue` methods `put` and `take`, respectively. Thus, the `Producer` and `Consumer` `Runnable`s are properly synchronized simply by calling the shared object's `set` and `get` methods.

Line 17 in method `set` (Fig. 23.14, lines 15–20) calls the `ArrayBlockingQueue` object's `put` method. This method call blocks if necessary until there's room in the buffer to place the `value`. Method `get` (lines 23–30) calls the `ArrayBlockingQueue` object's `take` method (line 25). This method call blocks if necessary until there's an element in the buffer to remove. Lines 18–19 and 26–27 use the `ArrayBlockingQueue` object's **size** method to display the total number of elements currently in the `ArrayBlockingQueue`.

Class `BlockingBufferTest` (Fig. 23.15) contains the `main` method that launches the application. Line 12 creates an `ExecutorService`, and line 15 creates a `BlockingBuffer` object and assigns its reference to the `Buffer` variable `sharedLocation`. Lines 17–18 execute the `Producer` and `Consumer` `Runnable`s. Line 19 calls method `shutdown` to end the application when the threads finish executing the `Producer` and `Consumer` tasks.

```
1   // Fig. 23.15: BlockingBufferTest.java
2   // Two threads manipulating a blocking buffer that properly
3   // implements the producer/consumer relationship.
4   import java.util.concurrent.ExecutorService;
5   import java.util.concurrent.Executors;
6
7   public class BlockingBufferTest
8   {
9       public static void main( String[] args )
10      {
```

Fig. 23.15 | Two threads manipulating a blocking buffer that properly implements the producer/consumer relationship. (Part 1 of 2.)

```
11          // create new thread pool with two threads
12          ExecutorService application = Executors.newCachedThreadPool();
13
14          // create BlockingBuffer to store ints
15          Buffer sharedLocation = new BlockingBuffer();
16
17          application.execute( new Producer( sharedLocation ) );
18          application.execute( new Consumer( sharedLocation ) );
19
20          application.shutdown();
21      } // end main
22  } // end class BlockingBufferTest
```

```
Producer writes  1      Buffer cells occupied: 1
Consumer reads   1      Buffer cells occupied: 0
Producer writes  2      Buffer cells occupied: 1
Consumer reads   2      Buffer cells occupied: 0
Producer writes  3      Buffer cells occupied: 1
Consumer reads   3      Buffer cells occupied: 0
Producer writes  4      Buffer cells occupied: 1
Consumer reads   4      Buffer cells occupied: 0
Producer writes  5      Buffer cells occupied: 1
Consumer reads   5      Buffer cells occupied: 0
Producer writes  6      Buffer cells occupied: 1
Consumer reads   6      Buffer cells occupied: 0
Producer writes  7      Buffer cells occupied: 1
Consumer reads   7      Buffer cells occupied: 0
Producer writes  8      Buffer cells occupied: 1
Consumer reads   8      Buffer cells occupied: 0
Producer writes  9      Buffer cells occupied: 1
Consumer reads   9      Buffer cells occupied: 0
Producer writes 10      Buffer cells occupied: 1

Producer done producing
Terminating Producer
Consumer reads   10     Buffer cells occupied: 0

Consumer read values totaling 55
Terminating Consumer
```

Fig. 23.15 | Two threads manipulating a blocking buffer that properly implements the producer/consumer relationship. (Part 2 of 2.)

While methods put and take of ArrayBlockingQueue are properly synchronized, BlockingBuffer methods set and get (Fig. 23.14) are not declared to be synchronized. Thus, the statements performed in method set—the put operation (line 17) and the output (lines 18–19)—are *not atomic*; nor are the statements in method get—the take operation (line 25) and the output (lines 26–27). So there's no guarantee that each output will occur immediately after the corresponding put or take operation, and the outputs may appear out of order. Even if they do, the ArrayBlockingQueue object is properly synchronizing access to the data, as evidenced by the fact that the sum of values read by the consumer is always correct.

23.7 Producer/Consumer Relationship with Synchronization

The previous example showed how multiple threads can share a single-element buffer in a thread-safe manner by using the ArrayBlockingQueue class that encapsulates the synchronization necessary to protect the shared data. For educational purposes, we now explain how you can implement a shared buffer yourself using the synchronized keyword and methods of class Object. Using an ArrayBlockingQueue will result in more-maintainable and better-performing code.

The first step in synchronizing access to the buffer is to implement methods get and set as synchronized methods. This requires that a thread obtain the *monitor lock* on the Buffer object before attempting to access the buffer data, but it does not automatically ensure that threads proceed with an operation only if the buffer is in the proper state. We need a way to allow our threads to wait, depending on whether certain conditions are true. In the case of placing a new item in the buffer, the condition that allows the operation to proceed is that the *buffer is not full*. In the case of fetching an item from the buffer, the condition that allows the operation to proceed is that the *buffer is not empty*. If the condition in question is true, the operation may proceed; if it's false, the thread must wait until it becomes true. When a thread is waiting on a condition, it's removed from contention for the processor and placed into the *waiting* state and the lock it holds is released.

Methods wait, notify and notifyAll

Object methods wait, notify and notifyAll, which are inherited by all other classes, can be used with conditions to make threads *wait* when they cannot perform their tasks. If a thread obtains the *monitor lock* on an object, then determines that it cannot continue with its task on that object until some condition is satisfied, the thread can call Object method **wait** on the synchronized object; this releases the monitor lock on the object, and the thread waits in the *waiting* state while the other threads try to enter the object's synchronized statement(s) or method(s). When a thread executing a synchronized statement (or method) completes or satisfies the condition on which another thread may be waiting, it can call Object method **notify** on the synchronized object to allow a waiting thread to transition to the *runnable* state again. At this point, the thread that was transitioned from the *waiting* state to the *runnable* state can attempt to reacquire the monitor lock on the object. Even if the thread is able to reacquire the monitor lock, it still might not be able to perform its task at this time—in which case the thread will reenter the *waiting* state and implicitly release the monitor lock. If a thread calls **notifyAll** on the synchronized object, then *all* the threads waiting for the monitor lock become eligible to reacquire the lock (that is, they all transition to the *runnable* state).

Remember that only one thread at a time can obtain the monitor lock on the object—other threads that attempt to acquire the same monitor lock will be *blocked* until the monitor lock becomes available again (i.e., until no other thread is executing in a synchronized statement on that object).

Common Programming Error 23.1

It's an error if a thread issues a wait, a notify or a notifyAll on an object without having acquired a lock for it. This causes an **IllegalMonitorStateException**.

Error-Prevention Tip 23.2
It's a good practice to use notifyAll to notify waiting threads to become runnable. Doing so avoids the possibility that your program would forget about waiting threads, which would otherwise starve.

The application in Fig. 23.16 and Fig. 23.17 demonstrates a Producer and a Consumer accessing a shared buffer with synchronization. In this case, the Producer always produces a value *first*, the Consumer correctly consumes only *after* the Producer produces a value and the Producer correctly produces the next value only after the Consumer consumes the previous (or first) value. We reuse interface Buffer and classes Producer and Consumer from the example in Section 23.5, except that line 28 is removed from class Producer and class Consumer. The synchronization is handled in the set and get methods of class SynchronizedBuffer (Fig. 23.16), which implements interface Buffer (line 4). Thus, the Producer's and Consumer's run methods simply call the shared object's synchronized set and get methods.

```java
1   // Fig. 23.16: SynchronizedBuffer.java
2   // Synchronizing access to shared data using Object
3   // methods wait and notifyAll.
4   public class SynchronizedBuffer implements Buffer
5   {
6      private int buffer = -1; // shared by producer and consumer threads
7      private boolean occupied = false; // whether the buffer is occupied
8
9      // place value into buffer
10     public synchronized void set( int value ) throws InterruptedException
11     {
12        // while there are no empty locations, place thread in waiting state
13        while ( occupied )
14        {
15           // output thread information and buffer information, then wait
16           System.out.println( "Producer tries to write." );
17           displayState( "Buffer full. Producer waits." );
18           wait();
19        } // end while
20
21        buffer = value; // set new buffer value
22
23        // indicate producer cannot store another value
24        // until consumer retrieves current buffer value
25        occupied = true;
26
27        displayState( "Producer writes " + buffer );
28
29        notifyAll(); // tell waiting thread(s) to enter runnable state
30     } // end method set; releases lock on SynchronizedBuffer
31
```

Fig. 23.16 | Synchronizing access to shared data using Object methods wait and notifyAll. (Part 1 of 2.)

```
32        // return value from buffer
33        public synchronized int get() throws InterruptedException
34        {
35           // while no data to read, place thread in waiting state
36           while ( !occupied )
37           {
38              // output thread information and buffer information, then wait
39              System.out.println( "Consumer tries to read." );
40              displayState( "Buffer empty. Consumer waits." );
41              wait();
42           } // end while
43
44           // indicate that producer can store another value
45           // because consumer just retrieved buffer value
46           occupied = false;
47
48           displayState( "Consumer reads " + buffer );
49
50           notifyAll(); // tell waiting thread(s) to enter runnable state
51
52           return buffer;
53        } // end method get; releases lock on SynchronizedBuffer
54
55        // display current operation and buffer state
56        public void displayState( String operation )
57        {
58           System.out.printf( "%-40s%d\t\t%b\n\n", operation, buffer,
59              occupied );
60        } // end method displayState
61     } // end class SynchronizedBuffer
```

Fig. 23.16 | Synchronizing access to shared data using Object methods wait and notifyAll. (Part 2 of 2.)

*Fields and Methods of Class **SynchronizedBuffer***

Class SynchronizedBuffer contains fields buffer (line 6) and occupied (line 7). Methods set (lines 10–30) and get (lines 33–53) are declared as synchronized—only one thread can call either of these methods at a time on a particular SynchronizedBuffer object. Field occupied is used to determine whether it's the Producer's or the Consumer's turn to perform a task. This field is used in conditional expressions in both the set and get methods. If occupied is false, then buffer is empty, so the Consumer cannot read the value of buffer, but the Producer can place a value into buffer. If occupied is true, the Consumer can read a value from buffer, but the Producer cannot place a value into buffer.

*Method **set** and the **Producer** Thread*

When the Producer thread's run method invokes synchronized method set, the thread implicitly attempts to acquire the SynchronizedBuffer object's monitor lock. If the monitor lock is available, the Producer thread implicitly acquires the lock. Then the loop at lines 13–19 first determines whether occupied is true. If so, buffer is full, so line 16 outputs a message indicating that the Producer thread is trying to write a value, and line 17 invokes method displayState (lines 56–60) to output another message indicating that buffer is full and that the Producer thread is waiting until there's space. Line 18 invokes method wait (inherited from Object by SynchronizedBuffer) to place the thread that called method set (i.e., the Producer thread) in the *waiting* state for the SynchronizedBuffer object. The call to wait causes the calling thread to *implicitly* release the lock on the SynchronizedBuffer object. This is important because the thread cannot currently perform its task and because other threads (in this case, the Consumer) should be allowed to access the object to allow the condition (occupied) to change. Now another thread can attempt to acquire the SynchronizedBuffer object's lock and invoke the object's set or get method.

The Producer thread remains in the *waiting* state until another thread notifies the Producer that it may proceed—at which point the Producer returns to the *runnable* state and attempts to implicitly reacquire the lock on the SynchronizedBuffer object. If the lock is available, the Producer thread reacquires it, and method set continues executing with the next statement after the wait call. Because wait is called in a loop, the loop-continuation condition is tested again to determine whether the thread can proceed. If not, then wait is invoked again—otherwise, method set continues with the next statement after the loop.

Line 21 in method set assigns the value to the buffer. Line 25 sets occupied to true to indicate that the buffer now contains a value (i.e., a consumer can read the value, but a Producer cannot yet put another value there). Line 27 invokes method displayState to output a message indicating that the Producer is writing a new value into the buffer. Line 29 invokes method notifyAll (inherited from Object). If any threads are waiting on the SynchronizedBuffer object's monitor lock, those threads enter the *runnable* state and can now attempt to reacquire the lock. Method notifyAll returns immediately, and method set then returns to the caller (i.e., the Producer's run method). When method set returns, it implicitly releases the monitor lock on the SynchronizedBuffer object.

Method get and the Consumer Thread
Methods get and set are implemented similarly. When the Consumer thread's run method invokes synchronized method get, the thread attempts to acquire the *monitor lock* on the SynchronizedBuffer object. If the lock is available, the Consumer thread acquires it. Then the while loop at lines 36–42 determines whether occupied is false. If so, the buffer is empty, so line 39 outputs a message indicating that the Consumer thread is trying to read a value, and line 40 invokes method displayState to output a message indicating that the buffer is empty and that the Consumer thread is waiting. Line 41 invokes method wait to place the thread that called method get (i.e., the Consumer) in the *waiting* state for the SynchronizedBuffer object. Again, the call to wait causes the calling thread to implicitly release the lock on the SynchronizedBuffer object, so another thread can attempt to acquire the SynchronizedBuffer object's lock and invoke the object's set or get method. If the lock on the SynchronizedBuffer is not available (e.g., if the Producer has not yet returned from method set), the Consumer is blocked until the lock becomes available.

The Consumer thread remains in the *waiting* state until it's notified by another thread that it may proceed—at which point the Consumer thread returns to the *runnable* state and attempts to implicitly reacquire the lock on the SynchronizedBuffer object. If the lock is available, the Consumer reacquires it, and method get continues executing with the next statement after wait. Because wait is called in a loop, the loop-continuation condition is tested again to determine whether the thread can proceed with its execution. If not, wait is invoked again—otherwise, method get continues with the next statement after the loop.

Line 46 sets occupied to false to indicate that buffer is now empty (i.e., a Consumer cannot read the value, but a Producer can place another value in buffer), line 48 calls method displayState to indicate that the consumer is reading and line 50 invokes method notifyAll. If any threads are in the *waiting* state for the lock on this SynchronizedBuffer object, they enter the *runnable* state and can now attempt to reacquire the lock. Method notifyAll returns immediately, then method get returns the value of buffer to its caller. When method get returns, the lock on the SynchronizedBuffer object is implicitly released.

Error-Prevention Tip 23.3

Always invoke method wait in a loop that tests the condition the task is waiting on. It's possible that a thread will reenter the runnable *state (via a timed wait or another thread calling* notifyAll*) before the condition is satisfied. Testing the condition again ensures that the thread will not erroneously execute if it was notified early.*

Testing Class SynchronizedBuffer

Class SharedBufferTest2 (Fig. 23.17) is similar to class SharedBufferTest (Fig. 23.13). SharedBufferTest2 contains method main (lines 8–24), which launches the application. Line 11 creates an ExecutorService to run the Producer and Consumer tasks. Line 14 creates a SynchronizedBuffer object and assigns its reference to Buffer variable shared-Location. This object stores the data that will be shared between the Producer and Consumer. Lines 16–17 display the column heads for the output. Lines 20–21 execute a Producer and a Consumer. Finally, line 23 calls method shutdown to end the application when the Producer and Consumer complete their tasks. When method main ends (line 24), the main thread of execution terminates.

```
1   // Fig. 23.17: SharedBufferTest2.java
2   // Two threads correctly manipulating a synchronized buffer.
3   import java.util.concurrent.ExecutorService;
4   import java.util.concurrent.Executors;
5
6   public class SharedBufferTest2
7   {
8      public static void main( String[] args )
9      {
10        // create a newCachedThreadPool
11        ExecutorService application = Executors.newCachedThreadPool();
12
13        // create SynchronizedBuffer to store ints
14        Buffer sharedLocation = new SynchronizedBuffer();
15
16        System.out.printf( "%-40s%s\t\t%s\n%-40s%s\n\n", "Operation",
17           "Buffer", "Occupied", "---------", "------\t\t--------" );
18
19        // execute the Producer and Consumer tasks
20        application.execute( new Producer( sharedLocation ) );
21        application.execute( new Consumer( sharedLocation ) );
22
```

Fig. 23.17 | Two threads correctly manipulating a synchronized buffer. (Part 1 of 3.)

```
23          application.shutdown();
24      } // end main
25   } // end class SharedBufferTest2
```

Operation	Buffer	Occupied
---------	------	--------
Consumer tries to read. Buffer empty. Consumer waits.	-1	false
Producer writes 1	1	true
Consumer reads 1	1	false
Consumer tries to read. Buffer empty. Consumer waits.	1	false
Producer writes 2	2	true
Consumer reads 2	2	false
Producer writes 3	3	true
Consumer reads 3	3	false
Producer writes 4	4	true
Producer tries to write. Buffer full. Producer waits.	4	true
Consumer reads 4	4	false
Producer writes 5	5	true
Consumer reads 5	5	false
Producer writes 6	6	true
Producer tries to write. Buffer full. Producer waits.	6	true
Consumer reads 6	6	false
Producer writes 7	7	true
Producer tries to write. Buffer full. Producer waits.	7	true
Consumer reads 7	7	false
Producer writes 8	8	true
Consumer reads 8	8	false
Consumer tries to read. Buffer empty. Consumer waits.	8	false

Fig. 23.17 | Two threads correctly manipulating a synchronized buffer. (Part 2 of 3.)

```
Producer writes 9                      9              true

Consumer reads 9                       9              false

Consumer tries to read.
Buffer empty. Consumer waits.          9              false

Producer writes 10                    10              true

Consumer reads 10                     10              false


Producer done producing
Terminating Producer

Consumer read values totaling 55
Terminating Consumer
```

Fig. 23.17 | Two threads correctly manipulating a synchronized buffer. (Part 3 of 3.)

Study the outputs in Fig. 23.17. Observe that *every integer produced is consumed exactly once—no values are lost, and no values are consumed more than once.* The synchronization ensures that the Producer produces a value only when the buffer is empty and the Consumer consumes only when the buffer is full. The Producer always goes first, the Consumer waits if the Producer has not produced since the Consumer last consumed, and the Producer waits if the Consumer has not yet consumed the value that the Producer most recently produced. Execute this program several times to confirm that every integer produced is consumed exactly once. In the sample output, note the highlighted lines indicating when the Producer and Consumer must wait to perform their respective tasks.

23.8 Producer/Consumer Relationship: Bounded Buffers

The program in Section 23.7 uses thread synchronization to guarantee that two threads manipulate data in a shared buffer correctly. However, the application may not perform optimally. If the two threads operate at different speeds, one them will spend more (or most) of its time waiting. For example, in the program in Section 23.7 we shared a single integer variable between the two threads. If the Producer thread produces values faster than the Consumer can consume them, then the Producer thread *waits* for the Consumer, because there are no other locations in the buffer in which to place the next value. Similarly, if the Consumer consumes values faster than the Producer produces them, the Consumer *waits* until the Producer places the next value in the shared buffer. Even when we have threads that operate at the same relative speeds, those threads may occasionally become "out of sync" over a period of time, causing one of them to wait for the other. *We cannot make assumptions about the relative speeds of concurrent threads*—interactions that occur with the operating system, the network, the user and other components can cause the threads to operate at different and ever-changing speeds. When this happens, threads wait. When threads wait excessively, programs become less efficient, interactive programs become less responsive and applications suffer longer delays.

Bounded Buffers

To minimize the amount of waiting time for threads that share resources and operate at the same average speeds, we can implement a **bounded buffer** that provides a fixed number of buffer cells into which the Producer can place values, and from which the Consumer can retrieve those values. (In fact, we've already done this with the ArrayBlockingQueue class in Section 23.6.) If the Producer temporarily produces values faster than the Consumer can consume them, the Producer can write additional values into the extra buffer cells, if any are available. This capability enables the Producer to perform its task even though the Consumer is not ready to retrieve the current value being produced. Similarly, if the Consumer consumes faster than the Producer produces new values, the Consumer can read additional values (if there are any) from the buffer. This enables the Consumer to keep busy even though the Producer is not ready to produce additional values.

Even a *bounded buffer* is inappropriate if the Producer and the Consumer operate consistently at different speeds. If the Consumer always executes faster than the Producer, then a buffer containing one location is enough. Additional locations would simply waste memory. If the Producer always executes faster, only a buffer with an "infinite" number of locations would be able to absorb the extra production. However, if the Producer and Consumer execute at about the same average speed, a bounded buffer helps to smooth the effects of any occasional speeding up or slowing down in either thread's execution.

The key to using a *bounded buffer* with a Producer and Consumer that operate at about the same speed is to provide the buffer with enough locations to handle the anticipated "extra" production. If, over a period of time, we determine that the Producer often produces as many as three more values than the Consumer can consume, we can provide a buffer of at least three cells to handle the extra production. Making the buffer too small would cause threads to wait longer; making the buffer too large would waste memory.

Performance Tip 23.3

Even when using a bounded buffer, it's possible that a producer thread could fill the buffer, which would force the producer to wait until a consumer consumed a value to free an element in the buffer. Similarly, if the buffer is empty at any given time, a consumer thread must wait until the producer produces another value. The key to using a bounded buffer is to optimize the buffer size to minimize the amount of thread wait time, while not wasting space.

Bounded Buffers Using ArrayBlockingQueue

The simplest way to implement a bounded buffer is to use an ArrayBlockingQueue for the buffer so that *all of the synchronization details are handled for you*. This can be done by modifying the example from Section 23.6 to pass the desired size for the bounded buffer into the ArrayBlockingQueue constructor. Rather than repeat our previous ArrayBlockingQueue example with a different size, we instead present an example that illustrates how you can build a bounded buffer yourself. Again, using an ArrayBlockingQueue will result in more-maintainable and better-performing code.

Implementing Your Own Bounded Buffer as a Circular Buffer

The program in Fig. 23.18 and Fig. 23.19 demonstrates a Producer and a Consumer accessing a *bounded buffer with synchronization*. Again, we reuse interface Buffer and classes

Producer and Consumer from the example in Section 23.5, except that line 28 is removed from class Producer and class Consumer. We implement the bounded buffer in class CircularBuffer (Fig. 23.18) as a **circular buffer** that uses a shared array of three elements. A circular buffer writes into and reads from the array elements in order, beginning at the first cell and moving toward the last. When a Producer or Consumer reaches the last element, it returns to the first and begins writing or reading, respectively, from there. In this version of the producer/consumer relationship, the Consumer consumes a value only when the array is not empty and the Producer produces a value only when the array is not full. The statements that created and started the thread objects in the main method of class SharedBufferTest2 (Fig. 23.17) now appear in class CircularBufferTest (Fig. 23.19).

```java
1   // Fig. 23.18: CircularBuffer.java
2   // Synchronizing access to a shared three-element bounded buffer.
3   public class CircularBuffer implements Buffer
4   {
5      private final int[] buffer = { -1, -1, -1 }; // shared buffer
6
7      private int occupiedCells = 0; // count number of buffers used
8      private int writeIndex = 0; // index of next element to write to
9      private int readIndex = 0; // index of next element to read
10
11     // place value into buffer
12     public synchronized void set( int value ) throws InterruptedException
13     {
14        // wait until buffer has space available, then write value;
15        // while no empty locations, place thread in blocked state
16        while ( occupiedCells == buffer.length )
17        {
18           System.out.printf( "Buffer is full. Producer waits.\n" );
19           wait(); // wait until a buffer cell is free
20        } // end while
21
22        buffer[ writeIndex ] = value; // set new buffer value
23
24        // update circular write index
25        writeIndex = ( writeIndex + 1 ) % buffer.length;
26
27        ++occupiedCells; // one more buffer cell is full
28        displayState( "Producer writes " + value );
29        notifyAll(); // notify threads waiting to read from buffer
30     } // end method set
31
32     // return value from buffer
33     public synchronized int get() throws InterruptedException
34     {
35        // wait until buffer has data, then read value;
36        // while no data to read, place thread in waiting state
37        while ( occupiedCells == 0 )
38        {
39           System.out.printf( "Buffer is empty. Consumer waits.\n" );
```

Fig. 23.18 | Synchronizing access to a shared three-element bounded buffer. (Part 1 of 2.)

```
40              wait(); // wait until a buffer cell is filled
41          } // end while
42
43          int readValue = buffer[ readIndex ]; // read value from buffer
44
45          // update circular read index
46          readIndex = ( readIndex + 1 ) % buffer.length;
47
48          --occupiedCells; // one fewer buffer cells are occupied
49          displayState( "Consumer reads " + readValue );
50          notifyAll(); // notify threads waiting to write to buffer
51
52          return readValue;
53      } // end method get
54
55      // display current operation and buffer state
56      public void displayState( String operation )
57      {
58          // output operation and number of occupied buffer cells
59          System.out.printf( "%s%s%d)\n%s", operation,
60             " (buffer cells occupied: ", occupiedCells, "buffer cells:   " );
61
62          for ( int value : buffer )
63             System.out.printf( " %2d  ", value ); // output values in buffer
64
65          System.out.print( "\n                " );
66
67          for ( int i = 0; i < buffer.length; i++ )
68             System.out.print( "---- " );
69
70          System.out.print( "\n                " );
71
72          for ( int i = 0; i < buffer.length; i++ )
73          {
74             if ( i == writeIndex && i == readIndex )
75                System.out.print( " WR" ); // both write and read index
76             else if ( i == writeIndex )
77                System.out.print( " W  " ); // just write index
78             else if ( i == readIndex )
79                System.out.print( "  R  " ); // just read index
80             else
81                System.out.print( "      " ); // neither index
82          } // end for
83
84          System.out.println( "\n" );
85      } // end method displayState
86  } // end class CircularBuffer
```

Fig. 23.18 | Synchronizing access to a shared three-element bounded buffer. (Part 2 of 2.)

Line 5 initializes array buffer as a three-element int array that represents the circular buffer. Variable occupiedCells (line 7) counts the number of elements in buffer that contain data to be read. When occupiedBuffers is 0, there's no data in the circular buffer and the Consumer must wait—when occupiedCells is 3 (the size of the circular buffer), the circular buffer is full and the Producer must wait. Variable writeIndex (line 8) indicates the next location in which a value can be placed by a Producer. Variable readIndex (line 9) indicates the position from which the next value can be read by a Consumer.

CircularBuffer Method set

CircularBuffer method set (lines 12–30) performs the same tasks as in Fig. 23.16, with a few modifications. The loop at lines 16–20 determines whether the Producer must wait (i.e., all buffer cells are full). If so, line 18 indicates that the Producer is waiting to perform its task. Then line 19 invokes method wait, causing the Producer thread to release the CircularBuffer's lock and wait until there's space for a new value to be written into the buffer. When execution continues at line 22 after the while loop, the value written by the Producer is placed in the circular buffer at location writeIndex. Then line 25 updates writeIndex for the next call to CircularBuffer method set. This line is the key to the buffer's *circularity*. When writeIndex is incremented past the end of the buffer, the line sets it to 0. Line 27 increments occupiedCells, because there's now one more value in the buffer that the Consumer can read. Next, line 28 invokes method displayState (lines 56–85) to update the output with the value produced, the number of occupied buffer cells, the contents of the buffer cells and the current writeIndex and readIndex. Line 29 invokes method notifyAll to transition *waiting* threads to the *runnable* state, so that a waiting Consumer thread (if there is one) can now try again to read a value from the buffer.

CircularBuffer Method get

CircularBuffer method get (lines 33–53) also performs the same tasks as it did in Fig. 23.16, with a few minor modifications. The loop at lines 37–41 determines whether the Consumer must wait (i.e., all buffer cells are empty). If the Consumer must wait, line 39 updates the output to indicate that the Consumer is waiting to perform its task. Then line 40 invokes method wait, causing the current thread to release the lock on the CircularBuffer and wait until data is available to read. When execution eventually continues at line 43 after a notifyAll call from the Producer, readValue is assigned the value at location readIndex in the circular buffer. Then line 46 updates readIndex for the next call to CircularBuffer method get. This line and line 25 implement the *circularity* of the buffer. Line 48 decrements occupiedCells, because there's now one more position in the buffer in which the Producer thread can place a value. Line 49 invokes method displayState to update the output with the consumed value, the number of occupied buffer cells, the contents of the buffer cells and the current writeIndex and readIndex. Line 50 invokes method notifyAll to allow any Producer threads waiting to write into the CircularBuffer object to attempt to write again. Then line 52 returns the consumed value to the caller.

CircularBuffer Method displayState

Method displayState (lines 56–85) outputs the application's state. Lines 62–63 output the values of the buffer cells. Line 63 uses method printf with a "%2d" format specifier to print the contents of each buffer with a leading space if it's a single digit. Lines 70–82 output the current writeIndex and readIndex with the letters W and R, respectively.

Testing Class CircularBuffer

Class CircularBufferTest (Fig. 23.19) contains the main method that launches the application. Line 11 creates the ExecutorService, and line 14 creates a CircularBuffer object and assigns its reference to CircularBuffer variable sharedLocation. Line 17 invokes the CircularBuffer's displayState method to show the initial state of the buffer. Lines 20–21 execute the Producer and Consumer tasks. Line 23 calls method shutdown to end the application when the threads complete the Producer and Consumer tasks.

Each time the Producer writes a value or the Consumer reads a value, the program outputs a message indicating the action performed (a read or a write), the contents of buffer, and the location of writeIndex and readIndex. In the output of Fig. 23.19, the Producer first writes the value 1. The buffer then contains the value 1 in the first cell and the value –1 (the default value that we use for output purposes) in the other two cells. The write index is updated to the second cell, while the read index stays at the first cell. Next, the Consumer reads 1. The buffer contains the same values, but the read index has been updated to the second cell. The Consumer then tries to read again, but the buffer is empty and the Consumer is forced to wait. Only once in this execution of the program was it necessary for either thread to wait.

```
1   // Fig. 23.19: CircularBufferTest.java
2   // Producer and Consumer threads manipulating a circular buffer.
3   import java.util.concurrent.ExecutorService;
4   import java.util.concurrent.Executors;
5
6   public class CircularBufferTest
7   {
8      public static void main( String[] args )
9      {
10        // create new thread pool with two threads
11        ExecutorService application = Executors.newCachedThreadPool();
12
13        // create CircularBuffer to store ints
14        CircularBuffer sharedLocation = new CircularBuffer();
15
16        // display the initial state of the CircularBuffer
17        sharedLocation.displayState( "Initial State" );
18
19        // execute the Producer and Consumer tasks
20        application.execute( new Producer( sharedLocation ) );
21        application.execute( new Consumer( sharedLocation ) );
22
23        application.shutdown();
24     } // end main
25  } // end class CircularBufferTest
```

```
Initial State (buffer cells occupied: 0)
buffer cells:    -1   -1   -1
                ---- ---- ----
                WR

Producer writes 1 (buffer cells occupied: 1)
buffer cells:    1   -1   -1
                ---- ---- ----
                 R    W
```

Fig. 23.19 | Producer and Consumer threads manipulating a circular buffer. (Part 1 of 3.)

```
Consumer reads 1 (buffer cells occupied: 0)
buffer cells:    1    -1    -1
                ----  ----  ----
                       WR

Buffer is empty. Consumer waits.
Producer writes 2 (buffer cells occupied: 1)
buffer cells:    1     2    -1
                ----  ----  ----
                 R     W

Consumer reads 2 (buffer cells occupied: 0)
buffer cells:    1     2    -1
                ----  ----  ----
                       WR

Producer writes 3 (buffer cells occupied: 1)
buffer cells:    1     2     3
                ----  ----  ----
                 W           R

Consumer reads 3 (buffer cells occupied: 0)
buffer cells:    1     2     3
                ----  ----  ----
                 WR

Producer writes 4 (buffer cells occupied: 1)
buffer cells:    4     2     3
                ----  ----  ----
                 R     W

Producer writes 5 (buffer cells occupied: 2)
buffer cells:    4     5     3
                ----  ----  ----
                 R           W

Consumer reads 4 (buffer cells occupied: 1)
buffer cells:    4     5     3
                ----  ----  ----
                       R     W

Producer writes 6 (buffer cells occupied: 2)
buffer cells:    4     5     6
                ----  ----  ----
                 W     R

Producer writes 7 (buffer cells occupied: 3)
buffer cells:    7     5     6
                ----  ----  ----
                       WR

Consumer reads 5 (buffer cells occupied: 2)
buffer cells:    7     5     6
                ----  ----  ----
                 W           R

Producer writes 8 (buffer cells occupied: 3)
buffer cells:    7     8     6
                ----  ----  ----
                       WR
```

Fig. 23.19 | Producer and Consumer threads manipulating a circular buffer. (Part 2 of 3.)

```
Consumer reads 6 (buffer cells occupied: 2)
buffer cells:    7    8    6
                ---- ---- ----
                 R         W

Consumer reads 7 (buffer cells occupied: 1)
buffer cells:    7    8    6
                ---- ---- ----
                 R    W

Producer writes 9 (buffer cells occupied: 2)
buffer cells:    7    8    9
                ---- ---- ----
                 W    R

Consumer reads 8 (buffer cells occupied: 1)
buffer cells:    7    8    9
                ---- ---- ----
                 W         R

Consumer reads 9 (buffer cells occupied: 0)
buffer cells:    7    8    9
                ---- ---- ----
                 WR

Producer writes 10 (buffer cells occupied: 1)
buffer cells:   10    8    9
                ---- ---- ----
                 R    W


Producer done producing
Terminating Producer
Consumer reads 10 (buffer cells occupied: 0)
buffer cells:   10    8    9
                ---- ---- ----
                      WR

Consumer read values totaling: 55
Terminating Consumer
```

Fig. 23.19 | Producer and Consumer threads manipulating a circular buffer. (Part 3 of 3.)

23.9 Producer/Consumer Relationship: The Lock and Condition Interfaces

Though the synchronized keyword provides for most basic thread-synchronization needs, Java provides other tools to assist in developing concurrent programs. In this section, we discuss the Lock and Condition interfaces. These interfaces give you more precise control over thread synchronization, but are more complicated to use.

Interface Lock and Class ReentrantLock

Any object can contain a reference to an object that implements the **Lock** interface (of package java.util.concurrent.locks). A thread calls the Lock's **lock** method (analogous to entering a synchronized block) to acquire the lock. Once a Lock has been obtained by one thread, the Lock object will not allow another thread to obtain the Lock until the first thread releases the Lock (by calling the Lock's **unlock** method—analogous to exiting a `synchronized` block). If several threads are trying to call method `lock` on the same `Lock` object at the same time, only one of these threads can obtain the lock—all the others are placed in the *waiting* state for that lock. When a thread calls method `unlock`, the lock on the object is released and a waiting thread attempting to lock the object proceeds.

Class **`ReentrantLock`** (of package `java.util.concurrent.locks`) is a basic implementation of the `Lock` interface. The constructor for a `ReentrantLock` takes a `boolean` argument that specifies whether the lock has a **fairness policy**. If the argument is `true`, the `ReentrantLock`'s fairness policy is "the longest-waiting thread will acquire the lock when it's available." Such a fairness policy guarantees that *indefinite postponement* (also called *starvation*) cannot occur. If the fairness policy argument is set to `false`, there's no guarantee as to which waiting thread will acquire the lock when it's available.

Software Engineering Observation 23.3
Using a `ReentrantLock` with a fairness policy avoids indefinite postponement.

Performance Tip 23.4
Using a `ReentrantLock` with a fairness policy can decrease program performance.

Condition Objects and Interface `Condition`

If a thread that owns a `Lock` determines that it cannot continue with its task until some condition is satisfied, the thread can wait on a **condition object**. Using `Lock` objects allows you to explicitly declare the condition objects on which a thread may need to wait. For example, in the producer/consumer relationship, producers can wait on *one* object and consumers can wait on *another*. This is not possible when using the `synchronized` keywords and an object's built-in monitor lock. Condition objects are associated with a specific `Lock` and are created by calling a `Lock`'s **`newCondition`** method, which returns an object that implements the **`Condition`** interface (of package `java.util.concurrent.locks`). To wait on a condition object, the thread can call the `Condition`'s **`await`** method (analogous to `Object` method `wait`). This immediately releases the associated `Lock` and places the thread in the *waiting* state for that `Condition`. Other threads can then try to obtain the `Lock`. When a *runnable* thread completes a task and determines that the *waiting* thread can now continue, the *runnable* thread can call `Condition` method **`signal`** (analogous to `Object` method `notify`) to allow a thread in that `Condition`'s *waiting* state to return to the *runnable* state. At this point, the thread that transitioned from the *waiting* state to the *runnable* state can attempt to reacquire the `Lock`. Even if it's able to reacquire the `Lock`, the thread still might not be able to perform its task at this time—in which case the thread can call the `Condition`'s `await` method to release the `Lock` and reenter the *waiting* state. If multiple threads are in a `Condition`'s *waiting* state when `signal` is called, the default implementation of `Condition` signals the longest-waiting thread to transition to the *runnable* state. If a thread calls `Condition` method **`signalAll`** (analogous to `Object` method `notifyAll`), then all the threads waiting for that condition transition to the *runnable* state and become eligible to reacquire the `Lock`. Only one of those threads can obtain the `Lock` on the object—the others will wait until the `Lock` becomes available again. If the `Lock` has a *fairness policy*, the longest-waiting thread acquires the `Lock`. When a thread is finished with a shared object, it must call method `unlock` to release the `Lock`.

Common Programming Error 23.2

Deadlock occurs when a waiting thread (let's call this thread1) cannot proceed because it's waiting (either directly or indirectly) for another thread (let's call this thread2) to proceed, while simultaneously thread2 cannot proceed because it's waiting (either directly or indirectly) for thread1 to proceed. The two threads are waiting for each other, so the actions that would enable each thread to continue execution can never occur.

Error-Prevention Tip 23.4

When multiple threads manipulate a shared object using locks, ensure that if one thread calls method await *to enter the* waiting *state for a condition object, a separate thread eventually will call* Condition *method* signal *to transition the thread waiting on the condition object back to the* runnable *state. If multiple threads may be waiting on the condition object, a separate thread can call* Condition *method* signalAll *as a safeguard to ensure that all the waiting threads have another opportunity to perform their tasks. If this is not done, starvation might occur.*

Common Programming Error 23.3

An IllegalMonitorStateException *occurs if a thread issues an* await, *a* signal, *or a* signalAll *on a* Condition *object that was created from a* ReentrantLock *without having acquired the lock for that* Condition *object.*

Lock *and* Condition *vs. the* synchronized *Keyword*

In some applications, using Lock and Condition objects may be preferable to using the synchronized keyword. Locks allow you to *interrupt* waiting threads or to specify a *timeout* for waiting to acquire a lock, which is not possible using the synchronized keyword. Also, a Lock is *not* constrained to be acquired and released in the *same* block of code, which is the case with the synchronized keyword. Condition objects allow you to specify multiple conditions on which threads may wait. Thus, it's possible to indicate to waiting threads that a specific condition object is now true by calling signal or signalAll on that Condition object. With synchronized, there's no way to explicitly state the condition on which threads are waiting, and thus there's no way to notify threads waiting on one condition that they may proceed without also signaling threads waiting on any other conditions. There are other possible advantages to using Lock and Condition objects, but generally it's best to use the synchronized keyword unless your application requires advanced synchronization capabilities.

Error-Prevention Tip 23.5

Using interfaces Lock *and* Condition *is error prone—*unlock *is not guaranteed to be called, whereas the monitor in a* synchronized *statement will always be released when the statement completes execution.*

Using Locks *and* Conditions *to Implement Synchronization*

To illustrate how to use the Lock and Condition interfaces, we now implement the producer/consumer relationship using Lock and Condition objects to coordinate access to a shared single-element buffer (Fig. 23.20 and Fig. 23.21). In this case, each produced value is correctly consumed exactly once. Again, we reuse interface Buffer and classes Producer and Consumer from the example in Section 23.5, except that line 28 is removed from class Producer and class Consumer.

Class SynchronizedBuffer (Fig. 23.20) contains five fields. Line 11 creates a new object of type ReentrantLock and assigns its reference to Lock variable accessLock. The ReentrantLock is created without the *fairness policy* because at any time only a single Producer or Consumer will be waiting to acquire the Lock in this example. Lines 14–15 create two Conditions using Lock method newCondition. Condition canWrite contains a queue for a Producer thread waiting while the buffer is full (i.e., there's data in the buffer that the Consumer has not read yet). If the buffer is full, the Producer calls method await on this Condition. When the Consumer reads data from a full buffer, it calls method signal on this Condition. Condition canRead contains a queue for a Consumer thread waiting while the buffer is empty (i.e., there's no data in the buffer for the Consumer to read). If the buffer is empty, the Consumer calls method await on this Condition. When the Producer writes to the empty buffer, it calls method signal on this Condition. The int variable buffer (line 17) holds the shared data. The boolean variable occupied (line 18) keeps track of whether the buffer currently holds data (that the Consumer should read).

```java
1   // Fig. 23.20: SynchronizedBuffer.java
2   // Synchronizing access to a shared integer using the Lock and Condition
3   // interfaces
4   import java.util.concurrent.locks.Lock;
5   import java.util.concurrent.locks.ReentrantLock;
6   import java.util.concurrent.locks.Condition;
7
8   public class SynchronizedBuffer implements Buffer
9   {
10     // Lock to control synchronization with this buffer
11     private final Lock accessLock = new ReentrantLock();
12
13     // conditions to control reading and writing
14     private final Condition canWrite = accessLock.newCondition();
15     private final Condition canRead = accessLock.newCondition();
16
17     private int buffer = -1; // shared by producer and consumer threads
18     private boolean occupied = false; // whether buffer is occupied
19
20     // place int value into buffer
21     public void set( int value ) throws InterruptedException
22     {
23        accessLock.lock(); // lock this object
24
25        // output thread information and buffer information, then wait
26        try
27        {
28           // while buffer is not empty, place thread in waiting state
29           while ( occupied )
30           {
31              System.out.println( "Producer tries to write." );
32              displayState( "Buffer full. Producer waits." );
33              canWrite.await(); // wait until buffer is empty
34           } // end while
```

Fig. 23.20 | Synchronizing access to a shared integer using the Lock and Condition interfaces. (Part I of 3.)

```
35
36            buffer = value; // set new buffer value
37
38            // indicate producer cannot store another value
39            // until consumer retrieves current buffer value
40            occupied = true;
41
42            displayState( "Producer writes " + buffer );
43
44            // signal any threads waiting to read from buffer
45            canRead.signalAll();
46         } // end try
47         finally
48         {
49            accessLock.unlock(); // unlock this object
50         } // end finally
51      } // end method set
52
53      // return value from buffer
54      public int get() throws InterruptedException
55      {
56         int readValue = 0; // initialize value read from buffer
57         accessLock.lock(); // lock this object
58
59         // output thread information and buffer information, then wait
60         try
61         {
62            // if there is no data to read, place thread in waiting state
63            while ( !occupied )
64            {
65               System.out.println( "Consumer tries to read." );
66               displayState( "Buffer empty. Consumer waits." );
67               canRead.await(); // wait until buffer is full
68            } // end while
69
70            // indicate that producer can store another value
71            // because consumer just retrieved buffer value
72            occupied = false;
73
74            readValue = buffer; // retrieve value from buffer
75            displayState( "Consumer reads " + readValue );
76
77            // signal any threads waiting for buffer to be empty
78            canWrite.signalAll();
79         } // end try
80         finally
81         {
82            accessLock.unlock(); // unlock this object
83         } // end finally
84
85         return readValue;
86      } // end method get
```

Fig. 23.20 | Synchronizing access to a shared integer using the Lock and Condition interfaces. (Part 2 of 3.)

```
87
88      // display current operation and buffer state
89      public void displayState( String operation )
90      {
91         System.out.printf( "%-40s%d\t\t%b\n\n", operation, buffer,
92            occupied );
93      } // end method displayState
94   } // end class SynchronizedBuffer
```

Fig. 23.20 | Synchronizing access to a shared integer using the `Lock` and `Condition` interfaces. (Part 3 of 3.)

Line 23 in method `set` calls method `lock` on the `SynchronizedBuffer`'s `accessLock`. If the lock is available (i.e., no other thread has acquired it), this thread now owns the lock and the thread continues. If the lock is unavailable (i.e., it's held by another thread), method `lock` waits until the lock is released. After the lock is acquired, lines 26–46 execute. Line 29 tests `occupied` to determine whether `buffer` is full. If it is, lines 31–32 display a message indicating that the thread will wait. Line 33 calls `Condition` method `await` on the `canWrite` condition object, which temporarily releases the `SynchronizedBuffer`'s `Lock` and waits for a signal from the `Consumer` that `buffer` is available for writing. When `buffer` is available, the method proceeds, writing to `buffer` (line 36), setting `occupied` to `true` (line 40) and displaying a message indicating that the producer wrote a value (line 42). Line 45 calls `Condition` method `signal` on condition object `canRead` to notify the waiting `Consumer` (if there is one) that the buffer has new data to be read. Line 49 calls method `unlock` from a `finally` block to release the lock and allow the `Consumer` to proceed.

> **Error-Prevention Tip 23.6**
>
> *Place calls to Lock method `unlock` in a `finally` block. If an exception is thrown, `unlock` must still be called or deadlock could occur.*

Line 57 of method `get` (lines 54–86) calls method `lock` to acquire the `Lock`. This method waits until the `Lock` is available. Once the `Lock` is acquired, line 63 tests whether `occupied` is `false`, indicating that the buffer is empty. If so, line 67 calls method `await` on condition object `canRead`. Recall that method `signal` is called on variable `canRead` in the `set` method (line 45). When the `Condition` object is signaled, the `get` method continues. Line 72–74 set `occupied` to `false`, store the value of `buffer` in `readValue` and output the `readValue`. Then line 78 signals the condition object `canWrite`. This awakens the Producer if it's indeed waiting for the buffer to be emptied. Line 82 calls method `unlock` from a `finally` block to release the lock, and line 85 returns `readValue` to the caller.

> **Common Programming Error 23.4**
>
> *Forgetting to `signal` a waiting thread is a logic error. The thread will remain in the waiting state, which will prevent it from proceeding. Such waiting can lead to indefinite postponement or deadlock.*

Class `SharedBufferTest2` (Fig. 23.21) is identical to that of Fig. 23.17. Study the outputs in Fig. 23.21. *Observe that every integer produced is consumed exactly once—no values are lost, and no values are consumed more than once.* The `Lock` and `Condition` objects ensure that the `Producer` and `Consumer` cannot perform their tasks unless it's their turn.

The `Producer` must go first, the `Consumer` must wait if the `Producer` has not produced since the `Consumer` last consumed and the `Producer` must wait if the `Consumer` has not yet consumed the value that the `Producer` most recently produced. Execute this program several times to confirm that every integer produced is consumed exactly once. In the sample output, note the highlighted lines indicating when the `Producer` and `Consumer` must wait to perform their respective tasks.

```java
1    // Fig. 23.21: SharedBufferTest2.java
2    // Two threads manipulating a synchronized buffer.
3    import java.util.concurrent.ExecutorService;
4    import java.util.concurrent.Executors;
5
6    public class SharedBufferTest2
7    {
8       public static void main( String[] args )
9       {
10         // create new thread pool with two threads
11         ExecutorService application = Executors.newCachedThreadPool();
12
13         // create SynchronizedBuffer to store ints
14         Buffer sharedLocation = new SynchronizedBuffer();
15
16         System.out.printf( "%-40s%s\t\t%s\n%-40s%s\n\n", "Operation",
17            "Buffer", "Occupied", "---------", "------\t\t--------" );
18
19         // execute the Producer and Consumer tasks
20         application.execute( new Producer( sharedLocation ) );
21         application.execute( new Consumer( sharedLocation ) );
22
23         application.shutdown();
24      } // end main
25   } // end class SharedBufferTest2
```

Operation	Buffer	Occupied
---------	------	--------
Producer writes 1	1	true
Producer tries to write. Buffer full. Producer waits.	1	true
Consumer reads 1	1	false
Producer writes 2	2	true
Producer tries to write. Buffer full. Producer waits.	2	true
Consumer reads 2	2	false
Producer writes 3	3	true
Consumer reads 3	3	false

Fig. 23.21 | Two threads manipulating a synchronized buffer. (Part 1 of 2.)

Producer writes 4	4	true
Consumer reads 4	4	false
Consumer tries to read. Buffer empty. Consumer waits.	4	false
Producer writes 5	5	true
Consumer reads 5	5	false
Consumer tries to read. Buffer empty. Consumer waits.	5	false
Producer writes 6	6	true
Consumer reads 6	6	false
Producer writes 7	7	true
Consumer reads 7	7	false
Producer writes 8	8	true
Consumer reads 8	8	false
Producer writes 9	9	true
Consumer reads 9	9	false
Producer writes 10	10	true
Producer done producing Terminating Producer Consumer reads 10	10	false
Consumer read values totaling 55 Terminating Consumer		

Fig. 23.21 | Two threads manipulating a synchronized buffer. (Part 2 of 2.)

23.10 Concurrent Collections Overview

In Chapter 18, we introduced various collections from the Java Collections API. We also mentioned that you can obtain synchronized versions of those collections to allow only one thread at a time to access a collection that might be shared among several threads. The collections from the java.util.concurrent package are specifically designed and optimized for use in programs that share collections among multiple threads.

Figure 23.22 lists the many concurrent collections in package java.util.concurrent. For more information on these collections, visit

```
download.oracle.com/javase/6/docs/api/java/util/concurrent/
    package-summary.html
```

For information on the additional concurrent collections that are new in Java SE 7, visit

```
download.java.net/jdk7/docs/api/java/util/concurrent/
    package-summary.html
```

Collection	Description
ArrayBlockingQueue	A fixed-size queue that supports the producer/consumer relationship—possibly with many producers and consumers.
ConcurrentHashMap	A hash-based map that allows an arbitrary number of reader threads and a limited number of writer threads.
ConcurrentLinkedQueue	A concurrent linked-list implementation of a queue that can grow dynamically.
ConcurrentSkipListMap	A concurrent map that is sorted by its keys.
ConcurrentSkipListSet	A sorted concurrent set.
CopyOnWriteArrayList	A thread-safe ArrayList. Each operation that modifies the collection first creates a new copy of the contents. Used when the collection is traversed much more frequently than the collection's contents are modified.
CopyOnWriteArraySet	A set that's implemented using CopyOnWriteArrayList.
DelayQueue	A variable-size queue containing Delayed objects. An object can be removed only after its delay has expired.
LinkedBlockingDeque	A double-ended blocking queue implemented as a linked list that can optionally be fixed in size.
LinkedBlockingQueue	A blocking queue implemented as a linked list that can optionally be fixed in size.
PriorityBlockingQueue	A variable-length priority-based blocking queue (like a PriorityQueue).
SynchronousQueue	A blocking queue implementation that does not have an internal capacity. Each insert operation by one thread must wait for a remove operation from another thread and vice versa.
Concurrent Collections Added in Java SE 7	
ConcurrentLinkedDeque	A concurrent linked-list implementation of a double-ended queue.
LinkedTransferQueue	A linked-list implementation of interface TransferQueue. Each producer has the option of waiting for a consumer to take an element being inserted (via method transfer) or simply placing the element into the queue (via method put). Also provides overloaded method tryTransfer to immediately transfer an element to a waiting consumer or to do so within a specified timeout period. If the transfer cannot be completed, the element is not placed in the queue. Typically used in applications that pass messages between threads.

Fig. 23.22 | Concurrent collections summary (package java.util.concurrent).

23.11 Multithreading with GUI

Swing applications present a unique set of challenges for multithreaded programming. All Swing applications have a single thread, called the **event dispatch thread**, to handle interactions with the application's GUI components. Typical interactions include *updating GUI components* or *processing user actions* such as mouse clicks. All tasks that require interaction with an application's GUI are placed in an *event queue* and are executed sequentially by the event dispatch thread.

Swing GUI components are not thread safe—they cannot be manipulated by multiple threads without the risk of incorrect results. Unlike the other examples presented in this chapter, thread safety in GUI applications is achieved not by synchronizing thread actions, but by *ensuring that Swing components are accessed from only a single thread*—the event dispatch thread. This technique is called **thread confinement**. Allowing just one thread to access non-thread-safe objects eliminates the possibility of corruption due to multiple threads accessing these objects concurrently.

Usually it's sufficient to perform simple calculations on the event dispatch thread in sequence with GUI component manipulations. If an application must perform a lengthy computation in response to a user interface interaction, the event dispatch thread cannot attend to other tasks in the event queue while the thread is tied up in that computation. This causes the GUI components to become unresponsive. It's preferable to handle a long-running computation in a separate thread, freeing the event dispatch thread to continue managing other GUI interactions. Of course, to update the GUI based on the computation's results, you must update the GUI from the event dispatch thread, rather than from the worker thread that performed the computation.

Class SwingWorker

Class **SwingWorker** (in package `javax.swing`) perform long-running computations in a worker thread and to update Swing components from the event dispatch thread based on the computations' results. `SwingWorker` implements the `Runnable` interface, meaning that *a SwingWorker object can be scheduled to execute in a separate thread*. The `SwingWorker` class provides several methods to simplify performing computations in a worker thread and making the results available for display in a GUI. Some common `SwingWorker` methods are described in Fig. 23.23.

Method	Description
`doInBackground`	Defines a long computation and is called in a worker thread.
`done`	Executes on the event dispatch thread when `doInBackground` returns.
`execute`	Schedules the `SwingWorker` object to be executed in a worker thread.
`get`	Waits for the computation to complete, then returns the result of the computation (i.e., the return value of `doInBackground`).
`publish`	Sends intermediate results from the `doInBackground` method to the process method for processing on the event dispatch thread.

Fig. 23.23 | Commonly used `SwingWorker` methods. (Part 1 of 2.)

Method	Description
process	Receives intermediate results from the publish method and processes these results on the event dispatch thread.
setProgress	Sets the progress property to notify any property change listeners on the event dispatch thread of progress bar updates.

Fig. 23.23 | Commonly used SwingWorker methods. (Part 2 of 2.)

23.11.1 Performing Computations in a Worker Thread

In the next example, the user enters a number n and the program gets the nth Fibonacci number, which we calculate using a recursive algorithm. Since the algorithm is time consuming for large values, we use a SwingWorker object to perform the calculation in a worker thread. The GUI also provides a separate set of components that get the next Fibonacci number in the sequence with each click of a button, beginning with fibonacci(1). This set of components performs its short computation directly in the event dispatch thread. This program is capable of producing up to the 92nd Fibonacci number—subsequent values are outside the range that can be represented by a long. Recall that you can use class BigInteger to represent arbitrarily large integer values.

Class BackgroundCalculator (Fig. 23.24) performs the recursive Fibonacci calculation in a *worker thread*. This class extends SwingWorker (line 8), overriding the methods doInBackground and done. Method doInBackground (lines 21–24) computes the nth Fibonacci number in a worker thread and returns the result. Method done (lines 27–43) displays the result in a JLabel.

```java
1   // Fig. 23.24: BackgroundCalculator.java
2   // SwingWorker subclass for calculating Fibonacci numbers
3   // in a background thread.
4   import javax.swing.SwingWorker;
5   import javax.swing.JLabel;
6   import java.util.concurrent.ExecutionException;
7
8   public class BackgroundCalculator extends SwingWorker< Long, Object >
9   {
10      private final int n; // Fibonacci number to calculate
11      private final JLabel resultJLabel; // JLabel to display the result
12
13      // constructor
14      public BackgroundCalculator( int number, JLabel label )
15      {
16         n = number;
17         resultJLabel = label;
18      } // end BackgroundCalculator constructor
```

Fig. 23.24 | SwingWorker subclass for calculating Fibonacci numbers in a background thread. (Part 1 of 2.)

```
19
20      // long-running code to be run in a worker thread
21      public Long doInBackground()
22      {
23         return nthFib = fibonacci( n );
24      } // end method doInBackground
25
26      // code to run on the event dispatch thread when doInBackground returns
27      protected void done()
28      {
29         try
30         {
31            // get the result of doInBackground and display it
32            resultJLabel.setText( get().toString() );
33         } // end try
34         catch ( InterruptedException ex )
35         {
36            resultJLabel.setText( "Interrupted while waiting for results." );
37         } // end catch
38         catch ( ExecutionException ex )
39         {
40            resultJLabel.setText(
41               "Error encountered while performing calculation." );
42         } // end catch
43      } // end method done
44
45      // recursive method fibonacci; calculates nth Fibonacci number
46      public long fibonacci( long number )
47      {
48         if ( number == 0 || number == 1 )
49            return number;
50         else
51            return fibonacci( number - 1 ) + fibonacci( number - 2 );
52      } // end method fibonacci
53   } // end class BackgroundCalculator
```

Fig. 23.24 | SwingWorker subclass for calculating Fibonacci numbers in a background thread. (Part 2 of 2.)

SwingWorker is a *generic class*. In line 8, the first type parameter is Long and the second is Object. The first type parameter indicates the type returned by the doInBackground method; the second indicates the type that's passed between the publish and process methods to handle intermediate results. Since we do not use publish and process in this example, we simply use Object as the second type parameter. We discuss publish and process in Section 23.11.2.

A BackgroundCalculator object can be instantiated from a class that controls a GUI. A BackgroundCalculator maintains instance variables for an integer that represents the Fibonacci number to be calculated and a JLabel that displays the results of the calculation (lines 10–11). The BackgroundCalculator constructor (lines 14–18) initializes these instance variables with the arguments that are passed to the constructor.

> **Software Engineering Observation 23.4**
>
> *Any GUI components that will be manipulated by SwingWorker methods, such as components that will be updated from methods process or done, should be passed to the SwingWorker subclass's constructor and stored in the subclass object. This gives these methods access to the GUI components they'll manipulate.*

When method execute is called on a BackgroundCalculator object, the object is scheduled for execution in a worker thread. Method doInBackground is called from the worker thread and invokes the fibonacci method (lines 46–52), passing instance variable n as an argument (line 23). Method fibonacci uses recursion to compute the Fibonacci of n. When fibonacci returns, method doInBackground returns the result.

After doInBackground returns, method done is called from the event dispatch thread. This method attempts to set the result JLabel to the return value of doInBackground by calling method get to retrieve this return value (line 32). Method get waits for the result to be ready if necessary, but since we call it from method done, the computation will be complete before get is called. Lines 34–37 catch InterruptedException if the current thread is interrupted while waiting for get to return. This exception will not occur in this example since the calculation will have already completed by the time get is called. Lines 38–42 catch ExecutionException, which is thrown if an exception occurs during the computation.

Class FibonacciNumbers

Class FibonacciNumbers (Fig. 23.25) displays a window containing two sets of GUI components—one set to compute a Fibonacci number in a worker thread and another to get the next Fibonacci number in response to the user's clicking a JButton. The constructor (lines 38–109) places these components in separate titled JPanels. Lines 46–47 and 78–79 add two JLabels, a JTextField and a JButton to the workerJPanel to allow the user to enter an integer whose Fibonacci number will be calculated by the BackgroundWorker. Lines 84–85 and 103 add two JLabels and a JButton to the event dispatch thread panel to allow the user to get the next Fibonacci number in the sequence. Instance variables n1 and n2 contain the previous two Fibonacci numbers in the sequence and are initialized to 0 and 1, respectively (lines 29–30). Instance variable count stores the most recently computed sequence number and is initialized to 1 (line 31). The two JLabels display count and n2 initially, so that the user will see the text Fibonacci of 1: 1 in the eventThread-JPanel when the GUI starts.

```
1   // Fig. 23.25: FibonacciNumbers.java
2   // Using SwingWorker to perform a long calculation with
3   // results displayed in a GUI.
4   import java.awt.GridLayout;
5   import java.awt.event.ActionEvent;
6   import java.awt.event.ActionListener;
7   import javax.swing.JButton;
8   import javax.swing.JFrame;
9   import javax.swing.JPanel;
```

Fig. 23.25 | Using SwingWorker to perform a long calculation with results displayed in a GUI. (Part 1 of 4.)

```
10    import javax.swing.JLabel;
11    import javax.swing.JTextField;
12    import javax.swing.border.TitledBorder;
13    import javax.swing.border.LineBorder;
14    import java.awt.Color;
15    import java.util.concurrent.ExecutionException;
16
17    public class FibonacciNumbers extends JFrame
18    {
19       // components for calculating the Fibonacci of a user-entered number
20       private final JPanel workerJPanel =
21          new JPanel( new GridLayout( 2, 2, 5, 5 ) );
22       private final JTextField numberJTextField = new JTextField();
23       private final JButton goJButton = new JButton( "Go" );
24       private final JLabel fibonacciJLabel = new JLabel();
25
26       // components and variables for getting the next Fibonacci number
27       private final JPanel eventThreadJPanel =
28          new JPanel( new GridLayout( 2, 2, 5, 5 ) );
29       private long n1 = 0; // initialize with first Fibonacci number
30       private long n2 = 1; // initialize with second Fibonacci number
31       private int count = 1; // current Fibonacci number to display
32       private final JLabel nJLabel = new JLabel( "Fibonacci of 1: " );
33       private final JLabel nFibonacciJLabel =
34          new JLabel( String.valueOf( n2 ) );
35       private final JButton nextNumberJButton = new JButton( "Next Number" );
36
37       // constructor
38       public FibonacciNumbers()
39       {
40          super( "Fibonacci Numbers" );
41          setLayout( new GridLayout( 2, 1, 10, 10 ) );
42
43          // add GUI components to the SwingWorker panel
44          workerJPanel.setBorder( new TitledBorder(
45             new LineBorder( Color.BLACK ), "With SwingWorker" ) );
46          workerJPanel.add( new JLabel( "Get Fibonacci of:" ) );
47          workerJPanel.add( numberJTextField );
48          goJButton.addActionListener(
49             new ActionListener()
50             {
51                public void actionPerformed( ActionEvent event )
52                {
53                   int n;
54
55                   try
56                   {
57                      // retrieve user's input as an integer
58                      n = Integer.parseInt( numberJTextField.getText() );
59                   } // end try
60                   catch( NumberFormatException ex )
61                   {
```

Fig. 23.25 | Using SwingWorker to perform a long calculation with results displayed in a GUI. (Part 2 of 4.)

```
62                         // display an error message if the user did not
63                         // enter an integer
64                         fibonacciJLabel.setText( "Enter an integer." );
65                         return;
66                      } // end catch
67
68                      // indicate that the calculation has begun
69                      fibonacciJLabel.setText( "Calculating..." );
70
71                      // create a task to perform calculation in background
72                      BackgroundCalculator task =
73                         new BackgroundCalculator( n, fibonacciJLabel );
74                      task.execute(); // execute the task
75                   } // end method actionPerformed
76                } // end anonymous inner class
77             ); // end call to addActionListener
78             workerJPanel.add( goJButton );
79             workerJPanel.add( fibonacciJLabel );
80
81          // add GUI components to the event-dispatching thread panel
82          eventThreadJPanel.setBorder( new TitledBorder(
83             new LineBorder( Color.BLACK ), "Without SwingWorker" ) );
84          eventThreadJPanel.add( nJLabel );
85          eventThreadJPanel.add( nFibonacciJLabel );
86          nextNumberJButton.addActionListener(
87             new ActionListener()
88             {
89                public void actionPerformed( ActionEvent event )
90                {
91                   // calculate the Fibonacci number after n2
92                   long temp = n1 + n2;
93                   n1 = n2;
94                   n2 = temp;
95                   ++count;
96
97                   // display the next Fibonacci number
98                   nJLabel.setText( "Fibonacci of " + count + ": " );
99                   nFibonacciJLabel.setText( String.valueOf( n2 ) );
100                } // end method actionPerformed
101             } // end anonymous inner class
102          ); // end call to addActionListener
103          eventThreadJPanel.add( nextNumberJButton );
104
105          add( workerJPanel );
106          add( eventThreadJPanel );
107          setSize( 275, 200 );
108          setVisible( true );
109       } // end constructor
110
111       // main method begins program execution
112       public static void main( String[] args )
113       {
```

Fig. 23.25 | Using SwingWorker to perform a long calculation with results displayed in a GUI. (Part 3 of 4.)

```
114            FibonacciNumbers application = new FibonacciNumbers();
115            application.setDefaultCloseOperation( EXIT_ON_CLOSE );
116      } // end main
117 } // end class FibonacciNumbers
```

a) Begin calculating Fibonacci of 40 in the background

b) Calculating other Fibonacci values while Fibonacci of 40 continues calculating

c) Fibonacci of 40 calculation finishes

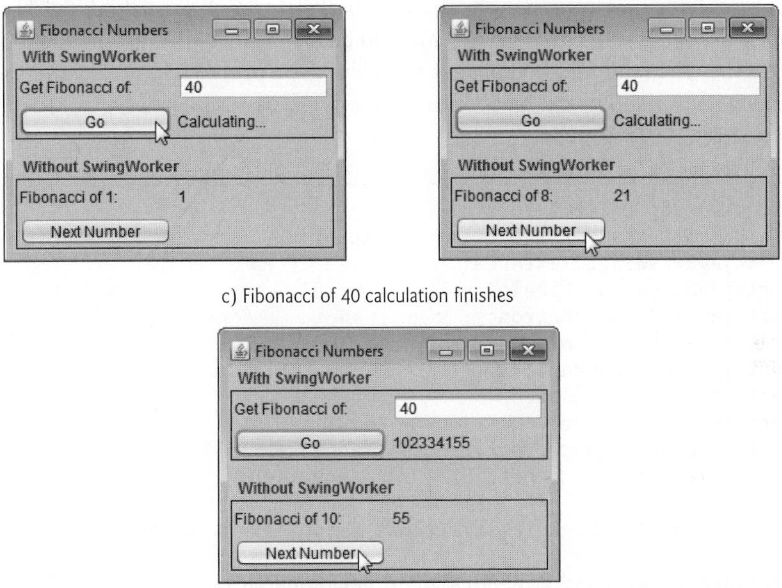

Fig. 23.25 | Using SwingWorker to perform a long calculation with results displayed in a GUI. (Part 4 of 4.)

Lines 48–77 register the event handler for the goJButton. If the user clicks this JButton, line 58 gets the value entered in the numberJTextField and attempts to parse it as an integer. Lines 72–73 create a new BackgroundCalculator object, passing in the user-entered value and the fibonacciJLabel that's used to display the calculation's results. Line 74 calls method execute on the BackgroundCalculator, scheduling it for execution in a separate worker thread. Method execute does not wait for the BackgroundCalculator to finish executing. It returns immediately, allowing the GUI to continue processing other events while the computation is performed.

If the user clicks the nextNumberJButton in the eventThreadJPanel, the event handler registered in lines 86–102 executes.Lines 92–95 add the previous two Fibonacci numbers stored in n1 and n2 to determine the next number in the sequence, update n1 and n2 to their new values and increment count. Then lines 98–99 update the GUI to display the next number. The code for these calculations is in method actionPerformed, so they're performed on the *event dispatch thread*. Handling such short computations in the event dispatch thread does not cause the GUI to become unresponsive, as with the recursive algorithm for calculating the Fibonacci of a large number. Because the longer Fibonacci computation is performed in a separate worker thread using the SwingWorker, it's possible to get the next Fibonacci number while the recursive computation is still in progress.

23.11.2 Processing Intermediate Results with SwingWorker

We've presented an example that uses the SwingWorker class to execute a long process in a *background thread* and update the GUI when the process is finished. We now present an example of updating the GUI with intermediate results before the long process completes. Figure 23.26 presents class PrimeCalculator, which extends SwingWorker to compute the first *n* prime numbers in a *worker thread*. In addition to the doInBackground and done methods used in the previous example, this class uses SwingWorker methods publish, process and setProgress. In this example, method publish sends prime numbers to method process as they're found, method process displays these primes in a GUI component and method setProgress updates the progress property. We later show how to use this property to update a JProgressBar.

```java
1   // Fig. 23.26: PrimeCalculator.java
2   // Calculates the first n primes, displaying them as they are found.
3   import javax.swing.JTextArea;
4   import javax.swing.JLabel;
5   import javax.swing.JButton;
6   import javax.swing.SwingWorker;
7   import java.util.Arrays;
8   import java.util.Random;
9   import java.util.List;
10  import java.util.concurrent.CancellationException;
11  import java.util.concurrent.ExecutionException;
12
13  public class PrimeCalculator extends SwingWorker< Integer, Integer >
14  {
15     private final Random generator = new Random();
16     private final JTextArea intermediateJTextArea; // displays found primes
17     private final JButton getPrimesJButton;
18     private final JButton cancelJButton;
19     private final JLabel statusJLabel; // displays status of calculation
20     private final boolean[] primes; // boolean array for finding primes
21
22     // constructor
23     public PrimeCalculator( int max, JTextArea intermediate, JLabel status,
24        JButton getPrimes, JButton cancel )
25     {
26        intermediateJTextArea = intermediate;
27        statusJLabel = status;
28        getPrimesJButton = getPrimes;
29        cancelJButton = cancel;
30        primes = new boolean[ max ];
31
32        // initialize all prime array values to true
33        Arrays.fill( primes, true );
34     } // end constructor
35
36     // finds all primes up to max using the Sieve of Eratosthenes
37     public Integer doInBackground()
38     {
```

Fig. 23.26 | Calculates the first *n* primes, displaying them as they are found. (Part 1 of 3.)

```
39          int count = 0; // the number of primes found
40
41          // starting at the third value, cycle through the array and put
42          // false as the value of any greater number that is a multiple
43          for ( int i = 2; i < primes.length; i++ )
44          {
45              if ( isCancelled() ) // if calculation has been canceled
46                  return count;
47              else
48              {
49                  setProgress( 100 * ( i + 1 ) / primes.length );
50
51                  try
52                  {
53                      Thread.sleep( generator.nextInt( 5 ) );
54                  } // end try
55                  catch ( InterruptedException ex )
56                  {
57                      statusJLabel.setText( "Worker thread interrupted" );
58                      return count;
59                  } // end catch
60
61                  if ( primes[ i ] ) // i is prime
62                  {
63                      publish( i ); // make i available for display in prime list
64                      ++count;
65
66                      for ( int j = i + i; j < primes.length; j += i )
67                          primes[ j ] = false; // i is not prime
68                  } // end if
69              } // end else
70          } // end for
71
72          return count;
73      } // end method doInBackground
74
75      // displays published values in primes list
76      protected void process( List< Integer > publishedVals )
77      {
78          for ( int i = 0; i < publishedVals.size(); i++ )
79              intermediateJTextArea.append( publishedVals.get( i ) + "\n" );
80      } // end method process
81
82      // code to execute when doInBackground completes
83      protected void done()
84      {
85          getPrimesJButton.setEnabled( true ); // enable Get Primes button
86          cancelJButton.setEnabled( false ); // disable Cancel button
87
88          int numPrimes;
89
90          try
91          {
```

Fig. 23.26 | Calculates the first *n* primes, displaying them as they are found. (Part 2 of 3.)

```
92                numPrimes = get(); // retrieve doInBackground return value
93            } // end try
94            catch ( InterruptedException ex )
95            {
96                statusJLabel.setText( "Interrupted while waiting for results." );
97                return;
98            } // end catch
99            catch ( ExecutionException ex )
100            {
101                statusJLabel.setText( "Error performing computation." );
102                return;
103            } // end catch
104            catch ( CancellationException ex )
105            {
106                statusJLabel.setText( "Cancelled." );
107                return;
108            } // end catch
109
110            statusJLabel.setText( "Found " + numPrimes + " primes." );
111        } // end method done
112 } // end class PrimeCalculator
```

Fig. 23.26 | Calculates the first *n* primes, displaying them as they are found. (Part 3 of 3.)

Class `PrimeCalculator` extends `SwingWorker` (line 13), with the first type parameter indicating the return type of method `doInBackground` and the second indicating the type of intermediate results passed between methods `publish` and `process`. In this case, both type parameters are `Integers`. The constructor (lines 23–34) takes as arguments an integer that indicates the upper limit of the prime numbers to locate, a `JTextArea` used to display primes in the GUI, one `JButton` for initiating a calculation and one for canceling it, and a `JLabel` used to display the status of the calculation.

Sieve of Eratosthenes

Line 33 initializes the elements of the `boolean` array `primes` to `true` with `Arrays` method `fill`. `PrimeCalculator` uses this array and the **Sieve of Eratosthenes** algorithm to find all primes less than `max`. The Sieve of Eratosthenes takes a list of integers and, beginning with the first prime number, filters out all multiples of that prime. It then moves to the next prime, which will be the next number that's not yet filtered out, and eliminates all of its multiples. It continues until the end of the list is reached and all nonprimes have been filtered out. Algorithmically, we begin with element 2 of the `boolean` array and set the cells corresponding to all values that are multiples of 2 to `false` to indicate that they're divisible by 2 and thus not prime. We then move to the next array element, check whether it's `true`, and if so set all of its multiples to `false` to indicate that they're divisible by the current index. When the whole array has been traversed in this way, all indices that contain `true` are prime, as they have no divisors.

Method *doInBackground*

In method `doInBackground` (lines 37–73), the control variable i for the loop (lines 43–70) controls the current index for implementing the Sieve of Eratosthenes. Line 45 calls the inherited `SwingWorker` method **isCancelled** to determine whether the user has clicked the **Cancel** button. If isCancelled returns true, method doInBackground returns the number of primes found so far (line 46) without finishing the computation.

If the calculation isn't canceled, line 49 calls setProgress to update the percentage of the array that's been traversed so far. Line 53 puts the currently executing thread to sleep for up to 4 milliseconds. We discuss the reason for this shortly. Line 61 tests whether the element of array primes at the current index is true (and thus prime). If so, line 63 passes the index to method publish so that it can be displayed as an intermediate result in the GUI and line 64 increments the number of primes found. Lines 66–67 set all multiples of the current index to false to indicate that they're not prime. When the entire array has been traversed, line 72 returns the number of primes found.

Method *process*
Lines 76–80 declare method process, which executes in the event dispatch thread and receives its argument publishedVals from method publish. The passing of values between publish in the worker thread and process in the event dispatch thread is asynchronous; process might not be invoked for every call to publish. All Integers published since the last call to process are received as a List by method process. Lines 78–79 iterate through this list and display the published values in a JTextArea. Because the computation in method doInBackground progresses quickly, publishing values often, updates to the JTextArea can pile up on the event dispatch thread, causing the GUI to become sluggish. In fact, when searching for a large number of primes, the *event dispatch thread* may receive so many requests in quick succession to update the JTextArea that it *runs out of memory in its event queue*. This is why we put the worker thread to sleep for a few milliseconds between calls to publish. The calculation is slowed just enough to allow the event dispatch thread to keep up with requests to update the JTextArea with new primes, enabling the GUI to update smoothly and remain responsive.

Method *done*
Lines 83–111 define method done. When the calculation is finished or canceled, method done enables the **Get Primes** button and disables the **Cancel** button (lines 85–86). Line 92 gets the return value—the number of primes found—from method doInBackground. Lines 94–108 catch the exceptions thrown by method get and display an appropriate message in the statusJLabel. If no exceptions occur, line 110 sets the statusJLabel to indicate the number of primes found.

Class *FindPrimes*
Class FindPrimes (Fig. 23.27) displays a JTextField that allows the user to enter a number, a JButton to begin finding all primes less than that number and a JTextArea to display the primes. A JButton allows the user to cancel the calculation, and a JProgressBar indicates the calculation's progress. The FindPrimes constructor (lines 32–125) sets up the application's GUI.

Lines 42–94 register the event handler for the getPrimesJButton. When the user clicks this JButton, lines 47–49 reset the JProgressBar and clear the displayPrimesJTextArea and the statusJLabel. Lines 53–63 parse the value in the JTextField and display an error message if the value is not an integer. Lines 66–68 construct a new PrimeCalculator object, passing as arguments the integer the user entered, the displayPrimesJTextArea for displaying the primes, the statusJLabel and the two JButtons.

```
1    // Fig 23.27: FindPrimes.java
2    // Using a SwingWorker to display prime numbers and update a JProgressBar
3    // while the prime numbers are being calculated.
4    import javax.swing.JFrame;
5    import javax.swing.JTextField;
6    import javax.swing.JTextArea;
7    import javax.swing.JButton;
8    import javax.swing.JProgressBar;
9    import javax.swing.JLabel;
10   import javax.swing.JPanel;
11   import javax.swing.JScrollPane;
12   import javax.swing.ScrollPaneConstants;
13   import java.awt.BorderLayout;
14   import java.awt.GridLayout;
15   import java.awt.event.ActionListener;
16   import java.awt.event.ActionEvent;
17   import java.util.concurrent.ExecutionException;
18   import java.beans.PropertyChangeListener;
19   import java.beans.PropertyChangeEvent;
20
21   public class FindPrimes extends JFrame
22   {
23      private final JTextField highestPrimeJTextField = new JTextField();
24      private final JButton getPrimesJButton = new JButton( "Get Primes" );
25      private final JTextArea displayPrimesJTextArea = new JTextArea();
26      private final JButton cancelJButton = new JButton( "Cancel" );
27      private final JProgressBar progressJProgressBar = new JProgressBar();
28      private final JLabel statusJLabel = new JLabel();
29      private PrimeCalculator calculator;
30
31      // constructor
32      public FindPrimes()
33      {
34         super( "Finding Primes with SwingWorker" );
35         setLayout( new BorderLayout() );
36
37         // initialize panel to get a number from the user
38         JPanel northJPanel = new JPanel();
39         northJPanel.add( new JLabel( "Find primes less than: " ) );
40         highestPrimeJTextField.setColumns( 5 );
41         northJPanel.add( highestPrimeJTextField );
42         getPrimesJButton.addActionListener(
43            new ActionListener()
44            {
45               public void actionPerformed( ActionEvent e )
46               {
47                  progressJProgressBar.setValue( 0 ); // reset JProgressBar
48                  displayPrimesJTextArea.setText( "" ); // clear JTextArea
49                  statusJLabel.setText( "" ); // clear JLabel
50
51                  int number; // search for primes up through this value
```

Fig. 23.27 | Using a SwingWorker to display prime numbers and update a JProgressBar while the prime numbers are being calculated. (Part 1 of 3.)

```
52
53                  try
54                  {
55                     // get user input
56                     number = Integer.parseInt(
57                        highestPrimeJTextField.getText() );
58                  } // end try
59                  catch ( NumberFormatException ex )
60                  {
61                     statusJLabel.setText( "Enter an integer." );
62                     return;
63                  } // end catch
64
65                  // construct a new PrimeCalculator object
66                  calculator = new PrimeCalculator( number,
67                     displayPrimesJTextArea, statusJLabel, getPrimesJButton,
68                     cancelJButton );
69
70                  // listen for progress bar property changes
71                  calculator.addPropertyChangeListener(
72                     new PropertyChangeListener()
73                     {
74                        public void propertyChange( PropertyChangeEvent e )
75                        {
76                           // if the changed property is progress,
77                           // update the progress bar
78                           if ( e.getPropertyName().equals( "progress" ) )
79                           {
80                              int newValue = ( Integer ) e.getNewValue();
81                              progressJProgressBar.setValue( newValue );
82                           } // end if
83                        } // end method propertyChange
84                     } // end anonymous inner class
85                  ); // end call to addPropertyChangeListener
86
87                  // disable Get Primes button and enable Cancel button
88                  getPrimesJButton.setEnabled( false );
89                  cancelJButton.setEnabled( true );
90
91                  calculator.execute(); // execute the PrimeCalculator object
92               } // end method ActionPerformed
93            } // end anonymous inner class
94         ); // end call to addActionListener
95         northJPanel.add( getPrimesJButton );
96
97         // add a scrollable JList to display results of calculation
98         displayPrimesJTextArea.setEditable( false );
99         add( new JScrollPane( displayPrimesJTextArea,
100           ScrollPaneConstants.VERTICAL_SCROLLBAR_ALWAYS,
101           ScrollPaneConstants.HORIZONTAL_SCROLLBAR_NEVER ) );
102
```

Fig. 23.27 | Using a SwingWorker to display prime numbers and update a JProgressBar while the prime numbers are being calculated. (Part 2 of 3.)

```
103        // initialize a panel to display cancelJButton,
104        // progressJProgressBar, and statusJLabel
105        JPanel southJPanel = new JPanel( new GridLayout( 1, 3, 10, 10 ) );
106        cancelJButton.setEnabled( false );
107        cancelJButton.addActionListener(
108           new ActionListener()
109           {
110              public void actionPerformed( ActionEvent e )
111              {
112                 calculator.cancel( true ); // cancel the calculation
113              } // end method ActionPerformed
114           } // end anonymous inner class
115        ); // end call to addActionListener
116        southJPanel.add( cancelJButton );
117        progressJProgressBar.setStringPainted( true );
118        southJPanel.add( progressJProgressBar );
119        southJPanel.add( statusJLabel );
120
121        add( northJPanel, BorderLayout.NORTH );
122        add( southJPanel, BorderLayout.SOUTH );
123        setSize( 350, 300 );
124        setVisible( true );
125     } // end constructor
126
127     // main method begins program execution
128     public static void main( String[] args )
129     {
130        FindPrimes application = new FindPrimes();
131        application.setDefaultCloseOperation( EXIT_ON_CLOSE );
132     } // end main
133  } // end class FindPrimes
```

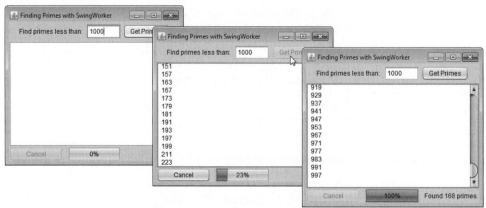

Fig. 23.27 | Using a SwingWorker to display prime numbers and update a JProgressBar while the prime numbers are being calculated. (Part 3 of 3.)

Lines 71–85 register a PropertyChangeListener for the PrimeCalculator object. **PropertyChangeListener** is an interface from package java.beans that defines a single method, propertyChange. Every time method setProgress is invoked on a PrimeCalculator, the PrimeCalculator generates a PropertyChangeEvent to indicate that the progress property has changed. Method propertyChange listens for these events. Line 78 tests whether a given PropertyChangeEvent indicates a change to the progress property. If so, line 80 gets the new value of the property and line 81 updates the JProgressBar with the new progress property value.

The **Get Primes** JButton is disabled (line 88) so only one calculation that updates the GUI can execute at a time, and the **Cancel** JButton is enabled (line 89) to allow the user to stop the computation before it completes. Line 91 executes the PrimesCalculator to begin finding primes. If the user clicks the cancelJButton, the event handler registered at lines 107–115 calls PrimeCalculator's method **cancel** (line 112), which is inherited from class SwingWorker, and the calculation returns early. The argument true to method cancel indicates that the thread performing the task should be interrupted in an attempt to cancel the task.

23.12 Interfaces Callable and Future

Interface Runnable provides only the most basic functionality for multithreaded programming. In fact, this interface has several limitations. Suppose a Runnable encounters a problem and tries to throw a *checked* exception. The run method is not declared to throw any exceptions, so the problem must be handled within the Runnable—the exception *cannot* be passed to the calling thread. Now suppose a Runnable is performing a long calculation and the application wants to retrieve the result of that calculation. The run method cannot return a value, so the application must use shared data to pass the value back to the calling thread. This also involves the overhead of synchronizing access to the data. The developers of the concurrency APIs recognized these limitations and created a new interface to fix them. The **Callable** interface (of package java.util.concurrent) declares a single method named **call**. This interface is designed to be similar to the Runnable interface—allowing an action to be performed concurrently in a separate thread—but the call method allows the thread to return a value or to throw a *checked* exception.

An application that creates a Callable likely wants to run it concurrently with other Runnables and Callables. The ExecutorService interface provides method **submit**, which will execute a Callable passed in as its argument. The submit method returns an object of type **Future** (of package java.util.concurrent), which is an interface that represents the executing Callable. The Future interface declares method **get** to return the result of the Callable and provides other methods to manage a Callable's execution.

23.13 Java SE 7: Fork/Join Framework

Java SE 7's concurrency APIs include the new fork/join framework, which helps programmers parallelize algorithms. The framework is beyond the scope of this book. Experts tell us that most Java programmers will benefit by this framework being used "behind the scenes" in the Java API and other third party libraries.

The fork/join framework is particularly well suited to divide-and-conquer-style algorithms, such as the merge sort, which uses a recursive algorithm to sort an array by *splitting* it into two equal-sized subarrays, *sorting* each subarray, then *merging* them into one larger array. Each subarray is sorted by performing the same algorithm on the subarray. For algorithms like merge sort, the fork/join framework can be used to create parallel tasks so that they can be distributed across multiple processors and be truly performed in parallel—the details of assigning the parallel tasks to different processors are handled for you by the framework.

To learn more about the fork/join framework and Java multithreading in general, please visit the sites listed in our Java Multithreading Resource Center at

```
www.deitel.com/JavaMultithreading
```

23.14 Wrap-Up

In this chapter, you learned that concurrency has historically been implemented with operating-system primitives available only to experienced systems programmers, but that Java makes concurrency available to you through the language and APIs. You also learned that the JVM itself creates threads to run a program, and that it also can create threads to perform housekeeping tasks such as garbage collection.

We discussed the life cycle of a thread and the states that a thread may occupy during its lifetime. Next, we presented the interface Runnable, which is used to specify a task that can execute concurrently with other tasks. This interface's run method is invoked by the thread executing the task. We showed how to execute a Runnable object by associating it with an object of class Thread. Then we showed how to use the Executor interface to manage the execution of Runnable objects via thread pools, which can reuse existing threads to eliminate the overhead of creating a new thread for each task and can improve performance by optimizing the number of threads to ensure that the processor stays busy.

You learned that when multiple threads share an object and one or more of them modify that object, indeterminate results may occur unless access to the shared object is managed properly. We showed you how to solve this problem via thread synchronization, which coordinates access to shared data by multiple concurrent threads. You learned several techniques for performing synchronization—first with the built-in class ArrayBlockingQueue (which handles *all* the synchronization details for you), then with Java's built-in monitors and the synchronized keyword, and finally with interfaces Lock and Condition.

We discussed the fact that Swing GUIs are not thread safe, so all interactions with and modifications to the GUI must be performed in the event dispatch thread. We also discussed the problems associated with performing long-running calculations in the event dispatch thread. Then we showed how you can use the SwingWorker class to perform long-running calculations in worker threads. You learned how to display the results of a Swing-Worker in a GUI when the calculation completed and how to display intermediate results while the calculation was still in process.

Finally, we discussed the Callable and Future interfaces, which enable you to execute tasks that return results and to obtain those results, respectively. We use the multithreading techniques introduced in this chapter again in Chapter 24, Networking, to help build multithreaded servers that can interact with multiple clients concurrently.

Networking

Objectives

In this chapter you'll learn:

- Java networking with URLs, sockets and datagrams.
- To implement Java networking applications by using sockets and datagrams.
- To implement Java clients and servers that communicate with one another.
- To implement network-based collaborative applications.
- To construct a simple multithreaded server.

24.1 Introduction

Java provides a number of built-in networking capabilities that make it easy to develop Internet-based and web-based applications. Java can enable programs to search the world for information and to collaborate with programs running on other computers internationally, nationally or just within an organization (subject to security constraints).

Java's fundamental networking capabilities are declared by the classes and interfaces of package **java.net**, through which Java offers **stream-based communications** that enable applications to view networking as streams of data. The classes and interfaces of package java.net also offer **packet-based communications** for transmitting individual **packets** of information—commonly used to transmit data images, audio and video over the Internet. In this chapter, we show how to communicate with packets and streams of data.

We focus on both sides of the **client/server relationship**. The **client** *requests* that some action be performed, and the **server** performs the action and *responds* to the client. A common implementation of the *request-response model* is between web browsers and web servers. When a user selects a website to browse through a browser (the client application), a request is sent to the appropriate web server (the server application). The server normally responds to the client by sending an appropriate web page to be rendered by the browser.

We introduce Java's **socket-based communications**, which enable applications to view networking as if it were *file I/O*—a program can read from a **socket** or write to a socket as simply as reading from a file or writing to a file. The socket is simply a software construct that represents one endpoint of a connection. We show how to create and manipulate *stream sockets* and *datagram sockets*.

With **stream sockets**, a process establishes a **connection** to another process. While the connection is in place, data flows between the processes in continuous **streams**. Stream sockets are said to provide a **connection-oriented service**. The protocol used for transmission is the popular **TCP** (**Transmission Control Protocol**).

With **datagram sockets**, individual **packets** of information are transmitted. The protocol used—**UDP, the User Datagram Protocol**—is a **connectionless service** and does *not* guarantee that packets arrive in any particular *order*. With UDP, packets can even be *lost* or *duplicated*. Significant extra programming is required on your part to deal with these problems (if you choose to do so). UDP is most appropriate for network applications that do not require the error checking and reliability of TCP. Stream sockets and the TCP protocol will be more desirable for the vast majority of Java networking applications.

Performance Tip 24.1

Connectionless services generally offer greater performance but less reliability than connection-oriented services.

Portability Tip 24.1

TCP, UDP and related protocols enable heterogeneous computer systems (i.e., those with different processors and different operating systems) to intercommunicate.

On the web at www.deitel.com/books/javafp2/, we present a case study that implements a client/server chat application similar to popular instant-messaging services. The application introduces **multicasting**, in which a server can publish information and *many* clients can *subscribe* to it. When the server publishes information, *all* subscribers receive it.

24.2 Manipulating URLs

The Internet offers many protocols. The **HyperText Transfer Protocol** (**HTTP**), which forms the basis of the web, uses **URIs** (**Uniform Resource Identifiers**) to identify data on the Internet. URIs that specify the locations of websites and web pages are called **URLs** (**Uniform Resource Locators**). Common URLs refer to files or directories and can reference objects that perform complex tasks, such as database lookups and Internet searches. If you know the URL of a publicly available web page, you can access it through HTTP.

Java makes it easy to manipulate URLs. When you use a URL that refers to the exact location of a resource (e.g., a web page) as an argument to the **showDocument** method of interface **AppletContext**, the browser in which the applet is executing will access and display that resource. The applet in Figs. 24.1–24.2 demonstrates simple networking capabilities. It enables the user to select a web page from a JList and causes the browser to display the corresponding page. In this example, the networking is performed by the browser.

Processing Applet Parameters
This applet takes advantage of **applet parameters** specified in the HTML document that invokes the applet. When browsing the web, you'll often come across applets that are in the public domain—you can use them free of charge on your own web pages (normally in exchange for crediting the applet's creator). Many applets can be customized via parameters supplied from the HTML file that invokes the applet. For example, Fig. 24.1 contains the HTML that invokes the applet SiteSelector in Fig. 24.2.

```html
1   <html>
2   <head>
3      <title>Site Selector</title>
4   </head>
5   <body>
6      <applet code = "SiteSelector.class" width = "300" height = "75">
7         <param name = "title0" value = "Java Home Page">
8         <param name = "location0"
```

Fig. 24.1 | HTML document to load SiteSelector applet. (Part 1 of 2.)

```
 9                    value = "http://www.oracle.com/technetwork/java/">
10             <param name = "title1" value = "Deitel">
11             <param name = "location1" value = "http://www.deitel.com/">
12             <param name = "title2" value = "JGuru">
13             <param name = "location2" value = "http://www.jGuru.com/">
14             <param name = "title3" value = "JavaWorld">
15             <param name = "location3" value = "http://www.javaworld.com/">
16       </applet>
17    </body>
18    </html>
```

Fig. 24.1 │ HTML document to load `SiteSelector` applet. (Part 2 of 2.)

The HTML document contains eight parameters specified with the **param element**—these lines must appear between the starting and ending `applet` tags. The applet can read these values and use them to customize itself. Any number of `param` elements can appear between the starting and ending `applet` tags. Each parameter has a unique **name** and a **value**. `Applet` method **getParameter** returns the `value` associated with a specific parameter name as a `String`. The argument passed to `getParameter` is a `String` containing the name of the parameter in the `param` element. In this example, parameters represent the title and location of each website the user can select. Parameters specified for this applet are named `title#`, where the value of # starts at 0 and increments by 1 for each new title. Each title should have a corresponding location parameter of the form `location#`, where the value of # starts at 0 and increments by 1 for each new location. The statement

```
     String title = getParameter( "title0" );
```

gets the value associated with parameter "title0" and assigns it to reference `title`. If there's no param tag containing the specified parameter, `getParameter` returns `null`.

Storing the Website Names and URLs
The applet (Fig. 24.2) obtains from the HTML document (Fig. 24.1) the choices that will be displayed in the applet's `JList`. Class `SiteSelector` uses a `HashMap` (package `java.util`) to store the website names and URLs. In this example, the *key* is the `String` in the `JList` that represents the website name, and the *value* is a `URL` object that stores the location of the website to display in the browser.

```
 1    // Fig. 24.2: SiteSelector.java
 2    // Loading a document from a URL into a browser.
 3    import java.net.MalformedURLException;
 4    import java.net.URL;
 5    import java.util.HashMap;
 6    import java.util.ArrayList;
 7    import java.awt.BorderLayout;
 8    import java.applet.AppletContext;
 9    import javax.swing.JApplet;
10    import javax.swing.JLabel;
11    import javax.swing.JList;
12    import javax.swing.JScrollPane;
```

Fig. 24.2 │ Loading a document from a URL into a browser. (Part 1 of 3.)

```
13   import javax.swing.event.ListSelectionEvent;
14   import javax.swing.event.ListSelectionListener;
15
16   public class SiteSelector extends JApplet
17   {
18      private HashMap< String, URL > sites; // site names and URLs
19      private ArrayList< String > siteNames; // site names
20      private JList siteChooser; // list of sites to choose from
21
22      // read parameters and set up GUI
23      public void init()
24      {
25         sites = new HashMap< String, URL >(); // create HashMap
26         siteNames = new ArrayList< String >(); // create ArrayList
27
28         // obtain parameters from HTML document
29         getSitesFromHTMLParameters();
30
31         // create GUI components and lay out interface
32         add( new JLabel( "Choose a site to browse" ), BorderLayout.NORTH );
33
34         siteChooser = new JList( siteNames.toArray() ); // populate JList
35         siteChooser.addListSelectionListener(
36            new ListSelectionListener() // anonymous inner class
37            {
38               // go to site user selected
39               public void valueChanged( ListSelectionEvent event )
40               {
41                  // get selected site name
42                  Object object = siteChooser.getSelectedValue();
43
44                  // use site name to locate corresponding URL
45                  URL newDocument = sites.get( object );
46
47                  // get applet container
48                  AppletContext browser = getAppletContext();
49
50                  // tell applet container to change pages
51                  browser.showDocument( newDocument );
52               } // end method valueChanged
53            } // end anonymous inner class
54         ); // end call to addListSelectionListener
55
56         add( new JScrollPane( siteChooser ), BorderLayout.CENTER );
57      } // end method init
58
59      // obtain parameters from HTML document
60      private void getSitesFromHTMLParameters()
61      {
62         String title; // site title
63         String location; // location of site
64         URL url; // URL of location
65         int counter = 0; // count number of sites
```

Fig. 24.2 | Loading a document from a URL into a browser. (Part 2 of 3.)

```
66
67          title = getParameter( "title" + counter ); // get first site title
68
69      // loop until no more parameters in HTML document
70      while ( title != null )
71      {
72          // obtain site location
73          location = getParameter( "location" + counter );
74
75          try // place title/URL in HashMap and title in ArrayList
76          {
77              url = new URL( location ); // convert location to URL
78              sites.put( title, url ); // put title/URL in HashMap
79              siteNames.add( title ); // put title in ArrayList
80          } // end try
81          catch ( MalformedURLException urlException )
82          {
83              urlException.printStackTrace();
84          } // end catch
85
86          ++counter;
87          title = getParameter( "title" + counter ); // get next site title
88      } // end while
89   } // end method getSitesFromHTMLParameters
90 } // end class SiteSelector
```

Fig. 24.2 | Loading a document from a URL into a browser. (Part 3 of 3.)

Class SiteSelector also contains an ArrayList (package java.util) in which the site names are placed so that they can be used to initialize the JList (one version of the JList constructor receives an array of Objects which is returned by ArrayList's toArray method). An ArrayList is a dynamically resizable array of references. Class ArrayList provides method add to add a new element to the end of the ArrayList. (ArrayList and HashMap were discussed in Chapter 18.)

Lines 25–26 in the applet's `init` method (lines 23–57) create a HashMap object and an ArrayList object. Line 29 calls our utility method getSitesFromHTMLParameters (declared at lines 60–89) to obtain the HTML parameters from the HTML document that invoked the applet.

Method getSitesFromHTMLParameters uses Applet method getParameter (line 67) to obtain a website title. If the `title` is not `null`, lines 73–87 execute. Line 73 uses Applet method getParameter to obtain the website location. Line 77 uses the `location` as the value of a new URL object. The URL constructor determines whether its argument represents a valid URL. If not, the URL constructor throws a **MalformedURLException**. The URL constructor must be called in a `try` block. If the URL constructor generates a MalformedURLException, the call to printStackTrace (line 83) causes the program to output a stack trace to the Java console. On Windows machines, the Java console can be viewed by right clicking the Java icon in the notification area of the taskbar. On a Mac, go to **Applications > Utilities** and launch the **Java Preferences** app. Then on the **Advanced** tab under **Java console**, select **Show console**. On other platforms, this is typically accessible through a desktop icon. Then the program attempts to obtain the next website title. The program does not add the site for the invalid URL to the HashMap, so the title will not be displayed in the JList.

For a proper URL, line 78 places the `title` and URL into the HashMap, and line 79 adds the `title` to the ArrayList. Line 87 gets the next title from the HTML document. When the call to getParameter at line 87 returns `null`, the loop terminates.

Building the Applet's GUI

When method getSitesFromHTMLParameters returns to `init`, lines 32–56 construct the applet's GUI. Line 32 adds the JLabel "Choose a site to browse" to the NORTH of the JApplet's BorderLayout. Line 34 creates JList siteChooser to allow the user to select a web page to view. Lines 35–54 register a ListSelectionListener to handle the JList's events. Line 56 adds siteChooser to the CENTER of the JFrame's BorderLayout.

Processing a User Selection

When the user selects a website in siteChooser, the program calls method valueChanged (lines 39–52). Line 42 obtains the selected site name from the JList. Line 45 passes the selected site name (the *key*) to HashMap method get, which locates and returns a reference to the corresponding URL object (the *value*) that's assigned to reference newDocument.

Line 48 uses Applet method **getAppletContext** to get a reference to an AppletContext object that represents the applet container. Line 51 uses this reference to invoke method showDocument, which receives a URL object as an argument and passes it to the AppletContext (i.e., the browser). The browser displays in the current browser window the resource associated with that URL. In this example, all the resources are HTML documents.

Specifying the Target Frame for Method **showDocument**

A second version of AppletContext method showDocument enables an applet to specify the **target frame** in which to display the web resource. This takes as arguments a URL object specifying the resource to display and a String representing the target frame. There are some special target frames that can be used as the second argument. The target frame **_blank** results in a new web browser window to display the content from the specified URL. The target frame **_self** specifies that the content from the specified URL should be displayed in the same frame as the applet (the applet's HTML page is replaced in this case).

The target frame _**top** specifies that the browser should remove the current frames in the browser window, then display the content from the specified URL in the current window.

> **Error-Prevention Tip 24.1**
> *The applet in Fig. 24.2 must be run from a web browser to show the results of displaying another web page. The* appletviewer *is capable only of executing applets—it ignores all other HTML tags. If the websites in the program contained Java applets, only those applets would appear in the* appletviewer *when the user selected a website. Each applet would execute in a separate* appletviewer *window.*

24.3 Reading a File on a Web Server

The application in Fig. 24.3 uses Swing GUI component **JEditorPane** (from package javax.swing) to display the contents of a file on a web server. The user enters a URL in the JTextField at the top of the window, and the application displays the corresponding document (if it exists) in the JEditorPane. Class JEditorPane is able to render both plain text and basic HTML-formatted text, as illustrated in the two screen captures (Fig. 24.4), so this application acts as a simple web browser. The application also demonstrates how to process **HyperlinkEvents** when the user clicks a hyperlink in the HTML document. The techniques shown in this example can also be used in applets. However, an applet is allowed to read files only on the server from which it was downloaded. [*Note:* This program might not work if your web browser must access the web through a proxy server. If you create a JNLP document for this program and use Java Web Start to launch it, Java Web Start will use the proxy server settings from your default web browser. See Chapters 20–21 for more information on Java Web Start.]

```
1    // Fig. 24.3: ReadServerFile.java
2    // Reading a file by opening a connection through a URL.
3    import java.awt.BorderLayout;
4    import java.awt.event.ActionEvent;
5    import java.awt.event.ActionListener;
6    import java.io.IOException;
7    import javax.swing.JEditorPane;
8    import javax.swing.JFrame;
9    import javax.swing.JOptionPane;
10   import javax.swing.JScrollPane;
11   import javax.swing.JTextField;
12   import javax.swing.event.HyperlinkEvent;
13   import javax.swing.event.HyperlinkListener;
14
15   public class ReadServerFile extends JFrame
16   {
17      private JTextField enterField; // JTextField to enter site name
18      private JEditorPane contentsArea; // to display website
19
20      // set up GUI
21      public ReadServerFile()
22      {
```

Fig. 24.3 | Reading a file by opening a connection through a URL. (Part 1 of 2.)

```
23              super( "Simple Web Browser" );
24
25              // create enterField and register its listener
26              enterField = new JTextField( "Enter file URL here" );
27              enterField.addActionListener(
28                 new ActionListener()
29                 {
30                    // get document specified by user
31                    public void actionPerformed( ActionEvent event )
32                    {
33                       getThePage( event.getActionCommand() );
34                    } // end method actionPerformed
35                 } // end inner class
36              ); // end call to addActionListener
37
38              add( enterField, BorderLayout.NORTH );
39
40              contentsArea = new JEditorPane(); // create contentsArea
41              contentsArea.setEditable( false );
42              contentsArea.addHyperlinkListener(
43                 new HyperlinkListener()
44                 {
45                    // if user clicked hyperlink, go to specified page
46                    public void hyperlinkUpdate( HyperlinkEvent event )
47                    {
48                       if ( event.getEventType() ==
49                          HyperlinkEvent.EventType.ACTIVATED )
50                          getThePage( event.getURL().toString() );
51                    } // end method hyperlinkUpdate
52                 } // end inner class
53              ); // end call to addHyperlinkListener
54
55              add( new JScrollPane( contentsArea ), BorderLayout.CENTER );
56              setSize( 400, 300 ); // set size of window
57              setVisible( true ); // show window
58           } // end ReadServerFile constructor
59
60           // load document
61           private void getThePage( String location )
62           {
63              try // load document and display location
64              {
65                 contentsArea.setPage( location ); // set the page
66                 enterField.setText( location ); // set the text
67              } // end try
68              catch ( IOException ioException )
69              {
70                 JOptionPane.showMessageDialog( this,
71                    "Error retrieving specified URL", "Bad URL",
72                    JOptionPane.ERROR_MESSAGE );
73              } // end catch
74           } // end method getThePage
75     } // end class ReadServerFile
```

Fig. 24.3 | Reading a file by opening a connection through a URL. (Part 2 of 2.)

```
 1   // Fig. 24.4: ReadServerFileTest.java
 2   // Create and start a ReadServerFile.
 3   import javax.swing.JFrame;
 4
 5   public class ReadServerFileTest
 6   {
 7      public static void main( String[] args )
 8      {
 9         ReadServerFile application = new ReadServerFile();
10         application.setDefaultCloseOperation( JFrame.EXIT_ON_CLOSE );
11      } // end main
12   } // end class ReadServerFileTest
```

Fig. 24.4 | Test class for ReadServerFile.

The application class ReadServerFile contains JTextField enterField, in which the user enters the URL of the file to read and JEditorPane contentsArea to display the file's contents. When the user presses the *Enter* key in enterField, the application calls method actionPerformed (lines 31–34). Line 33 uses ActionEvent method getAction-Command to get the String the user input in the JTextField and passes the String to utility method getThePage (lines 61–74).

Line 65 invokes JEditorPane method **setPage** to download the document specified by location and display it in the JEditorPane. If there's an error downloading the document, method setPage throws an IOException. Also, if an invalid URL is specified, a MalformedURLException (a subclass of IOException) occurs. If the document loads successfully, line 66 displays the current location in enterField.

Typically, an HTML document contains **hyperlinks** that, when clicked, provide quick access to another document on the web. If a JEditorPane contains an HTML document and the user clicks a hyperlink, the JEditorPane generates a **HyperlinkEvent** (package javax.swing.event) and notifies all registered **HyperlinkListeners** (package javax.swing.event) of that event. Lines 42–53 register a HyperlinkListener to handle HyperlinkEvents. When a HyperlinkEvent occurs, the program calls method **hyperlinkUpdate** (lines 46–51). Lines 48–49 use HyperlinkEvent method **getEventType** to determine the type of the HyperlinkEvent. Class HyperlinkEvent contains a public nested class called **EventType** that declares three static EventType objects, which represent the hyperlink event types. **ACTIVATED** indicates that the user clicked a hyperlink to change web pages, **ENTERED** indicates that the user moved the mouse over a hyperlink and **EXITED** indicates that the user moved the mouse away from a hyperlink. If a hyperlink was ACTIVATED, line 50 uses HyperlinkEvent method **getURL** to obtain the URL represented by the hyperlink. Method toString converts the returned URL to a String that can be passed to utility method getThePage.

Look-and-Feel Observation 24.1

A JEditorPane generates HyperlinkEvents only if it's uneditable.

24.4 Establishing a Simple Server Using Stream Sockets

The two examples discussed so far use *high-level* Java networking capabilities to communicate between applications. In the examples, it was not your responsibility to establish the connection between a client and a server. The first program relied on the web browser to communicate with a web server. The second program relied on a JEditorPane to perform the connection. This section begins our discussion of creating your own applications that can communicate with one another.

Step 1: Create a *ServerSocket*

Establishing a simple server in Java requires five steps. *Step 1* is to create a **ServerSocket** object. A call to the ServerSocket constructor, such as

```
ServerSocket server = new ServerSocket( portNumber, queueLength );
```

registers an available TCP **port number** and specifies the maximum number of clients that can wait to connect to the server (i.e., the **queue length**). The port number is used by clients to locate the server application on the server computer. This is often called the **handshake point**. If the queue is full, the server refuses client connections. The constructor establishes the port where the server waits for connections from clients—a process known as **binding the server to the port**. Each client will ask to connect to the server on this **port**. Only one application at a time can be bound to a specific port on the server.

Software Engineering Observation 24.1

Port numbers can be between 0 and 65,535. Most operating systems reserve port numbers below 1024 for system services (e.g., e-mail and World Wide Web servers). Generally, these ports should not be specified as connection ports in user programs. In fact, some operating systems require special access privileges to bind to port numbers below 1024.

Step 2: Wait for a Connection

Programs manage each client connection with a **Socket** object. In *Step 2*, the server listens indefinitely (or **blocks**) for an attempt by a client to connect. To listen for a client connection, the program calls ServerSocket method **accept**, as in

```
Socket connection = server.accept();
```

which returns a Socket when a connection with a client is established. The Socket allows the server to interact with the client. The interactions with the client actually occur at a different server port from the *handshake point*. This allows the port specified in *Step 1* to be used again in a multithreaded server to accept another client connection. We demonstrate this concept in Section 24.8.

Step 3: Get the *Socket's* I/O Streams

Step 3 is to get the OutputStream and InputStream objects that enable the server to communicate with the client by sending and receiving bytes. The server sends information to the client via an OutputStream and receives information from the client via an Input-Stream. The server invokes method **getOutputStream** on the Socket to get a reference to the Socket's OutputStream and invokes method **getInputStream** on the Socket to get a reference to the Socket's InputStream.

The stream objects can be used to send or receive individual bytes or sequences of bytes with the OutputStream's method write and the InputStream's method read, respectively. Often it's useful to send or receive values of primitive types (e.g., int and double) or Serializable objects (e.g., Strings or other serializable types) rather than sending bytes. In this case, we can use the techniques discussed in Chapter 17 to wrap other stream types (e.g., ObjectOutputStream and ObjectInputStream) around the Out-putStream and InputStream associated with the Socket. For example,

```
ObjectInputStream input =
    new ObjectInputStream( connection.getInputStream() );
ObjectOutputStream output =
    new ObjectOutputStream( connection.getOutputStream() );
```

The beauty of establishing these relationships is that whatever the server writes to the ObjectOutputStream is sent via the OutputStream and is available at the client's InputStream, and whatever the client writes to its OutputStream (with a corresponding ObjectOutputStream) is available via the server's InputStream. The transmission of the data over the network is seamless and is handled completely by Java.

Step 4: Perform the Processing
Step 4 is the *processing* phase, in which the server and the client communicate via the Out-putStream and InputStream objects.

Step 5: Close the Connection
In *Step 5*, when the transmission is complete, the server closes the connection by invoking the **close** method on the streams and on the Socket.

Software Engineering Observation 24.2
With sockets, network I/O appears to Java programs to be similar to sequential file I/O. Sockets hide much of the complexity of network programming.

Software Engineering Observation 24.3
A multithreaded server can take the Socket returned by each call to accept and create a new thread that manages network I/O across that Socket. Alternatively, a multithreaded server can maintain a pool of threads (a set of already existing threads) ready to manage network I/O across the new Sockets as they're created. These techniques enable multithreaded servers to manage many simultaneous client connections.

Performance Tip 24.2
In high-performance systems in which memory is abundant, a multithreaded server can create a pool of threads that can be assigned quickly to handle network I/O for new Sock-ets as they're created. Thus, when the server receives a connection, it need not incur thread-creation overhead. *When the connection is closed, the thread is returned to the pool for reuse.*

24.5 Establishing a Simple Client Using Stream Sockets

Establishing a simple client in Java requires four steps.

*Step 1: Create a **Socket** to Connect to the sServer*
In *Step 1*, we create a Socket to connect to the server. The Socket constructor establishes the connection. For example, the statement

```
Socket connection = new Socket( serverAddress, port );
```

uses the Socket constructor with two arguments—the server's address (*serverAddress*) and the *port* number. If the connection attempt is successful, this statement returns a Socket. A connection attempt that fails throws an instance of a subclass of IOException, so many programs simply catch IOException. An **UnknownHostException** occurs specifically when the system is unable to resolve the server name specified in the call to the Socket constructor to a corresponding IP address.

*Step 2: Get the **Socket**'s I/O Streams*
In *Step 2*, the client uses Socket methods getInputStream and getOutputStream to obtain references to the Socket's InputStream and OutputStream. As we mentioned in the preceding section, we can use the techniques of Chapter 17 to wrap other stream types around the InputStream and OutputStream associated with the Socket. If the server is sending information in the form of actual types, the client should receive the information in the same format. Thus, if the server sends values with an ObjectOutputStream, the client should read those values with an ObjectInputStream.

Step 3: Perform the Processing
Step 3 is the processing phase in which the client and the server communicate via the InputStream and OutputStream objects.

Step 4: Close the Connection
In *Step 4*, the client closes the connection when the transmission is complete by invoking the close method on the streams and on the Socket. The client must determine when the server is finished sending information so that it can call close to close the Socket connection. For example, the InputStream method read returns the value −1 when it detects end-of-stream (also called EOF—end-of-file). If an ObjectInputStream reads information from the server, an EOFException occurs when the client attempts to read a value from a stream on which end-of-stream is detected.

24.6 Client/Server Interaction with Stream Socket Connections

Figures 24.5 and 24.7 use stream sockets, ObjectInputStream and ObjectOutputStream to demonstrate a simple **client/server chat application**. The server waits for a client connection attempt. When a client connects to the server, the server application sends the client a String object (recall that Strings are Serializable objects) indicating that the connection was successful. Then the client displays the message. The client and server applications each provide text fields that allow the user to type a message and send it to the other application.

When the client or the server sends the String "TERMINATE", the connection terminates. Then the server waits for the next client to connect. The declaration of class Server appears in Fig. 24.5. The declaration of class Client appears in Fig. 24.7. The screen captures showing the execution between the client and the server are shown in Fig. 24.8.

Server Class

Server's constructor (Fig. 24.5, lines 30–55) creates the server's GUI, which contains a JTextField and a JTextArea. Server displays its output in the JTextArea. When the main method (lines 6–11 of Fig. 24.6) executes, it creates a Server object, specifies the window's default close operation and calls method runServer (Fig. 24.5, lines 57–86).

```
1    // Fig. 24.5: Server.java
2    // Server portion of a client/server stream-socket connection.
3    import java.io.EOFException;
4    import java.io.IOException;
5    import java.io.ObjectInputStream;
6    import java.io.ObjectOutputStream;
7    import java.net.ServerSocket;
8    import java.net.Socket;
9    import java.awt.BorderLayout;
10   import java.awt.event.ActionEvent;
11   import java.awt.event.ActionListener;
12   import javax.swing.JFrame;
13   import javax.swing.JScrollPane;
14   import javax.swing.JTextArea;
15   import javax.swing.JTextField;
16   import javax.swing.SwingUtilities;
17
18   public class Server extends JFrame
19   {
20      private JTextField enterField; // inputs message from user
21      private JTextArea displayArea; // display information to user
22      private ObjectOutputStream output; // output stream to client
23      private ObjectInputStream input; // input stream from client
24      private ServerSocket server; // server socket
25      private Socket connection; // connection to client
26      private int counter = 1; // counter of number of connections
27
28      // set up GUI
29      public Server()
30      {
31         super( "Server" );
32
33         enterField = new JTextField(); // create enterField
34         enterField.setEditable( false );
35         enterField.addActionListener(
36            new ActionListener()
37            {
38               // send message to client
39               public void actionPerformed( ActionEvent event )
40               {
```

Fig. 24.5 | Server portion of a client/server stream-socket connection. (Part 1 of 4.)

```
41                    sendData( event.getActionCommand() );
42                    enterField.setText( "" );
43                 } // end method actionPerformed
44              } // end anonymous inner class
45           ); // end call to addActionListener
46
47           add( enterField, BorderLayout.NORTH );
48
49           displayArea = new JTextArea(); // create displayArea
50           add( new JScrollPane( displayArea ), BorderLayout.CENTER );
51
52           setSize( 300, 150 ); // set size of window
53           setVisible( true ); // show window
54        } // end Server constructor
55
56        // set up and run server
57        public void runServer()
58        {
59           try // set up server to receive connections; process connections
60           {
61              server = new ServerSocket( 12345, 100 ); // create ServerSocket
62
63              while ( true )
64              {
65                 try
66                 {
67                    waitForConnection(); // wait for a connection
68                    getStreams(); // get input & output streams
69                    processConnection(); // process connection
70                 } // end try
71                 catch ( EOFException eofException )
72                 {
73                    displayMessage( "\nServer terminated connection" );
74                 } // end catch
75                 finally
76                 {
77                    closeConnection(); // close connection
78                    ++counter;
79                 } // end finally
80              } // end while
81           } // end try
82           catch ( IOException ioException )
83           {
84              ioException.printStackTrace();
85           } // end catch
86        } // end method runServer
87
88        // wait for connection to arrive, then display connection info
89        private void waitForConnection() throws IOException
90        {
91           displayMessage( "Waiting for connection\n" );
92           connection = server.accept(); // allow server to accept connection
```

Fig. 24.5 | Server portion of a client/server stream-socket connection. (Part 2 of 4.)

```
 93        displayMessage( "Connection " + counter + " received from: " +
 94           connection.getInetAddress().getHostName() );
 95     } // end method waitForConnection
 96
 97     // get streams to send and receive data
 98     private void getStreams() throws IOException
 99     {
100        // set up output stream for objects
101        output = new ObjectOutputStream( connection.getOutputStream() );
102        output.flush(); // flush output buffer to send header information
103
104        // set up input stream for objects
105        input = new ObjectInputStream( connection.getInputStream() );
106
107        displayMessage( "\nGot I/O streams\n" );
108     } // end method getStreams
109
110     // process connection with client
111     private void processConnection() throws IOException
112     {
113        String message = "Connection successful";
114        sendData( message ); // send connection successful message
115
116        // enable enterField so server user can send messages
117        setTextFieldEditable( true );
118
119        do // process messages sent from client
120        {
121           try // read message and display it
122           {
123              message = ( String ) input.readObject(); // read new message
124              displayMessage( "\n" + message ); // display message
125           } // end try
126           catch ( ClassNotFoundException classNotFoundException )
127           {
128              displayMessage( "\nUnknown object type received" );
129           } // end catch
130
131        } while ( !message.equals( "CLIENT>>> TERMINATE" ) );
132     } // end method processConnection
133
134     // close streams and socket
135     private void closeConnection()
136     {
137        displayMessage( "\nTerminating connection\n" );
138        setTextFieldEditable( false ); // disable enterField
139
140        try
141        {
142           output.close(); // close output stream
143           input.close(); // close input stream
144           connection.close(); // close socket
145        } // end try
```

Fig. 24.5 | Server portion of a client/server stream-socket connection. (Part 3 of 4.)

```
146              catch ( IOException ioException )
147              {
148                  ioException.printStackTrace();
149              } // end catch
150          } // end method closeConnection
151
152          // send message to client
153          private void sendData( String message )
154          {
155              try // send object to client
156              {
157                  output.writeObject( "SERVER>>> " + message );
158                  output.flush(); // flush output to client
159                  displayMessage( "\nSERVER>>> " + message );
160              } // end try
161              catch ( IOException ioException )
162              {
163                  displayArea.append( "\nError writing object" );
164              } // end catch
165          } // end method sendData
166
167          // manipulates displayArea in the event-dispatch thread
168          private void displayMessage( final String messageToDisplay )
169          {
170              SwingUtilities.invokeLater(
171                  new Runnable()
172                  {
173                      public void run() // updates displayArea
174                      {
175                          displayArea.append( messageToDisplay ); // append message
176                      } // end method run
177                  } // end anonymous inner class
178              ); // end call to SwingUtilities.invokeLater
179          } // end method displayMessage
180
181          // manipulates enterField in the event-dispatch thread
182          private void setTextFieldEditable( final boolean editable )
183          {
184              SwingUtilities.invokeLater(
185                  new Runnable()
186                  {
187                      public void run() // sets enterField's editability
188                      {
189                          enterField.setEditable( editable );
190                      } // end method run
191                  } // end inner class
192              ); // end call to SwingUtilities.invokeLater
193          } // end method setTextFieldEditable
194      } // end class Server
```

Fig. 24.5 | Server portion of a client/server stream-socket connection. (Part 4 of 4.)

```
 1   // Fig. 24.6: ServerTest.java
 2   // Test the Server application.
 3   import javax.swing.JFrame;
 4
 5   public class ServerTest
 6   {
 7      public static void main( String[] args )
 8      {
 9         Server application = new Server(); // create server
10         application.setDefaultCloseOperation( JFrame.EXIT_ON_CLOSE );
11         application.runServer(); // run server application
12      } // end main
13   } // end class ServerTest
```

Fig. 24.6 | Test class for Server.

Method runServer

Method runServer (Fig. 24.5, lines 57–86) sets up the server to receive a connection and processes one connection at a time. Line 61 creates a ServerSocket called server to wait for connections. The ServerSocket listens for a connection from a client at port 12345. The second argument to the constructor is the number of connections that can wait in a queue to connect to the server (100 in this example). If the queue is full when a client attempts to connect, the server refuses the connection.

Common Programming Error 24.1

*Specifying a port that's already in use or specifying an invalid port number when creating a ServerSocket results in a **BindException**.*

Line 67 calls method waitForConnection (declared at lines 89–95) to wait for a client connection. After the connection is established, line 68 calls method getStreams (declared at lines 98–108) to obtain references to the connection's streams. Line 69 calls method processConnection (declared at lines 111–132) to send the initial connection message to the client and to process all messages received from the client. The finally block (lines 75–79) terminates the client connection by calling method closeConnection (lines 135–150), even if an exception occurs. These methods call displayMessage (lines 168–179), which uses the event-dispatch thread to display messages in the application's JTextArea. **SwingUtilities** method **invokeLater** receives a Runnable object as its argument and places it into the event-dispatch thread for execution. This ensures that we don't modify a GUI component from a thread other than the event-dispatch thread, which is important since *Swing GUI components are not thread safe.* We use a similar technique in method setTextFieldEditable (lines 182–193), to set the editability of enterField. For more information on interface Runnable, see Chapter 23.

Method waitForConnection

Method waitForConnection (lines 89–95) uses ServerSocket method accept (line 92) to wait for a connection from a client. When a connection occurs, the resulting Socket is assigned to connection. Method accept blocks until a connection is received (i.e., the thread in which accept is called stops executing until a client connects). Lines 93–94 output the host name of the computer that made the connection. Socket method **getInet-**

Address returns an **InetAddress** (package java.net) containing information about the client computer. InetAddress method **getHostName** returns the host name of the client computer. For example, a special IP address (**127.0.0.1**) and host name (**localhost**) are useful for testing networking applications on your local computer (this is also known as the **loopback address**). If getHostName is called on an InetAddress containing 127.0.0.1, the corresponding host name returned by the method will be localhost.

Method getStreams
Method getStreams (lines 98–108) obtains the Socket's streams and uses them to initialize an ObjectOutputStream (line 101) and an ObjectInputStream (line 105), respectively. Note the call to ObjectOutputStream method **flush** at line 102. This statement causes the ObjectOutputStream on the server to send a **stream header** to the corresponding client's ObjectInputStream. The stream header contains such information as the version of object serialization being used to send objects. This information is required by the Object-InputStream so that it can prepare to receive those objects correctly.

> **Software Engineering Observation 24.4**
> *When using ObjectOutputStream and ObjectInputStream to send and receive data over a network connection, always create the ObjectOutputStream first and flush the stream so that the client's ObjectInputStream can prepare to receive the data. This is required for networking applications that communicate using ObjectOutputStream and ObjectInputStream.*

> **Performance Tip 24.3**
> *A computer's I/O components are typically much slower than its memory. Output buffers are used to increase the efficiency of an application by sending larger amounts of data fewer times, reducing the number of times an application accesses the computer's I/O components.*

Method processConnection
Line 114 of method processConnection (lines 111–132) calls method sendData to send "SERVER>>> Connection successful" as a String to the client. The loop at lines 119–131 executes until the server receives the message "CLIENT>>> TERMINATE". Line 123 uses ObjectInputStream method readObject to read a String from the client. Line 124 invokes method displayMessage to append the message to the JTextArea.

Method closeConnection
When the transmission is complete, method processConnection returns, and the program calls method closeConnection (lines 135–150) to close the streams associated with the Socket and close the Socket. Then the server waits for the next connection attempt from a client by continuing with line 67 at the beginning of the while loop.

Server receives a connection, processes it, closes it and waits for the next connection. A more likely scenario would be a Server that receives a connection, sets it up to be processed as a separate thread of execution, then immediately waits for new connections. The separate threads that process existing connections can continue to execute while the Server concentrates on new connection requests. This makes the server more efficient, because multiple client requests can be processed concurrently. We demonstrate a *multithreaded server* in Section 24.8.

Processing User Interactions
When the user of the server application enters a String in the text field and presses the
Enter key, the program calls method actionPerformed (lines 39–43), which reads the
String from the text field and calls utility method sendData (lines 153–165) to send the
String to the client. Method sendData writes the object, flushes the output buffer and
appends the same String to the text area in the server window. It's not necessary to invoke
displayMessage to modify the text area here, because method sendData is called from an
event handler—thus, sendData executes as part of the *event-dispatch thread*.

Client Class
Like class Server, class Client's constructor (Fig. 24.7, lines 29–56) creates the GUI of
the application (a JTextField and a JTextArea). Client displays its output in the text area. When method main (lines 7–19 of Fig. 24.8) executes, it creates an instance of class
Client, specifies the window's default close operation and calls method runClient
(Fig. 24.7, lines 59–79). In this example, you can execute the client from any computer
on the Internet and specify the IP address or host name of the server computer as a command-line argument to the program. For example, the command

```
java Client 192.168.1.15
```

attempts to connect to the Server on the computer with IP address 192.168.1.15.

```java
1   // Fig. 24.7: Client.java
2   // Client portion of a stream-socket connection between client and server.
3   import java.io.EOFException;
4   import java.io.IOException;
5   import java.io.ObjectInputStream;
6   import java.io.ObjectOutputStream;
7   import java.net.InetAddress;
8   import java.net.Socket;
9   import java.awt.BorderLayout;
10  import java.awt.event.ActionEvent;
11  import java.awt.event.ActionListener;
12  import javax.swing.JFrame;
13  import javax.swing.JScrollPane;
14  import javax.swing.JTextArea;
15  import javax.swing.JTextField;
16  import javax.swing.SwingUtilities;
17
18  public class Client extends JFrame
19  {
20     private JTextField enterField; // enters information from user
21     private JTextArea displayArea; // display information to user
22     private ObjectOutputStream output; // output stream to server
23     private ObjectInputStream input; // input stream from server
24     private String message = ""; // message from server
25     private String chatServer; // host server for this application
26     private Socket client; // socket to communicate with server
27
```

Fig. 24.7 | Client portion of a stream-socket connection between client and server. (Part 1 of 5.)

```
28      // initialize chatServer and set up GUI
29      public Client( String host )
30      {
31         super( "Client" );
32
33         chatServer = host; // set server to which this client connects
34
35         enterField = new JTextField(); // create enterField
36         enterField.setEditable( false );
37         enterField.addActionListener(
38            new ActionListener()
39            {
40               // send message to server
41               public void actionPerformed( ActionEvent event )
42               {
43                  sendData( event.getActionCommand() );
44                  enterField.setText( "" );
45               } // end method actionPerformed
46            } // end anonymous inner class
47         ); // end call to addActionListener
48
49         add( enterField, BorderLayout.NORTH );
50
51         displayArea = new JTextArea(); // create displayArea
52         add( new JScrollPane( displayArea ), BorderLayout.CENTER );
53
54         setSize( 300, 150 ); // set size of window
55         setVisible( true ); // show window
56      } // end Client constructor
57
58      // connect to server and process messages from server
59      public void runClient()
60      {
61         try // connect to server, get streams, process connection
62         {
63            connectToServer(); // create a Socket to make connection
64            getStreams(); // get the input and output streams
65            processConnection(); // process connection
66         } // end try
67         catch ( EOFException eofException )
68         {
69            displayMessage( "\nClient terminated connection" );
70         } // end catch
71         catch ( IOException ioException )
72         {
73            ioException.printStackTrace();
74         } // end catch
75         finally
76         {
77            closeConnection(); // close connection
78         } // end finally
79      } // end method runClient
```

Fig. 24.7 | Client portion of a stream-socket connection between client and server. (Part 2 of 5.)

```
80
81      // connect to server
82      private void connectToServer() throws IOException
83      {
84         displayMessage( "Attempting connection\n" );
85
86         // create Socket to make connection to server
87         client = new Socket( InetAddress.getByName( chatServer ), 12345 );
88
89         // display connection information
90         displayMessage( "Connected to: " +
91            client.getInetAddress().getHostName() );
92      } // end method connectToServer
93
94      // get streams to send and receive data
95      private void getStreams() throws IOException
96      {
97         // set up output stream for objects
98         output = new ObjectOutputStream( client.getOutputStream() );
99         output.flush(); // flush output buffer to send header information
100
101         // set up input stream for objects
102         input = new ObjectInputStream( client.getInputStream() );
103
104         displayMessage( "\nGot I/O streams\n" );
105      } // end method getStreams
106
107     // process connection with server
108     private void processConnection() throws IOException
109     {
110        // enable enterField so client user can send messages
111        setTextFieldEditable( true );
112
113        do // process messages sent from server
114        {
115           try // read message and display it
116           {
117              message = ( String ) input.readObject(); // read new message
118              displayMessage( "\n" + message ); // display message
119           } // end try
120           catch ( ClassNotFoundException classNotFoundException )
121           {
122              displayMessage( "\nUnknown object type received" );
123           } // end catch
124
125        } while ( !message.equals( "SERVER>>> TERMINATE" ) );
126     } // end method processConnection
127
128     // close streams and socket
129     private void closeConnection()
130     {
131        displayMessage( "\nClosing connection" );
132        setTextFieldEditable( false ); // disable enterField
```

Fig. 24.7 | Client portion of a stream-socket connection between client and server. (Part 3 of 5.)

```
133
134        try
135        {
136           output.close(); // close output stream
137           input.close(); // close input stream   1
138           client.close(); // close socket
139        } // end try
140        catch ( IOException ioException )
141        {
142           ioException.printStackTrace();
143        } // end catch
144     } // end method closeConnection
145
146     // send message to server
147     private void sendData( String message )
148     {
149        try // send object to server
150        {
151           output.writeObject( "CLIENT>>> " + message );
152           output.flush(); // flush data to output
153           displayMessage( "\nCLIENT>>> " + message );
154        } // end try
155        catch ( IOException ioException )
156        {
157           displayArea.append( "\nError writing object" );
158        } // end catch
159     } // end method sendData
160
161     // manipulates displayArea in the event-dispatch thread
162     private void displayMessage( final String messageToDisplay )
163     {
164        SwingUtilities.invokeLater(
165           new Runnable()
166           {
167              public void run() // updates displayArea
168              {
169                 displayArea.append( messageToDisplay );
170              } // end method run
171           }  // end anonymous inner class
172        ); // end call to SwingUtilities.invokeLater
173     } // end method displayMessage
174
175     // manipulates enterField in the event-dispatch thread
176     private void setTextFieldEditable( final boolean editable )
177     {
178        SwingUtilities.invokeLater(
179           new Runnable()
180           {
181              public void run() // sets enterField's editability
182              {
183                 enterField.setEditable( editable );
184              } // end method run
185           } // end anonymous inner class
```

Fig. 24.7 | Client portion of a stream-socket connection between client and server. (Part 4 of 5.)

```
186            ); // end call to SwingUtilities.invokeLater
187        } // end method setTextFieldEditable
188 } // end class Client
```

Fig. 24.7 | Client portion of a stream-socket connection between client and server. (Part 5 of 5.)

```
1  // Fig. 24.8: ClientTest.java
2  // Class that tests the Client.
3  import javax.swing.JFrame;
4
5  public class ClientTest
6  {
7     public static void main( String[] args )
8     {
9        Client application; // declare client application
10
11       // if no command line args
12       if ( args.length == 0 )
13          application = new Client( "127.0.0.1" ); // connect to localhost
14       else
15          application = new Client( args[ 0 ] ); // use args to connect
16
17       application.setDefaultCloseOperation( JFrame.EXIT_ON_CLOSE );
18       application.runClient(); // run client application
19    } // end main
20 } // end class ClientTest
```

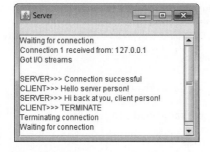 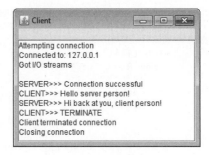

Fig. 24.8 | Class that tests the Client.

Method runClient

Client method runClient (Fig. 24.7, lines 59–79) sets up the connection to the server, processes messages received from the server and closes the connection when communication is complete. Line 63 calls method connectToServer (declared at lines 82–92) to perform the connection. After connecting, line 64 calls method getStreams (declared at lines 95–105) to obtain references to the Socket's stream objects. Then line 65 calls method processConnection (declared at lines 108–126) to receive and display messages sent from the server. The finally block (lines 75–78) calls closeConnection (lines 129–144) to close the streams and the Socket even if an exception occurred. Method displayMessage (lines 162–173) is called from these methods to use the event-dispatch thread to display messages in the application's text area.

Method *connectToServer*

Method connectToServer (lines 82–92) creates a Socket called client (line 87) to establish a connection. The arguments to the Socket constructor are the IP address of the server computer and the port number (12345) where the server application is awaiting client connections. In the first argument, InetAddress static method **getByName** returns an InetAddress object containing the IP address specified as a command-line argument to the application (or 127.0.0.1 if none was specified). Method getByName can receive a String containing either the actual IP address or the host name of the server. The first argument also could have been written other ways. For the localhost address 127.0.0.1, the first argument could be specified with either of the following expressions:

```
InetAddress.getByName( "localhost" )
InetAddress.getLocalHost()
```

Other versions of the Socket constructor receive the IP address or host name as a String. The first argument could have been specified as the IP address "127.0.0.1" or the host name "localhost". We chose to demonstrate the client/server relationship by connecting between applications on the same computer (localhost). Normally, this first argument would be the IP address of another computer. The InetAddress object for another computer can be obtained by specifying the computer's IP address or host name as the argument to InetAddress method getByName. The Socket constructor's second argument is the server port number. This *must* match the port number at which the server is waiting for connections (called the *handshake point*). Once the connection is made, lines 90–91 display a message in the text area indicating the name of the server computer to which the client has connected.

The Client uses an ObjectOutputStream to send data to the server and an ObjectInputStream to receive data from the server. Method getStreams (lines 95–105) creates the ObjectOutputStream and ObjectInputStream objects that use the streams associated with the client socket.

Methods *processConnection* and *closeConnection*

Method processConnection (lines 108–126) contains a loop that executes until the client receives the message "SERVER>>> TERMINATE". Line 117 reads a String object from the server. Line 118 invokes displayMessage to append the message to the text area. When the transmission is complete, method closeConnection (lines 129–144) closes the streams and the Socket.

Processing User Interactions

When the client application user enters a String in the text field and presses *Enter*, the program calls method actionPerformed (lines 41–45) to read the String, then invokes utility method sendData (147–159) to send the String to the server. Method sendData writes the object, flushes the output buffer and appends the same String to the client window's JTextArea. Once again, it's not necessary to invoke utility method displayMessage to modify the text area here, because method sendData is called from an event handler.

24.7 Datagrams: Connectionless Client/Server Interaction

We've been discussing connection-oriented, streams-based transmission. Now we consider **connectionless transmission with datagrams**.

Connection-oriented transmission is like the telephone system in which you dial and are given a connection to the telephone of the person with whom you wish to communicate. The connection is maintained for your phone call, *even when you're not talking.*

Connectionless transmission with datagrams is more like the way mail is carried via the postal service. If a large message will not fit in one envelope, you break it into separate pieces that you place in sequentially numbered envelopes. All of the letters are then mailed at once. The letters could arrive *in order, out of order* or *not at all* (the last case is rare). The person at the receiving end *reassembles* the pieces into sequential order before attempting to make sense of the message.

If your message is small enough to fit in one envelope, you need not worry about the "out-of-sequence" problem, but it's still possible that your message might not arrive. One advantage of datagrams over postal mail is that duplicates of datagrams can arrive at the receiving computer.

Figures 24.9–24.12 use datagrams to send packets of information via the User Datagram Protocol (UDP) between a client application and a server application. In the Client application (Fig. 24.11), the user types a message into a text field and presses *Enter.* The program converts the message into a byte array and places it in a datagram packet that's sent to the server. The Server (Figs. 24.9–24.10) receives the packet and displays the information in it, then **echoes** the packet back to the client. Upon receiving the packet, the client displays the information it contains.

Server Class

Class Server (Fig. 24.9) declares two **DatagramPackets** that the server uses to send and receive information and one **DatagramSocket** that sends and receives the packets. The constructor (lines 19–37), which is called from main (Fig. 24.10, lines 7–12), creates the GUI in which the packets of information will be displayed. Line 30 creates the Datagram-Socket in a try block. Line 30 in Fig. 24.9 uses the DatagramSocket constructor that takes an integer port-number argument (5000 in this example) to bind the server to a port where it can receive packets from clients. Clients sending packets to this Server specify the same port number in the packets they send. A **SocketException** is thrown if the DatagramSocket constructor fails to bind the DatagramSocket to the specified port.

Common Programming Error 24.2

Specifying a port that's already in use or specifying an invalid port number when creating a DatagramSocket results in a SocketException.

```
 1   // Fig. 24.9: Server.java
 2   // Server side of connectionless client/server computing with datagrams.
 3   import java.io.IOException;
 4   import java.net.DatagramPacket;
 5   import java.net.DatagramSocket;
 6   import java.net.SocketException;
 7   import java.awt.BorderLayout;
 8   import javax.swing.JFrame;
 9   import javax.swing.JScrollPane;
10   import javax.swing.JTextArea;
```

Fig. 24.9 | Server side of connectionless client/server computing with datagrams. (Part 1 of 3.)

```java
11   import javax.swing.SwingUtilities;
12
13   public class Server extends JFrame
14   {
15      private JTextArea displayArea; // displays packets received
16      private DatagramSocket socket; // socket to connect to client
17
18      // set up GUI and DatagramSocket
19      public Server()
20      {
21         super( "Server" );
22
23         displayArea = new JTextArea(); // create displayArea
24         add( new JScrollPane( displayArea ), BorderLayout.CENTER );
25         setSize( 400, 300 ); // set size of window
26         setVisible( true ); // show window
27
28         try // create DatagramSocket for sending and receiving packets
29         {
30            socket = new DatagramSocket( 5000 );
31         } // end try
32         catch ( SocketException socketException )
33         {
34            socketException.printStackTrace();
35            System.exit( 1 );
36         } // end catch
37      } // end Server constructor
38
39      // wait for packets to arrive, display data and echo packet to client
40      public void waitForPackets()
41      {
42         while ( true )
43         {
44            try // receive packet, display contents, return copy to client
45            {
46               byte[] data = new byte[ 100 ]; // set up packet
47               DatagramPacket receivePacket =
48                  new DatagramPacket( data, data.length );
49
50               socket.receive( receivePacket ); // wait to receive packet
51
52               // display information from received packet
53               displayMessage( "\nPacket received:" +
54                  "\nFrom host: " + receivePacket.getAddress() +
55                  "\nHost port: " + receivePacket.getPort() +
56                  "\nLength: " + receivePacket.getLength() +
57                  "\nContaining:\n\t" + new String( receivePacket.getData(),
58                     0, receivePacket.getLength() ) );
59
60               sendPacketToClient( receivePacket ); // send packet to client
61            } // end try
62            catch ( IOException ioException )
63            {
```

Fig. 24.9 | Server side of connectionless client/server computing with datagrams. (Part 2 of 3.)

```
64                displayMessage( ioException + "\n" );
65                ioException.printStackTrace();
66            } // end catch
67        } // end while
68    } // end method waitForPackets
69
70    // echo packet to client
71    private void sendPacketToClient( DatagramPacket receivePacket )
72        throws IOException
73    {
74        displayMessage( "\n\nEcho data to client..." );
75
76        // create packet to send
77        DatagramPacket sendPacket = new DatagramPacket(
78            receivePacket.getData(), receivePacket.getLength(),
79            receivePacket.getAddress(), receivePacket.getPort() );
80
81        socket.send( sendPacket ); // send packet to client
82        displayMessage( "Packet sent\n" );
83    } // end method sendPacketToClient
84
85    // manipulates displayArea in the event-dispatch thread
86    private void displayMessage( final String messageToDisplay )
87    {
88        SwingUtilities.invokeLater(
89            new Runnable()
90            {
91                public void run() // updates displayArea
92                {
93                    displayArea.append( messageToDisplay ); // display message
94                } // end method run
95            } // end anonymous inner class
96        ); // end call to SwingUtilities.invokeLater
97    } // end method displayMessage
98 } // end class Server
```

Fig. 24.9 | Server side of connectionless client/server computing with datagrams. (Part 3 of 3.)

```
1  // Fig. 24.10: ServerTest.java
2  // Class that tests the Server.
3  import javax.swing.JFrame;
4
5  public class ServerTest
6  {
7      public static void main( String[] args )
8      {
9          Server application = new Server(); // create server
10         application.setDefaultCloseOperation( JFrame.EXIT_ON_CLOSE );
11         application.waitForPackets(); // run server application
12     } // end main
13 } // end class ServerTest
```

Fig. 24.10 | Class that tests the Server. (Part 1 of 2.)

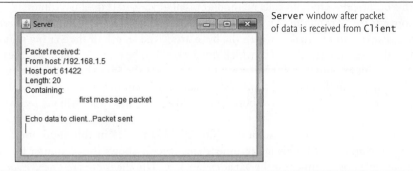

Server window after packet of data is received from Client

Fig. 24.10 | Class that tests the Server. (Part 2 of 2.)

Method waitForPackets

Server method waitForPackets (Fig. 24.9, lines 40–68) uses an infinite loop to wait for packets to arrive at the Server. Lines 47–48 create a DatagramPacket in which a received packet of information can be stored. The DatagramPacket constructor for this purpose receives two arguments—a byte array in which the data will be stored and the length of the array. Line 50 uses DatagramSocket method **receive** to wait for a packet to arrive at the Server. Method receive blocks until a packet arrives, then stores the packet in its DatagramPacket argument. The method throws an IOException if an error occurs while receiving a packet.

Method displayMessage

When a packet arrives, lines 53–58 call method displayMessage (declared at lines 86–97) to append the packet's contents to the text area. DatagramPacket method **getAddress** (line 54) returns an InetAddress object containing the IP address of the computer from which the packet was sent. Method **getPort** (line 55) returns an integer specifying the port number through which the client computer sent the packet. Method **getLength** (line 56) returns an integer representing the number of bytes of data received. Method **getData** (line 57) returns a byte array containing the data. Lines 57–58 initialize a String object using a three-argument constructor that takes a byte array, the offset and the length. This String is then appended to the text to display.

Method sendPacketToClient

After displaying a packet, line 60 calls method sendPacketToClient (declared at lines 71–83) to create a new packet and send it to the client. Lines 77–79 create a DatagramPacket and pass four arguments to its constructor. The first argument specifies the byte array to send. The second argument specifies the number of bytes to send. The third argument specifies the client computer's IP address, to which the packet will be sent. The fourth argument specifies the port where the client is waiting to receive packets. Line 81 sends the packet over the network. Method **send** of DatagramSocket throws an IOException if an error occurs while sending a packet.

Client Class

The Client (Figs. 24.11–24.12) works similarly to class Server, except that the Client sends packets only when the user types a message in a text field and presses the *Enter* key.

When this occurs, the program calls method `actionPerformed` (Fig. 24.11, lines 32–57), which converts the `String` the user entered into a byte array (line 41). Lines 44–45 create a `DatagramPacket` and initialize it with the byte array, the length of the `String` that was entered by the user, the IP address to which the packet is to be sent (`InetAddress.getLocalHost()` in this example) and the port number at which the `Server` is waiting for packets (5000 in this example). Line 47 sends the packet. The client in this example must know that the server is receiving packets at port 5000—otherwise, the server will *not* receive the packets.

The `DatagramSocket` constructor call (Fig. 24.11, line 71) in this application does not specify any arguments. This no-argument constructor allows the computer to select the next available port number for the `DatagramSocket`. The client does not need a specific port number, because the server receives the client's port number as part of each `DatagramPacket` sent by the client. Thus, the server can send packets back to the same computer and port number from which it receives a packet of information.

```java
1   // Fig. 24.11: Client.java
2   // Client side of connectionless client/server computing with datagrams.
3   import java.io.IOException;
4   import java.net.DatagramPacket;
5   import java.net.DatagramSocket;
6   import java.net.InetAddress;
7   import java.net.SocketException;
8   import java.awt.BorderLayout;
9   import java.awt.event.ActionEvent;
10  import java.awt.event.ActionListener;
11  import javax.swing.JFrame;
12  import javax.swing.JScrollPane;
13  import javax.swing.JTextArea;
14  import javax.swing.JTextField;
15  import javax.swing.SwingUtilities;
16
17  public class Client extends JFrame
18  {
19     private JTextField enterField; // for entering messages
20     private JTextArea displayArea; // for displaying messages
21     private DatagramSocket socket; // socket to connect to server
22
23     // set up GUI and DatagramSocket
24     public Client()
25     {
26        super( "Client" );
27
28        enterField = new JTextField( "Type message here" );
29        enterField.addActionListener(
30           new ActionListener()
31           {
32              public void actionPerformed( ActionEvent event )
33              {
34                 try // create and send packet
35                 {
```

Fig. 24.11 | Client side of connectionless client/server computing with datagrams. (Part 1 of 3.)

```
36                        // get message from textfield
37                        String message = event.getActionCommand();
38                        displayArea.append( "\nSending packet containing: " +
39                           message + "\n" );
40
41                        byte[] data = message.getBytes(); // convert to bytes
42
43                        // create sendPacket
44                        DatagramPacket sendPacket = new DatagramPacket( data,
45                           data.length, InetAddress.getLocalHost(), 5000 );
46
47                        socket.send( sendPacket ); // send packet
48                        displayArea.append( "Packet sent\n" );
49                        displayArea.setCaretPosition(
50                           displayArea.getText().length() );
51                     } // end try
52                     catch ( IOException ioException )
53                     {
54                        displayMessage( ioException + "\n" );
55                        ioException.printStackTrace();
56                     } // end catch
57                  } // end actionPerformed
58               } // end inner class
59            ); // end call to addActionListener
60
61            add( enterField, BorderLayout.NORTH );
62
63            displayArea = new JTextArea();
64            add( new JScrollPane( displayArea ), BorderLayout.CENTER );
65
66            setSize( 400, 300 ); // set window size
67            setVisible( true ); // show window
68
69            try // create DatagramSocket for sending and receiving packets
70            {
71               socket = new DatagramSocket();
72            } // end try
73            catch ( SocketException socketException )
74            {
75               socketException.printStackTrace();
76               System.exit( 1 );
77            } // end catch
78         } // end Client constructor
79
80         // wait for packets to arrive from Server, display packet contents
81         public void waitForPackets()
82         {
83            while ( true )
84            {
85               try // receive packet and display contents
86               {
87                  byte[] data = new byte[ 100 ]; // set up packet
```

Fig. 24.11 | Client side of connectionless client/server computing with datagrams. (Part 2 of 3.)

```
88                  DatagramPacket receivePacket = new DatagramPacket(
89                     data, data.length );
90
91                  socket.receive( receivePacket ); // wait for packet
92
93                  // display packet contents
94                  displayMessage( "\nPacket received:" +
95                     "\nFrom host: " + receivePacket.getAddress() +
96                     "\nHost port: " + receivePacket.getPort() +
97                     "\nLength: " + receivePacket.getLength() +
98                     "\nContaining:\n\t" + new String( receivePacket.getData(),
99                        0, receivePacket.getLength() ) );
100              } // end try
101              catch ( IOException exception )
102              {
103                  displayMessage( exception + "\n" );
104                  exception.printStackTrace();
105              } // end catch
106          } // end while
107      } // end method waitForPackets
108
109      // manipulates displayArea in the event-dispatch thread
110      private void displayMessage( final String messageToDisplay )
111      {
112          SwingUtilities.invokeLater(
113              new Runnable()
114              {
115                  public void run() // updates displayArea
116                  {
117                      displayArea.append( messageToDisplay );
118                  } // end method run
119              } // end inner class
120          ); // end call to SwingUtilities.invokeLater
121      } // end method displayMessage
122  } // end class Client
```

Fig. 24.11 | Client side of connectionless client/server computing with datagrams. (Part 3 of 3.)

```
1   // Fig. 24.12: ClientTest.java
2   // Tests the Client class.
3   import javax.swing.JFrame;
4
5   public class ClientTest
6   {
7       public static void main( String[] args )
8       {
9           Client application = new Client(); // create client
10          application.setDefaultCloseOperation( JFrame.EXIT_ON_CLOSE );
11          application.waitForPackets(); // run client application
12      } // end main
13  } // end class ClientTest
```

Fig. 24.12 | Class that tests the Client. (Part 1 of 2.)

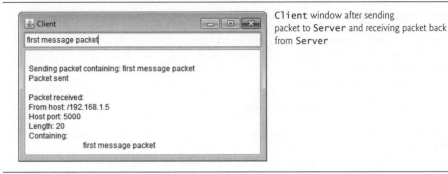

Client window after sending
packet to Server and receiving packet back
from Server

Fig. 24.12 | Class that tests the Client. (Part 2 of 2.)

Method waitForPackets

Client method waitForPackets (lines 81–107) uses an infinite loop to wait for packets from the server. Line 91 blocks until a packet arrives. This does not prevent the user from sending a packet, because the *GUI events are handled in the event-dispatch thread*. It only prevents the while loop from continuing until a packet arrives at the Client. When a packet arrives, line 91 stores it in receivePacket, and lines 94–99 call method displayMessage (declared at lines 110–121) to display the packet's contents in the text area.

24.8 Client/Server Tic-Tac-Toe Using a Multithreaded Server

This section presents the popular game Tic-Tac-Toe implemented by using client/server techniques with stream sockets. The program consists of a TicTacToeServer application (Figs. 24.13–24.14) that allows two TicTacToeClient applications (Figs. 24.15–24.16) to connect to the server and play Tic-Tac-Toe. Sample outputs are shown in Fig. 24.17.

TicTacToeServer Class

As the TicTacToeServer receives each client connection, it creates an instance of inner-class Player (Fig. 24.13, lines 182–304) to process the client in a *separate thread*. These threads enable the clients to play the game independently. The first client to connect to the server is player X and the second is player O. Player X makes the first move. The server maintains the information about the board so it can determine if a player's move is valid.

```
 1   // Fig. 24.13: TicTacToeServer.java
 2   // Server side of client/server Tic-Tac-Toe program.
 3   import java.awt.BorderLayout;
 4   import java.net.ServerSocket;
 5   import java.net.Socket;
 6   import java.io.IOException;
 7   import java.util.Formatter;
 8   import java.util.Scanner;
 9   import java.util.concurrent.ExecutorService;
10   import java.util.concurrent.Executors;
```

Fig. 24.13 | Server side of client/server Tic-Tac-Toe program. (Part 1 of 7.)

```
11   import java.util.concurrent.locks.Lock;
12   import java.util.concurrent.locks.ReentrantLock;
13   import java.util.concurrent.locks.Condition;
14   import javax.swing.JFrame;
15   import javax.swing.JTextArea;
16   import javax.swing.SwingUtilities;
17
18   public class TicTacToeServer extends JFrame
19   {
20      private String[] board = new String[ 9 ]; // tic-tac-toe board
21      private JTextArea outputArea; // for outputting moves
22      private Player[] players; // array of Players
23      private ServerSocket server; // server socket to connect with clients
24      private int currentPlayer; // keeps track of player with current move
25      private final static int PLAYER_X = 0; // constant for first player
26      private final static int PLAYER_O = 1; // constant for second player
27      private final static String[] MARKS = { "X", "O" }; // array of marks
28      private ExecutorService runGame; // will run players
29      private Lock gameLock; // to lock game for synchronization
30      private Condition otherPlayerConnected; // to wait for other player
31      private Condition otherPlayerTurn; // to wait for other player's turn
32
33      // set up tic-tac-toe server and GUI that displays messages
34      public TicTacToeServer()
35      {
36         super( "Tic-Tac-Toe Server" ); // set title of window
37
38         // create ExecutorService with a thread for each player
39         runGame = Executors.newFixedThreadPool( 2 );
40         gameLock = new ReentrantLock(); // create lock for game
41
42         // condition variable for both players being connected
43         otherPlayerConnected = gameLock.newCondition();
44
45         // condition variable for the other player's turn
46         otherPlayerTurn = gameLock.newCondition();
47
48         for ( int i = 0; i < 9; i++ )
49            board[ i ] = new String( "" ); // create tic-tac-toe board
50         players = new Player[ 2 ]; // create array of players
51         currentPlayer = PLAYER_X; // set current player to first player
52
53         try
54         {
55            server = new ServerSocket( 12345, 2 ); // set up ServerSocket
56         } // end try
57         catch ( IOException ioException )
58         {
59            ioException.printStackTrace();
60            System.exit( 1 );
61         } // end catch
62
63         outputArea = new JTextArea(); // create JTextArea for output
```

Fig. 24.13 | Server side of client/server Tic-Tac-Toe program. (Part 2 of 7.)

```
64              add( outputArea, BorderLayout.CENTER );
65              outputArea.setText( "Server awaiting connections\n" );
66
67              setSize( 300, 300 ); // set size of window
68              setVisible( true ); // show window
69          } // end TicTacToeServer constructor
70
71          // wait for two connections so game can be played
72          public void execute()
73          {
74              // wait for each client to connect
75              for ( int i = 0; i < players.length; i++ )
76              {
77                  try // wait for connection, create Player, start runnable
78                  {
79                      players[ i ] = new Player( server.accept(), i );
80                      runGame.execute( players[ i ] ); // execute player runnable
81                  } // end try
82                  catch ( IOException ioException )
83                  {
84                      ioException.printStackTrace();
85                      System.exit( 1 );
86                  } // end catch
87              } // end for
88
89              gameLock.lock(); // lock game to signal player X's thread
90
91              try
92              {
93                  players[ PLAYER_X ].setSuspended( false ); // resume player X
94                  otherPlayerConnected.signal(); // wake up player X's thread
95              } // end try
96              finally
97              {
98                  gameLock.unlock(); // unlock game after signalling player X
99              } // end finally
100         } // end method execute
101
102         // display message in outputArea
103         private void displayMessage( final String messageToDisplay )
104         {
105             // display message from event-dispatch thread of execution
106             SwingUtilities.invokeLater(
107                 new Runnable()
108                 {
109                     public void run() // updates outputArea
110                     {
111                         outputArea.append( messageToDisplay ); // add message
112                     } // end  method run
113                 } // end inner class
114             ); // end call to SwingUtilities.invokeLater
115         } // end method displayMessage
```

Fig. 24.13 | Server side of client/server Tic-Tac-Toe program. (Part 3 of 7.)

```
116
117     // determine if move is valid
118     public boolean validateAndMove( int location, int player )
119     {
120        // while not current player, must wait for turn
121        while ( player != currentPlayer )
122        {
123           gameLock.lock(); // lock game to wait for other player to go
124
125           try
126           {
127              otherPlayerTurn.await(); // wait for player's turn
128           } // end try
129           catch ( InterruptedException exception )
130           {
131              exception.printStackTrace();
132           } // end catch
133           finally
134           {
135              gameLock.unlock(); // unlock game after waiting
136           } // end finally
137        } // end while
138
139        // if location not occupied, make move
140        if ( !isOccupied( location ) )
141        {
142           board[ location ] = MARKS[ currentPlayer ]; // set move on board
143           currentPlayer = ( currentPlayer + 1 ) % 2; // change player
144
145           // let new current player know that move occurred
146           players[ currentPlayer ].otherPlayerMoved( location );
147
148           gameLock.lock(); // lock game to signal other player to go
149
150           try
151           {
152              otherPlayerTurn.signal(); // signal other player to continue
153           } // end try
154           finally
155           {
156              gameLock.unlock(); // unlock game after signaling
157           } // end finally
158
159           return true; // notify player that move was valid
160        } // end if
161        else // move was not valid
162           return false; // notify player that move was invalid
163     } // end method validateAndMove
164
165     // determine whether location is occupied
166     public boolean isOccupied( int location )
167     {
```

Fig. 24.13 | Server side of client/server Tic-Tac-Toe program. (Part 4 of 7.)

```
168        if ( board[ location ].equals( MARKS[ PLAYER_X ] ) ||
169           board [ location ].equals( MARKS[ PLAYER_O ] ) )
170           return true; // location is occupied
171        else
172           return false; // location is not occupied
173     } // end method isOccupied
174
175     // place code in this method to determine whether game over
176     public boolean isGameOver()
177     {
178        return false; // this is left as an exercise
179     } // end method isGameOver
180
181     // private inner class Player manages each Player as a runnable
182     private class Player implements Runnable
183     {
184        private Socket connection; // connection to client
185        private Scanner input; // input from client
186        private Formatter output; // output to client
187        private int playerNumber; // tracks which player this is
188        private String mark; // mark for this player
189        private boolean suspended = true; // whether thread is suspended
190
191        // set up Player thread
192        public Player( Socket socket, int number )
193        {
194           playerNumber = number; // store this player's number
195           mark = MARKS[ playerNumber ]; // specify player's mark
196           connection = socket; // store socket for client
197
198           try // obtain streams from Socket
199           {
200              input = new Scanner( connection.getInputStream() );
201              output = new Formatter( connection.getOutputStream() );
202           } // end try
203           catch ( IOException ioException )
204           {
205              ioException.printStackTrace();
206              System.exit( 1 );
207           } // end catch
208        } // end Player constructor
209
210        // send message that other player moved
211        public void otherPlayerMoved( int location )
212        {
213           output.format( "Opponent moved\n" );
214           output.format( "%d\n", location ); // send location of move
215           output.flush(); // flush output
216        } // end method otherPlayerMoved
217
```

Fig. 24.13 | Server side of client/server Tic-Tac-Toe program. (Part 5 of 7.)

```
218          // control thread's execution
219          public void run()
220          {
221             // send client its mark (X or O), process messages from client
222             try
223             {
224                displayMessage( "Player " + mark + " connected\n" );
225                output.format( "%s\n", mark ); // send player's mark
226                output.flush(); // flush output
227
228                // if player X, wait for another player to arrive
229                if ( playerNumber == PLAYER_X )
230                {
231                   output.format( "%s\n%s", "Player X connected",
232                      "Waiting for another player\n" );
233                   output.flush(); // flush output
234
235                   gameLock.lock(); // lock game to  wait for second player
236
237                   try
238                   {
239                      while( suspended )
240                      {
241                         otherPlayerConnected.await(); // wait for player O
242                      } // end while
243                   } // end try
244                   catch ( InterruptedException exception )
245                   {
246                      exception.printStackTrace();
247                   } // end catch
248                   finally
249                   {
250                      gameLock.unlock(); // unlock game after second player
251                   } // end finally
252
253                   // send message that other player connected
254                   output.format( "Other player connected. Your move.\n" );
255                   output.flush(); // flush output
256                } // end if
257                else
258                {
259                   output.format( "Player O connected, please wait\n" );
260                   output.flush(); // flush output
261                } // end else
262
263                // while game not over
264                while ( !isGameOver() )
265                {
266                   int location = 0; // initialize move location
267
268                   if ( input.hasNext() )
269                      location = input.nextInt(); // get move location
270
```

Fig. 24.13 | Server side of client/server Tic-Tac-Toe program. (Part 6 of 7.)

```
271                    // check for valid move
272                    if ( validateAndMove( location, playerNumber ) )
273                    {
274                       displayMessage( "\nlocation: " + location );
275                       output.format( "Valid move.\n" ); // notify client
276                       output.flush(); // flush output
277                    } // end if
278                    else // move was invalid
279                    {
280                       output.format( "Invalid move, try again\n" );
281                       output.flush(); // flush output
282                    } // end else
283                 } // end while
284              } // end try
285              finally
286              {
287                 try
288                 {
289                    connection.close(); // close connection to client
290                 } // end try
291                 catch ( IOException ioException )
292                 {
293                    ioException.printStackTrace();
294                    System.exit( 1 );
295                 } // end catch
296              } // end finally
297           } // end method run
298
299           // set whether or not thread is suspended
300           public void setSuspended( boolean status )
301           {
302              suspended = status; // set value of suspended
303           } // end method setSuspended
304        } // end class Player
305  } // end class TicTacToeServer
```

Fig. 24.13 | Server side of client/server Tic-Tac-Toe program. (Part 7 of 7.)

```
1   // Fig. 24.14: TicTacToeServerTest.java
2   // Class that tests Tic-Tac-Toe server.
3   import javax.swing.JFrame;
4
5   public class TicTacToeServerTest
6   {
7      public static void main( String[] args )
8      {
9         TicTacToeServer application = new TicTacToeServer();
10        application.setDefaultCloseOperation( JFrame.EXIT_ON_CLOSE );
11        application.execute();
12     } // end main
13  } // end class TicTacToeServerTest
```

Fig. 24.14 | Class that tests Tic-Tac-Toe server. (Part 1 of 2.)

Fig. 24.14 | Class that tests Tic-Tac-Toe server. (Part 2 of 2.)

We begin with a discussion of the server side of the Tic-Tac-Toe game. When the TicTacToeServer application executes, the main method (lines 7–12 of Fig. 24.14) creates a TicTacToeServer object called application. The constructor (Fig. 24.13, lines 34–69) attempts to set up a ServerSocket. If successful, the program displays the server window, then main invokes the TicTacToeServer method execute (lines 72–100). Method execute loops twice, blocking at line 79 each time while waiting for a client connection. When a client connects, line 79 creates a new Player object to manage the connection as a separate thread, and line 80 executes the Player in the runGame thread pool.

When the TicTacToeServer creates a Player, the Player constructor (lines 192–208) receives the Socket object representing the connection to the client and gets the associated input and output streams. Line 201 creates a Formatter (see Chapter 17) by wrapping it around the output stream of the socket. The Player's run method (lines 219–297) controls the information that's sent to and received from the client. First, it passes to the client the character that the client will place on the board when a move is made (line 225). Line 226 calls Formatter method **flush** to force this output to the client. Line 241 suspends player X's thread as it starts executing, because player X can move only after player O connects.

When player O connects, the game can be played, and the run method begins executing its while statement (lines 264–283). Each iteration of this loop reads an integer (line 269) representing the location where the client wants to place a mark (blocking to wait for input, if necessary), and line 272 invokes the TicTacToeServer method validateAndMove (declared at lines 118–163) to check the move. If the move is valid, line 275 sends a message to the client to this effect. If not, line 280 sends a message indicating that the move was invalid. The program maintains board locations as numbers from 0 to 8 (0 through 2 for the first row, 3 through 5 for the second row and 6 through 8 for the third row).

Method validateAndMove (lines 118–163 in class TicTacToeServer) allows only one player at a time to move, thereby preventing them from modifying the state information of the game simultaneously. If the Player attempting to validate a move is *not* the current player (i.e., the one allowed to make a move), it's placed in a *wait* state until its turn to move. If the position for the move being validated is already occupied on the board, validMove returns false. Otherwise, the server places a mark for the player in its local representation of the board (line 142), notifies the other Player object (line 146) that a move has been made (so that the client can be sent a message), invokes method signal (line 152) so that the waiting Player (if there is one) can validate a move and returns true (line 159) to indicate that the move is valid.

TicTacToeClient Class

Each TicTacToeClient application (Figs. 24.15–24.16; sample outputs in Fig. 24.17) maintains its own GUI version of the Tic-Tac-Toe board on which it displays the state of the game. The clients can place a mark only in an empty square. Inner class Square (Fig. 24.15, lines 205–261) implements each of the nine squares on the board. When a TicTacToeClient begins execution, it creates a JTextArea in which messages from the server and a representation of the board using nine Square objects are displayed. The startClient method (lines 80–100) opens a connection to the server and gets the associated input and output streams from the Socket object. Lines 85–86 make a connection to the server. Class TicTacToeClient implements interface Runnable so that a separate thread can read messages from the server. This approach enables the user to interact with the board (in the event-dispatch thread) while waiting for messages from the server. After establishing the connection to the server, line 99 executes the client with the worker ExecutorService. The run method (lines 103–126) controls the separate thread of execution. The method first reads the mark character (X or O) from the server (line 105), then loops continuously (lines 121–125) and reads messages from the server (line 124). Each message is passed to the processMessage method (lines 129–156) for processing.

```java
1   // Fig. 24.15: TicTacToeClient.java
2   // Client side of client/server Tic-Tac-Toe program.
3   import java.awt.BorderLayout;
4   import java.awt.Dimension;
5   import java.awt.Graphics;
6   import java.awt.GridLayout;
7   import java.awt.event.MouseAdapter;
8   import java.awt.event.MouseEvent;
9   import java.net.Socket;
10  import java.net.InetAddress;
11  import java.io.IOException;
12  import javax.swing.JFrame;
13  import javax.swing.JPanel;
14  import javax.swing.JScrollPane;
15  import javax.swing.JTextArea;
16  import javax.swing.JTextField;
17  import javax.swing.SwingUtilities;
18  import java.util.Formatter;
19  import java.util.Scanner;
20  import java.util.concurrent.Executors;
21  import java.util.concurrent.ExecutorService;
22
23  public class TicTacToeClient extends JFrame implements Runnable
24  {
```

Fig. 24.15 | Client side of client/server Tic-Tac-Toe program. (Part 1 of 6.)

```
25    private JTextField idField; // textfield to display player's mark
26    private JTextArea displayArea; // JTextArea to display output
27    private JPanel boardPanel; // panel for tic-tac-toe board
28    private JPanel panel2; // panel to hold board
29    private Square[][] board; // tic-tac-toe board
30    private Square currentSquare; // current square
31    private Socket connection; // connection to server
32    private Scanner input; // input from server
33    private Formatter output; // output to server
34    private String ticTacToeHost; // host name for server
35    private String myMark; // this client's mark
36    private boolean myTurn; // determines which client's turn it is
37    private final String X_MARK = "X"; // mark for first client
38    private final String O_MARK = "O"; // mark for second client
39
40    // set up user-interface and board
41    public TicTacToeClient( String host )
42    {
43       ticTacToeHost = host; // set name of server
44       displayArea = new JTextArea( 4, 30 ); // set up JTextArea
45       displayArea.setEditable( false );
46       add( new JScrollPane( displayArea ), BorderLayout.SOUTH );
47
48       boardPanel = new JPanel(); // set up panel for squares in board
49       boardPanel.setLayout( new GridLayout( 3, 3, 0, 0 ) );
50
51       board = new Square[ 3 ][ 3 ]; // create board
52
53       // loop over the rows in the board
54       for ( int row = 0; row < board.length; row++ )
55       {
56          // loop over the columns in the board
57          for ( int column = 0; column < board[ row ].length; column++ )
58          {
59             // create square
60             board[ row ][ column ] = new Square( ' ', row * 3 + column );
61             boardPanel.add( board[ row ][ column ] ); // add square
62          } // end inner for
63       } // end outer for
64
65       idField = new JTextField(); // set up textfield
66       idField.setEditable( false );
67       add( idField, BorderLayout.NORTH );
68
69       panel2 = new JPanel(); // set up panel to contain boardPanel
70       panel2.add( boardPanel, BorderLayout.CENTER ); // add board panel
71       add( panel2, BorderLayout.CENTER ); // add container panel
72
73       setSize( 300, 225 ); // set size of window
74       setVisible( true ); // show window
75
76       startClient();
77    } // end TicTacToeClient constructor
```

Fig. 24.15 | Client side of client/server Tic-Tac-Toe program. (Part 2 of 6.)

```
78
79      // start the client thread
80      public void startClient()
81      {
82         try // connect to server and get streams
83         {
84            // make connection to server
85            connection = new Socket(
86               InetAddress.getByName( ticTacToeHost ), 12345 );
87
88            // get streams for input and output
89            input = new Scanner( connection.getInputStream() );
90            output = new Formatter( connection.getOutputStream() );
91         } // end try
92         catch ( IOException ioException )
93         {
94            ioException.printStackTrace();
95         } // end catch
96
97         // create and start worker thread for this client
98         ExecutorService worker = Executors.newFixedThreadPool( 1 );
99         worker.execute( this ); // execute client
100     } // end method startClient
101
102     // control thread that allows continuous update of displayArea
103     public void run()
104     {
105        myMark = input.nextLine(); // get player's mark (X or O)
106
107        SwingUtilities.invokeLater(
108           new Runnable()
109           {
110              public void run()
111              {
112                 // display player's mark
113                 idField.setText( "You are player \"" + myMark + "\"" );
114              } // end method run
115           } // end anonymous inner class
116        ); // end call to SwingUtilities.invokeLater
117
118        myTurn = ( myMark.equals( X_MARK ) ); // determine if client's turn
119
120        // receive messages sent to client and output them
121        while ( true )
122        {
123           if ( input.hasNextLine() )
124              processMessage( input.nextLine() );
125        } // end while
126     } // end method run
127
128     // process messages received by client
129     private void processMessage( String message )
130     {
```

Fig. 24.15 | Client side of client/server Tic-Tac-Toe program. (Part 3 of 6.)

```
131         // valid move occurred
132         if ( message.equals( "Valid move." ) )
133         {
134            displayMessage( "Valid move, please wait.\n" );
135            setMark( currentSquare, myMark ); // set mark in square
136         } // end if
137         else if ( message.equals( "Invalid move, try again" ) )
138         {
139            displayMessage( message + "\n" ); // display invalid move
140            myTurn = true; // still this client's turn
141         } // end else if
142         else if ( message.equals( "Opponent moved" ) )
143         {
144            int location = input.nextInt(); // get move location
145            input.nextLine(); // skip newline after int location
146            int row = location / 3; // calculate row
147            int column = location % 3; // calculate column
148
149            setMark( board[ row ][ column ],
150               ( myMark.equals( X_MARK ) ? O_MARK : X_MARK ) ); // mark move
151            displayMessage( "Opponent moved. Your turn.\n" );
152            myTurn = true; // now this client's turn
153         } // end else if
154         else
155            displayMessage( message + "\n" ); // display the message
156      } // end method processMessage
157
158      // manipulate displayArea in event-dispatch thread
159      private void displayMessage( final String messageToDisplay )
160      {
161         SwingUtilities.invokeLater(
162            new Runnable()
163            {
164               public void run()
165               {
166                  displayArea.append( messageToDisplay ); // updates output
167               } // end method run
168            } // end inner class
169         ); // end call to SwingUtilities.invokeLater
170      } // end method displayMessage
171
172      // utility method to set mark on board in event-dispatch thread
173      private void setMark( final Square squareToMark, final String mark )
174      {
175         SwingUtilities.invokeLater(
176            new Runnable()
177            {
178               public void run()
179               {
180                  squareToMark.setMark( mark ); // set mark in square
181               } // end method run
```

Fig. 24.15 | Client side of client/server Tic-Tac-Toe program. (Part 4 of 6.)

```
182              } // end anonymous inner class
183            ); // end call to SwingUtilities.invokeLater
184      } // end method setMark
185
186      // send message to server indicating clicked square
187      public void sendClickedSquare( int location )
188      {
189         // if it is my turn
190         if ( myTurn )
191         {
192            output.format( "%d\n", location ); // send location to server
193            output.flush();
194            myTurn = false; // not my turn any more
195         } // end if
196      } // end method sendClickedSquare
197
198      // set current Square
199      public void setCurrentSquare( Square square )
200      {
201         currentSquare = square; // set current square to argument
202      } // end method setCurrentSquare
203
204      // private inner class for the squares on the board
205      private class Square extends JPanel
206      {
207         private String mark; // mark to be drawn in this square
208         private int location; // location of square
209
210         public Square( String squareMark, int squareLocation )
211         {
212            mark = squareMark; // set mark for this square
213            location = squareLocation; // set location of this square
214
215            addMouseListener(
216               new MouseAdapter()
217               {
218                  public void mouseReleased( MouseEvent e )
219                  {
220                     setCurrentSquare( Square.this ); // set current square
221
222                     // send location of this square
223                     sendClickedSquare( getSquareLocation() );
224                  } // end method mouseReleased
225               } // end anonymous inner class
226            ); // end call to addMouseListener
227         } // end Square constructor
228
229         // return preferred size of Square
230         public Dimension getPreferredSize()
231         {
232            return new Dimension( 30, 30 ); // return preferred size
233         } // end method getPreferredSize
```

Fig. 24.15 | Client side of client/server Tic-Tac-Toe program. (Part 5 of 6.)

```
234
235        // return minimum size of Square
236        public Dimension getMinimumSize()
237        {
238           return getPreferredSize(); // return preferred size
239        } // end method getMinimumSize
240
241        // set mark for Square
242        public void setMark( String newMark )
243        {
244           mark = newMark; // set mark of square
245           repaint(); // repaint square
246        } // end method setMark
247
248        // return Square location
249        public int getSquareLocation()
250        {
251           return location; // return location of square
252        } // end method getSquareLocation
253
254        // draw Square
255        public void paintComponent( Graphics g )
256        {
257           super.paintComponent( g );
258
259           g.drawRect( 0, 0, 29, 29 ); // draw square
260           g.drawString( mark, 11, 20 ); // draw mark
261        } // end method paintComponent
262     } // end inner-class Square
263  } // end class TicTacToeClient
```

Fig. 24.15 | Client side of client/server Tic-Tac-Toe program. (Part 6 of 6.)

```
1   // Fig. 24.16: TicTacToeClientTest.java
2   // Test class for Tic-Tac-Toe client.
3   import javax.swing.JFrame;
4
5   public class TicTacToeClientTest
6   {
7      public static void main( String[] args )
8      {
9         TicTacToeClient application; // declare client application
10
11        // if no command line args
12        if ( args.length == 0 )
13           application = new TicTacToeClient( "127.0.0.1" ); // localhost
14        else
15           application = new TicTacToeClient( args[ 0 ] ); // use args
16
17        application.setDefaultCloseOperation( JFrame.EXIT_ON_CLOSE );
18     } // end main
19  } // end class TicTacToeClientTest
```

Fig. 24.16 | Test class for Tic-Tac-Toe client.

If the message received is "Valid move.", lines 134–135 display the message "Valid move, please wait." and call method setMark (lines 173–184) to set the client's mark in the current square (the one in which the user clicked), using SwingUtilities method invokeLater to ensure that the GUI updates occur in the event-dispatch thread. If the message received is "Invalid move, try again.", line 139 displays the message so that the user can click a different square. If the message received is "Opponent moved.", line 144 reads an integer from the server indicating where the opponent moved, and lines 149–150 place a mark in that square of the board (again using SwingUtilities method invoke-Later to ensure that the GUI updates occur in the event-dispatch thread). If any other message is received, line 155 simply displays the message.

a) Player X connected to server.

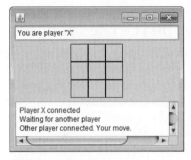

b) Player O connected to server.

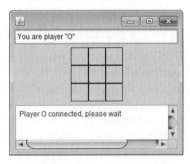

c) Player X moved.

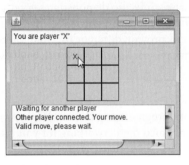

d) Player O sees Player X's move.

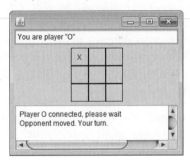

e) Player O moved.

f) Player X sees Player O's move.

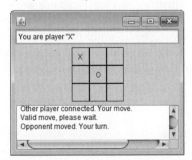

Fig. 24.17 | Sample outputs from the client/server Tic-Tac-Toe program. (Part 1 of 2.)

g) Player X moved.

h) Player O sees Player X's last move.

Fig. 24.17 | Sample outputs from the client/server Tic-Tac-Toe program. (Part 2 of 2.)

24.9 [Web Bonus] Case Study: `DeitelMessenger`

This case study is available at www.deitel.com/books/javafp2/. Chat rooms provide a central location where users can chat with each other via short text messages. Each participant can see all the messages that the other users post, and each user can post messages. This case study integrates many of the Java networking, multithreading and Swing GUI features you've learned thus far to build an online chat system. We also introduce **multicasting**, which enables an application to send `DatagramPackets` to *groups* of clients.

The `DeitelMessenger` case study is a significant application that uses many intermediate Java features, such as networking with `Sockets`, `DatagramPackets` and `MulticastSockets`, multithreading and Swing GUI. The case study also demonstrates good software engineering practices by separating interface from implementation and enabling developers to support different network protocols and provide different user interfaces. After reading this case study, you'll be able to build more significant networking applications.

24.10 Wrap-Up

In this chapter, you learned the basics of network programming in Java. We began with a simple applet and application in which Java performed the networking for you. You then learned two different methods of sending data over a network—streams-based networking using TCP/IP and datagrams-based networking using UDP. We showed how to build simple client/server chat programs using both streams-based and datagram-based networking. You then saw a client/server Tic-Tac-Toe game that enables two clients to play by interacting with a multithreaded server that maintains the game's state and logic. In the next chapter, you'll learn basic database concepts, how to interact with data in a database using SQL and how to use JDBC to allow Java applications to manipulate database data.

Accessing Databases with JDBC

It is a capital mistake to theorize before one has data.
—Arthur Conan Doyle

Now go, write it before them in a table, and note it in a book, that it may be for the time to come for ever and ever.
—The Holy Bible, Isaiah 30:8

Get your facts first, and then you can distort them as much as you please.
—Mark Twain

I like two kinds of men: domestic and foreign.
—Mae West

Objectives

In this chapter you'll learn:

- Relational database concepts.

- To use Structured Query Language (SQL) to retrieve data from and manipulate data in a database.

- To use the JDBC™ API to access databases.

- To use the `RowSet` interface from package `javax.sql` to manipulate databases.

- To use JDBC 4's automatic JDBC driver discovery.

- To create precompiled SQL statements with parameters via `PreparedStatement`s.

- How transaction processing makes database applications more robust.

25.1 Introduction[1]

A **database** is an organized collection of data. There are many different strategies for organizing data to facilitate easy access and manipulation. A **database management system** (**DBMS**) provides mechanisms for storing, organizing, retrieving and modifying data for many users. Database management systems allow for the access and storage of data without concern for the internal representation of data.

Today's most popular database systems are *relational databases* (Section 25.2). A language called **SQL**—pronounced "sequel," or as its individual letters—is the international standard language used almost universally with relational databases to perform **queries** (i.e., to request information that satisfies given criteria) and to manipulate data. [*Note:* As you learn about SQL, you'll see some authors writing "a SQL statement" (which assumes the pronunciation "sequel") and others writing "an SQL statement" (which assumes that the individual letters are pronounced). In this book we pronounce SQL as "sequel."]

Some popular **relational database management systems** (**RDBMSs**) are Microsoft SQL Server, Oracle, Sybase, IBM DB2, Informix, PostgreSQL and MySQL. The JDK now comes with a pure-Java RDBMS called Java DB—Oracles's version of Apache Derby. In this chapter, we present examples using MySQL and Java DB.

Java programs communicate with databases and manipulate their data using the **Java Database Connectivity** (**JDBC™**) **API**. A **JDBC driver** enables Java applications to connect to a database in a particular DBMS and allows you to manipulate that database using the JDBC API.

Software Engineering Observation 25.1

Using the JDBC API enables developers to change the underlying DBMS (for example, from Java DB to MySQL) without modifying the Java code that accesses the database.

---

1. Before using this chapter, please review the Before You Begin section of the book.

Most popular database management systems now provide JDBC drivers. There are also many third-party JDBC drivers available. In this chapter, we introduce JDBC and use it to manipulate MySQL and Java DB databases. The techniques demonstrated here can also be used to manipulate other databases that have JDBC drivers. Check your DBMS's documentation to determine whether your DBMS comes with a JDBC driver. If not, third-party vendors provide JDBC drivers for many DBMSs.

> **Software Engineering Observation 25.2**
> *Most major database vendors provide their own JDBC database drivers, and many third-party vendors provide JDBC drivers as well.*

For more information on JDBC, visit

```
www.oracle.com/technetwork/java/javase/tech/index-jsp-136101.html
```

which contains JDBC information including the JDBC specification, FAQs, a learning resource center and software downloads.

25.2 Relational Databases

A **relational database** is a logical representation of data that allows the data to be accessed without consideration of its physical structure. A relational database stores data in **tables**. Figure 25.1 illustrates a sample table that might be used in a personnel system. The table name is Employee, and its primary purpose is to store the attributes of employees. Tables are composed of **rows**, and rows are composed of **columns** in which values are stored. This table consists of six rows. The Number column of each row is the table's **primary key**—a column (or group of columns) with a *unique* value that cannot be duplicated in other rows. This guarantees that each row can be identified by its primary key. Good examples of primary-key columns are a social security number, an employee ID number and a part number in an inventory system, as values in each of these columns are guaranteed to be unique. The rows in Fig. 25.1 are displayed in order by primary key. In this case, the rows are listed in increasing order, but we could also use decreasing order.

Rows in tables are not guaranteed to be stored in any particular order. As we'll demonstrate in an upcoming example, programs can specify ordering criteria when requesting data from a database.

Number	Name	Department	Salary	Location
23603	Jones	413	1100	New Jersey
24568	Kerwin	413	2000	New Jersey
34589	Larson	642	1800	Los Angeles
35761	Myers	611	1400	Orlando
47132	Neumann	413	9000	New Jersey
78321	Stephens	611	8500	Orlando

Row { (34589 Larson 642 1800 Los Angeles)

Primary key   Column

Fig. 25.1 | Employee table sample data.

Each column represents a different data attribute. Rows are normally unique (by primary key) within a table, but particular column values may be duplicated between rows. For example, three different rows in the Employee table's Department column contain number 413.

Different users of a database are often interested in different data and different relationships among the data. Most users require only subsets of the rows and columns. Queries specify which subsets of the data to select from a table. You use SQL to define queries. For example, you might select data from the Employee table to create a result that shows where each department is located, presenting the data sorted in increasing order by department number. This result is shown in Fig. 25.2. SQL is discussed in Section 25.4.

Department	Location
413	New Jersey
611	Orlando
642	Los Angeles

Fig. 25.2 | Result of selecting distinct Department and Location data from table Employee.

25.3 Relational Database Overview: The books Database

We now overview relational databases in the context of a sample books database we created for this chapter. Before we discuss SQL, we discuss the *tables* of the books database. We use this database to introduce various database concepts, including how to use SQL to obtain information from the database and to manipulate the data. We provide a script to create the database. You can find the script in the examples directory for this chapter. Section 25.7 explains how to use this script. The database consists of three tables: Authors, AuthorISBN and Titles.

Authors *Table*
The Authors table (described in Fig. 25.3) consists of three columns that maintain each author's unique ID number, first name and last name. Figure 25.4 contains sample data from the Authors table of the books database.

Column	Description
AuthorID	Author's ID number in the database. In the books database, this integer column is defined as **autoincremented**—for each row inserted in this table, the AuthorID value is increased by 1 automatically to ensure that each row has a unique AuthorID. This column represents the table's primary key.
FirstName	Author's first name (a string).
LastName	Author's last name (a string).

Fig. 25.3 | Authors table from the books database.

AuthorID	FirstName	LastName
1	Paul	Deitel
2	Harvey	Deitel
3	Abbey	Deitel
4	Michael	Morgano
5	Eric	Kern

Fig. 25.4 | Sample data from the `Authors` table.

AuthorISBN *Table*

The `AuthorISBN` table (described in Fig. 25.5) consists of two columns that maintain each ISBN and the corresponding author's ID number. This table associates authors with their books. Both columns are foreign keys that represent the relationship between the tables `Authors` and `Titles`—one row in table `Authors` may be associated with many rows in table `Titles`, and vice versa. The combined columns of the `AuthorISBN` table represent the table's *primary key*—thus, each row in this table must be a *unique* combination of an AuthorID and an ISBN. Figure 25.6 contains sample data from the `AuthorISBN` table of the books database. [*Note:* To save space, we have split the contents of this table into two columns, each containing the `AuthorID` and `ISBN` columns.] The `AuthorID` column is a **foreign key**—a column in this table that matches the primary-key column in another table (i.e., `AuthorID` in the `Authors` table). Foreign keys are specified when creating a table. The foreign key helps maintain the **Rule of Referential Integrity**—every foreign-key value must appear as another table's primary-key value. This enables the DBMS to determine whether the `AuthorID` value for a particular book is *valid*. Foreign keys also allow related data in multiple tables to be selected from those tables for analytic purposes—this is known as **joining** the data.

Column	Description
AuthorID	The author's ID number, a foreign key to the `Authors` table.
ISBN	The ISBN for a book, a foreign key to the `Titles` table.

Fig. 25.5 | `AuthorISBN` table from the `books` database.

AuthorID	ISBN	AuthorID	ISBN
1	0132152134	2	0132575663
2	0132152134	1	0132662361
1	0132151421	2	0132662361
2	0132151421	1	0132404168
1	0132575663	2	0132404168

Fig. 25.6 | Sample data from the `AuthorISBN` table of `books`. (Part 1 of 2.)

AuthorID	ISBN	AuthorID	ISBN
1	013705842X	1	0132121360
2	013705842X	2	0132121360
3	013705842X	3	0132121360
4	013705842X	4	0132121360
5	013705842X		

Fig. 25.6 | Sample data from the AuthorISBN table of books. (Part 2 of 2.)

Titles Table

The Titles table described in Fig. 25.7 consists of four columns that stand for the ISBN, the title, the edition number and the copyright year. The table is in Fig. 25.8.

Column	Description
ISBN	ISBN of the book (a string). The table's primary key. ISBN is an abbreviation for "International Standard Book Number"—a numbering scheme that publishers use to give every book a unique identification number.
Title	Title of the book (a string).
EditionNumber	Edition number of the book (an integer).
Copyright	Copyright year of the book (a string).

Fig. 25.7 | Titles table from the books database.

ISBN	Title	EditionNumber	Copyright
0132152134	Visual Basic 2010 How to Program	5	2011
0132151421	Visual C# 2010 How to Program	4	2011
0132575663	Java How to Program	9	2012
0132662361	C++ How to Program	8	2012
0132404168	C How to Program	6	2010
013705842X	iPhone for Programmers: An App-Driven Approach	1	2010
0132121360	Android for Programmers: An App-Driven Approach	1	2012

Fig. 25.8 | Sample data from the Titles table of the books database .

Entity-Relationship (ER) Diagram

There's a one-to-many relationship between a primary key and a corresponding foreign key (e.g., one author can write many books). A foreign key can appear many times in its own table, but only once (as the primary key) in another table. Figure 25.9 is an **entity-relationship (ER) diagram** for the books database. This diagram shows the *database tables* and the *relationships* among them. The first compartment in each box contains the table's name and the remaining compartments contain the table's columns. The names in italic are primary keys. *A table's primary key uniquely identifies each row in the table.* Every row must have a primary-key value, and that value must be unique in the table. This is known as the **Rule of Entity Integrity**. Again, for the AuthorISBN table, the primary key is the combination of both columns.

Fig. 25.9 | Table relationships in the books database.

Common Programming Error 25.1
Not providing a value for every column in a primary key breaks the Rule of Entity Integrity and causes the DBMS to report an error.

Common Programming Error 25.2
Providing the same primary-key value in multiple rows causes the DBMS to report an error.

The lines connecting the tables (Fig. 25.9) represent the relationships between the tables. Consider the line between the AuthorISBN and Authors tables. On the Authors end of the line is a 1, and on the AuthorISBN end is an infinity symbol (∞), indicating a **one-to-many relationship** in which every author in the Authors table can have an arbitrary number of books in the AuthorISBN table. The relationship line links the AuthorID column in Authors (i.e., its primary key) to the AuthorID column in AuthorISBN (i.e., its foreign key). The AuthorID column in the AuthorISBN table is a foreign key.

Common Programming Error 25.3
Providing a foreign-key value that does not appear as a primary-key value in another table breaks the Rule of Referential Integrity and causes the DBMS to report an error.

The line between Titles and AuthorISBN illustrates another *one-to-many relationship*; a title can be written by any number of authors. In fact, the sole purpose of the AuthorISBN table is to provide a *many-to-many relationship* between Authors and Titles—an author can write many books and a book can have many authors.

25.4 SQL

We now overview SQL in the context of our books database. You'll be able to use the SQL discussed here in the examples later in the chapter and in examples in Chapters 27–28.

The next several subsections discuss the SQL keywords listed in Fig. 25.10 in the context of SQL queries and statements. Other SQL keywords are beyond this text's scope. To learn other keywords, refer to the SQL reference guide supplied by the vendor of the RDBMS you're using.

SQL keyword	Description
SELECT	Retrieves data from one or more tables.
FROM	Tables involved in the query. Required in every SELECT.
WHERE	Criteria for selection that determine the rows to be retrieved, deleted or updated. Optional in a SQL query or a SQL statement.
GROUP BY	Criteria for grouping rows. Optional in a SELECT query.
ORDER BY	Criteria for ordering rows. Optional in a SELECT query.
INNER JOIN	Merge rows from multiple tables.
INSERT	Insert rows into a specified table.
UPDATE	Update rows in a specified table.
DELETE	Delete rows from a specified table.

Fig. 25.10 | SQL query keywords.

25.4.1 Basic SELECT Query

Let us consider several SQL queries that extract information from database books. A SQL query "selects" rows and columns from one or more tables in a database. Such selections are performed by queries with the **SELECT** keyword. The basic form of a SELECT query is

```
SELECT * FROM tableName
```

in which the **asterisk (*)** *wildcard character* indicates that all columns from the *tableName* table should be retrieved. For example, to retrieve all the data in the Authors table, use

```
SELECT * FROM Authors
```

Most programs do not require all the data in a table. To retrieve only specific columns, replace the * with a comma-separated list of column names. For example, to retrieve only the columns AuthorID and LastName for all rows in the Authors table, use the query

```
SELECT AuthorID, LastName FROM Authors
```

This query returns the data listed in Fig. 25.11.

AuthorID	LastName
1	Deitel
2	Deitel
3	Deitel
4	Morgano
5	Kern

Fig. 25.11 | Sample AuthorID and LastName data from the Authors table.

Software Engineering Observation 25.3

In general, you process results by knowing in advance the order of the columns in the result—for example, selecting AuthorID *and* LastName *from table* Authors *ensures that the columns will appear in the result with* AuthorID *as the first column and* LastName *as the second column. Programs typically process result columns by specifying the column number in the result (starting from number 1 for the first column). Selecting columns by name avoids returning unneeded columns and protects against changes in the actual order of the columns in the table(s) by returning the columns in the exact order specified.*

Common Programming Error 25.4

If you assume that the columns are always returned in the same order from a query that uses the asterisk (*), the program may process the results incorrectly. If the column order in the table(s) changes or if additional columns are added at a later time, the order of the columns in the result will change accordingly.

25.4.2 WHERE Clause

In most cases, it's necessary to locate rows in a database that satisfy certain **selection criteria**. Only rows that satisfy the selection criteria (formally called **predicates**) are selected. SQL uses the optional **WHERE clause** in a query to specify the selection criteria for the query. The basic form of a query with selection criteria is

```
SELECT columnName1, columnName2, ... FROM tableName WHERE criteria
```

For example, to select the Title, EditionNumber and Copyright columns from table Titles for which the Copyright date is greater than 2010, use the query

```
SELECT Title, EditionNumber, Copyright
   FROM Titles
   WHERE Copyright > '2010'
```

Strings in SQL are delimited by single (') rather than double (") quotes.Figure 25.12 shows the result of the preceding query.

Title	EditionNumber	Copyright
Visual Basic 2010 How to Program	5	2011
Visual C# 2010 How to Program	4	2011
Java How to Program	9	2012
C++ How to Program	8	2012
Android for Programmers: An App-Driven Approach	1	2012

Fig. 25.12 | Sampling of titles with copyrights after 2005 from table Titles.

Pattern Matching: Zero or More Characters
The WHERE clause criteria can contain the operators <, >, <=, >=, =, <> and LIKE. Operator **LIKE** is used for **pattern matching** with wildcard characters **percent (%)** and **underscore** (_). Pattern matching allows SQL to search for strings that match a given pattern.

A pattern that contains a percent character (%) searches for strings that have zero or more characters at the percent character's position in the pattern. For example, the next query locates the rows of all the authors whose last name starts with the letter D:

```
SELECT AuthorID, FirstName, LastName
   FROM Authors
   WHERE LastName LIKE 'D%'
```

This query selects the two rows shown in Fig. 25.13—three of the five authors have a last name starting with the letter D (followed by zero or more characters). The % symbol in the WHERE clause's LIKE pattern indicates that any number of characters can appear after the letter D in the LastName. The pattern string is surrounded by single-quote characters.

AuthorID	FirstName	LastName
1	Paul	Deitel
2	Harvey	Deitel
3	Abbey	Deitel

Fig. 25.13 | Authors whose last name starts with D from the Authors table.

Portability Tip 25.1
See the documentation for your database system to determine whether SQL is case sensitive on your system and to determine the syntax for SQL keywords.

Portability Tip 25.2
Read your database system's documentation carefully to determine whether it supports the LIKE operator as discussed here.

Pattern Matching: Any Character
An underscore (_) in the pattern string indicates a single wildcard character at that position in the pattern. For example, the following query locates the rows of all the authors whose last names start with any character (specified by _), followed by the letter o, followed by any number of additional characters (specified by %):

```
SELECT AuthorID, FirstName, LastName
   FROM Authors
   WHERE LastName LIKE '_o%'
```

The preceding query produces the row shown in Fig. 25.14, because only one author in our database has a last name that contains the letter o as its second letter.

AuthorID	FirstName	LastName
4	Michael	Morgano

Fig. 25.14 | The only author from the Authors table whose last name contains o as the second letter.

25.4.3 ORDER BY Clause

The rows in the result of a query can be sorted into ascending or descending order by using the optional **ORDER BY clause**. The basic form of a query with an ORDER BY clause is

> **SELECT** *columnName1*, *columnName2*, ... **FROM** *tableName* **ORDER BY** *column* **ASC**
> **SELECT** *columnName1*, *columnName2*, ... **FROM** *tableName* **ORDER BY** *column* **DESC**

where ASC specifies ascending order (lowest to highest), DESC specifies descending order (highest to lowest) and *column* specifies the column on which the sort is based. For example, to obtain the list of authors in ascending order by last name (Fig. 25.15), use the query

> **SELECT** AuthorID, FirstName, LastName
>   **FROM** Authors
>   **ORDER BY** LastName **ASC**

AuthorID	FirstName	LastName
1	Paul	Deitel
2	Harvey	Deitel
3	Abbey	Deitel
5	Eric	Kern
4	Michael	Morgano

Fig. 25.15 | Sample data from table Authors in ascending order by LastName.

Sorting in Descending Order

The default sorting order is ascending, so ASC is optional. To obtain the same list of authors in descending order by last name (Fig. 25.16), use the query

> **SELECT** AuthorID, FirstName, LastName
>   **FROM** Authors
>   **ORDER BY** LastName **DESC**

AuthorID	FirstName	LastName
4	Michael	Morgano
5	Eric	Kern
1	Paul	Deitel
2	Harvey	Deitel
3	Abbey	Deitel

Fig. 25.16 | Sample data from table Authors in descending order by LastName.

Sorting By Multiple Columns

Multiple columns can be used for sorting with an ORDER BY clause of the form

> **ORDER BY** *column1 sortingOrder*, *column2 sortingOrder*, ...

where *sortingOrder* is either ASC or DESC. The *sortingOrder* does not have to be identical for each column. The query

```
SELECT AuthorID, FirstName, LastName
   FROM Authors
   ORDER BY LastName, FirstName
```

sorts all the rows in ascending order by last name, then by first name. If any rows have the same last-name value, they're returned sorted by first name (Fig. 25.17).

AuthorID	FirstName	LastName
3	Abbey	Deitel
2	Harvey	Deitel
1	Paul	Deitel
5	Eric	Kern
4	Michael	Morgano

Fig. 25.17 | Sample data from `Authors` in ascending order by `LastName` and `FirstName`.

*Combining the **WHERE** and **ORDER BY** Clauses*
The WHERE and ORDER BY clauses can be combined in one query, as in

```
SELECT ISBN, Title, EditionNumber, Copyright
   FROM Titles
   WHERE Title LIKE '%How to Program'
   ORDER BY Title ASC
```

which returns the ISBN, Title, EditionNumber and Copyright of each book in the Titles table that has a Title ending with "How to Program" and sorts them in ascending order by Title. The query results are shown in Fig. 25.18.

ISBN	Title	Edition-Number	Copy-right
0132404168	C How to Program	6	2010
0132662361	C++ How to Program	8	2012
0132575663	Java How to Program	9	2012
0132152134	Visual Basic 2005 How to Program	5	2011
0132151421	Visual C# 2005 How to Program	4	2011

Fig. 25.18 | Sampling of books from table `Titles` whose titles end with `How to Program` in ascending order by `Title`.

25.4.4 Merging Data from Multiple Tables: INNER JOIN

Database designers often split related data into separate tables to ensure that a database does not store data redundantly. For example, in the books database, we use an AuthorISBN table to store the relationship data between authors and their corresponding titles. If we did not separate this information into individual tables, we'd need to include author information with each entry in the `Titles` table. This would result in the database's storing *duplicate* author information for authors who wrote multiple books. Often, it's necessary to merge data from multiple tables into a single result. Referred to as joining the tables, this is specified by an **INNER JOIN** operator, which merges rows from two tables by matching values in columns that are common to the tables. The basic form of an INNER JOIN is:

```
SELECT columnName1, columnName2, ...
FROM table1
INNER JOIN table2
    ON table1.columnName = table2.columnName
```

The **ON clause** of the INNER JOIN specifies the columns from each table that are compared to determine which rows are merged. For example, the following query produces a list of authors accompanied by the ISBNs for books written by each author:

```
SELECT FirstName, LastName, ISBN
FROM Authors
INNER JOIN AuthorISBN
    ON Authors.AuthorID = AuthorISBN.AuthorID
ORDER BY LastName, FirstName
```

The query merges the `FirstName` and `LastName` columns from table `Authors` with the `ISBN` column from table `AuthorISBN`, sorting the result in ascending order by `LastName` and `FirstName`. Note the use of the syntax *tableName.columnName* in the ON clause. This syntax, called a **qualified name**, specifies the columns from each table that should be compared to join the tables. The "*tableName.*" syntax is required if the columns have the same name in both tables. The same syntax can be used in any SQL statement to distinguish columns in different tables that have the same name. In some systems, table names qualified with the database name can be used to perform cross-database queries. As always, the query can contain an ORDER BY clause. Figure 25.19 shows the results of the preceding query, ordered by `LastName` and `FirstName`. [*Note:* To save space, we split the result of the query into two columns, each containing the `FirstName`, `LastName` and `ISBN` columns.]

FirstName	LastName	ISBN	FirstName	LastName	ISBN
Abbey	Deitel	013705842X	Paul	Deitel	0132151421
Abbey	Deitel	0132121360	Paul	Deitel	0132575663
Harvey	Deitel	0132152134	Paul	Deitel	0132662361
Harvey	Deitel	0132151421	Paul	Deitel	0132404168
Harvey	Deitel	0132575663	Paul	Deitel	013705842X
Harvey	Deitel	0132662361	Paul	Deitel	0132121360
Harvey	Deitel	0132404168	Eric	Kern	013705842X
Harvey	Deitel	013705842X	Michael	Morgano	013705842X
Harvey	Deitel	0132121360	Michael	Morgano	0132121360
Paul	Deitel	0132152134			

Fig. 25.19 | Sampling of authors and ISBNs for the books they have written in ascending order by `LastName` and `FirstName`.

Software Engineering Observation 25.4

If a SQL statement includes columns with the same name from multiple tables, the statement must precede those column names with their table names and a dot (e.g., `Authors.AuthorID`*).*

Common Programming Error 25.5

Failure to qualify names for columns that have the same name in two or more tables is an error.

25.4.5 INSERT Statement

The **INSERT** statement inserts a row into a table. The basic form of this statement is

> **INSERT INTO** *tableName* (*columnName1*, *columnName2*, ..., *columnNameN*)
>   **VALUES** (*value1*, *value2*, ..., *valueN*)

where *tableName* is the table in which to insert the row. The *tableName* is followed by a comma-separated list of column names in parentheses (this list is not required if the INSERT operation specifies a value for every column of the table in the correct order). The list of column names is followed by the SQL keyword **VALUES** and a comma-separated list of values in parentheses. The values specified here must match the columns specified after the table name in both order and type (e.g., if *columnName1* is supposed to be the FirstName column, then *value1* should be a string in single quotes representing the first name). Always explicitly list the columns when inserting rows. If the table's column order changes or a new column is added, using only VALUES may cause an error. The INSERT statement

> **INSERT INTO** Authors (FirstName, LastName)
>   **VALUES** ('Sue', 'Red')

inserts a row into the Authors table. The statement indicates that values are provided for the FirstName and LastName columns. The corresponding values are 'Sue' and 'Smith'. We do not specify an AuthorID in this example because AuthorID is an autoincremented column in the Authors table. For every row added to this table, the DBMS assigns a unique AuthorID value that is the next value in the autoincremented sequence (i.e., 1, 2, 3 and so on). In this case, Sue Red would be assigned AuthorID number 6. Figure 25.20 shows the Authors table after the INSERT operation. [*Note:* Not every database management system supports autoincremented columns. Check the documentation for your DBMS for alternatives to autoincremented columns.]

AuthorID	FirstName	LastName
1	Paul	Deitel
2	Harvey	Deitel
3	Abbey	Deitel
4	Michael	Morgano
5	Eric	Kern
6	Sue	Red

Fig. 25.20 | Sample data from table Authors after an INSERT operation.

Common Programming Error 25.6

It's normally an error to specify a value for an autoincrement column.

Common Programming Error 25.7

SQL delimits strings with single quotes ('). A string containing a single quote (e.g., O'Malley) must have two single quotes in the position where the single quote appears (e.g., 'O''Malley'). The first acts as an escape character for the second. Not escaping single-quote characters in a string that's part of a SQL statement is a SQL syntax error.

25.4.6 UPDATE Statement

An **UPDATE** statement modifies data in a table. Its basic form is

```
UPDATE tableName
    SET columnName1 = value1, columnName2 = value2, ..., columnNameN = valueN
    WHERE criteria
```

where *tableName* is the table to update. The *tableName* is followed by keyword **SET** and a comma-separated list of column name/value pairs in the format *columnName = value*. The optional WHERE clause provides criteria that determine which rows to update. Though not required, the WHERE clause is typically used, unless a change is to be made to every row. The UPDATE statement

```
UPDATE Authors
    SET LastName = 'Black'
    WHERE LastName = 'Red' AND FirstName = 'Sue'
```

updates a row in the Authors table. The statement indicates that LastName will be assigned the value Black for the row in which LastName is equal to Red and FirstName is equal to Sue. [*Note:* If there are multiple rows with the first name "Sue" and the last name "Red," this statement will modify all such rows to have the last name "Black."] If we know the AuthorID in advance of the UPDATE operation (possibly because we searched for it previously), the WHERE clause can be simplified as follows:

```
WHERE AuthorID = 6
```

Figure 25.21 shows the Authors table after the UPDATE operation has taken place.

AuthorID	FirstName	LastName
1	Paul	Deitel
2	Harvey	Deitel
3	Abbey	Deitel
4	Michael	Morgano
5	Eric	Kern
6	Sue	Black

Fig. 25.21 | Sample data from table Authors after an UPDATE operation.

25.4.7 DELETE Statement

A SQL **DELETE** statement removes rows from a table. Its basic form is

> **DELETE FROM** *tableName* **WHERE** *criteria*

where *tableName* is the table from which to delete. The optional WHERE clause specifies the criteria used to determine which rows to delete. If this clause is omitted, all the table's rows are deleted. The DELETE statement

```
DELETE FROM Authors
    WHERE LastName = 'Black' AND FirstName = 'Sue'
```

deletes the row for Sue Black in the Authors table. If we know the AuthorID in advance of the DELETE operation, the WHERE clause can be simplified as follows:

```
WHERE AuthorID = 5
```

Figure 25.22 shows the Authors table after the DELETE operation has taken place.

AuthorID	FirstName	LastName
1	Paul	Deitel
2	Harvey	Deitel
3	Abbey	Deitel
4	Michael	Morgano
5	Eric	Kern

Fig. 25.22 | Sample data from table Authors after a DELETE operation.

25.5 Instructions for Installing MySQL and MySQL Connector/J

MySQL Community Edition is an open-source database management system that executes on many platforms, including Windows, Linux, and Mac OS X. Complete information about MySQL is available from www.mysql.com. The examples in Sections 25.8–25.9 manipulate MySQL databases using MySQL 5.5.8—the latest release at the time of this writing.

Installing MySQL
To install MySQL Community Edition on Windows, Linux or Mac OS X, see the installation overview for your platform at:

- Windows: dev.mysql.com/doc/refman/5.5/en/windows-installation.html
- Linux: dev.mysql.com/doc/refman/5.5/en/linux-installation-rpm.html
- Mac OS X: dev.mysql.com/doc/refman/5.5/en/macosx-installation.html

Carefully follow the instructions for downloading and installing the software on your platform. The downloads are available from:

> dev.mysql.com/downloads/mysql/

For the following steps, we assume that you're installing MySQL on Windows. When you execute the installer, the **MySQL Server 5.5 Setup Wizard** window will appear. Perform the following steps:

1. Click the **Next** button.

2. Read the license agreement, then check the **I accept the terms in the License Agreement** checkbox and click the **Next** button. [*Note:* If you do not accept the license terms, you will not be able to install MySQL.]

3. Click the **Typical** button in the **Choose Setup Type** screen then click **Install**.

4. When the installation completes, click **Next >** twice.

5. In the **Completed the MySQL Server 5.5 Setup Wizard** screen, ensure that the **Launch the MySQL Instance Configuration Wizard** checkbox is checked, then click **Finish** to begin configuring the server.

The **MySQL Instance Configuration Wizard** window appears. To configure the server:

1. Click **Next >**, then select **Standard Configuration** and click **Next >** again.

2. You have the option of installing MySQL as a Windows service, which enables the MySQL server to begin executing automatically each time your system starts. For our examples, this is unnecessary, so you can uncheck **Install as a Windows Service** if you wish. Check **Include Bin Directory in Windows PATH**. This will enable you to use the MySQL commands in the Windows Command Prompt. Click **Next >**, then click **Execute** to perform the server configuration.

3. Click **Finish** to close the wizard.

You've now completed the MySQL installation.

Installing MySQL Connector/J
To use MySQL with JDBC, you also need to install **MySQL Connector/J** (the J stands for Java)—a JDBC driver that allows programs to use JDBC to interact with MySQL. MySQL Connector/J can be downloaded from

```
dev.mysql.com/downloads/connector/j/
```

The documentation for Connector/J is located at

```
dev.mysql.com/doc/refman/5.5/en/connector-j.html
```

At the time of this writing, the current generally available release of MySQL Connector/J is 5.1.14. To install MySQL Connector/J, carefully follow the installation instructions at:

```
dev.mysql.com/doc/refman/5.5/en/connector-j-installing.html
```

We *do not* recommend modifying your system's CLASSPATH environment variable, which is discussed in the installation instructions. Instead, we'll show you how use MySQL Connector/J by specifying it as a command-line option when you execute your applications.

25.6 Instructions for Setting Up a MySQL User Account

For the MySQL examples to execute correctly, you need to set up a user account that allows users to create, delete and modify a database. After MySQL is installed, follow the steps below to set up a user account (these steps assume MySQL is installed in its default installation directory):

1. Open a Command Prompt and start the database server by executing the command `mysqld.exe`. This command has no output—it simply starts the MySQL server. Do not close this window—doing so terminates the server.

1. Next, you'll start the MySQL monitor so you can set up a user account, open another Command Prompt and execute the command

```
mysql -h localhost -u root
```

The -h option indicates the host (i.e., computer) on which the MySQL server is running—in this case your local computer (`localhost`). The -u option indicates the user account that will be used to log in to the server—`root` is the default user account that is created during installation to allow you to configure the server. Once you've logged in, you'll see a `mysql>` prompt at which you can type commands to interact with the MySQL server.

1. At the `mysql>` prompt, type

```
USE mysql;
```

and press *Enter* to select the built-in database named `mysql`, which stores server information, such as user accounts and their privileges for interacting with the server. Each command must end with a semicolon. To confirm the command, MySQL issues the message "`Database changed.`"

1. Next, you'll add the `deitel` user account to the `mysql` built-in database. The `mysql` database contains a table called `user` with columns that represent the user's name, password and various privileges. To create the `deitel` user account with the password `deitel`, execute the following commands from the `mysql>` prompt:

```
create user 'deitel'@'localhost' identified by 'deitel';
grant select, insert, update, delete, create, drop, references,
    execute on *.* to 'deitel'@'localhost';
```

This creates the `deitel` user with the privileges needed to create the databases used in this chapter and manipulate them.

1. Type the command

```
exit;
```

to terminate the MySQL monitor.

25.7 Creating Database books in MySQL

For each MySQL database we discuss, we provide a SQL script in a `.sql` file that sets up the database and its tables. You can execute these scripts in the MySQL monitor. In this chapter's examples directory, you'll find the script `books.sql` to create the `books` database. For the following steps, we assume that the MySQL server (`mysqld.exe`) is still running. To execute the `books.sql` script:

1. Open a Command Prompt and use the `cd` command to change directories to the location that contains the `books.sql` script.

2. Start the MySQL monitor by typing

```
mysql -h localhost -u deitel -p
```

The -p option prompts you for the password for the deitel user account. When prompted, enter the password deitel.

3. Execute the script by typing

```
source books.sql;
```

This creates a new directory named books in the server's data directory—located by default on Windows at C:\ProgramData\MySQL\MySQL Server 5.5\data. This new directory contains the books database.

4. Type the command

```
exit;
```

to terminate the MySQL monitor. You're now ready to proceed to the first JDBC example.

25.8 Manipulating Databases with JDBC

This section presents two examples. The first introduces how to connect to a database and query it. The second demonstrates how to display the result of the query in a JTable.

25.8.1 Connecting to and Querying a Database

The example of Fig. 25.23 performs a simple query on the books database that retrieves the entire Authors table and displays the data. The program illustrates connecting to the database, querying the database and processing the result. The discussion that follows presents the key JDBC aspects of the program. [*Note:* Sections 25.5–25.7 demonstrate how to start the MySQL server, configure a user account and create the books database. These steps *must* be performed before executing the program of Fig. 25.23.]

```java
1   // Fig. 25.23: DisplayAuthors.java
2   // Displaying the contents of the Authors table.
3   import java.sql.Connection;
4   import java.sql.Statement;
5   import java.sql.DriverManager;
6   import java.sql.ResultSet;
7   import java.sql.ResultSetMetaData;
8   import java.sql.SQLException;
9
10  public class DisplayAuthors
11  {
12     // database URL
13     static final String DATABASE_URL = "jdbc:mysql://localhost/books";
14
15     // launch the application
16     public static void main( String args[] )
17     {
```

Fig. 25.23 | Displaying the contents of the Authors table. (Part 1 of 3.)

```
18            Connection connection = null; // manages connection
19            Statement statement = null; // query statement
20            ResultSet resultSet = null; // manages results
21
22            // connect to database books and query database
23            try
24            {
25               // establish connection to database
26               connection = DriverManager.getConnection(
27                  DATABASE_URL, "deitel", "deitel" );
28
29               // create Statement for querying database
30               statement = connection.createStatement();
31
32               // query database
33               resultSet = statement.executeQuery(
34                  "SELECT AuthorID, FirstName, LastName FROM Authors" );
35
36               // process query results
37               ResultSetMetaData metaData = resultSet.getMetaData();
38               int numberOfColumns = metaData.getColumnCount();
39               System.out.println( "Authors Table of Books Database:\n" );
40
41               for ( int i = 1; i <= numberOfColumns; i++ )
42                  System.out.printf( "%-8s\t", metaData.getColumnName( i ) );
43               System.out.println();
44
45               while ( resultSet.next() )
46               {
47                  for ( int i = 1; i <= numberOfColumns; i++ )
48                     System.out.printf( "%-8s\t", resultSet.getObject( i ) );
49                  System.out.println();
50               } // end while
51            }  // end try
52            catch ( SQLException sqlException )
53            {
54               sqlException.printStackTrace();
55            } // end catch
56            finally // ensure resultSet, statement and connection are closed
57            {
58               try
59               {
60                  resultSet.close();
61                  statement.close();
62                  connection.close();
63               } // end try
64               catch ( Exception exception )
65               {
66                  exception.printStackTrace();
67               } // end catch
68            } // end finally
69         } // end main
70      } // end class DisplayAuthors
```

Fig. 25.23 | Displaying the contents of the Authors table. (Part 2 of 3.)

```
Authors Table of Books Database:

AuthorID        FirstName       LastName
1               Harvey          Deitel
2               Paul            Deitel
3               Andrew          Goldberg
4               David           Choffnes
```

Fig. 25.23 | Displaying the contents of the Authors table. (Part 3 of 3.)

Lines 3–8 import the JDBC interfaces and classes from package java.sql used in this program. Line 13 declares a string constant for the database URL. This identifies the name of the database to connect to, as well as information about the protocol used by the JDBC driver (discussed shortly). Method main (lines 16–69) connects to the books database, queries the database, displays the result of the query and closes the database connection.

In past versions of Java, programs were required to load an appropriate database driver before connecting to a database. JDBC 4.0 and higher support **automatic driver discovery**—you're no longer required to load the database driver in advance. To ensure that the program can locate the database driver class, you must include the class's location in the program's classpath when you execute the program. For MySQL, you include the file mysql-connector-java-5.1.14-bin.jar (in the C:\mysql-connector-java-5.1.14 directory) in your program's classpath, as in:

```
java -classpath .;c:\mysql-connector-java-5.1.14\mysql-connector-
java-5.1.14-bin.jar DisplayAuthors
```

If the period (.) at the beginning of the classpath information is missing, the JVM will not look for classes in the current directory and thus will not find the DisplayAuthors class file. You may also copy the mysql-connector-java-5.1.14-bin.jar file to your JDK's \jre\lib\ext folder. After doing so, you can run the application simply using the command

```
java DisplayAuthors
```

Connecting to the Database
Lines 26–27 of Fig. 25.23 create a **Connection** object (package java.sql) referenced by connection. An object that implements interface Connection manages the connection between the Java program and the database. Connection objects enable programs to create SQL statements that manipulate databases. The program initializes connection with the result of a call to static method **getConnection** of class **DriverManager** (package java.sql), which attempts to connect to the database specified by its URL. Method getConnection takes three arguments—a String that specifies the database URL, a String that specifies the username and a String that specifies the password. The username and password are set in Section 25.6. If you used a different username and password, you need to replace the username (second argument) and password (third argument) passed to method getConnection in line 27. The URL locates the database (possibly on a network or in the local file system of the computer). The URL jdbc:mysql://localhost/books specifies the protocol for communication (jdbc), the **subprotocol** for communication (mysql) and the location of the database (//localhost/books, where localhost is the host running the MySQL server and books is the database name). The subprotocol mysql

indicates that the program uses a MySQL-specific subprotocol to connect to the MySQL database. If the DriverManager cannot connect to the database, method getConnection throws a **SQLException** (package java.sql). Figure 25.24 lists the JDBC driver names and database URL formats of several popular RDBMSs.

RDBMS	Database URL format
MySQL	jdbc:mysql://*hostname*:*portNumber*/*databaseName*
ORACLE	jdbc:oracle:thin:@*hostname*:*portNumber*:*databaseName*
DB2	jdbc:db2:*hostname*:*portNumber*/*databaseName*
PostgreSQL	jdbc:postgresql://*hostname*:*portNumber*/*databaseName*
Java DB/Apache Derby	jdbc:derby:*dataBaseName* (embedded) jdbc:derby://*hostname*:*portNumber*/*databaseName* (network)
Microsoft SQL Server	jdbc:sqlserver://*hostname*:*portNumber*;databaseName=*dataBaseName*
Sybase	jdbc:sybase:Tds:*hostname*:*portNumber*/*databaseName*

Fig. 25.24 | Popular JDBC database URL formats.

Software Engineering Observation 25.5

Most database management systems require the user to log in before accessing the database contents. DriverManager method getConnection is overloaded with versions that enable the program to supply the user name and password to gain access.

Creating a *Statement* for Executing Queries

Line 30 invokes Connection method **createStatement** to obtain an object that implements interface Statement (package java.sql). The program uses the **Statement** object to submit SQL statements to the database.

Executing a Query

Lines 33–34 use the Statement object's **executeQuery** method to submit a query that selects all the author information from table Authors. This method returns an object that implements interface **ResultSet** and contains the query results. The ResultSet methods enable the program to manipulate the query result.

Processing a Query's *ResultSet*

Lines 37–50 process the ResultSet. Line 37 obtains the metadata for the ResultSet as a **ResultSetMetaData** (package java.sql) object. The **metadata** describes the ResultSet's contents. Programs can use metadata programmatically to obtain information about the ResultSet's column names and types. Line 38 uses ResultSetMetaData method **getColumnCount** to retrieve the number of columns in the ResultSet. Lines 41–42 display the column names.

Software Engineering Observation 25.6

Metadata enables programs to process ResultSet contents dynamically when detailed information about the ResultSet is not known in advance.

Lines 45–50 display the data in each ResultSet row. First, the program positions the ResultSet cursor (which points to the row being processed) to the first row in the ResultSet with method **next** (line 45). Method next returns boolean value true if it's able to position to the next row; otherwise, the method returns false.

Common Programming Error 25.8

Initially, a ResultSet cursor is positioned before the first row. A SQLException occurs if you attempt to access a ResultSet's contents before positioning the ResultSet cursor to the first row with method next.

If there are rows in the ResultSet, lines 47–48 extract and display the contents of each column in the current row. When a ResultSet is processed, each column can be extracted as a specific Java type. In fact, ResultSetMetaData method **getColumnType** returns a constant integer from class **Types** (package java.sql) indicating the type of a specified column. Programs can use these values in a switch statement to invoke ResultSet methods that return the column values as appropriate Java types. If the type of a column is Types.INTEGER, ResultSet method **getInt** returns the column value as an int. ResultSet *get* methods typically receive as an argument either a column number (as an int) or a column name (as a String) indicating which column's value to obtain. Visit

```
java.sun.com/javase/6/docs/technotes/guides/jdbc/getstart/
    GettingStartedTOC.fm.html
```

for detailed mappings of SQL data types to Java types and to determine the appropriate ResultSet method to call for each SQL data type.

Performance Tip 25.1

If a query specifies the exact columns to select from the database, the ResultSet contains the columns in the specified order. In this case, using the column number to obtain the column's value is more efficient than using the column name. The column number provides direct access to the specified column. Using the column name requires a search of the column names to locate the appropriate column.

Error-Prevention Tip 25.1

Using column names to obtain values from a ResultSet produces code that is less error prone than obtaining values by column number—you don't need to remember the column order. Also, if the column order changes, your code does not have to change.

For simplicity, this example treats each value as an Object. We retrieve each column value with ResultSet method **getObject** (line 48) then print the Object's String representation. Unlike array indices, ResultSet *column numbers start at 1*. The finally block (lines 56–68) closes the ResultSet, the Statement and the database Connection. [*Note:* Lines 60–62 will throw NullPointerExceptions if the ResultSet, Statement or Connection objects were not created properly. For code used in industry, you should check the variables that refer to these objects to see if they're null before you call close.]

Common Programming Error 25.9

Specifying column 0 when obtaining values from a ResultSet causes a SQLException.

Common Programming Error 25.10

A SQLException occurs if you attempt to manipulate a ResultSet after closing the Statement that created it. The ResultSet is discarded when the Statement is closed.

Software Engineering Observation 25.7

Each Statement object can open only one ResultSet object at a time. When a Statement returns a new ResultSet, the Statement closes the prior ResultSet. To use multiple ResultSets in parallel, separate Statement objects must return the ResultSets.

Java SE 7: Automatically Closing *Connections, Statements and ResultSets*

As of Java SE 7, the interfaces Connection, Statement and ResultSet each extend the AutoCloseable interface, so you can use objects that implement these interfaces with the new try-with-resources statement, which was introduced in Section 11.13. In the folder for the example of Fig. 25.23, the subfolder JavaSE7Version contains a version of the example that uses the try-with-resources statement to allocate the Connection, Statement and ResultSet objects. These objects are automatically closed at the end of the try block or if an exception occurs while executing the code in the try block.

25.8.2 Querying the books Database

The next example (Fig. 25.25 and Fig. 25.28) allows the user to enter any query into the program. The example displays the result of a query in a **JTable**, using a **TableModel** object to provide the ResultSet data to the JTable. A JTable is a swing GUI component that can be bound to a database to display the results of a query. Class ResultSetTable-Model (Fig. 25.25) performs the connection to the database via a TableModel and maintains the ResultSet. Class DisplayQueryResults (Fig. 25.28) creates the GUI and specifies an instance of class ResultSetTableModel to provide data for the JTable.

ResultSetTableModel Class

Class ResultSetTableModel (Fig. 25.25) extends class **AbstractTableModel** (package javax.swing.table), which implements interface TableModel. ResultSetTableModel overrides TableModel methods **getColumnClass**, **getColumnCount**, **getColumnName**, **getRowCount** and **getValueAt**. The default implementations of TableModel methods is-CellEditable and setValueAt (provided by AbstractTableModel) are not overridden, because this example does not support editing the JTable cells. The default implementations of TableModel methods **addTableModelListener** and **removeTableModelListener** (provided by AbstractTableModel) are not overridden, because the implementations of these methods in AbstractTableModel properly add and remove event listeners.

```
1   // Fig. 25.25: ResultSetTableModel.java
2   // A TableModel that supplies ResultSet data to a JTable.
3   import java.sql.Connection;
4   import java.sql.Statement;
5   import java.sql.DriverManager;
6   import java.sql.ResultSet;
7   import java.sql.ResultSetMetaData;
```

Fig. 25.25 | A TableModel that supplies ResultSet data to a JTable. (Part 1 of 5.)

```
 8   import java.sql.SQLException;
 9   import javax.swing.table.AbstractTableModel;
10
11   // ResultSet rows and columns are counted from 1 and JTable
12   // rows and columns are counted from 0. When processing
13   // ResultSet rows or columns for use in a JTable, it is
14   // necessary to add 1 to the row or column number to manipulate
15   // the appropriate ResultSet column (i.e., JTable column 0 is
16   // ResultSet column 1 and JTable row 0 is ResultSet row 1).
17   public class ResultSetTableModel extends AbstractTableModel
18   {
19      private Connection connection;
20      private Statement statement;
21      private ResultSet resultSet;
22      private ResultSetMetaData metaData;
23      private int numberOfRows;
24
25      // keep track of database connection status
26      private boolean connectedToDatabase = false;
27
28      // constructor initializes resultSet and obtains its meta data object;
29      // determines number of rows
30      public ResultSetTableModel( String url, String username,
31         String password, String query ) throws SQLException
32      {
33         // connect to database
34         connection = DriverManager.getConnection( url, username, password );
35
36         // create Statement to query database
37         statement = connection.createStatement(
38            ResultSet.TYPE_SCROLL_INSENSITIVE,
39            ResultSet.CONCUR_READ_ONLY );
40
41         // update database connection status
42         connectedToDatabase = true;
43
44         // set query and execute it
45         setQuery( query );
46      } // end constructor ResultSetTableModel
47
48      // get class that represents column type
49      public Class getColumnClass( int column ) throws IllegalStateException
50      {
51         // ensure database connection is available
52         if ( !connectedToDatabase )
53            throw new IllegalStateException( "Not Connected to Database" );
54
55         // determine Java class of column
56         try
57         {
58            String className = metaData.getColumnClassName( column + 1 );
59
```

Fig. 25.25 | A TableModel that supplies ResultSet data to a JTable. (Part 2 of 5.)

```
60              // return Class object that represents className
61              return Class.forName( className );
62          } // end try
63          catch ( Exception exception )
64          {
65              exception.printStackTrace();
66          } // end catch
67
68          return Object.class; // if problems occur above, assume type Object
69      } // end method getColumnClass
70
71      // get number of columns in ResultSet
72      public int getColumnCount() throws IllegalStateException
73      {
74          // ensure database connection is available
75          if ( !connectedToDatabase )
76              throw new IllegalStateException( "Not Connected to Database" );
77
78          // determine number of columns
79          try
80          {
81              return metaData.getColumnCount();
82          } // end try
83          catch ( SQLException sqlException )
84          {
85              sqlException.printStackTrace();
86          } // end catch
87
88          return 0; // if problems occur above, return 0 for number of columns
89      } // end method getColumnCount
90
91      // get name of a particular column in ResultSet
92      public String getColumnName( int column ) throws IllegalStateException
93      {
94          // ensure database connection is available
95          if ( !connectedToDatabase )
96              throw new IllegalStateException( "Not Connected to Database" );
97
98          // determine column name
99          try
100         {
101             return metaData.getColumnName( column + 1 );
102         } // end try
103         catch ( SQLException sqlException )
104         {
105             sqlException.printStackTrace();
106         } // end catch
107
108         return ""; // if problems, return empty string for column name
109     } // end method getColumnName
110
```

Fig. 25.25 | A TableModel that supplies ResultSet data to a JTable. (Part 3 of 5.)

```
111    // return number of rows in ResultSet
112    public int getRowCount() throws IllegalStateException
113    {
114       // ensure database connection is available
115       if ( !connectedToDatabase )
116          throw new IllegalStateException( "Not Connected to Database" );
117
118       return numberOfRows;
119    } // end method getRowCount
120
121    // obtain value in particular row and column
122    public Object getValueAt( int row, int column )
123       throws IllegalStateException
124    {
125       // ensure database connection is available
126       if ( !connectedToDatabase )
127          throw new IllegalStateException( "Not Connected to Database" );
128
129       // obtain a value at specified ResultSet row and column
130       try
131       {
132          resultSet.absolute( row + 1 );
133          return resultSet.getObject( column + 1 );
134       } // end try
135       catch ( SQLException sqlException )
136       {
137          sqlException.printStackTrace();
138       } // end catch
139
140       return ""; // if problems, return empty string object
141    } // end method getValueAt
142
143    // set new database query string
144    public void setQuery( String query )
145       throws SQLException, IllegalStateException
146    {
147       // ensure database connection is available
148       if ( !connectedToDatabase )
149          throw new IllegalStateException( "Not Connected to Database" );
150
151       // specify query and execute it
152       resultSet = statement.executeQuery( query );
153
154       // obtain meta data for ResultSet
155       metaData = resultSet.getMetaData();
156
157       // determine number of rows in ResultSet
158       resultSet.last(); // move to last row
159       numberOfRows = resultSet.getRow(); // get row number
160
161       // notify JTable that model has changed
162       fireTableStructureChanged();
163    } // end method setQuery
```

Fig. 25.25 | A TableModel that supplies ResultSet data to a JTable. (Part 4 of 5.)

```
164
165      // close Statement and Connection
166      public void disconnectFromDatabase()
167      {
168         if ( connectedToDatabase )
169         {
170            // close Statement and Connection
171            try
172            {
173               resultSet.close();
174               statement.close();
175               connection.close();
176            } // end try
177            catch ( SQLException sqlException )
178            {
179               sqlException.printStackTrace();
180            } // end catch
181            finally  // update database connection status
182            {
183               connectedToDatabase = false;
184            } // end finally
185         } // end if
186      } // end method disconnectFromDatabase
187   }  // end class ResultSetTableModel
```

Fig. 25.25 | A TableModel that supplies ResultSet data to a JTable. (Part 5 of 5.)

ResultSetTableModel *Constructor*

The ResultSetTableModel constructor (lines 30–46) accepts four String arguments—the URL of the database, the username, the password and the default query to perform. The constructor throws any exceptions that occur in its body back to the application that created the ResultSetTableModel object, so that the application can determine how to handle the exception (e.g., report an error and terminate the application). Line 34 establishes a connection to the database. Lines 37–39 invoke Connection method createStatement to create a Statement object. This example uses a version of method createStatement that takes two arguments—the result set type and the result set concurrency. The **result set type** (Fig. 25.26) specifies whether the ResultSet's cursor is able to scroll in both directions or forward only and whether the ResultSet is sensitive to changes made to the underlying data.

ResultSet constant	Description
TYPE_FORWARD_ONLY	Specifies that a ResultSet's cursor can move only in the forward direction (i.e., from the first to the last row in the ResultSet).
TYPE_SCROLL_INSENSITIVE	Specifies that a ResultSet's cursor can scroll in either direction and that the changes made to the underlying data during ResultSet processing are not reflected in the ResultSet unless the program queries the database again.

Fig. 25.26 | ResultSet constants for specifying ResultSet type. (Part 1 of 2.)

ResultSet constant	Description
TYPE_SCROLL_SENSITIVE	Specifies that a ResultSet's cursor can scroll in either direction and that the changes made to the underlying data during ResultSet processing are reflected immediately in the ResultSet.

Fig. 25.26 | ResultSet constants for specifying ResultSet type. (Part 2 of 2.)

Portability Tip 25.3
Some JDBC drivers do not support scrollable ResultSets. In such cases, the driver typically returns a ResultSet in which the cursor can move only forward. For more information, see your database driver documentation.

Common Programming Error 25.11
Attempting to move the cursor backward through a ResultSet when the database driver does not support backward scrolling causes a SQLFeatureNotSupportedException.

ResultSets that are sensitive to changes reflect those changes immediately after they're made with methods of interface ResultSet. If a ResultSet is insensitive to changes, the query that produced the ResultSet must be executed again to reflect any changes made. The **result set concurrency** (Fig. 25.27) specifies whether the ResultSet can be updated with ResultSet's update methods.

ResultSet static concurrency constant	Description
CONCUR_READ_ONLY	Specifies that a ResultSet cannot be updated (i.e., changes to the ResultSet contents cannot be reflected in the database with ResultSet's update methods).
CONCUR_UPDATABLE	Specifies that a ResultSet can be updated (i.e., changes to its contents can be reflected in the database with ResultSet's update methods).

Fig. 25.27 | ResultSet constants for specifying result properties.

Portability Tip 25.4
Some JDBC drivers do not support updatable ResultSets. In such cases, the driver typically returns a read-only ResultSet. For more information, see your database driver documentation.

Common Programming Error 25.12
Attempting to update a ResultSet when the database driver does not support updatable ResultSets causes SQLFeatureNotSupportedExceptions.

This example uses a ResultSet that is scrollable, insensitive to changes and read only. Line 45 invokes our method setQuery (lines 144–163) to perform the default query.

ResultSetTableModel Method getColumnClass

Method getColumnClass (lines 49–69) returns a Class object that represents the superclass of all objects in a particular column. The JTable uses this information to configure the default cell renderer and cell editor for that column in the JTable. Line 58 uses ResultSet-MetaData method **getColumnClassName** to obtain the fully qualified class name for the specified column. Line 61 loads the class and returns the corresponding Class object. If an exception occurs, the catch in lines 63–66 prints a stack trace and line 68 returns Object.class—the Class instance that represents class Object—as the default type. [*Note:* Line 58 uses the argument column + 1. Like arrays, JTable row and column numbers are counted from 0. However, ResultSet row and column numbers are counted from 1. Thus, when processing ResultSet rows or columns for use in a JTable, it's necessary to add 1 to the row or column number to manipulate the appropriate ResultSet row or column.]

ResultSetTableModel Method getColumnCount

Method getColumnCount (lines 72–89) returns the number of columns in the model's underlying ResultSet. Line 81 uses ResultSetMetaData method **getColumnCount** to obtain the number of columns in the ResultSet. If an exception occurs, the catch in lines 83–86 prints a stack trace and line 88 returns 0 as the default number of columns.

ResultSetTableModel Method getColumnName

Method getColumnName (lines 92–109) returns the name of the column in the model's underlying ResultSet. Line 101 uses ResultSetMetaData method **getColumnName** to obtain the column name from the ResultSet. If an exception occurs, the catch in lines 103–106 prints a stack trace and line 108 returns the empty string as the default column name.

ResultSetTableModel Method getRowCount

Method getRowCount (lines 112–119) returns the number of rows in the model's underlying ResultSet. When method setQuery (lines 144–163) performs a query, it stores the number of rows in variable numberOfRows.

ResultSetTableModel Method getValueAt

Method getValueAt (lines 122–141) returns the Object in a particular row and column of the model's underlying ResultSet. Line 132 uses ResultSet method **absolute** to position the ResultSet cursor at a specific row. Line 133 uses ResultSet method getObject to obtain the Object in a specific column of the current row. If an exception occurs, the catch in lines 135–138 prints a stack trace and line 140 returns an empty string as the default value.

ResultSetTableModel Method setQuery

Method setQuery (lines 144–163) executes the query it receives as an argument to obtain a new ResultSet (line 152). Line 155 gets the ResultSetMetaData for the new Result-Set. Line 158 uses ResultSet method **last** to position the ResultSet cursor at the last row in the ResultSet. [*Note:* This can be slow if the table contains many rows.] Line 159 uses ResultSet method **getRow** to obtain the row number for the current row in the Re-sultSet. Line 162 invokes method **fireTableStructureChanged** (inherited from class AbstractTableModel) to notify any JTable using this ResultSetTableModel object as its model that the structure of the model has changed. This causes the JTable to repopulate its rows and columns with the new ResultSet data. Method setQuery throws any exceptions that occur in its body back to the application that invoked setQuery.

ResultSetTableModel Method *disconnectFromDatabase*

Method disconnectFromDatabase (lines 166–186) implements an appropriate termination method for class ResultSetTableModel. A class designer should provide a public method that clients of the class must invoke explicitly to free resources that an object has used. In this case, method disconnectFromDatabase closes the ResultSet, Statement and Connection (lines 173–175), which are considered limited resources. Clients of the ResultSetTableModel class should always invoke this method when the instance of this class is no longer needed. Before releasing resources, line 168 verifies whether the connection is already terminated. If not, the method proceeds. The other methods in class ResultSetTableModel each throw an IllegalStateException if connectedToDatabase is false. Method disconnectFromDatabase sets connectedToDatabase to false (line 183) to ensure that clients do not use an instance of ResultSetTableModel after that instance has already been terminated. IllegalStateException is an exception from the Java libraries that is appropriate for indicating this error condition.

DisplayQueryResults Class

Class DisplayQueryResults (Fig. 25.28) implements the application's GUI and interacts with the ResultSetTableModel via a JTable object. This application also demonstrates the JTable sorting and filtering capabilities.

```
1   // Fig. 25.28: DisplayQueryResults.java
2   // Display the contents of the Authors table in the books database.
3   import java.awt.BorderLayout;
4   import java.awt.event.ActionListener;
5   import java.awt.event.ActionEvent;
6   import java.awt.event.WindowAdapter;
7   import java.awt.event.WindowEvent;
8   import java.sql.SQLException;
9   import java.util.regex.PatternSyntaxException;
10  import javax.swing.JFrame;
11  import javax.swing.JTextArea;
12  import javax.swing.JScrollPane;
13  import javax.swing.ScrollPaneConstants;
14  import javax.swing.JTable;
15  import javax.swing.JOptionPane;
16  import javax.swing.JButton;
17  import javax.swing.Box;
18  import javax.swing.JLabel;
19  import javax.swing.JTextField;
20  import javax.swing.RowFilter;
21  import javax.swing.table.TableRowSorter;
22  import javax.swing.table.TableModel;
23
24  public class DisplayQueryResults extends JFrame
25  {
26     // database URL, username and password
27     static final String DATABASE_URL = "jdbc:mysql://localhost/books";
28     static final String USERNAME = "deitel";
29     static final String PASSWORD = "deitel";
```

Fig. 25.28 | Displays contents of the database books. (Part 1 of 5.)

```
30
31        // default query retrieves all data from Authors table
32        static final String DEFAULT_QUERY = "SELECT * FROM Authors";
33
34        private ResultSetTableModel tableModel;
35        private JTextArea queryArea;
36
37        // create ResultSetTableModel and GUI
38        public DisplayQueryResults()
39        {
40           super( "Displaying Query Results" );
41
42           // create ResultSetTableModel and display database table
43           try
44           {
45              // create TableModel for results of query SELECT * FROM Authors
46              tableModel = new ResultSetTableModel( DATABASE_URL,
47                 USERNAME, PASSWORD, DEFAULT_QUERY );
48
49              // set up JTextArea in which user types queries
50              queryArea = new JTextArea( DEFAULT_QUERY, 3, 100 );
51              queryArea.setWrapStyleWord( true );
52              queryArea.setLineWrap( true );
53
54              JScrollPane scrollPane = new JScrollPane( queryArea,
55                 ScrollPaneConstants.VERTICAL_SCROLLBAR_AS_NEEDED,
56                 ScrollPaneConstants.HORIZONTAL_SCROLLBAR_NEVER );
57
58              // set up JButton for submitting queries
59              JButton submitButton = new JButton( "Submit Query" );
60
61              // create Box to manage placement of queryArea and
62              // submitButton in GUI
63              Box boxNorth = Box.createHorizontalBox();
64              boxNorth.add( scrollPane );
65              boxNorth.add( submitButton );
66
67              // create JTable based on the tableModel
68              JTable resultTable = new JTable( tableModel );
69
70              JLabel filterLabel = new JLabel( "Filter:" );
71              final JTextField filterText = new JTextField();
72              JButton filterButton = new JButton( "Apply Filter" );
73              Box boxSouth = Box.createHorizontalBox();
74
75              boxSouth.add( filterLabel );
76              boxSouth.add( filterText );
77              boxSouth.add( filterButton );
78
79              // place GUI components on content pane
80              add( boxNorth, BorderLayout.NORTH );
81              add( new JScrollPane( resultTable ), BorderLayout.CENTER );
82              add( boxSouth, BorderLayout.SOUTH );
```

Fig. 25.28 | Displays contents of the database books. (Part 2 of 5.)

```
83
84          // create event listener for submitButton
85          submitButton.addActionListener(
86
87             new ActionListener()
88             {
89                // pass query to table model
90                public void actionPerformed( ActionEvent event )
91                {
92                   // perform a new query
93                   try
94                   {
95                      tableModel.setQuery( queryArea.getText() );
96                   } // end try
97                   catch ( SQLException sqlException )
98                   {
99                      JOptionPane.showMessageDialog( null,
100                        sqlException.getMessage(), "Database error",
101                        JOptionPane.ERROR_MESSAGE );
102
103                     // try to recover from invalid user query
104                     // by executing default query
105                     try
106                     {
107                        tableModel.setQuery( DEFAULT_QUERY );
108                        queryArea.setText( DEFAULT_QUERY );
109                     } // end try
110                     catch ( SQLException sqlException2 )
111                     {
112                        JOptionPane.showMessageDialog( null,
113                           sqlException2.getMessage(), "Database error",
114                           JOptionPane.ERROR_MESSAGE );
115
116                        // ensure database connection is closed
117                        tableModel.disconnectFromDatabase();
118
119                        System.exit( 1 ); // terminate application
120                     } // end inner catch
121                  } // end outer catch
122               } // end actionPerformed
123            }  // end ActionListener inner class
124         ); // end call to addActionListener
125
126         final TableRowSorter< TableModel > sorter =
127            new TableRowSorter< TableModel >( tableModel );
128         resultTable.setRowSorter( sorter );
129         setSize( 500, 250 ); // set window size
130         setVisible( true ); // display window
131
132         // create listener for filterButton
133         filterButton.addActionListener(
134            new ActionListener()
135            {
```

Fig. 25.28 | Displays contents of the database books. (Part 3 of 5.)

```
136              // pass filter text to listener
137              public void actionPerformed( ActionEvent e )
138              {
139                  String text = filterText.getText();
140
141                  if ( text.length() == 0 )
142                      sorter.setRowFilter( null );
143                  else
144                  {
145                      try
146                      {
147                          sorter.setRowFilter(
148                              RowFilter.regexFilter( text ) );
149                      } // end try
150                      catch ( PatternSyntaxException pse )
151                      {
152                          JOptionPane.showMessageDialog( null,
153                              "Bad regex pattern", "Bad regex pattern",
154                              JOptionPane.ERROR_MESSAGE );
155                      } // end catch
156                  } // end else
157              } // end method actionPerfomed
158          } // end annonymous inner class
159      ); // end call to addActionLister
160  } // end try
161  catch ( SQLException sqlException )
162  {
163      JOptionPane.showMessageDialog( null, sqlException.getMessage(),
164          "Database error", JOptionPane.ERROR_MESSAGE );
165
166      // ensure database connection is closed
167      tableModel.disconnectFromDatabase();
168
169      System.exit( 1 ); // terminate application
170  } // end catch
171
172  // dispose of window when user quits application (this overrides
173  // the default of HIDE_ON_CLOSE)
174  setDefaultCloseOperation( DISPOSE_ON_CLOSE );
175
176  // ensure database connection is closed when user quits application
177  addWindowListener(
178
179      new WindowAdapter()
180      {
181          // disconnect from database and exit when window has closed
182          public void windowClosed( WindowEvent event )
183          {
184              tableModel.disconnectFromDatabase();
185              System.exit( 0 );
186          } // end method windowClosed
187      } // end WindowAdapter inner class
```

Fig. 25.28 | Displays contents of the database books. (Part 4 of 5.)

```
188          ); // end call to addWindowListener
189      } // end DisplayQueryResults constructor
190
191      // execute application
192      public static void main( String args[] )
193      {
194          new DisplayQueryResults();
195      } // end main
196  } // end class DisplayQueryResults
```

a) Displaying all authors from the Authors table

b) Displaying the the authors' first and last names joined with the titles and edition numbers of the books they've authored

c) Filtering the results of the previous query to show only the books with Java in the title

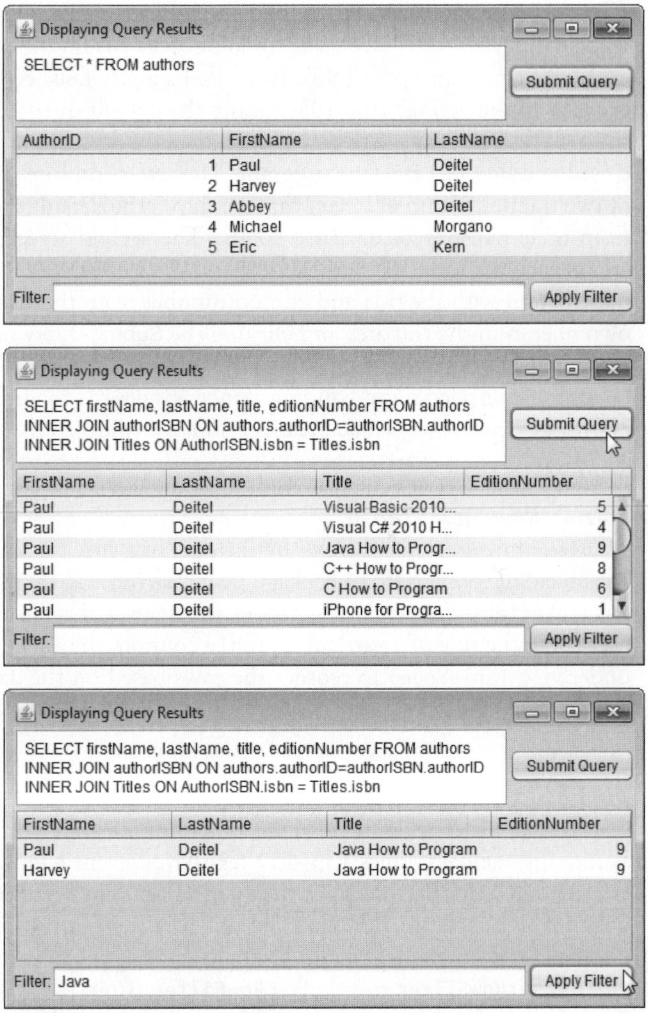

Fig. 25.28 | Displays contents of the database books. (Part 5 of 5.)

Lines 27–29 and 32 declare the URL, username, password and default query that are passed to the ResultSetTableModel constructor to make the initial connection to the database and perform the default query. The DisplayQueryResults constructor (lines 38–

189) creates a ResultSetTableModel object and the GUI for the application. Line 68 creates the JTable object and passes a ResultSetTableModel object to the JTable constructor, which then registers the JTable as a listener for TableModelEvents generated by the ResultSetTableModel.

The local variables filterText (line 71) and sorter (lines 126–127) are declared final. These are both used from an event handler that is implemented as an anonymous inner class (lines 134–158). Any local variable that will be used in an anonymous inner class *must* be declared final; otherwise, a compilation error occurs.

Lines 85–124 register an event handler for the submitButton that the user clicks to submit a query to the database. When the user clicks the button, method actionPerformed (lines 90–122) invokes method setQuery from the class ResultSetTableModel to execute the new query (line 95). If the user's query fails (e.g., because of a syntax error in the user's input), lines 107–108 execute the default query. If the default query also fails, there could be a more serious error, so line 117 ensures that the database connection is closed and line 119 exits the program. The screen captures in Fig. 25.28 show the results of two queries. The first screen capture shows the default query that retrieves all the data from table Authors of database books. The second screen capture shows a query that selects each author's first name and last name from the Authors table and combines that information with the title and edition number from the Titles table. Try entering your own queries in the text area and clicking the **Submit Query** button to execute the query.

Lines 177–188 register a **WindowListener** for the **windowClosed** event, which occurs when the user closes the window. Since WindowListeners can handle several window events, we extend class **WindowAdapter** and override only the windowClosed event handler.

Sorting Rows in a *JTable*

JTables allow users to sort rows by the data in a specific column. Lines 126–127 use the **TableRowSorter** class (from package **javax.swing.table**) to create an object that uses our ResultSetTableModel to sort rows in the JTable that displays query results. When the user clicks the title of a particular JTable column, the TableRowSorter interacts with the underlying TableModel to reorder the rows based on the data in that column. Line 128 uses JTable method **setRowSorter** to specify the TableRowSorter for resultTable.

Filtering Rows in a *JTable*

JTables can now show subsets of the data from the underlying TableModel. This is known as filtering the data. Lines 133–159 register an event handler for the filterButton that the user clicks to filter the data. In method actionPerformed (lines 137–157), line 139 obtains the filter text. If the user did not specify filter text, line 142 uses JTable method **setRowFilter** to remove any prior filter by setting the filter to null. Otherwise, lines 147–148 use setRowFilter to specify a **RowFilter** (from package javax.swing) based on the user's input. Class RowFilter provides several methods for creating filters. The static method **regexFilter** receives a String containing a regular expression pattern as its argument and an optional set of indices that specify which columns to filter. If no indices are specified, then all the columns are searched. In this example, the regular expression pattern is the text the user typed. Once the filter is set, the data displayed in the JTable is updated based on the filtered TableModel.

25.9 RowSet Interface

In the preceding examples, you learned how to query a database by explicitly establishing a Connection to the database, preparing a Statement for querying the database and executing the query. In this section, we demonstrate the **RowSet interface**, which configures the database connection and prepares query statements automatically. The interface Row-Set provides several *set* methods that allow you to specify the properties needed to establish a connection (such as the database URL, user name and password of the database) and create a Statement (such as a query). RowSet also provides several *get* methods that return these properties.

Connected and Disconnected RowSets

There are two types of RowSet objects—connected and disconnected. A **connected RowSet** object connects to the database once and remains connected while the object is in use. A **disconnected RowSet** object connects to the database, executes a query to retrieve the data from the database and then closes the connection. A program may change the data in a disconnected RowSet while it's disconnected. Modified data can be updated in the database after a disconnected RowSet reestablishes the connection with the database.

Package **javax.sql.rowset** contains two subinterfaces of RowSet—JdbcRowSet and CachedRowSet. **JdbcRowSet**, a connected RowSet, acts as a wrapper around a ResultSet object and allows you to scroll through and update the rows in the ResultSet. Recall that by default, a ResultSet object is nonscrollable and read only—you must explicitly set the result set type constant to TYPE_SCROLL_INSENSITIVE and set the result set concurrency constant to CONCUR_UPDATABLE to make a ResultSet object scrollable and updatable. A JdbcRowSet object is scrollable and updatable by default. **CachedRowSet**, a disconnected RowSet, caches the data of a ResultSet in memory and disconnects from the database. Like JdbcRowSet, a CachedRowSet object is scrollable and updatable by default. A Cached-RowSet object is also *serializable*, so it can be passed between Java applications through a network, such as the Internet. However, CachedRowSet has a limitation—the amount of data that can be stored in memory is limited. Package javax.sql.rowset contains three other subinterfaces of RowSet.

Portability Tip 25.5

A RowSet can provide scrolling capability for drivers that do not support scrollable ResultSets.

Using a RowSet

Figure 25.29 reimplements the example of Fig. 25.23 using a RowSet. Rather than establish the connection and create a Statement explicitly, Fig. 25.29 uses a JdbcRowSet object to create a Connection and a Statement automatically.

```
1   // Fig. 25.29: JdbcRowSetTest.java
2   // Displaying the contents of the Authors table using JdbcRowSet.
3   import java.sql.ResultSetMetaData;
4   import java.sql.SQLException;
```

Fig. 25.29 | Displaying the Authors table using JdbcRowSet. (Part 1 of 3.)

```
5   import javax.sql.rowset.JdbcRowSet;
6   import com.sun.rowset.JdbcRowSetImpl; // Sun's JdbcRowSet implementation
7
8   public class JdbcRowSetTest
9   {
10     // JDBC driver name and database URL
11     static final String DATABASE_URL = "jdbc:mysql://localhost/books";
12     static final String USERNAME = "deitel";
13     static final String PASSWORD = "deitel";
14
15     // constructor connects to database, queries database, processes
16     // results and displays results in window
17     public JdbcRowSetTest()
18     {
19        // connect to database books and query database
20        try
21        {
22           // specify properties of JdbcRowSet
23           JdbcRowSet rowSet = new JdbcRowSetImpl();
24           rowSet.setUrl( DATABASE_URL ); // set database URL
25           rowSet.setUsername( USERNAME ); // set username
26           rowSet.setPassword( PASSWORD ); // set password
27           rowSet.setCommand( "SELECT * FROM Authors" ); // set query
28           rowSet.execute(); // execute query
29
30           // process query results
31           ResultSetMetaData metaData = rowSet.getMetaData();
32           int numberOfColumns = metaData.getColumnCount();
33           System.out.println( "Authors Table of Books Database:\n" );
34
35           // display rowset header
36           for ( int i = 1; i <= numberOfColumns; i++ )
37              System.out.printf( "%-8s\t", metaData.getColumnName( i ) );
38           System.out.println();
39
40           // display each row
41           while ( rowSet.next() )
42           {
43              for ( int i = 1; i <= numberOfColumns; i++ )
44                 System.out.printf( "%-8s\t", rowSet.getObject( i ) );
45              System.out.println();
46           } // end while
47
48           // close the underlying ResultSet, Statement and Connection
49           rowSet.close();
50        } // end try
51        catch ( SQLException sqlException )
52        {
53           sqlException.printStackTrace();
54           System.exit( 1 );
55        } // end catch
56     } // end DisplayAuthors constructor
57
```

Fig. 25.29 | Displaying the Authors table using JdbcRowSet. (Part 2 of 3.)

```
58      // launch the application
59      public static void main( String args[] )
60      {
61          JdbcRowSetTest application = new JdbcRowSetTest();
62      } // end main
63  } // end class JdbcRowSetTest
```

```
Authors Table of Books Database:

AuthorID        FirstName       LastName
1               Paul            Deitel
2               Harvey          Deitel
3               Abbey           Deitel
4               Michael         Morgano
5               Eric            Kern
```

Fig. 25.29 | Displaying the Authors table using JdbcRowSet. (Part 3 of 3.)

The package **com.sun.rowset** provides Oracle's reference implementations of the interfaces in package javax.sql.rowset. Line 23 uses Sun's reference implementation of the JdbcRowSet interface—**JdbcRowSetImpl**—to create a JdbcRowSet object. We used class JdbcRowSetImpl here to demonstrate the capability of the JdbcRowSet interface. Other databases may provide their own RowSet implementations.

Lines 24–26 set the RowSet properties that the DriverManager uses to establish a database connection. Line 24 invokes JdbcRowSet method **setUrl** to specify the database URL. Line 25 invokes JdbcRowSet method **setUsername** to specify the username. Line 26 invokes JdbcRowSet method **setPassword** to specify the password. Line 27 invokes Jdbc-RowSet method **setCommand** to specify the SQL query that will be used to populate the RowSet. Line 28 invokes JdbcRowSet method **execute** to execute the SQL query. Method execute performs four actions—it establishes a Connection to the database, prepares the query Statement, executes the query and stores the ResultSet returned by query. The Connection, Statement and ResultSet are encapsulated in the JdbcRowSet object.

The remaining code is almost identical to Fig. 25.23, except that line 31 obtains a ResultSetMetaData object from the JdbcRowSet, line 41 uses the JdbcRowSet's next method to get the next row of the result and line 44 uses the JdbcRowSet's getObject method to obtain a column's value. Line 49 invokes JdbcRowSet method **close**, which closes the RowSet's encapsulated ResultSet, Statement and Connection. In a Cached-RowSet, invoking close also releases the resources held by that RowSet. The output of this application is the same as that of Fig. 25.23.

25.10 Java DB/Apache Derby

In this section and Section 25.11, we use Oracle's pure Java database **Java DB**. Please refer to the Before You Begin section after the Preface for information on installing Java DB. Section 25.11 uses the embedded version of Java DB. There's also a network version that executes similarly to the MySQL DBMS introduced earlier in the chapter.

Before you can execute the application in Section 25.11, you must set up the AddressBook database in Java DB. For the purpose of the following steps, we assume you're running Microsoft Windows with Java installed in its default location. Mac OS X and Linux will need to perform similar steps.

1. Java DB comes with several batch files to configure and run it. Before executing these batch files from a command prompt, you must set the environment variable JAVA_HOME to refer to the JDK's installation directory—for example, C:\Program Files\Java\jdk1.6.0_23. Be sure to use the exact installation directory of the JDK on your computer.

2. Open the batch file setEmbeddedCP.bat (typically located in C:\Program Files\Sun\JavaDB\bin) in a text editor such as Notepad. Locate the line

```
@rem set DERBY_INSTALL=
```

and change it to

```
@set DERBY_INSTALL=C:\Program Files\Sun\JavaDB
```

Save your changes and close this file. [*Note:* You might need to run Notepad as an Administrator to edit this file. To do so, open the Start menu and type Notepad in the **Search programs and files** field. Then, right click **Notepad** at the top of the menu and select **Run as administrator**.]

3. Open a Command Prompt as an administrator (as you did for Notepad in the previous step) and change directories to

```
C:\Program Files\Sun\JavaDB\bin
```

Then, type setEmbeddedCP.bat and press *Enter* to set the environment variables required by Java DB.

4. An embedded Java DB database must reside in the same location as the application that manipulates the database. For this reason, change to the directory that contains the code for Figs. 25.30–25.32. This directory contains a SQL script address.sql that builds the AddressBook database.

5. Execute the command

```
"C:\Program Files\Sun\JavaDB\bin\ij"
```

to start the command-line tool for interacting with Java DB. The double quotes are necessary because the path contains a space. This will display the ij> prompt.

6. At the ij> prompt type

```
connect 'jdbc:derby:AddressBook;create=true;user=deitel;
    password=deitel';
```

and press *Enter* to create the AddressBook database in the current directory and to create the user deitel with the password deitel for accessing the database.

7. To create the database table and insert sample data in it, we've provided the file address.sql in this example's directory. To execute this SQL script, type

```
run 'address.sql';
```

8. To terminate the Java DB command-line tool, type

```
exit;
```

You're now ready to execute the AddressBook application in Section 25.11. MySQL or any other database that supports JDBC PreparedStatements could also be used.

25.11 PreparedStatements

A **PreparedStatement** enables you to create compiled SQL statements that execute more efficiently than Statements. PreparedStatements can also specify parameters, making them more flexible than Statements—you can execute the same query repeatedly with different parameter values. For example, in the books database, you might want to locate all book titles for an author with a specific last and first name, and you might want to execute that query for several authors. With a PreparedStatement, that query is defined as follows:

```
PreparedStatement authorBooks = connection.prepareStatement(
   "SELECT LastName, FirstName, Title " +
   "FROM Authors INNER JOIN AuthorISBN " +
      "ON Authors.AuthorID=AuthorISBN.AuthorID " +
   "INNER JOIN Titles " +
      "ON AuthorISBN.ISBN=Titles.ISBN " +
   "WHERE LastName = ? AND FirstName = ?" );
```

The two question marks (?) in the the preceding SQL statement's last line are placeholders for values that will be passed as part of the query to the database. Before executing a PreparedStatement, the program must specify the parameter values by using the PreparedStatement interface's *set* methods.

For the preceding query, both parameters are strings that can be set with PreparedStatement method **setString** as follows:

```
authorBooks.setString( 1, "Deitel" );
authorBooks.setString( 2, "Paul" );
```

Method setString's first argument represents the parameter number being set, and the second argument is that parameter's value. Parameter numbers are *counted from 1*, starting with the first question mark (?). When the program executes the preceding PreparedStatement with the parameter values set above, the SQL passed to the database is

```
SELECT LastName, FirstName, Title
FROM Authors INNER JOIN AuthorISBN
   ON Authors.AuthorID=AuthorISBN.AuthorID
INNER JOIN Titles
   ON AuthorISBN.ISBN=Titles.ISBN
WHERE LastName = 'Deitel' AND FirstName = 'Paul'
```

Method setString automatically escapes String parameter values as necessary. For example, if the last name is O'Brien, the statement

```
authorBooks.setString( 1, "O'Brien" );
```

escapes the ' character in O'Brien by replacing it with two single-quote characters, so that the ' appears correctly in the database.

Performance Tip 25.2

PreparedStatements are more efficient than Statements when executing SQL statements multiple times and with different parameter values.

Error-Prevention Tip 25.2

Use PreparedStatements with parameters for queries that receive String values as arguments to ensure that the Strings are quoted properly in the SQL statement.

Interface PreparedStatement provides *set* methods for each supported SQL type. It's important to use the *set* method that is appropriate for the parameter's SQL type in the database—SQLExceptions occur when a program attempts to convert a parameter value to an incorrect type.

Address Book Application that Uses *PreparedStatements*

We now present an address book application that enables you to browse existing entries, add new entries and search for entries with a specific last name. Our AddressBook Java DB database contains an Addresses table with the columns addressID, FirstName, LastName, Email and PhoneNumber. The column addressID is a so-called *identity column*. This is the SQL standard way to represent an *autoincremented column*. The SQL script we provide for this database uses the SQL **IDENTITY** keyword to mark the addressID column as an identity column. For more information on using the IDENTITY keyword and creating databases, see the Java DB Developer's Guide at download.oracle.com/javadb/10.6.1.0/devguide/devguide-single.html.

Class *Person*

Our address book application consists of three classes—Person (Fig. 25.30), PersonQueries (Fig. 25.31) and AddressBookDisplay (Fig. 25.32). Class Person is a simple class that represents one person in the address book. The class contains fields for the address ID, first name, last name, email address and phone number, as well as *set* and *get* methods for manipulating these fields.

```java
1   // Fig. 25.30: Person.java
2   // Person class that represents an entry in an address book.
3   public class Person
4   {
5      private int addressID;
6      private String firstName;
7      private String lastName;
8      private String email;
9      private String phoneNumber;
10
11     // no-argument constructor
12     public Person()
13     {
14     } // end no-argument Person constructor
15
16     // constructor
17     public Person( int id, String first, String last,
18        String emailAddress, String phone )
19     {
20        setAddressID( id );
21        setFirstName( first );
```

Fig. 25.30 | Person class that represents an entry in an AddressBook. (Part 1 of 3.)

```
22          setLastName( last );
23          setEmail( emailAddress );
24          setPhoneNumber( phone );
25      } // end five-argument Person constructor
26
27      // sets the addressID
28      public void setAddressID( int id )
29      {
30          addressID = id;
31      } // end method setAddressID
32
33      // returns the addressID
34      public int getAddressID()
35      {
36          return addressID;
37      } // end method getAddressID
38
39      // sets the firstName
40      public void setFirstName( String first )
41      {
42          firstName = first;
43      } // end method setFirstName
44
45      // returns the first name
46      public String getFirstName()
47      {
48          return firstName;
49      } // end method getFirstName
50
51      // sets the lastName
52      public void setLastName( String last )
53      {
54          lastName = last;
55      } // end method setLastName
56
57      // returns the last name
58      public String getLastName()
59      {
60          return lastName;
61      } // end method getLastName
62
63      // sets the email address
64      public void setEmail( String emailAddress )
65      {
66          email = emailAddress;
67      } // end method setEmail
68
69      // returns the email address
70      public String getEmail()
71      {
72          return email;
73      } // end method getEmail
74
```

Fig. 25.30 | Person class that represents an entry in an AddressBook. (Part 2 of 3.)

```
75       // sets the phone number
76       public void setPhoneNumber( String phone )
77       {
78          phoneNumber = phone;
79       } // end method setPhoneNumber
80
81       // returns the phone number
82       public String getPhoneNumber()
83       {
84          return phoneNumber;
85       } // end method getPhoneNumber
86    } // end class Person
```

Fig. 25.30 | Person class that represents an entry in an AddressBook. (Part 3 of 3.)

Class *PersonQueries*

Class PersonQueries (Fig. 25.31) manages the address book application's database connection and creates the PreparedStatements that the application uses to interact with the database. Lines 18–20 declare three PreparedStatement variables. The constructor (lines 23–49) connects to the database at lines 27–28.

```
1     // Fig. 25.31: PersonQueries.java
2     // PreparedStatements used by the Address Book application.
3     import java.sql.Connection;
4     import java.sql.DriverManager;
5     import java.sql.PreparedStatement;
6     import java.sql.ResultSet;
7     import java.sql.SQLException;
8     import java.util.List;
9     import java.util.ArrayList;
10
11    public class PersonQueries
12    {
13       private static final String URL = "jdbc:derby:AddressBook";
14       private static final String USERNAME = "deitel";
15       private static final String PASSWORD = "deitel";
16
17       private Connection connection = null; // manages connection
18       private PreparedStatement selectAllPeople = null;
19       private PreparedStatement selectPeopleByLastName = null;
20       private PreparedStatement insertNewPerson = null;
21
22       // constructor
23       public PersonQueries()
24       {
25          try
26          {
27             connection =
28                DriverManager.getConnection( URL, USERNAME, PASSWORD );
29
```

Fig. 25.31 | PreparedStatements used by the Address Book application. (Part 1 of 4.)

```
30              // create query that selects all entries in the AddressBook
31              selectAllPeople =
32                 connection.prepareStatement( "SELECT * FROM Addresses" );
33
34              // create query that selects entries with a specific last name
35              selectPeopleByLastName = connection.prepareStatement(
36                 "SELECT * FROM Addresses WHERE LastName = ?" );
37
38              // create insert that adds a new entry into the database
39              insertNewPerson = connection.prepareStatement(
40                 "INSERT INTO Addresses " +
41                 "( FirstName, LastName, Email, PhoneNumber ) " +
42                 "VALUES ( ?, ?, ?, ? )" );
43           } // end try
44           catch ( SQLException sqlException )
45           {
46              sqlException.printStackTrace();
47              System.exit( 1 );
48           } // end catch
49        } // end PersonQueries constructor
50
51        // select all of the addresses in the database
52        public List< Person > getAllPeople()
53        {
54           List< Person > results = null;
55           ResultSet resultSet = null;
56
57           try
58           {
59              // executeQuery returns ResultSet containing matching entries
60              resultSet = selectAllPeople.executeQuery();
61              results = new ArrayList< Person >();
62
63              while ( resultSet.next() )
64              {
65                 results.add( new Person(
66                    resultSet.getInt( "addressID" ),
67                    resultSet.getString( "FirstName" ),
68                    resultSet.getString( "LastName" ),
69                    resultSet.getString( "Email" ),
70                    resultSet.getString( "PhoneNumber" ) ) );
71              } // end while
72           } // end try
73           catch ( SQLException sqlException )
74           {
75              sqlException.printStackTrace();
76           } // end catch
77           finally
78           {
79              try
80              {
81                 resultSet.close();
82              } // end try
```

Fig. 25.31 | PreparedStatements used by the Address Book application. (Part 2 of 4.)

```
83              catch ( SQLException sqlException )
84              {
85                 sqlException.printStackTrace();
86                 close();
87              } // end catch
88           } // end finally
89
90           return results;
91        } // end method getAllPeople
92
93        // select person by last name
94        public List< Person > getPeopleByLastName( String name )
95        {
96           List< Person > results = null;
97           ResultSet resultSet = null;
98
99           try
100          {
101             selectPeopleByLastName.setString( 1, name ); // specify last name
102
103             // executeQuery returns ResultSet containing matching entries
104             resultSet = selectPeopleByLastName.executeQuery();
105
106             results = new ArrayList< Person >();
107
108             while ( resultSet.next() )
109             {
110                results.add( new Person( resultSet.getInt( "addressID" ),
111                   resultSet.getString( "FirstName" ),
112                   resultSet.getString( "LastName" ),
113                   resultSet.getString( "Email" ),
114                   resultSet.getString( "PhoneNumber" ) ) );
115             } // end while
116          } // end try
117          catch ( SQLException sqlException )
118          {
119             sqlException.printStackTrace();
120          } // end catch
121          finally
122          {
123             try
124             {
125                resultSet.close();
126             } // end try
127             catch ( SQLException sqlException )
128             {
129                sqlException.printStackTrace();
130                close();
131             } // end catch
132          } // end finally
133
134          return results;
135       } // end method getPeopleByName
```

Fig. 25.31 | PreparedStatements used by the Address Book application. (Part 3 of 4.)

```
136
137     // add an entry
138     public int addPerson(
139        String fname, String lname, String email, String num )
140     {
141        int result = 0;
142
143        // set parameters, then execute insertNewPerson
144        try
145        {
146           insertNewPerson.setString( 1, fname );
147           insertNewPerson.setString( 2, lname );
148           insertNewPerson.setString( 3, email );
149           insertNewPerson.setString( 4, num );
150
151           // insert the new entry; returns # of rows updated
152           result = insertNewPerson.executeUpdate();
153        } // end try
154        catch ( SQLException sqlException )
155        {
156           sqlException.printStackTrace();
157           close();
158        } // end catch
159
160        return result;
161     } // end method addPerson
162
163     // close the database connection
164     public void close()
165     {
166        try
167        {
168           connection.close();
169        } // end try
170        catch ( SQLException sqlException )
171        {
172           sqlException.printStackTrace();
173        } // end catch
174     } // end method close
175  } // end class PersonQueries
```

Fig. 25.31 | PreparedStatements used by the Address Book application. (Part 4 of 4.)

*Creating **PreparedStatements***
Lines 31–32 invoke Connection method **prepareStatement** to create the Prepared-Statement named selectAllPeople that selects all the rows in the Addresses table. Lines 35–36 create the PreparedStatement named selectPeopleByLastName with a parameter. This statement selects all the rows in the Addresses table that match a particular last name. Notice the ? character that's used to specify the last-name parameter. Lines 39–42 create the PreparedStatement named insertNewPerson with four parameters that represent the first name, last name, email address and phone number for a new entry. Again, notice the ? characters used to represent these parameters.

*PersonQueries Method **getAllPeople***
Method getAllPeople (lines 52–91) executes PreparedStatement selectAllPeople (line 60) by calling method **executeQuery**, which returns a ResultSet containing the rows that match the query (in this case, all the rows in the Addresses table). Lines 61–71 place the query results in an ArrayList of Person objects, which is returned to the caller at line 90. Method getPeopleByLastName (lines 94–135) uses PreparedStatement method set-String to set the parameter to selectPeopleByLastName (line 101). Then, line 104 executes the query and lines 106–115 place the query results in an ArrayList of Person objects. Line 134 returns the ArrayList to the caller.

*PersonQueries Methods **addPerson** and **Close***
Method addPerson (lines 138–161) uses PreparedStatement method setString (lines 146–149) to set the parameters for the insertNewPerson PreparedStatement. Line 152 uses PreparedStatement method **executeUpdate** to insert the new record. This method returns an integer indicating the number of rows that were updated (or inserted) in the database. Method close (lines 164–174) simply closes the database connection.

*Class **AddressBookDisplay***
The AddressBookDisplay (Fig. 25.32) application uses a PersonQueries object to interact with the database. Line 59 creates the PersonQueries object. When the user presses the **Browse All Entries** JButton, the browseButtonActionPerformed handler (lines 309–335) is called. Line 313 calls the method getAllPeople on the PersonQueries object to obtain all the entries in the database. The user can then scroll through the entries using the **Previous** and **Next** JButtons. When the user presses the **Find** JButton, the queryButtonActionPerformed handler (lines 265–287) is called. Lines 267–268 call method getPeopleByLastName on the PersonQueries object to obtain the entries in the database that match the specified last name. If there are several such entries, the user can then scroll through them using the **Previous** and **Next** JButtons.

```
1    // Fig. 25.32: AddressBookDisplay.java
2    // A simple address book
3    import java.awt.event.ActionEvent;
4    import java.awt.event.ActionListener;
5    import java.awt.event.WindowAdapter;
6    import java.awt.event.WindowEvent;
7    import java.awt.FlowLayout;
8    import java.awt.GridLayout;
9    import java.util.List;
10   import javax.swing.JButton;
11   import javax.swing.Box;
12   import javax.swing.JFrame;
13   import javax.swing.JLabel;
14   import javax.swing.JPanel;
15   import javax.swing.JTextField;
16   import javax.swing.WindowConstants;
17   import javax.swing.BoxLayout;
18   import javax.swing.BorderFactory;
19   import javax.swing.JOptionPane;
```

Fig. 25.32 | A simple address book. (Part 1 of 9.)

```
20
21   public class AddressBookDisplay extends JFrame
22   {
23      private Person currentEntry;
24      private PersonQueries personQueries;
25      private List< Person > results;
26      private int numberOfEntries = 0;
27      private int currentEntryIndex;
28
29      private JButton browseButton;
30      private JLabel emailLabel;
31      private JTextField emailTextField;
32      private JLabel firstNameLabel;
33      private JTextField firstNameTextField;
34      private JLabel idLabel;
35      private JTextField idTextField;
36      private JTextField indexTextField;
37      private JLabel lastNameLabel;
38      private JTextField lastNameTextField;
39      private JTextField maxTextField;
40      private JButton nextButton;
41      private JLabel ofLabel;
42      private JLabel phoneLabel;
43      private JTextField phoneTextField;
44      private JButton previousButton;
45      private JButton queryButton;
46      private JLabel queryLabel;
47      private JPanel queryPanel;
48      private JPanel navigatePanel;
49      private JPanel displayPanel;
50      private JTextField queryTextField;
51      private JButton insertButton;
52
53      // no-argument constructor
54      public AddressBookDisplay()
55      {
56         super( "Address Book" );
57
58         // establish database connection and set up PreparedStatements
59         personQueries = new PersonQueries();
60
61         // create GUI
62         navigatePanel = new JPanel();
63         previousButton = new JButton();
64         indexTextField = new JTextField( 2 );
65         ofLabel = new JLabel();
66         maxTextField = new JTextField( 2 );
67         nextButton = new JButton();
68         displayPanel = new JPanel();
69         idLabel = new JLabel();
70         idTextField = new JTextField( 10 );
71         firstNameLabel = new JLabel();
72         firstNameTextField = new JTextField( 10 );
```

Fig. 25.32 | A simple address book. (Part 2 of 9.)

```
73         lastNameLabel = new JLabel();
74         lastNameTextField = new JTextField( 10 );
75         emailLabel = new JLabel();
76         emailTextField = new JTextField( 10 );
77         phoneLabel = new JLabel();
78         phoneTextField = new JTextField( 10 );
79         queryPanel = new JPanel();
80         queryLabel = new JLabel();
81         queryTextField = new JTextField( 10 );
82         queryButton = new JButton();
83         browseButton = new JButton();
84         insertButton = new JButton();
85
86         setLayout( new FlowLayout( FlowLayout.CENTER, 10, 10 ) );
87         setSize( 400, 300 );
88         setResizable( false );
89
90         navigatePanel.setLayout(
91            new BoxLayout( navigatePanel, BoxLayout.X_AXIS ) );
92
93         previousButton.setText( "Previous" );
94         previousButton.setEnabled( false );
95         previousButton.addActionListener(
96            new ActionListener()
97            {
98               public void actionPerformed( ActionEvent evt )
99               {
100                   previousButtonActionPerformed( evt );
101               } // end method actionPerformed
102            } // end anonymous inner class
103         ); // end call to addActionListener
104
105         navigatePanel.add( previousButton );
106         navigatePanel.add( Box.createHorizontalStrut( 10 ) );
107
108         indexTextField.setHorizontalAlignment(
109            JTextField.CENTER );
110         indexTextField.addActionListener(
111            new ActionListener()
112            {
113               public void actionPerformed( ActionEvent evt )
114               {
115                   indexTextFieldActionPerformed( evt );
116               } // end method actionPerformed
117            } // end anonymous inner class
118         ); // end call to addActionListener
119
120         navigatePanel.add( indexTextField );
121         navigatePanel.add( Box.createHorizontalStrut( 10 ) );
122
123         ofLabel.setText( "of" );
124         navigatePanel.add( ofLabel );
125         navigatePanel.add( Box.createHorizontalStrut( 10 ) );
```

Fig. 25.32 | A simple address book. (Part 3 of 9.)

```
126
127        maxTextField.setHorizontalAlignment(
128           JTextField.CENTER );
129        maxTextField.setEditable( false );
130        navigatePanel.add( maxTextField );
131        navigatePanel.add( Box.createHorizontalStrut( 10 ) );
132
133        nextButton.setText( "Next" );
134        nextButton.setEnabled( false );
135        nextButton.addActionListener(
136           new ActionListener()
137           {
138              public void actionPerformed( ActionEvent evt )
139              {
140                 nextButtonActionPerformed( evt );
141              } // end method actionPerformed
142           } // end anonymous inner class
143        ); // end call to addActionListener
144
145        navigatePanel.add( nextButton );
146        add( navigatePanel );
147
148        displayPanel.setLayout( new GridLayout( 5, 2, 4, 4 ) );
149
150        idLabel.setText( "Address ID:" );
151        displayPanel.add( idLabel );
152
153        idTextField.setEditable( false );
154        displayPanel.add( idTextField );
155
156        firstNameLabel.setText( "First Name:" );
157        displayPanel.add( firstNameLabel );
158        displayPanel.add( firstNameTextField );
159
160        lastNameLabel.setText( "Last Name:" );
161        displayPanel.add( lastNameLabel );
162        displayPanel.add( lastNameTextField );
163
164        emailLabel.setText( "Email:" );
165        displayPanel.add( emailLabel );
166        displayPanel.add( emailTextField );
167
168        phoneLabel.setText( "Phone Number:" );
169        displayPanel.add( phoneLabel );
170        displayPanel.add( phoneTextField );
171        add( displayPanel );
172
173        queryPanel.setLayout(
174           new BoxLayout( queryPanel, BoxLayout.X_AXIS) );
175
176        queryPanel.setBorder( BorderFactory.createTitledBorder(
177           "Find an entry by last name" ) );
178        queryLabel.setText( "Last Name:" );
```

Fig. 25.32 | A simple address book. (Part 4 of 9.)

```
179              queryPanel.add( Box.createHorizontalStrut( 5 ) );
180              queryPanel.add( queryLabel );
181              queryPanel.add( Box.createHorizontalStrut( 10 ) );
182              queryPanel.add( queryTextField );
183              queryPanel.add( Box.createHorizontalStrut( 10 ) );
184
185              queryButton.setText( "Find" );
186              queryButton.addActionListener(
187                 new ActionListener()
188                 {
189                    public void actionPerformed( ActionEvent evt )
190                    {
191                       queryButtonActionPerformed( evt );
192                    } // end method actionPerformed
193                 } // end anonymous inner class
194              ); // end call to addActionListener
195
196              queryPanel.add( queryButton );
197              queryPanel.add( Box.createHorizontalStrut( 5 ) );
198              add( queryPanel );
199
200              browseButton.setText( "Browse All Entries" );
201              browseButton.addActionListener(
202                 new ActionListener()
203                 {
204                    public void actionPerformed( ActionEvent evt )
205                    {
206                       browseButtonActionPerformed( evt );
207                    } // end method actionPerformed
208                 } // end anonymous inner class
209              ); // end call to addActionListener
210
211              add( browseButton );
212
213              insertButton.setText( "Insert New Entry" );
214              insertButton.addActionListener(
215                 new ActionListener()
216                 {
217                    public void actionPerformed( ActionEvent evt )
218                    {
219                       insertButtonActionPerformed( evt );
220                    } // end method actionPerformed
221                 } // end anonymous inner class
222              ); // end call to addActionListener
223
224              add( insertButton );
225
226              addWindowListener(
227                 new WindowAdapter()
228                 {
229                    public void windowClosing( WindowEvent evt )
230                    {
231                       personQueries.close(); // close database connection
```

Fig. 25.32 | A simple address book. (Part 5 of 9.)

```
232                       System.exit( 0 );
233                  } // end method windowClosing
234               } // end anonymous inner class
235            ); // end call to addWindowListener
236
237         setVisible( true );
238      } // end no-argument constructor
239
240      // handles call when previousButton is clicked
241      private void previousButtonActionPerformed( ActionEvent evt )
242      {
243         currentEntryIndex--;
244
245         if ( currentEntryIndex < 0 )
246            currentEntryIndex = numberOfEntries - 1;
247
248         indexTextField.setText( "" + ( currentEntryIndex + 1 ) );
249         indexTextFieldActionPerformed( evt );
250      } // end method previousButtonActionPerformed
251
252      // handles call when nextButton is clicked
253      private void nextButtonActionPerformed( ActionEvent evt )
254      {
255         currentEntryIndex++;
256
257         if ( currentEntryIndex >= numberOfEntries )
258            currentEntryIndex = 0;
259
260         indexTextField.setText( "" + ( currentEntryIndex + 1 ) );
261         indexTextFieldActionPerformed( evt );
262      } // end method nextButtonActionPerformed
263
264      // handles call when queryButton is clicked
265      private void queryButtonActionPerformed( ActionEvent evt )
266      {
267         results =
268            personQueries.getPeopleByLastName( queryTextField.getText() );
269         numberOfEntries = results.size();
270
271         if ( numberOfEntries != 0 )
272         {
273            currentEntryIndex = 0;
274            currentEntry = results.get( currentEntryIndex );
275            idTextField.setText( "" + currentEntry.getAddressID() );
276            firstNameTextField.setText( currentEntry.getFirstName() );
277            lastNameTextField.setText( currentEntry.getLastName() );
278            emailTextField.setText( currentEntry.getEmail() );
279            phoneTextField.setText( currentEntry.getPhoneNumber() );
280            maxTextField.setText( "" + numberOfEntries );
281            indexTextField.setText( "" + ( currentEntryIndex + 1 ) );
282            nextButton.setEnabled( true );
283            previousButton.setEnabled( true );
284         } // end if
```

Fig. 25.32 | A simple address book. (Part 6 of 9.)

```
285            else
286               browseButtonActionPerformed( evt );
287         } // end method queryButtonActionPerformed
288
289         // handles call when a new value is entered in indexTextField
290         private void indexTextFieldActionPerformed( ActionEvent evt )
291         {
292            currentEntryIndex =
293               ( Integer.parseInt( indexTextField.getText() ) - 1 );
294
295            if ( numberOfEntries != 0 && currentEntryIndex < numberOfEntries )
296            {
297               currentEntry = results.get( currentEntryIndex );
298               idTextField.setText("" + currentEntry.getAddressID() );
299               firstNameTextField.setText( currentEntry.getFirstName() );
300               lastNameTextField.setText( currentEntry.getLastName() );
301               emailTextField.setText( currentEntry.getEmail() );
302               phoneTextField.setText( currentEntry.getPhoneNumber() );
303               maxTextField.setText( "" + numberOfEntries );
304               indexTextField.setText( "" + ( currentEntryIndex + 1 ) );
305            } // end if
306         } // end method indexTextFieldActionPerformed
307
308         // handles call when browseButton is clicked
309         private void browseButtonActionPerformed( ActionEvent evt )
310         {
311            try
312            {
313               results = personQueries.getAllPeople();
314               numberOfEntries = results.size();
315
316               if ( numberOfEntries != 0 )
317               {
318                  currentEntryIndex = 0;
319                  currentEntry = results.get( currentEntryIndex );
320                  idTextField.setText( "" + currentEntry.getAddressID() );
321                  firstNameTextField.setText( currentEntry.getFirstName() );
322                  lastNameTextField.setText( currentEntry.getLastName() );
323                  emailTextField.setText( currentEntry.getEmail() );
324                  phoneTextField.setText( currentEntry.getPhoneNumber() );
325                  maxTextField.setText( "" + numberOfEntries );
326                  indexTextField.setText( "" + ( currentEntryIndex + 1 ) );
327                  nextButton.setEnabled( true );
328                  previousButton.setEnabled( true );
329               } // end if
330            } // end try
331            catch ( Exception e )
332            {
333               e.printStackTrace();
334            } // end catch
335         } // end method browseButtonActionPerformed
336
```

Fig. 25.32 | A simple address book. (Part 7 of 9.)

```
337    // handles call when insertButton is clicked
338    private void insertButtonActionPerformed( ActionEvent evt )
339    {
340       int result = personQueries.addPerson( firstNameTextField.getText(),
341          lastNameTextField.getText(), emailTextField.getText(),
342          phoneTextField.getText() );
343
344       if ( result == 1 )
345          JOptionPane.showMessageDialog( this, "Person added!",
346             "Person added", JOptionPane.PLAIN_MESSAGE );
347       else
348          JOptionPane.showMessageDialog( this, "Person not added!",
349             "Error", JOptionPane.PLAIN_MESSAGE );
350
351       browseButtonActionPerformed( evt );
352    } // end method insertButtonActionPerformed
353
354    // main method
355    public static void main( String args[] )
356    {
357       new AddressBookDisplay();
358    } // end method main
359 } // end class AddressBookDisplay
```

a) Initial **Address Book** screen.

b) Results of clicking **Browse All Entries**.

c) Browsing to the next entry.

d) Finding entries with the last name **Green**.

Fig. 25.32 | A simple address book. (Part 8 of 9.)

e) After adding a new entry and browsing to it.

Fig. 25.32 | A simple address book. (Part 9 of 9.)

To add a new entry into the AddressBook database, the user can enter the first name, last name, email and phone number (the AddressID will *autoincrement*) in the JText-Fields and press the **Insert New Entry** JButton. The insertButtonActionPerformed handler (lines 338–352) is called. Lines 340–342 call the method addPerson on the PersonQueries object to add a new entry to the database. Line 351 calls browseButtonActionPerformed to obtain the updated set of people in the address book and update the GUI accordingly.

The user can then view different entries by pressing the **Previous** JButton or **Next** JButton, which results in calls to methods previousButtonActionPerformed (lines 241–250) or nextButtonActionPerformed (lines 253–262), respectively. Alternatively, the user can enter a number in the indexTextField and press *Enter* to view a particular entry. This results in a call to method indexTextFieldActionPerformed (lines 290–306) to display the specified record.

25.12 Stored Procedures

Many database management systems can store individual or sets of SQL statements in a database, so that programs accessing that database can invoke them. Such named collections of SQL statements are called **stored procedures**. JDBC enables programs to invoke stored procedures using objects that implement the interface **CallableStatement**. CallableStatements can receive arguments specified with the methods inherited from interface PreparedStatement. In addition, CallableStatements can specify **output parameters** in which a stored procedure can place return values. Interface CallableStatement includes methods to specify which parameters in a stored procedure are output parameters. The interface also includes methods to obtain the values of output parameters returned from a stored procedure.

Portability Tip 25.6

Although the syntax for creating stored procedures differs across database management systems, the interface CallableStatement provides a uniform interface for specifying input and output parameters for stored procedures and for invoking stored procedures.

Portability Tip 25.7

According to the Java API documentation for interface CallableStatement, *for maximum portability between database systems, programs should process the update counts (which indicate how many rows were updated) or* ResultSets *returned from a* CallableStatement *before obtaining the values of any output parameters.*

25.13 Transaction Processing

Many database applications require guarantees that a series of database insertions, updates and deletions executes properly before the application continues processing the next database operation. For example, when you transfer money electronically between bank accounts, several factors determine if the transaction is successful. You begin by specifying the source account and the amount you wish to transfer from that account to a destination account. Next, you specify the destination account. The bank checks the source account to determine whether its funds are sufficient to complete the transfer. If so, the bank withdraws the specified amount and, if all goes well, deposits it into the destination account to complete the transfer. What happens if the transfer fails after the bank withdraws the money from the source account? In a proper banking system, the bank redeposits the money in the source account. How would you feel if the money was subtracted from your source account and the bank *did not* deposit the money in the destination account?

Transaction processing enables a program that interacts with a database to *treat a database operation (or set of operations) as a single operation*. Such an operation also is known as an **atomic operation** or a **transaction**. At the end of a transaction, a decision can be made either to **commit the transaction** or **roll back the transaction**. Committing the transaction finalizes the database operation(s); all insertions, updates and deletions performed as part of the transaction cannot be reversed without performing a new database operation. Rolling back the transaction leaves the database in its state prior to the database operation. This is useful when a portion of a transaction fails to complete properly. In our bank-account-transfer discussion, the transaction would be rolled back if the deposit could not be made into the destination account.

Java provides transaction processing via methods of interface Connection. Method **setAutoCommit** specifies whether each SQL statement commits after it completes (a true argument) or whether several SQL statements should be grouped as a transaction (a false argument). If the argument to setAutoCommit is false, the program must follow the last SQL statement in the transaction with a call to Connection method **commit** (to commit the changes to the database) or Connection method **rollback** (to return the database to its state prior to the transaction). Interface Connection also provides method **getAutoCommit** to determine the autocommit state for the Connection.

25.14 Wrap-Up

In this chapter, you learned basic database concepts, how to query and manipulate data in a database using SQL and how to use JDBC to allow Java applications to interact with MySQL and Java DB databases. You learned about the SQL commands SELECT, INSERT, UPDATE and DELETE, as well as clauses such as WHERE, ORDER BY and INNER JOIN. You learned the steps for obtaining a Connection to the database, creating a Statement to interact with the database's data, executing the statement and processing the results. Then you used a RowSet to simplify the process of connecting to a database and creating statements. You used PreparedStatements to create precompiled SQL statements. You also learned how to create and configure databases in both MySQL and Java DB by using predefined SQL scripts. We also provided overviews of CallableStatements and transaction processing. In the next chapter, you'll learn about web application development with JavaServer Faces.

25.15 Web Resources

www.oracle.com/technetwork/java/javadb/overview/index.html
Oracle Java DB home page.

db.apache.org/derby/papers/DerbyTut/index.html
Apache Derby tutorial. Includes Linux installation instructions.

download.oracle.com/javase/tutorial/jdbc/index.html
The Java Tutorial's JDBC track.

www.sql.org
This SQL portal provides links to many resources, including SQL syntax, tips, tutorials, books, magazines, discussion groups, companies with SQL services, SQL consultants and free software.

download.oracle.com/javase/6/docs/technotes/guides/jdbc/index.html
Oracle JDBC API documentation.

www.mysql.com
This site is the MySQL database home page. You can download the latest versions of MySQL and MySQL Connector/J and access their online documentation.

dev.mysql.com/doc/refman/5.5/en/index.html
MySQL reference manual.

download.oracle.com/javase/6/docs/technotes/guides/jdbc/getstart/rowsetImpl.html
Overviews the RowSet interface and its subinterfaces. This site also discusses the reference implementations of these interfaces from Sun and their usage.

JavaServer™ Faces Web Apps: Part 1

If any man will draw up his case, and put his name at the foot of the first page, I will give him an immediate reply. Where he compels me to turn over the sheet, he must wait my leisure.
—Lord Sandwich

Rule One:
Our client is always right.
Rule Two: If you think our client is wrong, see Rule One.
—Anonymous

A fair question should be followed by a deed in silence.
—Dante Alighieri

You will come here and get books that will open your eyes, and your ears, and your curiosity, and turn you inside out or outside in.
—Ralph Waldo Emerson

Objectives

In this chapter you'll learn:

■ To create JavaServer Faces web apps.

■ To create web apps consisting of multiple pages.

■ To validate user input on a web page.

■ To maintain user-specific state information throughout a web app with session tracking.

26.1 Introduction

In this chapter, we introduce web app development in Java with JavaServer Faces (JSF). Web-based apps create content for web browser clients. This content includes eXtensible HyperText Markup Language (XHTML), JavaScript client-side scripting, Cascading Style Sheets (CSS), images and binary data. XHTML is an XML (eXtensible Markup Language) vocabulary that is based on HTML (HyperText Markup Language). We discuss only the features of these technologies that are required to understand the examples in this chapter. If you'd like more information on XHTML, XML, JavaScript and CSS, please visit our Resource Centers on each of these topics at

> www.deitel.com/ResourceCenters.html

where you'll find links to introductions, tutorials and other valuable resources.

This chapter begins with an overview of how interactions between a web browser and web server work. We then present several web apps implemented with JSF. We continue this discussion in Chapter 27 with more advanced web applications.

Java multitier applications are typically implemented using Java Enterprise Edition (Java EE). The technologies we use to develop web apps here and in Chapter 27 are part of Java EE 6 (www.oracle.com/technetwork/java/javaee/overview/index.html). After you study this chapter and the next, you can learn more about JavaServer Faces 2.0 in Oracle's extensive Java EE 6 tutorial at download.oracle.com/javaee/6/tutorial/doc/.

We focus on the JavaServer Faces 2.0[1] subset of Java EE. JavaServer Faces is a **web-application framework** that enables you to build multitier web apps by extending the framework with your application-specific capabilities. The framework handles the details of receiving client requests and returning responses for you so that you can focus on your application's functionality.

Required Software for This Chapter

To work with and implement the examples in this chapter and Chapters 27–28, you must install the **NetBeans 6.9.1** IDE and the **GlassFish 3.0.1** open-source application server. Both are available in a bundle from netbeans.org/downloads/index.html. You're probably using a computer with the Windows, Linux or Max OS X operating system—install-

---

1. The JavaServer Faces Specification: http://bit.ly/JSF20Spec.

ers are provided for each of these platforms. Download and execute the installer for the **Java** or **All** version—both include the required **Java Web and EE** and **Glassfish Server Open Source Edition** options. We assume you use the default installation options for your platform. Once you've installed NetBeans, run it. Then, use the **Help** menu's **Check for Updates** option to make sure you have the most up-to-date components.

26.2 HyperText Transfer Protocol (HTTP) Transactions

To learn how JSF web apps work, it's important to understand the basics of what occurs behind the scenes when a user requests a web page in a web browser. If you're already familiar with this and with multitier application architecture, you can skip to Section 26.4.

XHTML Documents
In its simplest form, a web page is nothing more than an XHTML document (also called an XHTML page) that describes content to display in a web browser. HTML documents normally contain *hyperlinks* that link to different pages or to other parts of the same page. When the user clicks a hyperlink, the requested web page loads into the user's web browser. Similarly, the user can type the address of a page into the browser's address field.

URLs
Computers that run **web-server** software make resources available, such as web pages, images, PDF documents and even objects that perform complex tasks such as database lookups and web searches. The HyperText Transfer Protocol (HTTP) is used by web browsers to communicate with web servers, so they can exchange information in a uniform and reliable manner. URLs (Uniform Resource Locators) identify the locations on the Internet of resources, such as those mentioned above. If you know the URL of a publicly available web resource, you can access it through HTTP.

Parts of a URL
When you enter a URL into a web browser, the browser uses the information in the URL to locate the web server that contains the resource and to request that resource from the server. Let's examine the components of the URL

```
http://www.deitel.com/books/downloads.html
```

The `http://` indicates that the resource is to be obtained using the HTTP protocol. The next portion, `www.deitel.com`, is the server's fully qualified **hostname**—the name of the *server* on which the *resource* resides. The computer that houses and maintains resources is usually is referred to as the **host**. The hostname `www.deitel.com` is translated into an **IP (Internet Protocol) address**—a unique numerical value that identifies the server, much as a telephone number uniquely defines a particular phone line. This translation is performed by a **domain-name system (DNS) server**—a computer that maintains a database of hostnames and their corresponding IP addresses—and the process is called a **DNS lookup**. To test web apps, you'll often use your computer as the host. This host is referred to using the reserved domain name `localhost`, which translates to the IP address `127.0.0.1`. The fully qualified hostname can be followed by a colon (`:`) and a port number. Web servers typically await requests on port 80 by default; however, many development web servers use a different port number, such as 8080—as you'll see in Section 26.4.3.

The remainder of the URL (i.e., `/books/downloads.html`) specifies both the name of the requested resource (the HTML document `downloads.html`) and its path, or location (`/books`), on the web server. The path could specify the location of an actual directory on the web server's file system. For security reasons, however, the path normally specifies the location of a **virtual directory**. The server translates the virtual directory into a real location on the server (or on another computer on the server's network), thus hiding the resource's true location. Some resources are created dynamically using other information, such as data from a database.

Making a Request and Receiving a Response

When given a URL, a web browser performs an HTTP transaction to retrieve and display the web page at that address. Figure 26.1 illustrates the transaction, showing the interaction between the web browser (the client) and the web server (the server).

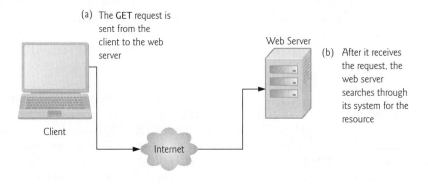

Fig. 26.1 | Client interacting with the web server. *Step 1:* The GET request.

In Fig. 26.1, the web browser sends an HTTP request to the server. Underneath the hood, the request (in its simplest form) is

```
GET /books/downloads.html HTTP/1.1
```

The word **GET** is an **HTTP method** indicating that the client wishes to obtain a resource from the server. The remainder of the request provides the path name of the resource (e.g., an HTML document) and the protocol's name and version number (`HTTP/1.1`). As part of the client request, the browser also sends other required and optional information, such as the `Host` (which identifies the server computer) or the `User-Agent` (which identifies the web browser type and version number).

Any server that understands HTTP (version 1.1) can translate this request and respond appropriately. Figure 26.2 depicts the server responding to a request.

The server first responds by sending a line of text that indicates the HTTP version, followed by a numeric code and a phrase describing the status of the transaction. For example,

```
HTTP/1.1 200 OK
```

indicates success, whereas

```
HTTP/1.1 404 Not found
```

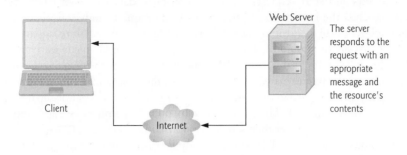

Fig. 26.2 | Client interacting with the web server. *Step 2:* The HTTP response.

informs the client that the web server could not locate the requested resource. On a successful request, the server appends the requested resource to the HTTP response. A complete list of numeric codes indicating the status of an HTTP transaction can be found at www.w3.org/Protocols/rfc2616/rfc2616-sec10.html.

HTTP Headers

The server then sends one or more **HTTP headers**, which provide additional information about the data that will be sent. If the server is sending an HTML text document, one HTTP header would read:

```
Content-type: text/html
```

The information provided in this header specifies the **Multipurpose Internet Mail Extensions (MIME)** type of the content that the server is transmitting to the browser. MIME is an Internet standard that specifies *data formats* so that programs can interpret data correctly. For example, the MIME type text/plain indicates that the sent information is text that can be displayed directly, without any interpretation of the content as HTML markup. Similarly, the MIME type image/jpeg indicates that the content is a JPEG image. When the browser receives this MIME type, it attempts to display the image. For a list of available MIME types, visit www.w3schools.com/media/media_mimeref.asp.

The header or set of headers is followed by a blank line, which indicates to the client browser that the server is finished sending HTTP headers. The server then sends the contents of the requested resource (such as, downloads.html). In the case of an HTML document, the web browser parses the HTML markup it receives and **renders** (or displays) the results.

HTTP GET and POST Requests

The two most common **HTTP request types** (also known as **request methods**) are GET and POST. A GET request typically asks for a resource on a server. Common uses of GET requests are to retrieve an HTML document or an image or to fetch search results from a search engine based on a user-submitted search term. A **POST** request typically sends data to a server. Common uses of POST requests are to send form data or documents to a server.

When a web page contains an HTML form in which the user can enter data, an HTTP request typically posts that data to a **server-side form handler** for processing. For example, when a user performs a search or participates in a web-based survey, the web server receives the information specified in the form as part of the request.

GET requests and POST requests can both send form data to a web server, yet each request type sends the information differently. A GET request sends information to the server in the URL, as in www.google.com/search?q=deitel. Here, search is the name of Google's server-side form handler, q is the name of a variable in Google's search form and deitel is the search term. A ? separates the **query string** from the rest of the URL in a request. A *name/value* pair is passed to the server with the *name* and the *value* separated by an equals sign (=). If more than one *name/value* pair is submitted, each is separated from the next by an ampersand (&). The server uses data passed in a query string to retrieve an appropriate resource. The server then sends a **response** to the client. A GET request may be initiated by submitting an HTML form whose method attribute is set to "get", by typing the URL (possibly containing a query string) directly into the browser's address bar or through a hyperlink when the user clicks the link.

A POST request sends form data as part of the HTTP message, not as part of the URL. The specification for GET requests does not limit the query string's number of characters, but some web browsers do—for example, Internet Explorer restricts the length to 2083 characters), so it's often necessary to send large pieces of information using POST. Sometimes POST is preferred because it hides the submitted data from the user by embedding it in an HTTP message.

Software Engineering Observation 26.1

The data sent in a POST request is not part of the URL, and the user can't see the data by default. However, tools are available that expose this data, so you should not assume that the data is secure just because a POST request is used.

Client-Side Caching

Browsers often **cache** (save on disk) web pages for quick reloading. If there are no changes between the version stored in the cache and the current version on the web, the browser uses the cached copy to speed up your browsing experience. An HTTP response can indicate the length of time for which the content remains "fresh." If this amount of time has not been reached, the browser can avoid another request to the server. Otherwise, the browser requests the document from the server. Thus, the browser minimizes the amount of data that must be downloaded for you to view a web page. Browsers typically do not cache the server's response to a POST request, because the next POST might not return the same result. For example, in a survey, many users could visit the same web page and answer a question. The survey results could then be displayed for the user. Each new answer changes the survey results.

When you use a web-based search engine, the browser normally supplies the information you specify in an HTML form to the search engine with a GET request. The search engine performs the search, then returns the results to you as a web page. Such pages are sometimes cached by the browser in case you perform the same search again.

26.3 Multitier Application Architecture

Web apps are **multitier applications** (sometimes referred to as *n*-**tier applications**). Multitier applications divide functionality into separate **tiers** (i.e., logical groupings of functionality). Although tiers can be located on the same computer, the tiers of web apps often reside on separate computers. Figure 26.3 presents the basic structure of a three-tier web app.

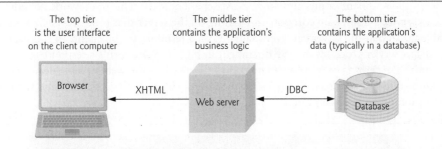

Fig. 26.3 | Three-tier architecture.

The **information tier** (also called the **data tier** or the **bottom tier**) maintains data pertaining to the application. This tier typically stores data in a *relational database management system* (*RDBMS*). We discussed RDBMSs in Chapter 25. For example, a retail store might have a database for storing product information, such as descriptions, prices and quantities in stock. The same database also might contain customer information, such as user names, billing addresses and credit card numbers. This tier can contain multiple databases, which together comprise the data needed for our application.

The **middle tier** implements **business logic**, **controller logic** and **presentation logic** to control interactions between the application's clients and the application's data. The middle tier acts as an intermediary between data in the information tier and the application's clients. The middle-tier controller logic processes client requests (such as requests to view a product catalog) and retrieves data from the database. The middle-tier presentation logic then processes data from the information tier and presents the content to the client. Web apps typically present data to clients as HTML documents.

Business logic in the middle tier enforces **business rules** and ensures that data is reliable before the server application updates the database or presents the data to users. Business rules dictate how clients can and cannot access application data, and how applications process data. For example, a business rule in the middle tier of a retail store's web app might ensure that all product quantities remain positive. A client request to set a negative quantity in the bottom tier's product-information database would be rejected by the middle tier's business logic.

The **client tier**, or **top tier**, is the application's user interface, which gathers input and displays output. Users interact directly with the application through the user interface (typically viewed in a web browser), keyboard and mouse. In response to user actions (e.g., clicking a hyperlink), the client tier interacts with the middle tier to make requests and to retrieve data from the information tier. The client tier then displays the data retrieved from the middle tier to the user. The client tier never directly interacts with the information tier.

26.4 Your First JSF Web App

Let's begin with a simple example. Figure 26.4 shows the output of our WebTime app. When you invoke this app from a web browser, the browser requests the app's default JSF page. The web server receives this request and passes it to the **JSF web-application framework** for processing. This framework is available in any Java EE 6-compliant application server (such as the GlassFish application server used in this chapter) or any JavaServer

Faces 2.0-compliant container (such as Apache Tomcat). The framework includes the **Faces servlet**—a software component running on the server that processes each requested JSF page so that the server can eventually return a response to the client. In this example, the Faces servlet processes the JSF document in Fig. 26.5 and forms a response containing the text "Current time on the web server:" followed by the web server's local time. We demonstrate this chapter's examples on the GlassFish server that you installed with Net-Beans locally on your computer.

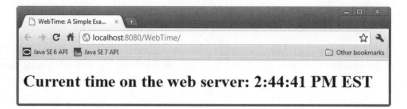

Fig. 26.4 | Sample output of the WebTime app.

Executing the WebTime App
To run this example on your own computer, perform the following steps:

1. Open the NetBeans IDE.

2. Select **File > Open Project...** to display the **Open Project** dialog.

3. Navigate to the ch29 folder in the book's examples and select WebTime.

4. Click the **Open Project** button.

5. Right click the project's name in the **Projects** tab (in the upper-left corner of the IDE, below the toolbar) and select **Run** from the pop-up menu.

This launches the GlassFish application server (if it isn't already running), installs the web app onto the server, then opens your computer's default web browser which requests the WebTime app's default JSF page. The browser should display a web page similar to that in Fig. 26.4.

26.4.1 The Default index.xhtml Document: Introducing Facelets

This app contains a single web page and consists of two related files—a JSF document named index.xhtml (Fig. 26.5) and a supporting Java source-code file (Fig. 26.6), which we discuss in Section 26.4.2. First we discuss the markup in index.xhtml and the supporting source code, then we provide step-by-step instructions for creating this web app in Section 26.4.3. Most of the markup in Fig. 26.5 was generated by NetBeans. We've reformatted the generated code to match our coding conventions used throughout the book.

```
1   <?xml version='1.0' encoding='UTF-8' ?>
2
3   <!-- index.xhtml -->
4   <!-- JSF page that displays the current time on the web server -->
```

Fig. 26.5 | JSF page that displays the current time on the web server. (Part 1 of 2.)

```
 5    <!DOCTYPE html PUBLIC "-//W3C//DTD XHTML 1.0 Transitional//EN"
 6        "http://www.w3.org/TR/xhtml1/DTD/xhtml1-transitional.dtd">
 7    <html xmlns="http://www.w3.org/1999/xhtml"
 8        xmlns:h="http://java.sun.com/jsf/html">
 9        <h:head>
10            <title>WebTime: A Simple Example</title>
11            <meta http-equiv="refresh" content="60" />
12        </h:head>
13        <h:body>
14            <h1>Current time on the web server: #{webTimeBean.time}</h1>
15        </h:body>
16    </html>
```

Fig. 26.5 | JSF page that displays the current time on the web server. (Part 2 of 2.)

Facelets: XHTML and JSF Markup

You present your web app's content in JSF using **Facelets**—a combination of XHTML markup and JSF markup. **XHTML**—the **Extensible HyperText Markup Language**—specifies the content of a web page that is displayed in a web browser. XHTML separates the **presentation** of a document (that is, the document's appearance when rendered by a browser) from the **structure** of the document's data. A document's presentation might specify where the browser should place an element in a web page or what fonts and colors should be used to display an element. The XHTML 1.0 Strict Recommendation allows only a document's structure to appear in a valid XHTML document, and not its presentation. Presentation is specified with Cascading Style Sheets (CSS). JSF uses the XHTML 1.0 Transitional Recommendation by default. Transitional markup may include some non-CSS formatting, but this is not recommended.

XML Declaration, Comments and the DOCTYPE Declaration

With the exception of lines 3–4, 10–11 and 14, the code shown in Fig. 26.5 was generated by NetBeans. Line 1 is an XML declaration, indicating that the JSF document is expressed in XML 1.0 syntax. Lines 3–4 are comments that we added to the document to indicate its file name and purpose. Lines 5–6 are a DOCTYPE declaration indicating the version of XHTML used in the markup. This can be used by a web browser to validate the syntax of the document.

Specifying the XML Namespaces Used in the Document

Line 7 begins the document's root html element, which spans lines 7–16. Each element typically consists of a starting and ending tag. The starting <html> tag (lines 7–8) may contain one or more xmlns attributes. Each **xmlns attribute** has a **name** and a **value** separated by an equal sign (=), and specifies an XML namespace of elements that are used in the document. Just as Java packages can be used to differentiate class names, XML namespaces can be used to differentiate sets of elements. When there's a naming conflict, fully qualified tag names can be used to resolve the conflict.

Line 7 specifies a required xmlns attribute and its value (http://www.w3.org/1999/xhtml) for the html element. This indicates that the html element and any other unqualified element names are part of the default XML namespace that's used in this document.

The xmlns:h attribute (line 8) specifies a prefix and a URL for JSF's **HTML Tag Library**, allowing the document to use JSF's elements from that library. A tag library defines a set of elements that can be inserted into the XHTML markup. The elements in the HTML Tag Library generate XHTML elements. Based on line 7, each element we use from the HTML Tag Library must be preceded by the h: prefix. This tag library is one of several sup-poorted by JSF that can be used to create Facelets pages. We'll discuss others as we use them. For a complete list of JSF tag libraries and their elements and attributes, visit

```
javaserverfaces.java.net/nonav/docs/2.0/pdldocs/facelets/
```

The h:head and h:body Elements

The **h:head** element (lines 9–12) defines the XHTML page's head element. In this example the head contains an HTML title element and a meta element. The document's title (line 10) typically appears in the browser window's title bar, or a browser tab if you have multiple web pages open in the browser at once. The title is also used when search engines index your web pages. The **meta** element (line 11) tells the browser to refresh the page every 60 seconds. This forces the browser to re-request the page once per minute.

The **h:body** element (lines 13–15) represent's the page's content. In this example, it contains a XHTML h1 header element (line 14) that represents the text to display when this document is rendered in the web browser. The h1 element contains some literal text (Current time on the web server:) that's simply placed into the response to the client and a **JSF Expression Language** (EL) expression that obtains a value dynamically and inserts it into the response. The expression

```
#{webTimeBean.time}
```

indicates that the web app has an object named webTimeBean which contains a property named time. The property's value replaces the expression in the response that's sent to the client. We'll discuss this EL expression in more detail shortly.

26.4.2 Examining the WebTimeBean Class

JSF documents typically interact with one or more Java objects to perform the app's tasks. As you saw, this example obtains the time on the server and sends it as part of the response.

JavaBeans

JavaBeans objects are instances of classes that follow certain conventions for class design. Each JavaBean class typically contains data and methods. A JavaBean exposes its data to a JSF document as **properties**. Depending on their use, these properties can be read/write, read-only or write-only. To define a read/write property, a JavaBean class provides *set* and *get* methods for that property. For example, to create a String property firstName, the class would provide methods with the following first lines:

```
public String getFirstName()
public void setFirstName( String name )
```

The fact that both method names contain "FirstName" with an uppercase "F" indicates that the class exposes a firstName property with a lowercase "F." This naming convention is part of the JavaBeans Specification (available at bit.ly/JavaBeansSpecification). A read-only property would have only a *get* method and a write-only property only a *set* method. The JavaBeans used in JSF are also **POJOs (plain old Java objects)**, meaning that—unlike prior versions of JSF—you do *not* need to extend a special class to create the beans used in JSF applications. Instead various annotations are used to "inject" functionality into your beans so they can be used easily in JSF applications. The JSF framework is responsible for creating and managing objects of your JavaBean classes for you—you'll see how to enable this momentarily.

Class *WebTimeBean*

Figure 26.6 presents the WebTimeBean class that allows the JSF document to obtain the web server's time. You can name your bean classes like any other class. We chose to end the class name with "Bean" to indicate that the class represents a JavaBean. The class contains just a getTime method (lines 13–17), which defines the read-only time property of the class. Recall that we access this property at line 14 of Fig. 26.5. Lines 15–16 create a Date object, then format and return the time as a String.

```
 1   // WebTimeBean.java
 2   // Bean that enables the JSF page to retrieve the time from the server
 3   package webtime;
 4
 5   import java.text.DateFormat;
 6   import java.util.Date;
 7   import javax.faces.bean.ManagedBean;
 8
 9   @ManagedBean( name="webTimeBean" )
10   public class WebTimeBean
11   {
12      // return the time on the server at which the request was received
13      public String getTime()
14      {
15         return DateFormat.getTimeInstance( DateFormat.LONG ).format(
16            new Date() );
17      } // end method getTime
18   } // end class WebTimeBean
```

Fig. 26.6 | Bean that enables the JSF page to retrieve the time from the server.

The *@ManagedBean* Annotation

Line 9 uses the **@ManagedBean annotation** (from the package **javax.faces.bean**) to indicate that the JSF framework should create and manage the WebTimeBean object(s) used in the application. The parentheses following the annotation contain the optional **name attribute**—in this case, indicating that the bean object created by the JSF framework should be called webTimeBean. If you specify the annotation without the parentheses and the name attribute, the JSF framework will use the class name with a lowercase first letter (that is, webTimeBean) as the default bean name.

Processing the EL Expression

When the Faces servlet encounters an EL expression that accesses a bean property, it automatically invokes the property's *set* or *get* method based on the context in which the property is used. In line 14 of Fig. 26.5, accessing the property webTimeBean.time results in a call to the bean's getTime method, which returns the web server's time. If this bean object does not yet exist, the JSF framework instantiates it, then calls the getTime method on the bean object. The framework can also discard beans that are no longer being used. [*Note:* We discuss only the EL expressions that we use in this chapter. For more EL details, see Chapter 6 of the Java EE 6 tutorial at download.oracle.com/javaee/6/tutorial/ doc/ and Chapter 5 of the JSF 2.0 specification at bit.ly/JSF20Spec.]

26.4.3 Building the WebTime JSF Web App in NetBeans

We'll now build the WebTime app from scratch using NetBeans.

Creating the JSF Web Application Project
Begin by opening the NetBeans IDE and performing the following steps:

1. Select **File > New Project...** to display the **New Project** dialog. Select **Java Web** in the **Categories** pane, **Web Application** in the **Projects** pane and click **Next >**.

2. In the dialog's **Name and Location** step, specify WebTime as the **Project Name**. In the **Project Location** field, specify where you'd like to store the project (or keep the default location). These settings will create a WebTime directory to store the project's files in the parent directory you specified. Keep the other default settings and click **Next >**.

3. In the dialog's **Server and Settings** step, specify **GlassFish Server 3** as the **Server** and **Java EE 6 Web** as the **Java EE Version** (these may be the default). Keep the default **Context Path** and click **Next >**.

4. In the dialog's **Frameworks** step, select **JavaServer Faces**, then click **Finish** to create the web application project.

Examining the NetBeans Projects Window
Figure 26.7 displays the **Projects** window, which appears in the upper-left corner of the IDE. This window displays the contents of the project. The app's XHTML documents are placed in the **Web Pages** node. NetBeans supplies the default web page index.xhtml that will be displayed when a user requests this web app from a browser. When you add Java source code to the project, it will be placed in the **Source Packages** node.

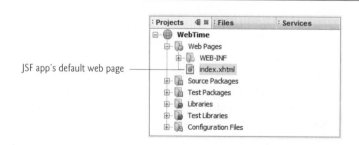

JSF app's default web page

Fig. 26.7 | **Projects** window for the WebTime project.

Examining the Default index.xhtml Page
Figure 26.8 displays index.xthml—the default page that will be displayed when a user requests this web app. We reformatted the code to match our coding conventions. When this file is first created, it contains elements for setting up the page, including linking to the page's style sheet and declaring the JSF libraries that will be used. By default, NetBeans

does not show line numbers in the source-code editor. To view the line numbers, select **View > Show Line Numbers**.

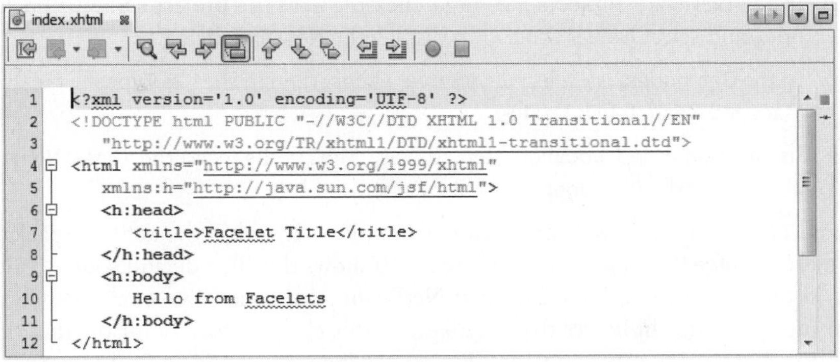

Fig. 26.8 | Default `index.xhtml` page generated by NetBeans for the web app.

Editing the h:head Element's Contents

Modify line 7 of Fig. 26.8 by changing the `title` element's content from `"Facelet Title"` to `"Web Time: A Simple Example"`. After the closing `</title>` tag, press *Enter*, then insert the `meta` element

```
<meta http-equiv="refresh" content="60" />
```

which will cause the browser to refresh this page once per minute. As you type, notice that NetBeans provides a code-completion window to help you write your code. For example, after typing "`<meta`" and a space, the IDE displays the code-completion window in Fig. 26.9, which shows the list of valid attributes for the starting tag of a `meta` element. You can then double click an item in the list to insert it into your code. Code-completion support is provided for XHTML elements, JSF elements and Java code.

```
content
dir
http-equiv
id
lang
name
scheme
xml:lang
```

Fig. 26.9 | NetBeans code-completion window.

Editing the h:body Element's Contents

In the `h:body` element, replace `"Hello from Facelets"` with the `h1` header element

```
<h1>Current time on the web server: </h1>
```

Don't insert the expression `#{webTimeBean.time}` yet. After we define the `WebTimeBean` class, we'll come back to this file and insert this expression to demonstrate that the IDE provides code-completion support for the Java classes you define in your project.

*Defining the Page's Logic: Class **WebTimeBean***

We'll now create the WebTimeBean class—the @ManagedBean class that will allow the JSF page to obtain the web server's time. To create the class, perform the following steps:

1. In the NetBeans **Projects** tab, right click the WebTime project's **Source Packages** node and select **New > Other...** to display the **New File** dialog.

2. In the **Categories** list, select **JavaServer Faces**, then in the **File Types** list select **JSF Managed Bean**. Click **Next >**.

3. In the **Name and Location** step, specify WebTimeBean as the **Class Name** and webtime as the **Package**, then click **Finish**.

NetBeans creates the WebTimeBean.java file and places it within the webtime package in the project's **Source Packages** node. Figure 26.10 shows this file's default source code displayed in the IDE. At line 16, notice that NetBeans added the **@RequestScoped** annotation to the class—this indicates that an object of this class exists only for the duration of the request that's being processed. (We'll discuss @RequestScoped and other bean scopes in more detail in Section 26.8.) We did not include this annotation in Fig. 26.6, because all JSF beans are request scoped by default. Replace the code in Fig. 26.10 with the code in Fig. 26.6.

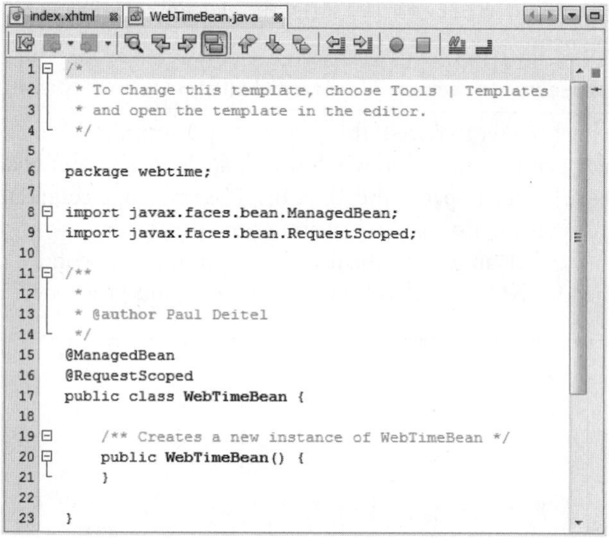

Fig. 26.10 | Default source code for the WebTimeBean class.

*Adding the EL Expression to the **index.xhtml** Page*

Now that you've created the WebTimeBean, let's go back to the index.xhtml file and add the EL expression that will obtain the time. In the index.xhtml file, modify the line

```
<h1>Current time on the web server: </h1>
```

by inserting the expression #{webTimeBean.time} before the h1 element's closing tag. After you type the characters # and {, the IDE automatically inserts the closing }, inserts the cursor between the braces and displays the code-completion window. This shows various items that could be placed in the braces of the EL expression, including the webTimeBean object (of type WebTimeBean). To insert webTimeBean in the code, you can type the object's name or double click it in the code-completion window. As you type, the list of items in the code-completion window is filtered by what you've typed so far.

When you type the dot (.) after webTimeBean, the code-completion window reappears, showing you the WebTimeBean methods and properties that can be used in this context (Fig. 26.11). In this list, you can double click the time property, or you can simply type its name.

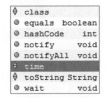

Fig. 26.11 | NetBeans code-completion window for the webTimeBean object.

Running the Application
You've now completed the WebTime app. To test it, right click the project's name in the **Projects** tab and select **Run** from the pop-up menu. The IDE will compile the code and deploy (that is, install) the WebTime app on the GlassFish application server running on your local machine. Then, the IDE will launch your default web browser and request the WebTime app's default web page (index.xhtml). Because GlassFish is installed on your local computer, the URL displayed in the browser's address bar will be

```
http://localhost:8080/WebTime/
```

where 8080 is the port number on which the GlassFish server runs by default. Depending on your web browser, the http:// may not be displayed (Fig. 26.5).

Debugging the Application
If there's a problem with your web app's logic, you can press <*Ctrl*> *F5* to build the application and run it in debug mode—the NetBeans built-in debugger can help you troubleshoot applications. If you press *F6*, the program executes without debugging enabled.

Testing the Application from Other Web Browsers
After deploying your project, you can test it from another web browser on your computer by entering the app's URL into the other browser's address field. Since your application resides on the local file system, GlassFish must be running. If you've already executed the application using one of the techniques above and have not closed NetBeans, GlassFish will still be running. Otherwise, you can start the server from the IDE by opening the **Services** tab (located in the same panel as the **Projects**), expanding the **Servers** node, right clicking **GlassFish Server 3** and selecting **Start**. Then you can type the URL in the browser to execute the application.

26.5 Model-View-Controller Architecture of JSF Apps

JSF applications adhere to the **Model-View-Controller** (**MVC**) **architecture**, which separates an application's data (contained in the **model**) from the graphical presentation (the **view**) and the processing logic (the **controller**). Figure 26.12 shows the relationships between components in MVC.

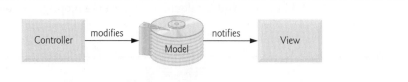

Fig. 26.12 | Model-View-Controller architecture.

In JSF, the controller is the JSF framework and is responsible for coordinating interactions between the view and the model. The model contains the application's data (typically in a database), and the view presents the data stored in the model (typically as web pages). When a user interacts with a JSF web app's view, the framework interacts with the model to store and/or retrieve data. When the model changes, the view is updated with the changed data.

26.6 Common JSF Components

As mentioned in Section 26.4, JSF supports several tag libraries. In this section, we introduce several of the JSF HTML Tag Library's elements and one element from the **JSF Core Tag Library**. Figure 26.13 summarizes elements discussed in this section.

JSF component	Description
h:form	Inserts an XHTML form element into a page.
h:commandButton	Displays a button that triggers an event when clicked. Typically, such a button is used to submit a form's user input to the server for processing.
h:graphicImage	Displays an image (e.g., GIF and JPG).
h:inputText	Displays a text box in which the user can enter input.
h:outputLink	Displays a hyperlink.
h:panelGrid	Displays an XHTML table element.
h:selectOneMenu	Displays a drop-down list of choices from which the user can make a selection.
h:selectOneRadio	Displays a set of radio buttons.
f:selectItem	Specifies an item in an h:selectOneMenu or h:selectOneRadio (and other similar components).

Fig. 26.13 | Commonly used JSF components.

All of these elements are mapped by JSF framework to a combination of XHTML elements and JavaScript code that enables the browser to render the page. JavaScript is a scripting language that's interpreted in all of today's popular web browsers. It can be used to perform tasks that manipulate web-page elements in a web browser and provide interactivity with the user. You can learn more about JavaScript in our JavaScript Resource Center at www.deitel.com/JavaScript/.

Figure 26.14 displays a form for gathering user input. [*Note:* To create this application from scratch, review the steps in Section 26.4.3 and name the application WebComponents.] The **h:form** element (lines 14–55) contains the components with which a user interacts to provide data, such as registration or login information, to a JSF app. This example uses the components summarized in Fig. 26.13. This example does not perform a task when the user clicks the **Register** button. Later, we demonstrate how to add functionality to many of these components.

```
1   <?xml version='1.0' encoding='UTF-8' ?>
2
3   <!-- index.xhtml -->
4   <!-- Registration form that demonstrates various JSF components -->
5   <!DOCTYPE html PUBLIC "-//W3C//DTD XHTML 1.0 Transitional//EN"
6      "http://www.w3.org/TR/xhtml1/DTD/xhtml1-transitional.dtd">
7   <html xmlns="http://www.w3.org/1999/xhtml"
8         xmlns:h="http://java.sun.com/jsf/html"
9         xmlns:f="http://java.sun.com/jsf/core">
10     <h:head>
11        <title>Sample Registration Form</title>
12     </h:head>
13     <h:body>
14        <h:form>
15           <h1>Registration Form</h1>
16           <p>Please fill in all fields and click Register</p>
17           <h:panelGrid columns="4" style="height: 96px; width:456px;">
18              <h:graphicImage name="fname.png" library="images"/>
19              <h:inputText id="firstNameInputText"/>
20              <h:graphicImage name="lname.png" library="images"/>
21              <h:inputText id="lastNameInputText"/>
22              <h:graphicImage name="email.png" library="images"/>
23              <h:inputText id="emailInputText"/>
24              <h:graphicImage name="phone.png" library="images"/>
25              <h:inputText id="phoneInputText"/>
26           </h:panelGrid>
27           <p><h:graphicImage name="publications.png" library="images"/>
28              <br/>Which book would you like information about?</p>
29           <h:selectOneMenu id="booksSelectOneMenu">
30              <f:selectItem itemValue="CHTP"
31                 itemLabel="C How to Program" />
32              <f:selectItem itemValue="CPPHTP"
33                 itemLabel="C++ How to Program" />
34              <f:selectItem itemValue="IW3HTP"
35                 itemLabel="Internet &amp; World Wide Web How to Program" />
```

Fig. 26.14 | Registration form that demonstrates various JSF components. (Part 1 of 2.)

```
36                    <f:selectItem itemValue="JHTP"
37                       itemLabel="Java How to Program" />
38                    <f:selectItem itemValue="VBHTP"
39                       itemLabel="Visual Basic How to Program" />
40                    <f:selectItem itemValue="VCSHTP"
41                       itemLabel="Visual C# How to Program" />
42                 </h:selectOneMenu>
43                 <p><h:outputLink value="http://www.deitel.com">
44                    Click here to learn more about our books
45                 </h:outputLink></p>
46                 <h:graphicImage name="os.png" library="images"/>
47                 <h:selectOneRadio id="osSelectOneRadio">
48                    <f:selectItem itemValue="WinVista" itemLabel="Windows Vista"/>
49                    <f:selectItem itemValue="Win7" itemLabel="Windows 7"/>
50                    <f:selectItem itemValue="OSX" itemLabel="Mac OS X"/>
51                    <f:selectItem itemValue="Linux" itemLabel="Linux"/>
52                    <f:selectItem itemValue="Other" itemLabel="Other"/>
53                 </h:selectOneRadio>
54                 <h:commandButton value="Register"/>
55           </h:form>
56        </h:body>
57     </html>
```

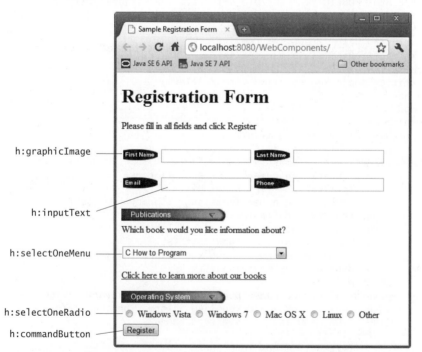

Fig. 26.14 | Registration form that demonstrates various JSF components. (Part 2 of 2.)

h:panelGrid Element

Lines 17–26 define an **h:panelGrid** element for organizing elements in the page. This element inserts an XHTML table in the page. The h: prefix indicates that panelGrid is from the JSF HTML Tag Library. The **columns attribute** specifies the number of columns in the `table`. The elements between the `h:panelGrid`'s start tag (line 17) and end tag (line 26) are automatically placed into the `table`'s columns from left to right in the order they appear in the JSF page. When the number of elements in a row exceeds the number of columns, the `h:panelGrid` creates a new row. We use the `h:panelGrid` to control the positions of the `h:graphicImage` and `h:inputText` elements in the user information section of the page. In this case, there are eight elements in the `h:panelGrid`, so the first four (lines 18–21) are placed in the table's first row and the last four are placed in the second row. The `h:panelGrid`'s **style attribute** specifies the CSS formatting for the `table`. We use the CSS attributes `width` and `height` to specify the width and height of the table in pixels (px). The `h:panelGrid` contains pairs of `h:graphicImage` and `h:inputText` elements.

h:graphicImage *Element and Resource Libraries*

Each **h:graphicImage** displays an image in the page. For example, line 18 inserts the image `fname.png`—as specified by the **name attribute**. As of JSF 2.0, you add resources that are used throughout your app—such as images, CSS files, JavaScript files—to your web apps by placing them in the app's **resources folder** within your project's **Web Pages** node. Each subfolder of `resources` represents a **resource library**. Typically, images are placed in an `images` library and CSS files in a `css` library. In line 18, we specify that the image is located in the `images` library with the **library attribute**. JSF knows that the value of this attribute represents a folder within the `resources` folder.

You can create any library you like in the `resources` folder. To create this folder:

1. Expand your app's node in the NetBeans **Projects** tab.

2. Right click the **Web Pages** node and select **New > Folder...** to display the **New Folder** dialog. [*Note:* If the **Folder...** option is not available in the popup menu, select **Other...**, then in the **Categories** pane select **Other** and in the **File Types** pane select **Folder** and click **Next >**.

3. Specify `resources` as the *Folder Name* and press *Finish*.

Next, right click the `resources` folder you just created and create an `images` subfolder. You can then drag the images from your file system onto the `images` folder to add them as resources. The images in this example are located in the `images` directory with the chapter's examples.

The `h:graphicImage` in line 18 is a so-called **empty element**—an element that does not have content between its start and end tags. In such an element, data is typically specified as attributes in the start tag, such as the `name` and `library` attributes in line 18. You can close an empty element either by placing a slash immediately preceding the start tag's right angle bracket, as shown in line 18, or by explicitly writing an end tag.

h:inputText *Element*

Line 19 defines an **h:inputText element** in which the user can enter text or the app can display text. For any element that might be accessed by other elements of the page or that might be used in server-side code, you should specify an **id attribute**. We specified these attributes in this example, even though the app does not provide any functionality. We'll use the `id` attribute starting with the next example.

h:selectOneMenu *Element*

Lines 29–42 define an **h:selectOneMenu** element, which is typically rendered in a web page as a drop-down list. When a user clicks the drop-down list, it expands and displays a list from which the user can make a selection. Each item to display appears between the start and end tags of this element as an **f:selectItem** element (lines 30–41). This element is part of the JSF Core Tag Library. The XML namespace for this tag library is specified in the html element's start tag at line 9. Each f:selectItem has itemValue and itemLabel attributes. The **itemLabel** is the string that the user will see in the browser, and the **item-Value** is the value that's returned when you programmatically retrieve the user's selection from the drop-down list (as you'll see in a later example).

h:outputLink *Element*

The **h:outputLink** element (lines 43–45) inserts a hyperlink in a web page. Its **value** attribute specifies the resource (http://www.deitel.com in this case) that's requested when a user clicks the hyperlink. By default, h:outputLink elements cause pages to open in the same browser window, but you can set the element's target attribute to change this behavior.

h:selectOneMenu *Element*

Lines 47–53 define an **h:selectOneRadio** element, which provides a series of radio buttons from which the user can select only one. Like an h:selectOneMenu, an h:selectOne-Radio displays items that are specified with f:selectItem elements.

h:commandButton *Element*

Lines 54 defines an **h:commandButton** element that triggers an action when clicked—in this example, we don't specify the action to trigger, so the default action occurs (re-requesting the same page from the server) when the user clicks this button. An h:commandButton typically maps to an XHTML input element with its type attribute set to "submit". Such elements are often used to submit a form's user input values to the server for processing.

26.7 Validation Using JSF Standard Validators

Validating input is an important step in collecting information from users. **Validation** helps prevent processing errors due to incomplete, incorrect or improperly formatted user input. For example, you may perform validation to ensure that all required fields contain data or that a zip-code field has the correct number of digits. The JSF Core Tag Library provides several standard validator components and allows you to create your own custom validators. Multiple validators can be specified for each input element. The validators are:

- **f:validateLength**—determines whether a field contains an acceptable number of characters.

- **f:validateDoubleRange** and **f:validateLongRange**—determine whether numeric input falls within acceptable ranges of double or long values, respectively.

- **f:validateRequired**—determines whether a field contains a value.

- **f:validateRegex**—determines whether a field contains a string that matches a specified regular expression pattern.

- **f:validateBean**—allows you to invoke a bean method that performs custom validation.

Validating Form Data in a Web Application

[*Note:* To create this application from scratch, review the steps in Section 26.4.3 and name the application Validation.] The example in this section prompts the user to enter a name, e-mail address and phone number in a form. When the user enters any data and presses the **Submit** button to submit the form's contents to the web server, validation ensures that the user entered a value in each field, that the entered name does not exceed 30 characters, and that the e-mail address and phone-number values are in an acceptable format. In this example, (555) 123-4567, 555-123-4567 and 123-4567 are all considered valid phone numbers. Once valid data is submitted, the JSF framework stores the submitted values in a bean object of class ValidationBean (Fig. 26.15), then sends a response back to the web browser. We simply display the validated data in the page to demonstrate that the server received the data. A real business application would typically store the submitted data in a database or in a file on the server.

Class ValidationBean

Class ValidationBean (Fig. 26.15) provides the read/write properties name, email and phone, and the read-only property result. Each read/write property has an instance variable (lines 11–13) and corresponding *set/get* methods (lines 16–25, 28–37 and 40–49) for manipulating the instance variables. The read-only property response has only a get-Result method (lines 52–60), which returns a paragraph (p) element containing the validated data. (You can create the ValidationBean managed bean class by using the steps presented in Fig. 26.4.3.)

```
1   // ValidationBean.java
2   // Validating user input.
3   package validation;
4
5   import java.io.Serializable;
6   import javax.faces.bean.ManagedBean;
7
8   @ManagedBean( name="validationBean" )
9   public class ValidationBean implements Serializable
10  {
11     private String name;
12     private String email;
13     private String phone;
14
15     // return the name String
16     public String getName()
17     {
18        return name;
19     } // end method getName
20
21     // set the name String
22     public void setName( String name )
23     {
24        this.name = name;
25     } // end method setName
```

Fig. 26.15 | ValidationBean stores the validated data, which is then used as part of the response to the client. (Part 1 of 2.)

```
26
27      // return the email String
28      public String getEmail()
29      {
30         return email;
31      } // end method getEmail
32
33      // set the email String
34      public void setEmail( String email )
35      {
36         this.email = email;
37      } // end method setEmail
38
39      // return the phone String
40      public String getPhone()
41      {
42         return phone;
43      } // end method getPhone
44
45      // set the phone String
46      public void setPhone( String phone )
47      {
48         this.phone = phone;
49      } // end method setPhone
50
51      // returns result for rendering on the client
52      public String getResult()
53      {
54         if ( name != null && email != null && phone != null )
55            return "<p style=\"background-color:yellow;width:200px;" +
56               "padding:5px\">Name: " + getName() + "<br/>E-Mail: " +
57               getEmail() + "<br/>Phone: " + getPhone() + "</p>";
58         else
59            return ""; // request has not yet been made
60      } // end method getResult
61   } // end class ValidationBean
```

Fig. 26.15 | ValidationBean stores the validated data, which is then used as part of the response to the client. (Part 2 of 2.)

index.xhtml

Figure 26.16 shows this app's index.xhtml file. The initial request to this web app displays the page shown in Fig. 26.16(a). When this app is initially requested, the beginning of the **JSF application lifecycle** uses this index.xhtml document to build the app's facelets view and sends it as the response to the client browser, which displays the form for user input. During this initial request, the EL expressions (lines 22, 30, 39 and 49) are evaluated to obtain the values that should be displayed in various parts of the page. Nothing is displayed initially as a result of these four EL expressions being evaluated, because no default values are specified for the bean's properties. The page's h:form element contains an h:panelGrid (lines 18–45) with three columns and an h:commandButton (line 46), which by default submits the contents of the form's fields to the server.

```
 1    <?xml version='1.0' encoding='UTF-8' ?>
 2
 3    <!-- index.xhtml -->
 4    <!-- Validating user input -->
 5    <!DOCTYPE html PUBLIC "-//W3C//DTD XHTML 1.0 Transitional//EN"
 6       "http://www.w3.org/TR/xhtml1/DTD/xhtml1-transitional.dtd">
 7    <html xmlns="http://www.w3.org/1999/xhtml"
 8       xmlns:h="http://java.sun.com/jsf/html"
 9       xmlns:f="http://java.sun.com/jsf/core">
10       <h:head>
11          <title>Validating Form Data</title>
12          <h:outputStylesheet name="style.css" library="css"/>
13       </h:head>
14       <h:body>
15          <h:form>
16             <h1>Please fill out the following form:</h1>
17             <p>All fields are required and must contain valid information</p>
18             <h:panelGrid columns="3">
19                <h:outputText value="Name:"/>
20                <h:inputText id="nameInputText" required="true"
21                   requiredMessage="Please enter your name"
22                   value="#{validationBean.name}"
23                   validatorMessage="Name must be fewer than 30 characters">
24                   <f:validateLength maximum="30" />
25                </h:inputText>
26                <h:message for="nameInputText" styleClass="error"/>
27                <h:outputText value="E-mail:"/>
28                <h:inputText id="emailInputText" required="true"
29                   requiredMessage="Please enter a valid e-mail address"
30                   value="#{validationBean.email}"
31                   validatorMessage="Invalid e-mail address format">
32                   <f:validateRegex pattern=
33                      "\w+([-+.']\w+)*@\w+([-.]\w+)*\.\w+([-.]\w+)*" />
34                </h:inputText>
35                <h:message for="emailInputText" styleClass="error"/>
36                <h:outputText value="Phone:"/>
37                <h:inputText id="phoneInputText" required="true"
38                   requiredMessage="Please enter a valid phone number"
39                   value="#{validationBean.phone}"
40                   validatorMessage="Invalid phone number format">
41                   <f:validateRegex pattern=
42                      "((\(\d{3}\) ?)|(\d{3}-))?\d{3}-\d{4}" />
43                </h:inputText>
44                <h:message for="phoneInputText" styleClass="error"/>
45             </h:panelGrid>
46             <h:commandButton value="Submit"/>
47             <h:outputText escape="false" value="#{validationBean.response}"/>
48          </h:form>
49       </h:body>
50    </html>
```

Fig. 26.16 | Form to demonstrate validating user input. (Part 1 of 3.)

a) Submitting the form before entering any information

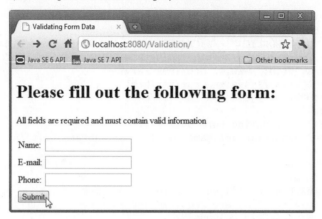

b) Error messages displayed after submitting the empty form

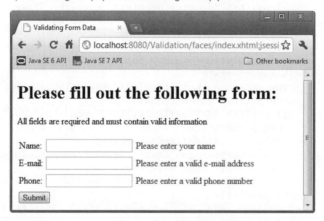

c) Error messages displayed after submitting invalid information

Fig. 26.16 | Form to demonstrate validating user input. (Part 2 of 3.)

d) Successfully submitted form

Fig. 26.16 | Form to demonstrate validating user input. (Part 3 of 3.)

First Row of the h:panelGrid

In this application, we demonstrate several new elements and attributes. The first new element is the **h:outputText** element (line 19; from the JSF HTML Tag Library), which inserts text in the page. In this case, we insert a literal string ("Name:") that is specified with the element's value attribute.

The h:inputText element (lines 20–25) displays a text box in which the user can enter a name. We've specified several attributes for this element:

- id—This enables other elements or server-side code to reference this element.

- **required**—Ensuring that the user has made a selection or entered some text in a required input element is a basic type of validation. When set to "true", this attribute specifies that the element *must* contain a value.

- **requiredMessage**—This specifies the message that should be displayed if the user submits the form without first providing a value for this required element.

- value—This specifies the value to display in the field or to be saved into a bean on the server. In this case, the EL expression indicates the bean property that's associated with this field.

- **validatorMessage**—This specifies the message to display if a validator is associated with this h:inputText and the data the user enters is invalid.

The messages specified by the requiredMessage and validatorMessage attributes are displayed in an associated **h:message** element (line 26) when validation fails. The element's **for attribute** specifies the id of the specific element for which messages will be displayed (nameInputText), and the **styleClass attribute** specifies the name of a CSS style class that will format the message. For this example, we defined a CSS style sheet, which was inserted into the document's head element at line 12 using the **h:outputStylesheet**

element. We placed the style sheet in the css library within the resources folder. The style sheet contains the following CSS rule:

```
.error
{
    color:red;
}
```

which creates a style class named error (the dot indicates that it's a style class) and specifies that any text to which this is applied, such as the error messages, should be red. We use this CSS style for all the h:message elements in this example.

Validating the *nameInputText* Element's Contents

If the user submits the form without a value in the nameInputText, the requiredMessage "Please enter your name" is displayed in the corresponding h:message element. If the user specifies a value for the nameInputText, the JSF framework executes the f:validate-Length validator that's nested in the h:inputText element. Here, we check that the name contains no more than 30 characters—as specified by the validator's **maximum attribute**. This might be useful to ensure that a value will fit within a particular database field.

Users can type as much text in the nameInputText as they wish. If the name is too long, the validatorMessage is displayed in the h:message element after the user submits the form. It's also possible to limit the length of user input in an h:inputText without using validation by setting its **maxlength attribute**, in which case the element's cursor will not advance beyond the maximum allowable number of characters. This would prevent the user from submitting data that exceeds the length limit.

Second and Third Rows of the *h:panelGrid*

The next two rows of the h:panelGrid have elements similar to those in the first row. In addition to being required elements, the h:inputText elements at lines 28–34 and 37–43 are each validated by h:validateRegex validators as described next.

Validating the e-Mail Address

The h:validateRegex element at lines 32–33 uses the regular expression

```
\w+([-+.']\w+)*@\w+([-.]\w+)*\.\w+([-.]\w+)*
```

which indicates that an e-mail address is valid if the part before the @ symbol contains one or more word characters (that is, alphanumeric characters or underscores), followed by zero or more strings comprised of a hyphen, plus sign, period or apostrophe and additional word characters. After the @ symbol, a valid e-mail address must contain one or more groups of word characters potentially separated by hyphens or periods, followed by a required period and another group of one or more word characters potentially separated by hyphens or periods. For example, bob's-personal.email@white.email.com, bob-white@my-email.com and bob.white@email.com are all valid e-mail addresses. If the address the user enters has an invalid format, the validatorMessage (line 31) will be displayed in the corresponding h:message element (line 35).

Validating the Phone Number

The h:validateRegex element at lines 41–42 uses the regular expression

```
((\(\d{3}\) ?)|(\d{3}-))?\d{3}-\d{4}
```

which indicates that a phone number can contain a three-digit area code either in parentheses and followed by an optional space or without parentheses and followed by a required hyphen. After an optional area code, a phone number must contain three digits, a hyphen and another four digits. For example, (555) 123-4567, 555-123-4567 and 123-4567 are all valid phone numbers. If the phone number the user enters has an invalid format, the validatorMessage (line 40) will be displayed in the corresponding h:message element (line 44).

Submitting the Form—More Details of the JSF Lifecycle
As we mentioned earlier in this section, when the app receives the initial request, it returns the page shown in Fig. 26.16(a). When a request does not contain any request values, such as those the user enters in a form, the JSF framework simply creates the view and returns it as the response.

The user submits the form to the server by pressing the **Submit** h:commandButton (defined at line 46). Since we did not specify an action attribute for this h:command-Button, the action is configured by default to perform a **postback**—the browser re-requests the page index.xhtml and sends the values of the form's fields to the server for processing. Next, the JSF framework performs the validations of all the form elements. If any of the elements is invalid, the framework renders the appropriate error message as part of the response.

If the values of all the elements are valid, the framework uses the values of the elements to set the properties of the validateBean—as specified in the EL expressions in lines 22, 30 and 39. Each property's *set* method is invoked, passing the value of the corresponding element as an argument. The framework then formulates the response to the client. In the response, the form elements are populated with the values of the validateBean's properties (by calling their *get* methods), and the h:outputText element at line 47 is populated with the value of the read-only result property. The value of this property is determined by the getResult method (lines 52–60 of Fig. 26.15), which uses the submitted form data in the string that it returns.

When you execute this app, try submitting the form with no data (Fig. 26.16(b)), with invalid data (Fig. 26.16(c)) and with valid data (Fig. 26.16(d)).

26.8 Session Tracking

Originally, critics accused the Internet and e-business of failing to provide the customized service typically experienced in "brick-and-mortar" stores. To address this problem, businesses established mechanisms by which they could *personalize* users' browsing experiences, tailoring content to individual users. They tracked each customer's movement through the Internet and combined the collected data with information the consumer provided, including billing information, personal preferences, interests and hobbies.

Personalization
Personalization enables businesses to communicate effectively with their customers and also helps users locate desired products and services. Companies that provide content of particular interest to users can establish relationships with customers and build on those relationships over time. Furthermore, by targeting consumers with personal offers, recommendations, advertisements, promotions and services, businesses create customer loyalty.

Websites can use sophisticated technology to allow visitors to customize home pages to suit their individual needs and preferences. Similarly, online shopping sites often store personal information for customers, tailoring notifications and special offers to their interests. Such services encourage customers to visit sites more frequently and make purchases more regularly.

Privacy

A trade-off exists between personalized business service and protection of privacy. Some consumers embrace tailored content, but others fear the possible adverse consequences if the info they provide to businesses is released or collected by tracking technologies. Consumers and privacy advocates ask: What if the business to which we give personal data sells or gives that information to another organization without our knowledge? What if we do not want our actions on the Internet—a supposedly anonymous medium—to be tracked and recorded by unknown parties? What if unauthorized parties gain access to sensitive private data, such as credit-card numbers or medical history? These are questions that must be addressed by programmers, consumers, businesses and lawmakers alike.

Recognizing Clients

To provide personalized services, businesses must be able to recognize clients when they request information from a site. As we have discussed, the request/response system on which the web operates is facilitated by HTTP. Unfortunately, HTTP is a *stateless protocol*—it *does not* provide information that would enable web servers to maintain state information regarding particular clients. This means that web servers cannot determine whether a request comes from a particular client or whether the same or different clients generate a series of requests.

To circumvent this problem, sites can provide mechanisms by which they identify individual clients. A session represents a unique client on a website. If the client leaves a site and then returns later, the client will still be recognized as the same user. When the user closes the browser, the session typically ends. To help the server distinguish among clients, each client must identify itself to the server. Tracking individual clients is known as **session tracking**. One popular session-tracking technique uses cookies (discussed in Section 26.8.1); another uses beans that are marked with the `@SessionScoped` **annotation** (used in Section 26.8.2). Additional session-tracking techniques are beyond this book's scope.

26.8.1 Cookies

Cookies provide you with a tool for personalizing web pages. A cookie is a piece of data stored by web browsers in a small text file on the user's computer. A cookie maintains information about the client during and between browser sessions. The first time a user visits the website, the user's computer might receive a cookie from the server; this cookie is then reactivated each time the user revisits that site. The collected information is intended to be an anonymous record containing data that is used to personalize the user's future visits to the site. For example, cookies in a shopping application might store unique identifiers for users. When a user adds items to an online shopping cart or performs another task resulting in a request to the web server, the server receives a cookie containing the user's unique identifier. The server then uses the unique identifier to locate the shopping cart and perform any necessary processing.

In addition to identifying users, cookies also can indicate users' shopping preferences. When a Web Form receives a request from a client, the Web Form can examine the cookie(s) it sent to the client during previous communications, identify the user's preferences and immediately display products of interest to the client.

Every HTTP-based interaction between a client and a server includes a header containing information either about the request (when the communication is from the client to the server) or about the response (when the communication is from the server to the client). When a Web Form receives a request, the header includes information such as the request type and any cookies that have been sent previously from the server to be stored on the client machine. When the server formulates its response, the header information contains any cookies the server wants to store on the client computer and other information, such as the MIME type of the response.

The **expiration date** of a cookie determines how long the cookie remains on the client's computer. If you do not set an expiration date for a cookie, the web browser maintains the cookie for the duration of the browsing session. Otherwise, the web browser maintains the cookie until the expiration date occurs. Cookies are deleted by the web browser when they **expire**.

Portability Tip 26.1
Users may disable cookies in their web browsers to help ensure their privacy. Such users will experience difficulty using web applications that depend on cookies to maintain state information.

26.8.2 Session Tracking with @SessionScoped Beans

The previous web applications used @RequestScoped beans by default—the beans existed only for the duration of each request. In the next application, we use a **@SessionScoped** bean to maintain selections throughout the user's session. Such a bean is created when a session begins and exists throughout the entire session. A @SessionScoped bean can be accessed by all of the app's pages during the session, and the app server maintains a separate @SessionScoped bean for each user. By default a session expires after 30 minutes of inactivity or when the user closes the browser that was used to begin the session. When the session expires, the server discards the bean associated with that session.

Software Engineering Observation 26.2
@SessionScoped beans should implement the Serializable interface. Websites with heavy traffic often use groups of servers (sometimes hundreds or thousands of them) to respond to requests. Such groups are known as server farms. Server farms often balance the number of requests being handled on each server by moving some sessions to other servers. Making a bean Serializable enables the session to be moved properly among servers.

Test-Driving the App
This example consists of a SelectionsBean class that is @SessionScoped and two pages (index.xhtml and recommendations.xhtml) that store data in and retrieve data from a SelectionsBean object. To understand how these pieces fit together, let's walk through a sample execution of the app. When you first execute the app, the index.xhtml page is displayed. The user selects a topic from a group of radio buttons and submits the form (Fig. 26.17).

Fig. 26.17 | `index.xhtml` after the user has made a selection and is about to submit the form for the first time.

When the form is submitted, the JSF framework creates a `SelectionsBean` object that is specific to this user, stores the selected topic in the bean and returns the `index.xhtml` page. The page now shows how many selections have been made (1) and allows the user to make another selection (Fig. 26.18).

Fig. 26.18 | `index.xhtml` after the user has submitted the form the first time, made another selection and is about to submit the form again.

The user makes a second topic selection and submits the form again. The app stores the selection in this user's existing `SelectionsBean` object and returns the `index.xhtml` page (Fig. 26.19), which shows how many selections have been made so far (2).

At any time, the user can click the link at the bottom of the `index.xhtml` page to open `recommendations.xhtml`, which obtains the information from this user's `SelectionsBean` object and creates a recommended books list (Fig. 26.20) for the user's selected topics.

Fig. 26.19 | `index.xhtml` after the user has submitted the form the second time and is about to click the link to the `recommendations.xhtml` page.

Fig. 26.20 | `recommendations.hxtml` showing book recommendations for the topic selections made by the user in Figs. 26.18 and 26.19.

@SessionScoped Class SelectionsBean

Class SelectionsBean (Fig. 26.21) uses the @SessionScoped annotation (line 13) to indicate that the server should maintain separate instances of this class for each user session. The class maintains a static HashMap (created at lines 17–18) of topics and their corresponding book titles. We made this object static, because its values can be shared among all SelectionsBean objects. The static initializer block (lines 23–28) specifies the Hash-Map's key/value pairs. Class SelectionsBean maintains each user's selections in a Set<String> (line 32), which allows only unique keys, so selecting the same topic multiple times does not increase the number of selections.

```
1   // SelectionsBean.java
2   // Manages a user's topic selections
3   package sessiontracking;
```

Fig. 26.21 | @SessionScoped SelectionsBean class. (Part I of 3.)

```
 4
 5    import java.io.Serializable;
 6    import java.util.HashMap;
 7    import java.util.Set;
 8    import java.util.TreeSet;
 9    import javax.faces.bean.ManagedBean;
10    import javax.faces.bean.SessionScoped;
11
12    @ManagedBean( name="selectionsBean" )
13    @SessionScoped
14    public class SelectionsBean implements Serializable
15    {
16       // map of topics to book titles
17       private static final HashMap< String, String > booksMap =
18          new HashMap< String, String >();
19
20       // initialize booksMap
21       static
22       {
23          booksMap.put( "java", "Java How to Program" );
24          booksMap.put( "cpp", "C++ How to Program" );
25          booksMap.put( "iphone",
26             "iPhone for Programmers: An App-Driven Approach" );
27          booksMap.put( "android",
28             "Android for Programmers: An App-Driven Approach" );
29       } // end static initializer block
30
31       // stores individual user's selections
32       private Set< String > selections = new TreeSet< String >();
33       private String selection; // stores the current selection
34
35       // return number of selections
36       public int getNumberOfSelections()
37       {
38          return selections.size();
39       } // end method getNumberOfSelections
40
41       // returns the current selection
42       public String getSelection()
43       {
44          return selection;
45       } // end method getSelection
46
47       // store user's selection
48       public void setSelection( String topic )
49       {
50          selection = booksMap.get( topic );
51          selections.add( selection );
52       } // end method setSelection
53
54       // return the Set of selections
55       public String[] getSelections()
56       {
```

Fig. 26.21 | @SessionScoped SelectionsBean class. (Part 2 of 3.)

```
57          return selections.toArray( new String[ selections.size() ] );
58      } // end method getSelections
59  } // end class SelectionsBean
```

Fig. 26.21 | @SessionScoped SelectionsBean class. (Part 3 of 3.)

Methods of Class *SelectionsBean*

Method getNumberOfSelections (lines 36–39) returns the number of topics the user has selected and represents the read-only property numberOfSelections. We use this property in the index.xhtml document to display the number of selections the user has made so far.

Methods getSelection (lines 42–45) and setSelection (lines 48–52) represent the read/write selection property. When a user makes a selection in index.xhtml and submits the form, method setSelection looks up the corresponding book title in the booksMap (line 50), then stores that title in selections (line 51).

Method getSelections (lines 55–58) represents the read-only property selections, which returns an array of Strings containing the book titles for the topics selected by the user so far. When the recommendations.xhtml page is requested, it uses the selections property to get the list of book titles and display them in the page.

index.xhtml

The index.xhtml document (Fig. 26.22) contains an h:selectOneRadio element (lines 19–26) with the options **Java**, **C++**, **iPhone** and **Android**. The user selects a topic by clicking a radio button, then pressing **Submit** to send the selection. As the user makes each selection and submits the form, the selectionsBean object's selection property is updated and this document is returned. The EL expression at line 15 inserts the number of selections that have been made so far into the page. When the user clicks the h:outputLink (lines 29–31) the recommendations.xhtml page is requested. The value attribute specifies only recommendations.xhtml, so the browser assumes that this page is on the same server and at the same location as index.xhtml.

```
1   <?xml version='1.0' encoding='UTF-8' ?>
2
3   <!-- index.xhtml -->
4   <!-- Allow the user to select a topic -->
5   <!DOCTYPE html PUBLIC "-//W3C//DTD XHTML 1.0 Transitional//EN"
6       "http://www.w3.org/TR/xhtml1/DTD/xhtml1-transitional.dtd">
7   <html xmlns="http://www.w3.org/1999/xhtml"
8       xmlns:h="http://java.sun.com/jsf/html"
9       xmlns:f="http://java.sun.com/jsf/core">
10      <h:head>
11          <title>Topic Selection Page</title>
12      </h:head>
13      <h:body>
14          <h1>Welcome to Sessions!</h1>
15          <p>You have made #{selectionsBean.numberOfSelections} selection(s)
16          </p>
17          <h3>Make a Selection and Press Submit</h3>
```

Fig. 26.22 | index.xhtml allows the user to select a topic. (Part 1 of 2.)

```
18        <h:form>
19           <h:selectOneRadio id="topicSelectOneRadio" required="true"
20              requiredMessage="Please choose a topic, then press Submit"
21              value="#{selectionsBean.selection}">
22              <f:selectItem itemValue="java" itemLabel="Java"/>
23              <f:selectItem itemValue="cpp" itemLabel="C++"/>
24              <f:selectItem itemValue="iphone" itemLabel="iPhone"/>
25              <f:selectItem itemValue="android" itemLabel="Android"/>
26           </h:selectOneRadio>
27           <p><h:commandButton value="Submit"/></p>
28        </h:form>
29        <p><h:outputLink value="recommendations.xhtml">
30           Click here for book recommendations
31        </h:outputLink></p>
32     </h:body>
33  </html>
```

Fig. 26.22 | `index.xhtml` allows the user to select a topic. (Part 2 of 2.)

recommendations.xhtml

When the user clicks the `h:outputLink` in the `index.xhtml` page, the browser requests the `recommendations.xhtml` (Fig. 26.23), which displays book recommendations in an XHTML unordered (bulleted) list (lines 15–19). The `h:outputLink` (lines 20–22) allows the user to return to `index.xhtml` to select additional topics.

```
1   <?xml version='1.0' encoding='UTF-8' ?>
2
3   <!-- recommendations.xhtml -->
4   <!-- Display recommended books based on the user's selected topics -->
5   <!DOCTYPE html PUBLIC "-//W3C//DTD XHTML 1.0 Transitional//EN"
6      "http://www.w3.org/TR/xhtml1/DTD/xhtml1-transitional.dtd">
7   <html xmlns="http://www.w3.org/1999/xhtml"
8      xmlns:h="http://java.sun.com/jsf/html"
9      xmlns:ui="http://java.sun.com/jsf/facelets">
10     <h:head>
11        <title>Recommended Books</title>
12     </h:head>
13     <h:body>
14        <h1>Book Recommendations</h1>
15        <ul>
16           <ui:repeat value="#{selectionsBean.selections}" var="book">
17              <li>#{book}</li>
18           </ui:repeat>
19        </ul>
20        <p><h:outputLink value="index.xhtml">
21              Click here to choose another topic
22        </h:outputLink></p>
23     </h:body>
24  </html>
```

Fig. 26.23 | `recommendations.xhtml` displays book recommendations based on the user's selections.

Iterating Through the List of Books

Line 9 enables us to use elements from the **JSF Facelets Tag Library**. This library includes the **ui:repeat element** (lines 16–18), which can be thought of as an enhanced for loop that iterates through collections JSF Expression Language. The element inserts its nested element(s) once for each element in a collection. The collection is specified by the **value attribute**'s EL expression, which *must* return an array, a List, a java.sql.ResultSet or an Object. If the EL expression does not return an array, a List or a ResultSet, the ui:repeat element inserts its nested element(s) only once for the returned Object. In this example, the ui:repeat element renders the items returned by the selectionsBean's selections property.

The ui:repeat element's **var attribute** creates a variable named book to which each item in the collection is assigned in sequence. You can use this variable in EL expressions in the nested elements. For example, the expression #{book} in line 17 inserts between the <li> and </li> tags the String representation of one item in the collection. You can also use the variable to invoke methods on, or access properties of, the referenced object.

26.9 Wrap-Up

In this chapter, we introduced web application development using JavaServer Faces in NetBeans. We began by discussing the simple HTTP transactions that take place when you request and receive a web page through a web browser. We then discussed the three tiers (i.e., the client or top tier, the business logic or middle tier and the information or bottom tier) that comprise most web applications.

You learned how to use NetBeans and the GlassFish Application Server to create, compile and execute web applications. We demonstrated several common JSF components. We also showed how to use validators to ensure that user input satisfies the requirements of an application.

We discussed the benefits of maintaining user information across multiple pages of a website. We then demonstrated how you can include such functionality in a web application using @SessionScoped beans.

In Chapter 27, we continue our discussion of Java web application development with more advanced concepts. You'll learn how to access a database from a JSF web application and how to use AJAX to help web-based applications provide the interactivity and responsiveness that users typically expect of *desktop* applications.

27

JavaServer™ Faces Web Apps: Part 2

Objectives

In this chapter you'll learn:

- To access databases from JSF applications.
- The basic principles and advantages of Ajax technology.
- To use Ajax in a JSF web app.

Whatever is in any way
beautiful hath its source of
beauty in itself, and is
complete in itself; praise
forms no part of it.
—Marcus Aurelius Antoninus

There is something in a
face, An air, and a peculiar
grace, Which boldest
painters cannot trace.
—William Somerville

Cato said the best way to
keep good acts in memory
was to refresh them with
new.
—Francis Bacon

I never forget a face, but in
your case I'll make an
exception.
—Groucho Marx

27.1 Introduction

This chapter continues our discussion of JSF web application development with two additional examples. In the first, we present a simple address book app that retrieves data from and inserts data into a Java DB database. The app allows users to view the existing contacts in the address book and to add new contacts. In the second example, we add socalled *Ajax* capabilities to the Validation example from Section 26.7. As you'll learn, Ajax improves application performance and responsiveness. This chapter's examples, like those in Chapter 26, were developed in NetBeans.

27.2 Accessing Databases in Web Apps

Many web apps access databases to store and retrieve persistent data. In this section, we build an address book web app that uses a Java DB database display contacts from the address book on a web page and to store contacts in the address book. Figure 27.1 shows sample interactions with the AddressBook app.

a) Table of addresses displayed when the AddressBook app is first requested

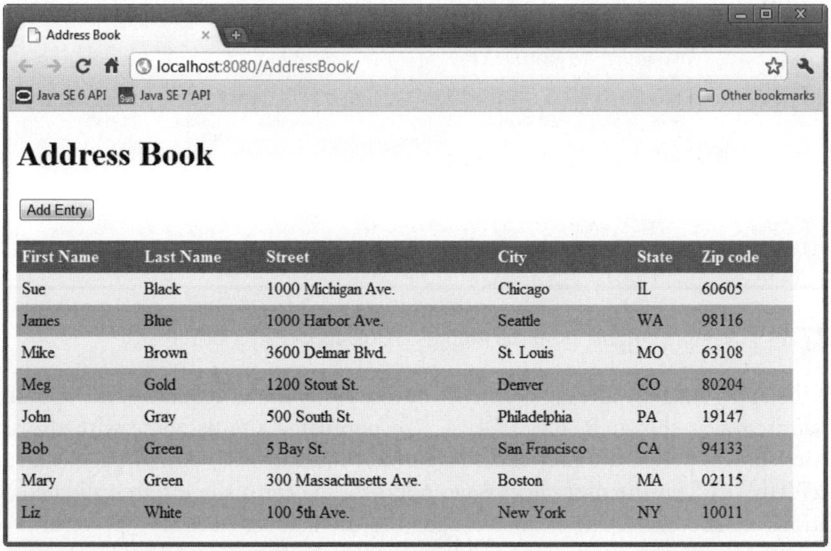

Fig. 27.1 | Sample outputs from the AddressBook app. (Part 1 of 2.)

b) Form for adding an entry

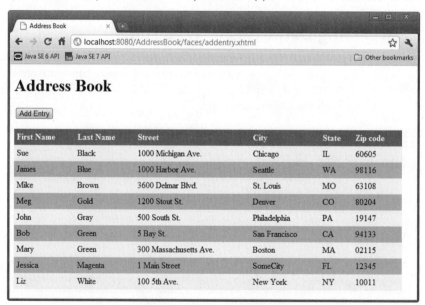

c) Table of addresses updated with the new entry added in Part (b)

Fig. 27.1 | Sample outputs from the AddressBook app. (Part 2 of 2.)

If the app's database already contains addresses, the initial request to the app displays those addresses as shown in Fig. 27.1(a). We populated the database with the sample addresses shown. When the user clicks **Add Entry**, the addentry.xhtml page is displayed (Fig. 27.1(b)). When the user clicks **Save Address**, the form's fields are validated. If the validations are successful, the address is added to the database and the app returns to the index.xhtml page to show the updated list of addresses (Fig. 27.1(c)). This example also introduces the h:dataTable element for displaying data in tabular format.

The next several sections explain how to build the AddressBook application. First, we set up the database (Section 27.2.1). Next, we present class AddressBean (Section 27.2.2), which enables the app's Facelets pages to interact with the database. Finally, we present the index.xthml (Section 27.2.3) and addentry.xhtml (Section 27.2.4) Facelets pages.

27.2.1 Setting Up the Database

You'll now create a *data source* that enables the app to interact with the database. As part of this process, you'll create the addressbook database and populate it with sample data.

Open NetBeans and Ensure that Java DB and GlassFish Are Running
Before you can create the data source in NetBeans, the IDE must be open and the Java DB and GlassFish servers must be running. Perform the following steps:

1. Open the NetBeans IDE.

2. On the **Services** tab, expand the **Databases** node then right click **Java DB**. If **Java DB** is not already running the **Start Server** option will be enabled. In this case, **Select Start** server to launch the Java DB server.

3. On the **Services** tab, expand the **Servers** node then right click **GlassFish Server 3**. If **GlassFish Server 3** is not already running the **Start** option will be enabled. In this case, **Start** server to launch GlassFish.

You may need to wait a few moments for the servers to begin executing.

Creating a Connection Pool
In web apps that receive many requests, it's inefficient to create separate database connections for each request. Instead, you should set up a **connection pool** to allow the server to manage a limited number of database connections and share them among requests. To create a connection pool for this app, perform the following steps:

1. On the **Services** tab, expand the **Servers** node, right click **GlassFish Server 3** and select **View Admin Console**. This opens your default web browser and displays a web page for configuring the GlassFish server.

2. In the left column of the page under **Common Tasks**, expand the **Resources** node, then expand its **JDBC** node to show the **JDBC Resources** and **Connection Pools** nodes (Fig. 27.2).

Fig. 27.2 | **Common Tasks** window in the GlassFish server configuration web page.

3. Click the **Connection Pools** node to display the list of existing connection pools, then click the **New...** button above the list to create a new connection pool.

4. In the **New JDBC Connection Pool (Step 1 of 2)** page (Fig. 27.3), specify Address-BookPool for the **Name**, select javax.sql.DataSource for the **Resource Type** and select **JavaDB** for the **Database Vendor**, then click **Next**.

5. In the **New JDBC Connection Pool (Step 2 of 2)** page (Fig. 27.4), scroll to the **Additional Properties** table and specify the following values (leave the other entries in the table unchanged):

- **ConnectionAttributes:** ;create=true (specifies that the database should be created when the connection pool is created)

- **DatabaseName:** addressbook (specifies the name of the database to create)

- **Password:** APP (specifies the password for the database—the **User** name is already specified as APP in the **Additional Properties** table; you can specify any **User** name and **Password** you like)

Fig. 27.3 | New JDBC Connection Pool (Step 1 of 2) page.

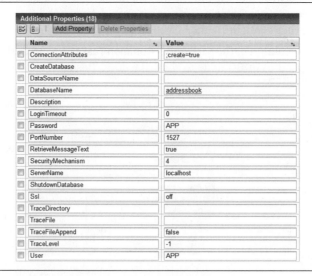

Fig. 27.4 | New JDBC Connection Pool (Step 2 of 2) page.

6. Click **Finish** to create the connection pool and return to the connection pools list.

7. Click `AddressBookPool` in the connection pools list to display the **Edit JDBC Connection Pool** page, then click **Ping** in that page to test the database connection and ensure that you set it up correctly.

Creating a Data Source Name

To connect to the database from the web app, you must configure a **data source name** that will be used to locate the database. The data source name must be associated with the connection pool that manages the connections to the database. Perform the following steps:

1. In the left column of the GlassFish configuration web page, click the **JDBC Resources** node to display the list of data source names, then click the **New...** button to display the **New JDBC Resource** page (Fig. 27.5).

2. Specify `jdbc/addressbook` as the **JNDI Name** and select `AddressBookPool` as the **Pool Name**. Then click **OK**. JNDI (Java Naming and Directory Interface) is a technology for locating application components (such as databases) in a distributed application (such as a multitier web application). You can now close the GlassFish configuration web page.

New JDBC Resource   OK   Cancel

Specify a unique JNDI name that identifies the JDBC resource you want to create. The name must contain only alphanumeric, underscore, dash, or dot characters.

JNDI Name: * `jdbc/addressbook`

Pool Name: `AddressBookPool`

Use the JDBC Connection Pools page to create new pools

Description:

Status: ☑ Enabled

Additional Properties (0)

Add Property Delete Properties

Name	Value	Description
No items found.		

Fig. 27.5 | New JDBC Resource page.

Populate the addressbook Database with Sample Data

You'll now populate the database with sample data using the `AddressBook.sql` SQL script that's provided with this chapter's examples. To do so, you must create a connection to the new `addressbook` database from NetBeans. Perform the following steps:

1. On the NetBeans **Services** tab, right click the **Databases** node and select **New Connection....**

2. In the **New Database Connection** dialog, specify `localhost` as the **Host**, 1527 as the **Port**, `addressbook` as the **Database**, APP as the **User Name** and APP as the **Password**, then select the **Remember password** checkbox and click **OK**.

The preceding steps create a new entry in the **Databases** node showing the database's URL (`jdbc:derby://localhost:1527/addressbook`). The database server that provides access to this database resides on the local machine and accepts connections on port 1527.

NetBeans must be connected to the database to execute SQL statements. If NetBeans is already connected to the database, the icon 🖥️ is displayed next to the database's URL; otherwise, the icon 🖥️ is displayed. In this case, right click the icon and select **Connect...**.

To populate the database with sample data, perform the following steps:

1. Click the + next to jdbc:derby://localhost:1527/addressbook node to expand it, then expand the database's **APP** node.

2. Right click the **Tables** node and select **Execute Command...** to open a **SQL Command** editor tab in NetBeans. In a text editor, open the file AddressBook.sql from this chapter's examples folder, then copy the SQL statements and paste them into the **SQL Command** editor in NetBeans. Next, right click in the **SQL Command** editor and select **Run File**. This will create the Addresses table with the sample data in Fig. 27.1(a). [*Note:* The SQL script attempts to remove the database's Addresses table if it already exists. If it doesn't exist, you'll receive an error message, but the table will still be created properly.] Expand the **Tables** node to see the new table. You can view the table's data by right clicking **ADDRESSES** and selecting **View Data...**. Notice that we named the columns with all capital letters. We'll be using these names in Section 27.2.3.

27.2.2 @ManagedBean Class AddressBean

[*Note:* To build this app from scratch, use the techniques you learned in Chapter 26 to create a JSF web application named AddressBook and add a second Facelets page named addentry.xhtml to the app.] Class AddressBean (Fig. 27.6) enables the AddressBook app to interact with the addressbook database. The class provides properties that represent the first name, last name, street, city, state and zip code for an entry in the database. These are used by the addentry.xhtml page when adding a new entry to the database. In addition, this class declares a DataSource (lines 26–27) for interacting with the database method getAddresses (lines 102–130) for obtaining the list of addresses from the database and method save (lines 133–169) for saving a new address into the database. These methods use various JDBC techniques you learned in Chapter 25.

```java
 1   // AddressBean.java
 2   // Bean for interacting with the AddressBook database
 3   package addressbook;
 4
 5   import java.sql.Connection;
 6   import java.sql.PreparedStatement;
 7   import java.sql.ResultSet;
 8   import java.sql.SQLException;
 9   import javax.annotation.Resource;
10   import javax.faces.bean.ManagedBean;
11   import javax.sql.DataSource;
12   import javax.sql.rowset.CachedRowSet;
13
14   @ManagedBean( name="addressBean" )
15   public class AddressBean
16   {
```

Fig. 27.6 | AddressBean interacts with a database to store and retrieve addresses. (Part 1 of 4.)

```
17      // instance variables that represent one address
18      private String firstName;
19      private String lastName;
20      private String street;
21      private String city;
22      private String state;
23      private String zipcode;
24
25      // allow the server to inject the DataSource
26      @Resource( name="jdbc/addressbook" )
27      DataSource dataSource;
28
29      // get the first name
30      public String getFirstName()
31      {
32         return firstName;
33      } // end method getFirstName
34
35      // set the first name
36      public void setFirstName( String firstName )
37      {
38         this.firstName = firstName;
39      } // end method setFirstName
40
41      // get the last name
42      public String getLastName()
43      {
44         return lastName;
45      } // end method getLastName
46
47      // set the last name
48      public void setLastName( String lastName )
49      {
50         this.lastName = lastName;
51      } // end method setLastName
52
53      // get the street
54      public String getStreet()
55      {
56         return street;
57      } // end method getStreet
58
59      // set the street
60      public void setStreet( String street )
61      {
62         this.street = street;
63      } // end method setStreet
64
65      // get the city
66      public String getCity()
67      {
68         return city;
69      } // end method getCity
```

Fig. 27.6 | AddressBean interacts with a database to store and retrieve addresses. (Part 2 of 4.)

```
70
71     // set the city
72     public void setCity( String city )
73     {
74        this.city = city;
75     } // end method setCity
76
77     // get the state
78     public String getState()
79     {
80        return state;
81     } // end method getState
82
83     // set the state
84     public void setState( String state )
85     {
86        this.state = state;
87     } // end method setState
88
89     // get the zipcode
90     public String getZipcode()
91     {
92        return zipcode;
93     } // end method getZipcode
94
95     // set the zipcode
96     public void setZipcode( String zipcode )
97     {
98        this.zipcode = zipcode;
99     } // end method setZipcode
100
101    // return a ResultSet of entries
102    public ResultSet getAddresses() throws SQLException
103    {
104       // check whether dataSource was injected by the server
105       if ( dataSource == null )
106          throw new SQLException( "Unable to obtain DataSource" );
107
108       // obtain a connection from the connection pool
109       Connection connection = dataSource.getConnection();
110
111       // check whether connection was successful
112       if ( connection == null )
113          throw new SQLException( "Unable to connect to DataSource" );
114
115       try
116       {
117          // create a PreparedStatement to insert a new address book entry
118          PreparedStatement getAddresses = connection.prepareStatement(
119             "SELECT FIRSTNAME, LASTNAME, STREET, CITY, STATE, ZIP " +
120             "FROM ADDRESSES ORDER BY LASTNAME, FIRSTNAME" );
121
122          CachedRowSet rowSet = new com.sun.rowset.CachedRowSetImpl();
```

Fig. 27.6 | AddressBean interacts with a database to store and retrieve addresses. (Part 3 of 4.)

```
123              rowSet.populate( getAddresses.executeQuery() );
124              return rowSet;
125         } // end try
126         finally
127         {
128              connection.close(); // return this connection to pool
129         } // end finally
130    } // end method getAddresses
131
132    // save a new address book entry
133    public String save() throws SQLException
134    {
135         // check whether dataSource was injected by the server
136         if ( dataSource == null )
137              throw new SQLException( "Unable to obtain DataSource" );
138
139         // obtain a connection from the connection pool
140         Connection connection = dataSource.getConnection();
141
142         // check whether connection was successful
143         if ( connection == null )
144              throw new SQLException( "Unable to connect to DataSource" );
145
146         try
147         {
148              // create a PreparedStatement to insert a new address book entry
149              PreparedStatement addEntry =
150                   connection.prepareStatement( "INSERT INTO ADDRESSES " +
151                        "(FIRSTNAME,LASTNAME,STREET,CITY,STATE,ZIP)" +
152                        "VALUES ( ?, ?, ?, ?, ?, ? )" );
153
154              // specify the PreparedStatement's arguments
155              addEntry.setString( 1, getFirstName() );
156              addEntry.setString( 2, getLastName() );
157              addEntry.setString( 3, getStreet() );
158              addEntry.setString( 4, getCity() );
159              addEntry.setString( 5, getState() );
160              addEntry.setString( 6, getZipcode() );
161
162              addEntry.executeUpdate(); // insert the entry
163              return "index"; // go back to index.xhtml page
164         } // end try
165         finally
166         {
167              connection.close(); // return this connection to pool
168         } // end finally
169    } // end method save
170 } // end class AddressBean
```

Fig. 27.6 | AddressBean interacts with a database to store and retrieve addresses. (Part 4 of 4.)

*Injecting the **DataSource** into Class **AddressBean***
A **DataSource** (package javax.sql) enables a web application to obtain a Connection to a database. Lines 26–27 use annotation **@Resource** to inject a DataSource object into the

AddressBean. The annotation's name attribute specifies java/addressbook—the JNDI name from the *Creating a Data Source Name* step of Section 27.2.1. The @Resource annotation enables the server (GlassFish in our case) to hide all the complex details of locating the connection pool that we set up for interacting with the addressbook database. The server creates a DataSource for you that's configured to use that connection pool and assigns the DataSource object to the annotated variable declared at line 27. You can now trivially obtain a Connection for interacting with the database.

AddressBean *Method* getAddresses
Method getAddresses (lines 102–130) is called when the index.xhtml page is requested. The method returns a list of addresses for display in the page (Section 27.2.3). First, we check whether variable dataSource is null (lines 105–106), which would indicate that the server was unable to create the DataSource object. If the DataSource was created successfully, we use it to obtain a Connection to the database (line 109). Next, we check whether variable connection is null (lines 112–113), which would indicate that we were unable to connect. If the connection was successful, lines 118–124 get the set of addresses from the database and return them.

The PreparedStatement at lines 118–120 obtains all the addresses. Because database connections are a limited resources, you should use and close them quickly in your web apps. For this reason, we create a CachedRowSet and populate it with the ResultSet returned by the PreparedStatement's executeQuery method (lines 122–123). We then return the CachedRowSet (a disconnected RowSet) for use in the index.xhtml page (line 124) and close the connection object (line 128) in the finally block.

AddressBean *Method* save
Method save (lines 133–169) stores a new address in the database (Section 27.2.4). This occurs when the user submits the addentry.xhtml form—assuming the form's fields validate successfully. As in getAddresses, we ensure that the DataSource is not null, then obtain the Connection object and ensure that its not null. Lines 149–152 create a PreparedStatement for inserting a new record in the database. Lines 155–160 specify the values for each of the parameters in the PreparedStatement. Line 162 then executes the PreparedStatement to insert the new record. Line 163 returns the string "index", which as you'll see in Section 27.2.4 causes the app to display the index.xhtml page again.

27.2.3 index.xhtml Facelets Page
index.xhtml (Fig. 27.7) is the default web page for the AddressBook app. When this page is requested, it obtains the list of addresses from the AddressBean and displays them in tabular format using an **h:dataTable element**. The user can click the **Add Entry** button (line 17) to view the addentry.xhtml page. Recall that the default action for an h:commandButton is to submit a form. In this case, we specify the button's **action attribute** with the value "addentry". The JSF framework assumes this is a page in the app, appends .xhtml extension to the action attribute's value and returns the addentry.xhtml page to the client browser.

The h:dataTable *Element*
The h:dataTable element (lines 19–46) inserts tabular data into a page. We discuss only the attributes and nested elements that we use here. For more details on this element, its attributes and other JSF tag library elements, visit bit.ly/JSF2TagLibraryReference.

```
 1   <?xml version='1.0' encoding='UTF-8' ?>
 2
 3   <!-- index.html -->
 4   <!-- Displays an h:dataTable of the addresses in the address book -->
 5   <!DOCTYPE html PUBLIC "-//W3C//DTD XHTML 1.0 Transitional//EN"
 6      "http://www.w3.org/TR/xhtml1/DTD/xhtml1-transitional.dtd">
 7   <html xmlns="http://www.w3.org/1999/xhtml"
 8      xmlns:h="http://java.sun.com/jsf/html"
 9      xmlns:f="http://java.sun.com/jsf/core">
10      <h:head>
11         <title>Address Book</title>
12         <h:outputStylesheet name="style.css" library="css"/>
13      </h:head>
14      <h:body>
15         <h1>Address Book</h1>
16         <h:form>
17            <p><h:commandButton value="Add Entry" action="addentry"/></p>
18         </h:form>
19         <h:dataTable value="#{addressBean.addresses}" var="address"
20            rowClasses="oddRows,evenRows" headerClass="header"
21            styleClass="table" cellpadding="5" cellspacing="0">
22            <h:column>
23               <f:facet name="header">First Name</f:facet>
24               #{address.FIRSTNAME}
25            </h:column>
26            <h:column>
27               <f:facet name="header">Last Name</f:facet>
28               #{address.LASTNAME}
29            </h:column>
30            <h:column>
31               <f:facet name="header">Street</f:facet>
32               #{address.STREET}
33            </h:column>
34            <h:column>
35               <f:facet name="header">City</f:facet>
36               #{address.CITY}
37            </h:column>
38            <h:column>
39               <f:facet name="header">State</f:facet>
40               #{address.STATE}
41            </h:column>
42            <h:column>
43               <f:facet name="header">Zip code</f:facet>
44               #{address.ZIP}
45            </h:column>
46         </h:dataTable>
47      </h:body>
48   </html>
```

Fig. 27.7 | Displays an h:dataTable of the addresses in the address book.

The h:dataTable element's **value attribute** (line 19) specifies the collection of data you wish to display. In this case, we use AddressBean's addresses property, which calls the getAddresses method (Fig. 27.6). The collection returned by this method is a CachedRowSet, which is a type of ResultSet.

The h:dataTable iterates over its value collection and, one at a time, assigns each element to the variable specified by the **var attribute**. This variable is used in the h:dataTable's nested elements to access each element of the collection—each element in this case represents one row (i.e., address) in the CachedRowSet.

The **rowClasses attribute** (line 20) is a space-separated list of CSS style class names that are used to style the rows in the tabular output. These style classes are defined in the app's styles.css file in the css library (which is inserted into the document at line 12). You can open this file to view the various style class definitions. We specified two style classes— all the odd numbered rows will have the first style (oddRows) and all the even numbered rows the second style (evenRows). You can specify as many styles as you like— they'll be applied in the order you list them one row at a time until all the styles have been applied, then the h:DataTable will automatically cycle through the styles again for the next set of rows. The **columnClasses attribute** works similarly for columns in the table.

The **headerClass attribute** (line 20) specifies the column header CSS style. Headers are defined with f:facet elements nested in h:column elements (discussed momentarily). The **footerClass attribute** works similarly for column footers in the table.

The **styleClass attribute** (line 21) specifies the CSS styles for the entire table. The **cellpadding** and **cellspacing** attributes (line 21) specify the number of pixels around each table cell's contents and the number of pixels between table cells, respectively.

The h:column Elements

Lines 22–45 define the table's columns with six nested **h:column elements**. We focus here on the one at lines 22–25. When the CachedRowSet is populated in the AddressBean class, it automatically uses the database's column names as property names for each row object in the CachedRowSet. Line 28 inserts into the column the FIRSTNAME property of the CachedRowSet's current row. To display a column header above the column, you define an **f:facet element** (line 23) and set its name attribute to "header". Similarly, to display a column footer, use an f:facet with its name attribute set to "footer". The header is formatted with the CSS style specified in the h:dataTable's headerClass attribute (line 20). The remaining h:column elements perform similar tasks for the current row's LASTNAME, STREET, CITY, STATE and ZIP properties.

27.2.4 addentry.xhtml Facelets Page

When the user clicks **Add Entry** in the index.xhtml page, addentry.xhtml (Fig. 27.8) is displayed. Each h:inputText in this page has its required attribute set to "true" and includes a maxlength attribute that restricts the user's input to the maximum length of the corresponding database field. When the user clicks **Save** (lines 48–49), the input element's values are validated and (if successful) assigned to the properties of the addressBean managed object. In addition, the button specifies as its action the EL expression

```
#{addressBean.save}
```

which invokes the addressBean object's save method to store the new address in the database. When you call a method with the action attribute, if the method returns a value (in this case, it returns the string "index"), that value is used to request the corresponding page from the app. If the method does not return a value, the current page is re-requested.

```
1   <?xml version='1.0' encoding='UTF-8' ?>
2
3   <!-- addentry.html -->
4   <!-- Form for adding an entry to an address book -->
5   <!DOCTYPE html PUBLIC "-//W3C//DTD XHTML 1.0 Transitional//EN"
6      "http://www.w3.org/TR/xhtml1/DTD/xhtml1-transitional.dtd">
7   <html xmlns="http://www.w3.org/1999/xhtml"
8      xmlns:h="http://java.sun.com/jsf/html">
9      <h:head>
10        <title>Address Book: Add Entry</title>
11        <h:outputStylesheet name="style.css" library="css"/>
12     </h:head>
13     <h:body>
14        <h1>Address Book: Add Entry</h1>
15        <h:form>
16           <h:panelGrid columns="3">
17              <h:outputText value="First name:"/>
18              <h:inputText id="firstNameInputText" required="true"
19                 requiredMessage="Please enter first name"
20                 value="#{addressBean.firstName}" maxlength="30"/>
21              <h:message for="firstNameInputText" styleClass="error"/>
22              <h:outputText value="Last name:"/>
23              <h:inputText id="lastNameInputText" required="true"
24                 requiredMessage="Please enter last name"
25                 value="#{addressBean.lastName}" maxlength="30"/>
26              <h:message for="lastNameInputText" styleClass="error"/>
27              <h:outputText value="Street:"/>
28              <h:inputText id="streetInputText" required="true"
29                 requiredMessage="Please enter the street address"
30                 value="#{addressBean.street}" maxlength="150"/>
31              <h:message for="streetInputText" styleClass="error"/>
32              <h:outputText value="City:"/>
33              <h:inputText id="cityInputText" required="true"
34                 requiredMessage="Please enter the city"
35                 value="#{addressBean.city}" maxlength="30"/>
36              <h:message for="cityInputText" styleClass="error"/>
37              <h:outputText value="State:"/>
38              <h:inputText id="stateInputText" required="true"
39                 requiredMessage="Please enter state"
40                 value="#{addressBean.state}" maxlength="2"/>
41              <h:message for="stateInputText" styleClass="error"/>
42              <h:outputText value="Zipcode:"/>
43              <h:inputText id="zipcodeInputText" required="true"
44                 requiredMessage="Please enter zipcode"
45                 value="#{addressBean.zipcode}" maxlength="5"/>
46              <h:message for="zipcodeInputText" styleClass="error"/>
47           </h:panelGrid>
48           <h:commandButton value="Save Address"
49              action="#{addressBean.save}"/>
50        </h:form>
```

Fig. 27.8 | Form for adding an entry to an address book. (Part I of 2.)

```
51               <h:outputLink value="index.xhtml">Return to Addresses</h:outputLink>
52        </h:body>
53    </html>
```

Fig. 27.8 | Form for adding an entry to an address book. (Part 2 of 2.)

27.3 Ajax

The term **Ajax**—short for **Asynchronous JavaScript and XML**—was coined by Jesse James Garrett of Adaptive Path, Inc., in 2005 to describe a range of technologies for developing highly responsive, dynamic web applications. Ajax applications include Google Maps, Yahoo's FlickR and many more. Ajax separates the *user interaction* portion of an application from its *server interaction*, enabling both to proceed *in parallel*. This enables Ajax web-based applications to perform at speeds approaching those of desktop applications, reducing or even eliminating the performance advantage that desktop applications have traditionally had over web-based applications. This has huge ramifications for the desktop applications industry—the applications platform of choice is shifting from the desktop to the web. Many people believe that the web—especially in the context of abundant open-source software, inexpensive computers and exploding Internet bandwidth—will create the next major growth phase for Internet companies.

Ajax makes **asynchronous** calls to the server to exchange small amounts of data with each call. *Where normally the entire page would be submitted and reloaded with every user interaction on a web page, Ajax allows only the necessary portions of the page to reload, saving time and resources.*

Ajax applications typically make use of client-side scripting technologies such as JavaScript to interact with page elements. They use the browser's **XMLHttpRequest** object to perform the asynchronous exchanges with the web server that make Ajax applications so responsive. This object can be used by most scripting languages to pass XML data from the client to the server and to process XML data sent from the server back to the client.

Using Ajax technologies in web applications can dramatically improve performance, but programming Ajax directly is complex and error prone. It requires page designers to know both scripting and markup languages. As you'll soon see, JSF 2.0 makes adding Ajax capabilities to your web apps fairly simple.

Traditional Web Applications
Figure 27.9 presents the typical interactions between the client and the server in a traditional web application, such as one that uses a user registration form. The user first fills in the form's fields, then *submits* the form (Fig. 27.9, *Step 1*). The browser generates a request to the server, which receives the request and processes it (*Step 2*). The server generates and sends a response containing the exact page that the browser will render (*Step 3*), which causes the browser to load the new page (*Step 4*) and temporarily makes the browser window blank. The client *waits* for the server to respond and *reloads the entire page* with the data from the response (*Step 4*). While such a **synchronous request** is being processed on the server, *the user cannot interact with the client web page.* If the user interacts with and submits another form, the process begins again (*Steps 5–8*).

This model was originally designed for a web of *hypertext documents*—what some people call the "brochure web." As the web evolved into a full-scale applications platform,

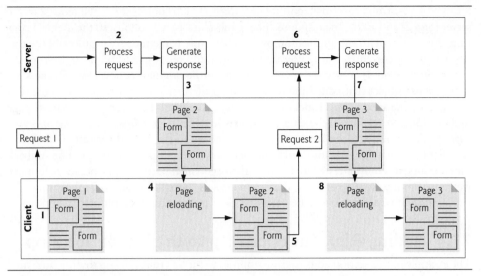

Fig. 27.9 | Classic web application reloading the page for every user interaction.

the model shown in Fig. 27.9 yielded "choppy" application performance. Every full-page refresh required users to reestablish their understanding of the full-page contents. Users began to demand a model that would yield the responsiveness of desktop applications.

Ajax Web Applications
Ajax applications add a layer between the client and the server to manage communication between the two (Fig. 27.10). When the user interacts with the page, the client creates an

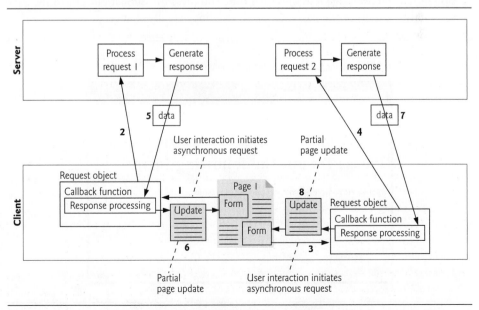

Fig. 27.10 | Ajax-enabled web application interacting with the server asynchronously.

XMLHttpRequest object to manage a request (*Step 1*). This object sends the request to the server (*Step 2*) and awaits the response. The requests are asynchronous, so the user can continue interacting with the application on the client side while the server processes the earlier request concurrently. Other user interactions could result in additional requests to the server (*Steps 3* and *4*). Once the server responds to the original request (*Step 5*), the XML-HttpRequest object that issued the request calls a client-side function to process the data returned by the server. This function—known as a **callback function**—uses **partial page updates** (*Step 6*) to display the data in the existing web page *without reloading the entire page*. At the same time, the server may be responding to the second request (*Step 7*) and the client side may be starting to do another partial page update (*Step 8*). The callback function updates only a designated part of the page. Such partial page updates help make web applications more responsive, making them feel more like desktop applications. The web application does not load a new page while the user interacts with it.

27.4 Adding Ajax Functionality to the Validation App

The example in this section adds Ajax capabilities to the Validation app that we presented in Section 26.7. Figure 27.11 shows the sample outputs from the ValidationAjax version of the app that we'll build momentarily. Part (a) shows the initial form that's displayed when this app first executes. Parts (b) and (c) show validation errors that are displayed when the user submits an empty form and invalid data, respectively. Part (d) shows the page after the form is submitted successfully.

As you can see, the app has the same functionality as the version in Section 26.7; however, you'll notice a couple of changes in how the app works. First, the URL displayed in the web browser always reads localhost:8080/ValidationAjax/, whereas the URL in the Section 26.7 changes after the form is submitted the first time. Also, in the non-Ajax version of the app, the page refreshes each time you press the **Submit** button. In the Ajax version, only the parts of the page that need updating actually change.

a) Submitting the form before entering any information

Fig. 27.11 | JSP that demonstrates validation of user input. (Part 1 of 2.)

b) Error messages displayed after submitting the empty form

c) Error messages displayed after submitting invalid information

d) Successfully submitted form

Fig. 27.11 | JSP that demonstrates validation of user input. (Part 2 of 2.)

index.xhtml

The changes required to add Ajax functionality to this app are minimal. All of the changes are in the index.xhtml file (Fig. 27.12) and are highlighted. The ValidationBean class is identical to the version in Section 26.7, so we don't show it here.

```
1   <?xml version='1.0' encoding='UTF-8' ?>
2
3   <!-- index.xhtml -->
4   <!-- Validating user input -->
5   <!DOCTYPE html PUBLIC "-//W3C//DTD XHTML 1.0 Transitional//EN"
6      "http://www.w3.org/TR/xhtml1/DTD/xhtml1-transitional.dtd">
7   <html xmlns="http://www.w3.org/1999/xhtml"
8      xmlns:h="http://java.sun.com/jsf/html"
9      xmlns:f="http://java.sun.com/jsf/core">
10     <h:head>
11        <title>Validating Form Data</title>
12        <h:outputStylesheet name="style.css" library="css"/>
13     </h:head>
14     <h:body>
15        <h:form>
16           <h1>Please fill out the following form:</h1>
17           <p>All fields are required and must contain valid information</p>
18           <h:panelGrid columns="3">
19              <h:outputText value="Name:"/>
20              <h:inputText id="nameInputText" required="true"
21                 requiredMessage="Please enter your name"
22                 value="#{validationBean.name}"
23                 validatorMessage="Name must be fewer than 30 characters">
24                 <f:validateLength maximum="30" />
25              </h:inputText>
26              <h:message id="nameMessage" for="nameInputText"
27                 styleClass="error"/>
28              <h:outputText value="E-mail:"/>
29              <h:inputText id="emailInputText" required="true"
30                 requiredMessage="Please enter a valid e-mail address"
31                 value="#{validationBean.email}"
32                 validatorMessage="Invalid e-mail address format">
33                 <f:validateRegex pattern=
34                    "\w+([-+.']\w+)*@\w+([-.]\w+)*\.\w+([-.]\w+)*" />
35              </h:inputText>
36              <h:message id="emailMessage" for="emailInputText"
37                 styleClass="error"/>
38              <h:outputText value="Phone:"/>
39              <h:inputText id="phoneInputText" required="true"
40                 requiredMessage="Please enter a valid phone number"
41                 value="#{validationBean.phone}"
42                 validatorMessage="Invalid phone number format">
43                 <f:validateRegex pattern=
44                    "((\(\d{3}\) ?)|(\d{3}-))?\d{3}-\d{4}" />
45              </h:inputText>
```

Fig. 27.12 | Ajax enabling the Validation app. (Part 1 of 2.)

```
46                    <h:message id="phoneMessage" for="phoneInputText"
47                       styleClass="error"/>
48               </h:panelGrid>
49               <h:commandButton value="Submit">
50                  <f:ajax execute="nameInputText emailInputText phoneInputText"
51                     render=
52                        "nameMessage emailMessage phoneMessage resultOutputText"/>
53               </h:commandButton>
54               <h:outputText id="resultOutputText" escape="false"
55                  value="#{validationBean.response}"/>
56          </h:form>
57       </h:body>
58    </html>
```

Fig. 27.12 | Ajax enabling the Validation app. (Part 2 of 2.)

Adding **id** *Attributes to Elements*

The Facelets elements that will be submitted as part of an Ajax request and the Facelets elements that will participate in the partial page updates must have id attributes. The h:inputText elements in the original Validation example already had id attributes. These elements will be submitted to the server as part of an Ajax request. We'd like the h:Message elements that show validation errors and the h:outputText element that displays the result to be updated with partial page updates. For this reason, we've added id attributes to these elements.

f:ajax *Element*

The other key change to this page is at lines 49–53 where the h:commandButton now contains an **f:ajax element**, which intercepts the form submission when the user clicks the button and makes an Ajax request instead. The f:ajax element's **execute attribute** specifies a space-separated list of element ids—the values of these elements are submitted as part of the Ajax request. The f:ajax element's **render attribute** specifies a space-separated list of element ids for the elements that should be updated via partial page updates.

27.5 Wrap-Up

In this chapter, we built an AddressBook application that allowed a user to add and view contacts. You learned how to insert user input into a Java DB database and how to display the contents of a database on a web page using an h:dataTable JSF element. We also demonstrated how to add Ajax capabilities to JSF web apps by enhancing the Validation app from Section 26.7. In Chapter 28, you'll use NetBeans to create web services and consume them from desktop and web applications.

Web Services

Objectives

In this chapter you'll learn:

- What a web service is.

- How to publish and consume web services in NetBeans.

- How XML, JSON, XML-Based Simple Object Access Protocol (SOAP) and Representational State Transfer (REST) Architecture enable Java web services.

- How to create client desktop and web applications that consume web services.

- How to use session tracking in web services to maintain client state information.

- How to connect to databases from web services.

- How to pass objects of user-defined types to and return them from a web service.

A client is to me a mere unit, a factor in a problem.
—Sir Arthur Conan Doyle

They also serve who only stand and wait.
—John Milton

...if the simplest things of nature have a message that you understand, rejoice, for your soul is alive.
—Eleonora Duse

Protocol is everything.
—Francoise Giuliani

28.1 Introduction

This chapter introduces web services, which promote software portability and reusability in applications that operate over the Internet. A **web service** is a software component stored on one computer that can be accessed by an application (or other software component) on another computer over a network. Web services communicate using such technologies as XML, JSON and HTTP. In this chapter, we use two Java APIs that facilitate web services. The first, **JAX-WS**, is based on the **Simple Object Access Protocol (SOAP)**—an XML-based protocol that allows web services and clients to communicate, even if the client and the web service are written in different languages. The second, **JAX-RS**, uses **Representational State Transfer (REST)**—a network architecture that uses the web's traditional request/response mechanisms such as GET and POST requests. For more information on SOAP-based and REST-based web services, visit our Web Services Resource Centers:

```
www.deitel.com/WebServices/
www.deitel.com/RESTWebServices/
```

These Resource Centers include information about designing and implementing web services in many languages and about web services offered by companies such as Google, Amazon and eBay. You'll also find many additional tools for publishing and consuming web services. For more information about REST-based Java web services, check out the Jersey project:

```
jersey.java.net/
```

The XML used in this chapter is created and manipulated for you by the APIs, so you need not know the details of XML to use it here. To learn more about XML, read the following tutorials:

```
www.deitel.com/articles/xml_tutorials/20060401/XMLBasics/
www.deitel.com/articles/xml_tutorials/20060401/XMLStructuringData/
```

and visit our XML Resource Center:

```
www.deitel.com/XML/
```

Business-to-Business Transactions

Rather than relying on proprietary applications, businesses can conduct transactions via standardized, widely available web services. This has important implications for **business-to-business (B2B) transactions**. Web services are platform and language independent, enabling companies to collaborate without worrying about the compatibility of their hardware, software and communications technologies. Companies such as Amazon, Google, eBay, PayPal and many others are benefiting by making their server-side applications available to partners via web services.

By purchasing some web services and using other free ones that are relevant to their businesses, companies can spend less time developing applications and can create new ones that are more innovative. E-businesses for example, can provide their customers with enhanced shopping experiences. Consider an online music store. The store's website links to information about various CDs, enabling users to purchase them, to learn about the artists, to find more titles by those artists, to find other artists' music they may enjoy, and more. The store's website may also link to the site of a company that sells concert tickets and provides a web service that displays upcoming concert dates for various artists, allowing users to buy tickets. By consuming the concert-ticket web service on its site, the online music store can provide an additional service to its customers, increase its site traffic and perhaps earn a commission on concert-ticket sales. The company that sells concert tickets also benefits from the business relationship by selling more tickets and possibly by receiving revenue from the online music store for the use of the web service.

Any Java programmer with a knowledge of web services can write applications that "consume" web services. The resulting applications would invoke web services running on servers that could be thousands of miles away.

NetBeans

NetBeans is one of many tools that enable you to *publish* and/or *consume* web services. We demonstrate how to use NetBeans to implement web services using the JAX-WS and JAX-RS APIs and how to invoke them from client applications. For each example, we provide the web service's code, then present a client application that uses the web service. Our first examples build simple web services and client applications in NetBeans. Then we demonstrate web services that use more sophisticated features, such as manipulating databases with JDBC and manipulating class objects. For information on downloading and installing the NetBeans and the GlassFish server, see Section 26.1.

28.2 Web Service Basics

The machine on which a web service resides is referred to as a **web service host**. The client application sends a request over a network to the web service host, which processes the request and returns a response over the network to the application. This kind of distributed computing benefits systems in various ways. For example, an application without direct access to data on another system might be able to retrieve the data via a web service. Similarly, an application lacking the processing power to perform specific computations could use a web service to take advantage of another system's superior resources.

In Java, a web service is implemented as a class that resides on a server—it's not part of the client application. Making a web service available to receive client requests is known as **publishing a web service**; using a web service from a client application is known as **consuming a web service**.

28.3 Simple Object Access Protocol (SOAP)

The Simple Object Access Protocol (SOAP) is a platform-independent protocol that uses XML to interact with web services, typically over HTTP. You can view the SOAP specification at `www.w3.org/TR/soap/`. Each request and response is packaged in a **SOAP message**—XML markup containing the information that a web service requires to process the message. SOAP messages are written in XML so that they're computer readable, human readable and platform independent. Most **firewalls**—security barriers that restrict communication among networks—allow HTTP traffic to pass through, so that clients can browse the web by sending requests to and receiving responses from web servers. Thus, SOAP-based services can send and receive SOAP messages over HTTP connections with few limitations.

SOAP supports an extensive set of types, including the primitive types (e.g., `int`), as well as `DateTime`, `XmlNode` and others. SOAP can also transmit arrays of these types. When a program invokes a method of a SOAP web service, the request and all relevant information are packaged in a SOAP message enclosed in a **SOAP envelope** and sent to the server on which the web service resides. When the web service receives this SOAP message, it parses the XML representing the message, then processes the message's contents. The message specifies the *method* that the client wishes to execute and the *arguments* the client passed to that method. Next, the web service calls the method with the specified arguments (if any) and sends the response back to the client in another SOAP message. The client parses the response to retrieve the method's result. In Section 28.6, you'll build and consume a basic SOAP web service.

28.4 Representational State Transfer (REST)

Representational State Transfer (REST) refers to an architectural style for implementing web services. Such web services are often called **RESTful web services**. Though REST itself is not a standard, RESTful web services are implemented using web standards. Each method in a RESTful web service is identified by a unique URL. Thus, when the server receives a request, it immediately knows what operation to perform. Such web services can be used in a program or directly from a web browser. The results of a particular operation may be cached locally by the browser when the service is invoked with a GET request. This can make subsequent requests for the same operation faster by loading the result directly from the browser's cache. Amazon's web services (aws.amazon.com) are RESTful, as are many others.

RESTful web services are alternatives to those implemented with SOAP. Unlike SOAP-based web services, the request and response of REST services are not wrapped in envelopes. REST is also not limited to returning data in XML format. It can use a variety of formats, such as XML, JSON, HTML, plain text and media files. In Sections 28.7–28.8, you'll build and consume basic RESTful web services.

28.5 JavaScript Object Notation (JSON)

JavaScript Object Notation (JSON) is an alternative to XML for representing data. JSON is a text-based data-interchange format used to represent objects in JavaScript as collections of name/value pairs represented as Strings. It's commonly used in Ajax applications. JSON is a simple format that makes objects easy to read, create and parse and, because it's much less verbose than XML, allows programs to transmit data efficiently across the Internet. Each JSON object is represented as a list of property names and values contained in curly braces, in the following format:

> { *propertyName1* : *value1*, *propertyName2* : *value2* }

Arrays are represented in JSON with square brackets in the following format:

> [*value1*, *value2*, *value3*]

Each value in an array can be a string, a number, a JSON object, true, false or null. To appreciate the simplicity of JSON data, examine this representation of an array of address-book entries:

```
[ { first: 'Cheryl', last: 'Black' },
  { first: 'James', last: 'Blue' },
  { first: 'Mike', last: 'Brown' },
  { first: 'Meg', last: 'Gold' } ]
```

Many programming languages now support the JSON data format. An extensive list of JSON libraries sorted by language can be found at www.json.org.

28.6 Publishing and Consuming SOAP-Based Web Services

This section presents our first example of publishing (enabling for client access) and consuming (using) a web service. We begin with a SOAP-based web service.

28.6.1 Creating a Web Application Project and Adding a Web Service Class in NetBeans

When you create a web service in NetBeans, you focus on its logic and let the IDE and server handle its infrastructure. First you create a **Web Application** project. NetBeans uses this project type for web services that are invoked by other applications.

Creating a Web Application Project in NetBeans
To create a web application, perform the following steps:

1. Select **File > New Project...** to open the **New Project** dialog.

2. Select **Java Web** from the dialog's **Categories** list, then select **Web Application** from the **Projects** list. Click **Next >**.

3. Specify the name of your project (WelcomeSOAP) in the **Project Name** field and specify where you'd like to store the project in the **Project Location** field. You can click the **Browse** button to select the location. Click **Next >**.

4. Select **GlassFish Server 3** from the **Server** drop-down list and **Java EE 6 Web** from the **Java EE Version** drop-down list.

5. Click **Finish** to create the project.

This creates a web application that will run in a web browser, similar to the projects used in Chapters 26 and 27.

Adding a Web Service Class to a Web Application Project
Perform the following steps to add a web service class to the project:

1. In the **Projects** tab in NetBeans, right click the **WelcomeSOAP** project's node and select **New > Web Service...** to open the **New Web Service** dialog.

2. Specify WelcomeSOAP in the **Web Service Name** field.

3. Specify com.deitel.welcomesoap in the **Package** field.

4. Click **Finish** to create the web service class.

The IDE generates a sample web service class with the name from *Step 2* in the package from *Step 3*. You can find this class in your project's **Web Services** node. In this class, you'll define the methods that your web service makes available to client applications. When you eventually build your application, the IDE will generate other supporting files for your web service.

28.6.2 Defining the WelcomeSOAP Web Service in NetBeans

Figure 28.1 contains the completed WelcomeSOAPService code (reformatted to match the coding conventions we use in this book). First we discuss this code, then show how to use the NetBeans web service design view to add the welcome method to the class.

```
1   // Fig. 28.1: WelcomeSOAP.java
2   // Web service that returns a welcome message via SOAP.
3   package com.deitel.welcomesoap;
4
5   import javax.jws.WebService; // program uses the annotation @WebService
6   import javax.jws.WebMethod; // program uses the annotation @WebMethod
7   import javax.jws.WebParam; // program uses the annotation @WebParam
8
9   @WebService() // annotates the class as a web service
10  public class WelcomeSOAP
11  {
```

Fig. 28.1 | Web service that returns a welcome message via SOAP. (Part 1 of 2.)

```
12        // WebMethod that returns welcome message
13        @WebMethod( operationName = "welcome" )
14        public String welcome( @WebParam( name = "name" ) String name )
15        {
16            return "Welcome to JAX-WS web services with SOAP, " + name + "!";
17        } // end method welcome
18    } // end class WelcomeSOAP
```

Fig. 28.1 | Web service that returns a welcome message via SOAP. (Part 2 of 2.)

Annotation import *Declarations*

Lines 5–7 import the annotations used in this example. By default, each new web service class created with the JAX-WS APIs is a POJO (plain old Java object), so you do *not* need to extend a class or implement an interface to create a web service.

@WebService Annotation

Line 9 contains a **@WebService annotation** (imported at line 5) which indicates that class WelcomeSOAP implements a web service. The annotation is followed by parentheses that may contain optional annotation attributes. The optional **name attribute** specifies the name of the service endpoint interface class that will be generated for the client. A **service endpoint interface (SEI)** class (sometimes called a **proxy class**) is used to interact with the web service—a client application consumes the web service by invoking methods on the service endpoint interface object. The optional **serviceName attribute** specifies the service name, which is also the name of the class that the client uses to obtain a service endpoint interface object. If the serviceName attribute is not specified, the web service's name is assumed to be the Java class name followed by the word Service. NetBeans places the @WebService annotation at the beginning of each new web service class you create. You can then add the name and serviceName properties in the parentheses following the annotation.

When you deploy a web application containing a class that uses the @WebService annotation, the server (GlassFish in our case) recognizes that the class implements a web service and creates all the **server-side artifacts** that support the web service—that is, the framework that allows the web service to wait for client requests and respond to those requests once it's deployed on an application server. Some popular open-source application servers that support Java web services include GlassFish (glassfish.dev.java.net), Apache Tomcat (tomcat.apache.org) and JBoss Application Server (www.jboss.com/products/platforms/application).

WelcomeSOAP Service's welcome *Method*

The WelcomeSOAP service has only one method, welcome (lines 13–17), which takes the user's name as a String and returns a String containing a welcome message. This method is tagged with the **@WebMethod annotation** to indicate that it can be called remotely. Any methods that are not tagged with @WebMethod are *not* accessible to clients that consume the web service. Such methods are typically utility methods within the web service class. The @WebMethod annotation uses the **operationName** attribute to specify the method name that is exposed to the web service's client. If the operationName is not specified, it's set to the actual Java method's name.

Common Programming Error 28.1

Failing to expose a method as a web method by declaring it with the @WebMethod anno-tation prevents clients of the web service from accessing the method. There's one excep-tion—if none of the class's methods are declared with the @WebMethod annotation, then all the public methods of the class will be exposed as web methods.

Common Programming Error 28.2

Methods with the @WebMethod annotation cannot be static. *An object of the web service class must exist for a client to access the service's web methods.*

The name parameter to welcome is annotated with the **@WebParam annotation** (line 14). The optional @WebParam attribute **name** indicates the parameter name that is exposed to the web service's clients. If you don't specify the name, the actual parameter name is used.

Completing the Web Service's Code

NetBeans provides a web service design view in which you can define the method(s) and parameter(s) for your web services. To define the WelcomeSOAP class's welcome method, perform the following steps:

1. In the project's **Web Services** node, double click WelcomeSOAP to open the file WelcomeSOAPService.java in the code editor.

2. Click the **Design** button at the top of the code editor to show the web service de-sign view (Fig. 28.2).

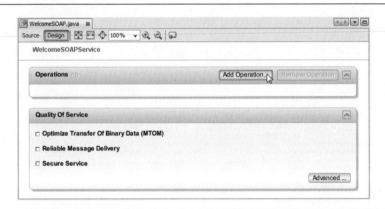

Fig. 28.2 | Web service design view.

3. Click the **Add Operation...** button to display the **Add Operation...** dialog (Fig. 28.3).

4. Specify the method name welcome in the **Name** field. The default **Return Type** (String) is correct for this example.

5. Add the method's name parameter by clicking the **Add** button to the right of the **Parameters** tab then entering name in the **Name** field. The parameter's default **Type** (String) is correct for this example.

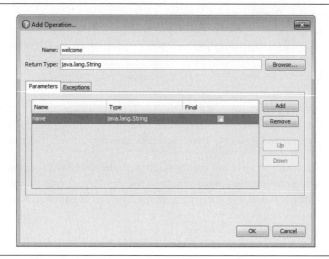

Fig. 28.3 | Adding an operation to a web service.

6. Click **OK** to create the welcome method. The design view should now appear as shown in Fig. 28.3.

7. At the top of the design view, click the **Source** button to display the class's source code and add the code line 18 of Fig. 28.1 to the body of method welcome.

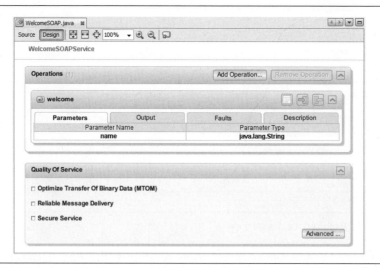

Fig. 28.4 | Web service design view after new operation is added.

28.6.3 Publishing the WelcomeSOAP Web Service from NetBeans

Now that you've created the WelcomeSOAP web service class, you'll use NetBeans to build and *publish* (that is, deploy) the web service so that clients can consume its services. Net-Beans handles all the details of building and deploying a web service for you. This includes creating the framework required to support the web service. Right click the project name WelcomeSOAP in the **Projects** tab and select **Deploy** to build and deploy the web application to the GlassFish server.

28.6.4 Testing the WelcomeSOAP Web Service with GlassFish Application Server's Tester Web Page

Next, you'll test the WelcomeSOAP web service. We previously selected the GlassFish application server to execute this web application. This server can dynamically create a web page that allows you to test a web service's methods from a web browser. To use this capability:

1. Expand the project's **Web Services** in the NetBeans **Projects** tab.

2. Right click the web service class name (WelcomeSOAP) and select **Test Web Service**.

The GlassFish application server builds the Tester web page and loads it into your web browser. Figure 28.5 shows the Tester web page for the WelcomeSOAP web service. The web service's name is automatically the class name followed by Service.

Fig. 28.5 | Tester web page created by GlassFish for the WelcomeSOAP web service.

Once you've deployed the web service, you can also type the URL

```
http://localhost:8080/WelcomeSOAP/WelcomeSOAPService?Tester
```

in your web browser to view the Tester web page. WelcomeSOAPService is the name (specified in line 11 of Fig. 28.1) that clients use to access the web service.

To test WelcomeSOAP's welcome web method, type your name in the text field to the right of the **welcome** button and click the button to invoke the method. Figure 28.6 shows the results of invoking WelcomeSOAP's welcome method with the value Paul.

Application Server Note
You can access the web service only when the application server is running. If NetBeans launches GlassFish for you, it will automatically shut it down when you close NetBeans. To keep it up and running, you can launch it independently of NetBeans before you deploy or run web applications. The GlassFish Quick Start Guide at glassfish.java.net/downloads/quickstart/index.html shows how to manually start and stop the server.

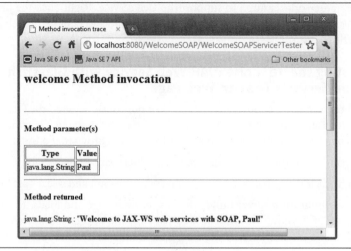

welcome Method invocation

Method parameter(s)

Type	Value
java.lang.String	Paul

Method returned

java.lang.String : "**Welcome to JAX-WS web services with SOAP, Paul!**"

Fig. 28.6 | Testing WelcomeSOAP's welcome method.

Testing the WelcomeSOAP Web Service from Another Computer
If your computer is connected to a network and allows HTTP requests, then you can test the web service from another computer on the network by typing the following URL (where *host* is the hostname or IP address of the computer on which the web service is deployed) into a browser on another computer:

```
http://host:8080/WelcomeSOAP/WelcomeSOAPService?Tester
```

28.6.5 Describing a Web Service with the Web Service Description Language (WSDL)

To consume a web service, a client must determine its functionality and how to use it. For this purpose, web services normally contain a **service description**. This is an XML document that conforms to the **Web Service Description Language** (WSDL)—an XML vocabulary that defines the methods a web service makes available and how clients interact with them. The WSDL document also specifies lower-level information that clients might need, such as the required formats for requests and responses.

WSDL documents help applications determine how to interact with the web services described in the documents. You do not need to understand WSDL to take advantage of it—the GlassFish application server generates a web service's WSDL dynamically for you, and client tools can parse the WSDL to help create the client-side service endpoint interface class that a client uses to access the web service. Since GlassFish (and most other servers) generate the WSDL dynamically, clients always receive a deployed web service's most up-to-date description. To access the WelcomeSOAP web service, the client code will need the following WSDL URL:

```
http://localhost:8080/WelcomeSOAP/WelcomeSOAPService?WSDL
```

Accessing the WelcomeSOAP Web Service's WSDL from Another Computer
Eventually, you'll want clients on other computers to use your web service. Such clients need the web service's WSDL, which they would access with the following URL:

```
http://host:8080/WelcomeSOAP/WelcomeSOAPService?WSDL
```

where *host* is the hostname or IP address of the server that hosts the web service. As we discussed in Section 28.6.4, this works only if your computer allows HTTP connections from other computers—as is the case for publicly accessible web and application servers.

28.6.6 Creating a Client to Consume the WelcomeSOAP Web Service

Now you'll consume the web service from a client application. A web service client can be any type of application or even another web service. You enable a client application to consume a web service by **adding a web service reference** to the application.

Service Endpoint Interface (SEI)

An application that consumes a web service consists of an object of a service endpoint interface (SEI) class (sometimes called a *proxy class*) that's used to interact with the web service and a client application that consumes the web service by invoking methods on the service endpoint interface object. The client code invokes methods on the service endpoint interface object, which handles the details of passing method arguments to and receiving return values from the web service on the client's behalf. This communication can occur over a local network, over the Internet or even with a web service on the same computer. The web service performs the corresponding task and returns the results to the service endpoint interface object, which then returns the results to the client code. Figure 28.7 depicts the interactions among the client code, the SEI object and the web service. As you'll soon see, NetBeans creates these service endpoint interface classes for you.

Requests to and responses from web services created with JAX-WS (one of many different web service frameworks) are typically transmitted via SOAP. Any client capable of generating and processing SOAP messages can interact with a web service, regardless of the language in which the web service is written.

We now use NetBeans to create a client Java desktop GUI application. Then you'll add a web service reference to the project so the client can access the web service. When you add the reference, the IDE creates and compiles the **client-side artifacts**—the framework of Java code that supports the client-side service endpoint interface class. The client then calls methods on an object of the service endpoint interface class, which uses the rest of the artifacts to interact with the web service.

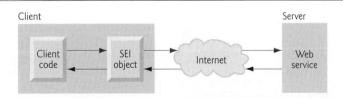

Fig. 28.7 | Interaction between a web service client and a web service.

Creating a Desktop Application Project in NetBeans

Before performing the steps in this section, ensure that the WelcomeSOAP web service has been deployed and that the GlassFish application server is running (see Section 28.6.3). Perform the following steps to create a client Java desktop application in NetBeans:

1. Select **File > New Project...** to open the **New Project** dialog.

2. Select **Java** from the **Categories** list and **Java Application** from the **Projects** list, then click **Next >**.

3. Specify the name WelcomeSOAPClient in the **Project Name** field and uncheck the **Create Main Class** checkbox. Later, you'll add a subclass of JFrame that contains a main method.

4. Click **Finish** to create the project.

Step 2: Adding a Web Service Reference to an Application

Next, you'll add a web service reference to your application so that it can interact with the WelcomeSOAP web service. To add a web service reference, perform the following steps.

1. Right click the project name (WelcomeSOAPClient) in the NetBeans **Projects** tab and select **New > Web Service Client...** from the pop-up menu to display the **New Web Service Client** dialog.

2. In the **WSDL URL** field, specify the URL http://localhost:8080/WelcomeSOAP/WelcomeSOAPService?WSDL (Fig. 28.8). This URL tells the IDE where to find the web service's WSDL description. [*Note:* If the GlassFish application server is located on a different computer, replace localhost with the hostname or IP address of that computer.] The IDE uses this WSDL description to generate the client-side artifacts that compose and support the service endpoint interface.

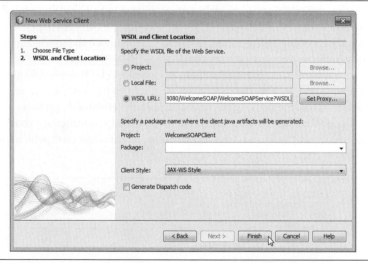

Fig. 28.8 | **New Web Service Client** dialog.

3. For the other options, leave the default settings, then click **Finish** to create the web service reference and dismiss the **New Web Service Client** dialog.

In the NetBeans **Projects** tab, the WelcomeSOAPClient project now contains a **Web Service References** folder with the WelcomeSOAP web service's service endpoint interface (Fig. 28.9). The service endpoint interface's name is listed as WelcomeSOAPService.

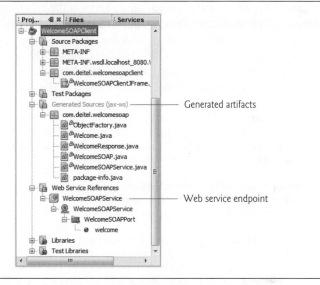

Fig. 28.9 | NetBeans **Project** tab after adding a web service reference to the project.

When you specify the web service you want to consume, NetBeans accesses and copies its WSDL information to a file in your project (named WelcomeSOAPService.wsdl in this example). You can view this file by double clicking the WelcomeSOAPService node in the project's **Web Service References** folder. If the web service changes, the client-side artifacts and the client's copy of the WSDL file can be regenerated by right clicking the Welcome-SOAPService node shown in Fig. 28.9 and selecting **Refresh....** Figure 28.9 also shows the IDE-generated client-side artifacts, which appear in the **Generated Sources (jax-ws)** folder.

28.6.7 Consuming the WelcomeSOAP Web Service

For this example, we use a GUI application[1] to interact with the WelcomeSOAP web service. To build the client application's GUI, add a subclass of JFrame to the project by performing the following steps:

1. Right click the project name (WelcomeSOAPClient) in the NetBeans **Project** tab and select **New > JFrame Form...** to display the **New JFrame Form** dialog.

2. Specify WelcomeSOAPClientJFrame in the **Class Name** field.

3. Specify com.deitel.welcomesoapclient in the **Package** field.

4. Click **Finish** to close the **New JFrame Form** dialog.

Next, use the NetBeans GUI design tools to build the GUI shown in the sample screen captures at the end of Fig. 28.10. The GUI consists of a **Label**, a **Text Field** and a **Button**.

The application in Fig. 28.10 uses the WelcomeSOAP web service to display a welcome message to the user. To save space, we do not show the NetBeans autogenerated initComponents method, which contains the code that creates the GUI components, positions

---

1. We assume you're already familiar with using the NetBeans GUI designer. If not, see Appendix H.

them and registers their event handlers. To view the complete source code, open the WelcomeSOAPClientJFrame.java file in this example's folder under src\java\com\deitel\ welcomesoapclient. NetBeans places the GUI component instance-variable declarations at the end of the class (lines 114–116). Java allows instance variables to be declared anywhere in a class's body as long as they're placed outside the class's methods. We continue to declare our own instance variables at the top of the class.

```java
1   // Fig. 28.10: WelcomeSOAPClientJFrame.java
2   // Client desktop application for the WelcomeSOAP web service.
3   package com.deitel.welcomesoapclient;
4
5   import com.deitel.welcomesoap.WelcomeSOAP;
6   import com.deitel.welcomesoap.WelcomeSOAPService;
7   import javax.swing.JOptionPane;
8
9   public class WelcomeSOAPClientJFrame extends javax.swing.JFrame
10  {
11     // references the service endpoint interface object (i.e., the proxy)
12     private WelcomeSOAP welcomeSOAPProxy;
13
14     // no-argument constructor
15     public WelcomeSOAPClientJFrame()
16     {
17        initComponents();
18
19        try
20        {
21           // create the objects for accessing the WelcomeSOAP web service
22           WelcomeSOAPService service = new WelcomeSOAPService();
23           welcomeSOAPProxy = service.getWelcomeSOAPPort();
24        } // end try
25        catch ( Exception exception )
26        {
27           exception.printStackTrace();
28           System.exit( 1 );
29        } // end catch
30     } // end WelcomeSOAPClientJFrame constructor
31
32     // The initComponents method is autogenerated by NetBeans and is called
33     // from the constructor to initialize the GUI. This method is not shown
34     // here to save space. Open WelcomeSOAPClientJFrame.java in this
35     // example's folder to view the complete generated code.
36
37     // call the web service with the supplied name and display the message
38     private void submitJButtonActionPerformed(
39        java.awt.event.ActionEvent evt )
40     {
41        String name = nameJTextField.getText(); // get name from JTextField
42
43        // retrieve the welcome string from the web service
44        String message = welcomeSOAPProxy.welcome( name );
```

Fig. 28.10 | Client desktop application for the WelcomeSOAP web service. (Part 1 of 2.)

```
45              JOptionPane.showMessageDialog( this, message,
46                 "Welcome", JOptionPane.INFORMATION_MESSAGE );
47          } // end method submitJButtonActionPerformed
48
49          // main method begins execution
50          public static void main( String args[] )
51          {
52             java.awt.EventQueue.invokeLater(
53                new Runnable()
54                {
55                   public void run()
56                   {
57                      new WelcomeSOAPClientJFrame().setVisible( true );
58                   } // end method run
59                } // end anonymous inner class
60             ); // end call to java.awt.EventQueue.invokeLater
61          } // end main
62
63          // Variables declaration - do not modify
64          private javax.swing.JLabel nameJLabel;
65          private javax.swing.JTextField nameJTextField;
66          private javax.swing.JButton submitJButton;
67          // End of variables declaration
68       } // end class WelcomeSOAPClientJFrame
```

Fig. 28.10 | Client desktop application for the WelcomeSOAP web service. (Part 2 of 2.)

Lines 5–6 import the classes WelcomeSOAP and WelcomeSOAPService that enable the client application to interact with the web service. Notice that we do not have import declarations for most of the GUI components used in this example. When you create a GUI in NetBeans, it uses fully qualified class names (such as javax.swing.JFrame in line 9), so import declarations are unnecessary.

Line 12 declares a variable of type WelcomeSOAP that will refer to the service endpoint interface object. Line 22 in the constructor creates an object of type WelcomeSOAPService. Line 23 uses this object's getWelcomeSOAPPort method to obtain the WelcomeSOAP service endpoint interface object that the application uses to invoke the web service's methods.

The event handler for the **Submit** button (lines 88–97) first retrieves the name the user entered from nameJTextField. It then calls the welcome method on the service endpoint interface object (line 94) to retrieve the welcome message from the web service. This object communicates with the web service on the client's behalf. Once the message has been retrieved, lines 95–96 display it in a message box by calling JOptionPane's showMessage-Dialog method.

28.7 Publishing and Consuming REST-Based XML Web Services

The previous section used a service endpoint interface (proxy) object to pass data to and from a Java web service using the SOAP protocol. Now, we access a Java web service using the REST architecture. We recreate the WelcomeSOAP example to return data in plain XML format. You can create a **Web Application** project as you did in Section 28.6 to begin. Name the project WelcomeRESTXML.

28.7.1 Creating a REST-Based XML Web Service

NetBeans provides various templates for creating RESTful web services, including ones that can interact with databases on the client's behalf. In this chapter, we focus on simple RESTful web services. To create a RESTful web service:

1. Right-click the **WelcomeRESTXML** node in the **Projects** tab, and select **New > Other...** to display the **New File** dialog.

2. Select **Web Services** under **Categories**, then select **RESTful Web Services from Patterns** and click **Next >**.

3. Under **Select Pattern**, ensure **Simple Root Resource** is selected, and click **Next >**.

4. Set the **Resource Package** to com.deitel.welcomerestxml, the **Path** to welcome and the **Class Name** to WelcomeRESTXMLResource. Leave the **MIME Type** and **Representation Class** set to application/xml and java.lang.String, respectively. The correct configuration is shown in Fig. 28.11.

5. Click **Finish** to create the web service.

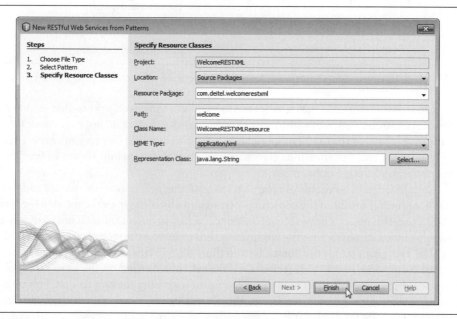

Fig. 28.11 | Creating the WelcomeRESTXML RESTful web service.

NetBeans generates the class and sets up the proper annotations. The class is placed in the project's **RESTful Web Services** folder. The code for the completed service is shown in Fig. 28.12. You'll notice that the completed code does not include some of the code generated by NetBeans. We removed the pieces that were unnecessary for this simple web service. The autogenerated putXml method is not necessary, because this example does not modify state on the server. The UriInfo instance variable is not needed, because we do not use HTTP query parameters. We also removed the autogenerated constructor, because we have no code to place in it.

```
 1   // Fig. 28.12: WelcomeRESTXMLResource.java
 2   // REST web service that returns a welcome message as XML.
 3   package com.deitel.welcomerestxml;
 4
 5   import java.io.StringWriter;
 6   import javax.ws.rs.GET; // annotation to indicate method uses HTTP GET
 7   import javax.ws.rs.Path; // annotation to specify path of resource
 8   import javax.ws.rs.PathParam; // annotation to get parameters from URI
 9   import javax.ws.rs.Produces; // annotation to specify type of data
10   import javax.xml.bind.JAXB; // utility class for common JAXB operations
11
12   @Path( "welcome" ) // URI used to access the resource
13   public class WelcomeRESTXMLResource
14   {
15      // retrieve welcome message
16      @GET // handles HTTP GET requests
17      @Path( "{name}" ) // URI component containing parameter
18      @Produces( "application/xml" ) // response formatted as XML
19      public String getXml( @PathParam( "name" ) String name )
20      {
21         String message = "Welcome to JAX-RS web services with REST and " +
22            "XML, " + name + "!"; // our welcome message
23         StringWriter writer = new StringWriter();
24         JAXB.marshal( message, writer ); // marshal String as XML
25         return writer.toString(); // return XML as String
26      } // end method getXml
27   } // end class WelcomeRESTXMLResource
```

Fig. 28.12 | REST web service that returns a welcome message as XML.

Lines 6–9 contain the imports for the JAX-RS annotations that help define the RESTful web service. The **@Path annotation** on the WelcomeRESTXMLResource class (line 12) indicates the URI for accessing the web service. This URI is appended to the web application project's URL to invoke the service. Methods of the class can also use the @Path annotation (line 17). Parts of the path specified in curly braces indicate parameters—they're placeholders for values that are passed to the web service as part of the path. The base path for the service is the project's resources directory. For example, to get a welcome message for someone named John, the complete URL is

```
http://localhost:8080/WelcomeRESTXML/resources/welcome/John
```

Arguments in a URL can be used as arguments to a web service method. To do so, you bind the parameters specified in the @Path specification to parameters of the web service method with the **@PathParam annotation,** as shown in line 19. When the request is received, the server passes the argument(s) in the URL to the appropriate parameter(s) in the web service method.

The **@GET annotation** denotes that this method is accessed via an HTTP GET request. The putXml method the IDE created for us had an @PUT annotation, which indicates that the method is accessed using the HTTP PUT method. Similar annotations exist for HTTP POST, DELETE and HEAD requests.

The **@Produces annotation** denotes the content type returned to the client. It's possible to have multiple methods with the same HTTP method and path but different @Produces annotations, and JAX-RS will call the method matching the content type requested by the client. Standard Java method overloading rules apply, so such methods must have different names. The **@Consumes annotation** for the autogenerated putXml method (which we deleted) restricts the content type that the web service will accept from a PUT operation.

Line 10 imports the **JAXB class** from package javax.xml.bind. **JAXB (Java Architecture for XML Binding)** is a set of classes for converting POJOs to and from XML. There are many related classes in the same package that implement the serializations we perform, but the JAXB class contains easy-to-use wrappers for common operations. After creating the welcome message (lines 21–22), we create a StringWriter (line 23) to which JAXB will output the XML. Line 24 calls the JAXB class's static method **marshal** to convert the String containing our message to XML format. Line 25 calls StringWriter's toString method to retrieve the XML text to return to the client.

Testing RESTful Web Services
Section 28.6.4 demonstrated testing a SOAP service using GlassFish's Tester page. Glass-Fish does not provide a testing facility for RESTful services, but NetBeans automatically generates a test page that can be accessed by right clicking the **WelcomeRESTXML** node in the **Projects** tab and selecting **Test RESTful Web Services.** This will compile and deploy the web service, if you have not yet done so, then open the test page. Your browser will probably require you to acknowledge a potential security issue before allowing the test page to perform its tasks. The test page is loaded from your computer's local file system, *not* the GlassFish server. Browsers consider the local file system and GlassFish as two different servers, even though they're both on the local computer. For security reasons, browsers do not allow so-called cross-site scripting in which a web page tries to interact with a server other than the one that served the page.

On the test page (Fig. 28.13), expand the **welcome** element in the left column and select **{name}.** The form on the right side of the page allows you to choose the MIME type of the data (application/xml by default) and lets you enter the name parameter's value. Click the **Test** button to invoke the web service and display the returned XML.

> **Error-Prevention Tip 28.1**
> *At the time of this writing, the test page did not work in Google's Chrome web browser. If this is your default web browser, copy the test page's URL from Chrome's address field and paste it into another web browser's address field. Fig. 28.13 shows the test page in Mozilla Firefox.*

The test page shows several tabs containing the results and various other information. The **Raw View** tab shows the actual XML response. The **Headers** tab shows the HTTP

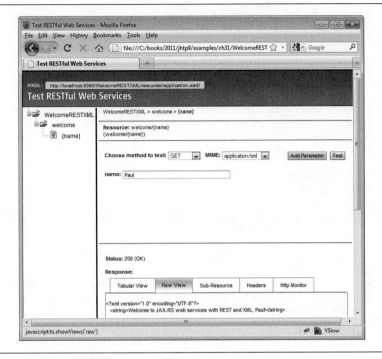

Fig. 28.13 | Test page for the WelcomeRESTXML web service.

headers returned by the server. The **Http Monitor** tab shows a log of the HTTP transactions that took place to complete the request and response. The Sub-Resource tab shows the actual URL that was used to invoke the web service

```
http://localhost:8080/WelcomeRESTXML/resources/welcome/Paul
```

You can enter this URL in any browser on your computer to invoke the web service with the value Paul.

The test page provides its functionality by reading a WADL file from the server—you can see the URL of the WADL file in the upper-left corner of the test page. **WADL (Web Application Description Language)** has similar design goals to WSDL, but describes RESTful services instead of SOAP services.

28.7.2 Consuming a REST-Based XML Web Service

As we did with SOAP, we create a Java application that retrieves the welcome message from the web service and displays it to the user. First, create a Java application with the name WelcomeRESTXMLClient. RESTful web services do *not* require web service references, so you can begin building the GUI immediately by creating a JFrame form called WelcomeRESTXMLClientJFrame and placing it in the com.deitel.welcomerestxmlclient package. The GUI is identical to the one in Fig. 28.10, including the names of the GUI elements. To create the GUI quickly, you can simply copy and paste the GUI from the **Design** view of the WelcomeSOAPClientJFrame class and paste it into the **Design** view of the WelcomeRESTXMLClientJFrame class. Figure 28.14 contains the completed code.

```
 1   // Fig. 28.14: WelcomeRESTXMLClientJFrame.java
 2   // Client that consumes the WelcomeRESTXML service.
 3   package com.deitel.welcomerestxmlclient;
 4
 5   import javax.swing.JOptionPane;
 6   import javax.xml.bind.JAXB; // utility class for common JAXB operations
 7
 8   public class WelcomeRESTXMLClientJFrame extends javax.swing.JFrame
 9   {
10      // no-argument constructor
11      public WelcomeRESTXMLClientJFrame()
12      {
13         initComponents();
14      } // end constructor
15
16      // The initComponents method is autogenerated by NetBeans and is called
17      // from the constructor to initialize the GUI. This method is not shown
18      // here to save space. Open WelcomeRESTXMLClientJFrame.java in this
19      // example's folder to view the complete generated code.
20
21      // call the web service with the supplied name and display the message
22      private void submitJButtonActionPerformed(
23         java.awt.event.ActionEvent evt)
24      {
25         String name = nameJTextField.getText(); // get name from JTextField
26
27         // the URL for the REST service
28         String url =
29            "http://localhost:8080/WelcomeRESTXML/resources/welcome/" + name;
30
31         // read from URL and convert from XML to Java String
32         String message = JAXB.unmarshal( url, String.class );
33
34         // display the message to the user
35         JOptionPane.showMessageDialog( this, message,
36            "Welcome", JOptionPane.INFORMATION_MESSAGE );
37      } // end method submitJButtonActionPerformed
38
39      // main method begins execution
40      public static void main( String args[] )
41      {
42         java.awt.EventQueue.invokeLater(
43            new Runnable()
44            {
45               public void run()
46               {
47                  new WelcomeRESTXMLClientJFrame().setVisible( true );
48               } // end method run
49            } // end anonymous inner class
50         ); // end call to java.awt.EventQueue.invokeLater
51      } // end main
52
```

Fig. 28.14 | Client that consumes the WelcomeRESTXML service. (Part 1 of 2.)

```
53        // Variables declaration - do not modify
54        private javax.swing.JLabel nameJLabel;
55        private javax.swing.JTextField nameJTextField;
56        private javax.swing.JButton submitJButton;
57        // End of variables declaration
58    } // end class WelcomeRESTXMLClientJFrame
```

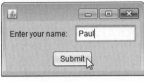
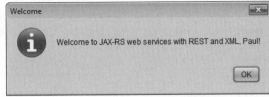

Fig. 28.14 | Client that consumes the WelcomeRESTXML service. (Part 2 of 2.)

You can access a RESTful web service with classes from Java API. As in the RESTful XML web service, we use the JAXB library. The JAXB class (imported on line 6) has a static **unmarshal** method that takes as arguments a file name or URL as a String, and a Class<T> object indicating the Java class to which the XML will be converted (line 82). In this example, the XML contains a String object, so we use the Java compiler shortcut String.class to create the Class<String> object we need as the second argument. The String returned from the call to the unmarshal method is then displayed to the user via JOptionPane's showMessageDialog method (lines 85–86), as it was with the SOAP service. The URL used in this example to extract data from the web service matches the URL used by the test page.

28.8 Publishing and Consuming REST-Based JSON Web Services

While XML was designed primarily as a document interchange format, JSON is designed as a *data* exchange format. Data structures in most programming languages do not map directly to XML constructs—for example, the distinction between elements and attributes is not present in programming-language data structures. JSON is a subset of the JavaScript programming language, and its components—objects, arrays, strings, numbers—can be easily mapped to constructs in Java and other programming languages.

The standard Java libraries do not currently provide capabilities for working with JSON, but there are many open-source JSON libraries for Java and other languages; you can find a list of them at json.org. We chose the Gson library from code.google.com/p/google-gson/, which provides a simple way to convert POJOs to and from JSON.

28.8.1 Creating a REST-Based JSON Web Service

To begin, create a WelcomeRESTJSON web application, then create the web service by following the steps in Section 28.7.1. In *Step 4*, change the **Resource Package** to com.deitel.welcomerestjson, the **Class Name** to WelcomeRESTJSONResource and the **MIME Type** to application/json. Additionally, you must download the Gson library's JAR file, then add it to the project as a library. To do so, right click your project's **Libraries** folder, select **Add JAR/Folder...** locate the downloaded Gson JAR file and click **Open**. The complete code for the service is shown in Fig. 28.15.

```java
 1   // Fig. 28.15: WelcomeRESTJSONResource.java
 2   // REST web service that returns a welcome message as JSON.
 3   package com.deitel.welcomerestjson;
 4
 5   import com.google.gson.Gson; // converts POJO to JSON and back again
 6   import javax.ws.rs.GET; // annotation to indicate method uses HTTP GET
 7   import javax.ws.rs.Path; // annotation to specify path of resource
 8   import javax.ws.rs.PathParam; // annotation to get parameters from URI
 9   import javax.ws.rs.Produces; // annotation to specify type of data
10
11   @Path( "welcome" ) // path used to access the resource
12   public class WelcomeRESTJSONResource
13   {
14      // retrieve welcome message
15      @GET // handles HTTP GET requests
16      @Path( "{name}" ) // takes name as a path parameter
17      @Produces( "application/json" ) // response formatted as JSON
18      public String getJson( @PathParam( "name" ) String name )
19      {
20         // add welcome message to field of TextMessage object
21         TextMessage message = new TextMessage(); // create wrapper object
22         message.setMessage( String.format( "%s, %s!",
23            "Welcome to JAX-RS web services with REST and JSON", name ) );
24
25         return new Gson().toJson( message ); // return JSON-wrapped message
26      } // end method getJson
27   } // end class WelcomeRESTJSONResource
28
29   // private class that contains the message we wish to send
30   class TextMessage
31   {
32      private String message; // message we're sending
33
34      // returns the message
35      public String getMessage()
36      {
37         return message;
38      } // end method getMessage
39
40      // sets the message
41      public void setMessage( String value )
42      {
43         message = value;
44      } // end method setMessage
45   } // end class TextMessage
```

Fig. 28.15 | REST web service that returns a welcome message as JSON.

All the annotations and the basic structure of the WelcomeRESTJSONResource class are the same as REST XML example. The argument to the @Produces attribute (line 17) is "application/json". The TextMessage class (lines 30–45) addresses a difference between JSON and XML. JSON does not permit strings or numbers to stand on their own—they must be encapsulated in a composite data type. So, we created class TextMessage to encapsulate the String representing the message.

When a client invokes this web service, line 21 creates the TextMessage object, then lines 22–23 set its contained message. Next, line 25 creates a **Gson** object (from package com.google.gson.Gson) and calls its **toJson** method to convert the TextMessage into its JSON String representation. We return this String, which is then sent back to the client in the web service's response. There are multiple overloads of the toJson method, such as one that sends its output to a Writer instead of returning a String.

RESTful services returning JSON can be tested in the same way as those returning XML. Follow the procedure outlined in Section 28.7.1, but be sure to change the MIME type to application/json in the test web page; otherwise, the web service will return an error stating that it cannot produce the desired response.

28.8.2 Consuming a REST-Based JSON Web Service

We now create a Java application that retrieves the welcome message from the web service and displays it to the user. First, create a Java application with the name WelcomeREST-JSONClient. Then, create a JFrame form called WelcomeRESTXMLClientJFrame and place it in the com.deitel.welcomerestjsonclient package. The GUI is identical to the one in Fig. 28.10. To create the GUI quickly, copy it from the **Design** view of the Welcome-SOAPClientJFrame class and paste it into the **Design** view of the WelcomeRESTJSONClient-JFrame class. Figure 28.16 contains the completed code.

```java
1   // Fig. 28.16: WelcomeRESTJSONClientJFrame.java
2   // Client that consumes the WelcomeRESTJSON service.
3   package com.deitel.welcomerestjsonclient;
4
5   import com.google.gson.Gson; // converts POJO to JSON and back again
6   import java.io.InputStreamReader;
7   import java.net.URL;
8   import javax.swing.JOptionPane;
9
10  public class WelcomeRESTJSONClientJFrame extends javax.swing.JFrame
11  {
12     // no-argument constructor
13     public WelcomeRESTJSONClientJFrame()
14     {
15        initComponents();
16     } // end constructor
17
18     // The initComponents method is autogenerated by NetBeans and is called
19     // from the constructor to initialize the GUI. This method is not shown
20     // here to save space. Open WelcomeRESTJSONClientJFrame.java in this
21     // example's folder to view the complete generated code.
22
```

Fig. 28.16 | Client that consumes the WelcomeRESTJSON service. (Part 1 of 3.)

```
23      // call the web service with the supplied name and display the message
24      private void submitJButtonActionPerformed(
25         java.awt.event.ActionEvent evt )
26      {
27         String name = nameJTextField.getText(); // get name from JTextField
28
29         // retrieve the welcome string from the web service
30         try
31         {
32            // the URL of the web service
33            String url = "http://localhost:8080/WelcomeRESTJSON/" +
34               "resources/welcome/" + name;
35
36            // open URL, using a Reader to convert bytes to chars
37            InputStreamReader reader =
38               new InputStreamReader( new URL( url ).openStream() );
39
40            // parse the JSON back into a TextMessage
41            TextMessage message =
42               new Gson().fromJson( reader, TextMessage.class );
43
44            // display message to the user
45            JOptionPane.showMessageDialog( this, message.getMessage(),
46               "Welcome", JOptionPane.INFORMATION_MESSAGE );
47         } // end try
48         catch ( Exception exception )
49         {
50            exception.printStackTrace(); // show exception details
51         } // end catch
52      } // end method submitJButtonActionPerformed
53
54      // main method begin execution
55      public static void main( String args[] )
56      {
57         java.awt.EventQueue.invokeLater(
58            new Runnable()
59            {
60               public void run()
61               {
62                  new WelcomeRESTJSONClientJFrame().setVisible( true );
63               } // end method run
64            } // end anonymous inner class
65         ); // end call to java.awt.EventQueue.invokeLater
66      } // end main
67
68      // Variables declaration - do not modify
69      private javax.swing.JLabel nameJLabel;
70      private javax.swing.JTextField nameJTextField;
71      private javax.swing.JButton submitJButton;
72      // End of variables declaration
73   } // end class WelcomeRESTJSONClientJFrame
74
```

Fig. 28.16 | Client that consumes the WelcomeRESTJSON service. (Part 2 of 3.)

```
75   // private class that contains the message we are receiving
76   class TextMessage
77   {
78      private String message; // message we're receiving
79
80      // returns the message
81      public String getMessage()
82      {
83         return message;
84      } // end method getMessage
85
86      // sets the message
87      public void setMessage( String value )
88      {
89         message = value;
90      } // end method setMessage
91   } // end class TextMessage
```

Fig. 28.16 | Client that consumes the WelcomeRESTJSON service. (Part 3 of 3.)

Lines 83–84 create the URL String that is used to invoke the web service. Lines 87–88 create a URL object using this String, then call the URL's **openStream** method to invoke the web service and obtain an InputStream from which the client can read the response. The InputStream is wrapped in an InputStreamReader so it can be passed as the first argument to the Gson class's **fromJson** method. This method is overloaded. The version we use takes as arguments a Reader from which to read a JSON String and a Class<T> object indicating the Java class to which the JSON String will be converted (line 92). In this example, the JSON String contains a TextMessage object, so we use the Java compiler shortcut TextMessage.class to create the Class<TextMessage> object we need as the second argument. Lines 95–96 display the message in the TextMessage object.

The TextMessage classes in the web service and client are unrelated. Technically, the client can be written in any programming language, so the manner in which a response is processed can vary greatly. Since our client is written in Java, we duplicated the TextMessage class in the client so we could easily convert the JSON object back to Java.

28.9 Session Tracking in a SOAP Web Service

Section 26.8 described the advantages of using session tracking to maintain client-state information so you can personalize the users' browsing experiences. Now we'll incorporate *session tracking* into a web service. Suppose a client application needs to call several methods from the same web service, possibly several times each. In such a case, it can be beneficial for the web service to maintain state information for the client, thus eliminating the need for client information to be passed between the client and the web service multiple times. For example, a web service that provides local restaurant reviews could store the client user's street address during the initial request, then use it to return personalized, localized results in subsequent requests. Storing session information also enables a web service to distinguish between clients.

28.9.1 Creating a Blackjack Web Service

Our next example is a web service that assists you in developing a blackjack card game. The Blackjack web service (Fig. 28.17) provides web methods to shuffle a deck of cards, deal a card from the deck and evaluate a hand of cards. After presenting the web service, we use it to serve as the dealer for a game of blackjack (Fig. 28.18). The Blackjack web service uses an HttpSession object to maintain a unique deck of cards for each client application. Several clients can use the service at the same time, but web method calls made by a specific client use only the deck of cards stored in that client's session. Our example uses the following blackjack rules:

> *Two cards each are dealt to the dealer and the player. The player's cards are dealt face up. Only the first of the dealer's cards is dealt face up. Each card has a value. A card numbered 2 through 10 is worth its face value. Jacks, queens and kings each count as 10. Aces can count as 1 or 11—whichever value is more beneficial to the player (as we'll soon see). If the sum of the player's two initial cards is 21 (i.e., the player was dealt a card valued at 10 and an ace, which counts as 11 in this situation), the player has "blackjack" and immediately wins the game—if the dealer does not also have blackjack (which would result in a "push"—i.e., a tie). Otherwise, the player can begin taking additional cards one at a time. These cards are dealt face up, and the player decides when to stop taking cards. If the player "busts" (i.e., the sum of the player's cards exceeds 21), the game is over, and the player loses. When the player is satisfied with the current set of cards, the player "stands" (i.e., stops taking cards), and the dealer's hidden card is revealed. If the dealer's total is 16 or less, the dealer must take another card; otherwise, the dealer must stand. The dealer must continue taking cards until the sum of the dealer's cards is greater than or equal to 17. If the dealer exceeds 21, the player wins. Otherwise, the hand with the higher point total wins. If the dealer and the player have the same point total, the game is a "push," and no one wins. The value of an ace for a dealer depends on the dealer's other card(s) and the casino's house rules. A dealer typically must hit for totals of 16 or less and must stand for totals of 17 or more. However, for a "soft 17"—a hand with a total of 17 with one ace counted as 11—some casinos require the dealer to hit and some require the dealer to stand (we require the dealer to stand). Such a hand is known as a "soft 17" because taking another card cannot bust the hand.*

The web service (Fig. 28.17) stores each card as a String consisting of a number, 1–13, representing the card's face (ace through king, respectively), followed by a space and a digit, 0–3, representing the card's suit (hearts, diamonds, clubs or spades, respectively). For example, the jack of clubs is represented as "11 2" and the two of hearts as "2 0". To create and deploy this web service, follow the steps that we presented in Sections 28.6.2–28.6.3 for the WelcomeSOAP service.

```
1   // Fig. 28.17: Blackjack.java
2   // Blackjack web service that deals cards and evaluates hands
3   package com.deitel.blackjack;
4
5   import com.sun.xml.ws.developer.servlet.HttpSessionScope;
6   import java.util.ArrayList;
7   import java.util.Random;
```

Fig. 28.17 | Blackjack web service that deals cards and evaluates hands. (Part 1 of 3.)

```
 8   import javax.jws.WebMethod;
 9   import javax.jws.WebParam;
10   import javax.jws.WebService;
11
12   @HttpSessionScope // enable web service to maintain session state
13   @WebService()
14   public class Blackjack
15   {
16      private ArrayList< String > deck; // deck of cards for one user session
17      private static final Random randomObject = new Random();
18
19      // deal one card
20      @WebMethod( operationName = "dealCard" )
21      public String dealCard()
22      {
23         String card = "";
24         card = deck.get( 0 ); // get top card of deck
25         deck.remove( 0 ); // remove top card of deck
26         return card;
27      } // end WebMethod dealCard
28
29      // shuffle the deck
30      @WebMethod( operationName = "shuffle" )
31      public void shuffle()
32      {
33         // create new deck when shuffle is called
34         deck = new ArrayList< String >();
35
36         // populate deck of cards
37         for ( int face = 1; face <= 13; face++ ) // loop through faces
38            for ( int suit = 0; suit <= 3; suit++ ) // loop through suits
39               deck.add( face + " " + suit ); // add each card to deck
40
41         String tempCard; // holds card temporarily during swapping
42         int index; // index of randomly selected card
43
44         for ( int i = 0; i < deck.size() ; i++ ) // shuffle
45         {
46            index = randomObject.nextInt( deck.size() - 1 );
47
48            // swap card at position i with randomly selected card
49            tempCard = deck.get( i );
50            deck.set( i, deck.get( index ) );
51            deck.set( index, tempCard );
52         } // end for
53      } // end WebMethod shuffle
54
55      // determine a hand's value
56      @WebMethod( operationName = "getHandValue" )
57      public int getHandValue( @WebParam( name = "hand" ) String hand )
58      {
59         // split hand into cards
60         String[] cards = hand.split( "\t" );
```

Fig. 28.17 | Blackjack web service that deals cards and evaluates hands. (Part 2 of 3.)

```
61        int total = 0; // total value of cards in hand
62        int face; // face of current card
63        int aceCount = 0; // number of aces in hand
64
65        for ( int i = 0; i < cards.length; i++ )
66        {
67           // parse string and get first int in String
68           face = Integer.parseInt(
69              cards[ i ].substring( 0, cards[ i ].indexOf( " " ) ) );
70
71           switch ( face )
72           {
73              case 1: // if ace, increment aceCount
74                 ++aceCount;
75                 break;
76              case 11: // jack
77              case 12: // queen
78              case 13: // king
79                 total += 10;
80                 break;
81              default: // otherwise, add face
82                 total += face;
83                 break;
84           } // end switch
85        } // end for
86
87        // calculate optimal use of aces
88        if ( aceCount > 0 )
89        {
90           // if possible, count one ace as 11
91           if ( total + 11 + aceCount - 1 <= 21 )
92              total += 11 + aceCount - 1;
93           else // otherwise, count all aces as 1
94              total += aceCount;
95        } // end if
96
97        return total;
98     } // end WebMethod getHandValue
99  } // end class Blackjack
```

Fig. 28.17 | Blackjack web service that deals cards and evaluates hands. (Part 3 of 3.)

Session Tracking in Web Services: @HttpSessionScope Annotation

In JAX-WS 2.2, it's easy to enable session tracking in a web service. You simply precede your web service class with the **@HttpSessionScope annotation**. This annotation is located in package com.sun.xml.ws.developer.servlet. To use this package you must add the JAX-WS 2.2 library to your project. To do so, right click the **Libraries** node in your Blackjack web application project and select **Add Library...**. Then, in the dialog that appears, locate and select **JAX-WS 2.2**, then click **Add Library**. Once a web service is annotated with @HttpSessionScope, the server automatically maintains a separate instance of the class for each client session. Thus, the deck instance variable (line 16) will be maintained separately for each client.

Client Interactions with the **Blackjack** *Web Service*
A client first calls the **Blackjack** web service's **shuffle** web method (lines 30–53) to create a new deck of cards (line 34), populate it (lines 37–39) and shuffle it (lines 41–52). Lines 37–39 generate **Strings** in the form "*face suit*" to represent each possible card in the deck.

Lines 20–27 define the **dealCard** web method. Method **shuffle** *must* be called before method **dealCard** is called the first time for a client—otherwise, deck could be **null**. The method gets the top card from the deck (line 24), removes it from the deck (line 25) and returns the card's value as a **String** (line 26). Without using session tracking, the deck of cards would need to be passed back and forth with each method call. Session tracking makes the **dealCard** method easy to call (it requires no arguments) and eliminates the overhead of sending the deck over the network multiple times.

Method **getHandValue** (lines 56–98) determines the total value of the cards in a hand by trying to attain the highest score possible without going over 21. Recall that an ace can be counted as either 1 or 11, and all face cards count as 10. This method does not use the **session** object, because the deck of cards is not used in this method.

As you'll soon see, the client application maintains a hand of cards as a **String** in which each card is separated by a tab character. Line 60 splits the hand of cards (represented by **hand**) into individual cards by calling **String** method **split** and passing to it a **String** containing the delimiter characters (in this case, just a tab). Method **split** uses the delimiter characters to separate tokens in the **String**. Lines 65–85 count the value of each card. Lines 68–69 retrieve the first integer—the face—and use that value in the **switch** statement (lines 71–84). If the card is an ace, the method increments variable **aceCount**. We discuss how this variable is used shortly. If the card is an 11, 12 or 13 (jack, queen or king), the method adds 10 to the total value of the hand (line 79). If the card is anything else, the method increases the total by that value (line 82).

Because an ace can have either of two values, additional logic is required to process aces. Lines 88–95 process the aces after all the other cards. If a hand contains several aces, only one ace can be counted as 11. The condition in line 91 determines whether counting one ace as 11 and the rest as 1 will result in a total that does not exceed 21. If this is possible, line 92 adjusts the total accordingly. Otherwise, line 94 adjusts the total, counting each ace as 1.

Method **getHandValue** maximizes the value of the current cards without exceeding 21. Imagine, for example, that the dealer has a 7 and receives an ace. The new total could be either 8 or 18. However, **getHandValue** always maximizes the value of the cards without going over 21, so the new total is 18.

28.9.2 Consuming the **Blackjack** Web Service

The blackjack application in Fig. 28.18 keeps track of the player's and dealer's cards, and the web service tracks the cards that have been dealt. The constructor (lines 34–83) sets up the GUI (line 36), changes the window's background color (line 40) and creates the **Blackjack** web service's service endpoint interface object (lines 46–47). In the GUI, each player has 11 **JLabels**—the maximum number of cards that can be dealt without automatically exceeding 21 (i.e., four aces, four twos and three threes). These **JLabels** are placed in an **ArrayList** of **JLabels** (lines 59–82), so we can index the **ArrayList** during the game to determine the **JLabel** that will display a particular card image.

```
 1    // Fig. 28.18: BlackjackGameJFrame.java
 2    // Blackjack game that uses the Blackjack Web Service.
 3    package com.deitel.blackjackclient;
 4
 5    import com.deitel.blackjack.Blackjack;
 6    import com.deitel.blackjack.BlackjackService;
 7    import java.awt.Color;
 8    import java.util.ArrayList;
 9    import javax.swing.ImageIcon;
10    import javax.swing.JLabel;
11    import javax.swing.JOptionPane;
12    import javax.xml.ws.BindingProvider;
13
14    public class BlackjackGameJFrame extends javax.swing.JFrame
15    {
16       private String playerCards;
17       private String dealerCards;
18       private ArrayList<JLabel> cardboxes; // list of card image JLabels
19       private int currentPlayerCard; // player's current card number
20       private int currentDealerCard; // blackjackProxy's current card number
21       private BlackjackService blackjackService; // used to obtain proxy
22       private Blackjack blackjackProxy; // used to access the web service
23
24       // enumeration of game states
25       private enum GameStatus
26       {
27          PUSH, // game ends in a tie
28          LOSE, // player loses
29          WIN, // player wins
30          BLACKJACK // player has blackjack
31       } // end enum GameStatus
32
33       // no-argument constructor
34       public BlackjackGameJFrame()
35       {
36          initComponents();
37
38          // due to a bug in NetBeans, we must change the JFrame's background
39          // color here rather than in the designer
40          getContentPane().setBackground( new Color( 0, 180, 0 ) );
41
42          // initialize the blackjack proxy
43          try
44          {
45             // create the objects for accessing the Blackjack web service
46             blackjackService = new BlackjackService();
47             blackjackProxy = blackjackService.getBlackjackPort();
48
49             // enable session tracking
50             ( (BindingProvider) blackjackProxy ).getRequestContext().put(
51                BindingProvider.SESSION_MAINTAIN_PROPERTY, true );
52          } // end try
```

Fig. 28.18 | Blackjack game that uses the Blackjack web service. (Part 1 of 10.)

```
53              catch ( Exception e )
54              {
55                 e.printStackTrace();
56              } // end catch
57
58              // add JLabels to cardBoxes ArrayList for programmatic manipulation
59              cardboxes = new ArrayList<JLabel>();
60
61              cardboxes.add( dealerCard1JLabel );
62              cardboxes.add( dealerCard2JLabel );
63              cardboxes.add( dealerCard3JLabel );
64              cardboxes.add( dealerCard4JLabel );
65              cardboxes.add( dealerCard5JLabel );
66              cardboxes.add( dealerCard6JLabel );
67              cardboxes.add( dealerCard7JLabel );
68              cardboxes.add( dealerCard8JLabel );
69              cardboxes.add( dealerCard9JLabel );
70              cardboxes.add( dealerCard10JLabel );
71              cardboxes.add( dealerCard11JLabel );
72              cardboxes.add( playerCard1JLabel );
73              cardboxes.add( playerCard2JLabel );
74              cardboxes.add( playerCard3JLabel );
75              cardboxes.add( playerCard4JLabel );
76              cardboxes.add( playerCard5JLabel );
77              cardboxes.add( playerCard6JLabel );
78              cardboxes.add( playerCard7JLabel );
79              cardboxes.add( playerCard8JLabel );
80              cardboxes.add( playerCard9JLabel );
81              cardboxes.add( playerCard10JLabel );
82              cardboxes.add( playerCard11JLabel );
83           } // end constructor
84
85           // play the dealer's hand
86           private void dealerPlay()
87           {
88              try
89              {
90                 // while the value of the dealers's hand is below 17
91                 // the dealer must continue to take cards
92                 String[] cards = dealerCards.split( "\t" );
93
94                 // display dealer's cards
95                 for ( int i = 0; i < cards.length; i++ )
96                 {
97                    displayCard( i, cards[i] );
98                 }
99
100                while ( blackjackProxy.getHandValue( dealerCards ) < 17 )
101                {
102                   String newCard = blackjackProxy.dealCard(); // deal new card
103                   dealerCards += "\t" + newCard; // deal new card
104                   displayCard( currentDealerCard, newCard );
```

Fig. 28.18 | Blackjack game that uses the Blackjack web service. (Part 2 of 10.)

```
105                    ++currentDealerCard;
106                    JOptionPane.showMessageDialog( this, "Dealer takes a card",
107                       "Dealer's turn", JOptionPane.PLAIN_MESSAGE );
108                 } // end while
109
110                 int dealersTotal = blackjackProxy.getHandValue( dealerCards );
111                 int playersTotal = blackjackProxy.getHandValue( playerCards );
112
113                 // if dealer busted, player wins
114                 if ( dealersTotal > 21 )
115                 {
116                    gameOver( GameStatus.WIN );
117                    return;
118                 } // end if
119
120                 // if dealer and player are below 21
121                 // higher score wins, equal scores is a push
122                 if ( dealersTotal > playersTotal )
123                 {
124                    gameOver( GameStatus.LOSE );
125                 }
126                 else if ( dealersTotal < playersTotal )
127                 {
128                    gameOver( GameStatus.WIN );
129                 }
130                 else
131                 {
132                    gameOver( GameStatus.PUSH );
133                 }
134              } // end try
135              catch ( Exception e )
136              {
137                 e.printStackTrace();
138              } // end catch
139           } // end method dealerPlay
140
141           // displays the card represented by cardValue in specified JLabel
142           private void displayCard( int card, String cardValue )
143           {
144              try
145              {
146                 // retrieve correct JLabel from cardBoxes
147                 JLabel displayLabel = cardboxes.get( card );
148
149                 // if string representing card is empty, display back of card
150                 if ( cardValue.equals( "" ) )
151                 {
152                    displayLabel.setIcon( new ImageIcon( getClass().getResource(
153                       "/com/deitel/java/blackjackclient/" +
154                       "blackjack_images/cardback.png" ) ) );
155                    return;
156                 } // end if
```

Fig. 28.18 | Blackjack game that uses the Blackjack web service. (Part 3 of 10.)

```
157
158            // retrieve the face value of the card
159            String face = cardValue.substring( 0, cardValue.indexOf( " " ) );
160
161            // retrieve the suit of the card
162            String suit =
163               cardValue.substring( cardValue.indexOf( " " ) + 1 );
164
165            char suitLetter; // suit letter used to form image file
166
167            switch ( Integer.parseInt( suit ) )
168            {
169               case 0: // hearts
170                  suitLetter = 'h';
171                  break;
172               case 1: // diamonds
173                  suitLetter = 'd';
174                  break;
175               case 2: // clubs
176                  suitLetter = 'c';
177                  break;
178               default: // spades
179                  suitLetter = 's';
180                  break;
181            } // end switch
182
183            // set image for displayLabel
184            displayLabel.setIcon( new ImageIcon( getClass().getResource(
185               "/com/deitel/java/blackjackclient/blackjack_images/" +
186               face + suitLetter + ".png" ) ) );
187         } // end try
188         catch ( Exception e )
189         {
190            e.printStackTrace();
191         } // end catch
192      } // end method displayCard
193
194      // displays all player cards and shows appropriate message
195      private void gameOver( GameStatus winner )
196      {
197         String[] cards = dealerCards.split( "\t" );
198
199         // display blackjackProxy's cards
200         for ( int i = 0; i < cards.length; i++ )
201         {
202            displayCard( i, cards[i] );
203         }
204
205         // display appropriate status image
206         if ( winner == GameStatus.WIN )
207         {
208            statusJLabel.setText( "You win!" );
209         }
```

Fig. 28.18 | Blackjack game that uses the Blackjack web service. (Part 4 of 10.)

```
210        else if ( winner == GameStatus.LOSE )
211        {
212           statusJLabel.setText( "You lose." );
213        }
214        else if ( winner == GameStatus.PUSH )
215        {
216           statusJLabel.setText( "It's a push." );
217        }
218        else // blackjack
219        {
220           statusJLabel.setText( "Blackjack!" );
221        }
222
223        // display final scores
224        int dealersTotal = blackjackProxy.getHandValue( dealerCards );
225        int playersTotal = blackjackProxy.getHandValue( playerCards );
226        dealerTotalJLabel.setText( "Dealer: " + dealersTotal );
227        playerTotalJLabel.setText( "Player: " + playersTotal );
228
229        // reset for new game
230        standJButton.setEnabled( false );
231        hitJButton.setEnabled( false );
232        dealJButton.setEnabled( true );
233     } // end method gameOver
234
235     // The initComponents method is autogenerated by NetBeans and is called
236     // from the constructor to initialize the GUI. This method is not shown
237     // here to save space. Open BlackjackGameJFrame.java in this
238     // example's folder to view the complete generated code
239
240     // handles dealJButton click
241     private void dealJButtonActionPerformed(
242        java.awt.event.ActionEvent evt )
243     {
244        String card; // stores a card temporarily until it's added to a hand
245
246        // clear card images
247        for ( int i = 0; i < cardboxes.size(); i++ )
248        {
249           cardboxes.get( i ).setIcon( null );
250        }
251
252        statusJLabel.setText( "" );
253        dealerTotalJLabel.setText( "" );
254        playerTotalJLabel.setText( "" );
255
256        // create a new, shuffled deck on remote machine
257        blackjackProxy.shuffle();
258
259        // deal two cards to player
260        playerCards = blackjackProxy.dealCard(); // add first card to hand
261        displayCard( 11, playerCards ); // display first card
262        card = blackjackProxy.dealCard(); // deal second card
```

Fig. 28.18 | Blackjack game that uses the Blackjack web service. (Part 5 of 10.)

```
263        displayCard( 12, card ); // display second card
264        playerCards += "\t" + card; // add second card to hand
265
266        // deal two cards to blackjackProxy, but only show first
267        dealerCards = blackjackProxy.dealCard(); // add first card to hand
268        displayCard( 0, dealerCards ); // display first card
269        card = blackjackProxy.dealCard(); // deal second card
270        displayCard( 1, "" ); // display back of card
271        dealerCards += "\t" + card; // add second card to hand
272
273        standJButton.setEnabled( true );
274        hitJButton.setEnabled( true );
275        dealJButton.setEnabled( false );
276
277        // determine the value of the two hands
278        int dealersTotal = blackjackProxy.getHandValue( dealerCards );
279        int playersTotal = blackjackProxy.getHandValue( playerCards );
280
281        // if hands both equal 21, it is a push
282        if ( playersTotal == dealersTotal && playersTotal == 21 )
283        {
284           gameOver( GameStatus.PUSH );
285        }
286        else if ( dealersTotal == 21 ) // blackjackProxy has blackjack
287        {
288           gameOver( GameStatus.LOSE );
289        }
290        else if ( playersTotal == 21 ) // blackjack
291        {
292           gameOver( GameStatus.BLACKJACK );
293        }
294
295        // next card for blackjackProxy has index 2
296        currentDealerCard = 2;
297
298        // next card for player has index 13
299        currentPlayerCard = 13;
300     } // end method dealJButtonActionPerformed
301
302     // handles standJButton click
303     private void hitJButtonActionPerformed(
304        java.awt.event.ActionEvent evt )
305     {
306        // get player another card
307        String card = blackjackProxy.dealCard(); // deal new card
308        playerCards += "\t" + card; // add card to hand
309
310        // update GUI to display new card
311        displayCard( currentPlayerCard, card );
312        ++currentPlayerCard;
313
314        // determine new value of player's hand
315        int total = blackjackProxy.getHandValue( playerCards );
```

Fig. 28.18 | Blackjack game that uses the Blackjack web service. (Part 6 of 10.)

```
316
317          if ( total > 21 ) // player busts
318          {
319             gameOver( GameStatus.LOSE );
320          }
321          else if ( total == 21 ) // player cannot take any more cards
322          {
323             hitJButton.setEnabled( false );
324             dealerPlay();
325          } // end if
326       } // end method hitJButtonActionPerformed
327
328       // handles standJButton click
329       private void standJButtonActionPerformed(
330          java.awt.event.ActionEvent evt )
331       {
332          standJButton.setEnabled( false );
333          hitJButton.setEnabled( false );
334          dealJButton.setEnabled( true );
335          dealerPlay();
336       } // end method standJButtonActionPerformed
337
338       // begins application execution
339       public static void main( String args[] )
340       {
341          java.awt.EventQueue.invokeLater(
342             new Runnable()
343             {
344                public void run()
345                {
346                   new BlackjackGameJFrame().setVisible( true );
347                }
348             }
349          ); // end call to java.awt.EventQueue.invokeLater
350       } // end main
351
352       // Variables declaration - do not modify
353       private javax.swing.JButton dealJButton;
354       private javax.swing.JLabel dealerCard10JLabel;
355       private javax.swing.JLabel dealerCard11JLabel;
356       private javax.swing.JLabel dealerCard1JLabel;
357       private javax.swing.JLabel dealerCard2JLabel;
358       private javax.swing.JLabel dealerCard3JLabel;
359       private javax.swing.JLabel dealerCard4JLabel;
360       private javax.swing.JLabel dealerCard5JLabel;
361       private javax.swing.JLabel dealerCard6JLabel;
362       private javax.swing.JLabel dealerCard7JLabel;
363       private javax.swing.JLabel dealerCard8JLabel;
364       private javax.swing.JLabel dealerCard9JLabel;
365       private javax.swing.JLabel dealerJLabel;
366       private javax.swing.JLabel dealerTotalJLabel;
367       private javax.swing.JButton hitJButton;
368       private javax.swing.JLabel playerCard10JLabel;
```

Fig. 28.18 | Blackjack game that uses the Blackjack web service. (Part 7 of 10.)

```
369        private javax.swing.JLabel playerCard11JLabel;
370        private javax.swing.JLabel playerCard1JLabel;
371        private javax.swing.JLabel playerCard2JLabel;
372        private javax.swing.JLabel playerCard3JLabel;
373        private javax.swing.JLabel playerCard4JLabel;
374        private javax.swing.JLabel playerCard5JLabel;
375        private javax.swing.JLabel playerCard6JLabel;
376        private javax.swing.JLabel playerCard7JLabel;
377        private javax.swing.JLabel playerCard8JLabel;
378        private javax.swing.JLabel playerCard9JLabel;
379        private javax.swing.JLabel playerJLabel;
380        private javax.swing.JLabel playerTotalJLabel;
381        private javax.swing.JButton standJButton;
382        private javax.swing.JLabel statusJLabel;
383        // End of variables declaration
384 } // end class BlackjackGameJFrame
```

a) Dealer and player hands after the user clicks the **Deal** JButton

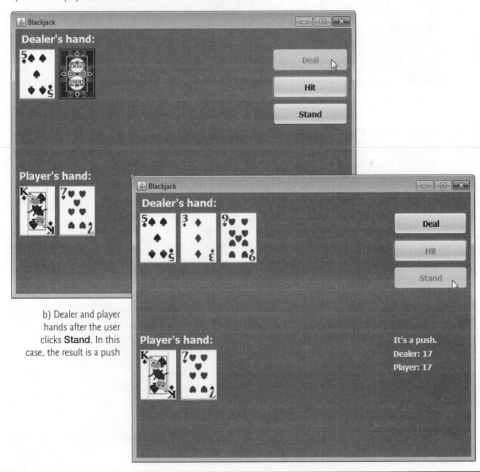

b) Dealer and player hands after the user clicks **Stand**. In this case, the result is a push

Fig. 28.18 | Blackjack game that uses the Blackjack web service. (Part 8 of 10.)

c) Dealer and player hands after the user clicks **Hit** and draws 21. In this case, the player wins

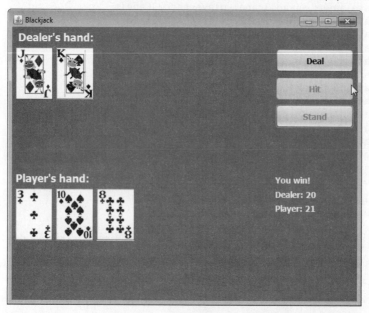

d) Dealer and player hands after the player is dealt blackjack

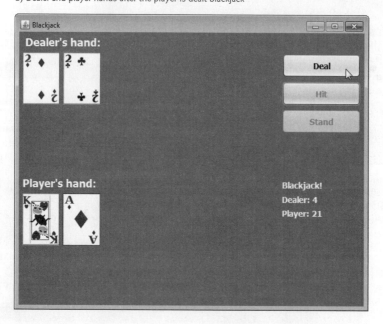

Fig. 28.18 | Blackjack game that uses the Blackjack web service. (Part 9 of 10.)

e) Dealer and player hands after the dealer is dealt blackjack

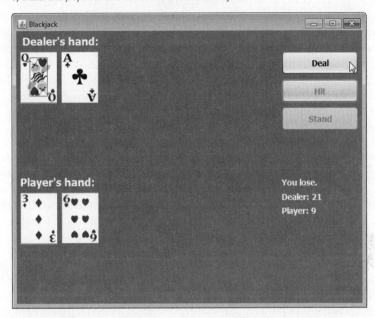

Fig. 28.18 | Blackjack game that uses the Blackjack web service. (Part 10 of 10.)

Configuring the Client for Session Tracking
When interacting with a JAX-WS web service that performs session tracking, the client application must indicate whether it wants to allow the web service to maintain session information. Lines 50–51 in the constructor perform this task. We first cast the service endpoint interface object to interface type BindingProvider. A **BindingProvider** enables the client to manipulate the request information that will be sent to the server. This information is stored in an object that implements interface **RequestContext**. The Binding-Provider and RequestContext are part of the framework that is created by the IDE when you add a web service client to the application. Next, we invoke the BindingProvider's **getRequestContext** method to obtain the RequestContext object. Then we call the RequestContext's **put method** to set the property

```
BindingProvider.SESSION_MAINTAIN_PROPERTY
```

to true. This enables the client side of the session-tracking mechanism, so that the web service knows which client is invoking the service's web methods.

Method gameOver
Method gameOver (lines 195–233) displays all the dealer's cards, shows the appropriate message in statusJLabel and displays the final point totals of both the dealer and the player. Method gameOver receives as an argument a member of the GameStatus enumeration (defined in lines 25–31). The enumeration represents whether the player tied, lost or won the game; its four members are PUSH, LOSE, WIN and BLACKJACK.

Method *dealJButtonActionPerformed*

When the player clicks the **Deal** JButton, method dealJButtonActionPerformed (lines 543–602) clears all of the JLabels that display cards or game status information. Next, the deck is shuffled (line 559), and the player and dealer receive two cards each (lines 562–573). Lines 580–581 then total each hand. If the player and the dealer both obtain scores of 21, the program calls method gameOver, passing GameStatus.PUSH (line 586). If only the dealer has 21, the program passes GameStatus.LOSE to method gameOver (line 590). If only the player has 21 after the first two cards are dealt, the program passes GameStatus.BLACKJACK to method gameOver (line 594).

Method *hitJButtonActionPerformed*

If dealJButtonActionPerformed does not call gameOver, the player can take more cards by clicking the **Hit** JButton, which calls hitJButtonActionPerformed in lines 605–628. Each time a player clicks **Hit**, the program deals the player one more card (line 609) and displays it in the GUI (line 613). If the player exceeds 21, the game is over and the player loses (line 621). If the player has exactly 21, the player is not allowed to take any more cards (line 625), and method dealerPlay is called (line 626).

Method *dealerPlay*

Method dealerPlay (lines 86–139) displays the dealer's cards, then deals cards to the dealer until the dealer's hand has a value of 17 or more (lines 100–108). If the dealer exceeds 21, the player wins (line 116); otherwise, the values of the hands are compared, and gameOver is called with the appropriate argument (lines 122–133).

Method *standJButtonActionPerformed*

Clicking the **Stand** JButton indicates that a player does not want to be dealt another card. Method standJButtonActionPerformed (lines 631–638) disables the **Hit** and **Stand** buttons, enables the **Deal** button, then calls method dealerPlay.

Method *displayCard*

Method displayCard (lines 142–192) updates the GUI to display a newly dealt card. The method takes as arguments an integer index for the JLabel in the ArrayList that must have its image set and a String representing the card. An empty String indicates that we wish to display the card face down. If method displayCard receives a String that's not empty, the program extracts the face and suit from the String and uses this information to display the correct image. The switch statement (lines 167–181) converts the number representing the suit to an integer and assigns the appropriate character to variable suitLetter (h for hearts, d for diamonds, c for clubs and s for spades). The character in suitLetter is used to complete the image's file name (lines 184–186). *You must add the folder blackjack_images to your project so that lines 152–154 and 184–186 can access the images properly.* To do so, copy the folder blackjack_images from this chapter's examples folder and paste it into the project's src\com\deitel\java\blackjackclient folder.

28.10 Consuming a Database-Driven SOAP Web Service

Our prior examples accessed web services from desktop applications created in NetBeans. However, we can just as easily use them in web applications created with NetBeans. In fact, because web-based businesses are becoming increasingly popular, it's common for web applications to consume web services. In this section, we present an airline reservation web service that receives information regarding the type of seat a customer wishes to reserve and makes a reservation if such a seat is available. Later in the section, we present a web application that allows a customer to specify a reservation request, then uses the airline reservation web service to attempt to execute the request.

28.10.1 Creating the Reservation Database

Our web service uses a `reservation` database containing a single table named `Seats` to locate a seat matching a client's request. Review the steps presented in Section 27.2.1 for configuring a data source and the `addressbook` database. Then perform those steps for the reservation database used in this example. Create a data source named `jdbc/reservation`. This chapter's examples directory contains the `Seats.sql` SQL script to create the seats table and populate it with sample data. The sample data is shown in Fig. 28.19.

number	location	class	taken
1	Aisle	Economy	0
2	Aisle	Economy	0
3	Aisle	First	0
4	Middle	Economy	0
5	Middle	Economy	0
6	Middle	First	0
7	Window	Economy	0
8	Window	Economy	0
9	Window	First	0
10	Window	First	0

Fig. 28.19 | Data from the seats table.

Creating the Reservation Web Service

You can now create a web service that uses the `Reservation` database (Fig. 28.20). The airline reservation web service has a single web method—`reserve` (lines 23–78)—which searches the `Seats` table to locate a seat matching a user's request. The method takes two arguments—a `String` representing the desired seat type (i.e., `"Window"`, `"Middle"` or `"Aisle"`) and a `String` representing the desired class type (i.e., `"Economy"` or `"First"`). If it finds an appropriate seat, method `reserve` updates the database to make the reservation and returns `true`; otherwise, no reservation is made, and the method returns `false`. The statements at lines 34–39 and lines 45–48 that query and update the database use objects of JDBC types `ResultSet` and `PreparedStatement`.

Software Engineering Observation 28.1

Using `PreparedStatements` to create SQL statements is highly recommended to secure against so-called SQL injection attacks in which executable code is inserted into SQL code. The site www.owasp.org/index.php/Preventing_SQL_Injection_in_Java provides a summary of SQL injection attacks and ways to mitigate against them.

```
 1   // Fig. 28.20: Reservation.java
 2   // Airline reservation web service.
 3   package com.deitel.reservation;
 4
 5   import java.sql.Connection;
 6   import java.sql.PreparedStatement;
 7   import java.sql.ResultSet;
 8   import java.sql.SQLException;
 9   import javax.annotation.Resource;
10   import javax.jws.WebMethod;
11   import javax.jws.WebParam;
12   import javax.jws.WebService;
13   import javax.sql.DataSource;
14
15   @WebService()
16   public class Reservation
17   {
18      // allow the server to inject the DataSource
19      @Resource( name="jdbc/reservation" )
20      DataSource dataSource;
21
22      // a WebMethod that can reserve a seat
23      @WebMethod( operationName = "reserve" )
24      public boolean reserve( @WebParam( name = "seatType" ) String seatType,
25         @WebParam( name = "classType" ) String classType )
26      {
27         Connection connection = null;
28         PreparedStatement lookupSeat = null;
29         PreparedStatement reserveSeat = null;
30
31         try
32         {
33            connection = DriverManager.getConnection(
34               DATABASE_URL, USERNAME, PASSWORD );
35            lookupSeat = connection.prepareStatement(
36               "SELECT \"number\" FROM \"seats\" WHERE (\"taken\" = 0) " +
37               "AND (\"location\" = ?) AND (\"class\" = ?)" );
38            lookupSeat.setString( 1, seatType );
39            lookupSeat.setString( 2, classType );
40            ResultSet resultSet = lookupSeat.executeQuery();
41
42            // if requested seat is available, reserve it
43            if ( resultSet.next() )
44            {
45               int seat = resultSet.getInt( 1 );
46               reserveSeat = connection.prepareStatement(
47                  "UPDATE \"seats\" SET \"taken\"=1 WHERE \"number\"=?" );
48               reserveSeat.setInt( 1, seat );
49               reserveSeat.executeUpdate();
50               return true;
51            } // end if
52
```

Fig. 28.20 | Airline reservation web service. (Part 1 of 2.)

```
53              return false;
54          } // end try
55          catch ( SQLException e )
56          {
57              e.printStackTrace();
58              return false;
59          } // end catch
60          catch ( Exception e )
61          {
62              e.printStackTrace();
63              return false;
64          } // end catch
65          finally
66          {
67              try
68              {
69                 lookupSeat.close();
70                 reserveSeat.close();
71                 connection.close();
72              } // end try
73              catch ( Exception e )
74              {
75                 e.printStackTrace();
76                 return false;
77              } // end catch
78          } // end finally
79      } // end WebMethod reserve
80  } // end class Reservation
```

Fig. 28.20 | Airline reservation web service. (Part 2 of 2.)

Our database contains four columns—the seat number (i.e., 1–10), the seat type (i.e., Window, Middle or Aisle), the class type (i.e., Economy or First) and a column containing either 1 (true) or 0 (false) to indicate whether the seat is taken. Lines 34–39 retrieve the seat numbers of any available seats matching the requested seat and class type. This statement fills the resultSet with the results of the query

```
SELECT number
FROM seats
WHERE (taken = 0) AND (type = type) AND (class = class)
```

The parameters *type* and *class* in the query are replaced with values of method reserve's seatType and classType parameters.

If resultSet is not empty (i.e., at least one seat is available that matches the selected criteria), the condition in line 42 is true and the web service reserves the first matching seat number. Recall that ResultSet method next returns true if a nonempty row exists, and positions the cursor on that row. We obtain the seat number (line 44) by accessing resultSet's first column (i.e., resultSet.getInt(1)—the first column in the row). Then lines 45–48 configure a PreparedStatement and execute the SQL:

```
UPDATE seats
SET taken = 1
WHERE (number = number)
```

which marks the seat as taken in the database. The parameter *number* is replaced with the value of `seat`. Method `reserve` returns `true` (line 49) to indicate that the reservation was successful. If there are no matching seats, or if an exception occurred, method `reserve` returns `false` (lines 52, 57, 62 and 75) to indicate that no seats matched the user's request.

28.10.2 Creating a Web Application to Interact with the Reservation Service

This section presents a `ReservationClient` JSF web application that consumes the Reservation web service. The application allows users to select `"Aisle"`, `"Middle"` or `"Window"` seats in `"Economy"` or `"First"` class, then submit their requests to the web service. If the database request is not successful, the application instructs the user to modify the request and try again. The application presented here was built using the techniques presented in Chapters 26–27. We assume that you've already read those chapters and thus know how to build a Facelets page and a corresponding JavaBean.

index.xhtml

`index.xhtml` (Fig. 28.21) defines two `h:selectOneMenu`s and an `h:commandButton`. The `h:selectOneMenu` at lines 16–20) displays all the seat types from which users can select. The one at lines 21–24) provides choices for the class type. The values of these are stored in the `seatType` and `classType` properties of the `reservationBean` (Fig. 28.22). Users click the **Reserve** button (lines 25–26) to submit requests after making selections from the `h:selectOneMenu`s. Clicking the button calls the `reservationBean`'s `reserveSeat` method. The page displays the result of each attempt to reserve a seat in line 28.

```
1    <?xml version='1.0' encoding='UTF-8' ?>
2
3    <!-- Fig. 28.21: index.xhtml -->
4    <!-- Facelets page that allows a user to select a seat -->
5    <!DOCTYPE html PUBLIC "-//W3C//DTD XHTML 1.0 Transitional//EN"
6        "http://www.w3.org/TR/xhtml1/DTD/xhtml1-transitional.dtd">
7    <html xmlns="http://www.w3.org/1999/xhtml"
8        xmlns:h="http://java.sun.com/jsf/html"
9        xmlns:f="http://java.sun.com/jsf/core">
10       <h:head>
11           <title>Airline Reservations</title>
12       </h:head>
13       <h:body>
14           <h:form>
15               <h3>Please select the seat type and class to reserve:</h3>
16               <h:selectOneMenu value="#{reservationBean.seatType}">
17                   <f:selectItem itemValue="Aisle" itemLabel="Aisle" />
18                   <f:selectItem itemValue="Middle" itemLabel="Middle" />
19                   <f:selectItem itemValue="Window" itemLabel="Window" />
20               </h:selectOneMenu>
21               <h:selectOneMenu value="#{reservationBean.classType}">
22                   <f:selectItem itemValue="Economy" itemLabel="Economy" />
23                   <f:selectItem itemValue="First" itemLabel="First" />
24               </h:selectOneMenu>
```

Fig. 28.21 | Facelets page that allows a user to select a seat. (Part 1 of 2.)

```
25              <h:commandButton value="Reserve"
26                 action="#{reservationBean.reserveSeat}"/>
27           </h:form>
28           <h3>#{reservationBean.result}</h3>
29        </h:body>
30    </html>
```

a) Selecting
a seat

b) Seat reserved
successfully

c) Attempting to
reserve another
window seat in
economy when
there are no such
seats available

d) No seats
match the
requested seat
type and class

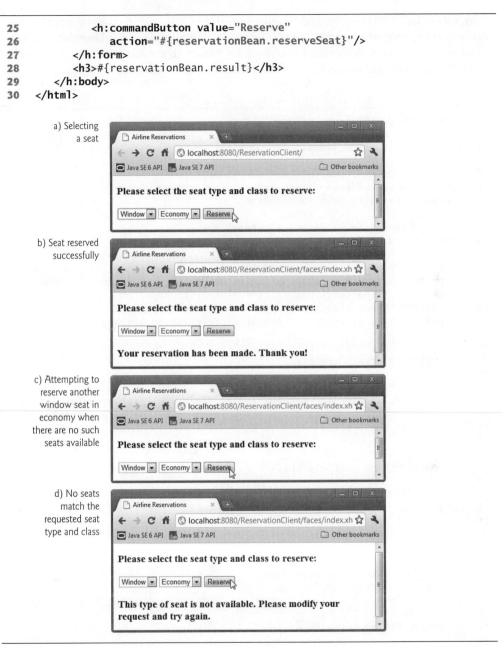

Fig. 28.21 | Facelets page that allows a user to select a seat. (Part 2 of 2.)

ReservationBean.java

Class ReservationBean (Fig. 28.22) defines the seatType, classType and result properties and the reserveSeat method that are used in the index.xhtml page. When the user clicks the **Reserve** button in index.xhtml, method reserveSeat (lines 57–74) executes. Lines 61–62 use the service endpoint interface object (created in lines 22–23) to invoke the web service's reserve method, passing the selected seat type and class type as arguments. If reserve returns true, line 65 sets result to a message thanking the user for making a reservation; otherwise, lines 67–68 set result to a message notifying the user that the requested seat type is not available and instructing the user to try again.

```java
1   // Fig. 28.22: ReservationBean.java
2   // Bean for seat reservation client.
3   package reservationclient;
4
5   import com.deitel.reservation.Reservation;
6   import com.deitel.reservation.ReservationService;
7   import javax.faces.bean.ManagedBean;
8
9   @ManagedBean( name = "reservationBean" )
10  public class ReservationBean
11  {
12     // references the service endpoint interface object (i.e., the proxy)
13     private Reservation reservationServiceProxy; // reference to proxy
14     private String seatType; // type of seat to reserve
15     private String classType; // class of seat to reserve
16     private String result; // result of reservation attempt
17
18     // no-argument constructor
19     public ReservationBean()
20     {
21        // get service endpoint interface
22        ReservationService reservationService = new ReservationService();
23        reservationServiceProxy = reservationService.getReservationPort();
24     } // end constructor
25
26     // return classType
27     public String getClassType()
28     {
29        return classType;
30     } // end method getClassType
31
32     // set classType
33     public void setClassType( String classType )
34     {
35        this.classType = classType;
36     } // end method setClassType
37
38     // return seatType
39     public String getSeatType()
40     {
41        return seatType;
42     } // end method getSeatType
43
44     // set seatType
45     public void setSeatType( String seatType )
46     {
```

Fig. 28.22 | Page bean for seat reservation client. (Part 1 of 2.)

```
47          this.seatType = seatType;
48       } // end method setSeatType
49
50       // return result
51       public String getResult()
52       {
53          return result;
54       } // end method getResult
55
56       // invoke the web service when the user clicks Reserve button
57       public void reserveSeat()
58       {
59          try
60          {
61             boolean reserved = reservationServiceProxy.reserve(
62                getSeatType(), getClassType() );
63
64             if ( reserved )
65                result = "Your reservation has been made. Thank you!";
66             else
67                result = "This type of seat is not available. " +
68                   "Please modify your request and try again.";
69          } // end try
70          catch ( Exception e )
71          {
72             e.printStackTrace();
73          } // end catch
74       } // end method reserveSeat
75    } // end class ReservationBean
```

Fig. 28.22 | Page bean for seat reservation client. (Part 2 of 2.)

28.11 Equation Generator: Returning User-Defined Types

Most of the web services we've demonstrated received and returned primitive-type instances. It's also possible to process instances of class types in a web service. These types can be passed to or returned from web service methods.

This section presents a RESTful EquationGenerator web service that generates random arithmetic equations of type Equation. The client is a math-tutoring application that accepts information about the mathematical question that the user wishes to attempt (addition, subtraction or multiplication) and the skill level of the user (1 specifies equations using numbers from 1 through 9, 2 specifies equations involving numbers from 10 through 99, and 3 specifies equations containing numbers from 100 through 999). The web service then generates an equation consisting of random numbers in the proper range. The client application receives the Equation and displays the sample question to the user.

Defining Class Equation

We define class Equation in Fig. 28.23. All the programs in this section have a copy of this class in their corresponding package. Except for the package name, the class is identical in each project, so we show it only once. Like the TextMessage class used earlier, the server-side and client-side copies of class `Equation` are unrelated to each other. The only requirement for *serialization* and *deserialization* to work with the JAXB and Gson classes is that class `Equation` must have the same `public` properties on both the server and the client. Such properties can be public instance variables or private instance variables that have corresponding *set* and *get* methods.

```java
1   // Fig. 28.23: Equation.java
2   // Equation class that contains information about an equation.
3   package com.deitel.equationgeneratorxml;
4
5   public class Equation
6   {
7      private int leftOperand;
8      private int rightOperand;
9      private int result;
10     private String operationType;
11
12     // required no-argument constructor
13     public Equation()
14     {
15        this( 0, 0, "add" );
16     } // end no-argument constructor
17
18     // constructor that receives the operands and operation type
19     public Equation( int leftValue, int rightValue, String type )
20     {
21        leftOperand = leftValue;
22        rightOperand = rightValue;
23
24        // determine result
25        if ( type.equals( "add" ) ) // addition
26        {
27           result = leftOperand + rightOperand;
28           operationType = "+";
29        } // end if
30        else if ( type.equals( "subtract" ) ) // subtraction
31        {
32           result = leftOperand - rightOperand;
33           operationType = "-";
34        } // end if
35        else // multiplication
36        {
37           result = leftOperand * rightOperand;
38           operationType = "*";
39        } // end else
40     } // end three argument constructor
41
42     // gets the leftOperand
43     public int getLeftOperand()
44     {
45        return leftOperand;
46     } // end method getLeftOperand
```

Fig. 28.23 | `Equation` class that contains information about an equation. (Part 1 of 3.)

```
47
48      // required setter
49      public void setLeftOperand( int value )
50      {
51         leftOperand = value;
52      } // end method setLeftOperand
53
54      // gets the rightOperand
55      public int getRightOperand()
56      {
57         return rightOperand;
58      } // end method getRightOperand
59
60      // required setter
61      public void setRightOperand( int value )
62      {
63         rightOperand = value;
64      } // end method setRightOperand
65
66      // gets the resultValue
67      public int getResult()
68      {
69         return result;
70      } // end method getResult
71
72      // required setter
73      public void setResult( int value )
74      {
75         result = value;
76      } // end method setResult
77
78      // gets the operationType
79      public String getOperationType()
80      {
81         return operationType;
82      } // end method getOperationType
83
84      // required setter
85      public void setOperationType( String value )
86      {
87         operationType = value;
88      } // end method setOperationType
89
90      // returns the left hand side of the equation as a String
91      public String getLeftHandSide()
92      {
93         return leftOperand + " " + operationType + " " + rightOperand;
94      } // end method getLeftHandSide
95
96      // returns the right hand side of the equation as a String
97      public String getRightHandSide()
98      {
```

Fig. 28.23 | Equation class that contains information about an equation. (Part 2 of 3.)

```
99          return "" + result;
100     } // end method getRightHandSide
101
102     // returns a String representation of an Equation
103     public String toString()
104     {
105         return getLeftHandSide() + " = " + getRightHandSide();
106     } // end method toString
107 } // end class Equation
```

Fig. 28.23 | Equation class that contains information about an equation. (Part 3 of 3.)

Lines 19–40 define a constructor that takes two ints representing the left and right operands, and a String representing the arithmetic operation. The constructor stores this information, then calculates the result. The parameterless constructor (lines 13–16) calls the three-argument constructor (lines 19–40) and passes default values.

Class Equation defines *get* and *set* methods for instance variables leftOperand (lines 43–52), rightOperand (lines 55–64), result (line 67–76) and operationType (lines 79–88). It also provides *get* methods for the left-hand and right-hand sides of the equation and a toString method that returns the entire equation as a String. An instance variable can be serialized only if it has both a *get* and a *set* method. Because the different sides of the equation and the result of toString can be generated from the other instance variables, there's no need to send them across the wire. The client in this case study does not use the getRightHandSide method, but we included it in case future clients choose to use it.

28.11.1 Creating the EquationGeneratorXML Web Service

Figure 28.24 presents the EquationGeneratorXML web service's class for creating randomly generated Equations. Method getXml (lines 19–38) takes two parameters—a String representing the mathematical operation ("add", "subtract" or "multiply") and an int representing the difficulty level. JAX-RS automatically converts the arguments to the correct type and will return a "not found" error to the client if the argument cannot be converted from a String to the destination type. Supported types for conversion include integer types, floating-point types, boolean and the corresponding *type-wrapper classes*.

```
1   // Fig. 28.24: EquationGeneratorXMLResource.java
2   // RESTful equation generator that returns XML.
3   package com.deitel.equationgeneratorxml;
4
5   import java.io.StringWriter;
6   import java.util.Random;
7   import javax.ws.rs.PathParam;
8   import javax.ws.rs.Path;
9   import javax.ws.rs.GET;
10  import javax.ws.rs.Produces;
11  import javax.xml.bind.JAXB; // utility class for common JAXB operations
12
```

Fig. 28.24 | RESTful equation generator that returns XML. (Part 1 of 2.)

```
13    @Path( "equation" )
14    public class EquationGeneratorXMLResource
15    {
16        private static Random randomObject = new Random();
17
18        // retrieve an equation formatted as XML
19        @GET
20        @Path( "{operation}/{level}" )
21        @Produces( "application/xml" )
22        public String getXml( @PathParam( "operation" ) String operation,
23            @PathParam( "level" ) int level )
24        {
25            // compute minimum and maximum values for the numbers
26            int minimum = ( int ) Math.pow( 10, level - 1 );
27            int maximum = ( int ) Math.pow( 10, level );
28
29            // create the numbers on the left-hand side of the equation
30            int first = randomObject.nextInt( maximum - minimum ) + minimum;
31            int second = randomObject.nextInt( maximum - minimum ) + minimum;
32
33            // create Equation object and marshal it into XML
34            Equation equation = new Equation( first, second, operation );
35            StringWriter writer = new StringWriter(); // XML output here
36            JAXB.marshal( equation, writer ); // write Equation to StringWriter
37            return writer.toString(); // return XML string
38        } // end method getXml
39    } // end class EquationGeneratorXMLResource
```

Fig. 28.24 | RESTful equation generator that returns XML. (Part 2 of 2.)

The getXml method first determines the minimum (inclusive) and maximum (exclusive) values for the numbers in the equation it will return (lines 26–27). It then uses a static member of the Random class (line 16) to generate two random numbers in that range (lines 30–31). Line 34 creates an Equation object, passing these two numbers and the requested operation to the constructor. The getXml method then uses JAXB to convert the Equation object to XML (line 36), which is output to the StringWriter created on line 35. Finally, it retrieves the data that was written to the StringWriter and returns it to the client. [*Note:* We'll reimplement this web service with JSON in Section 28.11.3.]

28.11.2 Consuming the EquationGeneratorXML Web Service

The EquationGeneratorXMLClient application (Fig. 28.25) retrieves an XML-formatted Equation object from the EquationGeneratorXML web service. The application then displays the Equation's left-hand side and waits for user to submit an answer.

```
1    // Fig. 28.25: EquationGeneratorXMLClientJFrame.java
2    // Math-tutoring program using REST and XML to generate equations.
3    package com.deitel.equationgeneratorxmlclient;
4
5    import javax.swing.JOptionPane;
```

Fig. 28.25 | Math-tutoring program using REST and XML to generate equations. (Part 1 of 4.)

```
 6   import javax.xml.bind.JAXB; // utility class for common JAXB operations
 7
 8   public class EquationGeneratorXMLClientJFrame extends javax.swing.JFrame
 9   {
10      private String operation = "add"; // operation user is tested on
11      private int difficulty = 1; // 1, 2, or 3 digits in each number
12      private int answer; // correct answer to the question
13
14      // no-argument constructor
15      public EquationGeneratorXMLClientJFrame()
16      {
17         initComponents();
18      } // end no-argument constructor
19
20      // The initComponents method is autogenerated by NetBeans and is called
21      // from the constructor to initialize the GUI. This method is not shown
22      // here to save space. Open EquationGeneratorXMLClientJFrame.java in
23      // this example's folder to view the complete generated code.
24
25      // determine if the user answered correctly
26      private void checkAnswerJButtonActionPerformed(
27         java.awt.event.ActionEvent evt)
28      {
29         if ( answerJTextField.getText().equals( "" ) )
30         {
31            JOptionPane.showMessageDialog(
32               this, "Please enter your answer." );
33         } // end if
34
35         int userAnswer = Integer.parseInt( answerJTextField.getText() );
36
37         if ( userAnswer == answer )
38         {
39            equationJLabel.setText( "" ); // clear label
40            answerJTextField.setText( "" ); // clear text field
41            checkAnswerJButton.setEnabled( false );
42            JOptionPane.showMessageDialog( this, "Correct! Good Job!",
43               "Correct", JOptionPane.PLAIN_MESSAGE );
44         } // end if
45         else
46         {
47            JOptionPane.showMessageDialog( this, "Incorrect. Try again.",
48               "Incorrect", JOptionPane.PLAIN_MESSAGE );
49         } // end else
50      } // end method checkAnswerJButtonActionPerformed
51
52      // retrieve equation from web service and display left side to user
53      private void generateJButtonActionPerformed(
54         java.awt.event.ActionEvent evt)
55      {
56         try
57         {
```

Fig. 28.25 | Math-tutoring program using REST and XML to generate equations. (Part 2 of 4.)

```
58            String url = String.format( "http://localhost:8080/" +
59                "EquationGeneratorXML/resources/equation/%s/%d",
60                operation, difficulty );
61
62            // convert XML back to an Equation object
63            Equation equation = JAXB.unmarshal( url, Equation.class );
64
65            answer = equation.getResult();
66            equationJLabel.setText( equation.getLeftHandSide() + " =" );
67            checkAnswerJButton.setEnabled( true );
68        } // end try
69        catch ( Exception exception )
70        {
71            exception.printStackTrace();
72        } // end catch
73    } // end method generateJButtonActionPerformed
74
75    // obtains the mathematical operation selected by the user
76    private void operationJComboBoxItemStateChanged(
77        java.awt.event.ItemEvent evt)
78    {
79        String item = ( String ) operationJComboBox.getSelectedItem();
80
81        if ( item.equals( "Addition" ) )
82            operation = "add"; // user selected addition
83        else if ( item.equals( "Subtraction" ) )
84            operation = "subtract"; // user selected subtraction
85        else
86            operation = "multiply"; // user selected multiplication
87    } // end method operationJComboBoxItemStateChanged
88
89    // obtains the difficulty level selected by the user
90    private void levelJComboBoxItemStateChanged(
91        java.awt.event.ItemEvent evt)
92    {
93        // indices start at 0, so add 1 to get the difficulty level
94        difficulty = levelJComboBox.getSelectedIndex() + 1;
95    } // end method levelJComboBoxItemStateChanged
96
97    // main method begins execution
98    public static void main(String args[])
99    {
100        java.awt.EventQueue.invokeLater(
101            new Runnable()
102            {
103                public void run()
104                {
105                    new EquationGeneratorXMLClientJFrame().setVisible( true );
106                } // end method run
107            } // end anonymous inner class
108        ); // end call to java.awt.EventQueue.invokeLater
109    } // end main
110
```

Fig. 28.25 | Math-tutoring program using REST and XML to generate equations. (Part 3 of 4.)

```
111      // Variables declaration - do not modify
112      private javax.swing.JLabel answerJLabel;
113      private javax.swing.JTextField answerJTextField;
114      private javax.swing.JButton checkAnswerJButton;
115      private javax.swing.JLabel equationJLabel;
116      private javax.swing.JButton generateJButton;
117      private javax.swing.JComboBox levelJComboBox;
118      private javax.swing.JLabel levelJLabel;
119      private javax.swing.JComboBox operationJComboBox;
120      private javax.swing.JLabel operationJLabel;
121      private javax.swing.JLabel questionJLabel;
122      // End of variables declaration
123  } // end class EquationGeneratorXMLClientJFrame
```

a) Generating a simple equation.   b) Sumbitting the answer.   c) Dialog indicating correct answer.

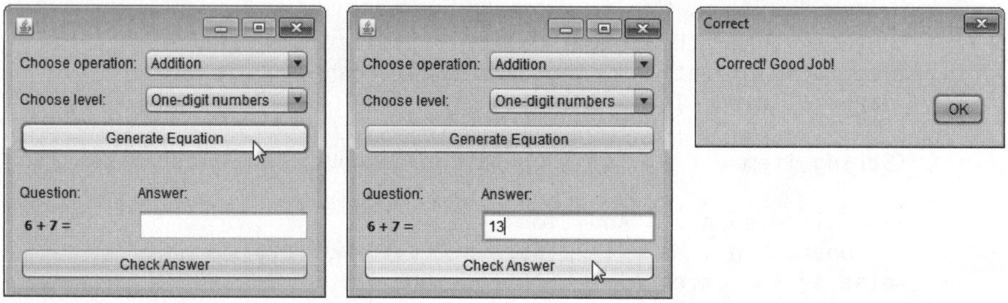

Fig. 28.25 | Math-tutoring program using REST and XML to generate equations. (Part 4 of 4.)

The default setting for the difficulty level is 1, but the user can change this by choosing a level from the **Choose level** JComboBox. Changing the selected value invokes the level-JComboBoxItemStateChanged event handler (lines 208–213), which sets the difficulty instance variable to the level selected by the user. Although the default setting for the question type is **Addition**, the user also can change this by choosing from the **Choose operation** JComboBox. This invokes the operationJComboBoxItemStateChanged event handler in lines 194–205, which assigns to instance variable operation the String corresponding to the user's selection.

The event handler for generateJButton (lines 171–191) constructs the URL to invoke the web service, then passes this URL to the unmarshal method, along with an instance of Class<Equation>, so that JAXB can convert the XML into an Equation object (line 181). Once the XML has been converted back into an Equation, lines 183–184 retrieve the correct answer and display the left-hand side of the equation. The **Check Answer** button is then enabled (line 185), and the user must solve the problem and enter the answer.

When the user enters a value and clicks **Check Answer**, the checkAnswerJButtonAc-tionPerformed event handler (lines 144–168) retrieves the user's answer from the dialog box (line 153) and compares it to the correct answer that was stored earlier (line 155). If they match, lines 157–161 reset the GUI elements so the user can generate another equation and tell the user that the answer was correct. If they do not match, a message box asking the user to try again is displayed (lines 165–166).

28.11.3 Creating the EquationGeneratorJSON Web Service

As you saw in Section 28.8, RESTful web services can return data formatted as JSON as well. Figure 28.26 is a reimplementation of the EquationGeneratorXML service that returns an Equation in JSON format.

```
1   // Fig. 28.26: EquationGeneratorJSONResource.java
2   // RESTful equation generator that returns JSON.
3   package com.deitel.equationgeneratorjson;
4
5   import com.google.gson.Gson; // converts POJO to JSON and back again
6   import java.util.Random;
7   import javax.ws.rs.GET;
8   import javax.ws.rs.Path;
9   import javax.ws.rs.PathParam;
10  import javax.ws.rs.Produces;
11
12  @Path( "equation" )
13  public class EquationGeneratorJSONResource
14  {
15     static Random randomObject = new Random(); // random number generator
16
17     // retrieve an equation formatted as JSON
18     @GET
19     @Path( "{operation}/{level}" )
20     @Produces( "application/json" )
21     public String getJson( @PathParam( "operation" ) String operation,
22        @PathParam( "level" ) int level )
23     {
24        // compute minimum and maximum values for the numbers
25        int minimum = ( int ) Math.pow( 10, level - 1 );
26        int maximum = ( int ) Math.pow( 10, level );
27
28        // create the numbers on the left-hand side of the equation
29        int first = randomObject.nextInt( maximum - minimum ) + minimum;
30        int second = randomObject.nextInt( maximum - minimum ) + minimum;
31
32        // create Equation object and return result
33        Equation equation = new Equation( first, second, operation );
34        return new Gson().toJson( equation ); // convert to JSON and return
35     } // end method getJson
36  } // end class EquationGeneratorJSONResource
```

Fig. 28.26 | RESTful equation generator that returns JSON.

The logic implemented here is the same as the XML version except for the last line (line 34), which uses Gson to convert the Equation object into JSON instead of using JAXB to convert it into XML. The @Produces annotation (line 20) has also changed to reflect the JSON data format.

28.11.4 Consuming the EquationGeneratorJSON Web Service

The program in Fig. 28.27 consumes the EquationGeneratorJSON service and performs the same function as EquationGeneratorXMLClient—the only difference is in how the

Equation object is retrieved from the web service. Lines 181–183 construct the URL that is used to invoke the EquationGeneratorJSON service. As in the WelcomeRESTJSONClient example, we use the URL class and an InputStreamReader to invoke the web service and read the response (lines 186–187). The retrieved JSON is *deserialized* using Gson (line 191) and converted back into an Equation object. As before, we use the getResult method (line 194) of the deserialized object to obtain the answer and the getLeftHandSide method (line 195) to display the left side of the equation.

```
1   // Fig. 28.27: EquationGeneratorJSONClientJFrame.java
2   // Math-tutoring program using REST and JSON to generate equations.
3   package com.deitel.equationgeneratorjsonclient;
4
5   import com.google.gson.Gson; // converts POJO to JSON and back again
6   import java.io.InputStreamReader;
7   import java.net.URL;
8   import javax.swing.JOptionPane;
9
10  public class EquationGeneratorJSONClientJFrame extends javax.swing.JFrame
11  {
12     private String operation = "add"; // operation user is tested on
13     private int difficulty = 1; // 1, 2, or 3 digits in each number
14     private int answer; // correct answer to the question
15
16     // no-argument constructor
17     public EquationGeneratorJSONClientJFrame()
18     {
19        initComponents();
20     } // end no-argument constructor
21
22     // The initComponents method is autogenerated by NetBeans and is called
23     // from the constructor to initialize the GUI. This method is not shown
24     // here to save space. Open EquationGeneratorJSONClientJFrame.java in
25     // this example's folder to view the complete generated code.
26
27     // determine if the user answered correctly
28     private void checkAnswerJButtonActionPerformed(
29        java.awt.event.ActionEvent evt)
30     {
31        if ( answerJTextField.getText().equals( "" ) )
32        {
33           JOptionPane.showMessageDialog(
34              this, "Please enter your answer." );
35        } // end if
36
37        int userAnswer = Integer.parseInt( answerJTextField.getText() );
38
39        if ( userAnswer == answer )
40        {
41           equationJLabel.setText( "" ); // clear label
42           answerJTextField.setText( "" ); // clear text field
43           checkAnswerJButton.setEnabled( false );
```

Fig. 28.27 | Math-tutoring program using REST and JSON to generate equations. (Part 1 of 3.)

```
44              JOptionPane.showMessageDialog( this, "Correct! Good Job!",
45                 "Correct", JOptionPane.PLAIN_MESSAGE );
46           } // end if
47           else
48           {
49              JOptionPane.showMessageDialog( this, "Incorrect. Try again.",
50                 "Incorrect", JOptionPane.PLAIN_MESSAGE );
51           } // end else
52        } // end method checkAnswerJButtonActionPerformed
53
54        // retrieve equation from web service and display left side to user
55        private void generateJButtonActionPerformed(
56           java.awt.event.ActionEvent evt)
57        {
58           try
59           {
60              // URL of the EquationGeneratorJSON service, with parameters
61              String url = String.format( "http://localhost:8080/" +
62                 "EquationGeneratorJSON/resources/equation/%s/%d",
63                 operation, difficulty );
64
65              // open URL and create a Reader to read the data
66              InputStreamReader reader =
67                 new InputStreamReader( new URL( url ).openStream() );
68
69              // convert the JSON back into an Equation object
70              Equation equation =
71                 new Gson().fromJson( reader, Equation.class );
72
73              // update the internal state and GUI to reflect the equation
74              answer = equation.getResult();
75              equationJLabel.setText( equation.getLeftHandSide() + " =" );
76              checkAnswerJButton.setEnabled( true );
77           } // end try
78           catch ( Exception exception )
79           {
80              exception.printStackTrace();
81           } // end catch
82        } // end method generateJButtonActionPerformed
83
84        // obtains the mathematical operation selected by the user
85        private void operationJComboBoxItemStateChanged(
86           java.awt.event.ItemEvent evt)
87        {
88           String item = ( String ) operationJComboBox.getSelectedItem();
89
90           if ( item.equals( "Addition" ) )
91              operation = "add"; // user selected addition
92           else if ( item.equals( "Subtraction" ) )
93              operation = "subtract"; // user selected subtraction
94           else
95              operation = "multiply"; // user selected multiplication
96        } // end method operationJComboBoxItemStateChanged
```

Fig. 28.27 | Math-tutoring program using REST and JSON to generate equations. (Part 2 of 3.)

```
97
98      // obtains the difficulty level selected by the user
99      private void levelJComboBoxItemStateChanged(
100        java.awt.event.ItemEvent evt)
101     {
102        // indices start at 0, so add 1 to get the difficulty level
103        difficulty = levelJComboBox.getSelectedIndex() + 1;
104     } // end method levelJComboBoxItemStateChanged
105
106     // main method begins execution
107     public static void main( String args[] )
108     {
109        java.awt.EventQueue.invokeLater(
110           new Runnable()
111           {
112              public void run()
113              {
114                 new EquationGeneratorJSONClientJFrame().setVisible( true );
115              } // end method run
116           } // end anonymous inner class
117        ); // end call to java.awt.EventQueue.invokeLater
118     } // end main
119
120     // Variables declaration - do not modify
121     private javax.swing.JLabel answerJLabel;
122     private javax.swing.JTextField answerJTextField;
123     private javax.swing.JButton checkAnswerJButton;
124     private javax.swing.JLabel equationJLabel;
125     private javax.swing.JButton generateJButton;
126     private javax.swing.JComboBox levelJComboBox;
127     private javax.swing.JLabel levelJLabel;
128     private javax.swing.JComboBox operationJComboBox;
129     private javax.swing.JLabel operationJLabel;
130     private javax.swing.JLabel questionJLabel;
131     // End of variables declaration
132  } // end class EquationGeneratorJSONClientJFrame
```

Fig. 28.27 | Math-tutoring program using REST and JSON to generate equations. (Part 3 of 3.)

28.12 Wrap-Up

This chapter introduced web services—a set of technologies for building distributed systems in which system components communicate with one another over networks. In particular, we presented JAX-WS SOAP-based web services and JAX-RS REST-based web services. You learned that a web service is a class that allows client software to call the web service's methods remotely via common data formats and protocols, such as XML, JSON, HTTP, SOAP and REST. We also benefits of distributed computing with web services.

We explained how NetBeans and the JAX-WS and JAX-RS APIs facilitate publishing and consuming web services. You learned how to define web services and methods using both SOAP protocol and REST architecture, and how to return data in both XML and JSON formats. You consumed SOAP-based web services using proxy classes to call the web service's methods. You also consumed REST-based web services by using class URL to invoke the services and open `InputStreams` from which the clients could read the services' responses. You learned how to define web services and web methods, as well as how to consume them both from Java desktop applications and from web applications. After explaining the mechanics of web services through our `Welcome` examples, we demonstrated more sophisticated web services that use session tracking, database access and user-defined types. We also explained XML and JSON serialization and showed how to retrieve objects of user-defined types from web services.

Operator Precedence Chart

Operators are shown in decreasing order of precedence from top to bottom (Fig. A.1).

Operator	Description	Associativity
++ --	unary postfix increment unary postfix decrement	right to left
++ -- + - ! ~ (*type*)	unary prefix increment unary prefix decrement unary plus unary minus unary logical negation unary bitwise complement unary cast	right to left
* / %	multiplication division remainder	left to right
+ -	addition or string concatenation subtraction	left to right
<< >> >>>	left shift signed right shift unsigned right shift	left to right
< <= > >= instanceof	less than less than or equal to greater than greater than or equal to type comparison	left to right

Fig. A.1 | Operator precedence chart. (Part 1 of 2.)

Operator	Description	Associativity
== !=	is equal to is not equal to	left to right
&	bitwise AND boolean logical AND	left to right
^	bitwise exclusive OR boolean logical exclusive OR	left to right
|	bitwise inclusive OR boolean logical inclusive OR	left to right
&&	conditional AND	left to right
||	conditional OR	left to right
?:	conditional	right to left
= += -= *= /= %= &= ^= |= <<= >>= >>>=	assignment addition assignment subtraction assignment multiplication assignment division assignment remainder assignment bitwise AND assignment bitwise exclusive OR assignment bitwise inclusive OR assignment bitwise left-shift assignment bitwise signed-right-shift assignment bitwise unsigned-right-shift assignment	right to left

Fig. A.1 | Operator precedence chart. (Part 2 of 2.)

B

ASCII Character Set

	0	1	2	3	4	5	6	7	8	9
0	nul	soh	stx	etx	eot	enq	ack	bel	bs	ht
1	nl	vt	ff	cr	so	si	dle	dc1	dc2	dc3
2	dc4	nak	syn	etb	can	em	sub	esc	fs	gs
3	rs	us	sp	!	"	#	$	%	&	'
4	(	)	*	+	,	-	.	/	0	1
5	2	3	4	5	6	7	8	9	:	;
6	<	=	>	?	@	A	B	C	D	E
7	F	G	H	I	J	K	L	M	N	O
8	P	Q	R	S	T	U	V	W	X	Y
9	Z	[	\	]	^	_	'	a	b	c
10	d	e	f	g	h	i	j	k	l	m
11	n	o	p	q	r	s	t	u	v	w
12	x	y	z	{			}	~	del		

Fig. B.1 | ASCII character set.

The digits at the left of the table are the left digits of the decimal equivalents (0–127) of the character codes, and the digits at the top of the table are the right digits of the character codes. For example, the character code for "F" is 70, and the character code for "&" is 38.

Most users of this book are interested in the ASCII character set used to represent English characters on many computers. The ASCII character set is a subset of the Unicode character set used by Java to represent characters from most of the world's languages.

Keywords and Reserved Words

Java Keywords				
abstract	assert	boolean	break	byte
case	catch	char	class	continue
default	do	double	else	enum
extends	final	finally	float	for
if	implements	import	instanceof	int
interface	long	native	new	package
private	protected	public	return	short
static	strictfp	super	switch	synchronized
this	throw	throws	transient	try
void	volatile	while		
Keywords that are not currently used				
const	goto			

Fig. C.1 | Java keywords.

Java also contains the reserved words true and false, which are boolean literals, and null, which is the literal that represents a reference to nothing. Like keywords, these reserved words cannot be used as identifiers.

Primitive Types

Type	Size in bits	Values	Standard
boolean		true or false	
[*Note:* A boolean's representation is specific to the Java Virtual Machine on each platform.]			
char	16	'\u0000' to '\uFFFF' (0 to 65535)	(ISO Unicode character set)
byte	8	-128 to $+127$ $(-2^7$ to $2^7 - 1)$	
short	16	$-32{,}768$ to $+32{,}767$ $(-2^{15}$ to $2^{15} - 1)$	
int	32	$-2{,}147{,}483{,}648$ to $+2{,}147{,}483{,}647$ $(-2^{31}$ to $2^{31} - 1)$	
long	64	$-9{,}223{,}372{,}036{,}854{,}775{,}808$ to $+9{,}223{,}372{,}036{,}854{,}775{,}807$ $(-2^{63}$ to $2^{63} - 1)$	
float	32	*Negative range:* $-3.4028234663852886E{+}38$ to $-1.40129846432481707e{-}45$ *Positive range:* $1.40129846432481707e{-}45$ to $3.4028234663852886E{+}38$	(IEEE 754 floating point)
double	64	*Negative range:* $-1.7976931348623157E{+}308$ to $-4.94065645841246544e{-}324$ *Positive range:* $4.94065645841246544e{-}324$ to $1.7976931348623157E{+}308$	(IEEE 754 floating point)

Fig. D.1 | Java primitive types.

For more information on IEEE 754 visit grouper.ieee.org/groups/754/.

Using the Java API Documentation

E.1 Introduction

The Java class library contains thousands of predefined classes and interfaces that programmers can use to write their own applications. These classes are grouped into packages based on their functionality. For example, the classes and interfaces used for file processing are grouped into the java.io package, and the classes and interfaces for networking applications are grouped into the java.net package. The **Java API documentation** lists the public and protected members of each class and the public members of each interface in the Java class library. The documentation overviews all the classes and interfaces, summarizes their members (i.e., the fields, constructors and methods of classes, and the fields and methods of interfaces) and provides detailed descriptions of each member. Most Java programmers rely on this documentation when writing programs. Normally, programmers would search the API to find the following:

1. The package that contains a particular class or interface.

2. Relationships between a particular class or interface and other classes and interfaces.

3. Class or interface constants—normally declared as public static final fields.

4. Constructors to determine how an object of the class can be initialized.

5. The methods of a class to determine whether they're static or non-static, the number and types of the arguments you need to pass, the return types and any exceptions that might be thrown from the method.

In addition, programmers often rely on the documentation to discover classes and interfaces that they have not used before. For this reason, we demonstrate the documentation with classes you know and classes you may not have studied yet. We show how to use the documentation to locate the information you need to use a class or interface effectively.

E.2 Navigating the Java API

The Java API documentation can be downloaded to your local hard disk or viewed online. To download the Java API documentation, go to www.oracle.com/technetwork/java/ javase/downloads/index.html/ scroll down to the **Additional Resources** section and click the **Download Zip** button to the right of **Java SE 6 Documentation**. You'll be asked to accept a license agreement. To do this, click **Accept**, then click **Continue**. Click the link to the ZIP file to begin downloading it. After downloading the file, you can use a program such as WinZip (www.winzip.com) to extract the files. If you're using Windows, extract the contents to your JDK's installation directory. To view the API documentation on your local hard disk in Microsoft Windows, open C:\Program Files\Java*YourJDKVersion*\docs\api\index.html page in your browser. To view the API documentation online, go to download.oracle.com/javase/6/docs/api/ (Fig. E.1).

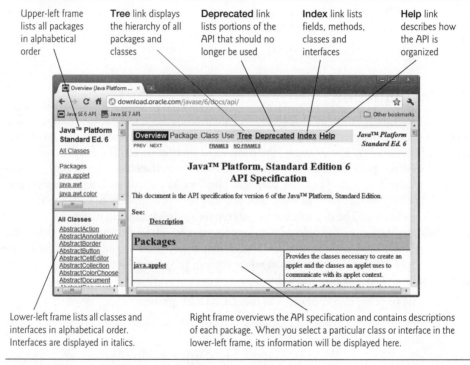

Upper-left frame lists all packages in alphabetical order

Tree link displays the hierarchy of all packages and classes

Deprecated link lists portions of the API that should no longer be used

Index link lists fields, methods, classes and interfaces

Help link describes how the API is organized

Lower-left frame lists all classes and interfaces in alphabetical order. Interfaces are displayed in italics.

Right frame overviews the API specification and contains descriptions of each package. When you select a particular class or interface in the lower-left frame, its information will be displayed here.

Fig. E.1 | Java API overview. (Courtesy of Oracle Corporation)

Frames in the API Documentation's index.html Page

The API documentation is divided into three frames (see Fig. E.1). The upper-left frame lists all of the Java API's packages in alphabetical order. The lower-left frame initially lists the Java API's classes and interfaces in alphabetical order. Interface names are displayed in italic. When you click a specific package in the upper-left frame, the lower-left frame lists the classes and interfaces of the selected package. The right frame initially provides a brief description of each package of the Java API specification—read this overview to become familiar wth the general capabilities of the Java APIs. If you select a class or interface in the lower-left frame, the right frame displays information about that class or interface.

Important Links in the `index.html` Page

At the top of the right frame (Fig. E.1), there are four links—**Tree**, **Deprecated**, **Index** and **Help**. The **Tree** link displays the hierarchy of all packages, classes and interfaces in a tree structure. The **Deprecated** link displays interfaces, classes, exceptions, fields, constructors and methods that should no longer be used. The **Index** link displays classes, interfaces, fields, constructors and methods in alphabetical order. The **Help** link describes how the API documentation is organized. You should probably begin by reading the **Help** page.

Viewing the Index Page

If you do not know the name of the class you're looking for, but you do know the name of a method or field, you can use the documentation's index to locate the class. The **Index** link is located near the upper-right corner of the right frame. The index page (Fig. E.2) displays fields, constructors, methods, interfaces and classes in alphabetical order. For example, if you're looking for `Scanner` method `hasNextInt`, but do not know the class name, you can click the **H** link to go to the alphabetical listing of all items in the Java API that begin with "h". Scroll to method `hasNextInt` (Fig. E.3). Once there, each method named `hasNextInt` is listed with the package name and class to which the method belongs. From there, you can click the class name to view the class's complete details, or you can click the method name to view the method's details.

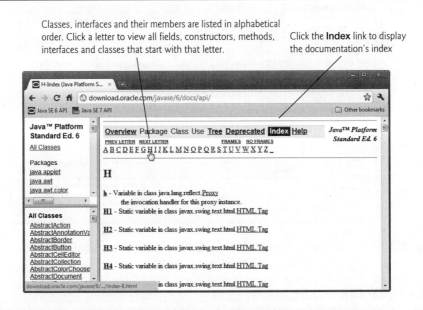

Classes, interfaces and their members are listed in alphabetical order. Click a letter to view all fields, constructors, methods, interfaces and classes that start with that letter.

Click the **Index** link to display the documentation's index

Fig. E.2 | Viewing the **Index** page. (Courtesy of Oracle Corporation.)

Viewing a Specific Package

When you click the package name in the upper-left frame, all classes and interfaces from that package are displayed in the lower-left frame and are divided into five subsections—**Interfaces**, **Classes**, **Enums**, **Exceptions** and **Errors**—each listed alphabetically. For example, the contents of package `javax.swing` are displayed in the lower-left frame (Fig. E.4) when you click `javax.swing` in the upper-left frame. You can click the package name in the lower-left frame to get an overview of the package. If you think that a package contains several classes that could be useful in your application, the package overview can be especially helpful.

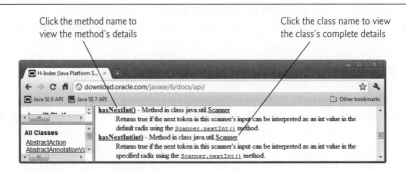

Fig. E.3 | Scroll to method `hasNextInt`. (Courtesy of Oracle Corporation)

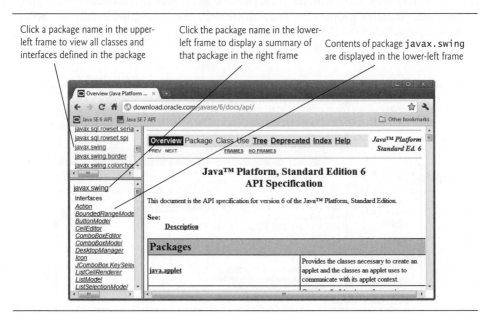

Fig. E.4 | Clicking a package name in the upper-left frame to view all classes and interfaces declared in this package. (Courtesy of Oracle Corporation)

Viewing the Details of a Class

When you click a class name or interface name in the lower-left frame, the right frame displays the details of that class or interface. First you'll see the class's package name followed by a hierarchy that shows the class's relationship to other classes. You'll also see a list of the interfaces implemented by the class and the class's known subclasses. Figure E.5 shows the beginning of the documentation page for class JButton from the javax.swing package. The page first shows the package name in which the class appears. This is followed by the class hierarchy that leads to class JButton, the interfaces class JButton implements and the subclasses of class JButton. The bottom of the right frame shows the beginning of class JButton's description. When you look at the documentation for an interface, the right frame does not display a hierarchy for that interface. Instead, the right frame lists the interface's superinterfaces, known subinterfaces and known implementing classes.

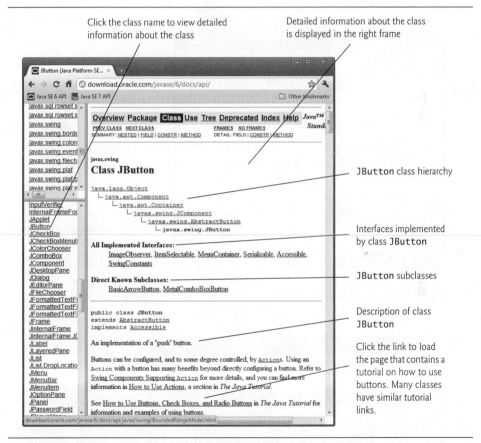

Fig. E.5 | Clicking a class name to view detailed information about the class. (Courtesy of Oracle Corporation)

Summary Sections in a Class's Documentation Page
Other parts of each API page are listed below. Each part is presented only if the class contains or inherits the items specified. Class members shown in the summary sections are public unless they're explicitly marked as protected. A class's private members are not shown in the documentation, because they cannot be used directly in your programs.

1. The **Nested Class Summary** section summarizes the class's `public` and `protected` nested classes—i.e., classes that are defined inside the class. Unless explicitly specified, these classes are `public` and non-`static`.

2. The **Field Summary** section summarizes the class's `public` and `protected` fields. Unless explicitly specified, these fields are `public` and non-`static`. Figure E.6 shows the **Field Summary** section of class `Color`.

3. The **Constructor Summary** section summarizes the class's constructors. Constructors are not inherited, so this section appears in the documentation for a class only if the class declares one or more constructors. Figure E.7 shows the **Constructor Summary** section of class `JButton`.

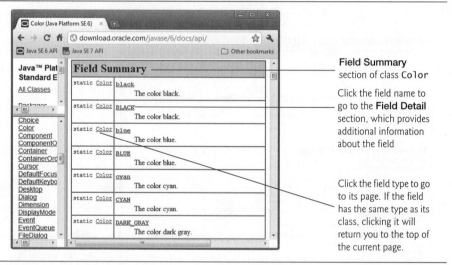

Fig. E.6 | **Field Summary** section of class `Color`. (Courtesy of Oracle Corporation)

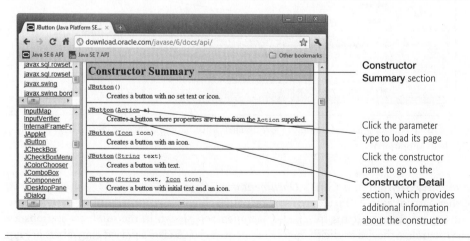

Fig. E.7 | **Constructor Summary** section of class `JButton`. (Courtesy of Oracle Corporation)

4. The **Method Summary** section summarizes the class's `public` and `protected` methods. Unless explicitly specified, these methods are `public` and non-`static`. Figure E.8 shows the **Method Summary** section of class `BufferedInputStream`.

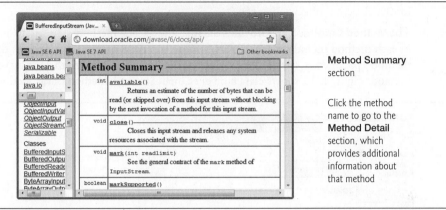

Fig. E.8 | **Method Summary** section of class `BufferedInputStream`. (Courtesy of Oracle Corporation)

The summary sections typically provide only a one-sentence description of a class member. Additional details are presented in the detail sections discussed next.

Detail Sections in a Class's Documentation Page

After the summary sections are detail sections that normally provide more discussion of particular class members. There isn't a detail section for nested classes. When you click the link in the **Nested Class Summary** for a particular nested class, a documentation page describing that nested class is displayed. The detail sections are described below.

1. The **Field Detail** section provides the declaration of each field. It also discusses each field, including the field's modifiers and meaning. Figure E.9 shows the **Field Detail** section of class `Color`.

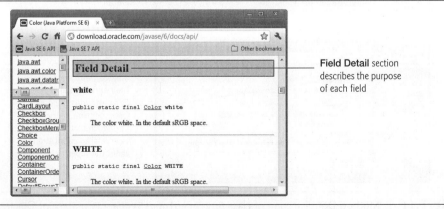

Fig. E.9 | **Field Detail** section of class `Color`. (Courtesy of Oracle Corporation)

2. The **Constructor Detail** section provides the first line of each constructor's declaration and discusses the constructors. The discussion includes the modifiers of each constructor, a description of each constructor, each constructor's parameters and any exceptions thrown by each constructor. Figure E.10 shows the **Constructor Detail** section of class JButton.

3. The **Method Detail** section provides the first line of each method. The discussion of each method includes its modifiers, a more complete method description, the method's parameters, the method's return type and any exceptions thrown by the method. Figure E.11 shows class BufferedInputStream's **Method Detail** section.

Fig. E.10 | **Constructor Detail** section of class JButton. (Courtesy of Oracle Corporation)

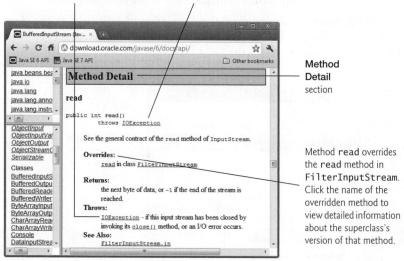

Fig. E.11 | **Method Detail** section of class BufferedInputStream. (Courtesy of Oracle Corporation)

The method details show you other methods that might be of interest (labeled as **See Also**). If the method overrides a method of the superclass, the name of the superclass method and the name of the superclass are provided so you can link to the method or superclass for more information.

As you look through the documentation, you'll notice that there are often links to other fields, methods, nested-classes and top-level classes. These links enable you to jump from the class you're looking at to another relevant portion of the documentation.

F

Using the Debugger

And so shall I catch the fly.
—William Shakespeare

We are built to make mistakes, coded for error.
—Lewis Thomas

What we anticipate seldom occurs; what we least expect generally happens.
—Benjamin Disraeli

Objectives

In this appendix you'll learn:

- To set breakpoints to debug applications.

- To use the **run** command to run an application through the debugger.

- To use the **stop** command to set a breakpoint.

- To use the **cont** command to continue execution.

- To use the **print** command to evaluate expressions.

- To use the **set** command to change variable values during program execution.

- To use the **step**, **step up** and **next** commands to control execution.

- To use the **watch** command to see how a field is modified during program execution.

- To use the **clear** command to list breakpoints or remove a breakpoint.

F.1 Introduction

In Chapter 2, you learned that there are two types of errors—syntax errors and logic errors—and you learned how to eliminate syntax errors from your code. Logic errors do not prevent the application from compiling successfully, but they do cause an application to produce erroneous results when it runs. The JDK includes software called a **debugger** that allows you to monitor the execution of your applications so you can locate and remove logic errors. The debugger will be one of your most important application development tools. Many IDEs provide their own debuggers similar to the one included in the JDK or provide a graphical user interface to the JDK's debugger.

This appendix demonstrates key features of the JDK's debugger using command-line applications that receive no input from the user. The same debugger features discussed here can be used to debug applications that take user input, but debugging such applications requires a slightly more complex setup. To focus on the debugger features, we've opted to demonstrate the debugger with simple command-line applications involving no user input. For more information on the Java debugger visit download.oracle.com/javase/6/docs/technotes/tools/windows/jdb.html.

F.2 Breakpoints and the run, stop, cont and print Commands

We begin our study of the debugger by investigating **breakpoints**, which are markers that can be set at any executable line of code. When application execution reaches a breakpoint, execution pauses, allowing you to examine the values of variables to help determine whether logic errors exist. For example, you can examine the value of a variable that stores the result of a calculation to determine whether the calculation was performed correctly. Setting a breakpoint at a line of code that is not executable (such as a comment) causes the debugger to display an error message.

To illustrate the features of the debugger, we use application AccountTest (Fig. F.1), which creates and manipulates an object of class Account (Fig. 3.13). Execution of AccountTest begins in main (lines 7–24). Line 9 creates an Account object with an initial balance of $50.00. Recall that Account's constructor accepts one argument, which specifies the Account's initial balance. Lines 12–13 output the initial account balance using Account method getBalance. Line 15 declares and initializes a local variable depositAmount. Lines 17–19 then print depositAmount and add it to the Account's balance using its credit method. Finally, lines 22–23 display the new balance. [*Note:* The Appendix F examples directory contains a copy of Account.java identical to the one in Fig. 3.13.]

```
 1    // Fig. F.1: AccountTest.java
 2    // Create and manipulate an Account object.
 3
 4    public class AccountTest
 5    {
 6       // main method begins execution
 7       public static void main( String[] args )
 8       {
 9          Account account = new Account( 50.00 ); // create Account object
10
11          // display initial balance of Account object
12          System.out.printf( "initial account balance: $%.2f\n",
13             account.getBalance() );
14
15          double depositAmount = 25.0; // deposit amount
16
17          System.out.printf( "\nadding %.2f to account balance\n\n",
18             depositAmount );
19          account.credit( depositAmount ); // add to account balance
20
21          // display new balance
22          System.out.printf( "new account balance: $%.2f\n",
23             account.getBalance() );
24       } // end main
25
26    } // end class AccountTest
```

```
initial account balance: $50.00

adding 25.00 to account balance

new account balance: $75.00
```

Fig. F.1 | AccountTest class creates and manipulates an Account object.

In the following steps, you'll use breakpoints and various debugger commands to examine the value of the variable depositAmount declared in AccountTest (Fig. F.1).

1. *Opening the* Command Prompt *window and changing directories.* Open the **Command Prompt** window by selecting **Start > Programs > Accessories > Command Prompt**. Change to the directory containing the Appendix F examples by typing cd C:\examples\debugger [*Note:* If your examples are in a different directory, use that directory here.]

2. *Compiling the application for debugging.* The Java debugger works only with .class files that were compiled with the **-g** compiler option, which generates information that is used by the debugger to help you debug your applications. Compile the application with the -g command-line option by typing javac -g AccountTest.java Account.java. Recall from Chapter 3 that this command compiles both AccountTest.java and Account.java. The command java -g *.java compiles all of the working directory's .java files for debugging.

3. *Starting the debugger.* In the **Command Prompt**, type **jdb** (Fig. F.2). This command will start the Java debugger and enable you to use its features. [*Note:* We modified the colors of our **Command Prompt** window for readability.]

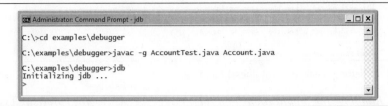

Fig. F.2 | Starting the Java debugger.

4. *Running an application in the debugger.* Run the AccountTest application through the debugger by typing **run** AccountTest (Fig. F.3). If you do not set any breakpoints before running your application in the debugger, the application will run just as it would using the java command.

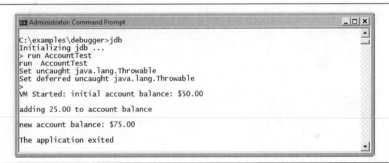

Fig. F.3 | Running the AccountTest application through the debugger.

5. *Restarting the debugger.* To make proper use of the debugger, you must set at least one breakpoint before running the application. Restart the debugger by typing jdb.

6. *Inserting breakpoints in Java.* You set a breakpoint at a specific line of code in your application. The line numbers used in these steps are from the source code in Fig. F.1. Set a breakpoint at line 12 in the source code by typing stop at AccountTest:12 (Fig. F.4). The **stop command** inserts a breakpoint at the line number specified after the command. You can set as many breakpoints as necessary. Set another breakpoint at line 19 by typing stop at AccountTest:19 (Fig. F.4). When the application runs, it suspends execution at any line that contains a breakpoint. The application is said to be in **break mode** when the debugger pauses the application's execution. Breakpoints can be set even after the debugging process has begun. The debugger command stop in, followed by a class name, a period and a method name (e.g., stop in Account.credit) instructs the debugger to set a breakpoint at the first executable statement in the specified method. The debugger pauses execution when program control enters the method.

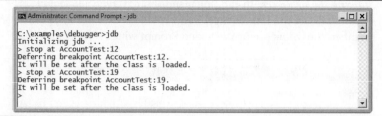

Fig. F.4 | Setting breakpoints at lines 12 and 19.

7. *Running the application and beginning the debugging process.* Type run AccountTest to execute the application and begin the debugging process (Fig. F.5). The debugger prints text indicating that breakpoints were set at lines 12 and 19. It calls each breakpoint a "deferred breakpoint" because each was set before the application began running in the debugger. The application pauses when execution reaches the breakpoint on line 12. At this point, the debugger notifies you that a breakpoint has been reached and it displays the source code at that line (12). That line of code is the next statement that will execute.

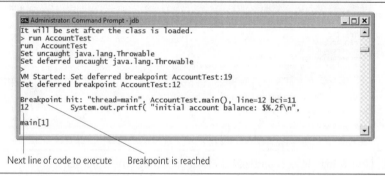

Next line of code to execute   Breakpoint is reached

Fig. F.5 | Restarting the AccountTest application.

8. *Using the cont command to resume execution.* Type cont. The **cont command** causes the application to continue running until the next breakpoint is reached (line 19), at which point the debugger notifies you (Fig. F.6). AccountTest's normal output appears between messages from the debugger.

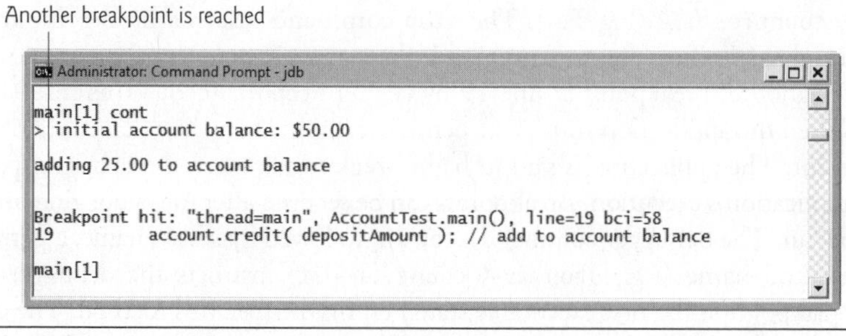

Another breakpoint is reached

```
Administrator: Command Prompt - jdb

main[1] cont
> initial account balance: $50.00

adding 25.00 to account balance

Breakpoint hit: "thread=main", AccountTest.main(), line=19 bci=58
19          account.credit( depositAmount ); // add to account balance
main[1]
```

Fig. F.6 | Execution reaches the second breakpoint.

9. *Examining a variable's value.* Type `print depositAmount` to display the current value stored in the depositAmount variable (Fig. F.7). The **print command** allows you to peek inside the computer at the value of one of your variables. This command will help you find and eliminate logic errors in your code. The value displayed is `25.0`—the value assigned to depositAmount in line 15 of Fig. F.1.

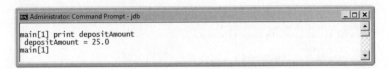

```
main[1] print depositAmount
 depositAmount = 25.0
main[1]
```

Fig. F.7 | Examining the value of variable `depositAmount`.

10. *Continuing application execution.* Type `cont` to continue the application's execution. There are no more breakpoints, so the application is no longer in break mode. The application continues executing and eventually terminates (Fig. F.8). The debugger will stop when the application ends.

```
 depositAmount = 25.0
main[1] cont
> new account balance: $75.00

The application exited

C:\examples\debugger>
```

Fig. F.8 | Continuing application execution and exiting the debugger.

F.3 The print and set Commands

In the preceding section, you learned how to use the debugger's print command to examine the value of a variable during program execution. In this section, you'll learn how to use the print command to examine the value of more complex expressions. You'll also learn the **set command**, which allows the programmer to assign new values to variables.

For this section, we assume that you've followed *Step 1* and *Step 2* in Section F.2 to open the **Command Prompt** window, change to the directory containing the Appendix F examples (e.g., `C:\examples\debugger`) and compile the AccountTest application (and class Account) for debugging.

1. *Starting debugging.* In the **Command Prompt**, type `jdb` to start the Java debugger.

2. *Inserting a breakpoint.* Set a breakpoint at line 19 in the source code by typing `stop at AccountTest:19`.

3. *Running the application and reaching a breakpoint.* Type `run AccountTest` to begin the debugging process (Fig. F.9). This will cause AccountTest's main to execute until the breakpoint at line 19 is reached. This suspends application execution and switches the application into break mode. At this point, the statements in lines 9–13 created an Account object and printed the initial balance of the Ac-

count obtained by calling its getBalance method. The statement in line 15 (Fig. F.1) declared and initialized local variable depositAmount to 25.0. The statement in line 19 is the next statement that will execute.

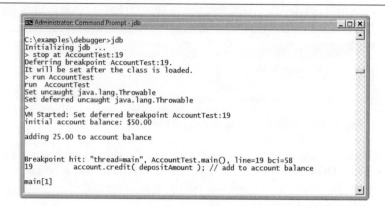

Fig. F.9 | Application execution suspended when debugger reaches the breakpoint at line 19.

4. *Evaluating arithmetic and boolean expressions.* Recall from Section F.2 that once the application has entered break mode, you can explore the values of the application's variables using the debugger's print command. You can also use the print command to evaluate arithmetic and boolean expressions. In the **Command Prompt** window, type print depositAmount - 2.0. The print command returns the value 23.0 (Fig. F.10). However, this command does not actually change the value of depositAmount. In the **Command Prompt** window, type print depositAmount == 23.0. Expressions containing the == symbol are treated as boolean expressions. The value returned is false (Fig. F.10) because depositAmount does not currently contain the value 23.0—depositAmount is still 25.0.

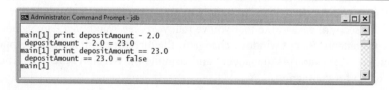

Fig. F.10 | Examining the values of an arithmetic and boolean expression.

5. *Modifying values.* The debugger allows you to change the values of variables during the application's execution. This can be valuable for experimenting with different values and for locating logic errors in applications. You can use the debugger's set command to change the value of a variable. Type set depositAmount = 75.0. The debugger changes the value of depositAmount and displays its new value (Fig. F.11).

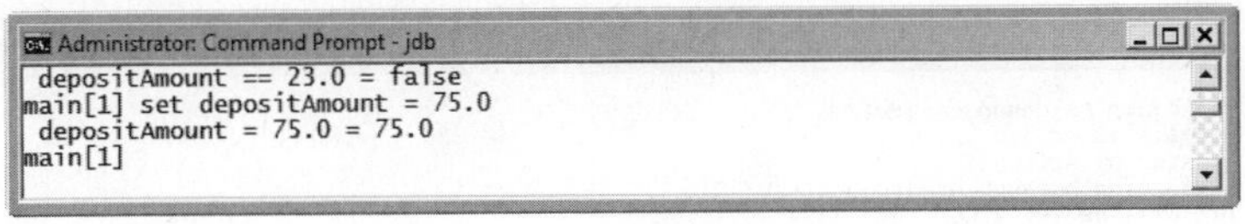

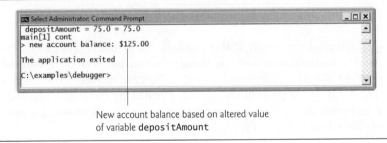

Fig. F.11 | Modifying values.

6. *Viewing the application result.* Type cont to continue application execution. Line 19 of AccountTest (Fig. F.1) executes, passing depositAmount to Account method credit. Method main then displays the new balance. The result is $125.00 (Fig. F.12). This shows that the preceding step changed the value of depositAmount from its initial value (25.0) to 75.0.

```
 Select Administrator: Command Prompt                              _ □ X
  depositAmount = 75.0 = 75.0
main[1] cont
> new account balance: $125.00

The application exited

c:\examples\debugger>
```

New account balance based on altered value
of variable depositAmount

Fig. F.12 | Output displayed after the debugging process.

F.4 Controlling Execution Using the step, step up and next Commands

Sometimes you'll need to execute an application line by line to find and fix errors. Walking through a portion of your application this way can help you verify that a method's code executes correctly. In this section, you'll learn how to use the debugger for this task. The commands you learn in this section allow you to execute a method line by line, execute all the statements of a method at once or execute only the remaining statements of a method (if you've already executed some statements within the method).

Once again, we assume you're working in the directory containing the Appendix F examples and have compiled for debugging with the -g compiler option.

1. *Starting the debugger.* Start the debugger by typing jdb.

2. *Setting a breakpoint.* Type stop at AccountTest:19 to set a breakpoint at line 19.

3. *Running the application.* Run the application by typing run AccountTest. After the application displays its two output messages, the debugger indicates that the breakpoint has been reached and displays the code at line 19 (Fig. F.13). The debugger and application then pause and wait for the next command to be entered.

4. *Using the step command.* The **step command** executes the next statement in the application. If the next statement to execute is a method call, control transfers to the called method. The step command enables you to enter a method and study

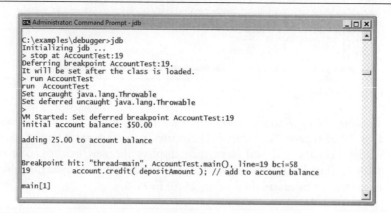

Fig. F.13 | Reaching the breakpoint in the `AccountTest` application.

the individual statements of that method. For instance, you can use the `print` and `set` commands to view and modify the variables within the method. You'll now use the `step` command to enter the `credit` method of class `Account` (Fig. 3.13) by typing `step` (Fig. F.14). The debugger indicates that the step has been completed and displays the next executable statement—in this case, line 21 of class `Account` (Fig. 3.13).

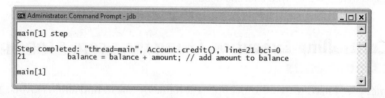

Fig. F.14 | Stepping into the `credit` method.

5. *Using the **step up** command.* After you've stepped into the `credit` method, type **step up**. This command executes the remaining statements in the method and returns control to the place where the method was called. The `credit` method contains only one statement to add the method's parameter `amount` to instance variable `balance`. The `step up` command executes this statement, then pauses before line 22 in `AccountTest`. Thus, the next action to occur will be to print the new account balance (Fig. F.15). In lengthy methods, you may want to look at a few key lines of code, then continue debugging the caller's code. The `step up` command is useful for situations in which you do not want to continue stepping through the entire method line by line.

6. *Using the **cont** command to continue execution.* Enter the `cont` command (Fig. F.16) to continue execution. The statement at lines 22–23 executes, displaying the new balance, then the application and the debugger terminate.

7. *Restarting the debugger.* Restart the debugger by typing `jdb`.

```
Administrator: Command Prompt - jdb                              _ □ ×
main[1] step up
>
Step completed: "thread=main", AccountTest.main(), line=22 bci=63
22          System.out.printf( "new account balance: $%.2f\n",

main[1]
```

Fig. F.15 | Stepping out of a method.

```
Administrator: Command Prompt                                    _ □ ×
main[1] cont
> new account balance: $75.00

The application exited

C:\examples\debugger>
```

Fig. F.16 | Continuing execution of the AccountTest application.

8. *Setting a breakpoint.* Breakpoints persist only until the end of the debugging session in which they're set—once the debugger exits, all breakpoints are removed. (In Section F.6, you'll learn how to manually clear a breakpoint before the end of the debugging session.) Thus, the breakpoint set for line 19 in *Step 2* no longer exists upon restarting the debugger in *Step 7*. To reset the breakpoint at line 19, once again type stop at AccountTest:19.

9. *Running the application.* Type run AccountTest to run the application. As in *Step 3*, AccountTest runs until the breakpoint at line 19 is reached, then the debugger pauses and waits for the next command (Fig. F.17).

```
Administrator: Command Prompt - jdb                              _ □ ×
C:\examples\debugger>jdb
Initializing jdb ...
> stop at AccountTest:19
Deferring breakpoint AccountTest:19.
It will be set after the class is loaded.
> run AccountTest
run  AccountTest
Set uncaught java.lang.Throwable
Set deferred uncaught java.lang.Throwable
>
VM Started: Set deferred breakpoint AccountTest:19
initial account balance: $50.00

adding 25.00 to account balance

Breakpoint hit: "thread=main", AccountTest.main(), line=19 bci=58
19          account.credit( depositAmount ); // add to account balance

main[1]
```

Fig. F.17 | Reaching the breakpoint in the AccountTest application.

10. *Using the next command.* Type **next**. This command behaves like the step command, except when the next statement to execute contains a method call. In that case, the called method executes in its entirety and the application advances to the

next executable line after the method call (Fig. F.18). Recall from *Step 4* that the step command would enter the called method. In this example, the next command causes Account method credit to execute, then the debugger pauses at line 22 in AccountTest.

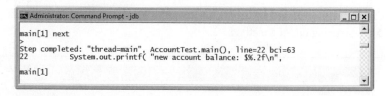

Fig. F.18 | Stepping over a method call.

11. *Using the* **exit** *command.* Use the **exit command** to end the debugging session (Fig. F.19). This command causes the AccountTest application to immediately terminate rather than execute the remaining statements in main. When debugging some types of applications (e.g., GUI applications), the application continues to execute even after the debugging session ends.

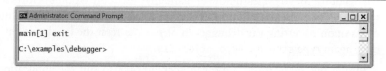

Fig. F.19 | Exiting the debugger.

F.5 The watch Command

In this section, we present the **watch command**, which tells the debugger to watch a field. When that field is about to change, the debugger will notify you. In this section, you'll learn how to use the watch command to see how the Account object's field balance is modified during the execution of the AccountTest application.

As in the preceding two sections, we assume that you've followed *Step 1* and *Step 2* in Section F.2 to open the **Command Prompt**, change to the correct examples directory and compile classes AccountTest and Account for debugging (i.e., with the -g compiler option).

1. *Starting the debugger.* Start the debugger by typing jdb.

2. *Watching a class's field.* Set a watch on Account's balance field by typing watch Account.balance (Fig. F.20). You can set a watch on any field during execution of the debugger. Whenever the value in a field is about to change, the debugger enters break mode and notifies you that the value will change. Watches can be placed only on fields, not on local variables.

3. *Running the application.* Run the application with the command run Account-Test. The debugger will now notify you that field balance's value will change

```
C:\examples\debugger>jdb
Initializing jdb ...
> watch Account.balance
Deferring watch modification of Account.balance.
It will be set after the class is loaded.
>
```

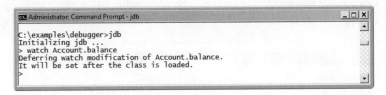

Fig. F.20 | Setting a watch on `Account`'s `balance` field.

(Fig. F.21). When the application begins, an instance of `Account` is created with an initial balance of $50.00 and a reference to the `Account` object is assigned to the local variable `account` (line 9, Fig. F.1). Recall from Fig. 3.13 that when the constructor for this object runs, if parameter `initialBalance` is greater than `0.0`, instance variable `balance` is assigned the value of parameter `initialBalance`. The debugger notifies you that the value of `balance` will be set to `50.0`.

```
It will be set after the class is loaded.
> run AccountTest
run  AccountTest
Set uncaught java.lang.Throwable
Set deferred uncaught java.lang.Throwable
>
VM Started: Set deferred watch modification of Account.balance

Field (Account.balance) is 0.0, will be 50.0: "thread=main", Account.<init>(), l
ine=15 bci=12
15          balance = initialBalance;

main[1]
```

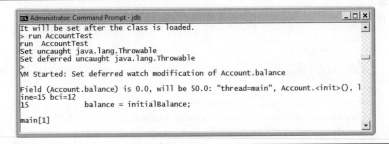

Fig. F.21 | `AccountTest` application stops when `account` is created and its `balance` field will be modified.

4. ***Adding money to the account.*** Type `cont` to continue executing the application. The application executes normally before reaching the code on line 19 of Fig. F.1 that calls `Account` method `credit` to raise the `Account` object's `balance` by a specified `amount`. The debugger notifies you that instance variable `balance` will change (Fig. F.22). Although line 19 of class `AccountTest` calls method `credit`, line 21 in `Account`'s method `credit` actually changes the value of `balance`.

```
main[1] cont
> initial account balance: $50.00

addi
ng 25.00 to account balance

Field (Account.balance) is 50.0, will be 75.0: "thread=main", Account.credit(),
line=21 bci=7
21          balance = balance + amount; // add amount to balance

main[1]
```

Fig. F.22 | Changing the value of `balance` by calling `Account` method `credit`.

5. *Continuing execution.* Type cont—the application will finish executing because the application does not attempt any additional changes to balance (Fig. F.23).

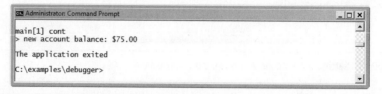

Fig. F.23 | Continuing execution of AccountTest.

6. *Restarting the debugger and resetting the watch on the variable.* Type jdb to restart the debugger. Once again, set a watch on the Account instance variable balance by typing the watch Account.balance, then type run AccountTest to run the application (Fig. F.24).

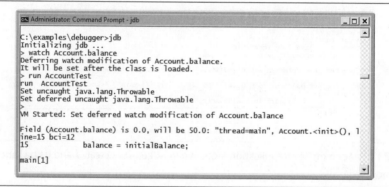

Fig. F.24 | Restarting the debugger and resetting the watch on the variable balance.

7. *Removing the watch on the field.* Suppose you want to watch a field for only part of a program's execution. You can remove the debugger's watch on variable balance by typing **unwatch** Account.balance (Fig. F.25). Type cont—the application will finish executing without reentering break mode.

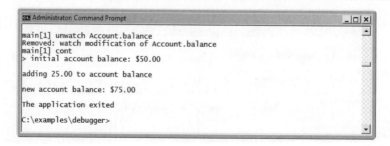

Fig. F.25 | Removing the watch on variable balance.

8. *Closing the* Command Prompt *window.* Close the **Command Prompt** window by clicking its close button.

F.6 The clear Command

In the preceding section, you learned to use the unwatch command to remove a watch on a field. The debugger also provides the clear command to remove a breakpoint from an application. You'll often need to debug applications containing repetitive actions, such as a loop. You may want to examine the values of variables during several, but possibly not all, of the loop's iterations. If you set a breakpoint in the body of a loop, the debugger will pause before each execution of the line containing a breakpoint. After determining that the loop is working properly, you may want to remove the breakpoint and allow the remaining iterations to proceed normally. In this section, we use the compound interest application in Fig. 5.6 to demonstrate how the debugger behaves when you set a breakpoint in the body of a for statement and how to remove a breakpoint in the middle of a debugging session.

1. *Opening the* Command Prompt *window, changing directories and compiling the application for debugging.* Open the **Command Prompt** window, then change to the directory containing the Appendix F examples. For your convenience, we've provided a copy of the Interest.java file in this directory. Compile the application for debugging by typing javac -g Interest.java.

2. *Starting the debugger and setting breakpoints.* Start the debugger by typing jdb. Set breakpoints at lines 13 and 22 of class Interest by typing stop at Interest:13, then stop at Interest:22 (Fig. F.26).

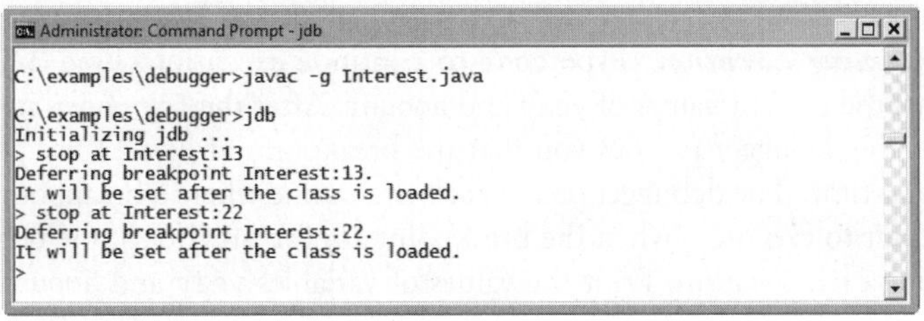

Fig. F.26 | Setting breakpoints in the Interest application.

3. *Running the application.* Run the application by typing run Interest. The application executes until reaching the breakpoint at line 13 (Fig. F.27).

4. *Continuing execution.* Type cont to continue—the application executes line 13, printing the column headings "Year" and "Amount on deposit". Line 13 appears before the for statement at lines 16–23 in Interest (Fig. 5.6) and thus executes only once. Execution continues past line 13 until the breakpoint at line 22 is reached during the first iteration of the for statement (Fig. F.28).

5. *Examining variable values.* Type print year to examine the current value of variable year (i.e., the for's control variable). Print the value of variable amount too (Fig. F.29).

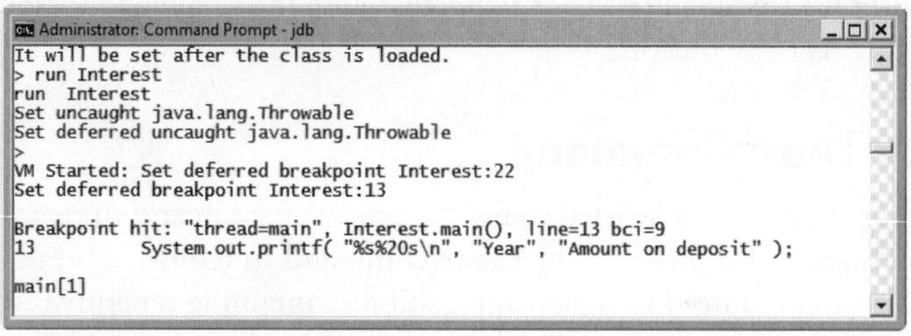

Fig. F.27 | Reaching the breakpoint at line 13 in the `Interest` application.

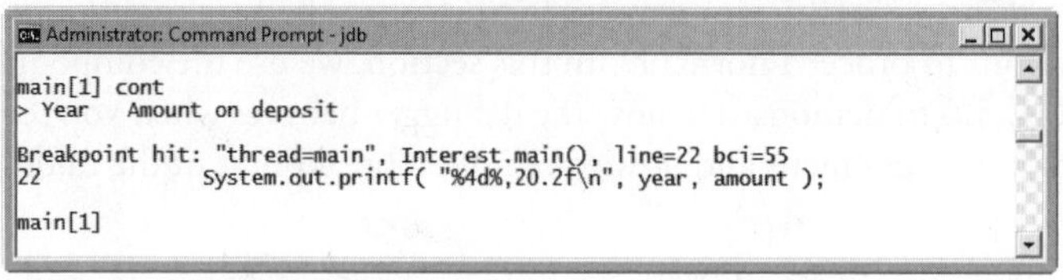

Fig. F.28 | Reaching the breakpoint at line 22 in the `Interest` application.

Fig. F.29 | Printing `year` and `amount` during the first iteration of `Interest`'s `for`.

6. *Continuing execution.* Type `cont` to continue execution. Line 22 executes and prints the current values of `year` and `amount`. After the `for` enters its second iteration, the debugger notifies you that the breakpoint at line 22 has been reached a second time. The debugger pauses each time a line where a breakpoint has been set is about to execute—when the breakpoint appears in a loop, the debugger pauses during each iteration. Print the values of variables `year` and `amount` again to see how the values have changed since the first iteration of the `for` (Fig. F.30).

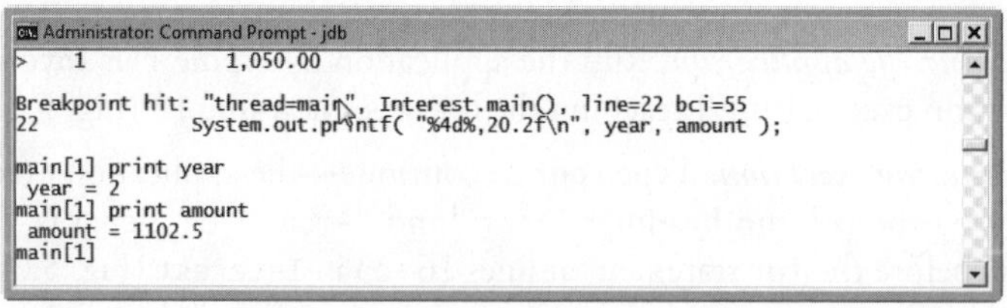

Fig. F.30 | Printing `year` and `amount` during the second iteration of `Interest`'s `for`.

7. *Removing a breakpoint.* You can display a list of all of the breakpoints in the application by typing **clear** (Fig. F.31). Suppose you're satisfied that the `Interest`

application's for statement is working properly, so you want to remove the breakpoint at line 22 and allow the remaining iterations of the loop to proceed normally. You can remove the breakpoint at line 22 by typing clear Interest:22. Now type clear to list the remaining breakpoints in the application. The debugger should indicate that only the breakpoint at line 13 remains (Fig. F.31). This breakpoint has already been reached and thus will no longer affect execution.

```
Administrator: Command Prompt - jdb                              _ □ ×
 amount = 1102.5
main[1] clear
Breakpoints set:
        breakpoint Interest:13
        breakpoint Interest:22
main[1] clear Interest:22
Removed: breakpoint Interest:22
main[1] clear
Breakpoints set:
        breakpoint Interest:13
main[1]
```

Fig. F.31 | Removing the breakpoint at line 22.

8. *Continuing execution after removing a breakpoint.* Type cont to continue execution. Recall that execution last paused before the printf statement in line 22. If the breakpoint at line 22 was removed successfully, continuing the application will produce the correct output for the current and remaining iterations of the for statement without the application halting (Fig. F.32).

```
Administrator: Command Prompt                                   _ □ ×
        breakpoint Interest:13
main[1] cont
>    2          1,102.50
     3          1,157.63
     4          1,215.51
     5          1,276.28
     6          1,340.10
     7          1,407.10
     8          1,477.46
     9          1,551.33
    10          1,628.89

The application exited

C:\examples\debugger>
```

Fig. F.32 | Application executes without a breakpoint set at line 22.

F.7 Wrap-Up

In this appendix, you learned how to insert and remove breakpoints in the debugger. Breakpoints allow you to pause application execution so you can examine variable values with the debugger's print command. This capability will help you locate and fix logic errors in your applications. You saw how to use the print command to examine the value of an expression and how to use the set command to change the value of a variable. You also learned debugger commands (including the step, step up and next commands) that can be used to determine whether a method is executing correctly. You learned how to use the watch command to keep track of a field throughout the life of an application. Finally, you learned how to use the clear command to list all the breakpoints set for an application or remove individual breakpoints to continue execution without breakpoints.

G

Formatted Output

Objectives

In this appendix you'll learn:

- To understand input and output streams.
- To use `printf` formatting.
- To print with field widths and precisions.
- To use formatting flags in the `printf` format string.
- To print with an argument index.
- To output literals and escape sequences.
- To format output with class `Formatter`.

All the news that's fit to print.
—Adolph S. Ochs

What mad pursuit? What struggle to escape?
—John Keats

Remove not the landmark on the boundary of the fields.
—Amenehope

G.1 Introduction

In this appendix, we discuss the formatting features of method `printf` and class `Formatter` (package `java.util`). Class **Formatter** formats and outputs data to a specified destination, such as a string or a file output stream. Many features of `printf` were discussed earlier in the text. This appendix summarizes those features and introduces others, such as displaying date and time data in various formats, reordering output based on the index of the argument and displaying numbers and strings with various flags.

G.2 Streams

Input and output are usually performed with streams, which are sequences of bytes. In input operations, the bytes flow from a device (e.g., a keyboard, a disk drive, a network connection) to main memory. In output operations, bytes flow from main memory to a device (e.g., a display screen, a printer, a disk drive, a network connection).

When program execution begins, three streams are created. The standard input stream typically reads bytes from the keyboard, and the standard output stream typically outputs characters to a command window. A third stream, the **standard error stream** (`System.err`), typically outputs characters to a command window and is used to output error messages so they can be viewed immediately. Operating systems typically allow these streams to be redirected to other devices. Streams are discussed in detail in Chapter 17, Files, Streams and Object Serialization, and Chapter 24, Networking.

G.3 Formatting Output with `printf`

Precise output formatting is accomplished with `printf`. Java borrowed (and enhanced) this feature from the C programming language. Method `printf` can perform the following formatting capabilities, each of which is discussed in this appendix:

1. Rounding floating-point values to an indicated number of decimal places.
2. Aligning a column of numbers with decimal points appearing one above the other.
3. Right justification and left justification of outputs.
4. Inserting literal characters at precise locations in a line of output.

5. Representing floating-point numbers in exponential format.

6. Representing integers in octal and hexadecimal format.

7. Displaying all types of data with fixed-size field widths and precisions.

8. Displaying dates and times in various formats.

Every call to printf supplies as the first argument a **format string** that describes the output format. The format string may consist of **fixed text** and **format specifiers**. Fixed text is output by printf just as it would be output by System.out methods print or println. Each format specifier is a placeholder for a value and specifies the type of data to output. Format specifiers also may include optional formatting information.

In the simplest form, each format specifier begins with a percent sign (%) and is followed by a **conversion character** that represents the data type of the value to output. For example, the format specifier %s is a placeholder for a string, and the format specifier %d is a placeholder for an int value. The optional formatting information, such as an argument index, flags, field width and precision, is specified between the percent sign and the conversion character. We demonstrate each of these capabilities.

G.4 Printing Integers

Figure G.1 describes the **integer conversion characters**. Figure G.2 uses each to print an integer. In lines 9–10, the plus sign is not displayed by default, but the minus sign is. Later in this appendix (Fig. G.14) we'll see how to force plus signs to print.

Conversion character	Description
d	Display a decimal (base 10) integer.
o	Display an octal (base 8) integer.
x or X	Display a hexadecimal (base 16) integer. X uses uppercase letters.

Fig. G.1 | Integer conversion characters.

```
 1    // Fig. G.2: IntegerConversionTest.java
 2    // Using the integer conversion characters.
 3
 4    public class IntegerConversionTest
 5    {
 6       public static void main( String[] args )
 7       {
 8          System.out.printf( "%d\n", 26 );
 9          System.out.printf( "%d\n", +26 );
10          System.out.printf( "%d\n", -26 );
11          System.out.printf( "%o\n", 26 );
12          System.out.printf( "%x\n", 26 );
```

Fig. G.2 | Using the integer conversion characters. (Part 1 of 2.)

```
13          System.out.printf( "%X\n", 26 );
14     } // end main
15  } // end class IntegerConversionTest
```

```
26
26
-26
32
1a
1A
```

Fig. G.2 | Using the integer conversion characters. (Part 2 of 2.)

The printf method has the form

```
printf( format-string, argument-list );
```

where *format-string* describes the output format, and the optional *argument-list* contains the values that correspond to each format specifier in *format-string*. There can be many format specifiers in one format string.

Each format string in lines 8–10 specifies that printf should output a decimal integer (%d) followed by a newline character. At the format specifier's position, printf substitutes the value of the first argument after the format string. If the format string contains multiple format specifiers, at each subsequent format specifier's position printf substitutes the value of the next argument in the argument list. The %o format specifier in line 11 outputs the integer in octal format. The %x format specifier in line 12 outputs the integer in hexadecimal format. The %X format specifier in line 13 outputs the integer in hexadecimal format with capital letters.

G.5 Printing Floating-Point Numbers

Figure G.3 describes the floating-point conversions. The **conversion characters e** and E display floating-point values in **computerized scientific notation** (also called **exponential notation**). Exponential notation is the computer equivalent of the scientific notation used in mathematics. For example, the value 150.4582 is represented in scientific notation in mathematics as

$$1.504582 \times 10^2$$

and is represented in exponential notation as

```
1.504582e+02
```

in Java. This notation indicates that 1.504582 is multiplied by 10 raised to the second power (e+02). The e stands for "exponent."

Values printed with the conversion characters e, E and f are output with six digits of precision to the right of the decimal point by default (e.g., 1.045921)—other precisions must be specified explicitly. For values printed with the conversion character g, the precision represents the total number of digits displayed, excluding the exponent. The default is six digits (e.g., 12345678.9 is displayed as 1.23457e+07). **Conversion character f** always prints at least one digit to the left of the decimal point. Conversion characters e and E print

Conversion character	Description
e or E	Display a floating-point value in exponential notation. Conversion character E displays the output in uppercase letters.
f	Display a floating-point value in decimal format.
g or G	Display a floating-point value in either the floating-point format f or the exponential format e based on the magnitude of the value. If the magnitude is less than 10^{-3}, or greater than or equal to 10^7, the floating-point value is printed with e (or E). Otherwise, the value is printed in format f. When conversion character G is used, the output is displayed in uppercase letters.
a or A	Display a floating-point number in hexadecimal format. Conversion character A displays the output in uppercase letters.

Fig. G.3 | Floating-point conversion characters.

lowercase e and uppercase E preceding the exponent and always print exactly one digit to the left of the decimal point. Rounding occurs if the value being formatted has more significant digits than the precision.

Conversion character **g** (or **G**) prints in either e (E) or f format, depending on the floating-point value. For example, the values 0.0000875, 87500000.0, 8.75, 87.50 and 875.0 are printed as 8.750000e-05, 8.750000e+07, 8.750000, 87.500000 and 875.000000 with the conversion character g. The value 0.0000875 uses e notation because the magnitude is less than 10-3. The value 87500000.0 uses e notation because the magnitude is greater than 10⁷. Figure G.4 demonstrates the floating-point conversion characters.

```
1   // Fig. G.4: FloatingNumberTest.java
2   // Using floating-point conversion characters.
3
4   public class FloatingNumberTest
5   {
6      public static void main( String[] args )
7      {
8         System.out.printf( "%e\n", 12345678.9 );
9         System.out.printf( "%e\n", +12345678.9 );
10        System.out.printf( "%e\n", -12345678.9 );
11        System.out.printf( "%E\n", 12345678.9 );
12        System.out.printf( "%f\n", 12345678.9 );
13        System.out.printf( "%g\n", 12345678.9 );
14        System.out.printf( "%G\n", 12345678.9 );
15     } // end main
16  } // end class FloatingNumberTest
```

```
1.234568e+07
1.234568e+07
-1.234568e+07
```

Fig. G.4 | Using floating-point conversion characters. (Part 1 of 2.)

```
1.234568E+07
12345678.900000
1.23457e+07
1.23457E+07
```

Fig. G.4 | Using floating-point conversion characters. (Part 2 of 2.)

G.6 Printing Strings and Characters

The c and s conversion characters print individual characters and strings, respectively. **Conversion characters c** and **C** require a char argument. **Conversion characters s** and **S** can take a String or any Object as an argument. When conversion characters C and S are used, the output is displayed in uppercase letters. Figure G.5 displays characters, strings and objects with conversion characters c and s. Autoboxing occurs at line 9 when an int constant is assigned to an Integer object. Line 15 outputs an Integer argument with the conversion character s, which implicitly invokes the toString method to get the integer value. You can also output an Integer object using the %d format specifier. In this case, the int value in the Integer object will be unboxed and output.

> **Common Programming Error G.1**
>
> *Using %c to print a String causes an IllegalFormatConversionException—a String cannot be converted to a character.*

```java
1   // Fig. G.5: CharStringConversion.java
2   // Using character and string conversion characters.
3   public class CharStringConversion
4   {
5      public static void main( String[] args )
6      {
7         char character = 'A';   // initialize char
8         String string = "This is also a string";   // String object
9         Integer integer = 1234;   // initialize integer (autoboxing)
10
11        System.out.printf( "%c\n", character );
12        System.out.printf( "%s\n", "This is a string" );
13        System.out.printf( "%s\n", string );
14        System.out.printf( "%S\n", string );
15        System.out.printf( "%s\n", integer ); // implicit call to toString
16     } // end main
17   } // end class CharStringConversion
```

```
A
This is a string
This is also a string
THIS IS ALSO A STRING
1234
```

Fig. G.5 | Using character and string conversion characters.

G.7 Printing Dates and Times

The **conversion character t** (or T) is used to print dates and times in various formats. It's always followed by a **conversion suffix character** that specifies the date and/or time format. When conversion character T is used, the output is displayed in uppercase letters. Figure G.6 lists the common conversion suffix characters for formatting **date and time compositions** that display both the date and the time. Figure G.7 lists the common conversion suffix characters for formatting dates. Figure G.8 lists the common conversion suffix characters for formatting times. For the complete list of conversion suffix characters, visit java.sun.com/javase/6/docs/api/java/util/Formatter.html.

Conversion suffix character	Description
c	Display date and time formatted as day month date hour:minute:second time-zone year with three characters for day and month, two digits for date, hour, minute and second and four digits for year—for example, Wed Mar 03 16:30:25 GMT-05:00 2004. The 24-hour clock is used. GMT-05:00 is the time zone.
F	Display date formatted as year-month-date with four digits for the year and two digits each for the month and date (e.g., 2004-05-04).
D	Display date formatted as month/day/year with two digits each for the month, day and year (e.g., 03/03/04).
r	Display time in 12-hour format as hour:minute:second AM|PM with two digits each for the hour, minute and second (e.g., 04:30:25 PM).
R	Display time formatted as hour:minute with two digits each for the hour and minute (e.g., 16:30). The 24-hour clock is used.
T	Display time as hour:minute:second with two digits for the hour, minute and second (e.g., 16:30:25). The 24-hour clock is used.

Fig. G.6 | Date and time composition conversion suffix characters.

Conversion suffix character	Description
A	Display full name of the day of the week (e.g., Wednesday).
a	Display the three-character name of the day of the week (e.g., Wed).
B	Display full name of the month (e.g., March).
b	Display the three-character short name of the month (e.g., Mar).
d	Display the day of the month with two digits, padding with leading zeros as necessary (e.g., 03).
m	Display the month with two digits, padding with leading zeros as necessary (e.g., 07).

Fig. G.7 | Date formatting conversion suffix characters. (Part 1 of 2.)

Conversion suffix character	Description
e	Display the day of month without leading zeros (e.g., 3).
Y	Display the year with four digits (e.g., 2004).
y	Display the last two digits of the year with leading zeros (e.g., 04).
j	Display the day of the year with three digits, padding with leading zeros as necessary (e.g., 016).

Fig. G.7 | Date formatting conversion suffix characters. (Part 2 of 2.)

Conversion suffix character	Description
H	Display hour in 24-hour clock with a leading zero as necessary (e.g., 16).
I	Display hour in 12-hour clock with a leading zero as necessary (e.g., 04).
k	Display hour in 24-hour clock without leading zeros (e.g., 16).
l	Display hour in 12-hour clock without leading zeros (e.g., 4).
M	Display minute with a leading zero as necessary (e.g., 06).
S	Display second with a leading zero as necessary (e.g., 05).
Z	Display the abbreviation for the time zone (e.g., EST, stands for Eastern Standard Time, which is 5 hours behind Greenwich Mean Time).
p	Display morning or afternoon marker in lowercase (e.g., pm).
P	Display morning or afternoon marker in uppercase (e.g., PM).

Fig. G.8 | Time formatting conversion suffix characters.

Figure G.9 uses the conversion characters t and T with the conversion suffix characters to display dates and times in various formats. Conversion character t requires the corresponding argument to be a date or time of type long, Long, **Calendar** (package java.util) or **Date** (package java.util)—objects of each of these classes can represent dates and times. Class Calendar is preferred for this purpose because some constructors

```
1   // Fig. G.9: DateTimeTest.java
2   // Formatting dates and times with conversion characters t and T.
3   import java.util.Calendar;
4
5   public class DateTimeTest
6   {
7      public static void main( String[] args )
8      {
9         // get current date and time
10        Calendar dateTime = Calendar.getInstance();
```

Fig. G.9 | Formatting dates and times with conversion characters t and T. (Part 1 of 2.)

```
11
12          // printing with conversion characters for date/time compositions
13          System.out.printf( "%tc\n", dateTime );
14          System.out.printf( "%tF\n", dateTime );
15          System.out.printf( "%tD\n", dateTime );
16          System.out.printf( "%tr\n", dateTime );
17          System.out.printf( "%tT\n", dateTime );
18
19          // printing with conversion characters for date
20          System.out.printf( "%1$tA, %1$tB %1$td, %1$tY\n", dateTime );
21          System.out.printf( "%1$TA, %1$TB %1$Td, %1$TY\n", dateTime );
22          System.out.printf( "%1$ta, %1$tb %1$te, %1$ty\n", dateTime );
23
24          // printing with conversion characters for time
25          System.out.printf( "%1$tH:%1$tM:%1$tS\n", dateTime );
26          System.out.printf( "%1$tZ %1$tI:%1$tM:%1$tS %tP", dateTime );
27      } // end main
28  } // end class DateTimeTest
```

```
Wed Feb 25 15:00:22 EST 2009
2009-02-25
02/25/09
03:00:22 PM
15:00:22
Wednesday, February 25, 2009
WEDNESDAY, FEBRUARY 25, 2009
Wed, Feb 25, 09
15:00:22
EST 03:00:22 PM
```

Fig. G.9 | Formatting dates and times with conversion characters t and T. (Part 2 of 2.)

and methods in class Date are replaced by those in class Calendar. Line 10 invokes static method **getInstance** of Calendar to obtain a calendar with the current date and time. Lines 13–17, 20–22 and 25–26 use this Calendar object in printf statements as the value to be formatted with conversion character t. Lines 20–22 and 25–26 use the optional **argument index** ("1$") to indicate that all format specifiers in the format string use the first argument after the format string in the argument list. You'll learn more about argument indices in Section G.11. Using the argument index eliminates the need to repeatedly list the same argument.

G.8 Other Conversion Characters

The remaining conversion characters are **b**, **B**, **h**, **H**, **%** and **n**. These are described in Fig. G.10. Lines 9–10 of Fig. G.11 use %b to print the value of boolean (or Boolean) values false and true. Line 11 associates a String to %b, which returns true because it's not null. Line 12 associates a null object to %B, which displays FALSE because test is null. Lines 13–14 use %h to print the string representations of the hash-code values for strings "hello" and "Hello". These values could be used to store or locate the strings in a Hashtable or HashMap (both discussed in Chapter 18, Generic Collections). The hash-code values for these two strings differ, because one string starts with a lowercase letter and the other with an uppercase letter. Line 15 uses %H to print null in uppercase letters. The last two printf statements (lines 16–17) use %% to print the % character in a string and %n to print a platform-specific line separator.

Conversion character	Description
b or B	Print "true" or "false" for the value of a boolean or Boolean. These conversion characters can also format the value of any reference. If the reference is non-null, "true" is output; otherwise, "false". When conversion character B is used, the output is displayed in uppercase letters.
h or H	Print the string representation of an object's hash-code value in hexadecimal format. If the corresponding argument is null, "null" is printed. When conversion character H is used, the output is displayed in uppercase letters.
%	Print the percent character.
n	Print the platform-specific line separator (e.g., \r\n on Windows or \n on UNIX/LINUX).

Fig. G.10 | Other conversion characters.

```
 1   // Fig. G.11: OtherConversion.java
 2   // Using the b, B, h, H, % and n conversion characters.
 3
 4   public class OtherConversion
 5   {
 6      public static void main( String[] args )
 7      {
 8         Object test = null;
 9         System.out.printf( "%b\n", false );
10         System.out.printf( "%b\n", true );
11         System.out.printf( "%b\n", "Test" );
12         System.out.printf( "%B\n", test );
13         System.out.printf( "Hashcode of \"hello\" is %h\n", "hello" );
14         System.out.printf( "Hashcode of \"Hello\" is %h\n", "Hello" );
15         System.out.printf( "Hashcode of null is %H\n", test );
16         System.out.printf( "Printing a %% in a format string\n" );
17         System.out.printf( "Printing a new line %nnext line starts here" );
18      } // end main
19   } // end class OtherConversion
```

```
false
true
true
FALSE
Hashcode of "hello" is 5e918d2
```

Fig. G.11 | Using the b, B, h, H, % and n conversion characters. (Part 1 of 2.)

```
Hashcode of "Hello" is 42628b2
Hashcode of null is NULL
Printing a % in a format string
Printing a new line
next line starts here
```

Fig. G.11 | Using the b, B, h, H, % and n conversion characters. (Part 2 of 2.)

Common Programming Error G.2

Trying to print a literal percent character using % rather than %% in the format string might cause a difficult-to-detect logic error. When % appears in a format string, it must be followed by a conversion character in the string. The single percent could accidentally be followed by a legitimate conversion character, thus causing a logic error.

G.9 Printing with Field Widths and Precisions

The size of a field in which data is printed is specified by a **field width**. If the field width is larger than the data being printed, the data is right justified in that field by default. We discuss left justification in Section G.10. You insert an integer representing the field width between the % and the conversion character (e.g., %4d) in the format specifier. Figure G.12 prints two groups of five numbers each, right justifying those numbers that contain fewer digits than the field width. The field width is increased to print values wider than the field and that the minus sign for a negative value uses one character position in the field. Also, if no field width is specified, the data prints in exactly as many positions as it needs. Field widths can be used with all format specifiers except the line separator (%n).

```
1   // Fig. G.12: FieldWidthTest.java
2   // Right justifying integers in fields.
3
4   public class FieldWidthTest
5   {
6      public static void main( String[] args )
7      {
8         System.out.printf( "%4d\n", 1 );
9         System.out.printf( "%4d\n", 12 );
10        System.out.printf( "%4d\n", 123 );
11        System.out.printf( "%4d\n", 1234 );
12        System.out.printf( "%4d\n\n", 12345 ); // data too large
13
14        System.out.printf( "%4d\n", -1 );
15        System.out.printf( "%4d\n", -12 );
16        System.out.printf( "%4d\n", -123 );
17        System.out.printf( "%4d\n", -1234 ); // data too large
18        System.out.printf( "%4d\n", -12345 ); // data too large
19     } // end main
20  } // end class RightJustifyTest
```

Fig. G.12 | Right justifying integers in fields. (Part 1 of 2.)

```
   1
  12
 123
1234
12345

  -1
 -12
-123
-1234
-12345
```

Fig. G.12 | Right justifying integers in fields. (Part 2 of 2.)

Common Programming Error G.3

Not providing a sufficiently large field width to handle a value to be printed can offset other data being printed and produce confusing outputs. Know your data!

Method `printf` also provides the ability to specify the precision with which data is printed. Precision has different meanings for different types. When used with floating-point conversion characters e and f, the precision is the number of digits that appear after the decimal point. When used with conversion characters g, a or A, the precision is the maximum number of significant digits to be printed. When used with conversion character s, the precision is the maximum number of characters to be written from the string. To use precision, place between the percent sign and the conversion specifier a decimal point (.) followed by an integer representing the precision. Figure G.13 demonstrates the use of precision in format strings. When a floating-point value is printed with a precision smaller than the original number of decimal places in the value, the value is rounded. Also, the format specifier %.3g indicates that the total number of digits used to display the floating-point value is 3. Because the value has three digits to the left of the decimal point, the value is rounded to the ones position.

The field width and the precision can be combined by placing the field width, followed by a decimal point, followed by a precision between the percent sign and the conversion character, as in the statement

```
printf( "%9.3f", 123.456789 );
```

which displays 123.457 with three digits to the right of the decimal point right justified in a nine-digit field—this number will be preceded in its field by two blanks.

```
1   // Fig. G.13: PrecisionTest.java
2   // Using precision for floating-point numbers and strings.
3   public class PrecisionTest
4   {
5      public static void main( String[] args )
6      {
7         double f = 123.94536;
8         String s = "Happy Birthday";
```

Fig. G.13 | Using precision for floating-point numbers and strings. (Part 1 of 2.)

```
 9
10          System.out.printf( "Using precision for floating-point numbers\n" );
11          System.out.printf( "\t%.3f\n\t%.3e\n\t%.3g\n\n", f, f, f );
12
13          System.out.printf( "Using precision for strings\n" );
14          System.out.printf( "\t%.11s\n", s );
15      } // end main
16  } // end class PrecisionTest
```

```
Using precision for floating-point numbers
        123.945
        1.239e+02
        124

Using precision for strings
        Happy Birth
```

Fig. G.13 | Using precision for floating-point numbers and strings. (Part 2 of 2.)

G.10 Using Flags in the `printf` Format String

Various flags may be used with method `printf` to supplement its output formatting capabilities. Seven flags are available for use in format strings (Fig. G.14).

Flag	Description
− (minus sign)	Left justify the output within the specified field.
+ (plus sign)	Display a plus sign preceding positive values and a minus sign preceding negative values.
space	Print a space before a positive value not printed with the + flag.
#	Prefix 0 to the output value when used with the octal conversion character o. Prefix 0x to the output value when used with the hexadecimal conversion character x.
0 (zero)	Pad a field with leading zeros.
, (comma)	Use the locale-specific thousands separator (i.e., ',' for U.S. locale) to display decimal and floating-point numbers.
(	Enclose negative numbers in parentheses.

Fig. G.14 | Format string flags.

To use a flag in a format string, place it immediately to the right of the percent sign. Several flags may be used in the same format specifier. Figure G.15 demonstrates right justification and left justification of a string, an integer, a character and a floating-point number. Line 9 serves as a counting mechanism for the screen output.

Figure G.16 prints a positive number and a negative number, each with and without the **+ flag**. The minus sign is displayed in both cases, the plus sign only when the + flag is used.

```
 1   // Fig. G.15: MinusFlagTest.java
 2   // Right justifying and left justifying values.
 3
 4   public class MinusFlagTest
 5   {
 6      public static void main( String[] args )
 7      {
 8         System.out.println( "Columns:" );
 9         System.out.println( "0123456789012345678901234567890123456789\n" );
10         System.out.printf( "%10s%10d%10c%10f\n\n", "hello", 7, 'a', 1.23 );
11         System.out.printf(
12            "%-10s%-10d%-10c%-10f\n", "hello", 7, 'a', 1.23 );
13      } // end main
14   } // end class MinusFlagTest
```

```
Columns:
0123456789012345678901234567890123456789

     hello         7         a  1.230000

hello     7         a         1.230000
```

Fig. G.15 | Right justifying and left justifying values.

```
 1   // Fig. G.16: PlusFlagTest.java
 2   // Printing numbers with and without the + flag.
 3
 4   public class PlusFlagTest
 5   {
 6      public static void main( String[] args )
 7      {
 8         System.out.printf( "%d\t%d\n", 786, -786 );
 9         System.out.printf( "%+d\t%+d\n", 786, -786 );
10      } // end main
11   } // end class PlusFlagTest
```

```
786      -786
+786     -786
```

Fig. G.16 | Printing numbers with and without the + flag.

Figure G.17 prefixes a space to the positive number with the **space flag**. This is useful for aligning positive and negative numbers with the same number of digits. The value -547 is not preceded by a space in the output because of its minus sign. Figure G.18 uses the **# flag** to prefix 0 to the octal value and 0x to the hexadecimal value.

```
 1   // Fig. G.17: SpaceFlagTest.java
 2   // Printing a space before non-negative values.
 3
```

Fig. G.17 | Printing a space before nonnegative values. (Part 1 of 2.)

```
 4    public class SpaceFlagTest
 5    {
 6       public static void main( String[] args )
 7       {
 8          System.out.printf( "% d\n% d\n", 547, -547 );
 9       } // end main
10    } // end class SpaceFlagTest
```

```
 547
-547
```

Fig. G.17 | Printing a space before nonnegative values. (Part 2 of 2.)

```
 1    // Fig. G.18: PoundFlagTest.java
 2    // Using the # flag with conversion characters o and x.
 3
 4    public class PoundFlagTest
 5    {
 6       public static void main( String[] args )
 7       {
 8          int c = 31;       // initialize c
 9
10          System.out.printf( "%#o\n", c );
11          System.out.printf( "%#x\n", c );
12       } // end main
13    } // end class PoundFlagTest
```

```
037
0x1f
```

Fig. G.18 | Using the # flag with conversion characters o and x.

Figure G.19 combines the + flag the **0 flag** and the space flag to print 452 in a field of width 9 with a + sign and leading zeros, next prints 452 in a field of width 9 using only the 0 flag, then prints 452 in a field of width 9 using only the space flag.

```
 1    // Fig. G.19: ZeroFlagTest.java
 2    // Printing with the 0 (zero) flag fills in leading zeros.
 3
 4    public class ZeroFlagTest
 5    {
 6       public static void main( String[] args )
 7       {
 8          System.out.printf( "%+09d\n", 452 );
 9          System.out.printf( "%09d\n", 452 );
10          System.out.printf( "% 9d\n", 452 );
11       } // end main
12    } // end class ZeroFlagTest
```

Fig. G.19 | Printing with the 0 (zero) flag fills in leading zeros. (Part 1 of 2.)

```
+00000452
000000452
      452
```

Fig. G.19 | Printing with the 0 (zero) flag fills in leading zeros. (Part 2 of 2.)

Figure G.20 uses the comma (,) flag to display a decimal and a floating-point number with the thousands separator. Figure G.21 encloses negative numbers in parentheses using the (flag. The value 50 is not enclosed in parentheses in the output because it's a positive number.

```
 1   // Fig. G.20: CommaFlagTest.java
 2   // Using the comma (,) flag to display numbers with thousands separator.
 3
 4   public class CommaFlagTest
 5   {
 6      public static void main( String[] args )
 7      {
 8         System.out.printf( "%,d\n", 58625 );
 9         System.out.printf( "%,.2f", 58625.21 );
10         System.out.printf( "%,.2f", 12345678.9 );
11      } // end main
12   } // end class CommaFlagTest
```

```
58,625
58,625.21
12,345,678.90
```

Fig. G.20 | Using the comma (,) flag to display numbers with the thousands separator.

```
 1   // Fig. G.21: ParenthesesFlagTest.java
 2   // Using the ( flag to place parentheses around negative numbers.
 3
 4   public class ParenthesesFlagTest
 5   {
 6      public static void main( String[] args )
 7      {
 8         System.out.printf( "%(d\n", 50 );
 9         System.out.printf( "%(d\n", -50 );
10         System.out.printf( "%(.1e\n", -50.0 );
11      } // end main
12   } // end class ParenthesesFlagTest
```

```
50
(50)
(5.0e+01)
```

Fig. G.21 | Using the (flag to place parentheses around negative numbers.

G.11 Printing with Argument Indices

An **argument index** is an optional integer followed by a $ sign that indicates the argument's position in the argument list. For example, lines 20–22 and 25–26 in Fig. G.9 use argument index "1$" to indicate that all format specifiers use the first argument in the argument list. Argument indices enable programmers to reorder the output so that the arguments in the argument list are not necessarily in the order of their corresponding format specifiers. Argument indices also help avoid duplicating arguments. Figure G.22 prints arguments in the argument list in reverse order using the argument index.

```
1   // Fig. G.22: ArgumentIndexTest
2   // Reordering output with argument indices.
3
4   public class ArgumentIndexTest
5   {
6      public static void main( String[] args )
7      {
8         System.out.printf(
9            "Parameter list without reordering: %s %s %s %s\n",
10           "first", "second", "third", "fourth" );
11        System.out.printf(
12           "Parameter list after reordering: %4$s %3$s %2$s %1$s\n",
13           "first", "second", "third", "fourth" );
14     } // end main
15  } // end class ArgumentIndexTest
```

```
Parameter list without reordering: first second third fourth
Parameter list after reordering: fourth third second first
```

Fig. G.22 | Reordering output with argument indices.

G.12 Printing Literals and Escape Sequences

Most literal characters to be printed in a printf statement can simply be included in the format string. However, there are several "problem" characters, such as the quotation mark (") that delimits the format string itself. Various control characters, such as newline and tab, must be represented by escape sequences. An escape sequence is represented by a backslash (\), followed by an escape character. Figure G.23 lists the escape sequences and the actions they cause.

Escape sequence	Description
\' (single quote)	Output the single quote (') character.
\" (double quote)	Output the double quote (") character.
\\ (backslash)	Output the backslash (\) character.
\b (backspace)	Move the cursor back one position on the current line.

Fig. G.23 | Escape sequences. (Part 1 of 2.)

Escape sequence	Description
\f (new page or form feed)	Move the cursor to the start of the next logical page.
\n (newline)	Move the cursor to the beginning of the next line.
\r (carriage return)	Move the cursor to the beginning of the current line.
\t (horizontal tab)	Move the cursor to the next horizontal tab position.

Fig. G.23 | Escape sequences. (Part 2 of 2.)

Common Programming Error G.4

Attempting to print as literal data in a printf statement a double quote or backslash character without preceding that character with a backslash to form a proper escape sequence might result in a syntax error.

G.13 Formatting Output with Class Formatter

So far, we've discussed displaying formatted output to the standard output stream. What should we do if we want to send formatted outputs to other output streams or devices, such as a JTextArea or a file? The solution relies on class Formatter (in package java.util), which provides the same formatting capabilities as printf. Formatter is a utility class that enables programmers to output formatted data to a specified destination, such as a file on disk. By default, a Formatter creates a string in memory. Figure G.24 demonstrates how to use a Formatter to build a formatted string, which is then displayed in a message dialog.

Line 11 creates a Formatter object using the default constructor, so this object will build a string in memory. Other constructors are provided to allow you to specify the destination to which the formatted data should be output. For details, see java.sun.com/javase/6/docs/api/java/util/Formatter.html.

```
1   // Fig. Fig. G.24: FormatterTest.java
2   // Formatting output with class Formatter.
3   import java.util.Formatter;
4   import javax.swing.JOptionPane;
5
6   public class FormatterTest
7   {
8      public static void main( String[] args )
9      {
10         // create Formatter and format output
11         Formatter formatter = new Formatter();
12         formatter.format( "%d = %#o = %#X", 10, 10, 10 );
13
14         // display output in JOptionPane
15         JOptionPane.showMessageDialog( null, formatter.toString() );
16      } // end main
17   } // end class FormatterTest
```

Fig. G.24 | Formatting output with class Formatter. (Part 1 of 2.)

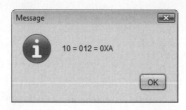

Fig. G.24 | Formatting output with class `Formatter`. (Part 2 of 2.)

Line 12 invokes method **format** to format the output. Like `printf`, method `format` takes a format string and an argument list. The difference is that `printf` sends the formatted output directly to the standard output stream, while `format` sends the formatted output to the destination specified by its constructor (a string in memory in this program). Line 15 invokes the `Formatter`'s `toString` method to get the formatted data as a string, which is then displayed in a message dialog.

Class `String` also provides a `static` convenience method named `format` that enables you to create a string in memory without the need to first create a `Formatter` object. Lines 11–12 and line 15 in Fig. G.24 could have been replaced by

```
String s = String.format( "%d = %#o = %#x", 10, 10, 10 );
JOptionPane.showMessageDialog( null, s );
```

G.14 Wrap-Up

This appendix summarized how to display formatted output with various format characters and flags. We displayed decimal numbers using format characters d, o, x and X; floating-point numbers using format characters e, E, f, g and G; and dates and times in various format using format characters t and T and their conversion suffix characters. You learned how to display output with field widths and precisions. We introduced the flags +, -, space, #, 0, comma and (that are used together with the format characters to produce output. We also demonstrated how to format output with class `Formatter`.

GroupLayout

H.1 Introduction

Java SE 6 introduced a powerful layout manager called **GroupLayout**, which is the default layout manager in the NetBeans IDE (www.netbeans.org). In this appendix, we overview GroupLayout, then demonstrate how to use the NetBeans IDE's **Matisse GUI designer** to create a GUI using GroupLayout to position the components. NetBeans generates the GroupLayout code for you automatically. Though you can write GroupLayout code by hand, in most cases you'll use a GUI design tool like the one provided by NetBeans to take advantage of GroupLayout's power. For more details on GroupLayout, see the list of web resources at the end of this appendix.

H.2 GroupLayout Basics

Chapters 14 and 22 presented several layout managers that provide basic GUI layout capabilities. We also discussed how to combine layout managers and multiple containers to create more complex layouts. Most layout managers do not give you precise control over the positioning of components. In Chapter 22, we discussed the GridBagLayout, which provides more precise control over the position and size of your GUI components. It allows you to specify the horizontal and vertical position of each component, the number of rows and columns each component occupies in the grid, and how components grow and shrink as the size of the container changes. This is all specified at once with a GridBagConstraints object. Class GroupLayout is the next step in layout management. GroupLayout is more flexible, because you can specify the horizontal and vertical layouts of your components independently.

Sequential and Parallel Arrangements

Components are arranged either sequentially or in parallel. The three JButtons in Fig. H.1 are arranged with **sequential horizontal orientation**—they appear left to right in sequence. Vertically, the components are arranged in parallel, so, in a sense, they "occupy the same vertical space." Components can also be arranged sequentially in the vertical direction and in parallel in the horizontal direction, as you'll see in Section H.3. To prevent overlapping components, components with parallel vertical orientation are normally arranged with sequential horizontal orientation (and vice versa).

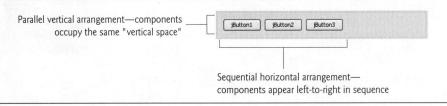

Fig. H.1 | JButtons arranged sequentially for their horizontal orientation and in parallel for their vertical orientation.

Groups and Alignment

To create more complex user interfaces, GroupLayout allows you to create **groups** that contain sequential or parallel elements. Within a group you can have GUI components, other groups and gaps. Placing a group within another group is similar to building a GUI using nested containers, such as a JPanel that contains other JPanels, which in turn contain GUI components.

When you create a group, you can specify the **alignment** of the group's elements. Class GroupLayout contains four constants for this purpose—LEADING, TRAILING, CENTER and BASELINE. The constant BASELINE applies only to vertical orientations. In horizontal orientation, the constants LEADING, TRAILING and CENTER represent left justified, right justified and centered, respectively. In vertical orientation, LEADING, TRAILING and CENTER align the components at their tops, bottoms or vertical centers, respectively. Aligning components with BASELINE indicates they should be aligned using the baseline of the font for the components' text. For more information about font baselines, see Section 15.4.

Spacing

GroupLayout by default uses the recommended GUI design guidelines of the underlying platform for spacing between components. The **addGap** method of GroupLayout nested classes **GroupLayout.Group**, **GroupLayout.SequentialGroup** and **GroupLayout.ParallelGroup** allows you to control the spacing between components.

Sizing Components

By default, GroupLayout uses each component's getMinimumSize, getMaximumSize and getPreferredSize methods to help determine the component's size. You can override the default settings.

H.3 Building a ColorChooser

We now present a ColorChooser application to demonstrate the GroupLayout layout manager. The application consists of three JSlider objects, each representing the values from 0 to 255 for specifying the red, green and blue values of a color. The selected values for each JSlider will be used to display a filled rectangle of the specified color. We build the application using NetBeans. For an more detailed introduction to developing GUI applications in the NetBeans IDE, see www.netbeans.org/kb/trails/matisse.html.

Creating a New Project

Begin by opening a new NetBeans project. Select **File > New Project....** In the **New Project** dialog, choose **Java** from the **Categories** list and **Java Application** from the **Projects** list then click **Next >.** Specify ColorChooser as the project name and uncheck the **Create Main Class** checkbox. You can also specify the location of your project in the **Project Location** field. Click **Finish** to create the project.

Adding a New Subclass of **JFrame** to the Project

In the IDE's **Projects** tab just below the **File** menu and toolbar (Fig. H.2), expand the **Source Packages** node. Right-click the **<default package>** node that appears and select **New > JFrame Form.** In the **New JFrame Form** dialog, specify ColorChooser as the class name and click **Finish.** This subclass of JFrame will display the application's GUI components. The NetBeans window should now appear similar to Fig. H.3 with the Color-Chooser class shown in **Design** view. The **Source** and **Design** buttons at the top of the ColorChooser.java window allow you to switch between editing the source code and designing the GUI.

Fig. H.2 | Adding a new **JFrame Form** to the ColorChooser project.

Design view shows only the ColorChooser's client area (i.e., the area that will appear inside the window's borders). To build a GUI visually, you can drag GUI components from the **Palette** window onto the client area. You can configure the properties of each component by selecting it, then modifying the property values that appear in the **Properties** window (Fig. H.3). When you select a component, the **Properties** window displays three buttons—**Properties, Bindings, Events, Code** (see Fig. H.4)—that enable you to configure various aspects of the component.

Projects tab   ColorChooser.java shown in **Design** view   Client area   **Palette** window

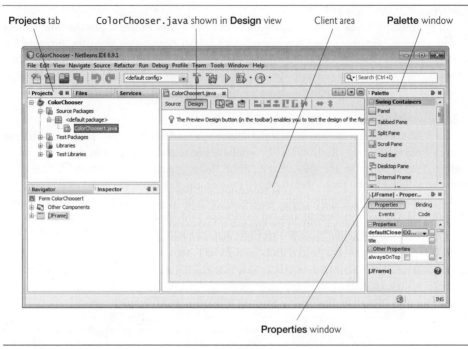

Properties window

Fig. H.3 | Class ColorChooser shown in the NetBeans **Design** view.

Fig. H.4 | **Properties** window with buttons that enable you to configure various aspects of the component.

Build the GUI

Drag three **Slider**s (objects of class JSlider) from the **Palette** onto the JFrame (you may need to scroll through the **Palette**). As you drag components near the edges of the client area or near other components, NetBeans displays **guide lines** (Fig. H.5) that show you the recommended distances and alignments between the component you're dragging, the edges of the client area and other components. As you follow the steps to build the GUI, use the guide lines to arrange the components into three rows and three columns as in Fig. H.6. Next, re-name the JSliders to redJSlider, greenJSlider and blueJSlider. To do so, select the first JSlider, then click the **Code** button in the **Properties** window and change the **Variable Name** property to redSlider. Repeat this process to rename the other two JSliders. Then, click the **Properties** button in the **Properties** window, select each JSlider and change its **maximum** property to 255 so that it will produce values in the range 0–255, and change its **value** property to 0 so the JSlider's thumb will initially be at the left of the JSlider.

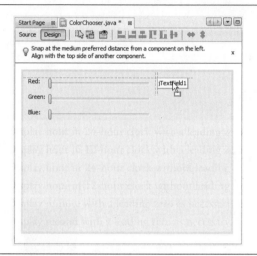

Fig. H.5 | Positioning the first JTextField.

Fig. H.6 | Layout of the JLabels, JSliders and JTextFields.

Drag three **Labels** (objects of class JLabel) from the **Palette** to the JFrame to label each JSlider with the color it represents. Name the JLabels redJLabel, greenJLabel and blueJLabel, respectively. Each JLabel should be placed to the left of the corresponding JSlider (Fig. H.6). Change each JLabel's **text** property either by double clicking the JLabel and typing the new text, or by selecting the JLabel and changing the **text** property in the **Properties** window.

Add a **Text Field** (an object of class JTextField) next to each of the JSliders to dis-play the value of the slider. Name the JTextFields redJTextField, greenJTextField and blueJTextField, respectively. Change each JTextField's **text** property to 0 using the same techniques as you did for the JLabels. Change each JTextField's **columns** property to 4. To align each **Label**, **Slider** and **Text Field** nicely, you can select them by dragging the mouse across all three and use the alignment buttons at the top of the Design window.

Next, add a **Panel** named colorJPanel to the right of this group of components. Use the guide lines as shown in Fig. H.7 to place the JPanel. Change this JPanel's **background** color to black (the initially selected RGB color). Finally, drag the bottom-right border of the client area toward the top-left of the **Design** area until you see the snap-to lines that show the recommended client area dimensions (which are based on the components in the client area) as shown in Fig. H.8.

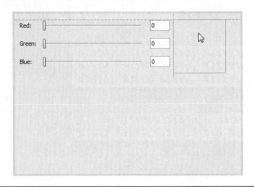

Fig. H.7 | Positioning the JPanel.

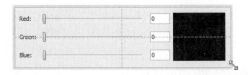

Fig. H.8 | Setting the height of the client area.

Editing the Source Code and Adding Event Handlers
The IDE automatically generated the GUI code, including methods for initializing components and aligning them using the GroupLayout layout manager. We must add the desired functionality to the components' event handlers. To add an event handler for a component, right click it and position the mouse over the **Events** option in the pop-up menu. You can then select the category of event you wish to handle and the specific event within that category. For example, to add the JSlider event handlers for this example, right click each JSlider and select **Events > Change > stateChanged**. When you do this, NetBeans adds a ChangeListener to the JSlider and switches from **Design** view to **Source** view where you can place code in the event handler. Use the **Design** button to return to **Design** view and repeat the preceding steps to add the event handlers for the other two JSliders. To complete the event handlers, first add the method in Fig. H.9 following the class's constructor. In each JSlider event handler set the corresponding JTextField to the new value of the JSlider, then call method changeColor. Figure H.10 shows the completed ColorChooser class as it's generated in NetBeans. We did not restyle the code to match our coding conventions that you've seen throughout the book. You can now run the program to see it in action. Drag each slider and watch the colorJPanel's background color change.

Method initComponents (lines 39–162) was entirely generated by NetBeans based on your interactions with the GUI designer. This method contains the code that creates and formats the GUI. Lines 41–93 construct and initialize the GUI components. Lines 95–161 specify the layout of those components using GroupLayout. Lines 108–136 specify the horizontal group and lines 137–159 specify the vertical group. Notice how complex the code is. More and more software development is done with tools that generate complex code like this, saving you the time and effort of doing it yourself.

We manually added the changeColor method in lines 25–30. When the user moves the thumb on one of the JSliders, the JSlider's event handler sets the text in its corresponding JTextField to the JSlider's new value (lines 166, 172 and 178), then calls method changeColor (lines 167, 173 and 179) to update the colorJPanel's background color. Method changeColor gets the current value of each JSlider (lines 28–29) and uses these values as the arguments to the Color constructor to create a new Color.

```
1    // changes the colorJPanel's background color based on the current
2    // values of the JSliders
3    public void changeColor()
4    {
5       colorJPanel.setBackground( new java.awt.Color(
6          redJSlider.getValue(), greenJSlider.getValue(),
7          blueJSlider.getValue() ) );
8    } // end method changeColor
```

Fig. H.9 | Method that changes the colorJPanel's background color based on the values of the three JSliders.

```
1    /*
2     * To change this template, choose Tools | Templates
3     * and open the template in the editor.
4     */
5
6    /*
7     * ColorChooser.java
8     *
9     * Created on Feb 8, 2011, 9:20:27 AM
10    */
11
12   /**
13    *
14    * @author Paul Deitel
15    */
16   public class ColorChooser extends javax.swing.JFrame {
17
18      /** Creates new form ColorChooser */
19      public ColorChooser() {
20         initComponents();
21      }
22
23      // changes the colorJPanel's background color based on the current
24      // values of the JSliders
25      public void changeColor()
26      {
```

Fig. H.10 | ColorChooser class that uses GroupLayout for its GUI layout. (Part 1 of 6.)

```
27          colorJPanel.setBackground( new java.awt.Color(
28             redJSlider.getValue(), greenJSlider.getValue(),
29             blueJSlider.getValue() ) );
30       } // end method changeColor
31
32       /** This method is called from within the constructor to
33        * initialize the form.
34        * WARNING: Do NOT modify this code. The content of this method is
35        * always regenerated by the Form Editor.
36        */
37       @SuppressWarnings("unchecked")
38       // <editor-fold defaultstate="collapsed" desc="Generated Code">
39       private void initComponents() {
40
41          redJSlider = new javax.swing.JSlider();
42          greenJSlider = new javax.swing.JSlider();
43          blueJSlider = new javax.swing.JSlider();
44          redJLabel = new javax.swing.JLabel();
45          greenJLabel = new javax.swing.JLabel();
46          blueJLabel = new javax.swing.JLabel();
47          redJTextField = new javax.swing.JTextField();
48          greenJTextField = new javax.swing.JTextField();
49          blueJTextField = new javax.swing.JTextField();
50          colorJPanel = new javax.swing.JPanel();
51
52          setDefaultCloseOperation(javax.swing.WindowConstants.EXIT_ON_CLOSE);
53
54          redJSlider.setMaximum(255);
55          redJSlider.setValue(0);
56          redJSlider.addChangeListener(new javax.swing.event.ChangeListener()
{
57             public void stateChanged(javax.swing.event.ChangeEvent evt) {
58                redJSliderStateChanged(evt);
59             }
60          });
61
62          greenJSlider.setMaximum(255);
63          greenJSlider.setValue(0);
64          greenJSlider.addChangeListener(new
javax.swing.event.ChangeListener() {
65             public void stateChanged(javax.swing.event.ChangeEvent evt) {
66                greenJSliderStateChanged(evt);
67             }
68          });
69
70          blueJSlider.setMaximum(255);
71          blueJSlider.setValue(0);
72          blueJSlider.addChangeListener(new javax.swing.event.ChangeListener()
{
73             public void stateChanged(javax.swing.event.ChangeEvent evt) {
74                blueJSliderStateChanged(evt);
75             }
76          });
```

Fig. H.10 | ColorChooser class that uses GroupLayout for its GUI layout. (Part 2 of 6.)

```
77
78          redJLabel.setText("Red:");
79
80          greenJLabel.setText("Green:");
81
82          blueJLabel.setText("Blue:");
83
84          redJTextField.setColumns(4);
85          redJTextField.setText("0");
86
87          greenJTextField.setColumns(4);
88          greenJTextField.setText("0");
89
90          blueJTextField.setColumns(4);
91          blueJTextField.setText("0");
92
93          colorJPanel.setBackground(new java.awt.Color(0, 0, 0));
94
95          javax.swing.GroupLayout colorJPanelLayout = new
javax.swing.GroupLayout(colorJPanel);
96          colorJPanel.setLayout(colorJPanelLayout);
97          colorJPanelLayout.setHorizontalGroup(
98
colorJPanelLayout.createParallelGroup(javax.swing.GroupLayout.Alignment.LEADIN
G)
99             .addGap(0, 100, Short.MAX_VALUE)
100         );
101         colorJPanelLayout.setVerticalGroup(
102
colorJPanelLayout.createParallelGroup(javax.swing.GroupLayout.Alignment.LEADIN
G)
103            .addGap(0, 91, Short.MAX_VALUE)
104         );
105
106         javax.swing.GroupLayout layout = new
javax.swing.GroupLayout(getContentPane());
107         getContentPane().setLayout(layout);
108         layout.setHorizontalGroup(
109
layout.createParallelGroup(javax.swing.GroupLayout.Alignment.LEADING)
110            .addGroup(layout.createSequentialGroup()
111
.addGroup(layout.createParallelGroup(javax.swing.GroupLayout.Alignment.LEADING
)
112                .addGroup(javax.swing.GroupLayout.Alignment.TRAILING,
layout.createSequentialGroup()
113                   .addContainerGap()
114                   .addComponent(redJLabel)
115                   .addGap(20, 20, 20)
116                   .addComponent(redJSlider,
javax.swing.GroupLayout.PREFERRED_SIZE, javax.swing.GroupLayout.DEFAULT_SIZE,
javax.swing.GroupLayout.PREFERRED_SIZE)
```

Fig. H.10 | ColorChooser class that uses GroupLayout for its GUI layout. (Part 3 of 6.)

```
117
.addPreferredGap(javax.swing.LayoutStyle.ComponentPlacement.UNRELATED)
118                    .addComponent(redJTextField,
javax.swing.GroupLayout.PREFERRED_SIZE, javax.swing.GroupLayout.DEFAULT_SIZE,
javax.swing.GroupLayout.PREFERRED_SIZE))
119                .addGroup(layout.createSequentialGroup()
120                    .addContainerGap()
121                    .addComponent(greenJLabel)
122
.addPreferredGap(javax.swing.LayoutStyle.ComponentPlacement.UNRELATED)
123                    .addComponent(greenJSlider,
javax.swing.GroupLayout.PREFERRED_SIZE, javax.swing.GroupLayout.DEFAULT_SIZE,
javax.swing.GroupLayout.PREFERRED_SIZE)
124                    .addGap(10, 10, 10)
125                    .addComponent(greenJTextField,
javax.swing.GroupLayout.PREFERRED_SIZE, javax.swing.GroupLayout.DEFAULT_SIZE,
javax.swing.GroupLayout.PREFERRED_SIZE))
126                .addGroup(layout.createSequentialGroup()
127                    .addContainerGap()
128                    .addComponent(blueJLabel)
129                    .addGap(19, 19, 19)
130                    .addComponent(blueJSlider,
javax.swing.GroupLayout.PREFERRED_SIZE, javax.swing.GroupLayout.DEFAULT_SIZE,
javax.swing.GroupLayout.PREFERRED_SIZE)
131
.addPreferredGap(javax.swing.LayoutStyle.ComponentPlacement.UNRELATED)
132                    .addComponent(blueJTextField,
javax.swing.GroupLayout.PREFERRED_SIZE, javax.swing.GroupLayout.DEFAULT_SIZE,
javax.swing.GroupLayout.PREFERRED_SIZE)))
133
.addPreferredGap(javax.swing.LayoutStyle.ComponentPlacement.RELATED)
134            .addComponent(colorJPanel,
javax.swing.GroupLayout.PREFERRED_SIZE, javax.swing.GroupLayout.DEFAULT_SIZE,
javax.swing.GroupLayout.PREFERRED_SIZE)
135            .addContainerGap(javax.swing.GroupLayout.DEFAULT_SIZE,
Short.MAX_VALUE))
136        );
137        layout.setVerticalGroup(
138
layout.createParallelGroup(javax.swing.GroupLayout.Alignment.LEADING)
139        .addGroup(layout.createSequentialGroup()
140            .addContainerGap()
141
.addGroup(layout.createParallelGroup(javax.swing.GroupLayout.Alignment.TRAILIN
G, false)
142                .addComponent(colorJPanel,
javax.swing.GroupLayout.DEFAULT_SIZE, javax.swing.GroupLayout.DEFAULT_SIZE,
Short.MAX_VALUE)
143                .addGroup(javax.swing.GroupLayout.Alignment.LEADING,
layout.createSequentialGroup()
144
.addGroup(layout.createParallelGroup(javax.swing.GroupLayout.Alignment.CENTER)
```

Fig. H.10 | ColorChooser class that uses GroupLayout for its GUI layout. (Part 4 of 6.)

```
145                          .addComponent(redJSlider,
javax.swing.GroupLayout.PREFERRED_SIZE, javax.swing.GroupLayout.DEFAULT_SIZE,
javax.swing.GroupLayout.PREFERRED_SIZE)
146                          .addComponent(redJTextField,
javax.swing.GroupLayout.PREFERRED_SIZE, javax.swing.GroupLayout.DEFAULT_SIZE,
javax.swing.GroupLayout.PREFERRED_SIZE)
147                          .addComponent(redJLabel))
148
.addPreferredGap(javax.swing.LayoutStyle.ComponentPlacement.UNRELATED)
149
.addGroup(layout.createParallelGroup(javax.swing.GroupLayout.Alignment.CENTER)
150                          .addComponent(greenJSlider,
javax.swing.GroupLayout.PREFERRED_SIZE, javax.swing.GroupLayout.DEFAULT_SIZE,
javax.swing.GroupLayout.PREFERRED_SIZE)
151                          .addComponent(greenJLabel)
152                          .addComponent(greenJTextField,
javax.swing.GroupLayout.PREFERRED_SIZE, javax.swing.GroupLayout.DEFAULT_SIZE,
javax.swing.GroupLayout.PREFERRED_SIZE))
153
.addPreferredGap(javax.swing.LayoutStyle.ComponentPlacement.UNRELATED)
154
.addGroup(layout.createParallelGroup(javax.swing.GroupLayout.Alignment.CENTER)
155                          .addComponent(blueJLabel)
156                          .addComponent(blueJSlider,
javax.swing.GroupLayout.PREFERRED_SIZE, javax.swing.GroupLayout.DEFAULT_SIZE,
javax.swing.GroupLayout.PREFERRED_SIZE)
157                          .addComponent(blueJTextField,
javax.swing.GroupLayout.PREFERRED_SIZE, javax.swing.GroupLayout.DEFAULT_SIZE,
javax.swing.GroupLayout.PREFERRED_SIZE))))
158                    .addContainerGap())
159       );
160
161       pack();
162    }// </editor-fold>
163
164    private void redJSliderStateChanged(javax.swing.event.ChangeEvent evt)
165    {
166       redJTextField.setText( String.valueOf( redJSlider.getValue() ) );
167       changeColor();
168    }
169
170    private void greenJSliderStateChanged(javax.swing.event.ChangeEvent
evt)
171    {
172       greenJTextField.setText( String.valueOf( greenJSlider.getValue() )
);
173       changeColor();
174    }
175
176    private void blueJSliderStateChanged(javax.swing.event.ChangeEvent
evt)
177    {
178       blueJTextField.setText( String.valueOf( blueJSlider.getValue() ) );
```

Fig. H.10 | ColorChooser class that uses GroupLayout for its GUI layout. (Part 5 of 6.)

```
179            changeColor();
180        }
181
182        /**
183         * @param args the command line arguments
184         */
185        public static void main(String args[]) {
186            java.awt.EventQueue.invokeLater(new Runnable() {
187                public void run() {
188                    new ColorChooser().setVisible(true);
189                }
190            });
191        }
192
193        // Variables declaration - do not modify
194        private javax.swing.JLabel blueJLabel;
195        private javax.swing.JSlider blueJSlider;
196        private javax.swing.JTextField blueJTextField;
197        private javax.swing.JPanel colorJPanel;
198        private javax.swing.JLabel greenJLabel;
199        private javax.swing.JSlider greenJSlider;
200        private javax.swing.JTextField greenJTextField;
201        private javax.swing.JLabel redJLabel;
202        private javax.swing.JSlider redJSlider;
203        private javax.swing.JTextField redJTextField;
204        // End of variables declaration
205
206    }
```

Fig. H.10 | ColorChooser class that uses GroupLayout for its GUI layout. (Part 6 of 6.)

H.4 GroupLayout Web Resources

download.oracle.com/javase/6/docs/api/javax/swing/GroupLayout.html
API documentation for class GroupLayout.

wiki.java.net/bin/view/Javadesktop/GroupLayoutExample
Provides an Address Book demo of a GUI built manually with GroupLayout with source code.

www.developer.com/java/ent/article.php/3589961
Tutorial: "Building Java GUIs with Matisse: A Gentle Introduction," by Dick Wall.

Java Desktop Integration Components

1.1 Introduction

The **Java Desktop Integration Components (JDIC)** are part of an open-source project aimed at allowing better integration between Java applications and the platforms on which they execute. Some JDIC features include:

- interacting with the underlying platform to launch native applications (such as web browsers and e-mail clients)

- displaying a splash screen when an application begins execution to indicate to the user that the application is loading

- creating icons in the system tray (also called the taskbar status area or notification area) to provide access to Java applications running in the background

- registering file-type associations, so that files of specified types will automatically open in corresponding Java applications

- creating installer packages, and more.

The JDIC homepage (jdic.dev.java.net/) includes an introduction to JDIC, downloads, documentation, FAQs, demos, articles, blogs, announcements, incubator projects, a developer's page, forums, mailing lists, and more. We discuss several of these features here.

1.2 Splash Screens

Java application users often perceive a performance problem, because nothing appears on the screen when you first launch an application. One way to show a user that your program is loading is to display a **splash screen**—a borderless window that appears temporarily while an application loads. The command-line option **-splash** for the java command enables you to specify a PNG, GIF or JPG image that should display when your application begins loading. To demonstrate this new option, we created a program (Fig. 1.1) that sleeps for 5 seconds (so you can view the splash screen) then displays a message at the command line. The directory for this example includes a PNG format image to use as the splash screen. To display the splash screen when this application loads, use the command

```
java -splash:DeitelBug.png SplashDemo
```

```java
1   // Fig. I.1: SplashDemo.java
2   // Splash screen demonstration.
3   public class SplashDemo
4   {
5      public static void main( String[] args )
6      {
7         try
8         {
9            Thread.sleep( 5000 );
10        } // end try
11        catch ( InterruptedException e )
12        {
13           e.printStackTrace();
14        } // end catch
15
16        System.out.println(
17           "This was the splash screen demo." );
18     } // end method main
19  } // end class SplashDemo
```

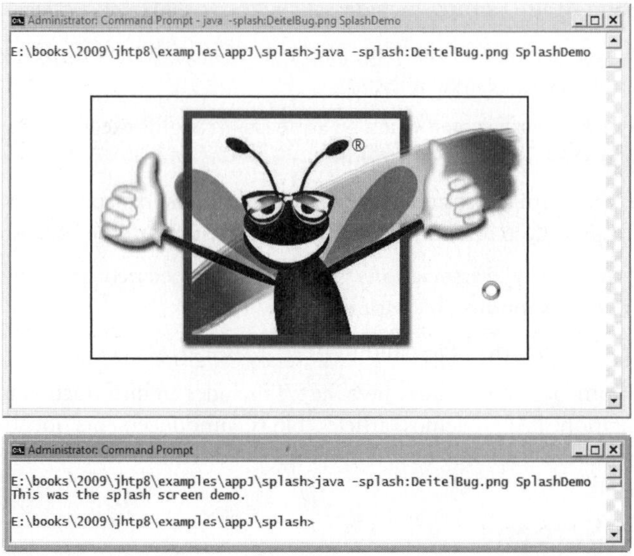

Fig. I.1 | Spash screen displayed with the -splash option to the java command.

Once you've initiated the splash screen display, you can interact with it programmatically via the **SplashScreen** class of the java.awt package. You might do this to add some dynamic content to the splash screen. For more information on working with splash screens, see the following sites:

I.3 Desktop Class

The **Desktop** class enables you to specify a file or URI that you'd like to open using the underlying platform's appropriate application. For example, if Firefox is your computer's default browser, you can use the Desktop class's browse method to open a website in Firefox. In addition, you can open an e-mail composition window in your system's default e-mail client, open a file in its associated application and print a file using the associated application's print command. Figure I.2 demonstrates the first three of these capabilities.

The event handler at lines 86–116 obtains the index number of the task the user selects in the tasksJComboBox (line 89) and the String that represents the file or URI to process (line 90). Line 92 uses Desktop static method **isDesktopSupported** to determine whether class Desktop's features are supported on the platform on which this application runs. If they are, line 96 uses Desktop static method **getDesktop** to obtain a Desktop object. If the user selected the option to open the default browser, line 101 creates a new URI object using the String input as the site to display in the browser, then passes the URI object to Desktop method **browse** which invokes the system's default browser and passes the URI to the browser for display. If the user selects the option to open a file in its associated program, line 104 creates a new File object using the String input as the file to open, then passes the File object to Desktop method **open** which passes the file to the appropriate application to open the file. Finally, if the user selects the option to compose an e-mail, line 107 creates a new URI object using the String input as the e-mail address to which the e-mail will be sent, then passes the URI object to Desktop method **mail** which invokes the system's default e-mail client and passes the URI to the e-mail client as the e-mail recipient. You can learn more about class Desktop at

```
1   // Fig. I.2: DesktopDemo.java
2   // Use Desktop to launch default browser, open a file in its associated
3   // application and an email in the default email client.
4   import java.awt.Desktop;
5   import java.io.File;
6   import java.io.IOException;
7   import java.net.URI;
8
9   public class DesktopDemo extends javax.swing.JFrame
10  {
11     // constructor
12     public DesktopDemo()
13     {
14        initComponents();
15     } // end DesktopDemo constructor
```

Fig. I.2 | Use Desktop to launch the default browser, open a file in its associated application and compose an e-mail in the default e-mail client. (Part 1 of 3.)

```
16
17    // To save space, lines 20-84 of the NetBeans autogenerated GUI code
18    // are not shown here. The complete code for this example is located in
19    // the file DesktopDemo.java in this example's directory.
20
21    // determine selected task and perform the task
22    private void doTaskJButtonActionPerformed(
23       java.awt.event.ActionEvent evt)
24    {
25       int index = tasksJComboBox.getSelectedIndex();
26       String input = inputJTextField.getText();
27
28       if ( Desktop.isDesktopSupported() )
29       {
30          try
31          {
32             Desktop desktop = Desktop.getDesktop();
33
34             switch ( index )
35             {
36                case 0: // open browser
37                   desktop.browse( new URI( input ) );
38                   break;
39                case 1: // open file
40                   desktop.open( new File( input ) );
41                   break;
42                case 2: // open email composition window
43                   desktop.mail( new URI( input ) );
44                   break;
45             } // end switch
46          } // end try
47          catch ( Exception e )
48          {
49             e.printStackTrace();
50          } // end catch
51       } // end if
52    } // end method doTaskJButtonActionPerformed
53
54    public static void main(String[] args)
55    {
56       java.awt.EventQueue.invokeLater(
57          new Runnable()
58          {
59             public void run()
60             {
61                new DesktopDemo().setVisible(true);
62             }
63          }
64       );
65    } // end method main
66
```

Fig. I.2 | Use `Desktop` to launch the default browser, open a file in its associated application and compose an e-mail in the default e-mail client. (Part 2 of 3.)

```
67      // Variables declaration - do not modify
68      private javax.swing.JButton doTaskJButton;
69      private javax.swing.JLabel inputJLabel;
70      private javax.swing.JTextField inputJTextField;
71      private javax.swing.JLabel instructionLabel;
72      private javax.swing.JComboBox tasksJComboBox;
73      // End of variables declaration
74   }
```

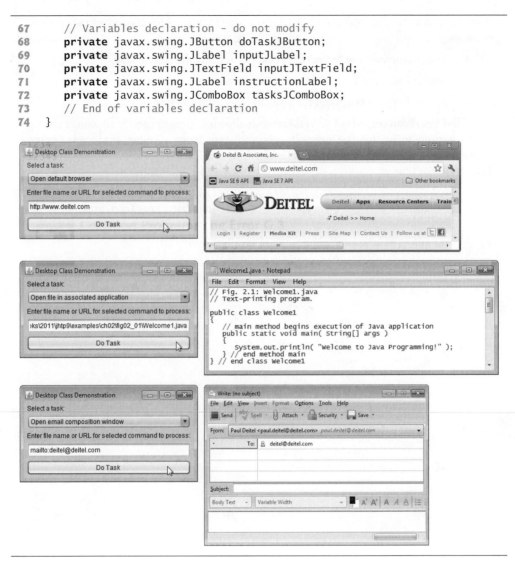

Fig. I.2 | Use Desktop to launch the default browser, open a file in its associated application and compose an e-mail in the default e-mail client. (Part 3 of 3.)

I.4 Tray Icons

Tray icons generally appear in your system's system tray, taskbar status area or notification area. They typically provide quick access to applications that are executing in the background on your system. When you position the mouse over one of these icons, a tooltip appears indicating what application the icon represents. If you click the icon, a popup menu appears with options for that application.

Classes SystemTray and TrayIcon (both from package java.awt) enable you to create and manage your own tray icons in a platform independent manner. Class **SystemTray** provides access to the underlying platform's system tray—the class consists of three methods:

- static method **getDefaultSystemTray** returns the system tray
- method **addTrayIcon** adds a new TrayIcon to the system tray
- method **removeTrayIcon** removes an icon from the system tray

Class **TrayIcon** consists of several methods allowing users to specify an icon, a tooltip and a pop-up menu for the icon. In addition, tray icons support ActionListeners, MouseListeners and MouseMotionListeners. You can learn more about classes System-Tray and TrayIcon at

```
download.oracle.com/javase/6/docs/api/java/awt/SystemTray.html
download.oracle.com/javase/6/docs/api/java/awt/TrayIcon.html
```

UML 2: Additional Diagram Types

J.1 Introduction

If you read the optional Software Engineering Case Study in Chapters 12–13, you should now have a comfortable grasp on the UML diagram types that we use to model our ATM system. We limit our discussion to a concise, subset of the UML. The UML 2 provides a total of 13 diagram types. The end of Section 12.2 summarizes the six diagram types that we use in the case study. This appendix lists and briefly defines the seven remaining diagram types.

J.2 Additional Diagram Types

The following are the seven diagram types that we chose not to use in our Software Engineering Case Study.

- **Object diagrams** model a "snapshot" of the system by modeling a system's objects and their relationships at a specific point in time. Each object represents an instance of a class from a class diagram, and there may be several objects created from one class. For our ATM system, an object diagram could show several distinct Account objects side by side, illustrating that they're all part of the bank's account database.

- **Component diagrams** model the **artifacts** and **components**—resources (which include source files)—that make up the system.

- **Deployment diagrams** model the runtime requirements of the system (such as the computer or computers on which the system will reside), memory requirements for the system, or other devices the system requires during execution.

- **Package diagrams** model the hierarchical structure of **packages** (which are groups of classes) in the system at compile-time and the relationships that exist between the packages.

- **Composite structure diagrams** model the internal structure of a complex object at runtime. Composite structure diagrams are new in UML 2 and allow system designers to hierarchically decompose a complex object into smaller parts. Composite structure diagrams are beyond the scope of our case study. Composite structure diagrams are more appropriate for larger industrial applications, which exhibit complex groupings of objects at execution time.

- **Interaction overview diagrams**, which are new in UML 2, provide a summary of control flow in the system by combining elements of several types of behavioral diagrams (e.g., activity diagrams, sequence diagrams).

- **Timing diagrams**, also new in UML 2, model the timing constraints imposed on stage changes and interactions between objects in a system.

If you're interested in learning more about these diagrams and advanced UML topics, please visit our UML Resource Center at www.deitel.com/UML/.

Index